NORTH CAROLINA
AT THE BEGINNING OF
1800

Showing Approximate County Divisions
within Present State Boundaries.

Map by
L. Polk Denmark

(From *The Formation of North Carolina Counties 1663-1943*,
by David Leroy Corbitt, Raleigh, 1950)

INDEX TO
THE 1800 CENSUS
OF NORTH CAROLINA

Compiled by

ELIZABETH PETTY BENTLEY

CLEARFIELD

Library of Congress Catalog Card Number 76-53969

Reprinted for Clearfield Company by
Genealogical Publishing Company
Baltimore, Maryland
2012

ISBN 978-0-8063–0751-0

Made in the United States of America

FOREWORD

Microfilm copies of the Federal Census of North Carolina for the year 1800 may be purchased from the Publication Sales Branch (NATS), National Archives (GSA), Washington, D.C. 20408. Their catalogue lists it as Micropublication number M32, rolls 29-34, presently priced at $12.00 per roll. The branch libraries of the Church of Jesus Christ of Latter-day Saints can also order microfilm copies of the census to be viewed at the branch for a fee of 55¢ for a two-week period. For the address of the branch nearest you, you may write to The Genealogical Society, 50 E. North Temple, Salt Lake City, Utah 84150. Photocopies of single pages may be obtained from either of the above agencies.

The microfilm copy is available for viewing by the public in the National Archives. However, some of it is out of focus, or faint, or difficult to read because of a tear in the page from which the photograph was made. In cases where the film is unreadable, the researcher may request permission to examine the bound negative photostatic copies of the original returns in the Central Search Room. These are especially useful as some tears occurred after the photostats were made, and many faint entries are much clearer. However, some names, particularly at the top and bottom of the page, have been written over in ink, obliterating the photo, and a few entries are obscured by what appears to be transparent tape, making the photo image indistinct.

I was fortunate enough to be able to view the original returns, which have been mounted on new sheets and rebound. These are on deposit with the Archives but are not readily accessible. Every effort has been made, using both sets of bound volumes, to interpret names which are not clear on the film. No visible entry has been intentionally omitted from this index.

An attempt has been made in the case of questionable interpretations of handwriting to refer the reader to the index entry. For example, "see Fruman" appears at the conclusion of the *Freeman* entries. Similar notations refer the reader to alternative phonetic spellings such as *Jiles* for *Giles,* or to entries where the surname was used as a given name or the order of the names has been inverted. The reader should be aware that some enumerators employed the British order of inversion: last name, middle name, first name, instead of the usual American convention: last name, first name, middle name.

In addition, the enumerator may have made no attempt whatever to discover the proper spelling of a name, simply spelling it as he heard it pronounced. For instance, one man used *Jeams* for *James* consistently, while another wrote

v

Federick for *Fredrick* and *Partrick* or *Pattrick* for *Patrick*. We can only imagine the variations in the spelling of unfamiliar surnames. The reader ought to try to imagine possible misinterpretations by substituting double letters for single ones, and vice versa, and replacing letters with similar sounds such as *ph* for *f*, *d* for *t*, and *y* for *i*, or with similar shapes such as *e* for *i* and *L* for *S*. No attempt has been made in this index to correct spellings. Abbreviations, too, have been transcribed as they appear. Superscripts, such as <u>*Jon*</u>*ⁿ*, appear as *Jonn.* in the index. Some names are followed by notations such as Senr., Junr., Terts. (meaning the third), Deep Creek, Ovr. (overseer), son of, or Dumb, whose meanings are clear. Others can be guessed at, such as BS (blacksmith or Bachelor of Science), JP (justice of the peace), BR (Back River). Still others, such as B or HR, may be clear only to the student of the area or era.

In addition to searching for various spellings of a name, the reader should also check for possible illegible entries, especially for names beginning with *B*, *C* or *D* in Beaufort County. When one or more letters had to be omitted, the gap is filled with ellipses (. . .), for example *C* . . . appears before names beginning with *Ca*, and *Cha* . . . *t* appears before the name *Chace*. Totally illegible names or intentional omissions by the enumerator are also denoted by ellipses. Most of the latter were free colored persons. These entries appear at the very beginning of the index.

It should be held in mind by the researcher that the Federal Census of 1800 listed only the heads of families by name. Your subject may be listed among a family of a different surname as a boarder, laborer, or student. He may have avoided enumeration because of fear, suspicion, or superstition, or he may simply have been left out because of his remote residence or absence from home.

Along with the name of the head of household, in the original census enumerations, the following twelve columns were filled in with an appropriate entry, left to right: White males under 10 years of age, white males from 10-16 years of age, white males from 16-26 years of age, white males from 26-44 years of age, white males from 45 and upwards (then the same five categories for white females), all other free persons (except Indians who were not taxed), and slaves. These headings usually appear in the original census only on the first page of each county.

Table I, following, contains a list of abbreviations used in this index and the roll number for each county. Table II lists the counties in the order they appear on the microfilm, the page numbers covered (machine stamped, unless otherwise stated), and any other information which might be helpful to the reader.

Thanks are due my patient family, who also helped alphabetize, and Dr. Michael Tepper for his technical advice.

It is hoped that this index will save the user many hours of tedious research.

Elizabeth Petty Bentley

TABLE I

County	Abbreviation	Roll no.
Anson	Ans	29
Ashe	Ash	29
Beaufort	Bfr	30
Bertie	Brt	30
Bladen	Bld	31
Brunswick	Brn	29
Buncombe	Bnc	29
Burke	Brk	29
Cabarrus	Cbr	29
Camden	Cmd	30
Carteret	Crt	31
Caswell	Csw	31
Chatham	Cht	31
Chowan	Chw	30
Craven	Crv	31
Cumberland	Cmb	31
Currituck	Crr	30
Duplin	Dpl	31
Edgecomb	Edg	30
Franklin	Frn	31
Gates	Gts	30
Granville	Grv	31
Greene	Grn	31
Guilford	Glf	31
Halifax	Hlf	30
Hertford	Hrt	31
Hyde	Hde	34
Iredell	Ird	29
Johnston	Jhn	31
Jones	Jns	31
Lenoir	Lnr	32
Lincoln	Lnc	29
Martin	Mrt	34
Mecklenburg	Mck	33
Montgomery	Mnt	33
Moore	Mre	32
Nash	Nsh	32
New Hanover	Nwh	33
Northampton	Nrt	34
Onslow	Ons	32

Orange	Orn	34
Pasquotank	Psq	34
Perquimans	Prq	34
Person	Prs	32
Pitt	Ptt	32
Randolph	Rnd	32
Richmond	Rch	33
Robeson	Rbs	32
Rockingham	Rck	32
Rowan	Rwn	33
Rutherford	Rth	33
Sampson	Smp	32
Stokes	Stk	32
Surry	Srr	32
Tyrrell	Trl	34
Wake	Wke	32
Warren	Wrr	32
Washington	Wsh	34
Wayne	Wne	32
Wilkes	Wlk	33

TABLE II

ROLL 29

Anson Co., pp. 198-241. Page 240A on the film is numbered 241 in the index.

Ashe Co., pp. 72-92.

Brunswick Co., pp. 13-22A. The original pages were cut in half in a volume, the bottom half being numbered with an A. Thus the pages appear to be in the following order: 13, 14, 13A, 14A, 15, 16, 15A, 16A, etc. Pages 13A and 17A do not have an A on the film. Page 14A is numbered 14B on the film.

Buncombe Co., pp. 158-194. The first six names on page 158 are Asheville Town.

Burke Co., pp. 720-808 and 279. Page 279 is Morganton and follows immediately after page 808.

Cabarrus Co., pp. 676-718. Pages 681½ and 681¾ on the film are numbered 681 in the index. Page 718A on the film is Concord and is numbered 718 in the index. The original copy of page 718A appears on roll 29 on page 282 of Lincoln County below.

Iredell Co., pp. 608-675 (handwritten numbers). Page 674A on the film is numbered 674 in the index. The original copy of page 674A appears on roll 29 between Burke and Cabarrus Cos. above. Page 675 is Statesville.

Lincoln Co., pp. 281 and 809-908. Page 281 is Lincolnton.

ROLL 30

Beaufort Co., pp. 1-24. Pages 22 through part of 24 are Town of Washington. Part of page 24 is Bath Town.

Bertie Co., pp. 26-91. Pages 88 through part of 90 are Windsor. Part of page 90 through page 91 are Colerain.

Camden Co., pp. 93-110.

Chowan Co., pp. 113-131. Pages 113-117 are Town of Edenton.

Currituck Co., pp. 137-169.

Edgecombe Co., pp. 171-173, 178-259. Pages 171-173 are Town of Scarborough.

Gates Co., pp. 261-281.

Halifax Co., pp. 286-359. Page 358 is Halifax Town.

ROLL 31

Bladen Co., pp. 2-52.

Capt. Nance's Dist.	pp. 2, 13-16.
Capt. Barfield's Dist.	pp. 3-6.
Capt. Powell's Dist.	pp. 6-10.
Capt. Greene's Dist.	pp. 11, 12, 17.
Capt. Lewis' Dist.	pp. 18-23.
Capt. M'Kay's Dist.	pp. 23-28.
Capt. Ashford's Dist. (including Elizabeth)	pp. 28-33.
Capt. Robison's Dist.	pp. 33-37.
Capt. Lock's Dist.	pp. 38-40.
Capt. Bryan's Dist.	pp. 40-46.

Capt. Ander's Dist.   pp. 47-50.
Elizabeth (see Capt.
   Ashford's Dist.)   p. 52.
Carteret Co., pp. 56-93.
Caswell Co., pp. 95-149.
Chatham Co., pp. 151-226. Part of page 225 is Pittsborough. Page 226 is Haywood.
Craven Co., pp. 229-345. Pages 229-257 are Newbern.
Cumberland Co., pp. 351-394.

Capt. Buie's Company	pp. 360-362.
Capt. Munroe's Company	pp. 362-366, 392-394.
Capt. Gibson's Company	pp. 366-367.
Capt. Dickson's Company	pp. 368-371.
Capt. McAllister's Company	pp. 371-374.
Capt. Shaw's Company	pp. 374-376.
Capt. McCain's Company	pp. 376-379.
Capt. Theames' Company	pp. 379-383.
Capt. Coles' Co.	pp. 383-386.
Capt. Graham's Company	pp. 387-389.
Capt. Pergram's Company	pp. 389-392.

Duplin Co., pp. 397-442.
Franklin Co., pp. 445-495. The six families of Louisburg appear on pages 445, 451, 483 and 487.
Granville Co., pp. 505-585.
Greene Co., pp. 587-617.
Guilford Co., pp. 619-693.
Hertford Co., pp. 696-738.

Capt. Foster's Captaincy	pp. 696-703.
Capt. Jones' Captaincy	pp. 703-707.
Capt. Barrow's Captaincy	pp. 708-715.
Capt. Moore's Captaincy	pp. 715-719.
Capt. Langston's Captaincy	pp. 719-722.
Capt. Lewis' Captaincy	pp. 722-727.
Capt. Brett's Captaincy	pp. 728-729.
Capt. Wiggin's Captaincy	pp. 730-733.
Capt. Spiers' Captaincy	pp. 734-737.
Murfreesboro	pp. 737-738.

Johnston Co., pp. 746-777.
Jones Co., pp. 779-819. Pages 823-825 are Trenton.

ROLL 32

Lenoir Co., pp. 1-35. Part of page 35 is Kinston.
Moore Co., pp. 39-77.
Nash Co., pp. 86-130, 133.
Onslow Co., pp. 135-182.
Person Co., pp. 187-219.

Pitt Co., pp. 224-295. Part of page 293 through page 295 are Greenville Town.
Randolph Co., pp. 297-353.
Robeson Co., pp. 358-430. Page 432 is Town of Lumberton.
Rockingham Co., pp. 436-492.
Sampson Co., pp. 494-536.
Stokes Co., pp. 544-628.

Salem	page 525 and part of 526.
Bethabara	part of page 526.
Huntsville	part of page 526.
Bethany	part of page 527.
Rockford	part of page 527.
Germantown	page 528.

Surry Co., pp. 631-711.
Wake Co., pp. 714-778.
Warren Co., pp. 784-841. Pages 784 through part of page 786 are Warrenton.
Wayne Co., pp. 843-874. There are two each of pages 871-873 on the film. This numbering is retained in the index.

ROLL 33

Montgomery Co., pp. 461-521.
Mecklenburg Co., pp. 522-606. Pages 606A and 606B on the film are numbered 606 in the index. The original copy of page 606A appears on roll 29 between Cabarrus and Iredell Cos. The original copy of page 606B appears on roll 29 between Burke and Cabarrus Cos. Page 606B is Charlotte.
New Hanover Co., pp. 1-12A. Pages 1 through part of page 4 are Town of Wilmington. The numbering of these pages is similar to Brunswick Co., roll 29, above: 1, 2, 1A, 2A, 3, 4, 3A, 4A, etc.
Richmond Co., pp. 242-271.
Rowan Co., pp. 276-278, 284-460 (handwritten numbers). Pages 276-278 are Salisbury.
Rutherford Co., pp. 93-156. Part of page 93 is Rutherfordton Town.
Wilkes Co., pp. 24-69.

ROLL 34

Hyde Co., pp. 362-381. Part of page 381 is Germanton. The original copy of page 362 appears on roll 30 between Beaufort and Bertie Cos.
Martin Co., pp. 383-416. Page 388 is Williamston. Page 416 is Jameston.
Northampton Co., pp. 423-487. The four families in Princeton are listed on pages 431, 457, 485 and 487.
Orange Co., pp. 490-619. Pages 490 through 494 are Town of Hillsboro. Page 496 is the University of North Carolina.
Pasquotank Co., pp. 624-641. Including Elizabeth City and Nixonton.
Perquimans Co., pp. 642-663. Including Hertford.
Tyrrell Co., pp. 668-694. Part of page 694 is Elizabeth Town. The original copy of page 668 appears on roll 34 at the end of Washington Co.
Washington Co., pp. 700-716. Part of page 714 through part of page 716 are Plymouth.

INDEX TO THE 1800 CENSUS
OF NORTH CAROLINA

..., ...	Crv 231
...	Crv 235
... (2)	Crv 237
...	Crv 239
...	Crv 243
... (4)	Crv 245
... (8)	Crv 247
...	Crv 249
... (9)	Crv 253
... (3)	Crv 255
... (2)	Crv 297
... (2)	Crv 299
... (3)	Crv 301
...	Crv 303
... (2)	Crv 305
... (4)	Crv 309
... (2)	Crv 325
...	Crv 329
...	Crv 333
...	Crv 337
... (3)	Crv 341
... (3)	Crv 343
...	Jns 809
... (8)	Jns 819
...	Ptt 294
Balam	Brn 16A
Ben	Nrt 469
Benjamin	Grv 528
Dinco	Wrr 801
Free Dick	Cht 197
Green	Ans 198
Jemboy	Bld 27
Joseph	Lnc 901
Joshua	Chw 116
Lewis (a Free Neagro)	Mck 555
Longfield	Crv 255
Moose	Crr 138
Old Lydia	Crr 162
Plumb (a Free Neagro)	Mck 565
Roror	Crr 138
Sam	Hlf 344
Scott, the estate of	Smp 523
Simpson	Brn 17
Tom	Hlf 346
Zachariah	Orn 591
...ace, J...	Nwh 1A
...al...nt, Joshua	Ans 202
...lds, John	Bld 2
...lker, ...	Nwh 10A
...man, ...	Nwh 10A
...nnel, James	Nwh 8A
...rinson, Joseph	Nwh 4A
...well, Thoma	Bld 2

-- A --

A..., 111	Rnd 300
Christopher	Rnd 297
Aaron, Elizabeth	Hlf 286
Henry	Nrt 423
Henry	Stk 595
Abanatha, Joshua	Frn 462
Abanathy, Buckner	Frn 478
Smith	Frn 478
Abberson, Archd.	Csw 107
Abbet, Bettey	Wrn 786
John	Rch 263
George	Bnc 159
William	Cht 160
Abbett, Eliza	Grv 579
John	Orn 542
Abbington, Hardeman	Nrt 423
Abbits, James	Ird 654
Jonathan	Brk 723
Abbot, John	Ons 141
Abbots, Absalom	Brk 721
Abbotson, Joshua	Rwn 363
Abbott, Abram	Wke 714
John	Rck 445
Abedles, Basil	Ird 654
Abel, John	Bnc 159
Thomas	Bnc 159
see Asbel	
Abercromby, Isaac	Ans 206
Aberella, Wikers	Brk 805
Abernathy, Battee	Lnc 845
Billy	Lnc 835
Charles	Lnc 851
David	Lnc 835
David (2)	Lnc 845
David	Lnc 851
Harbert	Lnc 858
Henson	Lnc 845
John (3)	Lnc 845
Jonas	Lnc 845
Joseph	Lnc 852
Jms.	Lnc 835
Martha	Lnc 809
Miles	Lnc 835
Nathan	Lnc 835
Robert	Lnc 845
Robert	Lnc 858
Sally	Lnc 845
Sarah	Lnc 845
Smith	Lnc 835
Sterling	Lnc 845
Turner	Lnc 845
Wm.	Lnc 845

see Abanathy	
Abert, John Geo.	Stk 544
Martin	Stk 625
Abets, Joseph	Brk 720
Abett, Joseph	Cmd 95
Abia, Joseph	Ird 666
Abington, Bowles	Stk 586
Littleberry	Hlf 288
Abot, Martin	Stk 598
Abram, Tamer	Crt 73
Abrams, Job	Ptt 230
Robert	Smp 507
William	Ptt 246
Absalom, Langston	Lnr 1
Abshare, John	Wlk 25
William	Wlk 25
Absher, Christopher	Brk 72
James	Brk 720
Achlen, Phillup	Crr 147
Achor, Cornelius	Rth 93
Achra, John	Rnd 297
William	Rnd 300
Ackis, Elisabeth	Crv 289
Ackiss, Thomas	Psq 641
Acklin, Jeams	Crr 140
Ackling, Charles	Bfr 1
Isaac	Bfr 1
Joshua	Bfr 1
Ormont	Bfr 1
see Alling	
Aclin, Christopher	Crv 331
Acock, Abner	Wrr 787
Britain	Wke 716
Brittian	Wrr 788
Edmond	Wke 716
John	Wke 716
Jonathan	Rwn 406
Robert	Wrr 787
William	Rbs 360
Acre, Abreham	Wrr 788
Edward	Brt 26
Hendley	Brt 26
Isaac	Wrr 788
Isaac, Junr.	Wrr 788
John, Junr.	Brt 26
John, Senr.	Brt 26
Joshua	Wrr 788
Leonard	Brt 26
William	Brt 26
Acton, John	Bnc 158
Robert	Rck 489
Adam, George	Rwn 417
John	Rwn 414
Robert	Cmb 351
Shroate	Rwn 290

Adams, ...min	Ptt 226	Mathew	Wlk 24	Ephraim	Ans 205
Abednego	Rth 94	Michael	Jns 789	Francis	Crr 167
Abednigo	Lnc 894	Mss	Srr 631	Harrison	Ons 136
Abigail	Wsh 700	Nathan	Crt 79	Henry	Bnc 158
Abraham, junior	Ptt 252	Peter	Prq 658	Howel	Hlf 286
Abraham, Senr.	Ptt 252	Philip	Wsh 700	John	Brn 14A
Abraham	Rwn 440	Phillip	Wke 716	John, Senr.	Mnt 495
Abram	Bfr 1	Polly	Rth 94	Richd.	Wlk 25
Absalom	Ptt 257	Reading	Edg 179	Thomas	Cmd 102
Absalom	Rbs 359	Reuben	Smp 498	Thos.	Hlf 286
Anne	Wlk 25	Reubin	Lnc 872	William	Brn 14
Archibald,		Richart	Rch 251	William	Crr 167
Junr.	Ptt 285	Samuel	Bfr 1	William	Xrr 631
Archibald,		Samuel	Brn 575	Wm.	Csw 107
Senior	Ptt 250	Samuel	Mck 598	Adkinson, Benjn.	Nwh 12
Benjamin	Bld 19	Simon	Csw 99	Britt	Rbs 358
Benjamin	Brk 721	Spencer (2)	Wlk 25	Danl.	Nwh 12
Benja.	Hlf 286	Susanna	Jns 789	Elisha	Jns 815
Benjn.	Wlk 25	Thomas	Hde 362	James	Nrt 423
Betey	Jhn 774	Thomas	Ptt 249	Joel	Rbs 359
Bryan	Jhn 773	Thomas	Stk 544	John	Cmb 380
Charles	Wlk 24	Thos.	Wlk 24	John	Nsh 86
Charles	Wlk 25	William	Ans 212	John	Nwh 11A
Daniel	Rwn 440	William	Bfr 1	Joseph	Rbs 359
Elijah	Brt 26	William	Brk 722	Saml.	Nwh 12
Elijah	Mck 567	William	Edg 179	Thomas	Ans 234
Elisha	Brk 722	William	Glf 667	William	Rbs 359
Elizabeth	Rbs 360	William	Hde 362	William	Ash 72
Enos	Stk 615	William	Jns 789	Adkison, John	Mre 49
George	Rck 451	William	Orn 497	Adkisson, James	Jhn 750
George	Srr 631	William	Ptt 250	Josiah	Jhn 751
Henry	Wlk 25	William	Rwn 406	Thomas	Jhn 754
Isaac	Bfr 1	William	Stk 544	Admire, Elisabeth	Rwn 435
Isaac	Rwn 440	William	Wlk 24	Adom, John	Mck 549
Jacob	Jhn 769	William, Jr.	Srr 631	Adoms, Elizebeth	Crr 149
Jacob	Rwn 315	William, Son of		Wm.	Mrt 383
Jacob	Rwn 440	Abm.	Ptt 257	Adrage, William,	
Jacob	Wlk 25	William, Sr.	Srr 631	Senr.	Rwn 414
James	Edg 179	Willoughby	Rbs 359	Adydelett, Obedh.	Glf 620
James	Ird 638	Adamson see Shaw		Aford, William	Wlk 25
James	Orn 497	Adcason, William	Rth 94	Agenor, David	Rwn 295
James	Rwn 406	Adcock, Andrew	Grv 575	Henry	Rwn 294
James	Srr 631	Henry	Ans 201	Ager, Cherry	Brt 26
James	Wsh 700	Jesse	Grv 572	Agers, Daniel	Ash 72
Jane	Wlk 24	John	Orn 499	Landrine	Ash 72
Jesse	Nsh 87	John, Senr.	Grv 571	William	Ash 72
Jesse	Rwn 430	Roland	Grv 572	Agerton, Charles	Ons 155
Jesse	Wlk 24	Seeny	Grv 571	James	Ons 155
Jno.	Lnc 836	Tabutha	Grv 577	Joseph	Rnd 298
John	Ash 72	Adcok, John, jur.	Grv 571	Agle, George	Rwn 311
John	Brk 720	Addcock, Joshua	Cht 166	John	Rwn 300
John	Crt 83	Adderholt, Fred-		Philip	Rwn 312
John	Cmb 374	erick	Lnc 809	Agness, Francis	Lnc 837
John	Glf 653	George	Lnc 809	Agnew, John	Orn 497
John	Orn 497	Jacob	Lnc 809	Ahling see Ackling	
John	Orn 499	Adderson, James	Rnd 298	Ahurt, Jacob	Csw 128
John	Ptt 285	Thomas	Rnd 298	Aimes, Edwd.	Mrt 383
John	Rwn 284	Adderton, Jeromiah	Rwn 377	Elisabeth	Mrt 383
John	Rwn 304	John	Rwn 377	Thos.	Mrt 383
John	Rwn 406	Addeson, Elijah	Crr 137	Aingel, George	Hlf 286
John	Wlk 24	Adenger, Frederick	Rwn 346	Ainsly, William	Rwn 417
John	Wlk 25	Aderage, Nicholas	Rwn 414	Ainsworth, James	Rth 93
John, junr.	Wlk 25	William	Rwn 414	Airs, David, Senr.	Wsh 700
John, Senr.	Rwn 406	Aderman, John	Dpl 407	Isaac, Junr.	Wsh 700
Jonathan	Srr 631	Aderson, John	Rnd 298	Isaac, Senr.	Wsh 700
Joseph	Crt 87	Aderton, Isaac	Hrt 722	John	Ash 72
Joseph	Grv 575	Adge, Disa	Bld 6	John	Wsh 700
Joseph	Psq 625	Elizabeth	Bld 43	Nathan	Wsh 700
Joseph	Wke 714	James	Bld 43	Ajah, Noah	Ans 207
Joshua	Bfr 1	John	Bld 43	Akeles, John	Rwn 360
Joshua	Wke 714	John, Senr.	Bld 43	Akem, Jacob, Junr.	Crv 319
Levi	Ans 212	Adkerson, Ann	Rck 447	Akeman, Anny	Cht 152
Levisa	Rch 265	John	Rck 485	Akin, Godfrey	Grv 561
Lewis	Jhn 771	Adkin, Jesse	Nwh 7A	Isham	Grv 560
Martha	Wsh 700	Mary	Rth 94	James	Rck 436
Mary	Hde 362	William	Rth 94	John	Grv 534
Mary	Ons 161	Adkins, ...	Nwh 10A	Joseph	Grv 513

Taply	Stk 595
William	Grv 567
William	Glf 631
Akins, John	Rth 94
Joseph	Rth 94
Thomas	Rth 94
Akles, Henry	Rwn 361
Alberson, John	Ons 168
Samuel	Ptt 279
Solomon	Ptt 265
Tany	Rnd 350
Yerley	Ptt 265
Albert, Joseph	Wne 849
Mary	Orn 499
Richard	Bfr 1
see Abert	
Albertson, Benja-	
min, sen.	Prq 646
Benjn., Jun.	Prq 658
Chalkley	Prq 645
David	Dpl 439
Edward	Dpl 439
Francis	Prq 658
John	Rnd 300
Joseph	Prq 650
Mary	Prq 644
Mary	Prq 662
Phinehas	Prq 646
Samuel	Dpl 439
Samuel	Prq 649
Samuel	Prq 658
Samuel	Rnd 300
Sarah	Dpl 403
Thomas	Prq 651
Tinea	Prq 650
William	Dpl 439
William	Psq 629
Alberty, Frederick	Srr 631
Albright, Daniel	Orn 498
George (2)	Orn 498
Henry	Orn 498
Jacob	Orn 499
Jacob	Rwn 344
John (2)	Orn 498
John	Rwn 345
John, Junr.	Orn 498
Joseph	Orn 498
Ludwick	Orn 499
Ludwick, Junr.	Orn 498
Michael	Rwn 339
Peter	Rwn 344
Philip	Orn 498
William	Psq 630
William	Glf 648
Albriton, Adam	Ptt 226
Joel	Ptt 226
Albritton, Enoch	Ptt 257
Henry	Ptt 253
James	Grn 602
Jonathan	Ptt 251
Luke	Ptt 227
Peter	Ptt 256
Albrooks, Jesse	Rch 262
Saml.	Ans 238
Willis	Ans 238
Albud, Solomon	Rth 94
Alckerson, Peter	Rck 446
Alcock, Shadrach	Trl 690
Solomon	Crr 155
Stephen	Trl 690
Vilany	Jns 799
William	Trl 690
Alcorn, John	Glf 657
Widow	Mck 569
Alday, Seth	Stk 589
Alder, Margret	Brk 721
Alderage, Ruth	Srr 706

Alderman, Daniel	
(2)	Dpl 408
David (2)	Dpl 408
John, Jr.	Dpl 407
Tho.	Nwh 7
Alderson, John,	
Jur.	Hde 362
John, Ser.	Hde 362
Simon	Hde 362
Thomas	Bfr 24
Aldise, Wm.	Csw 144
Aldrage, John	Mnt 467
Aldred, Finias	Rch 254
John	Ans 239
Aldridge, Isham	Prs 216
John	Grn 611
John	Lnr 1
John	Rck 485
Joseph	Prs 216
Joseph	Srr 633
Peter	Prs 216
Thomas	Grn 610
Thos.	Lnr 1
William	Grn 611
William	Srr 633
Aldrige, Calib	Mck 588
Alems, Charles	Mck 546
Alerden, Isaac	Cmd 100
Ales, Jeams	Crr 157
see Oles	
Alexander, Abdin	Mck 545
Abijah	Ird 666
Abner	Mck 546
Abner	Trl 676
Abram	Cbr 681
Abram Ird 638	Ird 638
Abram	Trl 676
Absalom	Mck 546
Alexander	Mnt 474
Alin	Mck 554
Allin	Ird 643
Amos	Mck 551
Amos	Mck 560
Andrew	Cbr 680
Anthony	Trl 668
Augustus	Mck 542
Benjamin	Trl 670
Benjn.	Cvr 681
Charles	Mck 572
Charles, Junr.	Mck 542
Charles, Senr.	Mck 542
Charles T.	Mck 573
Cornelius	Trl 676
Dan	Brk 722
Dann	Mck 554
Dann	Mck 557
David	Rck 460
Edward	Trl 668
Elias	Mck 545
Elias	Mck 556
Elias	Rth 93
Elijah	Mck 557
Elijah	Rck 459
Elisha	Rck 459
Enoch	Crv 241
Evan	Mck 559
Evan	Rwn 276
Even	Rwn 284
Everet, Sr.	Jhn 769
Ezekiel	Mck 549
Ezekiel	Trl 686
Ezra	Mck 546
Francis	Mck 569
Gabriel	Ird 643
George	Cbr 680
George	Glf 620
George, Esq.	Mck 542

Gideon	Trl 684
Henry	Trl 676
Hezekiah	Cbr 681
Hezekiah, Jun.	Mck 543
Isaac	Mck 526
Isaac	Trl 676
James	Bnc 158
James	Brk 720
James	Cbr 681
James	Glf 621
James	Ird 638
James	Ird 643
James	Mck 542
James	Mck 550
James	Mck 551
James	Orn 498
James	Rwn 315
James, Junr.	Orn 498
James, R.R.	Mck 566
Jediah	Mck 547
Jesse	Trl 668
Jesse	Wlk 25
Joab	Mck 556
John	Bnc 159
John	Cbr 681
John	Glf 622
John	Lnc 809
John	Lnc 873
John (2)	Lnc 894
John	Mck 554
John	Trl 670
John	Trl 676
John, Senr.	Trl 676
John McN.	Mck 551
Joseph	Brk 720
Joseph	Cbr 681
Joseph	Ird 643
Joseph	Lnc 859
Joseph	Mck 550
Joseph	Rth 93
Josiah	Mck 567
Josiah	Mck 569
Josiah	Mck 572
Martha	Glf 634
Martha	Trl 674
Moses	Cbr 681
Moses (Red)	Cbr 681
Nathaniel	Mck 557
Nathl.	Mck 526
Noble	Brk 721
Ozea	Mck 555
Paris	Mck 545
Phineas	Mck 522
Prudence	Mck 570
Richard	Lnc 858
Robert	Brk 720
Robert	Cbr 681
Robert	Lnc 825
Robt., Junr.	Lnc 825
Rubin	Ird 638
Rubin	Lnc 858
Samuel	Brk 721
Samuel	Mck 542
Samuel	Rnd 300
Sarah	Trl 674
Silas	Mck 544
Stephen	Cbr 681
Thomas	Bnc 158
Thomas (2)	Mck 557
Thomas	Mck 565
Tibles	Hrt 708
Traverse	Wlk 25
Wallace	Lnc 809
Widow	Mck 545
Widow	Mck 557
Widow	Mck 561
Widow	Mck 573

3

Name	Ref	Name	Ref	Name	Ref
William	Brk 721	Ezekiel	Cmb 371	Shadrach	Crn 317
William	Mck 545	Fanny	Hrt 737	Shadrack	Ptt 247
William	Mck 553	George	Gts 261	Sherwood	Orn 540
William	Mck 554	George	Rck 440	Solomon	Rck 470
William	Mck 564	George	Wrr 786	Tabitha	Nrt 423
William	Trl 676	George, Junr.	Orn 497	Taply	Stk 544
William	Trl 686	George, Senr.	Orn 497	Thomas	Jhn 770
William	Trl 692	George, Sn.	Wrr 788	Thomas	Rth 94
William	Trl 694	Gideon	Jhn 776	Thomas	Srr 633
William	Wlk 25	Gray	Ans 207	Thos.	Wlk 24
William, Senr.	Mck 572	Henry	Cmb 351	Valentine	Rck 480
William, Senr.	Trl 670	Henry	Dpl 421	Vincent	Lnc 864
William B.	Mck 550	Henry	Wsh 700	Vinsent	Wrr 786
William B.	Mck 554	Jacob	Ans 231	Will.	Prs 192
William L.	Rwn 276	Jacob	Rbs 360	William (2)	Bnc 159
William L.	Rwn 284	James	Nwh 2	William	Cht 213
William Lm.	Cbr 676	James	Rnd 297	William	Grv 557
Willis	Wlk 25	James	Rch 258	William	Hlf 286
Zebn.	Mck 545	James	Wrr 786	William	Jhn 773
Zeanis	Mck 530	Jarves	Crr 141	William	Orn 497
Alexanders, Benjn.	Nwh 7A	Jeremiah	Nrt 423	William	Orn 540
Joseph	Nwh 7A	Jesse	Hde 362	William	Rbs 360
Alfin, Thomas	Jns 789	Jesse	Nrt 423	William	Trl 674
Alford, Benjamin	Wne 871	Jesse	Stk 544	William	Wlk 24
Cane	Wke 714	John	Bfr 1	William H.	Rck 484
Drury	Wke 716	John	Bld 29	William, (Car-	
Etheldrel	Wne 868	John	Bnc 158	penter)	Wrr 786
Gutridge	Frn 469	John	Brk 720	William, (so	
Hudson	Wke 716	John	Crv 317	Chs.)	Wrr 786
Isaac	Frn 469	John	Crr 142	William, (so	
James	Rbs 358	John	Frn 458	Jas.)	Wrr 788
Jobe	Wke 716	John	Hlf 286	Zachariah	Grv 534
John	Frn 469	John	Lnc 858	Zachh.	Bld 20
John	Frn 487	John	Nwh 2A	Allender, Betsey	Hlf 286
John	Trl 690	John	Nrt 423	Thomas	Rwn 370
Kinchen	Frn 452	John	Orn 498	Allerson, Charles	Prs 214
Kinchen	Frn 468	John	Rck 439	Alleson, John	Orn 491
Lodwick	Wke 714	John	Rth 94	Allexander, John	Orn 497
Lodwick	Wne 868	John	Srr 631	Alley, Rosser	Frn 482
Mary	Rbs 359	John, F.R.	Srr 633	Saml.	Wke 716
Sarah	Wne 859	John, H.F.	Orn 497	Shadrick	Ird 654
Sion	Rbs 358	Jonathan	Ash 72	Alligood, Hillory	Jns 795
Warren	Rbs 359	Jonathan	Srr 631	Allimong, Betsy	Rwn 284
Alfred, Jesse	Ptt 293	Jonathan	Wlk 26	Frederick	Rwn 284
Algea, Widow	Mck 528	Joseph	Crv 319	Allin, Alexander	Cbr 677
Alin, James	Mre 47	Joseph	Rck 452	Alexander	Mck 574
Aliskey, John	Stk 596	Joseph	Rck 473	Ananias	Brk 720
Alison, Hamilton	Orn 541	Juleus	Ans 207	Andrew	Mck 579
Joseph	Orn 541	Levicy	Rck 449	Bartlet	Wke 716
Alkins, James	Mnt 504	Lewis	Bnc 158	Benjamin	Mck 536
John	Mnt 485	Lucey	Ptt 277	Champain	Grv 564
Alkinson, John	Jns 748	Martha	Crv 317	David	Wke 716
Allan, Elkanah (2)	Brn 13	Mathew	Grv 529	Drury	Prs 203
Allay, Benjamin	Wke 717	Merriday	Ans 234	George	Ird 654
Joseph	Wke 717	Merryman	Ptt 273	George	Mck 555
Samuel	Wke 717	Moses	Rnd 353	George	Mnt 468
Allegood, Benjamin	Bfr 1	Nathan	Jhn 773	George	Mnt 495
Francis, Senr.	Bfr 1	Nathaniel	Chw 116	George	Wke 716
Jacob	Bfr 1	Porter	Orn 540	George, Senr.	Mck 557
John	Bfr 1	Raphel	Hde 362	Gideon	Brk 720
see Wollard		Reuben	Bnc 159	Hugh	Rwn 335
Allemong, Betsy	Rwn 276	Richard	Ans 210	James	Brk 720
Fredrick	Rwn 276	Richard	Crr 142	James	Lnc 873
Allen, ...	Trl 670	Richard	Grn 596	James	Mck 537
Ann	Rck 458	Richard	Wlk 24	James	Mnt 495
Anna	Brt 26	Richd.	Rth 93	Jesse	Wke 716
Ben	Frn 459	Robert	Grv 521	John	Mck 530
Benjamin	Ans 210	Robert	Orn 541	John	Mnt 468
Charles	Rth 93	Robert	Wrr 788	John	Rwn 455
Charles	Wrr 786	Rodger	Ptt 281	John, Junr.	Brk 720
Charles, Senr.	Wrr 786	Saml.	Wlk 24	Joseph	Mnt 476
Daniel, Senr.	Rck 473	Samuel	Bnc 159	Joseph	Mre 71
Darlen	Ans 207	Samuel	Grv 521	Joseph	Rwn 455
David	Prs 203	Samuel	Rnd 297	Josiah	Wke 716
Drury	Ans 234	Samuel	Rck 470	Kinsman	Wke 716
Drury	Rth 93	Sarah	Nrt 423	Moses	Ird 638
Elwen	Dpl 421	Sarey	Ptt 282	Reynolds (2)	Ird 608

Name	Ref
Rubin	Mnt 468
Rubin	Rwn 455
Ruthey	Wke 714
Samuel	Mnt 468
Samuel	Mnt 511
Thomas	Cbr 711
Thomas	Rwn 310
Thomas	Rwn 455
William	Bnc 158
William	Mnt 495
William, C.	Mnt 476
William, Senr.	Mck 533
William R.	Mnt 515
William S.	Mck 555
Young	Wke 714
Alling, Parryunon	Bfr 1
see Ackling	
Allirson, David	Orn 540
Allison, Adam	Ird 663
Alexander	Glf 666
Andrew	Mck 547
Andrew	Rwn 286
Anthony	Lnc 833
Archibald	Mck 547
Benjam	Brk 723
Benjamin	Brk 722
Benjn.	Wlk 24
Burch	Brk 722
Ephriam	Wlk 24
Esther	Ird 669
Ezekiel	Brk 723
Ezekiel	Glf 670
Francis	Brk 722
Henry	Brk 723
Henry	Nrt 423
Hugh	Ash 72
James	Orn 541
James	Wlk 24
John	Grv 537
John	Glf 629
John	Orn 541
Joseph	Ird 619
Martha	Orn 541
Perey	Brk 722
Richard	Ird 670
Robert	Cbr 681
Robert	Glf 621
Samuel	Glf 621
Theophilus	Ird 646
Thiophelus	Ird 663
Thomas	Brk 721
Thomas	Ird 664
Thos.	Wlk 24
William	Ash 72
William	Brk 722
William	Ird 619
William	Ird 663
William (2)	Wlk 24
Allred, Betty	Rnd 297
Eli	Rnd 297
Elias	Rnd 300
Francis	Rnd 300
Isaac	Rnd 297
James	Rnd 297
James	Rnd 300
John (3)	Rnd 297
John	Rnd 300
Jonathan	Rnd 298
Joseph	Rnd 300
Margarett	Rnd 300
Sarah	Rnd 300
Thomas	Rnd 300
William	Rnd 297
Allridge, Ezekiel	Rnd 300
Mariam	Rnd 300
Allsbrook, Bethena	Edg 180
Joseph	Edg 180
Samuel	Edg 180
Allspack, Henry	Stk 600
Allston, Peter	Bld 6
Allum, James	Lnc 899
Ally, Edmd.	Csw 128
Edwd.	Csw 112
Almeny, Benjamin	Ird 654
Almon, Edward	Mnt 511
Gideon	Cbr 704
Nathan	Jhn 775
Nathan	Mnt 510
Richard	Mnt 506
Thomas	Mnt 510
Almond, Canady	Wke 714
Almore, Athen	Cbr 684
Alnut, William	Srr 631
Alphen, Jesse	Wne 847
Alphin, Hezekiah	Gts 261
Joseph	Gts 261
Alran, John	Brk 722
Alred, Jonathan	Rch 249
William	Glf 621
Also, Elizabeth	Dpl 418
John	Dpl 418
Alsobrook, Celah	Hlf 288
David	Hlf 288
Drew	Hlf 286
Edward	Orn 493
Howel, Jr.	Hlf 288
Howel, Sr.	Hlf 288
James	Hlf 288
Jno., Jur.	Hlf 288
John, Sen.	Hlf 288
William	Hlf 288
Willie	Hlf 288
Wm., Sen.	Hlf 288
Alsop, Joseph	Ans 237
Alston, Ann	Hrt 696
George	Grv 537
Gideon	Hlf 286
James	Cht 223
James	Wrr 787
Jno., Senr.	Wke 716
John	Cht 223
John	Wrr 786
John, Junr.	Wke 717
John Jos.	Hlf 288
John Joseph	Cht 152
Jos. John	Hlf 286
Joseph Jno.	Cht 206
Martha	Wrr 787
Oran	Cht 153
Philip, jn.	Wrr 787
Philip, Sr.	Wrr 787
Robert W.	Hlf 286
Samuel	Wrr 787
Thomas	Wrr 787
Thomas, jr.	Wrr 787
Thomas, (so H.)	Wrr 786
W. Robert	Hlf 286
William	Hlf 286
William	Wrr 787
Willis, Jr.	Hlf 286
Willis, Senr.	Hlf 286
Altom, Charls	Rnd 297
Alves, Walter	Orn 499
Alvez, Andrew	Cmb 351
Alvy, Feilding	Wlk 25
William	Wlk 25
Always, Henry	Crv 335
John	Crv 339
Meshach	Crv 339
Obediah	Crv 339
Aman, Jesse	Ons 172
Philip	Ons 170
Ambers, Daniel	Ons 158
Amberson, Solomon	Bfr 1
William	Rwn 414
Ambres, Esther	Trl 676
James	Trl 676
James	Wsh 700
Micajah	Wsh 700
Shimee	Wsh 700
Ambrose, Sarah	Wke 716
Amburn, Leanea	Brk 721
Amek, John	Rnd 297
John, J.	Rnd 297
Nicholas	Rnd 298
Peter	Rnd 300
Amerson, Benjamin	Edg 179
Eli	Edg 179
Isaac (2)	Edg 179
John	Edg 179
Manoah	Edg 179
William	Edg 179
Amery, Aaron	Mrt 383
Ames, John	Grv 548
see Amis	
Amick, Mathias	Glf 633
Amis, Lewis	Grv 549
Mary	Bld 11
William	Grv 535
William	Grv 584
William	Nrt 423
William, Senr.	Grv 550
see Ames	
Ammon, Martin	Mnt 513
Ammonds, Isaac	Brk 720
Ammons, Howell	Rbs 359
Isam	Smp 533
Jesse	Wne 866
Joshua	Rbs 359
Joshua	Rbs 360
Vaughan	Smp 533
Amon, John	Bnc 158
Amond, Elisabeth	Rch 257
Amonds, Mark	Brk 720
Amos, Charles	Wke 714
James	Hlf 286
John	Rck 443
John	Stk 579
John	Wke 716
William	Wke 716
Amyst, Amos	Jns 785
Daniel	Jns 815
Darius	Jns 799
Enoch	Jns 797
John	Jns 809
Susanna	Jns 799
Anders, Anne	Bld 49
Elisha	Bld 47
Evan, Capt.	Bld 49
John, Senr.	Bld 47
Samuel	Bld 24
Thomas	Cht 214
Anderson, Abel	Bnc 159
Abraham	Orn 542
Abraham, Junr.	Orn 541
Andrew	Mrt 383
Ann	Mrt 383
Augustine	Grv 561
Campbell	380
Charles	Crv 271
Charles	Nrt 423
Churchwell	Nsh 86
Daniel	Stk 619
David	Cmb 351
David	Orn 540
David	Rwn 339
Eli C.	Bnc 159
Enoch	Rth 94
Francis	Grv 556
Franciss	Mrt 383
Frank	Wke 716

Name	Ref	Name	Ref	Name	Ref
Frederick	Crv 271	William	Cmb 379	Thomas	Cht 181
George	Ash 72	William	Cmb 380	Thomas	Rnd 300
George	Cmb 391	William	Cmb 391	Thos.	Mrt 383
George	Edg 179	William	Edg 171	Wallis	Bfr 1
George	Grv 583	William (2)	Edg 179	Warrin, Esqr.	Mrt 383
George	Prs 187	William	Ird 619	Whitdon	Edg 179
Henry	Mrt 383	William	Ird 638	Whitmel	Smp 508
Henry (Cohy.)	Edg 179	William	Orn 499	Wholston	Frn 466
Henry (TR)	Edg 179	William	Ptt 260	Widow	Rnd 297
Isaac	Crv 319	William, Sen.	Edg 179	William	Brt 26
Isaac	Grv 545	William, Senr.	Mck 562	William	Frn 493
Isaac	Grv 585	Winefred	Mrt 383	William	Jns 793
Isaac	Lnc 887	Wm.	Crr 159	William	Lnr 1
Isaac	Rwn 323	Andes, Andrew	Cmb 381	William	Orn 498
Jacob	Brn 17	James	Nwh 7	William	Stk 579
Jacob	Grv 543	Stephen	Nwh 4	William	Wke 714
James	Brn 21	William	Nwh 7	William	Wrr 787
James	Bnc 159	Andrew, Alfred	Cmb 376	William, Jur.	Frn 483
James	Crv 269	Daniel	Brk 720	Andrus, David	Mnt 485
James	Cmb 368	Daniel	Jns 799	James	Mnt 485
James	Cmb 378	Francis	Jns 797	Andstred, Henry	Hlf 286
James	Edg 179	George	Rwn 319	Ang...w, William	Rnd 297
James	Hlf 286	Hannah	Crt 80	Ange, Franciss	Mrt 383
James	Orn 497	Hugh	Ird 615	Thos.	Mrt 383
James	Rwn 339	James	Brt 56	Angel, John	Rth 94
James, S.	Bnc 158	James	Dpl 416	Nicholas	Bnc 158
Jas.	Prs 190	James	Ird 619	William	Bnc 158
Jean	Orn 499	James	Rwn 319	see Aingel	
Jesse	Bnc 159	James, Junr.	Rwn 445	Angle, Charles	Stk 590
Jinnett	Orn 499	John	Jns 797	James	Stk 588
John	Brn 16A	John	Rwn 445	John	Stk 544
John	Brn 17	John	Wlk 24	Joshua	Lnc 901
John	Csw 140	Joseph	Wlk 25	Lawrance	Stk 592
John	Ird 638	Mark	Glf 645	Peter	Brk 721
John	Nwh 5A	Moses	Cbr 681	Anglin, Nancey	Bnc 158
John	Orn 540	Robert	Cbr 681	Wm.	Csw 138
John	Ptt 284	Robert	Wlk 24	Ansell, Jeams	Crr 155
John	Rwn 371	Samuel	Rth 93	Jeams	Crr 161
John	Rth 94	Shadrach	Glf 645	Ansley, Elizabeth	Trl 668
Johnston	Ird 623	William	Cbr 679	Joseph	Trl 670
Joseph	Bfr 1	William	Orn 542	Nathan	Trl 668
Joseph	Orn 540	Andrews, Abigail	Ptt 261	Anthony, Arsla	Csw 125
Keneth	Orn 492	Abraham	Dpl 417	Benjamin	Lnc 887
Lawrence	Ptt 280	Abrum	Frn 488	Creasy	Rth 94
Levi	Bnc 158	Alexander	Mnt 488	Elijah	Csw 135
Lewis	Grv 542	Arden	Mrt 383	George	Lnc 887
Major	Glf 689	Benjamin	Wke 714	Henry	Orn 498
Major	Glf 693	Catey	Ptt 294	Jacob	Brk 721
Mary	Chw 117	Cullin, Orph.	Edg 180	Jacob	Glf 643
Mary	Psq 624	Daniel	Jns 795	Jacob, Senr.	Brk 720
Miles	Wne 845	David	Jns 809	James	Srr 633
Mourning	Edg 179	David	Rnd 297	John	Hlf 286
Nancy	Glf 640	David	Stk 579	Newnan	Rwn 289
Nanny	Dpl 411	David	Wke 714	Obediah	Glf 680
Peter	Grv 582	Dreury	Lnr 1	Paul	Brk 721
Rachel	Brk 722	Drury	Wrr 787	Paul	Lnc 809
Rachel	Edg 179	Elijah	Jns 795	Philip	Lnc 809
Rebekah	Grv 583	Eliza	Hrt 734	Thomas	Srr 633
Richard	Rwn 310	Ethelard	Rwn 455	William	Crv 253
Robert (2)	Bnc 158	Green	Frn 493	William	Srr 633
Robert	Glf 642	Henry	Wke 714	Anthton, John	Hlf 288
Robert	Orn 541	Hermon	Rnd 297	Aoin see Avin	
Robert	Rwn 276	Jesse	Wke 714	Aple, John	Stk 544
Robert	Rwn 284	John	Cht 181	Apley, Daniel	Lnc 809
Robert	Rth 94	John	Edg 179	John	Lnc 809
Samuel	Prq 651	John	Frn 470	John	Lnc 852
Samuel	Rwn 323	John	Jns 795	Aplin, Thomas	Grv 509
Samuel	Rth 94	John	Mnt 489	Apperson, Mary	Brt 26
Samuel	Wlk 24	John	Rwn 323	William	Srr 631
Stephen	Cmb 386	John	Rth 93	Apperty, Isaac	Crv 289
Thomas	Crv 271	Joseph	Grn 613	Apple, Adam	Glf 661
Thomas	Rwn 315	Laborn	Orn 499	Daniel	Glf 661
Thomas	Rwn 323	Lazaras	Cht 219	John	Glf 661
Thomas	Wne 845	Marke	Cht 187	Thomas	Glf 661
Thornberry	Orn 541	Philo	Brt 26	Appleton, John	Mck 583
Wiley	Cmb 392	Philo	Brt 88	John	Stk 544
Will.	Nwh 5A	Robbert	Rnd 300	Applewhite, Elisha	Wne 870

6

Name	Loc	Name	Loc	Name	Loc
Henry	Hlf 286	James	Nwh 3A	Mattiah	Jns 807
Isaac	Wne 871	James	Ptt 243	Richard	Brt 26
John	Wne 850	Jno.	Lnc 833	Richd.	Csw 134
John	Wne 870	John	Brk 720	Robert	Rnd 297
Robert	Wne 863	John	Cmb 386	Samuel	Srr 631
Thos	Hlf 286	John	Dpl 401	Smith	Rnd 297
Applin, Thomas	Srr 631	John	Ird 619	Solomon	Wrr 786
Wm.	Mrt 416	John	Orn 497	Thomas	Bfr 1
Arant, John	Lnc 873	John	Orn 541	Thomas, Senr.	Srr 631
Arcal, William	Prq 643	John	Trl 686	Whitlock	Rnd 298
Archbell, Ja...	Bfr 1	Joseph	Edg 179	William	Gts 261
John, Jur.	Bfr 1	Joseph (2)	Orn 541	William	Grv 566
John, Senr.	Bfr 2	Martin	Rth 94	William	Ptt 254
Nathan	Bfr 2	Martin	Srr 631	William	Srr 631
Archer, Armstrong	Hrt 703	Martin, Sr.	Stk 572	William	Srr 711
Caleb	Hrt 722	Mary	Ptt 254	William	Trl 676
Catharine	Glf 677	Mattw.	Lnc 833	William	Wke 716
David	Glf 664	Myles	Trl 686	Aron, Aquilla	Jhn 757
Ezekiel	Hrt 703	Nathaniel	Brk 721	Aronet, Nelly	Brk 721
Evans	Hrt 703	Robert	Hlf 288	Arpes, Valentine	Prq 655
Hezekiah	Hrt 722	Robt.	Lnc 832	Arrawood, James	Rwn 435
Jacob	Hrt 719	Russell	Trl 674	Arrendill, Thomas	Frn 454
Jesse	Nrt 423	Samuel	Rwn 323	Arrenton, Ezekial	Prq 643
John	Glf 675	Spence	Trl 688	Robert	Prq 656
John	Hlf 358	Thomas	Crv 319	Thomas	Prq 642
Josiah	Hrt 715	Thomas	Cmb 384	William	Prq 652
Peggey	Crr 164	Thomas	Dpl 431	William, Sen.	Prq 642
Redock	Hlf 286	Thomas	Orn 499	Arringdon, John	Ird 608
Relhh	Hrt	Thoma-	Orn 541	Arrington, Fred-	
Thomas	Hrt 715	Thomas	Stk 544	erick	Trl 668
Thomas	Nrt 423	Thomas	Stk 628	Henry	Nsh 86
William	Hrt 703	William	Orn 541	James	Bnc 159
William, jnr.	Hrt 703	William	Rch 266	James	Wrr 787
Zachariah	Mrt 383	William	Wke 775	James, jr.	Wrr 787
Archibald, Elisa-		William, Junr.	Orn 541	John	Nsh 86
beth	Ird 666	Armsworthy, John	Rwn 435	Joseph	Nsh 87
Robt.	Lnc 826	Arnal, Owen	Brn 17A	Joseph, Sr.	Nsh 87
Samuel	Ird 663	Arnald, Nelly	Brn 20A	Mary	Nsh 86
William	Ird 664	Arnat, Philemon	Rbs 359	Peter	Nsh 86
William	Ird 666	Zadok	Rbs 359	William	Nsh 87
Arden, Richard	Srr 710	Arnatt, Joseph	Csw 102	Willis	Hlf 286
Areniel, James	Nwh 2	Arnet, David	Ans 219	Arrinton, Henry	Frn 485
Arging, Margrat	Nwh 1A	David	Ans 234	Arriwood, Benjamin	Lnc 883
Argoe, Robert	Lnr 1	John	Ans 207	Arrowood, Henry	Rwn 430
Arington, John	Edg 179	Peter	Ans 217	James	Rwn 430
Arledge, Isaac	Rnd 297	William	Ans 207	James	Rth 94
Arline, Jesse	Gts 261	Arnett, Silas W.	Crv 239	John, Junr.	Rwn 430
Arliz, William		Vaulinetine	Stk 616	John, Senr.	Rwn 430
(Mulatto)	Edg 179	Arney, Lawrence	Brk 720	Arstin, Benjamin	Brk 721
Arm, Elijah	Ash 72	Arnol, Levy	Ons 140	Artes, Hardy	Wrr 784
Armfield, David	Glf 673	Arnold, Ambrous	Prs 216	Arther, James	Crt 72
Elizabeth	Glf 668	Arthur	Crv 311	John	Rch 247
Elizabeth	Glf 681	Asel	Rnd 300	Lois	Crt 72
Isaac	Glf 673	Clement	Rnd 298	Richard	Crt 72
Jacob	Glf 634	David	Hlf 286	Seth	Crt 72
James	Glf 635	Edward	Ptt 255	Arthur, Edwards	Rth 109
John	Glf 669	Elisabeth	Frn 487	James	Hde 362
Nathan	Glf 670	Elizabeth	Ptt 254	John	Crv 283
William	Glf 666	Field	Rnd 298	John	Orn 498
William	Glf 668	Francis	Rnd 300	Joseph	Ird 659
William, Jur.	Glf 668	Frederick	Mck 579	Losson	Crv 317
William, Senr.	Glf 673	Henry	Glf 676	William	Brk 722
Armistead, Anne	Wsh 714	Henry	Ptt 254	William	Rth 94
John	Wsh 714	Henry	Stk 544	Arthurs, John	Lnc 894
Robert	Wsh 714	Henry, Ser.	Stk 544	Mary	Lnc 894
Sarah	Brt 26	James	Crv 333	Artis, Elizabeth	Hrt 733
Armsted, Anthony	Cht 161	James	Ptt 254	Artur, Tempy	Hlf 286
Carver	Cht 161	Jeremiah	Rnd 297	Asbee, Saml.	Crr 151
William	Rnd 297	John	Crv 267	Asbel, Christian	Rnd 300
Armstrong, Able	Rwn 323	John	Crv 333	Imanuel	Rnd 300
Bennett	Trl 690	John	Gts 261	Nancy	Bfr 1
Edward	Dpl 418	Joseph	Wne 864	William	Rnd 300
Francis	Wsh 700	Joseph, Junr.	Trl 668	Asbell, Joseph	Brt 26
George	Bnc 159	Joseph, Senr.	Trl 716	Asberry, Daniel	Lnc 858
Hugh	Srr 631	Joshua	Psq 638	Asbey, James	Brn 16
Isaac	Rch 266	Linsay	Rth 94	Meady	Brn 16
James	Brk 721	Mary	Cev 283	Asborn, William	Bfr 2

Asbridge, James	Rck 468	John	Hrt 696	Atkirson, Thomas	Orn 499
Asbury, Benjn.	Mrt 383	Jonathan	Hrt 715	Atkison, Amos	Jhn 759
John	Hlf 286	Jonas	Hrt 715	Henry	Csw 98
Ascu, Josiah	Brk 721	Josiah	Brt 26	Atkisson, Barsheba	Jhn 760
Aseley see Onley		Josiah	Edg 179	Jordan	Brt 88
Asgue, William	Cmb 384	Mary (2)	Hrt 708	Nathan	Jhn 760
Ash, Charles	Hlf 286	Miles	Hrt 708	Atten, Richard	Rwn 335
Jesse	Nrt 423	Moses	Mrt 383	Attman, Joel	Wne 844
Kitt	Hlf 286	Nathan	Ons 179	Attom, William,	
Sarah	Hlf 286	Shadrach	Hrt 708	Junr.	Mnt 475
Thomas	Wke 714	Thomas	Brt 26	Atwater, Moses	Orn 499
Ashabarner, Henry	Lnc 901	William	Hrt 708	Moses	Orn 542
Ashbarner, Orban	Lnc 851	Zachry	Hrt 715	Atwell, Eliphat	Bld 48
Ashbee, Abel	Crr 151	see Ascu, Asque		John	Prs 210
Solomon	Crr 152	Askey, John	Orn 497	Atwood, William	Rwn 293
Ashbey, Halifax	Srr 631	Askin, Fanny	Cmb 373	Aubrey, Jarret	Srr 709
Ashburn, Baldy	Brt 88	Askings, Benjamin	Ons 147	Jesse	Rch 268
Lewis	Cht 169	Joseph	Ons 149	Audler, Francis	Rwn 284
William	Stk 544	William	Ons 147	Augdon, James	Jhn 766
Ashburne, Elisha	Brt 26	Askins, James	Crv 279	Aughtrey, Alexan-	
John	Brt 26	Aslin, Salley	Wrr 788	der	Smp 497
Thomas	Brt 26	Asque, John	Grv 527	Cornelius	Smp 530
William	Brt 26	Asten, John	Rck 455	Drury	Smp 531
Ashcraft, Benjamin	Ans 235	Aston, Richard	Rnd 298	Hardy	Smp 523
Thomas	Ans 235	Aston, Samuel	Rnd 300	Isam	Smp 497
William	Ans 235	Atbom see Altom		Isam	Smp 530
Ashe, B. John	Hlf 286	Atcherson, John	Rck 468	Rachel	Smp 530
John B.	Hlf 286	John	Rck 471	Aughtry, John	Smp 531
Saml., Coln.	Nwh 9	John	Rck 477	Newsam	Smp 531
Saml., Maj.	Nwh 9A	Nathan	Rck 466	Theophilus	Smp 530
Saml., Senr.	Nwh 12A	Nathan, Jur.	Rck 466	see Autery	
Samuel	Orn 499	Ates, Loyd	Grv 569	Auldridge, Aron	Cht 213
Ashford, Butlar	Nwh 11A	Atherly, Mary	Crv 287	Aulmon, John	Rch 244
Jno. S.S.	Nwh 8A	Athey, Horatio	Lnc 836	Ausley, David	Cht 162
Sarah	Csw 131	Atkins, Asa	Mnt 500	see Ousley	
Street, Capt.	Bld 28	Barbara	Cmb 392	Aust, Frederick	Stk 544
William	Mnt 477	Charles	Wke 714	Frederick	Stk 628
Ashley, Cairy	Srr 633	Daniel	Orn 497	Leonard	Stk 596
David	Wke 716	Elizabeth	Wke 714	Austan, John	Crv 339
Elizabeth	Chw 124	Ephraim	Mnt 500	Thomas	Crv 339
Francis	Mck 603	Ica	Cmb 374	Austen, Benjamin	Srr 633
James	Orn 540	Isaac	Wke 714	Briant	Mnt 506
Jeremiah	Chw 118	James	Cmb 368	David	Srr 633
Jeremiah	Chw 124	John	Cmb 376	Samuel	Rwn 422
John	Srr 633	Josiah	Wke 714	William	Srr 633
John	Wlk 26	Lewis	Cmb 392	Austill, Armajer	Srr 631
Jonathan	Chw 124	Lewis	Wke 714	Isaac, Junr.	Srr 633
Joseph	Prq 653	Martha	Csw 134	Isaac, Senr.	Srr 633
Joseph	Srr 707	Nicholas	Wke 714	Austin, ...	Hlf 288
Mary	Orn 540	Richard	Cmb 377	Asa	Jhn 768
Mead	Chw 124	Rodham	Wke 714	Drue	Ans 218
Myles	Chw 126	Silas	Rbs 359	Elisha, Junr.	Brk 722
Robert	Orn 541	Thomas	Cmd 110	Elizabeth	Crt 63
William	Chw 119	Thomas	Wke 714	James	Ans 217
William	Mrt 383	William	Wke 714	John	Ans 218
William	Rbs 359	see Alkins		John	Jhn 766
William	Srr 633	Atkinson, Aaron	Ptt 286	Michl.	Ans 233
Ashlin see Acklin		Allen	Ptt 293	Moses	Orn 542
Ashlock, Josiah	Rth 93	Benja.	Nsh 87	Nathan	Brk 722
Ashmore, Walter	Mre 43	Benjamin	Cmb 380	Philip	Brk 722
Ashworth, Aron	Bnc 158	Benjamin (2)	Ptt 276	Richard, Junr.	Ans 218
Elias	Mnt 468	Elijah	Nsh 87	Richd.	Ans 218
John	Bnc 158	Elizabeth	Edg 179	Richd.	Rck 461
John, J.	Bnc 158	Henry	Cmb 380	Samuel, Junr.	Brk 722
Askburn, Lewis	Csw 116	Henry	Nsh 87	Samuel, Senr.	Brk 722
Askeel, William	Rwn 422	James	Nsh 87	William	Ans 218
Askew, Aron	Brt 26	John	Orn 498	William	Brk 722
Benjamin	Jns 817	John	Prs 214	William	Orn 499
Cullin	Hrt 708	John	Rbs 360	Auston, Charles	Wke 716
David	Brt 26	John, Jur.	Nsh 86	Daniel	Crr 169
David	Ptt 267	Nancy	Cht 225	Joseph	Bnc 159
Elisha	Hrt 703	Newel	Nsh 87	Richard	Gts 261
Federick	Ons 179	Richd.	Prs 197	Robert	Bnc 158
George	Hrt 708	Saml.	Wne 852	Sally	Crr 167
James	Hrt 719	William	Cbr 685	Thomas	Bnc 158
Jesse	Mrt 383	William	Hlf 288	Thomas	Crv 287
John (2)	Brt 26	see Adkinson		Thos., Jur.	Crr 168

Thos., Ser.	Crr 168	Aytes, Jethro	Wke 714	Nathan	Jhn 776
Valentine	Wke 714	William	Wke 714	Baggett, Drury	Mnt 488
William	Wke 716	Azwil, Medy	Gts 261	Josiah	Nrt 427
Auten, Josiah	Mck 531			Thomas	Rbs 365
Autery, Alexr.	Mre 74			Baggette, Nathan	Nrt 425
Elijah	Mre 74	-- B --		Baggot, Allen	Ans 222
Frederick	Mre 74			Zeal	Ans 223
James	Mre 74			Baggs, Charles	
see Aughtry		B... see Barks		Frederick	Stk 625
Authridge, Robert	Rbs 359	B..., ...mes	Bld 4	Widow	Mck 568
Auton, Fulkard	Lnc 835	Ann	Bfr 3	Bagitt, Grambry	Nsh 89
Thomas	Bnc 159	Thomas	Bfr 3	Bagley, Benjn.	Cht 184
Autrey, Absalem	Rth 94	B...addy, Rachel	Bfr 3	Docton	Gts 262
Reddin	Ans 231	B...age, John	Bfr 3	Henry	Orn 549
Avan, Nancy	Cht 160	B...ck, Richard	Brf 3	Henry, jr.	Cht 168
William	Cht 161	B...d, William,		Henry, Ser.	Cht 168
Avent, Abner	Hlf 286	Junr.	Bfr 3	Isaiah	Cht 184
William	Nsh 87	William Lon-		John	Prq 645
Avera, Alexander	Cmb 371	...ire	Bfr 3	John, Jun.	Prq 653
David	Ptt 281	B...ddy, John	Bfr 3	Joseph	Prq 644
Richard	Cmb 375	B...ills, Joseph	Bfr 3	Mariam	Prq 654
Thomas	Cmb 374	B...ledge, Richard	Bfr 3	Nathan	Prq 650
Thomas	Cmb 379	B...lount, Nathan-		Nelly	Orn 549
William	Cmb 373	iel	Bfr 3	Robin	Jhn 760
William	Cmb 374	B...lroad, Henry	Bfr 2	Sarah	Prq 650
Averet, David	Crv 269	B...ner, John, S...	Bfr 3	Thomas	Prq 663
John	Crv 269	B...nt, Kathrine	Bfr 3	Wasmon	Wke 722
Samuel	Crv 269	B...ow, John	Bfr 3	William	Prq 643
Solomon	Mck 585	John, Junr.	Bfr 3	William	Prq 663
William	Bld 37	B...own, Ephraim	Bfr 3	William	Wke 722
Averett, Abner	Jns 815	B...t, Bryan	Bfr 3	William	Wrn 789
Hannah	Jns 815	B...unt, Michael	Bfr 3	William	Wlk 28
James	Edg 180	B...yd, Coleman	Bfr 3	Wm.	Mrt 386
James	Grn 597	Bab, John	Cht 202	Bagly, Elizabeth	Smp 497
Averit, Lewis	Bld 36	Moses	Cht 202	Bagnal, Joseph	Edg 183
Averitt, Thomas	Bld 29	Babb, Christopher	Wke 719	Bagwell, Daniel	Wke 722
Avery, Aventon	Jhn 769	Jesse	Wke 719	Lundford	Rth 95
Henry	Jhn 768	John	Frn 480	Nathan	Wke 722
James	Crv 319	Matthew	Wke 719	Nathaniel	Ird 617
James	Crv 335	Stephen	Bnc 163	William	Wke 722
James	Wke 716	Thomas	Frn 485	Bailes, John	Glf 672
John	Chw 119	Baber, Benjamin	Rth 100	John	Glf 691
John	Jhn 769	James	Rth 95	Stephen	Bnc 160
John	Mnt 476	John	Rth 95	Bailess, Thomas	Rwn 456
Robert	Prq 657	John	Rth 96	Bailey, Abner	Orn 547
Samuel	Jhn 769	William	Rth 100	Ancil	Brk 728
Thomas	Bld 46	Baccus, James	Gts 261	Benjamin	Crv 341
Thomas	Jhn 770	Thomas	Gts 261	Benjamin	Nrt 425
Thomas	Rwn 346	Bachford, Alixan-		Bethuel	Hde 363
Waightstel	Brk 723	der	Edg 187	Carr	Rwn 422
Aves, Penelope	Brt 26	Bachelor, Eliza-		Charles	Brk 730
Avin, John	Cht 207	beth	Dpl 415	David	Jhn 756
William	Cht 207	Bachus, Thomas	Chw 117	David	Psq 636
Awalt, Michael	Cbr 698	Backham, Charles	Glf 666	David	Srr 705
Awls, Alligood	Grn 601	Backhurst, Allen	Crt 90	Ephraim	Grv 524
Evan	Grn 604	Backnett, Uriah	Srr 635	Francis	Mck 560
Frederick	Grn 601	Bacus, John, Senr.	Mrt 385	Israel	Grv 524
Gideon	Grn 601	Baden, Lydda	Edg 186	Jane	Crv 255
Jolly	Grn 601	Badger, Joshua	Wlk 27	Jeremiah	Grv 524
Axiam, Matthew	Grn 617	Susanna	Crv 243	Jerry	Rnd 302
Axiem, Francis	Ans 200	Badget, Benton	Grv 559	John	Grv 570
Axton, Robert,		William	Grv 582	John	Orn 559
Jur.	Rck 443	william	Jns 787	John	Rnd 302
Axum, William	Ans 216	Badgett, James	Srr 635	John	Rwn 390
Aycock, James	Wne 850	Badgit, John	Grv 580	John	Rwn 423
Jesse	Wne 850	Badham, John	Chw 114	John, Senr.	Brk 726
Aydelett, Judiah	Glf 655	William	Chw 121	Jonathan	Crv 339
Zadoc	Glf 655	Badley, Charles	Crr 153	Joseph	Lnc 873
Aydolett, Benjamin	Glf 669	Bagby, Davis	Hlf 288	Joshua	Hde 362
Parker	Glf 670	John	Wld 28	Matthew	Nrt 423
Thomas	Glf 669	Thos.	Hlf 288	Noah Jesse	Hde 364
Ayers, Mary	Ans 225	Bagett, Peter	Prs 203	Polley	Hde 363
William	Glf 635	Thomas	Prs 212	Richard	Grv 523
Aylett, Henry	Cmd 102	Baggatt, Barton	Rbs 366	Robert	Stk 575
Ayres, Baker	Srr 631	Bagge, Charles F.	Stk 598	Samuel	Hde 363
John	Srr 633	Bagget, Drury	Wke 720	Samuel	Rwn 423
Ayrs, Robert	Brk 722	Josiah	Jhn 776	Simon	Hde 364

Stephen Mnt 484
Thomas Ird 619
Thomas Mck 548
William Brk 725
William Grv 541
William Hlf 292
William Hde 362
William Ird 623
William Lnc 871
William Lnc 888
William Orn 546
William Rnd 302
William Rwn 455
Wm. Prs 195
Yancey Prs 196
see Baley, Barley,
   Briley
Baily, Cathrine Rth 95
Charles Bnc 161
Gabriel Psq 641
James Dpl 438
Jesse Psq 641
John Psq 632
John Psq 641
Josiah Psq 641
Levi Bnc 160
Lewis Rth 94
Mary Smp 520
Patrick Psq 641
Robert Crt 89
Samuel Rth 98
Stephen Bnc 160
Thomas Psq 626
Thomas Psq 641
Thomas Rth 95
William Bnc 160
William Bnc 161
Bain, Daniel Cht 153
James Rnd 301
Jonathan Rnd 304
Robert Cbr 676
Thomas Orn 545
William Cbr 676
Baines, Joseph Ans 209
Bains, Absalom Frn 480
Demsey Cmd 107
Engabur Prq 654
George, Jun. Chw 121
George, Sen. Chw 121
John Crv 579
Labon Rsh 92
Sarah Chw 120
William Chw 121
Baird, Bedent Bnc 160
Jms. Lnc 836
Jno. (2) Lnc 836
Jno., Senr. Lnc 836
Saml. Lnc 836
Will. Prs 196
Wm. Lnc 836
Zebulon Bnc 160
see Biard
Baity, William Rth 98
Bak..., Archibald Cmb 365
Baken, William Gts 262
Baker, Abraham Lnc 810
Alexander Rth 96
Allen Nsh 92
Ambrose Mnt 485
Archd. Nsh 89
Archibald Cmb 372
Arthur Nwh 10A
Asa Ptt 265
Barnard Lnc 809
Benjamin Ptt 265
Benjamin Trl 676
Benjamin, Junr. Ptt 268

Benjn. Hrt 696
Blake Brt 30
Blake, Esqr. Edg 171
Blake, Esqr. Edg 181
Bruce Wlk 27
Bryant Cmb 391
Burrel Cmb 391
Conrod Stk 550
Conrod Stk 597
Daniel Cmb 363
Daniel Cmb 385
David Brk 730
David Stk 551
Dempsey Brt 28
Dempsey Grn 595
Dread Hrt 696
Edward Brt 32
Edmond Rch 248
Elijah Jhn 772
Elijah Lnr 1
Fanney Wrr 793
Francis Ans 235
Francis Brt 28
Frank Ans 237
Frederick Lnr 1
Frederick John Stk 598
George Bnc 163
George (2) Srr 637
George M. Srr 637
Harry Brk 726
Hector Rbs 366
Henry Brk 729
Henry Frn 466
Henry Frn 471
Henry Hlf 294
Henry Hrt 696
Henry Hde 364
Henry Stk 587
Henry, Junr. Brk 726
Isaac Dpl 413
Jacob Rwn 340
Jacob Rwn 422
James Ash 72
James Cht 225
James Frn 454
James Gts 262
James Hlf 290
James Hrt 697
James Lnc 810
James Lnc 873
James Ptt 265
Jesse Ptt 265
Job. Rck 443
John Ans 220
John Brt 32
John Cbr 699
John Cmb 384
John Lnr 1
John Lnc 901
John Mre 62
John Mre 64
John Orn 546
John Rwn 345
John Srr 636
John, Junr. Ans 235
Jonathan Ash 72
Jonathan Mrt 384
Jordan Hlf 294
Joseph Orn 500
Larra Hrt 715
Lawrence Gts 262
Levi Brt 32
M. George Srr 637
Malcom Mre 66
Mary Brt 30
Michael Brk 725
Michael Rwn 311

Morris Ash 72
Nathan Hlf 290
Nathan Hde 362
Nathan Ird 628
Nathan Lnc 837
Neill Rbs 360
Nicholass Srr 636
Obediah Srr 636
Peggey Wrr 792
Peter Lnc 901
Philip Lnc 846
Richard Brt 30
Robert Bld 30
Robert Bnc 161
Robert Orn 550
Rushe Rwn 335
Samuel Ash 74
Sarah Brt 26
Sarah Edg 183
Sarah Lnc 810
Sarah Trl 692
Sarah Wlk 27
Silvester Stk 551
Simmons Hlf 294
Simmons Mrt 387
Simon Hrt 708
Solomon Ash 73
Solomon Brn 16
Susanna Lnc 873
Susannah Gts 263
Susannah Orn 544
Sylvester Wlk 27
Thomas Ash 73
Thomas Ptt 267
Uriah Brt 30
William Ans 238
William Brt 28
William Brt 34
William Brk 730
William Chw 114
William Crr 141
William Hlf 296
William Hrt 709
William Lnr 1
William Mnt 484
William Nsh 92
William (2) Wne 851
William, Jer. Nsh 90
William, Junr. Gts 263
Winefred Hlf 292
Winnifred Brt 30
Zachariah Ash 72
Zebidee Wlk 27
Balam, ... Brn 16A
Balance, Laban Hde 363
Balch, Wm. Lnc 837
Baldree, Isaac Ptt 283
   William Ptt 225
Baldridge, Alexr. Lnc 846
Alexr. Rth 99
John Rth 99
Daniel Orn 550
James Orn 550
Michl. Lnc 846
William Orn 550
William Rth 99
Baldwin, Amos Rch 255
Charles Bld 11
Elisha Ash 72
Jacob Brk 723
John Ash 73
John Bld 6
John Rch 266
Jonathan Rch 252
Joseph Bld 17
Samuel Cht 162
Stephen Ash 73

William	Ash 73	William		Rwn 351	Balmer, William	Orn 493
William	Bld 12	William		Wlk 27	Balthrope, Gussey	Wrr 793
William	Ptt 228	Wilson		Orn 546	John	Wrr 793
William, Sr.	Bld 17	Ballad, Edward		Orn 549	William	Wrr 793
Baldwyn, Edwd.	Csw 102	Ballah, Moses		Rwn 311	Balton, Nathan	Jhn 760
Elizabeth	Csw 102	Ballance, Aron		Crr 168	Baltrip, Hannah	Wlk 29
Henry	Csw 101	Caleb		Crr 168	John	Wlk 27
Luke	Csw 102	Jeams		Crr 144	Banbury, Bryan	Hrt 737
Bale, Richard	Lnc 852	John		Crr 168	Bancroft, Jonathan	Jns 785
Thomas	Mck 571	Joshua		Crr 167	Bandenman, Wm.	Lnc 846
Baleeck, Jacob	Lnc 866	Thos.		Crr 168	Bandiford, John	Hrt 696
see Boleck		William		Edg 183	Bandy, David	Rth 98
Balenger, Henry	Glf 664	Wm.		Crr 168	George	Lnc 873
John	Rck 484	Ballane, Barbara		Crr 168	Bane, Charles	Cbr 685
Mary	Jhn 773	Charles		Crr 153	Danl.	Lnc 835
Balentine, Henery	Crr 163	John		Crr 144	Hugh	Rbs 368
Joseph	Crr 164	Joseph		Crr 139	John	Nsh 90
Bales, David	Rth 96	Leven		Crr 144	Banely, George	Lnc 810
Ferreby	Ans 234	Polley		Crr 162	Banes, Henry	Nsh 90
Jacob	Srr 634	Ballaner see Ballane			Bange, Thomas	Wlk 28
John	Rth 96	Ballard, Archabald		Srr 634	Banker, Jacob	Ird 660
Nathan	Srr 634	Benjamin		Edg 182	Banks, Benjn.	Hrt 734
Thomas	Srr 634	Biram		Srr 634	Charles	Hde 363
William	Stk 551	Dudley		Csw 143	Cotton	Crv 261
Baley, Arther	Jhn 755	Edward		Nsh 93	Dorcas	Hde 364
Henry	Wne 862	Elias		Wne 870	Edward	Wlk 26
Isham	Jhn 756	Elisha		Mrt 384	Elizabeth	Hde 363
Jacob	Ans 211	Elizabeth		Lnc 864	Geo. H.	Csw 133
Jacob	Ans 232	Ezekiel		Wne 863	Gerard	Cmb 373
Jesse	Jhn 754	Germon		Srr 634	Gracey	Crr 156
John	Ans 232	Gormon		Srr 638	Harmon	Bnd 161
John	Grv 521	James		Lnc 859	Harris	Stk 593
John	Hrt 728	James		Mck 555	Henry	Bfr 4
John	Ons 178	James		Mre 67	Hugh	Cht 193
John	Jhn 757	James		Ons 162	James	Psq 638
Lury	Jhn 757	Jesse		Mrt 387	James	Wke 720
Micajah	Jhn 754	Jesse		Rwn 377	Jenny	Chw 116
Thomas	Ans 229	Jesse		Rwn 397	John	Bnc 162
Thomas	Orn 546	Jethro		Gts 263	John	Crv 261
Thomas	Wrr 790	John		Bnc 160	John	Psq 633
Walter	Bnc 163	John		Mnt 489	John	Rwn 423
William	Ans 229	Joseph		Ons 167	John	Stk 593
William	Hrt 729	Kedar		Gts 262	John	Stk 594
William	Jhn 754	Levin		Trl 676	John	Wlk 29
William	Orn 548	Lott		Ons 174	Joseph	Psq 626
Balkam, Thomas	Stk 568	Onan		Csw 143	Lilleston	Bfr 4
Ball, Benjamin	Ird 609	Peter		Smp 508	Mary	Trl 688
Cassa	Rnd 298	Samuel		Bnc 163	Moses	Hde 364
Daniel	Ird 623	Silas, Junr.		Mrt 384	Nathl.	Wlk 29
Daniel	Wrr 789	Silas, Senr.		Mrt 384	Peter	Crv 261
Eligah	Ons 146	Solomon		Mnt 489	Peter	Crv 305
Elizabeth	Grv 527	Thomas		Stk 558	Samuel	Stk 594
Elizebeth	Crr 143	Thomas		Srr 634	Silas	Nrt 429
Hosey	Crr 143	Thomas		Srr 638	Solomon	Rwn 423
Jacob	Prs 200	Walter		Hlf 288	Thomas	Edg 182
James	Bfr 2	Walton		Mnt 489	Thomas	Hrt 734
James	Crv 275	Wilie		Lnc 859	Thomas	Psq 638
James	Ons 146	William		Glf 690	Thos.	Crr 165
John	Bfr 2	William		Hlf 288	William	Glf 673
John	Gts 263	William		Srr 634	William	Hlf 290
John	Ird 623	Wyot		Edg 181	William	Psq 628
John	Prs 190	Ballas see Millar			William	Wlk 29
Leven	Crr 143	Ballenger, Henry		Glf 684	Bankston, Andrew	Mnt 515
Levi	Crv 273	John		Glf 670	Richard	Mnt 515
Lewis	Bnc 160	John		Glf 675	Banneham, Richard	Orn 545
Mary	Crv 273	John		Wlk 28	Banner, Benjamin	Stk 545
Mary	Lnr 28	Ballentine, Alexr.		Bld 26	Charles	Stk 568
Orsbourn	Grv 527	Davise, Ser.		Crr 160	Ephraim	Stk 545
Orson	Grv 531	Jeams		Crr 157	Ezekiel	Grv 575
Richard	Orn 546	Marthy		Mrt 387	Joseph	Stk 545
Robt.	Nwh 2	Peter		Crr 157	Bannester, Henry	Stk 550
Sarah	Crv 275	Ballet, Benjamin		Rwn 364	Nanny	Stk 550
Shadrach	Crv 275	Balliard, Bland		Rth 97	Bar..., William	Rnd 301
Stephen	Crv 277	William		Rth 95	Barbar, Abram	Ons 176
Stephen	Ons 148	Ballinger, Jacob		Bnc 162	Barbary, Allen	Smp 500
Whittenton	Crv 277	Josiah		Bnc 162	Barbe, Going	Cht 202
William	Edg 182	Ballow, Merideth		Ash 72	Gray	Cht 202
William	Ird 674					

11

Name	Loc	Pg	Name	Loc	Pg	Name	Loc	Pg
Mary	Cht	202	John	Smp	529	William	Wke	721
Barber, Abraham	Ans	210	Lewis	Dpl	403	William, Jur.	Wke	721
Abraham	Ans	232	Lewis	Dpl	425	Wm.	Csw	110
Allen	Orn	542	Lewis, Jr.	Dpl	403	Wm.	Srr	710
Allen	Rck	472	Mary	Rbs	364	Barkham, James	Stk	620
Benjamin	Rch	268	Matthew	Grn	592	Barkley, James	Rth	97
Burwell	Jhn	772	Moses	Ons	176	Barkly, Andrew	Ird	608
Charles	Brt	30	Nathan	Ons	176	Henry	Rwn	319
Cullin	Brt	34	Sarah	Edg	181	James	Ird	609
D. William	Brt	28	Sarah	Rbs	364	James	Rwn	319
David	Wsh	700	Solomon	Wne	853	John	Lnc	810
Elias	Rwn	324	Stephen	Smp	530	John	Rwn	324
Elizabeth	Ons	172	Stephen, Capt.	Bld	3	Samuel	Rwn	402
George	Jhn	767	Thomas	Dpl	426	Samuel, Junr.	Rwn	319
Isaac	Prq	655	William	Edg	184	Samuel, Senr.	Rwn	319
James	Wlk	30	Willis, Jur.	Rbs	363	Thomas	Rwn	319
John	Ans	210	Willis, Sen.	Rbs	363	William	Ird	608
John	Ons	139	Barfoot, James	Bld	10	Barksdale, Benja.	Hlf	358
Jonathan	Rwn	315	Barge, George	Cmb	351	Sherod	Cmb	366
Joseph	Orn	542	Lewis, Junr.	Cmb	351	Barler, Sarah	Wke	722
Joseph	Prq	651	Lewis, Senr.	Cmb	351	Barley, Benjamin	Orn	549
Joseph	Wke	719	Barger, George H.	Rwn	299	Christopher	Orn	548
Luke	Cmd	105	John	Brk	724	James	Orn	549
Mathew	Orn	542	John	Cbr	712	John	Orn	548
Mitchell	Ons	138	John	Cbr	714	John	Orn	549
Moses	Prq	646	John	Rwn	299	Joseph	Orn	548
Owen	Jhn	773	Barham, Daniel	Stk	622	Mark	Orn	548
Plar	Wke	718	Hartwell	Glf	651	Barlow, Ambrose	Nwh	10
Pliar	Jhn	767	Newsom	Rck	483	Branson	Rbs	368
Reuben	Jhn	773	Thorn	Grv	579	Carey	Nrt	423
Richd.	Wlk	26	Barjoram, John	Grn	587	Elizabeth	Rbs	365
Sally	Lnr	1	Bark see Burk			Jacob	Brn	21
Sarah	Rth	100	Barkdale, Daniel	Hlf	292	John	Rbs	365
Thomas	Jhn	772	Barkdarks, Creasy	Hlf	290	John	Rwn	440
William	Ans	216	Barker, Abner	Rnd	298	John, junr.	Wlk	29
William	Orn	542	Adin	Crv	295	John, senr.	Wlk	29
Barbrick, Leonard	Cbr	703	Anne	Nrt	427	Lewis	Edg	187
Barby, Francis	Orn	547	Charles	Rbs	365	Marsh	Rbs	369
William	Orn	548	David	Csw	146	Mason	Rbs	369
William	Rnd	299	Drury	Wke	721	Ralph	Rbs	368
Barclay, John	Nwh	1	Edmond	Wke	720	Tho.	Nwh	11
Rhodes	Nrt	425	Edmond	Wke	721	Thomas	Ons	165
Samuel	Nrt	429	Elizabeth	Cht	219	Thomas	Orn	550
Barcley, Robert	Lnc	859	Elizabeth	Hlf	294	William	Rbs	369
Barclift see Bartclift			Elizabeth	Prq	660	Zac	Stk	606
Barco, Costen	Cmd	100	George	Csw	141	Barly, Martin	Rck	442
Selbey	Crr	138	George	Wlk	28	Barmer, John	Mnt	488
Barcoe, Bailey	Cmd	104	George, junr.	Wlk	28	Barna, Arthur	Ons	179
Barden, Arther	Wne	863	Gillum	Ird	608	Barnard, Abenah	Crr	164
Ephraim	Smp	512	Hezekiah	Wlk	28	Job	Bnc	160
James	Hrt	728	Hincher	Ird	608	Luke	Crr	164
James	Wne	850	Hosea	Wke	720	Robert	Crr	156
John	Wne	847	Howell	Ird	608	Samuel	Cmd	107
Mary	Hrt	728	Isaac	Rnd	303	Samuel	Crr	137
Richard	Hrt	728	Israel	Csw	140	Thos.	Crr	138
Wm., Esqr.	Mrt	387	Jerry	Rnd	299	Barncastle, Fred-erick	Rwn	414
Woodard	Wne	847	Joannah	Nrt	429	Barnecastle, Bev-erly	Brt	28
Bare, Henry	Ash	73	John	Csw	140	Richard	Brt	28
Barefoot, Ambrose	Cmd	104	John	Cht	172	Barned, Salley	Crr	157
Amy	Cmd	108	John	Mre	76	Barneman, Geo.	Nwh	4A
Jepthah	Edg	184	John	Ons	145	Barnes, Amos	Rbs	368
John	Edg	184	John	Rnd	303	Archelaus	Edg	183
Miles	Jhn	775	John	Wlk	28	Aziel	Edg	182
Noah	Jhn	774	John, Jur.	Mre	76	Benjn.	Gts	263
Stephen	Edg	184	John H.	Wrr	788	Grenesly	Wlk	26
William	Edg	184	Leonard	Rck	488	Britain	Edg	183
Bares, John	Cmd	98	Lewis	Wke	721	Brittain (2)	Rbs	362
Barfield, Abraham	Rbs	361	Lyna	Rck	485	Cadar	Brt	32
Archibald	Rvs	362	Mark	Wke	721	Charles	Edg	184
Aron	Ons	175	Mary	Rnd	299	Charles	Hrt	730
Blake	Wne	853	Mary	Wke	720	Chesly	Rck	485
Charles	Edg	185	Neoma	Wke	721	Chessley	Wlk	27
Charles	Rbs	361	Nicholas	Rnd	303	Crawford	Grv	558
Dempsey	Rbs	362	Robert	Rnd	304	Dempsey	Edg	183
Elijah	Rbs	366	Samuel	Rnd	299	Elias	Rbs	360
Fedrick	Dpl	433	Thomas	Orn	550			
John	Edg	184	William	Rnd	299			

Francis	Rth 95	Amos	Mnt 516	John	Orn 500
Gehue	Wlk 30	Artha	Srr 635	John	Ptt 233
Guttridge	Grv 556	Carter	Rch 242	Robert	Mck 546
Henry	Brt 32	Elijah	Mnt 511	Robert	Orn 499
Henry	Nrt 429	Francis	Wlk 30	William	Ptt 233
Jacob	Rbs 362	Jeromiah	Mnt 508	Wm.	Csw 133
Jacob (2)	Wne 863	John	Mck 559	Barnit, William	Rth 99
James	Ans 210	John, Junr.	Mck 538	Barnkill see Barnhill	
James	Edg 183	John, Senr.	Mck 538	Barnot, Able	Mck 601
James	Edg 187	Robert	Mck 539	Barns, Abraham	Lnr 28
James	Gts 262	Robert	Rth 99	Anthoney	Ons 148
James	Rbs 361	Syon, Overseer	Mck 525	Burrel	Rnd 298
James	Rck 470	Thomas	Mck 568	Charity	Nsh 89
James	Wlk 26	Tristam	Stk 618	Delilah	Wke 720
James, Junior	Rbs 362	Widow	Mck 531	Drury	Wke 720
James, Junr.	Edg 184	William	Wne 869	Edward	Ird 628
James, Sen.	Rbs 362 Barnett, Amos	Mnt 477	George	Ird 628
James, (TR)	Edg 183	Amos	Rwn 305	George	Rck 480
Jerusha	Brt 32	Andrew	Prs 196	Grace	Frn 473
Jesse	Brt 28	Asa	Stk 615	James	Brk 727
Jesse	Glf 639	Francis	Ird 623	James	Hlf 292
Jesse	Rbs 362	Francis, Junr.	Ird 623	James	Nsh 89
Jesse	Wne 862	James	Grv 534	James	Ons 179
Jesse	Wne 863	James	Jns 787	James	Wlk 26
Jesse (Tosnot)	Edg 184	Jas.	Prs 198	Jesse	Ptt 273
Jethro	Edg 183	Jesse	Cmd 104	Jonathan	Cht 223
John	Brk 728	Jesse	Grv 534	Jonathan, Sr.	Cht 223
John	Cht 220	Jesse	Jns 785	John	Wlk 26
John	Edg 183	John	Bnc 162	Joseph	Nsh 91
John	Glf 621	John	Cmd 98	Laml.	Nsh 87
John	Nrt 425	John	Grv 513	Lucey	Wke 720
John	Rbs 364	John	Prs 200	Mary	Nsh 89
John	Wsh 700	Joseph	Grv 534	Richard	Rwn 406
John	Wne 849	Joshua	Lnr 29	Samuel	Ash 74
John	Wne 862	Libery	Glf 683	Steven	Psq 633
John, Senr.	Wlk 30	Luke	Bnc 160	Widow	Mck 592
Joshua	Nrt 427	Margert	Prs 199	William	Frn 476
Joshua	Ptt 268	Matthew	Lnr 29	William	Nsh 89
Josiah	Rbs 361	Obedhl	Glf 626 Barnside, Robert	Orn 545
Josiah	Rbs 364	Pheebett	Glf 683	see Barside	
Leath	Cht 220	Robert	Hde 362 Barnwell, Robert	Csw 126
Malachi	Edg 185	Robert	Mck 523	Robert	Orn 542
Mary	Nrt 429	Sarah	Prs 205 Barr, David	Brk 727
Matthew	Hlf 294	Stephen	Trl 686	Frederick	Wne 844
Merach	Jhn 766	Thomas	Csw 119	John	Rwn 319
Merriman	Grv 529	Thomas	Prs 200	Mary	Stk 593
Michael	Rbs 364	Tully	Cmd 105	Robert	Rck 478
Mourning	Edg 183	William	Cmd 100	William	Gts 263
Nathaniel	Rck 488	William	Grv 513	Wm. Granfield	Brk 728
Ninivy	Brk 728	William	Mnt 477 Barred, John	Stk 600
Noah	Edg 185	William	Rnd 303	see Borrod	
Randol	Hrt 730	William	Rth 94 Barret, John	Nwh 2
Reddick	Edg 182	Wm.	Csw 100	Edward	Cmb 367
Reuben	Trl 676	Wm.	Csw 119	Jacob	Rwn 276
Richard	Gts 263	see Burnit		James	Bnc 159
Saml.	Rck 475 Barnette, Daniel	Srr 634	John	Bnc 161
Samuel	Ans 208 Barney, Benjamin	Hde 364	John	Nsh 89
Samuel	Wne 862	John	Ons 180	William	Bnc 159
Samuel	Wne 863 Barnhart, Charles	Cbr 690	William	Cmb 367
Sarah	Mrt 388	Christian	Cbr 697 Barrette, James	Nrt 423
Sarah	Rck 461	George	Cbr 697 Barricks, John	Csw 142
Simeon	Wne 863	Jacob	Cbr 690 Barringer, Christ-	
Solomon	Wlk 26	John	Cbr 690	opher	Ird 647
Stephen	Edg 185	Mathias	Cbr 712	George	Cbr 712
Thomas	Gts 263	Philip	Cbr 711	George	Rwn 390
Thomas	Rbs 365 Barnhill, David	Brn 19A	Henry	Ird 647
Thomas	Wlk 30	David	Mrt 386	John	Cbr 707
Turbafield	Rck 488	Edwd.	Csw 133	John	Cbr 712
William	Ans 223	George	Ptt 233	Mathias	Cbr 712
William	Brt 28	Henry	Ptt 233	Mathias	Lnc 867
William	Grv 518	Henry, Senr.	Ptt 233	Nicholas	Rwn 299
William	Hrt 730	James	Orn 499	Paul	Cbr 707
William	Rbs 362	James	Rth 99	Peter	Rwn 299
William	Wne 861	Jas.	Mrt 386 Barrington, Isaac	Crt 64
Williamson	Edg 185	Jesse	Ptt 233	Isaac	Crv 249
Zachariah	Wlk 30	John	Csw 133	John	Crt 63
Barnet, Alexn.	Cht 158	John	Nwh 6A	John	Crv 341

John	Ons 178	Bartlet, Allen	Wrr 791	Darling	Grv 545
Joseph	Nwh 3A	James	Wne 858	Dempsey	Grv 545
Lidda	Crt 75	John	Wne 858	Edmond	Srr 639
Richard	Crv 283	Saml.	Wne 850	Edward	Grv 545
Barrocks, Joseph	Smp 503	Samuel	Wrr 791	Elijah	Rbs 362
Barrod, Booz	Mrt 386	William	Jhn 771	Elisha	Wne 856
Barroll, William	Mre 50	William	Wrr 794	Elitha	Ans 204
Barron, Barnaby	Edg 185	Bartlett, Benjamin	Hde 363	Elizabeth	Nrt 427
Edmond	Frn 475	Edward	Bfr 4	Elsi	Wne 858
James	Brt 28	Elisabeth	Crv 243	Ewrel	Wne 852
James	Edg 183	Harton	Csw 128	Felix	Smp 500
James	Frn 464	John	Bnc 161	Frederick	Ans 204
Leonard	Orn 501	John	Glf 624	Hardin	Grv 585
Samuel G.	Crv 321	Bartlette, Samuel	Nrt 425	Hardy	Grv 545
Thomas	Bfr 3	Bartley, Henry	Brt 34	Harwood	Nrt 429
Barrons, John	Brk 729	Joseph	Brt 32	Herman	Cmb 351
Barrot, Alse	Gts 261	Rebecca	Brt 34	Isaac	Hlf 294
Dominick	Mnt 489	Bartly, John	Rwn 292	Jacob	Brt 30
John	Rth 98	Solomon	Edg 186	Jacob	Frn 475
Barroth, Jacob	Rwn 285	Barton, Betty	Rnd 301	Jarrott	Orn 546
Barrott, John	Brt 30	Betty	Rnd 304	Jesse	Nsh 91
John	Stk 560	David H.	Orn 549	Jesse	Wne 856
Joseph	Wke 719	Elijah	Csw 98	Jethro	Nsh 91
Nathan	Hrt 733	James	Orn 543	Jethro	Wne 861
Thos.	Crr 142	John	Orn 549	Johannah	Smp 504
Barrow, Arodiah	Prq 659	Thomas	Orn 490	John	Brt 32
Aron	Stk 620	Thomas	Orn 548	John	Cmb 351
Barthellomy	Hlf 294	William	Grn 537	John	Grv 583
Belzibub	Wrr 789	William	Rnd 302	John	Nsh 91
Benjamin	Ptt 284	see Baxton		John	Nsh 88
Bennet	Edg 171	Bartt, Elie	Chw 128	Jordan	Nsh 88
Bennet	Edg 181	Baruck, John	Rck 439	Jordan	Rnd 302
Bezer	Hde 363	Barwick, John	Ans 210	Joshua	Smp 515
Elizabeth	Hde 363	John	Ans 218	Mac.in	Hlf 290
Erie	Prq 653	Joshua	Lnr 3	Mar··	Jhn 775
Frederick	Hde 363	White	Nwh 8A	Matthew	Nrt 429
George	Bfr 2	Basby, James	Wne 854	Mid··	Nrt 427
George (2)	Hde 363	Basdell, Jacob	Glf 650	Mos··	Srr 639
Harrod	Grn 613	Basedin, Jessy	Ons 175	Nathan	Grv 527
James	Hde 362	see Bazedin		Nathan	Grv 562
James	Ptt 224	Basefoot, John	Wne 872	Neeuham	Wne 858
Jeremiah	Grn 612	Baseley, Benjamin	Ons 163	Olive	Ans 204
John	Hrt 708	Basell, David	Prs 218	Reuben	Wke 720
John	Ptt 268	Basford, Benson	Wrr 791	Rice	Cmb 384
John, Jun.	Prq 659	Pentney	Wrr 791	Richard	Smp 510
John, Sen.	Prq 659	Basham, Jerkins	Wke 721	Richard	Wne 854
Joseph	Lnr 4	William	Wke 722	Sampson	Srr 637
Joseph	Lnr 28	Basheer, Thomas	Ird 623	Simon	Ans 204
Joseph	Prq 643	Basinger, George	Rwn 292	Solomon	Hlf 294
Moses	Stk 559	Basket, Pleasant	Wrr 789	Thomas	Grv 563
Penelope	Grn 587	Thomas	Wlk 26	Thomas	Wne 856
Sarah	Ons 159	Basley, Polley	Wke 721	Uriah	Wne 868
Sharrod	Grn 612	Basman, Dred	Brn 21	Warren	Frn 475
Thomas	Hlf 294	Basnett, Archebel	Crr 168	William	Cmd 97
Thos.	Jhn 756	Mary	Crr 168	William	Grv 549
see Burrow		Robert	Crr 168	William	Grv 583
Barrs, John	Lnr 3	Willoughby	Crr 168	William (2)	Smp 500
John, Senr.	Lnr 2	Basnight, Jacob	Trl 676	Wright	Grv 527
Barrum, William	Hrt 697	James	Trl 676	Basset, Wiley	Hrt 728
Barrus, John S.	Jns 803	James Davis	Trl 676	Bassett, Mary	Cmb 366
Barry, Buck	Jns 805	Jonathan	Trl 676	Baster, David	Lnc 827
John	Crr 161	Joseph	Trl 676	Baswell, Jas.	Prs 204
Mark	Jns 779	Lemuel	Trl 676	Malachi	Psq 624
Barside, Benjamin	Orn 545	Nathan	Trl 676	Samuel	Prs 218
Bartclift, Demsey	Prq 657	Randol	Trl 676	Will.	Prs 204
Elizabeth	Prq 657	William (2)	Trl 676	Batchelor, Barnaby	Nsh 93
Err	Prq 655	Bass, Abraham	Nsh 88	Benjamin	Hde 364
Thomas	Prq 649	Absalom	Grv 583	Daniel	Nsh 91
Thomas	Prq 657	Agustian	Nsh 92	James	Nsh 92
William	Prq 645	Andrew	Smp 500	John	Nsh 92
Bartee, John	Edg 186	Andrew	Wne 843	Joseph	Nsh 92
Barter, Peter	Lnc 887	Ann	Nsh 88	Saml.	Nsh 91
Barthal, Matthew	Stk 568	Aron	Cht 210	Steven	Frn 464
Bartholemew, John	Frn 463	Arther	Wne 864	William	Hlf 292
Bartholumy, Lewis	Wrr 791	Benjamin	Grv 583	William	Nsh 91
Barthuly, Charles	Wrr 792	Burrel	Smp 501	Willm., Jer.	Nsh 92
Bartie, Dinah	Prq 656	Councill	Nrt 427	Batchilor, Solomon	Frn 481
				Batelet, Edward	Stk 549

Bateman, Andrew	Wsh 700	Jethro	Edg 182	Libon	Ons 176
Ann	Prq 649	Joel	Edg 185	William	Ons 177
Ann	Prq 657	John	Ans 234	Bazemore, Amelia	Brt 34
Bethiah	Trl 676	Josiah	Hrt 722	James	Brt 32
Evan	Trl 667	Lott	Crv 253	Jesse	Brt 32
Godfrey	Trl 667	Randal	Cht 207	John	Brt 30
Henry	Trl 667	Susannah	Ons 178	Stevens	Brt 32
Hopkins	Crv 305	William	Nsh 93	Bazen, John	Dpl 408
James	Edg 185	Battles, Holeman	Rth 99	Bazmore, Jesse,	
James	Rck 472	John	Rth 99	Junr.	Brt 34
Jeremiah	Crv 291	William	Rth 99	William	Brt 32
Jeremiah	Edg 182	Battley, Moses	Hlf 296	Beach, Benjamin	Mck 526
Jeremiah	Trl 694	Batts, Hannah	Dpl 417	Benjn.	Mrt 386
Jesse	Rck 442	James	Dpl 415	John	Brk 729
Jesse	Trl 670	John	Nwh 11A	Thos., Junr.	Mrt 384
John	Edg 183	Sarah	Dpl 415	Thos., Senr.	Mrt 386
John	Prq 642	Battz, Benjamin	Edg 186	Beachum, Alexander	Ans 235
John	Prq 653	Chasetty	Edg 184	John	Crr 168
John	Trl 668	Frederick	Edg 183	Beacon, Catharine	Mre 57
John	Trl 694	Jeremiah	Edg 185	Beaddy see Braddy	
Jonathan	Prq 652	Joseph	Edg 181	Beadley, Benjamin	Wrr 793
Levi	Trl 667	William	Edg 185	Beagle, Joseph	Rwn 319
Nathan	Trl 670	William	Edg 186	Beagles, John	Prs 200
Simeon	Trl 676	Bauch, John	Prs 213	Beaher, Frederick	
Solomon	Trl 688	Baucom, Asa	Wke 717	Jno.	Ird 625
Stephen	Trl 668	Britain	Wke 717	Isaac	Ird 628
Stephen, Junr.	Trl 676	Isham	Wke 717	John	Ird 628
Thos.	Mrt 384	John	Wke 717	William	Ird 628
Thos.	Prq 659	Josiah	Wke 717	Beal, John	Edg 183
William	Trl 668	Kedar	Wke 717	John	Lnc 846
Bates, Abrose	Cht 191	Lewis	Wke 717	Joseph	Rwn 446
Andrew	Crr 153	Bauges, Joel	Csw 103	Wm.	Lnc 845
Daniel	Wlk 26	Baugust, James	Wlk 28	Beales, Asa	Crr 138
George	Srr 637	Richd.	Wlk 28	Mecagey	Crr 138
Humphrey	Rth 96	Baukim, James	Glf 638	Micagey	Crr 138
James	Crr 153	Reece	Glf 638	Beals, Zepheniah	Cmd 106
James	Ptt 255	Baul, Nicholass	Srr 637	Beam, David	Lnc 887
Mary	Brt 32	Baum, Abraham	Crr 152	Jacob, Senr.	Rwn 304
Mathias	Wlk 29	Adam	Nrt 427	John	Lnc 810
Polly	Wlk 29	Ezeriah	Crr 150	John T.	Lnc 898
Richard	Rth 96	John	Nrt 427	Mathias	Cbr 715
Sarah	Brt 32	Morriss, Jur.	Crr 151	Beaman, Abraham	Jhn 765
Whitmill	Hlf 292	Morriss, Ser.	Crr 151	Charles	Rwn 450
Bathae, John	Cmb 378	Noah	Nrt 427	Cellin	Hrt 730
Bathane, John	Mnt 467	Bawdon, John, P.J.	Wrr 789	David	Jhn 766
Bathune, John	Mre 50	Bawls, John	Wrr 793	Francis	Mnt 475
Nicholas	Mnt 461	Bawstick, John	Stk 545	Isaac	Jhn 773
Baton, Jonathan	Jhn 753	Baxley, Caleb	Rbs 364	Jacob	Jhn 767
Peter	Rch 244	James	Rbs 364	John	Rwn 450
Batson, Batt	Nwh 12	Job	Rbs 364	John	Smp 510
Peter	Nwh 12	William	Rbs 365	Mourning	Hrt 737
Thomas	Hlf 292	Baxter, Benjamin	Crt 89	see Beeman	
Batt see Butt		Bennet	Crr 150	Beamon, Cornelias	Rnd 301
Battar see Buttar		Charles	Rwn 422	Francis	Rnd 301
Batten, Anguish	Mnt 461	Daniel	Rwn 315	Josiah	Rnd 301
Daniel	Mnt 461	David	Rwn 315	Osias	Smp 510
David	Hrt 730	James	Orn 550	Bean, Daniel	Cbr 677
James	Mnt 490	James	Wrr 793	David	Lnc 810
John, Junr.	Mnt 491	Jeremiah	Wrr 794	Elijah	Rwn 396
John, Senr.	Mnt 490	John	Rwn 422	Hugh	Cmb 385
Joshua	Mnt 489	John	Wrr 793	Jessay	Mre 52
Meredith	Mnt 490	John, jr.	Wrr 793	John	Bnc 160
Nathan	Mnt 489	Joseph	Crr 144	John	Mck 575
Peter	Mnt 461	Molley	Crr 154	Jonathan	Mnt 477
Battester, Sarah	Crt 75	Nathl.	Wrr 790	Mary	Rwn 396
Battin, William	Mnt 466	Reubin	Wrr 790	Peter	Brk 729
Battl, Josiah	Nsh 89	Saml.	Crr 155	Richard	Rwn 396
Battle, Davis	Edg 185	Saml.	Crr 161	Robert	Mck 575
Dempsey	Edg 186	William	Rth 95	Thomas	Rwn 446
Elisha, Junr.	Edg 185	Baxton, Lydia	Crr 154	Walter	Mnt 484
Elisha, Senr.	Edg 185	Bay, Christopher	Cmd 105	William	Bnc 159
Frances	Edg 185	Solomon	Cmd 101	William	Mnt 468
Isaac	Edg 185	Bayakin see Boyakin		William	Rwn 396
Jacob	Edg 182	Bayley, David	Crr 154	William, Junr.	Mck 576
James	Cmb 389	Bay, Christopher	Cmd 105	William, Senr.	Mck 565
James	Hrt 730	Bayner, John, Junr.	Bft 4	Beanblosom, Jacob	Rwn 384
James	Nsh 88	Baze, William	Stk 585	Beanblossom, Abra-	
		Bazedin, James	Ons 179		

15

ham	Rwn 397	Thomas	Gts 263	Aquilla	Rwn 450	
Beanefield, James	Ptt 257	Thomas	Stk 581	Calop	Wne 851	
Beanock, William	Rwn 435	Thomas	Wrr 794	Elizabeth	Dpl 432	
Beanson, Leonard	Grv 551	William	Crr 158	Frederich	Grv 567	
Bear, Kisiah	Srr 638	William	Stk 551	Frederick	Rwn 406	
Nathanil	Stk 610	William	Trl 676	George	Rwn 406	
Beard, Alexander	Mnt 461	William	Trl 686	Henry	Rwn 407	
Andrew	Brk 726	Beasly, Elisha	Crv 333	Jacob	Brk 724	
Anthony	Wrn 794	James	Crv 333	Jacob, Junr.	Rwn 406	
Benjamin	Cmb 392	Beason, Benjamin	Glf 678	James	Cht 219	
Benjamin	Stk 618	Edward	Glf 685	James	Rwn 450	
David	Glf 689	Frederick	Orn 500	James	Wne 853	
David	Ird 664	Henry	Orn 500	Jefry	Rnd 301	
David	Wke 717	Isaac	Glf 684	John	Brn 17A	
George	Glf 674	Isaac, Senr.	Glf 686	John	Cht 166	
Hannah	Rwn 402	John	Orn 500	John	Cmb 383	
James	Cmb 380	John, (Junr.	Orn 545	John	Dpl 433	
James	Cmb 382	Richard	Stk 618	John	Jns 815	
John	Bnc 163	Samuel	Glf 678	John	Rwn 396	
John	Brk 730	William	Glf 686	Michael	Rwn 377	
John	Rnd 304	see Beeson		Nathaniel	Wne 851	
John	Rwn 276	Beates, Charles	Crv 231	Peter	Rwn 406	
John	Rwn 284	Beatty, Wm. H.,		Philip, Junr.	Rwn 406	
John	Wne 855	Esq.	Bld 47	Philip, Senr.	Rwn 406	
John	Wne 857	see Bently		Sentleger	Rwn 446	
Joseph	Rwn 405	Beaty, Alexander	Mck 583	Stephen	Cmb 351	
Joshua	Smp 522	Charles	Rwn 335	William (2)	Dpl 432	
Lewis	Rwn 276	David	Ird 659	Becker, James	Rwn 435	
Lewis	Rwn 285	Francis	Ird 660	Becket, John	Rwn 315	
Margret	Rwn 284	Francis	Lnc 894	Beckham, Benjamin	Wrr 789	
Michael	Rwn 390	George	Rwn 450	Jesse	Wrr 789	
Miles	Mnt 467	Isaac	Bnc 163	Solomon	Wrr 788	
Neill	Cmb 380	James	Lnc 894	Solomon	Wrr 789	
Peggy	Mck 567	James	Mck 549	Stephen	Wrr 788	
Reubin	Glf 682	James G.	Lnc 894	William	Wrr 788	
Thomas	Ird 664	Jms.	Lnc 832	William, jr.	Wrr 788	
Thomas	Rnd 298	Jno.	Lnc 834	Beckley, Edmond	Crr 141	
Thomas	Rch 249	Jno.	Lnc 845	Beckman, Christo-		
William	Cmb 380	John	Ird 623	pher	Rwn 329	
William	Glf 690	John	Mck 527	Becknal, William	Srr 708	
William	Rwn 402	John	Mck 528	Becks, Nancy	Bfr 3	
Bearden, John	Prs 205	John	Rwn 276	Thomas	Psq 628	
Richd.	Prs 201	John	Rwn 285	Beckwith, Amos	Nsh 89	
Bearder, Benjamin	Grv 545	Joseph	Lnc 830	Bolling	Wke 721	
Bearfoot, Emelia	Brn 13A	Joseph	Mck 527	Burrel	Nsh 89	
Beaseley, Barnald	Wrr 794	Moses	Mck 526	Isaac	Wke 721	
Beasley, Abel	Crr 151	Robt.	Lnc 834	James	Nsh 88	
Benja.	Crv 333	Samuel	Mck 558	Sion	Nsh 88	
Benjaman	Stk 551	Thomas	Ird 659	Thomas	Nsh 88	
Cornelious	Crr 157	Thomas	Lnc 859	Becoy, Widow	Rch 270	
Fendal	Cht 202	William	Lnc 859	Becthel, Andrew	Rwn 344	
Francis	Chw 115	see Bealy		Becton, Edwin	Crv 315	
George	Chw 130	Beaufort, William	Ans 232	Sarah	Rbs 368	
Henery	Crr 151	Beaujest see Baugust		Bedford, James	Grv 505	
Henry	Crr 155	Beaver, Christian	Rwn 340	Jonas	Rth 95	
Jacob	Crr 153	Christopher	Cbr 712	Jonas, Sr.	Rth 99	
James	Bfr 4	Daniel	Mnt 515	Patsy	Rth 97	
James	Stk 551	Davolt	Rwn 335	Sith	Rth 99	
Jocuum	Crr 154	Davolt	Rwn 340	Stephen	Rth 97	
John	Chw 114	George	Rwn 340	William	Stk 586	
John	Crv 331	Henry	Rwn 340	Bedgood, Benjn.	Prq 649	
John, Sen.	Chw 130	Jacob	Rwn 335	Bedingfield, Henry	Wke 717	
Joseph	Chw 116	James	Ans 230	Sarah	Nrt 425	
Mary	Bfr 3	Jesse	Csw 122	Bedsalt, John	Bnc 162	
Mordacay	Crr 158	Nicholas	Rwn 299	Bedsole, Thomas	Bld 44	
Nancey	Crr 151	Nicholas	Rwn 340	Bedwell, Elijah	Rwn 450	
Polley	Crr 153	Peter	Rwn 299	James	Rwn 440	
Richard	Stk 581	Wm.	Csw 122	James	Rwn 450	
Robert	Chw 121	Beazley, Abraham	Bld 11	William	Rwn 450	
Robert	Stk 581	Robert	Bld 11	Beeber, John	Orn 548	
Samuel	Orn 500	Bebee, Asa	Cmb 367	Beedle, John	Wke 775	
Soloman	Crv 331	Bechel, Nathaniel	Stk 550	Beek see Beck		
Solomon	Crr 153	Becher, Henry	Rwn 396	Beel, Benjn.	Cht 178	
Stephen	Crr 151	Bechum, Lenanah	Hde 364	Samuel	Wke 719	
Stephen	Grv 506	Morris	Hde 362	Beeland, John	Edg 184	
Taylor	Crr 155	Sally	Bfr 2	Beele, Burwell	Nrt 425	
Thomas	Bfr 4	Beck, Andrew	Srr 704	Beelhart, Jacob	Lnc 901	

Beeman, Abraham	Gts 263	Belfour, William	Edg 184	John	Psq 624
Benjn.	Gts 263	Belk, Darling	Mck 589	John	Rnd 298
Edmond	Grn 587	John, Esqr.	Mck 588	John	Rnd 303
James	Frn 493	Bell, Abner, jr.	Crt 87	John	Wrr 791
Jeremiah	Grn 587	Abner, sr.	Crt 85	John, Junr.	Hlf 294
John	Hrt 709	Absalom	Crt 87	John, Jur.	Hde 363
Mary	Crv 325	Amey	Wrr 793	John, Senr.	Hlf 294
Parks	Frn 451	Andrew	Rnd 303	John, Senr.	Hde 363
Thomas	Edg 185	Archabald	Crt 68	John, Ters.	Hde 363
see Beman		Arthur	Hlf 294	Jonathan	Cht 205
Been, Charles	Rck 473	Azzel	Crt 56	Jonathan	Hde 363
John	Rnd 301	Benjamin	Edg 186	Joseph	Crt 69
Richard	Rnd 299	Benjamin	Frn 462	Joseph	Crt 83
Beens see Buns		Benjamin	Hlf 294	Joseph	Crt 85
Beeny, Thomas	Rbs 364	Benjamin	Mnt 477	Joseph	Crv 315
Beesley, Abram	Nwh 9A	Benjamin	Wke 721	Joseph	Edg 182
Charles	Stk 545	Benjamin	Wrr 794	Joseph	Mnt 477
Fielding	Wke 721	Billet	Crt 86	Joseph	Rnd 303
Henry	Wke 719	Branum	Crr 139	Joseph C.	Crt 76
James	Wke 718	Breckhouse	Crr 159	Joshua	Ans 228
James, Jur	Wke 718	Burwell	Wke 722	Joshua	Lnr 3
John	Nwh 8	Bythel, Esqr.	Edg 181	Josiah	Cmd 99
John	Nwh 9	Caleb	Crt 82	Josiah	Crt 85
John	Wke 718	Caleb	Crr 138	Lemuel	Ans 239
Jonathan	Wke 718	Caleb	Crr 162	Littleton	Hde 363
Oxford	Brn 15	Celah	Hlf 294	Lovett	Hde 363
Patsey	Wke 718	Charles	Ird 667	Malachi	Crt 85
Richard	Stk 581	Charles	Wrr 794	Mary	Crt 83
Solomon	Nwh 6A	Daniel	Chw 116	Mary	Rbs 361
Sterling	Wke 719	David	Ird 666	Micajah	Lnr 3
William	Wke 718	David	Jhn 768	Morris	Hde 362
Beesly, Abram	Nwh 10	David	Mnt 477	Nancy	Csw 120
Daniel	Rch 258	Dixon	Hde 362	Nathan	Crt 83
Beeson, Amasa	Stk 549	Dorcas	Hde 364	Nathaniel	Crt 83
Benjamin	Rnd 302	Duke	Crr 154	Nathl.	Brn 18
Edward	Rnd 302	Ebenezer	Hde 363	Newel	Crt 87
Elizabeth	Rnd 302	Eden	Ons 135	Pearce	Rnd 302
Isaac	Rnd 302	Edey	Crr 139	Penelope	Ptt 285
Isaac, J.	Rnd 302	Elijah	Crt 76	Reubin	Crv 235
Richard	Rnd 302	Elijah	Mck 554	Richard	Edg 185
William	Ird 633	Felix	Smp 511	Richard	Mnt 477
William	Rnd 302	Francis	Crt 68	Richard Dixon	Hde 381
Beffle, Adam	Rwn 329	Francis	Glf 668	Robert	Brn 18A
Begerley, David	Ird 666	Francis	Hrt 709	Robert	Cmd 100
Begerly, Henry	Ird 667	Francis	Rnd 298	Robert	Glf 691
Begg, Malcolm	Rch 260	Francis	Rnd 302	Robert	Orn 545
Beggerly, Benjamin	Ird 667	Frederick,		Robert (2)	Smp 511
Francis	Ird 619	Junr.	Edg 186	Salley	Wne 846
Beggers, John	Cbr 718	Frederick,		Salley	Wne 871
Begget, James	Cmb 376	Senr.	Edg 186	Saml.	Brn 16A
Beggs, Benjamin	Cbr 684	George	Crt 82	Samuel	Cmd 103
James	Cmb 351	George	Ons 141	Samuel	Smp 509
Begloe, Rodrick	Wrr 693	George	Wke 722	Shadrach	Hlf 294
Beimbridge, Thomas	Wsh 704	Hannah	Crt 83	Starkey	Ptt 251
Beisley, Presley	Wlk 27	Henry	Wke 722	Stephen J.	Ans 220
Belange, Elisha	Trl 684	Hesekiah	Dpl 407	Thomas	Brk 724
Elisha, Junr.	Trl 684	James	Cbr 682	Thomas	Cmd 99
Belaty, Amelia	Brt 30	James	Crt 81	Thomas	Cht 174
Belborough, Ber-		James	Hlf 292	Thomas	Cht 178
rinson	Nsh 92	James	Ird 666	Thomas	Dpl 406
Belch, Elisha	Hrt 696	James	Mnt 477	Thomas	Edg 181
James	Brt 28	James	Rwn 315	Thomas	Ird 667
Lewis	Brt 28	James	Rth 99	Thomas	Lnc 859
Mary	Hrt 697	Jeckoniah	Hde 363	Thomas	Ons 137
Miles	Nrt 427	Jenny	Brt 34	Thomas	Rnd 302
Ryan	Brt 28	Jeremiah	Wke 722	Thomas	Rwn 315
William	Rbs 369	Jesse	Wrr 790	Thomas	Wrr 793
Belcher, Bartlet	Stk 583	Jesse, jr.	Wrr 792	Tishey	Crr 147
Beverly	Edg 181	Jno.	Lnc 836	Walter	Cbr 682
Woods	Grn 597	John (2)	Cmd 102	Walter	Hlf 358
Belden, Simeon	Cmb 351	John	Cmd 103	Watson	Hde 363
Belemy, William	Edg 181	John (2)	Crr 140	Whitmal	Edg 188
Belew, Jesse	Bnc 160	John	Crr 141	Will	Prs 214
Beleyw, John	Ans 230	John	Crr 147	William	Crt 81
Belfield, John	Lnc 873	John	Edg 184	William	Crr 140
Belflower, Adonjah	Mrt 385	John	Mck 562	William	Nrt 425
Elisabeth	Mrt 385	John	Mnt 477	William	Rnd 298

17

William	Rnd 302	John	Bnc 161	Benny, Wm.	Srr 710
William	Rnd 304	John (2)	Smp 518	Bensean, Benigga	Stk 625
William	Rwn 315	John	Wrr 794	Berniga	Stk 598
William, Senr.	Wne 871	Joseph	Brn 21	Lewis Christ.	Stk 625
Wm.	Wne 848	Joseph	Wrr 788	Lewis Cris	Stk 598
Wright	Edg 181	Mary	Rch 256	Bensel, William	Wlk 29
Zadick	Hlf 290	Mosses	Wrr 792	Bensham, Saml.	Crr 148
Zadock	Wke 722	Patsey	Wrr 791	Benson, Alexander	Hde 363
see Belt, Bill		Philemon	Wrr 792	Alexander	Orn 545
Belley, Isaac	Wrr 789	Richard	Rch 266	Betey	Ans 200
Bellis, Elijah,		Richard	Wrr 791	Bridget	Wne 861
Jun.	Mre 49	Richd.	Bnc 161	Daniel	Rwn 371
Elissha, Jun.	Mre 49	Samuel	Dpl 427	Dred	Wne 852
Bellisle, Mary	Cmb 351	Sephen	Bnc 161	Elizabeth	Bld 39
Bellray, Isham	Cht 199	Thomas (2)	Dpl 429	Francis	Bld 39
Lawrence	Cht 199	William	Bnc 159	Henry	Rwn 285
Bellune, Danl.	Brn 17A	William	Bnc 161	Hestre	Wne 852
Bellyew see Belyew		William	Cht 225	James	Bld 39
Belote, Noah	Brt 34	William	Dpl 432	James	Bnc 161
Thomas	Brt 32	William	Edg 182	John	Bld 39
Belsh, Willis	Cmb 351	William	Wne 857	John	Glf 635
Belt, Benjamin	Ird 667	Bennett, Arterxer-		John	Glf 640
Chamberlyne	Lnc 846	xes	Orn 543	John	Hde 363
John	Lnc 845	Benjamin	Rnd 304	John	Mck 567
Thomas	Ird 667	Benjamin	Stk 546	John	Wne 852
Wm.	Lnc 829	Bowen	Nrt 425	Massy	Hde 363
see Bell		David	Bfr 4	Nathan (2)	Brn 19A
Belton, James	Rck 487	Fanney	Crr 157	Reuben	Hde 363
Belvin, Abram	Wke 720	George	Rnd 301	Robert	Rwn 335
John	Wke 720	James	Rck 457	Robert	Rwn 422
Priscilla	Wke 720	John	Csw 123	Willes	Wne 852
Belyew, Abraham	Ans 232	John	Rck 440	William	Brt 88
Abraham, Jr.	Ans 200	JOhn, Junr.	Crv 259	William	Bld 38
Henry	Ans 204	Josiah	Bfr 2	William	Wne 852
Jacob	Ans 204	Lewis	Grv 559	Benston, William	Glf 644
see Beleyw		Lydid	Orn 549	Bent, Thomas	Chw 116
Beman, Abraham	Jhn 772	Malner	Csw 138	Benthal, Daniel	Stk 611
David	Wne 853	Richard	Stk 611	Jacob	Crt 87
Noah	Grn 593	Richd.	Csw 109	John	Crt 83
see Beaman		Sarrah	Chw 114	Thomas	Crt 83
Bembery, Benjn.	Hrt 704	Solomon	Mnt 468	Benthall, Babel	Nrt 425
Bembridge, Caleb	Wsh 700	Thomas	Csw 126	Catherine	Hrt 734
Sarah	Chw 114	William	Chw 124	Joseph	Hrt 722
Beming, Benomi	Brk 730	William	Nrt 423	Bentley, Ann	Ptt 282
Bemmington, Mar-		William	Rbs 361	John	Ons 150
garet	Ird 621	William	Rbs 365	John, Junr.	Brt 30
Benbow, Benjamin	Glf 663	William	Stk 550	John, Senr.	Brt 30
Thomas	Glf 666	Bennit, Drury	Mnt 477	Thomas	Ptt 284
Benbury, Joseph	Chw 120	John	Ans 222	William	Brt 30
Richard	Chw 122	John	Bld 33	Bently, Benjamin	Ird 628
Sarah	Gts 263	John, Senr.	Crv 261	John	Mck 601
Bench, Daniel	Srr 638	Joseph	Ons 161	Martha	Edg 185
Bender, Daniel	Ons 148	Joseph	Rwn 446	Moses	Ird 628
John	Jns 809	Josiah	Ird 620	Squire	Ird 628
Bendors, John	Ons 153	Mark	Mnt 477	Benton, Abraham	Gts 262
Benefield, William	Glf 637	Mary	Rch 251	Absolom	Edg 187
William	Glf 665	Mildred	Ans 210	Alexander	Smp 503
Benett, Peter	Prs 208	Nevil	Ans 229	Ann	Orn 543
Benfield, John	Lnc 885	Peter	Rch 257	Augustine	Orn 495
Benge, Samuel	Srr 638	Samuel	Rch 249	Bailey	Bfr 2
Thos.	Srr 705	Solomon	Mnt 519	David	Gts 262
Bengle, Henry	Lnc 901	Tessey	Rch 249	David	Rck 473
Benne, Benjamin,		Thomas	Mre 39	David	Smp 513
Sr.	Nsh 91	William	Rch 248	Demsey	Brn 21
Benneman, Elizth.	Nwh 6A	William, Jr.	Ans 232	Elkenah	Psq 624
Benners, Lucas J.	Crv 251	William, N.	Ans 229	Frances	Brn 18A
Bennet, Charles	Wrr 788	Bennitt, John	Wke 719	Francis	Lnr 29
Christian	Gts 261	Julius	Wke 720	Jacob	Rwn 335
Danl.	Brn 14A	Rachel	Crr 138	James	Ans 225
Duke	Wrr 789	Bennitte, Amy	Mrt 384	James	Psq 624
Elisabeth	Rch 255	Jas., Senr.	Mrt 386	Jeremiah	Nrt 423
George	Gts 262	Roberte	Mrt 384	Jesse	Gts 263
Henney	Wrr 792	Silas	Mrt 387	Jesse B.	Gts 263
Isham	Wrr 792	Thos., Senr.	Mrt 384	Jethro	Gts 263
James	Cht 177	Wm., Junr.	Mrt 386	Job	Brn 18A
Jeremiah	Dpl 429	Wm., Senr.	Mrt 386	John	Mnt 494
John	Bnc 159	Bennott, Elisha	Glf 631	John	Psq 624

Jonathan	Lnr 28	Widow	Mck 529	Nathl.	Ans 221
Joseph	Csw 141	William	Mck 530	Bevel, Edward	Glf 654
Josiah	Gts 263	Berryman, Benjamin	Rwn 435	Bevell, Robert	Wrr 794
Joshua	Dpl 440	Bert see Bost		Bevely, Isaac	Cht 215
Mary	Gts 263	Bertt, Robert	Chw 128	Beverit, Jacob	Dpl 431
Miles	Gts 263	Berugah see Bungah		Beverley, John	Ans 232
Mills	Gts 262	Beryman, Edward	Gts 262	Beverly, Benjn.	Hrt 716
Molley	Wke 717	William	Gts 261	Bevers, Abe	Stk 611
Reason	Csw 111	Besom, Solomon	Lnc 894	Thomas	Wke 718
Robert	Wke 717	Bess, Christifur	Prs 199	Zachariah	Wke 718
Samuel	Orn 491	Michael	Trl 692	Bevill, Elisha	Orn 548
William	Dpl 440	Bessent, Abram	Brn 18A	Hezekiah	Glf 652
Berbara, Sally	Rth 97	Kpjm	Brn 18A	Joel	Glf 652
Berford, John	Cmd 106	Bessley, Joseph	Bnc 163	John	Orn 547
Berger, Charles	Rwn 414	Best, Absolam	Dpl 437	Robert	Glf 667
Bergin, Benjamin	Brk 729	Benjamin	Grn 609	Thomas	Glf 652
Jacob	Brk 784	Benjamin	Wne 871	Bewighouse, George	Stk 598
see Burgin		Benjmin	Dpl 424	George	Stk 625
Bergwin, John	Nwh 12	Bostian	Lnc 828	Beyan, Frederick	Ptt 259
Berkle, William	Rck 441	Catharine	Dpl 437	Bezet, David	Nsh 89
Berks, Hontiel	Lnc 904	Charles	Psq 627	Biard, Blodget	Ash 74
Berl see Bird		Christina	Lnc 841	Ezekiel	Ash 74
Bernard, David	Rck 447	Danl.	Lnc 828	Bibb, William	Wke 721
Germain	Hde 363	Fredk.	Lnc 841	Bibbins, Philip	Wsh 702
Isaac	Nwh 2A	Hannah	Dpl 437	Bibby, Billey	Frn 475
Jacob	Rck 475	Henry	Grn 610	Biby, Thomas	Rth 98
Jarratt	Glf 662	Henry	Hrt 722	William	Rth 95
Stephen	Brn 16A	Howel	Dpl 424	Bice, Abraham	Rth 97
Thomas	Rck 437	Jacob	Lnc 828	Bickerstaff, Aaron	Rth 97
Berraymon, John	Mre 58	Jeams	Crr 148	Molly	Rth 97
William	Mre 51	Jno.	Lnc 827	Rebekah	Rth 97
Berrey, John	Crr 141	John	Bld 5	Bickett, James	Mck 595
John	Wrr 789	John	Dpl 424	Bickman, John	Cht 167
Lamuel	Crr 162	John	Rbs 364	Bicton, Mary	Jns 817
William	Crr 140	John	Wrr 789	Biddix, John, j	Rth 96
Berrine see Borrine		Kader	Frn 449	John, S.	Rth 96
Berry, Andrew	Mck 551	Martin	Lnc 828	Biddle, David	Brk 731
Calib	Cmd 101	Nancy	Crt 91	Elijah	Ons 137
David	Orn 550	Patience	Rbs 364	Biddock, Samuel	Rnd 301
Eliza.	Bld 37	Peter	Lnc 828	Bider, William	Orn 491
Enoch	Mnt 494	Sion	Rbs 366	Bidford, William	Orn 500
Jacob	Cbr 712	Theophilus	Wne 844	Bierly, David	Rwn 396
James	Cmd 105	Thomas	Edg 182	David	Rwn 406
James	Rth 100	Thomas	Hrt 723	Martin	Rwn 396
Jesse	Wlk 29	Thos.	Crr 148	Biffle, Adam	Bnc 162
Jno.	Lnc 836	Thos.	Crr 150	Jacob	Bnc 163
John	Csw 129	William	Edg 182	John	Bnc 160
John	Csw 138	William	Grn 609	Big see Oliver	
John	Lnc 873	William	Hrt 719	Bigford, Jeremiah	Bld 39
John	Psq 633	Wm.	Crr 148	Bigger, James	Mck 606
John	Rwn 384	Wm.	Crr 150	Joseph	Cbr 706
Joseph	Brk 727	see Bost		Biggers, Robert	Cbr 682
Joshua	Orn 550	Bestrey, Timothy	Wlk 27	Biggs, Amariah	Wsh 700
Lot	Brk 725	Bethell, Saml.	Rck 449	Benjamin	Stk 545
Margt.	Lnc 833	William	Rck 436	Charles	Stk 578
Mary	Brn 14	Bethey, Mary	Gts 263	Elijah	Ptt 294
Mary	Crr 154	Bethune, Christo-		James	Edg 186
Mathias	Cbr 712	pher	Mre 58	James	Rbs 366
Miles	Ans 202	Colin	Cmb 389	James	Rbs 367
Richard	Mck 549	Daniel	Cmb 374	Jemimah	Mrt 386
Robert	Hde 364	David	Rbs 368	John	Crv 291
Robert	Orn 550	Jane	Cmb 363	John	Edg 185
Robert, Junr.	Orn 550	John	Cmb 365	John	Mrt 384
Rody	Orn 492	Murdock	Mre 69	Jos.	Mrt 385
Robt.	Lnc 830	Bettey, Geoge	Wrr 791	Kedar	Mrt 384
Salley	Bfr 4	Bettis, Elijah,		Mitchell	Rbs 367
Solomon	Hlf 294	Sr.	Mre 57	Reubin	Bfr 2
Thomas	Cmd 102	James	Cht 189	Samuel	Rbs 366
Thomas	Crt 78	Betts, Charles	Brn 16	Sarah	Mrt 385
Thomas	Orn 551	Mary	Psq 637	William	Crv 299
William	Orn 551	Sarah	Brn 16A	Willis	Orn 546
William G.	Crv 239	Betty, David	Srr 637	Wm., Junr.	Mrt 384
Wm.	Lnc 830	John	Cht 156	Wm., Senr.	Mrt 384
Wright	Brt 28	William	Srr 635	Zachariah	Grv 563
Berryhill, Andrew	Mck 532	Bevan, William	Dpl 406	Bigham, Hugh	Mck 538
John	Mck 529	Bevans, Abel	Ans 221	John	Mck 523
Samuel	Mck 529	John	Ans 221	Robert	Mck 539

19

Robert	Mck 571	
Samuel, Jur.	Mck 537	
Samuel, Senr.	Mck 537	
Widow	Mck 547	
William	Mck 538	
William	Mck 542	
Bilbo, Joseph	Orn 549	
Bilbrary, John	Brn 20A	
Bilbrew, Dewel	Edg 187	
Bilbry, John	Cht 191	
Biles, Charles	Lnc 887	
Charles	Rwn 329	
Daniel	Rwn 329	
John	Lnc 901	
John	Rwn 406	
Jonathan	Rwn 285	
Joseph	Rwn 285	
Thomas	Mnt 516	
Thomas, Junr.	Rwn 329	
Bilew, George	Brk 725	
Joseph	Brk 731	
Joshua	Brk 725	
Polly	Brk 730	
Bilk, James	Rth 96	
John	Rth 100	
Bill, Horatia	Ird 619	
John	Ird 647	
Thomas	Ird 619	
William	Crv 247	
Zachariah	Ird 619	
Billator, Zebideck	Stk 608	
Billetor see Biltor		
Billing, Benjamin	Rwn 396	
Frederick	Rwn 402	
John, Junr.	Rwn 397	
John, Senr.	Rwn 396	
Billings, James	Wlk 28	
Jasper	Wlk 28	
Peter	Wlk 28	
Thomas	Wlk 28	
Billingsby, Bas-		
dell	Glf 652	
Henry	Glf 652	
Billingsly, Bazil	Rwn 363	
Elias	Mnt 488	
Samuel	Rwn 363	
Silas	Mnt 489	
Billington, Ezeki-		
el	Jhn 771	
Billins, Jasper	Mre 77	
Billips, William	Edg 185	
Billops, John	Edg 181	
Ransome	Edg 185	
Thomas	Edg 182	
William	Edg 181	
Billpaugh, Matthew	Stk 606	
Billrue, Alexander	Edg 181	
Nathaniel	Edg 181	
Bills, Daniel	Srr 637	
Gershom	Srr 635	
Isaac	Ird 619	
William	Srr 634	
Billups, Anna	Brt 26	
Richard	Brt 28	
Biltor, Edward	Stk 596	
Bimmer, Jas.	Prs 201	
Binam, Abram	Bfr 2	
Benjamin	Ptt 268	
Binbury, Miles	Brt 32	
Bineau, Peter	Nwh 1A	
Binford, James,		
Junr.	Nrt 429	
James, Senr.	Nrt 429	
John M.	Nrt 423	
M. John	Nrt 423	
Martha	Nrt 429	
Bingham, Christo-		
pher	Rnd 301	
Elizah	Rnd 301	
Robert	Wlk 27	
Thomas	Rnd 303	
Thomas	Stk 567	
William	Cht 176	
William	Rnd 303	
Bingle, Henry	Lnc 810	
Binham, Jno.	Lnc 830	
Binkley, Frederick	Stk 606	
John	Srr 635	
Binton, Job	Mnt 489	
Binum, Gray	Stk 545	
Biot, John	Psq 625	
Biram, Abner	Brt 34	
David	Brt 32	
James	Brt 32	
William	Brt 34	
Birched, James	Mre 59	
Lazarus	Mre 63	
Bird, Arthur	Hrt 734	
Baylor	Csw 117	
Benjamin	Mnt 488	
Benjamin, Senr.	Brk 726	
Benjn.	Mre 50	
David	Hrt 728	
Edward	Hlf 292	
Edward	Smp 511	
Edward	Smp 529	
Empson	Orn 542	
George	Bnc 160	
Henry	Wrr 791	
Isaac	Rbs 361	
James	Csw 130	
James	Csw 138	
James	Mnt 506	
James	Nsh 90	
Jesse	Wke 719	
Jessee	Cht 203	
Joel	Wke 718	
Joel	Wke 719	
John	Brk 729	
John	Brk 730	
John	Dpl 432	
John	Grn 607	
John	Rwn 311	
John	Rth 95	
John	Wke 719	
John	Wlk 29	
Jonathan	Brk 723	
Joseph	Orn 547	
Joseph	Srr 637	
Mary	Rbs 365	
Michael	Dpl 432	
Patrick	Bnc 161	
Peter	Wke 718	
Richard	Orn 543	
Richard	Rnd 299	
Robert	Brk 729	
Robert	Dpl 432	
Robert	Hrt 703	
Robert	Mre 75	
Robert	Smp 512	
Sally	Bnc 159	
Sasanna	Hlf 292	
Thomas	Brk 724	
Thomas	Orn 543	
Valentine	Rwn 311	
William	Bnc 159	
William	Csw 138	
William	Rwn 329	
Wm.	Csw 130	
Birden, Capt. (Mas-		
ter Compy.)	Prs 197	
Bireley, David	Rnd 303	
Mary	Rnd 303	
Birk, Richard	Lnc 846	
Bisar, Peter	Rwn 435	
Bishop, Abraham	Wlk 27	
Ann	Cht 164	
Asa	Crt 63	
Beal	Lnc 852	
Benjamin	Cht 165	
Bowlin	Hlf 294	
Henry	Cht 167	
Isaac	Nwh 2A	
James	Hlf 288	
James	Nwh 8	
James	Wne 871	
Jeromiah	Lnc 852	
Jesse	Hrt 719	
John	Cht 176	
John	Hlf 294	
John	Hde 364	
Joseph	Rck 447	
Marcus	Hlf 294	
Nancy	Edg 185	
Philip	Grv 551	
Rebecca	Hrt 719	
Robert	Dpl 413	
Roger (2)	Wlk 29	
Samuel	Wlk 29	
Sarah	Crv 335	
Tho.	Nwh 11A	
William	Hde 364	
William	Lnc 852	
William, Junr.	Lnc 852	
see Bushop		
Bissell, Thomas	Chw 115	
Bissett, Duncan	Hlf 358	
Bitlater, Alex	Stk 613	
Bitner, Henry	Crv 233	
Bitt, John	Stk 575	
Bittater, Caleb	Stk 596	
Bittick, John	Stk 612	
Bitting, Anthoy	Stk 597	
Rachel	Stk 628	
Bittis, Elisha	Mre 42	
Bittle, Andrew	Brt 34	
Elizabeth	Ptt 263	
Jeremiah	Nrt 425	
Jesse	Rbs 367	
John	Ans 232	
John	Brt 30	
William	Nrt 427	
Biven, Corbin	Rwn 292	
Ellis	Brk 724	
Fielder	Rwn 293	
Joseph	Bld 47	
Leonard	Rwn 284	
Rachil	Brk 727	
Randle	Rwn 292	
Thomas	Bld 49	
Bivens, Benjamin	Lnc 901	
Thomas	Orn 546	
Bivins, Abraham	Brk 730	
Bizell, David	Hrt 709	
John	Hrt 709	
Solomon	Hrt 709	
Bizet, John	Nsh 90	
Lodrick	Nsh 90	
Bizzel, Ann	Wne 854	
Arther	Wne 856	
Hannah	Dpl 428	
Hardy	Dpl 428	
Isaac	Wne 853	
James	Dpl 430	
Jesse	Wne 854	
John	Wne 854	
Thomas	Wne 854	
William	Wne 854	
Black, Andrew	Stk 607	
Angus	Cmb 363	
Angus	Rbs 367	
	Mre 41	

Archabald	Mre 41	Sion	Smp 521
Archibald	Cmb 364	William	Edg 184
Carolina	Crt 81	William	Edg 186
Daniel	Cmb 363	William	Smp 521
Daniel	Cmb 393	William	Stk 574
David	Ird 643	William	Wlk 28
Duncan	Cmb 364	Blackenwelder, Ja-	
Edward	Crv 337	cob	Cbr 708
Ezekiel	Mck 606	Blackledge, Ann	Ptt 258
Frederick	Rwn 440	Benjamin	Crv 249
Fredk.	Rck 458	William	Crv 249
Fredrick	Ash 73	Blackley, Charles	Grv 526
George	Bnc 160	Blackman, Cullen	Wne 873
George	Mck 600	Elisabeth	Jhn 774
George	Prs 207	JOhn	Jhn 773
George	Rnd 304	William	Smp 500
George	Stk 589	William	Wne 845
Henry	Rwn 450	Blackmon, Acabut	Jhn 771
Hugh	Mre 52	Arther	Jhn 773
Hugh	Mre 54	Barnebas	Smp 529
Hugh	Rth 99	Barsella	Jhn 775
Jacob	Rwn 440	Edward	Dpl 438
Jacob	Stk 608	Esther	Smp 529
Jacob, Junr.	Rwn 351	James	Smp 505
Jacob, Senr.	Rwn 351	Joab	Smp 528
James	Cbr 705	John	Jhn 772
James	Cmb 363	Josiah	Smp 529
James	Mck 526	Blackshear, Elisha	
James	Mck 564	S.	Jns 817
James	Mck 600	Abraham	Smp 522
James	Rbs 367	Blackshore, Jacob	Jns 811
James	Rth 99	Blackston, Elisha	Cht 212
Jesse	Glf 681	Henry	Brt 88
John	Bnc 162	Prisscilla	Ptt 288
John	Ird 609	William	Cht 212
John	Ird 654	see Brackston	Ptt
John, Junr. (2)	Cbr 705	Blackstone, Thomas	Orn 544
John, Sen.	Mck 543	Blackwelder,	
Joseph	Bnc 162	Christian	Cbr 697
Joseph	Mck 553	Daniel	Cbr 711
Malcolm	Cmb 389	Isaac	Cbr 708
Malcolm	Mre 53	John	Rwn 335
Malcolm	Mre 55	Martin	Cbr 708
Martin	Ons 143	Blackwell, David	Srr 636
Matthew	Brk 727	Eliza.	Bld 42
Neill	Cmb 380	James (2)	Grv 558
Robert	Bnc 160	James	Rth 95
Robert	Brk 727	Joel	Rth 95
Robert	Prs 207	Joel	Rth 96
Samuel	Mck 604	John	Grv 537
Sarah	Cmb 351	John	Rwn 311
Thomas	Cbr 705	JOhn	Rth 95
Thomas	Glf 641	John	Rth 96
Thomas	Mck 564	John, jr.	Grv 506
William	Glf 670	John, senr.	Grv 506
William	Ird 617	Judith	Nrt 427
William	Mck 543	Levy	Csw 148
William	Mck 605	Molley	Bld 41
Wm. (2)	Lnc 845	Patience	Bld 46
Blackard, Charles	Glf 668	Pomfrell	Grv 506
Jean	Prs 216	Pumphrey	Grv 538
Blackart, Wilyoube	Rck 476	Reubin	Bld 45
Blackborn, Isarel	Stk 545	Robert	Csw 128
Yourger	Stk 566	Thomas	Grv 529
Blackbur, William	Lnc 809	William	Mnt 461
Blackburn, Absolen	Mrt 385	William	Rth 100
Benjn.	Ash 74	William	Smp 506
Bryson	Stk 608	Blackwood, Isaac	Rwn 446
Burrel	Smp 521	Jms.	Lnc 836
Elias	Lnc 809	Jms.	Lnc 837
Elias	Wrr 792	John	Orn 547
Elizabeth	Stk 545	Richard	Ird 633
James	Rth 97	Richard	Orn 546
John	Rck 477	Richard	Orn 548
Lacy	Stk 568	Richard	Rwn 445
Martha	Lnc 809	Saml.	Lnc 836
Robert	Rth 98	William	Orn 547

Blades, Tilman	Rck 465		
Bladsoe, George	Mnt 461		
Blagg, John	Rck 441		
William	Rck 456		
Blair, Andrew	Rwn 371		
Colbert	Brk 725		
George	Ans 234		
Jacob	Rwn 371		
James	Brk 727		
James	Mck 578		
James	Orn 544		
James	Rck 457		
James, (Senr.)	Rwn 402		
John	Brk 725		
John	Glf 670		
John	Wke 775		
Samuel	Cbr 705		
Thomas	Glf 650		
Thomas	Glf 672		
William	Chw 116		
William	Mck 573		
Blake, Archble.	Ans 237		
Asa	Wke 718		
Baker	Hrt 697		
Demsey	Wke 718		
Elizabeth	Hrt 709		
Elizabeth	Hde 364		
Hugh M., M.	Wlk 30		
Isham	Orn 548		
James	Brn 17A		
Jas.	Ons 171		
John	Nwh 9		
John	Prs 202		
John	Rwn 284		
John	Stk 545		
Joshua	Dpl 418		
Margaret	Bld 32		
Mary	Orn 549		
Randle	Mnt 469		
Saml., Jur.	Wke 719		
Samuel	Wke 719		
Thomas	Mnt 461		
Uriah	Crt 92		
William	Nwh 5		
William	Rck 487		
Blakely, James	Bnc 160		
Widow	Mck 564		
William	Brk 730		
Blakey, John	Crv 281		
Blakston, Elisha	Orn 543		
Blalack, John	Prs 187		
Millington	Prs 190		
Millington, Junr.	Prs 190		
Thomas	Prs 216		
Will.	Prs 190		
Blalock, David	Cht 189		
David	Grv 556		
David	Mnt 499		
David	Orn 543		
George	Cht 173		
Hardy	Cmb 390		
Isham	Mnt 500		
Jessee	Orn 500		
Jiles	Orn 543		
John	Mnt 490		
Julius	Cht 206		
William	Orn 500		
Wm.	Lnc 845		
Blalocks, Mary	Smp 502		
Blalook, Henry	Orn 543		
Blanchard, Ameriah	Gts 261		
Aron	Gts 262		
Barnaby	Gts 262		
Elizabeth	Gts 262		
Emelia	Chw 128		
Ephraim	Nrt 425		

Jeremiah	Dpl 401	Bledsoe, Moses	Cht 206	Sally	Bfr 2
Jesse	Wne 855	Abram	Wke 721	Sharpe	Ptt 243
Josiah	Nrt 423	Barnaby	Wke 720	Stevens	Wsh 700
Pallitiah	Gts 262	Benjamin	Srr 636	Thomas	Trl 676
Uriah	Dpl 401	Hezekiah	Wke 720	Thomas, Esqr.	Edg 171
Uriah	Wne 844	Jacob	Wke 718	Thomas, Esqr.	Edg 181
Blanchet, Edey	Wrr 792	Jacob	Wke 720	Thos.	Wrr 829
Edward	Cmb 377	Jacob, Senr.	Wke 720	William	Prq 643
Frederick	Orn 500	Jno., Mr.	Wne 868	William	Wsh 700
Henry	Bld 22	John	Wke 720	Wilson	Crv 241
John	Cmb 379	Larking	Srr 635	see B...lount, B...unt	
Philemon	Wrr 792	Lewis	Wke 720	Blounte, John	Mrt 384
Ruth	Nwh 10	Richmond	Wke 720	William	Nrt 425
Thomas (2)	Wrr 792	William	Srr 635	Blow, Benjamin	Grn 615
William (2)	Wrr 793	William	Wke 720	Benjn.	Hrt 730
Bland, Allen	Crv 267	Bless, Philip	Cbr 718	James	Hrt 730
Arthur	Glf 682	see Blew		Richard	Grn 615
Barshaby	Cht 205	Blessed, William	Glf 658	Bloyd, Jacob	Rck 448
Benjamin	Rnd 299	Blessing, John	Rwn 406	John	Rck 449
Charles	Glf 682	Blevens, William	Bnc 160	Pernal	Rck 448
Gabriel	Orn 544	Blevins, Wells	Ash 73	Bludworth, Ann	Nwh 9A
Jacob	Cht 205	Blew, James	Rwn 285	David	Nwh 5
Jane	Rnd 299	John	Mre 45	John	Nwh 7
Jemimah	Mrt 385	Robert	Brk 724	Rebecca	Nwh 9
John	Cht 152	Stephen	Brk 728	Tho.	Nwh 9
John	Cht 211	Stephen	Mck 589	Tho.	Nwh 9A
John	Crv 265	William	Brk 726	Blue, Daniel	Cmb 366
John	Mrt 386	Blewit, Eli	Rch 256	Dougald	Bld 18
John	Ptt 270	Morris	Ans 202	Dugal	Rch 261
Prudence	Ptt 279	William	Rch 256	Duncan	Bld 25
Stephen	Crv 267	William	Rch 267	Duncan	Cmb 364
Theophilus	Ptt 279	Blinn, James	Bfr 22	Duncan	Cmb 369
Thomas	Bfr 4	Joseph	Crv 335	Duncan	Smp 494
William	Rnd 299	William	Crv 237	Dunkin	Mre 54
Blaney, Benjn.	Brn 16	Blizard, Ezekiel	Cmb 369	Isabella	Mre 53
Blangow, Gabriel	Bfr 2	Joab	Mck 559	James	Cmb 368
Isaac	Bfr 2	Blizzard, John	Dpl 401	John	Cmb 370
Margeret	Bfr 2	Pernald	Stk 551	John	Rch 249
Sall	Bfr 2	Blocker, Esabella	Cmb 371	John, Senr.	Bld 18
Blankenship, Eli-		George	Smp 531	Malcolm	Cmb 365
jah	Rth 96	James	Cmb 393	Malcolm	Rch 254
Isham	Rth 96	Michael	Cmb 363	Margaret	Cmb 394
Isham	Rth 99	Bloiksome, Richard	Edg 181	Peter	Mre 53
Presly	Rth 96	Bloire, Colbert	Brk 729	see Blew	
Samuel	Ird 608	Bloodgood, Isaac	Crt 69	Bluit, Thomas	Mnt 495
Stephen	Mck 541	Blount, Ann	Brt 88	Blume, Henry	Stk 604
William	Ird 608	Ann	Chw 125	Jacob	Stk 598
Zachariah	Rth 96	Benjamin	Bfr 3	Jacob	Stk 625
Blankinship, Thom-		Benjamin	Brt 34	Lewis	Stk 544
as	Ird 614	Benjamin	Wsh 700	Blunt, Anne	Dpl 432
Blanks, James	Crv 257	Benjn., Negroes	Bfr 22	Benjamin	Jhn 770
John	Nwh 3A	Charles	Prq 656	Benjamin	Nsh 93
John	Nwh 12A	Edmund	Wsh 700	Benjamin	Smp 524
Richard	Grv 508	Elizabeth	Bfr 22	Fredrick	Psq 638
Will.	Nwh 11A	Ezekiel	Wsh 700	Isaac	Psq 638
Blann, James	Dpl 407	Gray John	Bfr 22	James	Psq 630
Mary	Smp 536	Hannah	Wsh 700	James	Psq 638
William (2)	Dpl 407	Isaac	Ptt 285	Richard	Nsh 91
Blanshard, Benjn.	Gts 262	Jacob	Chw 113	William	Smp 513
Mary	Gts 262	Jacob, Jur.	Rbs 365	Blurton, Edward	Bnc 160
Blanton, Burrel	Rth 98	Jacob, Sen.	Rbs 365	Blythe, James	Bnc 160
George	Rth 98	James	Chw 116	James	Bnc 162
James	Dpl 408	James	Psq 636	James	Mck 597
Jeremiah	Rth 100	John	Brt 34	John	Bnc 162
Joshua	Dpl 407	John	Chw 125	Joseph	Mck 595
Obediah	Rth 99	John	Rbs 365	Thomas	Bnc 162
Reuben	Rth 98	John B.	Chw 114	Boager, Jacob	Cbr 716
Richard	Dpl 408	Joseph	Hlf 290	Peter	Cbr 716
Thomas	Cht 164	Levi	Wsh 700	Boak, Robert	Rck 475
Blare, Enos	Rnd 302	Levi, Junr.	Wsh 700	Boatright, Daniel	Stk 545
Hugh	Rnd 304	Lewis	Bfr 2	James	Stk 544
Blatchford, John	Psq 627	Mary	Chw 122	Boatwright, Samuel	Mck 546
Blaze, Dawalt	Rwn 403	Nathan	Wsh 714	Tho.	Brn 16
George	Rwn 390	Phillip	Rbs 364	William	Brn 15
Lewis	Rwn 396	Reading, Col.	Bfr 2	Bob, Betty	Crt 63
Bledso, Aaron	Frn 449	Reading, Senr.	Bfr 3	Bobb, ...	Hlf 288
Rush	Frn 492	Rubin	Mck 584	Bobbet, Drewry	Wrr 791

`Harris	Wrr 794	Boiner, John	Stk 568	John, Junr.	Bfr 2
Joshua	Wrr 790	Bolan, Benjamin		John, Sen.	Chw 131
Lewis	Wrr 790	(2)	Rnd 301	John, Senr.	Bfr 2
Mary	Wrr 790	Charls	Rnd 298	Lewis	Brt 32
Randolph	Wrr 791	John, J.	Rnd 298	Lewis	Hlf 294
Stephen	Wrr 791	William	Rnd 303	Mary	Brt 32
Bobbett, Sherwood	Hlf 290	Boland, Justice	Ash 73	Mary	Ons 169
Bobbit, John	Frn 486	Bolarjack, John	Wlk 27	Pritlow	Prq 649
Turner	Frn 450	Bolden, Jesse	Rch 250	Richard	Bnc 162
William	Ans 211	John	Orn 501	Richard	Gts 261
William	Frn 450	Robert	Orn 501	Richard, Junr.	Gts 262
Bobbitt, James	Bnc 161	William	Orn 501	Robert	Bfr 4
Sion	Orn 549	Bolder, John	Orn 550	Samuel	Stk 551
Bobbt, John	Wrr 790	Boleboh, Nicholas	Rwn 396	Southy	Wke 775
Thomas	Wrr 790	Boleck, Adam	Lnc 873	Sweeton	Nwh 9A
Bobet, John	Wrr 791	Boston	Lnc 872	William	Gts 262
Bobit, William	Ans 216	Gasper	Lnc 867	see Bund
Boddie, Bennitt	Wke 717	Godfrey	Lnc 873	Bonds, George	Mck 595
George	Nsh 89	see Baleeck		John, Sr.	Nsh 93
William	Nsh 91	Bolejack, Joseph	Stk 545	Shadrick	Mck 597
Willie	Nrt 427	Matthew	Stk 551	William	Orn 494
Boden, Moses	Rch 250	Samuel	Stk 569	Wm.	Mrt 384
Bodenhamer, Wil-		Bolemboh, Abram	Rwn 384	Wright	Nsh 91
liam	Rwn 351	Bolen, Thomas	Csw 129	Bone, Archibald	Cmb 380
Bodiford, William	Rbs 363	Boles, Alexander	Stk 566	David	Ans 239
Bodine, Gabriel	Ird 608	Benjamin	Mnt 461	William	Ird 615
Vincent	Wke 718	James	Stk 546	Boner, Isaac	Stk 544
Bodkin, William	Mck 571	John	Stk 546	Joseph	Rwn 360
Bodolie see Boddie		Robert	Mre 62	Bones, James, Senr.	Brk 726
Boger, Daniel	Cbr 690	Robert, Sen.	Mre 62	William	Ird 670
Daniel	Rwn 299	Bolin, James	Cmb 376	Boney, Bimbrick	Dpl 423
Bogers see Bogus		Jesse	Mnt 468	Daniel	Dpl 422
Bogg, Robert	Brt 28	John, Junr.	Mnt 468	Jacob	Dpl 422
Boggan, James, Jr.	Ans 233	John, Senr.	Brk 726	James	Dpl 423
Jesse	Ans 233	John, Senr.	Mnt 468	John	Dpl 423
John (2)	Ans 233	Joseph	Brk 730	William	Dpl 423
Patrick	Ans 215	Suble	Mnt 475	Bonham, Rebecca	Lnc 810
William	Ans 233	William, Junr.	Mnt 475	Bonner, Amey	Ptt 274
William, D.	Ans 233	William, Senr.	Mnt 468	Hamilton	Wrr 784
Boggs, James	Lnc 846	Williba	Mnt 475	Henry	Bfr 3
Jean	Orn 543	Boling, Alex	Orn 548	James	Bfr 3
Wm.	Lnc 845	Baxter	Orn 548	Jesse	Grv 566
Bogie, Alexander	Crv 309	Jarrott	Rck 459	John	Edg 183
Bennajah	Crv 307	John	Grv 578	Joseph	Bfr 22
Bogle, Robert	Ird 628	Michael	Mnt 484	Leah	Prq 656
William	Ird 647	Robbert	Rnd 350	Mary	Bfr 3
Bogue, Benjamin	Wne 859	Bolkcom, John	Dpl 420	Mary	Mrt 387
Elizabeth	Prq 662	Boller, Elijah	Stk 545	Miles	Brt 26
Ichabud	Prq 662	Stark	Rwn 359	Nathan	Bfr 3
John	Prq 644	William	Rwn 359	Nathan	Hde 364
John	Prq 663	Boltin, Thomas	Brk 729	Richard	Bfr 3
Joseph	Prq 645	Bolton, Benjamin	Rch 244	Stapleton, Junr.	Mrt 384
Joseph	Prq 663	Benjamin	Wke 722	Stapleton, Senr.	Mrt 384
Josiah	Prq 658	Charles	Csw 111	Thomas, Ser.	Grv 569
Robert	Prq 648	James	Rch 255	see B...ner
Samuel	Psq 641	James	Wke 722	Bonum, Ezekiah	Nwh 6A
William	Prq 662	Richard	Edg 181	Booco, Abraham	Srr 637
Bogus, Wm.	Crr 137	Shearwood	Wke 722	Booe, George	Rwn 422
Bohannan, Abner	Cht 160	Thomas	Csw 111	Jacob	Rwn 422
Duncan	Rch 253	William	Csw 105	Booker, Isaac	Cmb 378
James	Stk 580	see Balton		James	Cht 210
John	Rch 254	Boly, John	Smp 506	John	Cht 207
Joseph	Cht 159	Boman, Andrew	Stk 628	Nomcy	Cht 209
Judith	Ans 229	Richard	Glf 683	Samuel	Cmb 378
Richard	Cht 197	Thomas	Csw 124	Bookout, John	Rnd 299
William	Rch 261	Bond, Benjamin	Glf 636	Joseph	Rnd 299
Thomas	Prs 194	Edea	Brt 30	Books, Jesse	Nwh 10
Boher see Baker		Edward	Srr 704	Jonathan	Dpl 400
Boice, Betty	Rnd 301	Elisha	Gts 261	see Rooks
David	Hrt 715	Elizabeth	Chw 123	Boomer, Ann	Hde 363
Boid, Phinehas	Rnd 298	Elizabeth	Rnd 353	Matthew	Hde 363
William	Rnd 303	Francis	Ptt 294	Boon, Allen	Hrt 728
Boikin, Smitic	Cmb 381	Isban	Crv 329	Benjamin	Ird 633
Boiler, Jacob,`j	Bnc 161	James	Chw 118	Benjamin	Nsh 88
Jacob, S.	Bnc 163	John	Brt 32	Benjamin	Nrt 423
Boiles, Peter	Cbr 718	John	Srr 639	Daniel	Glf 666
William	Stk 582	John, Jun.	Chw 123	Henry	Nrt 425

23

Jacob	Nrt 425	Borden, Benja.	Crv 339	Jesse	Wne 861
Jacob	Orn 543	Comfort	Crt 81	John	Glf 663
James	Frn 463	Joseph	Crt 81	John	Orn 501
James	Nrt 425	William	Crt 89	John	Psq 640
Jesse	Brk 726	Borders, Henry	Rwn 407	John	Wne 863
Jesse	Nrt 425	John	Lnc 893	Joshua	Rnd 298
John	Dpl 419	Bordman, William	Glf 654	Thomas	Bld 4
John	Glf 637	Boren, William	Rbs 364	Thomas	Wne 867
John	Glf 644	Boreshell, Thomas	Brk 723	Thomas, Sr.	Wne 861
John	Orn 501	Borine, Max	Crr 164	William	Bld 4
John	Rch 264	Salley	Crr 156	William	Psq 740
John, Junr.	Nrt 427	Born, Reubin	Stk 580	Zadock	Wne 861
John, Senr.	Nrt 427	Borney, Lucey	Ptt 282	Boswood, Thos.	Crr 154
Jonathan	Brk 726	Borough, James	Wke 720	Bosworth, Elisa-	
Jonathan, Junr.	Brk 730	Jones	Cht 213	beth	Mnt 487
Joseph	Jhn 746	Boroughs, Bryan	Mre 51	Jonathan	Mnt 485
Joseph	Nrt 423	Hardy	Hrt 696	Obediah	Prq 659
Joyner	Nrt 427	James	Hrt 697	Boten, Abram	Brn 15
Lewis	Nrt 429	Wright	Hrt 696	Botenhammer, Chris-	
Margrett	Orn 543	Borrine, Salley	Crr 163	tian	Rwn 363
Martin	Glf 644	Borrittz, William	Chw 122	David	Rwn 363
Martin	Glf 666	Borrod, Jacob	Stk 600	George	Rwn 363
Mary	Hrt 709	see Barred		Jacob	Rwn 363
Mary	Hrt 733	Borum, Jeams	Crr 164	John	Rwn 363
Nathan	Nrt 427	Bosdil, Rubin	Mck 579	Peter	Rwn 363
Nicholas	Hrt 728	Bosinger, Martin	Rwn 305	Both, Barthw.	Jhn 763
Nicholas	Nrt 427	Bosley, Edward	Rck 452	Bottom, John	Nsh 93
Phillip	Frn 462	Bosman, James	Hlf 292	Bottoms, L. Saml.	Nsh 87
Rachel	Brt 34	Boss, Aaron	Ird 647	Saml. L.	Nsh 87
Raford	Frn 465	Henry	Rwn 396	William	Nsh 87
Rebeca	Frn 478	Peter	Rwn 397	Botton, Thomas	Brn 16
Rhoderic	Hrt 709	Philip	Rwn 396	Botts, Bartholomew	Rth 94
Samuel	Smp 512	see Bass		William	Rth 100
Sarah	Nrt 429	Bosser, Joshua	Cht 171	Bottums, Sarah	Bld 12
Stephen	Smp 511	Bosswell, Ichabod	Wne 862	Bough, Josiah	Stk 606
Stephen	Smp 512	Simeon	Wne 863	Boughton, Enos	Wsh 700
Thomas	Brk 723	Thomas	Wne 861	Jared	Trl 692
Thomas	Hrt 708	Bost, Conrod	Lnc 867	Bouin, Alexr.	Rch 268
Thomas	Nrt 425	Daniel	Cbr 692	Boulton, Celia	Hrt 720
William	Brt 30	Elias	Cbr 691	John	Hrt 719
William	Brt 34	Elias	Lnc 866	Thomas	Hrt 728
William, Junr.	Nrt 429	George	Cbr 708	Bounds, George	Rch 242
William, Senr.	Nrt 427	John	Lnc 867	James	Bnc 163
Willis	Frn 478	Joseph	Cbr 707	James	Rch 243
Boone, John	Rwn 446	William	Lnc 867	Jesse	Rch 242
Joseph	Rwn 422	Bostain, Alias	Cbr 708	Jesse	Rch 262
Boonn, Elias	Nsh 88	Andrew	Rwn 311	Bouoen see Bowen	
Bootey, Charlotte	Bfr 4	Andrew, Cap.	Rwn 339	Bourdox, Isaiah	Chw 114
James	Bfr 4	Andrew, Jur.	Rwn 340	Boush, Elizabeth	Crt 62
Richard	Bfr 2	David	Rwn 339	Boushall, Thomas	Cmd 101
William, Jur.	Hde 363	Jacob	Rwn 339	Bowden, Avera	Crv 261
William, Ters.	Hde 363	Mary	Cbr 708	Avera	Crv 267
Booth, David	Rwn 414	Mathias	Rwn 339	Baker	Dpl 435
Elisabeth	Mrt 385	Michael	Rwn 339	Benjamin	Dpl 436
George	Brk 725	Philip	Rwn 340	Elias	Frn 462
Joel	Grv 528	Stophel	Rwn 340	John	Crv 265
John	Edg 182	Bostic, Absalam	Stk 588	John	Frn 464
John	Rwn 406	Richd.	Nwh 7A	John	Nwh 9
Lewis	Edg 184	Bostick, Charles	Dpl 411	Nicolas	Dpl 430
Zachariah	Rwn 406	Charles	Rth 97	Samuel	Dpl 430
Boothe, Andrew	Nsh 93	Chesley	Rth 97	Samuel	Dpl 436
Daniel	Orn 548	Ezra	Ans 227	William	Frn 485
David	Ans 207	Firdenand	Stk 545	Bowdon, Travis	Rnd 299
Geo. C.	Wrr 789	James	Rch 245	William	Rnd 299
Jesse	Nsh 90	John	Rwn 456	Bowel, Benj.	Rch 265
John	Ans 207	Reuben	Rth 97	Robt.	Rch 265
John, Junr.	Ans 207	Samuel	Dpl 413	Bowell, Abner	Cmb 351
Joseph	Orn 549	William	Rch 257	Bowen, Bartholomew	Lnc 872
Lewis	Nsh 90	William	Rch 267	Benjamin, Junr.	Brt 28
Moses	Wke 721	Boston, Joshua	Wsh 700	Benjamin, Senr.	Brt 28
Zachr.	Ans 207	Boswell, Barnaby	Rnd 298	David	Nwh 8A
Booty, Eleanor	Grn 589	Cornelius	Bld 5	Edward	Dpl 407
Boovy, Mathias	Lnc 871	David	Bld 5	Elijah	Dpl 403
Boox, Samuel	Orn 544	Edward	Orn 542	Elijah	Nwh 4A
Booze, George	Stk 551	Ezekah	Csw 144	Ezekiel	Rck 465
Boozman, Britain	Edg 183	Ezra	Rnd 303	Hardy	Brt 34
Bordel, John	Rth 100	Ichabod	Wne 861	Jeams	Crr 164

24

Name	Ref	Name	Ref	Name	Ref
John	Dpl 417	William	Srr 638	William	Grv 533
John	Edg 186	Bownds, George	Mnt 474	William	Mnt 516
John	Rwn 384	Bowns, Green	Orn 546	William	Ptt 253
John, Junr.	Bfr 4	Bowser, James	Hlf 288	William, Esq.	Bfr 3
John, Senr.	Bfr 4	Rachel	Crr 138	see B...d, Boy...	
Luke	Cmb 351	Randol	Hrt 716	Boyde, Burwell	Nrt 429
Matthw.	Rck 465	Thomas	Hlf 288	Boyds, Jacob	Chw 126
Nathan, Junr.	Brt 28	Bowstrot, Absolam	Stk 592	Joseph	Chw 119
Nathan, Sen.	Brt 28	Bowyer, John	Stk 608	William	Chw 117
Sarah	Dpl 406	Joseph	Stk 608	Boyer, Adam	Stk 613
Tennant	Bfr 22	Boxer, Marth	Orn 549	James	Bnc 160
William	Brk 723	Boy..., Thomas	Bfr 3	Boyet, Etheldrel	Wne 868
Bower, Andrew	Rwn 305	Boyakin, Hardy	Nsh 92	Boyet, Jacob	Wne 869
George	Ash 73	James	Nsh 93	Shadrach	Wne 871
Henry	Rwn 305	Jonathin	Nsh 92	Boyett, Joseph	Wne 869
John	Ash 73	Sary	Nsh 93	Thomas	Wne 869
Bowers, Adam	Rwn 351	William	Hlf 292	Boyette, George	Jhn 756
Adam, Junr.	Cbr 697	see Boikin		Thomas	Jhn 752
Adam, Senr.	Cbr 697	Boyas, John	Prq 648	Boykin, Benjamin	Ans 228
Anna	Ptt 237	Josiah	Prq 661	Edward	Edg 184
Benjamin	Ptt 259	Moses	Prq 661	Francis	Nrt 427
Creecy	Hrt 734	Obediah	Prq 663	James	Edg 187
Francis	Stk 545	see Boyds		Jesse	Nrt 429
George	Stk 581	Boyce, Christopher	Brt 30	John	Smp 517
Giles	Ans 203	Dempsey	Brt 28	Lucy	Nrt 429
Jacob	Rwn 351	Hardy	Brt 32	Mary	Smp 494
James	Frn 453	Isham	Brt 26	Mary	Smp 517
James	Frn 466	John	Hrt 696	Robert	Nrt 425
James	Rwn 329	Josiah	Gts 263	Sterling	Nrt 425
John	Csw 118	Judith	Brt 34	Tobias	Smp 518
John	Cht 208	Leah	Chw 125	William	Ans 206
John	Frn 460	Mills	Nrt 427	William	Smp 517
John, junior	Ptt 229	Moses	Gts 263	William	Wne 873
John, Senior	Ptt 260	Scion	Nrt 427	Williamson	Ans 206
Maxwell	Nsh 89	Wm. H.	Hrt 696	Boyl, Ransor	Csw 97
Rachal	Nsh 91	Boyd, Aaron	Ird 627	Boylan, John	Nwh 5A
Rebecca	Nrt 425	Abram	Ons 157	Will.	Nwh 11
Reuben	Ptt 232	Andrew	Mck 579	William	Wke 775
William	Frn 452	Andrew	Rck 480	Boyle, James	Orn 500
William	Ptt 259	Anna	Bfr 3	James	Rth 96
Bowher, Jacob	Rwn 305	Benjamin	Ird 627	James	Rth 100
Bowie see Buey		Bethany	Bfr 3	William	Orn 501
Bowin, Silas	Mrt 386	Francis	Mnt 516	William, Junr.	Orn 542
Bowlen, Alex	Orn 545	George	Crv 233	Boyles, Hugh	Stk 550
Henry	Wlk 27	Henary	Prs 207	John	Stk 550
Bowler, Thomas	Rwn 414	Isaac	Ptt 253	William	Mck 534
Bowles, Francis	Stk 618	Jacob	Nsh 90	Boys, James	Mck 543
James	Cht 166	James	Hlf 292	Boyster, Joseph	Prs 198
Bowlin, Joseph	Brk 723	James	Mck 606	Boyt, Arthur	Dpl 424
Bowls, Isaac	Wrr 793	James	Mnt 516	Daniel	Dpl 431
James	Orn 501	Jessy	Ons 157	Ephraim	Dpl 424
John	Grv 583	Jms.	Lnc 841	Fereby	Dpl 437
John	Orn 500	John	Bfr 2	Jones	Dpl 406
Thomas	Orn 501	John	Grn 547	William	Dpl 437
William	Rck 465	John	Lnc 810	Boyte, Solomon	Mrt 384
Zachariah	Rck 464	John	Mnt 469	Thos.	Mrt 385
see Bawls		John	Mre 60	Boytte, Micajah	Wne 844
Bowman, Andrew	Stk 545	John	Psq 632	Bozman, John	Brt 30
Daniel	Lnc 866	John	Ptt 253	Josiah	Bld 48
Daniel	Lnc 871	John	Srr 638	Joseph	Chw 113
Edward	Orn 544	Joseph	Ird 628	Levin	Wsh 714
Elisabeth	Ird 659	Joseph	Ptt 253	William	Bld 48
Gilbert	Brk 724	Josias	Wne 864	Bozwell, Charles	Brt 30
Groves	Brk 728	Mary	Csw 124	John	Brt 28
Jacob	Brk 730	Moses	Ird 638	William	Brt 30
James	Cmb 351	Robert	Ird 608	Thomas	Brt 30
James	Ird 659	Robert	Ird 627	Bozzel, Benjamin	Rth 97
John	Ird 774	Robert	Ird 628	Lewis	Srr 638
John	Lnc 871	Robert, junior	Ptt 253	Brable, John	Crr 143
Nancy	Brk 729	Robert, son of		Wm.	Crr 143
Peter	Glf 647	Chas.	Ptt 253	Brace, Sampson	Jhn 773
Robert	Csw 96	Robert, Senior	Ptt 253	Bracewell, Abner	Edg 183
Samuel	Mck 522	Robt.	Wlk 29	Isaac	Edg 184
Shered	Brk 730	Samuel	Mnt 520	Jacob	Edg 183
William	Ird 664	Widow	Mck 541	James	Edg 181
William	Rth 96	William	Brn 13	James, (H)	Edg 183
William	Stk 618	William	Crv 299	James, Junr.	Edg 182

Permenter	Edg 184	Joseph	Glf 628	Braford, Edward	Cmb 367
Samon	Edg 184	Mary	Cbr 682	Brag, Frances	Bfr 22
Solomon	Edg 183	Philemon	Grv 524	Jesse	Crt 59
Zadock	Edg 182	Thomas	Orn 501	Bragboy, John	Bfr 4
Bracey, James	Rbs 361	Thomas	Orn 545	Bragdin, David	Grv 567
Bracher, Field	Brk 724	William	Orn 500	Bragdon, Timothy	Brt 30
Isaiah	Brk 724	William	Orn 544	William	Wrr 789
Josiah	Brk 723	Bradley, ...	Nwh 1A	William, jr.	Wrr 789
Obadiah	Brk 727	Ansel	Rth 96	Bragg, Benjamin	Grv 549
William, Senr.	Brk 726	Burwell	Edg 182	Hugh	Grv 572
Bracie, Irby	Grv 576	Darlin	Wke 718	John	Crv 297
Brack, Benjamin	Cmb 369	Edmund	Rth 98	John	Orn 549
Burrel	Grv 519	Henry	Frn 457	William	Crv 295
Burrel, Jur.	Grv 584	Isaac	Rth 98	Bragham, John	Ons 175
George	Grv 518	James	Wne 868	Braising, Andrew	Stk 626
John	Ons 158	John (2)	Dpl 430	Brake, Jacob	Edg 185
Samuel	Grv 518	Joseph	Rth 98	Jesse	Edg 185
Bracker, James	Csw 100	James	Grv 573	John	Edg 188
Saml.	Csw 102	James	Hlf 292	Nattan	Edg 181
Bracket, Benjamin	Rth 97	James	Nrt 425	Priscilla	Edg 184
Burrel	Rth 97	James, Esqr.	Bld 28	Braley, Fredrick	Bnc 162
Brackfrend, George	Cbr 682	Jas.	Hlf 288	Braly, Hugh	Rwn 335
Brackin, Edward	Rwn 423	Jno.	Lnc 840	James	Rwn 335
Henry	Orn 501	John	Ptt 275	John	Rwn 335
Isaac	Orn 501	John	Rth 96	Mary	Ird 660
James	Rwn 423	John	Wlk 29	Neil	Ird 659
Samuel	Rwn 422	Joseph	Hlf 290	William	Rwn 335
Thomas	Rwn 423	Lawrance	Rnd 301	Bramble, William	Smp 517
William	Orn 500	Lawrence	Wlk 29	Brame, Richard	Grv 518
William	Rwn 423	Major	Wke 719	William	Grv 519
Brackson, William	Ptt 283	Rachel	Orn 544	Branan, Caren	Wke 717
Brackston, Jesse	Ptt 288	Richard	Dpl 442	Caren, Senr.	Wke 717
John, Junior	Ptt 288	Richard	Wne 853	William	Wke 717
John, Senior	Ptt 288	Sampson	Orn 549	Branch, Anderson	Brk 725
Levy	Ptt 288	Samuel	Hlf 296	Anne	Nrt 425
Mary	Ptt 287	Thomas	Hlf 292	Archilaus	Dpl 439
see Blackston		Walton	Rth 98	Arthur	Wne 846
Bradberry, George	Wne 866	Willis	Rth 96	Benjamin	Nrt 427
Solomon	Wne 866	see Brdley		Bowen	Nrt 425
William	Rck 467	Bradlove, Charles	Rth 97	Burrel	Dpl 427
Bradborn, John	Bnc 162	Bradly, Andrew	Rwn 422	Dred	Dpl 428
Bradburn, John	Brk 729	Benjamin	Edg 187	Edmond	Cht 173
John	Rwn 351	Josiah	Cbr 685	Issachar	Prq 643
Thomas	Brk 728	Mary	Brk 730	James	Ptt 243
Bradbury, James	Wne 855	Michael	Rwn 456	Jesse	Dpl 428
Joshua	Cht 175	Richard	Edg 187	Job	Prq 643
Braddum, Stephen	Dpl 412	Robert	Mck 582	John	Hlf 292
Braddy, Anne	Edg 182	Sherwood	Smp 535	Mary	Nrt 425
Anne	Nrt 429	Stephen	Edg 187	Moses	Rbs 363
Benjamin	Bfr 2	Thomas	Edg 187	Nicholas	Hlf 290
Blake	Jhn 759	Widow	Mck 550	Olive	Brk 727
Elisha	Ptt 282	William	Edg 187	Randolph	Wne 846
Henry	Bfr 2	Bradshaw, Charles	Lnc 835	Randolph, jr.	Wne 845
James	Gts 263	Ephraim	Smp 508	William	Dpl 431
James	Ptt 282	Fields	Lnc 852	Brand, John, ju-	
Job	Edg 182	James, Junr.	Cbr 706	nior	Grn 596
Mary	Gts 263	James, Senr.	Cbr 705	John B.	Grn 597
William	Bfr 2	John	Prs 211	Solomon	Grn 597
see B...addy		Jonas	Lnc 852	William	Grn 597
Braden, Margarett	Glf 634	Josiah (2)	Lnc 852	Brandon, Able	Rwn 324
Robert	Rth 96	Moses	Prs 211	Abram	Rwn 446
William	Grv 544	Robert	Rwn 406	Benjamin	Rwn 324
Bradey, Peter	Crr 167	Solomon	Mck 595	Christopher	Rwn 446
Thos.	Crr 166	Thomas	Orn 544	David	Bnc 161
Bradford, Benjamin	Mnt 516	William	Brk 727	Elizabeth	Rwn 310
Bennet	Brk 726	William	Mck 594	George	Rwn 446
David	Cbr 682	William	Orn 544	John	Lnc 873
David	Orn 500	William, Junr.	Orn 544	John	Rwn 315
Elijah	Grv 556	Brady, Archibald	Ird 638	John	Rwn 324
George	Orn 545	Brassel	Nsh 93	John	Rwn 446
Henry	Hlf 292	Charles	Mre 48	John, Col.	Rwn 310
James	Grv 524	James	Mre 76	Josiah	Brk 729
John	Brk 725	John	Rwn 305	Matthew	Rwn 310
John	Brk 727	Joseph	Edg 186	William	Rwn 324
John	Grv 555	Lewis	Rnd 299	Brank, Robert	Bnc 160
John	Glf 628	Tabitha	Rnd 299	Brann, John	Prs 199
John	Wke 718	William	Jhn 746	Thomas	Prs 199

Vinsin	Prs 209	Brasher, Asa	Glf 672	Littlebery	Srr 634	
Brannham, Benjn.	Wlk 26	seth	Brk 729	Maryann	Crr 161	
Brannock, Henry	Orn 501	Zaza	Rck 441	Mathias	Rnd 299	
William	Orn 501	Brasing, Andrew	Stk 577	Nathan	Srr 635	
Brannon, Andrew	Cmb 383	Brasington, Joseph	Nrt 427	Nicholas A.	Jns 803	
James	Csw 107	William	Nrt 429	Patrick	Wlk 30	
Thomas	Jhn 760	Brassel, David	Jhn 771	Richard	Cht 184	
Brannum, Barnabas	Stk 550	Drew	Hlf 294	Rubin	Brk 725	
John	Stk 544	George	Nrt 423	Samuel	Cmd 103	
Jonathan	Stk 546	Jacob	Jhn 748	Samuel	Cmd 105	
Maliche	Stk 566	James	Hlf 294	Soloman	Cht 185	
Bransby, John	Nwh 7	Richard	Jhn 772	Stogna	Srr 638	
Branson, Henry	Rnd 299	William	Jhn 773	Thomas	Cmd 103	
John	Stk 558	Brassell, Duke	Nrt 425	Walles	Crr 161	
Joseph	Cht 195	Brasser, James	Mnt 484	Will	Prs 199	
Leonard	Stk 566	Brasure, Elijah	Rwn 440	William	Cmd 105	
Levi	Cht 194	William	Rwn 440	William	Cht 183	
Levi	Cht 220	Braswell, Arthur	Rbs 361	William	Cht 215	
William	Stk 558	Benja.	Nsh 91	William	Srr 635	
Zacheriah	Stk 575	Brittin	Nsh 88	Brayboy, Jacob	Mrt 387	
Brant, Benjamin	Brk 731	David	Rbs 362	Brayson, Hugh	Mck 566	
Mary	Brk 731	Demsy	Nsh 88	James	Mck 565	
Brantle, Jesse	Csw 143	Jacob, Sr.	Nsh 93	Robert	Mck 565	
Solomon	Csw 143	John	Nsh 93	Brazdell, Jacob	Glf 663	
Wm.	Csw 143	Micajah	Rbs 362	Brazer, David	Ird 620	
Brantley, Ann	Hlf 296	Milly	Nsh 93	Brazier, Elijah	Cmb 389	
Dinah	Nsh 93	Nathan	Rbs 361	Brazington see Brasington		
Edward	Hlf 292	Robert	Nsh 88	Brchouse, John	Crr 149	
Edwin	Nsh 90	Sarah	Nsh 89	Brdley, James	Wlk 29	
Eli	Bld 22	William	Nsh 88	Richard	Rth 98	
Henry	Nrt 429	Wilson	Nsh 88	Brea, Henry	Psq 631	
Jacob	Nsh 90	Bratcher, Benjamin	Dpl 422	John	Psq 630	
James	Cmb 351	Christopher	Smp 536	Breading, Meshack	Bnc 161	
James	Frn 473	Ephraim	Smp 506	Samuel	Bnc 161	
John	Nsh 90	Jesse	Smp 506	Breadlove, John	Wrr 790	
Joseph	Cht 151	Mary	Crv 307	Breadon, Isaac	Cbr 696	
Josiah	Nsh 87	Sion	Smp 522	Breath, John	Grv 551	
Lewis	Mrt 386	Thomas	Crv 337	Samuel	Grv 551	
Lewis	Nsh 91	Bratels, Christian	Brk 725	Breece, Joseph	Jns 799	
Matthew	Brt 32	Bratley, Jesse	Brn 13	Breecheen, David	Prs 212	
Patsy	Hlf 294	Brattan, Benjn.	Prq 652	Breechen, Jno.	Prs 206	
Robert, Jr.	Hlf 294	Brattell, James	Hde 364	Wm.	Prs 203	
Robert, Sr.	Hlf 294	Bratton, Benjamin	Brk 724	Breedlove, Sarah	Rck 490	
Samuel	Hlf 292	Benjamin	Rnd 302	Breekes see Brukes		
Shewood	Nsh 94	John	Rnd 304	Brees, Cornels.	Ons 160	
Thomas	Bld 8	Robert	Rnd 301	James	Crt 91	
Willice	Nsh 90	Robert	Rnd 302	Rossetter	Crt 91	
William	Hlf 292	Thomas S.	Brk 724	Breeze, James	Orn 551	
Brantly, Benjn.,		William	Rnd 298	Robert	Orn 551	
Jn.	Hrt 708	Braudaway, John	Ans 218	see Brize		
Benjn., Sen.	Hrt 708	William	Ans 218	Brehon, James G.	Wrr 790	
Blake	Cht 177	Braughton, Abel	Crv 289	Brellison see Bullison		
Edward	Cht 177	John	Crv 289	Brem, Conrod	Rwn 276	
John	Cht 179	Braveboy, Jacob	Rbs 367	Conrod	Rwn 284	
John, Sen.	Cht 177	Stephen	Rbs 366	Jacob	Rwn 276	
Joseph	Cht 179	Brawdy, John	Cmb 359	Jacob	Rwn 285	
Lewis	Hrt 709	Brawell, Elisabeth	Wne 860	Bremigim, Asa	Rch 259	
Sarah	Cmb 371	Shadrach	Wne 860	Caleb	Ans 200	
Thomas	Cmb 386	Brawley, Pryer	Glf 663	Charles	Ans 227	
William	Cht 206	Brawly, Martha	Glf 663	Stephen	Ans 227	
William, Senr.	Cht 172	Brawner, James	Rnd 301	Bremmer, Isaac	Lnc 830	
Branton, Matturin	Bld 13	Bray, Briant	Srr 639	Saml.	Lnc 830	
Samuel	Crv 327	Daniel	Cmd 104	Brenda, Sabra	Ptt 280	
Thos.	Lnc 846	Daniel	Cmd 106	Breninger, Adam	Rwn 435	
Uriah	Bfr 2	David	Srr 635	Paul	Rwn 423	
William	Cht 209	Demsey	Cmd 103	Brennen, John	Edg 171	
William	Crv 327	Edmond	Cht 218	Patrick	Edg 171	
Branum, Christ.	Rck 458	Edward	Srr 635	Brenner, Christian	Lnc 810	
see Brannum		Hanan	Srr 635	Brenning, Patrick	Edg 181	
Brasewell, Jesse	Wne 860	Hannah	Dpl 420	Brennon, John	Edg 181	
Brasfield, George	Grv 526	Henry	Cht 183	Brenson, John	Glf 688	
George	Wke 721	Henry	Cht 218	John	Ons 171	
Jesse	Wke 720	Jesse	Cmd 99	Reubin	Glf 688	
John	Wke 718	Jessee	Cht 183	Brent, Charles	Psq 627	
Joseph	Wke 723	John	Cht 182	John	Stk 594	
Willie	Wke 720	Joseph	Srr 639	Thomas C.	Rck 485	
Brash, William	Brk 723	Lener	Crr 161	Brentle, William	Csw 121	

Brester, William   Orn 545
Bret, Joseph   Smp 515
Breton see Bicton, Buton
Brett, Arthur   Hrt 728
  Collin   Hrt 728
  Etheldred   Hrt 729
  Hardy   Hrt 728
  James, junr.   Hrt 728
  James, Senr.   Hrt 728
  Lydia   Hrt 728
  Marten   Hrt 728
  Silas   Hrt 728
  Thomas, Senr.   Hrt 728
Brettin, Martha   Nsh 93
Brevard, Adam   Ird 659
  Alexander   Lnc 852
  Benjamin   Ird 659
  Robert   Ird 659
  Thomas   Brk 726
Brever, William   Cht 154
  see Brwer
Brew, Thomas   Crv 239
Brewer, ...oell   Rnd 299
  Amos   Cht 182
  Ansil   Cht 220
  Arthur   Ptt 299
  Daniel   Cht 155
  Dorcus   Mrt 386
  Druray   Mre 46
  Drury   Jhn 777
  Edmond   Ptt 261
  Edward   Rnd 299
  Ezedekiah   Wrr 791
  Ezekiel   Orn 547
  Henry   Ash 73
  Henry   Cht 163
  Henry   Rnd 303
  Isaac   Mrt 387
  Isham   Orn 547
  Jacob   Wne 864
  James   Grv 582
  James   Rwn 455
  James, Junr.   Rwn 456
  Jas.   Mrt 385
  Jerry   Cht 181
  Jesse   Hlf 294
  Jesse   Wne 864
  John   Cht 181
  John   Nrt 423
  John   Rwn 455
  Jones   Cht 190
  Kinchen   Hrt 728
  Mary   Cht 186
  Mary, Senr.   Mrt 387
  Moses   Prs 192
  Nathaniel   Cht 156
  Nathaniel   Cht 173
  Nathaniel   Cht 181
  Nicholas   Cht 220
  Nicholas   Nrt 425
  Oliver   Cht 201
  Roberte   Mrt 387
  Sackfield   Orn 547
  Sampson   Cht 163
  Sampson   Cht 220
  Sarah   Edg 186
  Sarah   Wke 718
  Silas   Mrt 387
  Sylvanus   Orn 547
  Thomas   Cht 160
  Thomas   Cht 165
  Thomas   Orn 547
  Thomas   Rwn 455
  Thomas, Senr.   Rwn 455
  William   Cht 168
  William   Hlf 290
  William   Hrt 730

  William   Nrt 427
  William   Orn 547
  William   Psq 629
  Willis   Nrt 429
  Wm.   Mrt 387
  Zedekiah E.   Wrr 791
  see Brever, Bruer,
    Brwer
Brewor, Ambrus   Mre 46
  Cagor   Mre 42
  Elizabeth   Mre 73
  Harmen   Mre 42
  William   Mre 42
Brian, James   Grn 614
  Lewis Cox   Ptt 240
Briant, Alexander   Srr 636
  John   Grn 594
  Jonathan   Srr 705
  Lewis   Brt 28
  Reuben   Srr 639
  Sarah   Orn 551
  Thomas   Srr 637
  William   Stk 592
Briants, Nicholas   Srr 709
Brice, John   Dpl 436
  John, Junr.   Rwn 414
  Joseph   Dpl 440
  Margaret   Crv 313
  William   Srr 637
Brichouse, Elishey Crr 151
  George   Crr 151
  Harmon   Crr 153
  Henery   Crr 160
  Nedey   Crr 151
  Peter   Crr 153
  Wm.   Crr 160
  see Brchouse, Brick-
    house
Brickell, Jonathan Hrt 709
  Thos. Neil   Hrt 709
  William   Frn 445
  William   Hrt 723
Brickett, Eliza-
    beth   Cmd 109
Brickhouse, John,
    Senr.   Trl 670
  Matthew   Trl 670
  Peter   Trl 684
  Sarah   Trl 684
  William   Trl 684
  William, Junr.   Trl 692
Brickle, Benjamin,
    Esq.   Edg 171
  Benjamin, Esqr.   Edg 181
  James   Bfr 2
  Joseph   Bfr 22
  Nancy   Hlf 292
  Thomas   Frn 481
  Thomas   Gts 261
Brickman, Isaac   Rch 242
Bricks see Brukes
Bricton, William   Mnt 468
Bridgeman, Thomas   Hde 364
  see Bridgman
Bridgemon, William Stk 582
Bridger, Joseph   Hrt 719
  Josiah   Hrt 719
Bridgers, Benjamin Nsh 91
  Benjamin   Nrt 423
  Catharine   Nrt 425
  Drewry   Nsh 91
  James   Nrt 427
  John, Senr.   Nrt 425
  John, Junr.   Nrt 427
  Joseph   Nrt 425
  Rebeca   Rbs 365
  Sampson   Rbs 361

  Samuel, Jur.   Rbs 361
  Samuel, Senr.   Rbs 361
  William   Edg 182
  William   Nsh 88
  William   Nrt 429
  William, Jur.   Nsh 93
  Willis   Nrt 429
Bridges, Aaron   Rth 97
  Daniel   Grv 521
  Dorrel   Frn 455
  Drury   Grv 523
  Elizabeth   Rth 98
  George   Jhn 748
  Isaac   Rth 98
  James   Bnc 161
  James   Cbr 686
  James (4)   Rth 97
  James   Wne 850
  Joseph   Ans 241
  Joseph   Cht 214
  Joseph   Frn 455
  Joseph   Grv 523
  Josiah   Frn 462
  Lewis   Frn 455
  Micajah   Frn 465
  Moses   Rth 97
  Patience   Brt 32
  Robert   Ptt 227
  Samuel   Rth 98
  Shadreck   Frn 451
  Thomas   Rth 97
  William   Bnc 161
  William   Rth 97
  William   Rth 98
  William   Wke 721
  William, Sr.   Bnc 161
Bridgman, James   Hde 364
Bridgmon, John   Stk 583
  Matthew   Srr 638
Brien, Thomas   Ptt 258
Brient see Brunt
Brier, John   Hrt 723
Brierlay, Solomon   Ptt 228
Brierley, Jacob   Ptt 290
Brierly, Benjamin   Ptt 230
  Bethea   Ptt 280
  Isaac   Ptt 231
  Jonas   Ptt 230
  Joseph   Ptt 230
  Mary   Ptt 230
  William   Ptt 231
Brigfarmer, Martin Rwn 440
Briggman, Solomon   Bnc 160
Briggs, Ann   Stk 628
  Charles   Wke 719
  David   Lnc 873
  Elisha   Lnc 873
  Elizabeth   Stk 549
  George   Grv 544
  George   Grv 571
  Jacob   Lnc 852
  James   Rwn 315
  James   Rwn 384
  Jesse   Rth 98
  Jesse   Stk 546
  John   Crt 66
  John   Grv 521
  John   Stk 546
  John   Stk 566
  Josiah   Gts 262
  Mells   Prq 647
  Moses   Gts 262
  Myles   Prq 647
  Nancy   Rth 96
  Nathan   Rwn 384
  Rhodham   Grv 567
  Richard   Gts 263

Richard	Grv 583	Elier		Prq 642	Britt, Aaron	Grn 595
Solomon	Gts 263	Elisha		Brt 30	Alexander	Grn 593
Thomas	Rwn 397	Elisha		Gts 263	Benjamin (2)	Rbs 363
Thomas P.	Stk 546	Ely		Gts 262	David	Rch 246
William	Lnc 873	Ely		Orn 549	Edward	Rbs 361
William	Rwn 377	Henry		Gts 262	Edward	Wke 717
William	Rwn 384	James		Grv 544	Elizabeth	Brt 28
Bright, Aron	Crr 163	John		Gts 262	Henry	Cmd 93
Benjamin	Bld 15	John		Ons 140	Henry	Wne 871
Benn.	Psq 641	John		Ptt 281	Hezekiah	Cmd 96
Ephraim	Psq 630	Joseph		Gts 261	Hiceker	Cmd 96
Graves	Grn 608	Josiah		Hlf 290	Isaac	Cmd 98
Hanee	Crr 161	Myles		Prq 652	Jeremiah	Cmd 93
Isaac	Cht 155	Peter		Orn 544	Jesse	Brt 28
Jabez	Psq 636	Peter, Junr.		Orn 544	John	Rbs 363
James	Bld 15	Sarah		Edg 184	John, Jur.	Rbs 363
James	Glf 682	Simeon		Gts 263	Joseph	Grn 593
James	Lnr 3	William		Gts 263	Josiah	Edg 184
James, Senr.	Lnr 3	William		Grv 582	Kinchen	Wne 844
Jarvice	Cht 156	William		Hlf 290	Malichi	Cmd 98
Jesse	Psq 630	William		Orn 549	Mariam	Cmd 93
John	Crv 325	Brinkly, James, jr.		Grv 576	Mary	Cmd 93
Jonn.	Crr 154	Peter		Cht 196	Mary	Rbs 363
Joseph	Psq 624	Thomas		Cht 161	Mordecai	Cmd 93
Mary	Lnr 3	Brinn, James		Chw 128	Samson	Mrt 385
Nathan	Psq 636	John		Chw 119	Samuel	Rbs 364
Polley	Crr 157	John		Hde 363	Shadrick	Cmd 93
Polley	Crr 163	Mary		Chw 122	Simon	Grn 593
Richard	Bld 4	Nathaniel		Chw 123	Simon	Grn 611
Richard	Psq 636	Nicholas		Hde 363	William	Edg 183
Robert	Bld 24	Richard, Jur.		Hde 363	William	Grn 593
Robert	Cht 156	Richard, Ser.		Hde 363	William	Rbs 363
Samuel	Brk 728	Brinsfield, John		Glf 662	William, Senior	Grn 595
Simion	Cht 165	Thomas		Csw 145	see Bill	
Simon	Lnr 35	Brinson, Benjamin		Crv 261	Brittain, Benj.	Hrt 709
Simon	Bld 15	Cason		Crv 261	James	Bnc 162
Simon, Jur.	Bld 5	Daniel		Crv 267	James	Srr 636
Solomon	Psq 641	Elizabeth		Ons 167	John	Srr 635
Solomon	Rwn 371	Hilery		Dpl 412	Michael	Hrt 703
Willis	Psq 630	John		Crv 261	William	Bnc 162
Brightwell, John	Rth 95	Joseph		Crv 261	William	Glf 663
Brigs, Ann	Stk 568	Mathew		Brn 15	Britting, Mr.	Stk 568
Brikford, James	Edg 182	Mathew		Crv 259	Brittle, John	Nrt 425
Briles, Frederick	Rnd 303	Nathan		Cmd 110	Martha	Nrt 429
John	Rnd 303	Rachal		Ons 172	Micajah	Nrt 427
Briley, Abraham	Ans 226	Brint, Ciatra		Cbr 696	Phillip	Nrt 427
George	Ans 202	Briols, Francis		Chw 126	Britton, Benjamin	Ons 156
Henry	Edg 185	Brion, John		Crr 159	Catharine	Crv 337
Joseph	Ans 206	Brisco, Nathan		Rth 95	John	Ons 142
Samuel	Edg 184	Brisket, Henry		Rwn 414	John	Ptt 236
William	Ans 226	Brisko, Wesley		Gts 262	Brize, John	Orn 550
Brim, James	Rck 474	Brison, Andrew		Ird 654	Brizinger, Henry	Lnc 810
John	Rck 489	Jane		Lnc 830	Bro..., Mary	Bfr 2
Raleigh	Rck 453	John		Srr 637	Broach, Jas.	Prs 213
Rice	Rck 466	John, Ser.		Srr 636	Broadfoot, Andrew	Cmb 351
Richins	Rck 461	Bristol, John		Bnc 163	Broadstreet, Patty	Edg 184
Brimage, Elizabeth	Brt 26	Bristow, Warner		Nrt 423	William	Jhn 770
see B...age		Brit, Benjn.			Broadwater, Joshua	Crv 275
Brime, John	Grv 514	Joseph		Mre 70	Jesse	Crv 315
Brind, Nathaniel	Chw 131	Royal		Mre 70	Jesse	Prs 213
Brindle, Daniel	Srr 635	Britain, Edmund		Dpl 411	John	Prs 213
George	Srr 636	Elizabeth		Glf 684	Samuel	Rth 95
John	Lnc 901	Henry		Glf 681	Broadwell, David	Brt 28
Brine, Jas.	Rck 446	Jesse		Nrt 423	Wm.	Wke 722
Brines, Henry	Cbr 686	John		Brt 28	Brock, Beasant	Dpl 427
Bringham, Benjamin	Stk 545	John		Nrt 423	Benjamin	Ans 224
Brinklay, Nicey	Ptt 239	Joseph		Orn 550	Benjamin	Dpl 427
Brinkle, Casper	Rwn 351	William W.,			Benjamin	Jns 813
Christian	Rwn 351	Ovr.		Orn 547	David	Srr 636
Richard	Grv 571	Britchett, Thomas		Grv 560	Elias	Crt 87
Wm., Jur	Csw 144	Briton, Aaron		Brk 724	Francis	Stk 550
Brinkley, Abraham		Mark		Brk 724	Hannah	Dpl 436
(2)	Hlf 290	Philip		Brk 725	John	Bfr 2
Abram	Edg 184	Samuel		Brk 724	John	Rbs 365
Cherry	Hlf 290	Brits, George		Grn 599	John	Rbs 432
Daniel	Crv 331	James		Grn 599	Joseph	Jns 815
David	Gts 262	Samuel		Grn 599	Losson	Bfr 3

Moses	Lnc	893	Larkin	Prs	196	John	Ird	615
Nathaniel	Crr	165	Larking	Cht	185	John	Ird	618
Rubin	Lnc	893	Leah	Ash	73	Mary	Lnc	858
Rune	Wlk	30	Marke	Cht	186	Broton, Joseph	Jhn	756
Silas	Lnc	887	Mary	Crr	167	Brotton, Adam	Crt	81
Thomas	Lnc	892	Mathew	Prs	200	Brough, Christopher	Rwn	414
see B...ck, Brook			Matthew	Stk	611	Broughton, Jesse	Bnc	161
Brockell, Mary	Hlf	294	Philip	Rch	250	Job	Bnc	160
Brocket, Elizabeth	Cmd	110	Rachel	Lnc	899	Nathl.	Prq	646
Jabeth	Cmd	110	Samuel	Cht	225	Woodward	Bnc	161
John	Cmd	107	Samuel	Rwn	430	Brouncy, Susanna	Edg	182
John	Cmd	110	Spring	Crv	277	Brow, Daniel	Wlk	27
Jonathan	Cmd	110	Stephen	Cht	164	John	Ash	74
Brockett, Benjamin	Jns	779	Tabeth	Prs	195	John	Brk	727
Brockinan, Mayor	Csw	102	Terrell	Cht	206	Browder, Isam	Rck	442
Brodie, Alexander	Grv	533	Thomas	Ash	73	Tiletha	Rck	442
John	Grv	547	Thomas	Cht	153	Brower, Christian	Rnd	299
Brogden, William	Wsh	700	Thomas	Hde	363	Jacob	Rnd	304
Brogdon, Catharine	Brt	34	Thomas	Orn	493	John	Rnd	304
John	Wne	856	William	Ans	219	Nicholas	Rnd	304
Moses	Brt	32	William	Brk	729	Browin, John	Hlf	358
Susanah, Senr.	Mrt	384	William	Crv	277	Browing, John	Nwh	7
Thomas	Brt	30	William	Gts	262	Mary	Orn	548
Thomas	Wne	856	William	Hde	363	Browks, Artha,		
William	Brt	32	William	Mnt	506	Junr.	Prs	194
Willie	Wke	722	William	Orn	545	David	Prs	193
Brogton, John	Cht	209	William	Rwn	377	Jno.	Prs	194
Broils, George	Rwn	351	William	Rth	95	Brown, A. Joseph	Brk	28
Broker, Joseph	Grv	584	Woody	Prs	195	A.T.	Nwh	3A
Brokshire, Wm.	Wlk	29	Wm. B.	Csw	142	Aaron	Wlk	28
Brook, George	Lnc	887	see Browks			Abner	Mrt	385
Jhon	Stk	545	Brookshare, Hugh	Rwn	414	Abraham	Rbs	368
Major	Orn	544	Jesse	Rwn	414	Absalom	Brk	729
Robert	Prs	195	Manering	Rnd	302	Adam	Glf	647
Thomas	Rwn	446	Thomas	Rnd	298	Alexander	Rck	476
William	Ptt	244	Brookshire, Benj.	Bnc	163	Amea	Hlf	290
William	Stk	545	James	Bnc	162	Amos	Brk	729
see Brock			Broom, Hailey	Nrt	425	Amy	Wne	855
Brooke, William	Ans	224	Jacob	Mck	585	Andrew	Bfr	2
Brooker, John	Nrt	429	James	Mck	583	Andrew	Cht	160
Brooks, Aaron	Rwn	430	Lucy	Hlf	290	Andrew	Rwn	292
Andrew	Orn	491	Mark	Cmb	391	Anguist	Rch	262
Ann	Csw	142	Marke	Cht	208	Angus	Cmb	364
Arter	Prs	219	Mason	Grn	605	Angus	Rbs	360
Bebby	Mnt	477	Sarey	Grn	594	Ann	Bfr	2
Chas.	Csw	148	Walker	Mck	585	Anne	Bld	21
Christopher	Frn	475	William	Ptt	258	Anthony	Prs	190
David	Prs	195	Broon, Rachel	Crr	154	Archibald	Cmb	384
David	Stk	617	Brosher, John L.	Psq	633	Archibald	Wrr	789
Elizabeth	Dpl	411	Joseph	Psq	633	Archibaldd	Cmb	367
Ephraim	Ans	229	Simon	Psq	633	Arthur	Brt	34
Ezekiel B.	Ans	200	Brothers, Andrew	Psq	628	Arthur	Ptt	269
Fanney	Ptt	294	Ann	Psq	636	Arthur	Smp	502
George	Gts	262	Betsey	Psq	636	Asa	Edg	182
Gresey	Brk	728	Betsey	Psq	639	Barnaba	Brn	18
Humphry	Rck	486	Bryant	Psq	633	Barnet	Mnt	487
Isaac	Cht	185	David	Crv	279	Benjamin	Brt	28
Isaac	Cht	194	David	Psq	638	Benjamin	Bnc	162
Jacob	Jhn	762	Deborah	Psq	629	Benjamin	Cmd	98
James	Crt	71	Edmond	Crv	303	Benjamin	Chw	116
James, junior	Ptt	245	Jerry	Psq	638	Benjamin	Dpl	400
James, Senior	Ptt	245	Jesse	Psq	629	Benjamin	Hrt	704
Jereh.	Csw	117	John	Psq	636	Benjamin	Mck	568
Jesse	Ans	218	John	Psq	639	Benjamin	Nrt	429
Joab	Cht	194	Joseph	Bfr	4	Benjamin	Ptt	289
John	Crt	70	Josh.	Psq	636	Benjamin	Wke	717
John	Cht	195	Joshua	Psq	636	Benjamin	Wlk	30
John	Hlf	292	Malachi	Psq	627	Benjn.	Wlk	28
John	Ird	664	Malachi	Psq	629	Betsey	Wrr	793
John	Mnt	506	Miles	Psq	629	Bonwell	Csw	143
John	Prs	199	Nathaniel	Ird	623	Cannon	Rwn	423
John	Ptt	242	Ruth	Psq	629	Carter	Wke	719
John	Rnd	301	Saml., Junr.	Bfr	4	Celix	Edg	188
John	Rbs	367	Samuel, Senr.	Bfr	4	Charles	Brk	730
John	Stk	617	Sarah	Prq	654	Christian	Rwn	292
Joseph	Crv	275	Thomas	Psq	639	Christopher	Srr	636
Joseph	Crv	277	Brotherton, James	Lnc	859	Christopher	Wne	857

Name	Ref	Name	Ref	Name	Ref
Coleman	Rth 98	James	Edg 186	John	Rwn 299
Daniel	Brk 726	James	Frn 470	John	Rwn 359
Daniel	Cmd 104	James	Glf 624	John	Rwn 435
Daniel	Cht 180	James	Glf 686	John	Srr 635
Daniel	Jns 811	James	Hrt 730	John	Srr 638
Daniel	Rwn 292	James	Lnr 2	John	Srr 639
Danl.	Lnr 29	James	Lnr 28	John	Wlk 26
David	Gts 263	James	Mck 529	John	Wlk 28
David	Mrt 384	James	Mck 546	John	Wlk 29
David	Mck 544	James	Ptt 290	John, Esqr.	Bld 23
Dempsey	Grn 607	James	Rnd 304	John, Esqr.	Wlk 26
Drury	Wke 719	James	Rwn 384	John, j	Rth 98
Duncan	Rbs 366	James	Rwn 285	John, Junr.	Wke 721
Dunkin	Mre 55	James	Rwn 315	John, (of Tho.)	Hrt 734
Ebenezar	Cht 211	James	Rth 95	John, S.	Rth 98
Edmond	Bfr 2	James	Stk 544	John, Senr.	Brk 723
Edward	Jns 813	James	Stk 545	John, Senr.	Cht 181
Edwin	Wlk 27	James	Srr 634	John Erwin	Ird 647
Eli	Bfr 2	James	Srr 637	John N.	Nwh 2
Elias	Hlf 290	James	Srr 638	Jonah	Wn3 856
Elijah	Csw 146	James	Wke 718	Joseph	Ash 74
Elijah	Wne 855	James	Wrr 792	Joseph	Brt 30
Elisabeth	Mrt 386	James, Esqr.	Wlk 26	Joseph	Cht 169
Elizabeth	Hlf 290	James, Jur.	Csw 129	Joseph	Joh 764
Elizabeth	Nsh 90	James, Junr.	Wsh 700	Joseph	Rnd 298
Esther	Rwn 276	James, Senr.	Wsh 700	Joseph	Rnd 303
Esther	Rwn 285	James, Senr.	Wlk 26	Joseph	Srr 637
Ezekial	Lnc 846	Jas., Junr.	Mrt 386	Joseph	Wke 721
Ezekiel	Rwn 363	Jas., Senr.	Mrt 385	Joseph	Wlk 28
Ezekiel	Wne 857	Jeremiah	Cht 160	Joseph A.	Brt 28
Ezekiel	Wlk 28	Jeremiah	Hrt 723	Joshua	Brk 723
Francis	Hrt 708	Jeremiah	Rwn 276	Joshua	Mnt 489
Francis	Rth 98	Jeromiah	Mnt 521	Joshua	Srr 637
Franky	Rbs 364	Jeromiah	Rwn 284	Josiah	Brn 13
Frederic	Brt 28	Jesse	Brt 34	Josiah	Csw 116
Frederick	Rnd 301	Jesse	Dpl 412	Josiah	Cmb 391
Fredr.	Lnr 28	Jesse	Dpl 427	Josiah	Hrt 723
George	Bnc 162	Jesse	Hlf 296	Josiah	Prs 202
George	Csw 135	Jesse	Jhn 770	Josiah	Srr 634
George	Cht 189	Jesse	Mck 532	Katharine	Rbs 368
George	Cmb 367	Jesse	Mre 71	Leonard	Csw 138
George	Rck 440	Jesse	Srr 634	Leond.	Csw 137
George	Srr 636	Jesse	Srr 638	Lewis	Jns 787
George, Esqr.	Wlk 27	Jesse	Wke 717	Lewis, Esqr.	Hrt 709
Hardy	Bld 21	Jesse	Wne 856	Lewis, Junr.	Hrt 708
Hardy	Hrt 703	Jesse	Wne 865	Lucy	Wlk 29
Henry	Bfr 2	Jethro	Csw 97	Luke	Crr 149
Henry	Cht 175	Jno.	Nwh 2A	Malcom	Rbs 367
Henry	Jns 787	Joel	Brt 34	Margarett	Brt 28
Henry	Rnd 299	Joel	Orn 544	Margret	Ird 660
Henry	Wke 720	John	Brn 18	Martha	Glf 652
Hubbard	Rck 491	John	Cbr 682	Martha	Nrt 429
Hudson	Csw 123	John	Cbr 696	Martin	Hrt 734
Hudson	Csw 140	John	Csw 97	Mary	Glf 636
Hugh	Bnc 162	John	Cmb 371	Mary	Glf 685
Hugh	Rbs 367	John	Dpl 408	Mary	Psq 627
Isaac	Jns 791	John	Dpl 414	Mary	Ptt 289
Isaac	Jns 817	John	Frn 479	Matthew	Glf 663
Isaac	Mnt 494	John	Hlf 290	Michael	Rnd 302
Isaac	Ptt 274	John	Ird 647	Michael	Rwn 276
Isaac	Rnd 304	John	Jhn 759	Michael	Rwn 285
Isabel	Lnc 864	John	Jns 823	Michael	Rwn 414
Jacob	Bfr 2	John	Lnr 3	Michael, J.	Rnd 302
Jacob	Dpl 411	John	Mrt 384	Michael, Junr.	Rwn 359
Jacob	Ird 664	John	Mck 567	Mordicai	Mnt 489
Jacob	Jns 789	John	Mck 568	Moses	Crt 85
Jacob	Mrt 384	John	Nrt 427	Moses	Grv 566
Jacob	Ons 176	John	Ons 176	Moses	Grv 569
Jacob	Rwn 292	John	Orn 550	Moses	Jns 813
Jacob	Srr 704	John	Orn 551	Moses	Rwn 285
James	Bnc 159	John	Psq 629	Moses	Srr 639
James	Brk 724	John	Prs 213	Nathan	Rwn 446
James	Csw 120	John	Rnd 304	Neal	Wke 775
James	Csw 130	John	Rbs 360	Neill	Rbs 367
James	Csw 140	John	Rck 470	Neill	Rbs 368
James	Edg 185	John	Rck 478	Noah	Ans 204
James	Edg 186	John	Rwn 293	Patrick	Hrt 737

31

Name	Loc	Pg
Patsey	Dpl	412
Pattrick	Mck	529
Pearson	Wke	719
Peter	Hlf	358
Peter	Rwn	276
Peter	Rwn	285
Philip	Rwn	292
Phillip	Lnr	28
Polly	Rth	99
Prudence	Cmd	106
Randle	Srr	638
Rebecca	Cht	175
Rebekah	Wlk	27
Reding	Mrt	384
Reuben	Edg	181
Reynolds	Ptt	240
Rhoderic	Hrt	708
Richard	Bld	25
Richard	Jhn	776
Richard	Lnr	3
Richard	Lnc	853
Richard	Mck	523
Richard	Srr	711
Richard, Junr.	Hrt	708
Richard S.	Hrt	709
Richd.	Wlk	29
Robert	Bnc	162
Robert	Csw	95
Robert	Csw	137
Robert	Ird	647
Robert	Ird	654
Robert	Mck	532
Robert	Nrt	429
Robert	Rck	455
Robert	Wke	721
Saml.	Crr	151
Saml.	Mrt	384
Saml.	Rck	455
Samuel	Brk	726
Samuel	Cbr	682
Samuel	Gts	262
Samuel	Grv	566
Samuel	Grn	615
Samuel	Glf	673
Samuel	Hrt	709
Samuel	Hrt	723
Samuel	Jns	811
Samuel	Mck	568
Samuel	Ptt	281
Samuel	Rnd	303
Samuel	Stk	589
Samuel	Srr	634
Samuel	Srr	639
Samuel, Senr.	Gts	263
Sarah	Bfr	24
Sarah	Cmd	105
Sarah	Trl	676
Shadrach	Ash	74
Sherwood	Smp	502
Sion	Cht	175
Sion	Wke	721
Solomon	Csw	137
Sophia	Hrt	709
Spencer	Hrt	719
Spilliard	Rth	96
Stephen	Dpl	437
Stephen	Hrt	709
Tho.	Nwh	4
Tho., Genl.	Bld	23
Thomas	Brk	723
Thomas	Csw	137
Thomas	Crv	273
Thomas	Grv	569
Thomas	Rwn	435
Thomas (2)	Srr	637
Thomas	Srr	704
Thomas	Wke	718
Thomas	Wsh	714
Thomas, Jr.	Bld	31
Thomas, jr.	Cht	186
Thomas R.	Wne	856
Thos.	Crr	146
Thos.	Prs	193
Timothy, Jur.	Rwn	311
Timothy, Sr.	Rwn	311
Vincent	Stk	620
Walter	Hrt	723
Walter	Wlk	28
Will.	Prs	212
Will. (St. Jas. District)	Prs	188
William	Ash	74
William	Bfr	3
William	Cmd	101
William	Csw	96
William	Csw	140
William	Dpl	410
William	Frn	471
William	Glf	657
William	Glf	658
William	Glf	672
William	Hlf	290
William	Hrt	708
William	Ird	628
William (2)	Ird	647
William	Ird	653
William	Ird	659
William	Jhn	759
William	Jns	813
William	Lnc	885
William	Mck	543
William	Mck	544
William	Mck	568
William	Mck	584
William	Ons	154
William	Ons	158
William	Orn	500
William	Rnd	303
William	Rch	260
William	Rbs	366
William	Srr	637
William	Srr	638
William	Srr	639
William	Wke	718
William	Wke	720
William (2)	Wke	721
William	Wlk	26
William, Junr.	Brt	28
William, Junr.	Nrt	429
William, Senr.	Brt	28
William, Senr.	Nrt	429
William, Senr.	Wke	719
Willie	Wke	719
Willis	Gts	262
Wm.	Csw	137
Wm., Senr.	Csw	129
Zachariah	Lnr	29
see B...own, Brow, Hoquet		
Brownfield, William	Mck	531
Brownin, William	Dpl	423
Browning, Edmd.	Csw	133
Edward	Ptt	241
Elisha	Brk	731
George	Edg	183
Jas.	Csw	129
John	Bld	50
John	Orn	542
John, Junr.	Brk	728
John, Senr.	Brk	728
Levy	Hlf	292
Martin	Brk	730
Radford	Grn	604
Richard	Frn	452
Richard	Orn	542
Robt.	Csw	133
Thomas	Hde	364
Thomas	Orn	549
William	Orn	550
William	Ptt	241
Wm. (2)	Csw	138
Brownlaw, James	Cht	154
Brownrigg, Thomas	Chw	128
Thomas, Chr.	Psq	634
Bruce, Abner B.	Orn	491
Absalom	Rbs	368
Alex	Csw	144
Allen	Hrt	715
Alsa	Hlf	290
Aziel	Edg	182
Benjamin	Wlk	26
Bennet	Hrt	716
Bennett	Nrt	425
Charles	Glf	670
Corneslus	Nsh	87
David	Csw	144
George	Edg	185
George	Glf	668
James	Crv	253
James	Nsh	93
James	Wlk	26
Jeremiah	Brt	32
Jeremiah	Hrt	716
Moses	Nrt	427
Peter.	Ird	614
Robert	Wlk	28
Robt.	Csw	128
William	Csw	105
William	Cmb	361
Bruenton, Joshua	Nwh	8
Lewis	Nwh	8
Bruer, Henry	Smp	504
Hubbard	Smp	500
Lewis	Srr	639
Bruffeth, Arthur	Bfr	4
Bruqq, John	Orn	547
Bruice, Arnold	Ird	608
Peter	Ird	609
Wilson	Ird	608
Bruihen see Breichen		
Brukes, Elizabeth	Smp	526
Brumbelow, Edward	Ans	222
Edward, Jr.	Ans	223
Isaac	Ans	221
Isaac, Jr.	Ans	222
Lewis	Ans	208
William	Ans	209
Brumble, Gilbert	Rbs	363
John	Rbs	363
Brumfield, Obe	Stk	606
Brumit, John	Srr	635
Brumley, John	Wne	868
Brumly, Jean	Brk	727
John	Brk	727
Brummel, Jacob	Rwn	363
James	Stk	544
Brummett, Nimrod	Grv	529
Brumsey, John	Crr	144
Thos.	Crr	144
Wm.	Crr	140
Brune, Michal	Stk	597
Bruner, John	Rwn	276
Matthew	Stk	605
William	Stk	601
Bruninger, Elijah	Brk	727
Brunner, Henry	Rwn	305
John	Rwn	284
Brunson, Asahel	Hlf	292
Brunt, James	Hlf	292
John	Wne	865

Name	Ref	Name	Ref	Name	Ref
Thomas	Brk 725	Nicolas	Dpl 441	Mary	Brt 34
Brunte, Jeames	Crr 161	Philemon	Rbs 363	William	Bfr 2
Bruntfield, James	Bfr 2	Rachel	Bld 8	Buchan, David	Mre 49
Bruse, John, Senr.	Wlk 30	Reubin	Stk 558	John	Mre 54
Bruten, Joseph	Lnr 1	Robt.	Wne 846	Peter	Rbs 366
Bruton, George	Mnt 468	Saml.	Prs 189	Buchanan, Fanny	Cmb 368
Simon	Lnr 3	Stephen	Bld 30	Hector	Cmb 385
Bruwer, Adam	Rnd 299	Thomas	Rbs 363	John	Cmb 368
Brwer, Eli	Rnd 304	Timothy	Dpl 419	William	Cmb 366
Bryan, Andrew	Wlk 28	Walter	Dpl 422	Buchannon, James	Brk 723
Andw.	Csw 112	William	Crv 325	James	Brk 728
Arthur	Wne 849	William	Jhn 764	James A.	Grv 524
Asa	Jhn 777	William	Jhn 774	John	Mck 534
Austin	Dpl 410	William	Jns 809	Joseph	Brk 728
Barnabas	Bld 42	William	Wne 853	Thos.	Lnc 830
Bartm., Capt.	Bld 42	William, Esqr.	Bld 37	Buck, Appolo	Ptt 256
Benjamin	Ons 157	William H.	Lnr 31	Charles	Rwn 335
Benjn.	Bnc 161	Willis	Wne 859	Daniel	Rwn 371
Betey	Ans 220	Bryant, Abram	Cht 178	Francis	Crt 88
Blake	Jhn 769	Aron	Cht 168	Isaac	Ptt 257
Breson	Ons 172	Benagey	Ons 157	Isaac, Junr.	Bfr 3
Cato	Nwh 8	David	Orn 545	Isaac, Senr.	Bfr 3
Clemt.	Jhn 772	Dempsey	Edg 181	James	Bfr 4
Darbey	Crv 323	Elias	Edg 183	James, Senior	Ptt 253
David	Bld 42	Elizabeth (2)	Brt 32	John	Hlf 292
Dawson	Crv 251	Elizabeth	Rwn 435	Moses	Rwn 430
Edward	Bld 12	Evan	Edg 187	Polley	Crr 142
Edward	Jns 811	George	Edg 181	Buckanon, James	Glf 655
Elisabeth	Ans 231	Hardee	Edg 186	John	Csw 120
Eliza.	Bld 29	Isaac	Rbs 366	Buckhannon, Jas.	Prs 193
Ellen	Nrt 427	James	Edg 183	Mary	Brk 723
Francis	Ash 72	James	Hlf 294	Robert	Mck 559
Frederick	Crv 331	Jesse	Rwn 440	Buckhanon, Andrew	Prs 195
Frederick	Jns 811	Joel	Hlf 294	Artha	Prs 196
George	Crv 331	John	Brk 730	Benj.	Prs 219
Green	Crv 257	John	Cht 171	Benjn.	Prs 191
Hardy	Jhn 768	John	Edg 181	Mary	Prs 196
Henry	Wlk 26	John	Edg 187	Buckingham, Joshua	Orn 543
James	Bld 29	John	Grv 525	Levy	Glf 685
James	Bld 34	John	Rwn 360	Sion	Wke 719
James	Bld 36	John	Rth 95	William	Wke 719
James	Crv 233	Mary	Nsh 92	Willis	Csw 104
James	Rth 100	Michael	Mre 75	Bucklay, Thomas	Crv 251
James C.	Jns 801	Nicholas	Rwn 436	Buckley, Charles	Stk 615
Jas.	Mrt 385	Peter	Srr 637	Moses	Chw 123
Jas.	Prs 189	Redding	Cht 168	Bucklow, Isaac	Cmb 351
Jason	Nrt 427	Rhody	Edg 184	Bucknal, Samuel	Wlk 27
Jerusha	Mrt 385	Roland	Grv 536	Bucknell, Benjn.	Wlk 27
Jesse	Bld 11	Roundtree	Smp 536	John	Wlk 27
Joel	Chw 124	Saml.	Nsh 92	Buckner, Benjamin	Rwn 422
Joel	Wne 849	Samuel	Rwn 440	Elisha	Cht 192
John	Bld 28	Sarah	Cht 178	Robert	Cmb 351
John	Dpl 421	Smith	Edg 182	Thomas	Rck 450
John	Ptt 261	Suckey	Nsh 92	Bucknor, James	Brk 726
John	Rth 99	Thomas	Brk 729	Jesse	Rwn 430
John	Stk 606	Thomas	Cht 178	John	Rwn 430
John, Esqr.	Wlk 27	Thomas	Nsh 92	Bucks, Saml.	Csw 125
John, Jr.	Jhn 768	Thomas	Brt 30	Buckwith see Beckwith	
John, Senr.	Jhn 762	William	Cht 178	Bucner, Jessee	Cht 191
John, Senr.	Jns 811	William	Grv 530	Budd, Thos.	Lnr 3
John C.	Crv 241	William	Hlf 294	Buddard, William	Ptt 281
John F.	Jns 823	William	Nsh 92	Buerdite, Richard	Rnd 304
John H.	Jns 809	William	Rwn 390	Buey, Archd.	Bld 24
Johnston	Ons 171	William	Smp 535	Buff, John	Lnc 810
Jos., Esqr.	Mrt 387	Bryar, David	Rth 97	Martin	Bnc 162
Joseph	Jns 811	Bryart, Jacob	Cht 153	Michael	Lnc 810
Judah	Mrt 385	Bryat, Best	Rbs 366	Buffaloe, Steel	Wke 717
Kedar	Smp 535	Bryley, William	Bnc 160	Buffellowe, Sam.	Frn 452
Leml.	Mrt 384	Bryon, Matthew	Mck 541	Buffeloe, Henry	Wke 721
Lewis	Crv 321	Bryson, Abner	Srr 638	Buffenton, John	Ans 236
Lewis	Jhn 774	James	Bnc 163	Buffoon, Matthew	Nrt 423
Lewis	Mrt 384	James	Srr 638	Bufkin, William	Chw 127
Martha	Nrt 427	John	Bnc 162	Bugg, Samuel	Grv 506
Mary	Ons 157	Samuel	Bnc 163	William	Cbr 694
Nathan	Wne 858	William	Bnc 162	Buhannan, Arthur	Rth 99
Needam	Brt 32	Bucannon, James	Mck 573	William	Rth 99
Needham	Bld 45	Buch, Justice	Mck 535	Buickhouse, Wm.	Crr 139

Buie, Alexander	Cmb 362	Charles	Rbs 361	Henry	Orn 550
Anguish	Mrs 66	Daniel	Ptt 261	Isaac	Chw 125
Archabald	Rbs 368	David	Edg 183	Ishmael	Prq 646
Archibald	Cmb 360	David	Gts 262	Jeremiah	Brt 30
Archibald, P.	Cmb 361	David	Orn 550	Joseph	Chw 123
Archibald, Ser.	Rbs 368	Edward	Grv 568	Malichi	Chw 118
Daniel	Cmb 361	Edward	Glf 673	Micajah	Chw 122
Daniel	Cmb 366	Elizabeth	Grv 511	Micajah, Junr.	Brt 32
Daniel	Rbs 367	Edward	Ptt 234	Micajah, Senr.	Brt 32
Daniel	Mre 40	Edward	Stk 619	Nehemiah	Brt 32
Daniel	Mre 64	Elizabeth	Ptt 261	Priscilla	Chw 123
Duncan	Cmb 364	Francis	Mre 41	Sarah	Prq 645
Duncan	Cmb 392	George	Grv 574	Solomon	Chw 118
Duncan	Rbs 368	Henry	Rbs 361	Solomon, Sen.	Chw 124
Dunkin	Mre 66	James	Grv 574	Solomon, Sen.	Chw 126
Gilbert, Jur.	Mre 66	James	Wrr 790	Thomas	Orn 550
Gilbert, Ser.	Mre 64	John	Chw 131	Thompson	Wke 722
Hector	Cmb 382	John	Orn 543	William	Brt 32
John	Cmb 360	John	Ptt 292	William	Chw 128
John	Cmb 366	John	Stk 621	William	Glf 664
John	Mre 71	Jonathan	Mre 49	William	Prq 647
John	Rbs 366	Joshua	Grv 575	William	Prq 660
John	Rbs 367	Jremiah	Grv 574	Willis	Chw 117
Malcolm	Cmb 360	Martha	Edg 183	Bund, Wm.	Srr 706
Malcom	Mre 65	Marthy	Ons 145	Bunday, Aney	Crr 164
Malcom	Rbs 368	Micajah	Grv 547	Bundin, Levy	Prq 655
Malcolm, GS	Cmb 361	Obediah	Mrt 386	Bundle, John	Rwn 359
Neill	Cmb 365	Philip	Grv 547	Bundrant, Richd.	Rck 491
Neill, Jur.	Rbs 367	Richard	Wrr 790	Bundrent, Francis	Rck 486
Neill, Ser.	Rbs 367	Samuel	Grv 574	Bundy, Benjamin	Prq 650
William	Mre 64	Samuel	Rck 465	Caleb	Psq 640
William	Mre 65	Stephen	Edg 185	Caleb	Psq 641
Buise, John, Senr.	Rwn 390	Thomas	Cmb 371	Christopher	Rnd 350
Buk see Beck		Thos.	Mrt 384	David	Psq 638
Buknall, Henry	Rnd 304	William	Grv 511	Gideon	Rnd 301
Bukum, Simon	Orn 546	Bullon, George	Rwn 299	James	Psq 640
Bulard, Demsey	Cmb 375	George	Rwn 305	Jeremiah	Psq 641
James	Cmb 374	John	Rwn 300	John	Psq 640
Buler, Benjamin	Ird 632	Bulls, Barnaba	Jhn 745	Jonathan	Psq 634
Bull, Henry T.	Hlf 290	Elisabeth	Crv 323	Joseph	Psq 627
Jno.	Lnc 829	James	Crv 323	Joshua	Prq 650
John	Glf 682	William	Jhn 746	Josiah	Prq 650
Joseph	Rnd 301	Bully, Thomas	Glf 630	Mark	Wne 846
Mary	Dpl 434	William	Glf 630	Meriam	Psq 641
Mary	Hlf 290	William	Hlf 290	Moses	Psq 641
Mary	Lnc 841	Buman see Beeman		Nathan	Prq 650
Richard	Orn 545	Bumand see Burnam		Samuel	Psq 624
Sarah	Hlf 290	Bumgarden, David	Stk 568	Samuel	Rnd 303
T. Henry	Hlf 290	Bumgarner, Daniel	Ash 73	Samuel	Prq 651
Thomas	Glf 682	John	Lnc 809	William	Psq 635
Bullar, Isaac	Grv 544	John	Lnc 810	William	Prq 651
John	Grv 535	Leonard	Ash 73	William	Wne 859
Bullard, Elizabeth	Rbs 365	Mary	Ash 73	Bungah, Zephaniah	Cmd 101
Ephraim	Rbs 362	Moses	Lnc 809	Bunkin, Daniel	Ptt 261
James	Cht 203	Peter	Rth 99	Bunn, Benjamin	Wke 722
James	Rbs 360	Thomas	Lnc 809	Benjamin, Jur.	Nsh 89
James	Rwn 396	Bumpass, Gabriel	Prs 191	Burrell	Nsh 89
James, jr.	Cht 203	John	Prs 191	David	Nsh 89
John	Rck 472	John	Prs 201	David	Wke 722
Joshua	Ans 239	John	Prs 205	Etheldred	Nrt 423
Nathan	Ans 238	John, Junr.	Prs 187	Fredk.	Wne 871
Prissilla	Rbs 363	Saml.	Prs 191	George	Nrt 425
Shaderack	Rbs 365	Bumpis, Elizabeth	Cmb 372	Jacob	Nrt 423
Thomas	Rbs 362	Bumps	Srr 634	Jacob	Stk 604
Thomas	Smp 495	Bumpus, John	Hlf 290	Jesse	Wke 722
Thomas	Smp 532	Saml.	Hlf 288	John, Jur.	Wke 717
William	Ans 238	Bun see Been		Odam	Wke 722
Buller, Thomas	Rnd 303	Buncer, Reubin	Glf 681	Redmun	Nsh 91
Bullin, Ann	Bnc 163	Bunch, Abner	Chw 125	Wilie	Nsh 90
Conrod	Rwn 305	Abner	Chw 126	Bunnell, Edward	Crr 161
Jacob	Stk 584	Cullen	Chw 125	Embley	Crr 140
Bullinger, David	Lnc 810	David	Glf 664	Moses	Crr 161
Henry	Lnc 867	David	Prq 652	Buns, Sucky	Frn 486
Bullison, Margret	Wlk 30	David	Wke 722	Bunten, John	Edg 182
Bullock, Agness	Ptt 272	David	Chw 125	Buntin, Jeremiah	Nsh 92
Allen	Rnd 299	Elijah	Chw 127	Robert	Rwn 324
Charles	Grv 573	Frederic	Brt 32	William	Nsh 90

Bunting, David	Smp	528
Saml.	Nwh	11A
William	Jns	797
Bunton, David	Rnd	299
Ebenezer	Rnd	299
James	Wlk	26
John	Wlk	29
Nelly	Wlk	30
William	Nwh	2
Bunyard, James	Ash	72
Buras, Mary	Chw	126
Mary	Chw	130
Burbage, Joseph	Bld	49
Burbayge, Clinton	Bfr	22
Peter	Bfr	22
Burbeaux, Susan	Brn	13A
Burch, Baylor	Prs	214
George	Csw	116
George	Srr	636
Henary	Prs	213
Henry	Csw	117
Jacob	Crv	307
John	Srr	635
Joseph	Brn	18
Levi	Crv	281
Mary	Orn	542
Narzarth	Prq	642
Nicholas	Csw	117
Phillip	Prs	214
Richd.	Prs	201
Richd.	Prs	213
Thomas	Csw	104
Thomas	Prs	214
Thomas	Srr	635
Thomas	Srr	711
William	Srr	636
William, Cat.	Srr	635
William, Merch.	Srr	635
William, Ser.	Srr	636
Wm.	Csw	132
see Rurch		
Burcham, Henry	Srr	634
Henry	Srr	638
James	Stk	551
John	Srr	634
John	Srr	639
Burchard, Jedediah	Cht	163
Burcher, Daniel	Rck	460
Burchet, Patsey	Wrr	790
Burchett, Isaac	Grv	558
James	Grv	525
Burchfield, Michael	Brk	724
Nathan	Brk	727
Nathan	Brk	728
Burcoad, John	Stk	598
Burdeaux, Danl.	Nwh	9A
Isaac	Nwh	10A
Israel	NwH	12
John	Nwh	10A
Burden, ...	Edg	183
Burdill, James	Brt	30
William	Brt	30
Burds see Buras		
Burdsen, Levi	Dpl	425
Burfield, Mary	Grn	600
Burford, Benjamin	Mck	522
Burge, Abraham	Stk	581
Allin	Stk	579
Woody	Rth	97
Burger see Burges		
Burges, Agey	Crr	164
Akin	Wke	718
Edward	Wke	719
Francis	Wke	718
John	Wke	718
Peter	Crt	88
Richard	Brk	725
Richd. H.	Csw	100
Stephen	Crt	82
William	Rth	95
Burgess, Cornelius	Rck	463
Covatt	Hlf	292
Dinah	Cmd	109
Draper	Mnt	510
Ezekiah	Cmd	106
John	Hlf	294
Malachia	Cmb	370
Mary	Hde	364
Mary	Rnd	302
Rubin, Junr.	Rwn	422
Rubin, Senr.	Rwn	422
Thamar	Nrt	427
William	Rnd	302
Burgin, John	Brk	730
see Bergin		
Burgis, John	Cht	183
John	Wrr	791
Thomas	Rwn	423
William	Rwn	423
Burgiss, John	Brk	727
Burick, James	Jns	797
Mary	Jns	809
William	Jns	813
William, Jr.	Jns	815
Burk, Arnold S.	Prq	654
Casper	Rwn	371
Edward	Rwn	371
Henry	Orn	548
Jno.	Rck	451
Joab	Cht	164
John	Nrt	425
Mary	Nwh	3A
Mary	Nrt	425
Saml.	Prs	215
see Buck		
Burke, Judah	Chw	116
Milner	Cht	167
Pattrick	Lnc	900
Peter	Csw	102
Sarah	Jns	799
Burket, Caleb	Crr	158
John	Rwn	371
John	Rwn	414
John, Senr.	Rwn	371
Joseph	Crr	158
Burkett, Christian	Ash	72
Christian	Ash	73
David	Ash	72
Jacob	Ash	73
Joseph	Ash	73
Moses	Wne	764
Reubin	Wne	873
Burkhart, Eliazer	Rwn	377
George	Rwn	346
John	Rwn	397
Burkitt, Lemuel	Chw	121
Burkitte, Lemuel	Nrt	425
Wm.	Mrt	388
Burks, John	Brk	725
William	Cht	193
see David		
Burkshare, Henry	Rwn	351
Burleyson, David	Mnt	506
John	Mnt	506
Moses	Mnt	506
Burlingham, William	Brt	88
Burlinson, Agga	Bnc	161
Isaac	Bnc	161
Burlison, Isaac	Mnt	513
Joseph	Rth	94
Thomas	Brk	728
Burn, John	Brt	34
Richard	Brt	34
Burnam, William	Dpl	430
Burnap, Abraham	Ons	142
Ebenezar	Ons	143
Isaac	Ons	136
John	Ons	137
John	Ons	145
John	Ons	163
Burnes, James	Dpl	427
Burnet, Carter	Rch	268
Daniel	Cht	189
David	Frn	475
Isaiah	Cht	154
James	Hlf	292
James	Ird	628
Jeremiah	Cht	173
Littleberry	Brk	724
Burnett, John	Jns	807
Justice	Trl	692
Peter	Brt	30
Sandy	Orn	544
Thomas	Ird	659
Thomas	Wke	721
Burney, Hardee	Ptt	247
John	Glf	667
Joseph	Crv	277
Robert	Glf	667
Sarah	Bld	5
Simon	Ptt	247
William	Bld	6
William	Glf	672
William	Srr	635
Burnham, Ann	Cmd	109
Benjamin	Cmd	97
Elijah	Cmd	96
Elijah	Cmd	108
Elizabeth	Psq	637
Ivy	Rnd	304
Joseph	Cmd	97
Joshua	Cmd	96
Margaret	Cmd	109
Samuel	Cmd	97
see Burnam		
Burnit, Claburn	Rth	95
Fredrick	Rth	95
Jesse	Rth	97
see Barnett		
Burnitte, Jas.	Mrt	384
John	Mrt	384
Burns, Andrew	Bnc	161
Bartholomew	Dpl	428
Barthw.	Nwh	6
Conrad	Brk	729
Federick	Ons	143
Francis	Onx	144
James	Cbr	677
James	Cht	167
James	Orn	545
James	Stk	559
John	Cht	168
John	Nwh	6A
John	Rck	482
John	Wke	722
John, Senr.	Cht	165
Joseph	Ons	143
Lard	Mck	589
Levi	Rth	97
Manuel	Chw	114
Nicholas	Brk	725
Robert	Brk	728
Sampson	Mnt	516
Taurence	Stk	544
Thomas	Cht	168
Thomas	Crv	287
Thomas	Crv	303
Wm.	Crr	144
see Barns		

Burnside, Margaret		John	Ash 73	Chloe	Brt 30
S.	Cmb 351	John	Bnc 162	Christopher	Dpl 417
Burnsides, James	Srr 636	John	Csw 113	Gabriel	Smp 525
Burny, Elizabeth	Bld 18	John	Hlf 294	Henry	Bld 48
Burr, Bennoni	Psq 637	John	Hrt 723	Henry	Crv 257
Calib, Senr.	Brk 726	John	Prs 195	Isaac	Smp 529
Burrass, Ann	Srr 636	Mos.	Prs 195	Isaac	Stk 580
Jacob	Srr 636	Rebeckey	Prs 204	James	Smp 525
John	Stk 551	Richard, Jur.	Glf 650	Jesse	Cmb 381
John	Srr 636	Richd.	Glf 649	Jethro	Brt 30
Joseph	Srr 634	Richd.	Prs 202	John	Bld 28
M.	Srr 638	Robert	Prs 194	John	Grv 540
Moses	Srr 638	Sarah	Prs 196	John	Rch 271
Thomas	Srr 636	Thomas	Bnc 162	John	Wke 720
William	Stk 545	Thos. H.	Prs 219	John, Junr.	Brt 30
William	Stk 551	Watson	Dpl 437	John, Senr.	Brt 30
Burrell, Armstead	Grv 513	William	Dpl 418	Joseph	Bld 35
Burres, John, Jur.	Crr 168	William	Hlf 294	Joseph	Cmb 390
Richard	Glf 659	William	Wke 719	Joshua	Mnt 468
Burress, Daniel	Srr 634	William B.	Csw 98	Keziah	Grn 589
John	Brn 17	Busbee, Edmond	Wke 717	Micajah	Frn 470
John	Crr 168	Thomas	Wke 717	Rayner	Crv 235
John	Srr 634	Thomas, Jur.	Wke 717	Rewbin	Grv 551
John, Junr.	Srr 634	Busby, Ezekiel	Bld 21	Robert	Bld 28
Ruben	Crr 168	James	Grv 514	Robert	Smp 518
William	Srr 636	James	Grv 584	Robert	Smp 528
Wm.	Crr 168	William	Bld 21	Simon	Mrt 384
Burrett, Mary	Stk 592	Busey, Charles	Ird 623	Thomas	Dpl 414
Burris, Charles	Rwn 324	Matthew	Rwn 450	Thomas	Mnt 468
James	Grv 510	Bush, Abraham	Rck 463	William	Brt 30
James	Orn 548	Bibbee	Lnr 29	William	Cmb 368
Jonathan	Rwn 324	Hardy	Crv 235	William	Rwn 414
Reubin	Orn 548	James	Prq 645	Zac.	Rck 473
Solomon	Mnt 513	Jereh.	Csw 144	Zachariah	Cmb 381
Burriss, Daniel	Brt 28	Jereh., Jur.	Csw 144	see Bullar	
Burrough, William	Wrr 792	John	Csw 144	Butner, Christo-	
Burroughs, Anthony	Mrt 386	John	Cmb 377	pher	Stk 601
Benjn., Esqr.	Mrt 385	Jos.	Csw 131	Harmon	Stk 616
Jas.	Mrt 388	Levy	Nwh 6	Thomas	Stk 598
Burrow, Dobson	Rnd 301	Penelope	Jns 819	Thomas	Stk 625
Ephraim	Glf 646	Richard	Cht 189	Buton, Robert	Nsh 93
Freeman	Orn 543	William	Chw 127	Butrey see Bestrey	
Ishmall	Glf 648	William	Dpl 400	Butroner, Nile	Wlk 27
Jarrett	Glf 643	William	Hrt 716	Butt, David	Prq 658
Polly	Rnd 304	Bushee, Cosiderate	Lnr 29	Hazle	Rck 465
Thomas	Wrr 791	Bushell, Thomas	Brk 279	James	Psq 639
Burrows, William	Wrr 790	Bushop, Aron	Glf 658	Jesse	Jhn 768
Burrus, James	Wrr 790	Benjn.	Mre 68	Polley	Crr 141
Burt, Hailey	Nrt 427	John	Glf 657	Buttar, Arthur	Crv 267
Jesse	Hlf 290	Moses	Brt 34	Judy	Jns 817
John	Hlf 290	Robert	Glf 655	Stephen	Crv 309
John	Hlf 292	Salley	Wrr 790	see Bullar	
John	Wke 721	Bushship, Gray.	Ons 159	Butter, Charles	Crv 321
Joseph	Cmb 391	Busich, James	Rck 453	Robert	Smp 517
Joseph	Hlf 290	Busick, Caleb	Orn 501	William	Smp 517
William	Hlf 292	Nathan	Rck 453	see Butler	
William	Hlf 358	see Burick		Butterry, John	Mrt 387
William	Wrr 792	Busley, Austin	Dpl 418	John, Junr.	Mrt 387
William, Inspr.	Hlf 292	James	Crv 277	Thos.	Mrt 387
Young	Cmb 389	see Beesley		Wm.	Mrt 387
Burten, Elijah	Srr 638	Buson see Beeson		Butterton, Sarah	Brt 28
Henry	Stk 611	Buss, James	Brn 15	Buttler, Elias	Mnt 489
Peter	Stk 546	Bussell, Leml.	Crr 142	Feeby	Ird 633
Peter	Stk 590	Bustian, Martha	Hlf 290	John	Brn 19
Shatton	Nwh 5	Butcher, Benjamin	Wne 868	John	Bnc 159
Burton, Allen	Csw 116	James	Stk 586	John	Ird 633
Allen	Prs 204	Mary	Grn 615	John	Mnt 504
Arthur	Brn 18A	Thomas	Rbs 366	Mary	Chw 122
Cubbutt	Orn 550	Bute, Ann	Cmd 94	Samuel	Chw 115
Danl.	Prs 204	John	Cmd 97	Samuel	Ird 619
Edmond	Mnt 516	Buter see Buler		William	Rwn 422
Edward	Ird 617	Butlar, Charles,		Buttnor, David, Sr.	Rwn 293
Francis	Grv 519	Sen.	Crv 325	Thomas	Rwn 285
Henry	Csw 119	Butler, Anna	Hde 363	William	Rwn 293
Isaac	Glf 635	Arthur	Bld 28	Buttrell, William	Cmb 378
James	Csw 98	Barnaby	Nsh 91	Buttrum, Andrew	Ird 627
James	Csw 102	Charles	Smp 518	Jacob	Ird 608

John	Ird 628	Wm.	Mrt 384	Mary	Cbr 696
Nicholas	Ird 608	Byrly see Bierly		Mary	Mnt 509
William	Ird 608	Byrn, John	Rwn 351	Peater	Mre 47
Butts, Michael	Lnc 852	Lissom	Rwn 351	Wm.	Mre 46
Moses	Hlf 290	Mary	Glf 643	Cagoal, David	Wne 851
Buttz, Seth	Edg 185	Matt, Senr.	Bld 33	Cahill, Richard	Crt 70
Buxston, Bryan	Nwh 10A	Matthew	Rwn 351	Cahoon, Abel	Trl 688
Jane	Crv 249	Matthew, Jur.	Bld 33	Benjamin	Jns 793
Saml.	Nwh 10A	Peter	Bld 33	Benjamin	Trl 688
Buxton, Jarvis	Crv 239	Thomas	Glf 642	Catharine	Trl 688
Robert	Grv 514	Thomas	Rwn 351	Daniel	Jns 793
Buzzard, Jacob	Cbr 712	Byrns, Benjamin	Lnr 29	Dudley	Jns 791
Byarly, David	Rwn 346	Byrom, Archibald	Grv 528	Ezekiel	Trl 688
Byars, James	Ird 654	Henry	Hrt 696	Gedion	Trl 688
John	Lnc 866	James	Hrt 697	James	Trl 688
Joseph	Ird 654	John	Hrt 696	James, Junr.	Trl 688
Nicholas	Grv 569	Nicholas	Grv 528	John	Trl 684
Samuel	Rth 96	Thomas	Hrt 696	John, Senr.	Trl 684
William	Grv 567	Byrum, Archibald	Grv 572	Joseph	Trl 682
Byas, George	Rth 95	Henry	Wke 722	Joseph	Trl 690
James	Rth 95	Jacob	Wke 720	Reuben	Trl 690
John	Rth 96	John	Grv 545	Robert	Ird 633
John	Rth 98	William	Grv 557	Caid, Elizabeth	Cmb 393
Nathan	Rth 95	Byson, John	Rck 440	Mary	Grn 607
Robert	Rth 95	Peter	Rck 439	Cail, Nathaniel	Prq 652
Stripling	Rth 95			Caila, Thomas	Bfr 24
Byerly, Jacob, Jr.	Rwn 351			Cain, Abraham	Rwn 346
Margret	Rwn 351	-- C --		Allen	Orn 558
Peter	Rwn 396			Benjamin	Srr 642
see Byarly				Daniel	Rwn 451
Byers, Julemus	Grv 548	C...bell, Wm., B.		Duncan	Nsh 94
William	Grv 519	Creeke	Bfr 5	Elisha	Cht 205
Byly, Michal	Stk 606	C...er, Rachel	Bfr 5	Hugh	Orn 558
Bynam, Gray	Lnc 852	C...y, Beckham	Bfr 5	James	Bld 36
Samuel	Lnc 852	Ca..., Samuel	Lnr 2	James	Bld 46
William	Lnc 852	Cabe, Elizabeth	Orn 557	James	Orn 616
Bynum, Arthur	Lnc 852	John	Bnc 165	James, Jr.	Hlf 300
Cordall	Nrt 423	John	Orn 614	James, Sr.	Hlf 300
James	Cht 199	William	Bnc 165	John	Orn 556
James	Hlf 294	William	Orn 557	John	Rbs 372
Lewis	Jns 801	Cabial, John B.	Ans 199	Joseph	Bld 34
Luke	Cht 198	Cable, Adam	Glf 643	Joseph	Hlf 300
Marke	Cht 169	Anthony	Orn 502	Nancy	Bld 43
Taply	Cht 167	Anthony, Junr.	Orn 502	Rachel	Bld 41
Turner	Nrt 429	Casper	Ash 76	Russel	Srr 640
William	Hlf 294	John	Orn 502	Saml.	Bld 46
William	Hrt 728	Cables, Thomas	Rck 484	Susanna	Bld 34
Byram, Isaac	Chw 125	Cabral, John Jo-		Thomas	Rwn 451
James	Mck 546	seph	Cmb 353	Tice	Srr 642
John	Mck 546	Caddet, John	Rth 100	William	Cht 174
Oswell	Mck 546	Caddle, Daniel	Mre 41	William	Orn 557
Upton	Mck 546	James	Mre 51	Cairaway see Carraway	
William	Chw 125	William	Mre 50	Cairey, John	Mck 565
William	Mck 546	Cade, James	Rbs 370	Caisey, Hubert	Rwn 336
Byrd, Alexander	Bld 3	Robert	Rbs 370	Cakey, Thomas	Ons 150
Benjamin	Lnr 3	Weddell	Cmb 370	Cala, Samuel	Bfr 6
Edward	Lnr 2	see Caid		Caldin, John	Glf 691
Edwd.	Mrt 386	Cadey, Thomas	Bnc 165	Caldwell, Andrew	Ird 664
Elenor	Lnr 3	Cadham, Darling	Mck 589	Daniel	Lnc 873
Elijah	Lnr 29	Cadle, Andrew	Prs 217	Daniel	Mck 559
Esther	Lnr 3	Thoms	Srr 643	David	Glf 663
James	Frn 486	see Coddle		David	Ird 664
Jesse	Lnr 2	Cadwick, Joseph	Wlk 34	James	Glf 687
Jethro	Frn 489	Caffs, John	Bfr 6	John	Glf 687
John	Brt 28	Caffy, Michael	Rck 470	John	Orn 496
Joshua	Lnr 29	Cager, Jacob	Mre 75	John	Smp 534
Joshua, Jur.	Lnr 29	Cagle, Benjamin	Mnt 501	Joseph	Ash 76
Martin R.	Wsh 700	Catharine	Mre 70	Joseph	Glf 687
Phillip	Nrt 425	David	Mnt 506	Joseph	Orn 495
Richard	Lnr 3	George	Mnt 506	Kirtes	Rth 101
Richard, Jur.	Lnr 3	George	Mre 70	Robert	Grn 606
Samuel	Lnr 3	Hennery	Mre 46	Robert	Mck 558
Sarah	Mrt 387	Hennery, Jur.	Mre 48	Samuel	Mck 550
Thomas	Ans 210	Henry	Cbr 694	Saml.	Lnc 826
Thomas	Lnr 2	John	Mnt 505	Spencer	Grn 606
Thomas	Lnr 28	Leonard	Mnt 501	Thomas	Brk 737
William	Ans 215	Leonard	Mre 47	Tryon	Glf 687

William	Lnc 874	Calvert, William	Srr 643	Colin	Cmb 373
William	Mck 560	Calvett, Ruthey	Ons 176	Colin	Rch 253
Cale, John	Prq 642	Calvin, James	Cmb 366	Collin	Ird 615
John	Prq 652	William, junr.	Cmb 366	Collin	Ird 643
John, Sen.	Prq 652	Cam, Thomas	Stk 591	Collin	Wke 724
Joseph	Prq 645	Camel, Anguest	Rch 261	Daniel	Cmb 360
Robert, Jun.	Prq 653	Archibald	Ptt 254	Daniel	Cmb 364
Robert, Sen.	Prq 653	Archibald	Rch 260	Daniel	Cmb 379
Wm.	Mrt 392	John	Wsh 714	Daniel	Cmb 389
Caleb, Capps	Wrr 797	Lydia	Ptt 258	Daniel (2)	Rbs 374
Catherine M.	Bld 11	Robert	Rch 252	Danl.	Bld 23
Shadrack	Hlf 296	Cameron, Absalom	Rwn 377	Deicey	Wke 775
Calef, James	Hrt 729	Absalom, Senr.	Rwn 399	Dicey	Nrt 431
Calhoon, Charles	Mck 539	Allen	Cmb 362	Dugald	Cmb 374
Samuel	Mck 539	Daniel	Cmb 362	Duncan	Cmb 353
see Colquhoon		Daniel	Cmb 364	Duncan	Cmb 388
Calhorda, John	Nwh 2	John	Mre 60	Duncan	Rch 253
Calico, Able	Rck 472	John	Mre 77	Duncan	Rbs 371
William	Rck 472	Mary	Wsh 702	Dunkin	Mre 52
Calicoat, James	Mre 47	see Jay		Dunkin	Mre 54
Calisle, Widow	Mck 565	Cammel, Alexander	Smp 497	Edward	Cmb 374
Call, Daniel	Rwn 436	Mary	Prq 660	Edward	Rbs 373
Henry	Rwn 456	Cammeran, Alexan-		Elias	Nrt 433
John	Rwn 456	der	Rbs 374	Elisabeth	Brk 738
Sarah	Rnd 307	Effy	Rbs 369	Farquer	Ans 198
Callahan, Edmd.	Rck 483	Rhoderick	Rbs 369	Farquhard	Cmb 371
Ezekiel	Rck 463	Cameron, Allan	Cmb 361	Farquhard	Mnt 516
Pearce	Rbs 373	Allen	Cmb 360	Findly	Rbs 373
Calland, John	Mrt 391	Duncan	Cmb 361	George	Cbr 680
Callaway, John (2)	Stk 618	Duncan	Orn 490	Hugh	Ird 629
Saml.	Srr 711	Elizabeth	Cmb 393	Hugh	Rwn 276
Calleham, Bryan	Bld 20	Hugh	Mre 51	Hugh	Rwn 286
Cornelius	Bld 20	John (2)	Cmb 360	Isaac	Mck 555
Callender, Thos.	Nwh 1	John	Cmb 362	Israel	Rbs 371
Caller, James	Wrr 796	John, jur.	Mre 40	Jacob	Hlf 300
John	Wlk 35	Keneth	Cmb 360	James	Ans 218
Robert	Wrr 796	Mary	Cmb 360	James	Ash 76
Thomas	Wrr 796	Norman	Cmb 360	James	Bfr 22
Calles, James	Rch 258	Cammock, David	Cmb 353	James	Bld 18
Callicoat, Harri-		Camp, Abnor	Lnc 899	James	Hlf 296
son	Mnt 469	Clabon	Rth 101	James	Ird 609
John	Mnt 476	Edward	Rth 102	James	Ird 634
Pleasant	Mnt 482	Isaac	Wlk 33	James	Rwn 352
Callicoatt, John	Rnd 305	Joseph	Rth 102	Jas.	Mrt 391
Callicolle, Beav-		Margeret	Rth 100	John	Ans 225
erley	Rnd 308	Sarah	Rth 102	John	Ans 234
Callier, Freck.	Ans 227	Stephen	Rth 100	John	Ash 75
Callifer, Henry	Trl 682	William	Rth 103	John	Bld 20
John	Trl 682	William	Wke 775	John	Bld 24
Calliham, John	Wke 725	Zebulon	Cmd 108	John	Cht 154
Callihan, Henry	Rth 103	Campbel, Alexander	Mck 555	John	Cmb 363
James	Ird 616	James	Rwn 446	John	Cmb 372
John	Ird 615	John	Mnt 516	John	Cmb 377
Calliway, Elijah	Crv 283	Robert	Mck 567	John (2)	Cmb 387
Callom, Willis	Brt 40	Campbell, ...	Nwh 1A	John	Ird 609
Callon, Daniel	Orn 615	Adlai	Rwn 325	John	Ird 623
James	Cbr 680	Alexander	Bld 3	John	Lnc 811
John	Cbr 680	Alexander	Cmb 351	John	Mck 542
Leonard	Orn 615	Alexander	Cmb 353	John	Mre 54
Mary	Orn 615	Alexander	Cmb 363	John	Ons 166
William, Junr.	Cbr 680	Allen	Cmb 388	John	Orn 503
William, Senr.	Cbr 680	Andrew	Rth 101	John	Prs 208
Calloway, Charles	Bnc 164	Anguish	Mre 72	John	Rnd 309
Elisjah	Ash 75	Annanias	Ird 667	John (2)	Rbs 373
Isaac	Mnt 521	Anne	Cmb 353	John	Rwn 311
James	Ash 75	Archabald	Stk 547	John, Sr.	Bld 27
John	Ash 74	Archbald	Stk 567	John S.	Cmb 353
Thos.	Ash 74	Archibald	Cmb 353	Josep	Rwn 324
Callum, Elijah	Lnr 31	Archibald	Orn 554	Joseph	Crv 271
Callume, Stephen	Brn 14A	Armsted	Mck 527	Joseph, Senr.	Rwn 324
Cally, John	Orn 612	Casander	Nwh 11A	Keneth	Cmb 353
Calton, Elisha	Srr 640	Catlett	Orn 491	Lachlan	Cmb 362
George	Mre 56	Cevilia	Cbr 687	Malcolm	Cmb 368
Lindsey	Srr 640	Charles	Ans 203	Malcom	Rnd 309
see Callon		Charles	Cbr 680	Margret	Mre 72
Calvan, John	Nwh 12A	Charles	Mre 58	Martha	Cbr 689
Calver, James	Wrr 796	Colin	Cmb 373	Mary	Bld 2

Mary	Cmb 353	Cane, Catharine	Prq 651	Caphart, Francis	Brt 36
Mary	Cmb 366	John (2)	Brn 16A	Frederick	Brk 731
Mary	Cmb 377	Leonard	Stk 548	George	Brt 36
Mary	Glf 650	William	Bnc 166	John	Brt 36
Matthew	Cbr 679	Cannaday, Aaron	Wlk 34	Thomas	Brt 34
Murdoch	Cbr 688	Alexander	Mre 47	Caple, Thomas	Rth 103
Nancy	Mre 41	Andrew	Wlk 34	William	Rch 263
Neal	Cht 179	James	Wlk 34	Capley, John	Rwn 390
Neil	Bld 26	Archibald	Dpl 399	Capps, Caleb	Wrr 797
Neill	Cmb 360	David	Mre 48	Cason	Ons 168
Neill	Cmb 387	Henry	Lnr 4	Dempsey	Rnd 305
Neill	Cmb 388	Hugh	Orn 613	Francis	Mnt 478
Purcephul	Ird 623	Jesse	Lnr 4	Francis	Wrr 797
Ransom	Wne 859	John	Lnr 4	Henry	Wrr 797
Rebecca	Rck 455	Walter	Lnr 4	Hilliry	Wrr 797
Robert	Crv 269	Cannan, Joshua	Cmb 351	John	Wrr 797
Robert	Mck 531	Cannon, Abashi	Mck 552	Joshua	Wrr 797
Robert	Orn 612	Abraham	Ptt 244	Marmaduke	Hde 364
Robert	Rth 103	David	Dpl 400	Matthew	Wrr 796
Samuel	Cmb 351	Dennis	Dpl 419	Mosses	Wrr 798
Sarah	Nwh 3A	Dennis	Ptt 244	Ruth	Hde 364
Sarah	Orn 558	Edward	Ptt 242	Thomas	Hde 364
Theophilus	Wlk 34	Furnifold	Ptt 243	Wealthy	Hde 365
Thomas	Csw 122	Henry	Dpl 401	William (2)	Wrr 796
Walt	Wke 724	Jackson	Bld 49	William	Wrr 797
William	Bfr 4	James	Cbr 699	Zackeriah	Wrr 797
William	Cht 152	James	Crv 291	see Clapps	
William	Cmb 383	James	Lnc 851	Caps, Caleb (2)	Crr 157
William	Mck 531	James	Mck 549	Cason	Orn 552
William	Orn 558	James	Wrr 784	Dennis, Jur.	Crr 157
William	Orn 613	Jeremiah	Crt 92	Dennis, Ser.	Crr 157
William	Rth 103	Jesse	Crt 81	Jelathel	Crr 150
William	Stk 547	Job	Mck 551	Lewis	Crr 150
William	Stk 548	John	Cbr 681	Malachi	Crr 158
William	Wrr 798	John	Crv 249	Mary	Brt 38
William, /Mut-		John	Smp 497	Mary	Crr 159
ter/	Cht 153	Joseph	Mck 552	Matthew	Jhn 748
see C...bell, Campll		Lewis, junior	Ptt 242	Moses	Crr 139
Campden, Duncan	Rch 260	Lewis, Senior	Ptt 243	Moses	Crr 147
Campe, Jonathan	Crr 139	Mary	Wrr 798	Needham	Jhn 749
Campen, Joseph, Jr.	Bfr 4	Micajah	Dpl 401	Obdiah	Crr 153
Joseph, Senr.	Bfr 4	Nathaniel	Ptt 247	Obediah	Crr 159
Thomas	Bfr 6	Radford	Ptt 242	William	Jhn 746
Campers, Stefines	Cht 194	Rebecca	Ptt 248	Capshaw, William	Rth 104
Campin, James	Hde 365	Simcock	Bnc 166	Car, James	Rth 102
Camplain, Henry	Glf 676	Theophilus	Mck 549	Dempsey	Jhn 771
Henry	Glf 680	Thomas	Ptt 244	Samuel	Jhn 771
James	Glf 673	Wiley	Ptt 242	William	Rnd 307
Camplin, Jacob	Stk 592	Canseler, John	Rth 104	Caraday see Canaday	
Campll, Sarah	Ons 156	Cansy, Thomas	Brk 732	Caradine, Andrew	Rth 102
Camron, Duncan	Rch 244	Cant, James	Cmb 351	Caragin, James	Cbr 681
John	Rch 244	Canter, Edward	Rwn 440	James, Senr.	Cbr 685
John	Rch 261	Edward	Rwn 456	John	Cbr 685
Canaday, Elijah	Crt 84	Jonathan	Rwn 441	Widow	Cbr 682
Elizabeth	Crt 78	Thomas	Rwn 441	Carathers, Hugh	Orn 615
Gideon	Crt 83	Cantrall, Aron	Rck 445	Caraway, Edward	Crv 291
Jemina	Crt 82	Cantrel, Charles	Brk 736	Francis	Crv 293
Jethro	Crt 77	Jones	Rnd 306	Henry	Crv 291
Richard	Crt 87	William	Brk 736	Jacob	Crv 289
Willet	Crt 82	Wm.	Csw 132	Joseph	Crv 291
William	Wlk 34	Cantrell, Benjamin	Csw 142	Levi	Crv 291
Canady, George	Wsh 702	Isaac	Csw 142	Mary	Crv 289
Hilley	Wsh 702	Cantrill, Axy	Rck 468	Mary	Crv 291
James	Brt 40	Jacob	Rck 468	Carburrus, Stephen	Chw 125
James	Rwn 364	Joseph	Orn 502	Card, Abrahard	Grv 572
John	Rwn 364	Cape, Williamson	Wke 725	Benjamin	Wke 726
John, Senr.	Rwn 364	see Cope		Benson	Wke 775
Linney	Wke 724	Capehart, John	Brt 36	Joseph	Wke 726
Shered	Rwn 364	John	Brk 279	Cardan, John	Orn 556
Wagstaff	Wke 725	Michael	Brt 36	John, jr.	Orn 556
William	Lnc 874	William	Brt 34	Carden, Reubin	Orn 556
William	Srr 644	Capel, Charles	Rch 248	Robert	Grv 527
Cander, John	Cbr 698	Capell, John	Nrt 431	Carder, James	Grv 527
Candle, Bucknor	Rwn 430	Thomas	Nrt 431	Cardison, Jessy	Ons 164
Candy, James	Crv 237	Capely, David	Rwn 397	Cardwell, John	Stk 581
John	Wne 855	Henry	Rwn 397	Mary	Grv 564
Mary	Bfr 24	Capey see Cassey		Payren	Wlk 30

Name	Ref
Rebecah	Rck 490
Thomas	Stk 582
Cardwil, Daniel	Stk 595
Careel, Thomas	Smp 513
Career, Christian	Lnc 811
Carell, Williby	Smp 507
Carey, Solomon	Dpl 442
Cargile, William	Wlk 32
Williams	Wlk 31
Carigan, John	Glf 642
Cariker, Andrew	Cbr 690
George	Cbr 690
Philip, Junr.	Cbr 690
Philip, Senr.	Cbr 689
Carisey, Green	Ptt 247
Cark, Harris	Wke 724
Carkeete, Benjn.	Mrt 391
Wm.	Mrt 391
Carlib, Robert	Stk 590
Carlile, James	Frn 477
Simon	Csw 145
Carlin, Thomas	Hlf 298
Carlisle, Mary	Grn 610
Robert	Cht 177
Robert	Edg 189
Robert	Mre 65
Sanders	Rbs 373
Thomas	Cht 179
William	Rbs 373
see Cerlisle, Curlile	
Carlisles, William	Grn 611
Carlock, George	Cbr 689
John	Cbr 695
Carlos, Fencis	Csw 99
Wm.	Csw 99
Carloss, Archibald	Wke 723
Carlton, Blake	Crv 315
David	Dpl 425
Elisabeth	Crv 315
F. John	Wke 723
Hardy	Dpl 402
John	Dpl 402
John F.	Wke 723
Lewis	Dpl 420
Lewis	Wlk 35
Mary	Crv 341
Patsey	Dpl 425
Peter	Dpl 402
Richard	Crv 315
Thomas	Crv 315
Thomas	Wlk 31
Carmack, Elisabeth	Crv 311
James	Crv 331
John, Junr.	Crv 313
John, Senr.	Crv 313
Mary	Crv 311
Mary	Crv 313
Soloman	Crv 313
Carmalt see Carwalt	
Carman, Archibald	Brk 732
Samuel	Bld 9
William	Crv 335
Wm.	Csw 129
Carmer, Jas., Esqr.	Mrt 416
Carmical, Andrew	Glf 621
Archabald	Stk 547
Duncan	Csw 129
William	Glf 621
Wm.	Csw 129
Wm.	Csw 136
Carmichael, Daniel	Rch 253
Daniel	Rch 253
Gilbert	Cmb 364
Hugh	Rch 252
Carmichel, Grissa	Mre 64
Carmicle, Archi- bald	Rch 254

Name	Ref
Daniel	Rch 254
Duncan	Rch 254
Thomas	Orn 552
Carmon, Caleb	Csw 128
Elijah	Csw 127
Elijah	Csw 128
Hanah	Rck 474
John	Rnd 307
Philip	Csw 128
Carmot, Mariam	Psq 627
Carn, Leonard	Rwn 397
Peter	Rwn 397
Philip	Rwn 397
William	Srr 642
see Corn	
Carnal, William	Grv 581
Carnegie see Kornigay	
Carnel, Elija	Grn 615
Carnell, James	Rwn 441
Richard	Rwn 441
Carner, Edmond	Mnt 484
Joseph	Mnt 484
Carnes, Alexander, Senr.	Mck 597
John	Mck 554
Joseph	Mnt 478
Carney, Absalom	Ptt 229
Andrew	Rwn 360
Frederick	Crv 323
James, Senr.	Crv 241
John	Crv 301
Joseph	Prs 212
Josiah	Ptt 229
Richard	Hlf 300
Robartus	Prs 212
Stephen W.	Hlf 300
Thomas	Ptt 229
W. Stephen	Hlf 300
Carns, Alexander	Mck 593
Daniel	Mck 593
John	Rwn 377
Silas	Rwn 377
Caroon, John	Trl 686
Kesiah	Psq 641
Carosine, George	Cbr 685
Carpenter, Addam	Mre 48
Benja.	Wke 725
Christian	Lnc 810
David	Lnc 812
David	Rth 104
Elizabeth	Nrt 433
Frederick	Lnc 811
George	Ans 219
Gilbert	Cht 208
Harbert	Rth 100
Henry	Lnc 811
Henry	Lnc 841
Isaac	Wke 725
Jacob (2)	Lnc 811
Jacob	Lnc 812
Jacob	Lnc 888
Jesse	Wlk 34
John	Crv 305
John	Frn 469
John	Hde 365
John (2)	Lnc 812
John, Senr.	Lnc 812
Jonathan	Mnt 506
Jonathan	Rth 100
Joseph (2)	Rth 104
Mary	Wke 724
Mathias	Ash 75
Michael	Lnc 888
Peter	Lnc 811
Peter	Nwh 4
Reuben	Nsh 95
Samuel	Cmb 391

Name	Ref
Samuel	Rth 101
Stephen	Chw 116
Thomas	Nsh 95
Wiley	Mnt 501
Will.	Nsh 95
William	Wke 724
William	Wke 726
Carpinter, Owen	Mre 49
Carr, Benjamin	Hlf 298
Benjamin	Smp 505
Charles	Grn 603
David	Glf 645
David	Glf 666
David, Senr.	Glf 645
Elias	Frn 474
Elias	Ptt 265
Elizabeth	Hrt 730
James	Orn 614
John	Dpl 421
John	Frn 491
John, Ser.	Frn 479
Jonathan	Smp 523
Joseph	Lnc 865
Lawrence	Hrt 730
Mary	Smp 530
Nathaniel	Glf 646
Patience	Smp 522
Patrick	Smp 522
Robert	Frn 478
Robert	Hrt 730
Robert, Ser.	Frn 473
Solomon	Ptt 269
Thomas	Rbs 371
Thomas	Rbs 432
Thomas, D.	Stk 644
Titus	Grn 594
William	Dpl 422
William	Glf 645
Carraway, Adam	Wne 857
Adam, Jr.	Wne 857
Charles	Cmb 372
Dred	Smp 509
James	Cmb 373
Jas.	Mrt 391
John	Wne 856
Jonathan	Mrt 391
Joseph	Bfr 22
Joshua	Crv 275
Moses	Mre 41
Nathan	Crv 303
Thomas (2)	Crv 303
Thomas	Cmb 373
Thomas	Grn 613
Thomas (null)	Grn 613
William	Smp 523
Carrel, Alexander	Smp 536
Bejamin	Orn 613
Charles	Orn 553
Charles	Orn 557
Dempsy	Smp 527
Dennis	Rth 101
Elisha	Smp 535
Fedrick	Smp 512
Hardy	Dpl 400
James	Ash 75
James	Orn 615
James	Smp 525
Jesse	Smp 511
John	Ash 75
John	Bnc 164
John	Grv 523
John	Jhn 766
John (2)	Smp 512
John	Smp 526
John	Wlk 34
John, Jr.	Smp 512
John, Senr.	Ash 75

Name	Ref
Michael	Orn 558
Roan	Ans 213
Spencer	Grv 523
Stephen	Orn 557
Stephen	Smp 529
Thomas	Smp 527
Thomas	Smp 530
William	Ash 75
William	Wlk 34
Willis	Rth 102
see Carrol	
Carrell, Alexander	Mre 42
Benjamin	Orn 614
Charls	Orn 503
George	Csw 112
Henry	Mck 606
James	Jhn 767
Jesse	Mre 43
Jesse	Rbs 369
John	Wlk 33
John, Jun.	Mre 43
John, Sen.	Mre 42
Jos.	Csw 120
Starling	Csw 112
Starling	Csw 128
Thomas	Jhn 751
Thomas	Rbs 369
William	Jhn 767
William	Lnc 901
Carrels, George	Csw 109
Carrigan, James	Glf 639
Magary	Orn 546
Carrill, Dennis	Mnt 490
Carrin, Hugh	Grv 551
Carringer, David	Mre 48
George	Mre 58
Carrington, Ephra-	
im	Orn 555
George	Orn 555
James (2)	Orn 556
John	Orn 555
John	Orn 557
John	Orn 616
John	Prs 189
Nathan	Orn 555
Thomas	Orn 556
William	Orn 556
Carriway, William	Stk 547
Carrol, Ann	Brn 14
Benjamin	Rck 471
David	Frn 490
Geo.	Csw 126
Grief	Frn 460
John	Edg 190
Jos.	Csw 136
Luke	Ird 643
Sterling	Cht 222
Sterling	Cht 223
see Carrel	
Carroll, Edward	Rnd 305
Henry	Rck 446
Isaac, Senior	Ptt 251
John	Bld 43
Owen	Bld 15
Samuel	Lnr 2
Thomas	Wrr 798
William	Cmb 353
Carroon, Levi	Hde 365
Carrothers see Currathers	
Carrott, Jesse	Grv 526
Carrow, Henry, Jur.	Hde 365
Henry, Senr.	Hde 365
James	Hde 364
John, Jur.	Hde 365
John, Senr.	Hde 365
Thomas	Hde 366
Carroway, John	Crv 303
Carrowon, Francis	Hde 365
Green	Hde 365
John	Hde 365
Joseph	Hde 365
William	Hde 365
Carruth, Adam	Rth 101
Adam, Sr.	Rth 101
Alexr.	Rth 101
John	Lnc 894
Robert	Rth 101
Carrway, William	Nsh 96
Carry, John	Cmb 377
Nicholas	Crv 255
Carsey, Jeremiah	Prq 656
William	Brn 21
Carsie, John	Bnc 164
Carson, Andrew	Ird 633
Bartlet	Stk 551
Daniel	Rth 100
David	Bnc 166
Elizabeth	Lnc 837
Henry	Rwn 286
Hugh	Rwn 423
Jacob	Stk 551
James	Brk 735
James	Cbr 687
James	Nwh 1A
James	Orn 552
Jno.	Lnc 837
John	Mck 522
John	Orn 552
John	Rwn 325
John	Rth 103
John	Stk 551
Peter	Lnc 833
Robert	Ird 629
Robert	Orn 502
Rbt.	Lnc 837
Samuel	Ird 629
Samuel	Orn 557
Samuel	Stk 546
Sarah	Trl 684
Thomas	Rwn 390
Thomas, Senr.	Ptt 264
Walter	Rth 100
William	Mck 552
Carstarphen, James	Hlf 296
Robert	Hlf 298
Cart, John	Rnd 309
Cartee, John	Prq 657
Carter, Abraham	Cmb 293
Anguish	Rbs 372
Alexander	Dpl 440
Allin	Wke 724
Ann	Crv 341
Benjamin	Hlf 300
Benjamin	Nrt 433
Benjn.	Cht 202
Berry	Srr 641
Bitha	Rbs 372
Britain	Nrt 431
Charles	Cbr 714
Charles	Hlf 296
Charles	Nsh 96
Clem	Mnt 521
Cullen	Brt 38
Daniel	Rck 443
Davee	Dpl 440
David	Hde 365
Edward	Dpl 401
Elbridge	Mnt 474
Elijah	Mnt 520
Emanuel	Rbs 370
Ephraim	Srr 643
Feby	Prs 195
Francis	Hlf 296
Frederick	Nrt 433
Frusanna	Hrt 723
Gabriel	Bld 30
George	Bfr 6
George	Rth 104
Henry	Lnr 30
Henry	Mnt 511
Henry	Mnt 520
Henry	Smp 515
Isaac	Cht 192
Isaac	Gts 264
Isaac	Nrt 431
Isaac, Jun.	Hrt 723
Isaac, Jur.	Srr 644
Isaac, Senr.	Hrt 723
Isaac, Senr.	Srr 644
Jacob	Mnt 516
Jacob	Wrr 798
James	Ans 211
James	Bnc 164
James	Cht 179
James	Gts 264
James	Hlf 296
James	Lnr 31
James	Mck 603
James	Nsh 95
James	Rbs 370
James, Ser.	Rbs 372
Jesse	Csw 110
Jesse	Cmb 370
Jesse	Grv 514
Jesse	Hlf 296
Jesse	Nrt 431
Jesse	Wke 725
Jesse	Wrr 796
John	Crt 84
John	Cht 206
John	Cht 215
John	Hlf 300
John	Hrt 734
John	Lnr 30
John	Mnt 516
John	Nsh 95
John	Orn 552
John	Prs 200
John	Rnd 308
John	Rth 101
John	Srr 642
John	Glf 640
Jonan.	Csw 141
Jos.	Hlf 296
Joseph	Srr 644
Joseph	Mnt 516
Joshua, Junr.	Mnt 516
Joshua, Senr.	Hrt 704
Josiah	Smp 531
Josiah	Jhn 764
Kindred	Stk 590
Landen	Hrt 723
Lazarus	Bfr 4
Levi	Hrt 704
Lewis	Rbs 372
Luke	Dpl 403
Man	Lnr 31
Margret	Rbs 372
Mark	Nsh 96
Matthw	Wlk 32
Mildrid	Rbs 372
Milikin	Gts 264
Moor	Nrt 431
Moore	Srr 706
Moring	Smp 515
Moses	Smp 516
Namon	Hlf 296
Nancy	Rck 460
Nathan	Rck 463
Nathan	Orn 552
Nathaniel	Wrr 798
Pervey	

Name	Ref	Name	Ref	Name	Ref
Reuben	Jhn 756	Joseph	Psq 639	John	Ird 620
Richard	Chw 115	Joshua	Brn 21	John	Prs 188
Richard	Hlf 300	Josiah	Psq 631	John, Junr.	Prs 190
Robert	Hlf 296	Mark	Cmd 100	Margret	Ird 674
S. William	Nrt 433	Moses	Cmd 104	Moses	Prs 190
Samuel	Ans 206	Parthinia	Psq 631	Peter	Grv 567
Samuel	Cht 215	Robert	Cmd 96	Richard	Ird 620
Samuel	Cht 218	Saba	Cmd 97	William	Ans 224
Samuel	Hlf 298	Thomas (2)	Psq 631	William	Wlk 34
Samuel	Mnt 516	Timothy	Cmd 95	Cashig, Richard	Grv 567
Samuel	Orn 552	William	Cmd 103	Cashon, David	Ird 660
Samuel	Rth 101	Wm.	Psq 634	James	Ird 660
Samuel	Srr 640	Zelly	Cmd 103	Cashwell, James	Bld 43
Silas	Lnr 31	Caruth, Robert	Cmb 385	John	Bld 44
Silas, Jur.	Lnr 31	Caruthers, Edmond	Lnc 846	Caskin, Oliver	Mck 562
Simeon	Srr 641	Hugh	Cbr 699	Casome, John	Brn 14
Solomon	Dpl 404	James	Glf 644	Cason, Edward	Ird 643
Stephen	Crv 307	James	Glf 671	Henry	Ptt 239
Stephen	Hde 365	James	Mck 547	James	Ptt 228
Tench	Mnt 469	James	Rwn 320	John	Ans 214
Theo.	Csw 141	John	Cbr 695	Nathan	Hde 365
Thomas	Grn 613	John	Mck 547	Caspar, Thomas	Brt 38
Thomas	Nsh 96	Thomas	Cbr 699	Casper, Adam	Rwn 340
Thomas	Rck 465	Carver, Benj.	Prs 206	Cadar	Brt 36
Thomas	Rck 483	Chris	Stk 607	Henry	Rwn 299
Thos.	Prs 206	Cornelius	Rth 105	Cassaday, James	Srr 642
Walter	Hlf 296	Elizabeth (2)	Cmb 383	Cassel, Samuel	Wlk 31
Wilford	Rck 458	James	Psq 628	Cassell see Carrell	
William	Brk 736	Jesse	Cmb 383	Cassey, Caleb	Psq 629
William	Csw 97	John	Mnt 495	Demsey	Crr 157
William	Chw 114	John	Rth 105	Enoch	Psq 630
William	Crv 341	Josiah	Prs 199	Samuel	Ptt 287
William	Gts 264	Robert	Prs 197	William	Psq 630
William	Grn 615	Thomas	Prs 210	Casso, Peter	Wke 775
William	Hlf 296	William	Cmb 381	Cassock, Jacob	Cbr 716
William	Hlf 298	Carwalt, Robert	Ons 136	Cast, James	Ird 623
William	Jhn 757	Carwell, William	Rwn 364	James	Wlk 32
William	Orn 552	Cary, Elisha	Frn 477	John	Wlk 33
William	Rth 101	George	Orn 555	Samuel	Ird 623
William, Junr.	Brk 736	George	Orn 612	see Cash	
William S.	Nrt 433	Henry	Hde 364	Casteel, Lydia	Dpl 416
Willson	Hlf 300	Hezekiah	Rck 489	Caster, Henry	Rth 102
Wm.	Crr 150	John	Hrt 710	Jacob	Rwn 340
Wm.	Mrt 389	Joshua	Csw 116	John	Glf 689
see Curter		Leven	Grv 568	Peter	Lnc 811
Carteright, Joab	Crr 145	Michael	Orn 555	Castillo, Bartholo-	
Cartes, Elijah	Ash 76	Miles	Nwh 7A	mew	Brt 36
Cartey, Joseph	Brt 88	Samuel	Orn 555	James	Brt 36
Carthy, Daniel	Crv 239	Shadick	Ons 143	John (2)	Brt 36
Cartright, Fanny	Ons 159	Shadrick	Ons 150	Martha	Brt 38
Lemuel	Hde 365	Caryl, James	Mck 533	William	Brt 36
Cartrite, Claudius	Bld 4	Casaday, John	Rnd 306	Castillow, Miles	Mck 522
Joseph	Bld 4	Casber, George	Stk 608	Castles, Thomas	Mnt 514
Richard	Bld 4	Case, Elisabeth	Mrt 392	Castner, Henry	Stk 617
Cartwright, Calib	Cmd 104	Isaah	Wlk 31	Castright, William	Rck 468
Christopher	Psq 634	John	Bnc 163	Caswell, Francis	Lnr 31
Clement	Psq 634	John, j	Bnc 163	Lany	Lnr 31
Daniel	Cmd 97	Jonathan	Crr 138	Matthew	Grn 608
Elizabeth	Rth 104	Joseph	Crr 138	Samuel	Trl 676
Ezekiel	Psq 631	Thomas	Bnc 163	Samuel, Junr.	Trl 678
Hezekiah	Psq 635	Thomas	Brk 735	Uriah	Trl 676
Isaac	Cmd 96	Casebolt, Johne	Bnc 164	Caswill, Holland	Crv 247
Isare	Cmd 103	Casen, Cannon	Smp 513	Catchey, John	Rwn 293
James	Cmd 104	Jacob	Smp 515	Catchy, Frederick	Rwn 294
James	Psq 631	Miles	Smp 515	Cate, Abner	Orn 612
James	Rth 104	Helery	Smp 513	Isaih	Prs 202
Jehu	Psq 638	Casey, Isaac	Crr 143	Joshua, Junr.	Prs 201
Jesse	Cmd 104	Jerremiah	Rch 262	Joshua, Senr.	Prs 203
Joab	Cmd 105	John	Orn 491	Mathew	Prs 216
Job	Psq 635	Micajah	Wne 857	Richard	Orn 613
John	Cmd 104	Samuel	Lnc 865	Robert, Junr.	Prs 188
John	Edg 191	Samuel	Rwn 451	Robert, Senr.	Prs 188
John	Psq 630	Cash, Aaron	Prs 188	Thomas	Prs 203
John	Psq 631	Elkins	Grv 566	Will.	Prs 215
John	Psq 635	Ingoe D.	Ans 214	Cates, Elisha	Orn 554
John	Psq 637	James	Ans 212	Ephraim	Rwn 456
Joseph	Cmd 93	James	Ash 74	James	Orn 554

Jesse	Orn 554	
John	Orn 554	
John	Orn 613	
John, (C.C.)	Orn 555	
Lazurus	Orn 556	
Mary	Orn 556	
Milly	Orn 554	
Moses	Orn 554	
Richard	Cht 175	
Richard	Orn 554	
Robert	Orn 554	
Robert	Orn 557	
Robert, Junr.	Orn 552	
Stephen	Orn 616	
Thomas (2)	Orn 554	
Thomas (Hatter)	Orn 554	
William	Orn 556	
William	Orn 558	
Cathey, Alexander	Mck 534	
Archibald	Brk 738	
George	Bnc 165	
George	Lnc 827	
George	Mck 527	
George, S.	Bnc 165	
James	Ird 609	
John	Mck 527	
Richard	Rwn 407	
Samuel	Brk 738	
Widow	Mck 560	
William	Bnc 165	
William, J.	Bnc 165	
Cathy, Archibald	Mck 559	
Esther	Mck 527	
Henry	Mck 527	
Catlett, Clark	Grv 521	
Labourn	Grv 564	
Cato, Mary	Crt 74	
Moses	Trl 688	
William	Edg 191	
see Caytoe		
Catoe, Daniel	Mnt 498	
Needham	Ans 238	
Robinson	Crr 155	
Caton, Charles	Rwn 431	
James	Ird 633	
John	Crr 139	
JOhn	Rwn 431	
Joshua	Ird 634	
Moses	Crv 261	
Solomon	Crv 265	
William	Crv 263	
William	Crv 265	
Catril, Jinnet	Crv 267	
see Cutril		
Cattanch, Dollee	Mrt 391	
Catton see Callon		
Catts see Cutts		
Cauble, Adam	Rwn 294	
Adam	Rwn 300	
Jacob	Rwn 293	
John	Cbr 714	
John	Rwn 293	
Michael	Rwn 293	
Peter	Cbr 717	
Peter	Rwn 293	
Peter, (A. Son)	Rwn 306	
Peter, Junr.	Rwn 293	
Cauddle, John	Cbr 716	
Caudle, Absalom	Ans 217	
Blecher	Cht 163	
James	Cht 199	
James	Wlk 33	
James	Wlk 34	
Jeremiah	Wlk 33	
Jesse	Wlk 33	
Jessee	Cht 209	
John	Cht 176	
Joshua	Cht 177	
Lewis	Jhn 774	
Mathew	Wlk 33	
Moses	Srr 643	
Stephen	Wlk 33	
Caughorn, Jas.	Prs 189	
John	Prs 188	
William	Prs 188	
Caul, Benjamin	Jhn 763	
Causey, Isaac	Rnd 305	
James	Glf 671	
John	Glf 622	
John	Glf 670	
Nehemiah	Glf 633	
Robert	Glf 619	
Solomon	Glf 627	
Thomas	Glf 621	
Causway, Absalom	Crv 269	
Anne	Crv 271	
John	Crv 269	
Philip	Crv 269	
Cauthon, David	Wrr 796	
Henry	Wrr 794	
James	Wrr 795	
Cave, Jonas	Bnc 165	
Cavenas, Frederick	Rnd 308	
Cavender, Bryant	Grv 522	
John	Grv 522	
Lewis	Crv 337	
Thomas	Grv 526	
William	Dpl 436	
Caveness, John	Mre 48	
Caves, Elizebeth	Crr 164	
Cavey, John	Mck 570	
Caviness, Richard	Cht 214	
Cavus, Penny	Hlf 300	
Cavy, Leven	Glf 652	
William	Glf 655	
Cawley, Roderick	Lnr 31	
Cayson, Elijah	Crr 155	
Hillery	Crr 163	
Caytoe see Cato		
Cazert, Jesse	Grv 578	
Cearby, Thomas	Hlf 296	
Cearley, John	Wlk 34	
William	Wlk 34	
Cearly, John	Wlk 31	
Joshep	Wlk 31	
Larken	Wlk 31	
Patsy	Wlk 35	
Patsy, Mrs.	Wlk 35	
William	Wlk 31	
Cearsey, Walden	Wrr 795	
Cearson, John	Frn 488	
Samuel	Orn 614	
Ceaton, Charles	Rwn 436	
Joshua	Rwn 436	
Cecil, Philip	Rwn 364	
Ceede see Cude		
Ceely, Isham	Rbs 370	
Tobias	Rbs 370	
Cell, Thomas	Brk 732	
Thomas, Junr.	Brk 733	
Cellar, John	Brk 737	
Nicholas	Brk 737	
see Celler		
Celler, Christian	Brk 737	
Jacob	Brk 737	
Martin	Brk 737	
Michael	Brk 731	
see Cellar		
Celly, Alexander	Brk 737	
Cemboll, Harris	Rnd 305	
Cements, Mary	Grv 521	
Cemmins, Thomas	Glf 637	
Cemp, William	Hlf 296	
Cempe, John	Crr 155	
Cenah, ...	Hlf 300	
Center see Senter		
Cerby, Josiah	Brk 736	
Larkin	Brk 737	
Cerley, Henry	Brk 735	
James	Brk 735	
Cerlisle, Nathan-		
iel	Hlf 298	
Certain, Thomas	Rck 462	
Cester, William	Stk 617	
Cetton, Robert	Brk 738	
Ch..., J...h	Rnd 305	
Cha..., John, son		
Chars.		
Cha...t..., Henry	Bfr 5	
Chace, Gorton	Rbs 371	
Gorton	Rbs 432	
Chaddock, Martin	Rck 474	
Chadwick, Barney	Crt 69	
Bartholomew	Crt 76	
Gear	Crt 69	
Gear	Crt 75	
James	Crt 70	
John	Crv 251	
Joshua	Rwn 364	
Oliver	Crt 71	
Samuel	Crt 70	
Solomon	Crt 72	
Thaddeus	Crt 69	
Thomas	Crt 69	
Wheelor	Rwn 364	
Chaeney, John	Rnd 308	
Chaffin, Amos	Brk 737	
Christ.	Rck 438	
Nathan, Junr.	Rwn 285	
Nathan, Junr.	Rwn 441	
Nathan, Senr.	Rwn 441	
Stanly	Rwn 423	
Chaimberlain, T.	Srr 704	
Chain, Isaiah	Grv 575	
Chalk, Stephen	Hrt 710	
William	Psq 626	
Challis, John	Rck 450	
Martha	Rck 477	
Chalmers, Charles	Cht 225	
Chamberlain, Eli-		
jah	Ptt 295	
Joseph	Psq 628	
Malichi	Brt 38	
Ralph	Ptt 294	
see Chaimberlain		
Chamberlin, Henry	Cmd 95	
James	Cmd 95	
Joh	Cbr 697	
Joseph	Cmd 94	
Robert	Prs 196	
Seth	Cmd 95	
Chambers, Abner	Prs 194	
Arthur	Ird 664	
Daniel	Jns 795	
Davidson	Prs 197	
Edmund, junr.	Wlk 32	
Edmund, Senr.	Wlk 32	
Edward	Prs 198	
Edward, Junr.	Mnt 461	
Edward, Senr.	Mnt 461	
Elihu	Bnc 165	
Elijah	Brk 734	
Elisha (2)	Wlk 32	
Enoch	Ash 76	
Francis	Ons 137	
Henry	Ash 76	
Henry	Ird 664	
Henry	Rch 247	
Henry	Rch 265	
James (2)	Ash 76	
James	Bnc 165	

Note: "Chars." appears with Bfr 5, and "Cha...t..., Henry" with Bfr 5.

43

James	Brk 733	Nathan	Smp 498	Samuel	Crv 249
James	Dpl 437	Pernal	Glf 631	Samuel	Trl 688
James	Hde 364	Richard	Crv 301	Soloman	Cht 207
James	Ird 647	Thomas	Ptt 235	Weeks	Crv 321
James	Ird 664	Thomas	Rck 472	William	Rwn 285
James	Orn 558	Warner	Rch 242	Wm.	Rck 442
John	Ans 207	William	Glf 619	Chappel, Andrew	Srr 643
John	Bnc 164	Chancey, John	Bld 12	Gideon	Prq 660
John	Dpl 424	Thomas	Bld 11	James	Chw 128
John	Glf 640	Chancler, Philip	Lnc 853	James	Chw 130
John	Rch 265	Chancy, Demsy	Bld 7	Isaac	Prq 647
John	Rth 103	Zachh.	Bld 8	Joab	Prq 649
John (2)	Wlk 31	Chandler, Daniel	Wlk 32	Job	Prq 645
John, H.C.R.	Wlk 33	Danl.	Csw 109	Jobe	Chw 119
John, Jur.	Hde 364	David	Srr 640	John	Chw 128
John, Ser.	Hde 364	Joel	Wlk 31	John, Jun.	Chw 130
Jonas	Mnt 469	John	Crt 88	Joseph	Prq 660
Joseph	Bnc 165	Jos.	Csw 107	Josiah	Chw 128
Joshua	Rch 247	Jos.	Csw 137	Mark	Prq 647
Josias	Rch 265	Joseph	Rck 487	Micajah	Chw 128
Keziah	Wlk 33	Josiah	Csw 124	Ranier	Prq 648
Mary	Rwn 339	Richard	Stk 582	Robert	Prq 648
Maxwell	Rwn 286	Richd.	Bnc 163	Samuel	Prq 663
Moses	Rch 255	Robert	Rck 491	Stephen	Ash 75
Nancy	Wke 725	Shadrick	Orn 612	William	Chw 119
Nathl.	Wrr 795	Thomas	Glf 639	William	Chw 124
Obediah	Trl 688	Thomas	Trl 688	William	Mck 605
Prudence	Dpl 431	Timothy	Rnd 305	Chappell, Mallichi	Mrt 389
Samuel	Orn 503	William	Nrt 433	Chapple, Ambrose	Glf 629
Sarah	Hde 366	William	Rnd 304	Christopher	Mnt 466
Thomas	Chw 118	William	Srr 643	Parks	Mnt 461
Thomas	Prs 199	Wm.	Crr 149	Solomon	Glf 629
Thomas	Rck 442	Chandlor, David	Grv 540	Char..., John, son	
Will.	Prs 197	Jane	Grv 540	Chars.	Bfr 5
Will.	Prs 198	Chanee, Benjamin	Wne 873	Charice, Moses	Crv 271
William	Bnc 165	Stephen	Wne 762	Charis, Charles	Grv 543
William	Ird 628	Chaney, James	Rwn 415	Chark, William, Sr.	Wrr 794
William	Rck 449	Judith	Rwn 415	Charlcraft, Levy	Grn 596
William	Rwn 339	Samuel	Bfr 4	Charles, Benjn.	Prq 655
William	Wlk 31	Channell, John	Rbs 370	Chrenchaw	Grv 539
William	Wlk 32	Michael	Rbs 371	Elijah	Glf 671
William, H.C.	Wlk 33	Michael	Rbs 432	Elisha	Glf 686
Chambles, Joel	Grv 573	Thomas	Rbs 370	John	Cmb 351
Chambliss, Allen	Nrt 433	Chany, George	Rck 448	Laven	Rwn 372
Chambly, John	Rwn 424	Chapel, Amos	Srr 643	Leven	Glf 671
Chamlee, Gerard	Wke 726	James	Srr 643	Charlescraft, Eli-	
James	Wke 726	Chapell, Mary	Wke 724	sha	Ons 147
John	Wke 726	Samuel	Wke 725	Isaac	Ons 147
Robert	Wke 726	Polley	Wke 725	Isaac	Ons 160
Chamler, Clabourn	Ans 207	Chaple, Roadey	Crr 155	James	Ons 157
Chamles, James	Nsh 96	Robert	Ans 240	Charls, Joseph	Rnd 308
William	Nsh 96	Chaplen, John	Crr 143	Samuel	Rnd 305
Chamless, John	Bnc 163	Spine	Crr 143	Charlton, George	Crv 269
Ruebon	Bnc 163	Chaplin, David	Rnd 306	Jobe	Chw 131
Chamley, Clabourn	Ans 204	Jacob	Stk 555	Charters, John	Rck 436
John	Ans 204	Chapman, Benjamin	Cmb 353	Chase, Elidia	Brk 736
Chamness, Anthony	Rnd 305	Benjamin	Rwn 441	John	Nrt 431
Charity	Glf 691	Cortny	Nsh 95	Chason, Benjamin	Cmb 369
Joseph	Rnd 305	Daniel	Orn 553	Joseph	Cmb 368
Joshua	Cht 217	David	Cht 207	Joseph	Cmb 370
William	Rnd 306	Douglas	Chw 114	Chastain, James	Bnc 166
Champain, James	Rwn 372	Enoch	Wlk 31	Chasten, Richard	Dpl 423
Richard	Grv 523	Erasmus	Rwn 441	Chatman, Robert	Rth 104
Champen, Benjamin	Edg 191	George	Grv 514	Chavers, Batte	Nrt 431
Willis	Edg 191	Harrison	Nrt 433	Bud	Ans 224
Champion, Drury	Hlf 300	James	Brk 738	Dilila	Wrr 795
Elias	Cmb 368	James	Csw 148	Jordan	Wke 723
Esther	Chw 128	Jemima	Trl 688	Richard	Ans 224
Henry	Jhn 767	Jesse	Crv 321	William	Wke 724
Jeremiah	Dpl 409	John	Orn 553	Chaves, Albert	Rbs 370
Jesse	Edg 189	John	Wlk 31	Isaac	Grv 550
Joab	Brt 38	Nicholas	Lnc 901	Ishmael	Rbs 371
John	Cht 206	Paris	Glf 664	John	Rbs 370
Susanah	Chw 129	Paul	Csw 129	Chavis, Erasmus	Bld 19
William	Hlf 300	Releigh	Wlk 31	James	Grv 579
Chance, Alexander	Mnt 482	Richard	Brk 737	John	Bld 10
Charrity	Ons 171	Robert	Rck 471	Joseph	Rwn 339

Chavors, Richmond	Brn 13	Jos.	Mrt 391	James	Rwn 390
Chavus, Miles	Cht 206	Josiah (2)	Crr 163	John	Brk 737
Chears, Benjamin	Rch 249	Laml.	Nsh 95	John	Brk 739
Elijah	Rch 249	Lemuel	Bfr 4	John	Lnc 860
James	Brn 17A	Lemuel	Ptt 250	Robert	Lnc 866
John	Nwh 7A	Levi	Edg 189	Robert H.	Csw 123
Samuel	Rch 245	Luke	Ptt 262	William	Lnc 888
Samuel	Rch 250	Nathan	Ptt 224	Childres, Ann	Wrr 798
Vachel	Rch 246	Robert	Edg 189	Pleasant	Csw 144
Cheatham, B. Wil-		Robert	Lnc 899	Pleasant	Wrr 795
liam	Nrt 431	Robert	Rth 103	Reps	Rck 437
George	Orn 555	Samuel	Ptt 264	Childress, Armaja	Stk 547
William	Orn 555	Sarah	Dpl 430	Benjamin	Stk 548
William	Grv 576	Solomon	Brt 38	David	Wlk 35
William B.	Nrt 431	Solomon	Ptt 260	Elisha	Stk 584
Cheatom, Wyatt	Wrr 798	Thomas	Brt 40	Jame	Stk 555
Cheatum, THomas	Wlk 34	Thomas	Hlf 300	Matthews	Stk 548
Check see Cheek		William	Ptt 261	Nicholas	Grv 510
Cheek, Hartwell	Orn 555	William, Junr.	Brt 38	Stephen	Stk 548
James	Mre 73	William, junr.	Ptt 262	Thomas	Stk 547
James	Orn 552	William, Senr.	Brt 38	Thomas	Stk 590
Joab	Mre 43	Willie	Edg 189	William	Stk 548
John	Mnt 508	Willis	Edg 189	Childs, Francis	Orn 492
John	Mre 51	Wm., Junr.	Mrt 391	James	Orn 492
John	Orn 553	Wm., Senr.	Mrt 392	Thomas, Junr.	Mnt 461
John	Wrr 795	Cherton, Alphred	Chw 114	Thomas, Senr.	Mnt 465
Joshua	Cbr 696	Joe	Chw 114	Chiles, James	Ans 227
Martin	Orn 554	Chesher, John	Rwn 385	Matthew	Jhn 769
Mastin	Cht 168	William	Bld 34	Chill, Charles	Brk 735
Philip	Mre 39	Cheshire, Buck	Rwn 436	Chilly, Martin	Jns 823
Randolph	Mre 50	John	Rwn 436	Chiner, Perry	Srr 641
Randolph	Wrr 796	Jonathan	Rwn 436	Chiners, Benjn.	Brn 14
Richard	Mre 74	Tenneson	Rwn 436	Chiney, Sarah	Ons 140
Robert	Mre 73	Zachariah	Rwn 385	Chipman, John	Glf 686
Robert	Wrr 796	Chesnut, Alexander	Smp 502	Paris	Glf 686
Robert, Junr.	Orn 555	Alexander	Smp 530	Chisenhall, Burrel	Orn 613
Robert, Senr.	Orn 555	Arthur	Smp 515	Celia	Orn 556
Silas	Mck 538	Charity	Smp 514	Reubin	Orn 613
Thomas L.	Crv 341	Charles	Smp 534	Samuel	Orn 613
Cheeves, James	Wke 724	Driver	Smp 530	Chisholm, Anguish	Mnt 485
Thomas	Wke 725	Jacob (2)	Smp 515	Daniel	Mnt 467
Cheltron, James	Csw 100	James	Smp 513	Daniel, Junr.	Mnt 468
Chenault, Abner	Rck 490	Jonathan	Smp 515	Daniel, Senr.	Mnt 461
Chencraw, Abraham	Grv 541	Joshua	Smp 529	Finlay	Cmb 351
Cheney, Benjamin	Crt 73	Needham	Smp 514	John	Mnt 462
William	Mck 584	Samuel	Smp 515	John	Rth 101
Chenour, Christian	Rwn 286	see Chesnut		Malcolm	Mnt 467
Cherenhapet, Clan-		Chessare, James	Bnc 165	Murdoch	Mnt 467
ler	Brk 738	Chesser, Henry	Chw 115	Chisnut see Chesnut	
Cherlon, Elizabeth	Orn 615	James	Ash 74	Chitley, Hardin	Cbr 687
Chermon, Barbery	Stk 577	see Clusser		Chittam, Jno.	Lnc 835
Cherry, Aaron	Edg 189	Chessher, Randolph	Bld 34	Wm.	Lnc 835
Abner	Mrt 391	Richd.	Bld 35	Chittem, Sebby	Wne 866
Caleb	Psq 637	Chesson, Benjamin	Wsh 702	Winney	Crr 156
Charles, Senr.	Bfr 4	John	Wsh 714	Chitty, Joseph	Stk 608
Daniel	Lnc 846	Joseph	Wsh 702	Chitwood, Amos	Rth 103
Harrell	Mrt 391	Joshua	Wsh 702	James	Rth 103
Henry	Bfr 4	Samuel	Wsh 702	Chivers, Andrew	Rwn 300
Hillery	Ptt 224	William	Wsh 702	Chren, Paul	Brk 731
Isham	Ans 237	Chester, David	Brk 731	Chrisenhall, Wil-	
James	Hrt 704	Jacob	Ans 205	liam	Orn 613
Jeams	Crr 157	John	Ans 236	Chrisman, Jacob	Glf 637
Jeremiah	Mrt 388	John	Edg 190	Joseph	Glf 637
Jesse, Esqr.	Mrt 391	Matthew	Grn 587	Chrismass, John	Csw 122
Jesse, Junr.	Mrt 389	Samuel	Bfr 6	William	Frn 449
Jesse, son of		Thomas	Brk 736	Chrismon, Charles	Stk 551
Jonathan	Mrt 391	Thomas	Brk 738	Chrispan, George	Stk 547
Jo..., son Jno.	Bfr 5	Worsley	Bfr 6	Christenbury, Wil-	
Job, Junr.	Mrt 389	Chesterfield, A.	Srr 707	liam	Hlf 300
Job, Senr.	Mrt 392	John, Taner	Srr 640	Wm., Jr.	Hlf 300
Joel	Mrt 391	Chestoms, Rookius	Nsh 94	Christian, James	Orn 553
Joha...	Bfr 5	Chieves, John	Frn 452	John	Cht 226
John	Ptt 224	Thomas	Frn 483	John	Mnt 485
John, Junr.	Brt 38	Thomas, Jur.	Frn 454	John	Mnt 490
John, Senr.	Brt 38	Childers, Gabriel	Ans 213	John	Stk 583
Jonathan, Junr.	Mrt 391	Isham	Lnc 853	William	Mnt 488
Jonathan, Senr.	Mrt 392	Jackson	Brk 732	see Cristian, Puller	

Christie, David	Mrt 391	Claghorn, Benjamin Crv 283	George	Crr 152
Jesse	Hlf 298	Horse	Mrt 391	George	Mnt 461
John	Hlf 298	Clamon, John	Bfr 22	Gilbert	Cmb 362
Thomas	Hlf 298	Clampet, Jerry	Rwn 371	Hannah	Orn 558
Christley, Jere-		Richard	Stk 615	Hardy	Bld 43
miah	Wlk 31	Clampit, George	Stk 619	Henery	Crr 167
Christman, Adam	Lnc 853	Clancy, George	Orn 492	Henry	Bld 30
Conrod	Lnc 853	Clanton, Abreham	Wrr 797	Henry	Hde 364
Daniel	Stk 625	Benjamin, Jr.	Srr 642	Henry	Mrt 391
Christmas, Charles	Orn 555	Benjamin, Sen.	Srr 641	Isaac	Crv 329
James	Orn 552	Charles	Srr 643	Isaac	Psq 630
Richard	Orn 553	Dudley	Wrr 798	James	Bld 8
Thos.	Wrr 796	Eadey	Wrr 795	James	Brk 737
Thos., Jr.	Wrr 795	Edward	Srr 641	James	Crv 321
William	Wrr 795	Edward	Srr 642	James	Cmb 379
Christopher, David	Grv 534	Edward	Wrr 798	James	Dpl 433
James	Cbr 681	Edward, Ser.	Srr 641	James	Glf 631
John	Rck 463	Thomas	Srr 641	James	Ird 647
Joseph	Wsh 702	Thomas	Srr 642	James	Mck 552
Mary	Rth 105	Clap, John	Orn 553	James	Nrt 431
Simon	Glf 629	John	Rnd 308	James	Stk 551
Thomas	Glf 659	Clapp, Christiana	Glf 639	James	Wrr 794
Thomas	Lnc 886	Daniel	Glf 647	James W.	Nrt 431
William	Orn 501	Felta	Glf 647	Jas.	Mrt 389
William	Rth 105	Felty	Glf 669	Jeromiah	Brk 731
Christophus, Crist-		Fetty	Glf 627	Jesse	Mck 529
opr.	Wke 775	George	Glf 643	Jesse	Orn 558
Christwick, Mr.	Wrr 795	George	Glf 648	Jethro	Grn 602
Christy, Andrew	Ird 653	Jacob	Glf 638	Joanna	Brk 731
Daniel	Glf 667	Jacob	Glf 643	John	Bfr 4
Joseph	Ird 653	John	Glf 648	John	Bld 7
Chritchfield, John	Srr 640	Ludwick	Glf 643	John	Brn 20A
Nathl.	Srr 640	Ludwick	Glf 648	John	Bnc 166
Wm.	Srr 640	Philip	Glf 631	John	Crv 311
Chronister, James	Lnc 859	Clapps, Thomas	Ons 167	John	Cmb 360
Chsnut, David	Smp 514	Clapton, Archibald	Grv 572	John	Cmb 361
Chuk see Cheek		Magaret	Grv 572	John	Cmb 362
Chun, Silvester	Rch 254	Clardy, Benjamin	Grv 514	John	Crr 167
Thomas	Rwn 320	Elizabeth	Grv 550	John	Glf 678
Chunn, Samuel	Bnc 158	Penelope	Bld 17	John	Mrt 391
Church, Amous	Wlk 32	Clarence see Claurence		John	Ons 171
Elijah	Wlk 31	Clark, Aaron	Crv 257	John	Orn 552
Elisha	Wlk 32	Abraham	Rth 103	John	Rnd 305
John	Brk 734	Abraham, j	Rth 103	John	Srr 310
John	Crr 161	Alexander	Brk 735	John	Wrr 794
John	Wlk 30	Alexander	Cmb 379	John, Junr.	Hrt 710
John	Wlk 32	Alexander	Lnc 873	Jonah	Nwh 7
Philip	Ash 75	Ann	Glf 645	Jonas	Mck 522
Philip	Ash 76	Archibald (2)	Cmb 362	Joseph	Brn 21A
Philip	Bnc 164	Archibald	Cmb 374	Joseph	Crv 309
Robert	Brk 737	Archibald	Cmb 378	Joseph	Mck 571
Thomas	Brt 40	Arthur	Rth 102	Joseph	Rwn 414
Thomas	Brk 731	Baptist	Rnd 306	Keneth	Mrt 391
Thomas	Cmd 99	Benjamin	Bnc 165	Keneth	Mnt 469
Thomas	Prq 644	Benjamin	Brk 733	Kerney	Hrt 709
William	Wlk 32	Benjamin	Crv 279	Leonard	Wke 724
Churchell see Churchill		Benjamin	Mck 571	Levan	Crv 239
Churchewell, Simon	Ans 199	Benjamin	Wke 725	Luke	Cmb 382
Churchill, Benjn.	Gts 264	Benjamin, Senr.	Brk 736	Major	Nwh 10A
Charles	Crv 235	Benjn.	Brn 20A	Malcolm	Cmb 361
Churchwell, Allen	Brt 40	Carey	Ans 199	Malcolm	Cmb 377
Edward	Brt 38	Charles	Grv 535	Marrti	Brk 736
William	Dpl 425	Cornelius	Lnc 860	Mary	Bfr 22
Churn, Silver	Rch 264	Daniel	Cmb 362	Mary	Hlf 300
Ciff, James	Nsh 94	Daniel	Rnd 306	Moses	Ird 609
John	Cmd 93	David	Bld 8	Nancey	Mrt 392
Cildon, Mary	Psq 634	David	Cmb 361	Nancy	Brk 736
Cimmins, Samuel	Glf 638	David	Lnc 874	Nathaniel	Cht 225
Cirbey, William	Bnc 164	David	Mrt 389	Nathaniel	Orn 556
Cirles, Saml.	Prs 219	David	Smp 530	Nelly	Mck 571
Citheart, John	Mck 530	David	Srr 642	Nelly	Rth 103
Civils, Abel	Crv 309	Dianna	Dpl 432	Niven	Mnt 461
John	Crv 309	Dougald	Bld 26	Rebeckah	Crr 167
William	Crv 307	Drewry	Edg 190	Richard	Edg 190
Clack, Eldridge	Hlf 298	E...	Bfr 5	Robert	Csw 97
Clackston, Anson	Grv 571	Elijah	Crv 249	Robert	Rnd 305
Clagget, Henry	Ird 620	Francis	Glf 680	Robert	Rnd 307

Robert	Rwn 456	Richd.	Brn 14
Robert K.	Mck 529	Claurence, John M.	Ans 208
Rubin	Ons 173	Clawson, William	Wlk 31
Ruth	Psq 632	Clay, Dennis	Cbr 694
Salley	Crr 164	Edward, Senr.	Prs 217
Samuel	Brk 736	Isaac	Lnc 811
Samuel	Hde 364	Isham	Cbr 693
Samuel	Rnd 305	James	Cbr 694
Samuel	Rnd 306	Mary	Hlf 296
Susanna	Brk 739	Peter	Grv 544
Thomas	Cbr 689	Samuel	Grv 551
Thomas	Hde 365	Claybrooks, Moses	Rwn 423
Thomas	Nrt 431	Clayton, Colmon	Prs 199
Thomas	Orn 558	Daniel	↑Prs 202
Thomas	Rck 477	Daniel (Yabe)	Prs 197
Thomas	Wrr 796	Danl.	Prs 192
Thomas	Wrr 798	Danl., Senr.	Prs 191
Thomas	Wlk 33	George	Ird 647
Vachel	Mnt 488	James	Crv 303
W. James	Nrt 431	John	Hlf 298
William	Brk 739	John	Stk 612
William	Cmb 380	John	Trl 670
William	Edg 189	Lambert	Bnc 165
William	Hrt 809	Lucy	Stk 547
William	Hde 364	Lucy, Ser.	Stk 547
William	Orn 557	Sarah	Prs 192
William	Orn 558	Thomas	Crv 305
William	Rnd 305	Thomas	Prs 202
William	Wrr 794	Will.	Prs 188
William, (Cain)	Orn 557	Will.	Prs 192
William, (Eno)	Orn 558	William	Crv 291
Wm.	Crr 165	William	Rwn 372
Zadok	Hrt 710	William	Smp 505
see Cark, Chark		William	Trl 688
Clarke, Alexander	Cht 152	Cleaver, Friderick	Rwn 407
Anthony	Lnc 837	Lydia	Hde 364
Christopher	Brt 34	Cleaves, John	Hde 364
David	Lnc 865	Clegg, Thomas	Cht 166
David	Ptt 285	Cleghorn, James	Rth 102
Frances	Cht 159	John	Rth 101
Frank	Ans 201	Clem, Adam	Brk 737
James	Cht 220	Cleman, Mark	Cbr 697
Jethro	Ptt 285	Clemants, Thomas	Orn 613
John	Ans 201	Clement, Andrew	Rth 103
John	Brt 38	Cornelius	Rth 103
John	Rch 267	Henry, Senr.	Rwn 407
John	Rwn 329	James	Rth 682
Joseph	Ans 226	Johnson	Stk 551
Nathaniel	Cht 220	Clements, John	Grv 577
Nicholas	Rch 245	Mellekiah	Grv 566
Ozborn	Ptt 257	Peyton	Wke 725
Patrick	Cht 220	Richard	Grv 566
Peter	Stk 589	Samuel	Grv 577
Richard	Cht 193	Simon	Grv 579
Robert	Ans 201	Simon, jr.	Grv 525
Samuel	Ptt 290	Thomas	Grv 571
Samuel	Stk 575	William	Grn 591
Samuel	Stk 589	William	Nrt 433
Silas	Cht 191	William	Wke 725
Thomas	Stk 595	Clemmings, Edwd.	Brn 18
William	Cht 155	Timy.	Brn 18
William	Lnc 859	Clemmins, David	Ird 648
Clarks, Burton	Cht 188	Clemmons, Henry	Rwn 424
Samuel	Stk 547	John	Chw 131
Clary, Conner	Rwn 286	Thompson	Mnt 477
James	Prq 645	Clemons, Charleton	Ptt 236
John	Prq 656	Elisabeth	Crv 321
John, Junr.	Rwn 286	Elizabeth	Brt 38
John, Senr.	Rwn 286	George	Ptt 236
Jordan	Prq 662	James	Glf 679
Lemuel	Hlf 296	John	Rch 248
Sarah	Rwn 345	William	Prq 642
Clash, Joseph	Crv 265	William	Ptt 236
Clastor, Nimrod	Wne 856	Clenard, Daniel	Rwn 364
Claton, Asher	Prq 657	Lawrence	Rwn 371
Jemima	Hde 365	Clendening,	
John	Prs 198	Charles	Orn 553

Fisher	Orn 553		
James	Orn 553		
Joseph	Orn 503		
Mary	Orn 545		
Clendenning, John	Orn 553		
Clendenon, Matthew	Ird 648		
Clenney, Samuel	Orn 490		
Clenny, William	Orn 557		
Clepard, John	Lnc 853		
Clerk, Archd.	Mre 59		
Benjamin	Hrt 716		
Cornelius	Psq 632		
Daniel	Mre 54		
James	Hrt 716		
Malcolm	Mre 54		
Penelophy	Nsh 94		
Cleveland, Jeremiah	Bnc 158		
Robert	Wlk 32		
Cleves, John	Hlf 298		
Robert	Hlf 298		
William	Gts 264		
Clewis, Geo.	Brn 18A		
Clibourn, Brittain	Rbs 370		
John	Rbs 372		
Click, Nicholas	Rwn 423		
Cliffard, John	Rwn 456		
Cliffo..., Loucin-			
dia	Bfr 5		
Cliffo...t, John	Bfr 5		
Clift, Mary	Glf 678		
William	Glf 677		
Clifton, Azel	Wke 723		
Benjamin	Mnt 483		
Bozman	Bld 42		
Daniel	Jns 825		
David	Lnc 846		
Edwin	Hlf 296		
Ezekel	Frn 469		
Henry	Srr 641		
Jacob	Srr 643		
James	Lnc 846		
Joel	Wke 723		
John	Frn 492		
John	Wke 723		
Joseph	Orn 612		
Josiah	Orn 612		
Lemuel	Hlf 296		
Reuben	Wsh 702		
Robert	Wsh 702		
Sarah	Jns 799		
Wiley	Frn 469		
William	Csw 97		
William	Wke 723		
Clim, David	Rth 104		
Climer, Dudley	Glf 667		
James	Csw 123		
Thomas	Csw 123		
Climore, Margaret	Lnc 841		
Clinard, Jacob	Rwn 371		
Peter	Rwn 294		
Cline, Christr.	Glf 638		
Daniel	Cbr 698		
Daniel	Cbr 711		
Henry	Cbr 715		
Henry	Lnc 811		
Jacob	Lnc 867		
John	Lnc 867		
John, Senr.	Lnc 867		
Martin	Lnc 876		
Michael	Lnc 867		
Sally	Lnc 876		
Valentine	Lnc 811		
William	Lnc 812		
Clingerman, Alexan-			
der	Rwn 305		
Clinton, Jms.	Lnc 833		
Owen	Smp 527		

Name	Ref
Robert	Rth 101
Robert	Rth 105
William	Smp 505
Clixbey, John	Prs 201
Cloman, John	Edg 191
Cloninger, Adam	Lnc 829
Michael	Lnc 859
Clontz, George	Cbr 717
Clopton, Richard	Frn 448
Clore, Jacob	Lnc 811
Close, John	Stk 621
Joseph	Glf 639
Thomas	Rnd 304
Clotfelter, Elias	Rwn 352
Felix	Rwn 372
George	Rwn 320
Jacob	Rwn 372
John	Rwn 371
Peter	Rwn 352
Peter	Rwn 371
Rudolph	Rwn 352
Cloud, Daniel	Orn 612
George	Stk 621
Isaac	Rth 101
Jacob	Rnd 308
Jaremiah	Stk 582
John, Jr.	Stk 583
Joseph	Rnd 304
Joseph	Rnd 306
Joseph, Jur.	Stk 581
Samuel	Orn 612
Clouder, Charles	
Godfrey	Stk 625
Charles Godfry	Stk 598
Clover, Charles	Cbr 714
Cloyd, Clifton	Nrt 429
Clubb, Gasper	Lnc 853
George	Lnc 853
Cluck see Clark	
Clusser, John	Mnt 469
Cluttz, John	Cbr 718
Leonard	Cbr 718
Clutz, Conrod	Rwn 299
David	Rwn 300
Jacob	Rwn 299
Jacob, Senr.	Rwn 300
Martin	Rwn 300
Tobius	Cbr 692
Windle	Rwn 299
Clyde, Robert	Cmb 353
Coady, James	Rwn 385
Coaker, Benjamin	Nrt 431
Henry	Nrt 433
William	Nrt 431
Coakley, Benjamin	Nrt 433
Coal, Edward	Rch 245
Francis	Rch 242
George	Rch 246
James	Rch 243
James	Wne 852
Jesse	Rch 262
John (2)	Rch 246
John, Junr.	Rch 263
Mark	Rch 246
Peter	Rch 246
Peter H.	Rch 242
Robert	Wrr 796
Stephen	Rch 242
Thomas	Ans 199
Thomas	Wne 853
William	Rch 243
Willis	Jhn 775
Coale, Fanny	Grv 557
John	Orn 557
John, (W)	Grv 526
Levy	Orn 556
Samuel	Orn 613
Thomas	Orn 552
W. John	Grv 526
William	Grv 557
William	Grv 572
Coalman, Carter	Wrr 798
Jacob	Wrr 796
John	Orn 557
Coalmon, Samuel	Orn 558
Coalson, George	Rck 459
Coan, Jacob	Rwn 423
Coane, Jesse	Nrt 431
Coatney, May	Ans 213
Stephen	Ans 213
Coats, Benjamin	Jhn 766
Caleb	Crr 149
Elizabeth	Smp 508
John	Jhn 765
Jordan	Smp 508
Patsay	Mre 70
Solomon	Jhn 766
Solomon	Rwn 407
Wiley	Rwn 407
William	Rwn 407
Cobay, George	Rch 256
Cobb, Amos	Ptt 276
Benjamin	Brk 733
Benjamin	Nsh 96
Clisby	Brk 736
David	Ans 208
David	Lnc 829
David, Junior	Ptt 293
David, Senior	Ptt 293
Edward, (R)	Edg 190
Edward	189
Elizabeth	Brt 36
Gray	Ptt 272
Heartwell	Ptt 293
Henry	Brt 36
Henry	Glf 665
Henry, Jur.	Glf 640
Jacob	Stk 577
James	Csw 147
James	Lnc 829
James	Smp 506
James, (L)	Edg 189
Jesse	Lnr 35
Jesse	Mrt 391
John	Ans 208
John	Brt 36
John	Csw 100
John	Csw 147
John	Lnr 31
John	Rnd 309
Keziah	Ptt 291
Martha	Nrt 433
Moses	Ptt 271
Nathan	Brt 38
Noah	Csw 147
Patience	Wne 872
Perry	Csw 123
Reuben	Ptt 273
Robert	Cht 166
Robt., jr.	Cht 199
Sally	Edg 189
Samuel	Csw 123
Samuel	Psq 626
Stephen	Edg 189
Stephen	Wne 872
Tobias	Nwh 12A
William	Nrt 433
William	Ptt 293
Wm.	Lnc 829
Cobbett, Lewis	Csw 134
Cobble, David	Mnt 501
Henry	Mnt 510
Jacob	Glf 646
John	Brk 731
John	Rwn 384
Cobbles, George	Mnt 500
Cobey, George	Rch 265
Coble, Anthony	Rnd 306
Christopher	Mnt 510
David	Orn 551
George	Glf 629
George	Orn 551
Henry	Orn 551
Jacob	Glf 648
John	Orn 503
John	Orn 551
John	Rnd 308
John, Junr.	Orn 551
Nicholas	Glf 629
Peter	Glf 647
Peter, Senr.	Glf 647
Philip	Glf 633
Powell	Glf 633
Nicholas	Rnd 308
Cobler, Fredk.	Rck 461
Harvy	Rck 461
Mary	Rck 461
Nicholas	Rck 479
Thomas	Rck 463
Cobourn, John	Mck 522
Coburn, Abner	Mrt 391
Andrew	Mrt 389
Daniel	Ans 208
Elijah	Ans 208
Francis	Ans 208
Fredrick	Mrt 391
griffin	Mrt 389
Headley	Ans 208
Isaac	Mrt 391
James	Ans 209
Jesse	Mrt 389
John	Ans 209
Cochran, Ann	Orn 551
Benjamin	Brk 739
Benjamin	Cbr 706
Eliazer	Mck 579
Jas.	Prs 217
Jas.	Prs 219
John	Mck 579
John, C.C.	Mck 579
Robert	Mck 580
Robert	Rwn 336
Thomas	Mck 579
Thomas, Junr.	Mck 579
William	Mck 579
Cochren, Simeon	Prs 212
John	Cbr 677
Robert, Junr.	Cbr 677
William	Cbr 677
Cochron, Jno., Jur.	Csw 123
John	Csw 122
Reubin	Csw 121
Robert	Hlf 300
Robt.	Csw 136
Cockburn, Frances	Edg 191
Cockerham, Daniel	Srr 641
David	Srr 640
Moses	Srr 710
William	Srr 640
Cockerum, Eliza-beth	Rth 101
Cockmon, Joseph	Mre 50
Joseph	Mre 50
Cockram, Aaron	Mnt 469
Abram	Mnt 469
Jacob	Mnt 469
Cockran, James G.	Brn 17A
Robert	Cmb 351
Cockrel, William	Jhn 753
Cockrell, John	Nsh 95
Jonathan	Nsh 95

Name	Loc	No.	Name	Loc	No.	Name	Loc	No.
Samuel	Jhn	752	Cogdell, Anna	Wne	873	John, Junr.	Wke	726
Cockrum, Humphrey	Wlk	33	William	Rth	104	John, Sen.	Mre	61
James	Rth	102	Cogdill, Lydia	Crv	251	John, Senr.	Wke	723
James	Rth	103	Coggin, Barnwell	Mnt	477	Joseph	Cht	173
John	Rth	101	James	Frn	463	Joshua	Hlf	300
John	Rth	103	Joshua	Frn	454	Loid	Wke	723
Minor	Rth	100	Joshua	Frn	478	Mark	Rnd	306
Thomas	Rth	101	Jourdin	Mnt	521	Mark	Rwn	377
Cocks, John	Ans	200	Robert	Frn	462	Mary	Brt	40
John	Ans	211	Robert	Frn	464	Mathew	Bnc	165
John, Junr.	Ans	201	Simon	Mnt	482	Mathew	Rnd	307
Miles	Grn	597	Coggins, Jeromiah	Rwn	378	Reuben	Cht	170
Coddle, Benjn.	Mre	56	John	Srr	640	Richard	Bfr	4
Jonathan	Mre	56	Matthew	Srr	640	Robert	Dpl	417
Codey, Godfrey	Bnc	164	Zacharia	Rwn	377	Samuel	Bnc	165
Peirce	Bnc	166	Coggshall, Tristum	Srr	641	Sarah	Rnd	305
Conrod	Mnt	513	Coghill, Thomas	Grv	514	Shadrach	Wke	723
Coe, Avery	Glf	659	Cogwell, Isram	Wrr	795	Thomas	Cmd	100
Isaah	Srr	640	James	Wrr	795	Thomas	Cht	188
John	Glf	634	Reubin	Wrr	794	Thomas	Dpl	415
John	Glf	659	Coher, Joseph	Srr	643	Thomas	Mre	62
John	Srr	642	Cohern, John	Ird	616	Thomas	Rth	102
William	Srr	642	Coherse, Elisabeth	Lnc	888	Thomas	Rth	104
Cofer, William	Mre	62	Cohoon, Duncan	Rch	252	Thomas	Wke	723
Coffe, Benjamin	Brk	733	Etheldred	Edg	190	Thos.	Wlk	30
Joel	Brk	734	Gray	Edg	190	William	Brk	734
Lewis	Brk	733	Joel	Edg	190	William	Cht	170
Rubin	Brk	733	John	Rch	252	William	Smp	529
Rubin	Brk	734	Simon	Edg	189	William, Esq.	Rwn	377
Rubin	Brk	738	Solomon	Mnt	501	Willis	Mre	42
Coffee, Bethel	Glf	663	William	Hde	365	Colea, Frank	Cht	177
James	Stk	546	William	Srr	643	Coledg, Henry	Cbr	694
Joseph	Brt	36	William, Junr.	Edg	190	Coleman, Amos	Bld	16
Nathan	Crr	152	William, Senr.	Edg	190	Benjamin	Crv	329
Coffen, Adam	Srr	641	Cohran, Robert	Lnc	859	Benjamin	Lnr	30
Coffer, John	Crr	147	Coil, Richard	Wke	775	Charles	Edg	189
Coffey, Ambrose	Wlk	30	Cok, George	Brk	731	David	Ash	76
Benjamin	Wlk	30	Coker, David	Wke	725	Dempsey	Bld	14
Ely	Wlk	35	Ezekiel	Edg	191	Elijah	Wne	859
James	Wlk	34	Jacob	Edg	189	Ethelred	Bld	13
John	Wlk	30	John	Bnc	163	Hardee	Edg	190
John, junr.	Wlk	34	Joseph	Brk	734	Hardy, T.C.	Edg	190
John, Senr.	Wlk	34	Nathaniel	Edg	189	Honor	Wne	872
Levy	Wlk	30	Richard	Edg	192	James	Mnt	511
Micajah	Stk	547	Colbert, John	Bnc	165	James	Rch	242
Thomas	Wlk	30	Matthew	Crt	69	John	Bld	13
Thomas, senr.	Wlk	34	Thomas	Frn	494	John	Bld	16
William	Hde	364	Colbreath, Arch-			John	Edg	192
William	Wlk	34	bald	Smp	523	John	Hlf	298
Coffield, Benjamin	Chw	121	Daniel	Smp	518	Jonathan	Ash	76
Benjamin	Edg	192	John	Smp	518	Lasania	Bld	13
Charles	Hlf	298	Kneal	Smp	519	Mary	Crv	329
David	Brt	36	Colburn, Revil	Cht	163	Moses	Bld	13
Elizabeth	Hrt	697	Colby, Creed	Srr	644	Philip	Rwn	336
Frederick	Chw	121	Coldiron, George	Rwn	293	Robert	Rck	439
Jethro	Brt	36	Jacob	Ird	670	Robert, Junr.	Edg	189
John	Chw	124	Coldmon, Richd.	Prs	191	Robert, Senr.	Edg	189
Josiah	Brt	36	Cole, Abraham	Mre	59	Sarah	Ash	76
Mary	Hlf	300	Alexander	Brk	738	Spill.	Rck	439
Sarah	Chw	124	Andrew	Mre	60	Spilsby	Csw	127
William (2)	Brt	36	Anna	Cmb	353	Stephen	Edg	190
Coffin, Aron	Glf	627	Captn.	Cmd	109	Theolus	Bld	16
Barnabas	Glf	690	Charles	Ons	141	Thomas	Brk	734
Elizabeth	Glf	692	David	Bnc	165	William	Rbs	371
Joseph, Jur.	Glf	690	George	Cht	193	Merriman	Orn	556
Mary	Glf	690	Hannah	Crt	84	Colemon, Sarah	Wke	725
Matthew	Glf	635	Harbert	Mre	61	Coleolaugh, John	Wrr	798
Peter	Glf	629	Isaac	Crv	235	William	Wrr	797
Peter	Glf	683	Jacob	Bfr	4	Coleron, Koonrod	Ash	74
Seth	Stk	614	James	Glf	652	Colescott, Thomas	Glf	662
Coffman, Leonard	Rwn	329	Jessee	Cht	200	Coleson, David	Stk	595
Cofiel, David	Edg	190	Joab	Wlk	30	James	Hrt	734
Thomas	Edg	190	John	Cht	190	Coleston, Betheny	Rck	459
Cofield, Thos.	Mrt	391	John	Cmb	383	Coley, Charles, Jr.	Hlf	296
Cogans, John	Ptt	274	John	Mck	544	Charles, Sr.	Hlf	296
Zacharia	Ptt	274	John	Mre	61	Francis	Wrr	796
Cogdal, Richard	Bfr	6	John, Jun.	Mre	60	James	Hlf	296

Jeffery	Hlf 296	James	Mre 39	Colquett, Ranson	Rck 437
Julias	Cht 178	James	Mre 44	Colquhoon, Anguish	Mre 52
Patsy	Hlf 296	James	Nwh 7A	Archibald	Cmb 385
Susanna	Hlf 296	James, Jur.	Frn 478	John	Cmb 385
William	Hlf 296	James, Ser.	Frn 478	Malcolm	Cmb 384
William	Mnt 501	Jaremiah	Stk 586	Colquohoune, Archi-	
William	Smp 536	Jas.	Mrt 391	bald	Smp 495
Colins, John	Psq 627	Jeremiah	Prq 652	Colson, John	Rch 270
Roger	Stk 583	Jesse	Nwh 6A	Joseph	Ans 228
Color, Peter	Stk 600	John	Cmd 104	Mary	Ans 206
Collands, Samuel	Mck 548	John	Grv 514	Sander	Nrt 429
Collans, William	Stk 579	John	Jns 805	Colston, Chester	Nsh 94
Collens, Caleb	Crt 89	John	Nwh 8A	James	Nsh 95
Jesse	Nsh 95	John	Nwh 10A	James	Nsh 96
Obediah	Srr 643	John	Orn 552	Colter, Hannah	Rch 255
William	Orn 555	John	Orn 558	Martin	Lnc 901
Coller, Charles	Orn 615	John	Orn 614	Philip	Lnc 901
Hencon	Orn 615	John	Rth 102	Coltharp, Norwell	Hlf 298
Collet, Charles	Rwn 364	John, Junr.	Mrt 389	Colton, Pellam	Brn 18A
Samuel	Rwn 364	John, senr.	Mrt 391	Coltrain, David	Rnd 305
Collett, James	Rnd 305	Joseph	Brt 38	Jacob	Rnd 305
Collharp see Coltharp		Joseph	Rth 104	James	Rnd 305
Colliar, Arthur	Lnc 866	Joseph	Ons 138	Jas.	Mrt 392
Lightfoot	Mnt 498	Josiah	Chw 114	John	Mrt 392
Collier, Ann	Rnd 307	Josiah	Ptt 280	William (2)	Rnd 305
Doctor	Frn 488	Kedar	Wke 724	Colvard, John	Srr 644
Drury	Ans 206	Kizah	Cmd 108	William	Wlk 33
Drury	Lnc 846	Lewis	Wke 724	Colvell, George	Lnc 812
Francis	Lnc 841	Lucy	Brt 36	James	Lnc 812
Hannah	Rch 255	Luke	Brt 36	Colven, Francis	Rbs 372
Herbert	Cht 188	Martha	Wke 724	Colver see Calver	
Herbert	Cht 200	Mary	Lnc 894	Colvert, Benjamin	Srr 642
James	Lnr 2	Mary	Rth 104	Joseph	Srr 642
Jesse	Nrt 431	Matthew	Wke 724	Colvin, Archibald	Cmb 367
John	Cht 188	Merrill	Wke 724	William	Cmb 366
Joseph	Nrt 431	Mical	Nsh 94	Colyar, James	Brk 733
Joshua	Nrt 431	Noah	Psq 624	John	Wne 864
Probate	Jhn 777	Noey	Crr 160	Samuel	Wne 864
Robert	Lnr 2	Peter	Frn 479	Colyerhouse, Lach-	
Thomas	Lnr 2	Reddick	Wke 724	lan	Cmb 365
William	Mck 592	Ricd.	Ons 150	Coman, James	Wke 775
William	Nrt 433	Salley	Mrt 391	Comb, Ebenezer	Wne 849
William	Wke 723	Samuel	Lnc 894	Combes, Thomas	Crv 301
Zacehariah	Wne 864	Shadrack	Hlf 300	William	Jns 791
see Colyar		Solomon	Nsh 96	Combo, Rheubin	Brn 14
Collieur, Henry	Cht 161	Stephen	Mre 61	Solomon	Brn 14
Colliham, Daniel	Stk 617	Tho.	Brn 18A	Combs, Aron	Orn 503
Collings, Sarah	Gts 263	Thomas	Ash 74	George	Wlk 33
Thomas	Gts 264	Thomas	Mre 44	James	Wlk 33
Collins, Abraham	Lnc 894	Thomas	Rwn 324	Jesse	Csw 105
Abraham	Rth 102	Thomas	Wsh 700	Jesse	Wsh 702
Ambrose	Ash 76	Thomas, Jun.	Mre 45	John, FR.	Orn 616
Andrew	Jhn 777	Timothy	Mrt 391	John, RH.	
Andrew	Orn 560	Tulley	Crr 160	Patsy	Rck 447
Anthony	Stk 547	Urias	Wke 724	Robert	Hlf 300
Benjamin	Jns 805	Vadery	Ash 75	Sarah	Srr 644
Brice	Brk 735	Valentine	Ash 75	Thomas	Trl 676
Daniel	Lnc 887	Watson	Rth 101	William	Trl 684
Daniel	Rch 252	William	Frn 478	Comecal, John	Rch 270
David	Ans 203	William	Grv 514	Comer, Amos	Rnd 307
David	Jhn 749	William	Lnc 900	Jesse	Rnd 307
David, Junr.	Brt 38	William	Mck 582	Robet	Rnd 308
David, Senr.	Brt 38	William	Mck 604	Thomas	Rnd 308
Deal	Jhn 749	William	Prq 657	William	Stk 580
Elisha	Rch 252	William (2)	Rth 102	Comly see Conely	
Elisha	Rth 102	William	Wsh 700	Commander, Alesbury	Psq 633
Ely	Orn 503	Willis	Wke 723	John	Psq 629
Ely	Orn 553	Wm.	Mrt 389	Jos.	Psq 640
Ely	Orn 558	Collis, James	Rth 103	Joseph	Prq 654
Enoch	Orn 502	Collit, Ezekiel	Rwn 352	Tukes	Psq 629
Gasper	Rwn 424	Collon, Ambrose	Brk 736	Common, John	Rch 264
Hannah	Brt 38	Collons, John, Ser.	Orn 616	William	Rnd 308
Henry	Frn 483	Collson, John	Mnt 499	Compton, Aquila	Csw 131
Henry	Lnc 871	Colner, David	Orn 551	Aquild.	Csw 120
Isaac	Lnc 894	David	Orn 552	see Cumpton	
Isaac	Rth 104	Colony, Thomas	Wke 725	Comwell, Mecajah	Rth 104
James	Hlf 298	Colquahoun, Duncan	Rbs 370	Con, Joseph	Stk 546

Name	Loc		Name	Loc		Name	Loc
Con..., John	Bfr 5		William	Brt 40		Hanah	Nwh 3A
Con...y, John	Bfr 5		William	Hlf 298		Harrison	Wrr 795
Conder, Lewis	Mck 606		William	Ird 655		Henry	Cht 175
Condie, William	Frn 471		William	Lnc 865		Henry	Cmb 375
Condra, Claben	Rth 103		William	Mck 561		Henry	Ird 609
Dennis	Jhn 761		William	Rck 441		Henry	Orn 503
Condrey, Calib	Ird 620		William H.	Crv 311		Henry	Orn 551
Cone, Archeles	Mrt 391		Wright	Brt 40		Henry	Stk 590
James	Nsh 95		Connerly, Cullen	Dpl 431		Henry	Wke 725
Jesse	Mrt 391		John	Orn 615		Henry	Wke 775
Lewis	Mrt 392		Conners, Thomas	Bfr 4		Isaac	Brk 732
Neal, senr.	Mrt 389		Conningham, Nathan-			Isaac	Glf 675
Stephen	Bfr 5		iel	Rnd 350		Isaac	Mck 525
Thomas	Edg 190		Connolly, Daniel	Rbs 374		Isaac	Mck 606
Thomas, Junr.	Brt 40		Connoly, Mary	Cmb 367		Jacob	Crv 241
Thomas, Senr.	Brt 38		Connor, Darby	Brk 737		Jacob	Wne 850
Conelly, Neill	Cmb 378		Connoway, James	Hlf 298		James	Dpl 418
Conely, Alexander	Cmb 378		John	Crr 146		James	Glf 691
Duncan	Cmb 366		Thomas	Csw 107		James	Orn 502
James	Brk 732		Conoly, Anne	Nrt 431		James	Rck 450
William	Mnt 469		John	Cmb 368		James	Rth 103
William, Junr.	Brk 733		Conrad, John	Stk 627		James	Smp 518
Cong...ton, Daniel	Bfr 5		Tac	Stk 596		James	Stk 548
James	Bfr 5		see Coonrod			James, Sr.	Smp 518
Jane	Bfr 5		Conrod, Adam, Junr.	Rwn 346		Jarvis	Mck 541
Conger, Eli	Mck 561		Jacob	Stk 606		Jehu	Dpl 422
Congleton, Abraham	Ptt 225		John	Lnc 887		Jesse	Nrt 433
David	Ptt 238		John	Stk 596		Joel	Cht 204
John	Bfr 22		Peter	Rwn 431		John	Cbr 704
Moses	Bfr 6		Peter	Rwn 436		John	Cht 196
Thomas	Bfr 6		Rudolph	Lnc 811		John	Cht 204
William	Bfr 5		Conrode, John	Stk 611		John	Cmb 353
William	Ptt 237		Constable, William	Brk 737		John	Dpl 422
Conklin, David	Bnc 164		Constantine, Edward	Rth 102		John	Frn 482
Conley, Hugh	Brk 739		Conway, Gunbey	Ons 140		John	Ird 655
John	Orn 546		Lezenah	Ons 142		John	Nrt 433
William	Brk 732		Conyears, Ephraim	Frn 455		John	Orn 503
William	Crv 333		Ross	Frn 476		John	Orn 553
Conly, Edmund	Wlk 33		William	Frn 476		John	Rbs 371
George	Csw 111		Cook, Abraham	Ird 643		John	Rwn 377
Henry	Ash 74		Abram	Cht 169		John	Rth 102
John	Ash 74		Adam	Brk 735		John	Stk 603
Sarah	Ash 85		Aimy	Smp 532		John (2)	Srr 641
Thomas	Ash 74		Alexander	Rwn 320		John	Wne 861
William	Ash 74		Alexander	Rwn 364		John	Wne 872
Conn, Edward	Frn 490		Allin	Ird 609		John, Junr.	Orn 502
William	Lnc 874		Ann	Grn 557		John, Sen.	Orn 502
Connal, John	Stk 546		Archibald	Orn 502		John D.	Grv 568
Connaway, James	Jns 793		Arther	Wne 858		Johnson	Rwn 378
Connel, Thomas	Nsh 94		Astage	Srr 741		Joiles	Nrt 433
Connell, Robert	Nrt 433		Benjamin	Brt 36		Joseph	Ird 660
Connelly, Catey	Ptt 294		Benjamin	Rth 100		Joseph	Rck 448
Connely, John	Mck 562		Blanton	Wke 724		Josiah	Psq 632
Conner, Andrew	Rck 456		Britain	Psq 637		Keren	Wke 724
Asa	Cmd 97		Catherine	Lnc 888		Lazarus	Smp 514
Burwell	Nrt 431		Charles	Bfr 22		Lee	Nrt 433
Charles	Mck 559		Charles	Frn 447		Leml.	Wke 723
Cornelius	Lnc 865		Charles	Stk 586		Lucy	Hrt 734
Daniel	Ash 76		Charles, Jr.	Ans 222		Mary	Ans 198
George	Crt 81		Charles, Senr.	Ans 223		Mathias	Cbr 704
George	Rth 100		Christopher	Nrt 433		Matthew	Srr 642
James	Cmd 95		Clayton	Grv 559		Michael	Brk 734
James	Cmd 109		Cullen	Brt 38		Nathan	Glf 691
James	Glf 673		Daniel	Lnc 901		Nathan	Nwh 4A
James	Hlf 298		David	Srr 641		Nehemiah	Orn 502
James	Mnt 483		Dempsey	Brt 38		Perigrine	Smp 514
James	Nwh 8		Edmund	Cmb 353		Peter (2)	Srr 641
James	Rth 101		Edward	Rth 103		Philip	Csw 120
James, Esqr.	Mck 559		Elisabeth	Crv 301		Philip	Stk 603
James, Jr.	Hlf 298		Elisabeth	Frn 488		Phillip	Srr 740
John	Rck 456		Elisha	Brt 38		Randle	Ird 616
Margret	Lnc 888		Eliza	Orn 612		Ransom	Rwn 377
Michael	Rbs 373		Elizabeth	Nrt 431		Richard	Ird 609
Moses	Nwh 8		Ephraim	Orn 551		Richard D.,	
Nancy	Hde 366		Francis	Cht 177		Capt.	Grv 572
Thomas	Hrt 716		George	Stk 603		Robert	Ans 223
Thomas	Lnc 899		Grove	Srr 641		Robert	Mck 546

Robert	Orn 502	Cooper, Absolum	Prs 217	Phillip	Wke 723
Robt.	Nwh 6A	Adam	Bnc 164	Polly	Rth 101
Roland	Grv 555	Alexander	Rth 102	Rachel	Stk 617
Sally	Wne 861	Allen	Csw 119	Risdon	Csw 142
Samuel	Brt 36	Ann	Crt 80	Risdon	Rck 467
Samuel	Crv 299	Barnet	Rwn 407	Robert	Frn 476
Shadrick	Smp 512	Benjamin	Cmd 107	Salley	Ptt 229
Shamuel	Frn 462	Benjamin	Dpl 437	Samuel	Cmd 107
Shem	Grv 555	Benjamin	Nsh 96	Seth	Cmd 94
Stephen	Wne 859	Benn.	Psq 637	Stansill	Mrt 389
Stephen, Senr.	Wne 859	Blount	Brt 34	Sterling	Frn 495
Thomas	Frn 455	Caleb	Prq 661	Thomas	Csw 142
Thomas	Glf 691	Core	Smp 527	Thomas	Rbs 370
Thomas	Ird 660	Cornelius	Grv 528	Thomas	Rck 467
Thomas	Mnt 521	David	Brt 40	Thomas	Rwn 311
Thomas	Orn 556	David	Glf 630	Thomas	Stk 607
Thomas	Orn 612	David	Rwn 316	Thomas	Trl 684
Thomas	Rwn 320	David	Trl 688	William	Frn 489
Thomas	Smp 530	Dinah	Lnc 846	William (2)	Grv 562
Thomas	Wne 859	Edmond	Nsh 95	William	Mck 532
Thomas	Wlk 31	Edward	Mrt 392	William	Nwh 3
William	Brt 34	Edward	Nsh 95	William	Ptt 234
William	Cht 197	Elizabeth	Glf 633	William	Rch 265
William	Cmb 353	Elizabeth	Smp 524	William	Rck 492
William	Cmb 375	Elzabeth	Nsh 96	William	Rwn 311
William	Dpl 421	Fleet	Smp 529	William	Rth 105
William	Frn 455	George	Jhn 761	William	Smp 527
William	Grv 558	George	Ptt 229	Willis	Orn 547
William	Ird 660	Griffin	Mrt 392	Willis	Orn 615
William	Mnt 461	Hardy	Wne 871	Willis	Trl 688
William	Orn 495	Henry	Rwn 407	Wm.	Mrt 392
William	Smp 514	Henry	Wke 723	Wm.	Rck 485
William, Junr.	Srr 640	Henry, Junr.	Mrt 392	Wm.	Rck 492
William, Jur.	Srr 641	Henry, Senr.	Mrt 391	see Coope, Cupper	
William, preach-		Isaac	Ptt 239	Coore, Stephen	Wne 867
er	Frn 462	Isles	Hlf 298	Thomas	Wne 867
William, Senr.	Srr 640	Isles	Lnc 890	Cope, Horatio	Orn 501
William N.	Srr 641	Jacob	Mnt 513	Jacob	Rwn 407
Windle	Srr 643	Jacob	Smp 527	John	Rch 256
Winnefred	Brt 36	Jacob	Stk 555	John	Rwn 430
Wm.	Csw 127	James	Crv 271	Philip	Rwn 431
Wm. Silas	Crv 251	James	Hlf 298	Randol	Wke 723
Zephaniah	Crv 293	James	Stk 546	Richard	Orn 502
Cooke, David	Orn 502	James	Srr 640	Samuel	Rch 268
John	Lnc 846	Jesse	Ans 231	Thomas	Cht 220
Sarah	Hlf 300	Joel	Psq 637	Copehart, John	Brk 735
Cookeley, Alen.	Frn 483	John	Brk 734	Copeland, Charles	Jhn 762
Cooker, Ephraim	Mnt 475	John	Dpl 424	Charles	Prq 652
Cooksy, Eliza.	Rck 449	John	Gts 264	David	Orn 557
Cool, F. John	Srr 642	John	Grv 564	Demcey	Nrt 431
John F.	Srr 642	John	Glf 648	Eli	Hrt 716
Cooley, David	Grv 567	John	Hlf 298	Elisha	Hrt 710
David	Grv 570	John	Hrt 704	Esther	Gts 264
Edward	Frn 467	John	Lnc 887	Henry	Gts 264
Edward	Stk 546	John	Mck 532	Hollowell	Hrt 716
James	Stk 546	John	Mnt 511	Isaac	Srr 643
John	Frn 467	John	Nsh 94	Isaac	Srr 706
John	Wke 725	John	Ons 149	Issac, Jur.	Srr 640
Perrin	Stk 546	John	Ons 164	Jacob	Wne 865
Rice	Stk 547	John	Prs 216	James	Cht 196
Steven	Frn 487	John	Stk 609	James	Cht 197
Cooly, John	Stk 546	John	Stk 613	John	Cht 167
Coombs, Sarah	Jns 817	John	Wke 723	John	Cht 196
Coomer, John	Stk 580	John, Junr.	Prs 193	John	Hrt 710
Richard	Stk 580	John, Sr.	Nsh 96	John	Rbs 372
Coon, Anthony	Rwn 299	Jonathan	Srr 642	John	Srr 642
Jacob	Rwn 451	Joseph	Brk 736	Jonah	Cht 203
Widow	Rch 270	Joseph	Mck 524	Joseph	Chw 128
Coonrod, Adam	Rwn 346	Joseph	Mnt 501	Joshua	Wne 865
Henry	Rwn 346	Josiah	Ons 165	Josiah, jr.	Cht 198
Coons, Henry	Wne 852	Lourton	Mrt 391	Lott	Srr 644
Michael	Rwn 346	Mariom	Nsh 95	Marke	Cht 191
Coonse, John	Rwn 346	Mark	Orn 552	Martha	Ird 617
Coonz, Christopher	Lnc 888	Martha	Crv 271	Samuel	Srr 640
Nicholas	Lnc 888	Martin	Prs 205	Samuel	Wne 866
Coop, Henry	Stk 547	Michael	Rwn 372	Sarah	Chw 129
Coope, John	Frn 492	Nathaniel	Srr 641	Stephen	Hrt 730

Thomas	Chw 128	see Pender		Cosley, John	Brk 736		
Thomas	Hrt 716	Corell, Adam	Rwn 311	William	Brk 736		
Thomas	Hrt 730	Jacob	Rwn 340	Cosly, William	Brk 734		
Thos.	Mrt 392	James	Brk 735	Cosner, Anthony	Stk 621		
William	Cht 198	Peter	Rwn 300	John	Stk 621		
William	Hrt 704	Philip	Rwn 340	Cosnit, Hew Bird	Cht 196		
William	Nrt 429	William	Cbr 699	Costen, Christian	Gts 264		
William	Rbs 375	Corey, John, Junr.	Mrt 392	Elizabeth	Gts 264		
Copelands, Abel	Cht 175	John, Senr.	Mrt 392	Isaac	Gts 264		
Copeley, James	Orn 613	Joseph	Ptt 251	James	Gts 264		
John	Orn 613	Martin	Mrt 392	Thomas	Gts 264		
Copelin, ...	Hlf 358	Nancey	Mrt 392	Costephens, John	Srr 642		
James	Brk 733	Corfers, Godfray	Rwn 300	Coster, Robert	Ons 146		
James	Brk 739	Cork, Joseph	Wrr 795	Costin, Anne	Ons 160		
John	Glf 638	Lever	Glf 652	Joseph	Ons 165		
Copeny, Albert	Brk 734	Will.	Prs 216	Marthey	Ons 161		
Copes, Stephen	Crt 67	Corkings, Mary	Nwh 1A	Rachel	Dpl 441		
Copher, Thomas	Stk 574	William	Brn 16A	Thomas	Ons 160		
Copland, David	Lnc 899	Corlew, Lemuel	Hlf 300	William	Ons 171		
Duglass	Orn 557	Sarah	Hlf 300	Costly, Widow	Ans 236		
Copley, Thomas	Orn 613	Cormack, John	Mnt 485	Costner, Adam	Lnc 841		
Coplin, Henry	Prq 644	Lewis	Mnt 485	David	Lnc 811		
Mary	Mre 64	Corman, Elisabeth	Jns 823	David	Lnc 841		
Coppage, Charles	Frn 490	Corn, B. Robert	Wke 723	Jacob	Lnc 841		
Charles	Wrr 797	Findle	Stk 590	Michl.	Lnc 841		
Jessey	Frn 490	John	Wlk 31	Thomas	Lnc 811		
William	Frn 490	Julius	Wke 723	Coston, Isaac	Nwh 11		
William	Prq 654	Peter	Wlk 31	Jacob	Nwh 12		
Wilmouth	Edg 190	Robert	Wke 723	John	Nwh 12		
Coppersmith, An-thony	Psq 638	Robert B.	Wke 723	Stephen	Nwh 6		
Micaja	Psq 633	Cornall, Moses	Grv 581	Cosway, Greenberry	Edg 191		
Thos.	Psq 633	Cornbarm see Common		Phillip, Junr.	Edg 189		
Coppis, Adam	Rwn 372	Cornealas, George	Stk 547	Phillip, Senr.	Edg 190		
Peter	Rwn 372	Cornegay, Daniel	Wne 858	Cota...h, Malachi	Bfr 5		
Copple, Jacob, Jr.	Rwn 352	Joseph	Smp 522	Cothan, Nathan	Mnt 485		
Jacob, Senr.	Rwn 352	Cornelies, Jere-miah	Stk 548	Cothern, William	Grv 546		
John	Rwn 352	Cornelious, John	Mnt 476	Cotiston, Gilbert	Prq 658		
Philip	Rwn 352	Cornelius, John	Ash 75	Cotner, Daniel	Glf 647		
Copps see Clapps		John	Stk 548	George, Senr.	Glf 647		
Corah, Benjamin	Brt 38	West	Stk 548	Mathias	Glf 646		
Coram, Richd.	Rck 464	William	Lnc 859	Peter	Orn 551		
Corbet, Abel	Cmb 381	Cornet, Joel	Bld 10	Cotral, Benjm.	Prs 196		
Samuel	Wne 866	Cornish, Benjamin	Rbs 371	Cotreel, Thomas	Grv 533		
Corbett, ...anl.	Nwh 2A	Cornitage, Caty	Rwn 430	Cots, Joseph	Rth 104		
Elias	Wne 867	John	Rwn 430	Cottel, Charles	Brk 735		
Elisha	Brt 36	Cornodel, George	Glf 661	Cotten, Elijah	Wne 850		
James	Brt 40	Cornwal, John	Prq 659	Henry	Nrt 431		
James	Brn 21	Cornwall, Benjamin	Nrt 431	James	Srr 643		
John	Brt 38	Cornwell, Edward	Rth 102	John	Nrt 433		
John	Nwh 4A	Jesse	Bnc 163	Rhoderick	Cht 153		
John	Ptt 272	Corouze, John	Lnc 812	Roderick	Nrt 433		
Medreth	Ptt 272	Corpage, Charles	Mnt 504	Solomon	Wrr 797		
Corbin, Benjamin	Hlf 300	Isaac	Mnt 504	Timothy	Psq 625		
Nancy	Hlf 300	Rodeham	Mnt 501	William	Cht 207		
Corbit, John	Edg 190	Corpe..., Thomas	Bfr 5	Cottle, Abner	Dpl 413		
John	Ons 168	Corprew, John	Wsh 700	Josiah	Cmb 391		
Josiah	Edg 190	Joshua	Wsh 700	Josiah	Dpl 411		
Merodith	Edg 190	Malachi	Wsh 700	Thomas	Dpl 411		
Richard	Edg 190	Samuel	Wsh 700	William	Cht 207		
Corbitt, Joshua	Edg 190	Correll, John	Ird 638	William	Crv 299		
Cord, William	Orn 501	Corry, Benn.	Psq 633	Cotton, Ann	Hrt 723		
Cordell, Benjamin	Rwn 423	Davison	Psq 633	Barnaba	Wne 844		
David	Rwn 423	Cortis, Moses	Mnt 477	Charles	Orn 558		
Corden see Corder		Russil	Mnt 477	Ephraim	Wne 844		
Corder, John	Csw 129	Coruthers, John	Cbr 682	Frederick	Edg 189		
Joseph	Srr 642	Robert	Brk 737	George	Glf 643		
Thomas	Bfr 5	William	Brk 731	Goodwin	Hrt 716		
Cording, Hosea	Hde 366	Corvin, Stephen	Ird 670	James	Hrt 723		
Joseph	Hde 366	Corzine, Elijah	Lnc 874	Jesse	Brt 40		
Ufamy	Hde 366	Samuel	Cbr 686	Jesse	Cmb 372		
William, Jur.	Hde 366	Corzort, William	Rwn 286	John	Edg 192		
William, Ser.	Hde 366	Cosand, Benjn.	Prq 651	John	Hrt 734		
Cordwell, William	Stk 546	Gabriel	Prq 646	Lemuel	Hlf 300		
Core, Daniel	Smp 532	Gabriel	Prq 651	Noah	Hrt 723		
Rachel	Wne 872	John	Prq 651	Randal	Edg 189		
Robert	Glf 652	Cosh (2)	Rnd 307	Randolph	Edg 171		
				Right	Wke 724		

Samuel	Edg 190	John	Nwh 9	Elisha	Rnd 306		
Sarah	Chw 113	John	Rwn 320	Elizabeth	Hde 366		
Seth	Cht 209	Joseph	Brk 731	Elkanah	Bfr 5		
Whitmell	Hlf 300	Magnes	Nwh 9A	Ephraim	Mck 780		
Willie	Edg 192	Mary	Rwn 324	Ezekiah	Crv 313		
Wright	Edg 192	Robert	Rwn 316	George	Cmb 378		
see Collon, Powell		Robert	Rwn 329	George	Grv 519		
Cottrel, Thomas	Wlk 31	Tho.	Nwh 3	George	Lnc 826		
Cottrell, William	Rck 489	Thomas	Rwn 320	George	Mre 41		
Cottril, John	Wlk 34	Widow	Rwn 315	Gilbert	Rbs 371		
Cotvill, Tamar	Jns 799	Widow	Rwn 324	Hanah	Ons 180		
Couch, Jacob	Wlk 34	William	Ird 609	Henery	Mre 67		
John	Ash 75	William	Rwn 315	Henry	Rwn 451		
Joseph	Ash 76	William	Rwn 320	Hermon	Brk 735		
Mesheck	Glf 679	William	Rwn 324	Levi	Rbs 371		
Thomas	Orn 615	Cowand, Ann	Brt 40	Lewis	Csw 126		
William	Orn 614	George	Brt 36	Lewis	Crr 157		
Couden, James	Brk 734	James	Brt 36	Lucy	Nrt 431		
Coudre, Nathaniel	Crv 241	John	Brt 38	Marion	Chw 116		
Council, Charles	Edg 191	Jonathan	Brt 36	Marmaduke	Jns 799		
Charles	Rbs 374	Mary	Brt 38	Martha	Wrr 795		
David	Bld 7	William (2)	Brt 36	Mary	Crr 155		
Hardy	Rbs 374	William	Brt 38	Mathew	Wlk 35		
Hodge	Ash 76	Coward, Cullen	Crv 329	Matthew	Brk 737		
John	Edg 189	Demsey	Mrt 391	Micajah, Senr.	Wne 855		
John	Rbs 374	Edward	Grn 602	Mildred	Stk 587		
Jose	Rbs 374	Elisha	Grn 603	Morris	Lnc 811		
Jourdon	Ash 76	Frederick	Grn 603	Moses	Cbr 713		
Mary	Bld 35	James	Rth 101	Moses	Mre 67		
Matthew	Rbs 374	John	Grn 603	Moses	Orn 553		
Robt.	Cht 204	John	Jns 785	Mourning	Crv 257		
Willie	Edg 191	Reuben	Wsh 702	Mourning	Jns 789		
Councilman, Mary	Orn 552	Sarey	Grn 603	Iavan	Crr 153		
Counsel, David	Hlf 300	Solomon	Rth 101	Isaac	Brk 735		
Counsil, Mary	Brn 21	Cowden, John	Ird 616	Isaac	Cht 217		
Countz, Adam	Bnc 166	Cowdry, Peggie	Mrt 388	Isham	Rbs 371		
Coupee, Francis	Rwn 286	Cowe, William	Bfr 5	Jacob	Rnd 307		
Court, John	Wsh 702	Cowell, Bernard	Edg 190	James	Lnr 31		
Courtice, David	Bfr 6	Jeams	Crr 144	James	Rck 480		
Richard	Bfr 6	Cowen, Elias	Glf 629	James	Rwn 384		
Courtney, James	Lnc 887	Solomon	Edg 190	James, (Senr.	Mnt 516		
Joseph	Orn 492	Cowing, David	Hrt 730	Javner	Mnt 517		
William	Orn 503	Cowper, Joel	Nrt 431	Jehue	Glf 691		
Cousins, Richard	Hde 366	William	Hrt 734	Jerry	Rnd 307		
Coventon, John	Rth 105	Cox, Aaron	Jns 787	Jesse	Cmd 104		
Josiah	Rth 102	Aaron	Lnc 812	Jesse	Hde 365		
Thomas	Rth 105	Aaron, Senior	Ptt 247	John (2)	Ash 75		
William	Rth 104	Abel	Ash 76	John	Cbr 712		
Covernton, Rosannah	Hde 365	Abel	Brk 738	John	Cht 219		
Covington, Asa	Rch 249	Abel	Rnd 307	John	Crr 163		
Benjamin	Rch 255	Abner	Jns 791	John	Jns 817		
Eleven	Dpl 415	Amos	Bnc 164	John	Lnr 4		
Elijah M.	Rch 255	Andrew	Jns 789	John	Lnr 31		
Fannen	Jhn 776	Ann	Crv 317	John	Lnc 812		
Henry	Rch 249	Benjamin	Brt 40	John	Prq 658		
Henry	Rch 255	Benjamin	Jns 817	John	Rnd 306		
John	Rch 255	Benjamin	Ptt 248	John (2)	Rnd 307		
John	Rck 476	Benjn.	Crr 141	John (2)	Rnd 308		
Matthew	Rch 249	Braxton	Wlk 32	John	Rbs 371		
Nancy	Rck 490	Caleb	Crr 163	John	Stk 586		
Peter	Rch 249	Caleb	Rnd 306	John	Srr 642		
Philip	Ons 162	Canaan	Bfr 4	John	Wne 871		
Sarah	Ans 200	Celah	Bfr 5	John C.	Rck 482		
Sarah	Rch 256	Charles	Jns 787	John H.	Jns 781		
Simon	Ans 213	Charles	Lnc 866	Jonathan	Crr 154		
William	Rch 249	Charles	Rnd 308	Joseph	Edg 191		
Cowan, Alexander	Rwn 320	Charmack	Grv 519	Joseph	Rnd 307		
Benjamin	Rwn 315	Daniel	Ptt 247	Joseph	Rck 469		
David	Mck 525	Daniel	Rnd 305	Joshua	Ash 74		
David	Mck 606	David	Brk 738	Joshua	Rnd 307		
David	Rwn 320	David	Rwn 377	Joshua	Stk 548		
David	Rwn 324	Duke	Crr 163	Josiah	Ons 181		
Henry	Rwn 316	Edmond	Cht 210	Josiah	Wne 856		
Isaac	Rwn 324	Edward	Mre 57	Nathan	Lnr 4		
James	Lnc 874	Eli	Rnd 308	Nathan	Rnd 308		
James	Rwn 324	Elisha	Brn 20	Nathaniel	Rnd 306		
John	Bld 30	Elisha	Lnc 833	Nicholas	Rnd 306		

Oxborn	Brk 735	Joseph, Junr.	Trl 688	Crane, Enoch	Trl 676
Osburn	Brk 732	Joseph, Senr.	Trl 688	Joseph	Trl 676
Paul	Lnc 811	Stevens	Trl 670	Cranford, Elias	Rnd 304
Philip	Csw 126	William	Trl 670	Kid	Rnd 353
Port	Cmb 379	Craddock, John	Orn 553	Leonard	Mnt 483
Presly	Cht 224	Thomas	Wne 854	Mary	Rnd 304
Reubin	Csw 109	Crader, Abraham	Lnc 901	Sally	Rnd 353
Richard	Rnd 308	Craderick, John	Grv 524	Samuel	Rnd 306
Richard	Stk 551	Cradick, Thomas	Smp 521	William	Mnt 478
Richard	Wne 856	Crafford, Eave	Rnd 306	William	Rnd 304
Richard, Junr.	Wne 868	Henry	Nrt 433	William	Rnd 306
Robert	Lnc 827	James	Gts 264	Crankfield, Jona-	
Samuel	Brn 17A	John	Ptt 281	than	Rwn 451
Samuel	Cht 181	Samuel	Orn 502	Thomas	Rwn 451
Samuel	Prs 200	Solomon	Jhn 772	William	Rwn 451
Sarah	Lnr 31	William	Gts 264	Crankford, John	Dpl 441
Shadrach	Hde 365	Craft, Archilus	Wlk 33	Cranston, Abram	Mck 603
Simon	Rbs 371	Easter	Ons 154	Cratch, George	Brt 38
Simon, Jur.	Rbs 371	Esther	Jns 813	Crater, Jacob	Rwn 415
Smisson	Wne 856	Frederick	Ans 238	Craven, Daniel	Rnd 308
Soloman	Crv 253	Herod	Brt 38	Henry	Rnd 306
Solomon, Jur.	Crr 163	John	Orn 555	John	Ird 647
Solomon, Ser.	Crr 163	John	Ptt 283	John	Rnd 306
Thomas	Bfr 5	John C.	Nwh 5	John	Wke 775
Thomas	Chw 114	Moses	Brt 38	Joseph	Rnd 308
Thomas	Crv 317	Crage, Abigal	Orn 554	Joshua	Rnd 306
Thomas	Rnd 307	Elinor	Orn 614	Peter	Rnd 306
Thomas (2)	Rnd 308	John	Orn 615	Peter	Rnd 307
Thomas, Jr.	Wne 855	Johnson	Orn 614	Richard	Rnd 308
Thomas, Senr.	Wnd 855	Mary	Orn 614	Robert	Ird 648
Thos.	Crr 163	William	Orn 614	Samuel	Ird 648
Thos., Ser.	Crr 156	William, jr.	Orn 614	Samuel	Rnd 307
Vincent	Lnc 846	Cragg, Benjn.	Nwh 7A	Thomas	Rnd 306
William	Bnc 165	Elias	Nwh 7	William	Ird 648
William	Cbr 713	Lewis	Nwh 7A	Craver, Jacob	Rwn 372
William	Cht 184	Roger	Rth 103	John	Rwn 371
William	Crv 317	Tho.	Nwh 7A	Michael	Rwn 372
William	Grv 519	William	Rth 104	Philip	Rwn 371
William	Hlf 298	Craig, Adam	Cmb 353	Cravey, Hugh	Jhn 750
William	Lnr 31	David	Orn 546	Crawford, ...	Bfr 5
William	Lnc 864	Edward	Bnc 164	Adam	Rck 489
William	Mre 41	James	Bnc 164	Anne	Cmb 351
William	Nrt 431	James	Orn 546	Arther	Wne 866
William	Ons 176	James, Junr.	Orn 614	Charles	Wne 866
William	Rnd 307	James, Senr.	Orn 614	Charles, Jur.	Bfr 6
William	Rnd 308	John	Ans 222	David	Brk 735
William	Wne 866	John	Bnc 165	David	Cbr 680
Zacha.	Cht 217	Joseph	Csw 134	Duncan	Rbs 373
see Brian		Craige, Allexander	Mck 584	George	Brk 732
Coxeter, James	Nwh 3	Elijah	Brk 734	James	Ird 648
Coxey, John	Rth 103	Henry	Brk 732	James	Mck 557
William	Rth 103	Hugh	Rwn 364	James, H.R.	Orn 502
Coyl, Nicholas	Rwn 385	Jno.	Lnc 837	John	Ird 629
Cozart, Anthony	Orn 555	John	Brk 739	John	Ird 647
Benjm.	Prs 188	John	Mck 593	John	Rth 102
Jacob	Grv 559	Mary	Rwn 286	John	Wne 866
James	Grv 559	Moses	Mck 582	Lazarus	Wne 866
Jas.	Prs 191	Nancy	Rwn 286	Michael, Jr.	Ans 228
Jas., Senr.	Prs 218	Robert	Brk 279	Michael, Senr.	Ans 229
Williamson	Grv 576	Ruth	Brk 739	Peter	Rbs 373
Crab, Ausey	Frn 484	Samuel	Brk 732	Robert	Wne 868
Jarrit	Ird 623	Thomas	Brk 733	Samuel	Rth 100
John	Hrt 720	Widow	Mck 553	William	Cmd 109
John	Ird 627	Widow	Mck 582	William	Ptt 235
Susanna	Hlf 298	William	Brk 734	William	Rch 251
Crabb, Benjamin	Wne 864	William	Mck 598	Crawley, Benjamin	Wrr 797
Crabtree, Abraham	Orn 614	see Robert		David	Hlf 296
Benjamin	Wlk 32	Craigg, James	Hde 381	James	Frn 467
Edward	Orn 616	John	Rwn 364	John	Frn 466
James	Orn 614	Crain, Demsy	Rth 102	John	Jhn 767
James	Rnd 305	Mafield	Rth 104	Thomas	Srr 640
James	Rnd 306	Craine, Stephen	Wrr 797	Crawly, Benjamin	Mck 578
James, Jr.	Orn 614	Crainer, Moses	Glf 673	John	Mck 577
Thomas	Orn 546	Cramis, Samuel, Jr.	Stk 612	Simon, Junr.	Mck 577
Thomas	Orn 556	Crandal, Christo-		Simon, Senr.	Mck 577
William (2)	Orn 614	pher	Ptt 237	Widow	Mck 592
Craddick, Azer	Trl 688	James	Bfr 4	Cray, Fanny	Ons 153

John	Ons 154	Thomas	Stk 620	Crocker, Arthur	Rth 100
Craysell, Andrew	Lnc 812	William	Smp 508	Eley	Frn 490
Crayton, Elizabeth	Bnc 164	Crezer, Conrad	Stk 625	Ira	Chw 116
Thomas	Cht 215	Criad, Cors.	Ons 152	Jacob	Frn 482
William	Cht 211	Crib, Jonathn. (2)	Brn 20A	John	Psq 634
Craze, Peggy	Srr 640	Crichlow, Eliza-		Mary	Frn 482
Creach, Benjamin	Lnr 4	beth	Hrt 730	Robert	Wrr 796
Ezekiel	Lnr 4	James	Hrt 720	Samuel	Nrt 431
Ezekiel, Senr.	Lnr 4	Crickman, Caleb	Hlf 298	Crockit, Archibald	Mck 601
John	Lnr 5	see Creekman		Robert	Mck 534
Creaf, Martha	Crt 71	Crickmon, Ballen-		Crofford, William	Wne 852
Creal, William	Rck 464	tine	Nsh 96	Crofton, Ambrose	Ptt 254
Creaton, James	Mck 528	David	Nsh 94	Matthew	Ptt 254
Creatton, James	Cbr 460	Robert	Nsh 94	Croker, Nathan	Brn 16
Creaves, Jno.	Lnc 833	Timothy	Nsh 95	Crolts, Valentine	Rth 103
Credle, Francis,		Criddleborough, Til-		Cromartie, Alexr.	Bld 48
Jur.	Hde 364	man	Glf 687	James	Bld 48
Francis, Senr.	Hde 364	Crider, Conrod	Lnc 874	Wm.	Bld 48
James	Hde 364	Fredrick	Brk 733	Cromer, Gotlip	Stk 546
John	Hde 364	Jacob	Brk 734	Cromwell, Ann	Brt 38
William	Hde 365	Jacob	Lnc 901	Elisha	Edg 189
Cree...er, James	Bfr 5	Jacob	Prs 212	John	Cbr 706
Creech, Betsey	Psq 639	John	Brk 733	Selah	Edg 189
Jesse	Jhn 750	Michael	Ash 75	Cron...ney, John	Bfr 5
Joshua	Jhn 750	Valentine	Brk 733	Crone, Mary	Orn 615
Creecy, Eliazor	Prq 645	Crigman, Elizabeth	Stk 577	Croner, Jacob	Cbr 698
Frederick	Chw 131	Crim, Jacob	Stk 567	William	Cbr 698
Levy	Prq 656	Criscow, George	Mnt 509	Crook, Allin	Rwn 385
Nathan	Chw 127	Crisenberry, Nicholas,		Bignal	Stk 608
Samuel	Chw 120	Senr.	Mck 570	Diannah	Rth 102
Thomas	Prq 642	Crisenbury, James	Mck 570	Dudley	Srr 711
William	Prq 642	Crish, John	Csw 116	George	Lnc 887
Creed, Barnett	Srr 643	Crisman, Daniel	Glf 662	Jeremiah	Stk 613
Bartlet	Srr 642	Daniel	Rwn 311	John	Bnc 163
Margrett	Srr 643	Elizabeth	Stk 626	John	Rwn 385
Mary	Crr 162	Henry	Glf 662	John	Rth 102
Matthew	Srr 643	Jacob	Rwn 311	Philip	Lnc 887
Ozwell	Srr 643	John	Glf 637	William	Stk 611
Solomon	Crr 167	Crismon, Daniel	Stk 598	Crooke, Stevens	Wsh 714
Creeger, John H.	Rwn 384	Jacob	Rth 104	Crookham, John	Psq 630
Creekman, Edward	Bfr 4	Crison, Margrit	Rwn 306	Croom, Charles	Wne 845
Elizebeth	Crr 163	Samuel	Rwn 305	Daniel	Wne 845
John	Crv 291	Crisp, Benjamin	Edg 189	Hardy	Lnr 4
Saml.	Crr 154	Charles	Brk 738	Jesse	Nwh 6A
Southy	Bfr 6	Frances	Edg 191	Jesse	Wne 845
see Crickmon		Jesse	Edg 190	Lott	Lnr 31
Creel, Nathan	Lnr 31	Joel	Brk 738	Lukey	Lnr 31
Solomon	Rbs 370	John	Brk 738	Major	Lnr 4
Creerkman, Betsy	Csw 138	Samuel	Edg 191	Mary	Lnr 4
Creese, Gideon	Grv 551	William	Brk 734	Nancy	Lnr 4
Cregar, Jacob	Stk 554	Crispin, Joseph	Crv 249	Richard	Wne 846
Cremain, Ann	Ptt 226	Crist, Rudolph	Stk 598	Thomas	Cht 181
Crenshaw, Freeman	Wke 725	Rudolph	Stk 625	William	Lnr 2
James	Wke 724	Cristian, Thomas	Ans 221	William, Jur.	Lnr 4
Robert	Wke 725	Cristy, Daniel	Glf 635	Croose, Henry	Rwn 301
Creps, John	Mnt 506	John	Glf 634	Peter	Rwn 301
Cresimore, John	Lnc 867	Nathan	Brn 16	Crops, William	Stk 597
Cresmore, Henry	Lnc 812	Criswell, Andrew	Rwn 407	Wm.	Stk 627
Creson, Joshua	Srr 642	James	Ird 654	Cropwhite, William	Stk 547
Cress, Daniel	Rwn 276	John	Orn 503	Crosbey, James	Bnc 166
Daniel	Rwn 286	Joseph	Orn 503	Crosby, George	Glf 638
Henry	Cbr 716	William	Ird 654	George	Rwn 456
Tobius	Cbr 715	William	Rwn 407	William	Rwn 336
Cretz, John	Lnc 865	Critchfield, Wil-		Croslin, John	Frn 451
Cretze, John	Lnc 859	liam	Orn 553	Nath.	Frn 451
Peter	Lnc 859	see Crutchfield		Cross, Abel	Gts 264
Crew, Andrew	Nrt 433	Criter, Micah	Crv 331	Abram	Lnc 812
James	Nrt 433	Crittenden, Henry	Nrt 433	Benjamin	Rwn 436
Robert	Nrt 431	Robert	Nrt 433	Charles	Stk 558
Crews, Benj.	Prs 218	Crittendon, Wil-		Cyprian	Gts 264
Benjamin	Wke 725	liam	Mnt 500	David	Gts 264
Caleb	Grv 546	Critz, Daniel	Lnc 846	David	Rwn 397
David	Stk 618	Critzfeezer, Henry	Rwn 360	David, Junr.	Rwn 397
David, Jur.	Stk 620	see Feezer		David, Senr.	Rwn 397
Hardy	Prs 192	Crizer, Conrod	Stk 599	Elijah	Bnc 164
James	Stk 619	Crochlaw, James	Brk 733	Elisabeth	Mrt 389
John	Nwh 9	see Crouchlow		Elisha	Gts 264

Name	Ref	Name	Ref	Name	Ref
Hardy	Gts 264	Matthew	Orn 556	Cruther, John	Rnd 308
Ja...	Bfr 5	Robert	Rth 104	Cruthers, George	Prq 648
Jacob, Junr.	Rwn 397	Stephen	Bnc 165	George	Prq 660
Jacob, Senr.	Rwn 397	Thomas	Nrt 433	James	Prq 646
James	Edg 191	Thomas	Wke 724	William	Crt 68
John	Brt 38	William	Mnt 466	William	Prq 648
John	Bnc 164	William	Rth 104	Cry, William	Brk 735
John	Brk 732	Crowel, Edward	Nsh 95	Crye, David	Mck 590
John	Brk 735	James	Nsh 95	John	Mck 590
John	Edg 189	John	Nsh 96	John	Mck 593
John	Gts 264	Peter	Mck 581	Samuel	Mck 594
Jonathan	Cmb 370	Crowell, Benjamin	Hlf 300	Cryer, Sarah	Nrt 431
Joseph	Rth 104	Edward	Hlf 300	Cubertson, Wm.	Csw 134
Joseph, j.	Rth 104	George, (Senr.	Mnt 516	Cuddy, James	Stk 547
Judah	Mrt 389	John	Mnt 517	James	Stk 593
Mosses	Bnc 164	Martha	Hlf 300	Cude, Timothy	Rnd 306
Mosses	Bnc 166	Peter	Rwn 293	Cudlepah, Thomas	Rwn 364
Nathan	Rwn 451	Peter (2)	Rwn 305	Cudworth, John	Crr 152
Parish	Cht 207	Peter	Rwn 403	Cuff, John	Gts 264
Peter	Rwn 397	Samuel	Hlf 300	Smith	Gts 264
Reddick	Gts 264	William	Mnt 521	Culberson, Andrew	Cht 215
Richard	Cmb 372	William	Rwn 305	David	Ans 222
Solomon	Bnc 165	Crowson, Elijah	Rch 242	James	Cht 224
Solomon	Lnc 841	Jacob	Bld 16	John	Rwn 330
Stephen	Edg 191	John	Rch 263	Samuel	Cht 215
Tho...	Bfr 5	William	Rch 262	Samuel	Rwn 330
William	Bnc 163	Crudup, John	Wke 726	William	Brk 731
William	Wke 725	Josiah	Wke 726	Culbreath, Angus	Rbs 373
Crosser, Leonard	Rwn 276	Crull, Peter	Rwn 293	Archibald	Rbs 374
Leonard	Rwn 285	Crum, David	Rwn 352	Daniel	Rbs 374
Crosset, Andrew	Brk 738	John	Stk 607	Culbreth, William	Rch 266
Crossland, Edward	Hlf 296	Crump, Adam	Cmb 353	Cullens, Jacob	Chw 129
Joshua	Hlf 298	Charles	Nrt 431	Cullifer, Henry	Trl 670
Crosslin, Salley	Wrr 798	James	Mnt 477	Isaac	Trl 670
Crossnore, George	Bnc 164	John	Stk 593	James	Trl 688
John	Bnc 164	John, Junr.	Mnt 485	Jerenah	Brt 36
Thomas	Bnc 165	John, Senr.	Mnt 477	John	Trl 688
Crosswell, Rich-		Josias	Nrt 431	Nathaniel (3)	Brt 34
mond	Ans 218	Polly	Cht 210	Thomas	Brt 36
Croswell, Nimrod	Mnt 485	Robert	Stk 594	Culligan, William	Wlk 34
Crouch, James	Ans 228	Silas	Stk 593	Cullin, Seth	Frn 457
John	Rch 249	William	Rck 490	Cullings, Thomas	Gts 264
John	Rck 445	Crumpler, Benjamin	Jhn 755	Cullum, Jeremiah	Hlf 298
John	Wlk 35	Cager	Smp 528	Jesse	Hlf 298
Crouchlow, James	Brk 738	Jacob	Smp 529	Matthew	Hlf 298
see Crochlaw		John	Smp 518	Thomas	Hlf 298
Croup, Koonrod	Ash 75	Mathew (2)	Smp 525	William, Jr.	Hlf 298
Crouse, Adam	Ash 74	West	Jhn 755	William, Sr.	Hlf 298
Andrew	Wlk 33	West	Jhn 757	Cullumber, Barbara	Wlk 32
George	Wlk 33	William	Nrt 431	Henry	Wlk 32
Gotlib	Stk 577	Crumpton, Ezekiel	Wlk 30	Cully, Francis	Crv 299
Gotlieb	Stk 626	Thomas	Dpl 418	Joseph	Crt 87
Henry	Ash 75	William	Bnc 164	Philip	Crt 87
Jacob	Ash 75	Crumwell, James	Cbr 677	Richard	Crt 87
Jacob	Rwn 430	John, Senr.	Cbr 705	Thomas	Crt 87
John	Rwn 377	Crunkleton, James	Lnc 859	Culp, George	Cbr 713
John	Stk 547	John	Lnc 859	Henry	Rwn 305
John, Junr.	Rwn 431	Cruon, Andrew	Brk 738	John	Cbr 712
John, Senr.	Rwn 430	Adam	Cbr 717	Culpepeper, Eliza-	
Wendle	Ash 75	Andrew	Cbr 717	beth	Nsh 96
William	Brk 736	Hyram	Glf 679	Culpeper, John	Cbr 686
William	Rwn 430	Jacob	Rwn 335	Joshua	Crr 157
Crow, Abel	Cht 205	James	Glf 683	Culpepper, Henery	Crr 163
Abner	Cht 173	Rice	Stk 574	Jerimiah	Nsh 94
Abraham	Rth 103	Crutch, John	Crt 77	John	Nsh 94
Ann	Rnd 307	Richard	Crt 68	Matthew	Nsh 94
James	Rnd 305	Crutcher, John	Grv 520	Patience	Nsh 96
John	Cht 171	Crutchfield, Eure-		Peter	Crr 163
Reuben	Rnd 304	bius	Crv 329	Culper, Nicholas	Cmd 107
Sarah	Wne 853	James	Orn 554	Thomas	Cmd 107
Stephen	Cht 173	John	Orn 616	Culppeper, Christo-	
Thomas	Wne 853	John	Wrr 798	pher	Nsh 96
Crowden, Ewel	Grv 527	Martin	Cht 153	Culppepper, John	Ans 218
Crowder, Abraham	Rth 104	Milly	Cht 191	Culpppper, Ausborn	Nsh 94
Absalom	Mnt 461	Sarah	Wrr 798	Culver, Ann	Chw 117
George	Wke 723	Thos.	Cht 193	Joseph	Ird 622
Hezekiah	Nrt 433	see Critchfield		Joseph	Ird 623

57

Culverhouse, John	Rwn 276	Cupples, Anne	Mnt 493	Mary	Csw 127
John	Rwn 286	Curd	Stk 607	Mary	Csw 133
Thomas	Grv 567	Cureton, Jeromiah	Mck 588	Mary	Rbs 370
Cumbo, Aaron	Rbs 372	Curkman, Robert	Rck 473	Murdock	Mre 51
Cannon	Rbs 372	Curl, Abraham	Hrt 723	Randal	Rbs 373
Elisha	Rbs 371	Benjamin	Lnr 2	Robert	Cbr 679
Gibby	Rbs 372	Elizabeth	Nsh 94	Robt.	Lnc 825
John	Rbs 372	James	Gts 264	Thompson	Frn 480
Matthew	Hrt 716	Lewis	Nsh 94	William	Wlk 32
Stephen	Rbs 371	Milly	Gts 264	Curstiphens, Thos.	Wlk 31
Cumboe, Jacob	Cht 180	William	Cht 192	Curter, Abraham	Rck 491
Cumming, John	Rck 456	Willis	Edg 189	Curtes, Henary	Prs 193
Robert	Rck 456	Curlee, John	Ans 217	Curtice, Caleb	Rnd 307
Cummings, Benjamin	Crv 297	John	Ans 219	Lovel	Rnd 305
Henry	Nwh 2A	Obadiah	Ans 221	Nancy	Rnd 305
James	Hde 365	William	Ans 219	Samuel	Rnd 309
John	Crv 297	Curlen, Josiah	Crr 143	Curtin, Thomas	Orn 552
Levi	Crv 301	Curlile, Clark	Mrt 391	Curtine, John	Orn 615
William	Orn 492	Curlis see Curtis		Curtis, Bennet	Mnt 482
Cummins, Casper	Ird 647	Curls, Samuel	Lnr 5	Boling	Orn 555
Jane	Glf 682	Curly see Cerley		Christopher	Wke 723
John	Glf 652	Curmeans, Moses	Glf 641	David	Ash 76
John	Ird 629	Curnal, Archebal	Prs 207	Edward	Brk 736
John	Mck 529	Hubbard	Prs 206	Elijah, Junr.	Ans 225
John	Prs 218	Pattriark	Prs 207	Elijah, Senr.	Ans 224
John	Rck 468	Richd., Capt.	Prs 206	George	Ons 164
Joseph	Glf 683	Currathers, Clay-		Hezekiah	Grv 581
Lucy	Rwn 441	ton	Crv 273	James	Mck 605
Robert	Glf 644	Samuel	Orn 554	John	Lnc 888
Samuel	Glf 653	Currell, Wm.	Mrt 391	John	Orn 554
Stephen	Srr 643	Curren, William	Wke 725	John	Wke 723
Thomas	Dpl 422	Current, John	Ird 620	Jonathan	Brk 732
William	Rck 468	Currett, Jms.	Lnc 840	Joseph	Brk 732
Cumpton, William		Currie, Anguest	Rch 245	Joshua	Ash 76
(2)	Orn 502	Duncan	Rch 257	Joshua	Brk 732
Cunen see Curren		Lohlin	Rch 244	Joshua	Rck 462
Cuningham, Jean	Rck 454	Curruthers, Alexan-		Joshua	Wlk 34
Jms.	Lnc 832	der	Crv 275	Laban	Glf 661
Jno.	Rck 454	John, Junr.	Crv 275	Nathaniel	Ans 225
Jno.	Rck 455	John, Senr.	Crv 275	Reubin	Rck 437
John	Glf 663	Curry, Abram	Glf 636	Saml.	Prs 208
Jos.	Rck 454	Angus	Rbs 373	Saml., Junr.	Ans 225
Matthew	Glf 662	Angus	Rbs 375	Samuel	Ash 76
Nathanl.	Mck 546	Angush	Mre 51	Samuel	Wlk 34
Widow	Rwn 339	Archd.	Mre 61	Samuel, Senr.	Ans 225
William	Csw 106	Archd.	Mre 66	Thomas	Ans 224
Cunmeaus, Scade	Glf 637	Danl.	Brn 14	Thomas	Brk 733
Cunnigan, John	Rch 252	David	Brt 36	Thomas	Brk 733
Cunnigham, John	Stk 628	Dugald	Rbs 374	Thomas	Crv 235
Cunningham, Abra-		Duncan	Rbs 374	William	Brk 738
ham	Srr 642	Duncan J.	Rch 259	Curzine, Levi	Cbr 689
Alexr.	Rth 101	Ebenezer	Orn 558	Margret	Cbr 689
Ashley	Orn 553	Edward	Rbs 373	Nicholas	Cbr 689
Chester	Grn 608	Edward	Smp 520	Cushing, Elizabeth	Wsh 714
George	Bnc 165	Ezekiel	Rck 468	Isaac	Mrt 391
George	Frn 474	Hugh	Csw 122	Cusic, William	Glf 632
George	Rwn 403	Hugh	Csw 131	Custer see Curter	
Hugh	Rwn 390	Jacob	Brt 36	Custis, Mary	Crv 253
Humphrey	Bnc 164	James	Bld 27	Cuswell, John	Brk 732
James, (B)	Chw 115	James	Csw 127	Robert	Brk 733
James, (S.)	Chw 116	James	Mck 564	Cuthbertson, John	Mck 577
Jesse	Grn 605	James (2)	Oln 613	Cuthizer, Henry	Cbr 715
Jesse	Wrr 795	James, Junr.	Brt 38	Cutl..., John,	
John	Bnc 164	James, Senr.	Brt 38	Senr.	Bfr 5
John	Rch 250	John	Bld 19	Robert	Bfr 5
John	Stk 555	John	Csw 120	Cutlar, Archd.	Nwh 1
John	Srr 709	John	Orn 551	Roger	Nwh 11A
John	Wlk 32	John	Rbs 373	Will.	Nwh 11A
Joseph	Rwn 390	John	Rbs 374	Cutler, Aaron	Bfr 5
Joseph, Sen.	Rwn 390	John	Wlk 32	John, Junr.	Bfr 5
Robert	Rth 101	Jos.	Csw 122	Moses, Junr.	Bfr 5
Roger	Mck 601	Jos.	Csw 127	Moses, Senr.	Bfr 5
Thomas	Rwn 390	Joseph	Srr 643	see Cutl...	
Timothy	Wsh 714	Lacklan	Rbs 369	Cutlin see Cutler	
Wm.	Srr 709	Lauchlin	Mre 51	Cutrel, Andrew	Hde 365
see Conningham		Malcom	Rbs 373	Benjamin, Jur.	Hde 365
Cupper, Willoughby	Crr 142	Malcum	Stk 546	Benjamin, Senr.	Hde 365

Charles Hde 365
Henry Hde 365
Jacob Hde 365
Jacob, Jur. Hde 365
John Bfr 4
Joseph Hde 365
Peter Hde 365
Rachel Hde 365
Solomon Hde 365
Stephen Hde 365
Cutril, Amos Crv 283
David Crv 265
Roger Crv 263
Cutter see Cuter
Cutts, Paul Cmb 374
Sherret Cmb 372
Will. Prs 210
William Cmb 374
Cyrus, Fredrick Wrr 797

-- D --

D..., ... (2) Bfr 6
..., Senr. Bfr 6
...hn Bfr 6
James Bfr 6
Polly Bfr 6
William Bfr 6
D...rden, Jacob Bfr 6
D...vis, Arthur Bfr 6
Dabb, David Rwn 360
Dabbs, John Ans 234
Nathl. Ans 234
William Ans 234
Dabney, John Cht 184
Dabs, David Stk 619
Daffin, John Hlf 302
Winnifred Brt 40
Dafford, Jeremiah Cht 151
Daffren, John Rnd 309
Dagenhart, Henry Lnc 874
Dagless, Jonathan Rwn 441
Dahins, Jesse,
Ctn. Prs 187
Dail, Abel Dpl 439
Thomas Dpl 438
Dailey, Ann Crv 249
Enoch Cmd 101
Pattrick Lnc 853
Thomas Cmd 109
William Hde 366
William Rwn 378
William Wke 726
Daily, Benjamin Rth 108
Dalbey, Jarratt Nrt 435
Dale, Bery Rck 491
Chas. Rck 491
Isaac Orn 505
John Hlf 304
Richard Nrt 435
Thomas Nrt 435
William Hlf 304
William Nrt 435
Daley, John Cmd 110
John Crr 147
Dalrymple, Archa-
bald Mre 40
James Mre 65
John Mre 65
Dalton, John Rck 484
John Stk 579
Samuel, Senr. Rck 486
Dameron, George Csw 101
James, Jur. Csw 128
Jos. Csw 103

Thomas Psq 632
Damic, John Rwn 365
Joseph Rwn 365
Damison, Barthw. Csw 126
Christopher Csw 126
John Csw 126
Damron, George Lnc 826
Jno. Lnc 830
Tigner Hlf 302
Dance, Barzillai Nrt 435
Etheldred Nsh 98
Dancey, Francis Nrt 435
James Nrt 435
see Demcey
Dancy, Benjamin Grv 532
Edward Rwn 391
Edwin Edg 193
John, Junr. Rwn 390
John, Senr. Rwn 391
WIlliam Rwn 391
William, Junr. Edg 194
William, Senr. Edg 193
Danelly, James Orn 504
John Orn 504
Daney, James Edg 195
Dangins, William Stk 594
Daniel, Alexander Dpl 440
Allen Hlf 304
Archibald Hlf 302
Arthur Bfr 6
Asa Edg 194
Belcher Crr 152
Benjamin Mnt 517
Benjamin Rwn 365
Britain Hlf 302
Bucknor Rwn 372
Charles Ash 77
Chesley Grv 508
Christopher Orn 561
David Crr 152
David Nsh 98
David Rwn 378
David Wke 726
Duke Cht 189
Edward Hlf 302
Edward Wsh 702
Elias Smp 524
Elias Wne 861
Elijah Grn 590
Elisha Rwn 372
Elizabeth Rwn 391
Ephraim Edg 193
Ephraim Wne 860
George Grv 560
George Ptt 238
Gideon Crr 152
Gillam Cht 190
Hannah Ptt 239
Hardy Rth 107
Hiram Rth 105
Isaac Smp 503
Isaac Wne 844
Isham Cht 197
Jacob Smp 498
Jacob Smp 506
Jacob Wne 850
James Bfr 7
James Bld 7
James Nrt 435
James Rwn 378
James Rwn 424
James Stk 591
James Wne 845
Jas. Mrt 392
Jas. Prs 201
Jas. K. Prs 195
Jessee Cht 197

John Bld 7
John Crr 152
John Orn 559
John Orn 561
John Rbs 376
John Rwn 372
John Rwn 424
John Rth 107
John Wrr 800
John, Senr. Grv 505
John W. Wrr 799
Joseph Cmd 99
Joseph Crr 152
Joseph Edg 194
Joseph Hrt 724
Josiah Edg 194
Josiah Rwn 424
Lanier Ptt 238
Lemuel Edg 194
Leonard Rth 107
Lewis Hlf 302
Mary Wne 850
Mathew Prs 193
Nancy Crr 152
Nathan Wne 844
Nathaniel Wne 843
Nichles Crr 152
O. Reubin Hlf 304
Overton Bld 24
Owen Dpl 440
Paul Rwn 365
Peter Bfr 7
Phillip Frn 463
Randle Rwn 372
Reubin O. Hlf 304
Richard Wrr 800
Robert Cht 190
Robert Grn 612
Roger Orn 561
Samuel Mck 522
Sarah Hlf 302
Shadrach Bld 7
Silas Rwn 372
Stephen Bld 27
Stephen Grn 590
Sterling Hlf 302
Thomas Ptt 238
Thomas Wne 853
Thomas, Junr. Grv 509
Wenny Rwn 372
Widow Wne 873
William Brt 40
William Hlf 302
William Hrt 723
William Rth 107
William Stk 591
William Wke 775
William Wne 847
William Wne 871
Willis Hlf 304
Woods Crr 152
Wm. Crr 152
Wm. Mrt 392
Wm., Jur. Crr 152
Wyley Ptt 238
Zadock Wrr 799
see O'Daniel
Danielly, John Mre 52
John Rbs 375
Daniels, Asa Crt 60
Barton Mnt 507
Jacob Crt 61
James Hde 366
Job Crt 91
John Crt 60
Paul Mnt 506
Randal Hde 366

Randol	Crt 60	Mary	Orn 559	George, Senr.	Mnt 495
Shadrach	Trl 684	Samuel	Glf 657	George L.	Ird 655
Simon	Mrt 392	William	Glf 667	Hugh	Bnc 166
Syon	Rwn 372	see Doherty		J. John	Edg 175
Thomas	Crt 60	Daughhety, Absalom	Rbs 376	J. John	Edg 193
Thomas	Hde 366	Daughtery, Miles	Hrt 731	James	Orn 504
Danier, John	Rwn 407	Samuel	Edg 193	James	Wlk 35
Dankins, John	Srr 705	Wm. Mills	Hrt 731	John	Brt 40
Dannel, Josiah	Grv 542	Daughton, Joseph	Wlk 36	John (2)	Bnc 167
William	Grv 542	Daughtre, Elijah	Brt 42	John	Mck 572
Dannil, Joseph	Grv 519	Laurence	Brt 42	John	Mnt 495
Daphin, Darling	Dpl 414	Daughtrey, Arther	Wne 866	John, (Majr.)	Mck 559
Darbey, George	Prs 209	Daughtridge, Benja.	Nsh 97	John J.	Edg 193
John	Prs 208	Daughtry, Abraham	Smp 499	Robert	Mck 561
Darby, Benjamin	Rth 106	Benjamin	Smp 499	Samuel	Mck 566
Daniel	Csw 115	Elisha	Nrt 435	Sarah	Mnt 495
John	Rbs 375	Jacob	Jhn 748	Thomas	Ird 655
Nicholas	Mck 604	James	Nrt 435	Widow	Mck 525
William	Rnd 309	Jeremiah	Nrt 435	Widow	Mck 561
Darcas, Hannah	Wsh 702	Jesse	Nrt 435	Widow	Mck 606
Darcy see Dancy		Joseph	Nrt 433	William	Bnc 166
Darden, Abraham	Nrt 433	Lawrence	Nrt 435	William	Ird 655
Allen	Hrt 731	Lewis	Nrt 433	William	Mck 525
Charles	Dpl 417	Lydia	Smp 499	William	Mck 606
Elias	Nrt 435	Rhody	Nrt 435	William	Orn 504
Henry	Hrt 731	William	Nrt 433	Wm. H.	Ans 205
Isaac	Nrt 437	Daughty, Henry	Gts 265	Davie, Jno.	Prs 207
Jesse	Smp 525	William	Gts 265	R. William	Hlf 304
Jethro	Hrt 731	Daugtry, Lawrance	Wne 845	R. William	Hlf 358
John, Junr.	Nrt 435	Dauley, John	Orn 504	William R.	Hlf 304
John, Senr.	Nrt 437	William	Orn 504	William R.	Hlf 358
Joseph	Smp 525	Dautridge, James	Edg 194	Davis, Aaron	Mre 45
Mary	Gts 265	Davenport, Abraham	Lnc 834	Abraham	Ans 225
Pleasent	Hrt 731	Daniel	Wsh 702	Abraham	Grv 551
Riddick	Nrt 433	David	Wsh 702	Abraham	Mck 559
Robert	Hrt 731	Ephraim	Wsh 702	Abram	Ird 609
Sisha	Hrt 730	Ezra	Trl 688	Abram	Psq 639
William	Smp 505	Frederick	Trl 684	Absalom	Ird 614
Willis	Nrt 435	George	Lnc 834	Absalom	Rbs 376
Dardin, Jonas	Prq 653	Hezekiah	Trl 678	Adam	Stk 613
Darel, Joseph	Mck 538	Isaac	Trl 688	Allin	Lnc 902
Darell, John	Cmb 369	Isaac	Wsh 702	Ally	Jhn 758
Darick, John	Rck 467	Ishmael	Trl 692	Amey	Wke 727
Dark, Samuel	Mre 39	Jacob	Wsh 702	Andrew	Cbr 676
Darke, Joseph	Cht 166	James	Wsh 714	Andrew	Srr 648
Oliver	Cht 187	Jesse	Wsh 702	Andrew, (Cap.)	Mck 588
Samuel	Cht 179	John	Wsh 702	Andrew, Junr.	Cbr 677
Samuel	Cht 187	Joseph	Trl 780	Anney	Mrt 392
William	Cht 154	Moses	Trl 684	Archabald	Crt 61
Darlen, Thomas	Rwn 403	Myles	Wsh 702	Archibald	Frn 486
Darlett, Ann	Brt 88	Nathan	Trl 670	Archibald	Hlf 304
Darling, Mary	Chw 113	Stephen	Wsh 702	Archibald	Psq 629
Darnal, Joseph	Stk 549	William (2)	Wsh 702	Archibald	Psq 635
Darnald, John	Wrr 800	Wm.	Lnc 835	Aron	Ons 177
Darnall, David	Wke 727	see Deavenport,		Arthor	Rnd 311
Darnel, John	Mck 532	Debenport, Devenport		Arthur	Nrt 437
Roylly	Stk 549	Daves, John	Edg 195	Arthur	Psq 635
Darnell, George	Lnr 5	Samuel	Edg 195	Augustine	Grv 534
Jordan	Lnc 841	Davey, Elisebeth	Prs 192	B. Henry	Edg 193
Moses	Lnc 841	Elizebeth	Prs 205	Baily	Psq 628
Darner, John	Rwn 398	Gabriel	Prs 188	Bartlett	Rth 107
Darnold, John	Ash 77	Robert	Prs 192	Baxter	Bld 40
Wm.	Csw 144	Wm.	Prs 191	Baster	Bnc 167
Darrach, John	Bld 24	David, Burks	Brk 728	Baxter	Grv 511
John	Cmb 360	L. Claudius	Hlf 304	Benjamin	Bfr 6
Darret, Francis	Brk 743	Lewis	Stk 548	Benjamin	Cmd 101
Darris, Mary	Orn 504	Matthew	Wrr 800	Benjamin	Crt 65
Daryan, William	Mnt 495	Davidson, Alexan-		Benjamin	Hde 366
Dasdins, Celia	Wne 861	der	Ird 648	Benjamin	Mnt 485
Daster, James	Mck 585	Amos	Brt 40	Benjamin	Rth 106
Samuel	Mck 585	Benjn.	Bnc 167	Benjamin	Wke 728
Thomas	Mck 585	Daniel	Ans 230	Benjamin, Senr.	Rwn 378
Dauge, Dorcy	Crr 140	David	Edg 195	Benjamin, Senr.	Wke 728
Josiah	Bfr 6	Ephraim	Ird 655	Benn.	Psq 626
Josiah	Hde 366	George	Ans 203	Berges	Mre 51
Dauger, Willis	Cmd 104	George	Bnc 166	Blake	Hrt 734
Daugherty, John	Wlk 35	George (2)	Ird 655	Buckner	Wrr 800

Burwell	Wrr 799	Henry	Lnc 826	John	Rbs 375
C. Edward	Wke 728	Henry	Rth 106	John	Rck 450
Calep	Brn 15A	Henry	Stk 603	John	Rwn 360
Catharine	Lnr 7	Henry	Stk 606	John	Rwn 365
Charles	Cht 216	Henry B.	Edg 193	John	Rwn 378
Charles	Rwn 378	Henry W.	Glf 672	John	Rwn 391
Charles	Stk 549	Hepsibah	Glf 676	John	Rwn 446
Charles	Wrr 800	Hezekiah	Bld 24	John	Rth 107
Chloe	Jhn 746	Ichabud	Rbs 376	John (2)	Stk 548
Clark	Rwn 378	Immer	Rnd 309	John	Srr 648
Claudius L.	Hlf 304	Isaac	Brn 16A	John	Wke 727
Clement	Brk 742	Isaac	Bnc 167	John	Wke 728
Daffren	Rnd 311	Isaac	Ird 609	John	Wne 859
Daniel	Grn 599	Isaac	Mnt 500	John	Wne 870
Daniel	Mck 562	Isaac	Nwh 3A	John	Wne 873
Daniel	Ptt 230	Isaiah	Crt 67	John, Junr.	Ans 216
David	Brt 40	Isham	Ans 226	John, Senr.	Ans 225
David	Dpl 408	Isham	Bnc 166	John, Son Wm.	Hde 366
David	Gts 265	Isham	Hlf 302	John, Ters.	Hde 366
David	Hde 366	Isham	Stk 621	John B.	Lnc 894
David	Mck 562	James	Ash 77	John L.	Mck 540
David	Mck 568	James	Cmd 94	Jonathan	Dpl 408
David	Orn 504	James	Crt 65	Jonathan	Mck 558
David	Rth 106	James	Crv 313	Jonathan	Mnt 505
David	Stk 549	James	Grn 601	Jonathan	Srr 648
David	Stk 588	James	Glf 658	Jonathan	Wrr 799
David	Srr 646	James	Hde 366	Joseph	Bld 23
Dedrick	Psq 632	James	Ird 610	Joseph	Crt 80
Devotion	Psq 628	James	Lnr 7	Joseph	Cht 211
Dolphin	Cmb 353	James	Mck 591	Joseph	Gts 265
Durant	Psq 628	James	Mre 50	Joseph	Glf 653
Edward	Bld 2	James	Nrt 435	Joseph	Prs 193
Edward	Rwn 378	James	Orn 504	Joseph	Rwn 391
Edward	Rwn 385	James	Orn 561	Joseph	Stk 605
Edward, Junr.	Nrt 437	James	Rnd 309	Joseph	Srr 705
Edward, Senr.	Nrt 437	James	Stk 549	Joseph P.	Grv 551
Edward C.	Wke 728	James	Stk 616	Joshua	Bld 40
Elijah	Srr 647	James	Srr 647	Joshua	Brk 740
Elisha	Trl 692	James	Srr 648	Joshua	Ird 609
Elizabeth	Lnc 837	James, Senior	Grn 611	Joshua	Wne 865
Elnathan	Cht 175	Jane	Crv 341	Joshua	Wne 873
Enoch	Hlf 302	Jane	Nwh 12A	Josiah	Nsh 98
Enoch	Rnd 311	Jean	Rwn 378	L. Nathan	Edg 193
Ephraim	Wlk 36	Jemima	Bld 24	Larkin	Srr 647
Etheldred	Brt 42	Jeremiah	Ons 168	Leonard	Srr 646
Evan	Rwn 360	Jesse	Bld 44	Leonard	Srr 648
Ezekias	Rth 107	Jesse	Nrt 435	Levi	Cht 184
Fanny	Srr 649	Jesse	Rnd 309	Levi	Psq 633
Frances	Bld 42	Jesse	Rwn 306	Levi	Stk 594
Francis	Bld 49	Jesse	Rwn 391	Levin	Trl 688
Francis	Cmd 94	Jesse	Stk 603	Lewis	Ans 216
Frederick	Rbs 376	Jesse	Wke 728	Lewis	Dpl 413
Fredrick	Frn 494	Jessey	Frn 460	Lewis	Wke 727
Fredrick	Psq 631	Job	Rnd 309	Lewis, junior	Ptt 268
Freeman	Crt 65	Joel	Lnr 7	Lewis, Senior	Ptt 267
Gabrial	Srr 647	John	Ans 215	Logan	Crt 90
Gabriel	Rwn 391	John	Bld 40	Maelacha	Lnr 7
Gelis	Wrr 799	John	Bld 41	Major	Cht 210
George	Ash 76	John	Brn 17	Martin	Grn 601
George	Brn 13A	John	Bnc 166	Mary	Csw 140
George	Cbr 678	John (2)	Bnc 167	Mary	Psq 631
George	Ird 629	John	Cbr 676	Mary	Trl 686
George	Psq 627	John	Csw 137	Matha	Srr 711
George	Rwn 306	John	Cht 197	Mathew	Cht 162
George, Senr.	Mck 555	John	Cht 216	Mathew	Mre 45
Glafrey	Wke 728	John	Crv 247	Mathew	Ons 175
Good	Hlf 358	John	Cmb 384	Matthew	Mnt 478
Goodman	Rth 106	John	Jhn 751	Matthew	Srr 646
Goodorum	Nrt 437	John	Lnc 846	Maxey	Trl 678
Grace	Lnr 7	John	Mck 555	Meredith	Mrt 392
Harday	Mre 47	John	Mnt 505	Merit	Hlf 302
Hardeman	Rwn 378	John	Nrt 435	Meshach	Ash 77
Henry	Bld 42	John	Orn 561	Micajah	Bld 41
Henry	Csw 127	John	Psq 631	Micajah	Frn 483
Henry	Csw 139	John	Prq 657	Miles	Mrt 392
Henry	Cht 176	John	Prs 192	Miles	Psq 628
Henry	Jhn 759	John	Ptt 230	Morris	Rwn 403

Moses	Gts 265	Thomas	Orn 504	John	Crr 149
Myrick	Rwn 391	Thomas	Orn 504	Lewis	Crr 159
Nancy	Hlf 358	Thomas	Ptt 230	Mark	Crr 146
Nancy	Rck 461	Thomas	Rch 265	Neal	Crr 163
Nathan	Crt 65	Thomas	Rbs 376	Davison, Jesse	Hlf 302
Nathan L.	Edg 193	Thomas	Rwn 378	John	Rnd 311
Nathaniel	Stk 548	Thomas (2)	Rth 106	Robert	Wsh 702
Patsy	Hlf 304	Thomas	Rth 107	Daviss, Abel	Nsh 98
Pattrick	Brk 743	Thomas	Rth 108	John	Nsh 98
Patty	Rch 265	Thomas	Srr 646	Davisson, James,	
Peter	Mnt 495	Thomas	Wrr 800	Jur.	Hde 366
Peter	Wrr 801	Thomas	Wne 865	James, Ser.	Hde 366
Peter R.	Wrr 784	Thomas, Jur.	Rbs 376	William	Hde 366
Philip	Rth 107	Thomas, Ser.	Rbs 375	Dawalt, Jacob	Cbr 715
Philip, junr.	Wlk 36	Trustan	Glf 678	Dawdy see Dowdy	
Philip, Senr.	Wlk 36	Upshear	Lnc 874	Dawe, Ann	Crv 281
Polly	Prs 202	Uriah	Ird 629	James	Crv 263
Ralph	Mre 45	Walter	Mck 600	John, Senr.	Crv 265
Ralph	Mre 51	Wendal	Lnr 7	Jonathan	Crv 263
Reuben	Psq 632	Weymouth	Psq 631	Nathan	Crv 285
Rich.	Brn 13	Widow	Mck 540	William	Crv 265
Richard	Brk 739	Widow	Srr 649	Dawkins, John	Rch 263
Richard	Mnt 495	Will.	Nwh 7A	John, Jr.	Rch 264
Richard	Orn 561	William	Ash 76	John, Sr.	Rch 264
Richard	Rwn 286	William	Ash 77	Samuel	Rch 243
Richard	Rwn 306	William	Bld 28	Samuel	Rch 264
Richard	Trl 670	William	Bld 33	William	Rch 243
Richard	Wne 859	William	Bnc 166	Dawl, Joseph	Rwn 300
Riteson	Edg 193	William	Brk 740	Dawns, Leven	Rch 480
Robert	Cbr 678	William	Brk 742	Daws, Jacob	Chw 128
Robert	Mck 591	William	Crt 65	James	Rwn 286
Robert	Mnt 485	William	Csw 138	Dawson, Daniel	Rnd 309
Robert	Mre 76	William	Cht 161	David	Hlf 304
Robert	Wke 727	William	Crv 289	Elizabeth	Hlf 304
Robert, Senr.	Wke 727	William	Cmb 371	Henry	Wrr 801
Ruth	Psq 639	William	Frn 461	Isaac	Dpl 403
Sally	Frn 484	William	Grv 517	James	Ird 629
Sampson	Bld 44	William	Hlf 302	Jennet	Crv 245
Samuel	Bnc 167	William	Hde 366	Joel	Rbs 376
Samuel	Brk 740	William	Ird 629	John	Lnr 5
Samuel	Cmd 101	William	Jhn 758	John	Nrt 437
Samuel	Crt 92	William	Mck 582	John	Wlk 35
Samuel	Dpl 408	William	Psq 631	Jonathan	Brk 741
Samuel	Hde 366	William	Psq 634	Joseph	Smp 495
Samuel	Orn 560	William	Ptt 231	Joshua	Rnd 309
Samuel	Ptt 268	William	Ptt 276	Levi	Crv 279
Samuel	Rwn 391	William	Rnd 309	Patience	Wne 871
Samuel	Srr 646	William	Rnd 311	Primus	Hrt 737
Samuel	Srr 647	William	Rch 262	Robt.	Ons 170
Samuel	Wke 726	William	Rwn 364	Sarah (2)	Hlf 304
Samuel, Junr.	Rwn 365	William	Rth 107	Solomon	Hlf 304
Sarah	Crt 65	William	Stk 548	Thomas	Lnr 7
Sarah	Gts 265	William	Stk 549	William	Mck 541
Sarah	Rck 438	William	Stk 591	William, jr.	Wne 848
Sarah	Rwn 446	William	Srr 647	Wm., Senr.	Wne 848
Shadrach	Psq 632	William (2)	Srr 648	Dawten, Anthony	Wrr 800
Simon	Rth 107	William	Wsh 702	John	Wrr 801
Smith	Brt 40	William	Wlk 36	Day, David	Hlf 304
Solomon	Bld 42	William, Esq.	Hde 366	Edmond	Mrt 392
Solomon	Cbr 707	William, Senr.	Brk 743	Edward	Brk 743
Solomon	Grv 533	William, son Esq.		Francis	Prs 204
Solomon	Ird 610	Wm.	Hde 366	Henary	Prs 191
Solomon	Rwn 364	William, Sr.	Crt 67	Henry	Stk 575
Stephen	Mre 72	Willm.	Bld 41	Isaac	Prs 192
Syrus	Grv 568	Wilson	Brn 16A	James	Brk 741
Tho. F.	Nwy 3	Wilson	Nrt 437	James	Stk 575
Thomas	Ash 77	Winfield	Hde 366	John	Brk 741
Thomas	Bld 42	Winny	Lnc 888	John	Crt 59
Thomas	Bnc 166	Wm.	Lnc 837	John	Prs 191
Thomas	Brk 740	Wm.	Mrt 392	John	Srr 647
Thomas	Cbr 679	Wm. Duke	Wke 727	Laban	Brk 741
Thomas	Crt 65	Zachariah	Lnr 7	Lewis	Nrt 437
Thomas	Cht 216	Zepheniah	Wsh 702	Lucy	Nrt 437
Thomas	Cmb 353	see Basnight		Michael	Rwn 346
Thomas	Cmb 371	Davise, Acquiler	Prs 216	Nicholas	Brk 740
Thomas (2)	Hlf 304	Cornelious	Crr 154	Richard	Glf 688
Thomas	Mre 46	Demsey	Crr 156	Thomas	Nrt 437

Name	Ref
Thomas	Stk 549
Thomas	Stk 575
Thomas, Junr.	Brk 739
Thomas, Senr.	Brk 739
Valentine	Rwn 346
William	Brk 739
William	Glf 688
William	Srr 648
Willis	Mrt 392
Wm.	Mrt 392
Dayley, Ted.	Crr 157
Dayton, James	Cht 221
Nathan	Bnc 166
Deadman, William	Rwn 456
Deal, Abel	Grn 595
Abner	Prq 652
Adam	Nwh 5
Adam	Psq 639
Andrew	Grn 600
George	Brk 742
George	Lnc 867
George	Lnc 874
Jacob	Brk 742
Jacob	Lnc 867
James	Edg 193
James	Wke 728
John	Brk 739
John	Dpl 417
John	Dpl 439
John	Psq 637
John	Prq 646
Joseph	Prq 653
Joseph	Prq 660
Lewis	Grn 598
Malicha	Prq 652
Mary	Brk 741
Moses	Prq 663
Peter	Lnc 874
Thomas	Grn 601
William	Chw 124
William	Grn 598
William (2)	Lnc 874
William	Prq 654
William	Prq 656
William	Lnc 884
Dealy, Charles	Rwn 316
Dean, Alsey	Wke 727
Daniel	Nrt 435
Farmer	Grn 610
Francis	Glf 685
Frederick	Hlf 302
Gaius	Hlf 358
Hardy	Wke 727
Hardy, Jur.	Wke 727
Howel	Srr 648
Isaac	Hlf 302
James	Hrt 710
Jean	Brk 743
Jeremiah	Mre 72
Moses	Wne 852
Samuel	Brt 42
Solomon	Brt 42
Solomon	Stk 620
Thomas	Wke 727
William	Lnr 7
Deane, Marey	Crr 146
Deanes, Cornelius	Hrt 724
James	Hrt 723
James	Wne 865
Jesse	Hrt 716
Judith	Hrt 724
Matthias	Hrt 697
Thomas	Hrt 720
William	Hrt 723
Deans, Dempsy	Wne 852
George	Wne 870
John	Wne 870

Name	Ref
Dearcer, Samuel	Rwn 456
Dearing, Anthony	Stk 578
John	Stk 549
William	Rck 489
Deas, Daniel, jr.	Jhn 749
Hilyard	Jhn 749
Deason, Enoch	Ans 236
William	Ans 236
Deatherage, Wm.	Stk 549
see Detherage, Duth-	
erage	
Deatheridge, Eliza-	
beth	Rck 470
George	Rck 458
Deaton, Birrell	Mre 48
Elias	Mnt 521
John	Cht 220
John	Mnt 469
Joseph	Mnt 469
Levy	Mre 59
Marthew	Mre 47
Mary	Mnt 469
Deatz, Jacob	Stk 549
Deavenport, Austin	Rwn 385
Martin	Brk 741
William	Brk 739
Deaver, Thomas	Edg 195
Deaves, John	Dpl 406
Sander	Dpl 406
Debard, Jacob	Ird 624
Debenport, Martha	Orn 561
Deberry, Benjamin	Nrt 437
Charlotte	Nrt 437
Henry	Mnt 485
Henry	Nrt 437
Lemuel	Ptt 267
Peter	Nrt 435
Susanna	Nrt 437
Deboard, Isaac	Srr 648
James	Srr 647
James, Jr.	Srr 647
John	Srr 647
John	Srr 648
Debrulah, Micagah	Orn 505
Deburner, John	Cht 224
Debusk, Jacob	Nwh 10
Deck, Cooper	Ans 203
Decker, Christian	Lnc 884
Michael	Lnc 874
see Duker	
Deckerson, Isham	Ans 220
Deckey, Robert	Brk 742
Deckins, Richard	Ird 624
DeClugny, Stephen	Hlf 358
DeCoine, Edward	Cmb 353
Dedman, Edmond	Rwn 456
Mark	Rth 106
Thomas	Rwn 424
Dednam, Charles	Frn 445
Dedurn, David	Crv 285
Deel, Jams	Nsh 97
Deem, H.	Lnc 902
Deemus, Andrew	Rch 245
Deen, James	Nsh 99
John	Srr 649
John	Wne 853
Richard	Rch 255
Deens, Bartley	Nsh 98
William	Nsh 98
Williss	Nsh 98
Deer, Charles	Rck 453
Stephen	Ans 198
Dees, Daniel	Smp 532
Daniel, Jr.	Jhn 750
Edmond	Jhn 771
Gabriel (2)	Rch 270
Hardy	Smp 532

Name	Ref
James (2)	Rch 270
Jesse	Ird 609
Levi	Rbs 376
Morris	Rch 270
Moses	Rbs 375
Sampson	Rch 270
Sampson	Smp 518
William	Rch 253
Deese, Drury	Jhn 749
Deeton, Dyson	Mnt 474
Deffnell, William	
H.	Ons 182
Deggs, ...	Ans 198
John	Ans 198
John	Ans 201
John	Ans 224
Marshall	Ans 223
Pleasant	Ans 223
Solomon	Ans 198
William	Ans 225
Dehart, Elijah	Wlk 36
Elisha	Brk 742
Rubin	Brk 742
Dehorty, James	Edg 194
Deifrece, James	Srr 646
Deitz see Duty	
Deiu see Dew	
Dejanet, Mumford	Ans 203
Dejernett, Daniel	Srr 649
DeKeyser, Leehayn-	
sius	Cmb 353
Delamar, Francis	Crv 291
Hearty	Crv 289
Nelson	Crv 289
Smith	Crv 305
Thomas	Crv 291
Delamoth, Henry	Mnt 478
Delaney, James	Mck 578
Mary	Frn 452
Thomas	Ons 152
Delap, Daniel	Rwn 373
John	Rwn 373
Delastatiors, Rebec-	
ca	Crv 231
Delay, Bird	Rck 455
James	Rck 455
Delk, David	Wke 726
John	Rnd 311
Jordon	Bnc 166
Dell, George	Brk 741
Dellard, Ozbourn	Cht 172
Delleny, James	Mck 597
Deller, Widow	Lnc 812
Delling, John	Lnc 860
George (2)	Lnc 853
Henry	Lnc 812
Jacob	Lnc 853
Jacob	Lnc 888
John	Brk 744
John	Lnc 902
Martin	Lnc 853
Philip	Lnc 853
William	Lnc 853
Deloach, Francis	Nrt 435
John	Jhn 766
Joseph	Jhn 770
Michael	Nrt 435
Sarah	Nrt 437
Deloah, Samuel	Jhn 766
Delon, Rachel	Psq 638
Delph, Peter	Ash 77
Demby, Joshua	Mre 67
Demcey, Henry	Nrt 435
see Dancey	
Dement, John	Grv 536
Mary	Brk 743

Demeritte, Aaron	Mrt 392	William, Jur.	Srr 646	Thomas	Smp 507
Peggey	Mrt 392	Wm.	Rck 452	Devebaugh, Philip	Lnc 812
Demery, Jehu	Bld 10	Zachariah	Ash 77	Devenny see Divinny	
Rinda	Bld 28	Zachariah	Grv 520	Devenport, ...	Brk 742
Dempsey, Ann	Brt 40	Denson, Benjamin	Frn 454	Absalom	Ptt 235
James	Hlf 304	James	Mck 553	Edmond	Ptt 234
James	Hlf 306	Jesse	Nsh 98	Elisha	Srr 648
Johnston	Brt 40	John	Frn 454	Isaac	Ptt 234
Joshua	Brt 40	John	Nsh 97	Jesse	Rnd 311
Susannah	Ons 156	John	Nsh 99	Joel	Ird 638
Thomas	Brt 40	John	Rch 243	Joel	Rnd 309
Thorogood	Brt 40	Jordan	Frn 481	Joel	Srr 648
Thurogood	Hlf 306	Joseph	Ans 206	John	Rth 106
William	Brt 40	Massey	Nsh 98	Reuben	Wlk 35
Demsy, Allen	Ans 203	Shadrach	Ans 212	Thomas	Brk 740
Micajah	Ans 207	William	Wrr 799	William	Lnr 5
Wiley	Ans 207	Wilson	Frn 486	William	Rwn 316
Denby, Asa	Frn 470	Dent, John, Jur.	Frn 459	William	Srr 647
Benn.	Psq 632	John, Ser.	Frn 459	William	Srr 648
Elijah	Frn 488	Michal	Frn 458	Dever, Nathan	Bnc 167
Jeremiah	Nsh 97	Thomas H.	Rwn 330	Richd.	Bnc 167
Patience	Frn 488	William	Rbs 376	William	Bnc 167
Denes, William	Rck 455	Denton, Ann	Frn 479	William, jr.	Bnc 166
Denham, Michael	Glf 679	Benjamin	Grv 518	Devereux, John	Crv 229
Denial, William	Orn 505	Edward	Frn 479	Devine, John D.	Jhn 775
Denison, Philendia	Hde 366	James	Hlf 304	Rachel	Brk 741
Denkins, Susanna	Wrr 801	Jessey	Frn 479	Dew, Allen	Hlf 302
Denley see Denby		John	Ans 232	Arthur	Edg 193
Denmark, John	Dpl 430	John	Grv 518	Duncan	Nsh 96
Denn see Dunn		John	Hrt 734	James	Frn 455
Denna, Barbara	Prs 193	John	Rth 106	John	Edg 193
Barbara	Prs 217	Samuel	Grv 514	Mary	Edg 193
James	Nwh 1A	Silas	Mck 552	Samuel	Edg 194
Dennen, Robert	Wne 852	William	Cmb 379	Thomas	Hlf 304
Denney, Abraham	Grn 604	see Smart		William	Edg 193
Dennis, Anderson	Rch 250	Depoister, John	Ird 634	Dewalt, Valentine	Lnc 846
Andrew	Mnt 480	Depriest, William	Rth 107	Dewbury, Daniel	Hlf 304
Devern	Brt 42	Derberry, Andrew	Brk 739	William	Hlf 302
Francis	Crt 85	Ann	Brk 740	William	Hlf 304
James	Crt 85	Daniel	Brk 740	Deweast, Josiah	Cbr 685
James	Wke 726	George	Brk 742	Dewees, Hezekiah	Mck 566
Jeremiah	Wke 727	Jacob	Brk 741	Dewkes, Jesse	Crv 301
John	Ptt 288	Michael	Brk 742	Dewlin, Amus	Wrr 801
John	Rnd 309	see Durberry		Mary	Wrr 801
John	Wke 728	Dercherson, Nancy	Stk 588	Dewty, Thomas	Wrr 799
Joseph (2)	Bnc 167	Dermen, William	Wne 851	Dewy, John	Crv 245
Joseph	Crt 67	Dermot, John	Rwn 431	Dial, Joseph	Rwn 456
Mary	Crt 83	DeRoset, Amt. J.	Nwh 2A	Shaderick	Rwn 456
Mary	Cht 208	Desart, James	Brk 740	Simes	Wlk 64
Morris	Crv 255	Margret	Brk 739	Dicason, William	Stk 584
Nancy	Crt 84	Descern, Martha	Srr 646	Dice see Due	
Reuben	Ptt 285	Desearn, Martha	Srr 648	Dick, Adam	Lnc 813
William	Brn 15A	Desern, James	Orn 561	Elizabeth	Rwn 391
William	Crt 84	Deshaso, Clemon	Prs 207	Free	Cht 197
William	Glf 651	Edmond	Prs 193	George	Lnc 813
William (2)	Rnd 309	Richd.	Prs 193	Jacob	Rth 107
William	Wke 727	Robert	Prs 199	James	Cmb 353
see Dinnis		Deson, Elzabeth	Nsh 98	James	Glf 639
Denny, Benjamin	Grv 523	Dessaux, Leonard	Bfr 22	John	Brk 741
Edmund	Wlk 36	Detherage, John,		Old	Chw 122
Elijah	Wlk 36	Sr.	Stk 548	Samuel	Glf 653
George (2)	Glf 641	Lewis	Stk 548	Thomas	Glf 660
George	Glf 666	Matthew	Stk 548	William	Cmb 353
George	Wlk 36	Detucker, George	Brk 741	William	Glf 653
Hezekiah	Srr 646	Deutch see Doitch		see Duck	
James	Ash 77	Devail, John	Crr 153	Dickard, Clark	Lnc 864
James	Glf 641	Devalt, Valentine	Lnc 828	Dickason, Martin	Wrr 799
James	Srr 646	Devane, James	Nwh 4	Nathl.	Wrr 799
James	Srr 648	John	Bld 50	William	Wrr 799
James, Senr.	Glf 642	Tho.	Nwh 4A	Winifred	Wrr 799
Jms.	Lnc 837	Thos.	Nwh 4	Dickay, William	Rnd 309
Joshua	Srr 646	William	Nwh 4A	Dicken, Anne	Hlf 304
Samuel	Srr 646	Devany, Jenkins	Frn 445	Benjamin	Hlf 302
Walter	Rck 452	Devaughan, Saml.	Nsh 97	Benjamin	Hlf 302
William	Glf 634	Will.	Nsh 98	Bennett	Hlf 302
William	Glf 642	Devaul, Samuel	Rnd 311	James	Hlf 302
William	Srr 646	Devawn, George	Smp 520	Jesse	Hlf 302

John	Hlf 302	James	Crt 61	John	Prs 204
Joseph, Jr.	Hlf 302	James	Dpl 400	Dillahurty, Susan-	
Joseph, Sr.	Hlf 302	James	Dpl 432	na	Jns 815
Lewis	Hlf 304	James	Lnc 853	Dillan, Nathan	Glf 668
Matthew	Hlf 302	Jedediah	Crv 263	Dillard, George	Srr 647
Richard	Edg 195	Jerremiah	Ans 211	Henry	Wke 727
William	Edg 193	Jno.	Lnc 825	Ismael	Rbs 375
William, Jr.	Hlf 302	Jno.	Lnc 837	James	Stk 579
William, Sr.	Hlf 302	Jno.	Lnc 842	John	Bnc 166
Dickens, Henry	Csw 144	John	Ans 225	John	Srr 647
Dickenson, Epaphrodi-		John	Crt 57	Joseph	Wke 726
tus	Grv 527	John	Cmb 368	Josiah	Wke 775
John	Grv 527	John	Lnc 900	Sukey	Wke 775
John	Grv 528	John	Prs 196	Thomas	Bnc 166
William	Mre 39	John	Ptt 252	William	Wke 727
Dicker, Frederick	Lnc 813	John	Rch 243	Willis	Cht 157
Dickermun, Barbary	Stk 626	John	Wlk 35	Dillen, Benjamin	Rck 482
Dickerson, Arther	Ans 206	Joseph	Dpl 438	Henry	Lnc 841
Daniel	Wne 860	Joseph	Lnc 825	John	Rck 439
David	Wlk 35	Joseph	Wlk 35	Dilliard, Eliza-	
Isaac	Wne 862	Jozel	Ons 142	beth	Edg 196
Isham	Ans 237	Lydia	Crv 265	John	Edg 194
Leonard	Ans 227	Michael	Dpl 438	Mary	Edg 195
Levan	Crv 289	Morris	Smp 533	Dillinger, Michael	Lnc 813
Matthew	Wne 861	Murphy	Grn 605	Dillion, Little-	
Shadrach	Wne 860	Richard	Rwn 276	berry	Stk 588
Thomas	Edg 193	Richard	Rwn 286	William	Glf 668
Wiley	Srr 647	Robert	Lnc 895	Dillon, Benjamin	Trl 678
William	Wne 858	Robert	Ons 140	James	Trl 678
Dickey, Anthony	Rth 105	Robert	Ptt 283	Jessee	Glf 674
D. James, Jun.	Orn 504	Samuel	Ans 199	John	Trl 670
David	Orn 561	Shadrak	Grn 605	Levin	Glf 656
David	Rth 105	Solomon	Crt 57	Mary	Trl 670
James	Orn 504	Sylvanus	Crt 57	Dillow, Jacob	Rwn 300
James	Rwn 325	Tabitha	Ptt 256	Peter	Rwn 300
Joel	Rwn 325	Thomas	Ash 77	Dills, Bartlett	Rth 105
John	Ird 660	Thomas	Lnc 895	Peter	Rth 105
Martha	Rth 105	Thos.	Lnc 841	Thomas	Rth 105
Samuel	Ird 660	Uriah	Crt 61	Dilworth, Benjamin	Rck 469
William	Orn 504	William	Crv 295	John	Rck 444
Zachariah	Orn 561	William	Dpl 432	Nancy	Rck 444
Dickie, Alexr.	Lnc 837	William	Grn 601	Dimmery, Richard	Nrt 435
Dickins, James	Wlk 36	Dicky, David	Csw 134	Dimond, William	Glf 654
John	Csw 144	John (2)	Csw 134	Dinco, ...	Wrr 801
William	Csw 144	John	Glf 632	Dinkin, Charles	Nrt 437
William, Capt.	Grv 580	Thomas	Rwn 325	Dinkins, James	Mck 538
Dickinson, ...	Trl 670	William	Glf 622	Jesse	Nsh 97
David	Nrt 435	William	Rwn 325	John	Wne 843
James	Crt 80	Dier, Mrs.	Chw 117	John, Junr.	Mck 538
John	Crt 81	Dietz, Jacob	Lnc 867	John, Senr.	Mck 538
John	Hrt 734	John	Lnc 867	Joshua	Ans 223
Samuel	Chw 114	Solomon	Lnc 867	Stephen	Srr 705
William	Grv 529	Dieu see Dew		Dinnis, Richard	Brk 741
Wm.	Nsh 97	Diffe, Moses	Rnd 309	Dirdent, William	Grn 594
Young	Grv 579	Diffee, Betty	Rnd 311	Disheroon, Waitman	Rth 106
Dickison, Mikel	Mre 39	Diffey, John	Mre 48	Dishion, Jacob	Orn 560
Robert	Mre 42	Diffin, Jesse	Rch 269	Dishman, Kizey	Ird 610
Willis	Mre 43	Diger, Von	Rch 270	Dishon, Augustine	Orn 503
Dickry, Michael	Rch 269	Diggins, William	Ptt 283	Augustine, Jun.	Orn 504
Dicks, James	Glf 627	Digh, Henry	Rth 107	Jacob	Orn 503
Jesse	Brk 742	Digner, John	Crv 245	Lewis	Orn 503
Joshua	Glf 664	Dilany, John	Gts 265	Luke	Orn 503
Nathan	Orn 505	Dilback, Jacob	Rth 106	Dismond, Daniel	Lnr 5
Peter	Glf 626	John	Rth 106	John	Lnr 5
William	Glf 625	Dilday, Jesse	Ptt 269	John, Senr.	Lnr 5
Zachariah	Orn 505	Joseph	Hrt 704	Dismukes, George	Cht 152
Dickson, Abia	Crv 255	Dildy, Amos	Gts 265	Dison, Leonard	Ird 617
Alexander	Dpl 437	Charles	Edg 195	Nathaniel	Orn 560
Benjamin	Crv 265	William	Gts 265	William	Wlk 36
David	Lnc 895	Dill, Balser	Psq 638	Ditto, Shadrach	Rch 257
Edward	Cmb 369	Edward	Crt 75	Zebulum	Cht 165
Elijah	Crv 263	John	Crt 75	Divan, E. Jeremiah	Brt 90
Frederick	Grn 605	John	Csw 146	Jeremiah E.	Brt 90
George	Crt 57	Owen	Stk 549	Divenny, Aaron	Rth 106
Jacob	Prs 194	Sarah	Crt 84	Divers, Francis	Cmd 102
James	Ash 77	Dillaha, Edmond	Prs 194	Diveux, Frederick	Crv 231
James	Bnc 167			Diving, Samuel	Glf 620

Divinny, Robert	Rth 106	John	Ird 620	Lem	Crr 137
Dix, James	Csw 101	John	Mck 541	Dolby, John	Grv 568
Peter	Rnd 309	John	Rwn 316	Knight	Grv 568
Wm.	Csw 126	John	Srr 646	William	Cmb 392
Dixan, William	Cht 214	John, Senr.	Rwn 316	Dolen, John	Stk 620
Dixon, Benjn.	Stk 596	Jonathan	Rth 107	Doles, Francis	Nrt 435
Charles	Csw 97	William	Rwn 316	Hannah	Nrt 437
Cofield	Edg 194	William (2)	Rth 106	Doling, William	Srr 707
Edmond	Prs 198	Dobbs see Dabbs		Dolison, Benjamin	Ird 616
Edward	Ptt 252	Dobins, Ann	Srr 704	Dollahide, Car.	Csw 124
Eli	Cht 163	Dobs, Chesle	Brk 740	Cornelius	Csw 132
Frederick	Bfr 6	William	Brk 740	James	Csw 124
George	Bfr 6	Dobson, Fanny	Wlk 35	Thomas	Csw 124
George	Cht 185	Henry	Stk 549	Dollar, Elisha	Orn 559
George	Hde 366	Hesekiah	Dpl 436	Henry	Orn 559
Green	Edg 195	John	Ird 617	James	Orn 559
Hannah	Cht 186	Joseph	Brk 740	Jonathan	Orn 559
Heckman	Edg 194	Joseph	Rth 107	William	Smp 527
James	Orn 505	Mary	Dpl 425	Dollarhide, Ezeki-	
James	Orn 561	Robert	Ird 617	ale	Rnd 311
Jessee	Cht 181	Thomas	Cbr 701	Francis	Rnd 311
John	Cht 219	William	Glf 622	Jas.	Prs 209
John	Prs 198	William	Stk 620	Dollars, William	Orn 560
John	Srr 647	Docherty, John	Brk 740	Dolleson, Wm.	Crr 153
Joseph	Cht 213	Dockery, Hasten	Rnd 311	Dollison, John	Glf 656
Joseph	Orn 559	Dockrey, John	Wke 728	Wm.	Crr 166
Joseph	Prs 197	Dodd, Aron	Wne 860	Dolton, Charles	Stk 548
Maria	Crv 231	Daniel	Smp 508	David	Rth 105
Mary	Orn 505	David	Smp 521	David	Rth 107
Milecent	Edg 195	Dempsey	Jhn 769	David	Stk 592
Nehemiah	Ptt 252	George	Ans 203	Isaac	Stk 549
Obadiah	Grn 604	John	Jhn 769	Isam	Csw 101
Olef	Edg 195	John	Rck 464	John	Rth 107
Robert	Orn 505	John	Smp 520	Nicholas	Rck 480
Samuel	Cht 163	Robert	Wke 775	Thomas	Rth 106
Samuel	Cht 191	William	Jhn 768	William	Rth 105
Samuel	Cht 219	William	Orn 561	Donaldson, Hugh	Bnc 167
Sarah	Edg 194	Dodson, Abe	Stk 586	John	Mck 605
Simon	Rnd 309	Charles	Grv 514	Robert	Csw 125
Solomon	Cht 163	Daniel	Rck 478	Robert	Chw 127
Stewart	Orn 505	James	Wlk 36	Robert	Cmb 353
Susanna	Prs 218	John	Rck 486	Robert	Mck 605
Thomas	Bfr 6	Pates	Wlk 35	Southwell	Edg 173
Thomas	Cht 219	Richard	Stk 586	Southwell	Edg 193
Thomas (2)	Edg 194	Stephen	Grv 513	Stokelay	Grn 591
Thomas	Orn 505	Thomas	Rwn 340	William	Brt 42
Walter	Ptt 252	Thos.	Cht 178	Donally, Henry	Hde 366
William	Cht 185	William	Cht 178	James	Srr 647
William	Glf 649	William	Grv 513	Donalson, Alexr.	Rwn 336
William	Orn 505	William	Rck 486	Andw.	Rwn 336
William, Jun.	Orn 505	William, jr.	Grv 514	John	Ird 634
William, junior	Ptt 252	Dogan, Sally	Wlk 36	Joseph	Rwn 336
William, Junr.	Edg 194	Dogged, Bushrod	Rth 105	Donaly, Nancy	Srr 647
William, Senior	Ptt 254	Doggett, Jeremiah	Hlf 304	Thomas	Srr 647
William, Senr.	Edg 194	Doherty, Andrew	Rth 106	Donathan, Eliza-	
Wynn	Csw 96	Daniel	Cbr 701	beth	Srr 648
see Bell		David	Mck 565	Hawkins	Srr 648
Dixson, Elisabeth	Frn 448	Edward	Brk 743	Done, Jacob	Cht 217
John	Frn 448	George	Brk 743	John	Cht 212
Jonathan King	Ons 173	George	Mck 567	Joseph	Cht 217
Dizer, John	Crt 80	George	Mck 592	Rachel	Bld 39
Do...son see Dobson		James	Brk 743	Donelson, Arthur	Cbr 681
Doak, Hanah	Glf 634	Jane	Glf 657	James	Ird 634
James	Glf 652	John (3)	Brk 743	William (2)	Ird 634
John	Glf 634	John	Rck 469	Donethan, Benjamin	Wlk 35
William	Glf 671	Pattrick	Rwn 424	Donlison see Dollison	
Doaty, John	Rwn 407	Richard	Rth 105	Donnall, Andrew	Glf 641
Dobb see Doub		Thomas	Brk 743	Daniel	Glf 641
Dobbing, Ann	Csw 115	William	Brk 743	George	Glf 620
Dobbins, Alexander	Rwn 325	Doitch, Lewis	Nsh 97	George	Glf 641
Cahtarine	Csw 112	Doity, Owen	Orn 557	John	Glf 669
Ezekiel	Rth 105	Dolahide, Francis	Rck 470	John, Senr.	Glf 641
Hugh	Rwn 316	Doland, Henry	Cbr 713	Letham	Glf 641
Hugh, Senr.	Rwn 316	Timothy	Cbr 713	Robert	Glf 641
James	Rth 106	Dolarhide, Mary	Csw 117	Robert	Glf 665
John	Csw 110	Dolbey, Absolem	Crr 142	Thomas	Glf 641
John	Csw 112			William	Glf 641

Name	Ref
Donoho, Thomas	Csw 109
William	Csw 105
Donohoe, Ann	Rwn 415
Donolson, Robert	Prs 200
Doram, Edward	Wke 727
Doremire, Andrew	Rwn 295
Dores, Susanna	Bld 14
Dority, Elisabeth	Crv 311
Ephraim	Crv 333
Richard	Crv 311
William	Crv 315
Willis	Crv 311
see Doity	
Dorman, Benjamin	Smp 495
Clary	Edg 195
Cullin	Edg 194
John	Smp 495
Mary	Edg 195
Michael	Orn 559
Dornbush, John	Ird 624
Doron, John	Rth 106
Dorsen, Henry	Brk 743
Dorset, Clement	Brk 741
John	Cht 194
Nancy	Cht 194
Dorsey, Barsil	Lnc 874
Benjamin	Lnc 874
Elizabeth	Nwh 3
James	Frn 474
Jerry	Frn 474
John	Brk 742
John	Frn 486
Robt.	Nwh 2A
Solomon	Frn 474
William	Frn 473
William, Ser.	Frn 474
see Elijah	
Dorson, John	Csw 144
Larkin	Hlf 302
Mary	Mnt 484
Rachel	Rck 447
Dorsy, Sally	Rck 460
William	Brk 742
Dorton, Charles	Cbr 705
Dosier, Josiah	Crv 323
Doss, Matthew	Stk 548
Dosset, Francis	Cht 173
Soloman	Cht 173
Dossett, Elizabeth	Orn 561
Thomas	Orn 560
William	Orn 560
William	Orn 561
Dotrey, Polley	Wke 775
Dotson, Isaac	Stk 549
Dotty, Pheby	Nwh 6
Doty, Isaac	Ans 226
James	Ons 154
Lemuel	Ons 159
Doub, John	Stk 611
Doudna, Henry	Edg 193
John, Junr.	Edg 194
John, Senr.	Edg 194
Douge, Isaac	Cmd 109
Joseph	Cmd 109
Douger, Benjamin	Cmd 104
Dough, Benjn.	Crr 151
Cornelious	Crr 165
Daniel	Crr 152
Demsey	Crr 152
Fed.	Crr 146
Jideon	Crr 146
Mary	Grr 151
Richard	Crr 145
Samuel	Crr 150
Susannah	Crr 151
Dougherty, James	Orn 557
Doughty, Daniel	Hrt 710
James	Hrt 697
William	Hrt 697
Douglas, Joseph	Mck 563
William	Csw 139
Douglass, Daniel	Rbs 375
Dorcas	Cht 205
James	Ans 232
John	Brt 42
John	Ird 648
Joseph	Mck 551
Solomon	Ird 648
Thos.	Prs 212
William	Cbr 683
Doup, Caleb	Cbr 692
Douthat, Thomas	Rwn 360
Douthet, Abraham	Rwn 360
John	Rwn 360
Joseph	Bnc 167
William	Rwn 360
Douthort, Isaac	Stk 605
Dove, Hugh	Bld 26
Dover, John	Bnc 167
Dow, John	Rbs 376
John	Rbs 432
Dowd, Charles	Cht 198
Conner	Cht 198
Cornelius	Mre 39
James	Mre 42
Owen	Cht 172
Patrick	Mre 63
Richard	Cht 173
Dowday, Jacob	Crr 138
John	Crr 138
John	Crr 151
Joseph	Crr 138
Josiah	Crr 138
Thos.	Crr 149
Thos., Jur.	Crr 149
Wm.	Crr 138
Wm.	Crr 139
Wm.	Crr 151
Dowden, Matthew	Edg 194
William	Crv 239
Ziphaniah	Wlk 36
Dowdie, Joseph	Crv 241
Dowdy, Bartly	Cht 212
Benjn.	Cht 179
Daniel	Mre 56
George	Cht 180
James	Mre 56
John	Cht 171
Lydia	Hde 366
Thomas	Cht 194
Thomas, Sr.	Cht 180
William	Cht 171
William	Cht 179
Dowel, John	Brk 741
William	Wlk 36
Dowell, George	Brk 741
James	Mck 541
James	Rwn 436
John	Rwn 436
John, Senr.	Rwn 436
Peter	Rwn 436
Peter, Senr.	Rwn 436
Philip	Rwn 431
Dowey, James	Bld 23
Dowgen, Richd.	Brn 15A
Dowlas, William	Bld 29
Dowlen, Nancy	Bfr 22
Downer, John	Ans 224
Downey, Abraham	Srr 648
James	Grv 550
John	Grv 509
Peter	Srr 648
Samuel	Srr 648
Timothy	Hrt 737
William	Rck 467
William	Stk 549
William	Stk 628
Downie, Dan	Bld 23
Downing, Elisha	Grn 616
James	Nwh 2
James, Junr.	Edg 195
James, Senr.	Edg 193
Joseph	Grn 616
Richard	Wsh 702
Stevens	Wsh 702
William	Hrt 697
Downs, Caleb	Ptt 262
Elisha	Grn 615
Elizabeth	Ptt 273
Frederick	Ptt 255
Nathaniel	Cmd 109
Nehemiah	Ptt 261
Samuel	Mck 600
Thomas	Mck 599
William	Hlf 302
William	Rth 107
William	Wke 726
Wm., Senr.	Wke 726
Zachariah	Brk 743
Downy, Alexander	Rth 106
Charles	Rwn 336
James	Srr 647
Patrick	Rth 108
Dows, Ephraim	Edg 194
Dowthard, John	Stk 549
Dowty, Elijah	Bfr 6
John	Bfr 6
Lodewick	Bfr 6
Peter	Bfr 6
Thomas	Bfr 6
Doxey, Jeams	Crr 140
John	Crr 140
Sanford	Crr 155
Doxy, John	Jhn 750
Doyle, Adam	Grv 514
Allen	Rth 107
James	Rth 105
John	Rth 105
Joshua	Lnc 885
Dozier, Abner	Cmd 99
Averilah	Nsh 98
Calib	Cmd 99
Clouey	Crr 160
Dennes	Crr 156
Evan	Cmd 98
Griffen	Crr 154
Jeams (2)	Crr 160
John	Cmd 99
Joseph	Cmd 102
Peter	Cmd 107
Peter	Cmd 110
Peter	Crr 165
Phillip	Crr 160
Richard	Crr 160
Richard	Nsh 97
Saml.	Crr 160
Thomas	Nsh 97
Willes	Crr 164
William	Nsh 53
Willoughby	Cmd 98
Willoughby	Crr 156
Drake, Albritain	Rbs 375
Benjamin	Nsh 97
Britain	Frn 479
Caswell	Wrr 799
David	Orn 559
Drewry	Edg 193
Edmund	Nsh 97
Eli	Mck 587
Elizabeth	Ptt 275
Francis	Cht 164

Francis	Hlf 304	Matthew	Hrt 704	Ransom	Rwn 378
Harboard	Hlf 304	Shaw	Frn 470	Richard	Cmb 353
Henry	Wrr 799	Thomas	Wke 727	Robert	Srr 647
Hines	Nsh 98	Thomas, Jur.	Wke 727	Solomon	Ons 148
Jno.	Lnc 837	William	Cht 152	Stephen	Crr 155
Joel	Nrt 435	William	Nsh 98	Thomas	Crt 72
John	Ans 209	Droghan, George	Cmb 373	Thomas	Jns 805
John	Crr 165	Robert	Cmb 373	Thomas	Ons 136
John W.	Nsh 97	Drum, John	Ird 643	William	Crv 239
Jordan	Nrt 433	see Dreem		William	Srr 647
Magarett	Edg 193	Drumm, John	Lnc 885	Wm.	Crr 158
Martin	Rwn 436	Peter	Lnc 884	Dudney, John	Ans 213
Mary	Edg 194	Drummond, John	Nrt 437	Dudroe, Jno.	Lnc 841
Matthew	Nsh 97	Rachel	Hlf 304	Jno., Junr.	Lnc 842
Nathl.	Nsh 97	Drummund, Thomas	Edg 195	Due, Elly	Grv 561
Richard	Cht 160	Drumon, Philip	Lnc 875	John	Cmb 353
Silas	Rbs 375	Drury, Anne	Rbs 376	John	Mre 52
Tristram	Nsh 97	Charles	Wrr 799	Dueast, Hezekiah	Glf 655
Trustham	Hlf 304	Eve	Rbs 376	Duers, John	Brt 40
Tyre	Orn 559	Henry	Hlf 302	Duey, E., Estate	Bld 27
W. John	Nsh 97	James	Nrt 435	Duff, George	Rwn 320
William	Cht 159	John	Mck 531	John	Dpl 402
William	Edg 193	Michael	Rth 93	John	Mck 577
Zilpha	Nsh 97	Dry, Andrew	Cbr 708	Robert	Mck 576
Draper, Joseph	Psq 626	Christian	Cbr 688	William	Dpl 409
Joseph	Prq 659	Jacob	Cbr 708	Duffee, Frederick	Hlf 302
Joshua	Csw 146	Martin	Cbr 691	James	Cmb 391
Presly	Csw 110	Owen	Cbr 708	Patrick	Wke 726
Robert	Rwn 415	Philip	Cbr 691	Samuel	Ans 209
Solomon	Prs 199	Virgil	Nwh 4	Samuel	Hlf 306
Thomas	Prq 662	William	Brn 14	William	Orn 491
Thomas, Sen.	Prq 656	Duart see Desart		Duffin see Daffin	
William	Gts 265	Dubary see Dewbury		Dugan, Joseph	Rnd 309
Willis	Wsh 702	Dubberly, Sacker	Crv 271	Duggan, John, Junr.	Mrt 392
Draughon, George	Smp 497	Duberry, Erby	Nrt 437	John, Senr.	Mrt 392
Hardy	Smp 497	see Deberry		Susanah	Mrt 392
Drawhon, James	Edg 194	Dubery, William	Wrr 801	Duggar, Benjamin	Wlk 36
Miles	Edg 193	DuBreetz, Gabriel	Cmb 353	Dugger, John	Brn 20A
Richard	Edg 193	Duck, John	Ash 77	Duggins, John	Stk 595
Thomas	Edg 193	John	Jhn 758	Duglas, Abel	Frn 488
William	Edg 194	John	Wke 726	John	Frn 488
Drawhorn, Jacob	Stk 622	John, Junr.	Mck 566	John	Orn 504
Dreding, John	Ptt 289	Robert	Mck 566	Duglass, Alexander	Srr 648
Dreem, John	Lnc 866	Simon	Mck 566	Anthony	Crr 152
Philip	Lnc 866	Timothy	Jhn 761	Charles	Crr 165
William .	Lnc 866	William	Wke 726	Jeams	Crr 143
William	Lnc 874	Duckett, Christo-		John	Orn 560
Drescall, Moses	Rck 470	pher	Wsh 702	Roadham	Jhn 775
Dresser, Manasah	Cbr 703	Duckey, Saml.	Csw 125	Thomas	Srr 648
Sarah	Psq 637	Duckry, Ann	Rch 255	Dugless, Demsey	Crr 157
Drew, Anthony	Dpl 431	Anna	Rch 255	Duglis, Thomas	Glf 645
Edward	Hrt 729	Matthew	Rch 263	Duice see Duier	
John	Ans 228	Thomas	Rch 264	Duier, James	Rwn 397
John	Brt 40	see Dickry		Duke, Andrew	Crr 146
John	Brn 17A	Ducksworth, John	Brk 742	Ann	Frn 476
John, Junr.	Hlf 304	Joseph	Mre 44	Burwell	Wrr 799
Joshua	Hlf 304	Duckworth, Able	Lnc 860	Daniel	Gts 265
Sarah	Smp 499	Absalom	Mck 563	Felitha	Hde 366
Solomon	Hlf 306	George	Brk 740	Green	Wrr 800
Thomas	Hlf 304	George	Mck 563	Hardiman	Orn 560
Wilson	Smp 522	John	Mck 560	Harrel	Grv 535
Drewry, James	Nsh 97	Jonathan	Brk 739	Jacob	Rwn 311
Dringe, Prissiler	Crr 167	William	Mck 563	James	Cmd 101
Drinkwater, Daniel	Rbs 375	Dudley, Abraham	Jns 805	James	Mnt 499
Drisdale, Jno.	Nwh 2A	Ann	Ptt 291	Jesse	Cmb 370
Drisdell, John	Brt 42	Charles	Srr 647	John	Cbr 716
Driskell, Dennis	Grv 551	Christopher	Ons 145	John	Cmb 371
Driskil, John, jr.	Rth 105	Daniel	Smp 507	John	Orn 559
John, Sr.	Rth 105	Edward	Ons 146	John, Junr.	Gts 265
Driskill, Elisha	Glf 660	George	Hde 366	John, Senr.	Gts 265
Jonan.	Glf 660	James	Ptt 239	Josiah	Hlf 306
Driver, Elzabeth	Nsh 98	Jeams (2)	Crr 158	Mary	Wrr 800
Jiles	Frn 470	John	Crt 72	Matthew	Wrr 800
John	Frn 494	John	Mnt 461	Robert	Orn 559
John	Hrt 704	Levi (2)	Smp 507	Simon	Wrr 800
John	Wke 727	Malachi	Crr 159	William	Orn 559
Martha	Hrt 716	Polly	Wke 775	William	Wrr 800

William	Wrr 801	Peter	Rck 445	Robert		Mck 583
William P.	Wrr 800	Robert	Orn 505	Samson		Mnt 507
Duker, Abraham	Ird 660	Sarah	Rck 442	Samuel		Dpl 432
Dukes, Harwood	Nrt 435	Thomas	Crt 74	Samuel		Mre 40
Hezekiah	Trl 684	Thomas	Ird 655	Silas		Rwn 295
John	Lnr 5	William	Dpl 428	Stephen		Crv 235
see Dewkes		William	Grv 540	Stephen		Rbs 375
Dukins, Wm., (GC.)	Prs 190	William	Rth 108	Thomas		Mre 46
Dula, Benett	Wlk 35	Duncom, Blanch	Wrr 800	Thomas		Wne 854
William	Wlk 35	Charles	Rnd 311	Walter		Lnr 5
Dulany, Benjamin	Dpl 412	John	Rnd 311	Widow		Mck 535
Dulin, David	Rwn 407	Kissey	Wrr 800	Widow		Mck 582
John	Mck 578	Duncun, Seamon	Grv 536	William		Frn 483
Lewsey	Wrr 801	Dunford, John	Hrt 730	William		Mck 530
Sugar	Mck 578	Phillip	Edg 193	William		Mre 45
Dull, John	Stk 578	William	Edg 194	William		Mre 70
Dullon, William	Grv 509	William	Gts 265	William		Wne 873
Dum, Bartholomue	Mre 69	Dunham, Henry	Rth 106	Dunnafin, John		Orn 504
Dumas, David, Junr.	Mnt 493	Joseph	Rth 106	Dunnagan, Elijah		Srr 646
David, Senr.	Mnt 490	Michael	Glf 688	Jesse		Srr 646
Zachariah	Mnt 490	William	Crv 239	John		Srr 646
Dumass, William	Wlk 35	Wm. R.	Bld 33	John, Se.		Srr 646
Dumen, George	Wne 851	Dunian, Elijah	Ans 239	Joseph		Srr 646
Dumis, Obadiah	Rch 254	Dunken, James	Stk 587	Justice		Srr 646
Richard	Rch 254	Dunker, Thos.	Crr 168	Thomas		Srr 646
Dumus, Amos	Rch 255	Dunkham, Thomas	Stk 595	William		Srr 646
Benjamin	Rch 263	Dunkin, Andrew H.	Grv 582	Dunnaven, Abrm.		Prs 208
Benjamin	Rch 268	Edmund	Dpl 426	Dunneway, Abram		Csw 107
Jerry	Rch 257	James	Cht 220	Dunnicks, William		Rch 258
Silus	Rch 257	William	Cht 220	Dunning, Elisha		Ptt 266
see Ditto		Dunkins, Joshua	Wlk 36	Ezekiel		Ptt 265
Dun, Anne	Edg 194	Dunlap, Alexander	Ird 670	Hardy		Brt 42
Edwin	Stk 621	Gilbert	Rth 107	James		Glf 666
Nicholas	Edg 194	Henry	Csw 95	Jeremiah		Brt 40
Simeon	Bnc 167	Henry	Lnc 888	Jesse		Ptt 266
Stephen	Edg 193	James	Cmd 102	Jesse, Senior		Ptt 265
Thomas	Hlf 304	James	Orn 504	John R.		Hrt 716
Dunagin, Ashley	Orn 560	James	Stk 549	Ladock		Grn 593
Charles	Orn 560	James	Mre 63	R. John		Brt 40
Dici	Orn 560	John	Stk 549	R. John		Hrt 716
James	Orn 560	John	Stk 591	Samuel		Brt 42
Sarah	Orn 560	John	Stk 592	Samuel		Hrt 716
Thomas	Orn 560	Robert	Mck 564	Shadrach		Brt 42
William	Orn 560	Sophia	Cmd 109	Uriah		Cht 170
Dunbar, Chrispan	Rnd 309	Will.	Nwh 3A	William		Hrt 716
John	Lnc 864	William	Lnc 888	Dunnington, Wil-		
Nathaniel	Mck 580	Dunm see Dunn		liam		Cht 174
Patsey	Ans 230	Dunn, Andrew	Mck 582	Dunscomb, James		Chw 116
Robert	Bfr 6	Aron	Ans 216	Dunsemore, James		Bnc 167
Thomas	Trl 692	Aron	Ans 234	Dunsmore, Adam		Bnc 167
Dunbarr, Milly	Rck 465	Barna	Mnt 478	Dunson, Winney		Wke 727
Dunbibin, Junie	Nwh 4	Bartholomue	Mre 70	Dunston, Abram		Trl 670
Duncan, Abner	Prs 209	Benjamin	Wne 854	Edmund		Brt 40
Abner	Prs 218	Bolling	Wke 728	Wm.		Crr 147
Absalom	Lnc 860	Drury	Ons 172	Dunton, Daniel		Crr 145
Cresy	Rck 462	Elizabeth	Bnc 166	Jacob		Crr 143
David	Cmd 106	Francis	Bfr 6	Jeam		Crr 167
Demsey	Brn 20A	George	Rwn 276	Dunwoodey, Jno.		Lnc 837
Elias	Brn 20A	George	Rwn 286	Dupe, William		Brk 740
Elijah	Rth 107	Hardy	Crv 335	Dupree, Benjamin		Ptt 274
George	Dpl 426	Hardyman	Wke 728	Bird		Ptt 273
Henry	Jhn 769	Henry	Ons 173	Cordall		Nrt 435
James	Ird 624	Hezekiah	Mnt 493	Jacob		Nrt 435
James	Rbs 375	Isaac	Ans 230	James		Nrt 435
James	Wrr 800	James	Mck 535	Thomas		Nrt 435
Jas.	Prs 209	Jeremiah	Wke 727	Thomas		Ptt 274
John	Ans 227	John	Bfr 24	Duprey, Hailey		Wke 726
John	Bnc 166	John	Brt 42	Jesse		Hlf 302
John	Grv 514	John	Brk 740	Duquid, Alexander		Crv 241
John	Grv 536	John	Mre 49	Dural, David		Dpl 426
John	Ird 609	John	Mre 70	Durberry, Hannah		Brk 742
John	Ird 655	John	Ons 171	see Derberry		
John	Lnc 853	John	Wne 846	Durdan, Mills		Prs 190
John	Rbs 375	Patrick	Orn 505	Richard		Edg 193
Mary	Bld 20	Richard	Bld 6	Durden, Absilla		Wne 860
Mary	Brk 743	Richard	Mnt 490	Jethro		Nwh 4
Peter	Brk 742	Robert	Mck 535	Durdins, Dempsey		Wne 863

Henry	Wne 861	William	Csw 108	John	Rwn 294
John	Wne 864	William	Csw 144	Killian	Rwn 306
Micajah	Wne 868	Dyer, Anthony	Bfr 22	Philip	Rwn 300
William	Wne 862	Caleb	Ash 77	Philip	Rwn 306
see Dasdins		Elijah	Wlk 35	Earp, Burwell	Wke 729
Dure, Leven	Gts 265	Jeromiah	Lnc 900	Edward	Wke 728
Durgan, Ann	Brt 40	John	Rth 107	Earston, Sarah	Crr 137
William	Brt 42	Jonathan	Srr 649	Earwood, Benjamin	Rth 108
Durham, Anna	Jhn 770	Manoah	Wlk 35	Daniel	Lnc 813
Charles	Rth 106	Nathan	Srr 710	Edmund	Rth 109
Henry	Csw 148	Robert	Cmb 383	John	Lnc 813
Isaac	Csw 103	Samuel	Lnc 895	Mary	Rth 109
James	Jhn 770	Sarah	Wlk 36	Thomas	Lnc 813
James	Srr 646	Shaderach	Rth 107	William	Lnc 813
James (2)	Wlk 36	Thomas	Ptt 294	William, Junr.	Lnc 813
Jno.	Csw 148	William	Lnc 895	Eary, Abraham	Rwn 295
John	Bnc 166	Dyke, John	Brk 741	John	Rwn 295
John	Brk 744	Dyson, Barton	Ird 634	Zacharias	Rwn 295
John	Orn 559	Isaac	Rbs 375	Easley, Daniel	Mnt 501
John	Rwn 398	Solomon	Bld 5	Joseph	Stk 550
John	Wrr 801			Wakeham	Stk 584
Lucius	Orn 559			Easlick, Francis	Ons 143
Mark	Orn 559	-- E --		Isaac	Crt 91
Mary	Jhn 770			Easly, David	Rwn 365
Masten	Wlk 36			Fanny	Hlf 306
Richard	Rth 106	Eacks, Mary	Csw 141	William	Srr 650
Saml.	Wrr 801	Eadins, Ann	Nsh 99	Easom, Will	Nsh 99
Susanna	Wrr 801	Richard	Nsh 100	Eason, Abner, Capt.	Edg 197
William	Brk 741	Eadleman, Peter	Rwn 300	Cobern	Edg 197
William	Jhn 771	Eads, Charles	Bnc 168	Elijah	Jhn 749
William	Wrr 801	George	Rnd 311	Fredrick	Gts 265
see Doram, Durram		Lindsey	Stk 550	George	Gts 265
Durhom, John	Wrr 801	Eagenor, Mathias	Lnc 884	Hardy	Gts 265
Durkin, Michael	Wke 726	Eagle, Leven	Edg 197	Isaac, Junr.	Edg 197
Durley, Charles	Edg 193	Sarah	Brn 15	Isaac, Senr.	Edg 197
Horatio	Wke 727	Eagleton, John	Hde 367	Isaiah	Nsh 99
Durmir, Samuel	Ird 643	Mary	Hde 367	Jacob	Gts 265
Durmin, James	Orn 560	Noah	Hde 367	Jacob	Nwh 9A
Durnel, William	Ird 660	Eaker, Christian	Lnc 813	John	Jhn 768
Durr, Adam	Lnc 874	Michael	Lnc 813	John	Orn 506
Durram, John	Prs 214	Peter	Lnc 813	Joseph	Stk 550
Joseph	Stk 591	Peter	Lnc 895	Levie	Gts 265
Dusenberry, Samuel	Rwn 391	Eakins, John	Mck 568	Mary	Gts 265
Dutherage, George	Stk 548	Samuel	Mck 568	Mills	Mrt 393
Duton, Eldridge	Rnd 309	Eakre, Christian	Lnc 887	Moses	Jhn 758
Jackson	Rnd 309	Eaks, Zachariah	Grv 551	Obed.	Edg 197
James	Rnd 309	Ealbeck, Mont, Jr.	Hlf 306	Saml.	Nsh 99
Dutton, Elenor	Lnr 5	Mont, Sr.	Hlf 306	Sanders	Jhn 759
Zachariah	Grv 507	Eanes, Ezeriah	Brk 745	Seth	Gts 265
Duty, George	Prs 211	Earhart, Abraham	Lnc 853	Shadrach	Jhn 762
Littleton	Prs 198	Earle, John	Rth 108	Solomon	Gts 265
Richd.	Prs 211	Earles, Joshua	Rth 109	East, Asa	Stk 550
Will.	Prs 197	William	Lnc 895	Isham	Stk 550
William	Cht 182	William	Rth 109	Joseph	Stk 550
William, jr.	Cht 182	Earley, Benjamin	Srr 650	Thomas, Jur.	Stk 550
Duval, Forme, Dr.	Bld 7	Jerry	Srr 650	Thomas, Ser.	Stk 550
Duvall, Bailey	Bnc 166	William	Hrt 724	Easter, David	Hde 367
Duveast see Deweast		Earls, Bennet	Lnc 900	James	Bfr 7
Dweir, Winnifred	Brt 42	Francis	Cmd 102	James	Hde 367
Dwier, Elisabeth	Mrt 392	Nancy	Wrr 801	John	Hde 367
Dwiggins, James	Glf 674	see Erls		Robert	Cht 159
Lydia	Glf 674	Early, Benjamin	Brt 42	Thomas (2)	Hde 367
Robert	Stk 575	John	Brt 42	William	Hde 367
Dwight, William	Wsh 702	John	Rth 108	Easterling, Wil-	
Dwinny see Divenny		Mary	Psq 641	liam	Lnr 7
Dwyer, Partrick	Hlf 302	Thomas	Rth 108	Eastes, John	Grv 527
Dyal, Robert	Rwn 424	Earnest, Andrew	Lnc 813	William	Grv 525
Dyanet see Dejanet		Danuel	Lnc 813	Eastham, Edward	Rck 490
Dyar, James	Rck 470	George	Rwn 407	Eastice, Bartlett	Csw 141
William	Rwn 340	Henny	Ash 78	Richd.	Csw 107
Dycas, Edward	Rth 107	Earney, Charles	Lnc 813	Richd.	Csw 124
Larkin	Rth 108	Earonhart, Abraham	Rwn 294	Richd.	Csw 137
William	Rth 108	George	Rwn 286	Eastis, John	Grv 520
Dyce, Jacob	Csw 142	George, Jur.	Rwn 306	Laban	Brk 745
Dye, Abram	Rck 465	George, Sr.	Rwn 306	Leonard	Brk 744
Jacob	Csw 130	Henry, Junr.	Rwn 294	Lot	Brk 745
Mary	Cmb 353	Henry, Senr.	Rwn 294	William	Crv 239

Name	Ref	Name	Ref	Name	Ref
Easton, Abner	Brt 42	Eccleston, Mary	Hrt 698	Samuel	Bnc 167
George	Ptt 229	Echols, Mary	Bfr 7	Edney, John	Cmd 93
George	Rwn 451	William	Bfr 7	John	Cmd 96
John	Crt 73	Eckard, Adam	Lnc 875	Newton (2)	Cmd 93
John	Ptt 268	Martin	Lnc 875	Robert	Cmd 95
Joseph	Brt 42	Simon	Lnc 875	Ednley, Andrew	Stk 615
Michael	Rwn 346	Eckles, Abner	Crv 325	Edridge, Burres	Orn 562
Samuel	Crt 76	William	Mck 548	Edson, Creighton	Edg 197
Stephen	Grn 589	see Akeles, Akles		Edward, Moses	Cmb 381
Whitmill	Wke 728	Ecord, Joseph	Brk 745	Edwards, Able	Stk 550
Eastridge, Aron	Cht 188	Ector, Samuel	Orn 506	Allen	Orn 506
John	Wlk 37	Ecum, James	Nrt 439	Ancel	Glf 675
Henry	Grv 510	Eddin, Jos.	Csw 106	Anthony	Hlf 306
Nathan	Wlk 37	Edding, Thel.	Stk 603	Aron	Cht 198
Eastub, Abraham	Rwn 442	Eddings, Joseph	Glf 681	Asa	Jns 781
Isaac	Rwn 441	Eddleman, Bostain	Lnc 854	Benjamin	Cmb 391
Jacob	Rwn 442	David	Lnc 854	Benjamin	Jhn 748
Thomas	Rwn 441	John	Lnc 847	Benjamin	Rbs 377
William	Rwn 431	Eddlemon, Alia (2)	Srr 650	Benjamin	Mnt 499
Eastwood, Alexander	Rth 108	Jacob	Srr 650	Benjamin	Nrt 439
Israel	Hde 367	Eddridge see Eldridge		Britain, Junr.	Edg 197
James	Bfr 7	Eddy, Jacob	Cmb 354	Britain, Senr.	Edg 197
John	Grv 559	Edens, Ezekeal	Ons 165	Brittin	Bfr 7
Mary	Grv 579	Jacob	Nwh 12	Burwell	Ans 220
William	Ptt 251	James	Ons 162	Burwell	Ans 231
see Eestwood, Estwood		Margreat	Nwh 12	Catharine	Chw 114
Eatmon, Irvin	Nsh 100	Oziah	Nwh 8	Charles	Bld 10
John	Nsh 100	Sarah	Ons 164	Charles	Grv 507
Noel	Nsh 100	Edey, Saml.	Crr 146	Charles	Lnc 895
Thophilus	Nsh 100	Edgar, Partrick	Frn 458	Charles	Rth 108
Eaton, Charles R.	Grv 530	Edgare, Julia	Crv 241	Christopher	Edg 198
Christopher	Stk 550	Edge, Jeremiah	Orn 561	Colin	Rbs 377
Daniel	Rwn 457	Edgenton, Ransom	Rth 109	Daniel	Frn 484
Henry	Lnc 847	Edgerton, Sarah	Wne 864	David	Ash 77
Isaac	Bnc 168	Edging, John	Glf 633	David	Glf 677
John	Hlf 306	Edgler, John	Lnr 7	David	Rth 108
John	Hlf 358	Edinger, Christian	Rwn 373	David	Rth 109
John	Lnc 813	Christopher	Rwn 373	David	Wke 729
John	Lnc 846	Edins, William	Mnt 462	David	Wne 858
Jonathan	Mrt 388	Edkin, John	Brn 21	David, Junr.	Bfr 7
Peter	Stk 626	Edleman, John	Cbr 717	David, Senr.	Bfr 7
Peter	Srr 650	Edlow, David	Nrt 439	Edmund	Edg 197
Robert	Orn 492	Edminson, Bazel B.	Bnc 168	Edwards	Stk 550
Thomas	Nrt 439	Moses	Bnc 167	Elizabeth	Edg 198
Thomas, Genl.	Wrr 802	Moses	Bnc 168	Emanuel	Bfr 7
William	Hlf 306	Robert	Bnc 168	Ephraim	Crv 323
William	Rck 488	Samuel	Bnc 168	Gideon	Srr 650
Wm.	Lnc 847	Edmiston, George	Brk 746	Gracy	Nsh 99
Eaverhart, Peter	Rwn 346	James	Brk 745	Gray	Edg 197
Eaves, Andrew	Rth 108	Edmond, Thomas	Jhn 756	Griffith	Lnc 875
Bartlett	Rth 109	Edmonds, John	Ird 648	Henry	Grn 614
Benjamin	Frn 450	Edmondson, Bryant	Crv 241	Heny	Orn 506
Buckner	Rth 109	Elisabeth	Mrt 393	Hugh	Cht 163
Burrel	Rth 108	Mary	Mrt 393	Isaac	Ans 204
David	Rth 109	Micajah	Mrt 393	Isaac	Bfr 7
Graves	Rth 109	Nathan	Mrt 393	Isaac	Mnt 485
Isaac	Ons 143	Edmons, Nelly	Bnc 168	Isaac, Junr.	Nrt 439
Solomon	Rth 109	Edmonson, James	Ons 154	Isaac, Senr.	Nrt 439
Ebelen, Lewis	Rwn 415	John	Rck 446	Isaac, Ters.	Nrt 439
Eborn, Edmund	Hde 367	William	Brk 745	Isham	Prs 197
Henry	Bfr 7	William	Ons 154	Israel	Ptt 275
Henry	Hde 367	Edmoston, John	Cbr 717	Jacob	Jhn 747
James	Hde 367	Edmunds, Charles	Hlf 306	Jacob	Trl 678
John	Bfr 7	Hannah	Hlf 306	Jacob	Rnd 310
John	Hde 367	Howell, Junr.	Nrt 439	James	Bnc 167
Kathrine	Bfr 7	Howell, Senr.	Nrt 437	James	Cht 183
Littleton	Hde 367	Sarah	Hlf 306	James	Glf 675
Margeret	Hde 367	William	Hlf 306	James	Nrt 437
Nathaniel	Hde 367	William	Nrt 437	James	Ptt 272
Samuel	Hde 367	Edmundson, Anne	Edg 198	James	Rbs 377
William, Jur.	Hde 367	Cullen	Wne 850	James	Rck 461
William, Ser.	Hde 367	John	Edg 197	James	Rck 491
Zachariah	Hde 366	John	Wne 849	Jeremiah	Wrr 802
Eccles, Gilbert	Cmb 354	John	Wlk 36	Jesse	Brn 20A
John	Cmb 353	Penelope	Wne 849	Jesse	Jhn 746
John	Orn 505	William	Edg 197	John	Ans 211
William	Orn 506	Edna, Essa	Bnc 167	John	Bfr 7

John	Bld 4	Thomas	Jhn 747	Elixon, William	Grv 508
John	Bnc 167	Thomas	Jhn 749	Elkin, Benjamin	Rth 108
John	Cht 191	Thomas	Rbs 377	James	Mre 73
John	Cht 199	Thomas	Rth 108	Elking, Owen	Cmb 390
John	Edg 197	Titus	Frn 481	Elkins, Agness	Bld 24
John	Grv 507	Urias	Wke 729	Benjn.	Mre 76
John	Lnc 846	Walker, Junr.	Bfr 7	Gabrile	Bnc 168
John	Lnc 860	Walker, Senr.	Bfr 7	Jesse	Bnc 167
John	Mnt 474	West	Grn 591	John	Bld 36
John	Nsh 99	William	Ans 201	John	Mnt 481
John	Orn 506	William	Ash 77	John	Srr 650
John (2)	Orn 562	William	Bfr 7	Joshua	Wke 729
John	Ptt 249	William	Brt 42	Nathl.	Rch 267
John	Ptt 256	William	Bnc 168	Saml.	Bld 31
John	Rnd 310	William	Cht 174	Samuel	Mre 73
John	Rwn 456	William	Cht 191	Samuel, Jur.	Bld 14
John	Wke 728	William	Grv 507	Shadrick	Mck 593
John	Wne 857	William	Grn 613	Stephen	Mre 39
John, J.	Bnc 167	William	Glf 675	Elks, Samuel	Ptt 255
John, Junr.	Nrt 439	William	Hlf 306	Uriah	Ptt 256
John, Senr.	Nrt 437	William	Ird 653	William	Ptt 256
Jonathan	Cht 182	William	Orn 507	Ellen, Dempsy	Hlf 306
Jonathan	Hlf 306	William	Orn 562	Hawil	Nsh 99
Jonathan	Rnd 310	William	Ptt 255	Ellener, James	Edg 197
Jordan	Nrt 437	William	Rth 108	Thomas	Edg 197
Joseph	Jhn 750	William	Rth 109	Eller, Elizabeth	Ash 77
Joshua	Cht 182	William	Srr 650	John	Ash 77
Joshua	Glf 678	William, Junr.	Nrt 439	Elleson, Isaiah	Glf 631
Joshua, jr.	Cht 183	William, Senr.	Nrt 437	Ellet, John	Smp 522
Josiah	Ons 157	Wm.	Csw 143	Peter	Bfr 7
Lewis	Lnc 860	Young	Ash 77	William	Bfr 7
Littleton	Frn 450	Eestis, Nathaniel	Grv 568	Elletson, Richd.	Bld 45
Martha	Nrt 437	Eestwood, Abraham	Grv 577	Ellett, George	Prs 208
Martin	Rth 108	Effrand, David	Orn 506	John	Glf 647
Mary	Wke 729	Effrit, Jacob	Cbr 691	John	Glf 681
Mathew	Dpl 411	Egerton, John, J.	Wrr 803	Ellexander, Simeon	Mrt 416
Matthew	Lnc 875	Martha	Wrr 802	Ellicot, John	Mre 62
Matthew	Nrt 439	Wilmot	Wrr 802	William	Mre 62
Meredith	Bnc 168	Egman, Lott	Csw 106	Ellicott, Robert	Grv 579
Micaja	Grn 599	Eicles see Eccles		William	Grv 539
Micajah	Jhn 748	Eights, Charles	Nsh 100	Ellicut, William,	
Michael	Jhn 747	Eirry, Zachariah	Hde 367	Jur.	Srr 650
Nancy	Grv 530	Eivy, Edward	Frn 456	Ellidge, Jacob	Wlk 37
Nathan	Brn 21	Elam, Danl.	Csw 109	John	Rth 108
Nathan	Edg 197	Elbeck, Henry	Chw 127	John	Wlk 37
Nathaniel	Cht 212	Elbeheart, John		Joseph	Wlk 37
Nathaniel	Lnc 860	Lewis	Stk 625	Joshua	Wlk 37
Nathaniel	Mnt 485	Elbephant, John		Elliff, John	Orn 506
Nathaniel	Nrt 439	Luis	Stk 598	Ellin, Obadiah	Wke 729
Nuet	Grn 602	Elcott, Mary	Rck 475	Elliner, Thomas	Edg 173
Oliver	Cht 191	Elder, James	Rnd 310	Ellington, Danl.	Wrr 802
Philip	Mnt 490	John	Ird 629	James	Wrr 802
Pumphrey	Wke 729	John	Rnd 310	Jesse	Wke 728
Ransom	Hlf 306	Peter, Senr.	Srr 650	Stephen	Wrr 802
Rebecah	Grv 540	William	Srr 650	William	Grv 519
Rial	Ans 204	Elders, Jeromiah	Lnc 895	Ellior, Leonard	Rnd 310
Riel	Bfr 7	Eldridge, Nathan	Crt 75	Elliot, Alexander	Frn 450
Robert	Cmb 381	Saml.	Jhn 775	Elisha	Crt 85
Robert	Orn 562	Elea, Sarah	Chw 117	Isaac	Rwn 437
Rowland	Rbs 377	Eley, Benjamin	Nsh 100	James	Mnt 478
Ruth	Bnc 168	Edward	Hrt 724	John	Ans 235
Saml.	Wrr 801	Eley, Jur.	Frn 463	John	Ans 240
Smpson	Jhn 748	Eley, Ser.	Frn 463	John	Rwn 407
Sampson	Wne 857	Josiah	Frn 487	Joseph	Lnr 35
Samuel	Rbs 377	Laurence	Frn 462	Lamuel	Frn 455
Sily	Edg 197	Michael	Hrt 724	Marvell	Rth 109
Simon	Edg 197	Michal	Frn 464	Nimrod	Brk 744
Sion	Hlf 306	Eli, Abner	Crt 65	Robert	Ans 235
Solomon	Nsh 99	Elias	Lnc 869	Thomas	Rwn 352
Stephen	Jhn 751	Elijah, Dorsey	Brk 740	Thomas	Rwn 398
Sterling	Ash 77	Elim, Robert	Csw 98	William	Rwn 407
Stokes	Cht 193	Elington, John F.	Jhn 762	William (2)	Rth 109
Stokes	Orn 506	Elinore see Elmore		William	Srr 650
Theophilus	Grn 613	Eliot, Rachel	Psq 640	see Ellior	
Tho.	Brn 20A	Eliott, Abel	Cht 217	Elliott, Abraham	Prq 648
Thomas	Brn 20A	Ebenezer	Cht 174	Abraham	Rnd 310
Thomas	Grn 613	John	Cht 174	Andrew	Mck 549

Axem	Rnd 310	Fanny	Ons 155	Willis	Rwn 403
Benjamin	Prq 655	Francis	Rth 109	Wm.	Mrt 393
Caleb, Jun.	Prq 646	Freeman, jr.	Crt 76	Zachariah	Mck 522
Calib, sen.	Prq 645	Freeman, Sr.	Crt 70	Ellisbarger, John	Lnc 886
Demsey	Prq 663	George	Crv 229	Ellison, Alderson	Bfr 7
Elizabeth	Prq 646	Isaac	Rwn 457	Cornelius	Crt 88
Enoch	Rnd 310	Jacob	Edg 198	Henry	Bfr 7
Francis	Nrt 439	Jacob	Wke 729	Jesse	Dpl 439
Gabriel	Chw 119	James	Bld 17	John	Csw 114
George	Cmb 366	James	Brn 14	John	Rnd 310
George	Mck 549	James	Grv 519	John	Rth 108
Hussha	Prq 648	James	Ird 614	Robert	Grv 556
Isaac	Prq 646	James	Rwn 378	Thomas	Bfr 7
Isaac	Rnd 311	James	Rwn 457	Thos.	Crr 163
Jesse	Prq 648	James	Wrr 802	Elliss, Benjamin	Nrt 439
Job	Prq 648	James, J.	Rth 109	Martha	Nrt 439
John	Frn 490	James, S.	Rth 109	Mary	Nrt 439
John	Ird 644	James D.	Brn 19	Robert, Junr.	Nrt 437
John	Prq 647	Joel	Smp 529	Robert, Senr.	Nrt 437
John, Jun.	Prq 656	Joel	Wne 873	Rowland	Nrt 439
Joseph	Prq 656	John	Cht 204	William	Nrt 439
Joseph (3)	Rnd 310	John	Cmb 353	Ellmore, Morgan	Rbs 377
Joseph, Sen.	Prq 653	John	Hrt 720	Ellor, Christian	Rwn 294
Joshua	Prq 646	John	Hrt 734	Christian, J.	
Josiah, elder	Prq 654	John	Jhn 764	Son	Rwn 295
Josiah, sen.	Prq 655	John	Lnr 6	Christian, Junr.	Rwn 294
Mary	Rnd 310	John	Orn 562	Frederick	Rwn 294
Mordecai	Prq 646	John	Rwn 457	George	Rwn 346
Myles	Chw 124	John	Wke 728	Henry	Rwn 294
Myles	Prq 644	John	Wrr 803	Jacob	Bnc 168
Myles, Jun.	Prq 656	John, Esqr.	Bld 32	Jacob	Rwn 294
Nathan	Rnd 311	John, Junr.	Rwn 378	John	Rwn 294
Nixon	Prq 648	John, (of Jo)	Gts 265	John	Rwn 306
Obediah	Rnd 311	John, Senior	Ptt 277	John (Jacob Son)	Rwn 294
Peter	Rnd 310	John, Senr.	Edg 197	John Melchor	Rwn 294
Pritlow	Prq 645	John, Senr.	Rwn 378	Ellsberry, John	Ash 77
Robert	Mck 523	Joseph	Orn 561	Ellsworth, Will. T.	Brn 18A
Robert	Mck 540	Joshua	Ird 620	Ellums, Mary	Smp 521
Samuel	Mck 523	Joshua	Wrr 803	Elmore, Abijah	Stk 618
Samuel	Rnd 310	Josiah	Wne 863	Absalom	Lnr 7
Solomon	Chw 125	Jossey	Gts 266	Archalus	Stk 621
Thomas	Mck 523	Lemuel	Gts 266	David	Bnc 168
Thomas	Prq 647	Lewis	Ons 173	Elijah	Wlk 37
Thomas	Prq 655	Lucy	Bld 17	Elizabeth	Orn 506
Thomas	Rnd 310	Margaret	Wne 861	George	Wlk 37
Townsend	Prq 642	Mathew	Crr 160	Jesse	Csw 114
William	Orn 506	Michael	Mrt 393	John	Csw 113
William	Prq 663	Mills	Gts 265	John, H.F.	Orn 506
Winslow	Prq 647	Mourning	Gts 265	John, Jun.	Orn 506
Wm.	Rck 463	Nancy	Wke 729	Osten	Stk 615
Zacharia	Grn 598	Nathen	Orn 506	Peter	Csw 99
see Ellicot		Nimrod	Orn 562	Peter	Orn 506
Ellis, Absalom	Wne 860	Obediah	Wrr 802	Randolph	Orn 506
Anne	Crv 243	Ozell	Hrt 710	Susanna	Hlf 306
Aron	Gts 266	Richard	Wrr 802	Susanna	Wne 853
Benjamin	Dpl 439	Robert	Bld 21	Thomas	Stk 616
Benjamin	Hde 367	Samuel (2)	Ird 720	Thomas	Wlk 37
Benjamin	Rwn 361	Sarah	Rwn 403	William	Bnc 168
Brition	Ons 173	Sherwood	Ans 208	William	Lnc 824
Charles	Ons 159	Stephen	Bld 42	Elms, Edward	Hlf 306
Charles	Wrr 803	Stephen	Rwn 361	John	Rth 109
Christopher	Ird 634	Stephen (2)	Wrr 802	Eloquence, Abraham	Rbs 377
Daniel	Edg 198	Taphiniah	Ird 667	Elrod, Adam, Junr.	Rwn 360
Dehorty	Edg 198	Thomas	Chw 120	Adam, Senr.	Rwn 360
Dellino	Crt 71	Thomas	Hlf 306	Christopher	Rwn 360
Edwin	Grn 590	Thomas	Ird 667	Conrod	Brk 744
Elijah	Orn 562	Widow	Mnt 505	Jacob	Rwn 360
Ebinezar	Rbs 377	Wiley	Rwn 361	John	Rwn 360
Elisha	Edg 197	William	Ans 202	Robert	Stk 607
Elizabeth	Ptt 277	William	Bld 23	Elsberry, Isaac	Srr 650
Ely	Ons 169	William	Edg 197	Jacob	Srr 650
Ephraim	Wrr 803	William	Ird 610	Elston, Elias	Rwn 398
Etheddron	Srr 650	William	Rwn 457	Jesse	Rwn 398
Etheldred	Ptt 277	William	Rth 109	Johnathan	Rwn 379
Evan	Cmb 383	William	Wrr 802	William	Rwn 398
Evan	Rbs 377	William, Esqr.	Edg 197	Elum, Mary J.	Csw 130
Even	Rwn 436	Willis	Prs 215	Elwell, Benja.	Bld 38

John	Cmb 381	Reece	Csw 139	William	Bnc 168
Ely, Katy	Bfr 7	Enry see Eirry		William (2)	Brk 745
Emberson, Benjn.	Cht 185	Ensley, Abram	Glf 672	William	Ird 639
James	Mck 561	Henry	Hde 367	William	Ird 644
James	Cht 214	John	Brk 744	William (2)	Rnd 311
James	Wrr 802	John, Senr.	Hde 367	William	Rwn 320
Margret	Cht 214	Solomon	Hde 367	William	Rwn 336
William	Cht 185	Ensly, John, Jur.	Hde 367	Esary, James	Rnd 311
Embry, William	Wke 729	Epdon, John	Crv 281	Esburn, John	Rwn 441
Bolley	Wke 729	Eperson, Robert	Wlk 36	Escam, William	Wne 847
Emburgy, John	Wlk 37	Robert, junr.	Wlk 36	Escum, Benjmen	Wne 848
Emerson, Henry	Mck 526	Epherson, James	Wlk 36	Esig, John	Stk 601
James	Psq 627	Epperson, John	Mrt 393	Eskredge, George	Prs 218
Wilson	Psq 627	Eppes, John	Nrt 437	Eskridge, Richd.	Csw 114
Emery, James R.	Crv 321	William	Nrt 437	Richd.	Prs 211
John	Rwn 325	Epps, Isom	Grv 568	Esley, Jesse	Mnt 506
Lewis	Grv 568	Nede	Mnt 517	Eslip see Estip	
Emler, John	Rwn 352	Pleasant	Rwn 378	Espie, Samuel	Lnc 895
William	Rwn 352	Eps, Edward	Mre 42	Esrry see Eirry	
Emmerry, Shadrach	Crt 61	Equals, Mary	Ptt 224	Estep see Estip	
Emmery, Aaron	Hlf 306	Erexcon, Jonathan	Ons 152	Ester, David	Cht 198
Edmund	Grv 569	Erexeson, Mary	Ons 152	Peter	Rwn 415
John	Hlf 306	Samuel	Ons 152	Estes see Eestis	
Emmet, Richard	Brk 746	Erls, Obediah	Wrr 802	Estip, Elijah	Ash 89
Emmett, Margaret	Cmb 354	Ervin, Edward	Jns 791	John	Ash 78
Emmison, Elisabeth	Crv 245	Garvin	Rth 108	Shadrach	Ash 89
Emmory, Amy	Rbs 377	James	Rth 108	Estis, Burriss	Orn 562
Endsley, H.	Stk 622	James	Rth 109	Elizabeth	Orn 493
J.	Stk 622	John	Jns 789	Wiley	Cht 182
see Ednley		Samuel	Hrt 710	Estwood, Charles	Grv 577
Enesly, Alexander	Lnc 888	Shadrac	Lnr 6	Etchison, Edmond	Rwn 441
Archibald	Lnc 888	William	Lnr 6	Henry	Rwn 457
John	Lnc 888	Ervine, Benjamin	Srr 650	James	Rwn 441
England, Daniel	Brk 744	Zacha.	Cht 168	James, Junr.	Rwn 441
John (2)	Brk 745	Erwin, Alexander	Brk 745	John	Rwn 441
Joseph	Brk 744	Alexander, Junr.	Brk 744	Walter	Rwn 441
Joseph, Senr.	Brk 745	Andrew	Wlk 37	William	Rwn 442
Mary	Cmb 354	Anne	Ird 648	Etherage, Caleb	Edg 198
Thomas	Brk 744	Anne	Wlk 37	Maryan	Edg 173
William	Brk 744	Ansel	Mnt 482	Maryan	Edg 197
William, Senr.	Brk 744	Arthur	Brk 745	Nathan	Edg 197
Engle, Barney	Glf 633	Catherin	Ird 667	Phillip	Edg 198
Jacob	Lnc 854	Christopher	Ird 670	Willoughby	Edg 197
John	Lnc 854	Elenor	Cbr 681	Etheridge, Abel	Crr 162
Martin	Lnc 854	George	Ird 639	Abel, Ser.	Crr 162
Michael	Lnc 854	George	Ird 648	Adam	Crr 151
English, Anne	Cmb 354	George	Rwn 325	Alphes	Crr 162
James	Ans 209	James	Brk 745	Andey	Crr 164
James	Hde 367	James	Mck 605	Asa	Cmd 106
James	Lnc 895	James	Rck 439	Asa	Crr 150
Jean	Rwn 451	Jane	Nwh 10	Barneby	Crr 151
John	Rwn 352	John	Brk 744	Caleb	Crr 162
John	Srr 650	John	Brk 745	Daniel	Crr 153
Joseph	Hde 367	John	Ird 639	Demsey	Crr 164
Peter	Crt 91	John	Ird 649	Elizebeth	Crr 165
Sarah	Nrt 437	John	Nwh 5A	Elsey	Crr 153
Thomas	Crt 91	John	Rwn 325	Franes	Crr 163
Thomas	Ptt 250	John	Rwn 447	Gise	Crr 151
William	Rwn 352	John, Senr.	Brk 744	Henery	Crr 162
Engly, John	Brk 744	Joseph	Glf 649	Holloway	Crr 138
Enlow, Abraham	Rth 108	Joseph	Ird 648	Isaac	Brn 21
Anthony	Rth 108	Joseph	Rwn 320	James	Ans 240
Ennett, Benjamin	Ons 164	Michael	Ird 635	Jeams	Crr 139
Joseph	Ons 161	Nancy	Brk 745	Jeams	Crr 140
Nat.	Ons 162	Nathaniel	Ird 670	Jeams	Crr 157
Thomas	Ons 161	Pattrick	Ird 654	Jean	Crr 162
Whitus	Ons 164	Richd.	Csw 125	John	Brn 21A
Ennis, Ezekiel	Brk 744	Richd.	Csw 133	John	Crt 81
James T.	Edg 197	Robert	Cbr 681	Jonathan	Bfr 7
Sarah	Dpl 406	Robert	Glf 655	Joseph	Crr 139
T. James	Edg 197	Robert	Ird 635	Mallechi	Mrt 393
Enochs, Benjamin	Csw 137	Robert	Mck 537	Marmaduke	Rbs 377
David	Rwn 437	Samuel	Glf 676	Mary	Psq 637
Isaac	Rwn 437	Samuel	Mck 560	Miriam	Wsh 704
John	Csw 125	Thomas	Cbr 682	Mitchel	Crr 162
John	Csw 139	Thomas	Ird 648	Nathan	Crr 151
Mary	Csw 139	Thomas	Wlk 37	Peter	Crr 162

Richard	Crr 152	Elisha	Csw 135	Thomas	Wke 729
Ruben	Crr 153	Etheldred	Wne 862	Timy.	Nwh 11
Saml.	Crr 140	Evan	Psq 640	William	Brt 42
Saml.	Crr 157	Ezekel	Crr 142	William	Bnc 168
Saml.	Crr 162	Ferreby	Wne 861	William	Cmb 372
Solomon	Ans 240	Francis	Hrt 697	William	Hrt 710
Sampson	Crr 143	George	Cmb 372	William	Wke 728
Thomas, Jun.	Cmd 102	George	Ird 667	William, Jur.	Wke 728
Thomas, Senr.	Cmd 101	George	Rnd 310	William, Senr.	Hrt 698
William	Wsh 714	Gilbert	Wke 728	Willie	Nrt 437
Willes	Crr 147	Henery	Crr 142	Winey	Hrt 710
Wilson	Crr 162	Henery	Crr 147	Zadoc	Ptt 277
Wm.	Crr 139	Isaac	Rnd 310	Evens, David	Nsh 99
Wm.	Crr 147	Isham	Wne 863	Ephraim	Brk 744
Wm.	Crr 148	Jacob	Ans 221	James	Nsh 99
Wm.	Crr 151	James	Chw 126	John	Mck 536
Etherngain, George	Hlf 306	James	Dpl 400	Richard	Mnt 493
Etherridge, Thomas	Wke 728	James	Dpl 417	Thomas	Prq 645
Etherton, Chris-		James	Rwn 365	William	Prq 645
tian	Rwn 403	James, Senr.	Rwn 365	Everage, Edward	Cmb 372
Ethridge, Abner	Wlk 37	Jesse	Glf 663	Milley	Cmb 373
David	Cmd 101	Jesse	Jhn 776	Everet, Alexander,	
Henry	Nsh 99	Joel	Hlf 306	Jr.	Jhn 769
Jeremiah	Nsh 99	Joel	Wne 863	Daniel	Jhn 764
Jeremiah, Jur.	Nsh 99	John	Brn 14	David	Hlf 306
Jerrod	Nsh 99	John	Cht 160	Demsey	Cmb 382
Peter	Nsh 99	John	Cht 164	John	Hlf 306
Willis	Cmd 101	John	Chw 117	Joseph	Wne 872
Etter, John	Nrt 439	John	Chw 126	Laurens	Rch 263
Eubank, Elisebeth	Prs 214	John	Crr 145	Thomas	Ans 199
George	Prs 214	John	Dpl 400	Everett, Henry	Cmb 382
Jas.	Prs 214	John	Mre 49	James	Ptt 235
Eubanks, Daniel	Ons 149	John	Nwh 6	Keeten	Edg 197
see Ewbanks		John	Nrt 439	Nathaniel	Ons 162
Eure, Benjn.	Gts 266	John	Ons 171	Everhart, Chris-	
Blake	Gts 266	John	Prq 646	tian	Rwn 346
Charles	Gts 266	John	Rch 262	Everidge, Demsey	Cmd 101
David	Gts 265	John	Smp 536	Everit, Elisabeth	Rch 256
Dempsey	Brt 42	John	Rnd 311	Epaphroditus	Csw 126
John	Gts 266	John	Rwn 446	John	Ons 161
Levy	Gts 266	John	Wke 728	John	Wne 873
Mills	Gts 266	John	Wne 861	Lawrence	Rch 256
Samuel	Gts 265	John, Junr.	Ans 221	Martin	Cbr 708
Stephen	Gts 266	John, Senr.	Ans 221	Rheubin	Nwh 8A
Uriah	Gts 266	John, Ser.	Crr 146	Thomas	Rch 249
Whitmill	Gts 266	Jonathan	Nwh 11	Everitt, Elizabeth	Bfr 7
Evans, ...	Ptt 282	Joseph	Trl 678	Hugh	Bfr 7
Abram	Edg 198	Josiah	Cmb 370	James	Bfr 7
Absalom	Hrt 704	Josiah	Hrt 710	James	Rck 468
Alexander	Rbs 377	Lewis	Csw 122	Jeresiah	Wsh 704
Amos	Ptt 290	Lewis	Csw 130	Jesse	Wsh 702
Anthony	Grv 514	Lydia	Ptt 290	Jesse's Estate	Brt 42
ARchabald	Rbs 377	Margarett	Orn 561	John	Bfr 7
Aron	Cht 164	Mark	Cbr 679	John	Wsh 702
Azariah	Psq 637	Martha	Grv 563	Joseph	Ons 161
Banister	Nrt 437	Martha	Stk 551	Joseph	Wsh 702
Barnabas	Ash 78	Mede	Brt 42	Mary	Brt 42
Bartholemy	Psq 633	Morris	Wke 728	Micajah	Bfr 7
Benjamin	Grn 608	Morris	Wke 728	Nathaniel	Wsh 704
Benjamin	Hlf 306	Peter	Hrt 710	Robert	Bfr 7
Benjamin	Prq 645	Philimon	Cmb 379	Saml.	Csw 133
Benjamin, jr.	Hrt 710	Rebecca	Cht 218	Spooner	Ons 161
Burrel	Grv 524	Richard	Cht 205	Thomas	Wsh 704
Caleb	Bfr 22	Richard	Ptt 282	see Evitt	
Charles	Ans 199	Robert	Psq 641	Everitte, Jas.,	
Charles	Orn 505	Saml.	Csw 116	Junr.	Mrt 393
Clement	Cmb 390	Samuel	Dpl 421	Jas., Senr.	Mrt 393
Cornelius	Brt 42	Samuel	Ird 664	Mary	Mrt 393
Daniel	Grv 565	Samuel	Ons 174	Miles	Mrt 393
Daniel	Glf 684	Solomon	Rnd 311	Nathaniel	Mrt 416
Danl.	Csw 117	Stephen	Edg 198	Simon	Mrt 393
David	Jhn 758	Theophelus	Cmb 383	Turner	Mrt 393
David	Nwh 7	Thomas	Csw 116	Wm.	Mrt 393
David	Rwn 437	Thomas	Crv 339	Evers, Elizabeth	Rbs 377
Eden	Hrt 698	Thomas	Dpl 421	Issabella	Rbs 377
Edwd.	Nwh 11	Thomas	Hrt 697	James	Bld 37
Elisha	Csw 126	Thomas	Lnr 7	Eversol, Jacob	Ash 77

Everton, Elisabeth	Crv 267	Stephan	Mrt 393	see Full	
Ezekiel	Crv 279	Thomas	Wsh 704	Faller see Fuller	
Hannah	Crv 281	William	Wsh 704	Falls, Andrew	Lnc 838
John	Chw 114	Fagans, Lachlan	Cmb 354	George	Lnc 899
Leml.	Crr 147	Fagg, Joseph	Wrr 805	James	Lnc 895
Soloman	Crv 281	Faggot, Daniel	Cbr 692	Jms.	Lnc 838
Thomas	Srr 650	Jacob	Cbr 691	John	Ird 649
Thos.	Crr 146	Valentine	Cbr 707	John	Lnc 895
Every, Henry	Brk 745	Fagins, William	Nsh 101	Sarah	Lnc 838
Evines, John	Nsh 100	Fagon, John	Mre 56	William	Ird 649
Evins, Daniel	Stk 550	Richardson	Mre 50	Fanchard, Ryland	Crr 161
Jacob	Stk 577	William	Mre 59	Fancher, Cancey	
James	Stk 615	Faigan, William	Rnd 313	Hillery	Crr 154
James	Srr 650	Fail, Dickson	Jhn 774	Moses	Crr 156
James	Wrr 802	John	Jhn 777	Faneer, Henery	Crr 162
Jesse	Prs 214	Osborn	Jhn 776	Faniher see Fancher	
John	Crt 79	Fair, Michal	Stk 575	Fann, Mark	Orn 563
John	Rth 108	Fairbanks, Mary	Glf 655	Nancy	Orn 564
John	Stk 550	Faircloth, Allen	Smp 525	Fannan, Anne	Rbs 378
John	Stk 618	Benjamin	Cmb 369	Fanney, John	Gts 266
Joseph	Prq 662	Benjamin	Grn 612	Fanning, John	Crv 311
Owen	Stk 620	Benjamin	Smp 531	William	Rck 458
Sherwood	Nsh 100	Benjamin	Wne 871	Fannoy, Jean	Fnd 312
Walter	Prs 206	Caleb	Smp 519	Fanny, William	Hrt 698
William	Cmd 93	Frederick	Grn 612	Fanoher see Fancher	
Evit, James	Mnt 495	Hardy	Smp 531	Fansher, Moses	Crr 160
Evitt, John, Senr.	Bfr 7	John (2)	Smp 517	Fansler, Adam	Stk 552
Lot	Bfr 7	Jonathan	Grn 612	Faquason, John	Csw 98
Thomas	Bfr 7	Kinchin	Grn 611	Farbur, Hugh	Mck 595
see Everitt		Mary	Grn 616	Farchild, Abijah	Wlk 38
Ewart, Joseph	Mck 568	Newsom	Grn 592	Farchilds, Abi-	
Ewbanks, Eligah	Ons 139	Richard	Cmb 369	neser	Ash 78
Elisha	Ons 139	Samuel	Smp 518	Biud	Ash 78
Isaac	Ons 138	Smedia	Smp 519	Cyrus	Ash 78
John	Ons 138	Solomon	Smp 531	Fare, Jonathan	Bnc 168
Thomas	Ons 137	Thomas	Ans 226	Farecloth, Edward	Cmd 104
Zekiel	Ons 138	Thomas	Srr 652	FareCloth, Isaac	Cmd 104
see Eubanks		Fairfax, Micajah	Bld 16	Farel, Leah	Bfr 7
Ewel, Thomas	Rwn 325	Walter	Csw 146	Farenge, William	Psq 636
Ewell, Catey	Ptt 232	Fairlee, Alexander	Rch 254	Farguson, Alexander	Cbr 686
Conner	Ptt 231	Peter	Rch 254	Alexander	Glf 636
James	Ptt 290	Fairleigh, Archble	Rch 269	Elizabeth	Rwn 330
John	Ons 146	John	Rch 269	Isaac	Rwn 408
Thomas	Ons 147	Fairless, Charlton	Hrt 698	James	Ird 670
Ewins, Alexander	Mck 595	Lydia	Hrt 698	James	Lnc 895
Robert	Mck 595	Nicholas	Hrt 698	John	Lnc 895
Exium, Prissilla	Nsh 99	Willm., jr.	Hrt 698	Martha	Cbr 686
Exum, Etheldred	Edg 198	William, sen.	Hrt 698	Moses	Lnc 895
John	Edg 197	Zadok	Hrt 698	Robert	Lnc 895
John	Edg 198	Fairley, John	Brk 746	Robert	Lnc 899
Susanna	Edg 198	Robert	Rbs 379	Robert	Rwn 385
William	Edg 198	Fairly, John	Csw 111	Samuel	Cbr 686
Ezards, Betty	Rnd 311	Faison, Edward	Nrt 441	William	Rwn 352
Ezel, Frederick	Mck 580	Elish	Smp 512	Farley, Steward	Lnc 838
Ezell, Benjn.	Hrt 734	Harwood	Nrt 439	Farlow, George	Rnd 312
Frederick	Wke 729	Henry	Nrt 443	George	Rnd 313
Henry	Dpl 420	James	Smp 513	Isaac	Rnd 312
John	Hrt 720	James	Smp 514	Joseph	Rnd 312
Myel	Hlf 306	Rebecca	Nrt 439	Michael	Rnd 312
Reuben	Dpl 420	Thomas	Nrt 439	Nathan	Rnd 312
Sarah	Dpl 420	William	Nrt 443	William	Rnd 312
Ezzel, Archebald	Ans 215	Faithfull, William	Edg 173	Farly, Catharine	Csw 118
Ezzell, Jalem	Nrt 437	William	Edg 199	Danl. S.	Csw 110
		Falcon, John	Wrr 804	James	Csw 119
		Falconae, Moses	Orn 563	John J.	Csw 113
-- F --		Falconer, Eliza-		Farmer, Asael	Edg 199
		beth	Lnr 8	Benjamin	Edg 199
F..., ...	Ons 166	James	Lnr 6	Conrod	Orn 562
F...uffum, Will.	Nwh 10A	James, Jur.	Lnr 6	Danl.	Prs 218
Fabre, Peter	Crv 237	John	Glf 659	Elizabeth	Mnt 462
Faddis, John	Orn 491	John	Lnr 8	Felty	Orn 508
Fadloch, Sumner	Wne 854	Ollive	Lnr 8	Frederick	Rnd 313
Fagan, Daniel	Mnt 478	Faling, Agnes	Rck 44	Henry	Stk 552
Enoch	Wsh 704	Falkener, Bettey	Wrr 803	Isaac	Edg 199
Richard	Wsh 704	John	Wrr 803	James	Ans 231
Shadrach	Wsh 704	William	Wrr 784	James	Orn 563
		Fall, Christian	Glf 660	James	Rnd 313

James	Wlk 38	John	Dpl 412	see Wills	
Jenkins	Jhn 777	Will.	Nwh 9	Febbs, William	Glf 655
Jesse, Junr.	Edg 199	Farris, John	Cmb 354	Fedit, William	Wne 859
Jesse, Senr.	Edg 199	Nathan	Orn 563	Fedrick, John	Prs 187
John	Rnd 313	Shadrick	Orn 563	Feezer, George	Rwn 398
John	Rwn 379	Silas	Orn 564	John	Rwn 398
John	Rth 111	Stephen	Orn 563	see Critzfeezer	
John	Stk 586	William	Bfr 8	Feggs, John	Rch 261
John	Srr 707	Farrow, Christon	Crr 167	Feilds, Demsey	Bnc 169
Joseph	Brt 44	Christopher	Crr 168	George, Jur.	Rbs 379
Joseph	Edg 199	Edward	Crr 167	George, Ser.	Rbs 379
Joseph	Rnd 313	Elijah	Crr 166	Lewis	Bnc 169
Josiah	Grv 540	Ezekiah	Crr 166	Felaw, James	Wsh 704
Joshua	Edg 199	Farrow	Crr 166	Jesse	Trl 670
Moses	Rnd 312	Frances	Crr 166	John	Wsh 704
Nathan	Rnd 313	Francis	Crr 166	William	Wsh 704
Nathan	Rth 111	Fredrick	Gts 266	Felch, William	Orn 564
Nathan	Srr 704	Isaac	Crr 166	Felker, John	Rwn 312
Robert	Glf 651	Jacob	Crr 168	Michael	Lnc 854
Samuel	Edg 199	Jeremiah	Hde 368	Peter	Lnc 854
Samuel	Rth 111	John	Crr 166	Fell, Samuel	Crv 235
Sarah	Brt 44	John	Hde 368	Thomas	Brt 44
Thomas	Glf 651	Joseph	Crr 167	Fellers, Susanna	Smp 502
Thomas	Ird 629	Thos.	Crr 166	Fellet, Marey	Crr 142
Thomas	Stk 587	William	Rck 479	Fellett, Avery	Crr 148
Thomas	Wlk 38	Wm.	Csw 134	Leml.	Crr 147
Thomas, junr.	Wlk 39	Farwell, Rebeccah	Lnr 8	Thos.	Crr 149
Will.	Prs 206	Fason, Henry	Wke 731	Fellow, Robert	Wne 763
William	Brt 44	Jesse	Wke 731	Robert, Senr.	Wne 866
William	Jhn 751	Fate, James	Rck 484	Fellowes, Jonathan	Crv 243
Zilpah	Edg 199	Faucet, Robert	Grn 617	Fellows, John	Nwh 4A
Farney, John	Rnd 313	Faucett, Henry	Orn 494	Kesiah	Jhn 773
Farnol, Benjamin	Ons 149	James	Orn 564	Fells, John	Hrt 724
Mekegey	Ons 146	Thomas	Orn 490	Felman, Martha	Chw 115
Thomas	Ons 154	Faughan, John	Hrt 735	Felmuth, Theo-	
Farquhar, Jas.	Prs 203	William	Hrt 735	dorous	Rth 111
Farr, ...	Ons 166	Fauker, Ann	Crv 233	Felps, Amby	Csw 104
David	Cbr 682	Faulcon, Jesse	Hlf 306	Amos	Orn 563
John	Bnc 169	Faulk, Isaac	Rbs 378	Isaac	Rwn 415
John	Lnc 858	Jennet	Bld 13	John	Ird 626
John	Ons 155	Joel	Bld 13	John	Rwn 415
Joseph	Brk 746	John, Senr.	Bld 12	Littleton	Ird 626
Samuel	Mck 567	Richard	Bld 14	Obadiah	Csw 104
Samuel	Mck 568	Simon	Bld 13	Samuel	Rwn 415
Walter	Cbr 678	William	Bld 13	Thomas	Csw 104
Farra, John	Lnc 847	Faulkner, Sugar	Grv 580	Thomas	Csw 116
Nathaniel	Lnc 836	Thomas	Grv 548	Felton, Cabah	Chw 125
John	Prs 212	Fauly, David	Rwn 385	Elisha	Hrt 710
Joseph	Cht 153	Faurett, John	Hlf 308	James	Frn 459
Obadiah	Wke 730	Fausell see Fausett		Job	Edg 199
Will	Prs 206	Fauset, George	Orn 509	John	Chw 125
Farrel, William	Frn 471	Fausett, David	Orn 508	Leah	Chw 125
Farrell, Alsey	Frn 481	Deborah	Orn 508	Noah	Gts 266
Francis	Cht 155	Ralph	Orn 508	Thomas	Gts 266
James	Frn 454	Richard	Orn 564	William	Chw 125
John	Frn 468	Richard, Hon.	Orn 563	Felts, Aaron	Wlk 39
John	Lnc 875	Robert	Orn 508	Aaron, junr.	Wlk 39
Patty	Frn 487	Thomas	Orn 564	Caid	Frn 455
William	Csw 113	Faust, Charistiana	Glf 647	Cary	Wrr 803
William	Chw 113	Daniel	Orn 562	Elizabeth	Dpl 437
William	Wne 861	Peter	Orn 562	Grufferd	Wrr 804
Farrer, Clement	Cht 200	Peter	Rwn 276	Isham	Wrr 804
John	Cht 200	Peter	Rwn 287	James	Wrr 804
John	Cht 226	Faw, Samuel	Ird 642	Jesse	Nrt 443
Peter	Cht 207	Fawlin, Redman	Rck 468	John	Wke 731
Peter, Ser.	Cht 164	Fawn, William	Frn 488	John	Wlk 38
William	Cht 191	Zacha.	Cht 190	Nathl.	Wrr 804
Farres, Charles	Bnc 168	Faylor see Taylor		Nathl.	Wrr 805
Elizabeth	Orn 565	Fayne, Ann	Wrr 804	Roland	Wrr 804
Farrington, Abra-		Daniel	Wrr 804	William	Wrr 804
ham	Rwn 373	Joel	Wrr 804	William	Wlk 38
Benjamin	Orn 564	Feagurson, James	Edg 173	see Fitts	
John	Cht 190	Feamster, William	Ird 639	Fencher, Richard	Stk 552
John	Glf 684	Fearling, Benjamin	Stk 626	Fender, Bosten	Bnc 169
Samuel	Rwn 373	Featherston, Isaac	Lnc 834	Gabriel	Ash 78
William	Glf 680	Susanah	Lnc 833	Henry	Srr 652
Farrior, James	Nwh 8	Wm.	Prs 200	John	Ash 78

M.	Srr 708	Hezekiah	Wke 730	Samuel	Wlk 39
Nimrod	Ash 78	Jacob, Jr.	Jhn 764	William	Crv 327
Fenders, C.	Srr 708	James (2)	Wke 731	Fifer, Felton	Glf 648
Fennel, Frederick	Rwn 306	John	Crr 156	Henry	Rwn 332
Joseph	Orn 563	Micajah	Wke 730	Jacob	Lnc 902
Michael	Cmd 101	Solomon	Wke 730	Fig, James	Gts 266
Morris	Smp 536	Thomas	Cmd 101	Figgins, Gracey	Prs 215
Nicholas	Nwh 4A	Widow	Ans 206	Figgs, Joseph	Nrt 443
see ...nnel		William	Wke 731	Fight, George	Lnc 836
Fennell, Anne	Nrt 439	see Terrell		Figinwinder, Christo-	
James	Nrt 441	Ferril, Edey	Brk 747	pher	Rwn 330
John	Nrt 439	Gabriel	Mck 571	Figures, Elizabeth	Hrt 737
Fenner, Doctor	Frn 482	John	Ird 667	Martha	Hrt 735
Elizabeth	Lnc 861	William, Senr.	Mck 571	Richard	Hrt 734
Robert	Hlf 308	Ferrill, John	Mrt 393	Fike, John	Cht 187
Robert	Hlf 358	William	Mnt 500	Josiah	Prs 216
Fenners, Robert	Nrt 443	Ferroll, Thomas	Wrr 784	Tyre	Cht 170
Fenning, James	Crv 267	Fersher, Joseph	Cht 157	File, George	Cbr 715
Fenny, Charity	Ans 222	Fervile, Ben.	Stk 591	John	Cbr 717
Fenster, Sarah	Lnc 864	Fesinger, Ruthey	Ons 163	Philip	Cbr 718
Fenton, Joseph	Cht 162	Fesler, Peter	Stk 552	Files, James	Ons 174
Fentress, Pharoah	Rnd 313	Fesperman, Henry	Cbr 714	Filgaw, James	Ons 179
Ferbush, Aaron	Cmd 103	Michael	Cbr 714	Filgs, William	Jhn 762
Joshua	Cmd 103	Fessenden, Benja-		Filhour, Nicholas	Rwn 323
Ferckle see Fuckle		min	Wsh 714	Fillary, Thaddeus	Ans 199
Ferebee, George	Crr 139	Festerman, John	Rwn 345	Fillett, Saml.	Crr 150
Herney	Crr 144	Fetherston, Meri-		Fillingham, Enoch	Crv 269
Joseph	Crr 144	man	Bnc 168	Fillyaw, Cullen	Nwh 9A
Saml.	Crr 159	Fews, Lucretia	Bfr 8	Filpot, William	Ash 78
Thos.	Crr 157	Fich, Nathan	Mre 77	Finanon, William	Brk 746
Thos.	Crr 160	Fichpatrick, Hugh	Stk 614	Fincanen, Peter	Brk 747
Thos. C.	Crr 140	Fidler, Peter	Stk 602	Fincannon, John	Brk 747
Ferell, Paul	Wke 731	Field, Jesse	Glf 679	Finch, Adam	Cht 207
Fergeson, William	Crt 77	John	Stk 582	Allen	Nsh 100
Fergurson, Slocumb	Crv 295	Mills R.	Gts 266	Charity	Ans 222
see Feagurson		Nelson	Rck 474	Claborn	Nsh 100
Fergus, John	Bnc 169	Peter	Glf 679	Edward	Frn 456
Ferguson, Alexan-		Robert	Glf 620	Edward, Jur.	Frn 457
der	Bnc 158	Robert	Glf 621	Harry	Frn 450
Andw.	Lnc 837	Samuel	Stk 582	Henry	Wke 729
Heander	Brt 42	Fielder, Samuel	Orn 562	Isham	Nsh 100
James	Edg 199	see Fulder		John	Grv 530
James	Ird 675	Fielding, John	Ans 229	John	Ird 655
James	Wlk 39	Fields, Allen	Rck 487	John	Mck 561
Jeremiah	Bnc 168	Ansel	Rck 480	William	Grv 510
Jeremiah	Wlk 38	Aron	Ons 139	Fincher, Abraham	Mck 548
Jms.	Lnc 838	Benjamin	Glf 677	Benjamin	Mck 595
John	Bnc 169	Charity	Rnd 312	Benjamin	Rnd 312
John	Cmb 377	David	Cht 163	James	Mck 595
John	Cmb 379	Isaac	Srr 653	Jesse	Mck 596
John	Stk 553	Jacob	Ons 140	John	Mck 595
John	Wlk 38	James	Ons 139	John	Rnd 312
Joseph	Wlk 39	Jeremiah	Grn 616	Jonathan, Junr.	Mck 596
Mary	Crv 297	Jeremiah	Glf 677	Jonathan, Senr.	Mck 595
Richard	Crv 231	Jerremiah	Rnd 315	Joseph	Mck 595
Richard	Wlk 38	John	Lnc 847	William	Mck 595
Sarah	Lnc 838	John	Ptt 267	William	Rnd 312
Stephen	Stk 587	John	Rck 478	Finder, Christian	Lnc 875
Thos.	Lnc 837	Joseph	Rnd 312	Findle, Mary	Mnt 520
William	Mck 539	Martha	Grn 596	Findley, Alexr.	Lnc 830
Fergusson, Angus	Cmb 375	Mary	Lnr 8	Isabela	Lnc 830
Duncan	Dpl 399	Moses	Ons 139	James	Orn 563
John	Rch 260	Richard	Cht 178	Jms.	Lnc 830
Ferrand, William	Ons 135	Robert	Stk 620	John	Orn 563
Ferreby, Benjamin	Rwn 365	Samuel	Rnd 313	Thomas	Dpl 401
Ferree, Daniel	Rnd 312	Thomas, Esqr.	Wlk 38	Fine, John	Rwn 385
Ferrel, Charles	Ans 205	William	Glf 677	Finger, Catherin	Lnc 854
Jacob	Jhn 764	William	Nrt 443	Daniel	Lnc 814
James	Cmd 96	William	Rnd 313	Henry	Lnc 854
James	Nsh 100	William	Rnd 315	Jacob	Lnc 854
Samuel	Cmd 108	William	Rck 456	Fink, David	Cbr 690
Sarah	Ans 206	William	Srr 652	Frederick	Rwn 341
Ferrell, Anselum	Nsh 100	William	Wlk 37	George	Cbr 692
Christina	Wke 731	see ...lds, Feilds		John	Rwn 341
Cornelius	Rbs 379	Fife, Ebenezer	Crv 319	Finlason, Daniel	Cmb 363
Ephraim	Wke 729	John	Chw 115	John	Cmb 386
Henry	Csw 129	Joseph	Wlk 38	Finley, Andrew	Glf 632

Charles	Brk 746	Jonathan	Glf 664	Mansfield	Ptt 230
George	Glf 658	Jonathan	Glf 685	Samuel	Ans 200
Hugh	Orn 508	Joshua	Rth 110	Flammon, George	Rth 111
Jno.	Lnc 830	Lewis	Cbr 691	Flanacan, John	Ons 174
John	Glf 632	Littleton	Mnt 517	Flanagan, Eliza-	
John	Glf 647	Michael, Cap.	Rwn 379	beth	Ptt 265
John	Mck 571	Moleston	Glf 679	Philip	Lnc 813
Robert	Rth 110	Rerden	Rwn 431	William	Ans 230
William	Glf 632	Samuel	Crv 251	Flanegen, Dennis	Mck 579
William	Orn 507	Southy	Smp 519	Flangen, William	Mck 542
Finly, Charles	Brk 748	Spencer	Smp 526	Flanigan, Samuel	Mck 579
George	Glf 658	Paul	Mck 587	Flanigen, Charles	Mck 568
James	Glf 658	Richard	Lnc 860	David	Mck 543
Finn, Elizebeth	Prs 212	Thomas	Lnc 868	John	Mck 543
Gabriel	Prs 213	Thomas	Smp 519	Flanigun, John	Wlk 37
Finney, John	Mck 594	Thos.	Csw 130	Flanner, William	Nrt 441
John	Wke 730	William	Crt 82	Fleaming, Leonard	Wrr 803
Thomas	Hrt 735	William	Crr 141	Peter	Wrr 803
Thomas	Mck 603	William	Lnc 860	Peter, jr.	Wrr 803
Finnie, Robert	Nrt 441	William	Mck 587	Thomas	Wrr 804
William	Nrt 441	William, jr.	Crt 76	William	Wrr 803
Finny, Drury	Hlf 308	Fisherman see Fesperman		Fleetwood, Ashley	Brt 44
Finsley, Christn.	Ptt 252	Fiskus, Frederick	Stk 553	Edmund	Brt 42
Fintress, William	Rnd 313	Fistler, Andrew	Stk 552	Hardy	Brt 44
Fippitt, Jonathan	Grv 535	Fitch, John	Orn 507	Henry	Brt 44
Fipps, Benjamin	Glf 646	Thomas	Orn 507	James	Bfr 8
James	Glf 646	William	Orn 507	John	Brt 90
John	Brk 747	Fitchet, Michael	Bld 11	William	Brt 44
Fips, Ann	Glf 629	Fite, Conrod	Rwn 295	Flefestert, Fred-	
Aron	Glf 633	Henry	Cbr 692	erick	Lnc 872
Joseph	Glf 632	Henry	Rwn 295	Fleming, Agnes	Rck 438
Jourdon	Wlk 39	Peter	Rwn 295	Agnes	Rck 484
Fish, James	Jhn 768	Widow	Rwn 295	Alexander	Smp 503
John	Jhn 766	Fits, Jas.	Rck 446	Allen	Dpl 438
John	Lnc 875	Fitts, Conny	Rck 453	Benjamin	Ptt 231
William	Lnc 875	Henry	Wrr 804	Daniel	Lnc 847
Fishe, Nathan	Crv 319	Henry, jr.	Wrr 804	David	Ptt 230
William	Crv 317	Oliver	Wrr 805	George	Ptt 252
Willie	Crv 319	Susana	Rck 453	Henry	Grv 515
Fisher, Adam	Mck 605	see Felts		John	Ptt 230
Adam	Stk 603	Fitzgerald, David	Ird 667	John	Smp 503
Amy	Bld 32	John	Hlf 306	John	Srr 652
Anne	Rwn 295	John	Ird 667	Joseph	Rck 438
Baily	Smp 526	John, Junr.	Ird 667	Pleasant	Csw 131
Beritle T.	Trl 678	Peter	Srr 653	Robert	Wke 730
Betty	Crt 69	Thomas	Csw 102	Samuel	Orn 563
Bowlen	Stk 591	Thos.	Nwh 1A	Wm.	Csw 126
Bowlin	Stk 614	Fitzgerrald, Wil-		Wm.	Srr 709
Caleb	Rck 470	liam	Ird 620	see Fluming	
Charles	Mck 589	Fitzmire see Fizmire		Flemings, Charles	Edg 199
Edward	Hlf 358	Fitzpatrick, Mary	Rwn 277	William	Edg 199
Elijah	Cmb 369	Thos.	Wlk 38	Flemming, Abram	Brk 746
Ezekiel	Lnc 860	see Fichpatrick		Alison	Rwn 336
Frederick	Mck 587	Fitzpattrick, Ed-		Andrew	Hlf 358
Frederick	Rwn 306	ward	Rwn 325	Archibald	Lnc 860
George	Cbr 717	James	Lnc 814	John	Ird 649
George	Crr 143	Mary	Rwn 287	John	Ird 660
George	Crr 144	Fitzrandolph, Ben-		John	Rwn 320
George	Hde 368	ja.	Bld 28	Robert	Brk 746
George	Lnr 8	FitzWilliams see Williams		Samuel (2)	Ird 649
George	Mck 605	Fiveash, Dempsey	Rbs 378	Samuel	Ird 654
George	Rwn 306	Frederick	Hrt 735	Flemmon, Catherine	Cbr 681
George	Stk 604	John	Rbs 378	Mitchel	Cbr 682
George, Esq.	Rwn 306	Fizer, Peter	Stk 552	Flemmons, John	Cht 213
Jacob	Cbr 717	Fizmire, William	Brk 746	Flemon, David	Cht 214
Jacob	Rwn 295	Flack, Andrew	Glf 660	Flenton, John (2)	Orn 564
Jacob	Rwn 300	Andrew	Rth 110	Fler, Nicholas	Lnc 889
Jacob	Stk 603	Andrew	Rth 111	Fleshman, Perten-	
John	Crr 144	George	Rth 111	ent	Brk 747
John	Lnc 860	James	Glf 660	Fletcher, Edward	Frn 465
John	Lnc 902	James	Rtk 438	Elizabeth	Wlk 39
John	Mck 587	Jane	Glf 660	Elizabeth	Prs 204
John	Ons 170	John	Ird 639	Francis	Psq 636
John	Rwn 301	Michael	Ird 639	George	Cmb 354
John	Rwn 316	Polly	Rth 110	James	Brk 748
John	Rth 110	William	Rth 111	James	Rck 484
John	Smp 519	Flake, John,Senior	Ptt 230	James	Wne 849

James	Wlk 38	Jacob	Jhn 767	Oliver	Orn 564		
James, Esqr.	Wlk 38	Jacob, jr.	Cht 164	Usley	Rth 109		
James, Junr.	Rwn 361	Jacob, Sr.	Cht 200	Folforde, William	Crr 156		
James, Senr.	Rwn 361	James	Brn 13A	Folger, Latham	Stk 552		
Jesse	Prq 645	John	Ans 199	Folh, Peter	Stk 553		
John	Nsh 100	John	Rbs 378	Folk, Benjamin	Brt 44		
John	Psq 629	John	Rck 468	John	Brt 44		
John	Stk 604	John	Wne 856	John	Stk 596		
John	Srr 652	Simon	Rbs 378	John	Stk 613		
John	Wlk 38	Uriah	Bld 13	William	Cbr 708		
Joseph	Frn 465	William	Rbs 378	William	Hlf 308		
Joshua	Psq 633	William	Wne 853	Folkener, John	Frn 465		
Joshua	Prq 644	Floyd, Barthw.	Brn 20A	Folkner, Asa	Ans 227		
Leven	Grv 576	Elizabeth	Hrt 698	Francis	Ans 212		
Ralph	Wne 849	Francis	Rwn 398	Isaac	Srr 652		
Rubin	Brk 747	Caleb	Stk 581	Job	Ans 214		
Rubin	Ird 624	George	Grv 530	John	Srr 652		
William	Bnc 169	Griffin	Mrt 393	Jonathan	Ans 214		
William	Rwn 361	Griffus	Bfr 8	Joseph	Srr 652		
William	Srr 652	Grissom	Bfr 8	Nathan	Ans 214		
William	Wlk 37	Hukmon	Grv 535	Folks, John W.	Grn 587		
Flewellin see Fluellin		John	Bfr 8	Josiah	Ird 644		
Flibus, Archibald	Crv 335	John	Brt 44	Martha	Nrt 441		
Flight, Peter	Lnc 832	John	Rwn 385	Follis, William	Stk 553		
Fliming, Robert	Orn 507	John	Rwn 398	Folman, Phebe	Crv 243		
Flin, Daniel	Bld 6	Josiah	Mnt 501	Folsom, George	Cmb 375		
Delphy	Rth 111	Lee	Lnc 860	Israel	Cmb 379		
James	Brn 13A	Morris	Brn 20A	Thomas	Jhn 768		
John	Rth 109	Peter	Bfr 8	William	Dpl 424		
John	Rth 111	Randolph	Brt 44	William	Mre 64		
Mary	Bld 6	Stephen	Wlk 39	Wm. W.	Mre 40		
Flinn, Benjamin,		Thomas	Frn 485	Folth, Adam	Stk 553		
Ser.	Hde 368	William	Grv 535	see Folh, Foth			
Enoch	Hde 368	William, jr.	Grv 530	Foltz, Jacob	Stk 613		
John	Srr 653	Winny	Grv 561	John	Stk 599		
Joseph	Mck 557	Floyed, Halsey	Prq 654	John	Stk 603		
Linn	Srr 652	John	Chw 123	John	Stk 626		
Mary	Srr 653	William	Chw 123	Peter	Stk 601		
Rebekah	Hde 368	Fluellin, Archble.	Jhn 768	Fones, John	Mrt 393		
Thos.	Srr 707	Sarah	Jhn 768	Mary	Ptt 257		
Flint, David	Stk 552	Fluman, Julius	Wke 730	Thos.	Mrt 388		
Hastin	Stk 552	Fluming, Christian	Bld 23	Fontaine, Frances	Nwh 2		
John	Stk 552	Flury, Henry	Chw 113	Fonveille, Ann	Crv 271		
Martin	Stk 552	Fly, Enoch	Nrt 441	Brice	Ons 150		
Perry	Stk 552	John	Nrt 441	Hatcher	Ons 163		
Rhoderick	Stk 589	Margarett	Nrt 443	William B.	Crv 285		
Thomas	Orn 564	Foddery, William	Crt 81	Fonvielle, Jere-			
Thomas	Stk 552	Foddry, Thomas	Hde 368	miah	Crv 311		
William	Stk 552	Fogartie, Edm.,		John, Junr.	Crv 309		
Flinton, John	Orn 508	Estate	Bld 27	Lewis	Crv 311		
Flitcher, Stephen	Hde 368	Fogleman, David	Glf 627	Fonville, Fredrick	Crv 327		
Floid, Fedrick	Nsh 100	Henry	Orn 508	John, Senr.	Crv 307		
Margaret	Dpl 410	John	Orn 508	Richard	Crv 307		
Newel	Nsh 100	Maillicah	Orn 508	Fookes, Joseph	Crv 335		
Flood, Benjamin	Hlf 308	Melchor	Cbr 691	Foot, Geo.	Rck 449		
Enoch	Nsh 101	Michael	Orn 508	Henry	Wrr 804		
Jesse	Hlf 308	Peter	Orn 508	William	Srr 653		
Josiah	Hrt 710	Fogler, Christian	Stk 599	Forbes, Adam	Cmd 110		
Patty	Edg 199	Christopher	Stk 626	Arthur	Glf 645		
William	Hrt 710	Samuel	Stk 610	Arthur	Ptt 259		
William	Hrt 724	Foile, Peter	Rwn 373	Baley	Cmd 106		
Flora, Wingfred	Edg 199	Foiles, James	Ons 173	David	Rth 110		
Florance, Obe.	Csw 125	James, Senr.	Ons 173	Demsey	Cmd 104		
Florence, Obeh.	Csw 139	Foils, Jacob	Mck 595	Eliza	Glf 645		
Florey, Richd.	Crr 161	Fokes, Elizabeth	Bld 3	George	Glf 639		
Wm.	Crr 160	John	Bld 12	Henry	Ptt 267		
Floridy, Pattrick	Brk 749	Jonah	Bld 3	Hubh	Glf 634		
Flough, Thomas	Mck 575	Margaret	Bld 12	Isaac	Cmd 104		
Flow see Floid, Flower		Fokle see Fuckle		Isaac, Jun.	Cmd 105		
Flower, Benjamin	Nsh 100	Folar, Caleb	Crv 257	Jacob	Cmd 104		
Flowers, Christo-		Folbert, John	Glf 679	Jacob	Cmd 110		
pher	Crr 166	Folcanon, Hardy	Grv 531	James	Cmd 100		
Goldsbury	Bld 3	Folconer, Alexan-		James, Jun.	Cmd 110		
Hardee, Esqr.	Edg 199	der	Frn 447	James, Sen.	Cmd 110		
Henry	Brn 18A	Foley, Elisabeth	Crv 233	Jesse	Glf 632		
Henry	Wne 853	Flood	Bld 16	John	Ptt 277		
Humphrey	Wne 844	Jeremiah B.	Dpl 437	John, Jur.	Glf 645		

Name	Ref	Name	Ref	Name	Ref
Joshua	Crv 301	John	Rwn 424	Thomas	Rwn 431
Lemuel	Cmd 106	Joshua	Hde 367	Thomas, Sr.	Bnc 169
Malichi	Cmd 100	Michael	Bfr 8	William	Rwn 431
Malichi	Cmd 110	Prudence	Ptt 276	Forsyth, John	Brk 747
Richard	Crv 253	Rebecca	Crt 79	John	Ird 667
Saml. W.	Cmd 105	Russel	Crt 79	William	Orn 563
Sampson	Cmd 104	Thomas	Rwn 447	Forsythe, Benjamin	Stk 552
Sarey	Ptt 267	Foress, George	Wne 859	Benjamin	Stk 628
Thomas	Cmd 104	Forest, Edmond	Brk 746	James	Grv 576
William	Glf 632	Samuel	Grn 594	Fort, Benjamin	Wne 859
William	Rth 110	William	Grn 594	Elias	Nrt 443
Forbis, Jeremiah	Glf 632	Forester, Edward	Orn 564	Elizabeth	Edg 199
John, Senr.	Glf 632	James	Srr 652	Frederick	Wke 730
Forbison, Peter	Rth 111	John	Wlk 38	French	Wke 730
Forbs, Demsey	Crr 153	Forgason, Eli	Stk 553	George	Edg 199
Enoch	Crr 151	George	Rnd 312	Geralders	Edg 199
Jeams	Crr 149	John	Rnd 312	Jacob	Edg 199
Wm.	Crr 150	Nancy	Orn 562	James	Wke 730
Forchand, James	Dpl 439	Forgeson, John	Crt 67	John	Bld 44
Nehemiah	Dpl 438	Forguson, Alexan-		John	Wke 730
Ford, Absalom	Grv 578	der	Glf 686	John, Esquire	Rbs 378
Archd.	Lnc 836	Benjamin	Lnr 6	John, Junr.	Wke 730
Arthur C.	Brt 44	Joel	Wke 730	Lewis	Edg 199
C. Arthur	Brt 44	John	Rck 470	Nancy	Edg 200
Danl.	Lnc 833	Richard	Rnd 310	Patsey	Smp 505
David	Csw 119	Robert	Srr 652	Sherewood	Cmb 381
David	Csw 135	Forhand, John	Lnr 8	Sugar	Nrt 441
Elias	Hlf 308	Forist, Abram	Mnt 517	Thomas	Brk 748
Francis	Prs 198	Nathan	Mnt 517	Turner	Smp 508
Gabriel	Mck 554	Forister, Hezekiah	Srr 653	William	Wke 730
George	Mck 595	Fork see Fort		Winsor	Bld 44
George	Rch 244	Forker, George	Crr 163	Fortenberry, Eliza-	
Henry	Glf 675	Forkner, Ford	Ird 674	beth	Rth 111
Henry	Mck 533	Fornes, Thomas	Crv 321	James	Rth 109
James	Bld 7	Forney, Abraham	Lnc 860	John	Rth 110
Jno.	Lnc 830	Jacob	Brk 746	Fortescue, Elijah	Hde 367
John	Ans 240	Jacob	Lnc 847	John, Jur.	Hde 368
John	Ash 78	Peter	Lnc 847	John, Ser.	Hde 367
John	Brk 748	Forrest, John	Orn 600	Moses	Hde 368
John	Cbr 694	Shadrick	Orn 562	Richard	Hde 367
John	Hlf 308	Wm.	Csw 118	Simon	Hde 367
John (2)	Rwn 391	Forrester,Feilding	Wlk 38	William, Dumb	Hde 367
Larkin	Csw 103	John	Rth 109	William, Jur.	Hde 368
Nathan	Lnc 830	William., S.	Bnc 168	Fortesiue, Simon	Bfr 7
Rabeckah	Cbr 696	Forrifet, William	Cmd 106	Fortner, Dred	Wlk 37
Sally	Brk 749	Forrist, John	Mnt 517	Flood	Wlk 39
Susanna	Rwn 391	Forrister, John	Rwn 361	Keziah	Wlk 37
Teady	Lnc 830	John	Srr 653	Levi	Wlk 39
Thomas	Rch 245	William	Srr 653	Lewis	Srr 652
William	Chw 127	William	Wlk 38	Lewis	Srr 653
William	Rwn 391	Forshee, Elijah		Plesant	Srr 652
Wyatt	Rwn 424	(2)	Cht 157	Robert	Wne 857
Zebulon	Mck 604	Joseph	Cht 157	William	Brk 746
see Fort		Joseph	Cht 167	William	Rth 111
Fordham, Benjamin	Jns 817	Forsher, Simeon,Sr.	Cht 175	William	Srr 652
John	Jns 815	William	Cht 205	Fortune, Ezekiel	Brk 748
Fore, Francis	Rck 489	Forster, Benjn.	Bnc 168	Hanah	Mrt 393
Julius	Rck 488	David	Mck 583	Jesse	Brk 746
Forehand, Anthony	Psq 637	David	Rwn 320	John	Rth 110
Daniel	Cmd 95	David, Senr.	Rwn 321	Prudence	Brk 746
John	Cmd 102	Edison	Rwn 336	Prudence	Brk 747
John	Rnd 350	Henry	Lnc 854	Richard	Brk 747
Jordan	Cmd 96	Henry	Mck 576	Foscue, Arthur A.	Jns 785
Joseph	Hrt 698	Hezekiah	Rwn 424	Frederick	Jns 779
Lambert	Cmd 96	John	Mck 588	Luke	Crv 337
Lemuel	Hrt 698	John	Rwn 431	Richard	Jns 803
Solomon	Edg 199	John, Senr.	Rwn 432	Simon, Senr.	Jns 783
Thomas	Chw 129	Joseph	Rwn 316	Fosgashar, William	Lnc 900
Wm.	Wne 848	Mark (2)	Bnc 168	Foshe, John	Prs 216
Wm.	Wne 849	Richard	Rwn 316	Foshee, Drucilla	Cht 200
see Fourhand		Robert	Rwn 320	John	Cht 158
Foreman, Benjamin	Hlf 308	Robert	Rwn 424	Joseph, Senr.	Cht 165
Benjamin	Hde 368	Robert	Rwn 431	Simeon	Cht 165
Elizabeth	Hde 368	Samuel	Lnc 814	see Forshee	
George	Edg 200	Samuel	Rwn 325	Fossett, Edward	Orn 507
James	Crt 80	Thomas	Bnc 169	Henry	Orn 507
John	Ptt 276	Thomas (2)	Brk 748	James	Orn 507

John	Hlf 308	Founton, Jonathan	Crr 149	James, Junr.	Brk 749
Lydda	Hlf 308	Fourhand, David	Edg 199	John	Brk 748
Mary	Hlf 306	see Forehand, Forhand		John	Cht 167
Mary	Hlf 308	Fourkom, Thomas	Rwn 442	John	Cht 216
Robert	Orn 507	Fouse, Christian	Cht 219	John	Mck 540
Robert, Junr.,		Foust, David	Rwn 408	John	Rwn 457
JG	Orn 507	Jacob	Rnd 313	Joseph	Mnt 482
William (2)	Orn 507	John	Rnd 313	Lance	Mnt 517
Foste, George	Orn 508	William	Rnd 313	Leonard	Rnd 310
Foster, Anthony	Srr 653	see Faust		Michael	Rnd 310
Anthony	Wlk 39	Fouster see Forester		Moses	Ons 172
Arthur, Jun.	Hrt 698	Foute see Fouts		Nathan	Brk 747
Asa	Orn 563	Fouts, Andrew	Ash 78	Nicholas	Cht 172
Asay	Frn 491	Andrew	Rnd 310	Palser	Lnc 854
Asey	Wrr 804	Daniel	Rnd 315	Samuel	Brk 747
Christopher	Frn 472	David	Ash 78	Samuel	Stk 553
Christopher	Nrt 443	David (2)	Rnd 312	Thomas	Cmb 390
Edward	Rth 111	David	Rwn 347	Thomas	Rnd 312
Elkin	Rth 110	Elizabeth	Rnd 312	Thomas	Rwn 352
Francis	Cht 195	Frederick	Rnd 313	William	Brk 748
Francis	Prq 649	Henry	Rnd 310	William	Nrt 443
George	Wlk 37	Jacob	Rnd 312	William	Rnd 310
Haskew	Rth 110	Jacob	Rnd 315	Wm., E.	Prs 215
Henry C.	Wrr 803	John	Rnd 310	Zenith	Wrr 804
James	Glf 676	John (2)	Rnd 312	Foxhall, Anne	Edg 200
James	Rwn 431	John	Rnd 315	Foy, Andrew	Stk 586
Jno.	Csw 122	John	Rwn 353	Anne M.	Jns 801
Joel	Gts 266	Lewis	Cbr 712	Barbary	Rwn 330
Joel	Rck 491	Michael	Rnd 312	Enoch	Jns 801
John	Frn 445	Peter	Ash 78	Frederick	Crv 341
John	Grv 563	Peter	Rwn 353	James	Nwh 8A
John	Rck 485	Fowlar, Mark	Orn 562	James	Ons 170
John	Rth 110	Fowler, Abraham	Rth 110	Thomas	Bfr 22
John	Rth 111	Ann	Wke 731	Fraeley, George,	
John	Trl 678	Ashley	Orn 564	Junr.	Rwn 403
John	Wrr 803	Batt	Wke 729	Fraezier, Alexan-	
John	Wlk 37	Bullard	Wke 729	der	Nsh 100
John, Ser.	Frn 473	Bullard	Wke 731	Frager, James	Bnc 169
Josh.	Psq 636	Cloey	Grn 609	Frailey, George	Rwn 295
Lewis	Csw 141	David	Wke 729	Jacob, Junr.	Rwn 295
Richard	Wke 730	Edmond	Frn 474	Jacob, Senr.	Rwn 295
Robert	Wlk 37	Esther	Bfr 7	Fraizer, Benjamin	Rnd 313
Sarah	Orn 508	George	Edg 200	David	Rnd 313
Thomas	Csw 141	John	Frn 491	Ellender	Crt 91
Thomas	Wlk 38	John	Grv 529	George (2)	Rnd 313
William	Cmd 105	John	Smp 532	James	Rnd 313
William	Hlf 308	John	Wke 731	Jonathan	Rnd 312
William	Ons 182	John	Wrr 803	Samuel	Rnd 313
William	Wsh 704	Joseph	Rch 245	Solomon	Rnd 312
Wm.	Mrt 393	Joseph	Wke 729	Fraley see Fraeley	
Wm.	Psq 628	Pleasant	Wrr 784	Frame, James	Wrr 804
Foten, Samuel	Glf 658	Richard	Grv 581	France, David	Rth 110
Foth, John	Stk 553	Richard	Rth 109	Edward	Rth 111
Joseph	Stk 553	Samuel	Stk 552	Elizabeth	Stk 553
see Folth		William	Grv 537	John	Stk 553
Fotherly, Stephen	Bfr 7	William	Wke 731	Joseph	Rth 111
Fouch, John	Rth 111	William, Junr.	Wke 731	William	Wlk 38
Jonathan	Rth 111	William, Senr.	Wke 729	Frances, Mary	Stk 553
William	Rth 111	Wm.	Rck 441	Francis, Charles	
Fouler, Danl.	Brn 20	see Fouler		(2)	Ash 78
David	Mnt 490	Fox, Abraham	Lnc 854	Mathew	Wlk 38
Ferriby	Brk 748	Allin	Brk 747	Thomas	Trl 670
Rabeckah	Rwn 381	Barny	Cht 172	see Agness	
Will.	Brn 20	Benjn.	Bnc 169	Francom, David	Brk 748
Foulk, Phillip	Brn 19	David	Cht 215	Joseph	Brk 748
Sherwood	Brn 18	Elijah	Brk 747	William	Brk 748
Fountain, Frances	Psq 635	Francis	Wlk 37	Francy, William	Stk 552
Henry	Dpl 414	Gatuss	Wlk 37	Frank, Frederick	Cbr 698
James	Edg 199	George	Cht 217	Frederick	Rwn 341
Joab	Dpl 412	Hugh, Junr.	Brk 749	Frederick	Rwn 345
John	Edg 200	Isam	Frn 456	Jacob	Rwn 341
Mary	Dpl 412	Jacob	Cht 172	John	Rwn 398
Mary	Edg 199	Jacob	Frn 456	Martin	Rwn 398
Nathan	Dpl 416	Jacob	Lnc 814	Tho.	Brn 19A
Samuel	Glf 629	James	Brk 747	William	Rwn 408
Solomon	Edg 200	James	Brk 749	William, Junr.	Rwn 398
Stephen	Stk 552	James	Ird 629	William, Senr.	Rwn 398

Name	Loc	Name	Loc	Name	Loc
Frankcom, Joshua	Brn 16	William	Bnc 169	Jesse	Hrt 698
Franklin, Barnard	Srr 653	William	Grv 546	Jesse	Ird 630
Betey	Ans 214	William	Grv 550	Jesse	Jns 785
Ephriam	Rth 110	William	Rth 110	John	Bld 28
Henry	Rth 110	William	Stk 615	John	Grn 605
James	Srr 653	William	Srr 652	John	Wke 730
Jesse	Srr 652	Frazier, Daniel	Mnt 463	Joseph	Frn 482
John (2)	Brk 746	James	Jns 805	Joseph	Gts 266
John	Rth 111	John	Wsh 704	Joshua	Brt 44
John	Srr 653	Joseph	Mck 570	Joshua	Ird 629
John	Wlk 39	Richard	Wsh 704	Josiah	Edg 199
Jonas	Gts 266	Urbane	Jns 805	Keziah	Wsh 704
Jonathan	Brk 747	Frederick, Felix	Dpl 431	Kinchen	Frn 489
Laurence	Ans 226	Weatherington	Lnr 8	Lewis	Cht 166
Lewis	Rnd 313	William	Dpl 400	Lukey	Bld 27
Mal	Srr 653	Fredrick, Eliza-		Malone	Rth 111
Margaret	Nrt 441	beth	Mnt 509	Martha	Brt 44
Mary	Bnc 168	see Fedrick		Mary	Rwn 431
Mary	Rth 110	Free, Andrew	Brk 748	Michael	Mck 528
Moses	Brk 747	Moses	Brk 747	Moses (2)	Brt 44
Noah	Nrt 441	Freear, Richard W.	Nrt 441	Moses	Ird 629
Shadrack	Srr 653	Freebody, Rebecca	Crv 297	Nathan	Nrt 441
Walter	Srr 653	Freedle, Casper	Rwn 353	Needham	Wke 729
William	Wke 730	Casper	Rwn 398	Patsey	Grv 564
Franks, Ann	Jns 789	John	Rwn 347	Patsey	Wke 730
Anthony	Wke 730	Freeland, Andrew	Ird 670	Patty	Grv 558
Edward	Jns 789	John	Brn 17	Peter	Brk 749
Henry	Rth 110	John	Orn 564	Richardson	Grv 557
Joseph	Wke 730	Joseph	Orn 562	Robert	Wrr 803
Lewis	Wke 730	Freeling, Henry	Rwn 424	Roger	Brn 14
Peter	Rth 110	Freeman, Aanderson	Grv 544	Roland	Frn 453
William	Cht 174	Aaron	Srr 653	Rubin	Mck 531
Fransaw, Abraham	Stk 572	Aaron	Ird 610	Rusell	Mnt 517
John	Stk 611	Aaron	Ird 630	Sally	Lnr 8
Rosina	Stk 599	Abram	Brn 13A	Sally	Lnr 35
Franum, Wm.	Rck 448	Agness	Rwn 408	Saml.	Brn 13A
Fraser, Henry	Mnt 469	Allin	Mck 574	Samuel	Orn 564
James	Dpl 411	Andrew	Cbr 696	Sarah (2)	Brt 44
James	Hrt 717	Aron	Brt 44	Sarah	Orn 563
John	Rwn 330	Benjamin	Rbs 379	Thomas	Wke 729
John	Rwn 385	Benjamin	Rth 110	Timothy	Gts 266
Simon	Mnt 462	Benjm., S.	Rbs 378	William	Brt 44
Widow	Mck 551	Charles	Brt 44	William	Frn 470
William	Cbr 702	Charles	Cbr 696	see Fruman	
Frasor, Alexander	Mnt 462	Clabour	Grv 573	Freemas, Jesse	Rth 111
Phebe	Ons 138	Daniel	Grv 565	Freemon, Elizabeth	Srr 652
Frater, David	Bfr 7	Daniel	Orn 562	John	Stk 552
Frazell, John	Ons 155	David	Mck 529	John	Stk 575
Frazer, Abraham	Srr 653	Douglas	Rth 110	Joshua	Srr 652
Alexander	Rth 110	Edmund	Grv 573	Robert	Srr 704
Alexr.	Wne 858	Edward	Ans 205	Rubin	Mre 47
Aron	Glf 683	Edward	Frn 454	William	Srr 652
Arthur, Capt.	Grv 576	Elisebeth	Ons 137	Freeson, John	Mnt 486
Barnett	Grv 582	Elisha	Jns 787	Freeze, Henry	Rwn 341
Charles	Srr 652	Evan	Grv 584	Jacob, Junr.	Rwn 336
David	Glf 677	Faithy	Rth 110	Jacob, Senr.	Rwn 336
Ephraim	Grv 582	Francis	Lnr 8	John, Junr.	Rwn 340
Francis	Glf 624	Gideon	Ans 209	John, Senr.	Rwn 344
Isaac	Glf 624	Gideon	Grv 571	Peeter, (Long)	Rwn 344
James	Glf 624	Hardy	Brk 44	Peter, Senr.	Rwn 344
James	Srr 652	Henry	Frn 461	Peter, (Short)	Rwn 344
James	Wne 857	Henry	Frn 490	Samuel	Rwn 341
Jeremiah	Grv 542	Henry	Wke 730	French, John	Srr 652
Jeremiah	Grv 546	Howell	Cht 209	William	Ons 152
John	Glf 624	Jacob	Brt 44	William	Stk 552
John	Glf 678	Jacob	Rbs 379	William	Stk 575
Joshua	Rth 110	James	Brt 44	Frene, King	Rch 268
Mary	Grv 550	James	Bld 8	Frensler, Phillip	Stk 603
Matthew	Glf 625	James (2)	Brn 13A	Freo, John D.	Crv 235
Robert	Grv 543	James	Frn 486	Freon, John	Crt 75
Robert	Stk 620	James	Gts 266	Freshwater, Thad-	
Samuel	Stk 621	James	Mck 528	deus	Psq 635
Sarah	Grv 547	James	Orn 508	William	Orn 563
Sarah	Wne 858	James	Stk 553	Freshwaters, Thom-	
Shadreck	Grv 539	James	Wsh 704	as	Ons 144
Stephen	Grv 549	Jeptha	Wke 730	Fretwell, William	Rck 445
Thomas	Srr 652	Jeresiah	Brt 44	Friar, Willice	Brt 44

83

Frick, Henry	Rwn 306	William	Glf 638	Isaih	Prs 196
Jacob	Rwn 307	Fuckle, Ann	Stk 603	Jacob	Prs 197
Mathias	Rwn 306	Fuget, Esom	Wlk 38	Jas.	Prs 203
Fricker, Valentine	Ird 618	Randol	Bnc 169	John	Prs 205
Friday, Andrew	Lnc 842	Reubin	Bnc 169	John, Senr.	Grv 532
James	Lnc 814	Fugler, Richard	Mrt 393	Jonathan	Grv 530
Martin	Lnc 814	Fulbright, Jacob	Lnc 875	Jones	Frn 485
Frier, Daniel	Rth 110	John	Lnc 875	Jones	Grv 531
Fries, John	Crv 339	William	Lnc 875	Margaret	Rbs 378
Frilick, Mary	Crv 235	Fulcher, Ephraim	Crv 291	Moses	Crt 75
Frishley, William	Rwn 385	Henary	Prs 206	Moses	Csw 119
Frishly, Abraham	Rwn 385	Jesse	Crt 67	Nathan	Crt 76
Frissel, John	Brk 748	John	Grv 576	Patsey	Dpl 417
Frits, George	Rwn 347	Joseph	Crt 57	Peter	Prs 209
Frizell, William	Lnc 875	Joseph	Crv 259	Richd. C.	Prs 205
Frizzle, Daniel	Mrt 393	Levi	Crv 287	Robert	Nrt 443
Jonathan	Crv 329	Thomas, jr.	Crt 57	Samuel	Grv 532
Frohock, Alexander	Rwn 403	Thomas, sr.	Crt 57	Scion	Nrt 443
John	Ird 654	Fulchire, Cason	Crv 305	Solomon	Hde 368
Fronebarger, Jacob	Lnc 814	Church	Crv 323	Washington	Grv 530
John	Lnc 814	Fulder, Saml.	Rck 451	Will.	Prs 200
William	Lnc 814	Wm.	Rck 451	Will.	Prs 211
Frorey, Curry	Ird 649	Fulenwider, Henry	Rwn 306	Will.	Prs 217
Frost, Ebenezer	Rwn 457	John	Lnc 814	William	Grv 533
James	Csw 119	Fulford, Abigail	Crt 69	Wm.	Csw 119
James	Jhn 770	Absalom	Crt 69	Fullerton, Andrew	Bfr 8
James	Jns 783	Benjamin	Hde 368	Peter	Bfr 22
Jonas	Rck 481	Daniel	Crr 161	Thomas	Ird 629
Miller	Jns 783	James	Crt 70	Fullford, John,	
Peter	Crt 57	John, junior	Ptt 244	Senior	Ptt 289
Robert	Lnc 814	Joseph	Crt 69	Joseph	Ptt 259
William	Rwn 457	Joseph	Crt 74	Fullington, James	Csw 110
see Snow		Obadiah	Crt 69	John	Chw 119
Fruit, James	Rnd 313	Sarah	Crv 249	Fulmore, Andrew	Rbs 378
John	Rnd 313	Stephen	Crt 69	Fulmwider, John	Rwn 304
Fruman, John	Orn 508	Stephen, jr.	Crt 69	Fulp, Michal	Stk 575
see Freeman		William	Crt 69	Peter	Stk 575
Fry, Daniel	Rwn 379	Fulforde, Daniel	Crr 156	Fulton, David	Orn 507
David	Rwn 415	Fulgham, Elias	Nrt 443	Francis	Stk 552
George	Lnc 867	Matthew	Nrt 441	James	Orn 564
George	Mre 52	Matthew	Wke 730	Jessee	Orn 508
George	Rwn 415	Michael	Nrt 443	Robert	Stk 558
Henry	Rwn 398	Fulghum, Jacob	Wne 849	Samuel	Glf 658
Henry	Stk 553	Fulgum, Arther	Wne 853	Samuel	Glf 659
Jacob	Lnc 868	Benj.	Wne 852	Samuel	Orn 507
Jacob	Lnc 871	John	Hlf 306	Thomas	Orn 563
James	Mnt 517	John	Wne 873	Fultz, Frederick	Rwn 373
James	Mre 43	Winney	Wne 853	Henry	Rwn 287
John	Stk 553	Fulham, Mary	Cbr 681	Peter	Rwn 287
John	Stk 583	Fulks, Charles	Lnc 889	Fulweder see Fulmwider	
John	Stk 597	Full, Christian	Glf 665	Fulwood, John	Ons 163
John	Stk 605	Fullar, Willson	Ons 136	William	Brk 748
Joseph	Mre 57	Fullenton, Adam	Brk 748	Fum.Vill, Jeremiah	Nwh 8A
Joseph	Rwn 415	Fuller, Alexander	Ird 674	Fuqua, William	Cht 208
Michael	Stk 553	Ann	Brn 15	Fuquire, Will.	Prs 209
Nathan	Mre 59	Ann	Nwh 1A	Furchies, Tobius	Rwn 457
Nicholas	Lnc 902	Archable	Rnd 313	Furer, Henry	Cbr 697
Peter	Lnc 902	Arther	Frn 457	John, Junr.	Cbr 692
Peter	Rwn 415	Barnaba	Nwh 4A	Paul	Cbr 691
Philip	Lnc 868	Bartholemew	Frn 459	Furfree, William	Chw 125
Philip	Lnc 890	Bathsheba	Crt 77	Furgason see Forgason	
Thomas	Mre 58	Benjamin	Grv 532	Furges, John	Nwh 8
Vincen	Rwn 353	Benjamin	Rnd 315	Furgeson, Margreat	Nwh 3A
Volentine	Stk 553	Britain	Grv 561	Furgesson, William	Frn 491
William	Mnt 517	Britten	Rnd 313	Furgher, William	Lnc 854
William	Mre 51	Britten, J.	Rnd 315	Furguson, Angus	Rbs 378
Fryar, John	Smp 535	Crafford	Grv 572	Duncan	Rbs 378
Jonathan	Smp 515	Crawford	Lnr 8	James	Rbs 379
William	Hrt 724	Darling	Rnd 315	John, Jur.	Rbs 378
William	Smp 535	David	Grv 558	John, S.	Rbs 379
Fryer, Henry	Glf 621	Ellimore	Csw 118	Malcom	Rbs 378
Isaac	Gts 266	Ezekel	Grv 528	Neill	Rbs 378
Isaac	Glf 638	Ezekiel	Rnd 310	Furloinsurlines,	
Isaac	Glf 666	Ezekiel, junr.	Grv 562	Abm.	Csw 117
John	Nrt 441	Henry	Csw 118	Furlow, David	Crv 231
Mary	Edg 199	Henry	Grv 532	Furnwell, Richard	Cbr 677
Thomas	Gts 266	Isaac	Prs 204	Furr, Leonard	Mre 48

Name	Ref
Furrer, John	Cbr 691
Fury, Martha	Csw 133
Fushire, Benjamin	Crv 291
Fussel, Benjamin	Dpl 420
Elizabeth	Dpl 409
John	Grv 518
Fussell, Aaron	Wrr 803
Futch, Jacob	Bld 45
John	Nwh 8A
Martin	Dpl 432
Futcher, William	Crv 231
Futral, Lawrence	Wne 851
Futrel, Danl.	Nwh 8A
Tho.	Nwh 8A
Futrell, Arthur	Nrt 441
Benjamin	Nrt 441
Daniel	Edg 199
David	Nrt 441
Demcey, Junr.	Nrt 441
Demcey, Senr.	Nrt 441
Elizabeth	Nrt 441
Elliott	Nrt 441
Ephraim	Nrt 439
Henry	Nrt 441
Jehu	Nrt 439
John, (Captain)	Nrt 439
John, Senr.	Nrt 441
Nathan, Junr.	Nrt 441
Nathan, Senr.	Nrt 439
Sampson	Nrt 441
Sander	Nrt 441
Sarah	Nrt 441
Shadrach	Nrt 441
William	Nrt 441
Futril, Matthew	Orn 563
Futsil, Moor	Dpl 412
Fuzer see Feezer	
Fuzzell, John	Ptt 286
Fuzzle, Moses	Orn 564
Wyate	Orn 564
Fyke, John	Cht 162

-- G --

Name	Ref
G..., William	Lnr 9
G...ns, John	Ptt 285
John R.	Mck 564
Gabie, John M.	Nwh 3
Gable, Thomas	Bnc 170
Gabrial, Benjamin	Crt 79
Gabriel, Jacob	Lnc 861
James	Crt 79
Gadberry, Nathaniel	Rwn 408
Gaddis, Alex	Orn 565
Archable	Rnd 314
Archibald	Rwn 385
Israel	Orn 565
Jacob	Rnd 314
James	Orn 566
James (2)	Rnd 316
John	Orn 565
Mary	Rth 112
Randal	Rth 112
Thomas	Rth 112
Gadds, Joseph, Senr.	Rch 265
William	Rch 265
Gaddy, Fredrick	Ans 211
Ithamer	Rbs 379
Jerry	Ans 211
Jerry	Ans 211
Thomas	Ans 211
Thomas, Jr.	Ans 239
Thomas, Senr.	Ans 211
William	Ans 240
Gaffen, John	Hlf 310
William	Hlf 310
Gafing, William	Stk 607
Gag see Gage	
Gage, Jacob	Rth 112
James	Brk 749
James (2)	Rth 112
Lucy	Rth 112
Reuben	Rth 112
William	Brk 750
Gaglard, Benjamin	Bfr 8
Gail, Sarah	Cmd 107
Gailer, James	Cbr 684
see Gasler	
Gainer, Henry	Nsh 101
Jesse	Edg 201
Johnothan	Edg 201
Martha	Crv 247
Polley	Mrt 394
Thomas	Hlf 310
William	Nsh 101
Gaines, James	Cht 187
Moses	Hlf 308
Gainey, Jacob	Smp 524
Gains, Kesiah	Crv 323
Rebecca	Brt 90
Richard	Stk 583
Richd.	Wlk 40
Thomas	Stk 592
William	Mck 548
Gainy, Abraham	Smp 504
Bartholomew	Smp 503
Noel	Smp 503
William	Smp 504
Galbraith, Daniel	Cmb 382
David	Cmb 370
Duncan	Cmb 384
John	Cmb 382
John	Cmb 384
John	Cmb 385
Neill	Cmb 383
Nevin	Cmb 386
Peter	Cmb 370
Torquill	Cmb 384
Galbreath, James	Bnc 170
Lachlan	Cmb 363
Gale, Christopher	
H.	Hrt 698
Christr., Sen.	Hrt 698
Isaac	Hrt 699
William	Hlf 310
Gales, Richd.	Csw 104
Galimore, John	Rnd 315
Gallaway, Nathl.	Brn 17A
Neel	Brn 16
Rachel	Glf 642
Sarah	Brn 16
William	Bfr 8
Galleway, James	Rwn 345
Gallimore, Asel	Rnd 315
Elisha	Rwn 386
James (2)	Rwn 386
John	Cbr 703
John	Rwn 386
William	Rwn 386
William, Jur.	Rwn 386
William, Senr.	Rwn 386
Gallin, Jesse	Rnd 315
Gallion, Thomas	Srr 657
Galliway, Charles	Rwn 457
Thomas	Cht 171
Thomas	Mck 572
Galloher, William	Csw 118
Gallop, Ann	Chw 113
Anthoney	Crr 147
Enoch	Cmd 103
Isaac	Cmd 103
Isaac	Cmd 110
Jones	Crr 147
Joshua	Cmd 104
Josiah	Cmd 103
Peter	Crr 150
Shadrick	Crr 148
Solomon	Cmd 105
Willes	Crr 147
Galloway, Elizabeth	Rck 484
Henry	Ptt 243
James	Grn 593
Job	Bld 5
Noah	Ptt 249
Robert	Rck 484
Thomas	Ird 668
Gallyon, Amos	Srr 709
Jacob	Srr 709
John	Srr 709
Saml.	Srr 709
Galteney, Nathan	Lnc 855
Gamache, John B.	Brn 18
Gamarn, William	Ptt 272
Gambal, James	Glf 620
John	Glf 623
Mary	Glf 623
William	Glf 632
Gambald, John	Stk 598
Gambell, Jesse	Wlk 41
John	Wlk 41
John, junr.	Wlk 41
Martin	Ash 79
William	Ash 79
Gambled, Joseph	Stk 598
Gambley, Joshua	Cmd 94
Gambold, John	Stk 625
Joseph	Stk 625
Gamborille, James	Prq 649
Gamey, Jno.	Lnc 841
Gammon, Isaiah	Stk 554
James	Hlf 310
Jesse	Hlf 308
Jno. Gordon	Brn 13
Joshua	Hlf 308
Gamud, Mehernel	Crr 150
Gamuell, Joshua	Crr 148
Gamwell, Jeams	Crr 148
Gandy, Amos	Nsh 101
Edward	Nsh 101
Gane, Westley	Stk 591
Ganey, James	Brn 14
Micajah	Rch 258
Stephen	Brn 14
Gann, Saml.	Rck 487
Gannon, Mark	Glf 631
William	Glf 631
Gans? George	Rwn 312
Gant, Charles	Frn 489
James	Glf 659
John	Mck 548
John	Orn 510
John	Stk 592
John, Junior	Orn 510
Widow	Mck 589
William	Frn 476
see Ghant	
Gapin, William	Orn 510
Gappins, Stephen	Orn 565
Gapton, Abner	Frn 465
Garden, Charles	Glf 690
Gardener, Jesse	Ptt 241
Mary	Ptt 247
Sebra	Ptt 241
Gardenor, Jacob	Lnc 824
Robert	Mck 572
William	Cbr 681
Gardin, John	Mck 594

Name	Code	Name	Code	Name	Code
Gardiner, James		Garmer, Walter	Csw 141	Elizebeth	Crr 162
(2)		Garmon, George	Cbr 696	Enoch	Bfr 8
Jason	Brt 46	John	Cbr 695	Jacob	Brt 44
Mary	Edg 202	Michael	Cbr 695	Jacob	Cmd 110
Marttha	Edg 202	Garnard, John	Lnr 11	James	Bfr 8
William	Brt 46	Garnen, John	Rnd 315	James	Cmd 107
William	Edg 201	Garner, Book	Wke 732	Jeams	Crr 163
Gardner, Brasilla	Glf 682	Bradly	Mre 48	Jemima	Trl 688
Dinah	Edg 201	Daniel	Hrt 711	Jesse	Brt 44
Edward	Ptt 249	Daniel	Rth 113	John	Bnc 169
Edward, Son of		Elisha	Jhn 759	John	Cmd 110
Jesse	Ptt 248	Francis, jr.	Crt 83	John	Crr 148
Eliab	Glf 681	Francis, sr.	Crt 82	John	Wsh 704
Elias	Bld 41	Gideon	Hrt 711	Joseph	Gts 267
George	Nsh 102	Henry	Rnd 315	Joseph	Wsh 704
Hardy	Mrt 395	Henry	Rwn 399	Lenonton	Grn 589
Henry	Chw 114	James	Rnd 315	Richard	Chw 116
Isaac	Glf 674	James	Rth 114	Sarah	Wsh 704
Isaac, Junr.	Mrt 395	Jesse	Rnd 314	Severen	Chw 125
Isaac, Senr.	Mrt 395	John	Cmb 375	Thomas	Brt 46
Jacob	Srr 656	John	Mnt 484	Thomas	Ptt 287
James	Bld 40	John	Nrt 445	Thos.	Crr 148
Jas.	Mrt 395	John	Stk 554	Welcomb	Srr 705
Jeremiah	Lnc 847	John	Srr 656	William	Bnc 171
John	Bld 41	Joseph	Wke 732	William	Rnd 314
John	Csw 141	Lucy	Crt 85	William	Wsh 704
John	Csw 144	Nancy	Lnr 9	Garrette, David	Hrt 711
John	Mrt 395	Needham (2)	Dpl 435	Garrick, Mary	Cmb 374
John	Orn 509	Randolph	Hrt 735	Garriner, Andrew	Glf 688
John	Rwn 442	Sabea	Edg 173	Garris, Alcy	Lnr 9
Jonathan	Glf 674	Sabra	Edg 201	John	Grn 592
Josiah	Hlf 308	Samuel	Crt 85	Joshua	Wne 870
Leticia	Bfr 22	Samuel	Cht 199	Patience	Wke 732
Richard	Glf 677	Samuel	Nrt 445	Thomas	Hrt 729
Richd.	Mrt 416	Shubel	Rnd 316	William	Dpl 404
Saml.	Mrt 395	Simeon	Dpl 435	Garrish, Elizabeth	Crt 59
Stephen	Glf 682	Thomas	Rth 113	Garrison, Absalom	Bnc 169
Stephen	Glf 692	Thomas	Rth 115	Adinih.	Nwh 11A
Susanah	Mrt 416	Wiley	Lnr 8	Comfort	Bnc 170
Sylvanius	Glf 692	William	Crt 82	Ebenezar	Dpl 411
Thaddius	Glf 690	William	Cht 199	Garrott	Orn 509
Thomas	Hlf 310	William	Jhn 759	George	Orn 509
Thomas	Wrr 806	William	Mre 47	Henry	Brk 751
thos.	Mrt 395	William	Nrt 445	Jacob	Orn 509
Valentine	Grv 566	William	Rth 114	James	Brk 753
William	Crv 289	William	Stk 615	John	Mck 550
William	Glf 690	William, jr.	Crt 85	Levy	Rck 447
William	Srr 656	Willis	Jhn 759	Moses	Rck 445
William T.	Jns 801	Willis	Wne 846	Richd.	Rth 114
Wm., Senr.	Mrt 416	Garnett, John	Lnc 851	Samuel	Rck 474
see Garden		Garnor, John	Mre 59	Solomon	Stk 554
Gardnor, Benjamin	Rwn 457	Lewis	Mre 59	Thomas	Dpl 437
David	Rwn 408	Mary	Csw 141	Thomas	Rwn 353
George	Lnc 854	Garrall, Abram	Nwh 5	William	Bnc 170
James	Rwn 312	Garratt, James	Rbs 381	Garriss, Henry	Nrt 445
John	Lnc 855	Garrawood, Jacob	Rwn 431	James	Nrt 443
John	Mck 571	Thomas	Rwn 431	Joseph	Nrt 445
John	Rwn 287	Garregus, Ann	Hlf 308	Joshua	Wne 845
John	Rwn 386	Garrel, James	Dpl 417	Garrit, Botar	Stk 554
John	Rwn 437	John	Jhn 751	Edmund	Rth 113
Mathias	Rwn 312	John	Jhn 758	Mary	Rwn 408
Philip	Rwn 386	Garrell, ...y	Ptt 243	William	Rth 113
Philip, Junr.	Rwn 391	Charles	Bfr 8	Garritt, John	Rwn 408
Robert	Rwn 287	Thomas	Jhn 754	Garron, Andrew	Rwn 353
William	Rwn 344	Garren, Garge	Rnd 314	James	Rwn 353
Garganus, Mary	Dpl 424	Jacob	Rnd 314	Garrot, Green	Wrr 805
Garish, Benjamin	Brk 749	John	Rnd 353	Nicholas	Mnt 483
Garison, Aron	Rck 443	Garret, Ebenezer	Crt 84	William	Wrr 805
Garland, John	Wne 871	James	Ans 230	Garrott, Ann	Grv 565
John, Senior	Grn 611	John	Edg 203	Henry	Orn 510
Kinchin	Grn 611	Margaret	Edg 203	Henry	Rck 482
Zilpah	Hrt 720	Garrett, Amos	Ptt 287	Jacob	Orn 566
Garlin, Jacob	Lnc 876	Benjamin	Bfr 8	Jesse	Grv 563
Garlington, Wm.	Mrt 394	Bradley	Wsh 704	John	Orn 566
Garman, Charles	Wlk 41	Daniel	Wsh 704	Milly	Orn 566
Nancey	Ons 157	David	Brt 44	Thomas	Wke 732
Garmany, Hugh	Bnc 171			William	Grv 531

William	Ons 156	Burges	Ird 634	Jonathan	Rnd 316
Garrotte, Thos.	Mrt 395	Eli	Ird 634	Judy	Frn 487
Garsett, Mary	Chw 115	Jeromiah	Ird 635	Lueresa	Frn 481
Gartner, Jacob	Lnc 902	Jeromiah	Ird 667	Mary	Edg 202
Jacob, Senr.	Lnc 902	John	Rwn 447	Nancy	Rbs 381
John	Lnc 902	John	Ird 634	Richard	Edg 201
Martin	Lnc 902	John, Senr.	Ird 634	Richard	Grn 589
William, Senior	Ptt 284	Nicholas	Rwn 457	Richard, Junr.	Edg 202
see Guartner		Walter	Rwn 457	Robert	Rwn 277
Garven, Hugh	Rnd 314	Zachius	Ird 634	Robert	Rwn 287
Garvey, Patrick	Cmd 109	Gathings, Charles	Ans 212	Solomon	Nrt 445
Garvis, Semu.	Ons 159	Philip, Junr.	Ans 212	Thomas	Frn 471
Garvy, Thomas	Dpl 425	Philip, Senr.	Ans 212	William	Edg 203
Gary, George	Ons 138	Gatinton, James	Cmd 103	Willis	Nrt 443
John	Hlf 308	Gatlin, Bryan	Crv 281	Zerobabel	Edg 202
William	Hlf 310	David	Crv 261	Gaylard, Hosea	Bfr 8
Gasaway, Nicholas	Rwn 410	Enoch	Crv 263	James	Hde 369
Gascoins, David,		Hardy	Crv 327	Jeremiah	Hde 369
Junr.	Brt 46	James	Crv 307	John	Hde 381
David, Senr.	Brt 46	John	Lnr 35	Mary	Hde 368
John	Brt 46	John	Crv 281	Rebekah	Hde 369
Gash, John	Bnc 169	John, Senr.	Crv 283	William	Hde 368
Joseph D.	Bnc 169	Sarah	Crv 283	Gear, David	Rth 114
Martin	Bnc 169	William	Crv 285	Solomon	Rth 114
Martin, Sr.	Bnc 169	Gatling, Arthur	Hrt 735	Gearin, David	Rck 444
Gasiway, John	Rwn 336	David	Hrt 735	Gearous, Federick	Ons 167
Gaskil, Jacob	Hde 368	Edward	Edg 201	Geddie, James	Cmb 385
Gaskill, James	Crt 57	Edward	Hrt 735	James, jr.	Cmb 385
John	Crt 58	Ferriba	Hrt 720	Gee, Charles	Nrt 443
Thomas	Crt 58	George	Gts 267	George	Cht 166
Gaskins, Abram	Crt 62	James	Gts 267	James	Cmb 393
Adam	Crv 273	James	Hrt 731	James	Hlf 310
Adam	Hde 368	Jethro	Hrt 720	Joseph	Crr 165
Benjamin	Crt 63	Miles	Gts 267	Nevil	Hlf 310
Delilah	Crt 62	Patrick	Hrt 737	Sarah	Nwh 11
Fisher	Crv 285	William	Edg 202	Geer, Cyrus	Nwh 2A
Harmon	Crv 279	William	Nrt 445	Frederick	Wke 732
James	Crv 281	William, Jr.	Gts 267	Gilbert	Nwh 1
James	Hlf 310	William, Senr.	Gts 267	John	Wlk 40
James, Senr.	Crv 281	Gattey, Nancey	Prs 217	Geler, Robert	Grv 521
John	Crt 58	Rachel	Prs 217	Gell, John	Wrr 805
John	Crv 279	Gattin see Gatlin		Gellam, Mason	Cht 172
John, jr.	Crt 59	Gatton, Hezekiah	Ird 634	William	Cht 173
Joseph	Crt 63	Gatts, John	Nrt 445	Gellespie, David	Brk 752
Nathaniel	Lnc 834	Gause, Bryan	Brn 20	Gellom, Drury	Rwn 353
Redden	Crv 281	Charles	Brn 14A	Hincha	Prq 644
Sarah	Chw 115	John (2)	Brn 18	John	Rwn 353
Thos.	Lnc 834	Nedom	Brn 18A	Gelmer, John	Glf 633
Thos.	Psq 636	Samuel	Bld 31	Gelsbreath, John	Orn 510
William	Crv 283	Will. (2)	Brn 18	Genkins, John	Rch 257
Williams	Crt 62	Gaut, Richard	Orn 509	William	Rch 257
Wm.	Psq 636	Gautier, J. R.,		Gennett, Abram	Trl 678
Zipporah	Crv 279	Esqr.	Bld 32	Hezekiah	Trl 670
Zorobabel	Hde 368	Mr.	Bld 32	Joseph	Trl 688
see Askins		Peter W.	Bld 25	Gentery, Athe	Srr 657
Gasler, Philip	Lnc 814	T. N., Esqr.	Bld 28	Richard	Srr 656
Gasper, Richard	Rwn 400	Gauvey, David	Lnc 902	Gentle, George	Rwn 442
Gass, Shearmon	Wke 732	Jacob	Lnc 902	John	Rwn 442
Gaster, Henery	Mre 65	Joseph	Lnc 902	Samuel	Rwn 442
Gaston, William	Crv 245	Gaven, Charles	Smp 511	Gentrey, Shadrack	Prs 195
Gatchey, Henry	Cbr 715	James	Bfr 22	Gentry, Allen	Srr 656
Michael	Cbr 715	Lewis	Smp 512	Clayburn	Stk 609
Gateley, Joseph	Rch 265	Samuel	Smp 525	John	Srr 655
Gater, Samuel	Edg 201	Gawf, Hugh	Wke 776	Jonathan	Srr 656
Gates, David	Srr 655	Sterling	Wke 731	Joseph	Srr 657
Edward	Bld 35	Gawin, Richard	Bld 39	Mashack	Srr 655
John	Bld 35	Gay, Charles	Hrt 731	Matthew	Srr 657
Joseph	Wke 776	Dempsey	Edg 202	Nicholass	Srr 656
Philip	Rck 484	Elias	Nrt 445	Samuel	Srr 657
Widow	Rwn 325	Henry (3)	Edg 202	Shelton	Srr 657
see Cates		Henry	Nrt 443	Simon	Srr 656
Gatewood, Gabriel	Mnt 511	James	Hrt 731	Watson	Rck 487
Griffin	Ans 212	Jesse	Nrt 445	William	Srr 656
Gather, Barsil	Ird 634	John	Edg 201	Georg, Old	Crr 165
Barsil	Ird 668	John	Edg 202	George, Abner	Wke 731
Barsil, Esqr.	Rwn 457	John, Senr.	Edg 202	Celia	Edg 201
Benjamin	Rwn 451	Jonathan	Nrt 445	David	Jhn 774

Name	Loc	Name	Loc	Name	Loc
David	Lnr 9	John	Mck 597	James	Glf 639
David	Orn 567	Gibble, Dedrick	Hde 368	Jinnings	Orn 565
Deborah	Chw 115	Frederick	Crt 79	Joel	Ash 78
Isaac	Stk 593	Gibbons see McGibbons		John	Csw 122
James	Stk 594	Gibbs, Bathsheba	Dpl 425	John	Glf 663
Jesse	Dpl 422	Benjaman, Ters.	Hde 369	John	Ird 616
Jesse	Stk 593	Benjamin	Crv 327	John	Ird 634
Jesse	Wke 731	Benjamin, Jur.	Hde 369	John	Mck 602
John	Edg 203	Benjamin, Ser.	Hde 369	John	Mnt 470
Mary	Cht 199	Casen	Hde 368	John	Ons 169
Mary	Chw 115	Cassandra	Hde 369	John	Rnd 314
Mary	Rbs 380	Catharine	Hlf 310	John	Rnd 315
Michael	Edg 201	Daniel	Hde 368	John	Rnd 316
Moreus	Wrr 784	Elisha	Dpl 428	John	Rck 437
Presley	Stk 554	Henry	Hde 369	Joseph	Brk 753
Richard	Stk 554	James (2)	Rth 113	Joseph	Rck 459
Samuel	Stk 589	Jesse	Brn 15A	Joseph	Rwn 337
Solomon	Wke 731	Jesse	Hde 369	Mary	Brk 753
Sukman	Brk 792	Jesse	Rth 113	Moses	Mnt 469
Thomas	Rch 266	John (2)	Dpl 428	Nathan	Brk 753
William	Cht 213	John, Jur.	Hde 369	Nelson	Rch 242
William	Jns 803	John, Ser.	Hde 369	Nimrod	Rch 264
William	Wke 731	Joseph, Jur.	Hde 369	Pricilla	Rck 447
Gepson, David	Crr 139	Joseph, Ser.	Hde 369	Robert	Brk 753
Jacob	Crr 139	Nathaniel	Bfr 22	Robert	Stk 555
Rebekah	Crr 138	Peter	Wrr 805	Robert	Stk 590
Gerald, Jacob	Nwh 7A	Rebecca	Brn 16A	Samuel	Trl 684
Mary	Nwh 7A	Richard	Brk 752	Stephen	Brk 753
Gerard, Burchet	Crr 148	Robert	Brn 13A	Stephen	Crv 243
Elizabeth	Edg 201	Robert	Hde 368	Stephen	Mnt 478
Germain, Nancy	Hde 368	Samuel, Jur.	Hde 369	Stephen	Rnd 315
German, Henry	Orn 567	Samuel, Ser.	Hde 368	Thomas	Rnd 315
John	Ans 240	Selby	Hde 369	Thomas	Rch 264
John	Jns 787	Stephen	Wke 732	Thomas	Rch 270
John, Senr.	Jns 789	Thomas	Smp 504	Thos.	Lnc 831
Mary	Ptt 226	Thomas, Jur.(2)	Hde 369	Volitame	Stk 554
Rachel	Jns 787	Thomas, Ser.	Hde 368	Walter	Ans 222
Reubin	Jns 789	Thomas, Ters.	Hde 368	Widow	Mck 524
Robert	Ans 214	Uriah	Hde 369	William	Brk 752
William	Jns 815	Visia	Crt 78	William	Cmb 366
Gerney, Luke	Rch 269	Washington	Hde 368	William	Ird 670
Gernigan, Joseph	Jhn 776	William	Brn 15A	William	Mnt 469
Lewis	Jhn 777	William	Lnc 876	William	Ons 156
William	Ans 199	William	Wrr 805	William	Orn 565
Gerock, Samuel	Crv 341	William, Jur.	Hde 369	William	Rch 262
Gerral, William	Glf 676	William, Senr.	Hde 368	William	Rch 268
Gerrard, Alexander	Bfr 22	Willis	Smp 504	William	Stk 554
George	Bfr 8	Gibbson, Archable	Ons 137	William	Srr 655
Gerrile, John	Cmd 106	Thomas (2)	Ons 139	see Guibson	
Gest, Joseph	Cmb 362	William (2)	Ons 139	Giddens, John	Wne 856
Gethings, John	Ans 229	Gibirt, Silas	Ptt 233	Moses	Bfr 8
Gettey, Jno.	Prs 201	Giboney, Nicholas	Mck 522	Giddings, Abram	Ons 168
Gettys, William	Rth 112	Gibs, Jiles	Crr 146	Giddins, Gilbert	Wlk 41
Gewin, Asa	Ans 236	John	Frn 474	Giddons, Benjn.	Nwh 6
Cristopher	Ans 200	Raborn	Frn 474	Jacob	Nwh 6
Hardy	Ans 238	Richard	Grn 603	Tho.	Nwh 6
John	Ans 200	Gibson, Abner	Rck 459	Tho.	Nwh 6A
Kedar	Ans 236	Andrew	Ash 79	Gideon, Edward	Wlk 40
Ghant, Henry	Lnc 884	Andrew	Glf 639	Edward	Wlk 41
John	Lnc 875	Archd.	Ash 78	Lewis	Wlk 51
Gheen, Elisabeth	Rwn 345	Benjamin	Csw 96	Margret	Wlk 40
James	Rwn 330	Benjan.	Csw 145	Rueben	Wlk 41
Joseph	Rwn 330	Bidy	Rck 462	Gier, Philip	Brk 751
Thomas	Rwn 330	Charles	Nrt 445	Giffin, Levy	Orn 510
Gherkins, Benjamin,		David	Lnc 842	Gifford, Unis	Glf 690
Jur.	Bfr 8	David	Orn 510	William	Glf 690
Benjm., Senr.	Bfr 8	David	Rnd 314	Gift, Nicholas	Glf 662
Jeremiah	Bfr 8	Elijah	Ons 140	Giger, Adam	Stk 619
Gholsberry, Igna-		Ezekel	Stk 554	John	Stk 555
tious	Frn 490	Ezekiel	Ash 78	Peter	Brk 751
Gholson, John	Frn 490	George	Mck 530	Gilaspie, Robert	Wrr 784
Gibart, Conrod	Lnc 814	George	Rnd 314	Gilbard, William	Crt 56
Gibbens, Francis	Mck 580	George	Rwn 337	Gilbert, Abraham	Smp 502
John	Crr 148	Gilbert	Rnd 314	Alexander	Rth 93
Gibbins, George	Dpl 397	Gilbert	Rch 242	Benjamin	Cmd 110
James	Rwn 391	Gilbert, Sr.	Rch 242	Benjn.	Mre 77
John	Dpl 431	Isaac	Jns 805	Elenear	Rbs 380

Name	Ref	Name	Ref	Name	Ref
Elijah	Brk 752	Joseph	Frn 447	Rebecca	Ans 209
James	Brk 750	Mary	Brt 46	Gillis, Archd.	Mre 55
James	Cmd 103	Robert	Frn 493	Archibald	Cmb 362
James	Cmd 108	Robert	Prs 192	Benjamin	Hde 369
James (2)	Cmb 376	Thomas	Brt 46	Daniel	Mre 44
James	Hlf 310	William	Grv 583	Daniel	Mre 55
Jeremiah	Psq 624	Gillam, Drury	Frn 477	Daniel	Rch 244
Jesse	Jns 813	Ephraim	Frn 489	Danl.	Bld 33
Jesse	Mnt 508	Joshua	Frn 453	Danull	Mnt 462
John	Brk 749	Joshua	Frn 458	John	Cmb 389
John	Cmd 103	Mangard	Brk 750	John	Mnt 470
John	Crr 137	Marcus	Frn 476	John	Rbs 381
John	Mnt 508	Moses	Brt 46	Murdock	Rbs 381
John	Ptt 276	Samson	Frn 488	Neill	Rbs 381
John	Smp 500	William	Frn 457	Norman	Rbs 381
John, Junr.	Jns 813	William	Frn 477	Gillispie, David	Bld 27
John, Senr.	Jns 813	Gillands, Richard	Srr 655	Gillom, Conrod	Rwn 287
Joseph	Jns 815	Gillaspie, Daniel	Glf 634	Gillon, Widow	Mck 590
Joseph	Prq 642	Daniel	Glf 641	Gillum, David	Glf 660
Joseph	Prq 663	James	Csw 126	Edmund	Glf 660
Joshua	Cht 223	James	Glf 634	Harbert	Grv 555
Josiah	Psq 625	James S.	Glf 653	Harris	Wke 731
Mary	Rbs 381	John	Bnc 170	John	Mre 47
Matthew	Hlf 310	John	Bnc 171	John, Ser.	Mre 49
Michael	Brk 750	John	Glf 642	Joshua	Grv 564
Nathan	Nsh 101	John	Rbs 381	William	Grv 520
Nicholas	Wsh 704	Robert	Bnc 170	William	Wlk 41
Robert	Jns 813	Silas	Bnc 169	Gilly, Charles	Ash 79
Sampson	Mnt 509	Widow	Bnc 170	Gilman, John	Dpl 421
Sebley	Cht 223	Gillchrist, Allen	Hlf 358	Gilmer, Joseph	Glf 633
William	Prq 646	gillekin, Ann	Mrt 394	Gilmon, Herbert	Jhn 756
William	Rbs 380	Gilleland, James	Glf 688	Gilmore, Archebald	Cbr 682
Wilson	Cht 223	John	Rck 466	Daniel	Rth 114
Wm.	Crr 151	Rebecca	Lnc 838	John	Cbr 681
see Gibirt		Robert	Rck 466	Pattrick	Mck 563
gilberte, Jas.	Mrt 394	Thomas	Lnc 860	Robert	Glf 647
John	Mrt 395	Gillem, Conrod	Rwn 277	Samuel	Cht 165
Lucy	Mrt 394	Gillespie, Alexan-		Stephen	Cmb 367
Wm.	Mrt 395	der	Mck 566	Thomas	Mre 44
Gilbreath, John	Glf 638	Alexander	Rwn 321	William	Mck 563
John	Glf 644	Charles	Mck 591	Gilmour, William	Hlf 310
Robert	Glf 634	David	Rwn 321	William	Hlf 358
Thomas	Rwn 341	Duncan	Smp 523	Gilreath, Alexr.	Wlk 40
Gilchrist, Anguest	Rch 262	Henry	Brk 753	John	Wlk 40
John	Glf 671	Isaac	Rwn 321	William (2)	Wlk 40
John	Mre 60	James	Dpl 400	Gilson, David	Orn 566
John	Rbs 381	Robert	Rwn 321	Wilburn	Brk 751
Malcolm	Mre 43	Saml.	Lnc 834	Gilstrap, Benjamin	Rwn 403
William	Glf 667	Thomas	Rwn 321	Bright	Rwn 403
William	Rbs 381	Thomas, Senr.	Rwn 321	Hardy	Dpl 402
Giles, Charity	Jhn 768	William	Ird 648	James	Orn 510
Henry	Rwn 277	Gillet, Philaney	Jns 807	Lewis	Dpl 402
Henry	Rwn 287	Rachel	Rth 112	Richard	Rwn 403
Jeremiah	Rth 112	Gillett, Thomas	Jns 805	Widow	Rwn 403
John	Bnc 171	Gilliam, Anne	Nrt 445	Gimbler, Barnibas	Rwn 347
John	Brk 750	Ephraditus	Bnc 170	Gimnilion, Absalam	Jhn 774
John	Jns 791	Wyatt	Nrt 447	Ginger, Henry	Brk 751
Meadow	Bnc 170	Gillian, Widow	Ans 222	Ginins, William	Stk 582
Richard	Brk 752	Gillican, Alexan-		Ginking, Henry	Nwh 2
Wi...m	Nwh 2	der	Crt 71	Ginn, Elisha	Edg 202
William	Bnc 170	Alexander, jr.	Crt 71	Ginnings, Anthony	Srr 655
William	Jhn 771	Arnnon	Crt 69	John	Srr 657
William	Rck 469	Charles	Crt 73	Gintle, Leddy	Rwn 437
Gilespie, James	Mck 566	Eanoch	Crt 71	Ginwright, Elias	Brn 18A
Gilford, Jacob	Crr 160	Elizabeth	Crt 73	Gipson, Henery	Crr 142
Surrey	Ptt 240	George	Crt 71	Lemule C.	Orn 509
Gilgo, Sarah	Crt 70	James	Crt 71	Peter	Crr 140
Gilky, Robert	Rth 114	Jesse	Crt 71	Robert	Crr 140
Gill, Allin	Ird 618	Joseph	Cht 182	Thomas	Edg 201
Catharine	Crv 249	Mary	Crt 71	Thos.	Crr 142
David	Ird 610	Thomas	Crt 71	William	Stk 590
Francis	Wrr 805	William	Crt 71	Giren, Simeon	Rnd 315
Isaac	Wke 732	Gilliham, Abraham	Rwn 316	Girkin, John	Wsh 704
James	Hlf 310	Gilliland, Aaron	Mck 568	Zachariah	Wsh 704
James	Orn 509	John	Mck 567	Girkins, Charles	Ptt 249
Jesse	Wke 732	Samuel	Mck 570	Girtin, Robert	Rnd 314
John	Crv 253	Gillion, Burrel	Orn 509	Gisborn, Thomas	Wne 864

Githings, George	Ans 222	Will.	Prs 201	Godly, Elias	Bfr 8
Gittel see Gillet		William	Orn 567	Joseph	Bfr 8
Given, Josiah	Smp 517	see Glinn		Robert	Bfr 8
Givens, Obediah	Rnd 315	Glinn, Thompson	Srr 656	Thomas	Bfr 8
William	Brk 753	Glisson, Daniel	Dpl 404	Godsey, William	Rck 437
William	Mck 596	Isaac	Mrt 395	godward, Ellender	Mrt 394
see G...ns		Jas.	Mrt 395	Fredrick	Mrt 394
Gladden, Aaron	Lnc 896	John	Dpl 440	george	Mrt 394
George	Crt 82	John	Mrt 394	Godwin, Alexr.	Brn 16A
Jarret	Bnc 170	Michael	Dpl 440	Aron	Jhn 776
Joseph	Lnc 896	Sarah	Mrt 395	Barnaby	Hrt 711
Moses	Lnc 899	Thomas	Hrt 724	David	Bld 16
Gladish, William	Nrt 443	Gloster, Thomas	Wrr 806	Edmond	Jhn 759
Gladson, Dempsey	Bfr 8	Glover, Abraham	Grv 515	Ephraim	Jhn 752
Gladston, Nathan	Glf 656	Daniel	Grv 512	George	Hrt 711
Glan, James	Ons 179	Darwald	Wrr 806	Isam	Brn 16A
Thomas	Ons 179	Frances	Nrt 447	James	Hrt 704
Glanden, Joshua	Rwn 353	Henry	Wrr 806	Jesse	Bld 15
Major	Edg 203	Hezekiah	Cbr 700	Jonas	Brn 20
Mary	Rwn 353	John	Nsh 101	Jonas	Brn 19A
Glandon, James	Rwn 365	John	Nrt 445	Mary	Ans 199
Glantz, Charles	Lnc 842	Jones	Nrt 445	Nathan	Rnd 314
Jeromiah	Mck 574	Joseph	Wke 732	Pearce	Bld 14
Glascock, Daniel	Grv 552	Nathaniel	Hlf 308	Peggy	Jns 809
Feling	Rwn 451	Pate	Cht 186	Reddick	Bld 15
Peter	Rwn 451	Person	Edg 201	Saml., Senr.	Jhn 752
William	Rwn 425	Ransom	Grv 515	Samuel	Hrt 711
Glascow, William	Grv 571	Silvey	Nsh 101	Samuel	Jhn 752
Cabb	Psq 631	Thomas	Grv 534	Stephen	Bld 14
James, junr.	Grn 616	Thomas	Nsh 101	Theophelus	Jhn 759
James, Senr.	Grn 616	Thomas	Nrt 447	Goelet, John	Wsh 704
Lemuel	Psq 630	William	Cbr 702	Goff, Frances	Bnc 170
Thos.	Crr 162	William	Nrt 443	Gates	Bld 9
Wm.	Crr 162	William	Rbs 381	James	Glf 654
Gloson, Josiah	Glf 628	Goach, David	Csw 129	John	Dpl 420
Glass, Alexander	Brk 751	Thomas	Csw 105	John, Sr.	Dpl 406
Daniel	Cht 219	William	Csw 106	Samuel	Dpl 404
George	Glf 631	Goald, John B.	Wlk 39	Thomas	Dpl 406
George	Rwn 307	Goat, Michael	Wlk 41	Thomas	Ptt 277
Henry	Brk 749	Gobble, Corbin	Ird 630	William	Dpl 406
James	Brk 749	Cornelius	Lnc 886	William	Ptt 282
Josiah	Cht 221	Jacob	Rwn 408	see Poff	
Mary	Cht 185	John	Lnc 876	Goffigon, Eliza-	
Powel	Glf 631	John	Rwn 408	beth	Crt 83
Robert	Mck 576	Gober, John	Grv 560	Goforth, Ezekiel	Rth 114
Thomas	Brk 749	John	Wrr 805	Preston	Lnc 896
Ulcan	Glf 631	Martha	Grv 560	Thomas	Wlk 40
William	Cht 179	Mary	Grv 560	William	Mck 548
Glasscock, Patsay	Mre 76	Godden, Alise	Smp 499	Gogg, William	Grv 575
Glassnore, George	Bnc 171	Jacob	Smp 499	Goile, Nicholas	Csw 125
Glasson, James	Cht 190	James	Smp 495	Goin, Allen	Prs 218
Sally	Cht 190	Nathen	Smp 495	Edward	Prs 196
Glaze, Alexander	Rwn 447	Richard	Smp 494	Godrich	Prs 209
Glemps, George	Grv 570	Solomon	Smp 504	Hennery	Mre 60
Glendening, Wm.	Wke 776	William	Smp 497	John	Rbs 379
Glenn, Abram	Rck 466	Goddes, Thomas	Csw 128	Levy	Mre 62
Beverly	Prs 188	Goddin, Ezekiel	Trl 688	Oliva	Rbs 381
Charles	Prs 187	Selbey	Trl 678	Samuel	Brk 751
David	Orn 566	William	Jhn 771	Susanna	Prs 205
David	Orn 567	Godebb, Abraham	Ans 241	William	Mnt 469
Gideon, Jur.	Frn 476	Godelt see Godebb		William	Mre 60
Gideon, Sr.	Frn 445	Godett, William	Hde 368	Going, Alexander	Rth 114
James	Frn 445	Godfray, John	Brk 753	Anthony	Srr 709
Jeremiah	Srr 655	Godfrey, Ann	Brt 46	Burges	Rnd 353
Jerimiah	Orn 567	Francis	Prq 651	Jacob	Stk 587
John	Lnc 831	James	Orn 510	James	Stk 607
John	Lnc 889	James	Wrr 805	Jesse	Srr 705
John	Orn 567	Jesse	Cmd 110	John	Rth 113
John	Stk 555	John	Cmd 103	William	Srr 655
Joseph	Glf 658	John	Mre 68	Goings, Jesse	Srr 655
Robert	Lnc 889	Joseph	Prq 658	Goins, Judith	Nsh 102
Robert, Junr.	Lnc 889	Juley	Prq 649	Gold, Daniel	Rth 112
Susanna	Prs 189	Lemuel	Cmd 103	Joseph	Prs 197
Terry	Orn 567	Samuel	Cmd 107	Will	Prs 206
Thomas	Srr 655	William	Cmb 354	Golden, John	Stk 554
Thompson	Frn 494	William, Senr.	Cmb 354	William	Srr 655
Warrick	Orn 568	Godley, John	Ons 159	Golding, Lemuel	Crv 301

Goldman, Henry	Lnc 842	Jacob	Smp 507	Goose, John	Rwn 451
John	Lnc 855	James	Lnr 9	Goostree, Absalom	Rck 436
Martin	Lnc 855	Job	Brn 19A	Gopage, Danl.	Csw 99
Goldsby, Wade	Rwn 386	John	Cbr 686	Gordan, Anthony	Psq 641
Goldsmith, John	Brk 751	John	Rwn 321	Isaac	Frn 447
Samuel	Brk 751	John	Rwn 353	James	Bfr 8
Thomas	Grv 515	Luke	Brn 20	James	Bfr 22
Golewood, Dudly	Csw 102	Michael	Cbr 714	Joshua	Frn 456
Gollihar, Hugh	Rwn 341	Michael, (Big)	Cbr 716	Joshua	Frn 464
James	Ird 648	Peter	Ash 79	Lemuel	Hde 369
Gollihon, Joseph	Wke 732	Solomon	Rwn 353	Willey	Frn 447
Golsby, William	Brk 751	Thomas	Cbr 718	William	Orn 565
Golson, Charles	Cht 158	William	Frn 485	William	Psq 635
William	Cht 224	William	Lnr 11	Gorden, Betsey	Crr 159
Golt, David	Srr 656	William	Rwn 353	George	Stk 619
Gooch, Amos	Grv 578	William	Rth 113	James	Glf 687
Daniel	Grv 559	William, Jr.	Gts 267	James	Orn 565
Daniel	Grv 581	William, Sr.	Gts 267	James	Stk 604
Gideon, Jur.	Grv 549	Goodmon, Ansylm	Stk 581	John	Orn 565
Gideon, Ser.	Grv 549	William	Stk 554	John	Stk 554
Gidon	Grv 511	Goodner, Henry	Glf 637	Jonathan	Glf 687
John	Grv 511	Walter	Glf 665	Nancy	Crr 138
John	Grv 548	Goodnight, Chris-		Thomas	Stk 554
Joseph, Senr.	Grv 579	tian	Cbr 698	William	Stk 604
Mary	Grv 511	Goodrich, George	Ans 210	Gordin, William	Cbr 690
Roland	Grv 576	James	Ans 210	Gording, Betsey	Crr 155
William	Grv 576	Goodrick, John	Glf 653	Gordon, Benjamin	Gts 267
William	Grv 579	Goodrum, James	Rch 248	Chapman	Wlk 39
Gooche, John	Bnc 170	Thomas	Grv 577	Charles	Csw 120
Mary	Bnc 169	Goodson, Dempsey	Rbs 380	Charles	Wlk 41
Good, Charles	Stk 555	George	Grn 613	Frederick, Capt.	Ans 230
Edward	Hlf 308	Joshua	Grn 613	Frederick, Junr.	Ans 235
Elizabeth	Hlf 310	Mandew	Nrt 443	George (2)	Ird 630
Henry	Hlf 308	Mary	Rth 114	Jacob	Gts 267
James	Hlf 308	Matthew	Lnc 855	James	Gts 281
John	Wne 763	Goodwin, Abraham	Lnc 883	James	Rwn 353
Joseph	Hlf 308	Axiom	Chw 130	Jeams	Mck 538
Joseph	Rch 248	Caleb	Prq 644	John	Mck 603
Patsy	Hlf 308	Crecey	Wke 774	John	Rth 115
Peter	Wlk 40	David	Frn 486	John	Wlk 41
Solomon	Brk 749	Dempsey	Cht 205	Jonathan	Mck 595
Solomon	Brk 750	Drury	Ons 176	Langston	Cht 178
William	Crv 229	George	Rbs 381	Mary	Rch 261
Goodbread, Joseph	Brk 752	Gideon	Wke 731	Nathaniel	Wlk 39
Philip	Brk 752	Gidion	Cht 153	Nathaniel	Wlk 40
Goodbred, John	Rth 114	Isham	Mnt 484	Nathl.	Prq 655
Goode, Abraham	Rth 112	Jacob	Prq 644	Polly	Wlk 40
Joseph	Rth 112	James	Prq 650	Robert	Cmb 377
Judith	Rth 112	Jesse	Hlf 310	Robert	Ird 670
Mary	Stk 592	John	Chw 120	Samuel	Mck 596
Polly	Rth 112	John	Psq 630	Sarah	Wlk 41
Richard	Rth 112	John	Prq 653	Solomon	Wke 776
Richard	Stk 554	John	Prq 654	Stewart	Ptt 244
Robert	Rth 112	Joseph	Chw 129	Thomas	Cht 178
Thomas	Rth 112	Josiah	Wlk 41	Thomas	Mnt 470
Goodin, Wiley	Ans 203	Lewis	Chw 129	Thomas	Psq 635
William	Jhn 776	Mourning	Chw 120	William	Csw 113
Gooding, James	Lnr 9	Nathan	Prq 653	Wm.	Csw 114
John	Crv 311	Rachel	Wke 732	see Gammon	
Jonathan	Crt 75	Robert	Lnc 883	Gordy, Jacob	Ons 145
Moses	Jns 817	Robinson	Lnc 875	Joshua	Ons 153
Richard	Jns 797	Samuel	Cmb 354	Gore, James	Brn 19
Thomas	Crt 61	Samuel	Grv 584	John	Brn 20
Goodline, John	Ons 162	Tabitha	Edg 173	John	Dpl 401
Goodloe, Garrat	Frn 481	Tabitha	Edg 201	Jonathan	Brn 19A
Henry	Wke 731	Thomas	Chw 129	Joseph	Brn 19A
John	Csw 124	William	Cbr 711	Thomas	Wke 732
Goodman, Ambrose	Cht 223	William	Cht 153	Will.	Brn 19A
Amey	Brn 17	William	Chw 120	William	Dpl 430
Christian	Rwn 307	William	Rth 113	Gorham, C. James	Bfr 22
David	Trl 678	William	Wke 732	Hezekiah	Chw 113
Flammon	Rth 114	Young	Frn 486	James	Ptt 252
George, Junr.	Cbr 715	Goodwrick, Robert	Lnc 866	William	Ptt 253
George, Senr.	Cbr 717	Goof, Daniel	Rck 456	Gorish, Henry	Brk 750
Henry	Brn 15	Gooman, Joel	Wrr 806	Gorman, James	Brk 751
Henry	Gts 267	Goonto, David	Ons 170	Gorrell, Peter	Glf 656
Jacob	Rth 114	J.	Ons 171	Ralph	Glf 645

Robert	Glf 634	Jacob	Rnd 314	Granbery, James	Chw 116
Robert	Glf 668	William	Rnd 314	Granbury, David	Brt 46
William	Glf 655	Gragston, William	Orn 510	Langley	Brt 46
Gorton, Bowin	Crt 74	Graham, Alexander	Cmb 389	Samuel	Brt 46
Gosett, Abraham	Rnd 314	Archibald (2)	Cmb 387	Grandey, Frederick	Cmd 98
Elijah	Rnd 314	Archibald	Lnc 896	Grandy, Charles	Cmd 102
Margarett	Rnd 314	Archibald	Rch 261	Charles	Psq 626
Goslin, John	Crv 309	Archibald, Jur.	Lnc 896	Myles	Cmd 102
Goss, Benjn.	Nwh 4	Arthur	Lnc 895	Noah	Cmd 99
David	Rwn 386	Benjamin	Cmb 389	Sarah	Cmd 98
Frederick	Rwn 386	Benjan.	Mre 74	Sarah	Cmd 102
Frederick, Senr.	Rwn 398	Charles	Rwn 347	Grange, John P.	Bld 27
George	Rwn 379	Chauncy	Hrt 737	Molsey	Brn 16
Jacob	Rwn 379	Daniel	Cmb 365	Granger, David	Mck 590
Jacob	Rwn 399	Daniel	Cmb 384	John	Grn 604
John	Grv 579	Daniel	Cmb 388	Margarett	Rck 453
Joseph	Rwn 385	Daniel	Cmb 389	William	Grn 603
Shermon	Grv 570	Daniel	Rch 259	William	Rck 453
Susanah	Brn 17A	Dugal	Rch 261	Grant, Absalom	Nrt 443
Thomas	Grv 559	Duncan	Rch 261	Alexander	Ons 140
Gosset, Allison	Rwn 415	Edward	Crv 245	Alexander	Rth 114
Gossett, Henry	Rnd 314	Edward	Cmb 363	Andrew	Rth 113
Thomas	Glf 624	Edward	Rwn 457	Asa	Rck 456
Goswick, John	Frn 473	Elijah	Srr 705	Catey	Grn 615
Joseph (2)	Frn 473	Elisabeth	Ird 629	David	Wke 731
Nicholas	Frn 473	Fargus	Rwn 312	George	Mck 552
Gott see Golt		George	Mck 522	Isham	Orn 509
Gouch, Benjamin	Wke 732	George	Nrt 445	James	Glf 657
Nathl.	Csw 149	James	Cmb 381	James	Orn 509
Rowland	Wke 732	James	Cmb 387	James, Jur.	Csw 100
Goudy, James	Glf 654	James	Lnc 827	James, Senr.	Csw 100
Gouge, John	Brk 752	James, Senr.	Rwn 325	Jno.	Lnc 842
William	Brk 753	John	Bnc 170	John	Nrt 445
Gouger, Henry	Rwn 345	John	Cmb 365	John	Ons 156
Gough, Robert	Psq 638	John	Cmb 380	John	Wne 844
Gould, Daniel	Ans 203	John	Cmb 384	John	Wlk 40
Michael	Crt 87	John	Ird 610	Mary	Rth 112
Goulding, Elizabeth	Crt 64	John	Ird 670	Michael	Wne 843
George	Crt 63	John	Ird 675	Reuben	Stk 627
Thomas	Crt 63	John	Lnc 854	Reubin	Srr 656
Gour, Lewis	Wke 732	John	Lnc 900	Richard	Nrt 445
Gower, Thomas	Rch 266	John	Mck 561	William	Nrt 443
see Gour		John	Mnt 500	William	Orn 509
Gowers, George	Ans 228	John	Rnd 315	William	Wne 871
William	Jhn 765	John	Rch 261	Grante, John	Crr 149
William	Rch 244	John	Rwn 325	Grantham, David	Smp 509
Gowing, Isham	Orn 565	John, Cap.	Rwn 336	Edward	Rbs 379
Grabeal, Henry	Ash 79	Joseph	Rwn 316	Edward, Jur.	Rbs 380
Peter	Ash 79	Levi	Stk 555	James, Senr.	Hrt 729
Grace, Able	Srr 657	Marrian	Cmb 364	John	Bnc 170
Creenberry	Glf 620	Marry	Lnc 838	John	Prq 645
James	Wne 873	Neill	Cmb 380	Joseph	Rbs 379
John	Wne 848	Peter	Rch 269	Joshua	Rbs 379
Solomon	Glf 628	Richard, Cap.)	Rwn 326	Josiah	Rbs 380
Walker	Srr 657	Richard (litle)	Rwn 317	Mary	Edg 202
Gracey, Robert	Ird 668	Robert	Cmb 382	Moses	Rbs 380
Graddy, Alexander	Dpl 439	Robert	Mre 75	Richard	Rbs 379
Fedrick	Dpl 403	S. Zepheniah	Nrt 443	Richard	Rbs 380
Henry	Dpl 402	Samuel	Mck 557	William	Bnc 170
James	Dpl 406	Thos.	Lnc 838	Grants, Elisha	Wne 851
John	Dpl 439	William	Bnc 170	Grantum, Jacob	Wne 855
Nancy	Lnr 9	William	Mck 560	James	Wne 855
William	Dpl 440	William	Rwn 442	Joel	Wne 855
William	Lnr 9	William	Rth 113	Mary	Wne 855
see Gaddy		Zepheniah S.	Nrt 443	Sion	Wne 855
Gradless, John	Bfr 8	Grahame, Michael	Cmb 376	Solomon	Wne 854
Gradson, Eli	Wke 732	Grahams, Daniel	Mre 55	Grare, John	Ons 173
Grady, Betty	Rnd 316	George	Mre 58	John	Ons 178
Dennis	Wke 731	Robert	Mre 50	Grason, George (2)	Orn 565
James	Wke 731	Thomas	Mre 50	Grasy, William	Brk 753
Rachel	Rwn 387	Grainger, Jonathan	Cmd 101	William	Rwn 408
Salley	Wke 732	Gran, William	Cht 162	Graver, Samuel	Cbr 713
William	Rck 492	Granad, Martin	Ans 235	Graves, Azariah	Csw 95
Graff, William	Rch 267	Granberry, James	Nrt 445	Barzella	Csw 136
Graffin, William	Grv 538	Josiah	Gts 267	Benjamin	Rnd 314
Grag, William	Brk 749	Josiah	Nrt 445	Benjn.	Brn 13A
Grage, Aron	Rnd 314	William	Nrt 443	Boston	Orn 510

Conrod	Rwn 424	Jephtha	Hde 368	see Grare		
David	Grv 549	Jesse	Edg 202	Greaves, Absolem	Crr 150	
George	Rwn 424	Jesse	Glf 685	David	Crr 149	
Hanah	Csw 122	Jinnet	Rnd 316	Matthew	Crt 83	
Hanah	Csw 136	John	Ans 198	Greaway, Catherine	Grv 579	
Hardy	Rbs 379	John	Cbr 695	Gree, Joseph	Brk 750	
Jacob	Csw 136	John	Crr 147	Greeg, Moses	Srr 657	
James	Csw 135	John	Crr 161	Greeger, John Hen-		
James	Rnd 315	John	Lnr 8	ry	Rwn 399	
James	Srr 656	John	Mnt 469	Green, Aaron	Mnt 511	
Jno.	Csw 136	John	Nrt 445	Abel	Cht 187	
John	Csw 98	John	Prs 215	Abraham	Gts 266	
John	Cht 186	John	Wsh 704	Aggy	Hlf 308	
John	Grv 538	Joseph	Cbr 718	Allen	Wrr 805	
John	Rnd 315	Joseph	Crr 141	Amers	Rth 114	
John	Rnd 316	Joseph	Crr 165	Anthony	Stk 554	
Lampson	Bld 29	Joseph	Ird 660	Arthur	Bld 27	
Leonard	Rnd 316	Joseph	Lnr 11	Atha	Frn 461	
Mary	Grv 538	Joseph	Psq 637	Benjamin	Hlf 308	
Nathaniel	Grv 550	Joseph	Ptt 236	Caney	Wke 732	
Nathaniel	Srr 656	Joshua	Crr 166	Conrod	Stk 602	
Rachel	Grv 511	Keziah	Wsh 704	Daniel	Grv 567	
Ralph	Grv 539	Lodwick	Lnr 11	Daniel	Orn 567	
Ralph	Grv 548	Lovick	Mrt 388	David	Hde 368	
Richard	Rnd 314	Lydia	Glf 685	David	Mnt 462	
Samuel	Rnd 314	Nancy	Lnr 11	David	Orn 567	
Solomon	Csw 106	Nelson	Cbr 680	Edmond	Orn 510	
Thomas	Prs 218	Obediah	Cmd 99	Edward	Cmb 375	
William	Grv 539	Polly	Psq 638	Edward	Glf 661	
William	Grv 549	Rabeckah	Ird 661	Edward	Wke 732	
William	Lnc 875	Rachel	Lnr 35	Elijah	Brk 750	
Gravil, James	Mnt 500	Robert	Crr 166	Elijah	Grv 574	
Gravis, Ezekiel	Nrt 447	Robert	Orn 566	Elisabeth	Ans 209	
Henary	Prs 203	Robert	Psq 631	Elisabeth	Crv 331	
Gray, Abigail	Chw 115	Robert, Junr.	Orn 566	Elisha	Orn 567	
Alexander	Glf 640	Rubin	Ons 144	Elizabeth	Brt 46	
Alexander	Mnt 511	S. William	Brt 46	Elizabeth	Hlf 308	
Alexander	Rnd 315	Samuel	Glf 685	Ellison	Ans 208	
Alexander,(Cap.	Mck 593	Samuel	Wlk 41	George	Brt 46	
Alexr., Senr.	Prs 215	Sherred, Esqr.	Mck 593	George	Hlf 310	
Alixander	Brk 750	Thomas	Cbr 680	George	Nsh 102	
Andrew	Orn 566	Thomas	Dpl 421	George	Ptt 293	
Anthony	Psq 637	Thomas	Hlf 310	George	Rch 262	
Benjamin	Ans 213	Thomas	Ird 661	H. William	Brt 46	
Benjamin	Edg 202	Thomas	Lnr 11	Henry	Grv 574	
Benjamin	Rwn 442	Thomas	Orn 567	Henry	Glf 629	
Benjamin P.	Jns 797	Thornton	Cmd 95	Henry	Hlf 308	
Beverly	Cbr 695	Thornton	Psq 631	Henry (2)	Rth 113	
Bevine	Srr 656	Thos.	Crr 142	Isaac	Gts 267	
Calib	Cmd 103	Thos.	Crr 166	Isaac	Ird 620	
Charles	Edg 201	William	Brt 44	Isaac	Rwn 408	
Charls	Rnd 315	William	Bld 42	Jacob	Ans 209	
David	Ans 213	William	Bnc 170	Jacob	Ans 219	
David	Ird 661	William	Cbr 681	Jacob	Rnd 316	
David	Mnt 501	William	Glf 685	James	Nsh 101	
Edwin	Nrt 445	William	Lnr 9	James	Wne 859	
Enoch	Ird 624	William	Lnr 11	James	Wne 871	
Ephraim	Brk 749	William	Mck 601	James, Senr.	Jns 815	
Frederick	Wsh 704	William	Nrt 445	Jamimah	Crv 321	
George	Brt 46	William	Wlk 39	Jereh.	Rck 488	
Gilbert	Jns 797	William, Junr.	Jns 797	Jeremiah	Ash 79	
Gilbert	Rnd 314	William S.	Brt 46	Jeremiah	Bnc 171	
Griffin	Crr 137	William W.	Jns 801	Jeremiah, junr.	Ash 79	
Henry	Wsh 704	Willis	Mre 45	Jesse	Edg 202	
Hugh	Ird 660	Wm.	Crr 145	Jesse	Hlf 308	
Hugh	Ird 661	Wm.	Crr 165	Jesse	Jhn 761	
Isaac	Glf 685	see Grag		Jesse	Wrr 806	
James	Frn 482	Grayham, Alexander	Rbs 381	Job	Prs 187	
James	Glf 640	Alexr.	Prs 204	John	Ash 79	
James	Glf 685	Dugald	Rbs 379	John	Bld 27	
James	Rwn 330	Eli	Stk 555	John	Brk 750	
James	Rth 112	Nancy	Rbs 381	John	Brk 752	
James	Wlk 39	William	Hlf 310	John	Crv 321	
James	Wlk 41	Grayson, Drury	Lnc 838	John	Cmb 374	
James, Senr.	Mnt 511	William	Wlk 39	John	Dpl 409	
James, Senr.	Wlk 40	Grear, Margaret	Csw 132	John	Frn 461	
Jean	Orn 496	Peter	Brk 750	John	Grv 575	

John	Glf 675	William	Frn 483	Jerry	Cht 203
John	Jhn 761	William	Grv 575	Jno., Jr.	Ans 202
John	Orn 567	William	Glf 620	John	Ans 202
John (2)	Rck 473	William	Ird 620	John	Cmd 107
John	Rth 113	William	Lnr 9	John	Rth 113
John	Stk 554	William	Lnr 11	Joseph	Crr 140
John	Wrr 806	William	Mnt 462	Joseph	Rth 112
John	Wne 867	William	Rnd 315	Joseph	Wlk 40
John C.	Wrr 805	William	Rwn 399	Judith	Cht 203
Joseph	Brk 753	William (2)	Rth 113	Laben	Crr 137
Joseph	Crv 291	William	Wke 732	Leon	Crr 149
Joseph	Frn 476	William, Jur.	Frn 465	Lewis	Nrt 445
Joseph	Hrt 704	Zacheus	Crv 309	Lot	Smp 507
Joseph	Rnd 316	Greenaway, John	Grv 511	Luke	Crr 149
Joseph	Rth 113	Thomas	Grv 511	Malichi	Cmd 107
Joseph	Wrr 805	Greene, Caleb	Bld 11	Mary	Chw 127
Joseph, jr.	Wne 843	James	Bld 12	Mathew	Dpl 433
Joseph, Senr.	Wne 843	John	Bld 16	Matthew	Nrt 445
Lewis	Mnt 470	Simon	Bld 5	Matthew	Rbs 381
Lewis	Wke 776	William	Bld 17	Matthew	Rbs 432
Lissia	Crt 91	Greenfield, Adam	Dpl 429	Matthias	Cmd 107
Littleberry	Hlf 308	Mathias	Bnc 170	Mitchel	Crr 140
Lot	Dpl 409	Nathaniel	Bnc 171	Mitchel	Crr 156
Major	Prs 204	Greenlee, James	Rth 114	Molley	Crr 154
Mary	Lnr 8	Greenlie, David	Rth 113	Nancy	Cmd 101
Mills	Brk 752	Greens see Guins		Neale	Crr 141
Nathan	Crr 148	Greent, John	Lnc 875	Owen	Smp 512
Nathan	Mck 540	Greenwood, Bartlet	Stk 584	Penney	Crr 159
Nicholas	Grv 574	Hugh	Rth 114	Ratchel	Crr 154
Nickoles	Prs 188	Robert	Stk 588	Richard	Cmd 101
Obediah	Frn 461	Samuel	Srr 655	Richard	Cht 186
Philip	Stk 612	William	Stk 586	Richard, jr.	Cht 186
Rachel	Orn 510	Greer, Ananius	Rck 441	Saml.	Crr 137
Reuben	Smp 536	Benjamin	Ash 79	Samuel	Cmd 107
Richard	Ash 79	Benjn., junr.	Ash 79	Thomas	Smp 513
Richard	Brk 750	David	Bnc 170	Thos.	Crr 143
Richard	Brk 751	David	Nwh 3	Uz.	Jhn 764
Richard	Mnt 470	Equillar	Ash 79	William	Cmd 102
Richard	Mnt 514	Francis	Cbr 679	William	Chw 125
Richard	Srr 656	George	Bnc 169	William	Dpl 434
Richard, Senr.	Mnt 470	James	Csw 135	William, Jun.	Cmd 1o7
Robert	Brn 20A	John	Brn 15	Wilson	Cmd 110
Robert	Cht 170	John	Brk 751	see Grgrory, Grigory	
Robert	Frn 466	John	Mck 606	Greives, John	Psq 632
Robert	Glf 668	Martha	Glf 631	Grenade, John	Jns 803
Robert	Glf 681	Sarah	Wlk 39	Grenella, Patrick	Ptt 241
Robert	Hlf 308	Greeson, Isaac	Glf 648	Greneway, Josiph	Brk 750
Robert	Ird 661	Samuel	Glf 628	Grenstoff, Isaac	Brk 752
Robert	Mnt 462	Greewood, John	Stk 586	Gresard, Hardy	Ans 215
Robert	Rnd 316	Gregery, Hosea	Prq 607	Gresham, James	Cht 187
Robert	Stk 555	Gregg, Jacob	Crr 164	Oliver	Wrr 806
Samuel	Gts 266	Moses	Stk 554	Grey, George	Wlk 40
Samuel, Junr.	Gts 267	Greggs, Charles	Crr 141	James	Gts 266
Sela	Edg 202	Gregory, Abraham	Cmd 110	Grgrory, Saron	Ons 175
Shaderach	Rth 113	Absolen	Rth 112	Grible, John	Brk 752
Shaderach	Rth 114	Alexr.	Cmd 104	Grice, Alexander	Smp 511
Shadrrach	Rth 113	Arthur	Nrt 445	Benjamin	Rbs 379
Sherwood	Wrr 806	Asael	Brt 46	Charles	Psq 627
Silas	Wke 732	Bry	Cht 204	Francis	Psq 627
Simon	Frn 447	Caleb	Crr 154	James	Smp 531
Solomon	Brt 46	Calib	Cmd 101	Mary	Rbs 379
Solomon	Wrr 805	Cornelious,Ser.	Crr 144	Robert	Cmb 382
Stephen	Crv 313	David	Cmd 103	Thophilus	Nsh 102
Thomas	Brk 753	Demsey	Cmd 103	William	Bld 43
Thomas	Crv 273	Enoch	Crr 156	Grider, John	Brk 750
Thomas	Crv 321	Gideon	Crr 156	Grier see Greer	
Thomas	Gts 267	Hardy	Nrt 445	Griesell, George	Rnd 307
Thomas	Jhn 750	Henry	Rth 113	Grieves, Sally	Frn 477
Thomas	Mck 537	Holloway	Cmd 98	Griffee, Edward	Srr 657
Thomas	Wrr 805	Isaac	Cmd 99	Griffen, Abigel	Cbr 696
Thomas	Wlk 40	Isaac	Cmd 107	Griffey, Isaac	Brk 751
Turnifold	Crv 331	Jacob	Crr 137	John	Brk 750
Widow	Mck 528	James	Brt 46	John	Brk 753
Will.	Nwh 11	James	Chw 118	Griffice, Benjamin	Edg 201
William	Ans 235	James	Gts 266	John, Junr.	Edg 202
William	Brk 752	James	Jhn 763	William	Edg 201
William	Crv 305	Jerekins	Chw 128	Griffies, Mason	Orn 510

Griffin, Abraham Ans 217
Abraham Ans 217
Abraham Crv 337
Alee Mrt 395
Amasiah Bfr 8
Amos Prq 648
Amos Rck 436
Andrew Rbs 380
Andrew Rwn 361
Archd. Nsh 102
Asa Mrt 395
Benjamin Crv 315
Benjamin Lnr 11
Betsey Wke 732
Brinkley Chw 117
Caleb Wne 871
Calib Prq 661
Charity Nsh 101
Charles Ans 222
Darlen Wne 858
David Ans 222
David Wsh 704
Delilah Mrt 394
Dempsey Wne 857
Edward, (Mulat-
to) Edg 202
Edwd. Mrt 388
Eliab Prq 659
Eliab, Sen. Prq 661
Elisha Ans 217
Ellexander Mrt 395
Ezekiel Rwn 424
Frederick Edg 201
Gilford Nsh 101
Hardy Wne 858
Henry Edg 202
Humphrey Chw 128
Isaac Hlf 310
Jacob Rnd 316
James Orn 565
James Prq 645
James Prq 648
James Ptt 225
Jas. Mrt 394
Jehu Mrt 394
Jesse Nsh 101
Jesse Prq 650
John Cht 198
John Cht 209
John Cmb 354
John Cmb 372
John Edg 202
John Glf 622
John Orn 509
John Prq 659
John Rth 113
John Wlk 40
John, Junr. Mrt 394
John, Senr. Mrt 395
John, Terts. Mrt 394
Joseph Bld 22
Joseph Cmb 366
Joseph Edg 202
Joshua Grn 602
Josiah Prq 648
Lewis Rnd 315
Lewis Wne 871
Martin Mrt 394
Mary Cht 222
Mary Grn 601
Mary Lnr 8
Mary Nsh 101
Mary Rbs 380
Moses Crv 233
Nathan Prq 659
Pearce Nsh 101
Polley Mrt 394

Reuben Mrt 394
Richard Mck 588
Samuel Lnr 11
Southern Rck 457
Theophilus Rbs 380
Thomas Ans 221
Thomas Glf 642
Thomas Orn 565
Thos. Nsh 101
Wiley Cht 198
William Ans 220
William Brt 46
William Crv 315
William Prq 645
William Prq 648
William Rnd 316
William Rwn 442
Willis Edg 202
Willis, Jur. Chw 127
Willis, Sen. Chw 125
Yokely Rwn 361
Zachariah Edg 201
Zadock Rwn 326
Zilpha Wsh 704
see Graffin
Griffis, Alen Cht 210
Allin Wke 731
Ephraim Wke 732
Mason Cht 211
Thomas Cht 164
William Ans 199
William Mre 67
William Orn 509
Griffith, Arthur,
Junr. Nrt 445
Arthur, Senr. Nrt 445
Demcey Nrt 445
Edward Crv 321
Edward Ird 610
Elias Csw 121
Evan Lnr 9
George Stk 607
Hartwell Hrt 735
James Lnr 9
John Hrt 735
John Ird 610
John Nrt 445
Jonathan Rck 450
Matthew Nrt 443
Robert Nrt 443
Samuel Ash 79
Sarah Nrt 445
Thomas Grv 522
William Mck 553
William Stk 607
Zadok Rck 448
Griffon, Burwel Gts 267
Griffy, Azariah Stk 580
Benjamin Srr 656
Isaac Orn 509
see Griffee
Griger, George Stk 554
see Cregar
Grigery, Pheby Srr 655
Grigg, Patience Nrt 443
William (2) Stk 554
Griggory, Chris-
tian Mnt 515
James Ird 617
Griggs, Berell Rth 114
Henry Bnc 170
James Rth 114
Jesse Rth 112
Lee Grv 570
Mrs. Mck 527
Robert Grv 570
Thomas Grv 570

Wood Rth 111
Griggus, Johnston,
Jur. Bfr 8
Johnston, Senr. Bfr 8
Grigory, Benjamin Bnc 170
John Bnc 169
Thomas Bnc 170
William Bnc 170
William Bnc 171
see Gregory
Grigrea, Abraham Prs 200
George Prs 206
Grigson, Amos Rwn 399
Grim see Goins
Grimes, Adam Rwn 399
Alexander Rnd 314
Ann Ptt 255
Barnabas Orn 567
Benjamin Ash 79
Benjn. (Ashe) Wlk 41
Berryman Csw 121
C. John Edg 201
Feby Orn 566
George Rch 252
George Rch 254
George Rwn 373
Godlip Rwn 353
Jacob Brk 751
Jacob Brk 753
James Bfr 22
James Dpl 426
John Dpl 397
John Glf 656
John Orn 509
John C. Edg 201
Joseph Dpl 402
Lewelling Mrt 395
Luke Orn 565
Morris Rch 252
Peter Rwn 353
Richard (2) Rnd 314
Sampson Dpl 427
Thomas Stk 554
thos. Mrt 394
William Edg 201
William Jhn 769
William Orn 565
William Rch 269
Grimmer, Jacob Ptt 291
John Hlf 310
Nazarah Hlf 310
Thomas Hlf 310
Grimslay, Jeth-
rough Grn 598
Grimsley, Eliza-
beth Grn 600
George Rbs 380
Irwin Rbs 380
James Grn 600
Lewis Rbs 380
Thos. Wlk 41
Trida Grn 600
Grinaway, William Brk 751
Grinder, Mary Stk 590
Grindsted, John Hlf 310
Lydda Hlf 310
Griner, Catharine Stk 591
Grinsley, Ann Grn 598
Grisard, Thomas Grn 596
Grise, Jacob Jhn 752
Lewis Jhn 753
Stephen Jhn 752
Grisham, Fardenand Orn 567
George Orn 568
John Grv 552
Robert Orn 568
Grisom, Benjn. Wlk 41

Jesse	Wlk 41	Gualtney, John	Ird 610	Gumms, Abraham	Nrt 443
John	Brk 752	Robert	Ird 610	Nathan	Nrt 445
Grisset, Rheubin	Nwh 4	Guard, Joshua	Crv 299	Gun, Elizabeth	Hlf 308
Grissett, Geo. (2)	Brn 20A	Guardsan, Mary	Cht 199	Martin	Cbr 702
John	Brn 20	Guartner, Thomas	Ptt 290	Gunn, Daniel	Csw 127
Sarah	Brn 20	Guartney, Benjamin	Crv 269	Gabriel	Prs 209
William	Brn 19	John	Crv 269	James	Csw 106
Grissom, George	Grv 584	Gudger, Benjamin	Bnc 170	James	Cmb 366
Harris	Orn 510	William	Bnc 169	Jesse	Prs 203
Henry	Grv 519	Gudley, Betsey	Crr 168	John	Glf 628
John	Brk 752	John	Crr 168	John	Wrr 805
Phebe	Ons 163	Wm.	Crr 168	Starling	Csw 122
Grissome, Will.	Nwh 7A	Guess, George	Orn 566	Thomas	Csw 100
Grissum, George	Grv 534	John	Orn 566	Thomas, Jur.	Csw 123
James	Ans 228	Joseph	Orn 566	see Green	
Grist, Charles	Lnc 847	Moses	Orn 566	Gunstan, James	Srr 655
Frederick	Bfr 8	William	Orn 566	Gunter, Abner	Cht 157
John	Bfr 8	Gufey, William	Rth 114	Benjn.	Cht 161
Reading	Bfr 8	Guffey, John	Rwn 447	Charles	Jns 823
William	Rwn 379	Gufford, Andrew	Dpl 439	Charles, Junr.	Jns 809
Grizard, Jesse	Ptt 267	Guffy, James	Rth 114	Charnal	Mre 67
Mary	Ptt 267	John	Rth 114	Clayburn	Brk 749
Mary, Senior	Ptt 267	John, Sr.	Rth 114	Gust	Brk 753
Grizel, Arthur	Nsh 102	Thomas	Rth 114	Isham	Cht 176
Danil	Nsh 101	Guibson, Mos.,		James	Brk 749
Herrod	Nsh 102	Junr.	Prs 193	Jeptha	Cht 161
William	Nsh 102	Robert	Prs 219	Jesse	Wlk 39
Grizzard, Ambrose	Wke 732	Thomas	Prs 194	John	Cht 159
Groft, William	Mnt 498	Guier, John	Prq 645	John, Jun.	Mre 64
Grogan, Barthel	Rck 460	Guilder, Gilbert	Bnc 170	John, Sen.	Mre 64
Barthow., Jur.	Rck 460	Guilford, Isaac	Cmd 100	Richard	Cht 155
Daniel	Rck 460	Joseph	Bfr 8	Thomas	Cht 199
Francis	Rck 460	Guin, Henry	Crt 90	William	Cht 155
Henry	Rck 440	John	Prs 203	William	Rwn 365
Mary	Rck 440	Mace	Wne 849	Willie	Jns 825
Richd.	Rck 459	Rollen	Crt 89	Willis	Cht 176
Thomas	Rck 459	Thornton	Stk 592	Gupton, Cooper	Frn 477
Thomas	Rck 460	Will.	Prs 187	Games	Frn 474
Thomas, Jur.	Rck 460	Guine, John	Crr 155	James	Frn 463
Groslea, George	Brk 752	Willis	Crr 155	James	Frn 474
Gross, Christian	Lnc 814	Guinn, Daniel	Csw 97	John	Frn 477
Daniel	Lnc 902	Hugh	Rck 451	Steven	Frn 477
David	Srr 656	Iverson	Csw 145	gurganiss, Major	Mrt 394
Frederick	Rwn 326	Ivy	Rck 451	Gurganus, Aaron,	
Henry	Lnc 814	Joseph	Orn 567	Jur.	Hde 368
Jacob	Srr 655	Robert	Glf 661	Aaron, Ser.	Hde 369
Jacob	Srr 656	Thomas	Orn 566	David	Hlf 310
James	Cmb 354	Thomas	Orn 567	Elizabeth	Bfr 8
John	Lnc 902	Guinnes, William	Orn 509	John	Hde 369
John	Srr 655	Guinney, Stephen	Crv 301	John	Ons 168
John	Srr 656	Guins, George	Rch 258	Lydia	Bfr 8
Morning	Cht 206	Guion, Isaac	Crv 241	Mary	Hde 369
Peter (2)	Srr 655	Thomas, Esqr.	Edg 173	Reuben	Ptt 237
Simon	Srr 655	Thomas, Esqr.	Edg 201	Sarah	Hde 368
Tevault	Srr 655	Guire, George	Lnc 861	Willy	Bld 6
William	Srr 656	William	Lnc 860	Gurin, Nathan	Rck 469
Grove, William		Guise, Philip	Bnc 169	Gurley, Arther	Jhn 746
Barry	Cmb 354	Guisoop, Timothy	Prq 647	Charles	Jhn 747
Grover, James S.	Brt 46	Gullage, Joel	Ans 239	George	Wne 868
Mary	Crv 233	Thomas	Ans 240	Isham	Ans 219
Mary	Crv 297	William	Ans 240	Jacob	Ans 213
Groves, Abraham	Ird 661	William H.	Ans 230	James	Mnt 509
Daniel	Bfr 22	Gullet, Daniel	Wlk 40	Jerremiah	Jhn 746
Salmons	Rwn 341	Jesse	Wlk 40	Joel	Wne 858
Solomon	Rwn 343	Joshua	Glf 631	Lewis	Wne 872
William	Lnc 838	Gullett, John	Glf 655	Peterson	Hrt 711
Grub, Conrod	Rwn 347	Gulley, George	Jhn 761	William	Ans 218
George, Junr.	Rwn 347	John	Jhn 759	Willis	Ans 218
George, Senr.	Rwn 347	Meed	Jhn 759	Gutherie, Carter	Lnc 855
John	Rwn 347	Nathan	Jhn 764	Thomas	Lnc 855
Koonrod	Ash 78	Robert	Jhn 761	Guthery, Archabald	Crt 75
Grubb, George	Rwn 391	Robert, Jr.	Jhn 751	Charles	Crt 73
Grubs, Thomas	Stk 555	Gullimo, Travis	Cbr 695	Charles, sr.	Crt 74
Grunaway, Mary	Grv 565	Gully, Jesse	Dpl 430	Frederick	Crt 77
Grunt, Adam	Lnc 884	William	Dpl 428	Levi	Crt 57
Gruser, Joseph	Orn 510	William	Dpl 430	Samuel	Crt 57
Gryson, Joseph	Rth 113	Guman, William	Ans 226	Samuel	Crt 73

Samuel	Crt 75	Hadder, John	Brt 50	Hagins, John	Bnc 172
Stephen	Crt 67	Haddock, Charles	Ptt 249	Mills	Brk 759
Zilphia	Crt 57	Charles, Senior	Ptt 249	Obadiah	Wne 762
Guthree, William	Wke 732	Drury	Bld 8	William	Brk 759
Gutridge, Joseph	Hlf 310	John	Rnd 320	Hagler, Isaac	Wlk 42
Guthrie, Beverly	Cht 154	John, junior	Ptt 250	Jacob	Mnt 511
Carter	Lnc 851	John, Senior	Ptt 257	Jacob	Wlk 42
Francis	Lnc 889	John, Son of		John	Mck 574
James	Lnc 855	John	Ptt 257	John	Mnt 496
Jermon	Wke 776	Shadrack	Edg 206	John	Wlk 42
John	Lnc 847	William	Ptt 249	Peter, Junr.	Cbr 691
Samuel	Cht 174	see Hadoc		Philip	Mck 574
William	Bld 36	Haddox, William	Rwn 452	Haglor, John,Senr.	Cbr 691
William	Cht 154	Haden, John	Rth 116	Hagnes, Christian	Stk 600
William	Cht 163	Hadick, Andrew	Lnc 816	John	Stk 600
Guthrow, Lucretia	Wsh 704	Jonas	Lnc 815	Hagness, Alias	Srr 661
Gutterage, William	Srr 655	Hadley, Benjamin	Cmb 384	Jonathan	Srr 661
Guttle, George	Rwn 431	Isaac	Rwn 379	Joseph	Srr 661
Guttrey, Jarrot	Prs 195	Jerry	Cht 214	Hagood, Bird	Mnt 494
Guy, Henry	Jhn 748	Jerry	Cht 216	George	Wke 738
James	Cmb 385	John	Brk 761	Hague, Susana	Prs 189
James	Grv 561	John	Cmb 354	Haguewood, Jesse	Orn 572
James	Ird 639	Jonah	Glf 628	Tapley	Orn 572
James	Ird 664	Joseph	Cht 212	Hagwood, John	Wrr 807
John	Dpl 435	Joshua	Brk 760	John, jr.	Wrr 807
John	Ird 664	Joshua	Cht 211	Shadk.	Nsh 104
Joseph	Ird 639	Joshua	Cht 212	William	Wrr 808
Offy	Dpl 434	Lydda	Hlf 314	Hagy, Coonrad	Glf 630
Sarah	Dpl 435	Simeon	Cht 193	Haigdon, Charles	Cht 156
William	Dpl 434	Simon	Srr 663	Hail, Daniel	Cmb 390
William	Dpl 435	Simon, Ser.	Srr 663	Hosea	Wlk 45
William	Jhn 751	Thomas	Brk 760	Joel	Cmb 390
William	Orn 567	Thomas	Cht 211	Joel	Wlk 44
William	Psq 624	Thomas	Cmb 386	John	Cht 195
William	Orn 566	Thomas	Srr 663	Jonathan	Hlf 316
William, Junr.	Prq 662	William	Cht 212	Nathaniel	Edg 208
Guyar, Jesse	Prq 662	William	Rch 245	Thomas	Lnr 12
Mariam	Prq 662	Hadly, John	Mnt 520	Thomas	Srr 662
Guyther, John	Wsh 714	Hadnot, Aldredge	Ons 151	William	Hlf 312
Guyton, James	Bld 30	Elizabith	Ons 168	Williamson	Hlf 316
William	Bld 30	Lebieus	Ons 151	Haile, James	Nrt 447
Gwaltony, John	Rth 111	Obediance	Ons 151	John	Grn 605
William	Rth 111	Sarah	Ons 158	Jonas	Nrt 449
Gwin, Edward	Edg 202	Hadoc, Henry	Stk 609	Hailey, Ansel	Cmb 374
James	Edg 202	Haffort, John	Crv 277	Holliday	Nrt 449
Josiah	Smp 496	Zilpha	Crv 279	William	Nrt 447
Leah	Gts 267	Haga, Charles	Stk 611	Haills, Robert	Rbs 384
Gwyn, Humphry	Wlk 41	Hagah see Hagar		Robert	Rbs 432
James	Wlk 40	Hagan, Hezekiah	Cht 204	Saml.	Bld 45
gynn, Nancy	Mrt 395	James	Nrt 449	Haimore, Jonas B.	Rwn 374
		Lammy	Cht 204	Haines see Hayns	
-- H --		Hagans, Amy	Mrt 395	Hainey, Benja.	Bld 21
		Hagar, William	Srr 662	John	Cht 156
		Hage, Charles	Stk 596	Hainly, Jacob	Rwn 432
H..., Christian	Lnc 902	Hagee, Christopher	Stk 627	Hains, Jonathan	Brk 755
Habbs, James	Ird 656	Hagel, Ann Sofia	Nwh 11	Joseph	Wlk 45
Jesse	Ird 656	Hagen, Christopher	Bfr 9	Martin	Rwn 361
William	Ird 656	Derby	Bfr 9	Nathan	Srr 658
Hace, John	Cht 204	Hagens, Betsey	Wlk 44	Philip	Rwn 361
Hack, Mark	Orn 574	John	Wlk 44	Rafe	Ird 649
Hackels, Peggy	Crt 67	Mary	Wlk 45	Thomas	Srr 660
Hacker, John	Brk 761	Hager, Christian	Lnc 847	William	Srr 660
Hacket, Anna	Rth 115	George	Lnc 847	Hair, Eleanah	Ans 215
John	Jns 811	John	Lnc 847	Frusanna	Hrt 724
Thomas	Cmb 354	Johnn.	Lnc 847	John	Ans 215
Hackett, Oliver		Simon	Lnc 815	Rachel	Chw 120
(2)	Glf 620	Simon	Lnc 847	William	Ans 215
Hackney, Mary	Jns 791	Wm.	Lnc 847	Wilson	Ans 215
William	Edg 208	Hagerman, Joseph	Ash 81	Hairis see Harris	
Hacney, Daniel	Cht 166	Joseph	Wlk 44	Haisley, John	Glf 692
Joseph	Cht 198	Hagewood, Barsom	Orn 512	William	Nrt 447
Joseph, jr.	Cht 167	Hagey, Lazerus	Rwn 416	Haitsfield, Andrew	Wke 739
Lott	Cht 158	Haggard, Benjn.	Rck 441	Andw., Junr.	Wke 738
Robert	Cht 166	Haggins, John	Lnc 815	Hale, Ferriba	Hrt 725
William	Cht 165	John	Rwn 344	Jesse	Brt 50
Hacy, Benjamin	Ird 624	Hagin, Peter	Bnc 172	Joseph	Cht 165
Nathaniel	Glf 676	Williss	Nsh 102	Joseph	Grn 605

97

Nathan, Esqr.	Bld 46	James	Mck 576
Samuel	Cht 175	James, Jur.	Hde 370
Simon	Crt 93	James, Ser.	Hde 369
Thomas	Crv 255	James H.	Ird 671
Thomas	Hlf 312	Jesse	Ash 80
Hales, Chapman	Jhn 756	Jesse	Wne 846
John	Edg 207	Jesse	Wlk 42
John	Jhn 758	Jesse	Wlk 43
Haley, George	Rch 246	Jno.	Prs 202
Hugh	Glf 687	Joel	Wke 737
Isham	Rch 243	John	Brn 13A
James	Rck 481	John	Brk 755
John	Glf 678	John	Brk 761
John	Rch 243	John	Cbr 683
John	Rch 247	John	Cht 152
Jonathan	Rch 243	John	Cht 160
Randal	Rch 267	John	Crv 339
Sarah	Cmd 98	John	Grv 538
Silus	Rch 246	John	Glf 634
William	Rch 246	John	Ird 665
Hall, Abraham	Rwn 452	John	Ird 670
Adam	Ird 611	John	Lnc 889
Alexander	Ird 668	John	Mck 578
Allmand	Nwh 2A	John	Mnt 483
Allen	Bld 44	John	Mnt 504
Andrew	Rck 463	John	Nrt 447
Ann	Brk 753	John	Orn 511
Ann	Jns 793	John	Orn 575
Anne	Edg 208	John	Rwn 326
Armager	Smp 499	John	Rwn 415
Barnabas	Smp 519	John	Smp 532
Benjamin	Hde 370	John	Stk 555
Benjamin	Ons 162	John	Stk 628
Benjamin	Rnd 317	John	Wrr 811
Bejm.	Ons 144	John H.	Edg 205
Caleb	Wne 850	Johnston	Ons 142
David	Brk 760	Joseph	Crv 331
David	Cmd 97	Joseph	Edg 206
David	Crt 75	Joseph	Frn 484
David	Dpl 419	Joseph	Hrt 711
David	Ird 610	Joseph	Mnt 478
David	Nwh 12A	Joseph	Rwn 345
David	Orn 573	Joseph	Stk 609
David	Stk 581	Joseph	Wne 865
Dickenson	Edg 208	Joseph,(Sadler)	Rwn 326
Durant	Crv 303	Joseph, Senr.	Rwn 326
Ebenezer	Wlk 44	Joshua	Brk 758
Edward	Prq 654	Josiah	Smp 532
Edward, Esqr.	Edg 205	Judith	Csw 123
Elijah	Brk 758	Keze	Hlf 314
Elisha	Crv 333	Lazarus	Smp 519
Elizabeth	Bfr 10	Levi W.	Crr 142
Fargus	Ird 671	Levy	Orn 511
Garlender	Bld 44	Lewis	Smp 531
George	Bnc 173	Lydia	Smp 501
George	Ird 665	Martin	Nrt 451
George	Rwn 458	Martin	Wlk 46
Grace	Crr 164	Mary	Crv 305
H. John	Edg 205	Mary	Ons 142
Henry	Mnt 501	Mason	Nrt 449
Hezekiah	Wlk 45	McEgey	Brk 756
Hugh	Ird 671	Mecias	Ash 80
Isaac	Dpl 418	Morgan	Cbr 702
Isaac	Hrt 711	Nathan	Crr 143
Isaac	Psq 640	Owen	Wlk 45
Isaac	Rwn 326	Pattrick	Mck 569
Isaac	Wne 850	Penny	Dpl 411
Isaac	Wne 865	Pharoah	Smp 508
Isaac	Wlk 44	Philadelphia	Ons 142
Isaco	Orn 511	Phillip	Stk 583
Jacob	Rnd 320	Phillip, Junr.	Prs 206
Jacob	Wke 737	Phillip, Senr.	Prs 201
James	Dpl 412	Prisilla	Smp 531
James	Edg 206	Raiford	Bld 41
James	Frn 472	Randle	Stk 580
James	Ird 668	Rebecah	Hlf 312
James	Ird 671		

Robert	Hlf 314	Samuel	Rwn 326
Robert	Orn 575	Sarah	Gts 269
Robert	Wke 734	Sephen	Bnc 172
Robert	Wlk 44	Simon	Crt 57
Saml.	Brn 15	Spine	Crr 142
Samuel	Bnc 171	Thomas	Bld 41
Samuel	Crv 273	Thomas	Crv 281
Samuel	Ons 141	Thomas	Crv 337
Thomas	Grn 590		
Thomas	Hrt 724		
Thomas	Ird 671		
Thomas	Jns 801		
Thomas	Mck 577		
Thomas	Orn 573		
Thomas	Orn 574		
Thomas	Rnd 353		
Thomas	Stk 556		
Thomas	Stk 609		
Thomas	Wlk 42		
Thomas, Doctr.	Edg 173		
Thomas, Doctr.	Edg 205		
Thomas, j.	Rth 115		
Thomas, S.	Rth 115		
Thomas, Senr.	Crv 261		
Washach	Rth 115		
William (2)	Brn 13A		
William	Cht 152		
William	Chw 115		
William	Dpl 399		
William	Dpl 441		
William	Frn 492		
William	Hlf 312		
William	Hde 370		
William	Ird 665		
William	Mnt 478		
William	Mnt 483		
William	Orn 575		
William	Rwn 345		
William	Rwn 379		
William	Rth 120		
William	Smp 499		
William	Wke 737		
William	Wlk 45		
William, Junr.	Wke 737		
Wm.	Nsh 104		
see Hull, Stall			
Hallard, George	Rwn 326		
Halley, James	Brk 756		
Hallford, Achillis	Rth 119		
John	Rth 115		
Lucy	Rth 119		
Halliman, James	Mck 588		
Saml.	Bld 13		
Halling, Solomon	Nwh 4		
Hallom, John	Brt 48		
Judith	Brt 48		
Halloman, Ezekiel	Wne 851		
Halloway, Mallicah	Csw 105		
Hallowell, Edwin	Wne 850		
John	Psq 634		
Hallum, George	Rck 475		
Halmaker, Francis	Orn 569		
Halsey, Edmund	Prq 642		
Elizabeth	Chw 126		
Frederick	Prq 654		
Henry	Chw 126		
Henry	Nwh 5		
John	Chw 131		
Malichi	Chw 126		

Halstead, Joshua	Crr 169	John	Chw 117	William	Ans 211
Mary	Crr 169	John	Grv 515	William	Ans 233
Halton, Charles	Ird 630	John	Grn 595	see Hamorond	
Haltum, Joseph,		John	Glf 653	Hammonds, Ephraim	Cmb 354
Senr.	Mnt 470	Joseph	Mnt 500	Isaac	Cmb 354
Spencer, Senr.	Mnt 470	Joseph	Orn 571	Jerusa	Cmb 354
William	Mnt 470	Joseph	Rth 93	John	Crr 145
Ham, Diner	Frn 484	Keziah	Wke 735	John	Mck 597
Ezekel	Stk 557	Lazarus	Wsh 706	John	Mck 598
George P.	Psq 628	Lewis	Wke 735	John	Rnd 316
Hezekiah	Glf 635	Martha	Lnc 834	Moses	Rnd 319
Mordicai	Stk 558	Marthy	Rth 115	Paul	Bld 21
Nehemiah	Rnd 318	Reubin	Wke 735	Hammons, Ar...ilaus	Bld 2
Philip	Glf 680	Richard	Lnc 877	Cha...	Bld 2
Thomas	Stk 555	Robert	Rth 120	Charles	Frn 462
Widow	Rwn 365	Robert	Bnc 158	Edward	Ons 158
William	Frn 477	Rubin	Lnc 885	Edward	Orn 575
Wm.	Mrt 396	Sally	Rth 93	Enoch	Rbs 384
Zekiel	Stk 574	Thomas	Hde 370	George	Ons 158
Hamahan, Walter	Bfr 22	Thomas	Rnd 320	Harvey	Rbs 384
Hambelton, John	Nwh 8A	Walter	Mnt 482	Horatio	Rbs 384
Hamber, Ben	Stk 614	William	Cbr 702	James	Frn 480
Hamberry, Dinah	Edg 206	William	Mck 564	James	Rth 119
Samuel	Edg 206	William	Rwn 379	Jesse	Nsh 104
Hambey, Thomas	Bnc 173	Hamlet, Ann	Wrr 810	Jessey	Frn 480
William	Bnc 173	Augusten	Wrr 808	John	Bnc 172
Hamble, Daniel	Glf 628	Elizabeth	Hlf 312	John	Nsh 102
Hamblen, Peter	Srr 659	Francis	Prs 208	John	Ons 158
see Hampben		Jas.	Prs 208	John (2)	Rbs 384
Hamblet, Richd.	Csw 121	Richard	Hlf 312	Jordon	Cht 203
Hambleton, Ann	Nwh 9	Thomas	Csw 104	Joseph	Stk 557
Elisha	Crv 327	Thos. M.	Prs 219	Martin	Ons 158
Fereby	Brt 52	William	Cht 163	Samuel	Rbs 384
Hannah	Crv 311	Hamlett, Kitty	Csw 116	Sarah	Rbs 384
Horatia	Stk 604	Wm.	Csw 116	Wiley	Stk 579
James	Crt 62	Hamlin, Will.	Prs 202	Will.	Nsh 104
James	Crt 63	Will., Junr.	Prs 205	William	Srr 662
John	Lnr 11	Hamlit, John	Mck 600	Willis	Rbs 384
John, Junr.	Crv 293	Peter	Mnt 508	Hammontree, Peter	Crv 263
John, Senr.	Crv 293	Hamm, Benjamin	Grv 526	Reubin	Crv 279
Mark	Crv 293	Erestus	Wne 846	Hamorond, John	Cmb 354
Robert	Crt 63	Jessee	Cht 162	Hampben see Hamblen	
Robert	Stk 558	Richard	Wne 846	Hampblen, Thomas	Srr 659
William	Crv 293	William	Wne 846	Hampten, Jonathan	Rth 115
Hamblett, Richd.	Csw 126	Zacehariah	Wne 871	Hampton, Ahab	Bnc 171
Hamblin, Wood	Hlf 314	Hammack, Robert	Srr 661	Andrew	Rth 115
Hambrick, Enoch	Rth 117	Hammd, John	Bfr 9	Andrew, Sr.	Rth 116
Henry	Rth 118	Hammell, Jane	Hlf 310	Benjamin	Srr 663
Isaac	Rth 117	John	Hlf 310	Collans	Srr 662
James	Rth 117	Hammer, Abraham	Rnd 320	Darner	Wlk 43
Jeremiah	Rth 118	Elisha	Rnd 320	David	Rwn 361
John	Rth 118	John	Rnd 320	Edward	Cht 200
Nathan	Rth 118	Hammilton, Thos.	Nsh 103	Edward	Orn 612
Price	Rth 117	Hammind, William	Srr 661	Ephraim, Jr.	Rwn 361
Samuel	Rth 117	Hammock, Bettey	Wrr 807	Ephraim, Senr.	Rwn 361
Travis	Rth 118	John	Cht 203	Henry	Stk 611
Yelvaton	Rth 118	William	Cht 203	Henry	Srr 704
Hamby, JOhn	Mck 579	Hammon, Ambrose	Wlk 44	Jacob	Wlk 42
John (2)	Wlk 42	Benjn.	Wlk 45	James	Stk 556
Joseph	Prs 202	Joseph	Wlk 45	Jeremiah	Ash 81
Samuel	Wlk 42	Robert	Bnc 174	Joel	Wlk 42
Stephen	Wlk 46	Sarah	Wlk 46	John	Grv 545
William	Wlk 42	Hammond, B. John	Bfr 9	John	Rwn 277
Hamden, William	Mck 549	Burwell	Edg 209	John	Rwn 361
Hamelton, Jane	Orn 512	Elizebeth	Crr 154	John	Stk 557
Hamilton, Alexan-		George	Ans 211	John, Junr.	Rwn 287
der	Lnc 826	Jacob	Ans 198	John, Senr.	Rwn 301
Barnaba	Wne 859	Jacob	Ans 224	Johnson	Ash 81
Clodius	Wne 870	John	Hde 369	Joseph	Mck 573
Elizabeth	Bnc 174	John B.	Bfr 9	Micajah	Bnc 171
Hance	Glf 650	Levi	Bfr 9	Nolin	Orn 574
Hugh	Cbr 683	Philip	Bfr 9	Oliver	Rwn 437
Jacob	Rwn 425	Sally	Lnr 12	Polly	Rth 121
James	Hde 371	Shadrach	Edg 209	Ruben	Wlk 43
James	Wsh 706	Thomas	Ans 211	Ruth	Crv 337
Jean	Lnc 899	Uel	Bfr 9	Samuel	Stk 556
John	Bfr 10	Wiley	Stk 592	Smith	Cht 197

Stephen	Srr 662	Marster	Brn 17A	see Howard, Manning	
Thomas	Srr 660	Tho.	Brn 18	Harden, Abraham	Rth 117
Thomas	Wlk 44	Thomas	Chw 113	Benjamin	Rnd 319
William	Crv 335	Hanks, Francis	Grv 515	Benjamin	Rth 120
William	Rwn 277	James	Wlk 45	Benjamin	Smp 510
William	Rwn 301	John	Orn 575	Charles	Glf 677
William, Jur.	Rwn 287	John	Stk 627	David (2)	Rth 118
Hamrich, Henry	Srr 662	Luke	Hlf 314	David	Smp 501
Hamrick, Patrick	Wlk 43	Nathan	Lnr 12	Edward	Rth 118
Hamtel see Hamlet		Richd.	Lnc 832	Gabrile	Rnd 319
Hamur, John	Ans 201	Sovrin	Lnr 17	Hannah	Rnd 318
William	Ans 201	Thos.	Lnc 835	Henry	Csw 145
Hanah, Robert	Glf 667	Hanler, Andrew	Rwn 425	Henry	Smp 510
Rody	Glf 633	Hanna, James	Srr 710	Henry	Srr 661
Hanchy, Martin	Bld 4	Hannah, Andrew	Rnd 318	James	Brk 757
Martin	Dpl 422	Ann	Lnc 826	John	Rth 120
Hancock, Benjn.	Cht 180	James	Ird 656	John, Junr.	Brk 759
Bennett	Wlk 42	John	Rth 120	Jonathan	Rth 118
Enock	Ons 150	Rubin	Brk 761	Joseph	Rth 118
Gabriel	Ons 150	Samuel	Ird 656	Lucy	Smp 501
Herman	Ptt 244	Thomas	Lnc 825	Mark	Rck 484
Isaiah	Trl 678	William	Rnd 317	Robert	Rth 118
James, junior	Ptt 245	William	Rnd 320	Sion	Smp 510
James, Senr.	Jns 793	Hanner, Alexander	Stk 593	Solomon	Rth 118
James, Senr.	Ptt 245	Barton	Stk 595	Starling	Grv 538
Jehue	Glf 641	Hanners, Henery	Crr 159	Stewart	Glf 621
John	Jns 793	Hennery	Crr 160	Theo.	Rck 441
John	Rnd 318	Hannis, David	Ons 165	Thomas	Brt 50
Joshua	Rnd 316	Hannon, Asa	Mre 55	Thomas	Glf 645
Josiah	Ptt 245	Edwin	Rth 116	Thomas	Rth 117
Nathaniel	Ons 151	John	Hlf 358	Thomas	Smp 501
Samuel	Rnd 320	Thomas	Mre 56	Thomas	Srr 662
Stephen	Dpl 414	Thomas, Sr.	Mre 56	William	Crv 321
Vachel	Rnd 318	William	Rth 116	William	Ird 624
William	Crv 343	Hansel, Wm.	Lnc 848	Harder, John	Orn 570
William	Ons 152	Hansill, John	Mrt 397	John N.	Orn 511
William	Trl 678	Wm.	Mrt 396	Joseph	Orn 511
William	Trl 692	Hansley, John	Ons 163	Hardesly, David	Csw 100
Zebedee	Ons 152	Will.	Nwh 8A	Hardester, Thomas	Rnd 353
Hancy, Robert	Rth 120	Hany, Henry	Ons 160	Hardesty, Benjamin	Crt 81
Hand, Chrisr.	Rck 482	Harald, Adam	Glf 654	Joseph	Crt 81
Jeremiah	Nwh 11A	Adam	Orn 512	Hardeway, Joseph	Wrr 811
John, Junr.	Ans 200	Harawood, Henry	Rwn 432	Hardey, Edwd.	Crr 145
John, Senr.	Ans 200	Harberson, William	Lnc 877	Hardick, Allen	Bld 6
William	Rck 485	Harbin, Allin	Rwn 442	Hardin, Benjamin	Lnc 896
Handcock, Calvin	Crt 71	Edward V.	Stk 608	Elijah	Lnc 900
Caswel	Crt 71	Reason	Rwn 442	Elizabeth	Rbs 382
Crumwel	Crt 74	Villers	Rwn 442	Gabriel	Ans 219
Elizabeth	Mre 43	Harbison, Alexan-		Henry	Ash 81
Hardee	Ptt 245	der	Brk 754	James	Lnc 900
Isacoh	Rck 473	Matthew	Brk 755	James	Mre 76
James	Mre 42	Nancy	Lnc 877	John	Brk 758
Joseph	Crt 71	William	Brk 754	Joshua	Brk 761
Nehemiah	Hrt 717	William	Mck 577	Lucy	Brt 52
Patsay	Mre 63	Harboard, Charles	Rch 250	Solomon	Rbs 383
Peggy	Crt 67	John	Hlf 318	William	Mre 57
Sarah	Crt 67	William	Hlf 314	William	Rwn 326
Wm.	Rck 468	Harbunkee, Conrod	Ird 633	William	Rwn 452
Handdock, Richd.	Csw 101	Hardcastle, Bisha	Rth 120	Harding, Israel	Bfr 10
Handen, John	Brk 759	James	Rth 120	John	Nrt 449
Handley, James	Wne 849	Robert	Rth 121	Michael	Bfr 10
James, Jr.	Wne 870	Hardee, Abraham,		Stephen, Ser.	Bfr 10
Handlin, Stephen	Bnc 171	junior	Ptt 251	Hardins, Stephen,	
Handy, Matthias	Jhn 748	Abraham, Senr.	Ptt 252	Jur.	Bfr 10
Hanely, Abnor	Brk 760	Charles	Ptt 248	Hardison, Anna	Hde 371
Hanes, Andrew	Cht 198	Elizabeth	Ptt 251	Asa	Wsh 716
Ezekiel	Rth 119	Isaac	Lnr 10	Benjamin	Wsh 714
Sally	Rth 119	John	Edg 206	Benjn.	Mrt 396
Samuel	Cht 201	Joseph	Edg 207	Charles	Ons 163
William	Edg 205	Lemuel, Senior	Grn 616	Charles	Ons 165
William	Rth 119	Major	Lnr 10	Cullin	Bfr 9
Haney, Hezekiah	Hlf 316	Michaal	Edg 205	David	Mrt 396
Jesse	Edg 208	Robert	Edg 207	Ezekiel	Wsh 714
Lewis	Edg 209	Sutton, Senior	Grn 616	Frederick	Bfr 10
Sarah	Smp 520	Thomas, junior	Ptt 245	Isaac	Hde 371
Hankens, Dennes	Brn 18	William	Lnr 10	Jas., Senr.	Mrt 396
Hankins, Elizabeth	Brn 17	William, junior	Ptt 251	Jasper	Crv 261

Jasper	Wsh 706	Nathon	Prs 216	Nicholas	Brt 50
Jessey	Wsh 714	Sarah	Orn 571	William	Prq 651
John, Junr.	Mrt 396	Shadrach	Prs 216	Zachariah	Cht 151
John, Senr.	Mrt 396	Thos.	Prs 215	Harmon, Adam	Rwn 392
Joseph	Hde 369	Will.	Prs 205	Adam, Senr.	Rwn 373
Joshua	Mrt 397	Hargit, Henry	Mck 583	Andrew	Lnc 896
Lemuel	Hde 370	Henry, Senr.	Mck 584	Cutliff	Ash 81
Lucretia	Grn 597	John	Mck 584	George	Lnc 868
Luke	Mrt 396	Joseph	Mck 584	George	Lnc 872
Mark	Mrt 397	Hargnes, Jacob	Lnc 889	George	Rnd 317
Mary	Wsh 714	Hargrave, Dicy (Free		Henry	Lnc 896
Richd.	Mrt 396	Negro)	Edg 207	Jacob	Lnc 896
Thos.	Mrt 396	Etheldred	Edg 207	Jacob	Rnd 318
Wiggins	Mrt 397	George	Edg 206	John	Hlf 316
William	Bfr 8	Unity	Edg 207	John	Lnc 896
Hardman, Peter	Rwn 415	Hargraves, James	Csw 143	John	Wlk 42
Hardon, Jordon	Ird 630	Hargrove, Aaron	Smp 505	Joseph	Rth 120
Robert	Ird 633	Arthur	Smp 505	Leonard	Rnd 319
Hardoway, Joseph	Edg 207	Britton	Bld 6	Littleton	Wke 735
Hardrick, Thomas	Rck 489	John	Grv 515	Lydea	Lnc 896
see Hendrick		John	Smp 505	Mathias	Ash 81
Hardridge, Robert	Rwn 354	John S.	Grv 534	Mathias	Rnd 353
Hardsworth, Calib	Prq 659	Lamuel	Smp 505	Micajah	Rth 115
Hardtimes, Thomas	Rch 269	Martha	Glf 685	Michael	Lnc 868
Hardy, Andrew	Brn 20A	Moses	Smp 508	Peter	Ird 630
Curtis	Wrr 809	Richard	Grv 513	Peter	Lnc 872
David	Hlf 312	Robert	Grv 515	Peter	Lnc 896
Elizabeth	Brt 52	Samuel	Glf 663	Philip	Rwn 408
Henry	Srr 660	William	Hlf 314	Richard	Lnc 896
Humphrey	Brt 46	Hargroves, Freder-		Valentine, Cap.	Rwn 373
John	Brt 52	ick	Glf 664	William	Lnc 872
John	Wne 872	Haril, Ezekial	Prs 194	Harmons, Andrew	Ird 650
Myles	Wsh 706	Harilson, Anderson	Prs 194	Harmor, John	Glf 619
P. William	Brt 46	Will.	Prs 208	Harney, Jeffry	Rwn 366
Sarah	Brt 48	Haris, John	Ons 173	Laurania	Cmd 109
William	Crt 75	Harison, Andrew	Csw 106	Thomas	Cmd 110
William, Senior	Ptt 244	Andw.	Csw 130	Harny, John	Glf 676
William P.	Brt 46	James D.	Csw 111	Harol, Henry	Ans 218
Winnifred	Brt 48	Ninian	Csw 130	Harold, Abner	Prq 648
Hare, Ann	Hrt 699	Thomas	Csw 106	David	Prq 647
David	Ird 665	William	Srr 658	Harp, Alexr.	Jhn 757
Edward	Brt 50	Hariston, Peter	Stk 573	Isaiah	Brn 16A
Elisha	Gts 269	Harkels see Hackels		James	Stk 590
Felix	Smp 532	Harker, Belcher	Crt 61	John	Grv 531
Isaac	Smp 496	Ebenezer, jr.	Crt 61	John	Nsh 103
Jesse	Cmb 382	Ebenezer, sr.	Crt 61	John	Srr 660
Joel	Smp 525	James	Crt 61	Jonathan	Jhn 761
John	Gts 268	James	Crv 257	Keziah	Rbs 382
John	Grv 515	Zachariah	Crt 61	Sampson	Grv 528
John	Mre 47	Harket, Simon	Psq 625	Sherwood	Jhn 758
John	Smp 496	Harkey, Henry	Mck 606	William	Bnc 173
John	Smp 532	Jacob	Cbr 708	William	Grv 530
Joseph	Gts 269	John (2)	Mck 604	William	Wke 735
Joseph	Ird 665	Martin (2)	Cbr 708	Harpe, Ann	Grv 561
Martin	Smp 532	Martin	Cbr 709	John	Stk 556
Mary	Brt 48	Martin	Cbr 712	Harper, Abraham	Crv 267
Moses	Hrt 711	Harkman, George	Cbr 703	Abraham	Crv 305
Sarah	Wsh 706	Harley, Elisha	Cht 178	Alexander	Crv 329
Thomas	Cmb 386	George	Brk 762	Ambrose	Hlf 318
William	Hrt 699	John	Cht 179	Ann	Crv 305
William	Smp 532	Harlin, Eadath	Rwn 366	Blaney, Senior	Grn 608
Haregrove, Jacob	Grv 515	Elijah	Mck 536	Francis	Grn 602
William	Grv 515	John	Mck 535	George	Brn 20A
Harel, Elizabeth	Grn 609	Stephen	Rnd 316	Hannah	Cht 166
Harfmon see Hartmon		Stephen (2)	Rnd 321	Hughey	Grn 603
Harget, Ann	Jns 791	William	Rwn 366	Jacob	Hlf 312
Frederick,Junr.	Jns 811	Harlley, William	Brk 762	James	Edg 208
Frederick,Senr.	Jns 797	Harlly, Jacob	Brk 757	James	Nwh 7A
Sally	Bnc 173	Harlow, Thomas	Hlf 312	James	Rnd 320
William, Senr.	Jns 797	Harlowe, John	Brt 90	Jesse	Lnr 30
Hargett, William		Harman, Abram	Brt 52	John	Cht 221
Isler	Ons 169	Benson	Rth 119	John	Grn 598
Hargis, Abahem	Prs 205	Daniel	Lnc 824	John	Hlf 312
Amy	Orn 575	David	Lnc 816	John	Jns 805
Jean	Prs 203	Hezekiah	Cht 158	John	Lnr 32
Jonathan	Prs 216	John	Cht 226	John	Nwh 9A
Joseph	Prs 217	Joseph	Cht 152	John	Orn 569

John	Rck 477	Jesse	Hrt 705	Aaron	Ird 621
John	Rwn 392	Jesse	Rbs 385	Abraham	Chw 124
John	Wne 855	Jesse, Junr.	Gts 269	Abraham	Chw 126
John, Junr.	Brk 754	Jno.	Csw 136	Absalom	Wlk 42
John, Senr.	Brk 754	John	Ans 238	Alice	Crt 69
Jonathan	Rnd 321	John	Gts 269	Ann	Ptt 228
Joseph	Lnc 901	John	Lnr 32	Archbald	Orn 574
Joseph	Wrr 808	John	Ptt 271	Archble	Rch 266
Mary	Cht 221	John, Junr.	Mrt 397	Archor	Wrr 809
Meridy	Brk 757	John, Senr.	Mrt 397	Arthur, (Col.)	Mnt 462
Nancy	Crv 267	Josiah	Gts 269	Arthur, Junr.	Mnt 479
Nathan	Lnr 30	Josiah	Lnr 32	Arthur, Senr.	Mnt 478
Peter	Crv 275	Kedar	Jhn 774	Barness	Srr 661
Ruebin	Edg 209	Leml.	Mrt 396	Barnet	Stk 579
Saml.	Wrr 810	Levy	Mrt 396	Bedford	Wrr 809
Samuel	Rwn 393	Lewis	Grn 604	Benjamin	Ans 210
Samuel, jr.	Wrr 810	Lewis	Mrt 397	Benjamin	Ans 220
Thomas, Junr.	Rwn 393	Lott	Mrt 397	Benjamin	Ans 231
Thomas, Senr.	Rwn 392	Michael	Ptt 288	Benjamin	Brk 761
Thos.	Lnr 12	Mills	Ans 239	Benjamin	Grv 509
Tyrrel	Hlf 314	Moses	Mrt 396	Benjamin	Glf 692
Vinson	Hlf 318	Nathan	Hrt 699	Benjamin	Hlf 316
William	Brk 754	Noah	Gts 268	Benjn.	Cht 171
William	Grn 603	Patience	Mrt 397	Bettey	Wrr 809
William	Rwn 432	Peter	Gts 269	Bevel	Grv 584
Zepheniah	Stk 610	Peter, Sr.	Gts 269	Brantly	Mnt 478
Harral, John, Junr.	Wlk 46	Rasha.	Ons 148	Bridget	Wke 736
John, Senr.	Wlk 46	Reuben	Nsh 105	Britain	Frn 452
Tarbes	Csw 108	Reuben	Ptt 271	Casen	Dpl 427
Harramond, Henry	Brt 46	Saml.	Mrt 397	Charles	Cbr 681
Harrard, James	Wke 734	Samuel	Gts 268	Charles	Grv 509
John	Wke 734	Samuel	Gts 269	Charles	Grv 545
Martin	Wke 735	Stephen	Chw 128	Charles	Hlf 312
William	Wke 734	Sylus	Prq 662	Charles	Hlf 358
Wm., Junr.	Wke 734	Theophilus	Gts 269	Charles	Ptt 288
see Hopson		Thomas, Senr.	Gts 269	Charles	Rck 476
Harrawood, John	Rwn 432	thos.	Mrt 396	Ciller	Rck 463
see Arrawood		William	Gts 269	Clabourn	Ans 230
Harrel, Benjn.	Mrt 395	William	Hrt 711	Clabourn	Grv 523
Daniel	Smp 515	Willis	Hrt 717	Claebourn	Wke 737
Ephrim	Mrt 394	Willis	Wne 856	Claibourn	Wke 737
Howsend	Rth 117	Wm., Senr.	Mrt 397	Cuningham	Cbr 679
James	Dpl 421	Zachr.	Ans 238	Cyrus	Frn 445
John	Chw 127	Harrendon, James	Ird 665	Dabney	Srr 664
John	Rth 117	Harreson, Joseph	Ird 629	Daniel	Dpl 429
Kedar	Dpl 415	Harress, Elias	Crr 147	Daniel	Frn 472
Kedar	Jns 803	Hartwell	Nsh 105	Daniel	Hde 371
Mary	Edg 206	Mary	Gts 268	Daniel	Smp 504
Mason	Smp 505	Nehemiah	Nwh 3	David	Brk 757
Moses	Cmb 376	Randolph	Nsh 105	David	Grv 576
Samuel	Rth 117	Sarah	Crr 147	David	Grv 583
Stephen	Edg 206	Thos.	Crr 147	Dred	Cht 168
see Herral		Harril, Paul	Prs 199	Ebenezer	Hde 370
Harrell, Abraham	Gts 268	Wm.	Csw 110	Edith	Frn 469
Aron	Gts 269	Harrill, Cason	Ans 205	Edward	Crv 249
Asa	Gts 268	Matthew	Mnt 486	Edward	Frn 449
Charity	Mrt 396	Harrilson, Benjm.	Prs 187	Edward	Grv 521
David	Gts 267	Harrin, Hugh	Ird 633	Edward	Wrr 809
David, Jr.	Gts 268	Mary	Ird 633	Edwd.	Brn 20
David, (of SC)	Gts 269	Robert	Ird 633	Edwd.	Grv 507
Demey	Gts 269	William	Ird 633	Edwin	Wrr 809
Edward	Jhn 774	Harrington,		Elang	Hde 370
Elijah	Gts 269	Charles	Bfr 10	Eli	Hlf 316
Elisabeth	Mrt 396	Charles	Hde 369	Elijah	Grv 523
Elisha	Gts 269	Henry W.	Rch 270	Elisabeth	Crv 251
Elisha	Rbs 385	John	Ans 224	Elisabeth	Crv 261
Elisha, (of		Lurany	Hlf 314	Elizabeth	Cbr 676
Peter)	Gts 269	Marmaduke	Bfr 9	Elizabeth	Hlf 318
Francis (2)	Jhn 776	Nathan	Hde 369	Enoch	Crv 325
Henry	Jhn 775	Nathl.	Rch 248	Enoch	Hde 370
Isaac, Sr.	Gts 269	Nathl.	Rch 264	Etheldred	Mnt 479
Isham	Ans 221	Philaman	Cht 159	Ephraim D.	Cbr 713
Jacob	Cht 202	Sion	Mre 65	Ezekiel	Hde 369
Jacob	Mrt 397	Thomas	Ans 230	Ezekiel, Senr.	Hde 369
Jacob	Prq 663	Thomas	Cht 154	Francis	Mnt 495
James	Ans 220	Timothy	Bnc 172	Fredrick	Wrr 809
James	Ans 235	Harris, ...	Grv 518	George	Cbr 679

George	Grv 552	John, Jur.	Rck 473	Simon	Wke 734		
George	Mck 606	Jonathan	Mck 576	Solomon	Grv 563		
George	Rwn 386	Jonathan	Rch 266	Solomon	Hde 370		
George B.	Crt 79	Jonathan	Rth 116	Solomon	Mck 583		
Gibson	Grv 551	Joseph	Psq 626	Sovereign	Ptt 227		
Gibson	Hde 370	Joseph	Psq 630	Spears	Grv 543		
Hanah	Glf 651	Joseph	Psq 631	Stephen	Crv 269		
Hannah	Crv 251	Joseph	Ptt 288	Sterling	Orn 491		
Hardey	Wrr 809	Joseph	Rwn 443	Sterling	Wrr 809		
Hardy	Wke 734	Joseph	Srr 661	Stokely	Crt 79		
Henry	Chw 124	Joshua	Mnt 462	Susannah	Wlk 44		
Henry	Hlf 316	Josiah	Hde 370	Taylor	Mnt 462		
Henry	Ptt 277	L., Widow	Mck 576	Thomas	Brn 19A		
Henry	Wrr 809	Lewis	Rth 119	Thomas	Crt 67		
Holsea	Chw 118	Lucey	Ptt 290	Thomas	Crt 89		
Holsey	Chw 123	Lucy	Hlf 312	Thomas	Ptt 259		
Hood	Ptt 259	Major	Ptt 228	Thomas	Wke 736		
Howard	Wrr 809	Mary	Bnc 173	Thomas, Jur.	Hde 370		
Hugh	Wlk 44	Mary	Ird 639	Thomas, Maj.	Mck 565		
Ichabud	Ptt 234	Mary	Mnt 462	Thompson	Hlf 312		
Isaac	Hlf 312	Mary	Orn 610	Turner	Mnt 478		
Isaac	Rth 119	Matthew	Stk 581	Tyre	Cmb 391		
Isham	Lnc 889	Mical	Wrr 808	Tyree	Grv 583		
Isham	Mnt 496	Milley	Stk 580	Vaten	Rth 115		
Isham	Wke 736	Moses	Ptt 227	Warren	Hlf 318		
Isham	Wrr 807	Mosley	Grv 546	West	Cht 153		
Jacob	Ird 665	Nathan	Lnc 889	West	Mnt 478		
Jacob	Ptt 228	Nathan	Mnt 467	Widow	Mck 566		
James	Bnc 173	Nathan	Orn 574	Widow L.	Mck 576		
James	Cbr 679	Nathaniel	Rck 482	Wiley	Mnt 478		
James	Crv 275	Nathaniel	Wlk 44	William	Ash 80		
James	Mck 544	Ned	Mnt 484	William	Cbr 676		
James	Mck 567	Neusom	Wrr 806	William	Bfr 10		
James	Mnt 479	Newit	Wrr 810	William	Crv 287		
James	Rth 119	Norphteel	Hlf 316	William (2)	Dpl 429		
James	Rth 120	Obadiah	Glf 692	William	Grv 515		
James	Wke 737	Obadiah, Senr.	Glf 693	William	Grv 523		
James	Wrr 808	Oliver	Cbr 683	William	Grv 551		
James	Wlk 44	Phil.	Wrr 808	William	Mck 553		
James, Jr.	Wrr 808	Prissy	Hlf 316	William	Mnt 462		
James, Junr.	Rwn 326	Ransan	Wrr 807	William	Nwh 2A		
James, Senr.	Rwn 326	Richard	Lnc 877	William	Ptt 229		
James Edwd.	Grv 507	Richard	Ptt 277	William	Rck 472		
Jane	Wrr 809	Richard	Ptt 290	William	Rth 119		
Jesse	Bnc 172	Richd.	Brn 14A	William	Stk 579		
Jesse	Crt 81	Richmond	Orn 610	William	Srr 663		
Jesse	Grv 564	Robert	Brk 758	William	Wke 737		
Jesse	Grv 565	Robert	Cbr 677	William	Wrr 808		
Jesse	Wke 735	Robert	Dpl 411	William	Wrr 810		
Jesse, Junr.	Rwn 386	Robert	Mnt 484	William, Jur.	Hde 369		
Jno.	Lnc 831	Robert	Orn 610	William, Ser.	Hde 370		
Jno.	Prs 191	Robert	Prs 196	William, (Tay-			
Joel	Wrr 808	Robert	Srr 661	lor)	Cbr 681		
John	Bfr 10	Robert	Srr 663	Willie	Wrr 810		
John	Bld 41	Robert	Wrr 808	Wilmot E.	Wrr 809		
John	Cht 173	Robert, Esq.	Cbr 683	Wooten	Rth 119		
John	Cht 185	Robert, Junr.	Cbr 679	Zaphenia	Rwn 437		
John	Cht 187	Roland	Grv 518	Harrison, Abraham	Nrt 449		
John	Cht 214	Roland	Mnt 517	Alex	Crr 149		
John	Crv 285	Sally	Brk 758	Benjamin	Jns 795		
John	Dpl 429	Saml.	Prs 197	Charles	Nrt 447		
John	Grv 507	Samson	Brk 759	David	Ans 232		
John	Glf 630	Samuel	Bnc 172	Delany, Sen.	Srr 658		
John	Ird 633	Samuel	Cbr 677	Elisabeth	Jns 815		
John	Mck 596	Samuel	Grv 575	Elisha	Hrt 711		
John	Mnt 462	Samuel	Mck 557	Ely	Grv 528		
John	Psq 635	Samuel	Mck 566	Ephraim	Jns 797		
John	Prs 209	Samuel	Wke 736	George	Grv 537		
John	Ptt 228	Sarah	Orn 574	George	Stk 556		
John	Rnd 317	Shadrach	Crv 267	Gideon	Hlf 316		
John	Rck 471	Shadrach	Crv 285	Henry	Glf 651		
John	Rwn 326	Shadrick	Dpl 429	Isaac	Crr 138		
John	Stk 579	Shearwood	Wke 737	Isham	Nrt 451		
John	Wke 735	Sherwood	Grv 522	James	Ans 216		
John	Wke 736	Sherwood	Grv 546	James	Grv 526		
John	Wrr 809	Sherwood	Jhn 770	James	Hrt 704		
John, Esq.	Mck 565	Sherwood	Rch 266	James	Jns 779		

Jas.	Mrt 395	Thos.	Crr 162	James	Grv 548
Jesse	Bfr 9	Timothy	Edg 205	James	Ird 674
Jesse	Hlf 316	William	Edg 207	James	Ird 675
Jesse	Rck 446	William	Gts 268	James	Orn 511
Jethro	Nsh 103	William	Nrt 449	James, (Majr.	Mck 537
John	Ans 216	Wm.	Crr 150	James, (N.H.)	Orn 571
John	Ans 217	Harrisson, Benja-		Jesse	Nrt 449
John	Bnc 171	min	Wsh 704	John	Cht 181
John	Glf 652	Elisha	Trl 690	John	Cht 220
John	Jns 795	Elisha	Wsh 706	John	Hrt 729
John	Nsh 103	Elizabeth	Wsh 704	John	Nrt 447
John	Nrt 449	Harmon	Wsh 704	John	Ons 150
Josep	Ird 630	Jesse	Wsh 706	John	Stk 584
Joseph	Crv 327	John	Brt 50	Joseph	Brk 756
Joseph	Ird 614	John	Cmd 105	Joseph	Grv 541
Joseph	Jns 813	Joseph (2)	Prq 661	Lucretia	Grn 593
Joseph	Rth 120	King	Brt 52	Matthew, Cap.	Mck 565
Josiah	Mck 601	Lovick	Wsh 704	Michael	Brk 760
Levi	Jns 779	Peter	Cmd 105	Michael	Lnc 877
Lovel	Wke 737	Reuben	Brt 48	Nathan	Grn 593
Major	Prs 200	William	Wsh 706	Peter	Ash 79
Mary	Csw 106	Harrod, Christopher	Edg 206	Peter	Lnc 906
Mary	Hlf 316	David	Mrt 394	Peter	Orn 512
Moses	Wke 737	Jesse	Mrt 394	Richard S.	Edg 205
Nathaniel	Stk 610	John	Chw 123	Robert	Grn 595
Nathl.	Wrr 806	Theophls.	Brn 19	Robert	Ons 151
Nehemiah	Mck 574	see Harrard		S. Richard	Edg 205
Polley	Wke 737	Harrold, Amos	Brt 52	Stephen	Orn 512
Richard	Jns 797	Arthur	Brt 52	Thomas	Cht 180
Robert	Glf 628	Benjamin	Brt 52	Thomas	Cht 182
Robert	Wrr 806	Christopher	Brt 52	Thomas	Jhn 760
Samuel	Bfr 10	Gabriel	Brt 50	Thomas	Nsh 105
Samuel	Rwn 409	George	Brt 52	Thomas	Orn 571
Sarah	Rck 485	Guin	Brt 50	Varnal	Hlf 318
Sciles	Jns 811	Henry	Brt 52	Warrin	Nrt 447
Simmons	Jns 815	Hezekiah	Brt 52	William	Ash 79
Stephen	Bfr 9	Hodges	Brt 52	William	Cht 220
Stephen	Jns 797	Isaac, Junr.	Brt 48	William	Grn 587
Susanna	Prs 191	Isaac, Senr.	Brt 48	William	Hrt 731
Thomas	Bnc 171	Isham	Brt 52	William	Mck 560
Thomas	Csw 105	James	Brt 52	William	Mck 567
Thomas	Lnr 10	Jeresiah	Brt 52	William, Junr.	Grn 597
Thomas	Rnd 316	Jesse	Brt 50	Zachariah	Edg 207
William	Frn 450	Job	Brt 48	Harte, Moses	Ans 228
William	Frn 483	John	Brt 48	Hartes, Leonard	Mck 583
William	Ird 630	John, Senr.	Brt 48	Hartgrave, Heze-	
William	Jns 799	Joshua	Brt 50	kiah	Stk 556
William	Rbs 383	Josiah	Brt 48	Howel	Stk 556
William	Rck 478	Luois	Brt 50	Hartgraves, Rich-	
William	Rck 480	Thomas	Brt 52	ard	Orn 511
William	Rwn 379	William	Brt 48	Hartgroves, Benja-	
William	Srr 659	William	Brt 50	min	Mck 528
William K.	Csw 108	Harry, Barnard	Stk 587	Thompson	Mck 528
Winnifred	Hlf 314	Caleb	Glf 626	Hartis, Lewis	Mck 605
Zorobable	Crr 138	Isaac	Rwn 458	Hartley, Benjamin	Rwn 408
Harriss, Amos	Brt 46	John	Glf 671	John	Crv 281
Dawson	Nrt 449	Harse, Lewis	Brk 756	Joseph	Crv 323
Elizabeth	Trl 678	Harser, Lewis	Rnd 318	Joshua	Ans 203
Ephraim	Nrt 451	Hart, Agsolom	Ons 151	Laybon	Rwn 409
George	Edg 205	Adam	Glf 662	Martha	Bfr 10
James	Nrt 447	Andrew	Cht 183	Thomas	Rwn 409
Jesse	Hde 370	Andrew	Ird 674	see Harlley	
John	Brt 50	Barram	Grn 602	Hartlie, Joseph	Lnc 877
John	Edg 208	Benjamin	Edg 206	Hartline, Peter	Rwn 307
John	Nrt 447	Benjamin, Junr.	Edg 208	Widow	Rwn 307
Joseph	Trl 678	Carr	Grn 595	Hartly, James	Smp 510
Josiah	Mrt 397	Cruse	Wlk 43	Richard	Rwn 409
Mary	Nrt 451	David	Mck 537	see Harlly	
Mildred	Nrt 451	Elizabeth	Csw 96	Hartman, George	Cbr 690
Nathan	Edg 209	Heath	Cht 183	George	Rwn 416
Nathan	Nrt 449	Henry	Glf 662	Jacob	Nwh 1A
Nathan, Junr.	Nrt 447	Henry	Glf 662	Jacob	Rwn 399
Nathan, Senr.	Nrt 449	Henry, Junr.	Nrt 447	John (2)	Rwn 296
Rachel	Hrt 720	Henry, Senr.	Nrt 447	Michael	Rwn 312
Richard	Edg 207	Jacob	Brk 759	Hartmon, Harmon	Stk 557
Saml. P.	Mrt 395	Jacob A.	Csw 136	John	Stk 604
Thomas	Edg 207	James	Ash 79	Hartmuss, Petter	Psq 626

Hartness, James	Ird 611	John	Crt 57	Hasten, Henry	Orn 571
Harton, Burwell	Wrr 810	John	Hlf 314	Henry	Orn 609
Hardeway	Wrr 810	John	Rwn 321	Henry, Junr.	Orn 609
Hawell	Wrr 810	Jonas	Stk 594	James	Orn 609
Salley	Wrr 810	Joshua	Orn 569	John	Csw 143
Zachh.	Csw 123	Molley	Stk 588	John	Orn 512
Hartsaugh, John	Rwn 321	Oney	Hlf 312	Joseph	Csw 121
Hartsel, John	Mnt 507	Sarah	Stk 594	Joseph (2)	Orn 609
Hartsell, George	Cbr 691	Thomas	Psq 624	Joseph, jr.	Orn 609
Leonard	Cbr 691	Thomas	Stk 584	Robert	ORn 609
Hartsfield, Jacob.	Frn 472	Thomas	Srr 660	William	Orn 609
James	Wke 734	Thomas, Jr.	Hlf 312	Zacharah	Grv 536
John	Lnr 10	Thomas, Senr.	Hlf 312	Haster, Charles	Grv 554
John	Wke 734	William	Rnd 319	Hastie, Samuel	Nrt 447
Sally	Lnr 10	William, Jr.	Hlf 310	Hastiff, Laban	Jhn 765
Samuel	Lnr 10	William, Senr.	Hlf 310	Hasting, William	Rth 120
Hartsford, John	Lnr 10	William, T.S.	Hlf 312	Hastings, Carter	Cmd 98
Hartsoe, Isaac	Cht 161	Harwell, Abigel	Lnc 864	Devotion	Cmd 100
John	Cht 196	Gardner	Hlf 310	James	Csw 123
Phillip	Cht 162	Heartwell	Hlf 314	John	Cmd 99
Hartzell, Jonathan	Cbr 711	Jackson	Lnc 865	Joshua	Wne 866
Harvel, David	Srr 662	Joel	Frn 493	Haston, Archd.	Rck 456
John	Srr 662	John	Wrr 808	Hasty, Delilah	Wne 860
Harvell, Mason	Wke 736	Milley	Lnc 861	Elijah	Rch 256
Harvey, Caleb	Orn 512	Sterling	Hlf 312	James	Rch 243
Charles	Psq 626	William	Nrt 451	Joseph	Wne 859
David	Orn 511	Harwood, Absalom	Mnt 513	Mathew	Mrt 394
Elizabeth	Chw 117	Malicha	Mnt 513	Pebles	Mrt 397
Ely	Orn 569	Haselip, Surthy	Mrt 396	William	Wne 860
George	Ird 635	Thomas	Rth 116	Hatay, William	Cht 199
Henry	Bfr 10	Hashaw, Abram	Brk 756	Hatch, Anthony	Jns 823
Isaac	Orn 569	Haskel, Jessa	Prq 651	Asa	Ons 160
Isam	Wlk 44	Hasket, Abraham	Rnd 319	Charles	Crv 341
James	Frn 493	Joseph	Prq 646	Durant	Jns 781
James, Jur.	Bfr 9	Joseph	Rnd 319	Edmond	Jns 803
James, Ser.	Bfr 9	Nathan	Prq 651	Ivey	Crv 337
John	Bfr 9	Silas	Prq 651	John	Ons 177
John	Crv 235	Thomas	Crt 81	Joseph	Jns 783
John	Prq 654	Thomas	Prq 650	Lemuel	Jns 803
John	Ptt 279	William	Prq 650	Penelope	Jns 807
John	Rnd 317	Haskett, Joseph	Rnd 316	Sarah	Jns 803
John	Srr 704	Joshua	Prq 645	Hatcher, Alex	Orn 571
John, Jun.	Prq 657	Haskew, William	Rth 117	Benjamin	Jhn 758
Jonathan	Orn 511	Haskins, James	Grv 575	Hancock	Smp 499
Joseph	Prq 654	John	Lnc 855	Jameston	Bnc 171
Joshua	Bfr 9	Robt.	Lnc 848	John	Rnd 321
Markam	Ons 144	Hasley, Benjamin	Ird 630	Obediah	Nsh 103
Michael	Rnd 317	Haslin, William	Rnd 317	Thomas	Rwn 386
Michael	Rnd 319	Haslip, Andrew	Brk 754	Thomas	Rwn 386
Michael	Rnd 320	Hasman, James	Orn 610	Widow	Rwn 387
Nathan	Bfr 10	Hassel, Christina	Bfr 10	William	Jhn 758
Nathan	Hde 369	Hassell, Abraham	Chw 120	Hatchett, Edward	Orn 512
Nathan	Orn 569	Ann	Chw 120	William	Orn 512
Richard, Jur.	Hde 371	Anne (2)	Trl 678	Hately, Richard	Rwn 426
Richard, Ser.	Hde 371	Anne	Wsh 706	Hatfield, Jesse	Trl 674
Robert	Bld 32	Benjamin	Trl 688	John	Prq 656
Stephen	Hde 371	Benone	Trl 690	Priscilla	Prq 652
Travers	Bld 35	Caswell	Mrt 397	Sarah	Crv 253
Willeelmy	Hde 371	Isaac	Mrt 397	William	Trl 674
William	Orn 569	James	Trl 674	Hathaway, David	Ptt 273
William	Srr 661	Jesse	Chw 121	James	Chw 115
Wyriott	Bfr 10	Job	Cmb 354	James	Ptt 274
see Hawey, Hervey		John	Trl 690	John	Ans 214
Harvie, Samuel	Cmb 385	Joseph	Trl 674	John	Ptt 293
Harvill, Lemuel	Ird 656	Joseph	Trl 686	Nathan	Ptt 273
Nathaniel	Ird 656	Joseph, Senr.	Trl 674	Sarah	Ptt 273
Roland	Lnc 833	Joshua	Wsh 706	Thomas	Ptt 275
William	Wke 735	Levi	Wsh 706	William	Ptt 274
Harville, Ambrose	Ird 655	Solomon	Trl 690	Hathcock, Aaron	Nrt 449
Frederick	Ird 655	Solomon, Senr.	Trl 692	Celah	Hlf 318
Marow	Cmb 372	Stephen	Trl 690	Curtis	Hlf 316
Harvines, David	Glf 661	William	Trl 678	Deney	Mre 68
Jacob	Glf 661	Zebedee	Trl 670	G. Major	Hlf 314
Harvy, Caleb	Orn 575	Zebulun	Trl 674	James	Cht 189
Henry	Crt 75	Haste, Charlton	Hrt 699	Jesse	Hlf 312
Isaac	Stk 594	John	Hrt 699	John	Cht 167
Jean	Rnd 319	Samuel	Brt 48	John	Nrt 449

Major G.	Hlf 314	George	Stk 556	Samuel	Hlf 314
Mary	Hlf 318	George	Stk 627	Solomon	Hlf 318
Reuben	Hlf 312	George, Senior	Stk 627	Thomas	Brt 50
Stephen	Wke 734	Henry	Stk 627	Thomas	Rth 117
Surry	Hlf 318	Henry, Jr.	Stk 557	Thomas	Wsh 706
Thomas	Rch 258	John	Stk 556	Whitehurst	Ons 178
Toliver	Hlf 318	John	Stk 557	Will.	Prs 205
Hathen, William	Csw 98	John	Stk 627	William	Brk 757
Hathman, Hezekiah	Rwn 330	Joseph	Stk 627	William	Hlf 312
Jonathan	Wlk 43	Martin	Stk 610	William	Jns 791
Hatley, Luke	Cht 175	Michael	Stk 627	William	Mck 603
Hatly, Hardy	Mnt 514	Michal	Stk 557	William	Ons 142
John	Mnt 513	Peter	Stk 557	William	Rth 115
Hatmaker see Halmaker		Peter, Junior	Stk 627	William	Stk 584
Hatrick, Robert	Orn 512	Peter, Jur.	Stk 557	William, Jur.	Jns 791
Robert	Rck 452	Peter, Senior	Stk 627	Willibough	Bfr 10
Hatsel, Armstead	Crt 92	Simon P.	Stk 556	Wyatt	Wrr 807
Hannah	Crt 74	Simon Peter	Stk 627	see Spruill	
Herrod	Crt 92	Have, Benjamin	Hrt 724	Hawks, Fredrick	Wrr 811
William, jr.	Crt 91	John	Hrt 724	Jeremiah	Wrr 811
William, Sr.	Crt 91	Susanna	Hrt 724	Hawl, John	Ans 203
Willis	Crt 91	Havenor, Daniel	Rth 120	Martin, Jr.	Jhn 755
Zilphia	Crt 88	Havour, John	Cmd 97	Martin, Sr.	Jhn 755
Hatsell, Richard	Ons 142	Haward, Arthur	Cht 207	William	Rch 271
Hatsfield, William	Wke 736	Barnett	Lnr 30	see Harol	
Hatslow, Henry	Brk 760	James	Cht 166	Hawley, Isaac	Cmb 354
see Hetslow		William	Cht 155	Pearson	Grv 560
Hattaway, Edmund	Dpl 397	see Howard		Sarah	Crv 235
Edmund, jr.	Dpl 397	Hawell, John	Ird 655	Hawly, Nathan	Grv 550
Hatten, Francis	Edg 206	see Howell		Hawn, Christian	Lnc 871
Hattey, John	Cht 174	Hawey, George	Ird 621	Conrod	Lnc 871
John	Cht 203	see Harvey		Frederick	Lnc 903
John	Cht 211	Hawkes, Francis	Crv 243	Jacob	Lnc 871
Joshua	Cht 184	Samuel	Crv 341	John	Lnc 903
Richard	Cht 204	Hawkins, Augustine	Brk 762	see Haun	
Sherwood	Cht 204	Benjamin	Bfr 9	Hawood, Henry,	
Hatthaway, Woolsey	Trl 674	Benjamin	Bnc 171	Doctr.	Edg 173
Hattin, Lewis	Nsh 105	Benjamin	Brk 758	Haws, Ezekiel	Smp 521
Hatton, George	Glf 628	Benjamin	Dpl 413	Henry	Hlf 312
George	Prq 662	Benjamin	Wrr 806	John	Nwh 11A
John	Ptt 228	Benjamin, Jr.	Hlf 314	John	Rth 117
Moses	Ptt 224	Benjamin, Sr.	Hlf 314	Saml.	Nwh 4A
Robert	Ptt 227	David	Hlf 314	Sarah	Hlf 312
Stephen	Ptt 227	Edward	Rth 117	Hawthorn, Hardy	Ans 238
see Hutton		Eperum	Prs 201	John, Jur.	Rbs 385
Hatty, Mary	Cht 183	Ezeriah	Ons 144	John, Ser.	Rbs 383
Hatwood, Jane	Orn 572	Frances	Edg 206	Joshua	Rbs 383
Thomas (2)	Orn 572	Gideon	Dpl 411	Kedar	Rbs 384
Hauge, James	Nsh 103	Henry	Hlf 318	William	Rbs 383
Haughton, Charles	Chw 120	Isham	Hlf 312	Hay, Benjamin	Grn 590
David	Chw 115	James	Bnc 171	Charles	Crt 92
Edward	Chw 125	James	Brk 756	Edward	Nrt 449
Jeremiah	Chw 125	Jesse	Jns 791	George	Rth 116
John	Chw 118	John	Grv 544	Isaac	Grn 587
Johnathan, Sen.	Chw 121	John	Hlf 314	John	Cmb 354
Jonathan, Jun.	Chw 121	John	Jns 791	Mary	Grn 590
Richard	Chw 121	John	Rwn 354	Mary	Jns 807
Richard, Jun.	Chw 129	John	Wrr 807	Nancy	Grn 589
William	Prq 654	John	Wlk 45	Peter	Nwh 3A
Haukit, Mallin	Rwn 365	Joseph	Brk 755	Haycraft, Will.	Nwh 7A
Hauks, David	Lnc 842	Joseph	Edg 209	Haydock, John	Brn 21
Haul, John	Ans 201	Joseph	Hlf 314	Haydon, George	Ird 639
Haun, Benedict	Lnc 903	Joseph	Ons 158	Hayes, Benjamin	Grv 531
Henry	Cbr 709	Joshua	Rwn 425	Catharine	Brt 52
John	Rwn 354	Major	Bfr 10	Ezekiel	Hrt 699
Joshua	Lnc 903	Major	Jns 791	James	Brt 52
Peter	Lnc 903	Michael	Rth 120	James	Cht 196
see Hawn		Nancy	Hlf 314	Jerry	Cht 201
Hausar, Henry	Stk 557	Obediah	Ons 154	John	Cht 223
Jacob	Stk 608	Oziel	Dpl 412	John	Frn 466
Martin	Stk 613	Phil. (deep		Joseph	Cht 169
Hause, Christian	Lnc 816	Creek)	Wrr 808	Joseph	Cht 175
Dudley	Wrr 811	Phil., Jr.	Wrr 807	Moses	Mck 534
John	Lnc 816	Phil., Senr.	Wrr 807	Nice	Brt 50
Hauser, Daniel	Stk 596	Philemon	Wrr 807	Samuel	Brt 52
Frederick	Stk 557	Robert	Rth 120	Streator	Hrt 699
Frederick	Stk 627	Saml.	Lnc 842	Thomas	Frn 451

William	Frn 468	Sarah	Grv 512	Headrick, Adam	Rwn 347		
William, Ser.	Frn 491	Sarah	Grv 530	Francis	Rwn 387		
Hayese, James	Hde 370	Sarah	Grv 533	George	Rwn 399		
Hayman, Laben	Trl 690	Sarah	Rck 481	George	Rwn 409		
Haymand, Isbel	Crr 163	Solomon	Ird 635	Jacob	Rwn 392		
Haymon, Isbel	Crr 162	Solomon	Nrt 447	Jacob	Rwn 399		
Haynes, Bartholo-		Sothy	Bld 3	John	Lnc 877		
mew	Mck 528	Stephen	Grv 512	Peter	Rwn 399		
Bythel	Bld 19	Thomas	Brk 757	Headspeth, Richard	Grv 538		
Eaton	Nrt 451	Thomas	Wke 736	Heady, Daniel	Crt 57		
Henry	Lnc 889	Widow	Mck 544	John	Ons 136		
John	Smp 512	Willie	Nrt 449	Thomas	Crt 68		
John	Smp 513	William	Bld 4	Uriah	Crt 70		
Jonan.	Rck 476	William	Bnc 174	Heagy, George	Rwn 347		
Joseph	Smp 513	William	Brk 756	Henry	Rwn 347		
Leonard	Lnc 816	William	Crv 273	John	Rwn 347		
Lucy	Hlf 318	William	Gts 268	Valentine	Rwn 347		
Prissilla	Mrt 397	William	Rnd 320	Healle, Amey	Cmb 354		
Salley	Wrr 807	William	Rwn 312	Healoan, Nicholass	Srr 663		
William	Smp 509	Hayse, Cherry	Wke 736	Heare, Hugh	Cbr 685		
Hayney, Joseph	Smp 520	Henry	Wne 873	Hearn, Abner	Cht 176		
Hayns, James	Ird 661	Hugh	Wrr 808	Amos	Edg 205		
John	Glf 684	Zachariah	Wrr 806	Benjamin	Ptt 293		
John	Ird 661	Haywood, Adam J.	Wne 843	Ebenezer	Mnt 483		
Joseph	Ird 661	Egbert	Edg 205	Edmond	Rch 257		
Joshua	Glf 675	Henry W.	Hlf 316	Edward	Rth 118		
Hays, Andrew	Rwn 341	J. Adam	Wke 776	George	Rnd 318		
Archibald	Wlk 45	James, Junior	Edg 205	James	Edg 205		
Arthur	Rck 481	James, Senior	Ptt 235	John	Wrr 810		
Charles	Smp 533	James, Senior	Ptt 235	Joseph	Jhn 777		
David	Rwn 312	John	Ptt 272	Joseph	Rth 118		
Edmond	Rnd 318	John	Crv 247	Joshua	Lnc 825		
Elias	Nrt 447	John	Frn 492	Mason	Jhn 753		
Elisabeth	Psq 641	John (Judge)	Wke 776	Nehemiah	Mnt 514		
Ezekiel	Grv 531	Shearwood	Orn 575	Pernell	Mnt 479		
George	Brk 756	Stephen, Esqr.	Wke 776	Stephen	Mnt 483		
George	Wlk 42	W. Henry	Edg 207	Thomas	Mnt 482		
Hance	Gts 268	Hayworth, Fanny	Wke 776	William	Edg 205		
Henry	Brk 761	George	Glf 683	William	Rnd 318		
Henry	Grv 508	Micaijah, Jur.	Rwn 365	William	Mnt 481		
Henry	Wlk 43	Micaijah, Sr.	Rwn 366	Hearndon, Aron	Cht 206		
Jacob	Brn 14	Samuel	Rwn 366	Hearne, James	Grn 609		
Jacob	Gts 268	Hazard, John	Rwn 365	Heath, Adam	Grn 609		
James	Gts 268	Lewis	Wrr 806	Cader	Crr 159		
James	Glf 665	Haze, Martha	Wrr 784	Frederick	Crv 333		
James	Rck 462	Hazel, Alexander	Hlf 318	Henry	Lnr 32		
James	Rck 481	Hazelip, John	Stk 593	James	Dpl 400		
James	Wlk 46	Hazle, Ezakle	Mrt 395	Jarman	Brk 755		
Jesse	Grv 535	Hazleton, John	Stk 615	John	Crv 313		
Jesse	Wke 735	Hazlett, Ezkiel	Grn 595	John	Crr 158		
Jesse	Wlk 43	Hazlewood, Ann	Lnc 842	John	Lnr 30		
John	Brn 14	David	Wrr 808	John	Stk 556		
John	Bnc 171	Worwick	Wrr 810	John	Stk 594		
John	Brk 756	Hazwell, Thomas	Wrr 809	John, Junr.	Crv 315		
John	Brk 762	Hazzard, George	Frn 455	Martha	Crv 337		
John	Csw 146	Lucy	Jns 809	Martin	Stk 556		
John	Crv 273	Thomas	Orn 571	Mary	Crv 245		
John	Edg 208	Head, Abraham	Rch 269	Matthew	Grn 613		
John	Gts 268	Hazzel, Robert	Stk 593	Richard	Crv 317		
John	Grv 537	Alexander	Srr 663	Samuel	Rck 441		
John	Rch 242	David	Lnc 855	Stephen	Crv 317		
John	Rch 268	George	Wke 736	Thomas	Crv 317		
Jonathan	Wlk 43	George	Srr 659	Thomas	Dpl 400		
Joseph	Cmb 354	Robert	Srr 661	Thos.	Crr 140		
Joseph	Rwn 341	Sarah	Srr 661	Heathcock, George	Wrr 807		
Joshua	Wlk 44	William	Wke 735	Holladay	Orn 569		
Josiah	Grv 531	Headen, Andrew	Srr 663	Howel	Orn 571		
Kinchen	Nrt 447	John	Cht 170	John	Wrr 807		
Mary	Crv 325	William	Cht 164	William	Wrr 809		
Price	Rnd 319	Headin, Elisha	Cht 186	Heathen, Wm.	Rck 447		
Reuben	Wne 861	Headley, William	Brk 761	Heckerson, David	Wlk 43		
Reuben	Wlk 45	James	Lnc 885	Joseph	Wlk 43		
Richard	Crv 271	Headon, Douglas	Cbr 687	Heckly, Thos.	Nwh 3A		
Samuel	Grv 535	Joseph	Rwn 425	Heckstall, John	Brt 48		
Samuel	Orn 572	William	Rwn 425	Hed, Philip	Rth 116		
Samuel	Rck 481	William	Mck 553	Heddin, John	Brk 762		
Samuel	Rwn 458	William	Rwn 425	Hedgcock, Thomas	Lnc 889		

Hedgepeth, Abraham	Nsh 105	John	Hlf 312	Peggy	Rch 251
Charity	Rbs 382	John	Rwn 437	Pleasant	Orn 495
Hulin	Wke 735	Mary	Glf 636	Richard	Mck 529
John	Wne 872	Mary	Glf 683	Richd.	Rck 455
see Hodgepeth		Peter	Orn 568	Saml.	Csw 106
Hedgepith, Demcey	Nrt 451	Peter, Sr.	Orn 568	Saml.	Wlk 43
Willoughby	Nrt 449	Stephen	Glf 636	Samuel	Rck 466
Hedgman, Lewis	Dpl 400	Thomas	Srr 659	Shadrick	Rwn 379
Hedgpeth, Arthur	Rbs 382	William	Hlf 312	Stephen	Ons 148
Charles	Hrt 731	Wintrupt	Hlf 312	Thomas	Mck 525
James	Hrt 705	Hemby, Dennis	Ans 233	Thomas	Mck 606
James	Wke 735	James	Rch 265	Thomas	Ons 176
Mourning	Hrt 732	Joseph	Ans 206	Thomas	Ons 177
Peter	Wke 738	Thomas	Ans 230	Thomas	Rck 466
Hedgpith, Daniel	Wne 868	Hemphill, Hugh	Prs 208	Violet	Lnc 826
Hedley, Joshua	Cbr 686	James	Brk 761	Widow	Mck 551
Hedspeth, Solomon	Grv 585	Saml.	Glf 621	William	Bld 18
Hedustle, James	Jhn 763	Samuel	Glf 620	William	Cht 158
Heeks see Hicks		Thomas	Brk 755	William	Ird 611
Heern, Will	Orn 573	Thomas	Brk 761	William	Mck 560
Heese, Evan	Cht 182	Henby, James	Grn 596	William (2)	Rth 116
Heesly, Jacob,Junr.	Rwn 347	James	Psq 627	William, Jur.	Mck 551
Jacob, Senr.	Rwn 347	see Hemby		Zekial	Ons 147
Leonard	Rwn 347	Hencely, David	Csw 141	see Hinderson	
Heffin, Charles	Grv 555	Jno.	Csw 141	Hendley, Elenour	Wke 733
Hefflin, Fielden	Grv 522	Maxfield	Csw 141	John	Grv 524
John	Grv 561	Henchey, David	Orn 573	John	Grv 564
John, jr.	Grv 522	John	Orn 573	Thomas	Grv 578
William (of J.)	Grv 525	Lewis	Orn 573	William	Grv 521
see Hiflin		Michael	Orn 573	Hendly, John	Mnt 490
Heflin, James	Wke 735	Hencock, Dorson	Mnt 478	Hendon, Isham	Wke 736
William	Wke 737	John, Senr.	Mnt 479	Isham, Jur.	Wke 736
Hefner, John	Lnc 877	Samuel, Sr.	Mnt 478	James	Wke 736
Philip	Lnc 877	Henderson, Alexan-		Josiah	Bld 31
Hegerty, Patrick	Gts 269	der	Rbs 385	Hendracks, Jobe	Prq 649
Hegner, John	Bnc 174	Andrew	Mck 558	Seth	Prq 650
Heidel see Hudel		Archabald	Rbs 382	Solomon	Prq 651
Heins, Ann	Prq 656	Archd., Esqr.	Rwn 287	Hendren, Downing	Edg 206
Heinsley, Joseph	Chw 123	Archibald	Rwn 277	Oliver	Rwn 458
Heinze, Charles	Stk 625	Barnaby	Ons 139	Hendrick, Edmond	Stk 616
Heirs, Darius	Lnr 32	Carnes	Mck 555	Elizabeth	Nsh 103
Heister, Thomas	Rbs 385	Charles	Ons 149	Isaac	Nsh 103
Heith, John	Rth 121	Daniel	Rch 244	Isham	Ird 655
Helderman, Jacob	Lnc 861	Daniel	Rch 253	Tignal	Nsh 103
Nicholas	Lnc 861	Dunlap	Bld 18	William	Stk 621
Heldreth, Reuben	Ans 205	Edward	Srr 662	Willm.	Nsh 103
Helfer, Henry	Rwn 425	Herculus	Cht 158	Hendricks, Abraham	Rwn 458
Jacob	Rwn 425	Hezekiah	Cht 152	Abram	Rck 475
Helford, Henry	Rwn 452	Isaac	Cht 155	Daniel	Rwn 425
Jacob	Rwn 452	Isaac	Cht 187	Darby	Wlk 42
Jacob, Junr.	Rwn 452	James	Bnc 174	Ezekiel	Wlk 44
Hell see Hill		James	Glf 687	Frederick	Rwn 458
Hellard, Ezekiel	Cht 222	James	Lnc 826	Henry	Glf 625
Hellen, Brian	Crt 77	James	Mck 555	Henry	Rck 442
Sarey	Ptt 251	James	Mck 560	Henry	Rck 464
Helliard, James	Nsh 102	James	Rth 120	Isaac	Rwn 426
John	Nsh 105	James	Wlk 44	James	Rck 464
Hellin, William	Ons 139	John	Cht 153	James	Rwn 425
Hellums, Abraham	Mck 588	John	Cht 193	James	Rth 115
David	Ans 218	John	Hde 370	John	Crv 325
George, Junr.	Mck 585	John	Ird 630	John	Mck 537
George, Senr.	Mck 584	John	Lnc 889	John	Rck 475
Gracie	Orn 570	John	Mck 535	John	Rwn 425
Isaac	Mck 584	John	Mck 564	Jonathan	Wlk 43
Jacob, Junr.	Mck 584	John	Mck 565	Peter	Rwn 296
John, Senr.	Mck 584	John	Orn 611	Wm.	Lnc 836
Tilman	Mck 584	John	Psq 636	Hendrickson, Isaac	Brt 52
William	Mck 586	John	Rck 455	Salathiel	Bfr 23
Helmstetler, Adam	Rwn 392	John	Rth 115	Hendrix, Benjn.	Wlk 46
Christian	Rwn 392	Josiah	Ons 147	Samuel	Rnd 320
Peter	Rwn 392	Lawson	Lnc 825	Tobias	Rnd 321
Helsabeth, Jacob	Stk 557	Leonard	Grv 513	Hendron, David	Rwn 452
Helton, Abraham	Orn 568	Lewis	Cht 155	Henry	Rwn 452
Alexander	Glf 637	Mary	Crt 63	Margret	Rwn 452
Dicey	Wrr 808	Matthew	Mck 565	Hendry, Alexr.	Bld 49
Ebenezar	Smp 535	Moses	Rth 120	Henfrow, Widow	Ans 236
James	Orn 568	Nancy	Rbs 382	Heniger, Joshua	Mck 582

Henikle, John	Lnc 855	Hensley, Benjamin	Brk 760	Heron, Allice	Nwh 3A
Heninger, James	Mck 580	Colbret	Bnc 172	Herord, James	Rth 118
James	Mck 581	Henry	Bnc 172	Herral, Edmund	Cmb 376
Rabeckah	Cbr 692	Hickman	Bnc 172	Herrald, John	Stk 557
Henley, Burrel	Orn 610	James	Bnc 172	Herreld, Jonathan	Stk 621
Henry	Rnd 319	John	Bnc 172	Richard	Stk 618
Jesse, J.	Rnd 317	Washington	Bnc 172	Wm.	Srr 706
Jesse, S.	Rnd 317	Henson, Bartlet	Ans 211	Herrell, Jacob	Cht 202
John	Rnd 317	Bartlet	Brk 754	Herril, Hugh	Ird 611
John	Rnd 318	Bartlet	Brk 755	Herrile, Andrew	Stk 553
John (2)	Rnd 321	Charles	Ans 208	Herrin, Allin	Mck 530
John	Stk 596	Charles, Junr.	Ans 209	Andrew	Mck 530
Jos.	Prs 209	Daniel	Ans 209	Delany, Jur.	Srr 658
Joseph	Rnd 321	Henry	Ans 235	Delany, Sen.	Srr 658
Lillice	Prs 211	James	Ash 80	Edward	Mnt 514
Richard	Stk 611	Jesse	Rnd 319	Francis	Srr 662
Stephen	Rnd 317	John	Ash 80	James	Rwn 307
William	Rch 247	John	Rnd 318	Jesse	Cbr 711
Henly, Darby	Rwn 307	Joseph (2)	Rnd 318	Michael	Rbs 383
James	Mnt 513	Philip	Rth 115	Saml.	Rck 445
Jesse	Edg 207	Sally	Rth 117	William	Brk 756
Seipis	Psq 634	Thomas	Brk 754	William	Rbs 382
William	Orn 610	William (2)	Ash 80	William	Srr 658
William, Jr.	Rch 247	William	Rnd 317	Herring, Benjamin	Ans 227
Hennegamm, Darby	Rch 271	see Hinson		Benjamin	Dpl 404
Hennent, James	Jhn 754	Hensy, Alexander	Brk 754	Benjamin	Wne 843
Henning, Lewis	Grv 508	Richard	Rck 454	David	Wne 856
Hennis, Danl.	Nwh 6A	Henton, Dempsey	Bfr 9	Elizabeth	Lnr 12
Elisabeth	Crv 257	Hep, Robert	Mnt 476	Enoch	Smp 516
Hennisey, Sarah	Nwh 4A	Hepler, Christian	Rwn 354	Fedrick	Smp 511
Henry, Alexander	Rck 480	Christopher	Rwn 354	Gabriel	Smp 516
Catherine	Cmb 354	Henry	Rwn 354	George	Wne 873
David	Brk 760	Hepner, Henry	Lnc 871	Harris	Wne 873
Earonhart,Senr.	Rwn 294	Hepnor, George (2)	Lnc 816	Henry	Wne 843
Elisabeth	Crv 255	Hepp, Mathias	Brk 759	Ichabod	Wne 844
Frances	Nwh 7A	Heptenstall, Wil-		Isaac	Rnd 321
George	Ans 203	liam	Hlf 314	Jacob	Wne 843
Hart	Stk 579	Herald, Jacob	Srr 658	Jane	Wne 857
Henry	Mck 561	Herben, Joshua	Wlk 45	John	Jhn 750
Hugh	Hde 370	Herbert, Charles	Crr 145	John	Nwh 4
Isaac	Lnc 826	Ellender	Crt 87	John	Nwh 7A
Isabela	Lnc 826	John	Rch 248	John	Nwh 9A
Isham	Rch 251	William	Crt 87	John	Nwh 11
James	Brk 755	Herbet, John	Rch 264	John	Smp 516
James	Ird 654	Herbin, Joshua	Wlk 46	John	Smp 512
James	Mck 549	Wm.	Rck 451	Joshua	Smp 516
James	Nwh 7	Herbs, John H.	Stk 598	Katherine	Cmb 386
Jams.	Lnc 838	John H.	Stk 625	Lewis	Dpl 441
Jno.	Lnc 838	Jonas	Stk 598	Mary	Wne 869
Joel	Crt 77	Jonas	Stk 625	Matchet	Jhn 751
John	Brk 754	Herby, Moses	Rch 256	Michael	Wne 844
John	Crt 77	Herdell, Josiah	Chw 119	Nathl.	Lnr 30
John	Hde 370	Herdle, Benjn.	Chw 128	Richard	Smp 516
John	Lnc 889	Harmon	Chw 129	Sally	Lnr 32
John	Nwh 7A	Henry	Chw 128	Saml.	Nwh 9A
Joseph	Bnc 173	Henry	Chw 129	Samuel	Dpl 432
Joseph	Lnc 833	Reuben	Chw 129	Sarah	Dpl 432
Neil	Nwh 10A	Herin, Delany,Sen.	Srr 658	Sarah	Smp 514
Philip	Ans 203	Heriton, Matthew	Cmd 100	Simon	Wne 858
Richd.	Rck 467	Hermine, Andrew	Mck 601	Simon	Wne 873
Robert	Brt 48	Hermon, Ephraim	Glf 647	Stephen	Dpl 405
Robert, Jur.	Bfr 10	James	Wne 866	Stephen	Dpl 432
Robert, Jur.	Hde 370	Hernby see Hemby		Stephen	Lnr 32
Robertson	Rnd 319	Herndon, Benjamin	Orn 573	Stephen	Wne 857
Samuel	Hde 370	Edmund	Orn 611	Uzzel	Smp 511
Sarah	Hlf 358	Elias	Orn 573	Whitfield	Dpl 404
Stephen	Rck 456	Elizabeth	Wlk 46	Herrington, Henry	Ptt 225
Thomas	Ird 674	George	Wke 734	Isaac	Cmd 100
Will.	Nwh 10A	James	Orn 573	James	Bld 30
William	Ans 203	Larkin	Csw 131	James	Ptt 249
William	Brt 48	Lewis	Orn 611	James	Smp 526
William	Rwn 373	Mary	Orn 611	John	Crv 265
William	Stk 557	Pumphrey	Orn 572	Joshua	Ptt 226
Henrys, Joseph	Bfr 10	Tapley	Orn 573	Margaret	Ptt 226
Samuel	Bfr 9	Waller	Orn 572	Paul	Ptt 288
Hensil, Benjamin	Brk 755	Zachariah	Orn 611	Herrintine, John	Nwh 12A
Hensle, David	Csw 123	Herod, Jonathan	Brk 756	Herrit, James	Crv 307

Herritage, William		Robert	Brn 17A	John		Brk 754
H.	Crv 321	Saml.	Brn 17	John		Brk 279
Herrold, Edy	Orn 610	Will.	Brn 17A	John		Lnc 866
Herron, Hugh	Mck 539	Will. (2)	Brn 21A	John		Mre 46
Hersey, Isaac	Cht 205	Hewls, Thomas	Grn 597	John		Nrt 449
Hervey, Thos.	Crr 147	Hews, Delila	Dpl 438	John		Orn 512
Hervin, Henry	Cmd 98	Margaret	Rch 270	John		Prs 205
Hesber, S.	Stk 625	Samuel	Ans 216	John		Wrr 810
Hesby, Solomon	Stk 598	William	Cmd 105	Joshua		Srr 662
Hesler, Francis	Grv 537	William	Cmd 109	Labin, Ser.		Srr 662
Hess, George	Rwn 307	Hewson, Micajah	Smp 528	Lewis		Dpl 420
Henry	Rwn 296	Hewston, Daniel	Rbs 382	Lewis		Rwn 458
Jacob	Stk 578	Elizabeth	Rbs 382	Little B.		Rch 265
John	Rwn 307	Hiatt, Amariah	Glf 680	Matthew		Ans 214
Hester, Abraham	Wlk 43	Ann	Gts 269	Micajah		Cht 203
Ann	Frn 456	Asa	Wke 733	Miles		Frn 447
Barbary	Grv 541	Enos, Jur.	Glf 688	Moses		Wke 736
Benjamin	Grv 561	Enos, Senr.	Glf 687	Nathaniel		Orn 611
Benjamin, OW.	Grv 552	Ezekiel	Glf 687	Nathaniel, Jr.		Srr 658
Francis	Grv 540	George	Glf 679	Prudance		Ons 144
Francis	Glf 689	Isaac	Glf 687	Randol		Wke 738
Henry	Grv 530	Sarah	Glf 680	Robert		Grv 552
James	Glf 668	Thomas	Gts 269	Robert		Nrt 449
Jasper	Bld 29	William, Jur.	Glf 687	Robert		Wrr 808
John	Bld 31	Wm., Senr.	Glf 687	Rubin		Rwn 387
John	Frn 457	Hibbets, Robert	Ird 656	Samuel (2)		Ash 81
John	Stk 558	Hibbs, Elizabeth		Samuel		Srr 662
John	Stk 620	(2)	Crt 85	Stephen		Jhn 756
Joseph (2)	Bld 29	Wilkins	Ons 148	Thomas		Grv 543
Joseph	Grv 566	Hickerson, Samuel	Wlk 41	Thomas		Nrt 451
Mary	Grv 565	see Heckerson		Thomas		Smp 513
Michael	Grv 552	Hickes, Jesse	Grn 598	Thomas		Stk 619
Oney	Grv 539	Hickman, George	Wlk 46	Widow		Ans 210
Robert	Grv 509	Isaac	Brk 757	Will.		Prs 205
Robert	Prs 215	Jacob	Crv 269	William		Bnc 171
Robert	Stk 608	Jesse	Cmb 367	William		Chw 119
Stephen	Bld 31	John	Rwn 416	William		Grv 538
Stephen	Grv 573	Noah	Edg 208	William		Nrt 449
Stephen	Stk 609	Richard	Crv 341	William		Rth 115
Thomas	Bld 29	Saml.	Brn 18	William		Wrr 810
William	Bld 30	Saml.	Brn 20	Willis		Wke 736
William	Grv 584	Samuil	Brk 757	Zebedee		Wke 733
William, Ser.	Bld 29	Sarah	Edg 208	Hide, Benjamin		Mnt 478
Zachariah	Grv 550	Snowden	Edg 208	John		Orn 610
Hetchbey, Marma-		Thomas	Brn 21A	Margret		Rwn 316
duke	Ons 172	William	Brn 20	Surthey		Ons 180
Heth, John	Ird 635	William	Edg 207	Hiett, Sarah		Glf 665
William	Ird 635	William	Glf 623	Hifflin, John		Grv 565
Hethcock, Benjamin	Mnt 501	Hickmon, Edwin	Stk 557	Hiflin, William		Grv 521
Dempsy	Mnt 505	Mary	Rnd 320	Higdon, Daniel		Cht 180
Young	Mnt 510	William	Stk 590	John B.		Rwn 331
Hetslow, Joseph	Brk 760	Hicks, Allen	Rch 254	Leonard		Brk 757
see Hatslow		Asa	Frn 469	Phillip		Cht 178
Hettinger, Michael	Rwn 307	Benjamin	Srr 662	Thomas		Brk 758
Hewbank, Christian	Hlf 316	Charles	Ans 202	Higgee, William		Grv 538
Hewell, Solomon	Ptt 230	Daniel	Rwn 379	Higgins, Holland		Bnc 172
William	Crv 293	Daniel	Smp 514	James		Ons 140
Hewet, Josiah	Brt 52	Danl.	Prs 188	John		Crv 327
Hewett, Isaac	Nrt 449	Danl., Junr.	Prs 188	William		Bnc 172
Josiah	Nrt 449	Demsy	Wlk 43	William		Dpl 399
Nancy	Jns 779	Elihu	Brk 756	Higgs, Amelia		Brt 52
see Huet		George	Grv 554	Jacob		Hlf 318
Hewey see Henry		Hansil	Ird 630	John		Grv 538
Hewit, John	Ons 141	Harris	Grv 546	Jonathan		Grv 537
John	Ons 142	Henry	Rwn 447	Leonard		Grv 552
Hewitt, Daniel	Crv 237	Hezikiah	Brk 759	Reuben		Brt 50
David	Brn 17	Isaac	Orn 611	Samuel		Hlf 314
Ebinezer	Brn 17A	Isaac	Wke 737	William		Brt 52
Elijah	Brn 17	Jacob	Grv 568	Zachariah		Grv 537
Hiah	Brn 18	James	Brk 759	High, Alsey		Wke 737
Jacob	Brn 17	James	Edg 205	Esau		Bld 17
Jno.	Csw 123	James	Nrt 447	Gardner		Ans 241
Joseph	Brn 15A	James	Rck 447	Luke		Bld 3
Joshua	Brn 14	James	Srr 662	Mark		Wke 737
Joshua	Brn 17A	Jas.	Prs 193	Rachel		Wke 737
Phillip	Brn 17	John	Ans 204	Robert		Frn 459
Rheubin	Brn 17A	John	Ans 205	Saml., Junr.		Wke 738

110

Samuel, Ser.	Wke 735	Clemment	Crr 147	John	Orn 611
Thomas	Bld 20	David	Crt 63	John	Rnd 319
William	Wke 738	David	Crv 299	John	Rck 459
Highat, John	Rwn 373	David	Gts 267	John	Rwn 277
Higher, Rudolph	Rwn 361	Doctor	Frn 455	John	Rwn 287
Highett, Edward	Bnc 173	Dutten	Rck 459	John	Rwn 443
Masheck	Bnc 171	Edward	Brn 21	John	Rth 117
Highler, James	Ird 639	Ely	Orn 610	John	Stk 592
Highsaw, Andrew	Brk 757	Enoch	Cht 154	John	Srr 658
Friderick	Brk 757	F., Estate of	Smp 504	John	Srr 663
Highsenith, Solo-		Felix K.	Dpl 438	John, Esqr.	Hrt 720
mon	Nwh 9	Garland	Csw 130	John, Junr.	Brt 50
Highsmith, Danl.	Nwh 6A	George	Bfr 9	John, Senr.	Brt 50
Isaac	Nwh 4A	George	Crv 325	John S.	Hrt 724
Jacob	Ptt 233	George	Orn 610	Johnson	Hrt 711
John	Ptt 233	Green	Frn 448	Jordan	Frn 456
Moses	Dpl 407	Green	Frn 490	Joseph	Jns 783
Saml.	Nwh 6A	Green	Jhn 768	Joseph	Srr 660
Sarah	Ptt 232	Green	Wne 853	Joshua	Bfr 9
William	Dpl 407	Gustavs	Rth 117	Joshua	Crr 150
Hight, Carnal	Grv 562	Harbert	Cht 155	Judah	Hrt 705
Ezeriah	Brk 756	Harboard	Hlf 310	Julian	Crr 164
Herbert	Frn 484	Harmond	Bfr 9	Lazarus	Bfr 9
Jacob	Stk 584	Hartwell	Hrt 729	Leonard	Rwn 443
John	Brk 757	Hemerick	Mre 73	Margarett	Rck 459
John	Grv 561	Henrick	Gts 268	Martha	Frn 481
Jonathan	Grv 530	Henry	Ans 233	Martin	Mnt 490
Mary	Frn 450	Henry	Brk 758	Mary	Dpl 423
Nath.	Frn 484	Henry	Cht 169	Mathias	Grn 607
Read	Brk 756	Henry	Edg 206	Matthew	Stk 556
William	Frn 450	Henry	Frn 465	Matthew	Stk 584
Hightfield, Heze-		Henry	Frn 494	Matthias	Grn 607
kiah	Grv 530	Henry	Gts 268	Micajah	Bld 15
see Hight		Henry	Nrt 447	Micajah	Orn 611
Hightour, Leroy	Rwn 330	Henry	Wke 734	Micajah	Rnd 319
Hightower, Auston	Bnc 173	Henry, Esqr.	Hrt 731	Michael	Bfr 10
Ephaphroditus	Csw 113	Hermon	Nrt 447	Michael	Wke 736
Hezeh.	Csw 113	Isaac	Ans 218	Miles	Gts 268
Jonathan	Cht 187	Isaac	Edg 205	Moses	Rbs 382
Joseph	Csw 113	Isaac	Nsh 102	Nancy	Orn 610
Oldham	Bnc 173	Isaac	Rck 436	Nathan	Edg 208
Richd.	Csw 124	Isaac	Srr 705	Nathl.	Nwh 1
Richd.	Csw 134	Isaac	Wlk 46	Nathl., Exr.	Nwh 4
Robert	Frn 495	Isaac, jr.	Crt 90	Noah	Gts 267
Hiland, Henry	Brk 756	Isaac, sr.	Crt 90	Peter	Crt 61
Hilburn, Hamblin	Bld 2	J.	Srr 706	Prescilla	Rth 119
Henry	Bld 16	Jacob	Rwn 437	Rebeca	Frn 473
Van	Brn 20A	James	Cmd 95	Resh	Brk 757
Hilch, Henry	Rwn 312	James	Grv 584	Richard	Frn 488
Michael	Rwn 301	James	Hrt 729	Richard	Grn 607
Hildreth, David	Ans 212	James	Ird 639	Richard	Lnr 11
Nancy	Ans 212	James	Jns 781	Richard	Srr 658
Hileman, George	Rwn 301	James	Rwn 416	Richard, Jur.	Srr 658
Hilford, Matthew	Cmd 93	James	Rth 118	Richd.	Bnc 173
Hilhouse, James	Lnc 842	Jane	Lnc 847	Richd.	Csw 101
Hill, Abner	Cht 171	Jeromiah	Lnc 861	Robert	Frn 479
Abraham	Grn 607	Jesse	Crv 289	Robert	Grn 607
Abraham, Junr.	Rwn 312	Jesse	Rnd 317	Robert	Rth 118
Abraham, Senr.	Rwn 312	Jms.	Lnc 838	Robert	Stk 555
Abram	Ird 639	Jno.	Lnc 847	Sally	Lnr 12
Amous	Mre 61	Joel	Brn 21	Samuel	Orn 493
Aron	Rnd 321	John	Ans 218	Samuel	Rck 475
Asa	Trl 670	John	Ans 220	Samuel	Stk 556
Augusta	Ans 235	John	Bfr 9	Samuel	Stk 587
Bartlet	Srr 658	John	Brn 21	Seth	Rnd 319
Ben.	Frn 474	John	Bnc 173	Seth	Rwn 312
Benjamin	Jhn 761	John	Crt 61	Shadrick	Mnt 494
Benjamin	Rnd 320	John	Crt 65	Simon	Hlf 316
Bennet	Smp 504	John	Crt 66	Sion	Jhn 767
C. William	Hlf 314	John	Crt 89	Sion	Smp 503
Caleb	Stk 555	John	Cht 220	Slaughter	Rbs 383
Casander	Rth 119	John	Crr 148	Stephen	Ird 639
Celia	Trl 690	John	Crr 164	Susanna	Wne 860
Charles	Grn 607	John	Dpl 438	Swinfield	Brk 762
Charles	Rth 117	John	Edg 207	Thomas	Ans 239
Charles	Rth 118	John	Ird 670	Thomas	Dpl 434
Chas.	Srr 705	John	Nwh 11	Thomas	Frn 477

Thomas	Hlf 316	Hinderson, Samuel	Ird 624	John	Stk 617
Thomas	Lnc 848	Hinds, Daniel	Cmb 371	John, Ser.	Stk 617
Thomas	Nwh 5	George	Ird 630	Jonathan	Wlk 45
Thomas	Rnd 317	Joseph	Rnd 316	Joseph	Srr 704
Thomas	Rnd 319	Nelly	Rnd 318	Thomas (2)	Rnd 321
Thomas	Rbs 382	William	Ird 630	Thomas	Srr 664
Thomas	Stk 606	Hindze, Christo-		Thomas	Srr 704
Thomas	Srr 662	pher	Stk 598	William	Rnd 316
Thomas	Wsh 706	Hineman, Hellery	Rwn 373	William	Rnd 318
Thophilus	Wke 735	Hines, Absalom	Rch 256	William	Wlk 45
Walter	Mck 562	Alixander	Nsh 105	Hinson, Aron	Cht 186
Webb	Wne 870	Boling	Cht 206	Aron	Lnr 12
Whitmill	Hrt 711	Bryant	Nsh 104	Benjamin, Jr.	Ans 211
Whitmill	Rbs 383	Christopher	Mrt 394	Benjamin, Jr.	Ans 224
Widow	Mck 562	Daniel	Dpl 438	Charles	Ans 223
Wilie	Orn 611	Dempsey	Mrt 397	Elijah	Wne 871
Will. H.	Nwh 5	Elizabeth	Edg 207	Henry	Cht 184
William	Ash 79	Felix	Smp 506	Henry	Cht 214
William	Brk 762	Fredr.	Lnr 30	Isham	Ans 223
William	Crv 283	Hardy	Wne 843	James	Cht 186
William	Crv 331	Hartwell, Jur.	Nsh 104	James	Rbs 383
William	Jns 801	Hartwell, Sr.	Nsh 105	Jesse	Grn 610
William	Rnd 319	Henry	Nsh 105	Jesse	Rbs 383
William	Rnd 320	Isaac	Lnr 30	John	Lnr 12
William	Rbs 382	Isham	Edg 209	John, Junr.	Ans 198
William	Rbs 383	Jacob	Stk 601	John, Senr.	Ans 198
William	Rth 118	James	Mre 71	Lazarus	Cht 186
William	Wke 737	James	Wne 873	Moses	Lnr 32
William, Jr.	Crt 56	Joel	Lnr 30	Rainey	Rbs 383
William, Junr.	Mck 564	John	Crt 83	St. George	Ons 136
William, Senr.	Mck 564	John	Edg 205	Samuel	Cht 172
William, Senr.	Srr 658	John	Mrt 394	William	Grn 616
William, Senr.	Crt 56	John	Ons 160	William, Capt.	Ans 217
William, Sr.	Crt 56	John	Stk 578	Wm.	Mrt 396
William C.	Hlf 314	Joseph	Rch 257	Hinton, Christo-	
Zadoc	Rth 118	Kedar	Wne 873	pher	Csw 109
see Jones		Lewis	Nsh 104	David	Bnc 172
Hillard, Rightman	Wke 732	Moses	Gts 269	David	Wke 733
Thomas	Wrr 807	Owen	Wne 857	Dempsy	Hlf 314
Hillborn, John	Rbs 384	Peter	Wne 856	Elisabeth	Jhn 760
Hilldreath, James	Ash 80	Peter, Capt.	Edg 205	Hardy	Jhn 760
Hillebrand, Conrod	Lnc 903	Peter, Esqr.	Edg 205	Hardy	Jhn 763
Hilleman, John	Rwn 341	Philip	Lnc 825	James	Mck 552
Hilliard, Isaac	Hlf 358	Rachell	Mrt 397	Jesse	Jhn 755
Jeremiah, Esqr.	Edg 205	Sarah	Nsh 105	Jno., Junr.	Wke 734
John	Bld 37	Sharod	Ptt 286	John	Jhn 762
William	Grv 546	Thomas	Wke 737	John	Wke 737
see Helliard		Willis	Dpl 438	Jonas	Prq 661
Hillman, Jesse	Hlf 316	Zilpha	Wne 857	Kedar	Gts 268
Hills, Aaron	Bld 16	see Heins		Kimbro	Wke 733
Hillsman, Hynes	Frn 489	Hinesly, Benjn.	Cht 210	Malachi	Jhn 760
Hillyard, Wiley	Mnt 501	Nathaniel	Cht 206	Malachi, Jr.	Jhn 760
William	Grv 542	William	Cht 209	Mary	Jhn 756
Hilman, Ezekiel	Glf 651	Hingston, Francis	Grv 579	Noah	Brt 52
Hilson, Elias	Brn 19	Hinkle, Anthony	Rwn 374	Reuben	Brt 50
Hiltebrandt, Henry	Lnc 903	Benjamin	Rwn 437	Ruth	Rwn 354
Hiltebrunt, Canrod	Brk 758	Casper	Rwn 373	William	Gts 268
Hilton, Abraham	Rnd 320	George	Rwn 392	William	Jhn 755
Andrew	Ird 665	Henry	Rwn 425	William	Wke 737
Buckom	Brk 760	Jacob	Rwn 387	William, Senr.	Gts 267
Freeman	Ird 621	Nathan	Rth 120	William R.	Bnc 172
James	Ird 621	Peter	Rwn 373	Zadok	Hlf 314
James	Rwn 354	Windle	Brk 754	Hip, George	Brk 755
James	Rth 117	see Henikle		Joshua	Mnt 470
Margret	Brk 760	Hinnand, John	Jhn 760	William	Mnt 470
Thomas	Brk 760	Hinnant, William	Jhn 752	Hipp, Valentine	Mck 534
Hilyard, John	Mre 52	William	Jhn 758	Hipworth, Mary	Csw 130
Philip	Jhn 766	William	Jhn 761	Hise, Conrod	Cbr 715
Hinbee, Thomas	Prq 650	Hinsberry, Eliza-		George	Cbr 709
Thomas, Jun.	Prq 651	beth	Brn 17	Hiser, Rudolph	Rwn 416
Hinby, Sylvanus	Prq 651	Hinshaw, Absolom	Cht 195	Hisler, Abraham	Stk 596
Thomas, sen.	Prq 655	Absolom (2)	Rnd 318	Michael	Rwn 296
Hincher, William	Glf 627	Azra	Rnd 321	Hisley, Leonard	Rwn 415
Hinckle, Anthony	Lnc 827	Benjn.	Cht 195	Michael	Rwn 408
Christina	Lnc 828	Jacob	Srr 704	Hitchcock, Isaac	Ash 80
Jacob	Lnc 827	Jessee	Cht 216	John	Ash 80
Hinckley, Wyatt	Crv 251	John	Rnd 320	John	Glf 635
Hind, Frederick	Rwn 366				

Name	Ref	Name	Ref	Name	Ref
Joshua	Ash 80	George	Rnd 316	Richard, Ser.	Bfr 9
Thomas	Rwn 366	Isaac	Cht 219	Robert	Ptt 239
Hite, James	Nwh 3A	Joseph	Cht 217	Salley	Bfr 23
Nelson	Wke 736	Stephen	Cht 196	Thomas	Ans 211
Hiter, Abraham	Crr 149	Will	Prs 206	Thomas	Nrt 451
Hix, Fereby	Rnd 319	William	Cht 196	William	Brt 52
John	Stk 608	William (2)	Cht 217	William	Hlf 314
Joseph (2)	Rnd 317	Hobten, Sarah	Crv 279	William	Rwn 443
Josiah	Rnd 319	Hochcomb, Shader-		William	Wke 738
Reuben	Rnd 319	ick	Srr 660	Wm.	Srr 710
William	Rnd 321	Hockaday, James	Hlf 310	Hodgins, Benjamin	Rwn 426
Hoage, William	Bnc 174	Warwick	Hlf 312	David	Glf 625
Hobb, Robert	Nsh 104	William	Hlf 310	George (2)	Glf 625
Hobbs, Abagail	Hde 370	Hocott, Richard	Hrt 699	George	Glf 679
Aron	Gts 267	Hocut, Edward	Wke 732	H.	Stk 616
Barnaby	Rnd 353	Richard	Wke 733	Jesse	Glf 625
Charlton	Brt 48	Hocutt, Benjn.	Hrt 699	John	Glf 624
David	Wke 733	Hocy, John, Esqr.	Mck 590	Jonan.	Glf 625
Edmond	Gts 267	Hodart, William	Srr 708	Joseph	Glf 625
Elisha	Rnd 319	Hodeman, Jacob	Cbr 716	Joshua	Glf 624
George	Smp 498	Hoder, Wm.	Mrt 397	Robert	Glf 624
George	Wke 733	Hodg, George	Brk 759	Robert	Glf 625
Guy	Hrt 699	Robert	Brk 761	William	Glf 625
Henry	Smp 498	Hodge, Abraham	Hlf 358	see Hudgins	
Isaac	Bld 17	Airs	Bfr 9	Hodgson, James	Glf 679
Jacob	Hrt 731	David	Csw 121	Hodum, Alexander	Smp 502
John	Chw 127	Delana	Wlk 43	Dempsey	Smp 501
John	Orn 609	Francis	Mck 599	George J.	Dpl 426
John	Smp 498	Henry	Hlf 316	Jacob	Smp 510
John	Wke 733	James	Bfr 10	John	Smp 509
John, (H.K.)	Orn 572	James	Cmb 372	Silas	Smp 510
Joseph	Bld 11	James	Mck 599	Hoell, Elias	Bfr 22
Joseph	Chw 121	James	Rck 472	Elizabeth	Bfr 22
Leah	Gts 267	John	Bfr 10	Hoff, Richard	Wsh 706
Mary	Hrt 731	John	Mck 599	Thomas	Wsh 706
Mary	Wke 739	John	Rnd 321	Hoffer, Lewis	Lnc 815
Moses	Chw 118	John	Wlk 42	Hoffler, James	Gts 268
Mourning	Hrt 733	Joseph	Orn 511	John	Gts 268
Myles	Chw 126	Joseph	Rwn 307	Thomas	Gts 267
Reuben	Chw 121	Leah	Bfr 10	Hoffner, Frederick	Lnc 903
Reuben	Chw 126	Robert	Orn 513	George	Lnc 903
Samuel	Chw 129	Robert, Junr.	Brk 762	Jacob	Lnc 817
Samuel	Gts 267	Samuel	Orn 571	Martin	Lnc 815
Sarah	Hrt 711	Thomas	Ash 81	Nicholas	Lnc 815
Shadrach	Hrt 731	Thomas	Bfr 9	Samuel	Lnc 903
Simon	Smp 530	Thomas	Lnr 10	Hofner, Abram	Lnc 816
Simon	Smp 533	Thomas, Esqr.	Edg 206	Frederick	Lnc 816
Thomas	Gts 267	William	Rck 472	Martin	Rwn 301
William	Gts 267	Hodgen, Joseph	Rnd 317	Hog, William	Rwn 387
William	Orn 512	Hodgepeth, John	Edg 207	Hogan, Abram	Wke 735
William	Smp 499	Hodges, Benjamin	Bfr 10	Cathrine	Rth 120
William	Wke 733	Benjamin	Dpl 433	James	Mnt 483
William, Junr.	Hrt 731	Bertholomew	Srr 664	John	Mnt 462
see Habbs		Charles	Nrt 449	Jonathan	Glf 656
Hobby, Alexander	Jhn 769	Drury	Wke 738	Lemuel	Hlf 316
John	Rbs 383	Edmond	Srr 663	Sarah	Orn 612
Reuben	Jhn 772	Floyd	Ptt 225	Widow	Ans 207
William	Jhn 769	Francis	Rbs 383	William	Orn 572
Hobdy, John	Crv 243	Henry	Bfr 9	Zacharia	Mnt 466
Hobely, Lydia	Brt 52	Henry	Ptt 240	Hogans, Henry's	
Hobes, Ewd.	Ons 165	James	Bfr 9	Negroes	Rth 121
Simon	Ons 165	James	Gts 258	James	Brk 758
Hobey, Edmond	Ptt 271	John	Ptt 239	Mary	Brk 757
Hobgood, Elijah	Hlf 316	John	Rwn 452	Hogden, Nehemiah	Mck 536
Ezekiel	Grv 580	John	Srr 711	Hogens, James	Edg 208
Fanny	Hlf 316	John	Wke 735	Hoger, Leonard	Stk 605
Fowler	Grv 559	Joseph	Bld 44	Hogerly, John	Brk 759
Lemuel	Hlf 316	Joseph	Cmb 383	Hogg, Andw.	Csw 128
Micaijah	Hlf 316	Lemuel	Ptt 240	Charles	Nsh 103
Thomas	Grv 580	Mary	Hde 370	Cloe	Rbs 384
Hoboman, Christo-		Meachum	Nrt 451	James	Orn 571
per	Wne 852	Moses	Bfr 8	John	Frn 473
Hobs, Agustus	Crr 141	Peggy	Ptt 239	John	Wke 776
Daniel	Glf 668	Phillemon	Cmb 367	Nancy	Hlf 316
William	Grn 594	Port Lock	Ptt 271	Rebecah	Hlf 316
Hobson, Charles	Cht 213	Richard	Grn 606	Robert	Hlf 316
George	Cht 216	Richard, Jur.	Bfr 9	Samuel	Grv 551

Thomas	Cmb 368	Aron	Brt 50	James	Grn 602
Hoggard, Elisha	Brt 48	Billy	Smp 501	James	Glf 673
Jesse	Brt 50	Charles	Mre 47	James	Rth 120
John	Brt 48	Charles	Stk 596	James	Wke 736
Patrick	Brt 50	Charles	Stk 599	James	Wne 865
William	Brt 50	Charles	Stk 613	John	Ans 218
Hoggatt, Aron	Rnd 320	Charles	Stk 625	John	Bfr 22
David	Glf 692	Daniel	Orn 611	John	Brt 46
James	Glf 680	David	Orn 611	John	Rth 116
Jesse	Rnd 320	Davis	Srr 710	John	Smp 501
Joseph	Glf 689	Elijah	Glf 655	John	Stk 603
Moses	Rnd 320	Elisha, Junr.	Brt 50	Julias	Lnc 842
Philip	Glf 675	Elisha, Senr.	Brt 50	Keziah	Hrt 720
Phillip	Rnd 320	George	Stk 577	Lewis	Crv 329
Stephen	Rnd 321	George, M:C:	Stk 613	Margaret	Edg 207
William	Glf 626	Henry	Stk 607	Matthew	Wne 867
William	Rnd 320	Henry, Jr.	Stk 613	Mattw.	Lnc 838
Hoggins, William	Lnc 815	James	Orn 609	Niecy Ann	Rwn 339
Hoggott, Anthony	Stk 557	Jesse	Smp 494	Philemon	Crv 337
Hogiton, Archibald	Ird 610	John	Orn 611	Philip	Bfr 9
Hogsdale, John	Grv 539	John	Rck 488	Richard	Bfr 9
Hogshead, David	Ird 625	Levinah	Rnd 318	Richard	Edg 207
Samuel	Bnc 174	p.	Srr 708	Richard	Mnt 510
Walter	Bnc 174	Shadrach	Brt 52	Richard	Nsh 103
Hogue, Stephen	Rth 116	Thomas	Brt 50	Samson	Wke 736
Hogwood, John	Rch 266	William	Orn 611	Shadrach	Jhn 750
Hoin, Nicholass	Srr 658	William	Rck 490	Thomas	Glf 673
see Horn		William	Stk 578	Thomas	Smp 532
Hoke, Daniel	Lnc 815	William, jr.	Orn 611	Thomas	Wke 736
Frederick	Lnc 815	Holderfeild, Isaac	Rth 117	William	Crv 335
Henry	Lnc 815	Holderfield, Ele-		William	Rth 116
John	Lnc 815	nor	Rwn 457	Willie	Wke 736
Holbert, John	Stk 555	Jacob	Rth 120	Hollandshead, Ann	Crv 325
William	Stk 595	William	Rth 120	Hollandsworth,	
Holbrook, Colbret	Wlk 46	Holderness, Reubin	Mnt 470	Sarah	Bfr 10
Dargas	Wlk 45	Holding, Charles	Wke 737	Vinson	Ash 80
John	Wlk 44	Frederick	Wke 737	Wm.	Ash 80
Ralph	Wlk 46	John	Wke 737	Hollansworth, Saml.Bld 34	
Randolph	Wlk 45	Matthew	Wke 739	Hollar, John	Rwn 307
Robert	Srr 663	Saml., Junr.	Wke 737	Hollaway, James	Crv 331
William	Wlk 45	Samuel	Wke 737	John	Crv 319
Zachariah	Wlk 45	Holdman, Richard	Orn 575	Holleman, Henry	Lnc 815
Zekell	Stk 558	Holdmon, Charles	Prs 189	Hollemond, Hinchey	Hrt 731
Holbrooks, Henry	Bnc 171	Holdsombac, John	Prs 210	Hollen, Thomas	Glf 635
Vashel	Cbr 700	Richd.	Prs 189	Hollerday, Reuben	Mrt 396
William	Bnc 173	Holebrook, James	Stk 555	thos., Junr.	Mrt 397
Holbut, John	Rth 116	John	Stk 558	thos., Senr.	Mrt 396
Holchomb, D.George	Srr 660	Holeman, Anthony	Lnc 815	Holleway, William	Rwn 399
Drury	Srr 662	David	Rwn 451	Hollewell, John	Mrt 397
George	Srr 660	Henry	Lnc 868	Levi	Mrt 397
George, se.	Srr 659	Isaac	Rwn 452	Miles	Mrt 397
George D.	Srr 660	Jacob	Rwn 452	Holley, Absalom	Ans 236
Larrence	Srr 663	James	Rwn 451	Juleus	Ans 231
Machek	Srr 663	Rubin	Ird 635	Moore	Brt 48
Margret	Srr 660	William	Rwn 452	Richard	Crv 297
Philip	Srr 660	Holford, Matthew	Hlf 316	Thomas	Prq 658
Thomas	Srr 660	Holibaugh, George	Rwn 296	William	Wke 735
Thomas, Se.	Srr 660	Holifield, Vaul	Srr 661	Holleyman, Hermon	Hlf 316
William	Srr 663	Holladay, Henry	Orn 569	Holliday, Joshua	Rnd 320
see Hochcomb		Robert	Orn 569	Robert	Cmb 354
Holcom, James	Mre 44	William	Orn 569	Samuel	Cht 169
Holcomb, John	Bnc 172	Hollamond, John	Hrt 731	Thomas	Cht 211
May	Bnc 172	Holland, Anthony	Mnt 510	see Hailey	
Holcombe, Kinchen	Bnc 173	Benja.	Wke 736	Hollifield, Elisha	Ans 237
Holcum, George	Csw 106	Benjamin	Wke 736	John	Ans 238
Holden, Amos	Brn 17A	Charles	Bfr 9	Joseph	Wke 734
Benjn.	Brn 17A	Daniel	Edg 206	Holliman, Ecum	Nrt 447
Edmond	Rwn 437	Daniel	Rwn 425	William	Wke 738
George	Smp 525	Elisha	Wne 865	Hollimon, Amelia	Wke 776
Isaac	Orn 610	Henry	Edg 205	Holling, James	Nwh 8
James	Brn 15A	Henry	Rwn 425	Hollingsworth, Eliz-	
James	Mnt 490	Henry	Smp 501	abeth	Smp 511
Job.	Brn 15A	Isaac	Lnc 831	Enoch	Cmb 382
John	Orn 610	Jacob	Gts 268	Henry (2)	Smp 511
Josiah	Jhn 757	James	Cht 204	Stephen	Cmb 383
Thomas	Orn 610	James	Dpl 425	Hollinsworth, Abra-	
Holder, Anne	Smp 494	James	Edg 206	ham	Bnc 173

Isaac	Glf 686	John	Chw 127	John	Ash 81
Jacob	Bnc 171	Riddick	Prq 660	Holsey, Ann	Chw 119
John	Bnc 173	William	Wne 849	John	Psq 627
Saml.	Bnc 172	Hollowell, Abner	Chw 122	William	Chw 124
Hollis, Armit	Wsh 706	Arthur	Brt 52	Holshead, John	Glf 643
Edward	Wsh 706	Benjamin	Bfr 10	Holsner, Lemuel	Crv 233
Hudson	Rwn 392	Benjamin	Hde 370	Holstad, Malle-	
Isaac	Crv 305	Denson	Hde 369	theas	Orn 568
James	Wsh 706	Joel	Prq 655	Holstead, Edward	Psq 631
Jesse	Csw 129	John	Wne 848	Jonn.	Psq 631
Jesse	Csw 140	Joseph	Wne 872	Milisant	Psq 632
John	Rwn 409	Robt.	Wne 849	Holsted, Jesse	Crr 146
Marium	Crt 83	Samuel	Nrt 449	Joliff	Crr 139
Thomas	Crv 305	Silus	Wne 860	Jolley	Crr 164
William	Rwn 392	Thomas	Wne 849	Lemuel	Psq 637
Holliway, Abnor	Rwn 447	William	Brt 52	Malachi	Crr 163
Isaac	Ird 624	Zadok	Hde 370	Holt, Absalom	Orn 568
Isaac	Rwn 437	Holly, Charlotte	Smp 504	Ambrose	Wlk 43
Robert	Cht 202	Elisabeth	Cbr 702	Arrington	Hlf 312
Holliwel, Thomas	Prq 662	George	Brk 754	Benjamin	Wlk 46
Holloday, Samuel	Grn 601	Henry	Nwh 6A	Bird	Stk 593
Thomas	Grn 601	James	Crv 297	Christopher	Orn 568
Thomas	Hrt 737	James	Smp 504	Cornelius	Nwh 3A
William	Grn 601	Jesse	Hlf 312	David	Cmb 390
Holloman, Jedediah	Edg 207	John	Smp 496	Fatherston	Stk 581
William	Stk 609	John	Smp 502	Francis	Orn 570
Hollomon, Aaron	Hrt 705	Osburn	Smp 494	Franke	Stk 588
Celia	Hrt 705	Reddick	Smp 494	Frederick	Cmb 391
Christopher	Hrt 704	Sarah	Smp 494	George	Orn 570
Cornelius, jr.	Hrt 705	Sherwood	Smp 495	Isaac	Orn 568
Cornelius, senr.	Hrt 705	Zachariah	Rwn 337	Israel	Orn 511
Fredk.	Jhn 754	Holman, Jacob	Ash 81	James	Hlf 314
Goddin	Mre 77	Thos.	Wlk 46	James	Jhn 746
Isham	Edg 206	Holmes, Amy	Wne 872	James	Orn 570
John	Hrt 705	Ann	Chw 125	Jeremiah	Orn 570
John	Jhn 754	Bryan	Wne 873	Joel	Brk 760
John	Stk 608	Charles	Wne 873	John	Cmb 389
Josiah	Jhn 757	Edward	Grn 616	John	Mnt 488
Josiah	Mre 77	Elizabeth	Cmb 370	John	Orn 512
Penelope	Edg 206	Frederick	Wne 855	John	Orn 570
Samuel, jr.	Hrt 704	Fredk.	Jhn 756	John (2)	Orn 611
Samuel, sen.	Hrt 704	Gabriel	Brn 13A	John	Srr 659
Seth	Jhn 760	George	Mck 595	John,(son John)	Orn 570
Tobias	Jhn 755	Hardy	Wne 855	Joseph	Hlf 314
William	Hrt 705	Henry	Nrt 447	Joshua	Orn 568
William	Jhn 755	Henry	Trl 678	Michael	Orn 568
William, Jur.	Stk 608	Homer	Cmb 392	Nathan	Srr 658
Wright	Hrt 705	James	Grn 615	Nathan, Ser.	Srr 658
Hollon, Richard	Mre 71	Jeremiah	Cmb 392	Nelly	Wlk 43
Holloway, Asa	Rch 468	Jessey	Grn 614	Nicholas	Orn 570
Brim	Orn 574	John	Bld 27	Peter, Senr.	Brk 760
David	Glf 652	John	Brn 17A	Richard, Junr.	Mnt 488
Hannah	Prq 657	John	Lnc 889	Richard, (Senr.	Mnt 488
James	Trl 678	Joseph	Brn 17	Samuel	Nrt 451
James	Wlk 44	Moses	Bld 25	Solomon	Mnt 511
James	Wlk 46	Moses	Grn 614	Thomas G.	Ons 182
John	Prs 195	Richard	Bld 6	William	Crt 89
John	Wke 735	Stephen	Grn 616	William	Hlf 314
John	Wlk 45	Timothy	Grn 615	William	Jhn 774
Jos.	Prs 193	Holmesly, Benjamin	Lnc 896	William	Orn 570
Luke	Chw 118	John	Lnc 889	William	Rck 487
Major	Wke 738	Holms, Fargus	Ird 620	William, Junr.	Orn 570
Mary	Crr 155	Francis	Ird 621	Holte, Taylor	Crr 167
Moses	Trl 678	Gabriel	Smp 501	Holten, David	Bfr 10
Obadiah	Csw 99	George	Mck 598	James	Bfr 10
Richd.	Prs 198	Grace	Smp 527	Holton, Abel	Bld 37
William	Wke 735	Hardy	Smp 524	Bazel	Crv 259
William	Wsh 706	James	Ird 621	Isaac	Glf 677
Wm.	Crr 145	James	Lnc 896	James	Cmb 370
Hollowel, Abner,		James	Stk 591	John	Cmb 371
Jun.	Chw 127	John	Bfr 9	Joseph	Bnc 172
Abner, Sen.	Chw 127	John	Ird 635	Josiah	Crv 261
Frederick	Prq 660	Owen	Smp 502	Nathaniel	Cmb 386
Henry	Prq 649	Reubin	Rwn 399	Penelope	Brt 90
Hillm.	Prq 649	Richard	Wke 737	Samuel	Cmb 368
James	Prq 661	Robert	Ird 620	William	Cmb 371
Joel	Prq 661	Holsclaw, James	Ash 81	William	Cmb 381

Name	Loc	Name	Loc	Name	Loc
see Hotton		William	Wke 738	Elizabeth	Trl 684
Holtree, Margret	Lnc 877	Hooks, Amy	Mrt 397	Elizabeth	Wsh 706
Holtsclaw, Nathan	Ans 219	Charles	Dpl 434	Ellender	Orn 574
Holtshouser, Mich-		Charles, Senr.	Mrt 395	George	Grv 585
ael	Rwn 392	Daniel	Ans 215	George	Hde 370
Andrew	Rwn 312	Ephraim	Wne 865	Hezekiah	Hlf 316
Holtshowzer, An-		Hardy	Wne 865	Hezekiah	Mrt 397
drew	Rwn 301	Isaac	Ans 215	Hody	Trl 678
Jacob	Rwn 301	John	Ans 209	John	Brt 46
Michael	Rwn 301	John	Mrt 395	John	Wke 738
Holtzclaw, James	Lnc 861	John	Wne 866	Jonan.	Rck 439
Holwick, Conrod	Mnt 509	Lemuel	Bld 16	Joseph	Hlf 316
Holyfield, Daniel	Brk 762	Mourning	Mrt 397	Joseph	Ptt 292
Homer, Gashom	Bfr 24	Robert	Bld 13	Joseph	Stk 606
John	Lnc 885	Thomas	Dpl 434	Joseph	Wke 738
John W.	Cmd 109	William, Junr.	Wne 865	Joshua	Hlf 358
Homes, John	Orn 568	William, Senr.	Wne 865	Josiah	Ptt 293
Moses	Orn 569	Wiloughby	Rwn 399	Luis	Stk 606
Samuel	Wke 735	Hooper, Elijah	Ird 624	Peter	Nsh 104
William	Wke 776	Geo.	Nwh 2A	Peter	Wke 738
William	Wne 855	James	Ird 639	Richard	Rnd 318
Homseker, Devoll	Lnc 876	James	Ird 674	Robert	Hde 370
Honbarier, William	Ird 650	James	Rth 115	Samuel	Orn 495
Honeycut, Boling	Ans 235	John	Ird 671	Sarah	Mrt 397
David	Wke 733	Joseph	Rck 438	Thomas	Rck 441
Dempsy	Mnt 510	Mary	Rth 120	William	Cht 215
Elisha	Mnt 513	Susana	Csw 123	William	Hde 370
Oliver	Wke 733	Tho. H.	Brn 15	William	Orn 574
Rawell	Ird 655	Will.	Nwh 11	William	Ptt 261
Uriah	Glf 628	William	Orn 494	William	Wke 738
William	Smp 517	William	Rth 115	Willie	Wke 738
Wyke	Mnt 514	Hoot, John	Wlk 45	Hopper, Betsey	Wlk 45
see Hocut		Hooten, Caleb	Lnr 11	Charles	Brk 762
Honeycutt, Drury	Jhn 765	Caleb, Jur.	Lnr 11	Darby	Rck 478
Drury	Mnt 507	Charles	Hde 369	Harman	Orn 570
John	Mnt 508	Henry	Mrt 396	James	Rck 459
Lewis	Mnt 507	Richard	Lnr 32	John	Orn 511
Honseker, William	Lnc 877	Shadr.	Lnr 32	John	Wlk 43
Hood, A. Charles	Wke 733	William	Lnr 11	Joseph	Rck 459
Archibald	Nrt 449	Wm.	Mrt 397	Lewis	Rck 459
Basd Robin	Wne 851	Hoots, Anthony	Srr 661	Lewis	Rck 483
Charles A.	Wke 733	Jacob	Srr 661	Thomas	Bnc 172
Edward	Wne 861	Hoover, Andrew	Rnd 320	William	Rck 459
Jesse	Wke 733	Daniel (2)	Rnd 317	William	Wlk 44
John	Brk 759	David	Rnd 317	Hoppes, Adam	Lnc 855
John	Glf 645	Gasper	Rnd 321	George	Srr 664
John	Lnr 12	George	Rwn 354	John	Srr 664
Roland	Grv 572	Henry	Rnd 317	Hoppus, Daniel	Ash 80
Rubin	Mck 604	Jacob	Cbr 714	Hopson, Benja.	Wke 734
Solomon	Ird 639	Jacob	Crv 287	Benoni	Wlk 43
Thomas	Ans 217	Jacob	Rnd 317	Benoni	Wlk 46
Thomas	Grv 556	James	Crv 287	Charles	Mnt 501
Thos.	Prs 189	John	Crv 287	Daniel	Cht 197
Tunus	Mck 604	John	Rnd 317	David	Srr 664
William	Lnr 12	John	Rnd 321	George	Cht 181
William	Rck 491	Jonas	Rnd 316	Harrard	Wke 735
Hoodenpyle, Philip	Bnc 172	Peter	Rwn 354	Henry	Rth 115
Hoof, John	Frn 492	Samuel	Crv 287	John	Mnt 501
Reubin	Frn 447	Samuel	Crv 305	John	Srr 706
Hoofman, Henry	Stk 556	Shadrach	Crv 287	Lewis	Wke 734
Jacob, Capt.	Grv 565	Soloman	Lnc 816	Morning	Mnt 507
John	Orn 570	Thomas	Lnc 816	Reubin	Wke 734
George	Stk 556	William	Crv 305	Silass	Srr 664
Hoogg, James,Junr.	Orn 491	Hope, Robert	Cbr 681	Stephen	Cht 215
John	Orn 491	Hopeworth, John	Mck 530	Stephen	Srr 664
Hooker, Elizabeth	Grv 521	Hopff, Henry	Lnc 896	Stephen	Srr 704
Hardy	Ans 202	Hopgood, John	Grv 559	Thomas	Wke 734
Heymrick	Grn 602	Hopkins, Alexander	Wsh 706	William	Orn 572
Jacob	Rnd 317	Ann	Grv 585	William	Rth 115
John	Trl 678	Ann	Ptt 263	William	Wlk 44
Nathan	Trl 674	Arnold	Ptt 263	Younger	Orn 610
Robbert	Rnd 317	Casa	Orn 574	Hopston, Jinnit	Jns 813
Sarah	Mrt 397	Charls	Rnd 319	Hopton, Charles	Wne 871
Stephen	Trl 678	Daniel	Brt 48	Hopvines, Philip	Glf 642
Stephen, Senr.	Trl 678	Daniel	Ptt 263	Hopwood, James	Rnd 321
William	Stk 587	Elisabeth	Mnt 484	Hoquet, Wm. Brotn	Jhn 756
William	Trl 678	Elizabeth	Edg 207	Horah, Hugh	Rwn 277

Hugh	Rwn 287	
Horceends, Elijah	Crv 267	
Jesse	Crv 261	
Horilson, Heronton	Prs 208	
Horn, Abel	Wne 872	
Anne	Edg 207	
David	Rch 255	
Edward	Nsh 103	
Elias	Mnt 507	
Elijah	Edg 206	
Elijah	Edg 207	
Elisha	Edg 207	
Henry	Nsh 102	
Henry	Ons 177	
Howel	Grv 556	
Isaac	Jhn 758	
Jacob	Edg 205	
Jacob	Nsh 104	
James	Jhn 752	
James	Orn 512	
James	Orn 572	
Jerry	Wne 872	
Jesse	Stk 556	
Joab	Edg 210	
Joel	Jhn 753	
Jonah	Jhn 752	
Joseph	Cmb 369	
Joshua	Orn 572	
Luly	Edg 207	
Mary	Gts 269	
Mical	Nsh 102	
Nathan	Mnt 462	
Nathan	Rbs 382	
Robert	Rwn 442	
Ruth	Edg 210	
Ruthy	Edg 207	
Sarah	Frn 465	
Simeon	Edg 208	
Sion	Cmb 368	
Thomas	Frn 468	
Thomas	Ons 177	
Thomas	Orn 572	
Thomas	Orn 575	
Thomas	Wne 872	
Thomas, Jur.	Nsh 103	
Thos.	Nsh 103	
Will.	Nsh 102	
William	Edg 205	
William	Jhn 752	
William	Nsh 102	
William	Orn 572	
William A.	Csw 146	
see Hoin		
Hornaday, Lewis	Orn 569	
Nathan	Orn 568	
Simon	Orn 569	
Hornbarger, John	Rwn 301	
Valt.	Rwn 301	
Hornbarier see Honbarier		
Hornbee, William	Prq 644	
Hornbuckle, Gear	Csw 131	
Jas.	Csw 148	
Richd.	Csw 101	
Solomon, Sr.	Csw 149	
Thomas	Csw 96	
Horne, Celia	Nrt 449	
Howel	Orn 612	
James	Nrt 447	
Joseph	Brt 52	
William	Nrt 447	
Hornday, John	Orn 568	
Hornedy, Christo-		
pher	Orn 568	
Horner, Elizabeth	Orn 575	
George	Orn 512	
Joshua	Stk 556	
Robert	Orn 574	
Robert	Orn 610	
see Homer		
Horney, James	Glf 687	
John	Glf 687	
Paris	Glf 687	
Philip	Glf 677	
Horniblow, Eliza-		
beth	Chw 114	
Hornsbey, Ebenezer	Wke 733	
William	Wke 735	
Hornsby, James	Frn 458	
Leonard	Bnc 171	
Hornseker see Homseker		
Horny, Philip	Rwn 366	
Horre, James	Brk 761	
Horscends, Elijah	Crv 305	
Joseph	Crv 289	
Horser, Abner	Cmb 388	
Isaac	Cmb 388	
Joab	Cmb 388	
Horsey, James	Wke 736	
Horten, Abraham	Srr 658	
Mary	Nsh 105	
Horton, Abraham	Orn 572	
Amos	Wke 738	
Anthony	Csw 132	
Benjn.	Cht 198	
David	Mrt 395	
David	Wke 738	
Drury	Wke 738	
Elisha	Mrt 397	
Elizabeth	Bfr 22	
Elizabeth	Hrt 711	
Frederic	Brt 50	
Hartwell	Wke 738	
Henry	Orn 574	
Horton	Orn 574	
Hugh	Hrt 717	
James	Nrt 447	
Jesse	Nrt 449	
Jesse	Wke 738	
John	Csw 111	
John	Wsh 716	
Julius	Hlf 312	
Margrett	Stk 557	
Moses	Wke 733	
Nathl.	Ash 81	
Reuben	Rth 115	
Samuel	Wke 733	
Sarah	Orn 610	
Thomas	Hrt 717	
Thomas	Orn 574	
Townsend	Rth 119	
William	Brt 50	
William	Cht 200	
William	Nrt 449	
William	Orn 493	
William	Orn 574	
William	Ptt 292	
William	Rth 120	
William	Stk 557	
Williford	Hrt 717	
Willis	Frn 492	
Willis	Prs 216	
Ziphiniah	Bnc 172	
Hosa, Henry	Wne 860	
Salley	Wne 865	
Hose, Henry	Brk 760	
Henry	Grv 534	
Peter	Brk 760	
Hosea, Henry	Wne 865	
Thomas	Jhn 762	
Thomas	Prq 644	
Hoskins, Ann	Chw 126	
Ann, Sen.	Chw 130	
Baker	Chw 122	
Edmond	Chw 113	
George	Orn 492	
Henry	Nwh 12A	
James	Trl 694	
John	Chw 117	
Richard, Jun.	Chw 122	
Richard, Sen.	Chw 122	
Samuel	Chw 122	
Thomas	Trl 674	
Hosselbarger, John	Lnc 903	
Hossell, Jeremiah	Mrt 396	
Hossey, Clement	Cht 171	
Hott, Peter	Brk 755	
see Holt		
Hotton, Dempcy	Crv 259	
Jesse	Crv 263	
Lott	Crv 335	
Merrill	Crv 343	
Houck, David	Rwn 341	
Felix	Rwn 373	
Michael	Brk 758	
Houeson, Demsey	Cmd 94	
Hought, Hezekiah	Ans 203	
James	Ans 203	
Houk, George	Brk 762	
Henry	Rwn 287	
Jacob	Rwn 373	
Peter	Brk 762	
Hoult, Wyatt	Rwn 432	
Houpt, Catherine	Ird 671	
Jacob	Ird 670	
Valentine	Ird 671	
House, Andw.	Lnc 828	
Anthony	Lnc 815	
Baliss	Brt 50	
Brinkley	Wke 734	
Bucknor	Ons 177	
Elias	Cbr 689	
Elisha	Smp 509	
George	Hrt 720	
George	Lnc 868	
George	Smp 533	
Isaac	Edg 209	
Israel	Edg 209	
Jacob	Edg 209	
Jacob	Lnc 815	
Jacob	Nsh 104	
James	Brt 50	
James	Brk 757	
James	Wrr 806	
John	Brk 756	
John	Cbr 709	
John	Orn 512	
John	Smp 499	
Joseph	Grn 600	
Julius	Wke 732	
Laww.	Ons 175	
Mary	Cbr 709	
Peter	Orn 573	
Philip	Lnc 868	
Ransom	Wke 736	
Simon	Lnr 10	
Simon	Lnc 868	
Thomas	Wke 734	
William	Brt 52	
William	Ptt 262	
William	Wke 733	
see Hause		
Houseman, John	Cmb 367	
Houser, Abraham	Stk 604	
Jacob	Rwn 437	
Houston, Aaron	Cbr 686	
Anne	Wlk 46	
Archibald	Cbr 683	
Archibald,Junr.	Cbr 683	
Christopher	Ird 635	
David	Brk 755	
Edward	Dpl 403	

George	Dpl 425	James	Mck 587	Anna	Edg 206
Henry	Dpl 431	James (2)	Nwh 12	Archilus	Wne 869
Henry	Mck 556	James	Srr 659	Archless	Hrt 735
Hugh, Senr.	Mck 578	John	Crt 59	Arther	Wne 873
James	Crv 297	John	Grv 507	Benjamin	Csw 111
James	Crv 317	John	Lnr 32	Benjamin	Nrt 447
James	Ird 635	John	Lnc 868	Benjamin	Wne 867
James	Ird 639	John	Lnc 903	Charles C.	Rck 450
James	Ird 656	John	Nwh 12	Daniel	Wne 869
James	Mck 578	John	Prs 198	Dareass	Wne 871
James,(Ted)	Mck 580	John	Rwn 330	David	Rbs 383
John	Cbr 683	John	Rwn 432	Edmond	Jhn 750
John	Crt 90	John	Rwn 437	Edmund	Trl 674
John	Dpl 403	John	Rwn 447	Elisha	Brk 761
John	Jns 803	John	Srr 663	Elizabeth	Grn 613
John	Mck 580	John	Wlk 43	Francis	Lnc 861
John	Mck 582	Joseph	Cmd 107	Harbett	Lnc 861
Patsey	Dpl 405	Joseph	Ons 182	Henry	Cbr 693
Samuel	Dpl 403	Joshua	Wlk 46	Henry	Cbr 694
Samuel	Ird 649	Josiah	Jns 809	Henry	Wne 868
Samuel	Mck 569	Littleton	Grv 585	Henry	Wne 869
Samuel	Mck 572	Luke	Hrt 717	Hopton	Cmb 368
Thomas	Mck 527	Mark	Grv 573	James	Edg 206
Widow	Mck 536	Matthew	Rwn 330	James	Mnt 501
William	Cbr 681	Mincen	Smp 532	James	Rwn 399
William	Mck 582	Obediance	Ons 149	James	Wne 869
William	Mck 594	Oley.	Ons 160	Jas., Junr.	Mrt 397
William, Esqr.	Mck 578	Parmenius	Ash 79	Jas., senr.	Mrt 396
William, Senr.	Cbr 684	Philip	Srr 660	Jasper	Wne 870
William A.	Dpl 402	Richard	Lnc 865	John	Cbr 694
Houx, Thomas	Brt 52	Robert	Prs 198	John	Edg 206
Houzer, Peter	Lnc 814	Shadrick	Nsh 102	John	Grn 612
Hovey, Seth	Hde 369	Simon	Crt 59	John	Glf 675
Hovis, Benjamin	Lnc 855	Stephen	Hrt 699	John	Mnt 517
Fredk.	Lnc 842	Stevanus	Glf 674	John	Nrt 447
George	Lnc 842	Thomas	Cmd 107	John	Rwn 425
John	Lnc 855	Thomas	Hde 370	John	Rwn 443
Howard, Aaron	Edg 205	Thomas	Orn 571	John	Rwn 452
Allen	Grv 584	Thomas	Rwn 447	John	Rth 118
Ambrose	Brk 758	William	Lnc 864	John	Wne 871
Arthur	Crv 339	William	Mck 598	John	Wne 872
Barnett	Grv 584	William	Mnt 486	Jorden	Mnt 500
Benjamin	Brt 54	William	Ons 151	Joseph	Ans 225
Benjamin	Ons 137	William	Rwn 432	Joseph	Rwn 442
Benjn.	Wlk 42	William	Rwn 447	Joseph, Junr.	Cbr 694
Bradford	Mnt 486	William	Srr 660	Joseph, Senr.	Cbr 694
Christefer	Nwh 12	William, jr.	Crt 59	Lazarus	Wne 867
Christopher	Rwn 437	William, Jur.	Bfr 10	Lewis	Wne 869
Clabourn	Srr 662	William, Senr.	Bfr 10	Major	Wne 868
Cornelius	Hde 370	William, Senr.	Rwn 447	Mary	Nrt 449
Cornelius	Rwn 437	William, Sr.	Crt 59	Mills	Wne 864
Edmond	Rwn 432	Willis	Edg 208	Mills	Wne 867
Edmund	Smp 528	Willson	Edg 208	Mills	Wne 870
Edward	Mnt 462	see Haward		Nancy	Edg 173
Elenor	Lnr 32	Howatt, Thomas	Grv 544	Nancy	Edg 205
Elijah	Brt 54	Howcan, Jesse	Crv 275	Patience	Edg 207
Elisabeth	Crv 251	Howcott, Nathaniel	Chw 117	Paul	Mnt 505
Elisha	Hrt 717	Howe, Arthur	Chw 118	Ralph	Wne 867
Eliz.	Ons 142	Robert	Brn 21A	Richard	Ans 206
Elizabeth	Hrt 733	Robt.	Nwh 5A	Richard	Rch 267
George	Crt 59	Tho.	Nwh 8	Robert	Cht 214
George	Crr 140	Hcwel, Ann	Hlf 358	Robert	Cht 215
George	Grv 585	Arthur	Wne 849	Robert	Wne 871
George	Hde 381	Caleb	Wne 843	Samuel	Lnc 861
George	Rwn 438	Caleb	Wne 847	Stephen	Ans 225
George	Wlk 42	David	Srr 661	Stephen	Rwn 443
Graves	Csw 130	Elizabeth	Orn 493	Stephen	Wne 870
H. John	Bfr 22	James	Srr 660	Thomas	Cmb 354
Hardee	Edg 208	John Barten	Cmb 371	Thomas	Grn 612
Henry	Rwn 437	Joseph	Hlf 316	Thomas	Mnt 486
Henry B.	Nwh 1	Matthew	Hlf 316	Thomas	Wne 872
Isaac	Srr 661	Matthew, Jr.	Hlf 316	William	Edg 205
James	Ans 211	Nathaniel	Edg 205	William	Stk 621
James	Cmb 371	William	Grv 532	William	Wne 871
James	Edg 205	William P.	Crt 92	see Hawell	
James	Hde 371	Zachariah	Hlf 316	Howen, Winsmore	Glf 674
James	Lnr 32	Howell, Aaron	Nrt 449	Howerlin, John	Bfr 10

Name	Ref	Name	Ref	Name	Ref
Howerton, John	Rck 446	Hucher, Nathan	Prq 659	Hueh, Abraham	Cmd 97
Obah.	Rck 449	Hucheson, Wm.	Stk 587	Huek see Hueh	
Thomas	Edg 209	Huckabee, Richard	Cmb 378	Hues, Duncan	Rbs 385
Howes, Absalom	Rck 451	Huckaby, John	Mre 68	Huet, Lydea	Crr 155
Howett, Ann	Psq 634	Thomas	Mnt 517	Huey, John	Ird 624
Anne	Trl 684	Thomas	Mnt 520	Joseph	Ird 624
John	Grv 547	William	Cmb 374	Thomas	Ird 624
Richard	Trl 684	William	Mnt 520	William	Ird 624
Howington, Herod	Wke 734	Hucker, Benjamin	Grn 603	see Hacy	
Jesse	Wke 734	James	Grn 605	Huff, Daniel	Srr 704
Howlen, Annala-		Samuel	Grn 605	Elizabeth	Crt 65
tisha	Bfr 10	Hucketh, Nathaniel	Cht 200	Henry	Crt 65
Christopher	Crt 65	Huddleston, David	Rth 119	Jacob	Rwn 393
Martha	Crt 65	John	Rth 115	John	Stk 612
William	Crt 65	John, j.	Rth 119	Richard	Crt 65
Zepheniah	Crt 65	John, Sr.	Rth 119	Thomas	Crt 65
Howlet, John	Ans 206	Jonan.	Glf 683	Valentine	Rwn 451
Thomas	Ans 206	William	Rth 119	William	Wrr 810
Howlett, Harmon	Glf 667	Hudel, Abraham	Prq 661	Huffam, John	Lnr 12
William	Glf 652	Hudgin, Bely	Glf 644	Huffman, Barnet	Brk 758
Howson, John	Hlf 314	Hudgins, Abner	Dpl 424	Christopher	Ons 179
Howze, Edmund	Frn 447	Humphrey	Gts 269	Daniel	Rwn 399
Isaac	Frn 482	John	Orn 573	Jacob	Lnc 855
John	Frn 448	Thos.	Prs 215	Jacob	Lnc 877
William	Frn 449	William	Dpl 424	Jacob	Ons 179
Hoyer, Rhodolph	Stk 604	Hudler, David	Crv 307	Jacob	Rwn 416
Hoyle, Andrew	Rth 120	Henry	Jns 799	Jno.	Lnc 842
Andw.	Lnc 842	Hudleston, Robert	Wrr 807	Joseph	Lnc 872
Margaret	Lnc 842	Hudlestone, Fields	Prs 216	Lewis	Stk 622
Peter	Lnc 815	Hudley, Elisha	Brk 758	Luis	Stk 597
Hoywood, Henry,		Hudlin, Nathan	Bnc 174	Martin	Lnc 871
Doctr.	Edg 205	Hudlow, Andrew	Rth 117	Michael	Rwn 307
Hozel, Moses	Stk 590	Hudnal, Mary	Bfr 9	Palser	Lnc 868
Huart, Lewis	Lnc 816	Rebekak	Edg 208	Hufham, James	Bld 38
Huay, Andrew	Rth 116	Robert	Bfr 9	Martha	Bld 39
Hubank, Elijah	Jns 809	William	Bfr 9	Hufhines, Daniel	Orn 570
George	Jns 803	Hudson, Absalom	Rwn 447	Daniel	Stk 609
John	Jns 783	Daniel	Lnc 903	Hufkins, John	Stk 609
Hubanks, William	Ird 621	Daniel	Rwn 447	Hufman, George	Stk 556
Hubard, John	Nsh 103	Edward	Nrt 449	Samuel	Brk 755
Morning	Cht 223	Francis	Srr 664	Hufmire, Alexander	Psq 629
Hubbard, Benjn.	Ash 80	Henry	Wrr 810	Hufstetler, George	Lnc 816
Benjn.	Wlk 43	Jacob	Cbr 718	Henry	Lnc 816
Demsey	Wke 733	James	Rwn 296	John	Lnc 899
Henry	Wke 733	Joel	Rck 455	Michael	Lnc 824
James	Ash 80	John	Bnc 171	Michael	Lnc 896
James	Mre 47	John	Frn 463	Hufstettler, Luisa	Lnc 816
John	Glf 658	John	Glf 639	Huges, Starling	Prs 194
Mary	Brt 50	John	Lnc 903	Huggans, Isaac	Jns 785
Mary	Rck 466	John	Rnd 318	Jacob	Jns 785
Moses	Ash 79	John	Rwn 296	James	Jns 787
Moses	Ash 80	Joseph	Chw 119	Huggins, Esther	Dpl 399
Nathan	Hrt 711	Joseph	Rnd 320	Francis	Ons 149
Rachel	Brt 52	Joseph	Rwn 296	Jacob	Ons 146
Ralph	Csw 125	Joshua	Ans 216	Jacob	Orn 575
Samuel	Glf 641	Joshua	Ans 219	Jno.	Lnc 831
Solomon	Crt 79	Mary	Brt 48	John	Ird 661
Thomas	Ash 80	Nathun	Rnd 318	Luke	Bnc 174
Thomas, Senr.	Ash 80	Obediah	Rnd 319	Philip (2)	Bnc 173
William	Ash 80	Peter	Wke 738	Robert	Ird 661
Hubbart, John	Rch 266	Richard	Rnd 318	William	Rbs 383
Hubbell, William	Brt 90	Richard	Srr 664	Wm.	Lnc 831
Hubberd, Isham	Rwn 447	Richard	Wrr 808	Hugh, Isareal	Srr 660
Hubbert, Freeman	Csw 108	Sarah	Brt 50	Jesse	Srr 659
Hubbous, ...	Nsh 103	Seth	Rwn 296	John	Srr 663
Hubburd, Hardy	Prs 211	Sterling	Srr 664	William	Srr 663
Wooson	Prs 187	Thomas	Hlf 312	Hughes, Alexander	Ird 661
Hucaber, James	Wke 739	Thomas	Nrt 451	Charles	Orn 511
Hucaby, Joshua	Rth 117	Thomas	Prq 660	Hudson	Rwn 277
Huccaby, Fuller	Frn 455	Uriah	Prq 647	Hudson	Rwn 287
John	Frn 474	William	Srr 663	James	Csw 140
Huchardson, Rich-		William	Wke 735	James (2)	Ird 661
ard	Stk 587	Hudspeth, Ayres	Srr 659	James, Senr.	Ird 661
Huchens, John	Srr 659	Ayres, Jr.	Srr 660	Joel	Csw 103
Jonathan	Srr 659	Carter	Srr 660	John	Ird 624
Strangmon	Srr 659	Elisabeth	Srr 662	John	Rwn 337
William	Srr 659	George	Srr 660	John, Esq.	Brk 754

John, Junr.	Brk 754	Hullet, Martha	Rth 120
Joseph	Brk 755	Hulloms, William	Ash 79
Joseph	Crv 255	Hulm, Moses	Wlk 46
Samuel	Rwn 277	Hulme, George	Wlk 41
Samuel	Rwn 287	William	Wlk 42
Sarjeant	Rwn 432	Hulson, Abraham	Brk 759
William	Mck 598	Richard	Cht 201
William	Orn 511	William	Orn 573
William	Rwn 386	Humber, Henary	Prs 201
see Hews, Hues, Huges		Humble, David	Mnt 470
Hughey, Alexander	Cbr 677	Henry	Mnt 470
Anne	Ird 671	Jacob	Mnt 470
Anne	Ird 675	Mary	Mnt 470
George	Mck 596	Peter	Mnt 475
James	Bnc 171	Humet, Christopho	Stk 604
James	Cbr 687	Humpherys, Saml.	Srr 661
Jean	Rwn 326	Humpheys, Thomas	Stk 557
John	Mck 596	Humphrees, Josiah	Crr 148
Joseph	Bnc 171	Humphress, Ezekiel	Bfr 9
Mary	Rwn 326	Jacob	Bfr 10
Peter	Cbr 676	Humphrey, Benjamin	Rbs 385
Robert	Mck 597	George	Rch 252
Samuel	Cbr 686	George	Rch 264
Samuel	Cbr 718	Isaiah	Srr 660
Samuel	Mck 559	James	Rbs 384
Hughlett, William	Stk 555	John	Hde 370
Hughman, Edwin	Srr 661	John	Rbs 385
Thomas	Srr 661	John	Srr 662
William	Srr 661	John	Wne 868
Hughs, Benjamin	Jhn 747	Lucy	Rbs 384
Charles	Orn 490	Owen (2)	Wlk 42
David	Brt 48	Humphreys, Joseph	Brn 15A
George	Brt 48	Milley	Wlk 41
George	Bld 21	Robert	Rth 121
George, Junr.	Brt 48	William	Rth 148
George, Senr.	Brt 48	Humphries, Adam	Cmd 105
Jeams	Crr 145	George	Hlf 312
John	Bnc 172	H. John	Wke 738
John	Orn 512	Henry	Csw 121
John	Srr 663	Hinson	Rck 451
John Scott	Brk 761	Hinson	Rck 481
John Wiln.	Srr 658	Isaac	Cmd 99
Josiah	Brt 48	Jno.	Csw 148
Josiah	Jhn 747	John	Crr 144
Josuah	Bnc 172	John	Wke 738
Samuel	Brk 761	John H.	Wke 738
Solomon	Brt 48	Jonathan	Chw 123
Thomas	Bnc 173	Judith	Hlf 312
Thomas	Brk 762	Robert	Wke 737
Will.	Prs 212	Thomas	Rck 451
William	Brt 48	William	Prq 655
William	Mre 64	Humphrys, George	Csw 102
see Hughes		Samuel	Srr 658
Hugh's, William	Bnc 171	Thomas	Csw 146
Hughson, Shadrach	Brt 48	Wm.	Csw 99
Hughy, Henry	Rwn 316	see Umphrys	
Widow	Rwn 316	Humpry, William	Rbs 384
Hukins, Hardy	Crv 289	Hundley, Humphrey	Brt 48
Huks see Hicks		Hundly, Margaret	Crv 247
Hulean, John	Mck 557	Hunner see Hanner	
Hulen, Ambrose	Wlk 43	Hunneycut, Milly	Orn 569
John	Wlk 44	Hunnings, Philip	Trl 678
Hulet, Henry	Dpl 421	Thomas	Trl 678
James	Rch 245	Wm.	Crr 142
Hulett, Jeremiah	Nwh 8	Hunnycut, Robt.	Cht 189
John	Nwh 8	Hunsucker, George	Mre 46
Wm.	Csw 132	John	Brk 762
Hulin, Arthur	Rwn 287	John, Senr.	Brk 762
Hull, Abnor	Lnc 815	Hunsuker, Peter	Brk 759
Ann	Hlf 312	Hunt, Able	Rwn 403
Benjamin	Lnc 816	Absolem	Rth 116
Charity	Hlf 314	Alexander	Mnt 475
John	Hlf 312	Alexd.	Mre 67
John	Stk 621	Andrew	Rwn 443
Joseph	Rch 248	Arthur	Bnc 173
Moses	Rwn 392	Benjamin	Frn 462
see Hall		Celid	Orn 574

Charles	Rwn 442
Charles	Stk 626
Charles	Srr 659
Daniel	Rwn 392
Daniel	Rwn 408
Daniel	Rwn 443
David	Nsh 104
David	Rwn 392
David	Srr 658
Dempsey	Crr 141
Dicie	Nsh 104
Drury	Hrt 735
Edward	Grv 539
Eleazer	Glf 689
Elijah	Nrt 449
Elzabeth	Nsh 104
Enoch	Rwn 443
Gersham, Junr.	Rwn 392
Gershom	Rwn 393
Gershom, Sen.	Rwn 392
Hannah	Grv 529
Hardy	Frn 463
Henry	Frn 462
Henry	Lnc 847
Henry	Orn 574
Jacob	Glf 671
James	Rbs 382
Jas.	Prs 202
Jessey	Frn 463
Johathan	Grv 510
John	Frn 466
John	Frn 484
John	Grv 585
John	Glf 671
John	Glf 692
John	Hrt 735
John	Nwh 7
John	Rwn 408
Jonathan	Rwn 392
Lewis	Rbs 382
Littleburg	Hrt 720
Mary	Grv 579
Matthw	Nsh 104
Nathan	Rwn 354
Onerps.	Ons 160
Robert	Crv 233
Saml.	Nsh 103
Sarah	Grv 585
Shadrach	Wke 734
Sion	Frn 480
Thomas	Glf 682
Thomas	Orn 570
Thomas	Orn 573
William	Cbr 682
William	Grv 513
William	Glf 669
William	Glf 680
William	Rch 257
William	Rth 120
Zachariah	Lnc 893
see Hurst	
Hunte, Charles	Crr 149
Hunter, Abner	Orn 569
Alex	Orn 569
Alexander	Wke 734
Andrew	Brk 755
Andrew	Orn 572
Andrew	Rck 492
Archd.	Nsh 104
Charles	Rck 437
David	Trl 690
David	Wke 734
Demsey	Wke 733
Edward	Dpl 417
Elijah, Sr.	Cht 173
Elisha	Frn 492
Elisha	Gts 268

Eliza	Orn 610	Thomas	Ans 215	Stephen	Rnd 316
Ezekiel	Crv 259	Thomas	Ans 238	Thomas	Hde 369
Francis	Bnc 173	Hunton, Thomas	Prq 649	Hussy, Mary	Glf 690
George	Rck 486	Huntsinger, Jacob	Ash 79	Hust, John S.	Prs 217
Henry	Mck 569	Hupper, Ezekel	Crr 166	Hustin, Robert	Orn 513
Henry	Wke 734	Hurd, Josiah	Brk 759	Huston, George	Csw 117
Henry, Senr.	Mrt 388	Hurdle, Abraham	Gts 268	James	Bld 44
Humphery	Mck 569	Hardy	Orn 511	Jas.	Prs 193
Humphrey	Lnc 826	Martin	Orn 511	Thomas	Bnc 173
Isaac	Gts 268	Mary	Gts 269	Thomas	Lnc 816
Isaac	Wke 735	Mills	Gts 268	Will.	Prs 203
Isaac	Wke 736	Thomas	Gts 268	William	Mck 524
Isaac	Wrr 807	William	Gts 267	Hutchardson, James	Orn 511
Isaac, Jur.	Wke 734	Hurley, Amos	Cht 161	Hutchen, John	Bfr 9
Jacob	Wrr 807	Daniel	Crv 233	Hutchens, Anderson	Srr 664
James	Cht 194	Daniel	Mnt 482	Benjamin	Srr 664
James	Hlf 316	Edmond	Mnt 479	James	Srr 662
James	Mck 569	Jacob	Rwn 416	John	Stk 558
James	Rch 256	Joseph	Mnt 478	John	Stk 584
James	Rck 466	Joseph	Rch 248	Josiah	Srr 662
Jesse	Orn 570	Joshua	Mnt 479	Meridith	Srr 664
Jesse	Orn 571	Samuel	Ird 635	Patrick	Srr 659
John	Bnc 173	William	Mnt 479	Robert	Stk 574
John	Cht 167	Hurloher, Chris-		Samuel	Stk 556
John	Frn 453	tian	Cbr 709	Samuel	Stk 612
John	Gts 268	Christian,Junr.	Cbr 709	Strangemon	Srr 663
John	Mck 558	Hurly, James	Ash 80	Thomas	Srr 664
John	Mck 569	Nihemiah	Rwn 447	see Huchens	
John	Mck 601	Hurn, John	Cth 201	Hutcher see Hucher	
John B.	Mrt 388	Stephen	Cht 157	Hutcherson, Daniel	Stk 595
Joseph	Rth 119	Hurrswood, Zachari-		Daniel, Jur.	Stk 595
Lewis	Rth 93	ah	Rwn 408	James	Orn 571
Libbeus, jr.	Crt 93	Hurst, Corn...s	Nwh 2	Joshua	Grv 535
Libbeus, sr.	Crt 93	George	Srr 659	Richard	Stk 595
Mary	Rch 256	Memucan	Grv 542	Ross	Orn 571
Mary	Stk 556	William B.	Dpl 433	Hutcheson, Carey	Lnc 847
Osbourn	Jhn 762	Hurste, Hardy	Mrt 397	Daniel (2)	Stk 587
Peter	Rck 486	Jas.	Mrt 397	Johnathan	Lnc 847
Peter	Rth 116	John	Mrt 397	see Hucheson	
Prissilla	Nsh 104	Wm.	Mrt 395	Hutchins, Aaron	Hrt 711
Rachel	Brt 48	Hurt, James	Wlk 45	Elijah	Crv 319
Reubin	Wke 735	Jesse	Mnt 470	Elijah	Lnr 11
Richard	Lnc 865	Joel	Srr 659	Howell	Hrt 731
Robert	Brk 758	John	Srr 659	Isaac	Wke 733
Robert	Mck 530	Mary	Srr 659	James	Grv 531
Robert	Orn 571	Hurter, Drew	Nsh 104	James	Orn 610
Robert	Rth 116	Husbands, Elisa-		Jno., Jur.	Wke 733
Robert	Rth 119	beth	Brk 754	Jno., Senr.	Wke 733
Salley	Wke 736	Robert	Rwn 426	John	Crr 154
Samuel	Glf 621	Thomas	Ans 225	John H.	Grv 544
Samuel	Orn 573	Veasy	Brk 754	Miles	Lnr 10
Samuel	Rck 476	William	Brk 755	Moses	Orn 573
Samuel	Rth 116	William	Rnd 319	Moses	Wke 733
Sarah	Wke 733	Huse, John (2)	Rth 115	Nathl.	Crr 154
Theophilus	Gts 268	Johne, Sr.	Rth 115	Parker	Lnr 18
Theops., Jur.	Wke 733	Neeal	Mre 57	Purnel	Psq 630
Thomas	Ird 671	Owen	Rth 119	Richard	Crr 154
Thomas	Mck 601	Samuel	Rth 116	Simon	Lnr 10
Thomas	Rth 93	Theophilus	Rth 116	Thomas	Rth 119
Thomas	Stk 555	Thomas	Rth 116	William	Hrt 732
Thops.	Wke 734	William	Rth 117	William	Wke 733
Timothy, Es-		Husey, Christopher	Rnd 316	Hutchinson, Aaron	Dpl 422
quire	Brt 48	Gidire	Rnd 319	Elisabeth	Ans 200
Timothy, Junr.	Brt 48	Stephen	Rnd 316	Isaiah	Ans 202
Whitmill	Wke 736	Husk, Edward	Orn 571	John K.	Ans 202
Widow	Mck 530	John	Orn 611	Joseph	Dpl 423
William	Brt 50	Lewis	Nrt 449	Prisscilla	Ptt 256
William	Bnc 173	Huske, William	Lnr 32	Hutchison, Alexr.	Ash 80
William	Dpl 416	Husket, Nathaniel	Grv 524	David	Lnc 861
William	Gts 268	William	Grv 524	George	Mck 524
William	Mnt 495	Husketh, Isaac	Grv 523	James	Mck 523
see Hurter		Thomas	Grv 522	William	Mck 523
Huntington, Jona-		Huson, David	Lnc 831	Hutson, Abel	Hde 370
than (2)	Nwh 5	Edward	Lnc 831	Adlai	Rwn 452
Roswell	Orn 492	Thos.	Lnc 831	Anthony	Hde 370
Huntley, Isaac	Ans 239	Hussay, John	Dpl 413	Archabald	Hde 370
Robert	Ans 240	Hussey, John	Cmb 366	Elijah	Hde 370

Jacob	Cbr 687	John	Lnc 868	Merrit	Frn 469		
James	Crv 289	Lawrence	Lnc 868	Ings, Matthew	Brt 54		
James	Rwn 321	Peter	Lnc 868	Ingums, Thomas	Chw 130		
James	Smp 506	Ikenor, George	Rbs 387	Inman, Hardy	Rbs 385		
Jesse	Mrt 396	Ikner, Jacob	Nwh 9	James	Rbs 385		
Joakem	Ans 218	Iles, John	Hlf 318	John	Rbs 385		
Joel	Smp 498	Roadham	Hlf 318	Robert	Rbs 385		
John	Rwn 452	Ing, Christopher	Edg 211	Innes, Rhamon	Cmb 376		
Joseph	Smp 519	Joseph	Edg 211	Innis, William	Rwn 331		
Moses	Rth 119	Inge, Richard	Grv 512	Inol see Idol			
Richard	Rth 119	Inglar, David	Rwn 392	Inscon, Reuben	Grv 565		
Roland	Mnt 466	Ingle, George	Glf 647	Inscow, John	Grv 526		
Thomas	Rwn 321	Jacob	Glf 633	Reuben	Grv 526		
Thomas	Rwn 425	Jacob	Glf 648	Stephen	Grv 526		
Thomas	Smp 520	John	Lnc 856	William	Grv 527		
Thos. H.	Mrt 396	Ludwick	Glf 647	Insor, John	Mre 55		
William	Ans 219	Margarett	Glf 633	Summer	Smp 506		
William	Hde 370	Inglefinger, Chris-		Ipock, Jacob	Crv 279		
see Hulson		tiana	Lnc 853	Nancy	Crv 285		
Hutton, Arnal	Glf 629	Ingles, John	Edg 211	Peter, Junr.	Crv 285		
George	Glf 629	John, Colo.	Edg 173	Peter, Senr.	Crv 283		
James	Glf 628	Samuel	Ptt 283	Samuel	Crv 325		
John	Mck 563	Inglish, Henry	Brk 763	Senea	Crv 283		
see Hatton		see Robert		see Spock			
Hutts, Charles	Grv 515	Ingold, Peter	Glf 647	Irby, Peter	Grv 541		
Hux, Benjamin	Hlf 314	Peter	Orn 513	William	Mnt 502		
Polley	Hlf 314	William	Glf 631	Iredell, Hannah	Chw 114		
Hyatt, Elisha	Nrt 449	Ingraham, Isaac,		Ireland, Abednego	Glf 669		
Evan	Glf 677	Junr.	Lnr 15	Daniel	Crt 61		
Joseph	Glf 674	James	Lnr 15	Grafton	Hrt 735		
Hyde, Benjamin	Lnc 903	Ingram, Abraham	Cmb 384	John	Bnc 175		
Benjamin	Rth 118	Allin	Mnt 504	Samuel	Orn 513		
Heartwell	Hlf 312	Barnaba	Jhn 772	Sarah	Crt 60		
John	Bnc 173	Benjamin	Rch 248	Irion, Fredk.	Rck 475		
John	Lnc 903	Charles	Cmb 371	Irons, William	Bnc 174		
Robert	Grv 512	Chattan	Csw 102	Irton, Merrcah	Crr 154		
Stephen	Ans 206	Clement	Rnd 323	Irvin, Abraham	Rth 121		
William	Lnc 903	Dennis	Ans 228	Alexd. John	Edg 211		
Hyder, Benjamin	Rth 116	Edwin	Rch 245	Isaac	Lnc 835		
Hyett, Shaderach	Bnc 173	Feriby	Smp 502	Jno. Alixander	Edg 173		
Hyles, John	Rth 120	Goldman	Bnc 175	John Alexd.	Edg 211		
John, Sr.	Rth 120	Isaac	Lnr 15	Thomas P.	Crv 249		
Martin	Rth 116	Isham	Ans 228	Irwin, George	Glf 635		
Hyman, James	Crv 289	Jacob	Cmb 355	Isaac	Rch 249		
Joel	Brt 50	James	Crv 317	Isaac	Rch 250		
John, Esqr.	Mrt 396	James	Nrt 455	John	Mck 549		
John, Junr.	Mrt 397	John	Ans 203	John	Mck 551		
Sarah	Brt 50	John	Crv 317	Robert	Mck 606		
Thomas	Crv 287	John	Smp 503	Samuel	Mck 606		
thos., Esqr.	Mrt 396	John, Este.	Cmb 359	William	Mck 571		
thos., Senr.	Mrt 394	John, Junr.	Ans 199	Isaacs, Elisha	Srr 666		
William, Esqr.	Edg 205	John, Junr.	Nrt 453	John	Rwn 354		
William, Junr.	Edg 206	John, Senr.	Nrt 453	Richard	Ash 82		
Hynes, Alexr.	Nwh 8A	Joseph	Jhn 759	Isbel, Thomas	Wlk 46		
Benjamin	Hlf 314	Joseph, Junr.	Ans 207	William	Wlk 46		
Lewis	Nwh 9A	Joseph, Senr.	Ans 207	Isbell, Christo-			
Micheal	Nwh 5A	Larking	Ans 233	pher	Srr 666		
Stephen	Wne 857	Mary	Csw 105	Littleton	Srr 666		
Thomas	Hlf 314	Matthew	Ans 233	Richard	Srr 709		
William	Nwh 9A	Needham	Jhn 750	Thomas	Stk 579		
Hypock, Lucy	Lnr 32	Samuel	Smp 498	Isehour, George	Lnc 876		
Hyslep, James	Rnd 318	Shadrach	Jhn 772	John	Lnc 876		
		Simon	Cmb 370	John	Lnc 886		
		Thomas	Cbr 694	Valentine	Lnc 876		
-- I --		Walt.	Rck 477	Isenhour, Michael	Cbr 712		
		Widow	Ans 216	Peter	Cbr 712		
		William	Ans 225	Islar, Adam	Lnc 817		
Idelot, Levin	Psq 630	William	Bnc 175	Isler, John	Jns 783		
Idle, George	Rwn 366	William	Brk 763	John, Junr.	Jns 815		
Jacob	Stk 615	William	Jhn 759	Williams	Jns 791		
Mathias	Rwn 366	William	Jhn 776	Isley, Balsire	Glf 665		
Michael	Rwn 366	William	Rnd 322	George	Orn 513		
Idlett, Thomas	Cmd 104	Willian, Junr.	Nrt 453	Philip	Orn 513		
Idol, John	Crv 259	William, Senr.	Nrt 455	Israel, Jesse	Bnc 174		
Ijams, Beal	Rwn 453	Ingrum, Ben.	Frn 491	John	Bnc 174		
Ikard, George	Lnc 902	Chalton	Csw 121	Michael	Wlk 46		
Henry	Lnc 868	Mary	Frn 469	Isteal, Thompson	Brk 763		

Name	Ref		Name	Ref
Iszel, John	Rbs 386		Curtice	Srr 667
Lemuel	Rbs 386		Curtis	Smp 494
Ives, Isaac	Lnr 15		Daniel	Bfr 11
Jesse	Crr 163		Daniel	Nrt 453
Job	Lnr 15		David	Ans 214
John	Crv 275		David	Psq 636
John	Crv 335		David (2)	Rth 121
Josiah	Edg 211		Dianna	Crv 301
Josiah	Hlf 320		Dorcas	Smp 501
Robert	Lnr 15		Edward	Bfr 11
Thomas	Crv 279		Edward	Brk 765
Thos.	Crr 145		Edward	Hlf 318
William	Crv 291		Edward	Nsh 106
William	Crv 305		Edmund	Nrt 455
Ivester, Barbara	Rth 121		Eleazar	Bfr 11
Ivey, Adam	Rbs 386		Elias	Brk 765
Austin	Rbs 387		Elijah	Mre 44
Charles (2)	Rbs 386		Ephriam	Rth 121
Claborn	Crv 239		Francis	Crt 59
David	Jhn 771		Francis	Stk 594
Edith (2)	Rbs 386		Frederick	Wke 741
Francis	Rbs 386		Frederick (Mulat-	
Henry	Wke 741		to)	Edg 214
Isham	Rbs 387		Gabriel	Brk 763
James	Jhn 771		Gabriel	Rth 121
John	Wne 844		George	Mre 44
Josiah	Rbs 386		George	Smp 497
Lewis	Brn 21A		George	Stk 559
Lovel	Jhn 773		Gibson	Smp 599
Nathan	Wke 741		Henry	Rck 491
Peter	Wke 741		Hody	Bfr 11
Robert	Bld 20		Isaac	Ans 211
Sarah	Cmb 355		Isaac	Frn 481
Thomas	Rbs 386		Isaac	Hlf 318
Ivy, Benjamin	Rnd 322		Isaac	Orn 513
David	Orn 514		Isaac	Orn 576
George	Wsh 706		Isaac	Rnd 322
John	Orn 514		Isaac	Rnd 323
Olive	Orn 514		Isaac	Wrr 813
Robert	Hlf 318		Jacob	Orn 576
see Eivy			Jacob	Rnd 321
Izbell, Peter	Hlf 320		Jacob	Wke 740
Izion, Sarah	Rck 442		James	Ash 81
see Irion			James	Ash 82
Izzard, Buckner	Orn 609		James	Crv 313
Elizabeth	Grv 565		James	Cmb 382
James	Orn 609		James	Glf 623
James, jr.	Orn 609		James	Mre 44
Mary	Nsh 107		James (3)	Orn 576
Randoph	Orn 609		James	Psq 626
			James	Psq 636
			James	Prq 652
-- J --			James	Rnd 323
			James	Rbs 387
			James	Rwn 307
Jack, Old	Chw 131		James	Rwn 379
Jacks, Nicholass	Srr 668		James	Srr 668
Richard	Rth 121		James, junr.	Ash 82
Richard, Jur.	Srr 668		Jehu	Psq 624
Thomas	Srr 668		Jemima	Bfr 11
Jackson, Abner	Wsh 706		Jesse	Psq 631
Allen	Smp 510		Jethro	Rbs 385
Allin	Mnt 487		Jno.	Csw 141
Amor	Stk 559		Joab	Psq 628
Amos	Brk 765		Joel	Mrt 398
Andrew	Glf 657		John	Brk 765
Andrew	Mre 60		John	Cmb 383
Andrew	Rnd 322		John	Frn 486
Arthur	Psq 630		John	Glf 670
Asa	Psq 628		John	Lnr 13
Baily	Psq 630		John	Orn 577
Benjamin	Orn 576		John	Psq 634
Catharine	Lnr 13		John	Ptt 243
Charlotte	Edg 214		John (2)	Rnd 322
Christon	Mre 57		John	Rnd 323
Cloe	Mrt 388		John	Rbs 386
Coleby	Orn 513		John	Smp 494

Name	Ref
John	Smp 510
John	Wne 864
Joseph	Brk 765
Joseph	Glf 657
Joseph	Prq 652
Joseph	Prq 658
Joseph	Ptt 243
Joseph	Srr 667
Joseph, Jur.	Srr 667
Joshua	Psq 624
Josiah	Bfr 11
Josiah	Frn 487
Lemuel	Psq 632
Lemuel	Wke 740
Levi	Rth 122
Levy	Grn 602
Levy (2)	Orn 576
Lewis	Psq 640
Lewis	Smp 495
Lewis	Srr 668
Loe	Wke 740
Low	Frn 481
Lowe	Grn 594
Malach	Psq 628
Malachi	Psq 626
Margret	Mre 52
Mary	Bfr 11
Mary	Edg 214
Mary, Junr.	Mrt 398
Mary, Senr.	Mrt 398
Mathew	Nwh 3A
Matthew	Hlf 322
Micajah	Smp 515
Miles	Psq 641
Nancy	Crt 59
Nathan	Smp 497
Nathan	Wke 740
Nelson	Srr 667
Newman	Wke 739
Peggy	Rth 122
Peleg	Psq 624
Randol	Mre 60
Randolph	Mre 50
Reading	Ptt 243
Reuben	Rbs 386
Reubin	Wke 739
Richard	Smp 494
Rieuben	Srr 668
Robert S.	Rnd 322
Roberte	Mrt 398
Sally	Lnr 13
Samuel	Ans 240
Samuel	Grv 580
Samuel	Stk 559
Samuel	Srr 667
Samuel	Trl 678
Seth	Mre 66
Solomon	Csw 143
Stephen	Ans 214
Stephen	Bfr 11
Stephen	Rnd 323
Susannah	Orn 576
Thomas	Crt 59
Thomas	Csw 128
Thomas	Hde 371
Thomas	Psq 624
Thomas	Prq 654
Thomas	Rnd 323
Thomas	Rbs 386
Thomas (2)	Rbs 387
Thomas	Rwn 387
Thomas	Wke 740
Thomas, Jur.	Csw 135
Thomas, Senr.	Csw 135
Welbourn	Mnt 475
Widow	Rnd 321
Will.	Nsh 106

William	Ans 212	Elias	Smp 511	Thomas	Rnd 322
William	Chw 124	Elijah	Mck 573	see Jones	
William	Cmb 383	Elisha	Hlf 320	Janier, Henry	Rck 440
William	Edg 214	Elizabeth	Dpl 401	Janson, Charles W.	Chw 114
William	Frn 466	Emanuel	Rck 441	Jarman, John	Trl 690
William	Frn 480	Fredric	Brt 54	Jarmon, Liddleton	Ons 157
William	Frn 486	George	Wrr 812	Jarnagan, Needham	Hrt 705
William	Glf 623	Hardy	Hlf 320	Jarott, David	Wke 742
William	Glf 657	Henry	Ans 222	Jarrat, Deaverson	Frn 449
William	Hlf 320	Isaac	Dpl 423	John	Frn 485
William	Mre 59	Isaac	Hrt 699	Jarrel, Henry	Rch 258
William	Orn 493	Isaac	Nwh 5	Jarrell, Isaac	Jhn 760
William	Orn 576	Isaac	Wrr 813	Nancy	Lnr 13
William	Prq 658	James	Ons 166	Pugh	Ptt 242
William	Rnd 321	Jane	Brn 16	Jarret, John	Lnc 904
William	Rnd 322	Jeremiah	Nrt 453	Philip	Lnc 904
William	Rwn 374	Jesse	Orn 576	see Jarrit	
William	Smp 497	John	Brt 56	Jarrett, Daniel	Bnc 174
William	Smp 499	John	Crv 271	John	Bnc 174
William	Srr 707	John	Dpl 409	Richard	Cmb 355
William, Jr.	Hlf 322	John	Ons 165	Widow	Mck 606
William, Senr.	Glf 623	John	Prq 661	Jarrill, William	Brk 764
William, Sr.	Hlf 322	John	Ptt 224	Jarrit, Killian	Brk 764
Wm.	Psq 636	John	Rch 258	Margret	Rwn 288
Zecharia	Psq 632	John	Stk 559	Samuel	Lnc 904
Zechariah	Psq 627	John, junior	Ptt 238	Widow	Mck 525
Jacob, Black		Jonathan	Chw 120	Jarrott, John	Ons 152
David	Crr 158	Joseph	Crv 271	Thomas	Wke 742
Kents	Rwn 379	Joshua	Ptt 238	Wiliam	Orn 575
Petty	Nwh 10	Kent	Rwn 409	Zachariah	Wke 742
William	Nwh 3A	Kisia	Bfr 10	Jarves, Betsey	Crr 154
Jacobs, Abraham	Rwn 288	Mary	Dpl 442	Ephrim	Crr 142
Abraham	Smp 515	Mary	Mrt 398	Foster	Crr 141
Benj.	Prs 215	Matthew	Ptt 226	Jeams	Crr 156
Christian	Rwn 288	Muckey	Brk 768	Jeams	Crr 161
Daniel	Rwn 288	Nancey	Wrr 813	John	Crr 137
Ezekiah	Brn 13	Nicanor	Dpl 423	Levet	Crr 154
Henry	Ash 81	Nicholas	Rwn 416	Liday	Crr 142
Jacob	Nrt 453	Patsey	Dpl 399	Saml.	Crr 142
James	Bld 10	Pattey	Mrt 398	Solomon	Crr 154
James	Brn 13A	Peter	Lnc 889	Thos.	Crr 141
James	Cmb 392	Philip	Rch 242	Thos.	Crr 142
Jeromiah	Rwn 447	Rebecca	Brt 56	William	Crr 162
John	Bld 10	Richard	Dpl 409	Wm.	Crr 156
Joshua	Prs 203	Samuel	Brk 763	Jarvice, Elizabeth	Cmd 100
Josiah	Rbs 386	Thomas	Brk 764	Jarvis, Daniel	Srr 667
Primus	Nwh 9A	Thomas	Dpl 433	David	Hde 371
Richd.	Prs 217	Thomas	Nwh 5	Foster	Hde 371
Ruth	Crt 84	Thomas	Rck 448	Foster, Ser.	Hde 371
Samuel	Brt 54	Thomas	Rwn 366	Jabez	Bnc 174
Samuel	Bld 10	Thomas, junior	Ptt 239	Jabz., Senr.	Srr 667
Shadrach	Bld 10	Thomas, Senior	Ptt 238	James	Hde 371
Susanna	Nrt 453	William	Ans 222	James	Srr 708
Thomas	Smp 515	William	Bnc 175	James	Wlk 47
William	Nrt 451	William (2)	Brk 764	Jesse	Hde 371
Zachariah (2)	Ird 635	William (2)	Dpl 409	John	Srr 669
Zack	Nwh 10	William	Lnc 828	Josiah	Hde 371
Jacoby, Benj.	Nwh 1A	William	Ptt 238	Joseph	Hde 371
Jacocks, Charles	Brt 54	William, Senr.	Brk 764	Moses	Crv 235
John	Brt 54	Winnifred	Crv 325	Rezia	Srr 667
Jonathan	Brt 54	Zackh.	Nwh 5	S.	Srr 708
James, Abner	Orn 514	see Janes, Jeams		Saml.	Crr 140
Allice	Nwh 12A	Jameson, Bond	Chw 129	Samuel	Hde 371
Ann	Grv 578	David	Mck 552	Thomas	Rwn 362
Bartly	Mnt 475	Robert	Mck 541	Zachariah	Hde 371
Benjamin	Hlf 322	Jamison, James	Ans 230	Zadock	Rwn 362
Benjn.	Mrt 398	James	Rwn 365	see Jarvice	
Cary	Prs 193	Thomas	Mck 534	Jasop, John	Stk 559
Charles	Crv 271	Jammison, Salley	Crr 158	William	Stk 559
Charles	Crv 295	Jandus, Charles	Chw 116	Jasper, Dorcus	Crr 154
D.	Srr 706	Jane, Edmond	Stk 559	Jonathan	Bfr 11
Daniel	Dpl 409	JOhn	Wlk 47	Richard	Bfr 11
Daniel	Ptt 238	Joseph	Stk 559	Saml.	Crr 154
Darkis	Bnc 174	Mourning	Cht 160	Selden	Hde 371
David	Mrt 398	Westly	Stk 592	Jasperwhite, John	Crr 155
Edward	Brk 764	William	Stk 559	Jasup, Abraham	Cmb 381
Edward	Chw 121	Janes, Richard	Wrr 812	Jay, Jas., Senr.	Prs 217

John	Prs 218	Robinson	Ptt 263	Jessers, Henry	Cht 221
John Cameron	Mre 75	Ruben	Lnc 842	Jessip, Isaac	Bld 45
Joseph	Rth 122	Samuel	Rwn 317	Jessop, Caleb	Srr 667
Jeams, John	Crr 144	Sanford	Cht 203	Jacob	Srr 667
Jean, Mary	Nrt 453	Thomas	Edg 213	Joseph	Stk 559
Mildred	Nrt 455	Thomas	Grv 522	Pratt	Stk 582
Nathan	Frn 459	Thomas	Grv 573	Prisilla	Srr 667
Sally	Cht 197	Thomas	Mnt 470	Timothy	Stk 582
Jedkins, Thomas	Ans 227	Thomas (2)	Rnd 322	Timothy, Jr.	Stk 582
Jeffers, John	Csw 108	Webb	Hrt 721	William (2)	Stk 582
Samuel	Rth 122	William	Ans 211	Jessup, Isaac	Cmb 382
Jefferson, Martha	Bfr 23	William	Grv 558	James	Cmb 382
Obadiah	Bfr 11	William	Ird 730	Samuel	Cmb 382
Peggy	Ptt 269	William	Orn 575	see Jasop	
Jeffery, William	Srr 668	William	Orn 577	Jester, Jacob	Glf 665
Jefferys, Joshua	Csw 124	William	Rwn 403	Jacob	Glf 673
Thomas	Csw 110	Winborne	Nrt 451	Nimrod	Glf 673
Jeffreys, Ganer	Bnc 175	Winbourne	Brt 56	Jacob	Glf 663
Gray	Wke 741	Wyatt	Lnc 843	Jeter, Dudley	Wke 742
John	Bnc 175	see Genkins, Jinkins		Edmond	Wke 742
Orsborn	Prs 217	Jennett, Criston	Crr 167	Edmund	Nrt 453
Paul	Prs 206	Druselley	Crr 167	John	Hlf 318
Simon	Frn 491	Jelisho	Hde 371	Jethro, Thomas	Trl 670
William	Frn 492	Jesse	Nwh 3A	Jetton, Able	Csw 101
Jeffries, Simon	Nrt 453	Robert	Hde 371	Lewis	Mck 562
William	Grv 557	Sarah	Hde 371	see Jitton	
Jeffris, Enoch	Grv 555	Jenney, Able	Orn 576	Jewel, Ebenezer	Hde 371
Jeffrus, Lucey	Wrr 813	Jennings, Andrew	Mck 604	Stephen	Lnc 826
Jekia see Sekia		David	Psq 731	Thomas	Wrr 813
Jelks, Robert	Hlf 320	Demsey	Psq 636	Jewell, James	Crv 263
Samuel	Jhn 761	Ebenezer	Psq 630	John	Brk 764
William	Hlf 320	Elisabeth	Psq 633	Jiffries, Jacob	Orn 514
Jemboy, ...	Bld 27	Geo.	Nwh 2	Jiffris, Evan	Orn 513
Jemerson see Jameson		Isaac	Brk 765	Jiggetts, Ann	Hrt 737
Jenerite, Isaac	Bld 3	John	Ans 214	John	Hrt 737
Jenkens, Thomas	Orn 577	John	Mnt 466	Jiggitts, Mary	Hrt 735
Jenkins, Benjamin	Cmb 355	John	Psq 635	Jiles, Samuel	Brk 764
Benjamin	Nrt 451	Sherwood	Mnt 466	Thomas	Rnd 322
Benjn.	Hrt 720	Thomas	Mnt 468	William	Rnd 323
Benjn.	Lnc 843	Thos.	Nwh 2	Jim, Nanny	Crt 73
Cadar	Brt 56	Thos.	Psq 636	Jimeson, William	Rwn 337
Charles	Ptt 287	William	Rck 487	Jimison, Arthur	Mck 526
Demcy	Hrt 720	Jent, John	Wke 740	John	Ird 661
Dempsey	Edg 213	Thomas	Wke 740	Samuel	Mck 568
Edward	Lnc 817	Thomas	Wke 741	Jingles, James	Lnc 831
Edward	Lnc 843	Jerkins, Edmund	Bfr 23	John	Mck 574
Elias	Grv 555	Gray	Bfr 23	Saml.	Lnc 830
Elijah	Lnc 842	Joseph	Srr 668	Jinkens, Simons	Crr 161
Ervin	Hrt 705	Oarolus	Glf 682	Jinkings, Nathan	Orn 513
George	Brt 54	Jerman, Henry	Brk 763	Jinkins, Benjamin	Rbs 387
Henry	Ptt 262	Hezekiah	Brk 762	Cannon	Hlf 318
Henry, Jun.	Hrt 720	Nancy	Brk 763	Charles	Hrt 725
Henry, Senr.	Hrt 720	Jernagan, Elisha	Dpl 435	Daniel	Mrt 398
Hugh	Rwn 317	Jean	Smp 499	Daniel	Ons 166
Isaiah	Mnt 483	Jesse	Smp 514	David	Ons 166
Isam	Hrt 705	William	Smp 511	Dew	Nrt 453
James	Brt 54	Jernigan, Arthur	Brt 54	Edward	Rbs 387
James	Ons 162	Benjamin	Wne 868	Ford	Hlf 318
Jenkin	Lnc 817	Etheldred	Wne 867	Francis	Srr 667
Jesse	Rwn 403	Fereby	Brt 56	Francis	Srr 705
Jesse	Rwn 409	Godwin	Brt 54	Genky	Rth 122
John	Brt 56	James	Brt 54	Henry	Ons 165
John	Grv 555	Joseph	Wne 854	Jas.	Mrt 398
John (2)	Lnc 843	Josiah	Wne 867	Jesse	Nsh 106
John	Mck 551	Kedar	Wne 854	John	Mrt 398
John	Orn 575	Lewis	Brt 54	John	Ons 165
John	Rck 471	Mills	Wne 869	John	Wrr 813
Joseph	Lnc 842	Samuel	Brt 56	Jonathan	Smp 520
Josiah	Brt 56	Sarah	Wne 843	Joseph	Srr 669
Lewis	Rwn 453	William	Brt 56	Josiah	Hrt 720
Lewis, Jr.	Ons 170	Winnefred	Wne 868	Lewis	Ons 160
Lewis, Sr.	Ons 170	Jerrel, William	Hlf 318	Lewis, Jur.	Rbs 387
Mary	Nrt 455	Jerry, Anne	Cmb 355	Lewis, Ser.	Rbs 387
Moses	Lnc 827	Rachel	Crt 72	Mary	Orn 577
Noah	Brt 56	Jervis see Jarvis		Nancy	Wrr 812
Reuben	Nrt 451	Jesop see Jasup, Jisop		Ozben	Mrt 398
Rigdon	Brt 54	Jesse, Bartholomew	Crt 90	Thomas	Dpl 425

William	Bnc 175	Benjamin	Nrt 455	James	Orn 514
William	Hlf 318	Benjamin	Ons 157	James	Rnd 323
William	Ons 167	Benjamin	Rnd 323	James	Rck 437
William	Orn 513	Benjamin (2)	Srr 668	James	Trl 688
William	Wrr 812	Benjamin (2)	Wrr 811	James (2)	Wrr 812
Willie	Wrr 812	Benjamin S.	Srr 668	James	Wlk 47
Winbon	Gts 270	Benjan.	Wlk 47	Jane	Csw 117
Wm.	Mrt 398	Benjn.	Wlk 47	Jeffery	Hlf 318
see Jenkins		Bunn	Rnd 323	Jepthah	Nrt 451
Jinks, George	Cht 208	Burwell	Jhn 759	Jeremiah	Orn 576
Joseph	Cht 207	Caleb	Glf 691	Jesse	Grv 583
Mathew	Cht 210	Chalds	Wlk 47	Jesse	Wlk 48
Thomas	Wke 741	Charles	Chw 120	Jesse, Junr.	Mrt 398
William	Cht 210	Charles	Rth 121	Jesse, Senr.	Mrt 398
Jinnings, James	Srr 667	Charles	Srr 668	Jno.	Csw 117
Jinnins, Charles	Wlk 48	Charles	Wke 741	Jno.	Rck 448
Elijah	Ash 81	Daniel	Grv 536	Job	Trl 678
John	Wlk 48	Daniel	Mre 40	Joel	Rth 121
Luke	Wlk 48	Daniel	Rth 122	John	Bnc 174
Martha	Rth 122	Daniel	Wrr 812	John	Csw 97
Jisop, Thomas	Prq 662	Darden	Nrt 453	John	Csw 114
Jitton, John	Brk 763	David	Edg 213	John	Frn 474
Widow	Mck 563	David	Rnd 321	John	Grv 516
Joan, Wiley	Stk 597	David	Rth 122	John	Grv 548
Job, Samuel	Brt 56	Delilah	Ans 221	John	Glf 627
Thomas	Rwn 438	Demsey	Frn 465	John	Jhn 771
Jobe, Imes	Glf 643	Drury	Jhn 768	John	Mrt 398
John	Glf 643	Drury	Orn 577	John	Mre 55
Jobs, Samuel	Rwn 458	Dudley	Hlf 318	John	Nrt 451
Thomas	Rwn 458	Edward	Bnc 175	John	Orn 514
Jocelin, Thomas	Crv 301	Elias	Hlf 320	John (2)	Orn 576
Joeel, Anson	Brk 764	Elijah	Nrt 451	John	Prq 652
John, Dann	Mck 601	Elisha	Lnr 12	John	Rnd 321
David	Bfr 11	Elisha	Srr 668	John	Rnd 322
Henderson	Orn 611	Elisha, Sen.	Lnr 12	John	Rnd 323
Ingram, Senr.	Nrt 453	Esther	Edg 213	John	Rck 442
Lewy	Bfr 23	Etheldred (2)	Jhn 773	John	Rth 121
Mackey	Brk 776	Ezekiel	Lnr 12	John	Rth 122
William	Srr 707	Frances	Edg 213	John	Srr 667
see Little John		Fredrick	Rth 122	John	Wke 739
Johnes, John	Stk 601	General	Ans 238	John	Wke 741
Johns, Benjamin	Stk 558	Geoffrey	Wlk 47	John	Wlk 47
Eliza	Orn 576	George	Glf 627	John, C.	Ans 215
Henry	Orn 576	George	Orn 577	John, G.	Ans 225
John, Esqr.	Wlk 48	George	Rck 437	John, (Hatter)	Csw 114
John L.	Wlk 48	George	Wlk 48	John, R.	Wlk 47
Johnson, Aaron	Wke 739	Hanah	Csw 114	John, S.	Rnd 323
Abel	Jhn 767	Hannah	Trl 678	John, Senr.	Csw 113
Abraham	Stk 619	Hardee	Ptt 286	Jonathan	Grv 536
Abram	Mrt 398	Henry	Jhn 765	Joseph	Mre 61
Accrel	Hlf 318	Henry	Jhn 767	Joseph	Nrt 451
Alex	Rck 436	Henry	Rnd 321	Joseph	Prq 652
Alexander	Ash 81	Henry	Rth 122	Joseph	Prq 663
Alexander	Cmb 355	Henry	Stk 617	Joseph	Rnd 322
Alexander	Glf 622	Henry	Wlk 48	Joseph	Rch 271
Allen	Jhn 773	Hiram	Rnd 323	Joseph	Wrr 813
Amos	Glf 638	Holland	Ptt 259	Joshua	Glf 692
Amos	Jhn 767	Isaac	Csw 123	Joshua	Jhn 774
Amos, Esqr.	Edg 213	Isaac	Srr 707	Joshua	Prq 652
Anderson	Grv 543	Issack	Orn 513	Joshua	Trl 686
Andrw	Nsh 107	Isaiah	Lnr 13	Josiah	Hlf 320
Archa	Srr 707	Israel	Wke 741	Josiah	Nsh 107
Archd.	Mre 55	Jacob	Ans 221	Judkin	Crt 79
Archd.	Rwn 366	Jacob	Bnc 174	Lanelott	Csw 96
Archer	Grv 544	Jacob	Edg 214	Leviticuss	Orn 514
Archibald	Grv 542	Jacob	Hlf 320	Lewis	Wlk 47
Archibald	Rch 259	Jacob	Jhn 764	M. Duke	Wrr 812
Archy	Rch 250	Jacob	Nsh 105	Margaret	Nrt 453
Arthur	Rth 121	Jacob	Prq 662	Martha	Nrt 451
Ashley	Stk 616	Jacob, Sr.	Bnc 174	Martin	Jhn 766
Ashley	Srr 668	James	Ans 233	Mary	Grv 512
Barnaby, Junr.	Nrt 453	James	Bnc 175	Mary	Grv 538
Barnaby, Senr.	Nrt 451	James	Csw 117	Mary	Stk 559
Barsheby	Gts 269	James	Edg 214	Matthew	Ans 221
Ben.	Frn 466	James	Glf 691	Matthew (2)	Nsh 107
Benjamin	Edg 213	James	Glf 692	Merida	Wke 739
Benjamin	Grv 513	James	Hlf 320	Merredith	Ans 239

Moses	Jhn 765	William	Nrt 453	Gideon	Rck 483
Moses	Jhn 772	William	Rch 258	H. Alexander	Brt 54
Moses	Wlk 47	William	Rck 446	H. John, Junr.	Brt 54
Mourning	Nsh 107	William (2)	Rth 121	H. John, Senr.	Brt 54
Nathan	Edg 214	William	Rth 122	Hardy	Prs 204
Nathan	Wke 739	William (2)	Srr 667	Henry	Crv 299
Nathaniel	Bnc 175	William	Srr 668	Henry	Wne 846
Noblet	Bnc 175	William	Wrr 812	Henry, Junr.	Crv 299
Noel	Grv 536	William	Wne 855	Hugh	Wrr 811
Noel	Jhn 764	William (2)	Wlk 47	Isaac	Cht 184
Obed	Jhn 769	William	Wlk 48	Isaac	Ird 655
Oliver	Nrt 453	William, B.C.	Ans 221	Isaac	Jhn 766
Peter	Jhn 775	William, Junr.	Edg 213	Isabella	Rbs 387
Philemon	Jhn 772	William, Sr.	Jhn 764	Isham	Cht 171
Philip	Ans 221	Willis	Edg 214	Isham	Jhn 768
Philip	Grv 545	Willis	Hlf 318	Jacob	Cmb 376
Philip	Rth 121	Wm.	Mrt 398	Jacob	Jns 809
Phillip	Mre 63	Wm., Sen.	Srr 667	Jacob	Rwn 387
Rachael (2)	Wlk 48	Wylie	Rth 121	Jacob, Junr.	Crv 267
Randal	Ptt 277	Young	Nrt 455	Jacob, Senr.	Crv 325
Randol	Trl 678	see Joshua		Jacob J.	Dpl 414
Reubin	Rck 454	Johnston, A.B.	Jhn 757	James	Bfr 11
Richard	Rth 121	Abram	Bfr 11	James	Brt 54
Rigdon	Jhn 764	Absalom	Rbs 386	James	Cht 218
Robert	Jhn 760	Absolum	Prs 214	James	Crv 299
Robert	Nrt 451	Alexander	Cmb 364	James	Cmb 371
Robert	Rth 122	Alexander	Cmb 374	James	Dpl 430
Robert	Stk 617	Alexander	Rbs 387	James	Grn 611
Robert	Wrr 812	Alexander H.	Brt 54	James	Jhn 766
Saml.	Csw 114	Amey	Wke 739	James	Lnc 848
Saml.	Wlk 48	Amos	Dpl 415	James	Lnc 904
Samuel	Wke 739	Amos	Jns 791	James	Mck 572
Sarah	Frn 484	Anderson	Ird 625	James	Mnt 496
Semele	Ans 216	Andrew	Ird 665	James	Ptt 272
Silas	Nrt 451	Andw.	Lnc 827	James	Rwn 362
Sill	Jhn 762	Angus	Cmb 388	James	Wsh 716
Solomon	Jhn 755	Angus	Rbs 387	James	Wne 843
Solomon	Jhn 756	Archibald	Cmb 361	Jashua	Dpl 407
Stephen	Nsh 107	Archibald	Cmb 389	Jean	Prs 209
Stephen	Nrt 451	Arthur	Cmb 376	Jeremiah	Hde 372
Sterling	Hlf 318	Asa	Ird 618	Jeremiah	Cbr 679
Strangemon	Srr 668	Ban	Cht 185	Jesse	Bld 39
Susanna	Hlf 318	Barnabas	Cmb 392	Jessee	Cht 176
Susanna	Nrt 451	Benj., Junr.	Prs 210	Jessee	Cht 184
Sutherland	Edg 213	Benj., Senr.	Prs 210	Jessee	Cht 211
Tarlton	Glf 690	Benjamin	Cmb 376	Jno.	Prs 206
Theo.	Csw 108	Benjamin	Dpl 435	Jno.	Prs 210
Thomas	Csw 97	Benjamin	Ird 625	Joab	Cht 186
Thomas	Csw 114	Benjamin	Ird 668	Joel	Rwn 438
Thomas	Csw 145	Benjamin	Lnc 855	Joel	Smp 535
Thomas	Edg 213	Benjamin	Rwn 448	John	Brt 54
Thomas	Grv 532	Benjn.	Cht 176	John	Cht 218
Thomas	Grv 537	Benjn.	Cht 179	John	Cmb 360
Thomas	Grn 616	Charles	Bld 44	John	Cmb 388
Thomas	Glf 622	Cuff Levi	Bfr 11	John	Dpl 424
Thomas	Glf 636	Daniel	Bfr 11	John	Dpl 428
Thomas	Stk 559	Daniel	Brt 54	John	Ird 625
Thomas	Stk 581	David	Cht 212	John	Ird 649
Thomas	Stk 616	David	Hde 371	John	Lnc 861
Thomas	Srr 667	David	Lnc 904	John	Mck 534
Thomas	Srr 706	David	Mck 557	John	Mck 562
Thomas, Jr.	Stk 581	David	Rwn 458	John	Mnt 502
thos	Mrt 398	Dempsey	Ons 167	John	Ons 168
Walker	Wlk 48	Duncan	Cmb 388	John	Ons 181
Wiley	Jhn 767	Edwd.	Nwh 8A	John	Prs 209
Wiley	Srr 669	Eli	Cht 166	John (2)	Rbs 387
William	Ans 198	Elijah	Lnc 904	John	Rwn 327
William	Ash 82	Elisabeth	Crv 251	John	Rwn 379
William	Edg 213	Elisabeth	Lnc 904	John (2)	Rwn 409
William	Edg 214	Elizabeth	Cmb 392	John	Rwn 416
William	Frn 463	Elizabeth	Rwn 326	John	Rwn 447
William	Frn 493	Elizebeth	Prs 211	John	Smp 516
William	Grv 536	Ephraim	Smp 519	John	Smp 524
William	Grv 538	Esther	Crv 233	John	Smp 531
William	Hlf 318	Ezekiah	Mre 75	John	Wke 742
William	Jhn 752	Frederick	Crv 273	John, Junr.	Rwn 448
William	Jhn 762	George	Lnc 831	John H., Junr.	Brt 54

John H., Senr.	Brt 54	William	Ird 625	Jonekin, Shadrach	Hlf 320
Joseph	Cht 159	William	Ptt 272	Jones, Abel	Bnc 175
Joseph	Cht 194	William	Rwn 403	Abel	Dpl 416
Joseph	Dpl 424	William	Smp 536	Abey	Crr 163
Joseph	Lnc 904	William	Wke 739	Abigail	Crv 301
Joshua	Grn 589	William	Wne 845	Abijah	Stk 620
Josiah	Rwn 387	William E.	Wrr 812	Abraham	Ans 225
Judith	Rwn 426	Wm., Jur.	Wke 742	Abram	Edg 214
Kiddy	Prs 189	Joice, Thomas	Stk 583	Abram	Glf 648
Larkin	Prs 207	William	Stk 583	Abram	Hde 371
Levi	Brt 56	Joicelin, Amh.	Nwh 2A	Abram	Wke 742
Levi	Cht 183	Joiclyn, Sam. R.	Nwh 3	Acquilla, Jun.	Orn 514
Lewis	Brk 764	Joiner, Abraham,		Acquilla, Sen.	Orn 514
Lewis	Cht 156	Junior	Ptt 279	Aden	Crt 69
Lewis	Dpl 434	Abraham, Senior	Ptt 266	Albridgton	Wke 742
Lewis	Jhn 757	Abraham, Son of		Alexr.	Lnc 848
Lewis	Rbs 386	Wm.	Ptt 280	Allen	Frn 465
Lewis	Smp 524	Benjamin	Hlf 320	Allen	Grn 605
Martha	Ptt 265	Benjamin (2)	Smp 503	Allen	Grn 606
Mary	Smp 536	Blount	Hlf 320	Allen	Nrt 453
Mason, Junr.	Ons 166	Cordy	Cmb 367	Allen	Ptt 254
Mason, (Senr.)	Ons 166	David	Srr 668	Allen	Wne 860
Mathw.	Nwh 8A	Drewry	Edg 213	Allin	Rwn 393
Michael	Cht 194	Eli	Hlf 320	Allin	Wke 740
Nathaniel	Rwn 312	Elisha	Edg 213	Alston	Cht 169
Nathon	Ons 155	Elizabeth	Ptt 279	Ambrose	Hde 371
Needham	Mnt 465	Henry	Hlf 320	Ambrose	Lnr 35
Nehemiah	Bld 6	Isam	Smp 507	Ambrose	Wlk 47
Pattrick	Mck 562	James	Dpl 401	Ambrous	Prs 194
Perigrine	Smp 523	James	Smp 503	Amereed	Grv 571
Philip	Jhn 763	Joel	Hlf 320	Amos	Frn 475
Rachal	Ons 154	John	Srr 667	Andrew	Hrt 725
Rachel	Rwn 453	Jonas	Grn 597	Ann	Nsh 106
Randle	Cmb 389	Jonathan	Hlf 320	Anne	Smp 525
Rebecca	Brt 54	Joseph	Ans 213	Anthony	Dpl 426
Reuben	Dpl 430	Joseph	Srr 667	Aquilla	Rwn 366
Richard	Cht 155	Loddwick	Edg 213	Aron	Grv 574
Richard	Lnc 904	Mathew	Grn 597	Aron	Glf 629
Robert	Bld 36	Matthew	Wke 742	Arther	Wne 867
Robert	Cht 156	Mills	Srr 667	Arther	Wne 872
Robert	Lnc 855	Patience	Wke 740	Asia	Brt 54
Robert	Mck 554	Robert	Smp 507	Augusta	Dpl 406
Robinson	Lnc 904	Samuel	Frn 491	Bartholomew	Crt 83
Robt.	Lnc 827	Simon	Rnd 322	Basheba	Rbs 387
Robt., Junr.	Lnc 827	Threthaney	Grn 602	Benjamin	Nrt 453
Saesby	Smp 535	Turner	Hlf 320	Benjamin	Rch 258
Saml.	Bld 45	William	Ptt 266	Benjamin	Rwn 354
Saml., Esqr.	Mrt 398	William, Senr.	Ptt 246	Benjamin	Rth 122
Samuel	Brt 56	Willias	Srr 668	Benjamin	Smp 498
Samuel	Crv 257	Joines, Ezekiel	Wlk 48	Benjamin	Stk 619
Samuel	Mck 548	Joinom, Ann	Crt 85	Benjamin	Wke 740
Sarah	Dpl 416	Joinor, Druray	Mre 49	Benjamin	Wlk 48
Snowden	Brt 90	Joins, Edmund	Wlk 47	Benjn.	Prs 192
Soloman	Cht 177	Thomas	Wlk 48	Benn.	Psq 637
Solomon	Bld 38	Joleff, Davis	Wrr 813	Bennet	Smp 521
Solomon	Crv 265	Jolley, Elizabeth	Ptt 237	Bennet	Wne 851
Solomon	Mnt 466	Isom	Ptt 237	Benton	Chw 124
Solomon	Smp 516	James	Ptt 236	Betty (2)	Rnd 323
Stephen	Cht 194	Joseph	Wke 742	Bilson	Edg 213
Tapley	Cmb 392	Sarah	Ptt 237	Blake	Gts 270
Taply	Cmb 375	Jolly, Boling	Cht 188	Bracket	Hlf 320
Thomas	Brt 54	Caleb	Cht 188	Brice	Mnt 463
Thomas	Cnb 367	Charles	Ird 623	Bringer	Jns 803
Thomas	Dpl 397	James	Cmb 386	Britain	Edg 213
Thomas	Dpl 403	James	Orn 514	Britain	Hlf 318
Thomas	Mnt 496	Jesse	Ptt 236	Britan	Ptt 225
Thomas	Ons 155	John	Bfr 10	Briton	Cmb 390
Turner	Cht 213	John	Cht 190	Brinton	Grv 579
Urias	Mnt 484	John	Ptt 234	Brittin	Nsh 106
William	Bfr 11	John, Sr.	Cht 188	Buckner	Rck 483
William	Brt 54	Jonathan	Bfr 10	Burwell	Jhn 763
William	Brt 56	Matthew	Ptt 234	Byrom	Rth 121
William	Cbr 706	Sally	Hlf 320	Cadwallerder	Stk 620
William	Cht 155	William	Bfr 10	Calley	Nsh 107
William	Cht 177	William	Ird 625	Ceely	Rch 271
William	Crv 229	William	Rth 122	Celia	Cmb 355
William	Dpl 428	Jonas, John	Ash 81	Chalwin	Rwn 339

Charles	Brn 21	Evan	Edg 213	James (2)		Gts 270
Charles	Brk 763	Even	Cbr 689	James		Grn 597
Charles	Cht 191	Even	Srr 667	James		Hlf 318
Charles	Lnc 843	Ezekiah	Rck 443	James		Hlf 320
Charles	Mnt 517	Ezekiel	Bnc 175	James		Hlf 322
Charles	Nsh 107	Ezekiel	Csw 139	James		Hrt 699
Charles	Smp 504	Fanning	Wke 739	James		Hrt 725
Charlotte	Chw 116	Fedrick	Dpl 406	James		Hde 371
Charls	Rnd 323	Fowler	Orn 575	James		Ird 649
Christian	Ird 649	Francis	Cht 169	James		Jns 811
Claton	Csw 119	Francis	Grv 533	James		Lnr 13
Corbin	Trl 684	Frank	Frn 459	James		Orn 515
Cornelious	Crr 155	Frederick	Edg 213	James		Psq 637
Cornelius	Hde 371	Frederick	Grn 605	James		Rwn 443
Counsil	Frn 462	Frederick	Nrt 453	James		Rth 122
Daniel	Frn 449	Frederick	Wke 741	James		Smp 512
Daniel	Grv 574	Fredr.	Lnr 12	James (2)		Srr 668
Daniel	Grn 600	Fredr.	Lnr 13	James (4)		Wke 739
Daniel	Wke 742	Gabriel	Ash 81	James		Wke 741
Darling	Mrt 398	Gabriel	Stk 574	James		Wke 742
David	Bfr 11	Garderer	Cmd 104	James		Wsh 706
David	Chw 123	George	Ons 175	James		Wne 868
David	Cmb 390	George	Rck 480	James, D.Creeke		Bfr 11
David	Crr 155	George	Wlk 47	James, Esqr.		Hrt 705
David	Edg 214	Gideon	Crv 335	James, Junr.		Crv 295
David	Frn 454	Giles	Wke 739	James, (of Da-		
David	Frn 489	Griffin	Dpl 402	vid)		Gts 270
David	Mre 61	Hager	Trl 688	James, Senr.		Crv 295
David	Nwh 3	Hanswell	Nrt 455	Jamima		Stk 617
David	Nwh 10	Hardy	Bfr 11	Jarvis		Ons 151
David	Rnd 323	Hardy	Brt 54	Jas.		Prs 214
David	Rwn 366	Hardy	Rwn 438	Jesse		Bfr 11
David	Trl 688	Hardy	Wke 739	Jesse		Bld 23
David (2)	Wke 741	Hardy, Senr.	Wke 740	Jesse		Cmb 355
David, Sen.	Mre 61	Henery	Crr 167	Jesse		Cmb 390
David, Son Solo.	Bfr 11	Henry	Cht 196	Jesse		Edg 214
Delila	Smp 498	Henry	Cht 216	Jesse		Gts 270
Demey, Junr.	Gts 270	Henry	Hlf 320	Jesse		Grn 597
Demey, Senr.	Gts 270	Henry	Ptt 292	Jesse		Grn 614
Demey O.	Gts 270	Henry	Smp 504	Jesse		Hlf 322
Dempsey	Ons 141	Henry	Wrr 813	Jesse		Lnr 13
Demsey	Cmd 97	Henry	Wne 868	Jesse		Mrt 398
Dianna	Grv 570	Henry, Jr.	Hlf 320	Jesse		Mnt 462
Dickey	Mrt 398	Hesekiah	Ons 138	Jesse		Ptt 255
Drury	Frn 492	Hezekiah	Bld 42	Jesse		Wke 741
Drury	Prs 213	Hezekiah	Gts 270	Jno.		Csw 139
Edmend	Bfr 11	Hezekiah	Stk 617	Jno.		Rck 454
Edmond	Cht 185	Hezekiah, (of		Jno., Sr., P.		
Edmund	Bfr 11	S.H.)	Gts 270	Swamp		Bfr 11
Edmund	Hlf 320	Hill	Wrr 812	Joel		Brt 56
Edmund	Wlk 47	Hugh	Wlk 47	John		Ans 215
Edward	Crt 78	Humphrey	Grn 607	John		Ans 221
Edward	Cht 175	Isaac	Bld 46	John (2)		Bfr 11
Edward	Crv 283	Isaac	Jhn 763	John		Brn 17
Edward	Grv 538	Isaac	Psq 637	John (2)		Bnc 174
Edward	Grv 574	Isaac	Psq 637	John (2)		Brk 763
Edward	Orn 577	Isaac	Rbs 386	John		Brk 279
Edward	Psq 630	Isaac	Rwn 366	John		Cbr 681
Edward J.	Wrr 811	Isach	Cmd 93	John		Cmd 103
Elijah	Rth 122	Isham	Nrt 451	John		Crv 241
Elijah	Wrr 812	Jacob	Ans 225	John		Crv 251
Elisabeth	Crv 343	Jacob, Jur.	Frn 486	John		Crr 146
Elisabeth	Wne 857	Jacob, Ser.	Frn 486	John		Frn 482
Elisha	Dpl 435	Jacob P.	Gts 270	John		Frn 495
Elisha	Lnc 842	James	Ans 217	John		Grv 515
Elizabeth	Cht 159	James	Bfr 11	John		Grv 539
Elizabeth	Dpl 405	James	Bld 22	John		Grv 580
Elizabeth	Hrt 711	James	Brn 13	John (2)		Hlf 320
Elizabeth	Lnr 15	James	Brn 15A	John		Hrt 721
Elizabeth	Nwh 3	James	Brk 764	John		Ird 614
Elizabeth	Orn 513	James	Chw 123	John		Jhn 765
Elkin	Wke 741	James	Crv 257	John		Jhn 766
Ephriam	Rth 122	James	Cmb 355	John (2)		Lnr 13
Epps	Wrr 813	James (2)	Edg 214	John		Lnc 817
Etheldred	Wke 740	James	Frn 448	John		Lnc 848
Evan	Crr 137	James	Frn 454	John		Lnc 876
Evan	Crr 153	James	Frn 489	John		Mrt 398

John	Nsh 105	Keziah	Jns 819	Polly	Brk 764
John	Nwh 2	Latony	Wrr 811	Prudence	Dpl 402
John	Nwh 7A	Lazarus	Nsh 106	Rachel	Edg 213
John	Nwh 10	Lemuel	Cmd 97	Rachel	Gts 269
John	Nrt 453	Lemuel	Srr 711	Reading	Hde 372
John	Ons 172	Levey	Crr 140	Rebecca	Crt 80
John	Ons 175	Levi	Bld 11	Rebekah	Hde 371
John	Orn 514	Levi	Srr 668	Redding	Wke 743
John	Psq 639	Levy	Chw 120	Rewlen	Grv 509
John	Prq 654	Lewelling	Grv 532	Richard	Cht 182
John	Ptt 258	Lewis	Crv 285	Richard	Crv 327
John	Rnd 322	Lewis	Gts 270	Richard	Nrt 455
John	Rch 269	Lewis	Nrt 455	Richard	Ons 140
John	Rck 440	Lewis	Orn 514	Richard	Stk 617
John	Rck 480	Lewis	Rnd 322	Richard	Wke 741
John	Rck 481	Lewis	Rth 122	Richard	Wsh 706
John	Rwn 438	Lewis	Wke 740	Richd.	Csw 120
John	Rwn 453	Lewis	Wke 741	Richd.	Csw 139
John	Rwn 458	Lewis	Wke 742	Richd.	Lnc 848
John	Rth 121	Lewis, Jr.	Dpl 435	Robert	Bfr 11
John (3)	Rth 122	Lewis, Junr.	Crv 231	Robert	Bnc 174
John	Smp 523	Lewis, Jur.	Wke 740	Robert	Frn 464
John	Wke 741	Lewis, Senr.	Wke 741	Robert	Grv 511
John	Wke 743	Lewis, Sr.	Dpl 435	Robert	Hlf 320
John	Wne 857	Lucy	Mre 77	Robert	Prs 195
John, H.F.	Orn 514	Lukey	Lnr 15	Robert	Prs 213
John, H.R.	Orn 514	Lylved	Grv 563	Robert	Stk 601
John, Jr.	Rch 258	Malachi	Crr 155	Robert	Trl 690
John, junior	Grn 597	Margaret	Hlf 320	Robert	Wrr 811
John, Junior	Grn 608	Margaret	Nrt 453	Robert, Senr.	Prs 218
John, junior	Ptt 265	Margaret	Prq 644	Robert H.	Wrr 812
John, (of Jo)	Gts 270	Martin	Prs 194	Roger	Crv 287
John, (of John)	Gts 270	Mary	Crv 311	Roger	Frn 449
John, Senior	Grn 600	Mary	Dpl 406	Roger, Junr.	Crv 339
John, Senior	Ptt 279	Mary	Dpl 428	Roland	Rwn 438
John, Senr.	Rch 258	Mary	Dpl 436	Ruebin	Edg 214
John H.	Rth 121	Mary	Jns 819	Russell	Wke 740
Jonas	Jns 787	Mary	Lnr 15	Ruth	Cmb 371
Jonathan	Grv 577	Mary	Mrt 398	Saml.	Ons 171
Jonathan	Orn 514	Mary	Ons 141	Saml.	Prs 192
Jonathan	Prs 194	Mary (2)	Wke 741	Samuel	Frn 451
Jos.	Mrt 398	Matthew	Jhn 765	Samuel	Grv 523
Joseph	Brt 54	Matthew	Nsh 107	Samuel	Grv 565
Joseph	Brk 763	Matthew	Rbs 385	Samuel	Mck 594
Joseph	Cmd 95	Matthew	Wke 742	Samuel	Rnd 350
Joseph	Cmd 100	Matthew, Senr.	Jhn 765	Samuel (2)	Srr 669
Joseph	Crv 287	Michael	Dpl 402	Sarah	Brt 54
Joseph	Hrt 725	Morgan	Crv 239	Sarah	Csw 137
Joseph	Hrt 737	Morris	Bfr 11	Sarah	Gts 270
Joseph	Nwh 2	Morton	Wlk 47	Sarah	Nrt 453
Joseph	Prq 654	Moses	Bld 21	Servant	Nrt 453
Joseph	Rwn 374	Moses	Edg 213	Seth	Rwn 366
Joseph	Wke 743	Moses	Grv 570	Shadrach	Jns 793
Joseph	Wlk 47	Moses	Grv 574	Shadrick	Smp 497
Joseph, Jun.	Cmd 97	Moses	Orn 575	Shugars	Orn 513
Joseph, Junr.	Rwn 354	Moses	Wke 740	Silvanus	Grn 600
Joseph, Senr.	Cmd 101	Nathan	Bld 44	Simon	Bld 12
Joseph, Senr.	Rwn 354	Nathan	Grn 595	Simon	Gts 270
Joshua	Ash 81	Nathan	Jns 793	Slartin	Rth 122
Joshua	Bfr 11	Nathan	Mrt 398	Smith	Psq 639
Joshua	Bnc 174	Nathaniel	Brk 763	Solomon	Dpl 435
Joshua	Frn 489	Nathl., C.F.	Wke 776	Solomon	Glf 628
Joshua	Hlf 320	Nathl., (Cord.)	Wke 741	Solomon	Mrt 398
Joshua	Rwn 458	Nathl., Senr.	Wke 740	Solomon	Rwn 453
Joshua	Stk 615	Nath., (WP	Wke 740	Solomon	Wke 740
Joshua	Wke 742	Neal	Rch 271	Stephen	Brk 764
Joshua	Wsh 706	Obed.	Rwn 458	Stephen	Dpl 427
Josiah	Bld 8	Owen	Ons 141	Stephen	Prs 195
Josiah	Chw 124	Peter	Lnr 15	Stephen	Rnd 323
Josiah	Gts 270	Peter	Orn 515	Sugor	Wrr 811
Josiah	Prq 643	Peter	Wlk 48	Tamer	Wrr 811
Josiah	Prq 656	Philip	Stk 578	Temperence	Frn 491
Josiah, Jur.	Bfr 11	Philip, Jur.	Hlf 322	Thomas	Ans 215
Josiah, Ser.	Bfr 11	Philip, Senr.	Hlf 322	Thomas	Bfr 12
Judah	Wlk 48	Phillip	Wke 740	Thomas	Brt 56
Judith	Hlf 320	Pleasant	Grn 596	Thomas (2)	Cht 192
Kelly	Ons 141	Polley	Wke 742	Thomas	Chw 122

Thomas	Crv 259	to	Edg 213	Levi	Wne 863
Thomas	Crv 277	William, Jr.	Bfr 11	Mathew	Crv 317
Thomas	Cmb 385	William, Jr.	Jhn 766	Matthew	Wne 871
Thomas	Frn 479	William, junior	Grn 600	Nathan	Bld 7
Thomas	Hlf 318	William, (Mill		Philip	Smp 534
Thomas	Hde 371	Pond)	Nrt 453	Reubin	Wke 739
Thomas	Jhn 768	William, Senr.	Jhn 766	Richard	Grn 595
Thomas	Mck 564	William, Ser.	Bfr 11	Richard	Hde 371
Thomas	Nrt 453	William,(Short)	Lnr 12	Richard	Ptt 272
Thomas	Orn 514	William, Ters.	Bfr 11	Rothay	Hde 371
Thomas	Rnd 321	William, (Tug		Salley	Wke 739
Thomas	Rnd 322	Mutton)	Nrt 453	Sarah	Wke 739
Thomas	Rwn 354	William R.	Grv 573	Sarah	Wsh 706
Thomas	Rwn 379	Willie	Crv 329	Seth	Frn 475
Thomas	Stk 559	Willie	Hlf 318	Siles	Edg 213
Thomas	Wke 740	Willie	Wke 739	Thomas	Cmb 373
Thomas	Wlk 47	Willie	Wke 741	Thomas	Grv 515
Thomas, Jun.	Prq 643	Willie, Sr.	Hlf 320	Thomas	Hde 371
Thomas Hill	Cht 159	Willis	Hlf 320	Thomas	Nrt 453
Thos.	Crr 148	Willis	Wne 868	Thomas	Psq 627
Tignal	Wke 739	Willm.	Nsh 106	Thomas	Psq 628
Tignal, Junr.	Wke 740	Wilson	Prs 213	William	Brt 54
Timothy	Trl 682	Wm.	Mrt 398	William	Hrt 725
Tobias	Wne 865	Wyler	Prs 212	Willm.	Nsh 107
Uriah	Crt 69	Zachariah	Chw 122	Wm.	Psq 634
Venkler	Grv 519	Zadock	Wke 742	Wm., Estate	Brt 72
Venson	Ash 81	see Fones, James, Janes		Zachariah	Rbs 385
Viley	Nsh 106	Jonson, John	Orn 513	Zeblon	Hrt 725
Walter	Crv 327	Jonston, John	Psq 628	Jorden, Philip	Mnt 514
Walter, Junr.	Bfr 11	Joplin, James	Wke 742	William	Smp 536
Walter, Ser.	Bfr 11	Mark	Wke 742	Jordin, Thomas	Orn 576
Western	Wke 742	Wm.	Csw 134	Jordon, Baldey	Wrr 811
Wheeler	Rck 451	Jopling, Benj.	Prs 206	Benjamin	Rth 122
Wiley	Jhn 767	Jordam, Abram	Wke 739	Brittain	Bnc 175
Wilice	Csw 111	Jordan, Abram	Hde 372	Marcillus	Wrr 811
Wilie	Grv 578	Arthur	Nrt 451	Thomas P.	Bnc 175
Will.	Prs 218	Barbara	Wke 739	Jornigan, Abram	Bld 16
Will. Watts	Nwh 12	Batte	Nrt 453	Whitmil	Bld 14
William	Wke 739	Benjamin	Frn 452	Jorry, George	Rch 271
William	Brk 763	Benjamin	Frn 487	Joseph, Jones	Wke 743
William	Cmd 96	Benjamin	Nrt 453	Romea	Nsh 3A
William	Cht 216	Benjamin	Ptt 266	Josey, John	Hlf 320
William	Chw 123	Charles	Ans 212	John, Junr.	Rwn 301
William	Crv 297	Charles	Brt 54	John, Senr.	Rwn 301
William	Crv 333	Charles	Wne 871	Robert	Hlf 320
William	Edg 213	Cornelious	Edg 214	William	Edg 214
William	Edg 214	David	Hrt 725	Joshua, Johnson	Edg 214
William	Frn 493	Dickson	Jhn 757	Jourdan, Abraham	Chw 123
William	Gts 270	Dillon	Cmb 354	Aven	Wne 846
William	Grv 522	Drury	Smp 534	Britten	Rnd 323
William	Grv 569	Edge	Edg 214	Calib	Chw 123
William	Grn 597	Elias	Smp 534	Calib	Chw 130
William	Hrt 705	Elizabeth	Hrt 725	Demsey	Chw 119
William	Jhn 762	Elizabeth	Ptt 239	Fredirick	Wne 847
William	Jns 785	Ferreby	Nrt 453	Hance	Chw 119
William	Lnr 12	Gray	Edg 214	Ichabud	Chw 117
William	Nwh 5A	Hamblen	Frn 453	Jacob	Chw 118
William	Nwh 11	Hanah	Wke 742	Jacob, Jun.	Chw 119
William	Ons 140	Henry	Edg 214	Jacob, (son of	
William	Prq 643	Hezekiah	Nrt 453	William)	Chw 126
William	Prq 647	James	Ans 215	John	Glf 640
William	Prq 661	James	Brt 54	Joseph, Jun.	Chw 123
William	Ptt 227	James	Brt 56	Joseph, Sen.	Chw 123
William	Rch 260	James	Frn 451	Josiah	Chw 117
William	Rck 440	Jeremiah	Gts 270	Josiah	Prq 654
William	Rck 454	John	Ans 237	Meede	Rnd 323
William	Rwn 366	John	Frn 451	Mourning	Chw 118
William	Rth 121	John	Nrt 453	Nathan	Chw 119
William	Rth 122	John, Jur.	Hde 371	Nathan	Chw 123
William	Wke 740	John, Ser.	Hde 372	Nicholas	Chw 118
William (2)	Wke 742	Jonathan	Orn 513	Notley	Rck 447
William	Wrr 811	Joseph	Ans 227	Pegga	Rnd 323
William	Wlk 47	Joseph	Ans 231	Robert	Rck 486
William	Wlk 48	Joseph	Brt 54	William	Hlf 320
William, (Cap-		Joseph	Grn 595	William	Rnd 323
tain	Nrt 453	Joseph, Junr.	Ans 220	William, Jun.	Chw 123
William, (Cone-		Joshua	Edg 214	William, Sen.	Chw 123

Name	Loc	Name	Loc	Name	Loc
William, Sen.	Chw 126	William	Mck 572	Keagle, Jacob	Bnc 176
Winiford	Wne 848	Junior, Anthony	Rth 121	Valentine	Bnc 176
Zachary	Rnd 323	Junkens, William	Rch 265	Keais, Barbara	Bfr 23
Jourden, James	Glf 624	Jury, Edith	Rbs 432	William	Bfr 23
John	Mnt 510	Justice, Allen	Cht 187	Kean, Edward	Crv 241
John	Stk 618	Amos	Bnc 175	James	Brt 56
John, Junr.	Mnt 471	Benjamin	Hlf 318	John	Rwn 443
Joseph	Glf 624	David	Cht 187	Lenard	Stk 613
Jourdin, Emelius	Wne 851	David	Wke 740	Moses	Brt 58
Jourdon, John,		Elelijah	Ons 161	Nicholas	Rwn 443
Senr.	Mnt 470	Henry	Brk 763	William	Crv 237
Thomas	Chw 119	Henry	Brk 764	Kearney, Crawford	Frn 459
Jowars, James	Mnt 495	Henry	Rnd 322	Henry	Wrr 813
Jowers, John	Mnt 495	Isaac	Lnc 876	James	Wrr 814
Joy see Ivy		Jarard	Rth 122	Samuel	Frn 459
Joyce, Alexander	Stk 586	John	Bnc 174	Sarah	Wrr 814
Andrew	Rck 487	John	Brk 764	Kearns, Isaac	Rnd 324
Caleb	Mrt 398	John	Crv 237	Joseph	Rnd 324
Ebnijah	Mrt 398	John	Hlf 318	Thomas	Rnd 324
Elijah	Rck 487	John	Rth 121	Kearsey, William	Wrr 814
Elisha	Rck 458	John	Rth 122	Keas, John	Mre 69
George	Stk 586	Jonathan	Rnd 323	see Keeas	
Isaac	Stk 586	Joseph	Brk 763	Keaten, Alexander	Dpl 404
John	Rck 487	Joseph	Rwn 387	Keatly, JOnathan	Dpl 439
John, (BS)	Rck 490	Jules	Prs 198	Keaton, Allin	Ird 610
Joseph T.	Rck 443	Peter	Lnc 876	Elisha	Cmd 108
Martin	Mrt 398	Rebecca	Crv 237	John	Psq 634
Robert	Rck 476	Simeon	Bnc 175	John	Psq 638
Thomas	Rck 474	Stephen	Cht 187	John	Wlk 49
Thomas	Rck 488	Thomas	Bnc 175	John, junr.	Wlk 49
Joyner, Burrell	Nsh 107	Thomas	Brk 765	Jos.	Psq 634
Charles	Hrt 729	Thomas	Rth 121	Julias (2)	Ird 610
Cornealus	Nsh 105	William	Lnc 817	Peter	Ird 611
Curtin	Nsh 106	Justis, Dempcy	Crv 289	Reuben	Psq 638
Drew	NSh 107	Sylvanus	Crv 289	Samuel	Cmd 102
Edmund	Nsh 105	Justise, John	Orn 503	Slevin	Psq 636
Hardy	Nsh 107	Justiss, Martha	Nrt 455	William	Psq 626
Jacob	Nsh 105			Keator, Charles	Cmd 108
Jesse	Nsh 106			Kebler, David	Lnc 817
Jesse	Nrt 451	-- K --		Kecker, John	Frn 469
John	Nsh 107			Kedd, Whels	Ons 166
John	Ptt 266			Kedda, William	Nwh 1A
Joiles	Nrt 453	K..., John	Rnd 322	Kee, Benjamin	Wrr 814
Lewis	Nsh 106	Kaas see Keeas		Daniel	Grv 519
Lewis	Nrt 453	Kahcey, George	Rch 251	James	Smp 500
Mary	Mrt 398	James	Rch 251	Holloway	Wke 743
Matthw	Nsh 107	John	Rch 251	William	Wrr 814
Nathan (2)	Nsh 106	Kail, Catharine	Brt 56	Keeas, Cornelius	Mre 47
Nathan, Sr.	Nsh 106	Jeremiah	Hrt 700	Thomas	Mre 69
Nelson	Hrt 735	John	Brt 56	William	Mre 69
Thomas	Nrt 453	Rebecca	Brt 56	Keef, O. Patrick	Edg 173
Willm., Jur.	Nsh 106	William	Brt 58	O. Patrick	Edg 215
Wm., Sr.	Nsh 106	see Kale		Sarah	Crv 309
Jud, William	Mre 66	Kaile, Elias	Lnc 884	Keek, Henry	Orn 515
Judd, John	Wlk 48	Palser	Lnc 876	Keel, Delily	Edg 215
Nathaniel	Wlk 48	Kailor, Leonard	Rwn 307	Hardy	Bfr 12
Nathaniel, jur.	Wlk 48	Ludwick	Rwn 307	Jacob	Hrt 700
Roland	Ash 82	Kale, John	Grn 605	James	Ptt 237
Roland	Wlk 47	Thomas	Grn 605	Jesse	Ptt 237
Roland	Wlk 48	Kanady, John	Rwn 329	John	Bfr 12
Judge, Israel	Nwh 5	Kannon, Heningham	Stk 559	Mary	Ptt 237
James	Hlf 320	William	Rth 123	Monacha	Hrt 700
Judkins, E. John	Edg 213	Kariher, George	Rwn 344	Simon	Ptt 238
James	Nrt 451	Karney, Margarett	Rnd 324	William	Ans 214
Joel	Glf 674	Kaser, Spencer	Stk 607	William	Ptt 237
John	Hlf 320	Kashat, Jacob	Cht 169	Willie	Edg 215
John E.	Edg 213	Jacob	Cht 212	Keeland, William	Orn 577
Thomas	Wrr 812	John	Cht 211	William, Jur.	Orn 577
Juitt, Matthew	Srr 668	Thomas	Cht 217	see Keland	
Julick, John	Lnc 831	Katon, James	Ird 635	Keeling, Carlton	Wlk 49
Johnathan	Lnc 831	Nelly	Ird 635	Leonard	Wlk 49
Julien, Isaac	Rnd 322	Kay, John	Nrt 455	Thomas	Wlk 49
Jesse	Rnd 323	Kaylor, Jacob	Bnc 175	William	Wlk 49
Tobius	Rnd 322	Kea, Henry	Edg 215	Keen, Isaac	Jhn 753
Julin, David	Rwn 405	Robert	Bld 25	Jno.	Csw 147
George	Mck 523	William	Edg 215	John	Jhn 753
Jump, John	Lnr 13	Keach, Jasper	Hde 372	John	Smp 494

Lemuel	Gts 270	Charles	Bfr 12	James, Senr.	Mck 524
William	Smp 523	Charles	Jhn 764	Jno.	Lnc 838
Keener, John	Lnc 817	Custus	Bfr 12	John	Rwn 409
John	Lnc 856	Daniel	Rbs 388	Samuel	Mck 525
Martin	Lnc 817	Daniel	Wke 744	Samuel	Srr 671
Kees see Kus		Duncan	Rbs 388	Thomas	Mck 527
Keesler, Jacob	Rwn 317	Edward	Edg 215	William	Ird 616
John	Rwn 322	Effy	Cmb 355	William	Mck 575
Keeter, Henry	Rth 123	Enoch	Lnc 883	Kenan, James	Dpl 441
James	Rth 123	Hannah	Bfr 12	Lohlin	Rch 260
James, jr.	Rth 123	Hanson	Nwh 3A	Owen	Nwh 2A
John	Rth 123	Henry	Rth 123	Thomas	Dpl 425
Keever, Henry	Mck 533	Hugh	Cmb 388	Will.	Nwh 11A
Kegan, Richard	Csw 100	Hugh	Mre 63	Kenard, John	Dpl 429
Keger, Adam	Stk 560	Isaac	Rck 452	Michael	Dpl 427
Kegle, Charles	Bnc 176	Jacob	Smp 512	Nathaniel (2)	Dpl 429
Keiker see Kecker		James	Mnt 490	Kendal, John	Psq 634
Keilough, Samuel	Cbr 683	James	Rbs 388	Kendall, John	Rnd 324
William	Cbr 683	James	Rck 486	William	Rnd 324
Keith, Gabrile	Bnc 176	James	Stk 614	Kendrick, Isham	Ird 656
John	Ans 199	James, Senr.	Mnt 476	Kenedy, Alexr.	Cmd 105
Reubin	Bnc 176	Jeremy	Ptt 261	William	Grn 611
William (2)	Brn 13	John	Cmd 93	Kenly, Samuel	Cbr 681
Kelah, Abigail	Crv 255	John	Cmb 355	Kennaday, John	Grv 573
Keland, Thomas	Orn 577	John	Jhn 763	Danial	Dpl 410
Kelby, Nancy	Bfr 23	John	Mre 63	George	Crv 343
Sarah	Bfr 23	John	Rwn 405	Jacob	Crv 341
Kell, Richard	Orn 577	John	Rth 122	John	Orn 515
William	Orn 577	John	Wke 744	Joseph	Dpl 413
Kellam, Nash	Ons 137	Laban, Junr.	Bfr 12	Patrick	Smp 499
Kellem, Noah	Rwn 355	Laban, Senr.	Bfr 12	Rieuben	Srr 670
Keller, Jacob	Rwn 426	Mariam	Cmd 93	Thomas	Dpl 410
John	Rwn 426	Mark	Cmd 101	William	Srr 706
Michael	Lnc 876	Mary	Csw 133	Kennan, Domfort	Nwh 3
Kelley, Charles	Orn 516	Mary	Cht 202	Kennard, George	Wne 851
David	Gts 270	Mary	Cmb 355	Kenneair, James	Nwh 9A
Dempsey	Hlf 322	Mary	Mre 63	Kennedy, David	Brt 58
James	Bld 18	Patrick	Bld 38	David	Ptt 242
James	Hlf 322	Polly	Rth 122	Henry	Cmd 96
John	Bld 18	Rachel	Bfr 12	Henry	Chw 113
John	Orn 577	Rebe	Glf 680	Isaac	Rbs 388
John	Stk 560	Reuben	Rth 122	James	Csw 100
John	Srr 670	Samuel	Mnt 500	James	Glf 643
Joseph	Srr 670	William	Mnt 476	John	Cmd 93
Josiah	Hlf 322	William	Rth 123	John	Cmd 105
Matthew	Bld 18	William	Smp 511	John	Cmb 360
Patrick	Rbs 388	Wm.	Csw 134	John	Ptt 243
Patrick	Stk 579	Kelso, Alexander	Nwh 4A	John	Rck 462
Thomas	Bnc 175	Danl.	Nwh 4A	John	Rck 470
Thomas	Hlf 322	Kelson, Daniel	Stk 600	John, Esqr.	Mrt 399
William	Bld 39	Kelton, Robert	Ird 656	John, Ser.	Bfr 12
William	Gts 270	see Kellon		Leml.	Mrt 399
William	Hlf 322	Kemble, Green	Lnc 864	Samuel	Mck 606
Kellian, Henry	Brk 765	Kembrough, John	Ans 213	William	Bfr 23
Kellis, James	Mnt 494	Kemes, Christian	Rnd 324	William	Cmb 361
John	Mnt 494	David	Rnd 324	William	Ptt 243
Lewis	Mnt 493	Kemp, Barnet	Prs 213	Kenney, Christian	Rwn 399
Kelloe, Edward	Hlf 322	Benjamin	Srr 671	William	Rwn 380
Kellon, John	Grv 528	Burrel	Grv 564	Kennon, Charles	Wke 744
John, Junr.	Grv 526	Burrett	Grv 522	John	Wke 744
Kellow, Shadrach	Glf 663	Henry	Grv 521	William	Rck 490
Thomas	Glf 662	Isaac	Crv 273	Kennuch, John	Rwn 443
Kellum, John	Glf 663	Jesse	Wke 743	Kent, Burrel	Nsh 108
John	Glf 667	Jesse	Wke 744	James	Rwn 409
John	Rck 461	John	Ird 625	James	Rwn 416
Polley	Wke 744	Joseph	Cht 217	Jesse	Nsh 108
Spencer	Rck 461	Joseph, Jur.	Bld 30	Levi	Crv 315
William, Jur.	Rck 461	Joseph, Sr.	Bld 30	Samuel	Crv 315
William, Senr.	Rck 461	Murphey	Grv 522	Thomas	Crv 319
Kelly, Abner	Cmd 98	Richard	Grv 564	Thomas	Crv 333
Abraham	Cmd 93	Zebulon	Cmd 102	Kente, Wm.	Mrt 399
Angus	Cmb 362	Ken, James	Orn 577	Kenton, Francis	Grv 560
Archibald	Bld 18	Kenady, David	Mck 524	Kents, Jacob	Rwn 379
Barbe	Cht 202	David	Mck 527	Kenut, Jacob	Glf 622
Barnabass	Srr 670	Gilbert	Mck 597	Kenworthy, David	Rnd 324
Benjamin	Ird 610	Jacob	Srr 671	Kenyon, John	Prq 660
Catharine	Lnr 15	James, Junr.	Mck 525	Jos.	Psq 628

Levy	Prq 649	Woolrick	Ash 82	Philip	Lnc 904
Sarah	Prq 659	Kessey, Job	Bld 31	Samuel	Lnc 868
Thomas	Prq 658	Kessler, John	Rwn 293	Killin, William	Rch 258
Keply, George	Rwn 346	Keston, John	Grv 563	Killingsworth,
Kelin	Cbr 713	Ketcham, Isrele	Ons 173	John	Jhn 746
Peter	Cbr 713	Ketchem, Joel	Stk 592	William	Glf 656
Peter, Junr.	Cbr 713	Ketcher, Jesse	Nsh 108	William	Hlf 322
Keppel, John	Cbr 713	Ketchum, Jacob	Dpl 411	Killingworth, Tru-
Kerby, Francis	Srr 670	Kethly, Richard	Wne 843	man	Jhn 761
Joel	Srr 670	Ketor, Jesse	Hlf 322	Killion, George	Stk 600
Peter	Srr 670	John	Cmd 94	John	Stk 609
Philip	Srr 670	Levey	Cmd 95	Killit, John	Wne 852
Samuel	Stk 560	Mary	Hlf 322	Killpatrick, War-
William	Chw 129	Samuel	Cmd 95	ren	Crv 317
Kerhsey see Kirksey		Ketta, Nehemiah	Brn 13	Killson, William	Rth 123
Kerless, Archd.	Cht 160	Rebecca	Brn 13A	Kilman, Henry	Rck 468
Kerley, Will.	Nsh 107	William	Brn 13	Kilpatric, Hugh	Glf 672
Kern, Conrod	Rwn 296	Kettle, William	Rwn 380	Kilpatrick, Fran-
John	Rwn 296	Kettrelin, John	Ptt 286	cis	Grn 604
Kerner, Joseph	Stk 600	Ketts, George	Rwn 305	Hugh	Rth 123
Kerney, David	Ird 616	John	Rwn 305	Isler	Lnr 15
Kerr, Absolam	Srr 670	Kewel, John	Bfr 12	James	Rth 123
Alexander	Srr 670	Key, Elisha	Orn 578	Spencer	Wke 744
Benjamin	Srr 670	Garland	Rck 474	William	Rth 123
Danl.	Nwh 6A	James	Grv 571	William, junr.	Grn 604
David	Mck 575	John	Rck 474	William, Senr.	Grn 603
David	Rwn 337	Jonathan	Jns 805	Kilpattrick, An-
Jacob	Ird 650	Thomas	Rck 477	drew	Ird 671
James	Ird 656	Matthew	Nrt 455	David	Rwn 317
James	Mck 603	Keyher, Widow	Rwn 308	John	Rwn 321
James	Rwn 327	Keys, James Henry	Hrt 732	Joseph	Ird 671
Jean	Ird 654	William	Cmb 386	Joseph	Rwn 327
John	Csw 138	Keyse, John	Stk 559	Robert	Rwn 322
John	Rwn 327	Kicker, Dilley	Wrr 814	William	Rwn 321
John	Stk 559	Kid, James	Brk 765	Kilson, George	Stk 560
John F.	Stk 560	Kidd, Benjamin	Csw 128	Kimball see Cemboll
Joseph	Mck 534	James	Wrr 814	Kimbell, Benjamin	Wrr 814
Joseph, (Cap)	Rwn 317	Kidner, Francis	Stk 609	David	Wrr 813
Mary	Rwn 317	Frederick	Stk 609	Francis	Wrr 813
Nathaniel	Ird 661	Kieth, George	Wke 744	Leonard	Wrr 814
Richard	Mck 534	Kiff, Jas.	Mrt 399	Nathl.	Wrr 813
Rieuben	Srr 670	Kiger, Adam	Stk 560	Ranson	Wrr 815
Robert	Mck 534	John	Stk 560	Suger	Wrr 815
William (2)	Ird 649	Kight, David	Ptt 248	William	Wrr 814
William	Ird 650	Rosanna	Ptt 247	Kimble, Bucknor	Mnt 521
William	Mck 575	Samuel	Ptt 248	Drury	Lnc 848
William	Srr 670	Kiher, George	Mck 577	George	Rck 477
Wm.	Csw 138	Kilbee, Edward	Hrt 735	Hezek.	Rck 446
Kerrell, James	Cmb 373	Kilbreath, Bartrum	Ird 640	Jackson	Lnc 848
Kerry, Wm.	Csw 118	James	Glf 692	Peter	Lnc 848
Kersey, Drury	Stk 605	Kilby, Humphrey	Wlk 49	Robert	Stk 561
Elizabeth	Rbs 388	James	Wlk 49	Kimbol, Abington	Grv 554
George	Brn 13	Reuben	Wlk 49	Drury	Grv 554
James	Rbs 388	William	Wlk 49	Drury, Jur.	Grv 554
Jemima	Rbs 388	Kile, Daniel	Cmb 384	Sion	Grv 554
Richard	Crt 58	Kilgoe, Isaac	Wke 744	Kimboo, Fathy	Stk 560
Solomon	Rbs 388	James (2)	Wke 743	Kimbrel, Peter	Wlk 49
Thomas	Crv 295	William	Wke 743	Kimbro, James	Csw 136
Kershaw, Michal	Stk 560	Killebrew, Hinchy	Jns 781	Jeramiah	Rwn 367
Kersy, Amos	Glf 691	Rebeckah	Edg 215	John	Csw 105
Daniel	Glf 690	Killem, Theoples	Crr 143	Susanna	Rwn 367
David	Csw 112	Killen, James	Cmb 372	Thomas	Csw 106
James	Csw 111	William	Cmb 368	Kimbrough, Freder-
Jesse	Glf 691	Killeniworth, Pa-		ick	Orn 515
John	Csw 111	tience	Edg 215	George	Srr 670
John, Jur.	Csw 111	Killey, Timothy	Mrt 399	Goldmon	Srr 670
Saml.	Csw 111	Killian, Abraham	Lnc 868	Henry	Orn 515
Thomas	Glf 691	Adam	Lnc 817	James	Wke 743
William	Glf 690	Andrew	Lnc 861	Jeremiah	Glf 628
Kesby, Jesse	Stk 559	Andrew, Senr.	Lnc 861	Jno.	Csw 136
Kesey, Jacob	Bnc 176	Daniel	Bnc 176	John	Wke 743
Kesler, Daniel	Ash 82	David	Lnc 817	Leonard	Rwn 416
George	Lnc 818	Jacob	Lnc 817	Marmaduke	Srr 670
John	Ash 82	John	Lnc 868	Ormond	Srr 670
John	Cbr 703	John	Lnc 876	Wm.	Csw 135
Joseph	Ash 82	Mathias	Lnc 855	Kimer, Henry	Orn 515
William	Ash 82	Mathias	Lnc 861	James	Nrt 455

Kimmery, Henry	Mnt 505	David	Crv 267	Levy	Rck 454
Kimmey, Mason	Ons 172	David	Jns 787	Lucy	Stk 560
Kimmons, Thomas	Rth 123	David	Mrt 399	Lydia	Bld 9
Kimons, Hugh	Cbr 677	David	Wrr 814	M.	Srr 706
Kimsey, Xenja.	Bnc 176	David, Senr.	Wrr 815	Martin	Brk 766
Benjamin	Bnc 176	Drewry	Cmb 391	Mary	Crv 283
David	Bnc 176	Drury	Wke 744	Mary	Cmb 392
Kinady, Jethrew	Ons 174	Edward	Ash 82	Mary	Ons 164
Kincaid, Andrew	Rwn 331	Edward	Cmb 355	Massy	Dpl 406
Archibald	Brk 765	Edward	Hlf 322	Micajah	Stk 560
David	Lnc 848	Edward	Rnd 322	Mich.	Ons 168
Hannah	Lnc 848	Edward	Wrr 814	Michael	Mrt 399
James	Brk 765	Eleanore	Orn 578	Michael	Smp 506
James, Junr.	Rwn 331	Elisabeth	Mrt 399	Michael	Smp 514
James, Senr.	Rwn 331	Elisha	Ptt 253	Michael	Wsh 706
John	Brk 765	Eliza	Rck 454	Nathan	Cmb 366
John	Lnc 848	Elizabeth	Orn 515	Nathaniel	Orn 578
John	Rwn 331	Elizabeth	Trl 670	Nathaniel	Stk 561
Joseph	Rwn 331	Elizath	Orn 577	Nehemh.	Rck 455
Robert	Brk 765	Esther	Lnc 848	Peter	Rnd 324
Thomas	Rwn 331	Francis	Wke 744	Peter	Stk 560
Wm.	Lnc 848	Francis	Wlk 49	Priscilla	Rth 123
Kincey, Henery	Crr 140	George	Dpl 405	Ransom	Mnt 479
Kinchen, Leonard	Nrt 455	George	Grv 529	Richard	Ird 617
Kindal, John	Ans 205	George	Hlf 322	Richard	Wke 743
William	Wlk 49	H. John	Brt 58	Richard	Wke 744
Kindall, James	Wlk 49	Hallard	Hlf 322	Ricd.	Ons 173
John	Wlk 49	Hannah	Orn 578	Rigdon	Jns 787
Kinder, Conrod	Lnc 843	Henry	Brt 58	Robert	Ash 82
Conrod	Lnc 856	Henry	Cmb 384	Robert	Brt 58
Henry	Lnc 861	Henry	Nrt 455	Robert	Csw 102
Jacob	Lnc 843	Henry	Rck 454	Robert	Mnt 490
Kindle, Benjamin	Rwn 355	Henry	Wke 743	Robert	Mre 43
John	Mnt 496	Hugh	Gts 270	Robert	Orn 515
Samuel	Mnt 517	Iles	Wke 743	Roberte, Junr.	Mrt 399
William	Mnt 513	James	Edg 215	Roberte, Senr.	Mrt 399
William, Senr.	Mnt 502	James	Ird 640	Rodey	Wke 743
Kindley, John	Rwn 387	James	Lnc 848	Saml. (2)	Jns 787
Kindly, Shadrick	Rwn 387	James	Ons 170	Samson	Wke 743
Kindol, Ann	Bnc 175	James	Ons 177	Sampson	Wrr 814
Kindreck, William	Mck 538	James	Rnd 322	Samuel (2)	Bnc 176
Kindred, Elisha	Ans 204	James, Jr.	Stk 578	Samuel	Orn 515
Kindrick, Thomas	Csw 114	James, Ser.	Stk 578	Samuel	Rck 457
William	Cht 172	Janet	Smp 513	Samuel, Senr.	Jns 795
King, A. John	Wke 744	Jesse	Rnd 324	Sarah	Orn 515
Abraham	Ptt 271	Jno.	Wne 850	Sarah	Wke 743
Absilla	Rbs 388	Job	Lnc 876	Simon	Gts 270
Alexr.	Brn 13A	John	Crv 273	Smith	Wke 743
Allen	Wrr 814	John	Frn 445	Stephen	Ons 175
Allen	Wne 861	John	Ird 617	Stephen	Smp 530
Amos	Bld 14	John	Mck 522	Thomas (2)	Brk 765
Andrew	Srr 670	John	Orn 578	Thomas	Ird 650
Ann	Hlf 322	John	Ptt 271	Thomas	Nsh 108
Anthony	Hlf 322	John	Rck 438	Thomas	Ons 173
Anthony	Wrr 814	John	Rck 455	Thomas	Orn 516
Armor	Orn 515	John	Rck 461	Thomas	Orn 577
Arther	Wke 744	John	Rwn 355	Thomas	Ptt 271
Benagey	Ons 164	John	Stk 560	Thomas	Rnd 322
Benajah	Dpl 440	John (2)	Wke 743	Thomas, Jur.	Rck 455
Benjamin	Bnc 176	John, Junr.	Brt 58	Thomas, Senr.	Rck 454
Benjamin	Nrt 455	John, Junr.	Hlf 322	Thos.	Lnr 35
Betsey	Wke 743	John, Junr.	Nrt 455	Vincent	Wke 743
Britton	Ptt 285	John, Senr.	Brt 58	William	Gts 270
Burwell	Hlf 322	John, Senr.	Hlf 322	William	Mre 39
Cadar	Brt 58	John, Senr.	Nrt 455	William	Mre 41
Celia	Crv 239	John A.	Wke 844	William	Ons 164
Celia	Crv 329	John H.	Brt 58	William	Ons 176
Charles	Dpl 441	Johnson	Stk 560	William	Ons 180
Charles	Hlf 322	Johnston	Brk 765	William	Orn 515
Charles	Orn 578	Jonathan	Rth 123	William	Orn 578
Charles	Smp 505	Jonathan	Wrr 815	William	Psq 639
Charles	Wrr 814	Joseph	Crv 231	William	Ptt 251
Charles, Junr.	Brt 58	Joseph	Lnr 15	William	Rnd 324
Charles, Senr.	Brt 58	Joseph	Ons 162	William	Rck 469
Charlotte	Brt 58	Joseph	Rth 123	William	Rck 486
Culbert	Csw 142	Julian	Nsh 108	William	Rwn 443
Daniel	Rth 123	Jutius	Orn 577	William	Smp 507

William	Stk 559	Joseph	Cht 162	Jacob	Rnd 324
William	Srr 670	Lewis	Orn 516	John	Rnd 324
William, Jr.	Hlf 322	Patience	Hlf 322	Peter	Rnd 324
William, Jun.	Orn 515	William	Orn 515	Kizer, Adam	Lnc 817
William, Sr.	Hlf 322	Kirkham, James	Wke 743	Frederick	Cbr 695
Wm.	Lnc 835	William	Wke 743	George	Cbr 693
Wm. C.	Mrt 399	Kirkindall, Jesse	Lnc 891	John	Lnc 817
Wood	Wrr 814	Kirkland, Benjn.	Rth 123	John	Stk 560
Wyatt	Rck 441	Jesse	Rth 123	Lawrence	Lnc 817
Zachah.	Rck 486	Joseph	Orn 578	Philip	Stk 560
see Dixson		Shadreck	Grv 562	Kline, Michael	Rwn 296
Kingings, Anna	Rth 123	William	Orn 493	Knight, Able	Glf 684
Kings, Samuel	Ons 169	Kirkman, Daniel	Glf 625	Able, Senr.	Glf 685
Kingsbery, Nathanl.	Rwn 312	Elijah	Glf 623	Able, son of	
Kington, Bethia	Brt 56	Elisha	Glf 684	Able	Glf 685
Kinkannon, Andrew,		Ellender	Glf 623	Abner	Hlf 322
Sr.	Srr 670	George	Glf 622	Amey	Wke 744
James	Srr 670	George	Glf 649	Ann	Hrt 721
Kinlaw, Benjamin	Rbs 388	James	Glf 623	Arthur	Edg 215
James	Rbs 388	Levin	Glf 623	Benjamin	Cmb 378
Robert	Rbs 388	Roger	Glf 633	Ephraim	Hlf 322
Kinley, Edward	Rnd 324	Thomas	Glf 649	Francis	Edg 215
John	Rnd 350	Thomas	Rnd 324	Garrot	Edg 215
Kinnada, Jas.	Prs 190	Kirkpatrick, An-		Henry	Cmb 383
Kinnamon, John		drew	Bnc 176	James	Edg 215
Thos.	Stk 603	Elizabeth	Cmb 379	James	Gts 270
Samuel	Glf 686	Joseph	Bnc 176	Jesse	Edg 215
Samuel	Stk 604	Samuel	Orn 515	Jonathan	Grv 544
Walter	Glf 686	Kirkpattrick, John	Mck 543	Jonathan	Grv 560
Walter	Stk 604	Thomas	Mck 543	Jonathan	Glf 667
Kinneair, John	Nwh 9	Valentine	Cbr 677	JOhn (2)	Hlf 322
Kinnemon, Philemon	Wrr 813	Kirksea, John	Mnt 504	John	Rck 448
Kinnen, Celia	Cht 169	Kirksey, Elisha	Cht 200	Joshua	Edg 215
Kinney, John	Mre 61	Gidion	Cht 163	Kindred	Edg 215
Kinnie, William	Rbs 388	Gidion	Cht 175	Kiney	Hlf 322
Kinnin, Anthony	Bfr 12	John	Orn 516	Mary	Glf 685
Kinnion, Daniel	Crr 160	William	Cht 163	Merida	Hlf 322
Joel	Crr 160	Kirkwood, John	Nwh 3A	Milly	Grv 571
Kinns, George	Crv 233	Kirsey, Willis	Cht 195	Moses	Rch 247
Kinny, William	Rwn 377	Kirvin, Thomas	Cmb 371	Reuben	Brt 56
Kinsall, Frederick	Stk 603	Kirwan, James	Cmb 355	Richard	Ans 224
Kinsarel, John	Ptt 225	Kitcham, Jonathan	Ons 143	Saml.	Lnc 838
William	Ptt 225	Kitchen, Elizabeth	Edg 215	Samuel	Glf 684
Kinsey, Daniel	Smp 508	James	Csw 125	Silvanus	Edg 215
Elizabeth	Hrt 717	John	Ird 649	Solomon	Bnc 175
James	Jns 783	Joseph	Rbs 388	Stephen	Grv 573
Jesse	Lnr 15	Kinchin	Mre 40	Thomas	Ans 230
John	Jns 787	Matthew	Bld 25	Thomas	Brk 765
John	Jns 793	Oren	Edg 216	Thomas	Glf 685
Joseph	Jns 787	Stephen	Bnc 176	Thomas	Psq 632
Lewis	Jns 785	Kitchesides, Tho-		Walker	Edg 215
Martha	Jns 793	mas	Rth 123	William	Cmb 379
Solomon	Crr 167	Kiteral, Isaac	Grv 526	William	Cmb 390
Stephen	Jns 807	Kitner, George	Rwn 341	William	Rnd 324
William	Jns 789	Peter	Rwn 341	William	Srr 670
Kinsig see Kinsey		Kitt, John	Cmd 106	William	Wlk 49
Kinworthy, Elisha	Rnd 324	Malichi	Cmd 106	William, Capt.	Grv 538
Kipps, Seth	Hde 372	Wilie	Cmd 95	Willis	Edg 215
see Moore		Zepheniah	Cmd 104	Knighton, Jesse	Stk 560
Kirby, Isaac	Cht 201	Kitteral, Bryant	Grv 528	Jesse, Jr.	Stk 560
James	Cht 180	Eliza	Grv 563	Thomas	Mck 536
James	Jhn 754	Isham	Grv 531	Knipe, Christian	Lnc 891
James, jr.	Cht 190	John, jur.	Grv 564	Knocks, Joseph	Ans 217
Jesse	Jhn 751	Jonathan	Grv 529	Samuel	Ans 198
Sarah	Nrt 455	Jonathan	Grv 531	Knoles, William	Prq 655
Thomas	Jhn 753	Joshua	Grv 531	Knoosh see Knowls	
Wright	Cht 153	Samuel	Grv 562	Knot, Caty	Frn 460
see Cerby		Kitterall, Samuel	Grv 533	David	Frn 460
Kirk, Elisha	Orn 516	Kitterell, Eliza-		William	Frn 460
George	Cht 162	beth	Gts 270	Knote, Jas.	Mrt 399
George	Prs 191	Kittle, Barbard	Grv 558	Knott, James	Grv 509
Isaac	Orn 516	Joel	Grv 557	James	Grv 550
J. Alex Parham	Orn 515	Kittrell, Belson	Brt 56	James	Grv 581
James	Orn 516	John	Brt 56	John	Grv 508
John	Mck 558	Martha	Brt 56	Mary	Brt 56
John	Mnt 517	Stanley	Brt 58	Thomas	Grv 508
John	Orn 516	Kivett, Henry	Rnd 324	William	Rwn 355

Name	Loc	Name	Loc	Name	Loc
William	Stk 567	John	Wlk 49	John	Cht 188
William	Stk 570	Kornegay, David	Smp 536	Joseph	Prq 650
Knotts, Absalom	Ans 226	George (2)	Dpl 429	Josiah	Psq 640
John	Ans 201	Isaac	Dpl 404	Martha	Rck 485
Tabitha	Lnr 19	John	Dpl 428	Peter	Rnd 350
Knowes, Rhoda	Bfr 12	Martin	Dpl 429	Phillip	Cht 187
Willibough	Bfr 12	Mary	Dpl 427	Phillip, Sr.	Cht 188
Knowles, George	Bld 28	William	Dpl 404	Stephen	Ans 232
James	Dpl 409	William	Dpl 439	Thomas	Ans 217
John	Crv 251	Kornegy, Abraham	Jns 783	William	Rwn 380
John	Dpl 409	Abraham, Junr.	Jns 797	Ladd, Constantine	Stk 562
John	Dpl 410	Daniel	Jns 797	Constantine	Stk 628
William	Dpl 409	Kory, Reuben	Bfr 12	Jacob	Hlf 324
Knowlin, Kathrine	Bfr 23	Kratzer, David,		James	Hlf 358
Knowls, Richard	Brk 778	Junr.	Rwn 294	Joseph	Rck 440
Knox, Allison	Mck 562	Kreder, John	Rwn 340	Noble	Stk 561
Andrew	Psq 634	Kreeger, Jacob	Stk 560	William	Rch 252
Benjamin	Rwn 321	Kreger, Henry	Stk 560	Laddish, Richard	Rch 243
David	Bfr 12	Krider, Barnard	Rwn 288	Lae see Lee	
David	Ptt 280	Bernhart	Rwn 277	Laechon, Ferreby	Wne 854
George	Ptt 294	Christian	Rwn 296	Lafever, Elizabeth	Mck 525
Hugh	Psq 628	Daniel	Cbr 703	Lafferty, Thomas	Orn 517
James	Bfr 12	Jacob, Junr.	Cbr 703	Laffoon, Dennis	Srr 674
James	Hrt 735	Jacob, Senr.	Cbr 704	Lafforty, Vance	Orn 578
James	Mck 539	Leonard	Rwn 288	Laflor, Wm. C.	Crr 146
James	Rwn 321	Philip	Rwn 296	Lagle, Jacob	Lnc 885
Jesse	Crv 315	Kroblet, Robt.	Cht 212	John	Rwn 426
John	Crv 341	Krotzer, David	Rwn 293	Lagrand, John	Mnt 490
John	Ird 650	Philip	Rwn 293	Lagwin, Sarah	Nwh 12
John	Mck 539	Kus, John	Rnd 324	Lain, James	Ans 233
John	Nrt 455	Kuter, Samuel	Brt 56	John	Wne 860
John	Psq 627	William	Brt 56	Joral	Prq 648
John	Rwn 322	Kuykindol, Abraham	Rth 123	Josiah	Rch 262
Joseph	Ird 649	Kuykindoll, Abra-		Taler	Wlk 49
Mary	Ird 650	ham	Bnc 175	Lainback, John	Stk 599
Matthew	Mck 539	James	Bnc 175	Laird, John	Ird 617
Milly	Edg 215	John	Bnc 175	John	Stk 628
Noah	Bfr 12	Peter	Bnc 175	Nathaniel	Ird 618
Robert	Lnc 861	Simon	Bnc 176	Laire, Bartholomew	Lnc 818
Robert	Ptt 240	Kyle, Hamilton	Bnc 176	Peter	Lnc 869
Robert	Rwn 322	Hugh	Cmb 385	Laithem, Anthony	Rnd 325
Robert, junior	Ptt 229	John	Bnc 176	Charls	Rnd 325
Samuel	Mck 539	William	Bnc 176	Cornelas	Rnd 326
Thomas	Ird 650	Kyles, William	Ird 662	James (3)	Rnd 325
Widow	Mck 540			John	Rnd 325
William	Jns 819			John	Rnd 328
William	Lnc 876	-- L --		John, J.	Rnd 328
William	Ptt 234			William	Rnd 325
see Knocks		Laboytonex, Wil-		William	Rnd 326
Knoy, Christian	Rwn 355	liam	Psq 624	Laithinghouse, Richd.	
George	Rwn 355	Lacefield, Susanna	Srr 672	R.	Crv 325
John	Rwn 355	Laceter, Elijah	Jhn 769	Lake, Daniel	Bnc 177
Philip	Rwn 355	Lacey, Parker	Ptt 279	William	Jhn 770
Knup, Jacob	Rwn 300	Lacin, Jacob	Stk 561	Lakey, Manor	Srr 673
John	Rwn 300	Lackenow, Jacob	Stk 602	Laky, Joel	Srr 672
Knupp, William	Rwn 307	Lackey, Alexander	Orn 517	Simon	Srr 706
Koen, John	Psq 638	Elizabeth	Orn 517	Lale, Jacob	Prq 663
Kolby see Kelly		George (2)	Ird 611	Lam, Isaac	Bld 26
Koon, Nicholas	Rth 123	Hugh	Bnc 177	Jane	Bld 15
Koonce, Benjamin	Jns 781	James	Bnc 177	John	Bld 26
Daniel	Jns 795	Jean	Ird 611	see Lane	
Daniel	Jns 811	John	Bnc 177	Lamb, Abraham	Rbs 389
Emanuel	Jns 817	John	Edg 218	Abraham	Wne 862
George	Jns 813	Robert	Orn 517	Armijah	Prq 648
Jacob	Jns 781	Thomas	Ird 611	Arthur (2)	Rbs 389
John, Junr.	Jns 817	William	Ird 611	Barnabas	Rbs 389
John, Minor	Jns 815	William	Ird 631	Benjamin	Rnd 327
John, Senr.	Jns 817	Lackie, Alexander	Lnc 897	Betty	Rnd 325
Michael	Jns 815	Lacky, Francis	Srr 673	Caleb	Rwn 380
Richard	Jns 815	Lacoler, Eli	Cht 224	Campbell	Rbs 389
Tobias	Jns 781	Lacy, Adams	Hde 372	Cornelas	Rnd 327
Koone, Lucretia	Crv 255	Batt C.	Rck 438	Gideon	Cmd 98
Koons, Gasper	Rnd 324	Fanney	Hde 372	Henry (2)	Rnd 328
George	Ash 82	James	Prq 644	Isaac	Cmd 101
John	Ash 82	John	Bfr 12	Isaac	Gts 271
Koonze, George	Lnc 817			Isaac	Rbs 389
Koots, George	Wlk 49			Isaac	Wne 862

Jacob	Gts 271	Joseph	Rch 242
Jacob	Wne 863	William	Rch 263
Jacob	Wne 865	Lampnay, Wm.	Csw 128
James	Rbs 389	Lanair, Clemment,	
Jams	Rwn 313	Senr.	Rwn 380
John	Glf 626	Lancaster, Benja-	
John	Glf 676	min	Crv 273
John	Prq 646	Benjamin	Rbs 390
John	Rnd 326	Henry	Edg 218
Joseph	Nwh 6A	James	Edg 218
Joseph	Prq 660	Jesse	Mrt 401
Joseph	Rnd 328	Levi	Nrt 455
Joshua	Rnd 327	Levi	Wne 850
Joshua	Wne 863	Nanny	Wne 871
Joshua	Wne 865	Robert	Edg 218
Josiah	Orn 518	William	Frn 479
Luke	Cmd 98	Wright	Wne 850
Meedy	Rbs 389	Lance, Henry	Bnc 177
Nathan	Rnd 326	John	Bnc 177
Pethiah	Gts 271	Peter	Bnc 176
Phinehas	Prq 648	Samuel	Bnc 177
Restore	Prq 648	Lanchester, Hart-	
Reuben (2)	Rnd 328	well	Mre 60
Robert	Glf 626	Lanchister, Hart-	
Samuel	Glf 684	well	Mre 60
Simeon	Glf 626	Lancy, John	Ans 236
Thomas	Nwh 6A	Land, Charles	Edg 218
Thomas	Rnd 326	Elizabeth	Nrt 459
William	Cmd 101	Isaac	Bnc 177
William	Cmd 106	Jerimiah	Crr 145
William	Nwh 6A	Jonathan	Wlk 51
William	Rch 268	Lamentation	Nrt 459
Zachariah	Prq 647	Littleberry	Edg 218
Zachariah	Prq 660	Mary	Dpl 416
Lambard, Joseph	Cht 184	Nancy	Wlk 51
Lambart, John	Jhn 765	Ruben	Crr 138
Lambden, Daniel	Rch 259	Seth	Brt 90
Lambe, John	Crr 159	Landanham, Thomas	Cht 200
Joseph	Mre 39	Landen, Elisha	Edg 219
Lamberd, Shaderach	Rth 124	Landers, Barna	Bnc 177
Lambert, Benjn.	Brn 19	John	Csw 131
Coatney	Bld 8	John	Grv 578
Elizth.	Nwh 9	Thomas	Bld 5
Ishue	Cht 184	Thomas	Glf 682
James	Rnd 328	Landing, Henry	Bfr 12
John	Cht 152	James	Ons 169
John	Cht 185	James, Junr.	Gts 272
Samuel	Crv 315	James, Senr.	Gts 272
Uriah	Cmb 394	Mills	Gts 272
William	Glf 693	Phebe	Ons 168
Lamberte, Mary	Mrt 401	Richard	Bfr 12
Lambertson, James	Nrt 457	Stephen	Ons 169
Lambeth, John	Rwn 355	Landley, Simon	Stk 598
Levi	Lnc 896	Landman, John	Ans 212
Moses	Rwn 355	Landon, Richd.	Nwh 11A
Richard	Cht 152	Landor, Neach	Ird 636
Thomas	Cht 176	Landram, Abner	Cht 155
William	Cht 176	Richard	Wke 746
Lambethson, John	Bld 9	Landreth, Stephen	Ash 82
Lamboard, William	Rck 462	William	Ash 83
Lambourd, James	Glf 640	Landrith, Francis	Glf 623
Lamburt, Mary	Wrr 815	Martha	Glf 623
Lamkin, Lehanna	Wrr 815	Thomas	Glf 623
Lewis	Nsh 109	Landsdale, Benja.	Bld 33
Lammon, Angus, Jr.	Bld 20	Landsdown, Nathan-	
Angus, Ser.	Bld 30	iel	Wlk 50
Christian	Bld 20	Wm.	Wlk 50
Lamon, Alex.	Rck 462	Lane, Ann	Crv 317
Archibald	Cmb 355	Anne	Crv 341
Duncan	Nsh 109	Barzila	Prq 660
Hugh	Cmb 378	Benjamin	Chw 119
John	Cmb 355	Benjamin	Hlf 326
Kenith	Rbs 389	Brian	Grn 615
Malcom	Rbs 389	Calib	Prq 653
Nancy	Rbs 390	Charles	Bnc 158
Lampkins, Matthew	Wrr 815	Cordy	Edg 219
Lampley, Benjamin	Rch 246	Daniel	Crv 317

Daniel	Glf 636
Daniel	Nrt 457
David	Brt 58
Demsey	Prq 646
Eady	Prq 660
Ezekial	Prq 653
Ezekiel	Nwh 9
Frederick	Crv 255
Gallant	Rwn 458
George	Crv 311
George	Crv 317
Gilman	Rwn 416
Isaac	Hlf 326
Isaac	Rnd 325
Isham, jr.	Wne 847
James	Brt 58
James	Dpl 433
James	Nrt 457
James	Ons 164
James, Junr.	Wke 745
James, Senr.	Wke 744
Jesse	Glf 630
Joel	Wke 745
John	Bnc 177
John	Crv 317
John	Glf 649
John	Orn 517
John	Psq 627
John	Prq 653
John	Rnd 327
John	Wke 745
John, S.	Rnd 327
Jonathan	Glf 673
Jonathan	Lnr 15
Joseph	Prq 660
Joseph	Rnd 325
Joseph	Wke 745
Joseph	Wne 872
Julia	Prq 660
Levan	Jns 815
Lydia	Chw 129
Martin	Wke 745
Mathew	Grn 610
Mathew	Wne 848
Mordecai	Glf 683
Myles	Prq 648
Nathaniel	Wke 744
Owen	Glf 642
Polley	Wke 745
Randle	Brk 766
Reuben (2)	Prq 653
Ruth	Nrt 457
Sampson	Crv 329
Samuel	Chw 119
Samuel	Chw 130
Samuel	Rbs 389
Sarah	Ons 163
Thomas	Dpl 433
William	Brk 767
William	Crv 317
William (2)	Dpl 429
William	Glf 672
William	Hlf 324
William	Hrt 705
William	Psq 629
William	Prq 653
William	Rwn 400
William	Rwn 416
William	Rwn 458
William	Srr 673
Lanemoore, George	Grv 573
Laney, Peter	Ans 237
Lanfield, Daniel	Rth 124
Lang, James	Gts 272
John	Ptt 269
Josua	Gts 271
Langdale, Thomas	Brt 58

Langdon, James	Jhn 765	John, Junr.	Mrt 401	John H.	Stk 625
John	Rwn 277	John, Senr.	Mrt 401	Lary, Amwall	Lnr 14
John	Rwn 288	Lewis	Dpl 415	Lasater, Abner	Cht 196
Langerier, B.	Lnc 886	Rebecah	Wrr 815	Hardy	Cht 154
Langford, Stephen	Wke 745	Robert	Bfr 12	Hardy	Cmb 375
Langfort, Mary	Jhn 746	Sampson	Rck 483	Hezekiah	Cht 164
Langley, Allen	Rnd 327	Stephen	Dpl 415	Jacob	Cht 175
Amy	Nsh 108	Thomas	Ans 232	James	Cht 225
Ann	Ptt 224	William	Ans 207	Micajah	Rnd 325
George	Bfr 24	William	Bfr 12	Sarah	Rnd 326
Isaac	Jhn 753	Wm.	Mrt 401	William	Cht 169
Jacob	Wne 864	see Lanair, Lannier		Lasenberry, Joshua	Ird 668
James	Jhn 752	Lank, Mary	Gts 271	Lasewell, William	Cmb 355
James	Ptt 225	Lankaster, Hait	Nsh 109	Lash, Abraham	Stk 561
James, Jr.	Jhn 754	Robert	Nsh 109	Charles	Stk 561
John	Ons 172	Lankester, John	Wrr 816	Christian	Stk 627
John	Srr 705	Lankford, Elias	Nrt 455	George	Srr 672
Leml.	Crr 145	Elisha	Frn 464	Jacob	Stk 561
Lodwick	Wne 865	George	Grv 561	Jacob	Stk 627
M.	Srr 707	James	Bnc 177	John	Srr 674
Mary	Nsh 108	Jessay	Mre 72	Nathaniel	Stk 561
Miles	Wne 866	Jesse	Mre 69	Lashley, Baswell	Wke 746
Nathaniel	Bfr 13	Joab	Wrr 816	Benjamin	Nrt 459
Ostwell	Wne 865	John	Rth 124	Edmond	Wke 745
Samuel	Jhn 747	John	Wrr 815	Elizabeth	Nrt 457
Sarah	Wke 776	Nathan	Rth 124	Howell	Wke 746
Stephen, Jur.	Bfr 13	Realeigh	Wrr 816	Lewis, Senr.	Wke 746
Stephen, Ser.	Bfr 13	Robert	Rth 124	William	Frn 471
Thomas	Trl 670	Thomas	Stk 581	William	Nrt 459
William	Rnd 324	William	Hlf 324	William	Wke 745
Willm.	Nsh 108	William	Stk 581	Lashsmith, Elias	Stk 602
Langly, Azaniah	Edg 218	Lankister, Joel	Wrr 816	Laskley, Barny	Orn 579
Christopher	Mnt 514	John, Senr.	Wrr 816	Thomas	Orn 579
Hezekiah	Edg 218	Lawrance	Wrr 816	Lasley, Peter	Orn 578
Isaih	Edg 218	Willie	Wrr 816	Lasonberry, Thomas	Ird 668
Jesse	Rwn 409	Lannier, Nancey	Mrt 401	Laspeyre, Bernard	Nwh 8
Shadrach	Edg 218	Lannin, John	Bnc 177	Lassater, Jacob	Grn 606
Zachariah	Mnt 515	Lanning, Eanis	Rwn 393	James	Cmb 394
Langmon, William	Grv 542	Joseph	Rwn 393	Ruben	Grn 606
Langston, ...,Mrs.	Hrt 712	Lansdon, Robert	Ird 640	Silas	Grn 606
Absalom	Lnr 1	Sarah	Cmb 355	Lassel, Othneil	Psq 627
Isaac	Edg 218	see Lumsden		Lasser, Sylvia	Bld 6
Isaac	Gts 272	Lanson, David	Csw 131	Lasseter, Abner	Gts 271
Isaac	Hrt 721	Lantern, Joseph,		Amos	Gts 271
Jesse	Grn 608	Jr.	Hlf 324	Aron (2)	Gts 271
Joseph	Jhn 774	Joseph, Sr.	Hlf 324	Fredrick	Gts 271
Joseph	Jhn 775	Lanum, Jos.	Csw 138	George	Gts 271
Judith	Gts 272	Tabitha	Csw 138	James	Gts 271
Levi	Wne 864	Lap, Robert	Mnt 471	Jeremiah	Gts 271
Luke	Hrt 721	Laphel, Eliza	Brt 60	Jethro	Gts 271
Martha	Hrt 721	Lapp, Robert	Glf 669	Jonathan, Junr.	Gts 271
Mary	Hrt 725	Lapslie, James	Orn 578	Jonathan, Sr.	Gts 271
Seth	Grn 592	Lard, John	Stk 562	Josiah	Gts 271
Simeon	Wne 869	Joseph	Wlk 51	Michael	Gts 271
Simon	Lnr 15	Largent, Elisha	Brk 767	Miles	Gts 271
Uriah	Wne 869	James	Rth 124	Moses	Gts 272
Langwith, Reubin	Wrr 815	William	Mnt 486	Rebecah	Hlf 326
Lanier, Alexander	Bfr 13	Largin, Thomas	Brk 766	Robert	Gts 271
Anne	Dpl 418	Larimore, Hanee	Glf 653	Seth	Gts 271
Benjamin	Dpl 416	James	Rck 449	William	Gts 271
Benjamin	Dpl 418	Philip	Rck 450	William	Grv 505
Bird	Dpl 414	Philip, Jur.	Rck 450	Lassiter, Aaron	Nrt 455
Bird	Dpl 416	Larkford, Thomas	Stk 561	Abijah	Brt 58
Clement	Ans 241	Larkin, Thomas	Rck 447	Ann	Hrt 700
Daniel	Rwn 393	Larkins, Benjn.	Nwh 9A	Charles	Nrt 455
Edmond	Lnc 872	James	Bld 50	Elias	Nrt 457
Elisabeth	Mrt 401	James	Nwh 9A	Everard	Nrt 455
Fanny	Bfr 13	John	Nwh 11	George	Smp 498
Isaac	Ans 224	Pricilla	Bld 50	Greene	Nrt 457
Jacob	Dpl 414	Robert	Nwh 5A	Harmond	Rch 246
James	Dpl 415	Roger	Nwh 9A	Isaac	Wke 744
James	Dpl 416	Saml.	Nwh 9A	James, Junr.	Nrt 457
Jas.	Mrt 401	Thomas	Smp 526	James, Senr.	Nrt 457
Jesse	Dpl 415	William	Bld 40	Jasper	Wke 746
Jesse	Dpl 418	Laroque, James,Dr.	Hrt 712	Jesse	Hrt 717
John	Dpl 415	Larry, Jeremiah	Smp 530	Jesse	Nrt 457
John	Wrr 815	Lartman, John H.	Stk 599	John	Rch 263

Jonas	Wke 745	Lauley, Joseph	Rnd 324	John	Wke 746
Joseph	Nrt 457	Laumann, Lewis	Brk 768	John, (DC)	Edg 217
Josiah	Rch 262	Launders, Hardy	Crv 243	John, Senr.	Edg 217
Jotham	Wke 746	Laurance, Abigail	Crt 71	Joshua	Edg 219
LUke	Wke 746	Abraham	Grv 537	Josiah	Ptt 277
Mary	Brt 60	David	Crt 71	Michael	Gts 271
Mary (2)	Smp 502	James	Grv 532	Obedia	Psq 626
Moses	Wke 746	John	Crt 71	Paul	Edg 217
Shadrach	Nrt 457	John	Grv 532	Solomon, Senr.	Edg 217
Silas	Nrt 457	Peter	Rnd 328	Thos.	Nsh 108
Stephen	Lnr 14	Richard	Stk 561	Widney	Wke 746
Thomas	Wsh 706	Watson	Crt 71	William	Crv 233
William	Brt 58	William	Grv 522	Wm.	Nsh 108
Willie	Nrt 457	Laurence, Charles	Nrt 457	Lawros, Jacob	Glf 665
see Laceter		Elisha	Nrt 457	Laws, Abraham	Lnc 864
Lassitor, Reuben	Chw 124	Frederic	Brt 58	Berry Little	Wlk 50
Lasslie, Christian	Cmb 389	George	Ans 221	David	Wlk 51
Latchem, Jesse	Cmd 109	James	Brt 60	Elizabeth	Orn 580
Laten, Jacob	Stk 568	John	Ans 199	Ezekiel	Orn 580
Latham, Alexander	Ash 82	John	Nrt 457	George	Orn 581
Alexander	Bfr 12	Joseph	Brt 58	Joseph (2)	Wlk 50
Charles	Bfr 13	Lemuel	Nrt 457	Josiah	Rth 126
Daniel	Hde 372	Mary	Nrt 457	Little Berry	Wlk 50
James	Bfr 12	Reuben	Brt 58	William	Dpl 405
James	Bfr 13	Robert	Brt 58	William	Grv 570
Jesse	Hde 372	Robert	Nrt 457	William	Orn 580
John	Crv 259	William	Brt 58	William	Wlk 49
Noah	Bfr 13	Laury, Rachel	Chw 118	Lawsin, Francis,	
Pheneas	Bfr 13	Lauthorn, Daniel	Wlk 49	Capt.	Prs 193
Rothas	Bfr 12	Laven, Charles	Rwn 372	Jno., Junr.	Prs 194
Sarah	Hde 372	Lavender, Benjamin	Jns 803	John	Prs 193
Thomas	Bfr 12	Daniel	Jns 789	Sherrid	Stk 580
Lathom, Aaron	Rwn 426	Daniel	Jns 817	Lawson, Burrel	Stk 593
Robert	Rwn 426	John	Jns 789	Christopher	Dpl 406
Lathrum, Cornelius	Mre 47	Lemuel	Jns 817	David	Stk 580
Latimore, Eliza-		William	Jns 815	David	Wlk 49
beth	Crr 150	Laving, Andrew	Mck 535	Francis	Rbs 389
Lating, John	Srr 708	William	Mck 535	James	Orn 580
Laton, Isaac	Lnc 878	Law, Adam	Glf 627	Jonas	Stk 580
James	Smp 509	Andrew	Glf 643	Samuel	Stk 583
William	Cmb 368	John	Mck 562	Thomas	Ird 662
William	Smp 494	Samuel	Glf 580	Thomas	Stk 580
Latta, James	Orn 579	Thos.	Lnc 848	Thomas	Srr 673
James, jr.	Orn 579	William	Rwn 327	William	Bnc 177
John	Orn 579	Lawhon, Joel	Cht 223	Lax, William	Bnc 176
John, jr.	Orn 579	Lewis	Mre 43	William	Mnt 475
Joseph	Mck 566	Lawhorn, Thomas	Prs 188	William	Rnd 325
Thomas	Orn 579	Lawing, William	Rth 125	Laxton, Jesse	Bnc 176
Thomas, jr.	Orn 580	Lawler, Evan	Mre 44	Levy	Wlk 50
Latter, Henry	Lnc 878	John	Mre 76	Lay, David	Csw 102
Latterlock see Lutterlock		Levy	Mre 76	George	Orn 518
Latterstedt, Eric,		Lawless, Augustin	Srr 673	Henry	Orn 519
Esq.	Bld 36	Presley	Srr 672	John (2)	Brn 19
Lattimore, Daniel		Lawrance, Edward	Rnd 325	John	Orn 518
(2)	Rth 125	Henry	Srr 672	John, Jun.	Orn 518
John, j.	Rth 125	John	Ons 153	Joseph	Brn 18A
John, S.	Rth 125	John	Srr 672	Margaret	Orn 518
Lattinhouse, John	Ptt 291	John	Wlk 51	Martin	Orn 518
Latty, James	Mck 551	Joseph	Srr 673	Mary	Csw 142
Laughinghouse, An-		Nancy	Rnd 325	William	Ird 640
drew	Bfr 12	Obediah	Trl 686	see Loy	
Susannah	Bfr 13	Richard	Rnd 325	Laycock, William	Orn 580
Thomas	Bfr 12	Richard	Srr 672	William, jr.	Orn 580
Laughinhouse, John	Cmd 107	Samuel	Srr 672	Layden, Francis	Prq 646
Laughlin, Hugh	Rnd 326	Thomas	Wlk 51	Layfield, Josiah	Grv 573
John	Rnd 326	see Lourance, Lowrance		Layray, Loyad	Ons 167
John	Rnd 328	Lawrence, Abner	Brt 58	Layton, Henry	Rbs 389
Richard	Rnd 326	Comfort	Edg 217	Jas.	Prs 192
Robert	Rnd 326	Elisha	Hrt 735	John	Cht 219
see Lohlin		Isham	Glf 651	Lea, Abner	Prs 209
Laughner, Peter	Lnc 878	James	Cht 197	Abner	Prs 210
Laughter, James	Rth 125	James, Junr.	Edg 217	Absalom	Csw 134
James H.	Rth 125	Jesse	Nsh 109	Ambrous, Junr.	Prs 210
John	Wrr 815	Jesse	Ptt 278	Barnet	Prs 209
William	Wrr 815	Jesse	Wke 746	Benjamn.	Csw 138
Wiley	Rth 125	John (2)	Glf 651	Benjm.	Prs 210
Laughton, William	Brt 58	John	Nsh 108	Carter, Capt.	Prs 209

George	Prs 210	Isaac	Ans 227	James	Cht 194
Jas.	Prs 210	Joel	Mnt 502	James	Jhn 771
Jere.	Csw 126	Labon	Rth 125	James	Jhn 776
John	Orn 581	Richard	Rth 125	James	Mnt 502
John	Prs 210	Richd.	Rth 125	James	Nsh 108
Nancey	Prs 211	William	Cht 174	James	Nwh 4A
Richard	Orn 580	William	Cht 203	James	Prq 649
Richd.	Prs 210	Zedekiah	Mnt 486	James	Rth 123
Will	Prs 209	Leddenham, John	Brt 60	James	Wke 746
Will, Senr.	Prs 212	Ledford, Alexander	Brk 767	James, Sr.	Nsh 108
see Lee		Fourey	Lnc 890	James Bud	Wke 747
Leabaugh, Chris-		Frederick	Lnc 900	Jerremiah	Jhn 776
tian	Lnc 823	Frederick	Rnd 327	Jesse	Cmb 355
Leach, Alexander	Cmb 388	Henry	Stk 562	Jesse	Rbs 389
James	Glf 637	Henry	Stk 621	Jesse, (Cokey)	Edg 218
John	Cmb 387	James	Lnc 890	Jesse, (Coneto)	Edg 218
Richard	Rwn 393	John	Brk 767	Jesse, Junior	Rbs 389
William	Stk 561	John	Lnc 890	Jesse, Ser.	Rbs 389
Leagle, Henry	Brk 768	John	Rnd 326	Joel	Jhn 776
Leak, John	Hlf 326	John	Stk 603	John	Ans 216
John	Rck 482	Mary	Rth 126	John	Ans 234
Josiah	Nrt 457	Nelly	Brk 768	John	Brt 60
Walter	Rch 243	Nicholas	Stk 561	John	Cbr 689
William	Glf 654	Nimrod	Brk 768	John	Crv 263
Leake, William	Mck 555	Obadiah	Rwn 355	John	Edg 219
Leamon, John	Wrr 815	Obediah	Rnd 327	John	Jhn 767
Lean, John	Grn 610	Peter	Brk 766	John	Jhn 775
Leanard, Fredrick	Frn 478	Sally	Brk 768	John	Jns 801
Fredrick	Frn 479	Samuel	Rnd 327	John	Jns 817
John	Frn 489	Squire	Rwn 367	John	Nsh 108
John, Jur.	Frn 478	Thomas	Rth 125	John	Rnd 328
John, Ser.	Frn 478	William	Rwn 393	John, Capt.	Csw 109
William	Frn 478	Ledwell, John	Rwn 380	John, Jur.	Csw 109
Leaney, George,		Lee, Aaron	Smp 498	John, Senr.	Csw 108
Senr.	Mck 586	Andrew	Csw 110	Jos., Senr.	Csw 122
Leany, George,		Anthony	Ans 216	Joseph	Cht 179
Junr.	Mck 586	Batt	Wne 849	Joseph	Crv 263
Titas	Mck 587	Benjamin	Crv 265	Joseph	Edg 219
Leary, Cornelius	Wsh 706	Benjamin	Rbs 389	Joseph	Rbs 389
Enoch	Wsh 706	Bud James	Wke 747	Joshua	Bld 30
Ephraim	Hde 372	Burchet	Smp 502	Joshua	Glf 660
Ezekiel	Wsh 706	Burton	Jns 807	Josiah	Dpl 407
Frederick	Wsh 706	Cato	Smp 509	Lawrence	Csw 115
Job	Jns 785	Charity	Crv 265	Leven	Crv 261
John	Chw 131	Charles	Jhn 760	Levie	Gts 272
John	Wsh 706	Christopher	Edg 218	Linton	Crr 161
Joseph	Hde 372	Creasy	Rth 126	Michael	Bld 22
Joshua	Wsh 708	Daniel	Crr 161	Michael	Hde 372
Justus	Prq 646	David	Hrt 700	Mitdhel	Crr 139
Salathiel	Hde 372	David, Senr.	Jhn 775	Nathaniel	Cht 191
Samuel	Trl 694	David, Senr.	Jhn 776	Owen	Rth 124
Thomas	Wsh 708	Demsey	Crr 160	Peter	Smp 502
William	Brt 58	Dianna	Crv 247	Peter	Smp 524
William H.	Grv 542	Drury	Nrt 459	Richard	Orn 579
Leasure, Joseph	Ird 643	Edmund	Rth 123	Richard, Capt.	Ans 207
Leatch, Dugald	Cmb 389	Edward	Jhn 775	Richd., G.N.	Ans 217
Leath, Joel	Csw 141	Elijah	Bnc 176	Robert	Ans 234
Mason	Csw 142	Rverit	Rbs 389	Robert	Bnc 177
Leatherman, Chris-		Francis H.	Gts 272	Robert	Cbr 688
tian	Rwn 416	Frederick	Hlf 324	Rowland	Wke 746
Daniel	Rwn 416	Gabril	Csw 115	Sally	Brk 768
Jonas	Rwn 416	George	Bnc 177	Saml.	Crr 139
Leathers, James	Grv 523	George	Orn 517	Saml.	Rch 271
James	Grv 572	Heardon	Csw 121	Saml., Junr.	Jhn 775
John	Cmb 367	Henry	Brt 60	Sampson	Smp 524
Moses	Orn 574	Henry	Edg 217	Samuel	Cht 191
Susana	Rck 482	Henry	Gts 271	Samuel	Jhn 774
William	Orn 580	Henry	Rwn 458	Samuel, Senr.	Jhn 775
Leatherwood, Ed-		Hillery	Crr 160	Sarah	Mnt 505
ward	Bnc 177	Hopkins	Cmb 371	Stephen	Edg 218
Lecraft see Leecraft		Isaac	Rbs 389	Stephen	Jhn 776
Ledbatter, Isaac	Ans 214	Isaac	Rwn 380	Stephen	Jns 803
Ledbetter, Charles	Mnt 486	Isaac	Smp 500	Thomas	Jns 807
Coleman	Cht 200	Jacob	Rbs 389	Thomas	Rwn 409
George	Rth 125	James	Ans 234	Thos.	Crr 139
Gray	Mnt 496	James	Csw 109	Tishey	Crr 160
Henry	Mnt 496	James	Csw 115	Westbrook	Smp 508

Name	Loc	Name	Loc	Name	Loc
William	Cht 191	Jacob	Crr 146	Thomas	Glf 677
William	Crv 263	Jacob	Crr 158	Valentine	Rwn 348
William	Cmb 382	Levi	Crr 152	Leonear, Thomas	Cmb 390
William	Edg 219	Leith, James	Bfr 12	Leopard, William	Wke 747
William	Jhn 772	John	Hde 372	Lequer, John	Rth 124
William	Jhn 774	Lemare, Ozban	Rnd 327	Leroy see Laray	
William	Mnt 502	Lemay, John	Grv 552	Lesbry, Henry	Srr 674
William	Rbs 389	Lewis	Grv 554	Lescomb, William	Brt 60
William	Smp 525	Lemly, Henry	Rwn 308	Lesenberry, Henry	Ird 668
William	Srr 673	John	Rwn 308	Leslie, Joseph	Bld 22
Wm., Jur.	Csw 115	Joseph	Rwn 308	Lesly, James	Ird 650
Wm., Senr.	Csw 114	Philip	Rwn 308	John	Mck 582
Zebn.	Crr 160	Lemman, Ruben	Brk 767	Lesslie, Daniel	Cmb 362
see Lea, Leigh		Lemmon, Abraham	Lnc 818	Daniel	Cmb 388
Leech, Benjamin	Rwn 331	Dedrick	Ird 650	Duncan	Cmb 393
George	Crv 237	John	Rch 256	John	Cmb 361
Hugh	Rnd 326	Lemmons, James	Mnt 475	see Lasslie	
John	Jhn 766	John	Mck 604	Lester, Banister	Ons 159
John	Rnd 327	John	Mnt 463	Elias	Glf 671
Joseph	Crv 239	John	Mnt 471	James	Glf 673
Richard	Rwn 453	Moses	Ird 621	Jeremiah	Ptt 272
William	Rnd 326	Nancy	Mck 589	Jesse	Stk 627
Zadock	Rwn 453	Neil	Mnt 471	Jesse	Srr 672
Leeck, Edmond	Rnd 328	Robert	Mck 524	John	Brt 58
Leecraft, Susannah	Crt 85	Robert	Rth 126	Matthew	Ptt 287
Leek, Isaac	Psq 637	William	Mck 605	Moses	Edg 217
Joel	Psq 639	Lemon, David	Rck 440	William	Srr 673
Sarah	Psq 639	Jacob	Orn 578	Lestie, Alexander	Cmd 100
Leeman, Joseph	Frn 450	John	Rck 480	Leston, Levi	Stk 586
Lees, James	Mck 601	Joseph	Rck 470	Letchmore, Freder-	
William	Mck 543	Stophel	Brk 768	ick	Crv 269
Leezer, John	Rwn 337	William	Rck 478	Letcook, John	Cht 208
LeFever, Elizabeth	Mck 606	see Limon		Letten, Elijah	Lnc 878
Lefevre, Elias	Stk 579	Lenan, Thomas	Frn 451	James	Lnc 877
Lefew, Eliza.	Rck 491	Lence, Benjamin	Rwn 308	Thomas	Lnc 878
Joseph	Rck 491	Bostian	Rwn 302	Wesly	Lnc 878
Polly	Rck 491	Bostian, Senr.	Rwn 302	Letterman, John	Brk 766
Lefferd, Peter	Crv 255	Davolt	Rwn 302	Letton, Isaac	Lnc 878
Leffers, Samuel	Crt 74	Davolt, Senr.	Rwn 302	Levens, Arthur	Orn 518
Leftley, Christo-		John, Senr.	Rwn 308	Leveret, Robert	Rth 124
pher	Mnt 515	Michael	Rwn 302	Thomas	Rch 248
Leggate, David	Ptt 229	Peter	Rwn 397	Leverit, Robert	Mnt 463
Obediah	Ptt 227	Peter	Rwn 302	Leverton, ...	Nwh 4
Legget, Noah	Edg 218	Peter	Rwn 313	James	Srr 672
Leggett, Alexander	Brt 60	Lendlay, John	Orn 578	Levingston, An-	
Daniel	Wsh 706	Owen	Orn 578	guist	Ans 202
David	Rbs 390	Lendley, James	Cht 192	Duncan	Nwh 1
Elizabeth	Rbs 389	Jonathan	Cht 192	Duncan	Rch 260
Leah	Brt 60	Samuel	Cht 192	Levins, Jacob	Wke 745
Luke	Wsh 706	William	Cht 193	Mary	Cht 209
Leggitt, Hezekiah	Bfr 12	Lengo, George	Orn 580	Richard	Wke 745
Jeremiah	Bfr 13	Lenier, Thomas	Grv 516	Levistone, Cather-	
Leggitte, Anne	Mrt 401	Lennon, Dennis	Bld 21	ine	Cmb 355
Benjn. R.	Mrt 401	George	Bld 21	Levy, Alexander,	
David	Mrt 401	Lenoir, William	Wlk 49	junr.	Ptt 233
Elisha	Mrt 401	Lenox, John	Brt 60	Alexander,Senr.	Ptt 233
Josiah	Mrt 401	John	Rck 450	Henry	Ptt 232
Rachell	Mrt 401	Lent, Isaac	Orn 578	Lewallen, John	Rnd 325
Saml.	Mrt 401	Lenton, George	Wne 856	Jonathan	Rnd 325
Legiet, James,		Leoman, Aaron	Ird 621	Mary	Rnd 325
(Cap.)	Mck 583	Leonard, Ezekiel	Glf 677	Lewark, Jeams	Crr 148
Legrand, William	Rch 258	Henry (2)	Brn 14A	John	Crr 148
Leigh, Christopher	Cbr 711	Henry	Rwn 302	Timothy	Brt 58
James	Bfr 12	Jacob	Rnd 327	Lewell, Benjamin	Csw 129
John	Bfr 13	Jacob	Rwn 348	Lewellen, Jesse	Ans 236
Peter	Brk 768	Jacob, Junr.	Rwn 348	Thomas	Rck 482
Richard	Brk 768	James	Cmb 355	Thomas, Senr.	Rck 482
Richard	Prq 655	John	Glf 626	Lewellin, Anderson	Wke 745
Thomas	Trl 678	John	Glf 627	Francis	Wke 745
Leinbach, John	Stk 625	John	Stk 561	Jesse	Wke 745
Leiper, James	Lnc 835	Jos., Senr.	Glf 627	Lewes, Alvery	Lnc 831
Jno.	Lnc 833	Mary	Wrr 816	Lewings, Hugh	Orn 581
Mattw.	Lnc 832	Michael	Rwn 348	Lewis, Aaron	Bld 22
Leister, Elisha	Psq 633	Philip	Rwn 348	Abraham	Rth 126
Jacob	Psq 633	Robert	Rwn 337	Amos	Edg 217
Leitchfield, Elize-		Saml.	Brn 14	Ann	Rck 467
beth	Crr 158	Tho.	Brn 14A	Archabald	Bfr 13

Archabald   Crt 57
Barnhabee   Crv 273
Benja.   Bld 13
Benjamin   Edg 218
Benjamin   Lnr 14
Benjamin   Wlk 50
Benjn.   Mre 75
Catharine   Crv 343
Charity   Hrt 712
Charles   Csw 126
Charles   Grv 507
Charles   Grv 547
Charles   Hlf 324
Charles   Rth 123
Daniel   Ans 239
Daniel   Ird 674
Daniel, Junr.   Rwn 426
Daniel, Senr.   Rwn 426
David   Crv 307
David   Gts 272
David   Mre 50
David   Orn 578
Delphi   Cbr 704
Denrum   Bld 30
Edwd.   Csw 124
Egbert W.   Hlf 324
Eliphaz   Nrt 457
Elisha   Crv 321
Elizabeth   Bfr 13
Elizabeth   Edg 219
Elizabeth   Orn 580
Elizabeth   Wlk 50
Elkaner   Srr 674
Flkener, Jur.   Srr 674
Exum   Edg 217
Exum, (Mercht.)   Edg 217
Fanny   Edg 218
Federick   Dpl 437
Federick   Srr 674
Fedrick   Dpl 420
Fielden   Orn 581
Figurs   Edg 219
Frances   Nwh 10
Franes   Grv 541
George   Mnt 471
George   Nsh 109
George   Orn 517
George (2)   Wlk 51
Gideon   Ash 82
Gideon   Wlk 51
Gideon, Senr.   Ash 82
Guion   Hrt 699
Henry   Bnc 176
Henry   Cht 191
Henry   Lnc 831
Henry   Nsh 108
Henry   Nsh 109
Henry   Orn 581
Heny   Nsh 109
Herbert   Cht 164
Howel   Grv 550
Jacob   Cbr 698
James   Ash 82
James   Bfr 12
James   Brn 13
James   Edg 217
James   Grv 516
James   Mck 553
James   Nrt 457
James   Rnd 326
James (2)   Rbs 389
James   Stk 561
James   Wke 744
James   Wke 746
James   Wlk 51
James, junr.   Ash 83
James, Junr.   Wke 744

Jas.   Csw 124
Jeremiah   Bld 7
Jerremiah   Ans 239
Jesse   Wsh 706
Joel   Mre 50
Joel   Rwn 426
John   Crt 64
John   Crv 277
John   Gts 271
John (2)   Hlf 324
John   Mre 75
John   Nwh 10
John (2)   Rnd 327
John   Rnd 328
John   Rbs 389
John   Rck 452
John (2)   Rth 123
John   Wke 745
John   Wsh 706
Jonathan   Bfr 12
Joseph   Bfr 13
Joshua   Crv 273
Joshua   Ptt 292
Josiah, Esqr.   Bld 20
Josiah, Senr.   Bld 22
Judah   Bfr 13
Levy   Ptt 280
Lewton   Gts 271
Luke   Hrt 725
Magor   Nsh 109
Major   Crv 275
Manson   Bld 12
Martha   Wne 847
Martin   Brk 766
Mary   Grv 510
Mary   Hlf 324
Mary   Mnt 518
Mary   Prs 210
Matthew   Wke 745
Mills   Gts 271
Morgan   Hlf 324
Moses   Bld 21
Nancy   Hlf 324
Nanny   Crt 68
Nathaniel   Grv 506
Nehemiah   Crv 287
Nicholas   Grv 525
Nicholson   Nsh 109
P.M., Capt.   Bld 21
Peter   Rwn 331
Philip   Ans 231
Philip   Gts 271
Prudence   Crt 68
Ralph   Cmd 106
Richard   Ash 83
Richard   Rnd 327
Richard   Rwn 374
Richard   Rth 123
Robert   Brk 725
Robert   Grv 546
Robert   Nsh 109
Samuel   Ird 643
Samuel   Rwn 331
Shadrach   Rck 442
Sherod (2)   Nsh 109
Simon   Lnc 891
Susannah   Crt 68
Tho.   Nwh 9A
Thomas   Cht 192
Thomas   Mck 580
Thomas   Mnt 471
Thomas   Orn 581
Thomas, Jr.   Crt 57
Thomas, Sr.   Crt 57
Thos.   Nsh 109
W. Egbert   Hlf 324
Warner   Hlf 324

Will.   Prs 207
William   Bfr 13
William   Crv 277
William   Grv 516
William   Grn 606
William   Hlf 324
William   Ird 643
William   Mck 596
William   Mre 56
William   Nrt 457
William   Orn 578
William   Orn 580
William   Orn 581
William   Ptt 263
William   Rwn 374
William   Wke 745
William   Wne 853
William   Wlk 50
William, jr.   Crt 65
William, sr.   Crt 64
Willis   Grv 547
Willis   Ptt 263
Wm.   Nsh 109
Zachariah   Orn 517
Lewisclaugel, John   Hde 372
Leynback, Daniel   Srr 673
Lias, Jesse   Stk 593
Liberton, Daniel   Srr 674
Lick, Martin   Stk 596
Liday, Jacob   Rth 125
Liddleton, Heze-
   kiah   Ons 154
   Jarmon   Ons 157
   Peggy   Ons 154
   Suthey   Ons 154
Liddon, Benjamin   Dpl 399
   John   Nwh 12
   Tho.   Nwh 6
Lierly, Jacob   Rwn 296
Liftenburg, Abra-
   ham   Cbr 694
Ligget, Widow   Mck 585
   William   Mck 585
Liggit, William   Mck 605
Lightfoot, Barthol. Cht 225
   John   Mnt 486
   Sapley   Prq 646
   William   Nrt 457
Like, Christian   Lnc 862
   Jacob   Lnc 862
   Eada   Prq 661
Lila, Reuben   Prq 660
Liler, Kinchen   Jhn 761
Liles, Benjn.   Brn 14
   Brittain   Rth 124
   Burges   Rth 124
   David   Ans 226
   David   Rth 123
   Elijah   Ans 226
   Elizabeth   Chw 127
   Ephriam   Rth 126
   George   Chw 127
   Jacob   Wke 746
   James, G.   Ans 230
   James, Senr.   Ans 202
   John   Ans 227
   John   Rth 124
   John, Junr.   Ans 202
   Joseph   Ans 226
   Robert   Ans 202
   Samuel   Wke 745
   Thomas   Chw 127
   Thomas   Rth 124
   William   Ans 228
   William   Brn 14
Lillard, Moses   Rck 462
Lilley, Joseph   Bfr 13

Josiah	Mrt 401	John	Jhn 776	William	Stk 574
Kedar	Mrt 401	John	Rth 125	Linville, Abraham	Ash 83
Myles	Prq 644	John, H.	Ans 229	Linyard, Samuel	Chw 130
Stephan	Mrt 388	Jonothan	Crr 138	Lion, James	Stk 580
Timothy	Mrt 401	Joshua	Rth 125	James	Wlk 51
Lillibridge, Jo-		Micajah	Rth 125	John	Srr 673
seph	Ons 141	Nancy	Glf 685	Thomas	Srr 673
Lillie, James	Rbs 389	Precelley	Crr 142	William	Stk 561
Lillington, Sarah	Nwh 12A	Rachel	Ans 199	Lionson, Stephen	Stk 561
Lilly, Armsted	Mnt 496	Sam	Lnc 838	Lipe, Jacob	Mnt 514
Edmond, Junr.	Mnt 486	Samuel	Glf 642	Lipley, James	Orn 581
Edmond, Senr.	Mnt 496	William	Ans 202	Lippard, Christian	Mnt 518
John, Junr.	Mnt 486	William	Rth 125	Daniel	Rwn 342
John, Senr.	Mnt 496	Wm.	Crr 146	Henry	Rwn 301
Nathaniel	Mnt 486	Linebarger, Bar-		John	Cbr 714
Limback, Benjamin	Stk 561	bara	Lnc 828	John	Ird 650
Charles	Stk 597	Fredk.	Lnc 828	William	Ird 671
Joseph	Stk 595	Jno.	Lnc 828	Lippe, John	Mck 588
Joseph	Stk 597	John (2)	Lnc 862	Lips, John	Wlk 51
Lewis	Stk 597	Peter	Lnc 862	Lipse, Jonathan	Wlk 50
Limbaugh, Freder-		Peter	Rwn 308	Lipsey, Archibald	Crv 253
ick	Lnc 904	Linehart, Lawrence	Lnc 893	Isaac	Ons 148
Limeboh, Peter	Cbr 717	Liner, James	Cht 180	Lemuel	Jns 801
Henry	Cbr 716	Lines, Bostian,		Rasco, Junr.	Jns 783
Liming, Josiah	Lnc 818	Junr.	Rwn 301	Rasco, Senr.	Jns 795
Limon, David	Orn 579	Lingle, Anthony	Rwn 302	Lisby, Henry	Srr 673
see Lemon		Casper	Rwn 302	Liscomb, John	Bfr 13
Linager, Elizabeth	Glf 687	Francis	Rwn 302	Liscombe, Willson	Hlf 326
Linch, Bryan	Jhn 775	Jacob	Cbr 718	Lisenby, John	Ans 231
Cornelius	Jhn 757	Lingleton, Richard	Crv 341	Lish, Isaac	Srr 673
Elias	Rth 124	Lingo see Lengo		James	Srr 673
Ellinor	Jhn 774	Linibury, Jacob	Rnd 326	Jesse	Srr 673
Henry	Mrt 401	Link, Jacob, Junr.	Rwn 331	Thomas	Srr 673
Jesse	Mrt 401	Jacob, Senr.	Rwn 331	Listenbay, Agness	Cbr 678
John	Orn 517	Philip	Rwn 332	Lister, Abel	Crv 295
Joshua	Wke 744	William	Rwn 356	Jesse	Crv 291
Mary	Rck 443	William	Rwn 416	Laban	Crv 295
Nancy	Rth 124	Linker, Henry	Cbr 690	Robert	Rwn 426
Sarah	Crt 49	Linkhorn, Susanna	Bfr 13	Liston, John	Psq 624
Lincicum, Daniel	Glf 625	Linley, Simon	Stk 612	Litaker, Conrod	Cbr 709
Linck, Anne	Lnc 856	Zachary	Rnd 327	John	Rwn 313
Frederick	Lnc 856	Linn, John	Glf 631	Philip	Cbr 709
Jacob	Lnc 856	John	Wke 745	Litchfield, Eliza-	
John	Lnc 877	Linquist, George	Crt 67	beth	Hde 372
Linder, Jesse	Rck 468	Linsey, Elisabeth	Frn 464	Litchworth, Benjn.	Wlk 50
John	Rck 483	James	Cht 170	Litten, Abel	Cmd 109
Mary	Rck 437	Jeptha	Frn 464	Ann	Cmd 109
Lindlay, Joshua	Cht 158	Lamuel	Frn 494	see Letten	
Lindley, David	Cht 212	Wm.	Nsh 109	Litterell, John	Glf 641
John	Crr 139	Linster, Isaac	Rwn 426	Little, Alexander	
Jonathan	Orn 518	Lint, Isaac	Orn 517	(2)	Rbs 389
Thomas	Orn 518	Linte, Christopher		Archabald	Cht 158
Lindsay, Ann	Orn 581	L.	Crv 249	Archabald (2)	Rbs 390
Athy	Orn 579	Linter, Zach	Srr 711	Asa	Edg 217
Ely	Orn 581	Linthicum, Daniel	Glf 671	Benjamin	Rck 472
James	Nrt 455	Richard	Glf 671	Charles	Ash 82
John	Rwn 374	Linton, Daniel	Bfr 12	Crecy	Edg 219
John, Jr.	Hlf 324	James	Bfr 12	Daniel	Cbr 689
John, Sen.	Hlf 324	Joanna	Hlf 324	David	Rck 473
Mary	Orn 579	John	Cmd 99	David	Rck 492
Matthew	Orn 580	John	Dpl 420	Duncan	Rbs 390
Taylor	Rck 479	Joseph	Cmd 96	Edmond	Ptt 292
Walter	Mck 573	Lemuel	Brt 60	Elizabeth	Edg 217
Lindsey, Betsey	Crr 142	Luke	Bfr 12	Etheldred	Ptt 281
Calib	Wrr 815	Malachi	Hde 372	Exum	Edg 217
Calip	Rth 125	Michael	Hde 372	Frank	Rnd 325
Carlton	Rth 124	Salley	Crr 152	George	Ptt 240
Colin	Rbs 389	Thomas	Cmd 95	Gray	Edg 217
Daniel	Crr 137	Thos.	Crr 162	Isaac	Ans 233
David	Crr 142	see Lee		Jacob	Ans 216
George, Jr.	Ans 226	Linvil, John	Srr 672	James	Ans 230
George, Junr.	Ans 213	Moses	Srr 672	James	Cbr 693
George, Senr.	Ans 213	Linvill, Aaron	Stk 567	James	Crv 329
James	Lnc 843	David	Stk 567	Jeremiah	Brn 21
James	Rth 124	John	Stk 561	Jesse	Edg 217
James	Rth 125	Richard	Stk 567	John	Ans 230
James, Sr.	Rth 124	William	Rwn 438	John	Brn 21

Name	Ref	Name	Ref	Name	Ref
John	Brk 767	Livinstone, James	Grv 556	Lockey, Henry	Ons 141
John	Chw 113	John	Grv 556	Lockhard, John	Nrt 457
John	Edg 217	Livister, David	Grv 572	Lockhart, Adam	Ans 214
John	Mnt 490	Llewellin, Lyson	Nrt 457	Adam	Ans 232
John	Rth 126	Llewelling, John	Edg 217	Benjanin	Jhn 762
John	Wke 746	see Lewellen		Joseph	Rwn 438
John, Junr.	Rwn 453	Lloyd, David	Bld 39	Letty	Ans 214
John, Senr.	Rwn 453	James	Bld 30	Stephen	Jhn 764
John Eli	Brk 766	Loafman, Jane	Csw 103	Widow	Jhn 768
John Willm.	Brk 766	Loar, Valentine	Lnc 904	William	Orn 491
Joseph	Ptt 227	Loback, Charles	Stk 599	William	Srr 672
Joseph	Ptt 292	Christopher	Stk 625	Locklin, Robert	Rch 269
Josiah	Bfr 12	Localier, Thomas	Wke 746	Lockman, Christo-	
Lewis	Rwn 416	Lochan, Nathaniel	Cmb 375	pher	Glf 668
Lewis	Rwn 459	Lochran, Mary	Brk 767	David	Lnc 862
Margret	Rwn 367	Lochwood, Holland	Psq 628	John	Lnc 862
Mary Ann	Hrt 732	Lock, Alexander	Rwn 313	Lockwell, Francis	Glf 658
Michael	Ptt 289	Benjamin	Bld 23	Locus, Frank	Ans 221
Michael	Wke 745	David	Cmb 381	Locust, James	Nsh 108
Mincher	Rnd 327	Eliza.	Bld 34	John	Nsh 109
Nancy	Ans 230	Elizabeth	Ptt 224	Martin	Wke 745
Nancy	Rck 472	Ezekiel	Grv 537	Valentine	Wke 745
Nathan	Brn 21	Feancis	Ird 621	Wm.	Nsh 109
Nathan	Ptt 270	Francis	Rwn 313	Lodge, John	Edg 218
Noah	Edg 217	George	Ird 621	Josiah	Edg 218
Peter	Rwn 443	George, Junr.	Ird 621	Lewis	Edg 218
Pleasant	Ptt 289	Isaac	Bld 19	Robert	Edg 218
Presly	Rck 473	James	Bld 38	Loe, James	Wke 745
Reading	Ptt 275	James	Brk 766	Jesse	Wne 863
Rebecca	Crv 251	James	Rwn 313	Loflin, John	Rwn 380
Robert	Rbs 389	James	Rwn 322	Richard	Rwn 380
Tho.	Brn 18A	John	Cmb 381	Loft, William	Rck 472
Thomas	Bfr 12	John	Rwn 313	Loften, James	Lnr 14
Thomas	Brk 767	Jonathan	Grv 567	Jeremiah	Lnr 16
William	Ans 233	Joshua	Grv 510	John	Lnr 14
William	Ptt 239	Leonard	Cmb 368	Joseph	Lnr 14
William	Rck 472	Mary	Bld 34	Leonard	Lnr 14
William P.	Wrr 784	Mary	Bld 38	Loftin, Cornelius	Rwn 380
Winney	Wke 746	Matthew	Rwn 317	Daniel	Rwn 380
Littlejohn, John	Grv 510	Matthew, Esqr.	Rwn 313	Henry	Mnt 484
William	Chw 114	Matthew, Jur.	Rwn 313	Isaac	Cbr 688
Little John, Mar-		Matthew,		James	Lnc 865
gret	Brk 766	(Taylr.)	Rwn 313	Joseph	Crv 319
Littleton, Ozias	Brn 14	Richard	Rwn 313	Lewis	Jns 791
Surry	Edg 218	Robert	Rwn 313	Lewis	Rwn 380
Thomas	Jns 801	Thomas	Bld 36	Longfield	Crv 319
Litton, Abel	Cmd 101	William	Grv 531	Moses	Rwn 308
Lively, Lewis	Rth 125	William	Hlf 324	Shadrach	Crv 313
Livengood, Chris-		Lockalier, Mary	Hlf 324	Stephen	Brn 19
tian	Rwn 348	Lockalin, Maria	Hlf 324	William	Mnt 479
Christian,Senr.	Rwn 348	Lockart, Nathaniel	Crv 329	Loftley, Daniel	Wne 870
Hardman	Rwn 355	William	Crv 233	Lofton, Frederic	Bld 4
Hardman, Senr.	Rwn 374	William	Glf 657	John	Bld 3
Henry	Lnc 893	William	Rck 470	Lofty, William	Mck 570
John	Rwn 348	Locke, James	Grv 549	Log, Jesse	Prs 199
John	Rwn 374	Phillip	Stk 568	Logan, Andrew	Rth 125
Michl.	Rwn 348	Thomas	Hlf 326	Drury	Rth 124
Thomas	Rwn 374	Lockelear, Amy	Rbs 389	Esom	Rth 125
Liverett, William	Rth 126	B. Malcom	Rbs 389	Francis	Rth 124
Liverman, Hezekiah	Crv 305	Jacob	Rbs 389	Geo.	Nwh 3
Jethro	Trl 682	Joseph	Rbs 389	Hugh	Srr 672
John	Trl 682	Levi	Rbs 389	James	Srr 673
John, Son of		Malcom B.	Rbs 389	John	Brk 767
John	Trl 690	Penellope	Rbs 389	John	Ird 662
John, (son of		Robert	Rbs 389	John	Rwn 296
Willm.)	Trl 690	Rodeah	Rbs 389	John	Rth 124
Joseph	Trl 682	Samuel	Rbs 389	John	Srr 674
Justice	Trl 690	Sarah	Rbs 389	Mary	Rth 125
Thomas	Trl 670	William	Rbs 389	Moses	Rth 124
William	Trl 682	Lockenow, George	Stk 602	Thomas	Rth 125
William, Senr.	Trl 690	Lockerleer, Eliza-		William	Rwn 438
Livermon, Adamant	Hrt 735	beth	Grv 563	Loggins, Joseph	Ash 82
Liversage, Mary	Chw 120	Lockerman, Jacob	Smp 496	Logon, George	Srr 674
Livingston, Henry		Moses	Smp 495	Lohlin, John	Rch 270
B.	Crv 231	Lockermy, James	Smp 527	Lohon, James	Jhn 776
John	Wlk 51	James, Sr.	Smp 527	John	Ans 219
		William	Smp 527	Loid, Edward	Ans 207

Lokey, William	Orn 518	John	Prs 197	John	Rwn 355
Loles, Benjamin	Bld 4	John	Rch 256	John, Col.	Rwn 348
Lollar, Jacob	Lnc 883	John	Rch 268	John, Junr.	Rwn 347
James	Lnc 883	John	Rwn 374	Peter	Rwn 348
Loller, Isaac, jr.	Rth 124	John	Rth 125	Lopwaser, Adam	Rwn 308
Isaac, Sr.	Rth 124	John, (Smith)	Rwn 374	Lord, John	Nwh 2A
Lolly, Elisha	Rnd 325	Jonathan	Lnc 862	Lord	Prs 194
Lomack, William	Mnt 479	Joseph	Brn 19A	Moses	Glf 629
Lomax, Robert	Rck 441	Joseph	Rwn 341	William	Cmb 370
Thomas	Rck 443	Joseph	Trl 682	Loretz, Andrew	Lnc 818
William	Rwn 380	Joseph Jno.	Hlf 324	Lorrin, Duncan	Rch 270
Lomix, Benjamin	Rnd 325	Joshua	Prq 642	Lorton, THomas	Hlf 326
London, Amos, Jr.	Srr 707	Josias, Junr.	Ans 201	Losson, Esther	Crv 287
John	Cht 223	Josias, Senr.	Ans 201	John	Stk 583
John	Nwh 4	Joyce	Nrt 457	Tatmon	Stk 583
John	Wlk 51	Lemuel	Hlf 324	Thomas	Crt 81
Josiah	Cht 223	Lemuel	Prq 643	Loston, John	Srr 672
Nimshi	Rck 448	Leonard	Lnc 848	see Lofton	
Owen	Cht 182	Lunsford	Hlf 324	Lotham, Reuben	Stk 589
William	Stk 562	Martha	Nrt 457	Louder, Thomas	Mnt 514
Lone see Lane		Mary	Hlf 324	William	Cbr 713
Long, Alexander	Brk 721	Mary	Trl 670	Loudermilk, Jacob	Rnd 327
Alexander	Rwn 288	Nathan	Bfr 13	Loughery, William	Ird 621
Aquilla	Mrt 401	Nathan	Prq 657	Loughrea, Charles	Chw 115
Azariah	Hde 372	Nicholas	Frn 466	Lourance, William	Brk 766
Benjamin	Rch 242	Peter	Cbr 693	Lourey, William	Bld 9
Benjamin	Wsh 708	Prittyman	Lnc 862	Louton, Henry	Ans 231
Benjn.	Prs 207	Rachel	Lnc 862	Lovatt, Barney	Nsh 108
Charles	Stk 614	Rebecca	Wsh 708	Henry	Rbs 389
Coonrod	Orn 518	Reuben	Ans 200	Love, Alexander	Nrt 457
Daniel	Crr 159	Reubin	Prs 204	Angus	Rbs 389
Edward	Brk 766	Rheubin	Brn 19A	Aron	Rck 467
Elisebeth	Prs 200	Richard H.	Hlf 324	Charles	Rth 126
Elizabeth	Hlf 324	Richard H.	Hlf 358	Daniel	Mre 75
Federick	Srr 672	Robert	Ird 618	Dunkin	Mre 67
Felix	Rwn 374	Ruben	Lnc 848	Edmond	Mre 57
Francis	Rck 481	Samuel	Lnc 862	Edward	Rbs 389
Gabriel	Brn 19	Silas	Nrt 457	Elizabeth	Nrt 457
George	Cbr 697	Simeon	Prq 642	Frederick	Rwn 380
George	Orn 581	Solomon	Rnd 326	James	Cbr 693
George	Rwn 348	Susannah	Rnd 325	James	Orn 517
George	Smp 523	Thomas	Chw 115	James	Rth 93
George	Srr 672	Thomas	Prq 642	James	Stk 561
Gloud	Rth 124	Widow	Mck 535	James	Stk 562
Gloud	Rth 126	William	Prq 643	John	Csw 115
H. Richard	Hlf 324	William	Rch 262	John	Mre 67
H. Richard	Hlf 358	William	Rch 264	John	Rnd 328
Henry	Brn 16	William	Rth 125	John	Rnd 353
Henry	Mck 575	William	Wsh 706	John	Wlk 49
Henry	Orn 518	Longbottom, Joseph	Wlk 50	John	Wlk 51
Henry	Stk 596	Longe, John	Wsh 714	John, Ser.	Srr 672
Isaac	Wsh 708	Longens, Amos,Jur.	Srr 674	Joseph	Rnd 326
Isreal	Stk 566	Longest, Caleb	Crt 85	Kenan	Dpl 438
Jacob	Mck 575	Joshua	Crt 74	Michael	Smp 510
Jacob	Orn 518	Longmere, William	Grv 545	Neill	Cmb 355
Jacob	Rwn 348	Longmire, John	Wke 746	Ruth	Stk 558
Jacob	Rwn 367	Lonish, John	Stk 600	Saml.	Csw 115
James	Cbr 695	Lonsford, Anthony	Srr 673	Samuel	Brk 768
James	Nrt 457	Lonson, John	Stk 582	Samuel	Ird 671
James	Rch 243	Lontz, George	Lnc 818	Thomas	Orn 517
James	Mnt 510	Looell, Coleson	Orn 517	Thomas	Ptt 270
James	Trl 670	Look see Lock		Thomas	Srr 672
James, Junr.	Wsh 706	Lookenbil, Henry	Rwn 355	Thomas	Srr 673
James, Senr.	Wsh 706	Christian	Rwn 355	Thomas, Esqr.	Bnc 177
James, son of		John	Rwn 356	William	Cmd 98
Andrew	Wsh 706	Lookinbill, David	Rwn 409	William	Orn 517
Jas.	Prs 199	John	Rwn 409	William	Srr 672
Jno. Joseph	Hlf 324	Loolen, Henry	Ans 211	William	Wke 746
John	Ash 83	Loomer, Anthy. B.	Nwh 11A	Lovel, Edward (2)	Srr 672
John	Bld 41	Loomis, Nathaniel	Ons 160	Williams	Hlf 324
John	Cbr 698	Looper, Daniel	Ird 625	Lovelace, Archd.	Wlk 50
John	Edg 219	Looten, Henry	Ans 234	Elias	Csw 141
John	Ird 650	see Loolen, Louton		John	Wlk 50
John	Lnc 897	Lopewaser, Widow		Thomas	Ird 668
John	Mck 589	(2)	Rwn 308	Young	Rck 449
John	Nrt 457	Lopp, Jacob	Rwn 355	Lovelas, Rhodham	Rck 449
John	Orn 518	Jacob	Rwn 393	Lovell, David	Rck 475

INDEX TO THE 1800 CENSUS OF NORTH CAROLINA

Name	Loc	Name	Loc	Name	Loc
John	Rck 447	Lowman, Adam (2)	Glf 660	Zadock	Grv 510
Joseph	Glf 680	Lowrance, Abraham	Lnc 877	Loyhead, William	Wrr 815
Zachh.	Rck 447	Abram	Rwn 322	Loys, Moses	Ons 178
Lovet, William	Smp 506	Alexander	Lnc 883	Lucadoe, James	Rth 124
Lovett, Richard	Crv 303	Alexander	Rwn 317	Lucas, Elizabeth	Brt 58
Lovick, John	Crt 81	Andrew	Rwn 322	Geo., Esqr.	Bld 28
John	Lnr 35	Daniel	Lnc 878	George	Cht 205
Sarah	Crv 335	George	Wlk 50	George	Rnd 328
Thomas	Crv 335	Isaac (2)	Lnc 877	Henry	Bfr 13
William	Lnr 14	Jacob	Lnc 877	Henry	Bld 24
Lovil, William	Srr 672	John	Ird 665	John	Bld 23
Loving, Frederick	Ptt 284	John	Rwn 322	John	Mnt 471
Gabrieal	Wlk 51	Joshua	Rwn 322	John	Wne 861
Gabriel	Brk 767	Michael	Mck 535	Lewis	Smp 531
Isham	Wne 859	Peter	Wlk 50	Samuel	Hde 372
John (2)	Brk 767	Widow	Rwn 327	Sherwood	Wne 862
William	Brk 766	William	Lnc 892	William	Cht 157
William	Brk 768	Lowrie, Samuel	Mck 535	William	Rth 124
William	Ptt 287	William	Chw 114	William	Rth 126
Lovit, John	Ons 137	Lowry, Avery	Wke 746	Luck see Leech	
Lovitt, David	Lnr 14	Elijah	Ans 237	Luckey, Robert	Rwn 327
John	Lnr 14	James	Brk 767	William	Rwn 327
Moses	Lnr 14	Jehu	Wke 746	Luckie, George	Ird 621
Lovlace, Erasmus	Ird 635	Jesse	Wke 746	Hugh	Lnc 849
Low, Aaron	Psq 640	John	Ans 211	James	Lnc 849
Anna	Wne 872	John	Rck 482	Samuel	Rwn 448
Barnabas	Psq 641	John	Rwn 331	Samuel, Junr.	Rwn 448
Betsy	Rck 438	John	Stk 614	William	Mck 524
Daniel	Ans 202	John, Senr.	Rck 438	Lucky, Richard	Rwn 327
Daniel	Rbs 389	Joseph	Psq 626	Samuel	Rwn 327
David	Glf 668	Mary	Ans 237	Lucus, Daniel	Wne 861
Isaac	Rck 446	Mary	Rwn 459	Lucy, Avery	Ans 205
James	Rck 458	Matthew	Wke 746	Beerwell	Hlf 324
John	Hlf 324	Rachel	Lnr 15	John	Rwn 400
John	Rbs 389	Rachel	Lnr 35	Michael	Rwn 400
John	Rck 483	Robert	Ans 237	Ludford, Mary	Trl 678
Milicent	Psq 624	Robert	Psq 634	Ludrige, Kesiah	Ird 636
Peter	Glf 646	William	Ans 237	Ludwick, Daniel	Stk 574
Stephen	Srr 674	William	Brk 768	Henry	Cbr 718
Tempy	Ans 202	William	Rch 249	Jacob	Stk 558
Thomas	Psq 624	William	Rwn 331	Peter	Stk 561
Thomas	Psq 638	Lows, Shadrach	Wlk 50	Peter	Stk 562
Thomas	Rck 482	Lowther, Penelope,		Philip	Glf 637
William	Hlf 324	Grs.	Brt 58	William	Stk 558
Willis	Rbs 389	Penolope	Chw 114	Luffman, Isbel	Crr 139
Lowden, Samuel	Stk 580	Lowthorp, Francis	Crv 233	Lufman, Edward	Psq 635
Lowder, John	Glf 630	Lowthrop, Francis,		Lugh see Leigh	
Joseph	Stk 583	Junr.	Crv 257	Luker, Jacob	Mnt 494
William	Stk 580	Loy, Catharine	Orn 518	Lukeroy, John	Bnc 177
Lowdermilk, Jacob	Brk 768	see Lay		Lumans, William	Grv 533
John	Rnd 327	Loyd, Edward	Hde 372	Lumbley, Joseph	Wke 744
Lowdon, Caleb	Stk 562	Frederick	Orn 579	Lumkins, Anthony	Grv 512
Lowe, Caleb	Wlk 50	Hanah	Edg 219	Lumley, Jesse	Ans 203
Ezekiel	Wlk 50	Henry	Hde 372	Lumpeck, John	Stk 609
George	Prq 651	Isaac	Grv 564	Lumpkins, Richd.	Glf 644
Isaac	Rnd 326	Isham	Grv 522	William	Grv 560
Isaac, Senr.	Wlk 50	James	Brk 767	Lumpter, Anne	Lnc 834
James	Rnd 327	James	Orn 579	Lumsden, John	Cmb 355
John	Wlk 50	Jarrot	Grv 552	Lun, Nathan	Mre 61
Margarett	Rck 440	John	Grv 552	Lunce, Martha	Ird 611
Mary	Rnd 326	John	Orn 579	Martha	Frn 472
Nathan (2)	Rnd 327	John	Rwn 409	William	Frn 472
Samuel	Wlk 50	Joseph	Hrt 700	Lunceford, Elijah	Wlk 51
Tabitha	Rnd 326	Joseph	Srr 673	Elisha	Wlk 51
Thomas	Rnd 325	Margaret	Hrt 700	Henry	Wlk 51
Thomas	Rnd 327	Margret	Ons 140	James	Wlk 51
Thomas	Rck 442	Martha	Orn 579	John	Wlk 51
Thomas, Senr.	Wlk 50	Mary	Edg 173	William	Wlk 50
William	Rnd 326	Mary	Edg 217	Lunchford, Aries	Rch 256
William	Wlk 50	Neagle	Ird 615	Lundsford, Elias	Rnd 325
Lowell see Looell		Si	Srr 707	Lundy, James	Cmb 355
Lower, John	Lnc 843	Stephen	Orn 579	Lungino, Sarah	Srr 674
Lowery, James	Rbs 389	Susannah	Hde 372	Lunn, William	Nrt 457
Thomas	Rbs 389	Thomas	Csw 139	Wm.	Crr 138
Lowhorn, Adam	Ptt 245	William	Grv 508	Lunsford, Allin	Ird 625
Arthur	Ptt 245	William	Hrt 712	August	Stk 609
George	Ptt 244	William	Orn 579	Jesse	Prs 190

John	Ash 82	Lymback, Charles	Stk 602	Mabe, Nancy	Stk 592
Joseph	Prs 190	Jo.	Stk 605	Philip	Stk 584
Lamech	Ash 82	Lyn, Alexander	Stk 610	Robert	Stk 586
Lincen	Wne 848	Edla	Bnc 177	Mabee, Reubin	Stk 584
Martha	Frn 461	James	Bnc 177	Maberry, C.	Rck 479
Paton	Ans 213	John	Bnc 177	Cornelius	Rck 481
William	Mnt 474	John	Orn 518	Jno.	Lnc 827
Luper, William	Rbs 389	William	Bnc 177	John	Lnc 856
Lupo, James	Edg 217	Lynback see Leynback		Philips	Rck 442
Laban	Rbs 389	Lynch, Christopher	Grn 615	Philips	Rck 463
Lupton, John	Crt 60	Darling	Orn 580	Randolph	Wlk 53
Luroy, Lewis	Bfr 23	David	Nrt 457	Solomon	Mnt 500
Lurrey, Wm.	Crr 153	George	Edg 217	Thomas	Lnc 851
Lurry, John	Cmd 105	Hugh	Rck 477	Thomas	Lnc 856
Lemuel	Cmd 93	James	Orn 517	William	Lnc 856
Thomas	Cmd 93	James	Rck 468	Mabery, Owen	Rck 450
Lusk, Hugh	Lnc 883	Jesse	Glf 638	Mabray, Randolph	Cht 156
John	Rth 124	John	Orn 580	Mabrey, Benjamin	Wrr 820
Joseph	Bnc 177	John	Rwn 341	Charles	Wrr 818
Joseph	Rth 124	Jonas	Orn 518	David	Wke 748
Samuel	Rwn 355	Moses	Orn 517	Delk	Wrr 820
William	Bnc 177	Patsy	Hlf 324	Gray	Wrr 818
Luslie, Abraham	Brk 766	Sophy	Edg 219	John	Wrr 818
Luster, Archibald	Brk 767	William	Hlf 326	Matthew	Wrr 818
Lute, John	Grv 570	William	Wsh 714	Repps	Wrr 817
Luteman, John A.	Crv 237	Lyndon, Josiah	Rnd 328	Mabry, Sarah	Frn 455
Luten, Henderson	Hrt 700	Lyne, Henry	Grv 513	Wilkinson	Edg 221
Mary	Nrt 457	James	Grv 516	Macam, John	Orn 588
Luter, Elias	Nrt 455	Lynn, Allin	Rwn 448	MacArthur, Peter	Cmb 357
Hardy	Cht 204	David	Brk 767	Macatee, Samuel	Ird 646
Henry	Cht 203	John	Lnc 904	MacAuslan, Duncan	Cmb 356
John	Nrt 455	Robert	Rwn 302	Macauslin, John	Nwh 1A
Joiles	Nrt 455	Thornton	Rck 449	Maccane, Nancy	Edg 224
Thomas	Nrt 457	William	Rwn 393	Maccater, Abednigo	Mre 77
Lutes, John	Brk 766	Lyols, John	Hlf 324	MacCause, William	Cmb 357
Luther, Christian	Rnd 325	Jordan	Hlf 324	Macdaniel, Campbel	Edg 222
George	Rnd 326	Thomas	Hlf 324	Macdeed, John	Edg 222
Godfrey	Rnd 326	Lyon, Alex	Stk 614	Willis	Edg 222
Jacob	Rnd 326	Alexander	Glf 663	Macdonald, Geo.	Nwh 12A
Michael	Rnd 326	Capt. (Company)	Prs 215	MacDonald, Alexan-	
Michael	Rnd 327	Henry	Edg 173	der	Cmb 356
Luton, Absolum	Chw 115	Henry	Edg 217	Mace, Aquilla	Jhn 772
Constantine	Psq 638	Jacob	Wlk 51	John	Edg 222
Ellett	Csw 142	James	Stk 580	Jonas	Jhn 772
Frederick	Chw 121	Richard	Edg 218	Thomas	Rwn 277
Harvey	Psq 636	Richd.	Prs 188	Thomas	Rwn 288
Henry	Chw 113	Robert	Csw 102	Macefe, Robert	Brk 777
John	Csw 142	Thomas	Edg 218	William	Brk 777
John	Chw 121	William	Lnr 15	Macfarson, Eley	Lnr 17
King	Chw 113	William	Wlk 51	Macham, Edmond	Cht 166
Samuel	Brt 58	Wm.	Csw 122	Joseph	Cht 166
Lutral, Jas.	Csw 103	Lyons, Elijah	Rwn 448	Machen, Thomas W.	Crv 231
Presly	Csw 103	Leonard	Brk 766	Machleroy, Adam,	
Lutt, Robert	Orn 517	Nancey	Chw 117	Jur.	Bfr 13
Lutterlock,		Thomas	Trl 694	Adam, Sr.	Bfr 13
Charles	Cht 175	Lype, Barbary	Cbr 709	Hnry	Bfr 13
Lutts, William	Crr 141	Godfred	Cbr 711	William	Bfr 13
Lutz, Adam	Lnc 900	Jonas	Cbr 709	see McLeroy	
Daniel	Lnc 904	Lyro, B.	Srr 708	Machy, William	Bfr 14
David	Lnc 818	Lytle, Caterine	Rnd 353	MacIntire, James	Cmb-357
George (2)	Lnc 818	George	Lnc 862	Mack, James	Rck 464
Henry	Lnc 818	James	Lnc 848	MacKae, Duncan	Cmb 356
Jacob	Lnc 818	Jno.	Lnc 848	Mackdaniel,	
Jacob	Lnc 869	John	Lnc 848	Charles	Edg 223
Luvings see Lewings		Robert	Orn 580	Sally	Edg 223
Lyars, Enoch	Stk 588	Sarah	Lnc 849	Mackdowel, John	Edg 223
Lybork, Barbary	Stk 577	William	Lnc 862	Mackeel, Benjamin	Edg 222
Lyda, Andrew	Bnc 177	Lyttle, Peter	Lnc 878	Mackey, George	Brk 772
John	Bnc 177			James	Brk 772
Lydia, Old	Crr 162			John	Crr 159
Lyle, John	Stk 594	-- M --		Joseph	Prq 657
Peter	Rwn 301			Thomas	Wsh 708
Lyles, Edwin	Hrt 738			see John, Muckey, Wil-	
Jackson	Frn 457	M...l..., Ja...	Ird 611	liam	
Mark	Frn 459	M...ttel, Stephen	Jns 807	Mackings, Nimrod	Hde 373
Mary	Nrt 457	Mabane, David	Glf 677	Mackins, Michael	Mnt 515
Robert	Hlf 324	James	Orn 521	Macklin, Elizabeth	Cmb 373

Name	Loc	Name	Loc	Name	Loc
James	Wke 749	William	Orn 521	Malinder, Rosan	Lnr 16
Matthew	Wke 748	Madling, Jonathan	Rwn 453	Mallard, Comfort	Dpl 436
Mackmillan, Robert	Edg 223	Madox, Tarleton	Cht 162	Daniel	Dpl 400
Macky, John	Srr 677	William	Cht 156	Daniel	Jns 799
Robert	Hde 373	Madra, Joseph	Wke 749	James	Rwn 444
MacLean, Hugh	Cmb 356	Madren, Matthias	Psq 632	John	Dpl 422
Maclemore, Archi-		Madrey, William	Wrr 818	John	Hlf 326
bald	Smp 526	Madrin, John (2)	Psq 631	John	Jns 799
Hesekiah	Smp 526	Thomas	Psq 631	Joseph	Dpl 400
Saml.	Srr 708	Madsworth, Igna-		Losson	Jns 783
West	Smp 510	tious	Mre 41	Thornton	Grv 577
MacLeod, Donald	Cmb 357	Magee, Harmon	Glf 650	Mallary, Stephen	Csw 122
John	Cmb 357	Henry	Wke 747	Mallery, John	Csw 127
MacLeran, Duncan	Cmb 357	James	Jns 799	Stephen	Csw 140
Macley see Menley		Joseph	Wke 750	Thomas	Csw 140
Maclin, John	Wrr 817	Mial	Cmb 381	William	Grv 545
Maclinq, Edmund	Hlf 328	William	Glf 651	see Mullery	
MacMullan, James	Cmb 357	Magelin, Henry	Cht 177	Mallett, Danl.	Nwh 7A
Macom, John	Rth 129	Magempsey, William	Bfr 23	Peter	Cmb 356
Macon, G. Hunt	Wrr 817	Maget, John	Hrt 729	Mallison, Christo-	
Gideon	Frn 448	Maggett, William	Nrt 459	pher	Hde 373
Henry	Wrr 817	Magmess, Benjn.	Rth 129	Gideon	Hde 373
Hunt G.	Wrr 817	Magness, Perry G.	Rth 130	John	Hde 374
John	Rnd 330	Magnus, William	Lnc 897	Thomas	Hde 372
Nathl., Esquire	Wrr 820	Magrego, Cloe	Hlf 326	William	Crv 293
Macorich, Matthew	Brk 777	Maguffer, Jane	Wke 776	Mallory, William	Hlf 326
Macoy, James	Brk 771	John	Wke 749	Malone, Charles	Nrt 463
James	Rwn 403	Magv..fie, Hardy	Wke 747	Danl.	Csw 115
Jeromiah	Brk 774	M..nafey, James	Srr 678	David	Wke 750
Spruce, Esq.	Rwn 289	Mahaffy, William	Bnc 180	John	Nsh 110
Wilson	Rwn 404	Mahalay, William	Cht 218	John	Rck 451
MacPhael, Malcolm	Cmb 376	Maham, Wm.	Csw 139	John	Rth 132
Macphail, Cather-		Mahaney, Elizabeth	Wke 748	John, Capt.	
ine	Cmb 356	James	Wke 748	(Compy.)	Prs 212
Margaret	Cmb 356	Mahee, William	Rth 130	Lewis	Csw 115
MacPhaill, John	Cmb 383	Mahew, John	Ird 657	Mark	Prs 213
MacPherson, John	Cmb 357	Maholland, John	Wke 748	Mildred	Nrt 459
MacQueen, Alexan-		Mahon, Dennis	Rwn 313	Nathan	Csw 132
der	Cmb 356	Mahony, Elizabeth	Hlf 326	Robert	Rth 127
MacRackan, James	Cmb 357	Maide, John	Crv 339	Staples	Csw 116
MacSwain, Angus	Cmb 385	Maiden, Andrew	Ird 636	Thomas	Prs 214
Macy, Barakiel	Glf 689	James	Ird 636	William	Wrr 819
Enoch	Glf 689	John	Ird 636	Wm.	Csw 116
George	Glf 675	Lawrence	Ird 636	Malony, John	Rth 129
Henry	Glf 626	Maidens, John	Grn 611	Maloy, Hugh	Rbs 406
Henry, Jur.	Glf 626	Maiefe, William	Brk 777	John	Rbs 401
Hanah	Glf 682	Mailey, Eve	Rwn 277	John	Rbs 406
Joseph	Srr 676	Main, Henry	Wlk 53	Margaret	Rbs 407
Martha	Glf 630	Mainard, Drewry	Ash 83	Malpass, Hardy	Nwh 9
Matthew	Glf 691	Gibson	Wlk 54	James	Nwh 10
Nathaniel	Glf 689	Jesse	Wlk 55	Jeremiah	Nwh 6A
Paul (2)	Glf 676	William	Wlk 54	John	Nwh 10
Robert	Glf 689	Maine, Richard	Frn 468	Simon	Nwh 10
Robert	Hrt 738	Mainer, John	Cmb 381	Malsbey, Thomas	Ons 181
Rody	Glf 672	William	Orn 586	Malsby see Masley	
Rody	Glf 692	Mainey, Martin	Bnc 179	Malssass see Malpass	
Stephen	Glf 689	Mair, John	Brt 60	Maltbee, Jonathan	Chw 116
Thadius	Glf 680	Samuel	Brt 64	Maltsby, Margaret	Cmb 356
Timothy	Glf 692	Mairs, Timothy	Grn 600	Malven, John	Crv 267
William	Rnd 331	William	Grn 598	Man, Fredk.	Cht 218
Zacheus	Glf 689	Majers, Benjamin	Stk 563	Isam	Cht 218
Madcaff, Joel	Ans 209	John	Cht 201	Jesse	Rnd 331
John	Ans 222	Robert	Stk 591	Rober	Bnc 180
William	Ans 222	Makee, Aaron	Lnc 862	Roland	Cht 190
Madden, George	Orn 582	Makefashion, George,		William	Cht 190
Samuel	Orn 589	Ser.	Crr 162	Man..., Peggey	Crr 156
Stephen	Orn 520	Henery	Crr 162	Manaca, Joseph	Stk 564
Maddin, Daniel	Rth 128	Husse	Crr 162	Manard, Thomas	Mnt 507
Maddocks, William	Ptt 228	Makefashions, Ro-		Mandaville, Yelles	Cmd 109
Maddox, Benn.	Psq 634	bert	Crr 163	Mander, Burgess	Nrt 463
Maddrey, Nathaniel	Nrt 461	Malaby, John	Wke 750	Mandewel, David	Hde 374
Randolph	Nrt 459	William	Wne 846	John	Hde 374
William	Nrt 459	Malden, Claborn	Cht 225	Samuel, Jur.	Hde 374
Maden, Matthew	Prq 643	Malery, Barbara	Ird 646	Samuel, Ser.	Hde 374
Mades, Mary	Jns 807	Charles	Cht 196	Mandril, Solomon	Rth 133
Madinal, Axander	Srr 679	James	Wrr 819	Maner, Aaron	Edg 221
Madkins, John	Csw 145	Malford, Anne	Bld 25	Levi	Edg 221

Sarah	Edg 223	Joseph	Crr 159	Maraign, John	Rck 451
Manerd, John	Mnt 507	Mannering, Andrew	Srr 706	Marbury, Isaac	Mnt 520
Manes, John	Rth 126	Elisha	Srr 678	John	Mnt 518
Maney, James,Esqr.	Hrt 732	Jourden	Srr 679	Leonard	Mnt 518
Mangram, Henry	Rnd 350	Manners, Marry	Orn 589	Luke	Mnt 518
John	Rnd 328	Manney see Mauney		Tabitha	Mnt 519
Ordey	Cht 198	Mannig see Mannis		Marcam, Joseph	Orn 588
William	Mnt 479	Mannin, John	Stk 563	Josiah	Orn 588
Mangrum, Absalom	Grv 520	Samuel	Bnc 179	Richard	Orn 588
Gray	Grv 578	Manning, Benja.	Nsh 110	Thomas	Orn 588
Howel	Grv 577	Charles	Hlf 328	William	Orn 588
James	Grv 523	Edward	Brt 62	see Macam	
James	Orn 586	Hardee	Edg 221	March, Frederick	Rwn 432
John	Grv 522	Hillery	Edg 221	George	Rwn 432
Joseph	Grv 577	Isham	Brt 64	Jacob	Rwn 432
Josiah	Grv 577	Jams	Nsh 110	John	Rwn 432
Lucy	Orn 586	Jesse	Mrt 400	William	Gts 273
Samuel	Grv 523	John	Nsh 111	Marchant, Thos.	Crr 164
Samuel	Orn 586	John, Senr.	Mrt 402	Marchman, John	Crv 261
Manguem, William	Orn 583	Markham	Mrt 402	Marchment see Marcht.	
Mangum, Henry	Hlf 330	Matthew	Nsh 112	Marcht., Elizabeth	Ons 163
Joseph	Wrr 816	Matthew	Nsh 113	Marchus, Jane	Cht 174
Mark	Glf 669	Meriam	Mrt 416	Marcum, Saml.	Wke 748
Mark	Glf 669	Merit	Dpl 414	Marcus, William	Wrr 816
Maning, John	Ptt 261	Mical	Nsh 112	Mardre, James	Brt 60
Reuben	Ptt 262	Moses	Dpl 415	Joseph	Prq 644
Reuben, Senr.	Ptt 264	Pierce	Crv 235	Mardrey, Marey	Wrr 819
Richard	Ptt 264	Pridgion	Nsh 112	Richard	Wrr 818
Mank, Catharine	Brt 90	Reuben	Mrt 402	Maredlin, Charles	Mrt 400
Mankin, Stephen	Srr 708	Saml.	Nsh 113	Miles	Mrt 400
Mankins, Walter	Orn 521	Thos.	Nsh 110	Maremoon, David	Nrt 459
Manley, Aron	Wne 852	William	Edg 223	Francis	Nrt 459
Besel	Cht 158	Willis	Hlf 328	John	Nrt 459
Henry	Wne 852	Willoughby	Nsh 112	Peter	Nrt 459
James	Wne 852	Wm., Junr.	Mrt 402	Robert	Nrt 459
Manlove, George	Glf 676	Wm., Senr.	Mrt 402	Samuel	Nrt 459
Jonathan	Rwn 367	Wm., terts.	Mrt 402	Mares, Elizabeth	Glf 640
William	Rwn 367	Mannis, John	Orn 584	Joseph	Hlf 328
Manly, Asa	Hrt 738	Manns, Francis	Csw 120	William	Edg 222
Hardy	Hlf 330	Manor, Isaac	Smp 509	William	Glf 640
James	Bfr 13	Jacob	Dpl 405	Maress, Aron	Cht 192
John	Nrt 461	James	Mre 40	Marey, Mardrey	Wrr 819
Joseph	Hrt 712	Joseph	Smp 507	Mareysalley, Mrs.	Wrr 818
Moses	Hlf 330	Josiah	Smp 507	Margan, John	Stk 590
Moses	Hrt 712	Nanny	Dpl 404	Margit, John	Crt 66
Moses, Jur.	Hlf 328	Manos, William	Mre 45	Marideth, John	Rwn 356
Samuel	Ird 645	Manous, Abedinego	Mre 76	Maris, John	Cmb 361
Southerland	Nrt 461	Ambrus	Mre 46	John	Glf 691
William	Hlf 330	Daniel	Mre 46	Silas	Glf 681
Mann, Allen	Nsh 110	Meshack	Mre 47	Markam, John	Stk 595
Annal	Cmb 378	Mansfield, Thomas	Stk 585	Thomas	Stk 593
Benjamin	Smp 517	Thos., jr.	Hrt 700	William	Stk 593
Daniel	Nsh 110	Thos., Sen.	Hrt 700	Markett, Benjamin	Jns 801
Denton	Nsh 110	Wm.	Csw 119	Frederick	Jns 801
Edward	Trl 686	Manship, Elijah	Glf 623	Joseph	Jns 801
Fredk.	Cht 224	Mansill, Robert	Stk 564	Markham, Anthony	Psq 633
Jas.	Prs 205	Manson, William	Mck 542	Charles	Psq 638
Jesse	Mnt 515	Manuel, Christo-		Thomas	Psq 626
John	Chw 116	pher	Smp 517	Markison, Kinith	Mre 52
John	Crr 151	Farley	Stk 578	Markland, Jonathan	Rwn 362
John	Frn 448	Henry	Mnt 509	Joseph	Stk 605
Leonard	Crt 83	John	Smp 517	Matthew	Stk 606
Lucey	Wke 749	Levi	Smp 510	Nathaniel	Stk 605
Malachi	Mnt 511	Nicholas	Smp 524	Robert	Stk 606
Peter	Grv 520	William	Stk 578	Marks, Andrew	Lnc 905
Robert	Wrr 821	William	Stk 579	James	Cht 157
Samuel	Trl 684	Manus, John	Ans 216	John	Cht 156
Solomon	Trl 682	Richard	Ans 216	Thomas	Hlf 328
Theodorick	Nrt 459	William	Ans 216	William	Bld 25
Thomas	Hde 373	Mapler, Marmaduke	Glf 624	William	Cht 197
Thomas	Psq 628	Maples, Birrell	Mre 56	Marler, Boling	Edg 223
Thomas	Trl 686	James	Mre 45	Nathan	Edg 221
Thos.	Prs 205	John	Mre 45	Marley, Adam	Orn 584
Will.	Prs 204	Marmaduke	Rnd 331	Alexander	Rnd 329
William	Nrt 459	Thomas	Mre 44	Benjamin	Cht 164
Wm., Junr.	Prs 205	Mapson, Mary	Nwh 3	Caty	Rnd 328
Manner, John	Stk 594	Saml.	Nwh 12A	Henry	Cht 215

James	Smp 507	Isaac	Wrr 820	George	Brk 769
John	Rnd 329	James	Ans 206	George	Cht 169
Marlin, David	Rwn 332	James	Crt 79	George	Cht 195
James, Jur.	Rwn 332	James	Hlf 328	George	Mck 570
James, Senr.	Rwn 332	Jesse	Rwn 362	George	Rwn 404
John, Junr.	Rwn 332	John	Crt 79	George	Srr 677
John, Senr.	Rwn 332	John	Ons 146	George	Srr 678
Joseph	Rwn 332	John	Srr 704	George	Wke 750
Joshua	Ird 611	John	Wke 776	Henry	Orn 520
Robert	Lnc 831	Jonathan	Ons 147	Henry	Orn 521
Marlo, Smallwood	Wrr 819	Joseph	Ons 145	Henry	Wlk 54
Marlor, Thomas	Rth 130	Mary	Crv 257	Higlety	Lnr 17
Marlow, David	Bnc 180	Moses	Wke 748	Hosea	Hde 373
Elijah	Ird 636	Purnall	Ons 145	Hugh	Stk 594
James	Brk 778	Richard	Stk 562	Isbel	Rck 436
John	Hlf 326	Robert	Mck 573	Israel	Nrt 459
John, B.H.	Wlk 55	Saml.	Wrr 819	Jacob	Brk 771
Marcus	Ird 612	Stephen	Wrr 819	James	Bnc 181
Thomas	Ird 636	Sterling	Hlf 330	James	Cbr 703
Maroon, Jacob	Rth 130	Tabitha	Wrr 821	James	Glf 690
John	Rth 130	Thomas	Crv 231	James	Lnr 17
Marr, John	Rck 482	Thomas	Gts 272	James	Lnc 819
John	Wke 748	Thomas	Rwn 400	James	Lnc 825
Richard	Rck 482	William	Ans 206	James	Lnc 838
Marrice see Morice		William	Crt 77	James	Rck 436
Marrill, Jonathan	Rwn 410	William	Cht 216	James	Stk 562
Marriner, Dempsey	Trl 686	William	Grv 511	James	Stk 588
James	Trl 690	William	Srr 678	James	Stk 612
John	Trl 686	William T.	Rwn 417	James	Srr 675
John, Senr.	Trl 690	Marshel, Sack	Prs 212	James	Wlk 52
Peter (2)	Trl 686	Marshell, Charles	Wrr 816	Jeremiah	Crv 231
Tabitha (2)	Trl 686	Martin	Stk 566	Jesse	Ans 201
Marris, Willis	Crr 158	Marshwell, Robert	Stk 596	Jesse	Brk 769
Marsh, Charles	Cht 151	Marten, Richard	Srr 677	Jesse	Gts 273
Daniel	Bfr 23	Stephen	Srr 676	Jesse	Rth 133
David W.	Edg 221	Marthena, Amos	Ans 236	Jno.	Lnc 849
Ezekel	Srr 678	Edmond	Ans 223	Jobe, Se.	Srr 678
James	Cmb 380	James	Ans 217	John	Ans 223
John	Cmb 380	Martim, Asa	Stk 619	John	Brt 64
John, Senr.	Srr 675	Martin, Abraham	Stk 565	John (2)	Brk 771
Jonathan	Bfr 24	Abraham, Ser.	Stk 566	John	Crv 277
Thomas	Nrt 461	Abram	Dpl 440	John	Crv 297
Thomas	Smp 527	Absalom	Crt 82	John	Frn 468
W. David	Edg 173	Adam	Cht 183	John	Mck 575
W. David	Edg 221	Adam	Cht 195	John	Mck 586
Marshal, Benjamin	Stk 566	Alexander	Cmb 365	John	Mnt 518
David	Rth 130	Alexander	Cmb 388	John	Mre 56
Frederick Wm.	Stk 599	Alexander	Rck 457	John	Mre 58
John	Grv 570	Amy	Wne 872	John	Nwh 2A
John	Nwh 10A	Andw.	Rck 471	John	Nwh 5A
John	Rth 130	Ann	Jns 789	John	Orn 585
Joseph	Srr 704	Anna	Crv 297	John	Ptt 261
Richard	Stk 591	Anny	Rck 436	John	Rch 244
Sterling	Hlf 358	Asa	Rwn 417	John	Rch 270
Thomas	Hlf 326	Asa	Rwn 426	John	Rck 471
Will.	Nwh 10A	Baily	Rck 471	John (2)	Rth 132
William	Orn 581	Benjamin	Bfr 14	John	Stk 562
William	Rth 130	Benjamin	Crv 241	John	Stk 565
Marshall, Aaron	Srr 676	Benjamin	Lnr 16	John	Srr 677
Alexand.	Hlf 330	Benjamin	Rck 491	John	Srr 705
Allen	Rnd 328	Benjamin	Wlk 52	John	Wke 750
Anney	Wrr 819	Benjamin	Wlk 54	John (2)	Wlk 53
Benjamin	Hlf 328	Benjn. H.	Wlk 55	John	Wlk 54
Benjamin	Rnd 328	Bowes	Ptt 237	John, Junr.	Nrt 459
Benjn.	Cht 217	Caleb	Orn 585	John, Junr.	Wke 750
Charles	Wrr 819	Charles	Wne 873	John, Senr.	Nrt 459
David	Wrr 819	Clia	Brk 773	John, S.F.	Stk 563
Dixon	Wrr 818	Daniel	Rch 250	John, Ters.	Nrt 459
Elizabeth	Hlf 328	David	Crv 259	John H.	Ans 201
Ezekiel	Wrr 819	David	Stk 619	John P.	Rbs 395
Frederick Wm.	Stk 625	David	Wke 747	Jonathan	Stk 563
George	Ird 611	Edmd.	Mrt 400	Joseph	Rck 491
Hannah	Srr 679	Elizabeth	Bfr 14	Joseph	Wne 860
Humphrey	Rwn 277	Ephraim	Ird 656	Joshua	Glf 649
Humphry	Rwn 289	Etheldred	Nrt 459	Joshua	Wlk 53
Ichabad	Mnt 488	Francis X.	Crv 239	Josias	Lnc 839
Isaac	Ons 147	Gabriel	Gts 273	Kinchen	Ans 204

Leonard	Rck 450	Thomas	Mre 58	Jeremiah	Hde 373
Lewis	Rnd 330	Marting, Moses	Crr 158	Jesse	Nsh 111
Lewis	Rth 128	Martinlere, Lucy	Cmb 372	John	Crv 297
Lorcah	Csw 122	Masbey see Masley		John	Cmb 366
Martha	Glf 650	Mase, William	Crt 81	John	Hde 373
Martin	Mre 58	Masemore, James	Srr 676	John	Ons 165
Martin	Rch 271	Mash, Daniel	Srr 676	John	Prs 209
Martin	Rth 127	Derias	Rnd 330	John	Wrr 817
Mary	Rck 453	Ebenezer	Ans 235	Jones	Hde 372
Michael	Brt 64	Ezakel	Srr 675	Joshua	Crt 63
Moses	Bnc 178	George	Hrt 717	Josiah	Hde 373
Murdock	Mre 50	John, Jur.	Srr 676	Lidy	Brn 15A
Nancy	Lnr 17	Leonard	Glf 625	Lydda	Hlf 328
Nancy	Wlk 54	Minar	Srr 676	Maik	Nsh 110
Neal	Rch 270	Robert	Cht 174	Martha	Nwh 5A
Nicholas	Srr 677	Samuel	Srr 679	Mary	Hde 373
Obediah	Srr 678	Simson	Ans 236	Mathew	Smp 521
P. John	Rbs 395	Solomon	Ans 235	Nancy	Bfr 13
Partrick	Hlf 328	Thomas	Ans 235	Patrick	Prs 210
Paul	Wne 845	Thomas	Srr 676	Peter	Brk 772
Payton	Csw 125	William	Cht 195	Peter	Lnc 891
Peter	Rck 465	William	Glf 625	Philip	Orn 521
Philip	Brk 769	William	Glf 654	Ralph	Nsh 111
Philip	Brk 772	Wilson	Srr 676	Richard	Cht 168
Rhody	Stk 564	Mashaw, Matthew	Wsh 708	Richard	Hlf 328
Richard	Bfr 14	Mashboarn, Mathew	Cht 158	Richard	Ons 165
Richard	Cbr 699	Mashborn, Matthew	Hrt 735	Ruben	Rwn 375
Richd.	Csw 136	Mashburn, Benja.	Ons 170	Saml.	Nwh 4
Richd.	Rck 486	Benjamin	Ons 182	Solomon	Glf 661
Robert	Bld 28	Christopher	Dpl 441	Thomas	Ans 204
Robert	Cbr 684	Daniel	Wke 747	Thomas	Hlf 328
Robert	Rck 484	David	Brk 771	Thomas	Hde 372
Robert	Stk 565	David	Brk 774	Thomas	Rck 466
Robert	Wlk 54	Drury	Brk 771	Thomas, Jur.	Hde 373
Rothas	Hde 373	Elisha	Brk 774	Thomas, M. Shat	Hde 373
Salley	Mrt 402	James	Jns 811	Uriah	Crt 63
Saml.	Lnc 825	James	Ons 169	Widow	Mck 525
Samuel	Mck 571	James, Sr.	Brk 771	Widow	Mck 606
Sarah	Bld 33	Levi	Brk 774	William	Cht 201
Solomon	Ird 625	Mary	Dpl 428	William	Ird 652
Tamer	Crt 81	Mathew	Dpl 417	William	Rck 479
Thomas	Brk 776	Matthew	Brk 771	Wm.	Nsh 110
Thomas	Mck 535	Thos.	Ons 170	Masoy see Macoy	
Thomas	Nrt 459	William	Brk 770	Mass, Thomas	Srr 677
Thomas	Rth 132	Masheck, George	Srr 678	Massa, John	Jhn 747
Vale., Ser.	Srr 677	Mashham, Thomas	Stk 584	Massenburg, Cargil	Wke 776
Vaul	Stk 562	Masingell, Ann	Nsh 112	Massengale, Daniel	Brt 64
Vaul	Stk 590	Mask, Dudley	Rch 247	Etheldred	Jhn 772
Vaul	Srr 677	John	Mnt 465	George	Jhn 770
Vaulintine	Srr 677	John	Rch 265	George, Sr.	Jhn 771
Watt	Rck 476	John D.	Rch 265	Henry	Jhn 772
William	Bfr 14	Pleasant M.	Rch 255	Kinchin	Brt 90
William	Cht 187	Masley, Thomas	Ons 180	Robert	Jhn 772
William	Frn 467	Mason, Abner	Nsh 112	Massengill, Anny	Nsh 110
William	Glf 649	Abraham	Rwn 375	James	Nsh 110
William	Hlf 326	Archibald	Trl 686	John	Nsh 110
William	Ird 636	Benjamin	Crv 297	Massey, Adkins	Trl 694
William	Lnc 897	Benjamin	Hde 373	Demsey	Wke 747
William	Mre 77	Benjamin	Nsh 113	Frederick	Trl 684
William	Orn 520	Caleb, Jur.	Hde 373	Frederick	Wke 751
William	Orn 585	Caleb, Senr.	Hde 374	Henry	Wke 749
William	Rck 472	Christopher,		Hezekiah	Wke 751
William	Stk 563	Ser.	Hde 373	James	Cht 155
William	Stk 584	Daniel	Hlf 328	James	Nrt 461
William	Srr 675	David	Crt 63	John	Cht 185
William	Srr 679	Foster	Nsh 111	John	Wke 751
William	Wke 750	Frederick	Hde 372	Josiah	Wke 751
William	Wne 872	Henry	Cht 197	Lucey	Wrr 817
William J.	Grv 515	Henry	Nsh 112	Mark	Lnc 843
Woody	Wke 748	Henry	Orn 583	Mary	Frn 452
Wm.	Lnc 839	James	Hde 373	Nathan	Wke 751
Wm.	Mrt 401	James	Mck 540	Peggy	Cht 158
Zaccheus	Nrt 459	James	Orn 519	Raif	Jhn 749
Zacha.	Cht 167	James, Ser.	Hde 373	Richard	Frn 483
see Marlin		James, Ters.	Hde 373	Richard	Wke 747
Martindale, Samuel	Mre 57	Jeams	Crr 152	Richd., Senr.	Wke 749
Stephen	Dpl 414	Jemima	Nrt 461	Samuel	Wke 750

Name	Ref	Name	Ref	Name	Ref
Thomas	Wke 751	William	Dpl 402	Thos., Senr.	Mre 75
William	Jhn 748	William	Edg 173	Vines	Csw 125
William	Wke 751	William	Edg 221	William	Cmb 384
Massick, Richard	Srr 675	William	Rnd 330	William	Glf 622
Massingale, Henry	Nrt 461	William	Wlk 54	William	Glf 631
Joseph	Bld 7	see Methews		William	Glf 670
Joseph	Jhn 748	Mathew's, Juda	Grn 597	William, Esqr.	Mck 599
Massingell, Eliza-		Mathewson, Nathan,		William, Senr.	Gts 273
beth	Nsh 112	Esqr.	Edg 173	Wm.	Rck 439
Jams	Nsh 112	Nathan, Esqr.	Edg 221	Wm., Junr.	Gts 273
Masson, James	Cht 152	Mathias see Methias		Matthewson, Alexr.	Ird 631
Massy, Abner	Orn 589	Mathis, Claborn	Cht 187	Daniel	Ird 631
Ann	Csw 143	Kinchen	Cht 169	Daniel	Ird 644
Bethiah	Dpl 404	Lewis	Cht 160	Daniel	Mnt 463
Gier	Ird 636	Nancy	Cht 209	Daniel	Mnt 467
Howel	Csw 142	Mathus, James	Srr 679	George	Ird 625
James	Orn 582	Matins, James	Brk 775	Matthias, Isaiah	Prq 656
Jemima	Orn 589	Matlock, Nicholas	Csw 112	John	Prq 652
Jordan	Csw 130	Matterson, William	Orn 587	Thomas	Chw 123
Mackner	Rck 447	Matthew, Thomas	Stk 580	Matthis, Josiah	Rwn 379
Nathan	Rck 456	Matthew & Wright	Cmd 106	Luke	Mrt 400
Samuel	Orn 589	Matthews, Alexan-		Matthowes, Aaron	Srr 675
Thomas	Orn 589	der	Rbs 396	Matthus, Benjamin	Stk 606
Thomas	Rck 441	Andrew	Gts 273	William	Stk 606
Master, Aaron	Lnc 872	Andrew	Mck 596	Mattocks, John	Ons 140
John	Cbr 718	Anthony	Gts 272	Matton, James	Csw 134
Nicholass	Srr 708	Anthony, Junr.	Gts 272	Mattox, Samuel	Hlf 326
Masters, Barsheba	Wlk 54	Barlt.	Csw 96	William	Hlf 326
Enoch	Crv 293	Bartlett	Csw 148	Maucum, Agnis	Crv 245
George	Rwn 337	Cline W.	Gts 272	Maudlen, Jesse	Rnd 330
Henry	Brk 776	Cornelius	Wke 750	Joseph	Rnd 330
Hilery	Srr 679	Daniel	Rbs 403	Maudlin, Benjamin	Rnd 332
Jacob	Brk 776	David	Cmb 392	John	Rnd 332
James	Srr 677	David	Glf 621	Nathan	Mrt 402
John	Cbr 687	David	Wke 749	Maudling, Dempsey	Brt 62
John	Wlk 54	Dolly	Cmb 386	Maughon, John	Nrt 461
Joseph	Hde 373	Edmond	Hrt 721	Mildred	Nrt 461
M.	Srr 709	Eliza	Grv 567	Peyton	Nrt 459
Michael	Lnc 856	Elzekiak	Prs 210	Thomas	Nrt 461
Susanna	Crv 299	George	Rch 259	Maulden, Tucker	Jns 787
Thomas	Crv 241	George	Rch 269	Maultsby, Thomas	Bld 25
Mastin, John	Stk 597	Gilbert	Hlf 330	Maund, William	Crr 140
Matthew	Stk 597	Hardy	Cmb 392	Mauney, Adam	Lnc 894
Matthias	Stk 606	Isham	Hlf 328	Christian	Lnc 897
Mataris, Charles	Rwn 410	Jacob (2)	Cmb 375	George	Lnc 819
Mataw, John Peter	Rwn 417	James	Hlf 328	Jacob	Lnc 818
Matchet, John	Dpl 437	James	Mck 546	John	Lnc 818
William	Dpl 402	James	Mre 74	Valentine	Lnc 819
Mater, James	Rck 437	James	Mre 75	Mavis, William	Ird 651
Matheril, Saml.	Csw 119	James	Stk 562	Mawdrich, Bridgett	Hde 374
Matherly, John	Rwn 417	Jiles	Ptt 260	Maxfield, Eliza-	
Mathers, David	Mck 548	John	Cmb 366	beth	Glf 656
Mathew, Richard	Psq 635	John	Grv 582	Mary	Wne 873
Mathews, Ancel	Wlk 54	John	Mck 546	Robert	Glf 657
Arthur	Dpl 419	John	Mck 584	William	Glf 659
Daniel	Rth 126	John	Mck 603	Maxwell, Benjamin	Rwn 427
Jacob	Dpl 431	John	Nrt 461	Benjamin	Mck 562
James	Dpl 404	John	Rch 260	David	Rwn 427
James	Smp 516	John	Rch 267	Henry	Dpl 436
Jemima	Edg 222	John	Rbs 405	James	Ash 84
John	Dpl 402	John	Rck 470	James	Bfr 14
John	Dpl 419	Joseph	Ptt 273	James	Dpl 430
John	Lnc 878	Little	Grv 559	James, Senr.	Mck 606
John	Mre 62	Mary	Nsh 111	John	Ash 83
John	Nsh 111	Mathew	Gts 273	John	Dpl 405
John	Rth 132	Moses	Hlf 328	John	Glf 659
John, Jun.	Mre 67	Penelope	Gts 272	Joseph	Bnc 180
Lazarus	Smp 534	Richard	Hlf 328	Joseph	Mck 568
Mary	Smp 533	Richard	Hrt 721	Peter	Nwh 3
Musendine	Ird 672	Robert	Glf 646	Sidney	Ash 83
Nancy	Wlk 54	Robert	Ird 665	Thomas	Smp 523
Normon	Mre 58	Robert	Mck 540	Thomas, Junr.	Rwn 426
Reuben	Srr 678	Sally	Rch 261	Thomas, Senr.	Rwn 426
Stap	Wlk 53	Tandy	Stk 565	Widow	Mck 568
Stephen	Mre 40	Thomas	Jhn 762	William	Ash 83
Thomas	Smp 534	Thomas	Rck 456	May, Abnor	Rwn 427
Will.	Nwh 11A	Thomas	Stk 592	Absalom	Wke 747

Allen	Ptt 291	James	Bfr 14	McAlpin, Alexander	Rbs 396
Benjamin	Ptt 267	John	Crt 59	Daniel	Cmb 370
Benjamin	Ptt 292	John W.	Edg 221	Daniel	Cmb 386
Benjamin,Senior	Ptt 267	Jolly	Ptt 233	Duncan	Cmb 363
Charles	Wke 747	Joseph	Edg 221	John	Cmb 369
Danl.	Orn 583	Joseph	Prq 654	Malcom	Rbs 401
David	Ash 83	Joseph	Prq 656	Neill	Rbs 396
Enock	Wrr 819	Joseph, Senr.	Edg 222	Neill	Rbs 402
Frederick	Ptt 291	Levi	Edg 221	McAlroy, Wm.	Rck 469
George	Glf 643	Micajah	Edg 221	Mcaning, Lewis	Stk 625
Henry	Cht 157	Nathan, Colo.	Edg 223	McAnly, William	Mre 66
Isaac	Rwn 444	Peter	Ptt 233	McAnnel, Joseph	Stk 563
Jacob (2)	Ash 83	Peter, junior	Ptt 261	McAnully, William	Cbr 705
Jacob	Ptt 291	Robert	Csw 98	MCarn, Archibald	Rch 253
Jacob, junr.	Ash 83	Sinnington	Edg 221	John	Rch 253
James	Bnc 179	Sterling	Ptt 260	MCarren, Duncan	Rch 253
James	Cht 157	W. John	Edg 221	MCarrin, Daniel	Rch 254
James	Ptt 291	William	Ptt 267	Hugh, Jr.	Rch 254
James, Sr.	Bnc 180	Mays, Betty	Frn 452	Hugh, Sr.	Rch 254
John	Ans 204	David	Wlk 54	MCarson, Duncan	Rch 253
John	Bnc 179	Elijah	Mck 593	McArter, Alexander	Mnt 488
John	Orn 581	John	Brk 776	McArthur, Alexan-	
John	Ptt 292	John	Brk 777	der	Cmb 393
John	Rck 442	Matthew	Ans 204	Alexander	Rbs 398
John	Wke 747	Thomas	Brk 777	Alexander (2)	Rbs 403
John, B.	Ans 213	William	Frn 454	Daniel	Cmb 393
John, Junr.	Ans 211	William	Lnc 865	Daniel	Cmb 394
John, Junr.	Ans 228	Mayton, John	Wke 747	Daniel, (Mull.)	Cmb 363
John, Senr.	Ans 216	Maze, Benjamin	Ird 665	Duncan	Rbs 390
Joseph	Cht 177	Mazingo, Elizabeth	Lnr 16	James	Rbs 390
Joseph	Rwn 444	Pearce	Lnr 16	Jennet	Bld 37
Littlebury	Jhn 764	Mazy, Shephen	Cht 183	John	Rbs 397
Ludwick	Orn 581	McAdam, Hugh	Orn 519	John	Rbs 398
Mary) Danl.	Orn 584	Hugh, jn.	Orn 584	Peter	Cmb 392
Nathan, Junior	Ptt 280	Isaac	Orn 584	Peter	Rbs 390
Philip	Ans 212	James (2)	Orn 584	Peter	Rbs 398
Pleasant	Ans 214	John	Orn 584	MCartle, Malcolm	Rch 246
Richard	Wne 863	Joseph	Orn 584	McArty, James	Mre 70
Robert	Nsh 110	William	Orn 584	MCaskle, Daniel	Rch 243
Samuel	Orn 583	McAden, John	Csw 110	Daniel	Rch 246
Shadrach	Ptt 275	William	Csw 108	Daniel	Rch 252
Thomas	Bnc 179	McAdow, David	Glf 668	John	Rch 250
Thomas	Cht 177	James, Jur.	Glf 632	John	Rch 251
Thomas	Wke 747	James, Senr.	Glf 632	Peter	Rch 246
William	Ash 83	John	Glf 671	MCastle, Anguist	Rch 242
William	Bnc 179	William	Glf 621	Finley	Rch 263
William	Wke 747	McAlester, Ezekiel	Csw 149	John	Rch 263
William, C.P.	Ans 212	McAleston, John	Rck 457	John, Jr.	Rch 263
William, sgt.	Ans 212	MCall, Alexr.		Kenith	Rch 247
Maya see Moye		MCall, Alexr.	Rch 251	McAtee, Edmond	Rwn 410
Maybee, John	Stk 584	Daniel	Rch 251	McAthatan, William	Glf 666
Mayberry, Fredrick	Wlk 54	Daniel	Rch 270	McAtie, Zachariah	Rwn 381
Maye, William	Bfr 14	Daniel, Jr.	Rch 250	McAuley, John	Cmb 363
Mayfield, Abreham	Wrr 818	Duncan (2)	Rch 244	McCauley, Malcolm	Rch 261
Ben.	Frn 465	Duncan	Rch 253	McAuly, John	Mre 69
Edmond	Wrr 818	Duncan	Rch 270	Murdock	Mre 59
John	Grv 556	Hugh	Rch 244	Murdock	Mre 71
John	Wrr 818	Hugh	Rch 250	Nancy	Mre 40
John, jr.	Wrr 818	John	Rch 247	McBain, Daniel	Cht 224
Obey	Grv 557	John	Rch 250	McBane, Catharine	Orn 519
Stephen	Cbr 689	John	Rch 253	McBath, Walter	Mre 59
Thomas	Wrr 817	John, Jr.	Rch 268	McBeam, Andrew	Orn 588
Valentine	Grv 556	Nelly	Rch 244	McBean, William	Lnr 35
William	Wrr 819	Paul	Rch 250	McBee, Varadry	Rth 128
Maynard, Benja.	Wke 750	Paul	Rch 256	McBirth, John	Smp 523
George	Wke 748	MCaller, Neal	Rch 251	McBoyd, Pattrack	Mck 530
Jacob	Wke 748	McAllester, Alexr.	Nwh 10A	Thomas	Mck 532
Thomas	Ans 208	Charls.	Nwh 10A	McBrayer, David	Bnc 181
William	Ans 214	James	Cmb 367	Iccabud	Bnc 180
William	Wke 748	Janet	Cmb 376	James	Bnc 179
Wm., Senr.	Wke 747	McAllister, Alexan-		Samuel	Bnc 180
Mayner, Hannah	Hrt 738	der	Cmb 386	McBred, Elisha	Cmd 97
Mayo, Benjamin	Frn 451	Anne	Cmb 373	McBrian, John	Rwn 443
Benjamin	Ptt 254	Charles	Cmb 380	McBride, Angus	Rbs 400
David	Edg 221	Hector (2)	Cmb 368	Archd.	Bld 26
Drewry	Edg 221	McAllum, Dunkin	Mre 62	Archibald	Rbs 400
Frederick	Edg 221	McAlpan, Angus	Cmb 370	Archibald	Rbs 404

David	Bnc 178	Elizabeth	Dpl 432	McCisick, James	Ird 651		
Duncan	Rbs 401	McCamerlin, Daniel	Smp 498	John	Ird 650		
Edward	Wke 750	McCammon, Joseph	Mck 594	McClain, Darcis	Glf 646		
Francis	Rck 455	McCamon, Widow	Mck 591	Donald	Ird 646		
Isaiah	Glf 664	McCamy, Francis	Orn 582	John	Glf 633		
Isaiah	Rck 446	Robert	Glf 650	John	Ird 611		
James	Wlk 53	McCandless, John	Orn 588	John	Ird 646		
John	Ash 84	William	Orn 587	John	Psq 632		
John	Glf 635	McCane, Hance	Mck 591	John A.	Psq 626		
John	Glf 646	Hugh	Mck 591	Jos.	Rck 449		
John	Rck 481	Hugh, Junr.	Mck 591	Joseph, Jur.	Glf 634		
John	Rwn 410	John	Mck 591	Joseph, Senr.	Glf 634		
John	Stk 609	Joseph	Mck 592	Marshal	Glf 646		
Nevin	Rbs 407	William	Mck 591	Moses	Glf 661		
Peter	Bld 41	McCann, Hugh	Dpl 436	Robert	Glf 646		
Robert	Mck 602	Mary	Dpl 421	Smauel	Glf 642		
Samuel	Rck 470	Nathaniel	Dpl 436	William	Smp 507		
William	Ird 651	Thomas	Dpl 421	see McCain			
William	Srr 676	William	Dpl 422	McClaine, George	Mck 555		
William	Srr 679	McCannon, Cor-		McClakin, James	Mck 601		
William	Wlk 53	nelius	Rwn 453	McClaming, Elijah	Nwh 3		
MCbride, Archble	Rch 271	Mary	Prq 656	McClammey, Joshua	Ons 162		
Cristian	Rch 252	McCarew see McCoren		McClammy, Geo.	Nwh 12		
Isham	Wne 859	McCarney, Henry	Csw 99	Mark	Nwh 11A		
McBroom, James	Rwn 317	McCarrel, Izrael	Rck 453	Mary	Nwh 12		
McBryde, Alexd.	Mre 65	John	Orn 583	Wonny	Nwh 8		
Archd.	Mre 45	Margarett	Rck 453	McClanachan, Reu-			
McBryer, William	Rth 130	McCarroll, Thomas	Cht 226	bin	Ird 646		
McCabe, Elizabeth	Trl 686	William	Rck 462	McClane, Duncan	Mnt 463		
James	Wsh 708	McCarson, David	Bnc 178	George	Mck 570		
John	Chw 122	McCarter, Aaron	Stk 565	John	Ird 644		
John, Jur.	Bfr 13	Charles	Cmd 105	John	Rwn 322		
John, Senr.	Bfr 13	McCartey, Charles	Crr 164	John	Rwn 337		
Susannah	Trl 680	James	Bnc 178	Thos.	Lnc 833		
McCafferty, James	Crv 267	McCarty, Archabald	Hde 373	Widow	Cbr 681		
Jane	Crv 257	James	Srr 679	William	Rwn 337		
Samuel M.	Crv 283	John	Srr 679	Wm.	Lnc 831		
McCain, Alex	Csw 112	Mary	Hde 373	McClanhan, Ruth	Chw 124		
Hance	Glf 666	Timothy	Glf 652	McClannel, Phillip	Nrt 459		
John	Csw 112	McCarver, James	Lnc 843	McClannin, Enoch	Crr 162		
John, Senr.	Glf 646	Jno.	Lnc 843	George	Ons 164		
Michael	Rwn 400	McCaskey, Edwd.	Mrt 401	McClarahan, Wil-			
McCain, Agness	Prs 207	McCaskil, Alexan-		liam	Ird 615		
McCaleb, Andrew	Stk 563	der	Mnt 471	McClarin, Alex	Rck 440		
James	Ash 84	Daniel	Mnt 474	McClary, Alexander	Cbr 699		
James	Bld 35	Daniel, Junr.	Mnt 463	Andrew	Mck 538		
James	Cbr 683	Finly	Mnt 467	Andrew	Orn 519		
McCalep, Hugh	Stk 563	Francis	Mck 603	John	Mck 574		
McCall, Alax	Stk 611	John	Mnt 472	Samuel	Ird 656		
Alexr.	Lnc 849	John	Mnt 474	Thomas	Mck 559		
Dugald	Cmb 366	John, Junr.	Mnt 467	Widow	Mck 524		
Hugh	Cmb 364	John, Senr.	Mnt 464	Widow (2)	Mck 547		
James	Bnc 181	McCaskill, Anguish	Mre 57	Widow	Mck 574		
James	Glf 637	Danile	Mnt 463	William	Mck 532		
James	Mck 557	John	Mre 57	McClatchy, Hamil-			
Jno., Senr.	Lnc 826	Nehemiah	Mnt 491	ton	Ird 641		
John	Cmb 365	McCasland, Harman	Cht 183	McClaughlin, ...	Srr 678		
John	Lnc 849	John	Cht 183	Joseph	Srr 678		
John	Lnc 859	William	Lnc 819	McClea, Hugh	Srr 706		
Robert	Rth 131	McCaslin, Matthew	Lnc 819	McCleary, Michael	Mck 532		
Soloman	Rbs 392	McCaucha, John	Ird 662	Widow	Mck 606		
William, Esqr.	Mck 604	McCauley, Andrew	Orn 519	McCleland, John	Ird 672		
McCalla, Anguis	Mnt 491	John	Orn 495	McClellan, William	Rck 485		
Mary	Hlf 326	Mathew	Orn 490	McClelland, John	Ird 631		
McCalley, John	Orn 589	McCauly, Farquar	Mnt 491	John	Ird 674		
Matthew	Orn 585	John	Mnt 463	John	Rwn 289		
William	Orn 583	McCauslin, James	Mck 580	William	Ird 640		
McCallister, James	Lnc 826	James	Rnd 330	McClellon, Jno.	Lnc 839		
McCallom, James C.	Orn 520	McCawn, James	Stk 612	McClenchan, John	Grv 533		
McCallon, James	Lnc 893	McCay, Beaty	Mck 550	McClendal, James	Smp 521		
McCallum, David	Rck 477	James	Mck 523	Jesse	Smp 508		
Dunkin	Mre 53	John	Mck 551	McClendon, Burwell	Lnr 16		
Isaac	Wke 750	McCerny, Wilson	Brk 770	Edmond	Mnt 487		
John	Mre 53	McCharon, Hector	Cbr 677	John	Mnt 502		
McCally, Daniel	Mck 573	McChimon see McThimon		McClennen, William	Ons 165		
James	Orn 583	McCinery, George	Brk 775	McClennon, Alexan-			
McCalop, Archibald	Crv 241	Thomas	Brk 775	der	Mnt 463		

Isaac	Cbr	707	McComack, James	Wke	748	July	Prq	644
John	Cbr	707	McCombs, Alexander	Grn	591	Keziah	Cmd	94
Reneth	Mnt	463	James	Mck	576	Lewis	Crv	331
McCleod, Duncan	Mnt	463	James	Mck	606	Malichi	Cmd	93
Norman, M.	Mnt	463	Major	Rth	130	Malichi	Cmd	99
McClese, John	Trl	680	Robert	Lnc	830	Mary	Brn	19A
McClester, Betty	Lnc	827	Robert	Mck	606	Samuel	Cmd	108
Daniel	Mnt	515	Shaderach	Rth	129	Sarah	Cmd	94
Eliza	Lnc	827	Shaderach	Rth	130	William	Cmd	94
Jno.	Lnc	827	Widow	Mck	525	William, Jur.	Crv	331
John	Mnt	511	Widow	Mck	606	William, Senr.	Crv	331
Joseph	Mnt	498	McCommid, Isaac	Srr	677	see Macoy		
McClintick, John	Glf	666	McCon, John	Crt	77	McCracken, Abigal	Orn	583
Robert	Glf	635	McCondki, John	Smp	503	Robert	Glf	693
McClintock, John	Glf	672	McCone, William	Hrt	721	McCrackin, Ephraim	Rwn	317
Robert	Glf	671	McConkey, Ruth	Bld	31	George	Mck	573
William	Glf	672	McConnell, Benja-			James	Mck	534
McCloud, Catherine	Srr	679	min	Ird	657	Joseph	Rwn	327
Daniel	Mnt	464	Catherine	Ird	622	McCracking, Alexan-		
Daniel	Smp	514	John	Ird	622	der	Orn	520
Hugh	Mnt	467	John (2)	Ird	657	John	Orn	520
John	Mnt	466	John	Rwn	393	John	Orn	521
John	Mnt	472	William	Ird	612	Robbert	Rnd	332
John	Smp	496	William	Ird	615	Samuel	Orn	521
Kneal	Smp	497	William	Ird	616	Thomas	Orn	521
Murdoch	Mnt	468	McConoughy, James	Rwn	318	McCrady, John	Crt	92
Norman	Mnt	471	Samuel	Rwn	318	McCraine see McCranie		
Reuben	Hde	373	McCord, James	Ird	636	McCrakin, John	Rwn	327
McClure, Alexander	Brk	771	John	Mck	523	McCraking, William	Rnd	329
Andrew	Brk	771	Robert	Mck	533	McCraney, Daniel	Rbs	402
David	Brk	771	William (2)	Mck	533	John	Rbs	405
Francis	Brk	771	William	Mck	536	Mary	Cmb	393
Henry	Orn	520	McCoren, Daniel	Cmb	367	Neill	Rbs	397
John	Lnc	832	McCoriedale, Dan-			McCranie, Archi-		
John	Mck	533	iel	Cmb	384	bald	Cmb	375
John, Jur.	Mck	523	McCorkle, Alexander			Daniel	Cmb	363
John, Sen.	Mck	524	(2)	Rwn	322	Hugh	Cmb	377
Matthew	Mck	561	Francis	Lnc	864	Murdoch	Cmb	375
Thomas	Mck	523	John, Esqr.	Mck	594	Murdoch	Cmb	377
William	Brk	770	Matthew	Mck	595	McCrannie, Malcolm	Cmb	361
William	Crv	335	Robert	Ird	650	McCrarey, Boyd	Bnc	180
William	Mck	550	Samuel	Rwn	318	William	Bnc	179
Wm.	Lnc	832	Thomas	Mck	561	McCrary, Boyd	Rwn	367
McColister, Mal-			Widow	Rwn	322	Hugh	Rwn	393
colm	Dpl	407	McCormack, Cather-			John	Ird	617
McColl, Alexr.	Bld	18	ine	Lnc	878	McCraven, James,		
Daniel	Cmb	370	John	Cmb	367	Junr.	Mck	606
Dugald	Cmb	387	Robert	Mck	539	John, Junr.	Mck	606
Duncan	Bld	20	McCormaig, Duncan	Rbs	394	McCravin, John,		
McCollam, John	Srr	679	Gilbert	Rbs	394	Senr.	Mck	606
McCollester, Eliza-			John	Rbs	393	McCraw, Jacob	Srr	677
beth	Bfr	23	Nepsey	Rbs	393	Samuel	Srr	677
McColloch, Alexr.	Nwh	11	McCorquodale, Dan-			McCray, Alexander	Mnt	491
R.M.	Bld	34	iel	Smp	496	Collin	Mnt	491
McCollum, Alexr.	Bld	24	John	Smp	496	Daniel	Mnt	491
Andrew	Rwn	337	McCorvey, Findley	Rbs	396	Finly	Mnt	491
Angus	Rbs	393	John	Rbs	396	George	Orn	519
Daniel	Rbs	391	Neill	Rbs	396	Robert	Glf	637
Daniel	Rbs	393	McCotter, Ann	Crv	279	William	Cbr	702
Dougle	Mnt	463	Archibald	Crv	279	McCree, Arthur	Cbr	681
Duncan (2)	Rbs	399	Jesse	Crt	61	McCrery, James	Ird	615
Edward	Mnt	476	McCoulskey, Niel	Bld	19	McCresick, Thomas	Orn	583
Edward	Rbs	392	McCoulsky, Duncan	Bld	20	McCrimmin, Archa-		
Henry	Orn	491	James	Bld	15	bald	Rbs	392
Hugh	Rbs	393	McCoune, Thomas	Cbr	684	Daniel	Rbs	392
Isaac	Rnd	332	McCown, Thomas	Rth	133	McCrory, John	Orn	519
James	Ird	640	Mccoy, Sarah	Nsh	113	Robert	Orn	519
James	Rnd	331	McCoy, Edward	Grn	602	Samuel	Rth	129
James	Srr	680	Gideon	Crv	333	Thomas	Rth	130
John	Mnt	472	Hardy	Crv	331	McCrummen, Angus	Cmb	388
John	Orn	583	James	Brk	769	John	Cmb	387
Jonathan	Rnd	332	James	Cmd	108	McCubbin, Jas.	Rck	447
Malcolm	Mnt	467	James	Orn	494	Nichs.	Rck	447
Neil	Bld	24	Joel	Cmd	95	McCubbins, John	Rck	449
Rachel	Bld	41	John	Crv	331	McCublins, Nichos.	Rck	476
Stephen	Rnd	328	Joseph	Prq	644	McCullam, John	Orn	588
Widow	Mck	578	Joshua	Cmd	108	McCullen, John	Smp	521

McCullers, Mattw.	Wke 749	Jacob	Cht 213	Allin	Mnt 463
see MCullers		James	Cht 215	Angus	Cmb 363
McCullin, Bryant	Wne 851	James	Jns 781	Archibald	Cmb 383
John	Smp 513	James	Mre 72	Catherine	Lnc 819
McCulloch, Duncan	Bld 25	James, Jur.	Jns 783	Christian	Cmb 357
Robert	Wrr 817	Jasen	Rnd 329	Daniel	Cmb 377
McCullock, Andrew	Orn 521	Jno.	Glf 635	Daniel	Mre 74
James	Orn 587	John	Brk 772	Daniel	Rbs 403
John	Orn 520	John	Cht 178	Daniel	Rbs 405
Joseph	Orn 521	John	Cht 212	Daniel	Rbs 406
Robert	Orn 520	John	Cmb 369	David	Mck 529
Robert	Orn 587	John	Jns 783	Donald	Cmb 355
Thomas	Orn 521	John (2)	Jns 795	Donald	Cmb 364
McCulloh, George	Dpl 401	John	Mre 57	Edward	Rbs 395
George	Rwn 322	John	Rnd 332	Effy	Rbs 396
James	Rwn 344	John	Rth 129	Elizabeth	Bnc 179
James	Rwn 427	John, Jr.	Cmb 370	George	Bnc 178
John	Mck 603	Lenvell	Cht 177	Hugh	Cmb 388
Margret	Ird 672	Malcolm	Smp 495	Hugh	Cmb 393
Sarah	Dpl 425	Margarett	Orn 521	Isaac	Cmd 108
Thomas	Glf 622	Mary	Cmb 367	James	Bnc 182
McCullum, Duncan	Cmb 388	Milley	Srr 676	James	Lnc 897
McCully, John	Orn 520	Nancy	Wlk 55	James	Mnt 480
McCurday, James	Ird 612	Peter	Nrt 459	James	Rth 132
William	Ird 612	Randle	Rth 130	James	Wsh 714
McCurdey, Archi-		Reuben	Rth 129	John	Cmb 366
bald	Cbr 706	Reuben	Stk 567	John	Ird 618
McCurdy, Samuel	Cbr 705	Rhoderick	Csw 126	John	Ird 646
Thomas	Dpl 399	Risdon	Jns 795	John	Psq 628
William	Dpl 433	Risdon, Jur.	Jns 795	John	Rbs 391
see MCurdy		Samuel	Brk 775	John	Rbs 405
McCurry, John	Glf 678	Samuel	Cht 167	Jonathan	Mnt 499
John	Glf 684	Temperance	Brk 775	Joseph	Rth 130
John	Rth 132	William	Crt 88	Katherine	Cmb 361
M.	Lnc 897	William	Jns 809	Kenneth	Mre 75
Malcom	Bnc 178	William	Rth 130	Neill	Cmb 384
Micaijah	Lnc 900	William	Wlk 53	Randol	Bnc 178
William	Rth 131	MCdaniel, Anguest	Rch 257	Rencher	Psq 637
McCvey see MCvey		Anguist	Rch 253	Roderick	Cmb 388
McDade, Elenor	Orn 583	Anguist	Rch 260	Sibby	Cmb 356
John	Rnd 329	Daniel	Rch 256	Starling	Mnt 491
McDahnl, James	Orn 582	Daniel	Wne 853	Thomas	Mnt 493
McDamed, Leah	Hrt 738	Eli	Rch 256	McDonaugh, Andw.	Wke 776
Mcdaniel, Joel	Csw 100	Elisabeth	Ans 240	MCdonnel, Alexr.	Rch 251
Wm.	Csw 114	James	Rch 248	Alexr.	Rch 261
McDaniel, Absalom	Rnd 332	John	Ans 225	Ann	Rch 267
Alexd.	Mre 51	Liddy	Rch 248	Daniel	Rch 244
Allin	Mre 53	Widow	Rch 265	Danl.	Rch 267
Allin	Rwn 432	McDannel, Daniel	Orn 584	Donnel	Rch 242
Amos	Rnd 332	Ely	Orn 582	Eli	Rch 269
Anguish	Crv 309	Ely	Orn 585	Rodrick	Rch 245
Anguish	Mre 50	James	Grv 532	MCdormd., Malcolm	Rch 269
Arch	Crr 151	John	Orn 582	McDougald, Dugald	Bld 27
Archd.	Bld 45	John	Orn 585	McDowald, James	Cmb 360
Arthur	Cht 180	Melkijah	Orn 585	McDowel, William	Brk 770
Bethany	Bfr 23	William	Orn 584	McDowell, Ann	Brk 777
Clary	Hlf 358	see McDahnl		Charles	Brk 768
Daneil	Mre 39	McDaw, David	Rth 133	Daniel	Bnc 181
Daniel	Cmb 382	McDearman, Michael	Glf 676	George	Nrt 459
Daniel	Mre 54	McDearmead, Alexan-		James	Bnc 181
Daniel	Mre 69	der	Rbs 398	James	Nrt 459
Daniel	Mre 72	Farquad.	Rbs 402	John	Bnc 180
Daniel	Rth 130	John	Rbs 394	John	Brk 769
Daniel	Wlk 55	Sarah	Rbs 394	John	Mck 531
Danl.	Bld 18	McDears, Rice	Brk 775	Joseph	Brk 769
David	Brk 769	William	Brk 775	Joseph	Glf 670
David	Cmb 369	McDermaid, Angus	Cmb 394	Michael	Wlk 54
David	Cmb 370	MCdermet, John	Rch 261	Widow	Mck 531
David	Cmb 383	MCdermet, Malcolm	Rch 271	William	Bnc 181
Dicey	Cmb 383	McDermon, James	Nwh 8A	MCdowell, John	Rch 263
Elisha	Nrt 459	McDewil, Frederick	Wsh 708	William	Rch 263
Findley	Mre 53	James	Wsh 708	McDuel, Miles	Brt 62
George	Rnd 332	MCdiffee, Murdoch	Rch 249	Stevens	Brt 60
Henry	Rwn 432	McDill, Samuel	Glf 646	McDuffee, Anguis	Mnt 476
Henry	Srr 678	McDodle, Thomas	Ird 651	Angus	Cmb 364
Hugh	Mre 40	Mcdoel, Thos.	Mrt 402	Archibald	Cmb 365
Hugh	Mre 55	McDonald, Alexr.	Ird 631	Archibald	Cmb 367
Isaac	Rnd 332				

Dugal	Nwh 6	(2)	Smp 523	McGeachey, John	Rbs 403
Duncan	Cmb 361	Dugald	Smp 501	McGeachy, Alexan-	
Duncan	Cmb 365	McFalls, ...	Brk 776	der	Rbs 405
Duncan	Cmb 388	Arthur	Brk 774	John	Glf 681
Dunkin	Mre 65	John	Brk 776	McGee, Andrew	Glf 634
George	Cmb 393	McFarlan, James	Rth 131	Chiles	Cht 179
John	Nwh 7	John	Mre 65	David	Wlk 52
George	Cmb 373	Parlan	Mre 53	George	Rnd 331
Malcolm	Cmb 365	Patrick	Rth 129	Hall	Mck 600
MCduffee, Dugal	Rch 270	William	Rth 129	Holden	Dpl 399
John	Rch 252	Mcfarland, Benja-		Jessee	Cht 165
Norman	Rch 247	min	Rck 480	John	Ird 631
McDuffie, Danl.	Bld 43	McFarland, George	Bnc 181	John	Smp 501
Martha	Crv 315	Jacob	Bnc 177	Mary	Nwh 10
Neeal	Mre 62	James	Bnc 181	Mary	Rbs 393
McDuffy, Daniel	Rbs 395	John	Bnc 180	Merreman	Brk 775
McDugal, Archabald	Mre 41	John	Bnc 181	Micajah	Cht 158
Randal	Nwh 7A	John	Orn 586	Pattrick	Brk 776
McDugald, Alexan-		Reuben	Bnc 181	Ralph	Wlk 53
der	Cmb 378	William	Bnc 181	Robert	Smp 528
Alexander	Rbs 397	McFarlane, Walter	Hrt 700	Samuel	Rnd 332
Alexander	Rbs 402	Mcfarlin, Jno.	Csw 137	Solomon	Cmb 380
Angus	Cmb 379	McFarlin, Dugal	Mre 55	Thomas	Dpl 399
Archabald	Rbs 399	James	Ird 644	Thos.	Wlk 55
Daniel	Cmb 360	Malcom	Mre 65	William	Cmb 380
Daniel	Cmb 361	Robert	Rck 437	William	Dpl 399
Daniel	Cmb 376	MCfarlin, Alexr.	Rch 251	William	Rnd 331
Hugh	Cmb 378	Daniel	Rch 260	William	Wlk 52
Mary	Cmb 377	Dugal	Rch 244	Williams	Nwh 4A
Randal	Rbs 394	Dugal	Rch 249	Willis	Smp 529
Samuel	Rbs 403	Duncan	Rch 260	McGeegan, Malcom	Rbs 406
McDugil, Allin	Mre 65	John	Rch 251	McGehe, Nathan	Grv 558
McDugle, Duncan	Mre 64	John	Rch 260	Sehon	
John	Mre 64	Neal	Rch 261	Tabitha	Orn 587
McDuncan, Daniel	Cmb 373	MCfarling, John	Prs 199	see Megehe	
McEachern, Archi-		Jos. D.	Prs 198	MCgehe, Benjamin	Ans 208
bald	Rbs 405	Walter	Prs 199	James	Ans 209
Daniel	Rbs 397	William	Prs 197	John	Ans 209
Duncan	Rbs 392	Mcfarror, William	Jhn 774	MCghee, Momford	Prs 206
Elizabeth	Rbs 401	McFarson, Joseph	Rwn 342	McGibbons, James	Mck 580
John	Rbs 400	MCfassion, Daniel	Rch 246	McGibony, Patrick	Glf 664
John	Rbs 402	McFatridge, Samuel	Glf 684	McGihe, John	Prs 207
John	Rbs 406	McFatter, Alexr.	Bld 26	Joseph	Prs 207
Malcom	Rbs 397	Danl.	Bld 26	McGill, Archibald	Rbs 397
Neill	Rbs 390	Isabella	Bld 25	Danl.	Lnc 829
Neill	Rbs 400	Margaret	Bld 26	Elizabeth	Lnc 839
Peter	Rbs 399	McFattridge, Dan-		John	Cmb 356
Robert	Rbs 406	iel	Glf 678	Mary	Cmb 393
McEackern, Neill	Rbs 403	McFee, Hettk.	Mre 77	Neill	Rbs 397
McEackren, Peter	Mre 58	James	Bnc 179	Neill	Rbs 398
McEchron, Robert	Cbr 705	James	Ptt 232	Neill, Ser.	Rbs 399
McEFee, Abnor	Lnc 897	Malcolm	Mnt 463	Rhoderick	Rbs 398
James	Lnc 897	Nancy	Rbs 394	Thos.	Lnc 828
McEldemor, Lydia	Lnc 893	see McEFee		MCgill, Allen	Rch 260
McEleroy, John	Mck 589	MCfeel, John	Rch 252	Anguist	Rch 253
David	Brk 772	Mcferson, Joseph	Stk 578	Duncan	Rch 254
James	Mck 592	MCferson, Alexr.	Rch 245	McGilvery, John	Mre 60
William	Mck 591	Edward	Rch 260	McGine, Michal	Stk 578
William	Mck 592	John	Rch 260	McGinn, James	Mck 523
McElwain, John	Smp 527	William	Rch 252	John	Mck 535
McElwrath, David	Brk 771	McFeters, Charles	Rwn 313	Thomas	Mck 548
Jacob	Brk 774	McFetrich, John	Ird 646	McGinnes, Charles	Cbr 678
McEncharn, Archd.	Bld 26	Mcfide, Duncan	Rch 252	McGinnis, Isaac	Rth 129
McEntire see MEntire		McForsen, William	Orn 582	James	Cmb 370
McEwen, Anne	Bld 20	McForson, Ercock	ORn 582	James	Lnc 849
James	Ird 650	McGahah, William	Ash 83	John	Lnc 897
James	Mck 557	McGahee see McGahn		Miles	Cht 172
James	Rwn 377	McGahey, Alexander	Rth 128	Patrick	Rth 129
Matthew	Bld 20	Amos	Mck 577	McGinty, James	Ird 640
Robert	Bld 23	Daniel	Rth 129	McGirt, Archibald	Rbs 391
William	Bld 23	Jeremiah	Rth 129	John	Rbs 391
McEwin, James	Rwn 289	William	Mck 577	McGlimmery, George	Rth 131
McFaddon, Hannah	Cbr 706	William	Rth 128	Jesse	Rth 131
McFadin, Alexr.	Rth 128	McGahn, Samuel	Bnc 179	McGlohawn, John	Brt 90
McFadon, John	Mre 62	McGahy, Archibald	Rwn 327	McGlohlin, John	Rwn 318
McFadyan, Niel	Mre 65	McGaughey, James	Rth 133	Samuel	Rwn 317
McFail, Alexander		McGauhey, John	Ird 656	McGlohon, Elisha	Hrt 705

George	Hrt 705	McIintire, Daniel	Stk 579	Rory	Mre 62
McGound, Hannah	Trl 690	McIlhenny, John	Nwh 3	Vanderon	Cht 179
William	Trl 690	McInally, Eliza-		see McIwer	
McGoune, James	Hde 374	beth	Stk 563	MCiver, John	Rch 261
John	Hde 373	McInnis, Daniel	Rbs 391	McIwer, John	Cht 180
Joseph, Jr.	Hde 373	John	Cmb 361	McJinon, Murdoch	Smp 523
Joseph, Ser.	Hde 374	John	Rbs 392	McJintire see McIintire	
William	Hde 373	John, Jur.	Rbs 392	McJunis see McInnis	
McGowen, John	Dpl 400	John, Jur.	Rbs 393	McJustice, Mary	Cmb 355
Mary	Dpl 400	Malcom	Rbs 391	McK..., John	Cmb 362
Pady	Rnd 328	Mary	Rbs 393	McKae, Alexander	Cmb 360
Robert	Dpl 430	Murdoch	Rbs 392	Christopher	Cmb 361
William	Dpl 400	Neill	Rbs 392	Colin	Cmb 363
McGowin, William	Rnd 328	McInnish, Daniel	Mre 53	Daniel	Cmb 361
McGown see McGoune		McInon, Daniel	Smp 497	Daniel (2)	Cmb 363
McGowns, George	Ptt 250	McIntagart, Daniel	Rbs 401	Daniel	Cmb 393
John	Ptt 229	Gilbert	Rbs 403	Duncan	Cmb 393
William	Ptt 256	MCintere, William	Ans 218	Gilbert	Cmb 363
McGrady, David	Glf 664	McIntire, Andrew	Dpl 437	Murdoch	Cmb 365
Jacob	Wlk 55	Archy	Cht 179	Roderick	Cmb 393
Moses	Glf 664	Daniel	Stk 563	McKamon, Micaijah	Ird 664
McGraw, James	Cbr 688	Dugald	Cmb 364	McKane, Hugh	Srr 675
John	Cbr 685	Gilbert	Cmb 363	McKann, John	Rth 130
John	Crv 243	James	Mck 550	Mathew	Rth 126
William	Cbr 689	Jereh.	Csw 113	McKaskel, Daniel	Ird 646
McGray, Elizabeth	Cmd 102	John	Cmb 365	McKaskey, George	Ird 645
McGregor, William	Nrt 459	John	Mck 550	McKaskin, Daniel	Rbs 403
MCgregor, Anthony	Ans 210	Nicholas	Cmb 365	McKasters, John	Lnc 856
William	Ans 206	Thomas	Brk 769	McKay, Alexander	Cmb 367
McGrew, Robert	Rth 128	MCintire, Chris-		Alexander	Ird 644
McGrigor, Hector	Mre 62	tian	Rch 254	Alexander	Ird 651
McGufford, James	Nwh 5A	Duncan	Rch 247	Archibald	Bld 38
Nathl.	Nwh 10	Mary	Rch 254	Archibald	Rbs 390
Will.	Nwh 10	McIntosh, Alexan-		Christopher	Rbs 404
McGuffy, Edmund	Bnc 178	der	Cmb 365	Daniel (2)	Ird 651
McGugan, Archibald	Cmb 364	Alexander	Mr3 60	Daniel	Rbs 391
Hugh	Rbs 402	Alexd.	Mre 62	Danl.	Bld 23
John	Cmb 385	Christian	Mre 56	Donald	Ird 644
John	Cmb 386	Daniel	Mre 60	Dugald	Rbs 397
McGuin, Michael	Rth 128	Daniel	Rbs 400	Edward	Cmb 361
McGuire, Elijah	Rth 133	Dunkin	Mre 44	George (2)	Ird 644
McGuire, James	Rwn 448	James	Crv 271	Hugh	Rbs 404
John	Chw 125	John	Cmb 362	James	Ird 631
John	Ird 621	John	Mre 60	John	Bld 23
Michael	Chw 131	Peter	Mre 64	John	Ird 631
Pattrick	Ird 665	MCintosh, Duncan	Ans 212	John	Rbs 404
Phillip	Chw 123	George	Rch 260	John	Rbs 432
Samuel	Chw 131	John	Ans 198	John	Rck 446
Thomas	Ird 621	Levin	Rch 246	John, Jur.	Bld 20
Thomas	Ird 665	McIntyre, Aaron	Rth 132	John, Senr.	Bld 18
MCguire, Nathan	Rch 264	Alexander	Rth 130	John, (Taylr.)	Bld 26
Owen	Rch 264	Alexander	Rth 131	Katherine	Cmb 363
William	Rch 264	Daniel	Cmb 364	Lachlan	Cmb 387
McGuistan, Ann	Glf 667	Daniel	Cmb 379	Malcolm	Cmb 393
Thomas	Glf 667	Daniel	Rbs 392	Margaret	Cmb 393
McGuistion, Wil-		James	Brk 279	Margret	Ird 651
liam	Orn 490	James	Rth 132	Margret	Ird 653
McGuiston, Darcus	Glf 654	John	Cmb 364	Michael	Cmb 378
Elizabeth	Glf 652	John	Cmb 384	Murdoh	Ird 644
Robert	Glf 653	John	Cmb 386	Neill	Cmb 378
Thomas	Glf 671	John	Rbs 394	Robert	Ird 644
Thomas	Glf 677	Josiah	Rth 131	Robert	Rck 445
Walter	Glf 653	Rachael	Rth 132	Thomas	Ird 646
McHaffey, Joseph	Lnc 869	William	Rth 132	Thomas	Ird 662
McHargew see McHargue,		McInzie, John	Smp 501	William	Ird 631
MHargew		Peter	Cht 175	William	Ird 645
McHargue, James	Ird 612	McItosh, Daniel	Mre 40	McKean, Michael	Orn 588
James	Ird 616	McIver, Alexd.	Mre 57	McKee, Alexander	Ird 644
William	Ird 612	Alexd.	Mre 65	Isaac	Lnc 828
McHenry, Archibald	Ird 612	Alexn.	Cht 179	Jms.	Lnc 828
Henry	Rwn 327	Anguish	Cht 226	John	Ird 644
Isaac	Ird 651	Daniel	Mre 60	John	Mck 536
John	Rwn 332	Daniel	Mre 66	John	Orn 588
MChenry, Jesse	Ans 232	Dunkin	Mre 66	Martha	Csw 132
John	Rch 244	Isabella	Cmb 356	Robert	Csw 132
MChissock, Thos.	Prs 212	John	Cht 179	William	Ird 672
Will	Prs 212	John	Mre 41	William	Orn 587

McKeel, Ann	Bfr 14	Conny '	Lnc 856	Hugh	Rwn 337
James	Bfr 14	Joseph	Mck 547	James	Ird 662
John	Bfr 14	Saml.	Wlk 52	James	Mck 530
John	Grn 592	Samuel	Brk 773	John	Glf 635
Michael	Prq 648	Samuel	Brk 775	John	Glf 664
Salley	Bfr 14	Thomas	Brk 775	Liddy	Ird 618
Shadrach	Bfr 14	William	Brk 775	Robert	Glf 667
McKeen, Robert	Wrr 784	see MKinney		Robert	Mck 530
McKega, John	Glf 633	McKinnian, John	Mre 58	Roger	Rwn 362
McKeithen, John	Bld 20	Normon	Mre 71	Thomas	Ird 662
McKellar, John	Cmb 361	Normon	Mre 72	Thomas	Mck 561
John	Cmb 387	MCkinnis, Daniel	Rch 263	Thomas	Rwn 427
Archibald	Cmb 365	Hugh	Rch 253	William	Mck 565
John	Cmb 364	James	Rch 253	William	Rwn 337
MCkemis, Kenith	Rch 269	Murdock	Rch 256	McKoean, Francis	Crv 307
MCkenan, Alexr.	Rch 266	Murdock	Rch 264	McLachlan, Archi-	
Lohlin	Rch 253	McKinnon, Angus	Cmb 364	bald	Cmb 387
McKendley, William	Mck 533	Daniel	Cmb 387	Colin	Rbs 397
McKenner, Murdock,		Daniel	Mre 53	Dugald	Rbs 397
Sr.	Rch 266	Duncan	Cmb 363	Duncal	Rbs 399
MCkennis, Malcolm	Rch 270	Hector	Cmb 362	Duncan	Rbs 407
McKennish, Seth	Mck 540	John	Cmb 387	Hugh	Cmb 373
McKenny, Howel	Cmb 391	John	Mre 53	John	Rbs 399
Sarah	Cmb 391	John	Rbs 393	Nicholas	Rbs 395
McKenrie, George	Drn 18	John	Rbs 395	Robert	Rbs 399
McKenzie, Benjamin	Rwn 319	Peter	Rbs 405	McLain, Affa	Mre 53
Daniel	Cmb 364	Roderick	Cmb 387	Alexander	Mre 62
Daniel	Cmb 377	MCkinnon, Charles	Rch 247	Allin	Mre 71
Duncan	Cmb 388	Daniel (2)	Rch 254	Archd.	Mre 57
Dunkin	Mre 54	Hector	Rch 243	Daniel	Rbs 407
Gilbert	Cmb 380	Hugh	Rch 242	Hector	Mre 71
Hugh	Cmb 377	Neal	Rch 242	Hector	Mre 72
John	Nwh 10A	Robert	Rch 254	Jane	Rth 127
Sarah	Cmb 378	McKinny, Brukes	Ons 138	John	Mre 64
William	Mck 558	George	Rth 127	John	Rbs 392
McKerall, Will.	Nwh 2A	Henry	Rth 126	John	Rbs 393
McKesick, Danuel	Lnc 818	James	Rth 126	Lauchlin	Mre 65
McKethan, Malcolm	Cmb 362	James	Srr 675	Neill	Rbs 393
McKethen, Dugald	Wke 776	Jesse	Srr 677	Neill	Rbs 400
John	Cmb 366	John	Rck 444	MClain, Charles	Rch 259
Neill	Cmb 378	John	Rth 126	Duncan	Rch 271
see McKiethen		John, j.	Rth 126	Hugh	Rch 261
MCkethen, John	Rch 260	Samuel	Bnc 178	John	Rch 271
McKever, John	Glf 619	William	Rth 126	McLaine, Peter	Bld 46
Timothy	Glf 620	Wilson	Bnc 179	McLamore, Drury	Bld 43
McKibben, Alek	Mck 602	MCkinny, Barnaba	Wne 871	Drury	Bld 43
McKibbens, Thomas	Mck 580	John	Wne 854	Elias	Bld 42
McKibbin, Aughbrey	Mck 601	Mary	Wne 854	McLane, Joseph	Rnd 332
McKie, Elias	Bld 42	Richd.	Wne 873	MClane, Daniel	Rch 271
George	Bld 19	Sarah	Wne 855	McLaren, John	Bld 18
James	Bld 45	William	Wne 857	MClarin, Lohlin	Rch 247
Robert	Rwn 404	McKinron, Kenith	Rbs 402	MClarren, Duncan	Rch 260
Theodosia,		McKinsey, Hector	Rbs 406	MClarrin, Hugh	Rch 246
(Cap.)	Rwn 404	MCkinsey, Danl.	Rch 270	McLarty, Archd.	Cbr 700
William	Mck 600	John	Rch 248	McLawn, Andrew	Mck 564
McKiethen, Archd.	Bld 24	McKinsie, Jim boy	Brn 13A	Jonathan	Mck 564
Danl.	Bld 24	Mal...lm	Nwh 2	McLead, William	Ird 651
Duncan	Bld 25	McKinzey, George	Chw 116	McLean, Alexander	Cmb 377
McKight, George	Srr 675	Hines	Ird 631	Allen	Cmb 368
McKimmy, Joseph	Trl 680	Keneth	Brk 773	Anne	Cmb 379
Nathaniel	Glf 658	Kenith	Rbs 406	Archabald	Rbs 391
Nelly	Glf 658	Mckinzie, Wm.,		Archibald (2)	Cmb 377
Thomas	Trl 680	Esqr.	Mrt 402	Charles	Rth 127
McKimon see McThimon		McKinzie, Alexan-		Christiana	Rbs 392
MCkimon, Randal	Rch 247	der	Ird 631	Daniel	Cmb 362
McKinlay, James	Crv 229	James	Mre 62	Daniel	Cmb 379
John	Bnc 180	John	Cmb 355	Daniel	Cmb 382
McKinley, Daniel	Rbs 402	John	Mre 53	Daniel (2)	Rbs 391
Charles	Cbr 706	John	Mre 76	Duncan	Cmb 376
John	Cbr 688	Katherine	Cmb 393	Hector	Cmb 377
McKinly, David	Cbr 686	McKithan, Danl.	Brn 17A	Hector	Rbs 398
McKinne, Abraham	Srr 680	McKithin, Alexr.	Brn 21A	Hugh	Cmb 362
Isaac	Crv 273	Moses	Brn 21A	John	Bnc 180
John	Wke 751	McKiver, John	Ird 618	John	Cmb 360
MCkinnes, Daniel	Rch 269	McKnight, David	Ird 641	John	Cmb 376
McKinney, Andrew	Ird 672	George	Rwn 362	John	Cmb 378
Charles	Brk 773	Hugh	Ird 662	John	Cmb 387

Name	Ref	Name	Ref	Name	Ref
John	Cmb 388	Nancy	Rch 259	Nancy	Rnd 332
John	Rbs 390	Neal	Rch 258	Simeon	Rnd 329
John (2)	Rbs 391	Norman	Ans 198	William	Cht 217
John	Rbs 392	Norman	Rch 247	McMath, James	Cht 193
John	Rbs 396	Norman, Jr.	Rch 253	William	Cht 193
John	Rbs 400	Peter	Rch 263	William, jr.	Cht 193
Malcom	Rbs 392	Rodrick	Ans 224	MCmellan, James	Ans 237
Murdoch	Cmb 387	Rory	Rch 245	McMical, Archd.	Glf 651
Nancy	Rbs 391	McLeowd, Alexander	Mre 41	McMicken, Andrew	Mck 531
Neall	Cmb 377	Alexd.	Mre 61	McMickle, Duggle	Srr 676
Neill (2)	Cmb 377	Alexd.	Mre 66	McMillam, Iver	Bld 25
Roderick	Cmb 367	Anguish	Mre 67	McMillan, Alexander	Cmb 363
McLearen, Flora	Rbs 396	Charles	Mre 45	Alexander	Rbs 391
McLellan, Angus	Cmb 385	Daniel	Mre 51	Angus	Rbs 404
Daniel	Cmb 385	Daniel	Mre 59	Archibald	Rbs 396
Jno.	Nwh 3A	Daniel (2)	Mre 71	Archibald	Rbs 400
Malcolm	Cmb 384	John	Mre 53	Archibald	Rbs 405
McLelland, Andrew	Bld 32	Murdock	Mre 71	Daniel	Cmb 370
M'Clelland, Widow	Mck 545	Nancy	Mre 69	Daniel	Rbs 400
MClellin, John	Rch 246	Neeal	Mre 45	Daniel (2)	Rbs 405
McLemore, Atkins	Wrr 817	Neeal	Mre 61	David	Rth 128
Clem.	Mnt 479	Niel	Mre 66	Dugald	Cmb 370
James	Grv 566	Normon	Mre 40	Dugald (2)	Rbs 398
John	Brk 770	Normon	Mre 57	Dougl.	Bld 19
John	Mnt 463	Nual	Mre 49	Duncan	Bld 48
Nathaniel	Orn 584	Nual	Mre 71	Duncan	Rbs 400
Wright	Srr 677	McLeran, John	Cmb 383	Duncan	Rbs 404
MClendon, Bryan	Ans 230	Daniel	Cmb 383	Duncan	Rbs 406
Dennis	Ans 228	Duncan	Cmb 383	Duncan, Jur.	Rbs 400
Dennis	Ans 234	Neill	Cmb 384	Gilbert	Cmb 384
Ezekiel	Ans 232	Henry	Lnc 905	Jeremiah	Rth 127
John	Ans 219	McLeroy see Machleroy		John	Ash 83
Nancy	Ans 215	McLerron, John	Cmb 369	John	Bld 31
McLennon, Anne	Cmb 356	McLettan, Angus	Rbs 394	John	Bld 48
Isaac	Cbr 679	McLillan, Eliza	Bld 27	John	Bld 33
John	Mre 44	MClin, Duncan	Rch 253	John	Rbs 397
MClenny, William	Jhn 775	McLohlin, Widow	Rwn 337	John	Rbs 398
McLeod, Alexander	Cmb 364	MClohlin, Daniel	Ans 229	John	Rbs 404
Alexander	Rbs 401	Daniel	Rch 262	John	Rbs 405
Christian	Cmb 387	John	Rch 252	John, (Tweed Side)	Cmb 386
Daniel	Cmb 357	MClothen, Archble	Rch 269	Malcom	Rbs 391
Daniel	Cmb 385	McLow, William	Rck 462	Malcom	Rbs 397
Daniel	Cmb 389	McLoy, William	Mck 580	Malcom	Rbs 405
Daniel,/Tayler/	Cmb 389	McLure, Arthur	Rth 127	Mary	Cmb 356
John	Cmb 375	Charles	Bnc 181	Micajah	Rth 128
John	Cmb 387	James	Ird 657	Neil	Bld 19
John	Cmb 388	John	Bnc 181	Neill	Rbs 402
John, Senr.	Mnt 467	John, j.	Rth 127	Neill	Rbs 404
Malcom	Bld 27	John, Sr.	Rth 127	Neill	Rbs 406
Malcolm	Cmb 374	Joseph	Bnc 180	Robert	Bld 48
Malcolm	Mnt 491	Richd.	Rth 127	Thomas	Rbs 406
Malcom	Rbs 399	Robert	Bnc 181	MCmillan, Alexander	Rch 252
Mary	Rbs 401	Thomas (2)	Bnc 181	Amos	Ans 236
Murdoch	Rbs 404	McLurg, Nathaniel	Lnc 819	Duncan	Rch 270
Norman	Cmb 388	McLurhin, Nancy	Rth 132	Gilbert	Rch 261
Norman	Nwh 3A	McLuskey, John	Bnc 181	Hector	Rch 247
Norman	Rbs 391	McLusky, Jean	Cbr 702	John	Rch 270
Norman	Rbs 394	McMahan, Edmund	Bnc 179	McMillen, James	Cmb 386
Normand	Mre 74	James (2)	Bnc 178	McMillin, Anguish	Mre 54
Normon	Cmb 356	Redman	Bnc 179	Archd. (2)	Mre 51
Rodrick	Cmb 360	James	Cbr 713	Archd.	Mre 55
William	Cmb 360	John	Rwn 444	Daniel	Mre 54
MCleod, Alexr.	Ans 198	Morgan	Rwn 459	Neeal	Mre 55
Alexr.	Rch 270	Samuel	Rwn 459	McMillon, Alexander	Dpl 435
Alexr.	Rch 271	William	Rwn 459	McMin, Abraham	Rth 133
Alexr., Senr.	Rch 271	McMains, James	Crv 235	Daniel	Glf 664
Anguest, Sr.	Rch 271	McManas, Eli	Cht 224	Lihue	Glf 664
Archble	Rch 269	McManis, Aron	Cht 222	McMinimay, Alex	Csw 131
Daniel	Rch 258	John	Cht 177	Wm.	Csw 131
Daniel	Rch 266	Lawrance	Cht 177	McMinn, Jane	Bnc 178
James	Rch 270	Nathaniel	Cht 222	John	Bnc 178
John	Rch 257	McMann, James	Orn 588	McMorine, Robert	Psq 628
John	Rch 259	McMaster, Margt.	Bld 49	McMullen, Daniel	Cmb 389
Hugh	Rch 267	Wm.	Bld 33		
Malcolm	Rch 256	McMasters, Andrew	Rnd 329		
Murdock	Rch 260	Jonathan	Cht 216		
Murdock	Rch 263	Lewis	Rnd 331		

Hugh	Orn 587	Andrew	Mck 528	MCormac, Daniel	Rch 243
John	Orn 587	Archd.	Rwn 317	John	Rch 247
Neill	Cmb 389	Archibald	Rwn 322	MCormage, Duncan	Rch 269
Rachel	Bfr 24	David	Mck 590	MCormish, Hugh	Rch 258
Samuel	Orn 582	David	Rwn 318	MCoy, Alexr.	Rch 251
Mcmullin, Nathan	Frn 471	Henry	Mck 582	Archibald	Rch 252
McMullin, Griffith	Ird 651	James	Rck 470	Archibald	Rch 254
James	Rth 128	James	Rwn 317	Daniel	Rch 261
Jno.	Csw 117	James	Rwn 322	Duncan	Rch 257
Joseph	Ird 657	John	Mck 596	John	Ans 225
Robert	Rth 128	John	Mck 598	John	Rch 257
McMun, Wm.	Csw 116	John	Rwn 317	McPeak, John	Rck 480
McMunn, Angus	Cmb 365	John	Rwn 318	McPeters, David	Bnc 180
McMurphy, Archi-		John, Senr.	Rwn 317	Jonathan	Bnc 181
bald	Smp 513	Joseph	Cbr 707	McPhadan, Archi-	
Mcmurrey, Jas.	Prs 215	McNeider, John	Prq 651	bald	Cmb 365
Jas.	Prs 218	Thomas	Prq 652	McPhail, Dugald	Cmb 394
John	Prs 213	McNeil, ...	Nwh 1A	John (2)	Rbs 406
Saml.	Prs 212	Archl.	Nwh 5	see McPhaul	
MCmurrey, Will	Prs 214	George	Wlk 54	McPhaill, Dugald	Cmb 384
McMurry, Elenor	Cbr 676	James	Ash 84	McPharland, John	Cmb 387
James	Cbr 676	John	Bnc 178	McPharson, Daniel	Cht 212
James	Glf 639	William	Ash 84	John	Cht 212
James	Glf 667	McNeill, Alexander	Rbs 403	Joseph	Cmd 108
James	Rth 132	Anne	Cmb 385	Othniel	Cht 175
Robert	Cbr 680	Archabald	Rbs 398	McPhatter, Archi-	
Samuel	Rth 128	Archibald	Cmb 362	bald	Rbs 400
William	Glf 654	Archibald	Rbs 404	John	Rbs 400
McMurtrey, Samuel	Rth 128	Colin	Cmb 379	McPhaul, Daniel	Rbs 401
McNab, Sarah	Grv 560	Daniel	Cmb 384	James	Cmb 365
McNabb, Archd.	Bld 48	Daniel	Rbs 393	John	Rbs 399
James	Cmb 363	Duncan	Rbs 401	John	Rbs 406
James	Rbs 396	Elizabeth	Bld 19	McPherson, Alexan-	
William	Grv 510	Godfrey	Rbs 402	der	Cmb 393
McNair, Edward	Rbs 391	Hector	Cmb 362	Cartley	Cmd 95
Katharine	Rbs 407	Hector	Cmb 366	Colin	Cmb 393
Mary	Rbs 396	Hector	Rbs 398	Daniel	Cmb 394
Mary	Rbs 397	Hector (2)	Rbs 404	Daniel	Rbs 401
Rhoderick	Rbs 390	Henry	Cmb 379	Demsey	Cmd 94
MCnair, Edward	Rch 251	James	Cmb 364	Grice	Cmb 365
Malcolm	Rch 260	James	Cmb 384	James	Hrt 717
Neal (2)	Rch 261	James	Rbs 399	Jesse	Cmd 94
McNairy, Robert	Glf 653	James	Rbs 404	Jesse	Psq 637
McNare, Jms.	Lnc 839	John	Bld 19	John	Bld 14
McNarie, William	Wrr 784	John	Cmb 366	John	Cmd 93
McNatt, James	Rbs 395	John	Cmb 368	John (2)	Cmb 393
John	Rbs 395	John	Cmb 375	John	Ird 657
John	Rwn 417	John	Rbs 393	John M.	Cmb 364
Margret	Rwn 410	John	Rbs 395	John, (Skipper)	Cmb 356
McNaught, Alexan-		John	Rbs 397	Joseph	Lnr 17
der	Cmb 364	John	Rbs 400	Joshua	Cmd 93
Benjamin	Cmb 384	John	Rbs 402	Joshua	Cmd 94
McNaughton,		John	Rbs 432	Matthew	Ird 657
Charles	Bld 26	Joswet	Cmb 366	Neill	Cmb 364
Neill	Cmb 365	Lachlan	Cmb 386	Noah	Psq 636
McNeal, Jean	Brk 774	Malcolm	Cmb 361	Randal	Rbs 399
MCneal, Archibald	Rch 261	Malcolm	Cmb 382	Robert	Ird 656
Hector	Rch 249	Malcom	Rbs 403	McQqueen, Norman	Cmb 372
Lohlin	Rch 249	Neill	Cmb 361	McQuag, Alexander	Cmb 364
Neal	Rch 259	Neill	Cmb 377	McQuaig, Malcom	Rbs 393
MCnear, Alexr.	Rch 254	Neill	Rbs 398	McQuan, Donald	Cmb 365
Edward	Rch 253	Neill	Rbs 399	McQueen, Alexander	Smp 496
Edward	Rch 271	Neill, Miller	Rbs 399	Dond.	Mre 74
Gilbert	Rch 253	Turguill	Rbs 401	Hugh	Smp 495
John	Rch 253	William, Esq.	Rbs 399	James	Rbs 391
John	Rch 259	McNeley, Robert	Ird 657	John	Cmb 384
John	Rch 261	McNelond, Charles	Cbr 700	Malcom	Rbs 402
McNease, Sarah	Grn 607	McNicols, Daniel	Mre 60	Mary	Crv 247
McNeeal, Daniel	Mre 58	McNiel, Anguish	Rnd 331	Murdock	Cht 213
Hector	Mre 52	MCniel, Henary	Prs 213	Neill	Cmb 393
Hector	Mre 56	McNight, William	Ird 640	Norman	Smp 495
John	Mre 40	MCnish, John	Ans 229	MCqueen, John	Rch 260
John	Mre 52	John I.	Ans 229	Neal	Rch 251
John	Mre 54	MCollen, Archibald	Rch 261	see McQqueen	
Malcom	Mre 52	MCollester, John	Rch 262	McQuerry, John	Wlk 55
McNeely, Adam	Ird 656	MCollister, John	Rch 260	William	Wlk 55
Alexander	Rwn 327	MColn, Archibald	Rch 256	McQuilkin, Neill	Rbs 406

McQuin, Braxton	Wlk 54	MCuage, Alexr.	Rch 245	Benjamin	Rnd 332
McQuiston see McGuiston		Duncan	Ans 204	Robert	Rck 487
McRa, Goold Arthur	Hde 374	Duncan	Ans 213	William	Rck 486
McRae, John	Cmb 365	Malcolm	Ans 229	Mears, Duke	Ans 237
see McKae		MCuffee, Mary	Rch 259	James	Bld 19
MCrae, Alex, Big	Rch 266	Murdock	Rch 259	Jesse	Bld 19
Alexr. (3)	Rch 244	McUin, Danil	Wlk 55	Joab	Bld 19
Alexr.	Rch 250	MCullers, John	Jhn 765	Joel	Bld 19
Alexr., B.	Ans 229	MCullin, John	Wne 858	Jonathan	Bld 19
Cristopher	Ans 198	MCurdy, Alexander	Ird 614	Moses	Srr 675
Cristopher	Rch 244	McVail, Nail	Orn 582	Thomas	Srr 675
Cristopher	Rch 251	McVay, James	Orn 584	William	Mre 51
Daniel	Ans 229	McVea, Hamilton	Glf 626	Meas, Mathias	Brk 774
Daniel	Rch 244	McVey, Mathew	Cht 213	Measles, Jonas	Jhn 757
Daniel	Rch 257	Patrick	Orn 586	Meazle, Durante	Mrt 402
Duncan	Ans 199	MCvey, John	Prs 191	Edwd., Junr.	Mrt 416
Duncan	Ans 224	McVicar, William	Rbs 407	Edwd., Senr.	Mrt 401
Duncan	Rch 244	McVickar, John	Bld 26	Hardy	Mrt 401
Duncan	Rch 257	McWadsworth, Dan-		Jas., Junr.	Mrt 402
Farquer	Ans 198	iel	Mre 73	Jas., Senr.	Mrt 400
Farquer	Rch 260	McWhackin, George	Rth 127	Jesse	Mrt 402
John (2)	Ans 224	McWhorter, George,		Luke	Mrt 401
John	Rch 251	Junr.	Mck 589	Luke, Senr.	Mrt 402
Malcolm	Rch 257	George, Senr.	Mck 589	Luke R.	Mrt 402
Murdock	Ans 198	John	Mck 589	Mark	Mrt 402
Murdock	Rch 249	Moses	Mck 593	Wm.	Mrt 400
Peter	Rch 253	Moses, Junr.	Mck 589	Wm. L.	Mrt 401
William	Rch 250	McWilliams, John	Hde 374	Mebame, James	Orn 583
William	Rch 253	Meacham, Banks	Mck 538	Mebane, David	Orn 521
William	Rch 267	George	Cht 193	John	Cht 206
MCrag, Malcolm	Rch 263	James	Cht 153	Samuel	Orn 584
McRa Goold, Arthur	Hde 374	Jessee	Cht 169	William	Orn 583
McRandal, Joseph	Rth 131	JOhn	Cht 169	William	Orn 584
McRary, John	Mck 553	Paul	Srr 704	William, Junr.	Orn 584
McRea, Alexander	Rbs 392	William	Cht 193	Meccom, John	Stk 566
Jno.	Nwh 1A	William, Sr.	Cht 192	Mecham, Jacob	Hlf 330
Malcom	Rbs 393	Meachum, Henry	Ans 215	Joseph	Hlf 330
Mary	Rbs 393	Henry	Ans 226	Mecimmey see Muimmey	
Mary	Rbs 407	Henry, Junr.	Nrt 461	Meck see Meek	
MCreal, Duncan, B.	Rch 266	Henry, Senr.	Nrt 463	Meckens, Gedion	Rnd 330
MCrear, Neal	Rch 251	Henry R.	Ans 201	Meckleroy, Archd.	Ash 84
McRee, Andrew	Mck 522	James	Rch 254	Mecklijohn, George	Grv 507
David	Mck 523	William	Rch 254	William	Grv 507
Robert	Mck 539	Meader, Randle	Brk 775	Mecray, Alexander	Orn 581
Ruth	Mck 523	Meador, Elias	Crt 90	Medaris, John	Prs 190
Widow	Mck 531	Isaac	Crt 86	Medcalf, William	Mck 575
William	Bld 36	Joel	Crt 87	Medden see Medders	
William	Mck 539	Levi	Crt 90	Medder, Bartholo-	
McReonalds, Luvay	Mre 57	Meadows, Allen	Rnd 330	mew	Jns 805
MCrevain, Finley	Rch 268	Daniel	Ird 631	Jacob	Jns 805
McReynolds, Hugh	Lnc 890	Isham	Wrr 820	Jason	Jns 805
McRorie, John	Mck 580	James	Grv 577	Mary	Jns 805
McRory, David	Brk 776	Jesse	Grv 578	Thomas	Jns 805
McSharpe see Sharpe		John	Brk 770	Medders, Benjamin	Jns 807
McSparren, James	Mck 600	John	Grv 576	Edward	Crv 337
McSwain, Alexander	Rbs 403	Michael	Grv 578	Elias	Jns 807
Angus	Rbs 405	Meads, Benn.	Psq 638	Isham	Ans 220
Angus	Rbs 406	Meahs, Matthew	Stk 625	Isham, Jr.	Ans 237
Daniel	Cmb 363	Meakes, John	Ons 173	Isham, Senr.	Ans 237
Daniel	Mnt 499	Meakings, James	Hde 372	Jason	Ans 240
Daniel	Rbs 402	James, Jur.	Hde 373	Job	Ans 237
George	Mnt 499	Isaac	Trl 690	Levi	Ans 237
John	Rbs 407	John	Trl 690	Lewis	Ans 237
Katharine	Rbs 403	Thomas	Trl 684	Thomas	Ans 240
Malcone	Rbs 401	Meaks, Briton	Ans 214	Thomas, Jr.	Ans 237
Malcom	Rbs 403	Frank	Ans 214	Thomas, Senr.	Ans 221
Roger	Rbs 397	Matthew	Stk 599	Thomas, Senr.	Jns 807
MCswain, Anguist	Rch 256	Meal see Mial		William	Ans 240
Donnel	Rch 247	Mealer, James	Wrr 818	Meddow, Job	Jns 783
Roger	Rch 247	Mealy, Eve	Rwn 289	Medearis, John	Wke 748
McSwane, Nancy	Mre 56	Meanes, James	Cbr 700	Mederis, Rice	Brk 773
McSwine, Daniel	Cht 186	John	Cbr 700	Medford, Elisabeth	Mrt 402
Edmond	Cht 184	William	Cbr 699	Jeptha	Mre 73
John	Cht 171	Meaning, Lewis	Stk 599	John	Mnt 480
William	Rth 130	see Mcaning		Medin, William	Wke 747
McThimon, Malcolm	Mre 44	Means, Alexander	Ird 672	Medlay, James	Brk 777
McTimmon, Normon	Mre 53	Andrew	Rnd 329	Medley, John	Hlf 328

Joseph	Brk 774	Megrigor, William	Nsh 113	Jno.		Glf 635
William	Jhn 746	Mehaffey, James	Wlk 53	John		Glf 635
Medlin, Benjamin	Wke 747	Mehanes, Adam	Crv 299	Joseph		Glf 690
Bradley	Frn 467	Benjamin	Crv 299	Joseph		Stk 622
Britain	Frn 461	Mehens see Mekins		Mordea		Glf 688
Bryan, Jr.	Wne 860	Mehunes, Stephen	Crv 299	Mordea, Senr.		Glf 688
Bryan, Senr.	Wne 860	Mekane, John	Crt 87	Moses		Glf 635
Cade	Wke 747	Mekens, Penney	Crr 166	Moses, Senr.		Glf 688
Drury	Wke 747	Wm.	Crr 166	Nathan		Glf 688
Francis	Wke 750	Mekins, Jeremiah	Crr 165	Phenis		Glf 684
Hugh	Mre 75	Market	Crr 165	Richard, Jur.		Glf 688
James	Frn 491	Melare, John	Prs 211	Seth		Glf 688
James	Prq 645	Melchell see Mitchell		Stephen		Rch 271
Jemima	Frn 484	Melchor, Henry	Cbr 714	Mendinghall, Eli-		
Joel	Mre 75	John	Cbr 709	sha		Rnd 331
John	Mnt 507	Melemore, Abreham	Frn 447	Mendinhall, Ann		Rnd 329
John	Mre 75	Robert	Frn 445	Benjamin		Rnd 329
Joseph	Frn 453	Young, Jur.	Frn 448	Isaac		Rnd 329
Josiah	Frn 471	Young, Ser.	Frn 482	Menes, Alexander		Ird 675
Mathew	Frn 486	Meleroy, Jones	Frn 448	Menet, John		Frn 450
Michael	Cht 209	Melican, George	Cht 152	Menges, Conrod		Lnc 869
Neoma	Prq 660	Quaenton	Cht 151	George		Lnc 878
Nicholas	Rbs 394	Mellon, Abel	Orn 583	Menies, Frederick		Rwn 314
Shadrick	Frn 471	Melone, James	Brk 777	Menley, Samuel		Cmb 356
Thomas	Lnr 16	Melsom, Edmond	Ons 143	Menries, John		Rck 475
Medlock, Charles	Brk 776	Melson, Alexr.	Ons 148	Mensinger, William		Cbr 717
John	Brk 776	John	Crt 89	Menter, John, Sr.		Cht 161
Nancy	Brk 776	Robert	Wlk 52	Joseph		Cht 161
Nathaniel	Brk 772	Taylor	Crt 89	Margret		Cht 196
Nicholas	Brk 777	Melsor, Jenney	Crr 142	see Minter		
Richard	Brk 775	Melteus, Jethro	Gts 272	MEntire, William		Ird 662
Stephen	Brk 776	Melton, Benjamin	Ons 155	Menton, Jesse		Wlk 54
Medows, Danl.	Prs 188	Cooper	Nsh 112	Mentor, John		Hrt 738
Meek, Adam	Mck 570	David	Nsh 111	Menyard, Israel		Gts 272
James	Mck 565	Elzabeth	Nsh 111	Mercer, Christo-		
James, Junr.	Mck 561	Ewd.	Ons 145	pher		Rbs 396
Mark	Nwh 1A	Ewd.	Ons 149	Jacob		Cmd 110
Moses	Mck 570	Jesse	Ans 237	Jesse		Cmd 107
Samuel	Cbr 681	Jesse	Stk 563	John		Edg 222
Meeks, Allen	Grn 593	Jessy	Ons 155	Joshua		Rbs 396
David	Bld 45	John	Mck 588	Lott		Wke 749
Elizabeth	Ptt 276	John	Nsh 112	Noah		Rbs 396
Francis	Bld 40	Jonathan	Ons 168	Peter		Cmd 109
Jacob	Dpl 406	Joseph	Nsh 110	Sarah		Rbs 395
James	Crv 243	Joseph	Ons 144	William		Cmd 101
John	Ptt 275	Joseph	Ons 149	see Merur		
Jonas	Bld 45	Josiah	Nsh 111	Merchant, Caleb		Trl 680
Joshua	Ptt 275	Mary	Nrt 461	John Spiers		Ptt 240
Lurena	Ptt 275	Michl.	Ans 237	Mercy see Merscey		
Mary	Ptt 275	Phahaley	Nsh 112	Merden see Alerden		
Readen	Bld 40	Philip	Ans 240	Meredith, David		Glf 683
Rheuben	Nwh 5A	Richard	Ons 149	Eliza.		Bld 47
Robert	Edg 221	Richard	Srr 676	Lewis		Hrt 736
Meely, Charles	Rbs 397	Robert	Srr 679	Meret, William		Dpl 431
Megalyard, John	Brk 773	Solomon	Ons 155	Merett, Daniel		Prs 197
Megee, Charles	Wrr 817	Solomon	Ons 158	Old		Crr 146
Joseph	Mre 39	Thomas	Ons 149	Merideth, James		Wlk 55
Megehe, Benjamin	Grv 554	see Milton		John		Chw 118
Josiah	Grv 556	Melvan, John	Orn 520	Daniel		Srr 676
Nathan	Grv 537	Melven, Robert	Crr 140	Meridith, Elija		Stk 614
Osbour	Grv 556	Melvin, Caty	Stk 563	James		Bnc 181
Tabitha, jr.	Orn 586	Danl.	Bld 42	James		Stk 619
see McGehe		George	Bld 40	John		Stk 614
Megehee, Charles	Mnt 509	John	Bld 46	William		Srr 675
Drury	Srr 679	Levi	Bnc 181	Merit, Absolam		Smp 511
Megginson, Samuel	Mnt 494	Memory, George	Wne 858	Absolam		Smp 516
Thomas	Mnt 491	George	Wne 873	Burrel		Smp 535
Meggs, John	Ans 231	Memurry, William	Rth 133	Daniel		Smp 535
Megill, William	Wlk 52	Menche, John	Trl 686	David		Smp 533
Meginnis, Jones	Crt 56	Mendenhal, Jesse	Brk 777	Ephraim		Hlf 330
Meglocklin, Salley	Crr 149	Mendenhall, Caleb	Glf 689	Fedrick		Smp 534
Megonegel, John	Brk 773	Daniel	Glf 686	Frederick		Hlf 328
Megreger, William,		Feby	Glf 688	Jacob		Smp 535
Senr.	Mnt 518	George	Glf 690	John		Hlf 328
Megriger, Bartlett	Mnt 518	Isaac	Glf 688	Levi		Smp 528
William	Mnt 499	James	Glf 693	Madrick		Hlf 328
William, Junr.	Mnt 518	Jane	Glf 689	Mary		Hlf 328

Michael	Smp 528	see Merser		James	Dpl 425
Nathaniel	Smp 528	Messick, Hopkins	Ons 156	Robert	Rth 128
Philip	Dpl 419	Sarah	Nwh 8A	Thomas	Wsh 708
Robert	Smp 533	Messoc, Joseph	Bfr 13	William	Chw 120
Robert, Sr.	Smp 533	William	Bfr 13	William	Glf 670
Sarah	Hlf 330	Messor, Benjn.	Crr 138	Midget, Nathan	Cmd 109
Shadrack	Hlf 328	Jeremiah	Crr 153	Midlin, John	Cht 205
Thomas	Hlf 328	Jeremiah	Crr 159	Midyett, Banister	Hde 373
Thomas, Sr.	Hlf 330	John	Crr 139	Christopher	Hde 372
William	Hlf 330	John	Crr 142	George	Hde 373
Mermiduke, Elijah	Crr 151	Malachi	Crr 137	Jesse	Hde 373
Merns, William	Nsh 113	Thos.	Crr 147	Micajah	Hde 373
Meroney, Phillip	Cht 174	Winney	Crr 153	Timothy	Hde 373
William	Gts 272	see Melsor		Miers, John	Chw 120
Merrell, Daniel	Rnd 329	Metcalf see Mitcalf, Mid-		John	Grv 557
Merret, Ann	Mre 41	calf		Peter	Wlk 54
Merrick, Geo.	Nwh 11	Metehell, Isham	Ans 201	Thomas	Chw 130
Merriday, John	Jhn 764	Metheas, Burres	Crr 140	Uphama	Rck 478
Merril, Andrew	Rwn 410	Metheeny, Sims	Mnt 510	Miflin, John	Grv 565
Arther	Crt 81	Metheny, William	Mnt 502	Miham, Silan	Smp 518
Benjamin	Rwn 409	Methews, John	Mre 66	Mihorney, John	Crr 141
John	Bnc 179	Methias, Simon	Crr 155	John, Ser.	Crr 141
Merrill, Samuel	Rwn 400	see Mathias		Thos.	Crr 141
Merrin, Barthola-		Metton, Robert	Frn 481	Milam, James	Wrr 819
mew	Srr 675	Metts, Asa	Jns 791	John	Wrr 819
Merriott, William	Wke 751	Frederick,Senr.	Jns 819	Milander, Rosanna	Grn 603
Merrit, Hezekiah,		Mews, John	Bfr 14	Milbourne, Arnold	Brt 64
Junr.	Jns 783	Meyca, Malden	Brk 773	Milburn, Alexander	Hrt 705
Hezekiah, Senr.	Jns 783	Meyell, Hector	Mnt 463	Milchner see Mitchner
John	Mnt 489	Meyers see Majers, Miars		Mileham, Ann	Glf 655
John	Mre 59	Meze, Benjamin	Rwn 410	Eliza	Glf 649
Joseph	Wrr 817	Mezingo see Mazingo		Jacob	Glf 654
Mark	Mre 59	M'Farling, Jacob	Mck 529	Valentine	Rck 454
Sarah	Wrr 816	MGlauhon, William	Brt 60	Miles, Ann	Orn 588
Thomas	Stk 564	MHargew, Alexander	Ird 612	Jacob	Csw 122
Merritt, Benjamin	Mnt 489	Mial, Thomas	Wke 747	Jacob, Jur.	Csw 122
Benjamin	Wke 750	Mials, John, Junr.	Edg 223	James	Brk 769
Jesse	Trl 680	John, Senr.	Edg 223	Joab	Rnd 332
Joel	Stk 565	Mialz, John	Edg 221	John	Csw 115
John	Stk 564	Narsworthy	Edg 221	John	Csw 116
Solomon	Csw 105	Miars, David	Ans 238	John	Chw 117
Thos.	Nsh 113	Peter	Wlk 51	John	Prs 211
William	Stk 565	Thomas	Ans 239	John	Rwn 381
William	Cht 201	Mibender, John	Bnc 179	Mary	Nrt 463
Merritte, Elijah	Mrt 388	Michael, Barnebas	Rwn 348	Thomas	Csw 116
Merryman, Elisa-		Conrod	Lnc 819	Thomas	Psq 628
beth	Mnt 521	David	Rwn 410	William	Wlk 53
Isham	Mnt 502	Freaderick	Rwn 393	Milholland, James	Ird 662
Nicholas	Mnt 521	Frederick	Rwn 410	Mill, Fanny	Hlf 326
William	Mnt 518	Henry	Ash 83	Millan, John	Dpl 397
Merscey, Edward	Ons 142	Henry, Senr.	Ash 84	Millar, Christopher
Merser, Coy, Jun.	Cmd 107	John	Cmd 106	Ballas	Cmb 356
Coy, Sen.	Cmd 107	Nicholas	Rwn 393	Millard, Hesikiah	Dpl 434
Peter	Cmd 102	Peter	Rwn 348	Jacob	Dpl 441
William, Jun.	Cmd 103	Peter, Junr.	Rwn 348	Jesse	Dpl 428
see Messer		Robert	Brk 772	Millen, Alexander	Chw 114
Mershon, Andrew	Crv 327	William	Rwn 417	Miller, Abraham	Brk 777
Merter, Martin	Brt 64	Michease, John	Cmd 109	Adam	Rwn 288
Merur, Absolam	Brn 20A	Michel, Reuben	Cht 204	Adam	Srr 676
Meschent, Gidon	Crr 147	Michican, Richard	Cmd 102	Alexander	Rth 131
Meshaw, Joel	Bld 24	Mickey, Lewis	Stk 596	Amos	Brn 18
Sion	Bld 24	Mickle, John	Srr 676	Andrew	Bnc 180
see Mushaw		William	Stk 627	Andrew	Lnc 878
Messemer, Peter	Rwn 302	William	Srr 678	Andrew	Rth 127
Messer, Asa	Rwn 444	Midcalf, Absolam	Bnc 179	Buskr...ol	Nwh 10
Dannis	Ptt 268	Danza	Rth 127	Cader	Crr 156
Jacob	Cmd 100	James	Bnc 179	Calib	Crr 137
James	Rwn 444	Warner	Rth 127	Christian	Rwn 303
Jarred	Lnc 904	William	Bnc 178	Christian	Srr 676
Jerry	Ans 232	William	Rth 128	Christopher	Rwn 308
John	Jhn 768	see Mitcalf		Daniel	Mnt 521
John	Ptt 267	Middleton, Arm-		David	Ans 201
Joshua	Dpl 402	stead	Csw 106	David	Glf 653
Solomon	Lnc 905	Benjamin	Glf 654	David	Lnc 878
William	Jns 799	David	Dpl 397	David	Lnc 900
William	Jhn 768	Isaac	Dpl 397	David	Rwn 410
William	Jns 813	James (2)	Dpl 397	David	Rwn 417

Name	Code	Name	Code	Name	Code
David	Rth 127	John	Srr 676	William	Rck 441
Elizabeth	Rbs 394	John	Srr 678	William	Rwn 318
Ephraim	Brk 60	John	Wke 749	William	Rwn 342
Federick	Wlk 52	John, Jr.	Stk 610	William	Rth 131
Felty	Rwn 417	John, Junr.	Brt 64	Windle	Rwn 302
Frederick	Bld 36	John, Junr.	Rwn 302	Wm.	Crr 166
Frederick	Brk 777	John, Senr.	Brt 62	see Millr	
Frederick	Rwn 289	John, Senr.	Rwn 303	Milles, John	Frn 475
Frederick	Rwn 400	John, Sr.	Stk 610	Millican, Andrew	Bld 3
Frederick	Stk 610	John H.	Stk 601	Benjamin	Rnd 329
Frederick,Esqr.	Rwn 374	Jonathan	Brt 62	Samuel	Rnd 331
George	Ash 83	Joseph	Ash 73	William	Rnd 331
George	Brk 777	Joseph	Grv 525	see Milluan	
George	Cbr 711	Joseph	Rth 128	Milligan, Alexr.	Ird 640
George	Dpl 402	Joseph	Stk 610	David	Ird 640
George	Grn 603	Joshua	Ptt 291	Fargus	Ird 640
George	Jns 789	Katty	Ash 83	James	Ird 640
George	Rwn 277	Kedar M.	Ans 231	Milliken, James	Orn 582
George	Rwn 288	Malichi	Br5 60	John	Orn 582
Godfrey	Stk 563	Maney	Crr 147	Robert	Orn 582
Hamon (2)	Rnd 330	Marimagdalene	Dpl 399	Millikin, James	Nrt 461
Henry	Ans 200	Martin	Rch 482	John	Nsh 110
Henry	Brk 772	Mary	Rwn 417	Millin, Easter	Mrt 402
Henry	Ird 646	Mason	Chw 120	Millis, Edward	Glf 625
Henry	Rck 466	Michael	Rnd 330	Edward	Glf 670
Henry	Rwn 417	Michael	Rwn 417	John	Glf 670
Henry	Rwn 448	Mordica	Rth 129	Moses	Crt 88
Henry	Stk 604	Morris	Stk 564	Millison, John	Orn 582
Isaac	Bnc 181	Nathaniel	Brt 60	Millon, Edward	Lnc 831
Isaac, Junr.	Gts 272	Nicholas	Lnc 866	John	Lnc 832
Isaac, Senr.	Gts 272	Nicholas	Rwn 349	John	Mnt 487
Jacob	Cbr 709	Nicholas	Rwn 417	Millor, James	Mre 49
Jacob	Lnc 869	Peter	Cbr 684	Millr, Harmon	Stk 563
Jacob	Rwn 288	Peter	Mnt 496	Mills, Ambrose	Rth 127
Jacob	Rwn 400	Peter	Rnd 330	Anne	Dpl 401
Jacob	Stk 563	Peter	Rwn 433	Anthony	Crv 323
Jacob	Stk 600	Peter	Rwn 444	Anthony	Rbs 395
Jacob	Stk 610	Phebe	Ans 240	Benjn.	Brn 14A
Jacob	Srr 676	Philip	Lnc 869	Charles	Ird 650
Jacob, Jur.	Rwn 308	Philip	Rwn 302	Edward	Glf 670
Jacob, Senr.	Rwn 308	Phillip	Lnr 17	Elizabeth	Wlk 53
Jacob L.	Stk 606	Rachel	Gts 272	Frederick	Ptt 244
James	Brk 777	Rachel	Rwn 288	Frederick,Junr.	Ptt 257
James	Frn 461	Reuben	Brt 60	George	Ons 174
James	Jns 811	Richard	Rnd 330	George	Rnd 330
James	Mck 602	Richard	Wsh 708	Henry	Ans 225
James	Orn 583	Robert	Cbr 685	Henry, Senior	Ptt 246
James	Orn 588	Robert	Dpl 399	Hicks	Dpl 411
James	Orn 589	Robert	Dpl 401	Hugh	Rck 448
James	Rnd 330	Robert	Rth 130	Isaac, Senior	Ptt 246
James	Rwn 342	Robt. J.	Lnc 849	Jacob	Rth 129
James	Rth 93	Saml.	Crr 164	James	Glf 639
James	Rth 126	Saml., (Widow		James	Glf 670
James	Wne 854	Son)	Rwn 318	James	Mnt 493
Jane	Wlk 55	Samuel	Rth 131	James	Ons 178
John	Bnc 178	Samuel, (Sam.		Jesse	Rth 128
John	Brk 770	Son)	Rwn 318	John	Ans 210
John	Chw 116	Samuel, Senr.	Rwn 317	John	Ans 231
John	Cmb 362	Sarah	Crt 92	John	Brn 20
John (2)	Lnc 871	Sarah	Rnd 332	John	Crv 323
John	Lnc 905	Sarah	Rwn 410	JOhn	Cmb 385
John	Mck 602	Solomon	Brt 62	John	Glf 638
John	Mnt 515	Solomon	Crr 158	John, J.	Rth 128
John	Nwh 5A	Stephen	Dpl 405	Jonathan	Rwn 381
John	Orn 586	Stephen	Edg 221	Joseph	Glf 692
John	Orn 587	Stephen	Stk 597	Joseph	Ptt 246
John	Prq 649	Thomas	Frn 484	Joshua	Ons 166
John	Rnd 331	Thomas	Jns 813	Koziah	Ptt 246
John	Rck 477	Thos.	Crr 140	Leonard	Dpl 408
John	Rwn 289	Thos.	Crr 156	Marvel	Rth 128
John	Rwn 387	Tobias	Rwn 308	Mary	Hlf 326
John	Rwn 400	Widow	Rwn 308	Micajah	Stk 618
John	Rwn 417	William	Ash 84	Nahum	Edg 222
John	Rth 127	William	Grn 603	Naxeby, junior	Ptt 246
John	Rth 129	William	Mck 575	Naxeby, Senior	Ptt 246
John (4)	Rth 130	William	Mck 594	Nicason	Glf 670
John	Stk 610	William	Mck 601	Samuel	Ptt 246

Sarah	Ons 178	Nathan	Grn 589	William	Rth 131
Sarah	Rck 449	Nathan, Jr.	Grn 591	William	Wlk 52
Spyas	Ptt 246	Minshoe, John	Wne 860	William (2)	Wlk 53
Stephen	Crt 56	Minshrew, Aaron	Grn 592	Mitchell, Aaron	Brk 772
Thomas	Mnt 489	Abraham	Grn 592	Abraham	Ash 83
Waitman	Rck 467	Isaac, jr.	Grn 592	Adam	Glf 666
William	Ans 210	Isaac, Senr.	Grn 592	Alexander	Crv 251
William	Ans 231	Jacob	Grn 592	Andrew	Ird 636
William	Brn 15	Jacob, Senior	Grn 595	Billey	Wke 750
William	Bnc 178	John	Grn 591	Cadar	Brt 62
William	Ons 181	Philip	Grn 592	Charity	Hrt 721
William	Srr 677	Minster, Frederick	Cbr 698	Charles	Rck 449
William	Wlk 53	Minter, Jeremiah	Cht 162	Daniel	Ans 210
William, junior	Ptt 245	John	Cht 170	Daniel	Mck 592
William, SEnior	Ptt 245	see Menter		David	Csw 115
Millsapps, Jacob	Rnd 332	Minton, Benjamin	Brt 64	Easter	Mrt 402
Reuben	Rnd 332	Chloe	Nsh 110	Elijah	Grv 510
Thomas	Rnd 332	James	Brt 64	Elisha	Brt 62
Milluan, Elizth.	Brn 21	James	Wlk 52	Elizabeth	Brt 62
Millwood, M.	Stk 585	John	Nsh 110	Elizabeth	Nrt 461
Milne, Joseph	Nwh 1	Thomas	Brt 64	Ephraim	Orn 519
Milner, Jacobina	Frn 465	Mints, Frances	Brn 15A	Evan	Grv 556
Richard	Lnr 17	Henry	Brn 15A	George	Wne 865
Milone, Robert	Rwn 438	Mire, Philip	Stk 597	Hardy	Lnr 16
Milrany, James	Glf 684	Mires, Jacob	Stk 564	Hezekiah	Grv 576
Milring, Joseph	Rwn 417	Joseph	Srr 678	Ican	Grv 542
Milsaps, Joseph		Peter	Srr 676	Jacob	Ans 230
(2)	Ird 611	Peter, Jun.	Srr 677	Jacob	Cbr 698
Thomas	Ird 611	Miris, David	Rwn 417	Jacob	Grv 512
William	Ird 612	Mirit see Meret		Jacob	Lnc 869
Milton, Agness	Grv 507	Mise, Leonard	Cbr 695	James	Brt 62
Anson	Mre 69	Misemor, John	Rwn 297	James	Brt 64
Cornelius	Rth 132	Misenhamer, Abram	Cbr 709	James	Crv 273
Daniel	Rth 129	George	Cbr 709	James	Crv 323
Isham	Srr 678	John	Cbr 693	James	Grv 516
James	Hrt 725	John	Cbr 717	James	Nrt 461
James	Mre 58	Peter	Cbr 690	James	Orn 586
John	Grv 509	Jacob	Cbr 698	James	Wke 776
John	Rth 129	Misteller, Michael	Lnc 893	Jeresiah	Brt 64
Josiah	Hrt 725	Mistler, John	Rwn 410	Jesse	Ans 210
Nathaniel	Mre 58	Mitcalf, James	Bnc 178	Jesse	Grv 554
Reuben	Rth 133	see Midcalf		Jesse	Mrt 400
Stephen	Grv 506	Mitchael, John	Wne 844	Jesse	Nrt 461
William	Rth 132	William	Wne 845	Jno., Senr.	Wke 751
see Melton		Mitcham, James	Orn 588	Joab	Wke 749
Mimdine, James	Crv 247	John	Orn 588	John	Brk 773
Mimms, David	Cht 209	Limus	Prs 199	John	Frn 472
Mims, Britain	Wke 749	see Mileham		John	Frn 493
David	Bld 10	Mitchel, Andrew	Bnc 181	John	Grv 516
James	Bld 8	Andrew (2)	Rth 131	John	Grv 576
Needham	Cht 210	Archd.	Wlk 52	John	Jhn 749
Thomas	Bld 6	Charity	Edg 222	John	Mck 532
Mince, William	Rth 127	Charles	Prs 197	John	Mck 558
Minchew, Juda	Prs 189	Cornealus	Nsh 113	John	Orn 520
Thos.	Prs 189	Dempsey	Grn 610	John	Orn 584
Minchey, Richd.	Prs 215	Dred	Grn 611	John	Psq 635
Minchus, Bond	Gts 272	Edward	Edg 222	John	Stk 574
Mindenhall, Nathl.	Lnc 839	George	Rth 128	John	Wke 750
Miner, Henry	Brn 21A	Hugh	Stk 595	John, Jun.	Chw 119
Jacob	Chw 115	Isham	Prs 201	John, Jun.	Chw 126
Joseph	Cht 167	James	Rth 128	John, Junr. (2)	Brt 62
Minfrey, James	Grv 510	Jas.	Prs 196	John, Sen.	Chw 119
Ming, Delilah	Chw 127	John	Crr 158	John, Sen.	Chw 126
James	Chw 121	John (2)	Wlk 52	John, Senr.	Brt 62
Joseph	Orn 519	Leml.	Crr 141	Joseph	Nrt 461
Minges, Jacob	Lnc 886	Peter	Edg 173	Joshua	Crv 247
Mingy, Dudley	Grv 516	Peter	Edg 221	Josiah	Wke 747
Minish, James	Srr 678	Relph	Stk 580	Leven	Rck 463
Minist, Isaac	Srr 678	Salley	Crr 146	Lucretia	Brt 62
Minner, Richard	Glf 644	Saml.	Nsh 113	Mary	Wke 776
Richard	Glf 666	Susanah	Cmd 105	Mathias, Junr.	Cbr 698
Minor, Ansil	Wrr 820	Thomas	Bld 9	Mathias, Senr.	Cbr 698
John	Grv 547	Thomas	Wlk 52	Messenah	Grv 533
John Koonce	Jns 815	Thomas,Fr. Neg.	Edg 222	Mjor	Grv 552
Nicholas	Gts 272	Thos.	Crr 137	Nazara	Rbs 390
Mins, Jacob	Grv 572	Will.	Prs 213	Olliver	Mrt 402
Minshew, Briant	Grn 591	William	Rth 128	Rabeckah	Cbr 696

Rachael	Wlk 52	Darcas	Wke 750	Christopher	Wlk 53

Rachael Wlk 52
Reuben Wne 864
Richard Cmd 107
Richard Gts 272
Robert Csw 139
Robert Cmb 356
Robert Lnc 878
Robert Mck 558
Samuel Glf 634
Shadrack Orn 519
Solomn. Rck 436
Thomas Brt 62
Thomas Frn 494
Thomas Grv 516
Thomas Ptt 231
William Ans 210
William Chw 126
William Crv 243
William Frn 481
William Grv 563
William Ird 625
William Rck 461
William, Junr. Nrt 461
William, Senr. Nrt 463
Zadock Brt 62
  see Mitichell
Mitchels, Thomas Srr 678
Mitchiner, William Nrt 461
Mitchner, Thomas Brk 773
Mitechell, William Grv 579
Mitichell, John Orn 586
Mixon, Elijah,Jur. Bfr 14
  Elijah, Ser. Bfr 14
  George Bfr 14
  James Bfr 13
  Jeremiah Chw 125
  Zachariah Bfr 13
Mize, Frederick Orn 586
  Henry Orn 586
  Jean Grv 577
  John Orn 586
  John Wlk 53
  Lewis Grv 577
  Randolph Wke 750
Mizel, Levi Dpl 440
  Luke Dpl 442
  Mark Dpl 419
  William Dpl 420
Mizzell, Aron Brt 60
  Bersheba Brt 60
  Cadar (2) Brt 62
  Henry (2) Brt 62
  Isaac Brt 60
  James Brt 62
  John Brt 60
  John, Junr. Brt 62
  John, Senr. Brt 62
  Joseph Brt 62
  Judith Brt 64
  Mary Brt 60
  Moses Brt 62
  Thomas Brt 64
MKinney, John Brk 775
Moaney see Mooney
Moaning, Christo-
  pher Ptt 274
  Henry Grn 614
  John Ptt 289
  Sarey Ptt 290
  Thomas Grn 612
  William Ptt 259
Moary, James Mnt 521
Moats, Jethro Smp 520
Mobley, Allin Wke 750
  Benajah Dpl 416
  Bigars Smp 524
  Burrel Dpl 416

Darcas Wke 750
Elisabeth Mrt 400
Ezekiel Wke 748
Jesse Wke 750
Jona. Rck 468
Lazer Ptt 226
Ollen Smp 533
Surrell Jhn 775
Thomas Ptt 226
Wiley Smp 502
Wm. Mrt 400
Mobly, Alexander Ird 625
  Hammon Ird 626
  John Rck 475
  Loving Rwn 438
  William Rck 475
Mock, Henry Srr 679
  Jacob Rwn 374
  John Rwn 367
  John Rwn 444
  Peter Ird 645
  Peter Srr 679
  Philip Rwn 367
  Thomas Cbr 700
  Widow Rwn 375
Mocksley, Daniel Srr 680
Mocman see Morman
Mocton see Morton
Mode, John Rth 131
  William Rth 133
Modett, Joseph Orn 589
Modlin, Gideon Psq 629
  Mark Rnd 330
Moffet, David Rth 131
Moffett, James Rnd 328
Moffit, John Brk 777
  Robert Rwn 356
  Silas Rwn 367
  Widow Mck 569
  William Brk 777
  William Mck 571
Moffitt, Adam Rnd 329
  Charls Rnd 330
  Hugh Rnd 330
  Robbert Rnd 329
  Robbert Rnd 330
  Samuel Rnd 329
  William Rnd 330
Mohon, Wiley Ans 211
Mohun, James Brt 60
  Jesse Brt 60
  John Brt 64
Moler, Valentine Ird 636
  Abraham Lnc 905
  John Lnc 905
Mollay, Edward Glf 674
Molley, Thomas Hlf 328
Mollogue, William Glf 629
Molly, Thomas Mnt 513
Moloy, Charles Cmb 389
  Duncan Cmb 385
Molpus, John Dpl 425
Molten, Hannah Rch 265
Molton, Catherlin
  Motherlin Prs 200
  George Prs 200
  Michael Cmb 356
  Peter Ans 201
  Thos. Prs 200
  Will. Prs 200
Moman, John Ird 618
  William B. Ird 618
Momfort, William Edg 222
Mon, Hardy Brn 19A
  John Brk 777
Monday, Arthur Mnt 471
  Arthur Nrt 461

Christopher Wlk 53
Francis Wlk 55
James Mnt 479
Jeromiah Brk 777
Mary Mnt 484
Peter Wne 860
Thomas Ird 631
William Ird 631
William Mnt 479
  see Muddy, Munday
Monden, Mary Ptt 225
Money, Isaac Prs 202
  Jacob Prs 202
  Mangrom Prs 202
  Wm. Prs 197
Monfort, Richard Wrr 820
Monger, Smith Crt 89
Mongomer, Hugh Orn 587
  John Bnc 181
  William Orn 586
Monk, Jacob Smp 512
  Latitia Brt 64
  Nottingham Brt 62
  Willis Wke 747
Monny, John Bld 5
Monroe, David P. Nrt 463
  P. David Nrt 463
Monrow, George Rwn 289
  John, (Cap.) Rwn 367
  Thomas Rwn 410
Mons, Alexander Dpl 404
Monseau, Sarah Wke 776
Montague, Henry Rth 126
Monteeth, Widow Mck 570
Montford, William Ons 150
Montfort, Edward Hlf 328
  Richard Hlf 326
  Robartson Rwn 459
  Thomas Hlf 326
  William Hlf 326
Montgomery, Ann Brt 64
  Daniel Cmb 367
  David Brk 769
  Elender Hrt 712
  Hanah Glf 669
  James Brn 17
  James Csw 107
  James Csw 108
  John Cht 178
  John Glf 630
  John Glf 638
  John Ird 612
  John Mck 527
  John Wlk 52
  Michl. Csw 129
  Robert Hrt 712
  Robert Mck 559
  William Glf 629
  William Glf 665
  William Orn 586
  see Mongomery
Montiff, George Glf 682
Montigue, Salend Grv 511
Mony, William Rck 469
Moodey, Thomas Wrr 818
Moody, Benjamin Nrt 463
  Edward Brk 769
  Epps Frn 480
  Ezekial Cht 165
  Frederick Hlf 326
  George Brk 770
  Henry Mnt 488
  Isaac Bnc 180
  James Brk 769
  James Dpl 406
  James Jhn 765
  John Brk 769

John	Lnc 851	Burwell	Wne 862	James		Hlf 328
John	Wke 748	Camm	Glf 690	James		Hde 372
Joseph	Bnc 179	Catherine	Bld 34	James		Idd 641
McCayer	Brk 771	Charles	Prq 643	James		Ird 662
Nathaniel	Stk 566	Charles	Prs 187	James		Mck 552
Phillip	Nsh 113	Charles, Jun.	Prq 653	James		Mck 570
Rebecca	Nrt 463	Charles, Jur.	Grv 527	James		Mck 584
Samuel	Wke 750	Christian	Rth 127	James		Mnt 475
Surrell	Nrt 463	Clary	Orn 585	James		Nsh 112
Thomas (2)	Brk 769	Cornelius	Ans 210	James		Nwh 5
Thomas	Cmb 356	Cornelius	Prq 644	James		Nwh 9
Thomas	Stk 562	Cotila	Ptt 228	James		Ons 160
Thomas	Stk 565	Daniel	Brk 773	James (2)		Orn 520
Thomas	Srr 675	David	Mck 577	James		Orn 521
William	Bnc 179	David	Mck 580	James		Orn 585
William	Cht 165	David	Ons 148	James		Orn 587
William	Frn 461	David	Prs 189	James		Ptt 269
Moodye, John	Frn 480	David	Ptt 256	James		Rbs 394
Moon, Jacob	Cht 216	David	Stk 562	James		Rth 133
James	Cht 218	Dempsea	Prs 204	James		Stk 562
John	Cht 216	Dempsey	Ptt 227	James		Stk 564
Mooney, Elisabeth	Brk 769	Didgenira	Grn 589	James		Stk 566
Friderick	Brk 774	E. William	Nrt 461	James		Wke 750
Jeromiah	Brk 772	Edmond	Nwh 5A	James, Esqr.		Hrt 717
John	Bld 18	Edmond	Ptt 232	James, Junr.		Brk 772
Sarah	Brn 20	Edward	Brk 775	James, Junr.		Brk 776
Will.	Brn 19A	Edward	Rwn 288	James, Junr.		Hrt 717
William	Wlk 53	Edward	Wke 748	James, Senr.		Brk 776
Zediah	Hde 373	Edward	Wrr 816	Jas.		Mrt 401
Mooneyham, Hannah	Wke 747	Edward, Senr.	Ptt 232	Jeremiah		Grv 549
Jams	Nsh 111	Eli	Hrt 725	Jeremire		Prs 188
Thos.	Nsh 113	Elijah	Edg 222	Jesse		Csw 108
Moony, David	Rth 129	Elisabeth	Ird 651	Jesse		Mrt 402
David	Rth 131	Elisha	Ptt 266	Jesse		Nrt 461
George	Rth 131	Elisha	Ptt 281	Jesse		Ptt 260
James	Rth 131	Elisha, Senior	Ptt 280	Jesse		Rch 247
Peter	Rth 93	Elisha, Senior	Ptt 284	Jesse, junior		Ptt 266
Moor, Auston	Dpl 434	Eliz.	Ons 159	Jessy		Ons 145
Charles	Rck 486	Elizabeth	Cmb 357	Jms.		Lnc 834
Drury	Hrt 700	Elizabeth	Hrt 721	Jno., Senr.		Lnc 834
James	Hrt 700	Elizabeth	Ptt 233	Joel		Grv 527
Joseph	Smp 524	Enoch	Edg 221	John		Bfr 13
Lewis	Smp 510	Ephraim	Grn 604	John		Bfr 14
Martha	Dpl 433	Francis	Rth 130	John		Brt 62
Maurice	Dpl 434	Francis Kipps	Hde 381	John		Brt 64
Susanna	Rwn 288	Frederick	Brk 769	John		Brt 90
Thomas	Smp 498	Frederick	Crv 317	John		Bnc 179
Moore, ... (2)	Nwh 10A	George	Grv 567	John		Brk 772
...	Ptt 286	George	Hlf 328	John		Crv 287
Aaron	Cmb 373	George	Mrt 402	John		Crv 319
Aaron	Hrt 717	George	Orn 585	John		Crv 329
Aaron	Stk 564	George	Rbs 395	John		Grv 521
Abel	Cmb 371	George	Rbs 432	John		Grv 527
Abram	Prs 202	George	Rwn 444	John		Glf 653
Adam	Ird 657	George	Rwn 453	John		Hrt 721
Alexander	Cmb 365	George	Rth 129	John		Jhn 759
Alexander	Stk 565	George	Rth 130	John		Lnr 16
Alexr.	Cht 162	Gideon	Jns 787	John (2)		Lnc 819
Alexr.	Lnc 828	Goodrich	Ird 618	John		Lnc 883
Alexr. D.	Nwh 7	Grizey	Prs 187	John		Mrt 402
Alfred	Brn 15	Hardy	Cmb 372	John		Mnt 520
Allen	Hrt 721	Henry	Hrt 705	John		Mre 73
Andrew	Ans 239	Henry	Hde 372	John		Nrt 459
Andrew	Ird 644	Henry	Ptt 231	John		Orn 521
Andrew	Mck 554	Henry	Rch 255	John		Orn 585
Ann	Brt 64	Henry, Jur.	Hde 374	John		Orn 586
Anthony, Junr.	Nrt 459	Higdon	Wrr 818	John		Orn 589
Anthony, Senr.	Nrt 459	Hilory	Nwh 8	John		Prq 642
Arthur	Hrt 725	Jacob	Nwh 6	John		Prs 209
Audlin	Rwn 297	Jacob	Ptt 231	John		Ptt 225
Benj.	Rck 473	Jacob	Rwn 314	John		Rnd 329
Benjamin	Brk 774	Jacob, Junior	Ptt 256	John		Rck 446
Benjamin	Cmb 372	Jacob, junior	Ptt 266	John		Rwn 314
Benjamin	Rbs 394	James	Bld 34	John		Rwn 328
Benjamin	Rwn 367	James	Csw 108	John		Rth 128
Benjan.	Rck 452	James	Cht 201	John		Stk 564
Britton	Grn 589	James	Grn 601	John		Wke 747

Name	Ref
John	Wke 749
John	Wrr 820
John, Junior	Ptt 284
John R.	Cmb 372
Jordan	Cmb 373
Jordan	Ptt 268
Jos.	Mrt 402
Joseph	Brt 64
Joseph	Bnc 179
Joseph	Brk 772
Joseph	Crt 92
Joseph	Orn 589
Joseph	Orn 619
Joseph	Prq 644
Joseph	Rnd 329
Joseph	Rwn 327
Joseph	Rth 132
Joseph, Senr.	Mck 533
Joshua	Prq 644
Josiah	Brk 773
Judah	Hrt 717
Kellum	Frn 463
Kennidy	Ptt 260
Keziah	Hlf 328
Kezine	Ons 149
Lane	Grv 567
Latham	Crv 303
Laurence	Ans 210
Lemuel	Rth 129
Levi	Crv 243
Levi	Mrt 388
Levy	Grn 587
Lewis	Wke 748
Luke	Prs 187
M. William	Nrt 461
Mark	Wke 749
Martha	Bfr 14
Mary	Brn 17A
Mary	Hlf 326
Mary	Hlf 330
Mary	Lnr 16
Mary	Mrt 400
Mary	Rbs 393
Mary	Wne 855
Mathias	Mrt 416
Matthew	Cmb 372
Matthew	Stk 565
Matthias,junior	Ptt 227
Matthias,senior	Ptt 227
Morris	Hrt 717
Morriss	Mrt 402
Moses	Brt 64
Moses	Crt 91
Moses	Edg 222
Moses	Lnc 818
Moses	Mrt 400
Moses	Ptt 256
Moses, junior	Ptt 233
Moses, Junior	Ptt 272
Nancy	Brk 774
Nathan	Prq 656
Nathan (2)	Prq 662
Nathan	Rwn 367
Nathaniel	Glf 676
Natthaniel	Wne 862
Nimrod	Rck 473
Nuton	Ptt 251
Obadiah	Ptt 227
Penny	Wke 749
Peter	Rck 470
Peter	Rck 481
Philip	Mck 598
Philip	Rth 132
Phillip	Prs 187
Polly	Rth 132
Rachael	Rth 130
Randal	Jhn 759
Ratchell	Mrt 402
Reading	Ptt 232
Rebecca	Nrt 461
Redrick	Mnt 504
Reuben	Stk 562
Reubin	Hlf 328
Richard	Lnr 16
Richard	Ptt 227
Robert	Chw 128
Robert	Lnr 16
Robert	Orn 520
Robert	Orn 586
Robert	Prs 187
Robert	Prs 200
Robert	Rnd 329
Robt.	Cht 222
Roger	Nwh 5A
Samuel	Csw 96
Samuel	Prq 662
Samuel	Rck 469
Samuel	Rwn 313
Samuel, junior	Grn 604
Samuel, Senior	Grn 604
Samuel, Son of Wm.	Ptt 268
Sithe	Bnc 181
Smith	Glf 663
Sukey	Ptt 226
Thomas	Bnc 178
Thomas	Brk 772
Thomas	Crt 57
Thomas	Cht 200
Thomas	Cht 201
Thomas	Grv 506
Thomas	Grn 604
Thomas	Glf 663
Thomas	Ird 615
Thomas	Lnr 16
Thomas	Mck 533
Thomas	Mnt 471
Thomas	Mnt 488
Thomas	Orn 520
Thomas	Prq 662
Thomas	Prs 187
Thomas	Ptt 231
Thomas	Rck 456
Titus	Brt 64
Travers	Ans 198
Valentine	Mnt 471
Valentine	Orn 585
Wade	Nsh 111
Wallace	Crv 243
Widow	Mck 540
Widow	Mck 561
Widow	Mck 577
William	Bfr 13
William	Bfr 14
William	Brt 62
William (2)	Bnc 178
William	Brk 774
William	Csw 104
William	Crv 329
William (2)	Cmb 366
William	Edg 221
William	Grv 518
William	Grv 557
William	Grn 594
William	Hrt 725
William	Mck 567
William	Mnt 494
William	Orn 584
William	Orn 589
William	Prq 662
William	Ptt 287
William	Rnd 329
William	Rbs 393
William	Rbs 394
William	Rbs 397
William	Rwn 344
William	Rwn 404
William	Srr 675
William, junr.	Ptt 268
William, Senr.	Rwn 404
William E.	Nrt 461
William M.	Nrt 461
Willis	Nwh 6A
Willm.	Nsh 112
Wm.	Lnc 833
Wm.	Rbs 432
Wooda	Ptt 266
Zachariah	Lnr 16
Moorey, Jeremiah	Wrr 820
John	Wrr 820
Moorhead, James, Esq.	Bld 31
Moorin, Edward	Brk 776
Mooring, Henry	Wke 749
Mooris, Amanual	Ons 156
Moorison, Willm., Doctor	Mck 579
Moorland, William	Lnc 886
Moose, ...	Crr 138
George	Lnc 819
Jacob	Cbr 713
see Moore	
Mootray, James	Cht 170
Mootry, James	Cht 191
Moran, Henry	Hlf 330
William	Cht 169
Morce, Nathl.	Ans 212
Mordecai, Jacob	Wrr 784
More, Aaron	Srr 675
Edward	Srr 710
Joel	Srr 677
Joel	Srr 678
John	Srr 705
Moses	Srr 676
Rodeham	Srr 677
William	Stk 564
William	Srr 680
Morefield, John	Stk 582
Mary	Rwn 394
see Murfield	
Morehead, James	Rch 255
James	Rth 133
John	Rck 440
Joseph	Rch 255
see Moorhead	
Moreland, Edward	Hlf 328
Francis	Orn 588
Mary	Rth 133
Joseph	Srr 678
Joseph	Srr 679
William	Srr 678
Morene, Thomas	Csw 145
Morer, Joshua	Ans 202
Morfleet, Abraham	Chw 118
Morgan, ...	Brk 774
Abel	Nwh 10
Abraham	Gts 273
Ann	Cmd 100
Anne	Nrt 461
Arnold	Nrt 461
Asa	Psq 630
Benjamin	Frn 453
Benjamin	Glf 632
Benjamin	Rnd 332
Benjn.	Nwh 11
Benn.	Psq 640
Betty	Frn 461
Charles	Cht 157
David	Rnd 331
Edward	Smp 524
Elijah	Rwn 387

Name	Ref	Name	Ref	Name	Ref
Elisabeth	Crv 337	Sarah	Cmd 99	Morris, Aaron	Smp 499
Elizabeth	Hrt 733	Sarah	Psq 641	Abram	Brt 62
Elizabeth	Nrt 463	Sary	Orn 585	Absalom	Wlk 52
Elizth.	Nwh 10	Seth	Gts 272	Ann	Crv 315
Enoch	Cbr 678	Seth	Psq 641	Ann	Mnt 518
Ezekiel	Rnd 331	Susanna	Csw 114	Aquilla	Hlf 330
Fedrick	Smp 526	Theophilus	Ird 626	Benjamin	Cmd 103
George	Chw 113	Thomas	Mnt 463	Benjamin	Rwn 387
George	Srr 706	Thomas	Orn 589	Benjn.	Bnc 179
Habicock	Glf 632	Thomas	Wlk 52	Charles	Grn 599
Hambeton	Smp 504	Thomas, jr.	Orn 587	Christian	Cbr 711
Hannah	Wlk 55	Thophilus	Ird 625	David	Hde 373
Hardy	Hrt 700	Timothy	Nrt 461	Dunston	Hlf 326
Hardy	Nsh 111	William	Ans 230	Edward	Frn 490
Isaac	Rwn 387	William	Brn 16A	Edward	Wlk 52
Isaac, Mulatto	Edg 223	William	Csw 120	Elias	Mnt 471
Jacob	Hrt 700	William	Csw 127	Elijah	Rch 255
James	Brt 60	William	Cht 156	Esther	Dpl 432
James	Glf 641	William	Mnt 493	Faithy	Hlf 326
James	Rwn 380	William	Nrt 463	Francis	Hde 372
James, Junr.	Rwn 387	William	Orn 586	Francis	Stk 596
James, Senr.	Rwn 387	William	Wlk 54	Fredrick	Mre 64
Jesse	Jhn 773	William, Mulat-		George	Bnc 178
Jesse	Rnd 330	to	Edg 223	George, Jr.	Hlf 326
Joab	Brk 769	Willis	Hrt 700	George, Sen.	Hlf 326
Job	Psq 638	Wllm.	Nsh 111	Griffin	Cbr 679
John	Brt 60	Zacha.	Cht 157	Harmon	Stk 565
John	Crt 75	Morgen, Joseph	Crr 166	Haton, Senr.	Mnt 471
John	Cht 155	Morgin, George	Mre 48	Henry	Brk 771
John	Crv 283	James	Mre 70	Henry	Mre 64
John	Hlf 328	Jno.	Prs 208	Holoway	Hlf 330
John	Jhn 771	Joseph	Mre 46	Hezekiah	Hlf 330
John	Nsh 111	Nathan	Mre 70	Isaac	Orn 585
John	Nrt 461	Phillip	Prs 203	Isaac	Rwn 356
John	Orn 583	Susanna	Prs 219	Jacob	Ans 202
John	Orn 585	William	Mre 46	James	Ans 202
John	Psq 626	William	Mre 48	James	Brk 771
John	Rth 127	Morgon, Charles	Bnc 181	James	Hde 372
John	Smp 526	Morgrave, John	Srr 679	James	Mre 72
John	Stk 562	Morhead, James	Rch 268	James (2)	Rth 127
John	Wlk 52	Morice see Morrice		Jeptha	Ans 205
John (Moore)	Orn 589	Morine, John	Crt 88	Jeremiah	Wne 872
Jonathan	Mnt 507	William	Crt 88	John	Brt 62
Joseph	Brk 770	Moring, William	Wne 849	John	Cht 197
Joseph	Cmd 101	Morley, David	Bld 31	John	Crv 275
Joseph	Cht 153	Morman, Andrew	Rch 263	John	Crv 277
Joseph	Edg 221	Andrew	Rch 268	John	Hlf 328
Joseph	Gts 272	John	Rch 263	John	Ird 631
Joshua	Wlk 52	Thomas	Rch 263	John	Lnc 819
Josiah	Frn 458	William	Ans 211	John	Ons 149
Lewis	Glf 690	Williams	Ans 224	John	Orn 587
Mark	Mnt 493	Morningham, Shad-		John	Rwn 380
Martha	Hrt 738	erick	Srr 676	John	Wke 748
Martha	Rth 129	Morphet, James	Cht 183	John	Wlk 52
Martin	Ird 626	Morphus, John	Cht 173	John, jr.	Grv 543
Mary	Rnd 330	Morpus, James	Wke 751	John, Jun.	Mre 65
Matthew	Cmb 374	Joseph	Wke 751	John, Junr.	Mnt 475
Methias	Gts 273	Morr, George	Rwn 277	John, Senr.	Grv 546
Milicent	Psq 640	Morress, John	Stk 566	John, Ser.	Mre 64
Morgan	Rth 128	Morrice, Aaron	Psq 626	Joseph (2)	Brt 62
Nathan	Rwn 344	Benn.	Psq 627	Joseph	Cmd 109
Nathan, Junr.	Rwn 297	Betsey	Psq 632	Joseph	Orn 583
Patience	Frn 454	Charity	Psq 635	Joseph	Rwn 367
Paul	Orn 587	James	Psq 632	Joseph	Rwn 417
Peter	Hlf 330	Job	Psq 633	Joshua	Psq 633
Polly	Bnc 180	John	Psq 632	Jourden	Mnt 471
Prudence	Nrt 461	Joseph	Psq 626	Mary	Mnt 475
Rebecca	Nwh 3A	Joshua	Psq 632	Mary	Orn 585
Rebeckah	Lnr 17	Lydia	Psq 634	Mary	Rnd 332
Rebekah	Rnd 331	Mariam	Psq 633	Matthew	Cmb 362
Reuben	Smp 532	Mark	Psq 633	Micajah	Rth 133
Richard	Rbs 395	Nathan	Psq 624	Moses	Brt 62
Robert	Cmd 98	Nathan	Psq 640	Moses	Crv 277
Robert	Frn 458	Thomas	Psq 630	Nancy	Hlf 328
Robert	Rwn 313	Thomas	Psq 632	Nancy	Hde 374
Rubin	Ird 626	Thomas	Psq 633	Nathan	Ans 205
Sam.	Nwh 3	William P.	Psq 634	Nathaniel	Srr 678

Name	Code
Noah	Gts 273
Patey	Rth 132
Peter	Mre 64
Phebe	Bfr 14
Philemon	Hlf 326
Presley	Stk 565
Richard	Hde 374
Richard	Jns 795
Richard	Orn 586
Rubin	Mnt 471
Samuel	Wne 863
Shaderick	Stk 563
Solomon	Nwh 8A
Stephen	Grv 546
Stephen	Mre 65
Thomas	Bfr 13
Thomas	Bld 31
Thomas	Csw 131
Thomas	Grv 581
Thomas	Jns 795
Thomas	Mnt 471
Thomas	Rth 127
Thomas	Stk 566
Thomas	Wke 748
Thomas	Wke 750
Valentine	Rch 258
William	Ans 216
William	Bfr 13
William	Brt 60
William (2)	Brt 64
William	Brk 773
William	Cht 159
William	Grv 536
William	Hlf 326
William	Hrt 712
William	Hde 373
William	Rbs 394
William	Stk 563
William, Senr.	Brt 62
William G.	Ans 238
Zacehariah	Wne 859
see Mooris, Morice	
Morrisett, Peter	Crr 145
Morrisey, George	Smp 513
Morrison, Alexan-der	Mck 599
Alexander	Mre 59
Alexr.	Lnc 849
Andrew	Brk 770
Andrew	Ird 640
Andrew	Ird 672
Archabald	Rbs 396
Archibald	Bnc 180
Cain	Cmb 388
Daniel	Cmb 363
Daniel	Ird 646
Daniel	Rch 260
Daniel	Rbs 392
David	Rwn 327
Elisabeth	Brk 770
Henry	Ird 643
Hugh	Cmb 364
James	Cbr 678
James	Ird 641
James	Ird 646
James	Mck 574
James	Mck 599
James, (Cap.)	Mck 569
James, Junr.	Mck 574
John	Bld 36
John	Bnc 180
John	Brk 775
John	Cbr 678
John	Ird 672
John	Mck 574
John	Mre 54
John	Rch 257

Name	Code
Keaneth	Bld 37
Malcolm	Ans 229
Malcolm	Rch 263
Malcom	Mre 72
Malcom	Mre 74
Mordoch	Ird 645
Morris	Mre 41
Norman	Cmb 361
Norman	Rch 252
Norman	Rch 261
Norman	Rbs 398
Normon	Mre 59
Robert	Mck 574
Robert	Orn 582
Roderick	Cmb 368
Roderick	Cmb 379
Susanna	Cbr 702
Thomas	Ird 641
Thomas	Ird 672
William	Brk 770
William	Cbr 677
William	Cbr 678
William (2)	Ird 640
William	Ird 672
William	Rch 261
see Moorison	
Morriss, Adly	Edg 223
Catharine	Trl 680
Charity	Gts 272
Chislon	Nrt 459
Christian	Edg 222
Christian	Gts 272
Easter	Mrt 402
Elisabeth	Mrt 402
Hillery	Edg 222
John	Ird 662
John, Junr.	Nrt 461
John, Senr.	Nrt 461
John,(son John)	Edg 222
John,(son Wm.)	Edg 222
Jonathan	Trl 678
Nathaniel	Srr 676
Thomas	Edg 222
Thomas, Jr.	Nsh 112
Thos.	Nsh 112
William, Junr.	Edg 222
William, Senr.	Edg 222
Williss	Nsh 112
Willoughby	Crr 144
Morrow, Alex	Orn 583
Andrew	Orn 582
Daniel	Grv 516
Ezekiel	Lnc 906
George	Mck 563
Henry	Rth 131
Jabez	Rth 131
James	Brk 770
James	Brk 776
James	Csw 131
James	Orn 519
James	Orn 585
James (2)	Rth 126
James	Rth 131
Jesse	Rth 126
John	Bnc 179
John	Bnc 181
John	Bnc 182
John	Csw 131
John	Mck 563
John	Orn 581
John	Rwn 448
Patrick	Rth 132
Richard	Bnc 180
Robert	Brk 774
Robert	Glf 669
Widow	Mck 563
William	Bnc 180

Name	Code
William	Brk 773
William	Orn 585
William	Rwn 448
William	Rth 126
see Murrow, Rorrow	
Morse, Abigail	Crt 77
Arther	Crr 158
Blanding	Crt 73
Daniel	Crt 73
Elisha	Bld 25
Elizabeth	Crt 73
Francis	Ons 144
Franes	Crr 161
Hillery	Crr 161
Howel	Grv 516
Howel, jr.	Grv 516
Jacob	Crt 73
James, jr.	Crt 79
James, Sr.	Crt 73
John	Ons 144
Joseph	Crr 143
Joshua, jr.	Crt 79
Mary	Crt 73
Peggey	Crr 159
Peter	Crr 161
Ruben	Crr 158
Samuel	Grv 515
Theodore	Crt 73
Turner	Grv 516
William	Crt 73
Willoughby	Crr 159
Zachriah	Crr 139
Morset, Cason	Cmd 102
Morten, Jacob	Orn 519
Mortimore, David	Glf 672
William	Glf 672
Mortin, Samuel	Cbr 683
Morton, David	Mnt 467
Ezekiel	Ans 221
James	Lnc 856
James	Mnt 502
John	Brk 772
John	Crt 83
John	Cht 174
John (2)	Ird 651
John Peter	Rbs 432
Joseph	Crt 86
Joseph (2)	Ons 145
Micajah	Jns 805
Oliver	Wsh 708
Patrick	Srr 675
Peter	Ons 146
Richard	Ons 146
Richard	Ons 148
Richard	Srr 675
Samuel	Csw 127
Sarah	Ons 149
William	Ans 221
William	Bnc 180
William	Mnt 466
William	Ons 145
William	Srr 675
Moseby, Samuel	Srr 679
Moseley, David	Edg 222
Mosely, Benjamin	Dpl 397
Joel	Mnt 479
Jonathan	Ans 214
Mary	Psq 627
Shadrick	Ird 614
Taph	Ird 612
Tart	Srr 677
West	Srr 675
Moser, Adam	Rnd 329
Anthony	Lnc 818
Elizabeth	Lnc 886
Henry	Stk 564
Jacob	Lnc 878

Jacob	Lnc 878	Mouncy, Eli	Rwn 374	Mulion, Parrott	Lnr 16
Jacob	Orn 581	Mount, John	Rck 436	Mulky, James	Ash 84
Jacob	Rnd 328	Matthew	Rck 480	Mull, Elizabeth	Rwn 288
John	Orn 581	Thomas	Rck 471	Peter, Junr.	Brk 770
Michal	Stk 563	Mounteuce, Coleg	Crr 153	Peter, Senr.	Brk 770
Nicholas	Orn 522	Thos.	Crr 153	Thomas	Rwn 277
Peter	Stk 563	Mourer, Frederick	Rwn 303	Thomas	Rwn 288
Tobias	Rnd 329	Peter	Rwn 302	Mullen, Elizabeth	Prq 652
Moses, Abrum	Frn 451	Rudolph	Rwn 303	Jesse	Prq 649
James	Wke 776	Mouring, Burwell	Wne 871	John	Psq 638
Samuel	Ans 201	Mourning, William	Crv 309	Nancy	Crv 255
Slythe	Rwn 356	see Moaning		Richard	Prq 659
Mosier, Adam	Cht 218	Mouser, B.	Lnc 872	Thomas	Prq 659
Mosley, Elizabeth	Lnr 16	Francis	Lnc 878	William	Lnr 19
James	Wrr 820	George	Lnc 878	Zadoack	Prq 655
Jesse	Wrr 820	Michael	Lnc 905	Zadock	Prq 659
John	Crt 84	Moutray, Joseph	Cht 192	Mullenix, Green	Rnd 331
Matthew	Lnr 17	William	Cht 157	Jonathan	Rnd 331
Sarah	Nwh 11	Moxly, Joseph	Rwn 381	Susannah	Rnd 331
Tuley	Lnr 16	Nathal.	Rck 458	Mullens, Charles	Rth 129
Moss, Barbary	Rnd 331	William	Ash 83	William	Wlk 53
Benjamin	Wrr 784	Moyars, John	Lnc 869	Mullery, James	Csw 140
David	Rnd 331	Michael	Rwn 349	Mullican, Lewis	Rwn 362
David	Rth 131	Peter	Rwn 348	Mullin, Arthur	Brk 774
David	Wrr 818	Moye, Elizabeth	Grn 609	Charls	Rnd 331
Ephraim	Ptt 249	Elizabeth	Ptt 253	James	Hrt 729
Henry	Rth 132	Gardner	Ptt 250	John	Mck 551
Henry	Stk 601	George	Grn 601	Patrick	Rck 442
Howel	Rth 132	George, junior	Ptt 278	Robt.	Csw 147
Jacob	Ash 84	George, Senior	Ptt 285	Thomas	Rck 436
James	Mnt 521	George, Son of		Mullins, Abner	Bnc 178
James	Rth 131	John	Ptt 282	Baker	Brk 774
James	Wne 851	Gideon	Ptt 250	Budd	Frn 468
Jas.	Mrt 402	Jesse	Ptt 285	Champ	Wlk 54
John	Brk 761	Joell	Ptt 264	Daniel	Rth 126
John	Cht 208	John	Crv 313	Henry	Wlk 54
John	Grv 533	John, Senior	Ptt 252	John	Brk 773
John	Rnd 330	Marmaduke	Crv 315	John	Brk 775
Joseph	Ash 84	Mary	Ptt 245	Thomas	Rck 483
Martha	Mnt 518	Matthew	Ptt 285	Valentine	Rth 132
Mary	Cht 205	Richard	Ptt 285	Will.	Prs 210
Michael	Ans 212	Shadrach	Crv 313	William	Bnc 178
Obediah	Nsh 113	William	Ptt 259	William	Rck 483
Reubin	Grv 513	William, Junior	Ptt 264	Mullis, Ambrose	Ird 612
Reubin	Rbs 395	see Mayo		Ambrose	Ird 625
Richard	Wrr 816	Moyer, Abraham	Lnc 869	George	Ird 625
Richardson	Prq 658	Adam	Rwn 297	James	Ans 209
Robert	Mnt 518	Elias	Rwn 302	John	Ans 223
Samuel	Trl 680	Elisha	Lnc 819	Peggy	Ans 223
Spencer	Csw 101	Frederick	Lnc 862	Solomon	Ans 223
Stephen	Rwn 356	George	Cbr 711	Mullony, William	Lnr 17
William	Csw 101	Harmon	Cbr 692	Mullowaey, Jere-	
William, Jur.	Csw 101	Henry	Rwn 297	miah	Cmb 356
Willie	Wke 776	John	Lnc 905	Mulloy see Mulky	
Wm.	Mrt 401	Mathias	Cbr 708	Mulwee, William	Mck 541
Mossanan, Robert	Ird 662	Nicholas	Rwn 297	William	Mck 544
Mossey, Jno.	Lnc 839	Moyers, Elias	Lnc 856	Mumford, Elisabeth	Wne 861
see Massey		John (2)	Brk 773	James	Ans 224
Mosson, Sally	Hrt 738	John	Lnc 856	Jeffery	Hlf 326
Mosteller, David	Lnc 819	Rose	Brk 772	Jehew	Ons 141
George	Lnc 905	Muckelroy, Mich	Wke 748	Lydia	Ans 233
Peter	Lnc 819	Muckey see James		Robeson	Cmb 356
Moth, Simon	Rwn 453	Muckleroy, John	Crv 307	Muncy, Eli	Rwn 356
Motherlin see Molton		Muddy, James	Ash 84	Munday, Free	Wne 871
Motley, Harrison	Wke 747	Mudwell, John	Rnd 331	Peter	Wne 873
Henry	Hlf 328	Mugelin, Freeman	Ans 238	Robert	Wne 872
James	Wke 748	Henry	Ans 238	Thomas	Wne 873
John	Wke 748	Strangeman	Ans 238	Munden, Nathan	Psq 640
Motlon see Molton		Mugs, Eliza	Rck 453	Simon	Psq 641
Motly, William	Rck 486	Muimmey, Nevel	Crr 141	William	Psq 641
Motsinger, Daniel	Rwn 367	Mulder, James	Rwn 427	Mundin, Elisha	Prq 649
Jacob	Rwn 367	Kader	Crr 161	Joseph	Prq 650
John	Rwn 367	Thos.	Crr 161	William	Prq 658
Mott, ...	Nwh 10A	Mulford, David	Bld 38	Mundine, Elisabeth	Jns 779
Benjn.	Nwh 6	Ephm., Jur.	Bld 38	Munford, Elisabeth	Jns 803
Motton see Molton		Ephm., Senr.	Bld 49	Mungar, Peter	Wrr 817
Mottz, John	Lnc 819	Mulhollen, Martha	Orn 619	Munger, Burwell	Nrt 461

Henry	Nrt 461	Muroney, William	Cmb 356	Timothy	Dpl 420
Jesse	Nrt 461	Murph, Jacob	Cbr 704	William	Bnc 179
Julien	Nrt 461	Murphey, Archibald	Rbs 398	William	Brk 770
Samuel	Nrt 461	Duncan	Rbs 397	William	Dpl 410
Mungor, Spell	Wrr 816	Elcey	Orn 492	William	Rck 474
Tabetha	Wrr 817	James	Frn 487	William, Jur.	Csw 132
Munk, James	Mre 40	James	Ptt 249	William B.	Crv 271
Munn, Alexander	Cmb 361	James	Wlk 53	Murr, George	Rwn 288
Daniel	Cmb 363	Jesse	Ptt 249	Murrane, Elizah	Rnd 329
Duncan	Mnt 471	Jethra	Grn 599	Murrar, John	Csw 134
James	Mnt 472	John	Cmb 365	Murray, Adam	Nwh 9A
John	Mnt 471	John	Grn 599	Delilah	Grn 589
John	Rbs 402	John	Lnc 894	Dominick	Chw 114
Malcolm	Cmb 361	Joseph	Wlk 53	Hardy	Wke 749
Neill	Cmb 368	Margaret	Rbs 393	James	Crv 237
Munns, Jacob	Chw 126	Neill	Rbs 398	James	Orn 519
Thomas	Chw 126	Nicholas	Frn 473	James	Orn 520
William, Jun.	Chw 126	Samuel	Ird 646	James, Ser.	Frn 484
William, Sen.	Chw 126	Thomas	Ptt 249	Jane	Cht 214
Munroe, Alexander	Cmb 387	William	Frn 477	Jonathan	Ons 170
Archibald	Bld 33	William	Grn 599	Jonathan	Orn 520
Archibald	Cmb 364	William, junr.	Grn 599	Joshua	Nwh 9A
Archibald	Rbs 401	Murphrey, Angus	Rbs 407	Thos. (2)	Nwh 5
Colin	Rbs 403	Arther	Frn 477	Walter	Orn 519
Daniel	Mre 53	John	Rbs 405	Murrel, Barnaba	Brn 17
Donald	Cmb 387	Michael	Hde 373	Mirit	Dpl 433
John	Cmb 365	Neill	Rbs 405	Moses	Lnc 828
John	Mre 54	Parker	Frn 478	Sarah	Ons 156
John, (C)	Cmb 363	William	Frn 487	William	Brn 16A
Malcom	Mre 41	Murphy, Alex	Csw 100	Murrell, Jacob	Frn 485
Malcom	Rbs 401	Alex	Csw 130	John	Crr 150
Marian	Rbs 404	Archd.	Csw 108	Mark	Nrt 459
Neill	Cmb 362	Archibald	Grn 609	Sarah	Ons 178
Patrick	Cmb 365	Barbary	Dpl 410	William	Ons 177
Munteeth, Alexan-		Barthw.	Ans 228	Winborne	Nrt 461
der	Mck 568	Charles	Nwh 10A	Murret, Zachh.	Bld 8
Samuel	Mck 568	Daniel	Rwn 356	Murrey, John	Nsh 111
Munts, Mathew	Bld 29	Daniel, Jr.	Ans 223	John, Jur.	Nsh 111
Munyard, B.L. John	Bfr 13	Daniel, Senr.	Ans 223	Margerit	Wrr 816
Murchie, James	Crv 263	Edward	Hrt 738	Thadius	Wrr 820
Murchison, Alexan-		Elisabeth	Lnc 890	Thos.	Nsh 111
der	Cmb 356	Ezekiel	Rck 450	William	Nsh 111
Alexander	Cmb 362	Gabriel	Csw 121	Wm.	Crr 152
Keneth	Cmb 356	Gabriel	Csw 132	Murrow, Alexander	Rnd 329
Keneth	Cmb 363	Gabriel	Rck 464	Arthur	Dpl 414
Murckison, Chris-		Gabril, J.	Csw 132	Benjn.	Prs 191
tian	Mre 61	George	Brt 60	Daniel	Dpl 423
Murden, David	Hrt 721	Guilford	Crv 271	James	Dpl 423
John	Nrt 461	Hugh	Bld 40	John	Dpl 412
Robert	Psq 633	James	Brk 770	John	Dpl 425
Murder, John	Glf 636	James	Csw 132	Sarah	Dpl 422
Murdoch, John	Ird 665	James	Cmb 371	Will.	Prs 192
John	Ird 671	James	Hrt 732	William	Rth 131
Robert	Ird 640	John	Cmb 386	Murry, Barnabas	Stk 565
William	Ird 650	John	Cmb 393	Charles	Csw 133
Murdock, Andrew	Orn 521	John	Glf 682	Daniel	Hde 373
Eliza	Orn 587	John	Glf 683	James	Rth 127
James	Orn 587	John	Rck 439	Jane	Cht 186
Lewis	Cmb 390	John	Rwn 374	Jean	Orn 582
William	Orn 587	John	Rth 132	Jessee	Cht 171
Murdoh, James	Ird 672	John, Jr.	Ans 229	John	Brk 773
Murfey, Archabald	Cht 217	John, Sen.	Ans 230	John	Csw 124
Murfield, James	Stk 588	Jonathan	Glf 672	John	Frn 491
John	Stk 588	Joseph	Csw 103	John	Rwn 417
Murfree, Hardy	Hrt 738	Joseph	Srr 677	Johnson	Bnc 179
Hardy	Nrt 461	Maik	Ans 211	Joshua	Wlk 52
Malachi	Edg 222	Margaret	Dpl 422	Nathl. D.	Rck 438
Murkeson, Mordica	Cht 198	Mary	Cmb 357	Samuel, j.	Bnc 181
Murkison, Alexan-		Miles	Psq 641	Samuel, S.	Bnc 180
der	Mnt 467	Richard	Srr 677	Thomas	Stk 565
Alexander	Mnt 471	Robert	Cmb 356	Timothy	Hde 372
Daniel	Mnt 467	Robt.	Nwh 4A	William	Brt 60
Daniel	Mnt 475	Sidney	Crv 247	William	Bnc 180
Daniel	Mre 61	Spencer	Ptt 240	William	Hde 373
Dunkin	Mre 62	Thomas	Cmb 385	William	Orn 519
John	Mre 61	Thomas	Jns 803	Musaga, Lemuel	Bld 31
Kinnith	Mre 56	Thomas	Rth 129	Muse, Caleb	Crv 277

Name	Code	Name	Code	Name	Code
James	Crv 277	Nathan	Brt 62	Willis	Wrr 822
James	Mre 55	Nathan	Brt 64	Wm. N.	Wrr 822
Jesse	Mre 58	Samuel	Brt 62	Narvel, David	Grv 534
Kendrick	Mre 43	Myett, Frank	Crr 165	Nash, Demsy	Psq 630
Levi	Crv 275	Myhan, James	Hlf 330	George	Cmb 391
Thomas	Mre 43	Myles, Benjamin	Hlf 326	Greffin	Ans 205
William T.	Psq 628	Thomas	Hlf 326	John	Ans 217
Willis	Crv 275	Myres, Dartha	Stk 599	Joseph	Mnt 502
Musentine, James	Brk 768	David	Wlk 53	Josiah	Cmd 109
Musgrove, Abraham	Wne 868	Dorthy	Stk 625	Mary	Mnt 504
James	Wne 872	Mary	Srr 680	Michael	Ans 217
Jesse	Wne 872	Myrick, Charles	Wrr 819	Sully	Cmd 100
John	Wne 855	Charles, jr.	Wrr 820	William	Csw 96
Joshua	Wne 855	Edmunds	Hlf 328	Nashe, Widow	Mck 586
Richard	Wne 867	George	Wrr 817	Nasworthy, Samuel	Grn 595
Mushaw, Mary	Wke 749	John	Frn 492	Nation, Christo-	
William	Frn 494	John	Hlf 328	pher	Stk 564
Mushburn, Samuel	Mre 65	Mary	Cht 165	Nations, Abraham	Rnd 333
Music, Austin	Rth 128	Matthew	Mck 530	Naugle, George	Lnc 869
George	Rth 132	Matthew	Mck 540	Nave, Henry	Lnc 905
Musick, James	Srr 679	Moses	Cht 219	Neagle, John	Lnc 833
John	Crv 325	Mosses	Wrr 820	Neal, Adam	Lnc 897
Lenus	Stk 580	Owen	Wrr 817	Andrew	Ird 651
Musselwhite, Jesse	Rbs 395	Richard	Wke 749	Edward	Frn 445
Leonard	Rbs 395	Sterling	Wrr 820	Gelbreath	Brk 778
Mary	Rbs 395	Tranus	Mre 76	Gelbreath	Ird 674
Milby	Rbs 395	William	Cht 174	Henry	Rwn 427
Nathan	Rbs 396			James	Brk 778
Thomas	Rbs 395			James, Esq.	Mck 532
Musser, Eli	Wne 863	-- N --		Jeremiah	Rth 133
Musslewhite, Leo-				Jesse	Mck 574
nard	Ans 218			John	Brk 778
William	Jhn 748	Nadom, William	Mre 70	John	Mnt 518
Mustapher, Deborah	Chw 117	Nail, Henry	Orn 590	John	Rwn 427
Patty	Chw 115	James (2)	Orn 522	Joseph	Lnc 832
Mustell, George	Rwn 374	Martha	Orn 590	Margret	Ird 651
Muter, Robt.	Nwh 2	Nailinge, William	Grv 554	Moses	Frn 456
Mutter, Eliza	Grv 550	Nairon, Durante	Mrt 403	Paten	Rth 134
Thomas	Grv 540	Nalby, Isaac	Prs 204	Presly	Cht 186
Muzells, Polly	Bfr 23	Nall, James	Mnt 486	Samuel (2)	Brk 778
Muzzle, William	Csw 120	Martin	Mre 45	Samuel	Mck 537
Myars, Barbara	Rwn 404	Martin	Wke 751	Samuel	Mck 571
Christian	Rwn 349	Nathan	Cht 219	Thomas	Mck 573
George	Rwn 349	Nicholas	Mre 59	Thomas	Rck 489
George	Rwn 356	Robert	Ash 84	William	Brk 778
Jacob, Junr.	Rwn 356	Thomas	Cht 219	William	Cht 155
Jacob, Senr.	Rwn 356	Nance, Buckner	Rch 249	William	Ird 652
John	Rwn 356	Clem	Lnc 849	William	Rck 437
John	Rwn 432	Danl.	Bld 32	William	Rck 462
Peter	Rwn 349	Elizabeth	Lnc 849	William	Rck 489
Myatt, Alexander	Wke 749	Francis	Lnc 849	Neale, Abner	Crt 71
Britain	Wke 749	Frederick	Grv 525	Amos	Hde 374
John	Wke 749	George	Wke 751	Christopher	Hde 374
Mark	Wke 749	Herod	Grv 524	Daniel	Crv 297
Matthew	Wke 749	Hudson	Rck 443	Elisabeth	Crv 297
Nimrod	Cht 205	James	Wke 751	John	Hde 374
Willie	Wke 749	John	Rck 471	Milley	Bfr 23
Mydett, Berthamey	Crr 153	John	Wlk 56	Philip, Junr.	Crv 301
Christopher	Crr 167	Joseph	Bld 32	Philip, Senr.	Crv 301
Daniel	Crr 165	Milly	Grv 561	William	Hde 374
Dolley	Crr 165	Richd.	Rck 464	Nealey, Samuel	Srr 681
Jacob	Crr 165	Thomas	Rnd 333	Neally, Andrew	Bld 5
John	Crr 165	Thomas	Wke 751	Nealy, ...iah	Bld 4
Morress	Crr 151	Wiat	Ans 234	Nearling, Ben	Stk 599
Robert	Crr 165	William	Wlk 56	Nearn, John	Bfr 14
Saml.	Crr 151	Wynne, Esqr.	Bld 16	Nearns, Benjamin	Lnc 891
Saml.	Crr 152	Nancy, Dempsy	Hrt 733	Nease, Felty	Orn 522
Solomon	Crr 166	Nankin see Nonlin		George	Orn 522
Thos.	Crr 166	Nanny, Mary	Rth 133	Jacob	Orn 522
Wm.	Crr 167	Uriah	Rth 133	Martin	Orn 522
see Myett		Napper, Robert	Gts 273	Neat, Rudolph	Rwn 433
Mydgett, John	Trl 684	Robert	Rck 467	Neath, Solomon	Brk 779
Samuel	Trl 684	Naron, John	Nsh 113	Neavill, William	Cmd 106
William	Trl 684	Braswell	Nsh 113	Neblock, George	Rwn 328
Myers, Elizabeth	Brt 62	Narsworthy, Nathan	Nrt 463	Neddy, Reuben	Ans 206
Elizabeth, 2nd	Brt 62	Ozburn	Edg 225	Needham, Bailey	Rnd 333
Joseph	Frn 445	William	Nrt 463	Jesse	Rnd 333

John   Rnd 332
John (2)   Rnd 333
John, N.   Rnd 333
Lewis   Rnd 333
Thomas   Rnd 332
Thomas   Rnd 333
William   Rnd 332
Wm.   Csw 136
Needlen, William   Jhn 747
Neel, Brooks   Wrr 822
  Jeams   Crr 167
  John   Wrr 821
  Ralph   Wrr 822
  Ralph, Jr.   Wrr 822
  Thomas   Stk 587
Neele, Wm., Jur.   Crr 167
  see O'Neele
Neeley, Thos.   Prs 213
Neely, Francis,
  (Cap.)   Rwn 448
  Henry   Mck 572
  Hugh   Mck 548
  Isaac   Cbr 677
  Isaac   Mck 562
  Jno.   Lnc 839
  John   Mck 547
  Joshua   Rwn 448
  Moses   Mck 539
  Samuel   Mck 539
  Samuel   Rwn 448
  Sarah   Cbr 707
  William   Lnc 879
Neewell see Newell
Neil, Aaron   Trl 694
  George   Lnc 820
  John   Cbr 683
  John   Dpl 437
  John   Trl 690
  Samuel   Ird 652
  Widow   Cbr 683
  see Nuil
Neile, Fielden   Grv 522
  Joseph   Grv 525
Neill, John   Lnc 886
Neilson, William   Bnc 182
Neivill see Newill
Nelfon, Thomas   Orn 589
Nellenner, Henry   Orn 589
Nellums, Edmond   Brn 20
  Francis   Smp 521
  Jesse   Smp 526
  Josiah   Hlf 330
  Sarah   Hlf 332
Nelms, Eben   Frn 476
  Elias   Frn 463
  Presley   Frn 474
Nelson, Abraham,
  Junr.   Nrt 463
  Abraham, Senr.   Nrt 463
  Ann   Glf 660
  Asa   Crv 297
  Benjamin   Crv 297
  Charity   Ptt 255
  Cracia   Grn 604
  David   Crt 63
  Ebenezer   Rwn 427
  Edward   Crv 323
  Elizabeth   Ptt 256
  George   Crv 323
  George   Rwn 427
  Hardy   Crv 323
  Hugh   Mck 528
  Ichabud   Ptt 256
  James   Crv 293
  James   Nrt 463
  James   Stk 588
  Jarrett   Rck 439

Jesse   Rnd 333
Jiles   Ptt 255
Joab   Rch 262
Joel   Stk 564
John   Crv 323
John   Glf 640
John   Glf 660
John   Nrt 463
John   Orn 522
John   Ptt 255
John   Stk 582
John   Stk 583
John   Stk 588
John   Stk 596
John S.   Crv 303
Jonas   Nrt 463
Joseph   Crt 63
Joseph   Crv 289
Joseph   Stk 565
Joshua   Ird 662
Joshua (2)   Stk 565
Levi   Bfr 14
Levina   Glf 673
Martin   Ptt 255
Moses   Glf 635
Nancy   Crt 63
Nathan   Bfr 14
Nathaniel   Stk 588
Rachel   Crt 68
Rebecca   Crv 323
Samuel   Orn 522
Samuel   Ptt 255
Samuel   Rnd 333
Sarah   Jns 799
Sarah   Rnd 333
Sarey   Ptt 241
Shadrach   Nrt 463
Susanna   Stk 582
Thomas   Crv 293
Thomas   Crv 305
Thomas H.   Crv 303
Widow   Mck 606
William   Crt 63
William   Nrt 463
William   Rwn 427
William   Stk 565
William   Stk 585
William   Stk 592
William, Sr.   Stk 585
Nenlin see Nonlin
Nesbet, William   Lnc 883
Nesbit, Mary   Rwn 277
  see Nisbet
Nether, Robert   Brk 778
Nettle, John   Edg 225
Nettles, Shaderach   Rth 133
Nevel, Jessee   Orn 523
Nevels, Elizabeth   Grv 520
Neves, John   Orn 590
Nevil, Benjamin   Hlf 330
  Benjamin   Orn 523
  Benjamin, Sr.   Hlf 332
  Edmund   Hlf 332
  Goodman   Hlf 330
  Hardy   Hlf 330
  Jesse   Hlf 330
  John   Hlf 330
  Soloman   Orn 523
  Thomas   Hlf 330
  William   Hlf 330
Nevill, Yelvaton   Rth 133
Nevin, Alexander   Rbs 408
  Daniel   Rbs 408
  John   Mre 68
  Robert   Mre 68
Nevins, William   Rwn 318
New, George   Smp 510

John   Stk 612
Margaret   Dpl 401
William   Dpl 438
New..., William   Wne 873
Newbern, George   Edg 225
  Nicholas   Chw 122
  Rachel   Brt 66
  Thomas (2)   Brt 66
  William   Chw 125
  Wilson   Chw 120
Newberry, Isaac   Cmb 380
  James   Rch 263
  Jesse   Rbs 408
  John   Cmb 381
  John   Rbs 408
  Jonathan   Rch 244
  William   Rch 251
Newbey, Elizabeth   Wke 751
Newbold, Elijah   Ons 139
  Lovey   Ons 137
Newbould, Samuel   Psq 632
Newbury, John   Wsh 708
Newby, Alexander   Cmb 367
  Axiom   Prq 661
  Elizabeth   Prq 646
  Enoch   Prq 650
  Enoch   Prq 654
  Francis   Prq 649
  Francis, (Jai-
    lor)   Prq 662
  Francis, Jun.   Prq 647
  Frederick   Rnd 333
  Gabriel   Prq 645
  Gabriel   Rnd 333
  Gabriel   Rnd 333
  Gedion   Rnd 350
  James   Psq 636
  James   Psq 641
  Jesse   Prq 646
  Jesse   Wne 872
  Jessey   Frn 452
  John   Psq 624
  John   Psq 627
  Jonathan   Prq 650
  Joseph   Psq 627
  Joseph   Prq 647
  Joseph   Rnd 333
  Joshua   Rnd 333
  Kesiah   Psq 624
  Mary   Prq 656
  Milicent   Psq 640
  Nathan   Prq 647
  Peter   Rnd 350
  Samuel   Rnd 333
  William   Prq 644
  William   Prq 647
  William   Rnd 333
  William, Sen.   Prq 658
  see Newly
Newcomb, Wm., (Wew-
  comb)   Orn 590
Newel, Joshua   Brn 13
  Mary   Brn 13
  Thomas   Brn 13
Newell, Adan   Wne 857
  Anne   Cmb 357
  David   Wrr 821
  Edward   Wrr 821
  Francis   Cbr 706
  John   Wrr 821
  Peter   Wrr 821
  William   Cbr 706
  William   Wrr 821
  see Nuel
Newholster, James   Stk 588
Newill, John   Cbr 706
Newkam, Seel   Csw 125
Newkim, Thomas   Stk 564

Name	Ref	Name	Ref	Name	Ref
Newkirk, Abram	Nwh 11	John	Nwh 7A	John, (of	
Henry	Dpl 413	John	Ptt 271	Jonn.)	Orn 590
Newlal, John	Rnd 333	Joseph	Nwh 7	John, Senr.	Orn 590
Newland, Benjamin	Brk 778	Major	Hde 374	Jonathan	Gts 273
Frederick	Wne 859	Mary	Dpl 434	Jonathan, jr.	Orn 590
Newler, John	Prs 211	Mary	Orn 589	Joseph	Ash 84
Newly, Eley	Grv 564	Robert	Bnc 182	Joseph	Ird 616
Newmall, Ebenezer	Crv 233	Robert	Rth 133	Joseph	Trl 680
Newman, Austin	Rth 133	Saml.	Nwh 4A	Joshua	Ird 668
Avory	Wrr 821	Starling	Hde 374	Josiah	Wke 752
Daniel	Brk 778	William	Bld 31	Julius	Wke 751
Daniel	Wrr 821	William	Nrt 463	Julius, Senr.	Wke 752
John	Glf 626	William	Rth 134	Lurane	Nsh 113
John	Stk 564	see Nuton		Mary	Cmd 102
John, Jr.	Stk 564	Newum see Nucum		Nathaniel	Hrt 706
Robert	Stk 564	Nice, Cornelius	Brk 778	Nathaniel	Hrt 717
Sarah	Lnc 865	Nichelson, Josiah	Crr 146	Nathaniel	Hrt 726
Thomas	Wrr 821	Nicholas, Edmund	Nrt 463	Osbern	Wke 752
William	Orn 522	Elimelech	Nrt 463	Rhody	Glf 686
Newmans, John	Ptt 278	John	Nrt 463	Robt.	Crv 255
Newmon, Charles	Stk 564	Lemuel	Nrt 463	Thomas (2)	Orn 590
Charles	Stk 583	Nathaniel	Rbs 408	Thomas	Rck 452
Joel	Prs 198	Thomas	Brt 66	Thomas	Wke 752
Joseph	Stk 564	Nicholds, Jacob	Wlk 56	Walter	Nwh 8A
Payton	Stk 564	John (2)	Wlk 55	William	Ans 199
William	Smp 529	Williby	Rnd 333	William	Hrt 717
Newnan, Anthony	Rwn 277	Zachary	Rnd 333	William	Rck 452
Anthony	Rwn 289	Nicholdson, Alexd.	Mre 62	William	Wke 752
John	Rwn 277	Nicholes, Benjamin	Srr 681	Wright	Hrt 718
John	Rwn 289	Micajor	Prs 188	Nicholson, Abel	Wlk 56
Newsom, Benjn.	Gts 273	Willis	Prs 187	Alexander	Rch 258
Charles	Hrt 706	Wright	Prs 205	Archibald	Orn 522
David	Hrt 706	Nicholls, Benajah	Brt 64	Atkins	Frn 460
David	Wne 858	George	Brt 64	Benn.	Psq 632
Etheldred	Rbs 408	Jehu	Brt 64	Brittean	Wrr 821
Gillum	Hlf 330	John	Brt 64	Daniel	Rch 245
Henry	Rwn 381	Mary	Ptt 227	Elizabeth	Lnr 19
Hosea	Hrt 717	Noah	Brt 66	Ellick	Wrr 822
Joel	Hrt 706	Richard	Cmb 357	George	Grv 525
Joel	Jhn 752	Thomas	Brt 64	George	Wrr 822
Joseph	Edg 225	Nichols, Abraham	Rck 452	Geriesha	Psq 628
Joseph	Wne 862	Alex.	Rck 452	Griffin	Hlf 332
Lewis	Rwn 381	Amoss	Orn 590	Healy	Psq 634
Nathaniel	Gts 273	Averit	Bld 13	Irrey	Wrr 822
Nelsom	Smp 521	Becketh	Rwn 328	Jacob	Rwn 365
William	Rwn 381	Bidy	Rck 445	James	Orn 522
Willis	Wne 859	Boulden	Orn 590	James, Jun.	Orn 522
Winney	Wke 751	Coleman	Bld 14	Jane	Stk 587
Newsome, Amos	Nrt 463	David	Mck 593	Jeams	Crr 145
Booth	Nrt 465	David	Nsh 113	John	Bnc 182
Etheldred	Nrt 463	Elias	Bld 13	John	Frn 460
James (2)	Nrt 463	Ephraim	Bld 16	John	Mrt 403
Jesse	Nrt 465	Francis	Rth 134	John	Rch 258
Joab	Wne 850	Isaac	Ans 230	John	Stk 619
Moses, Junr.	Nrt 465	Isaac	Glf 687	Jonas	Psq 634
Moses, Senr.	Nrt 463	Jacob	Ird 668	Josiah	Nsh 113
Nathaniel	Nrt 463	James	Brk 778	Lamiell	Nsh 113
Sarah	Nrt 465	James	Hlf 330	Lucy	Rwn 410
Thomas	Edg 225	James	Rck 452	Malachi	Edg 225
Newson, Hosea,		James	Wke 751	Mary	Wrr 822
Senr.	Hrt 706	James, Sen.	Hlf 332	Nancy	Cmb 379
Jacob	Glf 668	Jereh.	Rck 452	Nathan	Prq 650
John	Hrt 706	Jeremiah	Nsh 113	Nicholas	Prq 651
Newton, Abraham	Dpl 407	Jeremiah	Psq 637	Nicholas, sen.	Prq 654
Benja.	Wke 751	Joel	Jhn 776	Orsburn	Wrr 821
Benjamin	Rth 134	Johathan	Orn 590	Penelope	Edg 225
Daniel	Ons 147	John	Ans 211	Peter	Rch 245
Ebenezer (2)	Rth 134	John	Bnc 182	Rodrick	Rch 247
Edwd.	Nwh 7	John	Hrt 718	Saml.	Prq 650
Elizabeth	Ons 147	John (2)	Ird 668	Samuel	Wlk 56
Enoch	Dpl 408	John	Mnt 472	Thomas	Psq 628
Geo.	Nwh 6A	John	Nwh 2A	Thos.	Prq 643
George	Bnc 182	John	Nwh 8A	Widow	Ans 236
Isaac	Nwh 6A	John	Rck 452	Nickelson, James	Stk 586
James	Orn 590	John	Rwn 289	Nickerson, Joseph	
John	Ans 207	John	Wke 752	W.	Hlf 330
John	Grv 516	John, Junr.	Orn 590	Nathaniel	Prq 642

Thomas Hlf 330
W. Joseph Hlf 330
Nickham, William Rwn 368
Nickins, Malichi Hrt 725
Prescott Hrt 725
Richard Hrt 712
Richard Hrt 725
Nickles, Frederick Grn 604
William Ptt 275
Nicks, George Glf 642
George Glf 666
George Prs 189
John Glf 642
Quinton Glf 666
Nickson, Charles Ons 175
Samuel Prq 643
Niddan, Matthias Stk 604
Niel, Honore Chw 113
James Chw 113
Nielis, William Wlk 55
Niell, William Jns 823
Nifong, Elizabeth Rwn 375
Night, Barremon Stk 589
Jonathan Bnc 182
Jonathan Mnt 483
Kedar Jns 801
Mil... Nwh 4
Patsey Wrr 821
Peggy Wke 777
Sampson Rck 438
William Stk 589
Nile, Thomas Brk 778
Niler, Susanna Crt 61
Nilson, Archibald Orn 523
Widow Mck 525
Nims, Benjamin Rch 263
Thomas Rch 263
Nipper, Allin Wke 752
Buckner Wke 752
Holley Wke 752
Nisbet, Mary Rwn 289
Ross Ird 645
Nishler, David Cbr 704
John Cbr 684
John, (Senr.) Cbr 698
Nison, Benjamin Wne 847
Nisteet, John Ird 672
Nivion, Charles Ans 212
Nix, John Rck 491
John Rth 134
William Rth 133
Nixon, Daniel Ons 170
Delight Prq 652
Henry Wne 869
James Lnc 849
James Psq 627
James Rwn 342
Jno. Lnc 849
John Chw 119
John Prq 654
John Wne 871
John, Sen. Prq 651
John, Sen. Prq 652
Joseph Prq 650
Nathan Prq 650
Nicholas Nwh 12
Osten Gts 273
Phinehas Rnd 333
Reuben Gts 273
Richd. Nwh 8A
Robt. Nwh 11A
Sarah Crv 309
Tho. Nwh 12
Thomas Wne 869
Wm. (2) Lnc 849
Zachariah Prq 654
Zachariah, Jun. Prq 658
Noah, John Orn 522
Peter Orn 523
Noals, Butler Wrr 822
Corbin Wrr 822
Susanna Wrr 822
Noble, Colemon Srr 681
John Jns 779
Simpson Mnt 511
Nobles, Anna Ptt 250
Benjamin Ptt 232
Benjamin Ptt 283
Drury Ptt 232
Elisabeth Mrt 403
Geo. Nwh 3A
George Lnr 19
Isaac, Jur. Bfr 14
Isaac, Ser. Bfr 14
Jarrott Nwh 11A
Jesse Bfr 14
Jesse Crv 285
John Bfr 14
John Lnr 19
John Ptt 250
Joseph Bld 2
Joseph Bld 4
Joshua Ptt 232
Lewis Lnr 19
Philemon Lnr 19
Richard Lnr 19
Sarey Ptt 232
Simon Ptt 284
Thomas Bld 15
William Lnr 19
William Mnt 521
Winifred Ptt 294
Noblet, John Brk 779
Joseph Brk 778
Joseph Srr 681
William Srr 681
Nobly, Josiah Smp 529
Noe, George Brk 778
James Crt 77
Laieticia Crt 77
Peter Crt 77
Noel, Edward Csw 123
Ephraim Csw 124
Gilbert Rwn 453
Joel Rwn 427
John Rwn 427
Noils, William Rck 462
Noland, James Rwn 459
Nolen, Henry Wlk 56
Pearce Wlk 55
Noles, Laurence Rck 450
William Csw 120
Nolgrass, Susannah Grv 569
Nolin, Philip Wlk 55
Nolly, Jacob Edg 225
Nolten, Joshua Smp 525
Nonlin, James Orn 522
Norcom, Deborah Chw 121
Edmond Chw 120
Frederick Chw 121
John Prq 654
John, Sen. Chw 121
Norcot, Nicholas Ans 235
Norden, Thomas Cmb 376
Nordin, John Cmb 374
Nordyke, Adin Stk 615
Norfleet, Benjamin Chw 113
Elisha Chw 113
James Brt 66
Nathaniel Prs 212
Reuben Brt 66
Norflett, Kinchen Gts 273
Noris, Will. Prs 201
Norman, Abner Bfr 14
Charles Glf 658
Charles Rck 476
Charles Trl 670
Forney G. Lnc 890
Francis Rck 471
George Grv 549
Hannah Orn 522
Henry Ans 204
Henry Trl 670
Henry Trl 684
Hezekiah Trl 670
Isaac Trl 670
Isaac Wlk 55
Isbell Wrr 821
James Grv 505
James Lnc 890
James Trl 686
James Wlk 55
Jemima Trl 672
John Cmb 371
John Lnc 890
John, Senr. Trl 672
Joseph Orn 522
Nathan Wsh 708
Nehemiah Wsh 708
Reubin Wrr 822
Richard Dpl 399
Sarah Lnc 890
Thomas Grv 531
Thomas Lnc 891
Thomas Lnc 892
Thomas Wrr 821
Thomas Wsh 708
Thomas Wlk 55
William Cht 194
William Cht 218
William Frn 488
William Grv 548
William Ons 172
William Wlk 55
Normand, John Ons 161
Norment, William Rbs 408
Normin, Henry Grv 548
Normon, Henry Srr 711
Norphleet, Marmaduke Hlf 332
Norrell, William Grv 555
Norrice, Malachi Psq 630
Norrington, John Mre 63
Norris, Elisabeth Jhn 769
Elisha Smp 519
Ephriam Ash 84
Francis Ash 84
Gilbert Ash 84
James Hde 374
James Jhn 768
Jeri. Rck 478
Jesse Dpl 423
John Ash 84
John Cmb 372
John Frn 471
John Ptt 277
John Rck 454
John Wke 751
John Wke 752
Joseph Frn 468
Matthew Crt 79
Nahor Jhn 768
Nancy Rck 457
Peyton Wke 751
Robert Frn 470
Thomas Wlk 56
Will. Brn 19A
William Ptt 280
William Rck 438
Norriss, Henry Edg 225
Jesse Trl 684

John	Edg 225	Shippe	Ash 84	Obrion, Asesanna	Rch 268	
Luke	Edg 225	Nowls, Sarah	Cbr 704	O'Bryan, David	Crv 313	
Mary	Lnr 19	Noxum, Benjamin	Crv 337	Pattrick	Lnc 820	
Norsworthy, James	Gts 273	Noyes, John	Rbs 408	Richard	Crv 313	
John	Hlf 330	John	Rbs 432	Obryant, Lawrence		
Willie	Hlf 330	Nuckuls, Honour	Wrr 822	O'Bryant, Lawrence	Edg 173	
North, Arthur	Mrt 403	Silvester	Wrr 821	Obsyan, Joseph	Prs 195	
Daniel	Srr 681	Nucum, Julius	Brk 778	Ocain, Elisabeth	Mrt 403	
John	Glf 636	Nudom see Nadom		Jenney	Mrt 403	
Richard	Brt 66	Nuel, Zeb.	Crr 159	John	Mrt 403	
Thomas	Rck 448	Nuil, Edward	Cbr 679	Thos.	Mrt 403	
see Neath		Nullus, John	Orn 590	Wm.	Mrt 403	
Northan, Demsey	Crr 164	Numans, James	Ptt 249	Ochilltree, Eliza-		
Northcut, Anthony	Hrt 712	Nuncasser, Adam	Rwn 349	beth	Cmb 393	
John	Hrt 712	Nuner, Nathan	Glf 620	Hugh	Cmb 377	
Northen, Carity	Crr 163	Preston	Glf 629	Odam, Benjamin	Gts 273	
John	Crr 157	Nunley, Anderson	Lnc 849	Charles	Wke 752	
Northern, Edmund	Wlk 56	Nunn, Francis	Lnr 19	Demey	Gts 273	
Samuel	Rwn 400	Joshua	Lnr 19	Feriby	Gts 273	
Samuel	Wlk 56	William	Lnr 19	Jacob	Nrt 465	
Northington, Jesse	Cmb 389	William	Orn 495	Jemima	Ptt 266	
Samuel	Cmb 389	Nunnerly, Archd.	Rth 133	Jerry	Frn 480	
William	Cmb 389	John	Rth 134	Jesse	Cmb 380	
Northom, Thomas	Hlf 332	Thomas	Rth 134	John	Gts 274	
Northron, John	Ash 84	Amos	Cmb 369	Josiah, Junr.	Nrt 465	
Northwood, John	Ird 662	Nuns, Elizabeth	Stk 565	Josiah, Senr.	Nrt 465	
Norton, Alexander	Rwn 362	John	Stk 581	Mills	Nrt 465	
David	Rth 133	William	Stk 565	Moses, Junr.	Nrt 465	
Enoch	Rth 134	Nurney, John	Gts 273	Moses, Senr.	Nrt 465	
George	Crr 150	Nicholas	Gts 273	Rachel	Nrt 465	
Isham	Rch 259	Nusom, Elizabeth	Grn 599	Thomas	Cht 190	
James	Glf 649	Moses	Grn 599	William	Ptt 269	
James	Rch 259	Nutall, John,Capt.	Grv 554	see Oldam		
James, Jr.	Rch 259	Nuton, John	Mre 69	Odaniel, Henry	Orn 523	
Martin	Rch 259	Mary	Mre 69	John	Orn 523	
Mary	Lnc 865	Nutt, David	Orn 589	John, Jun.	Orn 523	
Nathaniel	Glf 649	John	Nwh 2A	Samuel	Orn 523	
Nicholas	Rwn 362	John	Wke 752	O'Daniel, Labin	Cmd 99	
Normon	Rwn 362	Wi...m	Nwh 2	Odau, William	Rth 134	
Sarah	Rnd 333	William	Wke 751	William	Rth 135	
William	Rch 258	Nuttall, Wm. J.	Gts 273	Odear, James	Wke 752	
Willie	Hlf 330			John	Wke 752	
Norval, Theophs.	Nwh 4			Odell, Benjamin	Bnc 182	
Norvil, Benjn.	Hrt 701	-- O --		Benjamin	Bnc 183	
Winey	Hrt 701			Isaac	Glf 687	
Norvill, John	Rth 133			James	Glf 688	
Samuel	Rth 133	Oakey, Nathan	Stk 578	John	Bnc 182	
Norville, James	Frn 457	Thomas	Grv 580	Lewis	Rck 483	
Norwood, Benjamin	Grv 516	Oakley, John	Grv 581	Street	Rck 484	
George	Frn 474	MCferling	Prs 190	William	Rck 475	
George	Nrt 463	Richd.	Prs 187	Oden, Charles	Bfr 15	
Gillam	Cht 172	Walter	Prs 190	John	Bfr 15	
John	Frn 469	Will.	Prs 188	Richard	Bfr 15	
John, Ser.	Frn 475	Oakly, James	Rck 460	William	Bfr 15	
Jordan	Grv 512	Joseph	Grv 571	Odeneal, Sarah	Rck 479	
Joseph	Nrt 463	Joseph, Junr.	Grv 571	O'Deneal, Bartlet	Rwn 444	
Laban	Nrt 463	Richard	Rck 460	Odinel, Reubin	Hlf 332	
Moses	Nrt 463	Thomas	Rck 460	Odle, Caleb	Rnd 333	
William	Cht 200	Oaks, James	Brk 779	Isaac	Rnd 333	
William, Sr.	Cht 200	Oar, Wm.	Rck 465	Jesse	Rck 460	
Nosa, Sarah	Hlf 332	Oasteen, Isaac	Crt 87	John	Rwn 368	
Nott, Ephraim	Srr 681	Samuel	Crt 90	Uriah	Rck 444	
Notton see Nolten		William	Crt 87	Odom, Jacob	Mnt 476	
Nowall, David	Grv 551	Oates, John	Lnc 899	Jacob	Wne 851	
Nowe, George	Ash 84	William	Lnc 897	James, Junior	Ptt 236	
Nowel, Enos	Edg 225	Oats, James	Smp 504	James, Senior	Ptt 236	
Hardee	Edg 225	Jesse	Smp 528	Jethro	Wne 852	
Nowell, David	Ans 202	Jethro	Smp 508	Mary	Hrt 712	
Demcy	Hrt 701	John	Smp 522	Sampson	Bfr 15	
James	Csw 128	Michael	Mck 588	Theophelus	Nsh 114	
James	Jhn 761	Stephen	Mre 57	Theophelus, Sr.	Nsh 114	
John	Hrt 701	Obar, Samuel	Brk 779	William	Rbs 408	
John	Jhn 761	Obeijant, William	Grv 509	Odoon, George	Lnc 884	
John	Wne 867	Obrian, John	Grv 552	Odum, Dempsey	Edg 227	
Nowels, Isham	Edg 225	Patrick	Grv 506	Elisha	Edg 227	
Nowlen, David (2)	Rth 134	Tillotson	Rch 252	James	Jhn 752	
James	Rth 134	Obriant, Dennis	Grv 581	Michael	Jhn 754	

Richard	Edg 227	Jno.	Lnc 849	Wm., Ser.	Crr 167
Oferrell, Barnebas	Orn 491	John	Brt 66	see Neele	
Ogburn, Susanna	Hlf 332	John	Crv 231	Onger, Lawrence	Rwn 459
Ogden, Robert	Crv 239	John	Grv 506	O'Niel, Nathan	Crr 141
Ogdon, Benjamin	Mnt 489	John	Jhn 746	Peter	Chw 121
Ogelsby, Else	Brk 779	John	Nrt 465	Saml.	Crr 143
Ogelthorp, Richard	Brk 779	John	Rch 255	Onions, Susanna	Hlf 332
Oglesbea, John	Prs 209	John	Rwn 444	Onley, Edward	Gts 273
Oglesbee, Asa	Crt 86	John	Rth 134	Smith	Wne 853
Benjamin	Crt 86	John, Big	Rch 255	Only, Levy	Frn 476
Gideon	Crt 86	John M.	Crv 249	Onstat, John	Brk 779
John	Crt 86	Joseph	Crv 233	Onstock, Caty	Cht 213
Jonathan	Crt 86	Joseph	Trl 672	Onstott, George	Rnd 335
Joseph	Crt 86	Malichi	Brt 66	Ooutlaw see Outlaw	
Levi	Crt 86	Martha	Rck 484	Opits, Charles	Stk 599
Lidda	Crt 86	Martin	Brt 66	Charles	Stk 625
Richd.	Prs 219	Mary	Grv 506	Oquin, Hardy	Rbs 409
Oglesby, Micajah	Srr 681	Mitchell	Jhn 746	John	Rbs 409
Oguin, Patrick	Jhn 775	Moses	Mnt 480	Ozekiel	Rbs 408
O'Guinn see O'Quinn		Needham	Jhn 746	Tarlor	Rbs 409
Ogwin, Stephen	Ans 241	Peter	Nwh 3	O'Quinn, Alexander	Cmb 383
O'Hara, Charles	Mck 558	Peter	Rck 483	John	Cmb 357
O'Keef see Keef		Samuel	Crv 295	Orberry, John	Wlk 56
Okelly, William	Cht 169	Stephen	Jhn 747	Orbison, Agness	Ird 652
Okely, James	Cht 201	Stephen	Prs 207	Orear, Daniel	Ash 85
Okerman, Daniel	Lnc 894	Susannah (2)	Wlk 56	Orions, Peter	Smp 506
Okey, William	Grv 580	Thomas	Crv 229	Orm, Thomas	Stk 608
Old, Sarah Price	Crv 265	Thomas	Lnc 886	Orme, William	Jns 795
OLD, Edward	Cmd 97	William	Mck 602	Ormon, Andrew	Rnd 335
Oldam, Isham	Nrt 465	William	Rck 483	Michael	Rnd 335
Oldfield, Pitt	Jns 803	William	Stk 566	Ormond, Adam	Mck 600
Richard	Jns 801	Willis, Jun.	Mre 67	Benjamin	Lnc 897
William	Glf 674	Willis, Sen.	Mre 67	Jacob	Mck 596
Oldham, John	Cht 188	Olliphante, Sarah	Mrt 403	James	Grn 598
Richman	Cht 172	Olmond, Jacob	Brk 779	James	Mck 596
William	Cht 188	Olphan, William	Dpl 404	Thomas	Grn 598
Oldrage, Samuel	Brk 779	O'Malley, Myles	Chw 113	William, Senr.	Grn 598
Oldridge, Anna	Grn 617	Ombles, John	Hde 374	Ormsby, Geo.	Nwh 10
Drury	Grn 617	Omerry, Richard	Grv 571	Ornerry see Omerry	
OLDS, Arthur	Cmd 96	O'Merry, Jacob	Bfr 14	Orr, Alexander	Mck 597
Oles, Joel	Crr 164	Onails, Lemon	Edg 227	Bunyan	Mck 542
Olian, Peter	Stk 626	Oneal, Benjamin	Wke 752	David	Mck 596
Olifant, Ruth	Bnc 182	Charles	Rwn 427	James, (Here-	
Oliphant, Eupha.	Bld 27	Elizabeth	Orn 523	tick)	Mck 577
George	Ird 652	Ferreby	Jhn 759	James, (Jocky)	Mck 555
Jesse	Bld 35	Isham	Jhn 753	James, Senr.	Mck 555
Matthew	Ird 641	James	Glf 642	Jas.	Csw 147
William	Ird 652	John	Lnc 900	John	Bnc 182
Olison, Caleb	Ptt 255	Joseph	Orn 523	John	Lnc 893
Olive, Abel	Cht 226	Pattrick	Brk 779	John	Mck 598
Demsey	Wke 752	O'Neal, Charles	Bld 24	John H.	Mck 569
Isham	Wke 752	Christopher	Lnc 900	Nathan, Junr.	Mck 556
James, Jur.	Wke 752	Elizabeth	Prq 656	Nathan, Senr.	Mck 556
James, Senr.	Wke 752	John	Bfr 14	Robert	Bnc 182
Jesse	Wke 752	Sarah	Chw 113	Widow	Mck 596
John	Wke 752	Oneale, Francis	Crt 59	Orrac, Benjamin	Rnd 335
Southwell	Wke 752	John	Crt 59	Orrel, Isaac	Bfr 14
William	Wke 752	William	Crt 59	James (2)	Ons 155
Oliver, Abijah	Srr 681	O'Neale, John	Hde 374	John	Ons 156
Abraham	Rck 484	Robert	Hde 374	Stephen	Bfr 14
Alexander	Wsh 708	Oneals, Affey	Jhn 757	William	Bfr 14
Andrew (2)	Mck 602	Anna	Jhn 756	Orrell, Kirkam	Ons 160
Andrew	Wsh 708	Bridges	Jhn 755	Kirkham	Ons 171
Benjamin	Bnc 183	Isham	Jhn 755	Orrich, Benjamin	Mnt 480
Benjamin	Ons 178	Moses	Jhn 755	Orrick, Samuel	Rwn 332
Daniel	Crv 295	Patrick	Jhn 752	Orsborn, Arthur	Rth 134
Edward	Trl 672	Ross	Jhn 758	Philip	Wsh 708
Elijah	Srr 681	Saml.	Jhn 755	Orsburn, George	Orn 523
Francis	Dpl 428	Warren	Jhn 756	James	Orn 523
George	Lnc 826	Oneel, Edmund	Edg 227	John	Glf 635
Henry	Jhn 746	Elisha	Edg 227	William	Orn 523
Henry	Wne 872	Isham	Edg 227	Orsment, Richd.	Glf 630
Henry, Jr.	Jhn 747	O'Neel, Christopher,		Orton, Charles	Ird 653
James	Ons 174	Ser.	Crr 165	James	Ird 652
James	Rck 463	Nathan	Crr 165	James	Rwn 328
James	Rck 473	O'Neele, Christopher,		John	Rwn 328
James	Wne 872	Jur.	Crr 167	Joseph	Rwn 448

Name	Code	Name	Code	Name	Code
William	Ird 619	William	Brt 66	Jesse	Cmd 94
Osborn, Abner	Glf 626	Wright	Brt 66	John	Ash 85
Adlai	Ird 657	Outlieus, George	Crv 241	John	Hrt 712
Alexander	Mck 583	Outterbridge, Burr	Mrt 403	John	Mre 42
Alexander	Mck 593	Steven	Frn 482	Joseph	Cmd 95
Elias	Ash 85	Ovebey, David	Jhn 750	Joshua	Cmd 95
Elizabeth	Hrt 712	Ephraim	Jhn 750	Josiah	Cmd 94
James	Mck 543	Ovenshine, Rine-		Lazarus	Cmd 94
Jeremiah	Ash 85	hold	Cbr 714	Lemuel	Psq 634
Jeremiah (2)	Bnc 182	Overbey, Amy	Rck 442	Lemuel	Prq 659
John	Ash 84	Overby, Freemon	Stk 566	Moses	Frn 450
John	Bnc 182	Nics.	Rck 446	Nathaniel	Hrt 712
John	Glf 630	Overcarsh, George	Cbr 685	Obediah	Cmb 370
John	Mck 547	Overcash, Francis	Rwn 303	Osborn	Frn 450
John	Mck 568	Jacob	Cbr 704	Pathena	Prq 657
John	Mck 596	Michael	Cbr 703	Peter	Cmd 95
John C.	Crv 241	Michael	Cbr 704	Peter, Jun.	Cmd 95
Jonan.	Glf 681	Overcast, Jacob	Rwn 338	Rachel	Rck 441
Nancy	Hrt 712	John	Cbr 700	Richard	Cmd 95
Nathaniel	Brk 721	Overley, John	Rnd 335	Robert	Cmd 94
Noble	Mck 543	Overman, Aron	Wne 872	Samuel	Chw 118
Peter	Glf 624	Benn.	Psq 629	Thomas	Cmb 357
Reuben	Bnc 182	Benn.	Psq 636	Titus	Cmb 370
Robert	Ash 85	Charles	Psq 624	see Daniel	
Robert	Mck 599	Charles	Psq 640	Overwenter, Adam	Brk 779
Stephen	Rwn 368	Henry	Prq 651	Overwinters, Peggy	Rth 135
William	Glf 626	Isaac	Psq 631	Owell, Marmaduke	Rbs 409
William	Mck 596	James	Orn 523	Ralph	Rbs 409
Osborne, John	Ptt 275	James (2)	Psq 640	Owen, Andrew	Glf 654
Osburn, Joseph	Smp 536	Jesse	Wne 873	Aron	Glf 650
see Orsburn		John	Psq 640	DAniel	Cht 200
Oseas, Peter	Stk 620	John	Prq 650	David	Wlk 56
Osley, Isaac	Cmb 391	John	Wne 872	David, junr.	Wlk 56
Osmond, Henry	Bfr 14	John	Wne 873	Edward	Glf 649
Wyriott	Bfr 15	Jo-eph	Psq 641	Francis	Cmb 357
Ostean, Wallace	Ons 157	Morgan	Prq 660	George	Wlk 56
Osteen, Caleb	Dpl 418	Nathan	Psq 638	James	Wrr 822
Osten, Bartholomew	Ash 84	Othniel	Psq 635	Jeremh.	Rck 450
Oston, Wm.	Crr 157	Ozias	Psq 634	John	Rck 436
Ostree, Ch.	Ons 163	Robert	Psq 635	John	Rck 441
William	Ons 161	Thomas	Psq 624	John	Wrr 822
Otis, Nathaniel	Crv 285	Thomas	Wne 873	John	Wlk 56
Ottrey, Kathrine	Bfr 14	Wm.	Psq 633	Latitia	Brt 66
Ousley, Jessee	Cht 207	Overmon, Nathan	Rnd 335	Lawrance	Ash 85
Jessee	Cht 208	Zebulon	Rnd 335	Oliver	Cht 173
Outhouse, Israel	Brt 66	Overnton, David	Chw 128	Oliver	Cht 189
Outland, Axum	Wne 873	Overstreet, Ferri-		Samuel	Glf 650
Cornelius	Wne 872	by	Rch 252	Thomas	Stk 610
Jeremiah	Nrt 465	John	Rbs 409	Thomas, Esqr.	Bld 37
Jonathan	Wne 871	Moses	Rch 246	Wm.	Csw 148
Josiah	Nrt 465	Silus	Rch 253	Owenby, Thos.	Lnc 849
Thomas	Nrt 465	Overton, Aaron	Frn 450	Owens, Adam	Trl 680
Thomas	Wne 871	Abner	Psq 639	Ambrose	Rwn 400
William	Nrt 465	Abraham	Cmd 107	Barnett	Ash 85
William	Wne 871	Ahab	Cmd 108	Barsil	Rwn 433
Outlaw, Aron	Brt 66	Ann B.	Rck 488	Benjamin	Rwn 400
Edward	Brt 66	Anthony	Cmd 108	Bletha	Orn 590
Edward	Dpl 438	Benjamin	Cmd 94	Brannok	Bfr 15
George	Brt 66	Benjamin	Trl 672	Catharine	Grv 548
George	Gts 273	Christopher	Brt 66	Daniel	Nsh 114
Hardy	Bfr 14	David	Cmd 93	David	Rck 480
Jacob	Brt 66	David	Chw 118	Dempsey	Edg 227
Jacob	Gts 273	David	Mre 49	Effard	Rwn 394
James	Dpl 438	Devotion	Cmd 95	Elias	Edg 227
James, Junr.	Brt 66	Edward	Trl 686	Elias	Nsh 114
James, Senr.	Brt 66	Elijah	Cmd 95	Elijah	Edg 227
John	Dpl 440	Francis	Cmd 94	Elisha	Edg 227
Joshua	Brt 66	Francis	Prq 657	Elizabeth	Hde 374
Josiah	Dpl 426	Gehovah	Cmd 94	Frederick	Grv 548
Levi	Gts 273	George	Rck 466	Henry	Rwn 433
Lewis	Hrt 706	Gorshan	Cmd 108	Isaac	Trl 680
Luois	Brt 66	Henry	Cmd 94	James	Bnc 182
Morgan	Brt 66	Jacob	Hrt 712	James	Mck 528
Rachel	Hrt 706	James	Cmd 94	James	Rth 134
Ralph	Brt 66	James, Junr.	Hrt 712	James	Srr 681
Susanna	Hrt 706	James, Senr.	Hrt 712	James	Trl 680
Thomas	Brt 66	Jeconiah	Cmd 95	Jehu	Trl 680

Jesse	Bnc 182	James	Brk 779	Joab	Dpl 415
John	Brk 779	Samuel	Bnc 182	John	Rth 138
John	Grv 506	Samuel	Lnc 879	John	Wke 753
John	Grv 510	Oxley, John	Lnr 19	William	Dpl 415
John	Grv 511	John, Junr.	Brt 66	William	Rth 137
John	Grv 534	John, Senr.	Brt 66	Padgett, Ephaim	Srr 683
John	Nsh 114	Jonas	Crv 327	Jesse	Trl 672
John	Orn 590	Mary	Lnr 19	John	Trl 672
John	Rnd 335	Oydlott, John	Crr 149	John	Trl 684
John	Rwn 394	Mary	Crr 143	John	Wsh 708
John	Rwn 433	Wm.	Crr 149	Padqit, James	Wlk 59
John	Rth 135	Oyston, Thos.	Crr 157	William	Wlk 59
John	Srr 681	Ozbarn, Jesse	Rnd 335	Padjet, John	Stk 602
John	Trl 680	Mathew	Rnd 335	see Pagett	
John, H.D.	Wlk 56	Samuel	Rnd 335	Padrick, Abegail	Ons 153
John, Junr.	Edg 227	Seth	Rnd 353	Aron	Ons 145
John, Senr.	Edg 227	William	Rnd 335	Daniel	Crr 146
Joseph	Rwn 332	Ozburne, William	Stk 566	John	Crr 148
Josiah	Rwn 394	Ozier, Christopher	Mnt 506	Sarah	Crr 146
Lot	Edg 227	Jacob	Mnt 472	Pae, David	Cht 161
Lucrecy	Trl 680	Jerry	Rnd 335	James	Cht 162
Mosbey	Bnc 182	John	Glf 661	Reuben	Cht 158
Normon	Rwn 433	John	Mnt 472	William, Sen.	Cht 153
Only	Orn 590	William	Mnt 472	Paffard, William	Stk 567
Owen	Bnc 182	William, Senr.	Mnt 472	Paford, Samuel	Cmb 361
Owen	Smp 519	Ozment, James	Glf 672	Page, Absolem	Mrt 403
Owen	Trl 680	Ozsment, John	Glf 672	Benjamin	Rnd 334
Perry	Cmd 104			Benjamin, Sr.	Rnd 334
Peter	Bnc 182			Catharine	Brt 70
Peter	Rwn 394	-- P --		Daniel	Brk 782
Peter	Trl 680			Edward	Wke 753
Rachael	Wlk 56			Elizabeth	Ptt 234
Ralph	Rwn 400	P..., Zachariah	Orn 591	J...	Ptt 234
Richard	Rwn 394	P...rs, John	Ons 137	Jacob	Edg 230
Richd.	Wlk 56	Pac see Pae		Jesse	Wke 755
Robert	Rwn 394	Pace, Buckner	Wke 756	Jesse, Junr.	Wke 755
Samuel	Brk 779	Edmond	Srr 707	John	Bnc 184
Samuel	Rwn 394	James	Wke 756	John	Mrt 405
Stephen	Bfr 15	Jemima	Frn 471	John	Ptt 234
Stephen	Rwn 338	John	Frn 483	John	Rwn 375
Tabby	Ird 632	John	Wke 755	Jos.	Mrt 403
Thomas	Grv 508	Joseph	Glf 636	Joseph	Ptt 270
Thomas	Rwn 410	Joseph	Orn 523	Joseph	Rbs 410
Thomas	Rth 134	Richard	Cht 203	Joseph	Smp 536
Thomas	Smp 519	Samuel	Wsh 714	Joseph	Srr 683
Thomas	Trl 680	Solomon's, free		Lewis	Wke 753
Widow	Mck 531	Ben	Nrt 469	Melchisedec	Ptt 270
William	Edg 227	Stephen	Jhn 760	Nathan	Brt 68
William (2)	Ird 636	Stephen, Junr.	Ans 210	Nathaniel	Cht 187
William	Nsh 114	Stephen, Senr.	Ans 211	Samuel	Smp 495
William	Rwn 400	William	Ans 215	Thomas	Csw 107
William	Smp 519	William	Cht 224	Thomas	Edg 230
William	Wlk 56	William	Frn 462	Thomas	Jhn 767
William, (Son of		William	Hlf 334	Tobias	Jhn 767
Zach.)	Trl 680	Pacely, James	Glf 631	Uriah	Mnt 510
Wm.	Csw 117	John, Jur.	Glf 640	Whitehead	Csw 107
Zachariah	Trl 680	John, Senr.	Glf 640	William	Ptt 270
Owestwald, Henry	Cbr 709	William	Glf 645	William	Ptt 292
Owin, Richardson	Prs 201	Pack, Benjamin	Rth 135	Wm.	Csw 107
Owins, Markham	Mrt 403	John	Rth 135	Wm.	Csw 147
Shadrack	Prs 194	Ezeriah	Rwn 433	Wm., Jur.	Csw 103
Thomas	Ons 142	Reason	Rwn 433	Paget, John	Chw 123
William	Crt 79	Richard	Rwn 433	Pagett, Thomas	Stk 602
Ownsby, Arthur	Rth 134	William	Rwn 433	see Padjet	
James	Rth 134	Packer, Clenny	Jns 817	Paight, Nathaniel	Grn 603
John	Rth 134	David	Jns 817	Paihn, John	Srr 684
Porter	Rth 134	Paden, John W.	Edg 233	Pain, George	Wlk 57
Powell S.	Rth 134	William	Edg 232	John	Bnc 184
Thomas	Frn 449	Padget, Abraham	Rth 136	John	Csw 107
Thomas	Rth 134	Benjamin	Dpl 417	John	Srr 682
Oxendine, Benjamin	Rbs 409	Cornelius	Dpl 416	Thomas	Brk 780
Charles	Rbs 409	Edmund	Rth 137	Paine, Barnet	Brk 782
Charles, Jur.	Rbs 409	Isaac	Dpl 415	Caroline	Brk 785
David	Rbs 409	Isaac	Wne 872	Daniel	Brk 781
Jesse	Rbs 409	Jacob	Rth 138	Daniel	Brk 783
John	Cmb 357	James	Dpl 416	George	Brk 784
Oxford, Bashaba	Bnc 182	James	Dpl 422	James	Wrr 825

John	Rwn 375	Joseph	Wrr 822	Benjamin (2)	Rch 268	
Joseph	Brk 785	William	Wrr 823	Benjn.	Gts 276	
Robert	Brk 784	Pardiew see Pardue		Bramble	Dpl 434	
Thomas	Brk 784	Pardue, Patrum	Wrr 823	Britain	Nrt 465	
William	Brk 782	Pare, Jones	Hlf 336	Buckner	Rck 465	
William	Rwn 289	William	Cmd 101	Cader	Nrt 467	
see Poine		Parham, Avery	Grv 536	Charles	Lnc 820	
Painter, George	Rth 137	Avery	Wke 754	Cressy	Wlk 58	
John	Lnc 891	Ephraim	Grv 535	Cullin	Hrt 726	
Nathan	Prs 197	Isham	Grv 536	D. Solomon	Nsh 115	
Pair, Caleb	Crr 142	Isham, jr.	Grv 535	Daniel	Dpl 435	
Daniel	Crr 142	John	Cht 187	Daniel	Gts 275	
Jesse	Crr 160	John	Grv 535	Daniel	Hrt 721	
John	Wke 753	Kennon	Grv 535	Daniel	Rck 465	
John	Wlk 58	Lewis	Grv 535	Danl.	Rch 267	
John, Junr.	Wke 753	Mary	Grv 561	David	Grv 576	
Mathias	Wlk 57	Samuel	Grv 535	David	Lnc 865	
Richard	Crr 139	Thomas	Grv 536	David	Orn 591	
Wm.	Crr 142	Thomas, jr.	Grv 537	David	Rwn 428	
Paire, Iseah	Crr 140	William	Hlf 334	David, Junr.	Nrt 467	
Pait, William	Jns 779	Parhom, Lewis	Wrr 786	David, Senr.	Nrt 465	
Paiten, Henry	Lnc 863	Parick, Jacob	Cmd 102	Demey	Gts 274	
James	Lnc 863	Paridise, William	Dpl 414	Edward	Crr 150	
Paiton, Thomas	Cmb 367	Paris, George	Crv 291	Edward	Rwn 428	
Pake, Elizabeth	Crt 67	Samuel	Rth 135	Elijah	Grv 575	
John	Crt 67	Stephen	Grn 605	Elijah	Rch 246	
Pall, Jacob	Crv 267	Parish, Allen	Orn 591	Elisabeth	Mnt 518	
John	Crv 279	Ann	Grv 565	Elisha	Brt 70	
Joseph	Crv 279	Austing	Grv 552	Elisha	Chw 118	
Mary	Crv 279	Charles	Grv 552	Elisha	Prq 646	
Palmer, Daniel	Brk 784	Charles	Jhn 763	Elisha	Wne 859	
David	Psq 635	Charles	Wke 777	Elizabeth	Gts 275	
Demsey	Psq 634	Clabourn	Orn 591	Elizabeth	Hlf 336	
Edmond	Rwn 318	David	Cht 159	Elizabeth	Hrt 726	
Edmund	Bnc 184	Elijah	Grv 566	Enoch	Chw 119	
Elijah	Bfr 16	Elizabeth	Grv 561	Enoch	Lnc 900	
Isiah	Bnc 183	Elonor	Prs 194	Ephraim	Hrt 736	
Jacob	Crv 273	George	Jhn 767	Esther	Gts 275	
James	Cmb 358	Humphrey	Rth 135	Ezekiel	Bld 2	
James	Hrt 738	James	Chw 127	Felix	Ons 177	
James	Orn 525	Jestice	Jhn 766	Feriby	Gts 276	
James	Rwn 319	John	Chw 126	Francis	Nrt 467	
Jane	Crv 239	John	Grv 536	Francis	Wrr 825	
John	Psq 635	John	Grv 552	Gabriel	Jhn 760	
John	Stk 620	John	Prq 662	Gabriel	Lnr 33	
John, Senr.	Mnt 511	John	Rck 459	Gabril	Nsh 114	
Lemuel	Hde 374	Joseph	Chw 126	Garrit	Mnt 493	
Marquis	Mnt 512	Lewis	Grv 512	George	Bld 15	
Martin	Orn 526	Lewis	Grv 560	George	Grv 571	
Pat	Brk 786	Mary	Orn 591	Green	Crv 237	
Philip	Rwn 319	Mary	Rck 459	Hardy	Dpl 421	
Robert	Mnt 480	Noel	Glf 651	Hardy	Jhn 758	
William	Crv 331	Shadrech	Grv 526	Hardy	Nwh 8A	
William	Mnt 464	Susanna	Dpl 433	Hardy	Ons 176	
William	Mnt 496	Thomas	Rwn 411	Henderson	Wke 753	
William	Psq 635	Valentine	Grv 552	Henry	Bld 8	
Palmore, Ezekiel	Ptt 256	William	Mck 544	Howell	Glf 656	
Pane, Jessephy	Mre 60	William	Orn 591	Ica	Cmb 378	
Richard	Rth 135	Zachariah	Orn 591	Isaac	Brt 70	
Panegor, Mall	Stk 619	see Parrish		Isaac	Chw 122	
Panker, William	Rch 268	Parisher, Benjn.	Prq 656	Isaac	Nrt 467	
Panket, Stephen	Rch 264	Joseph	Prq 655	Isaac	Wne 848	
Pannel, Evan	Lnc 843	Park, James	Rwn 381	Isaac	Wne 849	
Pannell, William	Grv 542	John	Rwn 404	Isaac, Junr.	Gts 274	
Panter, Henry	Brk 781	Robert	Wrr 824	Isaac, Senr.	Gts 274	
John	Brk 783	Samuel	Rwn 362	Jacob	Dpl 421	
Samuel	Brk 780	Parker, Aaron	Bld 8	Jacob, Junr.	Nrt 467	
Paquinette, Eliza-		Aaron	Nrt 467	Jacob, Senr.	Mrt 405	
beth	Crt 80	Abner	Prs 218	Jacob, Senr.	Nrt 467	
John	Crt 80	Abraham	Orn 591	James	Cmd 102	
Paradice, William	Hlf 336	Abrahum	Gts 275	James	Gts 276	
William	Ons 178	Alexander	Nrt 467	James	Hlf 332	
Parc, Bethell	Hlf 336	Amos	Gts 275	James	Hrt 721	
Eli	Hlf 336	Amos	Ons 169	James	Nrt 467	
Parc...m, William	Ans 206	Amoss	Orn 591	James	Ons 157	
Parch, Seath	Wke 753	Andrew	Rth 136	James	Rwn 438	
Pardew, Bevill	Wrr 823	Arthur	Wne 852	Jas.	Mrt 405	

Name	Ref	Name	Ref	Name	Ref
Jas., Junr.	Mrt 405	Peter	Dpl 426	Asa	Lnc 897
Jeams	Crr 141	Peter	Edg 229	Benjamin	Brk 781
Jehu	Hlf 336	Peter, Junr.	Hrt 721	Benjn.	Wlk 57
Jeremiah	Nrt 467	Peter, Senr.	Hrt 721	Catharine	Nrt 467
Jeromiah	Ird 615	Powel	Prs 191	Daniel	Prq 650
Jesse (2)	Gts 275	Richard	Nrt 467	Darrel	Orn 524
Jesse	Wne 872	Richard	Rwn 309	David	Rwn 439
Jethro	Hlf 336	Richard	Smp 534	Ebenezer	Rwn 309
Jobe	Chw 122	Robert	Cht 164	Elisha	Nrt 465
John	Bld 45	Robert	Cht 197	Frances	Crv 231
John	Cmb 371	Robert	Gts 274	George	Bnc 183
John (2)	Dpl 409	Robert	Hrt 736	George	Brk 783
John	Frn 445	Rubin	Rwn 449	Henry	Wne 848
John	Gts 274	Samuel	Chw 130	Hiram	Csw 134
John	Gts 275	Samuel	Grv 520	Hugh	Mck 527
John	Hrt 713	Samuel	Nrt 467	Humphrey	Prq 645
John	Lnr 33	Samuel	Srr 682	James	Nrt 469
John	Mck 588	Sarah	Hlf 336	James	Rth 135
John	Mnt 493	Sarah	Hrt 736	Jean	Rwn 338
John	Nsh 116	Sarah	Nrt 467	Jeptha	Csw 134
John	Ons 158	Sarey	Ptt 270	John	Mck 556
John	Psq 640	Sessoms	Smp 532	John	Wlk 56
John	Prq 651	Seth	Chw 121	John, Senr.	Mck 556
John	Prq 662	Silas	Hrt 721	Jonathan	Wlk 57
John	Rwn 438	Silas, Senr.	Hrt 721	Joseph	Prq 645
John	Smp 531	Solomon	Rwn 453	Joseph	Rwn 349
John	Srr 708	Solomon D.	Nsh 115	Joshua	Mck 576
John	Wke 753	Stephen	Jhn 757	Larkin	Brk 781
John	Wne 847	Stephen	Ons 158	Major	Wne 871
John	Wlk 58	Stephen	Prs 218	Mary	Nsh 115
John, jr.	Hrt 736	Susannah	Wlk 56	Mary	Orn 524
John, Junr.	Nrt 465	Thomas	Brt 70	Moses	Mck 602
John, Senr.	Gts 276	Thomas	Gts 275	Noah, Jur.	Rwn 309
John, Senr.	Nrt 465	Thomas	Hlf 336	Noah, Senr.	Rwn 309
John, Ters.	Nrt 467	Thomas	Lnc 856	Reuben	Wlk 57
John, Gatling	Gts 276	Thomas	Nrt 467	Richd.	Wlk 57
Jonan.	Glf 624	Thomas	Prs 199	Robert	Csw 121
Jonas	Edg 232	Thomas	Rwn 453	Robert	Mck 558
Jonathan	Nsh 116	Thomas	Rth 137	Robert	Mck 580
Jonathan	Smp 500	Thomas	Smp 532	Robert	Mck 582
Jonathan	Smp 524	Weeks	Edg 173	Robert	Nrt 469
Jonathan	Srr 682	Weeks	Edg 229	Rueben	Wlk 56
Jonathan, Junr.	Gts 275	Wiley	Cmb 378	Rueben	Wlk 57
Jonathan, Sr.	Gts 275	Will	Brn 18A	Samuel	Bnc 183
Jos.	Mrt 405	Will.	Nsh 116	Samuel	Bnc 185
Joseph	Gts 274	William	Bld 8	Samuel	Brk 783
Joseph	Hlf 334	William	Edg 232	Samuel	Rnd 335
Joseph	Psq 629	William	Hlf 332	Solomon	Csw 122
Joseph	Srr 683	William	Hrt 736	Thomas	Brk 782
Joseph, Junr.	Brt 68	William	Lnc 856	Thomas	Mck 558
Joseph, Senr.	Brt 68	William	Nrt 467	Thomas	Wlk 57
Josiah	Gts 274	William	Prq 653	Will. (2)	Nsh 115
Josiah	Nrt 467	William	Rwn 454	William	Brk 782
Josiah	Mck 550	William	Smp 531	William	Mck 558
Kader	Cmb 378	William, Junr.	Mnt 491	William	Nrt 469
Kedar	Edg 232	William, Senr.	Mnt 493	William	Orn 592
Kedar (2)	Gts 275	Willis	Chw 123	William	Rth 137
Kesiah	Wne 871	Willis	Gts 275	Wm.	Csw 134
Lancaster	Nsh 114	Winborne	Nrt 467	Parlier, Isaac	Wlk 57
Lemuel	Hrt 726	Wm.	Mrt 405	John (2)	Wlk 57
Lemuel	Nrt 467	Zachri	Gts 276	Parmer, James	Lnc 865
Lewis	Nrt 467	see Packer		Jesse	Lnc 843
Luke	Brt 68	Parkes, David,		Jno.	Lnc 843
Mary	Hrt 736	Junr.	Mck 556	John B.	Rwn 444
Mary	Nrt 467	David, Senr.	Mck 556	Will.	Nwh 10
Mary	Ons 154	James	Srr 683	Parmerle, Jane	Hde 374
Mary	Orn 591	John	Grv 558	William	Hde 374
Matthew	Jhn 752	Robert	Mck 556	Parmoore, Augus-	
Matthew	Jhn 757	Thomas	Cht 214	tine	Orn 528
Miles	Gts 275	Thomas	Cht 215	David	Orn 528
Moses	Bld 2	Parket, Carter	Ird 662	Parnall, John	Wke 753
Nancy	Hlf 334	Parkins, Anna	Crv 267	John, Junr.	Wke 753
Nancy	Jns 813	Jesse	Csw 100	Parnel, Eliza.	Bld 40
Nancy	Ons 143	Parkinson see Perkinson		John	Hlf 332
Nicholas	Ans 219	Parks, Aaron	Wlk 58	Marget	Gts 274
Nicolas	Smp 528	Ambrose	Wlk 58	Widow	Rch 270
Peter	Crr 142	Andrew	Nrt 469	Parnell, Edward	Rwn 375

Parnold, Benjamin	Jhn 749	Mary	Hlf 334	Charls	Rnd 335
Henry	Jhn 757	Mary	Mnt 483	David	Orn 525
Jerremiah	Jhn 759	Nathaniel	Mnt 480	David	Stk 591
John	Jhn 758	Penelope	Hrt 733	Dunken	Mre 54
Parr, Arthur	Rwn 388	Randle	Mnt 480	Dunkin	Mre 53
Claiburn	Mck 592	William	Hlf 334	Elizabeth	Edg 232
Henry	Rwn 349	William	Wke 754	James	Wrr 825
John	Lnc 856	Partis, Peter	Glf 624	Joab	Srr 684
John	Mck 592	Parton, Charles	Orn 617	John (2)	Mre 55
Thomas	Mck 592	Leonard	Orn 617	John	Srr 684
Parr...m, William	Ans 206	William	Orn 617	John	Wrr 826
Parrack, James	Rth 137	Partrick, John	Hlf 332	Lewis	Wrr 824
Parram, John	Mre 68	Partridge, Thomas	Cht 208	Rebekah	Srr 684
Parris, John,Junr.	Crv 303	William	Cht 208	Thomas	Cht 187
William	Orn 527	Pary, John	Glf 678	William	Srr 684
Zadoch	Crv 303	see Perry		Young	Wrr 825
Parrish, Barsil	Rwn 388	Pascal, Ann	Frn 455	Patient see Pateint	
Daniel	Wrr 826	Elijah	Csw 146	Patilla, Henry	Brk 786
Edward	Rwn 388	Robt.	Cht 206	John	Brk 786
James	Nwh 2A	Saml.	Csw 146	Millington	Brk 785
Jesse	Lnc 884	Wm.	Csw 147	Rachel	Brk 785
Joel	Frn 458	Paschal, Alex	Csw 127	Patillo see Pattilloe	
John	Wrr 825	Paschall, Anderson	Wrr 823	Patisall, William	Cht 156
Leroy	Mre 69	Dennis	Wrr 823	Patison, Joseph	Stk 615
Richd.	Brn 14A	Elisha	Wrr 823	Patrick, Agnis	Wrr 826
Robert	Frn 485	John	Wrr 824	Armstead	Wke 755
Samuel, Sr.	Crt 79	John, jr.	Wrr 823	Benjamin	Ptt 294
Sharwood	Mre 69	Nicholson	Wrr 823	Cornelius	Bfr 15
Thomas	Mre 71	Samuel	Wrr 823	Courtney	Hrt 738
William	Wke 756	Thomas (2)	Wrr 824	Daniel	Grn 603
see Parish		Pasdon, Moses	Stk 615	Danl.	Bld 9
Parrom, Lewis	Mre 68	Pasely, William	Mck 603	Hugh	Rck 444
Parrot, Lewis	Prs 193	Paskel, Samuel	Grv 520	Isaac	Brt 68
Reuben	Rth 136	Paskell, John	Grv 525	Isaac	Trl 680
Parrott, Benja.	Lnr 20	Silas	Grv 565	Jas.	Rck 444
Elizabeth	Lnr 20	William	Grv 558	Joel	Ptt 241
Elizabeth	Rck 445	Pass, H. John	Edg 229	John	Crv 303
Jacob	Lnr 20	Nathl.	Csw 104	John, Junr.	Crv 303
John	Lnr 20	Nathl.	Csw 110	John, Junr.	Trl 692
Mary	Crt 76	Passens, Wm.	Crr 146	Joshua	Ptt 281
Parrow, Samuel	Ptt 224	Passmore, John	Nsh 116	Mary	Lnr 19
Parrum, William	Rth 136	Mary	Hlf 334	Matthias	Ans 216
Parry, John	Nrt 469	William	Wke 754	Reubin	Wrr 826
Parrymour, Joseph	Wsh 708	Pasteur, Abner	Crv 223	Solomon	Ptt 293
Thomas	Wsh 708	Edward	Crv 241	Thomas	Wsh 708
Parshall, James	Wke 777	John	Crv 235	William	Rck 440
Parsley, Robert	Crt 68	Pasture, Winnefred	Ons 136	see Padrick, Partrick	
Parson, Charles	Cht 190	Pasturs, Martha	Hlf 336	Patridge, Jesse	Crr 141
John	Jns 815	Pate, Anthony	Lnr 19	John	Crr 147
Parsons, Asa	Wsh 714	Asa	Ans 213	John	Lnr 18
Elisabeth	Crv 301	Benjamin	Bfr 15	Patrum, Peter	Wrr 823
Evans	Glf 624	Benjamin	Wke 755	Pats, John	Lnc 839
Francis	Ans 227	Catherine	Rwn 368	Pattegrew, John	Orn 591
George	Glf 624	Charles	Grn 596	Patten, Hance	Bfr 15
James	Crv 301	Charles	Rbs 412	Mathew	Orn 524
James	Glf 630	Frederick	Lnr 18	Wm.	Lnc 839
James (2)	Wlk 57	Isaac	Rch 271	Pattern, Dempsey	Crr 143
James	Wlk 58	Isham	Wne 870	James	Orn 527
John	Crv 301	James	Wne 869	John	Crr 145
John	Wlk 56	Jesse	Mre 73	John	Orn 525
Joseph	Hlf 336	Joseph	Grn 596	Margarett	Orn 600
Lydia	Wne 847	Parret	Bfr 15	Rebecah	Orn 525
Richard	Srr 683	Samuel	Bfr 15	Robert	Orn 527
Richard, Jur.	Srr 683	Samuel	Rch 259	Samuel	Orn 527
Samuel	Mnt 464	Shadrach	Wne 869	Patters, Robert	Brk 783
Thomas	Wne 847	Stephen	Rch 258	Patterson, Alexan-	
William	Glf 624	Thurrigood	Rch 259	der	Bnc 184
Wm.	Wne 850	Traves	Jhn 765	Alexander	Cbr 699
Partee, Abner	Grv 578	Travis	Jhn 767	Alexander	Rch 254
Charles	Grv 578	William	Bfr 15	Alexander,	
Parten, Charles	Orn 617	William	Bfr 17	Esquire	Rbs 413
Henry	Cmb 376	William	Lnr 18	Alexr.	Lnc 832
Henry	Nrt 469	William, Jur.	Lnr 18	Angus (2)	Rbs 414
Partin, Benjamin	Hlf 334	Pateint, Job	Grv 512	Arthur	Lnc 897
Drury	Wke 754	Pateman, Esais	Jhn 752	Benjamin	Nrt 467
Jesse	Hlf 334	Paterson, Archd.	Mre 54	Crecey	Wke 777
John	Mnt 480	Archd.	Mre 55	Daniel	Cmb 360

Name	Loc		Name	Loc		Name	Loc
Daniel	Cmb 388		William, Ters.	Nrt 467		James	Rwn 368
Daniel	Cmb 389		see Patters			Jas.	Prs 202
Daniel (2)	Rbs 413		Pattetgrew, James	Orn 591		Jesse	Csw 145
David	Nrt 467		Pattillo, John	Wrr 825		John	Csw 126
David	Rck 467		Pattilloe, Chath-			John	Crr 165
David	Rck 489		erine	Grv 511		John	Orn 526
David	Rth 135		Henry	Grv 511		John	Prs 202
Elisabeth	Cbr 701		Pattison, Simmons	Stk 615		John	Trl 686
Gideon	Csw 111		Patton, Aaron	Bnc 183		Joseph	Csw 96
Gordon	Ird 637		Ann	Cbr 700		Joseph, Senr.	Rck 443
Hanswell	Nrt 467		Benjamin	Cbr 700		Joshua	Rck 491
Hugh	Cbr 700		Catherine	Brk 780		Michael	Chw 116
Isaac	Cmb 358		Charles	Mck 550		Moses	Srr 684
Isaac	Orn 525		Elijah	Brk 782		Richard	Crr 165
Isabella	Orn 527		Elijah	Rth 135		Robert	Prs 196
Isham	Wke 754		Francis	Brk 780		Thomas	Trl 686
James	Bnc 184		George	Bnc 183		Thos.	Crr 153
James	Csw 109		Huston	Bnc 183		Thos.	Crr 165
James	Dpl 431		James	Bnc 183		Thos., Jur.	Crr 166
James	Ird 612		James	Wlk 57		Will.	Prs 211
James	Ird 657		John	Bnc 183		William	Rwn 278
James	Lnc 899		John	Lnc 820		Payner, Henery	Orn 525
James	Orn 526		John	Rwn 322		John	Cmd 105
James	Orn 591		Joseph	Cbr 702		Thomas	Rck 477
James	Rch 259		Mathew	Bnc 183		Paynie, Philip	Lnc 891
James	Rwn 323		Mathew, j.	Bnc 183		Payson, George	Ptt 291
James	Rwn 411		Robert	Bnc 183		Paysour, George	Lnc 841
James	Rth 135		Robert	Brk 782		Pea, James	Mck 545
Jane	Lnc 832		Samuel	Brk 781		Peabody, John	Nwh 3A
Jarratt	Rck 458		Thomas	Bnc 183		Peace, Clayburn	Mck 593
Jeremiah	Nrt 467		Thomas	Wlk 57		John	Frn 492
John	Bnc 184		Thomas, Sr.	Bnc 183		John	Grv 528
John	Cbr 700		Pattox, John	Rwn 404		John	Grv 557
John	Cbr 702		Pattrick, Jeromiah	Rwn 454		John	Mck 593
John	Cmb 360		Robert	Ird 622		Joseph	Wke 777
John	Cmb 386		William	Ird 637		Joseph, jr.	Grv 528
John	Ird 618		William, Jur.	Rwn 449		Joseph, sr.	Grv 528
John	Ird 632		William, Senr.	Rwn 449		Samuel	Grv 562
John	Mck 600		Paul, Abraham,			William H., jr.	Grv 564
John	Nrt 467		Jur.	Rbs 409		Peacock, Abraham	Rnd 334
John (2)	Rbs 414		Abrahm, Ser.	Rbs 409		Cisley	Wke 755
John	Rth 136		Benjamin	Brk 785		David	Jhn 774
Jonathan	Nrt 467		Elias	Brk 783		George	Wsh 708
Joseph	Ird 636		Elias	Brk 785		Isaac	Bfr 23
Joseph, Junr.	Nrt 467		Ezekiel	Ans 198		Jesse	Wne 859
Joseph, Senr.	Nrt 467		Ezra	Hde 374		John	Wne 865
Joseph, Ters.	Nrt 467		George	Rbs 409		John	Wne 869
Malcom	Rbs 413		Hosea	Bfr 15		Luke	Orn 525
Mann	Orn 616		Jacob	Hde 374		Micajah	Jhn 752
Mark	Orn 616		James, Jur.	Csw 102		Peter	Wne 849
Mary	Wsh 714		John	Orn 524		Seth	Wne 873
Mathew	Bnc 185		Lewis	Brk 782		Simeon	Wne 858
Michael	Glf 633		Margret	Brk 785		Stephen	Wne 858
Neill	Cmb 360		Pigg	Srr 682		William	Cmb 357
Neill	Rbs 413		Reading	Bfr 16		William	Mnt 491
Nicolas	Crt 78		Samuel	Csw 102		William	Wne 864
Robert	Bnc 184		Sarah	Ans 224		Peaden, William	Jhn 746
Robert	Cbr 701		Stephen	Rbs 409		Peal, Amos	Mrt 405
Robert	Lnc 899		Thomas	Srr 682		Edwd.	Mrt 405
Robert	Rth 138		William	Rbs 409		Henry	Bld 49
Robt.	Lnc 839		Pawel, Charles	Cht 190		Jas.	Mrt 405
Sally	Edg 173		see Powel, Powell			Jesse	Mrt 404
Sally	Edg 229		Paxton, Benjamin	Ptt 253		John	Edg 230
Samuel	Rth 135		John	Mck 580		John	Edg 231
Sarah	Cht 177		John	Mck 582		John	Mrt 405
Silmon	Frn 459		Payn, Charles	Rck 469		Jonathan	Mrt 405
Thomas	Bnc 185		James (2)	Orn 527		Moses	Mrt 405
Thomas	Lnc 897		Joseph	Rck 479		Reuben	Mrt 404
Thos.	Srr 705		Robert	Rck 457		Robert, Junr.	Edg 231
William	Csw 100		Thos.	Rck 469		Robert, Senr.	Edg 231
William	Glf 639		William	Rck 469		Thos.	Mrt 403
William	Mck 541		Payne, Barnebas	Rwn 368		William	Brt 70
William	Mck 606		Benjamin	Rwn 368		William	Ptt 281
William, Junr.	Mck 522		Charles	Rwn 411		Peale, Dempsey	Brt 70
William, Junr.	Nrt 467		Enoch	Crr 164		Henery	Crr 165
William, Senr.	Mck 525		Isaac	Prq 663		Hilary	Ptt 270
William, Senr.	Nrt 467		Isaac	Rwn 349		James	Ptt 270

James, Junr.	Mck 563	Preston	Wke 754	John, Junr.	Nrt 469
James, Senr.	Mck 563	Richmond	Rwn 427	John, Senr.	Nrt 469
John	Mck 563	Saml.	Wke 754	Thomas	Nrt 469
Jonah	Brt 70	Samuel	Rwn 368	see Puler	
Pealor, Anthony	Rwn 381	Simon	Wke 754	Peelor, Andrew	Rth 137
Michael	Cbr 703	Starling	Orn 617	Peter	Rth 137
Peanix, Gallant	Cbr 702	Stephen	Brk 780	Peels, Edward	Wne 854
Molly	Cbr 702	Sterling	Orn 617	Peeple, Joseph	Cmb 374
Pearce, Abner	Gts 274	Thomas	Brk 782	Peeples, Hubbard	Glf 673
Abraham	Gts 274	Thomas	Mnt 476	Pegg, James	Glf 686
Ansil	Frn 467	Thomas	Rwn 367	William	Rth 137
Arthur	Mnt 467	William	Brk 780	Peggs, Matthew	Rck 476
Benjamin	Hlf 334	William	Cht 189	Pegram, Richard	Cmb 390
Charles	Jhn 751	William	Rwn 368	William	Cmb 390
Christopher	Gts 274	Peartree, Holmes	Hde 375	Pegrom, Daniel	Wrr 825
Everit	Jhn 751	Mary	Bfr 16	George	Wrr 825
Francis	Wlk 59	Noah	Hde 375	Henry	Wrr 825
Hardy	Rch 265	Wilson	Hde 375	Peirce, Jacob	Nrt 465
Isaac	Ans 235	Peasely, James	Brk 785	Susanah	Mrt 404
Isaac	Gts 274	John	Brk 785	Wm.	Mrt 405
Isham	Mnt 482	William	Brk 784	Pelecoat, Eliza-	
Isham	Mnt 483	Peasinger, Thomas	Cbr 700	beth	Brk 780
James	Ird 645	Peasley, Nathan	Brk 785	Pelkinton, Anthony	Wke 755
James	Rwn 454	William	Orn 527	Pell, Jonathan	Srr 683
Jas.	Prs 218	Peasly, John	Brk 784	William	Rth 137
Jesse	Jhn 751	Peator, Ludwick	Rwn 299	Pellam, Peter	Nwh 3A
Jesse	Jhn 752	Michael	Rwn 299	Pellard, John	Grv 584
John	Ans 235	Peavy, Calep (2)	Brn 13	Samuel	Grv 583
John	Hlf 334	Charles	Brn 13A	Pellateis, Jerome	Crt 85
John	Jhn 753	Peaw, Samuel	Grv 541	Pelliford, William	Orn 616
John Jos.	Hlf 334	Peay, George	Rck 479	Pellmon, James	Rnd 334
Jos. John	Hlf 334	James	Rck 438	Pellovine, Richd.	Psq 634
Joseph	Hlf 334	George, Jur.	Rck 470	see Morrice	
Lazarus	Lnr 33	William	Rck 489	Pellson, Thomas	Ptt 295
Levi	Jhn 752	Peck, David	Crv 233	Pelly, James	Rwn 418
Mary	Jhn 751	David	Grv 569	Pemberton, John	Rch 248
Mary	Prs 218	Frederick	Cbr 713	Rebecca	Bld 27
Moses	Ans 221	Jacob	Rwn 388	Stitch	Mnt 464
Nathan	Cmb 357	Jacob, Senr.	Rwn 411	Pen, Stephen	Srr 711
Obediah	Prs 215	John	Lnc 891	Penawel, Price	Crt 83
Patty	Cht 207	Lewis	Rwn 459	Pence, Henry	Cbr 717
Philip	Jhn 746	William	Wke 777	Jacob	Cbr 717
Philip	Lnc 835	Peckett, Martin	Ans 208	Pender, B. Reddick	Edg 229
Phillip	Frn 468	Peckins, Beggin R.	Lnc 879	David	Edg 229
Shadrach	Jhn 748	Peddy, Andrew	Wke 755	Hardy	Wne 872
Sion	Mnt 472	Peden, Amos	Jhn 747	Jethro	Hrt 721
Steven	Frn 467	James	Jhn 746	John Core	Wne 872
William	Ans 222	Patience	Jhn 749	Joseph	Edg 230
William	Gts 274	Pedergrass, Luke	Csw 132	Josiah	Edg 230
William	Jhn 754	Peebles, Benjamin	Nrt 469	Needham	Wne 868
William	Mnt 481	George	Hlf 332	Paul	Wne 867
Winser	Rnd 334	Henry	Nrt 469	Reddick B.	Edg 229
see Peaw		Howell	Nrt 469	Thomas	Jhn 757
Pearcy, Abner	Orn 618	John	Wke 755	William	Brt 70
Philip	Brk 783	Nathan	Wrr 823	see Penter	
Peared, Henry	Mnt 464	Seth	Nrt 469	Pendergras, Spen-	
Pearmon, Celah	Hlf 334	Sterling	Nrt 469	cer	Ird 626
Pearry, John	Ash 85	Thomas	Wrr 823	Thomas	Csw 132
Pearsall, Edward	Dpl 424	William	Wke 755	Pendergrass, Ben-	
James	Dpl 405	Peed, James	Prq 651	ja.	Wke 756
Jeremiah	Dpl 433	Lamuel	Prq 651	Jesse	Grv 528
Pearson, Asa	Wke 754	Peede, John	Bfr 15	Job	Orn 617
Benjamin	Hlf 332	Tabitha	Bfr 16	John	Bnc 185
Christopher	Brk 782	Peeden, Patrick	Ptt 273	John	Cht 189
Cristopher	Wne 865	Peek, Samuel	Wke 756	John	Cht 200
Eliza	Rck 452	Peel, Ann	Hrt 706	Moses	Wke 756
George	Hlf 332	Daniel	Bfr 15	Richd.	Prs 198
Herbert	Ans 198	Demcy	Hrt 706	Richd., Jur.	Prs 198
Ichabod	Wne 864	Jesse	Jhn 754	Solo.	Wke 756
Isaiah	Orn 525	John	Cmb 357	William	Orn 617
John	Brk 781	Thomas	Hrt 713	Pendirgras, Thorn-	
John	Lnc 897	see Piel		ton	Brk 785
John	Rck 452	Peele, Christopher	Crr 165	Pendleton, Abijah	Psq 634
John	Rwn 427	Edmund	Nrt 469	Andrew	Psq 635
Lawrance	Wlk 58	Franes	Crr 165	Ann	Psq 629
Michael	Brk 782	Jethro	Nrt 469	Benjn.	Psq 633
Paris	Wke 754	John	Crr 165	Henry	Psq 629

Huram	Bld 31	Drury	Rwn 410	John	Edg 230
John	Psq 628	Edward	Rck 457	Nancy	Edg 229
John	Psq 632	Henry	Ptt 277	Nathanal	Edg 230
Martha	Psq 634	Jehugh	Cht 162	Theophilus	Edg 230
Micajah	Psq 638	Lewis	Rck 457	Pernall, John	Rwn 418
Nehemiah	Psq 634	William	Ptt 271	Pernel, Penelopy	Hlf 334
Timothy	Psq 633	Peper, John	Orn 591	William	Hlf 334
Pendygrass, Nimrod	Wlk 58	Samuel	Orn 591	Perois, Robert	Cht 181
Penelope, Clinton	Smp 527	Pepinger, Abraham	Rwn 400	Perrage, Lucindea	Rck 475
Penetent, Absalom	Brk 784	Cornelius	Rwn 400	Perrell, John	Rwn 418
Penex, Jno.	Csw 140	Pepper, Joshua	Crt 89	Tus	Rwn 418
Penick, Jeremiah	Rth 135	Richard	Frn 483	Perrett, Daniel	Cht 179
Peniger, Matthew	Stk 567	Stephen	Hlf 332	Isaac	Cht 167
Peninger, Asemus	Cbr 715	Perant, Charles	Mnt 512	Perriman, James	Brk 783
Penington, Benjn.	Ash 85	William	Mnt 511	William	Brk 783
Ephriam	Ash 85	Percy, Elisabeth	Brk 783	Perrimore, Benja-	
Ephriam, junr.	Ash 85	Perdew, Dennis	Lnr 32	min	Ans 233
Levi	Ash 86	Perdie see Pudie		Perrin, James	Rck 489
Mecajah	Ash 85	Perdue, George	Grv 518	Stephen	Wke 777
Micajah	Ash 86	Perett, Soloman	Cht 180	Perry, Aaron	Cbr 707
Reuben	Ash 85	Perinaut, Francis	Chw 116	Abner	Hrt 718
Wells	Ash 85	Perisher, Devotion	Trl 680	Abraham	Mnt 494
William (2)	Ash 85	James	Trl 686	Abreham	Frn 456
Penix, Overton	Srr 683	Perkins, Benjamin	Hlf 334	Adonijah	Jns 809
Penkirton, Robert	Orn 527	Calib	Cmd 101	Amos	Chw 119
Penkley, Michael	Brk 786	Elijah	Cmd 110	Amos	Crv 247
Penland, George	Bnc 184	Ephraim	Lnc 879	Ann	Brt 68
James	Brk 783	Henry	Csw 127	Benjamin	Brt 68
see Pintland		Henry	Csw 147	Benjamin	Frn 468
Penlee, Joshua	Brk 783	Henry	Hlf 336	Benjamin	Frn 470
William	Brk 783	Isaac	Bnc 183	Benjamin	Frn 489
Penley, Nancy	Brk 783	Isaac	Glf 664	Benjamin	Prq 661
Penly, Joshua	Brk 781	Jacob	Rch 243	Burrell	Frn 465
Penn, Will.	Prs 197	James	Ptt 234	Burrell, Ser.	Frn 476
Pennel, Eless	Wlk 58	Jesse	Brk 784	Burwell	Wke 756
Penner, Jno.	Lnc 843	Jesse	Csw 121	Cadar	Psq 641
Pennery, Thomas	Rwn 449	Jesse	Lnc 879	Civil	Jns 809
Thomas	Rwn 453	Jno.	Csw 123	Civil, (again)	Jns 809
Pennewell, Elisa-		Jno.	Csw 147	Daniel	Jns 781
beth	Mrt 405	John	Hlf 334	Daniel	Psq 641
Penney, Malachi	Edg 232	John	Lnc 879	Darlin	Wke 754
Thomas	Bld 12	John	Rch 262	David	Mrt 388
Penninger, Martin	Cbr 715	John	Rth 135	Dempsey	Jhn 760
Pennington, David	Mnt 518	John	Stk 591	Develly	Wsh 714
James	Rwn 444	Jos.	Csw 127	Ebenezer	Glf 683
Kinchin	Mnt 518	Joshua (2)	Bnc 183	Elijah	Orn 526
Neddy	Mnt 519	Joshua	Chw 120	Elisabeth	Psq 640
Noel	Dpl 434	Joseph	Brk 780	Elisha	Hrt 701
Patsay	Mre 77	Lemuel	Ptt 237	Enos	Frn 480
Pennly, James	Wlk 58	Moses	Rwn 375	Ephraim	Frn 472
Jonathan (2)	Wlk 58	Myles	Cmd 107	Etheldred	Brt 68
Penny, Alexander	Jhn 762	Peter	Stk 567	Francis	Wke 754
Alexander	Rwn 338	Polly	Bfr 23	Francis, Junr.	Wke 755
Caleb	Jhn 762	Richard	Lnc 879	Isaac	Prq 660
Charles	Wke 753	Richard	Lnc 884	Isaac, Junr.	Brt 68
David C.	Nwh 6	Robert	Chw 131	Isaac, Senr.	Brt 68
Edward	Cmb 375	Robert B.	Lnc 862	Jacob	Psq 640
Hardy	Wke 755	Simon	Brk 782	Jacob, Capt.	Mrt 405
Isaac	Jhn 762	Thomas	Psq 634	James	Brt 68
James	Jhn 762	Thomas	Rck 466	James	Frn 456
John	Lnc 886	Thomas	Rwn 433	James	Frn 466
Joshua	Nwh 6	Timothy	Ash 85	James	Hlf 336
Penwell	Jhn 762	Valentine	Rck 437	James	Hrt 726
Wm.	Lnc 836	William	Ans 235	James	Srr 683
Pennywell, John	Jns 811	William	Bfr 15	James	Wke 756
Penrice, Clark	Prq 642	William (3)	Hlf 336	Jerrimiah	Frn 451
Penright, John	Srr 683	William	Rth 137	Jerrimiah, C.C.	Frn 472
Penson, Aron	Grv 540	William	Wlk 57	Jerrimiah,Ridge	Frn 456
John	Csw 137	William, Jr.	Hlf 336	Jerrimiah,Capt.	Frn 451
Zachariah	Grv 540	see Peckins		Jesse	Crr 137
Penter, Henry	Prq 646	Perkinson, Eley	Wrr 826	Jesse	Prq 650
Penyon, Benjn.	Wlk 58	Levy	Wrr 826	John	Brt 68
Peobles, Nathaniel	Rwn 438	Page	Wrr 826	John	Bld 26
Peocock, Alexander	Rbs 412	Perknson, Jesse	Wrr 826	John	Chw 118
Peoples, Abener	Jhn 770	Permair, John	Rch 265	John	Crr 148
Abraham	Glf 673	Permenter, James	Ans 226	John	Frn 456
Balaam	Ptt 274	John	Ans 202	John	Frn 461

Name	Ref
John	Jns 799
John	Mnt 494
John	Orn 547
John	Orn 591
John	Prq 650
John	Stk 614
John, Capt.	Frn 447
John, Senr.	Jns 783
John, Speckle	Frn 452
Joseph	Wke 754
Joshua	Frn 456
Joshua	Frn 470
Joshua	Frn 493
Josiah	Brt 68
Josiah	Crr 148
Kinchen	Frn 471
Laurence	Prq 660
Lawrence	Prq 647
Levi	Cht 219
Mary	Frn 467
Mildred	Dpl 426
Mordacai	Gts 274
Mymy	Hlf 332
Nathaniel	Frn 449
Nathaniel	Wke 756
Nicholas	Wke 754
Noah	Mrt 405
Obediah	Wlk 58
Peter	Bnc 184
Peter	Bnc 185
Peter	Cmb 357
Phill	Frn 475
Phillip	Prq 661
Phillip	Rbs 411
Polly	Edg 175
Polly	Edg 229
Precilla	Gts 275
Randol	Wke 756
Redmon	Brk 785
Reuben	Jhn 761
Reuben	Prq 647
Richard	Hrt 703
Robert	Cmb 372
Samuel	Mre 73
Samuel, Jun.	Chw 127
Samuel, Sen.	Chw 129
Shadrach	Rch 248
Seth	Hrt 706
Seth	Prq 650
Shadrach	Ptt 229
Sion	Wke 756
Solomon	Frn 456
Stephen	Jhn 757
Thomas	Frn 480
Thomas	Prq 654
Thomas, Genl.	Wrr 825
Tilmon	Orn 617
Turner	Cht 193
Will.	Nsh 115
William	Ash 86
William	Brt 68
William	Cht 193
William	Frn 457
William	Prq 649
William	Rth 137
William	Stk 589
William	Wke 754
Winnefred	Edg 173
Winnefred	Edg 229
Wm.	Mrt 405
Perrycan, John	Grv 541
Robert	Grv 540
Perrygan, William	Grv 541
Perryman, Isaac	Rck 456
Jacob	Rck 457
Jas.	Rck 457
John	Rwn 375
Persey, William	Rch 255
Person, Benjamin	
E.	Grv 584
Frank	Frn 477
Jesse	Wrr 824
Joannah	Grv 560
John	Ons 151
Peterson	Wrr 825
Thomas	Grv 555
Thomas	Ons 151
William	Frn 455
William	Wrr 824
Personet, John	Srr 684
Persons, Aney	Crr 164
Charles	Rth 135
John	Mnt 472
John	Wlk 57
Joseph	Mnt 472
Joseph	Stk 567
Samuel	Mre 59
Pertillo, Little-ton	Lnc 862
Pervatt, Peter	Rbs 411
Thomas	Rbs 411
Pervo	Rnd 353
Pervs, Asel	Rnd 335
Pery, Josiah	Psq 627
Petchey, John H.	Rwn 278
Peteat, James	Brk 783
John	Brk 779
Peteel, William	Brk 781
Peter, John	Rbs 432
Old	Crr 157
Peterd, Samuel	Csw 108
Peters, Cullen	Hlf 334
Cullen	Hlf 336
Gilliam	Nrt 471
James	Wke 753
Mary	Hde 374
Nathaniel	Ptt 242
Reading	Ptt 241
Samuel	Bnc 184
Samuel	Smp 494
William	Lnr 18
William	Smp 498
Peterson, Aaron	Smp 516
Anne	Nrt 467
Batte	Nrt 469
Henry	Brt 68
Jno.	Csw 122
John	Rbs 413
John	Smp 512
John	Smp 520
Malcolm	Smp 527
Martha	Nrt 469
Mathias	Lnc 869
Moses	Smp 521
Nathan	Smp 526
Nual	Mre 72
Peter	Crv 231
Peter	Cmb 357
Thomas	Smp 533
Tobius	Brk 782
Williams	Nrt 469
Petery, Dorothy	Cbr 692
Petit, Gideon	Ptt 246
Petotman see Pittman	
Petre, Simon	Stk 568
Pett, Joseph	Edg 229
Pettecord, Wm.	Stk 611
Pettegon, John	Srr 683
Pettett, Rachel	Srr 682
Petticoat, John	Stk 602
Petticord, Bazsel	Stk 602
Greenberry	Stk 602
John, Ser.	Stk 602
William	Stk 602
Pettiford, Tabby	Wke 753
Pettigrew, Charles	Trl 672
Pettijohn, Abraham	Hrt 701
Jobe	Chw 120
John	Chw 120
Pettipool, Ander-son	Nrt 469
Pettis, William	Mck 540
Pettit, Robert	Crv 251
Thomas	Crv 237
Pettitt, George	Srr 683
Pettoway, Micajah	Edg 229
Petty, Ambrose	Cht 157
George	Rth 137
Haratia	Grv 539
Isaac	Cht 157
James	Cht 196
Jessee	Cht 165
John	Cht 154
Joseph	Rth 137
Lewis	Cht 171
Reubin	Cht 151
Theophilus	Ash 85
William	Wlk 57
William, jr.	Cht 153
William, Sen.	Cht 152
William, Senr.	Wlk 57
Zacheriah	Srr 682
see Ditto	
Pettycoat, Nathan	Stk 602
Pettyford, George	Grv 543
Pettypool see Pool, given name, middle initial P	
Petty Pool, Young	Grv 509
Peugh, John	Crt 74
Pew, Arnold	Jhn 756
Fletcher	Ird 637
John	Ird 636
Julin	Ash 86
Labon	Nsh 116
Richard	Jhn 756
Shadrick	Smp 529
Simeon	Jhn 755
see Peaw	
Pewils, Thomas	Ird 652
Pfah, Adam	Stk 605
Isaac	Stk 604
Jacob	Stk 605
Phaddis, Alexander	Orn 524
Andrew	Orn 524
Phares, Isaac	Cmb 369
John	Cmb 370
Samuel	Cmb 370
Pharis, James	Rth 135
Stephen	Rth 135
Pharoah, Joshua	Rbs 412
Phason, James	Bld 37
Phelan, Edmond	Ptt 282
Phelps, Anne	Wsh 708
Asa	Trl 672
Benjamin	Trl 672
Benjamin	Trl 680
Cuthbert	Wsh 708
Darias	Trl 680
Edward	Trl 672
Edward, Senr.	Trl 680
Enoch	Trl 672
Ephraim	Wsh 708
Evan	Wsh 708
Frederick	Wsh 708
George	Trl 690
George	Wsh 708
Godfrey	Trl 680
Henry	Brt 70
Isaac	Wsh 708
Jacob	Jns 805

James	Gts 276	John	Mck 587	Frederick	Edg 229
James	Trl 672	John	Mck 593	Gabril	Nsh 114
Jeremiah	Trl 672	John	Rwn 314	Hartwell	Edg 229
Jesse	Trl 680	John	Rwn 444	Henry	Edg 229
John	Mrt 403	John	Srr 682	Isaac	Mrt 405
John	Trl 680	John	Wne 867	James	Cht 177
John	Wsh 708	John, Senr.	Mck 593	James	Crv 327
John	Wsh 714	Jonas	Mnt 507	James	Lnr 6
John, Senr.	Trl 686	Jonathan	Srr 683	James	Rbs 412
John, (son of		Joseph	Mck 554	James	Wke 754
John)	Trl 680	Joseph	Orn 525	James, Jur.	Lnr 6
Jonathan	Rnd 334	L. Richard	Srr 682	Jane	Crv 327
Joseph	Trl 672	Laughlan	Smp 523	Jane	Edg 233
Joseph	Wsh 708	Lawrence	Brk 783	Jeams	Crr 154
Joseph, (Black-		Lazarus	Bnc 183	Jeremiah	Cht 221
smith)	Trl 672	Mark	Grn 607	Jesse	Rbs 412
Joshua	Wsh 708	Martha	Rwn 433	Jethro	Nsh 115
Josiah, Junr.	Wsh 708	Mary	Mnt 508	Joel	Cht 221
Josiah, Senr.	Wsh 708	Mary	Orn 528	John	Crv 327
Kedar	Gts 275	Mary	Ptt 271	John	Prs 217
Mary	Trl 680	Matthew	Srr 684	John	Stk 567
Mary	Trl 692	Miles	Hde 374	Jordan	Rbs 412
Micajah	Gts 274	Mordaica	Stk 567	Joseph	Nsh 115
Sarah	Gts 274	Nancy	Glf 629	Lazarus	Cht 221
Seth	Trl 672	Rachel	Orn 526	Lewis	Cht 221
Uriah	Trl 680	Reuben	Ans 239	Lewis	Mre 43
Urijah	Wsh 708	Reuben	Wlk 59	Mark	Bld 26
William	Gts 275	Richard	Srr 684	Mark	Lnr 6
William, junior	Grn 614	Richard L.	Srr 682	Mark	Mre 43
William, Senior	Grn 614	Robert	Bnc 184	Martha	Edg 233
see Felps		Robert	Lnc 879	Mathew	Cht 222
Phenel, Noah	Cmd 100	Robert	Lnc 884	Mereday	Cht 222
Pheobus, James	Bld 32	Robert	Mck 526	Milly	Rnd 335
Pherrel, George	Cmd 98	Robert	Wlk 59	Mitchel	Cmd 102
Richard	Cmd 98	Roberts	Srr 684	Nemrod	Orn 524
Phifer, Adam	Glf 628	Samuel	Ans 212	Nicy	Lnr 6
Calib	Cbr 700	Samuel	Smp 530	Patientz	Mre 43
Henry	Mck 605	Soloman	Srr 682	Renchall	Wke 754
Martin	Cbr 700	Solomon	Lnc 872	Reubin	Crv 327
Mathias	Cbr 687	Stephen	Rth 135	Richard	Crv 329
Paul	Cbr 701	Stephen	Rth 137	Richard	Stk 568
Philips, Abner	Srr 682	Stephen	Wlk 56	Richard	Stk 571
Abraham	Srr 684	Thomas	Crv 311	Robert	Rck 490
Abram	Rck 479	Thomas	Dpl 397	Robt.	Cht 222
Adam	Mck 606	Thomas	Orn 524	Saml.	Crr 145
Alexander	Ans 218	Thomas H.	Grv 552	Sion	Cht 221
Angus	Cmb 366	Thos.	Wlk 58	Stephen	Stk 509
Ann	Orn 524	Wade	Srr 683	Thomas	Crv 327
Ann	Orn 526	William	Ans 208	Thomas	Lnr 6
Bedder	Rwn 427	William	Crt 91	Urby	Wke 755
Benjamin	Glf 661	William	Mck 587	Will.	Nsh 115
Celah	Gts 276	William	Mck 590	William	Cht 221
Charles	Bnc 184	William	Mnt 507	William	Cmb 366
Cornelius	Srr 682	William	Orn 526	William	Edg 231
David	Lnc 829	William	Srr 683	William	Wke 755
David	Orn 526	William	Wlk 58	Willis	Cht 221
David	Rth 138	William, j.	Orn 526	Wm., Senr.	Wke 755
David, Junr.	Orn 526	Philipy, John	Glf 647	Philops, John	Cht 205
Dorithy	Dpl 397	Phillemon, Elijah	Rbs 413	Philpote, Charles	Mrt 405
Eben	Rth 138	William	Rbs 412	Saml.	Mrt 405
Elijah	Rwn 444	Phillingham, Benja-		Philpott, John	Grv 560
Ellender	Crt 68	min	Crv 271	Thomas	Grv 582
Ephraim	Srr 684	Samuel	Crv 271	William	Grv 559
Ezra	Ash 86	Phillips, Abner	Cht 222	Philyaw, Martin	Jns 813
Ezra	Brk 783	Benjamin	Cmd 102	Phipps, Nathaniel	Crv 273
Garland	Grv 565	Benjamin	Edg 231	Richardson	Wke 777
George	Ans 228	Cartwright	Cmd 102	see Fipps	
Jacob	Ans 238	Daniel	Cmd 102	Phips, Isaiah	Rwn 309
James	Cmb 385	David	Edg 230	Isiah	Bnc 183
James	Orn 490	Dennis	Cht 221	Josiah	Brk 780
James (2)	Rth 138	Drury	Nrt 465	Samuel	Ash 86
Joel	Glf 636	Duncan	Rbs 414	Phismire, John	Cht 181
John	Ans 212	Ephram	Nsh 115	Martin	Cht 181
John	Ans 229	Exum	Edg 229	Mary	Cht 181
John	Cht 176	Exum, Colo.	Edg 230	Phissioc, John	Hde 374
John	Hlf 334	Fanster	Stk 568	Pholl, Thomas	Stk 599
John	Mck 532	Frank	Wke 756	Thomas	Stk 625

Physic, Peter	Crv 337	Isaac	Hrt 713	William	Stk 616
William	Crv 335	Israel	Hde 374	William	Wrr 824
Pibus, Hannah	Jns 809	Jacob	Gts 274	Piland, Catharin	Gts 274
Pichard, Alex	Orn 527	Jacob	Hrt 713	Charity	Gts 275
Henery	Orn 527	Jehu	Mrt 403	David	Gts 274
Isaac	Orn 527	Jeremiah	Brt 70	Edward	Gts 274
Pick, John	Stk 597	Job	Hrt 713	Edwd., (of	
Pickard, Elisha	Orn 528	John	Prq 645	Edwd.)	Gts 274
James	Orn 528	John	Srr 683	James	Gts 274
John	Orn 528	John	Wke 756	John	Gts 274
John, Junr.	Orn 527	Joseph	Bfr 15	Willis	Gts 274
William	Cht 162	Joseph	Prq 645	Pilcher, Daniel	Srr 684
William	Cht 195	Lazarus	Bfr 15	Pile, Joseph	Cht 173
Pickell, Edward	Orn 527	Martha	Dpl 404	Pilerer, Isaac	Srr 707
Pickering, John	Edg 231	Mary	Crv 321	Piles, Caleb	Orn 524
Picket, Alexander	Dpl 418	Mary	Crv 333	Isaac	Orn 524
Benjamin	Lnc 850	Mary	Wsh 708	James	Orn 524
Donson (2)	Nwh 5	Mourning	Brt 68	James, Jun.	Orn 524
Elizabeth	Rth 136	Myles	Trl 680	Jeromiah	Ird 615
Frank	Dpl 414	Philip	Csw 123	Joshua	Ird 626
Henry	Nwh 11A	Richard	Hrt 713	Pilgford, Will.	Nwh 8A
Henry	Orn 616	Sarah	Wsh 708	Pilgreen, Priscil-	
Hozy	Brn 19	Snoden	Dpl 414	la	Ptt 236
James	Dpl 413	Stephen	Wsh 714	Pilgrim, John	Lnc 905
John	Rth 136	Thomas	Prq 645	Michael	Bnc 183
John	Wrr 823	Thomas	Rwn 418	William	Bnc 183
Joseph	Orn 616	Urania	Brt 68	William	Lnc 905
Margaret	Dpl 418	Piercen, Jonathan	Smp 511	Pilkenton, Richard	Cht 188
Micajah	Rth 137	Pierceson, William	Prq 648	Samuel	Cht 188
Prissilla	Dpl 416	Piercey, Andries	Ptt 236	Pilkerton, Nicanor	Glf 659
Sion	Nwh 11	Piercy, Cadar	Brt 68	William	Glf 659
Tho.	Nwh 11A	Zadock	Brt 68	Pilkington, John	Ird 668
William	Dpl 414	Pierse, Jacob	Stk 568	Richard, Jr.	Jhn 748
William (2)	Dpl 416	Piersel see Pursel		William	Cht 168
William	Rth 136	Piersin, John	Prs 208	William	Jhn 750
William, Jur.	Orn 619	Pierson, Jesse	Rnd 334	Pillaway, Patom	Ons 174
Pickett, Charles	Rwn 375	Jonathan	Prq 653	Pilleway, John	Ons 174
Henry	Ird 626	Nathan	Rnd 335	Pilley, Thomas	Bfr 16
James	Rch 244	Nathan (2)	Rnd 336	Thomas, Jur.	Bfr 15
Jesper	Crr 141	Pigford, Will.	Nwh 8A	William	Bfr 15
Joseph	Ans 214	see Pilgford		Pillows, John	Csw 133
Mark	Orn 616	Pigg, Nathan	Srr 682	Pinchback, John	Rwn 453
Thomas	Ans 201	Paul	Srr 682	Pinchley, Joseph	Stk 567
Thomas	Orn 616	Richard	Srr 682	Pincom, James	Bfr 15
William	Orn 618	Susannah	Wlk 57	Pinder, Joseph	Orn 592
William	Rwn 375	William	Srr 682	Pinegar, William	Stk 567
Wm. R.	Ans 232	William	Wlk 57	Pinenland, John	Brk 779
see Peckett		Piggot, Charrity	Cht 218	Piner, Joseph	Crt 66
Pickings, William	Mck 569	Jeremiah	Cht 216	Nancy	Crt 79
William	Mck 571	John	Crt 92	Patience	Jhn 747
William	Mck 574	John	Cht 217	Reuben	Crt 81
Pickins, Hugh	Cbr 681	Oliver	Crt 92	Thomas	Crt 71
Samuel	Cbr 683	William	Cht 214	Unis	Crt 77
Pickle, Frederick	Rwn 418	William	Cht 218	Will.	Prs 207
Henry	Orn 591	Piggott, Levi	Crt 70	Pines, John	Rwn 428
John	Rwn 411	Pigott, Culpepper	Crt 69	Pinion, Joshua	Ans 219
Michael	Lnr 33	Elijah	Crt 69	Reuben	Ans 208
Tobias	Rwn 418	Jechonias	Crt 75	William	Srr 682
Valentine	Rwn 418	Micajah	Crt 75	Wm.	Srr 707
Pickler, Jesse	Mnt 521	Ralph	Crt 76	Pinkerton, David	Rwn 394
Joseph	Rwn 418	Sevil	Crt 69	James	Rwn 394
Joseph	Rwn 428	William	Crt 69	John	Rwn 394
Pickott, Benjamine	Orn 525	Pigpen, Joshua	Ons 177	Robert	Rwn 394
Joshua	Orn 525	Pike, Benjn.	Mre 67	William, Junr.	Rwn 394
Picot, Julian	Wsh 714	Elizabeth	Stk 616	William, Senr.	Rwn 394
Pidgeon, Charles	Rwn 356	Ephraim	Hrt 706	see Penkirton	
Samuel	Rwn 356	James	Csw 146	Pinkett, Zacharia	Ptt 226
Piel, David	Wne 848	John	Orn 552	Pinkham, Job	Crt 70
Pasco	Wne 850	John	Psq 636	Nathaniel	Crt 70
Willis	Wne 846	John	Srr 707	Pinkley, Jacob	Stk 553
Pierce, Alexander	Dpl 414	Joseph	Srr 684	John	Stk 553
Archibald	Dpl 415	Lewis, Jur.	Csw 145	Peter	Stk 608
David	Crv 325	Lewis, Senr.	Csw 97	see Penkley	
David	Prq 648	Samuel	Orn 525	Pinkston, David	Rwn 289
Elisha	Nrt 469	Theodorick	Hlf 334	John	Rwn 290
Elisha	Stk 568	William	Hlf 334	Meshack	Rwn 290
H. George	Bfr 15	William	Orn 525	Thomas	Rwn 290

Turner	Rwn 314	James, H.S.	Rbs 410	Mary	Ons 136
William	Rwn 314	Jeremiah	Ons 157	Nancy	Hlf 334
William, Junr.	Rwn 290	Jesse	Edg 231	Noel	Nsh 114
Pinnell, John	Frn 494	Jesse	Rbs 410	Philip	Brk 781
Levy	Frn 494	Jethro	Jhn 761	Ridgon	Ons 139
Pinner, Arthur	Hrt 706	Joel	Rbs 410	Samuel	Stk 617
James	Nwh 6A	John	Edg 231	Walter	Nsh 114
John	Nrt 469	John	Nwh 5A	Pitty see Petty	
Joseph	Nrt 467	John	Orn 617	Pittz, Conrod	Lnc 869
Rachel	Hrt 706	Joseph	Crv 277	Piver, Daniel	Crt 79
Tho.	Nwh 6	Joseph	Crv 295	George	Crt 78
William	Bnc 184	Joseph	Edg 231	Johannes	Crt 78
Wright	Brn 18A	Joseph	Prs 196	Pivry, Drury	Rth 137
Pinnery, James	Rwn 332	Josiah	Orn 592	Plair, Sarah	Nwh 9
Pinninger, George	Rwn 314	Jurdan	Ons 180	Plaister, John	Rwn 338
John	Mck 596	Mary	Edg 230	Joseph	Rwn 338
Pinnington, Henry	Rwn 427	Micaijah	Rwn 309	Plaler, Paul	Ans 209
William	Rwn 428	Micajah, Jur.	Rwn 309	Plank, Jacob	Lnc 820
Pinson, John	Csw 107	Moses	Bld 17	Plant, Williamson	Ans 239
Richard	Srr 682	Nathan, Jur.	Rbs 410	Plast, Joseph	Ird 647
Pintland, Robert	Brk 781	Nathan, Ser.	Rbs 410	Joseph	Ird 652
William	Brk 782	Newit	Rbs 412	Plaster, Abraham	Cbr 710
see Penland		Noah	Rbs 411	John	Cbr 710
Pinx, Frances	Abr 686	Noah	Rbs 412	Plat, Joshua	Brn 13
Pipkin, Arther	Wne 853	Noah	Rbs 432	Platt, Adam	Dpl 423
Elisha	Wne 873	Rachal	Rbs 412	Pleasant, Bluford	Csw 132
Isaac	Ptt 265	Robert	Edg 231	John	Csw 132
Isaac, Jr.	Gts 276	Robert	Rbs 410	Micajah	Csw 132
Isaac, Sr.	Gts 276	Sampson	Rbs 410	Thomas	Cht 173
Jesse	Lnr 33	Sampson	Rbs 413	William	Csw 132
Jesse	Wne 851	Samuel	Ans 204	William	Frn 466
John	Nrt 469	Samuel	Edg 230	Pledger, Joseph	Trl 680
Philip	Wne 853	Silvia	Rbs 413	Joseph, Senr.	Trl 680
Stephen	Wne 854	Sion	Rbs 412	Stephen	Rch 260
Tabitha	Nrt 469	Thomas	Crv 293	Pleman, John	Brk 780
Willis	Wne 854	Thomas	Edg 230	Peter	Brk 780
Pipkins, Enos	Grn 593	Thomas	Mnt 464	Thomas	Brk 780
Pipluca, John	Srr 683	Thomas	Orn 592	Plenn, John	Rck 479
Pippin, Ama	Edg 231	Thomas, Jur.	Rbs 411	Pless, Henry	Cbr 716
Benagy	Edg 231	Thomas, Ser.	Rbs 411	Philip	Cbr 687
Benjamin	Edg 229	Timothy	Edg 230	Ploff, George	Lnc 820
John	Edg 229	William	Edg 232	Plomer see Plummer	
John	Frn 483	Pitmon, Jesse	Jhn 759	Plott, Henry	Cbr 704
Joseph	Edg 229	Samuel	Ash 86	John	Cbr 688
Joseph, Junr.	Edg 230	Pitney, Adam	Stk 611	Plowman, John	Rwn 297
Nelson	Frn 484	Pitre, Henry	Stk 567	Plumb, ..., (a Free	
Noah	Edg 230	Jacob	Stk 567	Neagro)	Mck 565
Soloman	Edg 231	Pitt, Anne	Edg 233	Plumer, Elisabeth	Brk 784
William	Edg 232	Davis	Edg 230	Phillimon	Rnd 335
Pirkle, John	Rck 444	James	Edg 230	Rachel	Brk 784
Pirtle, John	Rck 479	Joseph, Junr.	Edg 230	Thomas	Rck 489
Piser, Peter	Crt 77	Robert	Edg 230	Zureah	Brk 784
Pistole, Charles	Mnt 498	Thomas	Edg 230	Plumly, Able	Brk 780
Drury	Mnt 498	Thos.	Ons 171	Obadiah	Nrt 469
Pitchford, Daniel	Wrr 824	William	Glf 638	Plummer, Aaron	Bld 34
E. Zedeckiah	Wrr 824	Pittard, Elijah	Grv 548	Jeremh.	Bld 35
Thomas	Wrr 824	Pittit, Annead	Ons 167	John	Bld 35
Pitchy, John Henry	Rwn 289	Pittle, Thomas	Srr 684	John	Rwn 388
Pitcock, Stephen	Mnt 491	Pittman, Arthur	Hlf 336	Joseph	Rwn 357
Pitman, Abner	Edg 229	Celah	Hlf 336	Joseph	Rth 136
Amos	Ons 171	Elisha	Hlf 336	Judy	Grv 561
Arther	Ans 221	J. Robert	Hlf 336	Kemp	Wrr 784
Arthur	Dpl 414	Jesse	Rnd 335	Meshack	Rwn 356
Brittain	Rbs 311	John	Hlf 336	Richard	Cmb 371
Dempsey	Rch 251	John	Mck 546	Widow	Mck 523
Dempsey	Rch 266	Matthew	Hlf 336	William	Frn 491
Dempsy	Hlf 334	Robert J.	Hlf 336	William	Rwn 332
Edward	Edg 230	Samuel	Hlf 336	Plunk, Jacob	Lnc 879
Francis B.H.	Ons 158	Pitts, Andrew	Cht 170	John	Lnc 879
Grisham	Edg 229	David	Wne 854	Peter	Lnc 820
Hardy	Rbs 411	Henry	Hlf 334	Plunket, James,	
Hardy, Jer.	Rbs 410	Isaac	Stk 619	Junr.	Cbr 701
Harrison	Edg 229	Jesse	Mnt 491	James, Senr.	Cbr 676
Isham, Jur.	Rbs 410	John	Nsh 116	Plunkett, Thomas	Glf 628
Isham, Ser.	Rbs 411	John	Stk 617	William	Glf 628
Jacob	Rbs 410	Joseph	Cht 152	Plunter, William	Bfr 17
James, b. Smith	Rbs 410	Mark	Hlf 334	Ply, John	Rwn 418

Plylor, Frederick	Cbr 691	Pollock, Hannah	Ons 168	Elisha	Nsh 116
Henry	Cbr 690	John	Ons 168	Elizabeth	Ptt 267
Pockok, James	Psq 639	William	Dpl 401	George	Rwn 368
Podes, Woodhouse	Ons 172	Polly, James	Rth 137	Hardy	Wne 869
Poe, Edmund	Ash 85	Polson, Caleb	Grs 276	Harwood	Frn 452
Hastin	Cht 224	John	Gts 275	Henry	Lnc 879
Henry	Ash 85	Sarah	Gts 275	Henry	Rbs 411
James	Cht 199	William	Gts 274	Henry	Wne 862
Jessee	Cht 179	Polston, Peter	Orn 524	Jacob	Hlf 334
John	Wlk 57	Pond, Griffes	Wlk 58	Jacob	Rbs 411
Parsons	Bnc 183	Ponder, Daniel	Bnc 185	Jacob	Smp 516
Robert	Cht 175	Pone, David	Bld 10	Jacob	Smp 518
Stephen	Cht 155	Pooc, David	Stk 607	Jacob	Smp 518
Susanah	Cht 219	Pool, Alexander	Rth 135	Jeremiah	Smp 518
William	Ash 85	Betsey	Psq 636	Jesse	Edg 233
William	Wlk 57	Claybour P.	Grv 508	Jesse	Smp 534
see Pae		Darcas	Trl 692	John	Edg 234
Poff, Daniel	Rck 463	Elisabeth	Mrt 404	John	Grv 521
Pogue, James	Rth 135	George	Wke 753	John	Grn 602
John	Prs 201	Hardy	Wke 753	John	Nsh 116
Poindexter, Archa-		Jacob	Rwn 309	John	Wne 862
bl.	Srr 684	James	Lnr 18	John	Wne 869
David	Stk 567	James	Psq 636	Jonathan	Nrt 465
David	Stk 591	James	Psq 638	Jonathan	Smp 517
David	Srr 682	John	Psq 629	Joseph	Nsh 116
Francis	Srr 682	John	Prq 651	Joshua	Smp 517
John	Srr 683	John	Wke 753	Josiah	Wke 754
Pledge	Srr 683	John, Junr.	Wke 753	Lazarus	Jhn 757
Thomas	Srr 683	John P.	Grv 509	Mary	Lnr 20
William	Srr 682	Lewis	Wke 753	Micajah	Ans 227
William	Srr 683	Logustine P.	Grv 509	Mrs.	Wrr 826
Poine, Isaac	Psq 624	Matthew	Crt 67	Nathan	Ash 85
Pointer, Thomas	Stk 593	Patrick	Psq 629	Nithaniel	Rnd 334
William	Stk 588	Phillip P.	Grv 509	Osbourn	Grv 521
Poisson, John	Brn 15	Samuel	Rnd 335	Pharaby	Nsh 115
Lewis	Nwh 8	Sethe	Grv 509	Phillip	Edg 229
Poivers see Powers		Simon	Rnd 335	Poole	Cmb 373
Poke, Thomas	Ans 208	Stephen P.	Grv 508	Reading	Grn 602
Poland see Piland		Thomas	Psq 626	Samuel	Bld 14
Poleet, James	Csw 129	William	Grv 508	Simon	Jns 805
Thomas	Csw 109	William	Mnt 507	Solomon	Wne 870
Wm.	Csw 109	William (2)	Rnd 335	Stephen	Cmb 392
see Poteel		Young Petty	Grv 509	Thomas	Cmb 381
Poleson, Andw.	Wlk 57	Poole, Alexander	Mnt 507	Thomas	Smp 518
Poleston, James	Orn 524	Allexr.	Crr 145	Thomas	Smp 522
Polin, John	Nsh 115	Arther	Ans 209	Ufamy	Hlf 334
Will.	Nsh 116	Arther	Ans 219	Umphrey	Wrr 826
Polk, Charles	Mck 525	Henry	Mnt 472	West, great	Smp 518
Charles	Mck 526	James	Rnd 334	West, little	Smp 518
Charles, Senr.	Mck 574	John	Jhn 768	Wilis	Nsh 114
Ezekiel	Mck 542	John	Mck 593	William	Edg 233
John	Ans 210	Levi	Hde 374	William	Rwn 368
John	Cbr 696	Theophilus	Jhn 764	William	Wke 754
Samuel	Mck 542	William	Jhn 769	William	Wne 872
Thomas	Mck 542	Poll, William	Rnd 334	William, Senr.	Wke 754
Thomas	Mck 575	Poor, Edward	Glf 682	Will.	Nsh 116
William	Ans 210	Enoch	Ird 663	Winfield	Wne 870
William	Cbr 697	Jeremiah	Glf 684	Zedekiah	Rbs 411
William	Rth 138	John	Rck 464	Poperwell, Ann	Crr 149
William	Wke 777	see Pooc		John	Crr 149
Wm.	Mck 525	Poorce, Calib	Brk 780	Poplin, Daniel	Cht 174
Poll, William	Rth 135	Poore, David	Mnt 472	John	Mnt 505
Pollan, William	Grv 517	James	Mnt 474	Mary	Nsh 115
Pollard, Benjamin	Ptt 276	William	Rwn 418	William	Mnt 505
Easter	Ptt 258	Pope, Archabald	Edg 234	Popst, Henry	Rwn 289
Everett	Ptt 276	Arther	Jhn 755	Porch, Benjamin	Frn 480
Frederick	Crv 323	Atkin	Edg 232	Henry	Frn 479
George	Mrt 405	Benjamin	Hlf 334	James	Frn 480
Jacob	Crv 321	Blackmon	Smp 522	Solomon	Cmb 358
John	Ptt 290	Charles	Wke 754	Sucky	Frn 479
Major	Wke 753	Charles	Wne 870	William	Frn 479
Thomas	Crv 325	David	Nsh 116	Porten, James B.	Mck 581
Thomas	Mnt 499	Dimsy	Nsh 116	Porter, Absolam	Smp 525
Turner	Ptt 276	Elijah	Ans 228	Alexander	Mck 530
William	Grv 520	Elijah	Ash 85	Andrew	Brk 784
William	Wke 756	Elijah	Nrt 465	Barnaba	Ans 228
Poller see Potter		Elijah	Wke 754	Benjn.	Prs 190
				Brittain	Rbs 414

Caloson	Rck 448	Jos.	Rck 448	Nathan	Cmb 391
Charles	Ans 228	Joshua	Crv 301	Nathan	Nsh 114
Charles	Orn 525	Miles	Brn 14A	Nathan	Nsh 116
Christopher	Bnc 184	Nathaniel	Hde 374	Plolomy	Hlf 332
Daniel	Ans 203	Nelley	Wke 753	Robert	Gts 275
David	Rth 136	Richard	Prq 643	Ruth	Wrr 824
Dudly	Rck 458	Richard	Prq 656	Sarah	Orn 523
Edward	Hrt 732	Robert	Brn 14A	Sion	Nsh 115
Ezekiel	Mck 558	Stephen	Srr 684	Stephen	Edg 231
Hugh	Mck 530	Thomas	Grv 546	Thomas	Brk 781
James (2)	Glf 621	William	Bfr 15	Wilie	Nsh 116
James	Ird 665	Wm.	Lnc 832	Will.	Nsh 115
James	Mck 537	Potts, George	Rwn 428	William	Brt 68
John	Crv 303	Henry	Cbr 688	William	Gts 275
John	Crv 337	Henry	Ird 641	William	Wlk 58
John	Hrt 736	James	Brk 781	Willoughby	Nsh 116
John	Mck 531	James	Ird 641	Zilpha	Gts 276
John	Wke 777	James	Ird 672	Powell, Aaron	Hlf 332
John	Wrr 823	Jeromiah	Rwn 433	Able	Cbr 694
Joseph	Wlk 58	Jesse	Cmb 357	Abner	Csw 144
Lawrence	Rwn 381	John	Mck 602	Abram	Glf 622
Margarett	Rnd 334	Jonathan	Mck 560	Absolam	Bld 3
Mark	Jhn 749	Joshua	Nwh 2	Aden	Jhn 750
Martha	Hrt 736	Peter	Ird 612	Alexander	Hrt 718
Mary	Cmd 105	Peter	Rwn 433	Ambrose	Orn 526
Mathew	Smp 496	Phobe	Cmb 357	Ambrose	Rbs 413
Mathew	Smp 523	Pleasant	Lnr 18	Ambrose, Ser.	Rbs 413
Moody	Edg 229	Ralph	Bfr 23	Ann	Hrt 718
Robert	Bnc 184	Robert	Ird 641	Benjamin	Ptt 262
Robert	Rth 136	Robert	Mck 566	Benjamin	Rch 247
Samuel	Hlf 334	Stringer	Lnr 18	Benjamin	Rbs 413
Samuel (2)	Rth 136	William (2)	Ird 641	Benjamin	Wrr 825
Samuel	Smp 495	William	Mck 600	Benton	Wke 755
Silvia	Edg 233	William	Rwn 433	Caswell	Wke 755
Thomas	Edg 233	Poulis, Adam	Rwn 303	Charles	Cht 171
Thomas	Orn 525	Pound, Ally	Orn 617	Charles	Hrt 726
Widow	Mck 594	John	Csw 128	Cotton	Hrt 718
William	Bnc 184	Thomas	Rck 443	Daniel	Edg 231
William	Hde 374	Pounds, John	Ans 230	Daniel	Hlf 332
William	Mck 537	John (2)	Brn 14A	Daniel	Lnr 18
William	Rth 137	Samuel	Ans 230	David	Cbr 694
William	Smp 498	William	Grv 517	David	Csw 103
William, Senr.	Brk 785	Povel, John Turner	Brn 15	Demsey	Wke 755
Portes, Robert, (Mulat-		Pow, Rolley	Srr 682	Douglass	Rbs 411
to)	Edg 232	Powe, James, Jr.	Ans 236	Ecum	Nrt 469
Portevent, Isaac	Nwh 5A	James, Sr.	Ans 236	Edmond	Cht 170
Portevint, Jane	Nwh 10	Wiat	Ans 237	Eli	Rnd 334
Peter	Brn 19	Powel, Abram	Brn 20	Elias	Nrt 465
Portis, Ann	Hrt 701	Allinson	Nsh 116	Elijah	Jhn 777
Ann	Hrt 706	Beedy	Smp 521	Elijah	Rnd 334
James	Rnd 334	Britain	Dpl 407	Eliza.	Bld 9
Portiss, Irey	Nsh 114	Cadar	Brt 70	Elizabeth	Ptt 227
Jerimiah	Nsh 114	Charles	Bnc 185	Elizabeth	Rbs 410
Portlock, William	Cmd 98	Charles	Gts 274	Enos	Wne 864
Posey, Francis	Bnc 184	Daniel	Gts 274	Ferreby	Nrt 465
Post, Henry	Stk 568	Edward	Grv 531	George	Csw 98
Postin, Benjamin	Rwn 323	Elisha	Brk 781	George	Cht 167
Charles	Stk 606	George	Dpl 422	Hampton	Hlf 332
Postle, Henry	Ird 652	George	Hlf 332	Henry	Rnd 334
Poston, Elizath.	Csw 120	Hardy	Dpl 407	Isaac	Jhn 751
Sarah	Ird 657	Hardy	Nwh 4A	Isaac, Esqr.	Bld 9
Postwood, Benjn.	Crr 143	Honourias	Wrr 824	Jacob	Edg 230
Poteel, Miles	Csw 109	Jacob	Brn 20	Jacob	Jhn 777
see Poleet		Jacob	Gts 275	Jacob	Rnd 334
Poteet, James	Bnc 183	Jacob	Nwh 4A	James	Csw 101
James, Sr.	Bnc 184	Jacob	Nwh 6A	James	Cht 189
John	Bnc 183	James	Ons 162	James	Edg 232
Potter, Abraham	Ash 86	John	Cmd 109	James	Hlf 336
Absolam	Rth 135	John	Nsh 115	James	Hrt 726
Archibald	Grv 583	John	Wne 851	James	Ptt 258
Dreury	Lnr 32	John,(of Jacob)	Gts 275	James	Ptt 287
Henry	Rwn 400	John, Senr.	Gts 275	James	Wrr 825
Henry	Wke 777	Lemuel	Prq 661	Jane	Cht 219
James	Brn 14A	Lemuel	Prq 655	Jesse	Hlf 336
James	Crv 339	Lewis	Brk 781	John	Bld 47
John	Brn 14A	Lucy	Hlf 332	John	Cbr 695
John	Grn 603	Moses	Nsh 116	John	Csw 98

John	Lnr 18	John	Rbs 413	Prearce, Jesse	Srr 684	
John	Mrt 403	John	Wke 777	Precett, Thomas	Grv 522	
John	Orn 526	John	Wsh 708	Preisce, Nathan	Cmb 390	
John	Rbs 412	Joseph	Bld 16	Nicholas	Cmb 392	
John	Rwn 459	Joshua	Wsh 714	Prendergast, Luke	Csw 127	
John	Wrr 825	Josiah	Trl 690	Prescoat, Austan	Crv 333	
John, j.	Orn 526	Mark	Rbs 413	Frederick	Crv 265	
John O.	Crv 257	Mary	Brt 70	Prescot, Aaron	Crt 91	
Kader	Hrt 718	Mary	Crr 163	Matthew	Bfr 16	
Levi	Cht 170	Matthew	Rbs 413	Sarah	Bfr 16	
Lewis	Rbs 412	Michael	Mrt 416	William	Edg 231	
Mary	Cmb 386	Michael	Trl 692	Willsbee	Crt 92	
Matthew	Nrt 469	Moses	Hlf 334	Prescott, John	Ons 181	
Moses	Wke 753	Nancy	Rbs 413	Nancy	Ons 181	
Nathan	Mnt 464	Pegie	Mrt 388	Simon	Ptt 269	
Nicholas	Cht 157	Procy	Crr 162	Thomas	Ons 150	
Nicholas, Es-		Saml.	Crr 163	Presler, Thomas	Ans 209	
quire	Rbs 411	Samuel	Trl 692	Presley, Andrew	Bnc 184	
Ransom	Rth 137	Sarah	Hde 374	David	Bnc 184	
Restore	Bld 13	Susanna	Brt 68	John	Ans 209	
Rhoda	Ptt 239	Thomas	Rth 138	Presly, Andrew	Ird 645	
Richard	Edg 230	William	Cmd 102	Anthony	Mnt 510	
Richard	Rbs 412	William	Cmd 108	David	Mck 552	
Richard	Rbs 432	William	Hlf 332	Levi	Mck 586	
Robert	Rch 247	William	Jhn 750	Peter	Mck 589	
Robert	Wke 753	William	Wsh 708	Richard	Mck 587	
Roderick	Ptt 225	Powgh, Joseph	Stk 568	Thomas	Mck 587	
Samuel	Hlf 334	Powil, John,		William	Mck 587	
Silas	Nrt 465	(Junr.)	Orn 591	Pressler, Elias	Ans 226	
Solomon	Hlf 332	Poyner, Abey	Crr 144	John	Ans 216	
Stapleton	Ptt 235	Ann	Crr 143	Peter	Ans 222	
Starlin	Wne 858	Benj.	Crr 139	William	Ans 217	
Stephen	Jhn 750	David	Csw 128	Pressley, Elias	Ans 216	
Stephen	Jhn 777	Deney	Crr 160	Elijah	Ans 208	
Thomas	Cht 163	Diney	Crr 144	Pressnall, Absolom	Rnd 335	
Thomas	Mnt 464	Even	Crr 144	Curtice	Rnd 334	
Thomas	Wrr 824	George	Crr 144	James	Rnd 335	
Thompson	Rbs 410	Isbel	Crr 143	James, J.	Rnd 334	
Wiley	Cht 167	Jeams	Crr 144	William	Rnd 334	
William	Mnt 465	Joel, Jur.	Crr 145	Preston, David	Csw 104	
William	Rbs 410	Joel, Ser.	Crr 145	Prevat, Sarah	Crv 317	
William	Rbs 413	John	Crr 143	Prevet, Matthew	Ans 214	
William	Wke 753	John	Crr 144	Previtt, Miles	Wke 756	
William	Wne 871	Levi	Crr 145	Nehemiah	Wke 755	
William, Cons.	Hlf 332	Nathan	Crr 137	Polley	Wke 756	
William, Jr.	Hlf 332	Robert	Crr 139	Zach	Wke 756	
William, Senr.	Hlf 332	Robt., Ser.	Crr 146	Prewet, John	Grv 520	
Willice	Brt 68	Saml.	Crr 137	Joseph	Wlk 57	
Willie	Nrt 469	Sarah	Crr 156	Prewit, Doak	Grv 516	
Willis	Wke 755	Thos.	Crr 141	Wm.	Csw 119	
Wright	Wne 865	Wm.	Crr 139	Price, Absalom	Grn 591	
Zachariah	Hlf 332	Poynter, John	Bld 38	Aky	Csw 104	
see ...well		Poysland, Sebas-		Asa	Mrt 403	
Powen see Powers		tian	Nrt 467	Benjamin	Cmb 368	
Power, Edward	Edg 232	Poythress, Celia	Nrt 469	Benjamin	Prq 659	
John	Wrr 824	Odeham	Nrt 469	Charles	Csw 101	
Powers, Absalom	Hlf 332	Temperance	Nrt 471	David	Brk 785	
Arther	Rch 247	Praeter see Procter		David	Glf 653	
Barnaba	Rch 245	Prance, John	Cmb 368	Demsey	Cmd 97	
Benn.	Psq 633	Prat, Tabitha	Crt 89	Elias	Mrt 405	
Caleb	Crr 162	Prate, Robert	Stk 568	Enoch	Grn 591	
Charles	Bld 14	Prater, Archibald	Bnc 184	Gideon	Orn 617	
Cornelious	Crr 163	Prather, John	Rwn 448	Isaac	Mck 537	
David	Cht 162	William	Ird 622	Isaac	Rck 461	
Ephraim	Nwh 9A	William	Stk 568	Isaac	Rck 483	
Ephraim	Trl 690	Pratt, Elizabeth	Rck 485	Isabela	Lnc 839	
Hardy	Rck 479	George	Orn 591	James	Bfr 15	
Henry	Hlf 332	James	Orn 526	James	Crv 265	
James	Bnc 183	John	Rck 458	James	Dpl 441	
James	Rch 267	John	Rck 474	James	Mck 562	
Jeams	Crr 162	Lott	Wsh 708	James	Wlk 58	
Jeams	Crr 163	Mary	Orn 592	James	Wlk 59	
Jesse	Jhn 766	Richard	Stk 612	Jams.	Lnc 839	
Jesse	Ptt 228	William	Ans 224	Jesse	Edg 233	
Jesse	Ptt 270	William	Rck 457	Joel	Edg 233	
John	Crv 263	William	Rck 458	John	Csw 117	
John	Crr 163	Zebulon	Prq 651	John	Dpl 426	

Name	Ref	Name	Ref	Name	Ref
John	Frn 487	Joseph	Rnd 335	Jonathan	Brt 68
John	Jns 787	Pricket, Giddion	Bld 28	Joseph	Psq 632
John	Mck 537	Josiah	Bld 34	Martha	Psq 634
John	Orn 617	Priddy, George	Grv 564	Mary	Nrt 469
John	Rbs 411	Rrbert	Grv 557	Moses	Psq 634
John (2)	Rth 137	William	Grv 529	Pressley	Nrt 465
John	Wlk 59	William	Grv 556	Richard	Psq 631
John, Cap.	Mrt 405	William	Grv 572	Rigdon	Brt 68
John, Junr.	Brk 785	Pride, Edward	Wke 753	Ruth	Psq 635
John, Junr.	Mrt 405	Pridgen, Fedrick	Smp 535	Thomas	Cmd 98
John, Senr.	Brk 785	John	Bld 47	Thomas	Mnt 513
John, Senr.	Csw 103	Mathew	Smp 534	Thomas	Psq 628
John, Senr.	Mrt 404	Matthew	Bld 47	Thomas	Psq 631
Jonathan	Edg 233	Peter	Bld 47	William	Rwn 368
Jonathan	Mck 541	William	Mnt 520	Pritchart, Benja-	
Joseph	Edg 231	William	Smp 516	min	Cmd 94
Lemuel	Chw 122	Pridgeon, David	Nsh 114	Joseph	Cmd 94
Leney	Cht 192	Drewey	Nsh 115	Pritchel, Thomas	Orn 527
Lewis	Mre 65	Edwin	Grn 609	Pritchet, Christo-	
Lewis	Ptt 263	Frances	Nwh 10A	pher	Hlf 334
Luke	Frn 461	Hardy	Nsh 115	James	Cmb 373
Mary	Bfr 15	Jesse	Grn 609	Jesse	Orn 617
Mary	Mrt 403	Jesse	Nsh 115	Jessey	Frn 462
Meredith	Csw 98	John	Brn 13A	John	Nsh 114
Moses	Edg 231	Ruffian	Grn 609	Lewis	Wke 755
Nathaniel	Dpl 426	Thomas, Senior	Grn 609	Sarah	Hlf 334
Philip	Ird 612	Prier, John H.	Stk 609	William	Stk 583
Philip	Wlk 58	Priest, David	Lnr 33	see Prichet	
Reese	Rck 459	John	Cmb 387	Pritchett, Abraham	Bfr 16
Rice	Mck 567	Joseph	Brk 779	Alexander	Glf 649
Rice	Wne 864	Stephen	Rth 136	Ezekiel	Glf 639
Richard	Lnc 883	Priestly, John	Crv 299	Jacob	Bfr 15
Richard	Wrr 825	Joseph	Lnc 886	Jerimiah	Rck 480
Robert	Mck 562	Prim, Kitchen	Frn 480	Nathaniel	Jns 799
Samuel	Edg 232	Prime, John	Brk 784	Peter	Bfr 15
Samuel	Ons 163	Primrose, William	Grv 575	Rachel	Rck 480
Samuel	Rwn 404	Prince, Ann	Crv 237	Thomas	Glf 637
Sarah	Crv 261	Nicholas	Cht 157	William	Jns 823
Sarah	Crv 265	Richard	Ans 209	Zebulon	Glf 645
Sarey	Grn 614	see Preisce		Prittle, Peter	Stk 582
Shadrach	Bfr 16	Pringle, Charles	Crv 301	Pritymon, Thomas	Cmd 94
Stephen	Grv 542	Prinkle, Nicholas	Rwn 289	Private, James	Ird 612
Sterling	Rth 136	Prior, Celia	Crv 317	Noah	Ptt 269
Thomas	Dpl 426	David	Rwn 357	Privet, John	Prq 653
Thomas	Grn 591	John H.	Stk 615	William	Jhn 757
Thomas	Orn 592	Matthew	Stk 568	Privette, John	Ird 626
Thomas	Rck 488	Thomas	Crv 251	Prock, Christian	Brk 784
Thomas	Wke 753	Prise, Drury	Ans 237	Terah	Brk 782
Thos.	Mrt 403	Edward	Jhn 763	Procter, Henry	Jhn 767
William	Bfr 16	Etheldred	Jhn 756	Ira	Ans 233
William	Edg 233	Henry	Ans 233	Jacob	Edg 229
William	Grn 591	Isaac	Ans 222	John	Chw 115
William	Orn 617	James	Jhn 757	John	Jhn 771
William	Psq 635	Jerry	Jhn 770	Joseph	Grv 549
William	Rth 135	Kinchen	Jh- 770	Micager	Wrr 823
William	Rth 137	Mosceer	Ans 209	Moses	Rth 136
William	Wrr 824	Reddick	Ans 233	Reuben	Prq 652
William	Wne 866	Rial	Jhn 759	Reuben	Rth 136
Williamson	Hlf 332	Rias	Jhn 760	Richard	Wrr 824
Wm.	Lnc 839	Rice	Jhn 755	Selah	Nsh 114
Wm., Senr.	Csw 103	Rice	Jhn 756	Stephen	Jhn 773
Wm., Senr.	Mrt 405	Sherwood	Rch 268	Thomas	Wke 754
see Preisce		Simeon	Jhn 757	Proctor, Aaron	Edg 231
Prichard, Bazel	Jns 815	Thomas	Jhn 764	Anna	Edg 231
Cary	Mnt 486	William	Jhn 770	Frederick	Edg 231
Clement	Jns 815	Zacchariah	Jhn 747	Jesse	Edg 231
David	Psq 626	Prisson, John	Ans 215	Jiles	Rck 465
Henry	Psq 630	Prita, Ning	Brk 784	John	Edg 231
Phil	Srr 710	Pritchall, Thomas	Orn 617	Lucey	Ptt 231
Ruth	Psq 626	Pritchard, Absalom	Brt 68	Rubin	Rwn 459
Zach	Srr 710	Christopher	Brt 68	Sampson	Edg 231
Prichet, Elisha	Edg 230	David	Cmd 95	Sarah	Ptt 231
Sion	Hlf 334	Elisha	Psq 637	Thomas	Srr 684
Thomas	Cht 190	Hugh	Cmd 108	William	Rck 465
William	Edg 234	Hugh	Psq 639	Profet, James	Ash 86
Prichett, Edward	Cht 224	James	Brt 68	Profit, John,Senr.	Wlk 58
John	Rnd 334	James	Brk 781	William	Wlk 58

Prook, Christian	Rwn 418	William	Ptt 241	Pursell, George	Rck 456		
Propst, Henry	Cbr 703	Wm.	Crr 150	Purser, Coventan	Crv 307		
Proptz, Henry	Lnc 869	Pughe, Eaton P.	Wrr 825	John	Mck 575		
John	Lnc 820	Puit, Jesse	Brk 785	Neill	Cmb 386		
Sophia	Lnc 820	Josep	Brk 784	Purviance, James	Cbr 685		
Prosser, John	Nrt 469	Puler, Christiam	Orn 616	John	Cbr 701		
Proud, John	Hde 374	Christon	Orn 617	Joseph	Mck 575		
Provo, Benjamin	Ons 141	Samuel	Orn 616	Robert	Cbr 686		
Mark	Ons 143	Pullam, Alsa	Mnt 496	Samuel Deris-			
Pruden, David	Brt 68	Pulleam, John W.	Prs 199	more	Cmb 357		
Jacob	Gts 275	Pullem, Barnett	Grv 581	Purvis, Allen	Brt 70		
James	Gts 275	Pullen, William	Edg 231	Cullen	Brt 70		
Lodowick	Brt 68	Puller, Christian	Orn 612	Henry	Rbs 411		
Pruell, William	Stk 583	Pulley, Henry	Wne 870	Moses	Brt 70		
Pruett, Micajah	Stk 584	Wm.	Mrt 405	William	Brt 68		
William	Stk 585	Pulliam, Benjamin	Wke 777	Purviss, Lewis	Mrt 403		
see Precett		Bird	Prs 200	Purvoice, John	Grn 615		
Pruit, Abraham	Rwn 444	Pullim, James	Orn 526	Purygan see Perrycan			
Herod	Rwn 411	Pullin, John,Junr.	Wke 755	Putman, Benjn.	Rth 136		
Herod	Rwn 427	John, Senr.	Wke 755	Elias	Rth 136		
Hugh	Brk 780	Jonathan	Wke 756	Griggs	Rth 136		
John	Rth 137	Thomas	Wke 754	William	Rth 136		
Joseph, Junr.	Brk 782	Thomas	Wke 756	Willis	Rth 136		
Joseph, Senr.	Brk 782	Pullison, Jas.	Prs 198	Wilson	Rth 136		
Mackarias	Ird 632	Pullum, John	Frn 450	Putnel, John	Ptt 257		
Obadiah	Rwn 428	John	Grv 512	Stephen	Ptt 257		
Rothel	Brk 786	John	Rth 135	Putner, Adam	Stk 627		
Samuel	Brk 780	John B.	Grv 529	Putney, Richard	Nrt 469		
William	Rth 136	Nelson	Frn 453	Puvils see Pewils			
see Puit		Peggy	Rth 135	Pyburn, Christo-			
Pruitt, Willis	Stk 583	Pully, Ben.	Frn 459	pher	Bnc 184		
Pryer, Pleasant	Mnt 496	Charlotte	Hlf 334	Jacob	Bnc 184		
Pryor, John	Wrr 825	David	Hlf 334	Pybus, James	Dpl 412		
Thomas	Glf 653	Mary	Nrt 469	Pye, John	Rwn 418		
William	Hlf 336	Moses	Hlf 336	Pyke, Anne	Nrt 469		
Psalter, Henery	Crr 167	Spittle	Cht 203	Pyland, Stephen	Nrt 469		
Pucket, Benjamin	Srr 682	Pumphrey, Henry	Wlk 56	Thomas	Nrt 467		
John	Orn 495	Susanna	Ptt 281	Pylands, John	Cmb 390		
Mary	Nsh 115	Pumprey, Sylvanos	Frn 494	Pylant, Benjamin	Cht 176		
Parum	Dpl 420	Punch, Giles	Bfr 15	Robert	Cht 176		
Puckett, Isham	Srr 682	Lucy	Bfr 15	William	Cht 176		
Richard	Srr 682	Thomas	Lnc 869	Pyle, Jehsu	Cht 212		
Puct see Puit		Purcel, John	Rbs 414	Pyles, John	Lnc 905		
Pudie, Thomas	Wke 754	John	Rck 454	Leonard	Lnc 905		
Pue, Hinton	Wke 756	William	Rck 455	William	Lnc 905		
Tegnet	Jhn 754	Purcer, David	Bfr 15	Pyrant, Joshua	Csw 143		
Puff, Andrew	Rbs 414	James	Bfr 15	John	Csw 143		
Pugh, Betheney	Crr 166	Polley	Bfr 15	Mary	Csw 137		
Daniel	Orn 524	Robert	Bfr 15				
David	Hrt 706	Purde, Leonard	Brt 90				
Easter	Brt 70	Purden, Jean	Brk 781	-- Q --			
Eaton P.	Nrt 471	Purdey, Ester	Crr 152				
Elizabeth	Brt 68	Purdie, J.S.,Esqr.	Bld 37				
Elizabeth	Hlf 336	Mary	Chw 117	Quakenbush, John	Cht 192		
Elizabeth	Ptt 243	Purdin, John	Bnc 184	Peter	Cht 192		
Francis	Brt 68	Purdom, Elisha	Stk 609	Qualls, Abner	Csw 127		
Franes	Crr 165	Mary	Stk 609	Sarah	Grv 523		
George (2)	Crr 152	William	Stk 609	William	Ird 674		
Jacob	Cht 194	Purdu, Blackman	Grv 560	Quarles, Henry	Hlf 336		
James	Rnd 334	Purdue, John	Frn 465	Peter	Hlf 336		
Jeams	Crr 152	Purgason, Joel	Wke 755	Quawls, Barbary	Mrt 404		
John	Brt 70	John	Wke 755	Wm.	Mrt 404		
John	Hlf 336	Purkin, Edmond	Crv 307	Queen, Francis	Ird 612		
John	Orn 525	Purkins, Anne	Crv 285	Henson	Mnt 491		
John	Rnd 334	David	Nwh 8A	John	Rth 138		
Mary	Brt 68	Jacob	Crr 145	Merideth	Rth 138		
P. Eaton	Nrt 471	Jeremiah	Crr 147	Samuel	Rth 138		
Paul	Crr 152	Jonathan	Crv 305	Timothy (2)	Rth 138		
Paul	Crr 166	Nathan	Crr 150	William (2)	Rth 138		
Sampson	Orn 524	Purnell, Margaret	Rbs 412	Querie, Jonathan	Mck 578		
Stephen	Ptt 247	John	Rbs 412	Robert	Mck 578		
Theney	Crr 152	Purrce, Francis	Edg 229	William	Mck 578		
Thomas	Brt 70	Purree, Francis	Edg 175	William	Mck 606		
Thomas	Cht 194	Purrington, John		Querny, Lawrence	Rwn 342		
Thomas	Rnd 334	H.	Hlf 358	Query, Alexander	Cbr 681		
Thomas W.	Brt 68	Pursel, Daniel	Cmb 369	Francis	Mck 572		
William	Brt 68	Hardy	Nsh 114	Quickle, Michael	Lnc 820		

Quidley see Gudley		Ragland, Fredk.	Cht 210	Ralls, James	Frn 486
Quiet, David	Glf 622	Reuben	Grv 552	Ralph, Lewis	Rck 447
Robert	Glf 623	Robert	Cht 198	Thomas	Gts 278
William	Glf 622	Thomas	Cht 154	Raltz, Godfray,	
Quilling, John	Stk 578	William	Cht 171	Senr.	Rwn 411
Quilman, Peter (2)	Cbr 710	William	Grv 553	Ramage, Derias	Mre 71
Quimby, Henry	Hrt 701	Ragsdale, Baxter	Frn 473	Ramcke, Frederick	Chw 113
Quin, John	Brk 786	David	Grv 510	Ramsay, Henry	Hrt 736
John	Edg 235	Edward	Grv 506	John	Brt 70
Milly	Edg 235	Edward	Grv 547	Ramsey, Alexander	Bnc 185
Quinaly, Sarah	Glf 656	James	Grv 506	Ambrose	Cht 198
Quince, Richard.	Nwh 9A	John	Grv 585	Andrew	Ird 652
Quine, Benjamin	Csw 122	Jones	Grv 547	Benjn. (2)	Ons 180
Jacob	Csw 105	Mary	Bnc 185	Danl.	Prs 194
Quinn, Abner	Crt 82	Nimrod	Frn 484	Danl., Junr.	Prs 194
Caleb	Dpl 402	Ragsdall, Joel	Rnd 338	David	Brk 789
David	Dpl 399	Ragsdell, Thomas	Rch 250	David	Ird 652
George	Dpl 412	William	Wrr 828	David	Nwh 5A
James	Dpl 397	Ragsdil, Abnor	Mre 60	Isaac	Ons 180
Thomas	Dpl 412	Dan	Mre 52	Isaac	Ons 181
see Guinn		John	Mre 62	James	Bnc 187
Quinney see Guinney		Richd.	Mre 52	James	Brk 787
Quinny, John	Dpl 406	Ragsdon, Nathan	Ash 87	James	Glf 666
Quit, William	Ird 612	Raibey, Mary	Wke 758	James	Lnc 821
		Raibon, William	Wke 757	James	Mck 534
		William, Jur.	Wke 757	James	Brn 16
-- R --		Raiden, Jeremiah	Stk 569	James G.	Lnc 840
		Raiford, Philip	Cmb 358	Jno.	Bnc 186
		Railsback, David	Rwn 459	John	Bnc 187
Rabb, William	Mck 573	Henry	Rwn 459	John	Cht 198
Rabey, Blake	Brt 72	Raily, Etheldred	Hrt 718	John	Ons 181
Raboteau, John S.	Wke 777	Joseph B.	Rth 140	John	Rch 268
Raby, James	Grv 546	Raimer, George	Rwn 342	Mary	Cmb 358
James	Grv 582	Jacob	Rwn 342	Mathew	Cht 171
Martha	Gts 277	John	Rwn 342	Neill	Rbs 414
Mary	Wsh 712	Raimey, Thomas	Mck 547	Richard	Brk 789
Racket, Jno.	Lnc 835	Rainer, John	Edg 237	Robert	Ird 652
Rackley, Francss	Nsh 118	Samuel	Edg 237	Robert	Lnc 820
Matthw	Nsh 118	Raines, Allen	Cht 159	Robert	Mck 597
Persons	Nsh 117	Rainey, Henry	Bld 20	Samuel	Ans 205
Persons	Nsh 118	John	Prs 214	Samuel	Lnc 820
Siless	Nsh 117	Thomas	Prs 216	Samuel	Lnc 893
Rackly, James	Smp 514	Will.	Prs 215	Simon	Bnc 186
Jeremiah	Smp 534	Rainney, David	Orn 528	Simon	Brk 787
Joshua	Smp 534	Rains, Ambrose	Cht 181	Stark	Ans 205
Radford, Jesse	Stk 569	Ambrous	Jhn 747	Tho.	Nwh 5A
John	Bnc 186	Anthony	Rnd 337	Thomas	Lnc 820
John	Frn 474	Betty	Rnd 338	William	Bnc 185
Noah	Wne 849	Cay	Ans 236	William (2)	Bnc 186
Radier, Moses	Cht 221	Enouch	Wke 759	William	Cht 199
Radliff, Cornelius	Rnd 336	Gabriel M.	Crv 235	William	Lnc 820
Rae, Angus	Rbs 416	George	Rnd 336	William	Ons 135
Archibald	Rbs 416	George (2)	Rnd 339	William	Mck 534
Daniel	Rbs 416	Henry	Rnd 339	William, Junr.	Brk 787
Duncan	Cmb 393	James	Cht 160	Ramsour, Henry	Lnc 821
Jean	Nsh 118	Joab	Rnd 339	John	Lnc 821
John	Rbs 416	John	Rnd 338	John, Junr.	Lnc 821
Lachlan	Rbs 416	John	Rnd 339	Ramsower, Edward	Cht 181
Neill	Rbs 416	Lawrance	Rnd 336	Henry	Rnd 339
Raferty, Wm.	Rck 441	Oliver	Jhn 746	Michael	Cht 181
Rafferty, John	Rck 464	Robert	Rnd 336	Michael	Rnd 339
Raford, James	Mnt 466	William	Rnd 338	Ramsy, James	Mck 553
Jos.	Mrt 409	Willie	Wke 759	Ranca, David	Ans 229
Matthew	Mnt 466	Rainwater, James	Srr 687	Rancy, David	Orn 593
Ragan, David	Wke 757	Rainy, James	Csw 113	David, Junr.	Orn 593
Eli	Ash 86	James	Rth 140	Rand, Abraham	Stk 570
Isham	Rwn 375	Thomas	Csw 113	Walter	Wke 757
James	Rwn 375	see Rany		William	Stk 569
James	Wke 759	Raisden, James	Dpl 434	Randal, Ann	Crv 253
Joseph	Wke 759	Raker, Frederick	Rwn 375	William	Jns 811
Thomas	Orn 594	Rakestraw, Nancy	Rck 453	Randle, Benjamin	
Willis	Wke 759	Raleigh, Elijah	Glf 676	A.	Mnt 473
Ragdil, Benjn.	Mre 45	Jacob	Nrt 473	Colby	Mnt 499
Ragin, Jesse	Prs 194	James	Rck 445	George	Rth 139
Marth	Prs 195	see Roulhac		Isham	Mnt 502
Nathan	Prs 193	Raley, Robert	Grv 559	John	Mnt 497
Patsey	Prs 193	Ralley, Joshua	Grv 565	John, (Deaf)	Mnt 496

Name	Ref
Merrit	Mnt 496
Ozbin	Mnt 497
Parom	Mnt 502
Robert	Rth 139
Robert	Rth 141
Sarah	Mnt 500
Silas	Rth 140
Thomas	Brk 789
William	Mnt 496
William	Rth 141
Wilson	Mnt 497
Randlemon, John	Stk 569
Randles, Hugh	Ird 614
William	Ird 652
Randol, James	Rnd 337
Thomas	Rnd 337
Randolph, Green	Hrt 699
Griffin	Wke 758
James	Csw 104
James	Ptt 277
Jesse	Ptt 259
John	Nrt 473
John	Wrr 786
Malachi	Nrt 473
Mary	Csw 104
Oliver	Wrr 827
Paul	Edg 175
Paul	Edg 237
Peter	Wrr 827
William	Nrt 473
Willis	Ptt 291
Willobough	Srr 687
Raney, Daved	Orn 618
Edward	Bfr 23
William	Rwn 290
Rank, John	Stk 626
Michael	Stk 627
Michal	Stk 611
Ranken, Saml.	Lnc 829
William	Lnc 829
Rankham, Joshua	Psq 640
Rankhom, Demsy	Psq 627
Rankhon, Duncan	Rch 244
Joseph	Ans 238
Rankhorn, Amos	Prq 658
Rankin, George	Glf 664
John	Glf 640
Richard	Mck 549
Robert	Glf 634
Robert	Glf 664
Robert	Ird 657
Samuel	Mck 536
William	Glf 640
Rankins, David	Lnc 825
Rann, Michael	Nrt 473
Ransom, Charles	Nsh 118
James	Gts 277
James	Wrr 827
John	Frv 467
Reubin	Frn 449
Samuel	Frn 482
Seymour	Wrr 828
Simon	Rbs 414
William	Frn 445
Ranson, Thomas	Stk 569
Ransor, Richd.	Csw 107
Rany, Isaac	Csw 119
Wm.	Csw 113
Rap, James	Brt 72
Rape, Henry	Mck 581
Peter	Mck 598
Raper, Elizabeth	Prq 644
Henry	Prq 655
John	Prq 655
Joseph	Prq 644
Thomas	Stk 569
Thomas	Stk 570
William	Glf 686
Raphael, Southy	Dpl 441
Rarden, Nancy	Hrt 714
Rare, Martin	Grv 538
Rasberry, Francis	Grn 595
Jesse	Grn 595
John	Lnr 21
Joseph	Grn 592
Margaret	Hrt 707
Thos.	Hrt 707
William	Hrt 707
Rasbury, George L.	Dpl 435
Rascoe, Elizabeth	Brt 72
James	Brt 72
Peter	Brt 72
Thomas	Brt 72
Rascow, Daniel	Hde 375
John	Hde 375
Rash, Daniel	Wlk 60
James (2)	Wlk 61
John	Srr 686
Levi	Wlk 60
Thomas	Ird 626
Rasor, Josiah	Brt 70
Rath see Ruth	
Rathbone, John	Bnc 186
Ratlaff, James	Hde 375
Ratleff, Richard	Ans 202
Zachr.	Ans 199
Ratley, Cage	Frn 453
John	Rbs 415
Joseph	Rbs 414
Noah	Rbs 415
Ratlif, Thomas	Rnd 340
Ratliff, Abner	Cht 182
Abraham	Rnd 338
Amon	Cht 217
Aron	Lnr 21
Benjamin	Rnd 336
Duke	Ans 203
Edom	Cht 182
Jailes	Stk 569
John	Cht 182
John, Sen.	Cht 182
Moses	Rnd 338
Rebeca	Ans 203
Richard	Rnd 340
Sally	Lnr 21
Thomas	Ans 199
William	Ans 225
Ratly, Frederick	Mnt 491
Rattleiffe, Rachel	Nwh 7A
Ratts, Henry	Rwn 395
Rattz, Godfrey	Rwn 411
Rauley, John	Glf 645
Sarah	Glf 645
Raven, John	Csw 147
Ravins, Jno.	Csw 130
Jno.	Prs 202
John	Prs 215
Ravis, Thomas	Grv 519
Rawles, Ann	Hrt 713
Jesse	Hrt 707
Jesse, Senior	Hrt 713
Moses	Hrt 713
Rawls, Cornelius	Grn 594
David	Mrt 407
Jas.	Mrt 407
Jesse	Mrt 407
John	Mrt 407
Jonas	Brt 72
Josiah	Brt 72
Levi	Brt 72
Mary	Ptt 235
Mosiah	Brt 70
Rebecca	Brt 72
Richard	Gts 276
Silas	Ptt 265
William	Hlf 338
William	Hrt 713
Willis	Crv 265
Wm.	Mrt 409
Zebudee	Crv 261
Rawson, John	Rnd 336
Ray, Absalom	Rch 245
Andrew	Mck 581
Andrew	Rck 453
Andrew	Stk 615
Andrew, Senr.	Mck 602
Angus	Cmb 387
Archd.	Mre 45
Archd.	Mre 54
Archd.	Mre 55
Archibald	Cmb 365
Archibald	Cmb 369
Daniel	Cmb 358
Daniel	Cmb 365
Daniel	Cmb 369
Daniel	Cmb 388
Daniel	Wke 760
David	Mck 599
David	Orn 594
David	
Dougald	Bld 18
Duncan	Bld 18
Dunkin	Mre 54
Frederick	Ird 657
George	Orn 592
George	Stk 569
Hannah	Orn 530
Hugh	Cmb 360
James	Bld 12
James	Ird 657
James	Orn 593
James	Wke 758
James	Wlk 59
Jesse	Ash 86
Jesse	Bld 12
John	Brk 788
John (2)	Cmb 364
John	Cmb 369
John	Cmb 373
John	Cmb 387
John	Grv 584
John	Mck 553
John	Mck 581
John	Mre 54
John	Mre 55
John (2)	Orn 593
John	Orn 618
John	Wke 759
John, Senr.	Wke 759
Jos.	Csw 144
Joseph	Orn 618
Luke	Wke 759
Lydia	Orn 593
Nathan	Wke 759
Neill	Cmb 365
Neill	Cmb 393
Raymon	Smp 505
Robert	Bnc 187
Robert	Orn 529
Robert	Orn 593
Robert	Rck 453
Robertson	Smp 522
Saml.	Mrt 407
Samuel	Mck 603
Skipworth	Rck 476
Thomas	Bnc 186
Thomas	Cht 214
Thomas	Orn 593
Thomas	Rnd 336
Thomas, jr.	Bnc 186
Turner	Ird 658
William	Brk 788

William	Glf 664	John	Psq 624	Redditt, Constant	Brt 70
William	Wke 760	John	Psq 641	Job	Brt 70
William, Junr.	Orn 593	Robert	Psq 640	Jonah	Brt 70
William, Senr.	Orn 593	Reary, George	Rwn 333	Lewis	Bfr 16
Wilson	Cmb 392	Reasons, Rawly	Hrt 713	Theophilus	Brt 70
see Wray		Saml.	Mrt 409	Reddoch, William	Glf 688
Rayburn, Sil	Srr 711	Reau, Anthony	Ash 87	Reddock, John	Rnd 337
Thomas	Srr 711	John	Ash 87	Redenour, Joseph	Rwn 395
Rayfield, Isaac	Srr 685	Reav, Jerry	Frn 458	Redfaren, Isaac	Rnd 338
Rayford, Apsella	Wne 866	Reaves, D. John	Srr 685	Samuel	Rnd 338
Philip	Jhn 748	Edward	Cht 224	Redfearn, John	Ans 238
Philip	Wne 866	Edward	Srr 709	Nimrod	Ans 238
Robert	Jhn 747	Edward	Wrr 827	Redford, Jesse	Mck 598
Raymi, Joseph	Srr 709	Edwd.	Bld 45	John	Mck 598
Rayner, Amos	Hrt 713	George	Orn 593	John, Junr.	Mck 583
Enoch	Brt 72	Hamblen	Frn 454	John, Senr.	Mck 594
Joshua	Brt 70	Hardy	Dpl 425	William	Mck 581
Luke	Hrt 707	Jesse	Ash 86	Redick, Cornelius	Brk 790
Miles	Brt 90	Jesse	Dpl 429	James	Grn 600
Samuel	Brt 72	Jesse	Mnt 481	John	Brk 786
William	Brt 72	Jesse	Srr 709	John	Grn 596
Raynor, Daniel	Dpl 417	Jessee	Glf 672	William	Grn 596
David	Smp 500	John D.	Srr 685	Reding, Jesse	Psq 629
Richard	Smp 503	Josias	Mnt 482	Samuel	Psq 632
Seton	Cmb 358	Josph	Srr 685	Thomas	Psq 630
Razor see Rasor		Mark	Brn 19A	William	Cmb 390
Rea, Elizabeth	Brt 72	Richard	Frn 461	Redings, Nathaniel	Srr 707
Henry	Brt 70	Richard	Frn 491	Redling, George M.	Cbr 691
James	Brt 74	Solomon	Brn 20	Redly see Ridly
John	Brt 70	Thomas	Cht 212	Redman, Thomas	Ird 626
John	Prq 662	William	Ash 87	William	Lnc 900
Samuel	Chw 127	William	Frn 454	Redmon, Jacob	Stk 569
Thomas	Chw 127	William	Wrr 826	John	Orn 618
William	Brt 70	Reburn, Hodge	Brk 788	Redock, Pheba	Rnd 337
William	Hrt 738	Rece, Abraham	Srr 685	Redwine, Michael	Mnt 485
Reace, Volentine	Ash 87	Charrit	Cmb 367	Redwood, Jas	Prs 194
see Reav		Daniel	Srr 685	Redyard, Mary	Cht 184
Read, Christian	Brt 72	Levi	Srr 685	Reece, Caleb	Glf 635
D. John	Brt 72	Record, David	Cht 171	Calib	Rwn 357
David	Cht 170	John	Mre 41	David	Cbr 701
Dread	Cht 215	Sion	Cht 171	George	Glf 629
Ezekiel	Crv 289	Recraft, John	Jhn 762	George	Mck 606
George	Crt 75	Rector, Jacob	Rwn 445	John	Glf 641
George	Prq 645	John	Srr 686	see Riece
Jacob	Stk 570	Peter	Rwn 445	Reed, Abraham	Lnc 850
Jacob	Stk 601	Reddan, Rheam	Bld 31	Alexander	Ird 622
Jacob	Stk 604	John	Orn 618	Allin	Mck 542
James	Brn 15	Thomas	Orn 618	Andrew	Brn 13A
James	Crt 89	Reddett, Alexander	Bfr 16	Archd.	Mre 59
John	Prq 643	Peter	Bfr 16	Archibald	Bnc 188
John	Stk 570	Reddick, David	Mrt 407	Burwell	Nrt 473
John D.	Brt 72	Elisabeth	Mrt 407	Bluford	Csw 110
Lovet	Brk 788	Henry	Chw 127	Daniel	Rck 491
Robert	Crt 83	John	Mrt 407	David	Mck 550
Thomas	Prq 656	Josiah	Chw 121	David	Rwn 309
Tully	Prq 655	Josiah	Mrt 407	Dempsy	Mck 532
William	Ons 162	Kenith	Mrt 407	Eldad	Rwn 394
William	Ons 178	Mills	Mrt 409	Eldad, Senr.	Rwn 394
William	Prq 646	Noah	Mrt 409	Fredrick	Frn 470
see Reed		Rice	Mrt 409	George	Brk 788
Reader, Adam	Lnc 869	Robert	Brt 72	George	Rwn 411
William	Lnc 869	Thos.	Mrt 407	Henry	Brk 789
Ready, Frederick	Lnc 872	Whitmell	Mrt 407	Hugh	Rck 476
John R.	Srr 687	Willis	Mrt 409	Isaac	Gts 277
Reagan, John	Rck 463	Redding, Daniel	Wke 760	Isaac, Jur.	Bfr 16
Realeigh, Benjn.	Hrt 732	Francis	Cmb 392	Isaac, Senr.	Bfr 16
Reals, Mary	Ons 162	Francis	Wke 760	Jacob	Hrt 713
William	Jhn 773	John	Rnd 337	James	Brk 789
Reamer, Henry	Lnc 893	John	Wlk 59	James	Ird 669
Reames, John	Nrt 471	Joseph	Rnd 337	James	Lnc 850
Margaret	Nrt 471	Nathan	Cmb 391	James	Mck 599
William	Nrt 471	Robert	Cmb 391	James	Rwn 459
Rean, Caty	Jhn 773	Robert	Rnd 337	James, Junr.	Brk 786
Reanard, Joseph	Rwn 454	William	Rnd 337	James, Senr.	Brk 786
Reaper, Benn.	Psq 641	William	Wlk 59	Jenny	Nrt 473
Cornelius	Psq 636	Reddish, Betsey	Wke 760	Jeremiah	Hrt 726
David	Psq 636	William	Ans 217	Jeremiah,

(Scotch)	Hrt 726	Elisabeth	Crv 267	Rencher, Abraham	Brk 787
Jerry	Cht 209	Preter	Lnc 821	Rencker, Jean	Brk 788
Jesse	Brk 789	Rogers	Nsh 118	Rendleman, John	Rwn 303
John	Ans 210	Reeves, Betsey	Wke 777	John, Jur.	Rwn 314
John	Bfr 17	Colia	Grn 612	Reninger, Joseph	Srr 686
John	Brk 786	Elizabeth	Wke 759	Renn, Howel	Nsh 117
John	Brk 789	Isaac, junr.	Wlk 60	Joseph	Grv 518
John	Cbr 681	Isaac, Senr.	Wlk 60	Renninger, Henry	Srr 686
John	Cbr 697	James	Rwn 445	Renshaw, Elijah	Rwn 428
John	Csw 120	John	Rwn 454	James	Rwn 428
John	Crr 137	John	Wke 760	Samuel	Rwn 332
John	Ird 622	Joseph	Grn 611	Thomas	Rwn 449
John	Lnc 865	Malicah	Glf 650	William	Rwn 328
John	Lnc 869	Richard	Ptt 276	Rensor, Noel	Jhn 753
John	Mck 529	Samuel	Mnt 480	Rentfro, Everet	Wne 863
John	Psq 638	Samuel	Rwn 328	Jacob, Jr.	Wne 862
John	Rwn 318	Thomas	Rnd 340	James	Wne 862
John	Rwn 382	William	Rwn 278	Jacob, Senr.	Wne 862
John	Rth 141	William	Wke 760	Rentfroe, John	Bnc 186
John	Wrr 828	William, Jur.	Wke 760	Reonalds, Jeptha	Mre 40
John, Junr. (2)	Rwn 309	Zachariah	Cmb 382	Jeptha	Mre 60
John, Senr.	Rwn 309	Reevis, Samuel	Wke 758	Reph, Isaac	Glf 683
Joseph	Mck 599	Reevs, Benjamin	Rwn 382	Rese, John	Nsh 117
Lucy	Cmb 358	Ephraim	Rwn 339	Resner, John	Lnc 824
Malachi	Crr 164	William	Rwn 290	Rether, Conrod	Brk 786
Mary	Crv 255	Regan, John, Jur.	Rbs 416	Reu, Jacob	Ash 87
Micajah	Gts 277	John, Senr.	Rbs 415	Reuster, Sabrena	Ans 215
Noah	Rwn 309	Joseph	Rbs 415	Revel, Burrell	Rbs 416
Robert	Bnc 187	Martha	Csw 142	Elijah	Nsh 117
Robert	Grv 547	Regans, Charles	Ash 87	Henry	Nsh 117
Samuel	Brk 787	Joel	Wlk 60	Jonathan	Nsh 117
Sarah	Bfr 16	William	Wlk 60	Reveley, Thomas	Wke 758
Shadrach	Hrt 726	Regester, Ezekiel	Nwh 7	Revell, Edmond	Lnr 20
Thomas	Bfr 17	Josiah	Nwh 6A	Matthew	Hrt 736
Thomas	Brk 789	Josiah	Nwh 7	Peggy	Orn 618
Thomas	Csw 104	Pricilla	Bld 9	Revels, Elijah	Smp 525
Thomas	Csw 146	Shadrick	Brn 13A	Nathaniel	Rbs 415
Thomas	Wrr 827	William	Bld 9	Nathaniel	Smp 526
Widow	Mck 592	Wright	Nwh 7	Reves, Adam	Wne 857
Widow	Rwn 411	Reggin, Darby	Ptt 271	Elisabeth	Wne 857
William	Brk 789	Reggs, James	Bfr 17	George	Bnc 185
William	Mck 544	Register, David	Smp 534	Lewis	Grv 520
William	Mck 570	Benjamin (2)	Smp 536	Stephen	Wne 857
William	Rwn 411	John (2)	Smp 535	Thomas	Bnc 187
William, Senr.	Brk 789	John	Smp 536	Revil, Isham	Wne 847
Reede, Asia	Hlf 338	Joseph	Smp 536	Solomon	Wne 848
Clement	Hlf 338	Thomas	Smp 533	Revill, Lazarus	Nrt 471
James	Hlf 338	Thomas	Smp 534	Margaret	Nrt 471
Jesse	Hlf 338	Reich, Charles	Stk 599	Matthew	Nrt 471
Moses	Hlf 338	Christopher	Stk 625	Michael	Nrt 471
Rhesa	Hlf 338	Reid, Abraham	Wlk 60	Revins see Ravins	
William	Hlf 338	Archibald	Rth 138	Revis, George	Orn 618
William, Sen.	Hlf 338	James	Ash 87	Reviss, David (2)	Rth 140
see Rude		John	Rth 140	Edward	Rth 139
Reeder see Ruder		Samuel	Ird 618	see Riviss	
Reedmon, Harman	Stk 590	Samuel	Rth 140	Rew see Reau	
Reedwine, Jacob	Rwn 381	Si	Srr 705	Rex, George	Orn 530
John	Rwn 309	Stephen	Ash 86	John	Wke 777
Reeks, Phebe	Edg 238	Thomas	Wlk 60	Reynald, Hamilton	Prs 211
Reel, David	Grn 590	Reigns, William	Bnc 187	Reynalds, Francis	Wlk 60
John	Crv 283	Reigsbry, William	Ird 637	James	Wlk 60
Joshua	Bfr 17	Reilley, Gregory	Edg 237	Reynolds, Abraham	Bnc 187
Levi	Crv 281	Reilly, Gregory	Edg 175	Ann	Glf 626
Reele, Daniel	Lnc 857	Reives, Archibald	Orn 496	Anne	Bld 14
David	Lnc 857	John	Orn 529	Anne	Bld 15
George	Lnc 857	Relf, Elizabeth	Cmd 100	Anthony	Rnd 338
Godfrey	Lnc 857	Relfe, Benn.	Psq 632	Christopher	Jns 783
Reels, Isham	Jhn 763	Joseph	Psq 632	Daniel	Ash 86
William	Jhn 767	Josiah	Psq 634	David	Rnd 336
Reep, Adam	Lnc 820	Thomas T.	Psq 628	David	Rnd 338
Adolph	Lnc 890	Thos. T.	Psq 635	David	Stk 618
Michael	Lnc 891	William	Psq 626	Dempsy	Bld 7
Reeper, Luke	Rwn 369	Remey, William	Mck 541	Ebenezer	Rnd 338
Rees, Enoch	Rwn 368	Remswace, David	Crt 93	Edward	Rck 485
Thomas	Crt 73	Ren, Joseph	Jhn 765	Elijah	Csw 115
Reese, David	Bfr 16	Sherwood	Jhn 766	Elisha	Wlk 60
Easter	Rwn 449	Rench, John	Smp 494	Francis	Rnd 338

George	Stk 618	Susanah	Cht 173	Peter	Rnd 337
Henry	Mnt 464	Thomas	Bnc 187	Robert	Rth 140
James	Stk 614	Thomas	Hlf 338	Samuel	Stk 617
James	Srr 686	Thomas	Hde 375	Tymothy	Wke 757
Jerremiah	Rnd 338	Thomas	Nrt 473	Richard, Charles	Stk 603
John	Rnd 339	William	Dpl 408	Gasper	Rwn 400
Jonas	Srr 687	William	Mre 74	J...s.	Nwh 2A
Obedants	Grn 611	William (2)	Orn 612	John	Srr 687
Penelope	Jns 817	William	Rck 456	Solomon	Ptt 283
Peregrine	Lnc 892	Rhodrick, Philip	Stk 601	see Rickard	
Richard	Bld 7	see Rudrock		Richards, Abraham	Rwn 349
Sharpe	Jns 783	Rhodrock, Peter	Stk 601	Adam	Crt 63
Solomon	Srr 685	Rhods, Acquilla	Orn 594	Benjamin	Frn 447
Urania	Bld 8	Thomas	Orn 594	Durett	Csw 110
William	Rnd 338	Rhubottom, Ezekel	Mre 41	Evan	Nrt 471
Wm.	Lnc 832	Rhumyon, John	Srr 685	Felix	Srr 685
Wm.	Srr 708	Rial, Clement	Wke 759	Francis	Frn 467
see Runnalds, Rynalds		John	Lnc 863	George	Frn 491
Rhea, George	Stk 613	Riblin, Widow	Rwn 297	Isaac	Rnd 337
Rhem, Jacob, Senr.	Crv 313	Rice, Abigal	Csw 138	Jacob	Hde 375
William	Jns 781	Benjamin	Crv 263	James	Hde 375
Rhew, John	Orn 593	Edward	Csw 97	Jessey	Frn 468
Rhine, Jacob	Lnc 844	Evan	Crv 263	John	Jns 799
Jacob, Junr.	Lnc 844	Francis	Csw 137	John	Lnc 857
Martin	Lnc 844	Francis	Crv 277	John	Nrt 471
Michael	Lnc 844	George	Mck 525	John	Rwn 400
Peter	Lnc 844	Henry	Csw 97	Joshua	Frn 482
Philip	Lnc 844	Ibsun	Csw 107	Lucindia	Hde 375
Rhinehart, Jacob	Lnc 905	Isham	Rwn 332	Major	Frn 445
Rhoades, Ephraim	Brt 72	James	Brt 72	Morriss	Srr 686
Henry	Brt 72	James	Crv 281	Nancy	Bfr 16
Isaac	Brt 74	Jeptha	Csw 96	Richard	Hde 375
Jacob	Hrt 713	Jesse	Crv 291	Shadrach	Hde 375
James	Brt 72	John	Crv 263	Thomas	Hde 375
Jesse	Brt 72	John	Grv 553	Wherry	Ptt 257
John	Brt 72	John	Ptt 242	William	Nrt 471
John	Wne 851	Joseph	Bnc 187	William	Srr 685
Mary	Brt 74	Joshua	Crv 279	Willis	Frn 467
Robert, Junr.	Brt 72	Mary	Crv 255	Richardson, Alexr.	Wlk 59
Robert, Senr.	Brt 72	Mary	Glf 637	Andrew	Crv 307
Thomas	Brt 74	Nathan	Csw 96	Appewhite	Jhn 756
William (2)	Brt 72	Nathl.	Csw 137	Benjamin	Hlf 338
Rhoads, Arthur	Wsh 714	Prisley	Wke 760	Canaday	Ash 86
Christopher	Lnc 843	Spencer	Bnc 187	Charles	Rth 139
Henry	Lnc 821	Susana	Csw 137	Christian	Rnd 338
Isaac	Trl 684	Thomas	Csw 96	Coonrod	Rnd 336
Jacob	Lnc 843	Thomas	Grv 553	Daniel	Ash 87
Leven	Trl 684	Thomas	Mnt 519	Daniel	Psq 630
Rhodes, Alexander	Orn 618	William	Bnc 186	David	Mre 69
Andrew	Bnc 187	William	Csw 95	Drury	Mre 73
Benjamin	Dpl 403	William	Csw 97	Drury	Rnd 340
Benjamin	Dpl 417	William	Mck 606	Edward	Mck 587
Benjamin	Orn 618	William	Mnt 497	Edward	Mre 74
Felix	Dpl 403	William	Rwn 433	Elijah	Hlf 338
Fortune	Glf 650	Williams	Csw 140	Elizabeth	Cht 205
George	Lnc 844	Wm.	Lnc 840	Fany	Rnd 340
Hezekiah	Rck 454	see Price, Riece		George	Mck 587
Jacob	Jns 789	Rich, Christ.	Stk 603	Henry	Hlf 338
Jacob	Lnc 844	Christian	Stk 622	Jacob	Psq 639
Jacob	Rbs 415	Jacob	Wke 758	James	Ash 86
James	Brn 19	Jesse	Wke 759	James, Esqr.	Bld 37
James	Jns 785	John	Nrt 473	Jesse	Rth 138
James	Smp 523	John	Rnd 337	John	Bld 9
James	Wne 873	John	Rwn 369	John	Mnt 502
Jeremiah	Wke 760	John	Rth 140	John	Mre 57
Jesse	Wke 760	John	Rth 141	John	Mre 69
Jessee	Rck 455	John	Stk 577	John	Psq 626
John	Brn 19	Joseph	Rnd 337	John	Trl 690
John	Orn 612	Joseph	Smp 520	John	Jhn 759
John	Orn 618	Joseph	Stk 617	John	Wke 759
John	Rck 456	Joshua	Smp 526	John, Jr.	Hlf 338
John	Wke 757	Lot	Smp 526	John, Sr.	Hlf 338
John	Wke 759	Luis	Stk 600	Jonathan	Jhn 756
Joseph T.	Dpl 410	Matthew	Stk 600	Joseph	Cmd 95
Peter	Lnc 840	Matthew	Stk 626	Joseph	Jhn 757
Randol	Wke 759	Moses	Rnd 337	Labius	Psq 630
Sarah	Wlk 59	Nimrod	Wke 758	Mary	Wrr 827

Miles Psq 632
Moses Mck 587
Mr. Bld 52
Pharoby Hlf 338
Richard Crv 331
S.N. Bld 34
Samuel Rnd 336
Stephen Mre 58
Tho. Brn 13A
Thomas Bld 10
Thomas Bld 12
Thomas Psq 639
Will Nsh 117
William Hlf 338
William Jhn 754
William Mre 42
William Rwn 411
Richason, Richard Rnd 338
Richerdson, Wil-
  liam Crv 325
Richerson, Edward Rck 478
  Fesherd Cht 199
  Isaac Cht 187
  Isaiah Cht 172
  John Cht 199
  John Orn 529
  Samuel Cht 192
  Thomas Cht 199
Richeson, Joseph Rck 488
  Sabby Stk 569
  Samuel Rck 488
Richhman, Nicholas Stk 586
Richie, Anthony Rth 139
Richmon, John Stk 585
Richmond, Charles Mck 569
  Creesy Dpl 411
  Jno. Csw 125
  Rachel Ird 663
  Wm. Csw 125
Rickard, Jacob Lnc 892
  John Lnc 892
Rickerson, Dius Jns 803
Rickets, Francis Prs 189
  Reason Mnt 475
  Robert Brk 790
Ricketts, Ananias Glf 633
  John Ans 215
  Moses Rck 451
  William Ans 232
Rickitts, Anthony Orn 593
Rickles, Ananias Glf 620
Rickman, Jesse Rwn 394
Ricks, Abraham Nsh 117
  Edmond, Esqr. Ptt 292
  Isaac Hlf 338
  Jacob Nsh 117
  Joel Nsh 117
  John Grv 553
  Robert Nsh 118
  Sarah Nsh 117
  Thomas (2) Grv 553
  Will. Nsh 118
Riddick, Abraham Gts 277
  David Gts 277
  Edward Gts 277
  Isaiah Gts 276
  James Prq 659
  Job Gts 276
  John Gts 277
  Joseph Gts 276
  Lasseter Gts 276
  Micajah Gts 277
  Micajah, Senr. Gts 277
  Reuben Gts 276
  Robert Gts 277
  Robert, Jr. Gts 277
  Sarah Gts 277

Sarah Prq 661
Seth Prq 661
Solomon Prq 660
Thomas Gts 277
William Prq 659
Willis Prq 659
Willis Prq 661
Wm. W. Gts 277
  see Trotman
Riddle, Cato Cht 177
  James Mre 61
  James Rck 487
  James Rwn 428
  John Cht 170
  John Rwn 357
  John Stk 586
  Julius Cht 154
  Randle Stk 569
  Richard Cht 154
  Samuel Srr 711
  Thomas Cht 160
  Tyer Stk 569
  William Cht 156
  William Rck 487
  William Rth 140
Ride, Robert Lnc 830
Ridenhour, Nicho-
  las Cbr 708
Ridenour, Mary Rwn 395
Rider, Adam Rwn 388
  Frederick Brk 787
  Jacob Brk 787
Ridge, Caleb Rnd 336
  Jacob Orn 529
  James Rnd 337
  Robertson Rnd 336
  Samuel Rnd 339
  William Rnd 339
Ridging, Jacob Orn 530
Ridgway, Mary Rwn 362
Ridings, David Rth 139
  George Wke 757
  James Rth 138
  John Rth 139
  John Srr 686
  see Rigings
Ridley, John Cbr 692
  John Rck 491
  Thomas Ans 226
Ridly, Timothy Hrt 732
Riece, Richard Wke 759
Rigan, William Cht 218
Rigby, John Wne 856
  John Wne 871
  William Dpl 397
  William, Sr. Dpl 369
Rigdon, Benjamin Ons 163
Riger, Samuel Cht 196
Rigesbey, Arch Wke 758
Riggans, John Bld 16
Riggen, Charles Lnc 850
Rigger, Joel Rwn 368
Riggins, John Ons 144
  Jonathan Nrt 473
Riggon, Charles Wrr 827
  Daniel Wrr 726
  Francis Wrr 827
  Francis Wrr 827
  Jacob Wrr 828
  John Wrr 828
  Mary Wrr 826
  William Wrr 828
Riggs, David Srr 685
  Elizabeth Srr 687
  Evan Cmd 97
  Happy Ons 137
  Hiram Srr 687

Isaac Cmd 105
Isaac Crt 78
Isaac, Jun. Cmd 97
Jacob Crv 275
James Dpl 411
James Orn 594
John Bfr 16
John Crv 275
John Ons 140
John Orn 592
John Stk 579
John Srr 687
Lott Srr 687
Miller Crv 273
Nehemiah Cmd 97
Noha Cmd 96
Samuel Psq 631
Sarah Crv 275
Sarah Orn 594
Shadrach Bfr 16
Stephen Ons 148
Stephen Stk 593
Thomas Csw 115
William Bfr 16
William Ons 146
William Orn 592
Zadck Srr 685
Righley, Will. Prs 190
Right, James Wke 757
  James Wke 758
  John Rnd 339
  John Rth 140
  John Wke 757
  Joseph Wke 758
  Ralph Rnd 336
  Saml. Nsh 118
  Will. Nsh 118
  William Grv 578
  William (2) Srr 685
  see Wright
Rightcline see Riteclin
Righte, Jonn. Crr 160
Rights, John Stk 599
Rigings, Joel Orn 594
Rigsbey, Frederick Wke 758
  James Wke 757
  John Wke 758
  Susanah Wke 758
  Thomas Bnc 186
Rigsby, James Ans 223
  John Cht 188
  Josiah Brt 74
  Luke Cht 174
  Luke Cht 189
  Traverse Cht 188
Rigsley, Jesse Orn 618
Riley, Absalom Cmb 369
  Doyal Rwn 444
  Edward Chw 115
  George Rwn 381
  George Rwn 388
  James Ird 637
  James Rwn 388
  John Mck 535
  John Mck 559
  John Nwh 3
  John Wke 757
  John, Junr. Wke 757
  Nancy Orn 619
  Nathan Rwn 388
  Peter Rwn 388
  Rodius Rwn 388
  Widow Rwn 388
  William Hrt 726
  William Rwn 382
  Wm. Jordan Hrt 718
Rily, Charles Stk 574
  James Orn 593

John	Orn 618	Rivers, Joel	Wrr 826	Luke	Bfr 16
William	Orn 592	Joseph	Wlk 60	Marmaduke	Bfr 17
William	Orn 593	Joshua	Wrr 828	Thomas	Bfr 16
William	Orn 594	Richd.	Jhn 765	Thomas	Bfr 23
Rimer, Balser	Ash 86	Thomas	Stk 573	Thos.	Mrt 407
Jacob	Cbr 716	William	Jhn 770	William	Bfr 16
Rin, Shaderack	Rth 139	Rives, George	Nrt 471	Robb, Robert	Cbr 676
Rinberton, James	Bld 25	Sarah	Nrt 471	Robbin, George	Crt 81
Rinchart, Andrew	Cbr 691	Riviss, Edmund	Rth 139	Robbins, Absolem	Brn 14A
Rincher, John G.	Wke 757	Harris	Rth 139	Ann	Gts 276
Rindall, George	Mnt 499	James	Rth 139	Arther (2)	Brn 15
Rine, Elias	Lnc 885	John	Rth 139	Benjn.	Brn 15
Rinehart, Chris-		see Reviss		Betty	Rnd 336
tian	Lnc 821	Rix, Demcey	Nrt 473	Dorcas	Gts 276
David	Rwn 382	Jonas	Glf 689	Jacob	Rnd 339
Jacob	Cbr 710	Roach, Charles,		James	Gts 276
John	Lnc 820	Junr.	Crv 323	James	Rnd 337
William	Rwn 297	Charles, Senr.	Crv 323	Jethro	Bld 5
Ring, David	Mnt 499	Hannah	Crv 231	John	Frn 492
George	Rwn 357	James	Brk 787	John	Rnd 336
Jacob	Rwn 357	James	Grn 598	John	Rnd 337
John	Stk 612	James	Rck 480	Jonathn.	Brn 15
Martin	Rwn 357	John	Crv 321	Joseph (2)	Rnd 336
Martin	Stk 612	John	Rth 141	Moses	Rnd 339
Michael	Rwn 357	John	Smp 513	Philip	Rth 138
Stephen	Rwn 381	Reuben	Ptt 243	Richard	Rnd 337
Thomas	Lnc 870	Thomas	Stk 607	Sarah	Gts 276
Thomas, Jr.	Stk 612	Thomas	Stk 611	Simon	Bld 3
Thomas, Sr.	Stk 612	Thomas	Srr 685	William	Rth 138
William	Rch 264	William	Bfr 17	Robbs, Alexander	Orn 528
Ringstaff, Addam	Mre 49	Roadlander, Nicho-		Robe, Frederick	Brk 789
Conrod	Orn 529	las	Ans 215	Robenson, Alexan-	
Ripets, William	Brk 787	Peter	Ans 215	der	Mck 568
Ripley, William	Crt 79	Roads, Abram	Edg 237	James	Mck 559
Ripple, Henry	Stk 600	Adam	Rnd 339	John	Mck 566
Rippy, Edmund	Rth 140	Adam	Rwn 357	Joseph	Crt 76
Edward	Orn 529	Jacob	Rnd 339	Teningham	Crt 76
James	Ash 86	John	Rnd 337	Roberds, Will.	Prs 218
James	Orn 529	John	Rnd 339	Robertson, David	Prs 216
Jessee	Orn 528	John	Rwn 357	Robern, Danl.	Brn 20A
John	Orn 528	Joseph	Edg 237	Roberson, Amos	Glf 656
John	Rth 140	Richard	Brk 788	Andrew	Rck 462
Joseph	Orn 528	William	Brk 788	Andw.	Csw 141
Mathew	Orn 528	William	Jhn 771	Andw.	Rck 479
Thomas	Orn 528	William	Rnd 338	Annes	Edg 237
Rising, James	Bld 14	Roadsmith, George	Rwn 290	Annis	Edg 175
Riskman, Thomas	Cht 173	Paul	Rwn 290	Clayborn	Frn 473
Rispess, Langley	Bfr 17	Roan, Adam	Mck 586	Daniel	Rck 451
Richard	Bfr 17	Benjamin	Hlf 338	Edwd.	Rck 465
Thomas, Jur.	Bfr 17	Henry, Junr.	Mck 586	Elisha	Grv 518
Riston, Bazel	Wlk 59	Henry, Senr.	Mck 586	Henry	Stk 616
Ritch, Anna	Cmb 358	John	Wke 759	Higdon	Grv 529
Ritcherson, John	Rck 467	Judith	Hlf 338	James	Csw 105
William	Rck 466	Lewis	Hlf 338	James	Orn 529
Ritchey, George	Cbr 717	William	Hlf 338	James	Orn 594
John	Cbr 718	William	Wke 760	James	Rck 462
John	Mck 551	Roane, Thomas	Csw 116	Jeremiah	Grv 530
Ritchie, David	Mck 585	Roark, Elisha	Prs 211	Jesse	Csw 110
Edmund	Mck 585	James	Orn 593	John (2)	Brn 17A
James	Bnc 186	Timothy	Stk 569	John	Orn 618
James	Cmb 358	Roatrok, Jacob	Rwn 375	John	Rck 451
James	Mck 584	Frederick	Rwn 375	John	Rck 479
John	Mck 581	Robason, Amos	Mrt 409	Jones	Glf 628
Rite, Henry	Hrt 726	Benjn.	Mrt 409	Joseph	Nwh 1A
John	Prs 210	Daniel	Mrt 407	Joseph	Nwh 8
Ritecel, Christian	Rnd 337	David, Junr.	Mrt 407	Mark	Grv 517
Riteclin, Peter	Rwn 303	David, Senr.	Mrt 409	Mary	Nwh 6A
Ritter, James	Srr 685	Edward	Bfr 16	Mary	Orn 529
William	Edg 237	Esther	Wsh 710	Michael	Orn 594
Ritton, Samuel	Mck 548	Hardy	Mrt 409	Nathaniel	Glf 643
Rivels see Revels		Henry, Junr.	Mrt 407	Paschal	Wke 759
Rivenbark, Fedrick	Dpl 400	Henry, Senr.	Mrt 407	Rebecah	Rck 461
John	Nwh 7	Jas., Junr.	Mrt 409	Richd., Senr.	Wke 758
Phillip	Nwh 9	Jas., Senr.	Mrt 407	Stark	Orn 618
Saml.	Nwh 9	Jesse	Mrt 407	Susannah	Grv 580
Simon	Dpl 400	John	Bfr 16	Thos.	Nwh 8
Will.	Nwh 9	Joshua	Mrt 407	William	Edg 237

Name	Loc	Name	Loc	Name	Loc
William	Gts 276	John	Psq 626	Benjamin	Cmd 108
William	Nwh 4A	John	Prq 655	Burwell	Wrr 828
William	Ons 164	John	Prq 658	Charles	Bld 26
William	Orn 594	John	Prs 203	Christopr.	Wke 757
William	Rck 451	John	Rwn 328	Esther	Crt 62
Robert, Craige	Brk 731	John	Rth 140	Fanny	Cmd 94
Inglish	Brk 763	John	Srr 687	Gennet	Brt 72
Jno.	Csw 126	John	Wke 758	Harbert	Wke 757
John	Csw 97	John	Wne 845	Isham	Wrr 826
Thomas	Grv 573	John	Wlk 61	James	Bld 22
Roberts, Aaron	Rth 139	John, Senr.	Srr 686	James	Ons 136
Aaron	Wlk 61	Jonathan	Cmd 107	James	Wke 758
Abel	Crr 144	Jonathan	Gts 276	Jno.	Wke 760
Abner	Orn 592	Jonathan	Nrt 473	Jno., Junr.	Wke 760
Aron	Wke 757	Joseph	Wlk 59	John	Brt 74
Benjamin	Hrt 738	Joshua	Lnc 821	John	Bld 49
Benjamin	Ird 632	Joshua	Srr 686	John	Crr 159
Benjamin	Prq 655	Lawrence	Rwn 433	John	Nsh 117
Benjn.	Prq 655	Mark	Bnc 186	John	Nrt 473
Bill	Cmb 378	Marshal	Frn 488	John	Psq 624
Briton	Jhn 763	Martin	Rth 140	John	Psq 629
Charles	Bfr 16	Mary	Chw 116	Joseph	Rwn 449
Charles	Bfr 17	Mary	Lnr 20	Lott	Wke 760
Charles	Crt 61	Mary	Mck 559	Lucretia	Wke 760
Charles	Chw 114	Mary	Orn 492	Mark	Csw 135
Charles	Orn 592	Mary	Rbs 416	Nathan	Crr 140
Charles	Psq 641	Matthew	Ird 626	Peter	Nsh 117
Claxton	Nrt 473	Morris	Rth 141	Peter	Wrr 827
Curtis	Wke 757	Moses	Ird 641	Thomas	Crt 57
David	Ird 632	Moses	Wke 757	Thomas	Csw 97
David	Mck 553	Naman	Rck 477	Thomas	Cht 159
David	Prs 190	Peter	Bfr 23	Thomas	Nrt 471
Edward	Wlk 60	Philip	Mck 559	Thomas	Orn 530
Elias	Nrt 473	Phillip	Prs 189	Thomas	Prq 647
Eliza	Rck 477	Phlep	Grv 510	Thomas	Prq 662
Elizabeth	Grv 532	Piland	Rnd 336	Thomas	Wke 757
Ephraim	Orn 592	Polly	Wlk 61	Thomas	Wke 759
Esther	Nrt 473	Rebecca	Hrt 736	Upshaw	Cht 151
George	Ird 632	Richard	Jns 807	William	Bnc 186
George	Prs 188	Richard	Wlk 61	William	Crt 60
George	Wke 758	Right	Wne 873	William	Crt 62
George, (the R)	Prs 203	Robert	Bnc 185	William	Cht 217
Gideon	Bnc 185	Sabia	Crt 61	William	Frn 459
Henry	Bnc 185	Samuel	Frn 457	William	Prq 654
Henry	Rwn 409	Samuel	Ird 632	William	Wrr 826
Henry	Rwn 411	Samuel	Rwn 381	William	Wrr 827
Henry	Wne 843	Sarah	Chw 131	Wilie	Nsh 117
Hugh	Smp 515	Sarah	Wlk 60	Wyatt	Nrt 471
Humphry	Csw 134	Solomon	Brn 13A	Robeson, Alice	Smp 526
Humphry	Rwn 333	Solomon	Csw 148	Andrew	Stk 566
Isaac	Crr 144	Step	Rwn 394	Edward	Cmb 379
Isaac	Grv 532	Thomas	Bnc 186	Elizabeth	Cmb 358
Ishmael	Rbs 415	Thomas	Csw 136	Jacob	Stk 620
Jacob	Wlk 59	Thomas	Chw 126	James	Smp 516
James	Crt 87	Thomas	Glf 688	Joel	Cmb 390
James	Grv 546	Thomas	Lnc 898	Joel, jun.	Cmb 390
James	Hde 375	Thomas	Rck 459	John	Stk 569
James	Ird 632	Thos.	Crr 148	John	Srr 686
James	Mck 540	William	Brn 14A	John	Srr 687
James	Orn 593	William	Bnc 185	Littleberry	Stk 616
James	Rck 463	William	Brk 787	Mark	Cmb 390
James	Srr 686	William	Crt 88	Peter	Nwh 7A
James, Junr.	Nrt 473	William	Cht 223	Rudy	Stk 611
James, Jur.	Wke 758	William	Chw 123	Tho.	Nwh 3
James, Senr.	Nrt 473	William	Dpl 438	Thomas	Srr 685
Jas.	Prs 188	William	Nrt 473	William	Smp 520
Jemima	Crt 87	William	Orn 592	William	Smp 527
Jeptha	Rth 139	William	Prq 658	William	Srr 685
Jeremiah	Orn 592	Willis	Prs 188	Wm.	Srr 705
John	Bnc 185	William	Rch 242	Robey, George	Lnc 850
John	Bnc 187	William	Rwn 383	Leonard	Ird 672
John	Crt 87	William	Wlk 59	Tobias	Ird 668
John	Cht 161	William	Wlk 60	Robine, Old	Crr 162
John	Chw 128	Zachariah		Robines, Jesse	Mck 548
John	Crr 147	Robertson, Abner	Crr 156	Robinett, Allen	Wlk 61
John	Glf 688	Alex	Csw 135	Isaac	Wlk 59
John	Orn 592	Allen	Crt 60	James	Wlk 60

Jesse	Wlk 60	John	Lnc 906	Rodes, Benjamin	Ons 163
Samuel	Ash 86	John	Mck 557	Cornelius	Cmd 100
RobinHood, Basd	Wne 851	John	Mck 572	Cornelius	Cmd 108
Robins, Bersheba	Hde 375	John	Mck 599	Frederick	Lnc 857
Charles	Mnt 514	John	Mnt 509	John	Jhn 775
Daniel	Rnd 336	John	Ptt 292	Samuel	Cmd 96
George	Prq 657	John	Rwn 368	Rodey, John	Chw 124
Isaac	Lnc 891	John	Rwn 411	Rodgers, Absalom	Ptt 291
Isaac	Rnd 337	John	Wne 867	Absalom, Senr.	Ptt 269
Jacob	Edg 237	John, Junior	Ptt 281	Benjamin	Ptt 228
John	Ans 217	Jonathan	Lnc 906	Drurey, Junior	Ptt 278
John	Brk 790	Joseph	Rwn 278	Drurey, Senior	Ptt 278
John	Rck 469	Joseph	Rwn 290	Everett	Ptt 235
John	Wlk 59	Julius	Bnc 186	Frederick	Ptt 233
John, (Capt.)	Edg 237	Mary	Hlf 338	John	Ptt 278
Joseph	Brk 786	Matthew	Mck 523	John	Ptt 295
Joseph	Prq 659	Mattw.	Lnc 836	Shadrack	Ptt 225
Kidah	Chw 129	Moses	Mck 524	Stephen	Grn 587
Reuben	Wlk 59	Penty	Mnt 491	William	Ptt 235
Rowland	Edg 238	Peter	Mnt 464	William, junr.	Ptt 235
Saml.	Crr 138	Prissilla	Bnc 187	Rodin, Widow	Mck 526
Samuel	Prq 657	Richard	Mck 537	Rodrey, Uenjamin	Wke 757
Sarah	Edg 238	Richard	Rwn 349	Rodrock, Valentine	Stk 600
Stephen	Edg 237	Risden	Brk 786	Rodwell, John	Wrr 828
Thos.	Wlk 59	Robert	Mck 555	Thomas	Wrr 828
Wells	Edg 237	Robert	Mck 591	Rody, John, Jun.	Chw 128
William	Edg 238	Robert, Senr.	Mck 524	Roe, Charles	Wke 760
William	Prq 657	Samuel	Ird 637	Jos.	Csw 146
William, Senr.	Edg 238	Sarah	Cmb 379	Joseph	Rch 263
William, (son		Solomon	Lnc 857	Malachi	Jhn 754
Wm.)	Edg 238	Solomon	Lnc 864	Mary	Cht 187
Wm.	Mrt 388	Sovereign	Ptt 231	Mathew	Frn 453
Robinson, Adam	Lnc 865	Squire	Rch 265	Soloman	Cht 153
Alexander	Brk 788	Thomas	Ans 233	William	Frn 452
Alexr.	Lnc 839	Thomas	Rch 265	see Rae, Rowe	
Alexr., Junr.	Lnc 839	Thomas	Rwn 438	Roebuck, George	Mrt 407
Andrew G.	Lnc 879	Toddy	Ans 214	Raleigh	Mrt 409
Anne	Rwn 333	Tyre, Senr.	Mnt 502	Roes, Benjamin	Jhn 777
Arther	Rch 247	Widow	Mck 555	Rofe, See Rose	
Arthur	Brk 788	Widow	Rch 269	Rogans, Powel	Orn 618
Arthur	Mnt 519	William	Brk 788	Rogers, Agness	Prs 189
Boothy	Ans 204	William	Ptt 231	Airs	Wsh 710
Charles	Rch 247	William	Rch 262	Allin	Rwn 309
Charles	Rch 254	William	Rwn 333	Anne	Wsh 710
Daniel	Crv 309	William	Rwn 368	Anne Tissha	Trl 672
Daniel	Mck 606	William	Rth 138	Aron	Wke 759
David	Lnc 905	Wm.	Lnc 839	Bartlett	Bnc 186
David	Mck 537	Wm.	Lnc 840	Benajah	Wne 867
David, Senr.	Mck 524	Zachariah	Lnc 839	Benjamin	Mnt 515
Elijah	Lnc 879	Robison, Burtram	Bld 33	Benjamin	Rch 249
Elizabeth	Rwn 369	Charles	Rth 139	Benjn.	Gts 277
George	Brk 786	George	Rth 140	Bird	Prs 197
George	Ird 672	Isaac	Rth 140	Benjn.	Hrt 736
George	Ird 675	James	Rth 141	Bryan	Brn 19A
George	Rwn 333	John (2)	Rth 139	Daniel	Edg 238
Henry (2)	Rwn 333	Jona., Capt.	Bld 33	Daniel	Ons 143
Henry, Senr.	Rwn 332	Jonathan	Rth 140	David	Bnc 187
Hugh	Rwn 317	Samuel	Bnc 187	David	Mck 536
Hugh, Junr.	Rwn 333	Thomas	Rth 139	Dread	Wke 760
Hugh, Senr.	Rwn 333	Thomas	Smp 534	Drury	Cbr 714
Isaac	Lnc 863	Volentine	Bnc 187	Eli	Ans 240
Isaac	Lnc 879	William	Bld 36	Elisabeth	Ans 223
Isaac	Lnc 880	Roblin, Lewis	Rwn 411	Elizabeth	Orn 529
Isaac	Rth 140	Robly, John	Rwn 333	Elizabeth	Rwn 381
James	Mck 524	Robson, Archalas	Edg 237	Enos	Crv 329
James	Ptt 229	Benjamin	Lnr 15	Ezekiel	Wsh 710
Jane	Bld 36	Daniel	Mre 61	Frederick	Mnt 512
Jeremiah	Ans 198	Henry	Edg 237	George	Bnc 186
Jeremiah	Cmb 392	Jesse	Edg 238	George	Hlf 338
Jesse	Lnc 906	Joseph	Mre 56	Green	Wke 757
Jms.	Lnc 839	Rochel, Benjn.	Nwh 5A	Harden	Crt 56
Jno.	Lnc 839	Celia	Nrt 473	Hardy	Brn 19A
Job	Lnc 839	Rochell, Thomas	Wke 759	Henry	Cht 156
John	Brk 787	William	Wke 759	Hezekiah	Prq 653
John	Cbr 681	Rockford, Moses	Lnc 832	Hugh	Bnc 187
John	Hlf 338	Roddy, Wm.	Crr 159	Hugh	Mck 576
John	Lnc 863	Roden, Mary	Mck 527	Hugh	Mck 589

Humphrey	Ans 208	Sterling	Mrt 407	Mark	Edg 238
Isaiah	Dpl 430	Stephen	Wke 758	Richard	Gts 277
Isham	Ans 238	Theophiles	Lnr 21	William	Rnd 339
Isham	Wne 867	Thomas	Ans 223	Rollins, Charles	Ptt 234
Jacob	Glf 675	Thomas	Bnc 187	Edward	Dpl 420
Jacob	Nsh 117	Thomas	Cbr 702	George	Rth 139
James	Dpl 420	Thomas	Frn 483	James	Dpl 408
James	Hrt 701	Thomas	Stk 588	John	Cht 207
James	Mnt 512	Thomas	Wke 760	John	Ptt 234
James	Nwh 4A	Timothy	Nwh 5	Joseph	Trl 686
James	Orn 592	Widow	Mck 591	William	Rth 140
James	Stk 614	Willabay	Mre 56	Rolston, Vincent	Glf 650
James	Wne 865	William	Bnc 185	Rombough, William	Chw 113
Jesse	Edg 238	William	Dpl 427	Rominer, Jacob	Stk 569
Jesse	Nsh 117	William	Edg 237	Rominger, George	Lnc 857
Job	Ans 210	William (2)	Hlf 338	Jacob	Stk 600
Job	Wke 760	William	Mck 588	Rominor, Cornilus	Stk 601
Joel	Dpl 427	William	Mnt 512	Roney, James	Orn 528
John	Brn 19	William	Orn 529	John	Lnc 821
John	Cbr 699	William	Orn 592	Ronsley, James	Cht 213
John	Crr 147	William	Wke 757	Rook, Benjamin	Nrt 471
John	Dpl 425	Willie	Wke 759	John	Nrt 471
John	Grv 554	Wm.	Crr 159	Martin	Nrt 471
John	Jhn 763	Zekl.	Ons 156	Stephen	Glf 668
John	Mck 576	Rogerson, Daniel	Prq 653	Rooker, Presley	Wrr 827
John	Mck 591	David	Mrt 409	William	Rth 140
John	Mnt 515	Eliza.	Bld 35	William	Wrr 827
John	Prs 200	Esther (2)	Prq 660	Rooks, ..., Mrs.	Hrt 718
John (2)	Wke 760	Jesse	Prq 661	Cerena	Nwh 4A
Jonathan	Gts 277	Job	Mrt 407	Charity	Mrt 409
Joseph	Cbr 701	John	Orn 618	Charles	Gts 276
Joseph	Frn 485	John	Prq 656	Demcy	Hrt 701
Joseph	Mck 533	Josiah	Prq 648	James	Hrt 701
Joseph	Nrt 471	Josiah, Jun.	Prq 660	Joseph	Gts 277
Joseph, jr.	Grv 530	Josiah, Sen.	Prq 660	Levi	Hrt 701
Joseph, Senr.	Grv 531	Mary	Prq 653	Roots, Mary	Brn 14
Josiah	Cht 193	Mary	Prq 654	Rope, Ann	Grn 599
Josiah	Chw 125	Reuben	Mrt 407	Roper, Anne	Nrt 471
Josiah	Hde 375	Samuel	Prq 663	David	Wlk 60
Josiah	Wke 758	Simon	Mrt 407	Frederick	Hde 375
Judah	Edg 238	Solomon	Prq 663	James	Brk 789
John	Rbs 414	Thomas	Prq 653	James	Rch 244
Mark	Dpl 430	Roit, John	Stk 577	James	Rch 266
Martha	Rck 490	Roiter, Ephraim	Brk 787	John	Csw 112
Meede	Wne 867	Roland, Abraham	Ash 86	John	Rch 263
Milley	Gts 277	Andrew	Ash 86	William	Ans 223
Minutes	Brt 72	Auston	Mnt 514	Rora, William	Ans 240
Moses	Cbr 699	Charles	Bnc 186	Rorey see Rora	
Nathan	Wsh 710	Henry	Bnc 186	Roror, ...	Crr 138
Nicolas	Dpl 420	Henry	Grv 520	Rorrow, George	Orn 582
Niel	Mre 63	Hosa	Mnt 512	Rosa, Benjamin,	
Peleg	Dpl 431	James	Mnt 505	Junr.	Brk 787
Peleg, Junr.	Wke 758	Jerry	Cht 178	Ezekiel	Ans 239
Peleg, Senr.	Wke 758	Jessee	Cht 209	Rosborough, James	Rwn 328
Philip	Gts 277	Joseph	Ash 86	John	Rwn 328
Priscilla	Hrt 736	Mary	Mnt 514	Roscoe see Rascoe	
Randel	Rnd 336	Robert	Mnt 512	Rosdel, Richard	Lnc 850
Randolph	Dpl 441	Thomas	Grv 518	Rose, Aaron	Edg 238
Reubin	Frn 482	Thomas	Mnt 512	Aaron	Stk 570
Rheubin	Nwh 12A	Young	Cht 210	Abner	Srr 685
Richard	Rwn 438	Wiley	Frn 453	Amos	Edg 238
Richd.	Ans 208	Wiley	Frn 456	Amos	Nsh 118
Robert	Bnc 185	William	Wrr 827	Archey	Ons 142
Robert	Bnc 187	Rolen, Fendel	Csw 124	Base	Srr 685
Robert	Edg 237	Roler, George	Crr 147	Benjamin	Bnc 185
Robert	Glf 671	Rolleson, Christo-		Benjamin	Brk 787
Ruthe	Wlk 60	pher	Crr 168	Benjamin	Nsh 118
Saml.	Prs 189	Francis	Crr 168	Burrel	Nsh 118
Samuel	Dpl 441	John	Crr 168	Charles	Rck 477
Sarah	Dpl 430	Wm.	Crr 168	Duncan, Junr.	Prs 201
Seth	Cbr 701	Rollings, Agnes	Rnd 339	Edward	Hde 375
Shadrach	Hlf 338	Agness	Rnd 339	Francis	Bnc 188
Sion	Cht 176	David	Rnd 339	Francis	Brk 786
Solomon	Wke 759	George	Rnd 336	Jacob	Brk 788
Spine	Crr 150	James	Rnd 337	James	Nrt 471
Stephen	Dpl 427	John	Rnd 339	John	Bfr 16
Stephen	Mrt 407	Jonathan	Rnd 337	John	Bnc 186

John	Brk 788	Joseph, Senr.	Cbr 684	Rouse, Alexr.	Nwh 1A
John	Srr 705	Josiah	Bfr 16	Joseph	Mre 56
John	Wne 866	Joseph	Srr 687	Laben	Rnd 339
Jonathan	Brk 788	Judah	Ptt 241	Michl.	Rck 477
Joseph	Crt 62	Leven	Mrt 409	Peter	Nrt 473
Mathew	Edg 238	Luke	Ans 222	William	Dpl 422
Matthias	Crv 249	Martin	Prq 651	Roussau, Hilair	Wlk 60
Mitchell	Hde 375	Martin	Glf 660	Hiram	Wlk 59
Nancy	Bfr 23	Mary	Mrt 407	Routh, William,	
Peyton R.	Brt 90	Nathan	Orn 530	(Capt.)	Edg 237
Pheroby	Hlf 338	Nealby	Mrt 409	Routledge, Thomas	Dpl 399
Philip	Rck 478	Reuben	Glf 644	Row, ...	Nwh 10A
R. Peyton	Brt 90	Reubin	Rck 446	Christopher	Ons 138
Reddick	Nsh 118	Robert	Rck 478	James	Ons 159
Robert	Edg 238	Samuel	Stk 614	John	Brk 789
Reubin	Edg 238	Sarah	Grv 563	John	Nwh 10
Salley	Wrr 827	Silvey	Ans 201	Robert	Bfr 17
Samuel	Bnc 187	Solomon	Chw 126	Rowan, Appolus	Bld 29
Sterling	Wlk 59	Thomas	Glf 656	John	Brt 90
Theophilus	Wne 862	Thomas	Ptt 261	Roward, Elijah	Stk 569
Thomas	Cht 196	Thomas	Wke 757	Rowden, Jeremiah	Rth 139
Thos.	Nsh 117	Thos.	Mrt 409	Nathaniel	Rth 139
Tonkins	Nsh 117	Timothy	Glf 643	Rowe, Benjamin	Crv 287
Will.	Nsh 118	Walter	Ans 200	C.	Lnc 886
William	Edg 238	William	Chw 114	Jesse	Crv 281
William	Rwn 342	William	Frn 481	Joseph	Crv 231
Wm.	Psq 634	William	Glf 643	Joshua	Crv 281
Zachariah	Bnc 185	William	Rth 140	Mathew	Frn 456
Roseborough, Sam-		William	Rth 141	Rachael	Trl 672
uel	Rwn 328	Wm., Senr.	Mrt 409	Robert	Prq 642
William	Lnc 866	see Rose		Sarah	Crv 261
Rosel, James	Rck 444	Rosser, Alse	Jhn 770	William	Crv 337
Roseman, George	Rwn 303	Isaac	Jhn 770	William	Edg 238
George, Senr.	Rwn 303	Isham	Cht 207	Rowel, Benjn.	Brn 13
Jacob	Lnc 879	James	Jhn 770	Crusy	Smp 535
Peter	Rwn 303	John	Jhn 774	Jacob	Wne 848
Peter	Rwn 342	Joseph	Ans 233	Rowen, Hugh	Mck 539
Rosin, Binony	Csw 139	Rosson, Abner	Cht 170	Rowh, Daniel	Rwn 297
Ross, Andrew	Ans 201	John	Cht 158	John	Rwn 297
Anne	Cmb 358	John, Sr.	Cht 158	John	Rwn 310
Benjamin	Bfr 16	Roterson see Roberson		Rowland, Arick	Rbs 415
Charles	Srr 687	Rothwell, Jonathan	Bld 5	Jacob	Wke 759
Daniel	Ans 232	Rotin, William	Cmd 106	James	Rbs 415
Daniel	Edq 237	Rough, Nicholas	Cbr 714	James	Rth 139
David	Brn 19	Roughten, Anne	Trl 682	Jesse	Bfr 16
Edward	Frn 476	David	Srr 686	Jesse	Wke 758
Elijah	Hde 375	Isaiah	Srr 686	John	Rbs 415
Elisabeth	Crv 241	Roughton, Daniel	Trl 680	Joseph	Edg 238
Elsie	Orn 529	Richard	Trl 680	Lewis	Wke 758
Francis	Bfr 16	Roughty, Edward	Mnt 504	Mary	Nrt 471
Francis	Cbr 701	Roulhac, G.P.	Bfr 16	Needham	Rbs 415
George	Cbr 683	John	Mrt 409	Pleasant	Grv 518
Griffin	Ans 236	Rounberry, Lud-		Samuel	Rbs 415
Gustavus	Ans 214	wrick	Orn 530	Rowling, Mildred	Brn 17
Gustavus	Ans 239	Roundtree, Charles	Orn 594	Rowls, David	Wne 867
Henry	Ans 208	Francis	Wne 862	Rowminger, Michal	Stk 603
Henry	Grv 512	Jesse, J.P.	Ptt 290	Rows, Ebenezer	Dpl 422
Hugh	Ans 205	John	Prs 217	Rowsom, Hannah	Wsh 710
Hugh, Senr.	Ans 236	Kedar	Wne 861	Royal, Bigars	Smp 501
James	Ans 209	Moses	Bfr 16	Hardy	Smp 525
James	Bnc 187	Moses	Crv 327	Joseph	Crt 78
James	Frn 476	Moses	Edg 238	Larry	Smp 501
James	Mck 536	Thomas	Orn 594	Lewis	Smp 528
James	Orn 529	Rounsavall, John	Rwn 338	Marmaduke	Crt 56
James	Rth 140	Rounseval, David	Rwn 318	Marmaduke	Smp 528
James	Rth 141	Rountree, Abner	Gts 277	Orman	Smp 517
Jas.	Mrt 409	John	Gts 277	Owen	Smp 510
Jean	Cbr 684	Josiah	Gts 276	Simon	Smp 528
John	Cbr 684	Miles	Gts 277	William	Smp 510
John	Edg 238	Seth	Gts 276	Young	Smp 501
John	Mrt 409	Rous, Cloe	Lnr 20	Royale, John	Csw 99
John	Ptt 237	Henry	Lnr 20	Roycraft, Thomas	Wke 757
John	Rwn 303	John (2)	Lnr 20	Royen, Abraham	Ptt 287
John	Srr 687	Joshua	Lnr 20	Royster, Francis	Grv 539
Jos.	Mrt 407	Simon	Lnr 20	John	Grv 539
Joseph	Cbr 701	Simon, Senr.	Lnr 20	William	Grv 541
Joseph	Wlk 59	Solomon	Lnr 20	Roziar, David	Rbs 415

Name	Loc	Name	Loc	Name	Loc
Mary	Rbs 415	Rumple, Daniel	Rwn 318	David	Bld 28
Patience	Rbs 416	Frederick	Rwn 309	Eliazer	Bld 40
Reubin	Rbs 415	John	Cbr 685	James	Brn 18
Rubottom, Thomas	Cht 219	Runalds, James,		John	Bld 24
Ruby, William	Ans 204	Junr.	Mnt 472	John	Brn 21A
Rucker, Colbey	Wlk 61	Rundle, Lucri...	Nwh 1A	John, Senr.	Bld 31
Mordecai	Rth 139	Runian, John	Bnc 185	Joseph	Bld 38
Ruckmon, William	Stk 594	Runnalds, Anderson	Mnt 464	Sarah	Bld 39
Rucks, Josiah	Grv 544	Jacob	Mnt 472	William	Trl 690
Rudacil see Ritecel		John	Jhn 755	Russel, Abner	Grv 581
Rudd, John	Hlf 338	James, Senr.	Mnt 473	Abner	Wlk 60
William	Hlf 338	John	Mnt 472	Alexander	Rck 489
Rudder, Samuel	Trl 682	Runnals, Josiah	Ons 167	Charles	Gts 277
Rudduck, William	Glf 636	Runnels, Benjn.	Hrt 713	Charles (2)	Nwh 6
Rude, Arther	Rnd 338	David	Hrt 713	Charles	Srr 686
Ruder, Benjamin	Rnd 338	Fanny	Smp 517	Charna	Nwh 6
Rudesil, Jonas	Mck 531	Gideon	Rth 139	Charnal	Nwh 6
Rudesill, Henry	Lnc 857	James	Rwn 410	David	Bnc 187
Jacob	Lnc 843	James	Wke 760	David	Crt 89
John	Lnc 821	Jesse	Hrt 713	Delilah	Glf 649
Michael	Lnc 820	John	Rth 140	Edwd.	Nwh 1A
Philip (2)	Lnc 821	John	Wke 760	Elizabeth	Hde 375
Rudolph, Andrew	Rwn 381	Patience	Hrt 713	Enoch	Rck 460
John	Rnd 337	Richard	Rwn 449	George	Mre 76
Rudrock, Philip	Stk 601	Stephen	Rth 138	George	Rck 486
Rudwine, Frederick	Mnt 480	Will.	Brn 21	George	Wke 758
Rue, David	Gts 277	William	Hrt 713	Habbakkuk	Crt 89
Edward	Hde 375	Willis	Smp 516	Hannah	Hde 375
Elizabeth	Gts 277	Runniss, Richard	Jns 781	James	Glf 649
Frederick	Crv 295	Runyan, Jeremiah	Rth 140	James	Mnt 480
Frederick	Hde 375	Rupart, Peter	Rwn 438	James	Psq 630
Mark	Bfr 16	Rupe, Martin	Srr 686	James	Rbs 432
Mary	Crv 297	Michal	Srr 686	John	Bnc 187
Reuben	Hde 375	Rurch, Pemberton	Csw 117	John	Crt 79
Solomon	Hde 375	see Burch		John	Grv 581
Southy	Crv 293	Rusel, George	Rnd 338	John	Jhn 760
Southy, Jur.	Hde 375	Samuel	Rnd 339	John	Jns 825
Southy, Ser.	Hde 375	Rush, Abraham	Rth 138	John	Mre 76
Southy J.	Crv 297	Absalom	Frn 453	John	Psq 638
Suthy	Crt 90	Benjamin	Frn 495	John C.	Grv 583
Thomas	Rwn 411	Benjamin	Rnd 336	Jorden	Mnt 520
Vincent	Wke 757	George	Lnc 821	Malachi	Crv 319
Ruff, Charles	Wlk 61	John	Rnd 336	Mark	Cmb 358
Daniel	Grn 589	Mary	Rnd 336	Martin	Ash 87
James	Grn 590	Widow	Rwn 303	Mathew	Bnc 185
John	Grn 589	William	Mnt 464	Moses	Mnt 481
Ruffen, John	Prs 199	Rusher, Jacob	Rwn 297	Moses	Rth 139
Ruffian, Etheldred	Grn 614	Rushing, Abraham	Ans 240	Polly	Rth 140
Ruffin, Henry	Wsh 710	Abraham, B.C.	Ans 220	Talbout	Srr 686
James	Brt 72	David	Ans 220	Thomas	Crt 67
Jesse	Edg 237	Elijah	Ans 220	Thomas	Hrt 713
John, Junr.	Edg 237	Hardy	Ans 220	Thomas	Mnt 482
John, Senr.	Edg 237	Jacob	Ans 220	William	Crt 87
Joseph	Edg 237	Jason	Ans 227	William	Cmb 358
Samon	Edg 238	Jason	Ans 239	William	Glf 623
Samuel, (Capt.)	Edg 237	John	Ans 230	William	Glf 652
Samuel, Senr.	Edg 237	Joseph	Ans 220	William	Glf 655
Sarah	Edg 237	Mark	Ans 220	William	Rnd 336
William	Brt 72	Noah	Ans 240	Russell, Benjamin,	
Ruffs, John	Rth 140	Paul	Ans 221	Sr.	Hde 375
Ruhmon see Richmon		Philip	Ans 220	Celia	Cbr 703
Ruledge, Ben	Srr 704	Philip	Ans 239	James	Cbr 676
Rulk, Samuel	Brn 17A	Philip, J.	Ans 230	James	Rbs 415
Rumage, George	Mnt 500	Rowlen	Ans 227	James	Wke 759
George, Senr.	Mnt 520	Richard	Ans 220	John	Cbr 687
Rumley, Clement	Crt 72	Robert	Ans 220	Joseph	Cbr 703
Dennard	Crt 77	Solo.	Ans 220	Levi	Cbr 699
Gilbard	Crt 77	Solomon	Ans 215	Richard	Ans 232
James	Glf 620	William	Rch 267	Richard	Wrr 827
Joseph	Orn 529	William, Jr.	Ans 239	Robert	Glf 656
Maryan	Glf 632	William, Senr.	Ans 215	Sarah	Ons 172
Nancy	Crt 73	Rusk, Hanah	Brn 15A	Susanna	Cbr 681
Rachel	Crt 61	James	Brn 16A	Thomas	Mck 544
William	Crt 77	Simphronius	Brn 16	William	Ons 150
Rumly, Ann	Rwn 438	Thomas	Brn 16A	William	Prq 657
Henry	Orn 529	Russ, Anna	Bld 38	William	Stk 566
John	Orn 529			Russett, Alexander	Orn 530

Nathan	Rwn 381	Edward	Glf 679	Salls, Abram	Ird 653
Russle, David	Cbr 687	George	Brt 70	Salmon, Jacob	Stk 573
Henry	Rwn 459	John	Srr 686	Jacob	Stk 628
Jean	Cbr 688	John	Srr 687	James	Srr 692
Mary	Cbr 687	Margarett	Glf 669	Joseph	Srr 692
Richard	Mnt 497	Patrick	Srr 686	Richard	Smp 512
Russom, Wilson	Rwn 357	Thomas	Brt 72	William	Dpl 425
Russy, James	Rck 481	William	Glf 669	Sals, John	Ird 669
Rust, David	Brk 788	William	Hde 375	Salsberry, John	Rwn 376
Ezra	Brk 786	Ryans, Michael	Ans 238	Saltar, Anne	Bld 35
George	Wke 758	Rye, Deenn	Rch 245	Richard	Bld 37
Jeremiah	Grv 554	Robert	Rch 246	William	Bld 30
John	Grv 554	Ryel, John	Hlf 338	Willm., Senr.	Bld 40
John, Senr.	Grv 554	Ryland, Benoni	Ptt 279	Salter, Ann	Bfr 18
Margret	Brk 786	Ryle, John	Rwn 405	Christopher	Crt 64
Matthew	Grv 562	Ryley, James	Orn 603	James	Crt 63
Matthew	Grv 564	Rymer, Nicholas	Rwn 303	John	Ptt 228
Peter	Brk 787	Rymes, Jesse	Hlf 358	Margaret	Ptt 225
Samuel	Grv 529	Rynalds, John	Wlk 60	Peter	Prq 653
Samuel	Grv 562	Ryne, Thos.	Lnc 827	Richard	Crt 65
Samuel, Jur.	Grv 572	Ryner, Adam	Orn 530	Wilie	Orn 532
Vincent	Grv 556	Rynes, Patrick	Rch 248	William, jr.	Crt 64
Rustin, James	Rnd 338			William, Sr.	Crt 64
John (2)	Rnd 338			see Psalter	
William	Rnd 338	-- S --		Salterman, Aron	Jhn 770
Ruter, John	Brk 789			Saltonstall,	
Lewis	Ird 632			George	Cmb 358
Ruth, David	Grv 517	S..., Jehue	Glf 680	Salyer, Saml.,Jur.	Crr 137
Jacob	Rnd 338	Sack, John	Grv 559	Saml., Ser.	Crr 137
James	Rnd 339	Sadberry, John	Nwh 12	Sam, ...	Hlf 344
Sarah	Rnd 339	Stockly	Nwh 11A	Samford, William	Frn 447
Rutherford, David	Brk 789	Sadler, Henry	Lnc 850	Sammon, Edwd.	Csw 99
James	Bnc 185	Henry	Mck 536	Sammons, Rebecca	Crt 88
John	Brk 787	Jeromiah	Lnc 850	Robert	Crv 293
Thomas	Ash 87	John	Hde 376	Robert	Wke 766
Wm.	Lnc 834	Nathan	Lnc 829	see Simmons	
Rutherson, James	Csw 123	Philip	Mck 527	Sample, James	Mck 550
Ruthlidge, John	Rwn 323	Richard	Hde 377	John	Grv 559
Rutland, Abednego	Nrt 471	Samuel	Hde 377	Joseph	Mck 552
Elizabeth	Hlf 338	Stephen	Hde 376	Samuel	Bnc 189
James	Brt 72	Thomas	Hde 376	Sampson, Erving	Crv 293
John	Brt 72	William	Mck 604	Isaac	Crt 81
Meshech	Nrt 471	Wm.	Lnc 829	James	Crv 293
Reddick	Frn 468	Saeles, Thomas	Wrr 830	John	Lnc 885
Sarah	Nrt 471	Saels, William	Wrr 833	Mary	Nwh 3A
Scion	Nrt 471	Saferight, Jno.	Glf 624	Michl.	Nwh 11A
Watson	Nrt 471	Sage, Robert	Ons 182	Mrs., the Es-	
William	Hrt 726	Sagle, George	Lnc 906	tate	Smp 525
Wilson	Nrt 471	Sail, John	Stk 616	Polly	Crt 84
Rutledege, John	Srr 706	Sailor, John	Stk 572	Stephen	Hlf 342
Rutledge, Alex	Stk 610	Saint, Benjamin	Ans 216	Sams, Edmund	Bnc 188
Benjamin	Stk 569	Exum	Ans 216	James	Bnc 189
Charles	Lnc 829	Isham	Ans 226	John (2)	Bnc 189
George	Lnc 829	St. Clair, Alexan-		Rice	Rck 474
George, Junr.	Lnc 829	der	Bnc 190	William	Bnc 189
James	Srr 686	Duncan	Rch 269	Samuel, Andrew	Wrr 833
Jns.	Lnc 829	Thomas	Bnc 190	Edward	Stk 570
John	Lnc 897	St. George, Hinson	Ons 136	James, Senr.	Csw 111
Mary	Srr 686	Will.	Nwh 4	John	Stk 571
William	Stk 569	St. James, Phillip	Frn 495	John	Stk 577
William	Srr 685	St. John, James	Csw 118	Johnson	Grv 545
Rutlidge, James	Rwn 449	Richd.	Prs 216	Mordicai	Wlk 62
Johnson	Stk 569	William	Frn 490	Reaubin	Stk 570
Rutling, Reddin	Brn 16A	St. Lawrence, Eliza-		Simmons	Rwn 382
Ruttledge, William	Stk 570	beth	Cht 225	Standfield	Srr 693
Ryal, Whitmill	Ans 205	Saintsing, Bettey	Wrr 830	Samuels, Archd.	Csw 113
William	Cbr 716	John	Wrr 831	Jereh.	Csw 106
Ryall, Daniel	Crv 295	Sale, Ann	Wlk 61	Sandefer, Henry	Nrt 477
Wright	Cmb 380	Cornelious	Wlk 61	James	Wrr 829
Ryalls, Richard	Cmb 375	James	Wlk 61	John	Nrt 477
Ryals, Isham	Bld 30	Leonard	Wlk 61	William	Nrt 477
James	Bld 27	Thomas	Wlk 61	Sandeford, Noah	Cbr 704
Joseph	Cmb 376	Sales, Anthony	Wrr 830	Sanderlin, Agnes	Brt 74
Ryan, Cornelius	Brt 70	Saley, Aron	Ons 165	Calib	Cmd 103
Darby	Srr 687	Sallenger, Reuben	Mrt 410	Charles	Chw 123
David	Brt 70	Stephen	Mrt 410	David	Brt 74
Edward	Glf 669	Saller, Washington	Grv 517	Dolly	Brt 90

Elie	Cmd 101	Lawrence	Gts 279	Sanford, James	Mnt 466
Ezekial	Cmd 98	Leah	Dpl 426	James T.	Rch 257
Griffin	Cmd 99	Luke	Mnt 482	Sankston, John	Orn 537
Japath	Cmd 104	Lusey	Crr 149	Sansbury, Hilia	Chw 131
John	Cmd 109	Martha	Glf 675	Santee, John	Bld 27
Joseph	Cmd 99	Mary	Nsh 119	Michael	Orn 535
Josiah	Chw 122	Mason	Csw 146	Sap, Elizabeth	Stk 562
Josiah	Chw 123	Moses	Jns 785	John	Brk 795
Murria	Brt 74	Nimrod	Mnt 482	Milley	Stk 562
Nicolas	Dpl 413	Obadiah	Csw 113	Neeil	Rwn 369
Prince	Brt 74	Philip	Crt 82	Sapenfield, George	Rwn 350
Robert	Cmd 105	Prudence	Crt 91	John	Rwn 349
Samuel	Dpl 412	Rebh.	Ons 142	Saphel, James	Ird 637
Sanderline, Jacob	Crr 149	Reuben	Jhn 764	Sapinfield, Mi-
Sanderling, Isaac	Cmd 105	Richard	Bld 35	chael	Rwn 419
Sanders, Abraham	Ptt 266	Richard	Hlf 342	Sapp, Jesse	Rnd 344
Adam	Prs 208	Richard	Wne 862	Saratt, John	Rwn 382
Alexander	Dpl 413	Richd.	Csw 121	Joseph	Brk 798
Alexr.	Jhn 764	Richd.	Prs 192	Sarels, Jacob	Grn 614
Amry	Wlk 63	Robert	Csw 112	James	Grn 614
Aron	Csw 148	Robert	Ptt 278	Sargant, Danl.	Prs 209
Benja.	Mnt 482	Robert	Rck 464	John	Prs 201
Benjamin	Wne 872	Robert	Rwn 290	Will.	Prs 198
Benjn.	Cht 221	Sarah	Jns 793	Sargent, Shaderick	Stk 588
Benjn.	Nwh 9A	Shadrick	Brk 798	Sarjent, William	Stk 587
Bryon	Gts 279	Smith	Csw 146	Sarkins, Will.	Nwh 11
Christian	Edg 241	Solomon	Edg 240	Sarrat, Thomas	Rwn 389
Cornealus	Nsh 119	Starling	Ons 136	Sarsnett see Sasnut
Corpilas	Wlk 63	Stephen	Mnt 480	Sartler, David	Cmd 99
Daniel	Crt 91	Stephen	Rck 475	Sarzadas, Moses	Rwn 291
David	Glf 676	Susana	Rck 445	Sarzedas, Moses	Rwn 278
Disy	Wne 872	Susanna	Stk 562	Sasnut, Henritty	Edg 241
Edith	Wke 764	Taylor	Csw 146	John	Edg 239
Edward	Lnc 866	Thomas	Crt 89	Sasseman, Henry	Rwn 297
Elisha	Jhn 753	Thomas	Cht 221	Sasser, Abel	Jhn 754
Elizabeth	Crt 61	Thomas	Edg 242	Benjamin	Bld 11
Elizabeth	Ons 167	Thomas	Lnc 823	James	Wne 869
Ezekiel	Crt 83	Thomas	Nrt 479	John	Wne 864
Goolsby	Csw 112	Tilman	Cht 161	John	Wne 866
Hanah	Rck 439	Will.	Nsh 119	Joseph	Ans 213
Hardy	Wke 764	William	Ons 159	Joseph	Jhn 752
Hardy, Junr.	Wke 764	William	Ons 167	Richard	Ans 213
Henry	Gts 279	William	Rwn 334	Ruth	Wne 868
Henry	Rck 473	William	Wne 864	Stephen	Wne 867
Isaac	Edg 241	Wright	Wne 850	William	Jhn 753
Isaac	Ons 141	Sanderson, Ann	Crr 141	Satchwell, James	Hde 378
Jacob	Mnt 484	Benjamin	Jns 793	John	Hde 378
Jacob	Rwn 290	Caleb	Crr 142	Sater, John	Srr 692
James	Crt 88	Charles	Glf 688	Satherland, John	Edg 239
James	Cht 200	Elijah	Jns 793	Satterfield, Bed-
James	Lnr 22	John	Crr 138	well	Prs 191
James	Mnt 466	John	Crr 141	Elizabeth	Prs 190
James	Rck 475	Joseph	Jns 797	James	Chw 118
Jesse	Gts 279	Leml.	Crr 139	John	Prs 201
Jesse	Stk 614	Morey	Crr 141	Josiah	Prs 202
Jesse	Cht 186	Richardson	Prq 646	Thomas	Chw 114
Jessy	Ons 143	Samuel	Hde 376	William	Chw 115
Joel	Glf 681	Shadrack	Jns 793	Satterthaite, William,
John	Crt 90	Thomas	Rbs 418	Ser.	Hde 376
John	Cht 221	Thos.	Crr 138	Satterthwaite, Abram,
John	Grn 600	Thos.	Crr 141	Jur.	Hde 378
John	Glf 677	Thos., Jur.	Crr 159	Abram, Ser.	Hde 378
John	Jhn 768	Sandford, John	Wrr 828	Isaac	Hde 378
John	Nsh 119	Willis	Nrt 477	Jeremiah	Bfr 17
John	Ons 144	Sandifer, Eliza-		John	Hde 376
John	Rck 473	beth	Hrt 733	Jonathan	Hde 378
John	Rck 484	Hill	Wke 766	Samuel	Hde 378
John	Wke 766	Nancy	Hrt 733	William, Jur.	Hde 376
John	Wlk 63	Samuel	Wke 767	Wm., Ters.	Hde 378
John	Wlk 65	Sandiford, Joseph	Dpl 441	Zacheus	Hde 378
John, jr.	Grv 581	Robert	Mre 50	Satterwhite, James	Grv 553
John, Sr.	Nsh 119	Sandlin, Asa	Psq 631	Michael	Grv 507
Jonathan	Glf 675	Elisabeth	Frn 460	Stephen	Grv 507
Joseph	Crt 91	John	Frn 460	Saucerman, Daniel	Ird 671
Joseph	Gts 279	Sandy, James	Crv 233	Saul, Kindred	Jns 813
Joseph	Jns 781	Letty	Wke 766	Sauls, Abner	Jhn 763
Keziah	Wke 767	Thomas	Rnd 342	Benjamin	Wne 870

Name	Loc	Name	Loc	Name	Loc
Britain	Nrt 477	Jerry	Cht 215	Matthias	Cmd 108
David	Jhn 762	Jesse	Gts 278	Miller	Cmd 108
Henry	Nrt 477	Joel	Wne 847	Nancy	Psq 637
Henry	Wne 860	John	Edg 243	Nathan	Jns 785
John	Lnc 823	Kitchen	Edg 240	Newton	Psq 638
John	Wne 860	Lavin	Srr 692	Peter	Cmd 101
Raymon	Wne 847	Love	Dpl 436	Peter	Hde 377
Redden	Jhn 761	Loveless	Edg 240	Pharah	Cmd 96
Saunderlin, John	Trl 682	Mike	Nsh 121	Randal	Hde 377
Saunders, Abraham	Grv 569	Oliva	Ptt 239	Reuben	Cmd 102
Abraham	Prq 642	Patience	Nsh 118	Reubin	Cmd 109
Abraham	Prq 650	Randol	Nsh 119	Richard	Cmd 110
Benjamin	Hde 378	Rebecca	Dpl 413	Richard	Trl 694
Bray	Hrt 733	Sharrod	Edg 240	Roben	Trl 684
Charles	Crv 341	Tazy	Edg 243	Robert, Senr.	Trl 694
Eliz.	Csw 148	Warren	Edg 240	Samuel	Cmd 100
Elsey	Crv 287	Savern, Levi	Ird 632	Samuel	Cmd 109
Francis	Hrt 736	Savills, Seth	Cmd 106	Samuel	Psq 629
Goolsby	Csw 101	Savine, David	Crr 145	Sarah	Cmd 102
Isaac	Rnd 340	Savitz, George	Rwn 343	Stephin	Cmd 110
Jacob	Prq 647	Sawers, Jno.	Csw 140	Sylvanus	Cmd 98
James	Csw 111	Robert	Csw 140	Sylvanus	Cmd 99
James	Chw 128	Sawls, Jonathan	Wrr 833	Thomas	Cmd 93
James	Frn 468	Sawyer, Arther	Jhn 752	Thomas	Cmd 99
Jesse	Lnc 892	Benn.	Psq 626	Thomas	Cmd 101
John	Prq 648	Caleb	Psq 632	Tully	Cmd 99
John	Prq 661	Charles	Cmd 98	William	Cmd 96
John	Trl 692	Cornelius	Cmd 99	Willis	Cmd 98
John, Elder	Prq 645	Daniel	Trl 692	Willis	Hde 377
John, Sen.	Prq 645	Daniel	Trl 694	Zail	Cmd 98
John, Sen.	Prq 647	Demsey	Cmd 97	Zepaniah	Hde 377
John P.	Hrt 718	Demsey	Cmd 102	Zepheniah	Crr 143
Joseph	Grv 569	Ebenezer	Psq 635	Sawyers, William	Stk 573
Joseph	Prq 655	Elijah	Cmd 93	Saxon, John	Hlf 340
Joseph	Rnd 342	Elisha	Cmd 99	Saxton, Afeas	Crr 162
Joshua	Prq 663	Elisha	Trl 684	Thomas	Rnd 344
Josiah	Prq 654	Elizabeth	Cmd 98	Sayer, Absalom	Rwn 460
Julius	Csw 101	Enoch	Cmd 106	Sayers, Wm. Smith	Wne 871
Leah	Crv 315	Evin	Cmd 100	Sayne, Fredrick	Rwn 428
Mary	Bfr 18	Fredk. B.	Psq 635	George	Rwn 428
Mary	Prq 653	Fredrick	Psq 638	Jasper	Rwn 428
Matthew	Lnc 892	Griffin	Psq 631	John	Rwn 428
Micajah	Frn 468	Griffin	Trl 682	Joseph	Rwn 428
Miles	Rnd 341	Hollowell	Psq 630	Scaate, Jeams	Crr 154
Nathan	Hrt 701	Isaac	Cmd 102	Wm. Jer.	Crr 154
Nathan	Hrt 718	Isaac, Sen.	Cmd 100	Scaff, Joseph	Hlf 342
Nathan	Prq 645	Jabeth	Cmd 99	Scaging, Jno.	Csw 143
Nathan	Prq 660	Jabeth	Cmd 100	Scales, Abraham	Stk 579
Nathaniel	Frn 468	Jacob	Crr 137	Absalom	Rck 462
Phebe	Psq 635	James	Psq 626	Daniel	Rck 490
Priscilla	Hrt 722	Joab	Trl 694	David	Rck 478
Reuben	Mrt 388	Job	Cht 166	Henry	Rck 438
Richard	Prq 645	Jobe	Cmd 93	James	Rck 490
Robert	Csw 101	Joel	Cmd 96	John	Rck 490
Sally	Bfr 18	John	Cmd 96	Joseph	Rck 439
Sarah	Prq 662	John	Cmd 99	Mary	Rck 479
Stephen	Prq 651	John	Cht 209	Nathaniel	Stk 584
Thomas	Prq 647	John	Crr 153	Nathl.	Rck 479
Vinson	Frn 466	John	Hde 377	Thomas	Rck 490
William	Bfr 17	John	Psq 637	Scalf, John	Srr 690
William	Frn 467	John	Psq 639	Lewis	Srr 690
William	Frn 473	Joseph	Cmd 106	Scallion, Joab	Srr 693
William	Hrt 722	Joseph	Cmd 110	Scarber, Ayston	Crr 152
William	Psq 635	Joshua	Cmd 96	Chesterfor	Cmd 104
William	Prq 653	Keziah	Trl 692	Ezekiah	Crr 166
Saurey, Edward	Nrt 479	Lemuel	Cmd 96	Fanney	Crr 165
Henry	Nrt 475	Lemuel	Cmd 106	Nancy	Crr 166
Mildred	Nrt 479	Lemuel	Hlf 342	Scarbor, Auston	Crr 166
Sauther, Michael	Brk 797	Lemuel	Prq 657	Jeorge	Crr 166
Savage, Allen	Edg 242	Levin	Trl 694	John	Crr 166
Arthur	Nwh 7	Levy	Cmd 98	Patsey	Crr 166
Betty	Rnd 341	Lewis	Ans 224	Rosemond	Crr 167
Canvas	Rnd 343	Lodrick	Cmd 100	Scarborough, David	Grn 591
Francis	Nwh 7	Lucy	Cmd 93	Elisabeth	Lnc 864
Frederick	Edg 239	Malichi, Jur.	Cmd 99	Elizabeth	Crt 59
Hambleton	Srr 688	Mark	Cmd 100	Enos	Edg 175
James	Dpl 422	Masick	Crr 148	Enos	Edg 239

Hardee	Edg	241
James	Rck	473
James, Majr.	Edg	239
Jeorge	Crr	165
Joshua	Grn	596
Martha	Grn	591
Peter	Lnc	850
Sidney	Grn	591
William, Senr.	Mnt	492
Scarborow, Nathan	Dpl	415
Scarbrough, Benja-		
min	Mnt	487
Edward	Mnt	488
James	Mnt	487
John	Mnt	486
John	Wke	767
Miles	Cht	168
Saml., Senr.	Wke	767
Samuel	Wke	766
William, Jur.	Mnt	487
Scares, Caleb	Crr	155
Scarf, Israel	Crt	56
Scarloth, John	Orn	538
Scarlott, Eliza-		
beth	Orn	538
John (2)	Orn	538
John	Orn	540
Stephen	Orn	538
Thomas	Orn	540
Scars, Elizabeth	Orn	540
Henry	Orn	538
Mary	Orn	538
Scat see Seat		
Scavils, Solomon	Hlf	342
Scay, James	Brt	78
Sceter see Suter		
Schench, G.L. John	Edg	175
G.L. John	Edg	239
Schon, David	Crt	67
Schoolfield, Jesse	Ptt	242
William	Ptt	293
Schoolley, Samuel	Stk	618
Schultz, Samuel	Stk	625
Schutchens, Lydda	Edg	242
Mary	Edg	242
Samuel	Edg	241
Thomas	Edg	242
Schuttz, Samuel	Stk	599
Scidmore, Abraham	Srr	691
Abraham, Ser.	Srr	691
John	Brk	791
John	Srr	691
Scipper, Abram	Brn	14A
Isaac	Brn	14
Jesse	Brn	14A
John	Brn	14A
Moses	Brn	14A
Urius	Brn	14
Scoby, Lucy	Orn	539
Scofield, John	Glf	640
Scogans, Sally	Cmb	391
Scoggin, John	Wke	761
Scoggins, Anna	Rth	142
Benjn.	Rth	142
Francis	Rth	145
Jemima	Ptt	268
Joseph	Rth	141
Nicholas	Rth	142
Scogin, John	Prs	191
Scold, Joseph	Brk	793
Samuel	Brk	796
Scoles, John	Cbr	681
William	Hlf	342
Scoot, Michel	Crr	153
Nathan	Wlk	64
Samuel	Wlk	64
William	Glf	634

Scot, Hector	Hde	375
Henry	Hde	378
Nancy	Mre	62
Scote, John	Mrt	411
Luke	Mrt	411
Nancy	Mrt	411
Randol	Mrt	410
Scotland, ..., of		
Colour	Hde	378
Scott, ..., the Es-		
tate of	Smp	523
Abraham	Brk	793
Abraham	Hlf	344
Abram	Psq	639
Adam	Crv	255
Adam	Glf	622
Alexander	Cbr	678
Anemerah	Brk	791
Axiom	Cmb	392
Cason	Crv	261
Charles	Wne	870
Daniel	Rnd	341
Daniel	Srr	691
David, Junr.	Nrt	479
David, Senr.	Nrt	477
Demsey	Psq	630
Dorothy	Cbr	706
Edward	Srr	691
Edward	Srr	692
Elizabeth	Ons	148
Ellender	Ons	158
George	Brk	791
Hardy	Nrt	479
Henry	Csw	140
Henry	Orn	530
Henry	Prq	652
Isaac	Nrt	477
Isaiah	Ird	653
Isham	Hlf	342
Israel, free		
Negro	Edg	241
James	Bnc	190
James	Cbr	676
James	Cbr	698
James	Cht	222
James	Ird	613
James (2)	Psq	626
James	Psq	626
Jesse	Srr	692
John	Cbr	706
John	Csw	121
John	Cht	202
John	Crv	259
John	Hlf	338
John	Hrt	702
John	Hrt	736
John	Ird	632
John	Ird	642
John	Ird	663
John	Jhn	776
John	Nwh	1A
John	Orn	533
John	Rnd	343
John	Rwn	358
John	Rth	142
John	Rth	143
John	Wke	762
John, J.	Rnd	343
Jos.	Csw	130
Jos.	Psq	640
Joseph	Bnc	189
Joseph	Chw	119
Joseph	Prq	643
Joseph	Prq	648
Joseph, Sen.	Chw	129
Joshua	Ons	136
Levin	Ons	143

Lydia	Nrt	479
Manuel	Hlf	342
Margt.	Lnc	826
Marmaduke	Psq	626
Natthaniel	Ans	200
Nehemiah	Smp	518
Nelly	Ons	154
Obed.	Ons	173
Obed	Ons	174
Prissey	Hlf	340
Richard	Hlf	342
Richd.	Csw	139
Robert	Csw	134
Robert	Cmb	386
Robert	Psq	631
Robert, Esqr.	Bld	23
Samuel	Orn	531
Samuel	Psq	630
Samuel	Psq	631
Solomon	Ash	88
Solomon	Rnd	341
Stephen	Nrt	477
Stephen	Psq	632
Susanna	Mnt	483
Thomas	Brk	797
Thomas	Grv	581
Thomas	Hlf	342
Thomas	Orn	495
Thos.	Wlk	65
William	Grv	507
William	Ird	641
William	Lnc	825
William	Mck	536
William	Orn	536
William	Psq	626
William	Rck	474
William, free		
Negro	Edg	241
see Scote, Stott		
Screws, Benjamin	Ons	174
David	Dpl	415
James	Dpl	416
James	Nsh	119
John	Nsh	121
Joseph	Bld	22
Joseph	Dpl	416
Polly	Ons	175
Thomas	Rch	246
William	Ons	166
William	Rch	250
Scribner, Susana	Csw	148
Scriven, Thomas	Bld	35
Scrivner, Dolley	Wke	762
Lewis	Wke	762
Scrivnor, Benjamin	Rwn	401
Scroggs, David	Ird	641
James	Ird	652
Jeromiah	Ird	642
John	Ird	641
Scrug see Soyrug		
Scrugs, Richd. (2)	Rth	141
Scuday, Augustin E.	Rnd	344
Scuder, Moses	Srr	692
Scule, John	Brn	13A
Scull, Elisha	Hrt	702
Elizabeth	Hrt	714
Scurlock, Joseph	Grn	617
Scurry, Susana	Rck	453
Sea see Star		
Seabaugh, Jacob	Lnc	822
Seabolt, Adam	Ash	88
Jacob	Ash	87
John	Lnc	870
Seaborn, Frederick	Nrt	479
Joseph	Hde	377
Seabrook, Daniel	Hde	377
Seabry, Moses	Mck	526

Seafard, Leonard	Lnc 858	Sebrel, Joshua	Edg 243	Parish	Cht 168		
Seagle, John	Lnc 822	Sebret, John Dani-		Stephen	Cbr 696		
John, Senr.	Lnc 822	el	Grn 610	William	Lnc 892		
Seal, Jeromiah	Mnt 481	Secal, Sarah	Cmd 96	William	Rth 145		
Mollay	Mre 61	Sechler, Rudolph	Rwn 343	see Seff			
Solomon	Mnt 480	Secret see Suret		Sell, Jonathan	Stk 616		
Seales, Joseph	Stk 587	Secrignt, Abraham	Stk 585	Jonathan, Ser.	Stk 616		
Signe	Cbr 689	Secrist, Andrew	Mck 584	Philip	Mnt 515		
Sealey, George	Brk 797	Christian	Rwn 358	Winney	Wrr 829		
Seals, Joshua	Ans 206	Frederick	Rwn 357	Sellars, Abraham	Smp 535		
Peter	Rnd 340	George	Rwn 357	Ann	Brn 14A		
Thomas	Brt 76	J. Fredrick	Rwn 357	Archabald	Rbs 417		
Wm.	Mrt 410	Jacob	Mck 581	Conrod	Lnc 880		
Zachary	Rnd 340	Jacob	Mck 594	Edward	Brk 797		
Seamon see Duncun		Jacob	Rwn 358	Elijah	Brn 15A		
Seamons, Mary	Frn 453	John, (Cap.)	Mck 578	Elijah	Dpl 419		
Seamore, Daniel	Cmd 105	Thomas	Rwn 357	Elisha	Brn 21A		
Elizabeth	Cmd 105	Sedberry, George,		George	Lnc 821		
Peter	Crr 150	Junr.	Mnt 492	Isaac	Cht 199		
Robert	Ird 663	George, Senr.	Mnt 492	Isaac	Rth 144		
Seane, Owen	Rwn 454	John	Mnt 492	Jacob	Smp 528		
Searborow, Kinchen	Smp 519	Sedbury, Asa	Ons 160	James	Brn 21A		
Searcy, Richd.	Rth 144	James	Ons 160	James	Brk 791		
Rueben	Rth 144	See, Barrel	Rth 141	James	Brk 794		
Thomas	Orn 495	Seears, David	Mre 56	James	Cht 173		
William	Rnd 340	Seebrook, Thomas	Hde 375	John	Brk 790		
William	Rth 144	Seego, Joseph	Ans 226	John	Nwh 6A		
Willie	Rth 144	Seegoe, John	Ans 201	John	Smp 534		
see Sercy		Seelove, Philip	Rwn 375	Joseph	Smp 534		
Seares, John	Crr 154	Seeman, James	Frn 493	La...l	Cht 173		
see Scares		Seemore, John	Prs 198	Lewis	Brn 14A		
Searles, Edward	Bfr 17	Seers, James	Ans 229	Mathw.	Brn 19		
William	Crv 285	Seff, Ewell	Glf 670	Robert	Brk 792		
Searlet, John, J.	Rnd 344	Seffrid, Charles	Cbr 715	Robert	Brk 794		
John, Sen.	Rnd 344	George	Cbr 715	Robert	Brk 797		
Searlock, Sarah	Cht 157	Sefred, William	Cbr 714	Robert	Cht 166		
William	Cht 157	Segars, Southward	Smp 494	Simon	Nwh 7A		
Searls, Covernton	Bfr 17	Segers, Josiah	Wke 765	Tho.	Brn 16		
Sears, Abner	Wrr 831	Segle, Adam	Lnc 907	Tho.	Brn 18		
Barbe	Cht 202	Segrave, Feba	Wrr 830	Willid	Brn 18A		
Celia	Crv 329	Segraves, Daniel	Mnt 487	Sellers, Abraham	Smp 534		
Christian	Rwn 357	Henry	Wke 764	Arthur	Nsh 120		
George	Crv 239	Jacob	Wke 763	Catherine	Bld 48		
Henry	Wke 767	Jacob	Wke 764	Elizabeth	Rth 145		
Isham	Wrr 831	John (2)	Ans 234	James	Nsh 120		
Jacob	Rwn 358	John	Wke 764	John	Bld 50		
James, Senr.	Grv 553	Renchen	Mnt 465	John	Nsh 119		
John	Crv 237	Stephen	Wke 763	Joseph	Nsh 119		
John	Grv 553	William	Ans 226	Millifred	Bld 5		
John	Wke 762	William	Wke 763	Sampson	Rch 243		
Joseph	Grv 554	William	Wke 764	Sampson	Rch 266		
Joseph	Wke 762	Segrist, John	Mre 40	Silus	Rch 257		
Timothy	Lnr 23	Sehler, Fredrick	Rwn 338	Thomas	Orn 531		
William	Grv 517	Seigler, Philip	Ash 87	Sells, Enos	Rnd 344		
William	Grv 553	Sein, Jacob	Lnc 892	Selvey, Edward	Rwn 445		
William	Wke 766	Sein, Henry E.	Gts 279	Semmons see Simmons			
see Scars, Seears,		Sekia, Lott	Cmd 93	Semms, Job	Lnc 825		
Seirs		Selah, Joseph	Nsh 119	Semoore, Peter	Wne 848		
Searsey, Aquilla	Wke 763	Rebeckeh	Nsh 120	Sems see Sims			
Seary, John	Stk 573	Selby, Burridge	Hde 376	Senclar, Noah	Cht 157		
Seat, James	Nrt 475	Elizabeth	Hde 377	Senior, Peter	Rwn 363		
Joseph	Hlf 342	Henry	Hde 375	Sensing, John	Mck 606		
Nardy	Hlf 342	Jeremiah	Hde 377	Sentel, Samuel	Wrr 832		
Salley	Wke 766	John	Hde 377	Senter, Freeman	Wrr 832		
Thos.	Cht 170	Margan	Hde 376	Henry	Cmb 390		
Seatton, John	Rnd 344	Nathan	Hde 376	John	Srr 710		
Seavell, Edward	Grv 583	Samuel, Ser.	Hde 379	Stephen	Cmb 391		
Seawell, Henry	Wke 777	Samuel, Sen.	Hde 376	Stephen	Lnc 844		
James	Frn 482	Samuel, Ters.	Hde 376	William	Cmb 391		
Joseph	Frn 482	William	Brk 794	Senters, John	Srr 693		
Seay, William	Hrt 718	Self, Baxter	Orn 539	Seoles see Scoles			
see Scay		Bradley	Cht 170	Seps, Paul	Lnc 881		
Sebastian, Benjn.	Wlk 62	David	Cbr 695	Sercy, George	Cmb 375		
Elisha	Wlk 62	Jacob, (Junr.)	Cbr 695	Sergant, Jacob	Glf 629		
William	Wlk 61	Jacob, (Senr.)	Cbr 695	James	Csw 116		
Sebeston, David	Crt 78	Jobe	Frn 460	Sermon, Ann	Hde 377		
William	Crt 75	John	Lnc 893	David	Hde 377		

Joseph, Jur.	Hde	377	Samuel, Senr.	Nrt	479	Sharlington, Ann	Bfr	23
Joseph, Ser.	Hde	377	Tamar	Psq	630	Sharlocke, Samuel	Brt	78
Mary	Hde	377	William	Bfr	17	Stevins	Brt	78
Peter	Hde	377	Willis	Psq	638	Thomas	Brt	78
see Surman			Seymon, John	Lnc	885	Sharon see Shearrin	
Sertin, James	Wlk	62	Seymore, John	Wne	846	Sharp, Aron	Orn	533
Jobe	Wrr	830	John, jr.	Wne	846	Boston	Orn	533
John	Wrr	830	Thomas	Wne	871	Catharine	Rck	488
Serug, Bettey	Wrr	833	Shaccleford, Fran-			Ezekiel	Cbr	680
Charles	Wrr	829	cis	Rbs	419	Jacob	Hrt	714
Server, Henry	Orn	535	Shackleford, Brina	Crt	73	James	Mck	542
Sesames, Nathan	Brt	74	Francis	Cmb	393	James	Nrt	477
Seslow, George	Rwn	375	George	Ons	182	Jemima	Hrt	702
see Seelove			James	Crt	56	John	Mck	600
Sessions, Joseph	Bld	6	Nancy	Grn	592	John	Nrt	477
Joseph	Brn	20	Stephen	Crt	66	John, (Majr.	Mck	569
Richard	Smp	520	William	Ons	175	Joseph	Orn	493
Thomas, Esqr.	Bld	5	Willoughby	Grn	592	Joseph	Rwn	454
Sessoms, Isaac	Smp	531	Shaddock, Barton	Rck	472	Joshua	Edg	240
Jacob	Smp	531	Hardy	Rck	474	Mary	Rnd	343
Mary	Bld	41	Rebecah	Rck	474	Peter	Orn	533
Mary	Smp	531	Shaddy, Jacob	Orn	533	Richard	Mck	544
Samuel	Cmb	370	John	Orn	595	Richard	Rck	490
Sarey	Ptt	235	Shade, Thomas	Csw	123	Thomas	Brk	791
Solomon	Smp	531	Shadeing, James	Wne	848	Thomas	Edg	241
Sessums, Alexander	Edg	239	Shader, Mary	Csw	139	see Tharp	
George	Hrt	714	Shadmon, William	Wrr	831	Sharpe, Abnor	Ird	675
James	Edg	239	Shadrach, Thomas	Wke	766	Abnor	Ird	673
John	Edg	240	Shafer, John	Rwn	291	Adam	Orn	532
John	Hrt	702	Shaffer, Jacob	Rnw	412	Aron	Orn	535
Josiah	Edg	240	Shafner, George	Glf	628	Daniel	Rwn	412
Richard	Edg	241	Shake, Jeromiah	Brk	795	Grove	Jhn	774
Robert	Edg	240	Shaler, Daniel	Wsh	714	Henry	Jhn	747
Solomon	Edg	175	Shalloon, John	Srr	711	James	Ird	616
Solomon	Edg	239	Shambles, John	Stk	570	James, Cap.	Mck	549
William	Hrt	707	Shamblin, John	Stk	611	James M.	Ird	617
Sest, Joshua	Crt	80	William	Srr	693	John	Ird	617
Sethers, John	Rwn	338	Shambling, William	Stk	606	Joseph	Ird	613
Setliff, Sarah	Srr	691	William, Jr.	Stk	607	Nelly	Orn	539
Setser, Adam	Brk	794	Shamburger, John	Mre	49	Richd., Jur.	Rck	490
Settars see Sellars			Peter	Mre	49	Samuel	P⌐k	491
Settors, John	Mre	57	Shamwell, Elisha	Rwn	382	Silas	Ird	617
Setzer, Jacob	Lnc	870	Isaac	Rwn	382	Thomas, Junr.	Rwn	369
John	Lnc	870	James	Grv	527	Turner	Ans	235
John	Rwn	343	Jonathan	Rwn	382	William	Ans	222
Sevain see Swain			Mary	Grv	562	William	Ird	617
Sevall, John	Cmd	106	Samuel	Grv	562	William	Rck	490
Seve, Wm. Cock	Wlk	64	Shane, Levy	Orn	536	Sharples, Will.	Nwh	9A
Severe, Charles	Bnc	188	Shanee, William	Orn	536	Sharrod, John	Edg	241
Severn, John	Crt	75	Shankle, Abraham	Mnt	497	Joseph	Edg	241
Sevils, Robinson	Psq	627	George	Mnt	497	Sharrow, James	Rth	142
Sevims, John	Wlk	63	Jacob	Mnt	497	Shas, Jo	Srr	704
Sevrit, John	Mck	549	John	Mnt	497	Shatterly, Michael	Glf	647
Sewall, Elizabeth	Rwn	343	Valentine	Mnt	497	Shaver, Coonrod	Glf	638
Sewell, Asay	Mre	72	Shanks, Charles	Orn	532	Frederick	Mck	606
Bihu	Mre	70	James	Mck	599	Jacob	Glf	648
Charles	Mre	70	Thomas	Csw	125	John	Cbr	686
John	Mre	50	Thomas	Csw	139	John	Ird	616
Lewis	Mre	69	Thomas	Rbs	419	John	Rwn	310
Lewis, Jun.	Mre	70	Shannanhouse, James			John	Rwn	349
Mary	Mre	72	L.	Psq	628	Joseph	Ird	619
see Lewell, Sual			Susana	Psq	627	Joseph, Junr.	Ird	619
Sexton, Absalom	Cmb	372	Shannen, Charles	Cmd	109	Tunis	Mck	606
Anderson	Wke	762	Shanning, Charles	Cmd	100	William	Glf	638
Britain	Mnt	486	Shannon, Daniel	Crr	137	William	Glf	646
Dempsey	Wsh	710	Henery	Crr	148	William	Glf	648
Fredrick	Rth	145	James	Cmb	358	Shaw, Adamson	Ird	633
James	Mnt	486	James	Mck	590	Allen	Nwh	10A
John	Psq	637	Jms.	Lnc	834	Anguish	Mre	66
John	Wke	774	Levi	Crr	148	Angus	Bld	30
Mark	Nrt	477	William	Glf	627	Angus	Cmb	374
Mark	Wke	763	Shape, William	Ans	237	Angus	Cmb	375
Obadiah	Wke	764	Sharborough, Per-			Angus	Rbs	420
Peter	Cht	208	thenia	Glf	636	Archibald	Bld	19
Robt.	Psq	639	Sharbrough, Jehu	Psq	639	B. John	Wke	766
Samuel	Trl	694	Share, Michael	Rwn	445	Benjamin	Glf	671
Samuel, Junr.	Nrt	479	Shares, John	Srr	688	Daniel (2)	Cmb	375

Daniel	Mre 66	Shearman, Benjamin	Orn 532	Shelton, Ben	Stk 585
Daniel	Rbs 420	Charles	Csw 121	Beverley	Ans 217
Daniel, Jur.	Bld 11	Charles	Grv 580	Burwell	Ans 232
Danl.	Bld 32	William	Csw 121	Burwell	Hlf 342
Dashee	Cmb 375	Shearmon, Michael	Grv 559	David	Csw 112
David	Wke 763	Shearrin, Aaron	Wrr 831	Edmond	Prs 196
Duncan	Cmb 367	Amey	Wrr 832	Edward	Stk 570
Duncan	Cmb 377	Bettey	Wrr 832	Elijah	Rck 440
Edward	Cmb 387	Daniel	Wrr 831	Elizabeth	Bnc 188
Elliott	Hlf 340	Fredrick	Wrr 832	George	Bnc 189
Gabriel	Wke 764	Gardner	Wrr 831	George	Stk 613
Garden	Rnd 341	Hardridge	Wrr 831	James	Csw 124
Henry	Hlf 340	Isham	Wrr 832	Jerry	Srr 692
Hugh	Wke 761	John	Wrr 832	John	Rck 455
Hugh, Jur.	Glf 630	Lewis	Wrr 832	Joseph	Rth 144
Hugh, Senr.	Glf 630	Mosses	Wrr 833	Joseph	Stk 595
James	Hlf 340	Sterling	Wrr 831	Ma.	Stk 613
James	Nwh 6A	William (2)	Wrr 831	Martin	Bnc 188
James	Srr 689	William (2)	Wrr 832	Rabecca	Csw 101
James	Wke 761	Zackeriah	Wrr 832	Roderick	Bnc 189
Jennet	Cmb 375	Shears, George	Hrt 714	Ruth	Hlf 342
John	Bfr 18	George	Hrt 726	Salley	Wke 777
John	Brt 78	James	Rth 146	Sarah	Srr 688
John	Bld 29	John	Hrt 714	Spencer	Lnc 850
John	Cmb 375	Shearwood, Daniel		Thomas	Csw 100
John	Cmb 376	(2)	Glf 627	Thomas	Csw 111
John	Glf 671	Hugh	Glf 620	Thomas	Dpl 437
John	Orn 532	Sheats, Andrew	Ash 88	William	Edg 239
John	Psq 629	Sheawood, Thos.	Crr 152	William	Rth 144
John	Rnd 340	Sheecraft, Wm. C.	Hrt 727	William	Stk 572
John (2)	Rbs 420	Sheek, Adam	Rwn 460	William, Jr.	Stk 585
John	Wke 761	Sheen, Rebecker	Lnr 23	see Shel...n	
John	Rbs 421	Sheering, Abner	Hlf 342	Shelty, Peter	Lnc 829
John B.	Wke 766	Sheerly, Nancy	Hlf 344	Shenie, James	Psq 636
Joseph	Orn 539	Richard	Edg 240	Shenn see Shinn	
Joseph	Wke 761	Sheets, Andrew	Rnd 341	Shepard, Benjamin	Ons 172
Joseph, Junr.	Wke 761	Andrew	Rwn 439	Cipian	Ons 172
Lucy	Cmb 375	Frederick	Rnd 344	Daniel	Ons 170
Malcolm	Cmb 377	Jacob	Rwn 434	David	Crt 87
Malcom	Bld 19	John	Rnd 341	Elizabeth	Crt 83
Malcom	Rbs 420	Martin	Rwn 439	George	Ons 167
Maren	Cmb 358	see Streets		George	Ons 174
Murdoch	Rbs 421	Sheffield, Ephraim	Nrt 475	John	Ons 167
Neal	Rch 261	John	Rbs 418	Mariam	Crt 75
Neill	Cmb 376	Josiah	Nrt 475	Stephen	Ons 173
Norman	Cmb 363	Shehorn, John	Ans 210	Thomas	Dpl 399
Norman	Cmb 374	Morris	Mck 586	Shephard, John	Mre 63
Norman	Rch 253	Morris, Jur.	Mck 587	John	Ons 167
Patrick	Glf 667	Peggy	Mck 588	John, Jun.	Mre 68
Peter	Cmb 389	William	Ans 218	John, Sen.	Mre 66
Robert	Hlf 340	William	Nrt 477	Shepherd, Bird	Rch 251
Rodrick	Rch 244	Sheilds, Enos	Bnc 188	Charls	Rnd 341
Sanda	Brn 15	John	Stk 616	Cyprian	Psq 628
Simson	Wke 762	Shel...n, Saml.	Rck 492	Isaac	Ans 236
Stephen	Ons 181	Shelby, Even	Mck 572	Jacob	Ans 236
Thomas	Ans 239	Jacob	Ans 217	Jacob	Srr 688
Thomas	Hlf 340	Jonathan	Ans 208	James	Bfr 17
Widow	Rch 270	Sarah	Cbr 676	John	Gts 278
William	Cht 203	Thomas	Mck 585	John	Rck 481
William	Glf 633	see Shelly		Jordan	Ptt 227
William	Ird 637	Shelfer, Jesse	Jns 791	Peter	Rnd 341
William	Ons 181	Shelhouse, John	Cbr 703	Reading	Grn 614
William	Srr 689	Shell, Fredrick	Ash 89	Robert	Rch 250
William	Wke 761	Gasper	Lnc 906	Robert	Rch 267
William	Wke 763	Gasper, Senr.	Lnc 906	Stephanus	Grn 599
William	Wke 766	Henry	Lnc 870	Thomas	Ans 236
William	Wke 777	Joseph	Rwn 419	Thomas	Rch 267
Zachariah	Wke 764	Michael	Lnc 907	Valentine	Wne 855
She...her, John R.	Prq 652	Simon	Ash 89	William	Ans 236
Shealds, Able	Stk 620	Stephen	Wrr 832	William	Ird 663
Shearer, Christian	Ash 87	Shelley, Mary	Lnc 857	William	Lnc 880
Jacob	Glf 661	Shellton, John.	Stk 585	William	Stk 607
John	Glf 669	Shelly, Benjamin	Ird 615	William, Jr.	Ans 236
Sarah	Ash 88	John	Glf 684	Zeal	Glf 671
Shearing, Jno.,		Joseph	Ird 618	Sheple, Charles	Rck 473
Junr.	Wke 766	Richard	Ird 615	Sheppard, Benjn.	Nwh 8
John	Wke 766	Shelman, Thos.	Crr 156	David	Orn 495

Jacob	Nwh 5	Joel	Nrt 477	Jacob	Rwn 349		
James	Rwn 383	John	Mrt 408	Shoat, John	Bnc 189		
John	Brk 796	John	Nrt 477	Sabret, Senr.	Wlk 64		
John	Mnt 466	Lewis	Mrt 408	Sabrit	Wlk 63		
John	Rwn 401	Michel	Nrt 479	Shober, Godlip	Stk 570		
Thomas	Bnc 188	Randol	Mrt 410	Gotlieb	Stk 626		
Thomas	Edg 241	Roberte	Mrt 408	Shoe, John	Cbr 710		
William	Crv 229	Thomas	Frn 489	Philip	Glf 643		
Shepperd, David	Cmb 358	Sherwood, Benjamin	Hlf 344	Shoemaker, Ran-			
James	Orn 536	see Sheawood		dolph	Ird 627		
James	Rwn 389	Sheshan, M. Miles	Brt 78	Talton	Ird 627		
John	Orn 539	Shesson, John	Trl 670	Thomas	Ird 627		
John, Junr.	Rwn 389	Shewcraft, Abram	Hrt 721	William	Ird 626		
John, Senr.	Rwn 389	James	Hrt 726	Shoeman, Christian	Rwn 298		
Lewis	Csw 124	William	Hrt 722	John	Rwn 310		
Samuel	Orn 539	Shewmake, Susana	Glf 665	Shoes, Ann	Nsh 118		
William	Grv 533	Shickle, John	Glf 678	Shoffener, Freder-			
William	Orn 536	Shields, Benjamin	Mre 42	ick	Orn 533		
William	Orn 539	Cornelius	Mre 39	Shofner, Martin	Orn 533		
Sheppherd, Agnes	Rth 144	David	Mck 522	Michael	Orn 534		
James	Wlk 62	Elizabeth	Wsh 714	Peter	Orn 534		
John	Wlk 62	Reubin	Stk 621	Sholar, Benjamin	Brt 78		
John	Wlk 62	Rubin	Mre 69	James	Brt 78		
Lewis	Wlk 62	Thomas	Hlf 342	Joshua	Brt 76		
Robert	Wlk 62	William	Mck 569	Levi	Dpl 414		
Stephen	Wlk 63	Shifter, Christo-		Solomon	Dpl 414		
William	Ash 88	pher	Brk 794	Thomas	Dpl 414		
Sherbrough, Luke	Psq 632	Shilling, Elisa-		Sholars, Ephraim	Nwh 5		
Sherer, John	Chw 113	beth	Crv 343	John	Nwh 6		
Shergold, Wm.	Crr 147	Shilly, George	Glf 678	Moses	Nwh 5		
Sherlin, Isham	Mck 591	Shin, Samuel	Wlk 64	Sholders, Anny	Cht 204		
James	Mck 554	Shine, Daniel	Jns 811	Sholey, David	Grn 611		
John, Senr.	Mck 591	Franck	Jns 781	Sholtz, Gadfrey	Stk 625		
Sherlock, Michl.	Nwh 9	James	Hlf 340	Sholven, Anthony	Psq 627		
Sherlon, John,		James	Jns 811	Shook, Andrew	Lnc 880		
Junr.	Mck 591	John	Jns 781	Frederick	Lnc 881		
Sherly, Michael	Smp 513	William	Lnr 21	Jacob	Bnc 189		
Sherman, Edwd.	Nwh 4A	Shines, Daniel	Frn 486	John	Lnc 884		
Robert	Brk 792	Francis	Lnr 21	Shoole, Christian	Rwn 389		
Shermer, Peter	Srr 691	Shingleton, Beth-		Shooler, Adam	Rwn 358		
Sherod, Elisabeth	Crv 311	iah	Bfr 17	Michael	Rwn 358		
Jordan	Nsh 120	Lurreaney	Ons 181	Peter	Rwn 358		
Sherrard, Benjamin	Wne 847	William	Brn 16	Shools, George	Rwn 401		
Robt.	Wne 848	William	Bfr 17	Shoot, George	Lnc 906		
William	Wne 847	Willibough	Bfr 17	Shoote, James	Brk 794		
Sherrel, Jehu	Grv 569	Shinn, Catherine	Cbr 688	Shope, Jacob	Stk 572		
Sherrell, William	Brk 796	John	Srr 689	John	Stk 572		
Sherrill, Aaron	Lnc 863	Joseph	Cbr 686	Shopshire, John	Rck 459		
Adam	Lnc 880	Levi	Srr 689	Shore, David	Srr 691		
Alexander	Lnc 872	Shinpock, Lawrence	Mnt 521	Frederick	Srr 691		
Babel	Lnc 870	Ship, Anne	Smp 507	Heney	Stk 573		
Benjamin	Lnc 885	John	Ptt 241	Henry	Stk 605		
David	Lnc 880	Reading	Ptt 242	Henry, Sr.	Stk 627		
Elisha	Lnc 863	Robert	Srr 693	Jacob	Stk 572		
Enos	Lnc 881	Thomas	Stk 573	John	Stk 571		
Ephraim	Lnc 886	William	Ptt 242	Lewis	Hlf 338		
Evan	Lnc 886	Shipman, D., Minors		Peter	Stk 572		
Jacob	Lnc 870	of	Bld 11	Peter	Stk 577		
Jacob (2)	Lnc 881	Edward	Bnc 188	Rieuben	Srr 689		
James	Brk 790	James	Bld 18	Simeon	Wlk 62		
Joseph	Lnc 881	John	Rth 145	Shores, Frederick	Stk 572		
Joshua	Lnc 863	Shipp, Tiller	Wke 764	Short, Aron	Rck 457		
Moses	Lnc 863	William	Wke 762	Barwell	Wke 763		
Moses	Lnc 880	Shipton, Sarah	Rwn 383	Charles	Rth 142		
Nicholas	Lnc 880	Shirer, John	Ash 88	Daniel	Stk 570		
Rubin	Lnc 885	Shirley, Daniel	Psq 634	David	Lnc 898		
Thomas	Brk 792	Shirly, Marian	Rth 142	Jacob	Wrr 830		
Ute	Brk 794	Moses	Lnr 23	James	Hlf 340		
William	Brk 794	Thomas	Rth 144	John	Nrt 477		
William	Brk 796	Shive, Martin	Cbr 701	Jonan.	Glf 673		
Sherrod, Allen	Mrt 411	Philip	Cbr 703	Josiah	Wke 763		
Arthur	Nrt 477	Shivers, Jesse	Ptt 230	Judy	Rck 456		
Benjamin	Frn 448	Jonas	Ptt 230	Landman	Wke 763		
Henry	Nrt 477	Thomas	Edg 240	Manny	Wke 765		
James	Frn 458	Shivey, William	Smp 536	Moses	Rck 457		
James	Nrt 475	Shoaf, Christian	Rwn 349	Moses, Jur.	Rck 457		
Jas.	Mrt 410	Henry	Rwn 350	Needham	Wke 763		

Richard	Wrr 829	John	Mck 583	John	Nrt 479
Samuel	Glf 683	Sibly, Elijah	Mck 585	Lemuel	Nrt 477
Samuel	Stk 571	Robert	Mck 585	Silman, Benjn.	Rth 145
Sarah	Nrt 479	Siclove, Ahart	Rwn 376	Sils, David	Nsh 121
Sihon	Wke 763	John	Rwn 376	Silva, Antonia C.	Nwh 1A
William	Cht 206	Siddle, Job	Csw 106	Silver, Clous	Crr 159
William (2)	Rth 142	Siddon, Joseph	Rwn 434	Milly	Hlf 342
William, Junr.	Nrt 477	Side, John	Mnt 514	Silvers, Jacob	Brk 796
William, Senr.	Nrt 479	Sides, Andrew	Cbr 711	William	Rwn 382
William O.	Rck 481	Genges	Stk 602	Silversides, Wil-	
Willis	Nrt 479	George	Lnc 907	liam	Rth 142
Winnifred	Bfr 17	Henry	Ans 209	Silverthorn, Ro-	
Shorte, Daniel	Ans 224	Jacob	Lnc 906	bert	Hde 376
John	Ans 228	John	Ans 209	Southy John	Hde 376
Shote, Edward	Srr 688	Leonard	Cbr 710	William	Bfr 17
Shoulders, Thomas	Brt 78	Michal	Stk 602	Willis Joshua	Hde 376
Shoults, George	Rwn 389	Michael	Cbr 717	Simans, William	Wke 765
Shouse, Daniel	Stk 570	Sidz, Jacob	Lnc 828	Sime, Briggs	Frn 450
Philip	Stk 597	Thos.	Lnc 829	Simenton, Thomas	Ird 652
Shout, Peter	Lnc 907	Siers, James	Rck 487	Simeral, Samuel	Rth 142
Shovitts, Andrew	Rwn 297	Siffard, Abraham	Rwn 304	Simes, Dial	Wlk 64
Shroat, Christian	Rwn 396	Frederick	Rwn 314	Simeson, James	Mck 600
Shroate, Adam	Rwn 290	George	Rwn 303	John	Mck 599
Shrom, Henry	Lnc 822	Peter	Rwn 304	Simington, John	Ird 673
Jacob	Lnc 822	Sifferd, Barnard	Cbr 710	Theophilus	Ird 673
John	Lnc 871	Charles	Cbr 710	William	Ird 672
Peter	Lnc 822	George	Cbr 710	William	Ird 673
Shuffell, William	Wne 843	Siglar, Jacob	Rwn 454	Simmerman, Chris-	
Shuffield, Amos	Dpl 419	Sigman, Barnet (2)	Lnc 880	tian	Rwn 418
John	Crv 243	Christian	Lnc 870	Daniel	Rwn 419
John	Dpl 419	Christian	Lnc 880	Simmermon, Joseph	Stk 573
John	Mnt 474	George	Lnc 870	Simmon, William	Crv 303
Lincoln	Dpl 418	George	Lnc 881	Simmonds, Mary	Lnc 826
Shuffle, Everet	Mre 48	John	Lnc 870	Paul	Bld 44
Isom	Mre 46	Martin	Lnc 870	Sanders	Bld 43
John	Mre 46	Palser	Lnc 881	Simmones, Anthony	Crr 153
William	Rbs 419	William	Lnc 880	Simmons, Abraham	Rnd 345
Shufford, George	Bnc 190	Signer, Barnard	Lnc 907	Abraham B.	Jns 823
John	Lnc 822	Sikes, Abram	Crt 89	Amos	Jns 783
Shufford, Daniel	Lnc 906	Benjn.	Crr 146	Amy	Crr 145
David	Lnc 906	Cornelius	Smp 515	Aney	Crr 149
Jacob (2)	Lnc 906	Creasy	Hlf 342	Ann	Brn 19A
Shugars, Hannah	Orn 534	Harbord	Ons 179	Anthony	Crr 158
Isaac	Orn 535	Henry	Crt 89	Arthur	Brn 19A
Shugart, George	Srr 689	Jacob	Hlf 340	Benjamin	Frn 488
Leonard	Srr 693	Jacob	Nsh 119	Benjamin	Jns 795
Shulebarger, Freder-		James	Hlf 340	Benjamin	Mnt 473
ick	Rwn 343	Joab	Hlf 340	Benjamin	Orn 535
Garret	Rwn 343	Joel	Hlf 340	Benjn.	Brn 15A
Shuler, Henry	Rwn 418	John	Cmd 97	Benjn.	Brn 19
Isaac	Rwn 419	John	Crr 149	Caleb	Orn 532
Shulis, Mark	Rwn 389	John	Trl 692	Daniel	Jns 791
Shull, Charles	Lnc 892	Joshua	Hlf 340	Daniel	Jns 793
Frederick	Brk 790	Joshua (2)	Smp 515	Edward	Hde 375
Shuls, Jeremiah	Rth 142	Malichi	Cmd 108	Elias	Glf 650
Shumate, John	Wlk 61	Mary	Crv 257	Elizabeth	Smp 497
Joshua	Wlk 61	Needham	Smp 516	Emanuel	Jns 783
Shupe see Shape		Phillip	Nsh 118	Ephriah	Stk 570
Shuping, Andrew	Rwn 343	William	Cmd 100	Henry	Cbr 703
Jacob	Rwn 343	William	Cmb 373	Hillory	Nwh 9
Nicholas, Jr.	Rwn 304	William	Smp 516	Isaac	Brn 19
Nicholas, Senr.	Rwn 304	Siler, Adam	Cht 214	Isaac	Brn 21A
Shurer, Robert	Ash 88	Jacob	Cht 172	Isaac	Brk 791
Shut, Jacob	Stk 601	James	Cht 213	Isaac	Trl 694
Shute, Giles	Bfr 17	John	Cht 213	Isham	Srr 693
Joseph	Crv 243	Phillip	Cht 215	Isle	Crr 139
Thomas	Crv 319	Siles, James, R.	Ans 229	James	Brn 15A
Shuter, John	Nwh 1A	Silgreaves, John	Hlf 358	James	Brn 19
Saml.	Nwh 2A	Silis, William	Grv 521	James	Cht 168
Shutt, Henry	Ash 88	Sill, James	Mnt 483	James	Jns 801
Shy, Rachel	Csw 133	Priscilla	Nwh 8	James	Orn 537
Robert	Csw 137	Sillars, John	Rth 143	James	Rth 143
Shytle, Anthony	Lnc 890	Sillevent, Richard	Bfr 18	Jas.	Mrt 408
Martin	Lnc 890	Silliman, Robert	Rwn 319	Jehu	Orn 537
Sibbit, William	Bld 2	Sills, Isham, Jun.	Hlf 344	Jeremiah	Smp 528
Sibley, John	Cmb 358	Isham, Senr.	Hlf 344	Jeremh.	Bld 41
John	Mck 577	Jesse	Rth 145	Jesse	Bld 4

Jesse	Hlf 344	Simms, Ambrose	Cmb 373	Joseph	Mck 553	
Jesse	Mnt 473	Barnaba	Wne 872	Joshua	Crt 72	
Jesse	Orn 535	Benjamin	Edg 241	Joshua	Crr 138	
John	Bld 3	Isaac	Cmb 381	Joshua	Crr 150	
John	Brn 19A	James	Cmb 382	Josiah	Crr 150	
John	Brk 790	John	Rwn 402	Mary	Orn 531	
John	Cht 158	Martha	Edg 241	Moses	Glf 662	
John	Frn 490	Robert	Bld 36	Nancy	Bld 21	
John	Hlf 342	William	Edg 241	Nathan	Mnt 498	
John	Jns 793	Simon see Seymon		Nathl. (2)	Glf 657	
John	Lnc 821	Simons, ..., Mrs.	Hrt 726	Nicholas	Rwn 412	
John	Mck 570	Edward	Brk 792	Ralph	Brk 795	
John	Rnd 344	Enoch	Ptt 266	Richard	Ons 166	
John	Rwn 428	George	Brt 76	Richard	Ons 169	
John	Smp 526	John (2)	Rth 145	Richd.	Csw 96	
John	Smp 532	John, Jun.	Chw 120	Richd.	Glf 649	
John	Trl 694	John, Sen.	Chw 131	Richd.	Glf 657	
Jonathan	Crr 159	Joseph	Rth 145	Robert	Bld 17	
Joseph	Crr 143	Joseph, Junr.	Brt 76	Robt.	Psq 631	
Joseph	Ons 155	Joseph, Senr.	Brt 76	Robt.	Psq 640	
Joshua	Stk 570	Joshua	Bfr 18	Rossetter, jr.	Crt 73	
Josiah	Trl 694	Joshua	Hrt 702	Rosseter, sr.	Crt 73	
Lavender	Jns 795	Mark	Hrt 736	Saml.	Wlk 61	
Lemuel	Crv 329	Rachel	Chw 128	Samuel	Crv 235	
Malichi	Brt 76	Reuben	Chw 121	Samuel	Crv 319	
Mark	Mck 580	Sarah	Gts 279	Sarah	Chw 124	
Mary	Nwh 5A	Sarah	Nrt 479	Simon	Bld 12	
Mary	Rck 490	Thomas	Stk 570	Surrel	Bld 17	
Mitchel	Crr 139	W.	Srr 710	Thomas	Dpl 427	
Mitchel	Crr 144	William	Chw 121	Thomas	Mnt 500	
Molley	Wke 763	see Simans		William	Chw 124	
Moses	Brn 20A	Simonton, William	Ird 675	William	Mck 577	
Nacy	Cht 176	Simpkins, Able	Brk 795	Ziba	Crt 78	
Needham	Jns 803	Joseph	Crv 265	Sims, Abraham	Wne 863	
Patty	Frn 492	Joseph	Mnt 488	Adam	Wke 765	
Penelopy	Hlf 340	Joseph, Junr.	Crv 265	Anderson	Wke 763	
Peter	Cbr 718	Sarah	Brk 797	Benjamin	Ans 218	
Polly	Ons 151	Thomas	Mnt 503	Benjamin	Wne 863	
Pricella	Csw 138	William	Jhn 763	Bnjamin	Wrr 828	
Richd.	Rth 141	Simpson, ...	Brn 17	Breton	Wne 872	
Robert	Crr 157	Abram	Crt 72	Brittain	Rth 144	
Ruth	Orn 537	Alexander	Jns 813	Buck	Prs 205	
Saml.	Crr 139	Aron	Orn 532	Chesley	Wrr 829	
Saml.	Crr 146	Arthur	Bld 12	David	Chw 118	
Saml.	Crr 164	Axiom	Chw 124	Elisha	Wrr 829	
Samuel	Trl 694	Banj.	Orn 531	Fanny	Rck 462	
Sarah	Mrt 408	Benjamin	Rwn 412	Fanny	Rck 471	
Seml.	Crr 144	Charles	Brt 76	George	Csw 142	
Solomon	Mck 585	Easter	Ons 154	George	Wke 766	
Solomon	Wke 763	Edward	Bld 21	Herbert	Orn 538	
Susannah	Crr 149	Elisha	Bld 7	Irwin	Wke 765	
Thomas	Bld 44	Elisha	Crt 75	Isham	Wke 765	
Thomas	Csw 138	Elizabeth	Crt 72	Joel	Jhn 747	
Thomas	Crv 307	Elizabeth	Ptt 252	John	Rck 483	
Thomas	Mck 572	Enoch	Dpl 415	John	Wrr 830	
Thomas	Mnt 474	Evan	Chw 117	Leonard	Wrr 830	
Thomas	Prq 645	Fedrick	Nwh 4A	Littleton	Rth 142	
Vilet	Frn 473	Frederick	Prq 648	Mary	Brn 20A	
Will.	Brn 19	Hannah	Crv 245	Mary	Srr 693	
Willes	Crr 154	Jacob	Bld 11	Mrs.	Wrr 828	
Wiley	Frn 463	James	Csw 97	Nathaniel	Wke 766	
William	Brn 15A	James	Chw 124	Parish	Stk 573	
William	Crt 88	James	Chw 129	Sanders	Wrr 829	
William	Crv 291	Jane	Crt 77	Shadrach	Wne 863	
William	Crr 164	Jemima	Psq 640	Swepston	Wke 766	
William	Frn 483	Jesse	Psq 640	Thomas	Wrr 829	
William	Frn 487	John	Bfr 23	William	Jhn 771	
William	Frn 489	John	Brt 78	William	Srr 692	
William	Mck 570	John	Bld 17	William	Wke 765	
William	Orn 535	John	Crt 72	William	Wrr 829	
William	Rth 145	John	Cmb 358	William	Wlk 63	
William	Wke 761	John	Crr 157	Zackeriah	Wrr 829	
Wm.	Crr 139	John	Mck 577	Simson, Archd.	Mrt 408	
Zach	Srr 710	John	Ons 138	Benjamin, Junr.	Rwn 411	
Zadock	Ans 213	John	Psq 632	Simsoner, John	Cbr 701	
see Sammons, Semmons,		John	Ptt 252	Sinclair, John	Cmb 364	
Sinmons, Timmons		John	Rwn 412	John	Mre 61	

John	Wlk 61	Skiles, John	Brt 78	William	Chw 116
see Senclar, St. Clair		John	Rwn 318	William	Hde 376
Sinclaire, Andrew	Rbs 421	William	Brt 78	Wm.	Mrt 410
Sinclar, Daniel	Cht 180	Skiliton, Elisa-		Slagg, Judith	Orn 538
John	Cht 224	beth	Cbr 702	Slagle, Frederick	Lnc 890
Sinclare, Mary	Rbs 421	Skillcut, Rebecah	Glf 657	Henry	Lnc 890
Sarah	Ons 161	Skinner, Ann	Prq 643	John	Rwn 412
Sineath, James	Bld 14	Benjamin	Brt 78	Slankard, Joel	Lnc 863
Singletary, Benja.	Bld 33	Benjn.	Prq 643	Slanly see Stanly	
Benja., Jur.	Bld 35	Charles	Hrt 729	Slate, Saml.	Lnc 840
Benjn.	Brn 17A	Dempsey, Junr.	Edg 241	Slaten, Benjamin	Rth 142
Ithemar	Bld 31	Dempsey, Senr.	Edg 242	Nehemiah	Edg 239
James, Jr.	Bld 35	Dorothy	Chw 114	see Staten	
James, Senr.	Bld 35	Evan	Wsh 710	Slater, Allen	Ptt 250
John	Bld 34	Fredk.	Rck 450	Henry	Stk 602
John	Bld 39	Henry	Edg 242	John	Ptt 244
Jona.	Bld 31	James	Nrt 477	Sampson	Ptt 250
Joseph	Bld 32	James	Prq 642	Slatter, John	Bld 4
Joseph	Bld 34	James	Rch 266	Robert	Bld 4
Joseph	Brn 17A	John	Chw 125	Solomon	Hlf 344
Josiah	Bld 30	John	Edg 242	Slaturfield see Statur-	
Mary	Bld 32	John	Rch 266	field	
Richd.	Bld 33	Joseph	Prq 642	Slaubeck see Stanbeck	
Richd.	Bld 46	Joshua, Jun.	Prq 652	Slaughson, John	Brt 74
William	Bld 32	Joshua, Sen.	Prq 644	Slaughter, Abraham	Grv 580
Wm. C.	Bld 38	Judith	Nrt 477	Alexander	Brt 74
Singleton, Anne	Dpl 399	Martha	Nrt 479	George	Rch 251
Daniel	Rth 143	Nathan	Prq 642	Isaac	Grv 580
Edmond	Mnt 473	Nathan	Wsh 712	Jacob	Grv 580
Robert	Mnt 465	Rachel	Nrt 477	John	Edg 242
Spyers	Crv 343	Rachel	Prq 642	Owen	Rch 250
William	Wke 761	Richard	Chw 117	Peter	Jhn 750
Singular, James	Csw 107	Samuel	Chw 117	Sarah	Crr 139
Sink, John	Rwn 349	Stephen	Prq 646	Seilden	Rch 250
Michael	Rwn 350	Thomas	Rwn 459	Thomas	Brt 74
Philip	Rwn 350	William	Chw 124	Thomas	Edg 243
Sinkler, Archble	Rch 262	Skipper, Benjamin	Rch 245	Slausbery, Luke	Rck 479
James	Ans 211	Jacob	Brn 19A	Slavin, William	Ird 669
John	Ans 239	James	Lnr 23	Slawber, Christian	Stk 577
Wm.	Mrt 408	Thomas	Rch 245	Slay, Nathan	Rch 271
Sinks, George (2)	Rnd 340	William	Grv 570	Thomas	Ans 241
Jacob	Rnd 342	Skitor, Marget	Gts 279	Slead, John	Rbs 417
Sinmons, Hardy	Ons 152	Skittletharpe,		Sleagle, George	Lnc 891
Sinnitte, Isom	Mrt 410	Charles	Wsh 712	Sled, William	Ans 232
Sion, William	Stk 582	John	Wsh 710	Sledge, Archibald	Hlf 340
Sipps, Daniel	Lnc 884	Skrtor, Frederick	Stk 602	Hamblen	Frn 451
Sips see Seps		Skunk, Henry	Rth 142	James	Wrr 831
Siremore, Elize-		Slack, John	Rnd 344	Joel	Frn 448
beth	Stk 573	Slad, Mary	Bfr 18	Sherwood	Wrr 831
Sisemore, George	Wlk 643	Slade, David	Hde 376	Sleight, John	Wsh 712
Sishe, John	Crv 317	Ebenezer	Crv 331	Sleighter, Henry	Rwn 278
Sisk, Allin	Srr 693	Ebenezer	Hde 376	Henry	Rwn 291
Robert	Brk 792	Ebenzr., Esqr.	Mrt 411	Slevile, John H.	Brk 754
Robert (2)	Rth 145	Furnifer	Hde 376	Slime, William	Crv 291
Timothy	Brk 794	Henry	Bfr 18	Slinkard, Freder-	
Sissom, Elizabeth	Mre 40	Henry	Hde 376	ick	Lnc 881
Sitgraves, Jon.	Crv 247	Henry, Junr.	Mrt 410	Henry	Lnc 857
Widow	Crv 247	Henry, Senr.	Mrt 388	John	Lnc 857
Sitis, Philip	Stk 600	Jeremiah	Mrt 408	Sloan, Allen	Nwh 9
Sitterson, Isaac	Prq 643	John	Crv 265	David	Dpl 397
James	Prq 662	John	Hrt 721	David	Dpl 421
Joseph	Prq 655	John	Hde 376	Edward	Dpl 436
William	Prq 658	John	Hde 378	Elenor	Dpl 436
Sivers, Timothy	Cmd 103	Joshua	Wsh 710	Gibson	Dpl 436
Sizer, Jabez	Crt 77	Josiah	Csw 136	John	Dpl 421
Sizemore, George	Ash 87	Laban	Hde 375	John	Mck 565
Henry	Rbs 419	Mary	Crv 331	John	Mre 63
Newmon	Stk 573	Nancy	Hrt 722	John, Junr.	Rwn 404
Owen	Ash 87	Nathan	Csw 106	John, Senr.	Rwn 404
William	Stk 573	Philip	Crv 321	Robert	Dpl 419
Skeator see Skrtor		Reuben	Bfr 17	Robert	Ird 663
Skeen, Jacob	Rwn 383	Robert	Mck 553	Robert	Ird 672
John	Glf 634	Samuel	Bfr 17	Robert	Mck 565
Matthew	Rwn 382	Stephen	Hde 376	Widow	Mck 565
Sketer, John	Wne 872	Thomas	Hrt 729	Slocomb, Stephen	Smp 511
Skilcutt, Cair	Glf 656	William	Bfr 18	Slocumb, David	Wne 854
Skilenton, John	Cbr 681	William	Csw 106	Ezekiel	Wne 857

Saml.	Wne 858	Smelly see Smitty		Archabald, Ser.	Rbs 419
Slolcup see Stotcup		Smethwick, David	Mrt 410	Archd.	Mre 65
Slone, Alexn.	Cht 160	Ebenezar, Esqr.	Mrt 408	Archibald	Crv 335
Archibald	Brk 791	Edmd., Junr.	Mrt 410	Archibald	Cmb 361
Archibald	Ird 613	Edmd., Senr.	Mrt 408	Archibald	Cmb 366
Elisabeth	Ird 613	Edwd., Junr.	Mrt 408	Archibald	Rbs 420
James	Mck 528	Edwd., Senr.	Mrt 411	Archibald	Rwn 460
James	Mck 571	Joel	Mrt 408	Archibald, Jur.	Rbs 419
Jeromiah	Ird 613	John, Junr.	Mrt 410	Arnhart	Rwn 342
John	Mck 527	John, Senr.	Mrt 408	Aron	Jhn 766
Pattrick	Brk 791	John, Terts.	Mrt 410	Arther	Wne 871
Pattrick	Brk 793	Luke	Mrt 410	Arthor	Rnd 340
Robert	Mck 527	Saml., Esqr.	Mrt 410	Arthur	Bld 8
Samuel	Brk 796	Saml., Junr.	Mrt 408	Arthur	Nrt 475
William	Brk 797	Saml. S.	Mrt 410	Arthur	Smp 514
William	Lnc 880	Simon	Mrt 410	Arthur	Wke 764
Sloner, John	Ird 613	Wm.	Mrt 408	Asa	Mnt 514
Sloop, Conrod	Rwn 344	Smicegood, Eve	Rwn 411	Averet	Mre 46
Slough, Jacob	Cbr 718	see Swicegood		Bailey	Grv 532
Martin	Cbr 704	Smiely, James	Cmb 378	Barbara	Rwn 401
Philip	Rwn 338	Smiley, David	Grn 610	Barnet	Srr 693
Slover, James	Crv 237	James	Rch 269	Batson	Nsh 120
Slowers, Adam	Orn 538	Neil	Rch 271	Bazel	Jns 805
Slump, John M.	Lnc 823	Sally	Cmb 383	Benjamin	Ans 216
Slythe, Moses	Rwn 356	Smilley, James	Cmb 389	Benjamin	Brk 790
Small, Abraham	Cht 122	Smipes, John	Grv 543	Benjamin	Cmb 367
Benjamin	Crt 81	Smith, A.	Srr 708	Benjamin	Grn 610
Benjamin, Jun.	Chw 121	A. Richard	Wke 761	Benjamin	Hde 375
Benjamin, Sen.	Chw 121	A. Samule	Wke 761	Benjamin	Jhn 763
Elizabeth	Chw 113	A. William	Wke 761	Benjamin	Rch 254
Elizath.	Rck 455	Abeye	Rnd 343	Benjamin	Rwn 369
James, Senr.	Gts 278	Abner	Ash 88	Benjamin	Rwn 404
John	Cmb 360	Abner	Orn 537	Benjamin	Rwn 412
John	Gts 278	Abner	Ptt 251	Benjamin	Trl 682
John	Psq 624	Abraham	Ans 223	Benjamin	Wke 766
Joseph	Chw 120	Abraham	Bld 10	Benjamin	Wne 844
Myles	Prq 653	Abraham	Brk 797	Benjamin	Wlk 64
Nathan	Wne 864	Abraham	Ptt 248	Benjamin, Senr.	Wne 844
Night	Srr 688	Abraham	Ptt 258	Benjan.	Rck 460
Rewben	Chw 122	Abraham	Rck 483	Benjn.	Brn 15
Sarah	Psq 624	Abraham	Srr 692	Benjn.	Prq 643
William	Prq 644	Abram	Hrt 718	Bennet	Brk 279
William	Rbs 417	Abram	Psq 639	Bennet	Nsh 121
Smallwood, ...	Srr 690	Absolom	Cht 191	Bennet	Smp 520
Charles	Bfr 18	Absolom	Rnd 342	Bennet	Wrr 830
Elijah, Jr.	Srr 690	Adam	Brk 798	Betsey	Wlk 62
Elijah, Sr.	Srr 690	Adam	Orn 533	Bookcajah	Wne 845
John	Crv 231	Adam	Orn 534	Briant	Rnd 342
John	Srr 690	Adam	Rnd 342	Bryan	Jhn 773
William	Rwn 382	Adam	Rnd 344	Burn	Rch 258
Zadock	Rwn 389	Adam	Stk 558	Casper	Rwn 401
Smally, Andrew	Brk 790	Adam	Srr 691	Casper, Cap.	Rwn 401
Smar, Perril	Lnc 850	Adam, Senr.	Mnt 503	Chalet	Ons 138
Smart, George	Mck 538	Adam George	Lnc 881	Charity	Cmb 371
James Denton	Mck 592	Alexander	Ash 88	Charles	Ash 88
John	Mnt 481	Alexander	Cmb 368	Charles	Bld 45
John	Orn 535	Alexander	Rnd 343	Charles	Gts 278
Laban	Cht 176	Alexn.	Cht 197	Charles	Grv 508
Littleberry	Mck 541	Alexr.	Jhn 769	Charles	Mrt 408
Reuben	Rth 145	Alice	Wrr 830	Charles	Mck 550
Stephen	Mnt 482	Ambers	Dpl 408	Charles	Ptt 248
Thomas	Rwn 429	Ambrose	Cht 220	Charles	Srr 690
Widow	Mck 541	Ambrose	Cmb 381	Christian	Rwn 418
William	Rth 144	Amos	Brt 74	Clater	Rth 142
Smathers, Henry	Rwn 310	Andrew	Grv 561	Cloe	Rwn 405
Jacob	Rwn 310	Andrew	Glf 662	Daniel	Bnc 188
William	Rwn 310	Andrew	Mnt 515	Daniel	Brk 798
Smaw, Henry	Bfr 18	Andrew	Orn 530	Daniel	Cmd 108
John, Jur.	Bfr 18	Andrew	Orn 539	Daniel	Crv 297
John, Senr.	Bfr 17	Andrew	Rwn 404	Daniel	Cmb 361
Thomas	Bfr 17	Angus	Mck 559	Daniel	Cmb 386
Smedley, Moses	Nsh 119	Ann	Gts 278	Daniel	Lnc 899
Rebecah	Nsh 119	Ann	Hlf 344	Daniel	Lnc 907
Smeeton, Will.	Nwh 3	Ann	Nsh 121	Daniel	Mck 531
Smellege, John	Ons 147	Ann	Rnd 342	Daniel	Rch 261
Smelley, Francis	Wrr 831	Ann	Stk 610	Daniel	Rbs 419
Smellidge, Joseph	Ons 147	Anne	Dpl 405	Daniel	Rck 461

221

Daniel	Rwn 291	(Majr.)	Rwn 401	James	Bld 7	
Daniel	Stk 573	George	Ans 219	James	Bld 9	
Daniel	Srr 692	George	Ash 89	James	Bld 36	
David	Ash 88	George	Brn 14	James	Brn 18A	
David	Cmb 383	George	Brk 793	James	Brn 19	
David	Cmb 390	George	Cbr 687	James	Brk 791	
David	Gts 279	George	Cbr 693	James	Brk 793	
David	Ird 613	George	Cbr 718	James	Cbr 681	
David	Jhn 760	George	Dpl 405	James	Cmd 96	
David	Lnr 22	George	Lnc 881	James	Csw 149	
David	Mck 566	George	Orn 537	James	Cht 176	
David	Mck 600	George	Ptt 241	James	Cht 188	
David	Mnt 500	George	Rwn 382	James	Chw 125	
David	Nwh 6	George (2)	Rwn 401	James	Dpl 404	
David	Ptt 259	George, Senr.	Rwn 290	James	Edg 239	
David	Rnd 342	Goodman	Frn 484	James	Frn 475	
David	Rwn 401	Gorden	Rck 471	James	Grv 507	
David	Rth 143	Hannah	Hlf 342	James	Glf 636	
David	Smp 503	Hardy	Ptt 258	James	Hrt 718	
David, Junr.	Rwn 402	Hennick	Nwh 6	James (2)	Hde 378	
Davis	Mnt 492	Henry	Ash 88	James	Ird 613	
Davis	Psq 639	Henry	Brt 74	James	Jhn 774	
Dread	Grn 610	Henry	Bld 10	James	Jns 779	
Drew	Hlf 344	Henry (2)	Brk 793	James	Mck 590	
Drewry	Wne 845	Henry	Brk 795	James	Mnt 481	
Drury	Dpl 405	Henry	Crt 63	James	Mnt 486	
Drury	Mnt 508	Henry	Cht 213	James	Mnt 497	
Drury	Rck 450	Henry	Cht 215	James	Mre 72	
Drury	Rck 461	Henry	Cmb 360	James	Nwh 6	
Drury	Smp 520	Henry	Gts 278	James	Nwh 11	
Duncan	Cbr 681	Henry	Grv 510	James	Ptt 248	
Duncan	Cmb 387	Henry	Glf 652	James	Rch 242	
Duncan	Rbs 417	Henry	Lnc 822	James	Rbs 417	
Edmond	Mnt 505	Henry	Mnt 473	James	Rbs 419	
Edmond	Wrr 829	Henry	Mnt 476	James	Rbs 420	
Edward	Ans 229	Henry	Mnt 512	James	Rwn 369	
Edward	Lnc 898	Henry	Nrt 475	James	Rwn 404	
Edward	Ptt 286	Henry	Orn 533	James	Rwn 460	
Edward	Rch 258	Henry	Wne 847	James	Rth 143	
Edward	Rth 143	Henry, J.P.	Ptt 258	James	Rth 144	
Edward	Srr 688	Henry, Junr.	Cbr 696	James	Rth 146	
Edwin	Jhn 765	Henry, Junr.	Jns 797	James	Srr 690	
Eleazer	Rwn 369	Henry, Junr.	Wne 871	James	Srr 693	
Eli	Bld 8	Henry, Senior	Ptt 241	James (2)	Wke 762	
Eli	Wne 871	Henry, Senr.	Cbr 696	James	Wke 765	
Elihu	Wrr 831	Henry, Senr.	Jns 799	James	Wke 766	
Elijah	Dpl 431	Henry, Son of		James, Jun.	Hlf 344	
Elijah	Mnt 507	Henry	Ptt 248	James, L.R.	Rch 264	
Eliz.	Ons 153	Henry, Son of		James, Sen.	Hlf 344	
Elizabeth	Grn 598	John	Ptt 241	James, Senr.	Rck 471	
Elizabeth	Lnr 23	Hezekiah	Rwn 434	James, Ser.	Bfr 18	
Elizabeth	Ons 144	Hosea	Prq 646	James, Sr.	Cht 189	
Elizabeth	Ptt 278	Howell	Jhn 774	James W.	Grv 511	
Elizabeth	Rck 467	Hugh	Rbs 419	James W.	Grv 551	
Elizabeth	Trl 692	Isaac	Glf 654	Jarit	Brk 791	
Elsey	Crv 237	Isaac	Jhn 765	Jarvis	Wlk 62	
Enoch	Cmb 376	Isaac	Rbs 418	Jean	Bld 41	
Esther	Rbs 419	Isaac	Rwn 439	Jeremiah	Trl 694	
Etheldred	Jhn 765	Isaac	Trl 692	Jerry	Ans 234	
Etheldred	Nrt 475	Isaac	Wke 762	Jesse	Bld 10	
Everit	Mnt 476	Isaack	Mre 41	Jesse	Nrt 475	
Fedrick (2)	Dpl 405	Isaack	Mre 46	Jesse	Ptt 286	
Francis	Csw 97	Isham	Cht 189	Jesse	Rbs 417	
Francis	Cht 189	Isham	Hlf 340	Jesse	Trl 690	
Francis	Hlf 340	Isaiah	Dpl 405	Jesse	Wke 761	
Francis	Jns 809	Isaiah	Grv 532	Jiral	Prq 661	
Francis	Rck 460	Israel	Prq 660	Jno. L.	Rck 491	
Francis	Rck 492	Jabus	Trl 694	Job	Cmb 374	
Francis	Rth 146	Jacob	Cbr 707	Joel	Nrt 475	
Francis, Senr.	Csw 129	Jacob	Crt 63	Joel	Rth 146	
Frank	Csw 136	Jacob	Rwn 401	Johana	Bld 8	
Frank	Rck 460	Jacob	Rwn 439	Johanna	Trl 672	
Frederick	Glf 662	Jacob	Rth 143	John	Ans 198	
Frederick	Orn 536	Jacob	Srr 690	John	Ans 206	
Frederick	Rwn 382	Jacob	Srr 693	John	Ans 226	
Frederick	Rwn 401	James	Ans 226	John	Bld 9	
Fredrick,		James	Bfr 17	John	Bnc 188	

John	Bnc 189	John, L.R.	Mnt 472	Marian	Cmb 361
John	Brk 797	John, Senr.	Mnt 503	Mark	Wne 847
John	Cbr 699	John, Senr.	Rwn 401	Marke	Cht 189
John	Cbr 701	John, Son of		Martha	Lnc 844
John	Cht 214	John	Ptt 247	Martha	Rck 462
John	Cht 215	John, Sr.	Mnt 483	Martin	Cht 189
John	Cht 220	John F.	Crv 235	Martin	Wrr 786
John	Chw 115	John F.	Mnt 519	Mary	Crt 65
John	Chw 125	John G.	Brn 19	Mary	Grv 511
John	Crv 299	John P.	Grv 507	Mary	Hlf 340
John	Crv 329	John P.	Orn 530	Mary	Jhn 747
John	Crv 339	Jonath	Brt 74	Mary	Mnt 514
John	Crv 241	Jonathan	Bfr 23	Mary	Orn 531
John	Crv 253	Jonathan	Gts 278	Mary	Orn 537
John	Crv 255	Jonathan	Wke 765	Mary	Ptt 247
John	Crv 269	Jordan	Cht 190	Mary	Rnd 342
John	Crv 299	Joseph	Ans 216	Mary	Wke 762
John	Cmb 362	Joseph	Ans 226	Massey	Cht 185
John	Cmb 370	Joseph	Bnc 188	Matthew	Mck 583
John	Cmb 371	Joseph	Crt 64	Mecajah	Rth 143
John	Cmb 388	Joseph	Crv 261	Michael	Rwn 439
John	Grv 562	Joseph	Crv 303	Mildred	Nrt 475
John	Glf 639	Joseph	Cmb 358	Milly	Grv 519
John	Hlf 340	Joseph	Cmb 382	Molly	Stk 594
John	Hlf 342	Joseph	Dpl 442	Mordecai	Psq 635
John (2)	Hlf 344	Joseph	Frn 448	Morris	Cmb 373
John	Hrt 718	Joseph	Gts 279	Moses	Csw 139
John	Hrt 727	Joseph	Grv 558	Moses	Edg 240
John	Hde 376	Joseph	Glf 670	Moses	Rth 141
John (2)	Ird 613	Joseph	Hde 377	Moses	Stk 620
John	Ird 669	Joseph	Mnt 497	Myles	Hlf 342
John	Jhn 758	Joseph	Nrt 475	Nancy	Brk 795
John	Jhn 768	Joseph	Ptt 247	Nancy	Edg 240
John	Jhn 773	Joseph	Rnd 342	Nancy	Edg 242
John	Jhn 775	Joseph	Rch 248	Nancy	Hlf 344
John	Lnc 833	Joseph	Rwn 412	Nancy	Rck 490
John	Lnc 844	Joseph	Rwn 429	Nathan	Bnc 189
John	Lnc 884	Joseph	Rth 145	Nathan	Brk 792
John	Lnc 892	Joseph	Srr 692	Nathan	Crv 293
John	Mck 531	Joseph	Srr 707	Nathan	Jhn 754
John	Mck 543	Joseph	Wne 849	Nathan	Mnt 492
John	Mck 556	Joseph, (Cap)	Mck 573	Nathan	Mre 46
John	Mnt 503	Joseph, Jr.	Srr 707	Nathan	Rwn 412
John	Nrt 475	Joseph, Ser.	Hde 378	Nathaniel	Nrt 475
John	Ons 153	Joshua	Frn 468	Neeal	Mre 53
John	Orn 537	Joshua	Rck 443	Needham	Cht 191
John	Orn 539	Joshua	Wke 761	Needham	Jhn 762
John	Prq 651	Josiah	Mrt 408	Neill	Rbs 417
John	Rnd 341	Josiah	Nrt 475	Neinrod	Rth 141
John	Rnd 343	Josiah	Prq 644	Nelly	Cht 215
John	Rnd 344	Josiah	Rwn 369	Newit	Bld 7
John	Rch 255	Josiah	Wne 847	Nicholas	Wne 848
John	Rch 257	K. Stephen	Srr 690	Noah	Ptt 280
John	Rch 261	Kinnan	Grv 561	Noble	Bld 37
John (2)	Rbs 419	Lander	Rwn 412	Obadiah	Rwn 428
John	Rbs 420	Lannon	Ptt 240	Obid	Nwh 6
John	Rck 436	Lasries	Wne 851	Oliver	Ptt 294
John	Rck 458	Lazarus	Ptt 286	Patey	Stk 587
John	Rck 475	Laurence	Nrt 475	Patrick	Rbs 420
John	Rwn 401	Lemuel	Cht 185	Patsey	Hlf 340
John	Rwn 404	Leonard (2)	Rnd 340	Peggy	Bfr 18
John	Rwn 419	Leonard	Rwn 401	Peggy	Hde 375
John	Rwn 429	Levy	Mre 46	Peggy	Wlk 63
John	Rth 143	Lewis	Dpl 405	Penelope	Wsh 716
John	Rth 144	Lewis	Rbs 417	Peter	Bld 44
John	Smp 514	Lewis	Rwn 333	Peter	Csw 99
John	Smp 525	Lewis	Rth 144	Peter	Csw 133
John	Stk 610	Lewis	Wke 763	Peter	Cht 190
John	Srr 689	Littleberry	Nrt 475	Peter	Cmb 369
John	Srr 690	Lucretia	Bfr 18	Peter	Glf 643
John	Srr 691	Lucretia	Wne 871	Peter	Hlf 340
John	Wrr 832	Luke	Smp 509	Peter	Jns 793
John	Wrr 833	Lyus	Cht 189	Peter	Lnc 828
John	Wne 851	Mace	Csw 104	Peter	Rbs 420
John, jr.	Grv 528	Malachi	Jns 793	Peter	Rwn 400
John, Jr.	Jhn 766	Malcom	Cht 190	Peter	Stk 570
John, Junr.	Brk 797	Mallechi	Mrt 408	Peter	Stk 610

Name	Loc	Name	Loc	Name	Loc
Pheba	Rnd 340	Samuel, jr.	Crt 65	Watson	Grv 531
Philip	Ans 206	Samuel, Senr.	Mck 573	Wiley	Mnt 464
Philip	Bnc 189	Samuel, Senr.	Rwn 460	William	Ans 220
Philip	Cmb 376	Samuel, sr.	Crt 64	William	Ash 88
Philip	Rwn 401	Samuel A.	Wke 761	William	Brt 74
Plat	Ptt 241	Samul, Junr.	Mck 573	William	Bld 43
Pleasant	Cht 223	Sarah	Csw 118	William	Brk 798
Rachel	Brt 78	Sarah	Csw 135	William	Cbr 697
Ralph	Glf 656	Sarah	Crv 313	William	Csw 121
Ralph	Glf 658	Sarah	Crr 138	William	Cht 156
Ransom	Grv 555	Sarah	Edg 241	William	Cht 189
Rebecah	Hlf 342	Sarah	Hlf 340	William	Cht 220
Rebekah	Grv 563	Sarah	Rch 262	William	Cmb 373
Reuben	Cmb 376	Saul	Bld 22	William	Dpl 409
Reubin	Wrr 830	Sherwood	Grv 506	William	Dpl 439
Richard	Ans 217	Sherwood	Mnt 512	William	Grv 530
Richard	Gts 278	Sihon	Wke 762	William	Grv 549
Richard	Grn 610	Silas	Brt 78	William	Glf 639
Richard	Lnr 23	Simon	Bld 5	William	Glf 661
Richard	Mnt 497	Simon	Bld 27	William	Hlf 340
Richard	Rnd 344	Solomon	Brk 792	William	Hde 376
Richard	Wke 764	Solomon	Crt 64	William	Ird 632
Richard	Wke 766	Solomon	Hde 378	William	Jhn 758
Richard A.	Wke 761	Solomon	Nrt 475	William	Jhn 763
Richd.	Csw 99	Sparkman	Ptt 265	William	Jhn 774
Richd.	Csw 147	Stephen	Chw 130	William	Mck 591
Richd.	Glf 656	Stephen	Dpl 432	William	Mck 601
Ridley	Grn 598	Stephen	Hde 378	William	Mnt 497
Rigden	Jns 779	Stephen	Ird 666	William	Mnt 508
Robert	Bld 17	Stephen K.	Srr 690	William	Mnt 519
Robert	Cbr 681	Susanna	Ptt 247	William	Mre 48
Robert	Chw 125	Susanna	Ptt 286	William	Mre 67
Robert	Cmb 388	Tarleton	Rth 142	William	Mre 71
Robert	Grv 517	Temperanc	Edg 243	William	Nrt 475
Robert	Glf 645	Thomas	Ans 226	William	Ons 144
Robert	Glf 662	Thomas	Bfr 17	William	Ons 153
Robert	Hlf 344	Thomas	Bfr 23	William	Ons 155
Robert	Mnt 519	Thomas	Bld 45	William	Orn 537
Robert (2)	Orn 539	Thomas	Brk 794	William	Ptt 239
Robert	Rwn 404	Thomas	Brk 795	William	Ptt 248
Robert	Rth 143	Thomas	Brk 798	William	Rnd 341
Robert	Stk 570	Thomas	Chw 127	William	Rnd 344
Robert	Wke 764	Thomas	Crv 313	William	Rch 242
Robert, Junr.	Ans 201	Thomas	Edg 241	William	Rch 262
Robert, Senr.	Ans 211	Thomas	Gts 278	William	Rch 264
Robt.	Csw 129	Thomas	Grv 529	William	Rwn 291
Ruiben	Orn 530	Thomas	Grn 610	William	Rwn 328
Salley	Wrr 830	Thomas	Glf 664	William	Rwn 369
Sally	Brk 797	Thomas	Hlf 340	William	Rth 141
Saml.	Jhn 761	Thomas	Hrt 702	William (2)	Rth 142
Saml.	Nsh 121	Thomas	Ird 626	William	Rth 144
Saml.	Rck 436	Thomas	Jns 803	William (2)	Rth 145
Saml., Junr.	Jhn 751	Thomas	Mnt 498	William	Smp 505
Saml., (son of		Thomas	Rck 461	William	Smp 514
Saml.)	Mck 576	Thomas	Rwn 404	William	Smp 518
Saml., Sr.	Nsh 121	Thomas	Rwn 454	William	Srr 691
Sampson	Wne 851	Thomas	Rth 143	William	Srr 710
Samuel	Ans 218	Thompson	Stk 618	William	Trl 690
Samuel	Bld 7	Thomas	Srr 688	William	Wrr 832
Samuel	Bnc 189	Thomas	Wke 765	William	Wne 844
Samuel	Brk 793	Thomas	Wsh 710	William, Junr.	Mck 602
Samuel	Crv 337	Thomas, Esqr.	Bld 23	William, (m	Orn 536
Samuel	Crv 339	Thomas, Junr.	Nrt 475	William, (of	
Samuel	Gts 278	Thomas, Senr.	Mnt 508	Rob.)	Orn 539
Samuel	Grv 513	Thomas, Senr.	Nrt 475	William, Ser.	Mre 48
Samuel	Grv 550	Thos.	Psq 639	William A.	Wke 761
Samuel	Ird 613	Tobias	Rwn 343	William G.	Wrr 829
Samuel	Mck 605	Tobius	Orn 533	Wilie	Grv 585
Samuel	Mnt 519	Tulley	Crr 163	Willis	Cht 189
Samuel	Ons 156	Turner	Brt 78	Wily	Cht 189
Samuel	Orn 537	Turner	Wke 765	Wm.	Csw 107
Samuel	Prs 199	Tyra	Wke 764	Wm.	Csw 147
Samuel	Rbs 417	Umphrey	Crv 301	Wm.	Crr 150
Samuel	Rbs 419	Uriah	Edg 241	Wm.	Lnc 844
Samuel	Rwn 328	Uriah	Hlf 340	Wm.	Mrt 408
Samuel	Rwn 460	Uriah	Mnt 508	Wm.	Nwh 2
Samuel	Wrr 829	Vachel	Rch 258	Wm., Junr.	Mrt 411

Zach	Wke 762	Jesse	Wsh 710	Jacob	Rwn 412		
Zachariah	Bnc 188	John	Mck 576	Sockwell, Levin	Grv 573		
Zachariah	Hlf 342	John	Smp 508	Samuel	Grv 573		
Zachariah	Mre 75	John	Wsh 710	Solby, Thomas	Brk 795		
Zacheriah	Rth 143	Joseph	Trl 684	Sole, John	Brn 16A		
Zachriah, Sr.	Hlf 342	Roger	Smp 506	Soles, Armsted	Crr 146		
Zebedee	Trl 684	Roger	Wsh 712	Joseph	Bld 3		
Zedekiah	Brk 793	Sarah	Smp 508	Joshua	Brn 20A		
Smithe, Anne	Bld 25	Sarah	Wsh 710	Nathl.	Brn 20		
Benja.	Bld 49	Widow	Mck 573	Timothy	Brn 20		
James	Bld 49	William	Brn 15	Solgrove, James	Glf 666		
Jon.	Bld 25	Snelling, Barnett	Grv 563	Solice, James	Dpl 431		
Richd.	Bld 49	Snellinge, Hugh	Grv 558	Solmon, Thomas	Prs 216		
Stephen	Bld 48	Snellins, Curtis	Wke 762	Solomon, Elijah	Frn 481		
Tryon	Bld 25	Snider, Adam	Rwn 297	Goodwin	Frn 447		
see Smith		Barnet	Lnc 880	James	Frn 463		
Smithermon, Hugh	Rnd 341	Cornilus	Stk 601	Jordan	Wke 765		
Smithson, Aaron	Psq 631	David	Stk 601	Kunsbury	Brk 791		
Albert	Bnc 189	George	Srr 689	Lewis	Frn 464		
Samuel	Cmd 109	John	Lnc 881	Luke	Frn 445		
Thomas	Psq 629	Lewis	Rwn 389	Soloman	Glf 683		
Smithwick, John	Brt 76	Peter	Rth 143	William	Frn 445		
Lanier	Brt 76	Philip	Rwn 439	see Bennit			
Luke	Brt 76	Phillip	Stk 604	Somerland, Jonas	Brt 78		
Mary	Brt 76	William	Rth 143	Susanna	Brt 76		
William	Brt 76	Sniley, Saml.	Nwh 10	Sones, George	Stk 573		
Smithy, Ambrose	Wsh 710	Smiper, John	Cht 188	John	Mrt 408		
Elizth.	Csw 132	John	Wke 765	Stevens	Brt 78		
John	Csw 136	Thomas, Sr.	Cht 188	Soomer, Mary M.	Nwh 2A		
Saml.	Csw 132	Snipes, Benjamin	Dpl 404	Sorey, Robert	Hlf 344		
Smitty, Andrew	Grv 532	John	Nrt 475	Tulley	Crr 160		
Smoot, Ann	Rch 264	Matthew	Glf 683	Sorrel, Benjamin	Brt 74		
James	Wlk 64	Matthew	Stk 617	James	Brt 74		
Smothermon, John	Rnd 340	Nathan	Wne 868	James, jr.	Hrt 702		
Smothers, Gabreil	Wlk 63	Nathaniel	Grv 543	John	Cmb 368		
John	Orn 532	Needham	Jhn 763	William	Hrt 702		
Smoty, Abnor	Brk 793	Robert	Nrt 475	Edward	Wke 762		
Smoyer, John	Lnc 870	Thomas	Cht 167	Micajah	Wke 762		
Smyth, Samuel	Crv 307	William	Cht 166	Thomas	Wke 762		
William	Crv 233	William	Jhn 764	William	Wke 762		
Snapp, Lawrence	Cbr 687	William	Nrt 475	Sorrells, Samuel	Brk 795		
Lawrence	Cbr 718	see Smipes		Sorrels, John (2)	Rth 144		
Snawden, Nanny	Rth 143	Snips, Thomas	Prs 214	Joseph	Bnc 189		
Snead, Alex.	Rck 474	Snives, Britton	Jhn 762	Margret	Brk 795		
Benjamin	Srr 688	Snoden, Francis	Crr 146	Richard	Brk 790		
Charles	Ons 150	Snody, Samuel	Ird 645	Walter	Brk 790		
Harriott	Ons 153	Thomas	Ird 645	Walton	Rth 144		
Jacob	Brk 796	Snotterly, Eliza-		Sorrows, William	Grn 590		
John	Crv 241	beth	Orn 533	Sorsley, Alexander	Nsh 121		
Thomas	Nwh 4	Henry	Orn 533	Benjamin	Nsh 119		
William	Ons 153	Snow, Benjamin	Rnd 342	Sory, Andrew	Edg 241		
Sneed, Daniel	Rch 246	Ebenezer	Rnd 341	Malachi	Edg 243		
Henry	Rch 260	Fielding	Srr 693	Willoughby	Edg 242		
Jacob	Stk 580	Frost	Srr 689	Soseman, John	Cbr 711		
John	Prs 203	Frost, Jur.	Srr 690	Sotherland, Patsy	Hlf 342		
John	Rch 245	Frost, Ser.	Srr 690	Sotherlin, Robert	Prs 197		
Philip	Csw 115	Henry	Rwn 439	South, Andrew	Brt 76		
Philip	Rch 246	Jacob	Srr 689	Betsey	Crr 153		
Robert	Wke 764	James	Crv 267	Southall, Daniel	Gts 278		
Saml.	Prs 203	John	Crr 149	Furnca	Hlf 342		
Solomon	Rch 244	John	Ird 616	Henry	Nsh 119		
Solomon	Rch 267	John	Ird 618	Southan, Boze	Stk 573		
Stephen	Grv 517	John	Stk 568	Southard, Benjamin	Glf 662		
Thomas	Prs 203	John	Stk 612	Henry	Srr 692		
William	Rch 245	Leonard	Srr 689	John	Orn 531		
William	Rch 246	Mathew	Rnd 342	Southards, Abraham	Brk 794		
Zacheus	Stk 571	Obe	Srr 693	Souther see Sauther			
Zadock	Nsh 120	Spensor	Wrr 830	Southerland, Da-			
Sneedon, William	Crt 90	William	Rwn 439	niel	Dpl 441		
Sneel, James	Rck 460	William	Srr 693	George	Dpl 433		
Snell, Abijah	Wsh 710	Wm.	Crr 146	Jno.	Rck 454		
Asa	Wsh 710	Wm.	Crr 149	John	Dpl 433		
Charles	Smp 508	Snowden, Nathan	Cmd 108	John	Dpl 434		
Daniel	Mrt 408	see Snawden		Mordicai	Orn 538		
James	Cbr 679	Snugg, John	Mnt 497	Philip	Dpl 436		
James	Smp 506	Snuggs, Richd.	Ans 237	Robert	Dpl 414		
James	Wsh 710	Snyder, George	Rwn 412	Samuel	Orn 538		

Thomas	Stk 571	Jesse	Grn 590	Shaderick	Srr 688
William	Dpl 410	R. William	Brt 76	William	Srr 689
William	Orn 540	Ruebin	Edg 241	Willie	Edg 240
Southern, John	Stk 589	Solomon	Brt 78	Speers, John	Smp 520
Thomas	Stk 589	Thos.	Mrt 408	Speight, Alice	Grn 591
William	Stk 584	William	Brt 74	Ann, (Elder)	Gts 279
Soward, Thos.	Crr 145	William	Rbs 417	Ann, (Younger)	Gts 279
Sowars, Christian	Rwn 349	William R.	Brt 76	Aron	Gts 278
John, Senr.	Rwn 350	Sparkmond, Lewis	Gts 279	Elizabeth	Brt 74
Michael	Rwn 349	Willis	Gts 278	Elizabeth	Grn 615
Peter	Rwn 350	Sparks, Abel	Wlk 62	Fullenton	Gts 278
Philip	Rwn 350	Benjamin	Srr 689	Jeremiah	Gts 278
Valentine	Rwn 350	Charles	Wlk 64	John	Jns 785
Sowder, Henry	Wlk 64	George	Srr 707	Moses	Gts 278
Joshua	Wlk 63	James	Ans 207	Orpha	Grn 590
Sowel, Charles	Brt 76	James	Srr 692	Samuel	Grn 592
Chloe	Brt 76	Jeromiah	Brk 791	Sarcy	Grn 591
Demcy	Hrt 702	John	Srr 689	Seth	Grn 590
Ezekiel	Brt 74	John	Wlk 62	Sharpe	Jns 785
George	Cmb 390	Jonas	Rwn 439	Simon	Jns 785
John	Mnt 476	Joseph	Srr 692	William	Gts 278
John, Junr.	Brt 76	Mathew	Srr 692	William	Wke 763
John, Senr.	Brt 74	Reuben	Wlk 62	William, Esqr.	Grn 592
Lewis	Brt 74	Samuel	Srr 690	William, Junr.	Grn 591
Lewis	Cmb 392	William	Rwn 439	William, Junr.	Wke 765
Obadiah, Jur.	Brt 74	William	Srr 693	William, Jr.	Gts 278
Obadiah, Senr.	Brt 74	William, Senr.	Brk 791	William, Senr.	Grn 589
Samuel, Sr.	Dpl 403	see Parks		Speights, Mathew	Edg 242
William	Brt 76	Sparrow, Amy	Crv 263	Spell, John	Edg 239
William	Dpl 402	Ann	Crv 301	Spellar, Thos.	Mrt 410
William	Mnt 465	George	Crv 299	Spence, Ann	Cmd 97
William	Mnt 494	John	Crv 299	Caleb	Trl 694
Sowell, Charles	Hrt 714	John	Orn 538	Charles	Lnr 23
Claton	Jhn 765	Samuel	Crv 267	Demsey	Cmd 96
George	Hrt 707	Thomas	Crv 291	Demsey	Cmd 99
James	Hrt 714	William	Crv 291	Edward	Cmd 97
John	Mnt 473	William	Orn 538	Firb	Nrt 477
Mary	Hrt 701	Spaugh, Adam	Rwn 418	Guion	Cmd 96
Moses	Mrt 410	Jacob	Rwn 418	Isaac	Dpl 428
Shadrick	Ons 166	Speace, John	Stk 571	James	Cmd 96
Sowerby, Henry	Nrt 477	Speake, George	Cbr 716	James (2)	Cmd 97
Soyrug, William	Frn 482	Martin	Rwn 328	James	Psq 639
Spadlem, David	Brk 796	Speaks, Luckey	Ird 626	John	Cmd 96
James	Brk 796	Thomas	Ird 627	John	Cmd 97
Spadlum, Jesse	Brk 796	Spear, John	Brk 279	John	Cmb 390
Spady, Peter	Hde 378	Spears, Bird	Hlf 344	John	Lnr 22
Spagers, William	Stk 605	Christopher	Wke 766	John	Lnr 35
Spaight, Christo-		Elisha	Cbr 679	John	Srr 689
pher	Lnc 889	James	Ptt 226	John	Wlk 62
Richard D.	Crv 229	John	Brk 790	Jos.	Psq 639
Spain, Austin	Ptt 259	John	Cmb 378	Joseph	Nrt 477
Berry	Hlf 342	John	Grv 529	Joseph	Psq 639
Clabourn	Edg 240	John	Mre 68	Joseph	Trl 694
David	Wke 763	Joseph	Hlf 342	Lemuel	Cmd 93
Drury	Ptt 231	Josiah	Cbr 705	Mark	Psq 626
Frederick	Wke 766	Mary	Bfr 17	Nathan	Glf 655
John	Ptt 231	Phillip	Rbs 417	Nathan	Trl 692
John	Wke 763	Solomon	Cbr 678	Noah	Cmd 97
Thomas	Ptt 275	William	Bld 36	Rhody	Smp 514
Thomas	Wke 763	William	Cbr 678	Robert	Trl 694
Thomas, Junr.	Wke 765	William	Hlf 344	Robt. (2)	Psq 639
Thomas, Senr.	Wke 766	William W.	Cbr 678	Samuel	Cmd 98
William	Ptt 232	Speck, David	Cbr 716	Samuel	Psq 637
William	Wke 763	Speed, John	Rch 246	Thomas	Srr 689
Spainhour, Henry	Stk 573	Speer, Aaron	Srr 689	Timothy	Dpl 430
Spairhouse, Jacob	Stk 571	Andrew	Srr 692	Spencer, Anne	Lnc 834
Span, Frederick	Hlf 338	Eli	Srr 688	Arther	Crr 161
Richard	Hlf 340	George	Srr 692	Benjamin	Hde 376
William	Hlf 340	Henry	Srr 688	Benjamin	Mnt 504
William	Rth 142	Henry	Srr 691	Benjm., son	
Willis	Hlf 340	James	Srr 691	Richd.	Hde 376
Spangler, Peter	Lnc 891	John	Srr 688	Carcey	Crr 156
Spankling, James	Orn 536	John	Srr 691	Christopher	Hde 377
Spanyard, Susanna	Hrt 714	Joshua	Srr 692	Elias	Mnt 474
Sparkman, Charney	Ons 167	Leven	Srr 688	Elijah	Mnt 473
James	Brt 74	Levi	Srr 688	Frisbay	Hde 376
James	Grn 590	Samuel	Srr 690	George	Lnc 834

Isaac	Rnd 342	John	Jhn 751	Junr.	Mck 531
James	Lnc 834	Jonas	Rwn 358	James, Senr.	Mck 531
Jesse	Jhn 747	Jonathan	Brt 78	Sprouce, Aron	Glf 639
Jesse	Mck 566	Jonathan, Senr.	Brt 76	Sprouse, Chaney	Bnc 188
John	Brt 78	Judith	Gts 279	Spruce, Joseph	Glf 642
John	Brk 790	Matthew	Nrt 473	Quinton	Glf 642
John	Brk 793	William	Brt 76	William	Glf 641
John	Mnt 503	William	Mnt 464	Spruill, Abihu	Trl 672
John, Senr.	Brk 796	William	Nrt 473	Anne	Trl 674
Johnson	Rnd 343	William B.	Brt 76	Benjamin, Junr.	Trl 674
Jones	Hde 377	see Spvay		Benjamin, Senr.	Trl 672
Joseph	Brk 279	Spivry, James	Rth 114	Charles	Trl 674
Malachi, Jur.	Crr 156	Spivy, Benjn.	Cht 160	Dempsey	Trl 672
Malachi, Ser.	Crr 156	John	Chw 128	Ebenezer	Trl 672
Mary	Hde 376	William	Jhn 759	Evan	Wsh 710
Nanny	Rth 144	Splman, Salley	Crr 151	Hezekiah	Trl 672
Nathan	Hde 378	Spock, Gotlieb	Stk 605	James	Trl 674
Nathan	Stk 571	John	Stk 605	Jesse	Trl 672
Nathan	Stk 612	Joseph	Stk 605	John	Wsh 710
Peleg	Hde 376	see Ipock		John, Senr.	Wsh 712
Samuel	Brk 795	Spoon, Adam	Orn 533	Josiah	Trl 672
Thomas	Grv 543	Adam	Srr 693	Joshua	Trl 694
Thomas	Hde 376	Barbara	Orn 533	King	Wsh 710
Tucker	Hde 377	Christian	Rnd 344	Myles	Trl 672
Widow	Mck 563	John	Glf 636	Nehemiah	Trl 672
William	Ans 201	John	Orn 534	Obadiah	Wsh 712
William	Brk 793	John	Rnd 344	Richard	Trl 684
William	Grv 546	Peter	Orn 533	Samuel, Junr.	Trl 674
William	Trl 672	Spooner, John	Chw 116	Samuel, Senr.	Trl 682
Wm.	Lnc 827	Jonthn.	Nwh 8	Samuel, (Son of	
Zachariah	Lnc 834	Reubin	Jns 797	Joseph)	Trl 682
see Spener		Spoonhour, Henry	Stk 612	Stephen	Trl 672
Spendlove, Jennit	Bld 25	Michal	Stk 613	Thomas	Trl 672
Spener, Malachi	Crr 161	Spoonhow, John	Stk 613	Thomas Hawkins	Trl 672
Sperry, Jesse	Wlk 62	Sport, William	Rbs 420	William	Trl 672
Spiars, Betsy	Ans 231	Spraberry, John	Mck 590	William	Wsh 712
Spicer, Jeremiah	Ons 166	Spradlin, James	Wlk 63	Zebulun	Trl 674
John	Ons 162	James, junr.	Wlk 65	Spruit, John	Rth 145
William	Edg 239	Jesse	Wlk 63	Spry, John	Rwn 439
William	Wlk 61	John	Wlk 63	Mimey	Crr 141
Spiers, Elisha	Hrt 714	Spradly, Obediah	Rth 142	Spud, James	Rch 242
John, Merchant	Ptt 240	Spraker, George,		Spurgin, Isaac	Rwn 369
John, P.	Ptt 240	Junr.	Rwn 350	John	Rwn 376
Thomas	Hrt 736	George, Senr.	Rwn 413	Joseph	Rwn 369
William	Ptt 228	Sprall, Andrew	Mck 603	Josiah	Rwn 369
Spight see Speight		Sprat, Andrew	Rth 144	Samuel	Rwn 376
Spigle, Martin	Lnc 906	Sprate, Henery	Crr 158	Spurlen, Elijah	Lnc 899
Michael	Lnc 907	Spratt, Hugh	Lnc 892	Zachariah	Ash 87
Samuel	Lnc 906	Sprawls, Samuel	Rch 268	Spurlin, Asa	Rch 252
Spikes, Elisha	Wke 765	Solomon	Rch 257	Irvin	Rch 268
John	Crv 259	Sprayberry, Archd.	Mck 592	James	Rch 254
John	Rbs 418	James	Mck 592	John	Lnc 897
Spiller, Henry	Brt 76	Sprewel, Rebekah	Bfr 23	Spurling, William	Cht 162
Henry, Senr.	Brt 76	Sprewell, Saml.	Mrt 408	Spurlock, William	Wlk 63
Thomas	Brt 76	Spricle, Matthew	Stk 571	Zackeriah	Wrr 830
Spillmon, William	Srr 689	Sprigans, Thomas	Stk 592	Spurrier, John	Rck 478
Spilman see Splman		Spriger, Stephen	Glf 691	Thomas	Rck 478
Spin, Elizabeth	Ash 89	Spriggs, Jordan	Grv 574	Spurs, Joseph	Rth 142
Spinhour, Peter	Brk 794	Sprigh, James	Cmd 101	Spvays, James	Mre 47
Spink, Enock	Rnd 344	Sprinell, Moses	Cht 186	Spyers, Mary	Crv 325
Spinks, Lewis	Rnd 340	Spring, Aaron	Bfr 18	Squire, Roger	Nrt 479
Rolly	Rnd 340	Abraham	Bfr 18	Squires, Appleton	Bfr 18
Spircle, George	Stk 571	Albert	Rwn 333	Jeremiah	Crv 269
Spires, Absalom	Hrt 714	Samuel	Hde 377	John	Cmd 105
Spivay, John	Mre 49	Springer, George	Mnt 508	John	Crv 279
Spivey, Abraham	Gts 278	Margaret	Orn 534	John	Orn 532
Aron	Brt 78	Springfield, Mos-		Mary	Bfr 18
Aron	Jhn 751	ses	Prs 191	Reading	Bfr 18
B. William	Brt 76	Springle	Bfr 18	Roger	Brt 78
Daniel	Hrt 714	Dorcas	Bfr 18	Sreel, Enos	Ird 627
Elisha	Rwn 358	George	Bfr 18	Sroll, Arthur	Stk 573
Elizabeth	Rbs 418	Springs, Adam	Mck 526	Stacks, Ruth	Orn 531
Ephraim	Grn 594	John	Mck 526	Stacway, Barnet	Lnc 881
Esther	Brt 76	Sedgwick	Brn 16	Stacy, Charles	Chw 131
George	Mrt 408	Sprinkle, Moses	Srr 689	Malon	Csw 124
Jacob	Gts 278	Peter	Srr 689	Malon	Csw 141
James	Brt 76	Sproat, James,		Robert	Chw 131

Simon	Brk 793	James	Edg 243	Jesse	Glf 692
Steven	Rck 439	Jesse	Gts 279	Jesse	Stk 571
William	Chw 124	Jesse	Hrt 727	Jessee	Glf 668
William	Prq 652	Jesse	Mrt 410	Jessee	Glf 678
Staffer, Nelson	Grv 584	Jesse	Prq 655	John	Crr 147
Stafford, Adam	Csw 108	Jesse, Jun.	Prq 661	John	Stk 571
Cuthbert	Nrt 477	John	Prq 661	Jonathn.	Nwh 9
David	Hlf 342	Mary	Edg 243	Spirus	Nwh 11
Elexr.	Prq 642	Matthew	Ans 214	Samuel	Glf 692
Elijah	Crv 309	Mila	Prq 661	Thomas	Brn 21A
George	Mck 557	Mills	Edg 243	Wm.	Crr 147
Henry	Lnc 871	Mishack	Dpl 423	Standly, John	Grv 541
James	Cbr 679	Myles	Chw 130	Richd.	Glf 644
Jas.	Prs 212	Nichilas	Chw 127	William	Glf 654
John	Csw 113	Rachal	Nsh 119	Stanfield, Abram	Csw 109
John	Glf 676	Reuben	Brt 78	Isaac	Ans 227
John	Psq 635	Reuben	Prq 661	Jacob	Ans 199
John	Prq 658	Right	Cht 209	John	Ans 227
Jonah	Glf 684	Seth	Gts 278	John	Glf 684
Joseph	Orn 535	Shadrick	Dpl 431	Sampson	Ans 212
Josiah	Dpl 403	Shadrick	Gts 278	Solomon	Mck 563
Laban	Csw 114	Simon	Gts 278	William	Glf 671
Levi	Ash 88	Willis	Edg 243	William	Glf 681
Levy	Rwn 343	Zadock	Jhn 763	Stanfill, James	Ans 229
Malachi	Psq 631	Stallins, Philip	Brt 78	Stanford, John	Mck 552
Nathaniel	Bnc 189	Stallions, Jacob	Stk 571	Robert	Cbr 685
Rebekah	Rth 143	see Stalyans		Robert	Grv 508
Revel	Rnd 341	Stally, Christian	Cht 218	Samuel	Dpl 434
Samuel	Rnd 344	Stalyans, Rubin	Brk 794	Samuel	Mck 566
Sarey	Ptt 241	Abraham	Brk 791	Stanings, John	Chw 129
Stewart	Glf 669	Stamper, Jacob	Wlk 62	Rachel	Chw 129
Susana	Csw 108	Jesse	Wlk 62	Thomas	Chw 129
Thomas	Csw 114	Joel	Wlk 62	Stanlay, Anna	Grn 606
Thomas, Junr.	Prq 659	John	Ash 87	John	Grn 607
Thomas, Sen.	Prq 659	John	Hlf 344	Matthew	Grn 607
William	Csw 114	Jonathan	Ash 87	Shadrack	Grn 606
William	Psq 630	Richd.	Wlk 61	Stanley, Barnaba	Wne 873
William	Prq 654	Robert	Hlf 344	Charles	Brk 797
Stagnor, George	Rwn 328	William	Ash 87	Dancy	Cmb 368
Stags, Charles	Wlk 65	William	Grv 519	Elwin	Smp 521
Staiert, Sebastian	Cmb 358	Stanaland, Hugh	Brn 18A	Evin	Cmd 106
Stailey, Christian	Rnd 343	Nedom	Brn 18A	Isaac (2)	Ons 180
John (2)	Rnd 343	Saml.	Brn 18A	John	Smp 521
Martin	Rnd 343	Susan	Brn 18A	John, Jr.	Smp 522
see Staley		Stanback, Thomas	Rch 264	Jonathan	Brt 76
Staily, Coonrod	Rnd 343	John	Crv 277	Jonathan	Brt 78
Jacob	Rnd 343	Stanberry, Nathan	Wlk 64	Moses	Wne 871
Stalcup, John	Orn 531	Stancill, Hannah	Nrt 473	Perry	Brt 78
Solomon	Orn 531	John	Nrt 473	R.	Brk 795
Tobias	Orn 531	Samuel	Nrt 473	Richard	Wke 761
Stalen see Staten		Standard, Alice	Rck 472	Rubin	Brk 797
Staley, Bennet	Lnc 850	Standen, William	Prq 646	Sarah	Brt 78
Coonrod	Rnd 343	Standfield, Durrat	Prs 207	Stephen	Bld 19
Martin	Rnd 343	Henary	Prs 201	Stephen	Smp 522
see Stailey		Jas.	Prs 208	Thomas	Cmd 103
Stalhans see Stallians		John	Srr 693	William	Brt 76
Stalie, Benjamin	Lnc 850	Samuel	Srr 693	William	Jhn 772
Stalings, Mosses	Nsh 120	Thomas	Srr 690	Stanly, Elizabeth	Wlk 64
Stalions, Job	Edg 240	Thos. (2)	Srr 693	Ephraim	Crv 319
John	Edg 241	Will.	Prs 210	Hugh	Jns 817
Josiah	Edg 242	Will	Prs 219	James	Jns 783
Stall, Simon	Crv 297	Standford, Charles	Orn 531	Jesse	Lnr 22
Stallens, John	Nrt 477	Israel	Orn 539	John	Crv 241
Stallians, Ann	Frn 494	James	Orn 531	John	Jns 781
Elijah	Frn 491	Joshua	Orn 540	John	Wlk 63
Elisha	Frv 494	Richard	Orn 536	John, Senr.	Wlk 65
James	Frn 486	Standifer, John	Orn 530	Joseph	Brk 795
John	Frn 489	Standin, Elizabeth	Prq 656	Joseph	Rwn 376
Joseph	Frn 468	Henderson	Chw 115	Liza	Wlk 65
Reddick	Frn 494	Joseph	Chw 118	Moses	Lnr 22
Reubin	Frn 471	Lemuel	Chw 118	Richard	Crv 233
see Stalions		William	Chw 122	Rubin	Rwn 376
Stallings, Celia	Edg 243	Standley, A.	Srr 706	Shadrach	Wlk 64
Hardy, Esqr.	Mrt 410	Hutchens	Srr 711	Thomas	Brk 797
Henry	Prq 648	James	Nwh 9	Thomas	Rwn 449
Hugh	Nwh 2	James	Srr 706	William	Lnr 23
Isaac	Jhn 750	Jesse	Glf 679	William	Rwn 376

Stans, Hardy	Rch 248	Casper, Junr.	Rwn 363	John, Esqr.	Rwn 291	
Stansberry, Moses	Wlk 64	Casper, Senr.	Rwn 362	John, Senr.	Mck 570	
Stansel, John	Bnc 190	Henry	Stk 626	Joseph	Lnc 870	
John	Jhn 756	Henry	Trl 682	Mark	Mnt 480	
John	Ptt 262	Jacob	Lnc 870	Martin	Mck 564	
Jonathan	Jhn 755	Jacob	Rwn 460	Ninian	Ird 669	
Nathan	Jhn 757	John	Rwn 362	Ninian	Ird 673	
Noble	Ptt 232	Jonathan	Lnc 872	Ninion	Ird 666	
Peter	Cmb 372	Joseph	Dpl 403	Richard	Ird 673	
Peter	Rch 249	Margarett	Trl 682	Robert	Rwn 333	
Sarah	Jhn 756	Starrett, James	Glf 661	Robert J.	Rch 247	
Stansell, Godfrey	Ptt 292	Jno.	Lnc 827	Samuel	Rwn 333	
Nathan	Ptt 261	John	Glf 661	Thomas	Mnt 480	
Sarah	Ptt 264	Stasy, Joseph	Mnt 487	William	Brt 74	
William	Cmb 372	State, Sarah	Brt 78	William, J.	Orn 534	
Stansil, Jesse	Mck 579	Staten, Arthur,		Steeles, William	Lnc 865	
Stanton, Elizabeth	Nrt 475	Majr.	Edg 240	Steelman, Jeremiah	Trl 692	
Frederick	Nrt 475	Ezekiel	Edg 240	Steels, Jacob	Mre 73	
James	Crt 74	Keziah	Edg 240	Steely, Edmund	Wsh 712	
James	Wlk 64	Jesse	Edg 240	Elizabeth	Wsh 712	
James, Capt.	Edg 242	Thomas	Rwn 439	Frederick	Wsh 710	
John (2)	Bnc 188	William	Edg 242	Jeremiah	Wsh 714	
John	Prq 659	Zadock	Edg 242	John	Mck 562	
John	Rnd 343	Statlins, Jacob	Stk 613	Lovatt	Lnc 850	
Lewis	Grv 527	Staton, Frederick	Edg 239	Michael	Bfr 18	
Lewis	Grv 533	Thos.	Mrt 410	Steener, Benjamin	Lnc 870	
Mary	Crv 299	William	Hlf 344	Steert see Sturt		
Owin	Crt 80	Staturfield,		Stegall, Absalom	Ans 225	
Samuel	Rnd 342	George	Rch 267	George	Ans 223	
Thomas	Prq 659	Lurene	Rch 264	John	Rck 489	
Willie	Edg 242	Stauton see Stanton		Moses	Ans 210	
Staple, Thomas	Cmd 110	Stawber, Christo-		Solo.	Ans 223	
Staplefoot, Taylor	Bfr 23	pher	Stk 626	Solomon	Ans 210	
Stapleton, Roger	Rwn 278	Stawls, Jas.	Mrt 410	Thomas	Ans 199	
Roger	Rwn 290	Sarah	Mrt 410	William	Ans 222	
William	Rck 471	Steagan, Edward	Srr 708	Steickey see Stieckey		
Star, Jehue	Glf 680	Steal, William	Stk 572	Steickle see Shickle		
Starbow, James	Wlk 65	Stealley, Benja.	Mnt 475	Steiner, Jacob	Stk 599	
Starbuck, Edward	Stk 620	Stealmon, Charles	Srr 708	Jacob	Stk 625	
Gayer	Glf 692	George	Srr 708	Stell, Jeams	Crr 153	
George	Glf 689	James	Srr 704	Thomas	Crv 241	
Hezekiah	Glf 690	John	Srr 691	Stelley, Hezekiah	Hde 376	
Matthew	Glf 686	Steamy, Daniel	Lnc 907	Stelwell, Jeromiah	Lnc 891	
Paul	Stk 566	John	Lnc 823	Stem, George	Grv 574	
Stark, John	Grv 520	Peter	Lnc 822	Stenear, Abra	Stk 613	
William	Grv 518	Stear, Henry	Stk 577	Stener, Ann	Stk 602	
Starkes, George	Hlf 340	Stearman, Foxal	Rck 462	Stenson, Bird	Cht 210	
Starkey, Alcey	Ons 137	Stebbins, James	Nwh 5A	Step, James	Bnc 188	
Edward	Jns 805	Stedham, Jeremiah	Ash 88	James	Nrt 479	
Edward	Ons 182	Samuel	Ash 88	John	Brk 792	
Joel	Bnc 190	Stedman, Elisha	Cmb 358	Rebecka	Bnc 188	
Starks, Benjamin	Wke 765	Nathan	Cht 194	Thomas	Wlk 65	
Starling, Adam	Jhn 758	Steed, Claton	Rnd 340	William	Bnc 188	
Elisha	Wne 874	Collin	Rnd 344	Steph, Elesebeth	Prs 215	
John	Bld 2	Green	Rnd 340	Stephen, Joshua	Brn 20A	
John (2)	Bld 14	Helkiah	Mnt 483	Stephens, Anthony	Csw 126	
Robert	Wne 873	John	Rnd 341	Asa	Ons 145	
Seth	Smp 494	Moses	Mnt 480	Benjamin	Orn 532	
Stephen	Rbs 418	Samuel	Mnt 480	Benjn.	Crr 154	
Thomas	Bld 45	Thos.	Wlk 64	Benjn.	Mre 77	
Widow	Wne 874	Steedman, John	Rth 146	Bent	Csw 109	
William	Jhn 757	Steegall, Jesse	Hlf 342	Bettey	Wrr 830	
William	Rbs 418	Raimon	Hlf 340	Cornaba	Mre 40	
Starnes, James	Chw 122	Steel, Samuel	Brk 796	Daniel	Orn 537	
James	Chw 124	Thomas	Cht 172	Daniel	Orn 540	
Starns, Charles	Cbr 710	Thomas	Cht 192	David	Wke 763	
David	Mck 587	Steele, Andrew	Brk 796	Deborough	Grv 517	
Evan	Glf 674	Elijah	Jns 783	Edwin	Cmb 391	
Frederick	Cbr 692	Henry	Ird 666	Eli	Bld 20	
Frederick	Mck 587	Henry	Ird 669	Elisabeth	Brk 795	
Jacob	Mck 583	James	Brk 796	Evans	Glf 682	
Jacob	Mck 605	James	Rwn 333	Francis	Mnt 473	
John	Mck 605	John	Brk 796	George	Csw 110	
Joseph	Cbr 710	John	Ird 673	Hanah	Cht 197	
Joseph	Mck 605	John	Ird 675	Hardy	Wke 765	
Nicholas	Mck 605	John	Mck 567	Henry	Bld 26	
Starr, Adam	Glf 648	John	Rwn 278	Henry	Cmb 390	

Henry	Mnt 473	Charles	Smp 522	Daniel	Cmb 379
Henry	Wke 763	Edward	Smp 529	Daniel	Cmb 389
Isham	Wke 765	Edward	Wke 764	Daniel	Cmb 392
James	Cmb 374	Edward	Jhn 777	Daniel	Smp 495
James	Mnt 473	Emanuel	Mck 581	Elizabeth	Bfr 17
James	Nsh 120	George	Jns 809	Elizabeth	Rbs 418
James	Ons 158	Hardy	Smp 529	Francis	Crt 85
James	Rbs 420	Henry	Jhn 767	George	Cmb 390
James	Wke 765	Henry	Jhn 776	Hector	Cmb 385
Jane	Orn 536	Henry	Wne 866	Isaiah	Ans 223
Jarrott	Wke 765	Henry	Wne 872	James	Cht 151
Jeremiah	Nsh 120	Isaac	Jhn 766	James	Crv 237
John	Cht 188	Jacob	Jhn 758	James	Glf 657
John	Glf 679	Jamima	Smp 524	James	Hlf 342
John	Mnt 473	John	Crr 145	James	Ptt 225
John	Mre 77	John	Jhn 751	James	Wke 765
John	Nsh 120	John	Jhn 775	James	Wne 859
John	Ptt 243	John	Mck 581	James	Wlk 63
John	Rnd 341	John	Rwn 382	James, /Souple/	Cht 154
John	Smp 501	Joseph	Frn 476	Jehue	Glf 691
John	Srr 688	Joseph	Jns 807	Jeptha	Cht 154
John	Wke 765	Mathew	Crv 341	John	Crt 86
John	Wlk 63	Micajah	Smp 508	John	Cht 216
John, Senr.	Mnt 475	Michl.	Brn 21A	John	Cmb 362
Joseph	Cmd 107	Mildred	Smp 522	John	Cmb 377
Joseph	Wke 763	Sally	Lnr 23	John	Cmb 390
Levi	Cht 209	Samson	Rwn 434	John	Dpl 404
Lucy	Mre 68	Spencer	Rwn 433	John	Glf 622
Lydia	Bfr 18	Squire	Mck 581	John	Mrt 410
Marcus C.	Crv 243	William	Bld 14	John	Rch 266
Moses	Srr 690	William	Dpl 433	John (2)	Rbs 417
Richard	Mre 68	William	Jhn 766	John	Rbs 420
Richard	Ons 142	William	Ptt 251	John (2)	Rbs 421
Robert	Mnt 493	William	Rwn 434	John	Rck 486
Salley	Wke 765	Stevenson, Abraham	Nrt 473	John	Smp 524
Samuel	Cht 171	Arthur	Nrt 473	John	Srr 691
Sherwood	Wlk 63	David	Jhn 767	Joseph	Cht 225
Simon	Brn 19A	James	Cbr 684	Joseph	Cmb 374
Thomas	Srr 688	James	Ird 613	Lydia	Crv 241
William	Grv 517	James	Ird 673	Malcom	Rbs 420
William	Mnt 473	James	Jhn 768	Margaret	Cmb 358
William	Ons 159	James, Junr.	Ird 613	Norman	Cmb 387
William	Rnd 341	John	Ird 613	Peter	Nrt 477
William	Rck 482	John (2)	Ird 673	Peter	Orn 534
William	Srr 688	Joseph	Lnc 881	Randol	Mre 66
William	Wlk 63	Martin	Crv 249	Rape	Orn 530
Zach	Wke 764	Mary	Crv 321	Rhoderick	Rbs 421
Stephenson, James	Jns 807	Nancy	Jns 799	Robert	Glf 630
James	Jns 811	Nathaniel	Nrt 473	Robert	Orn 534
James	Prq 657	Robert	Ird 641	Robert	Orn 538
James	Rck 485	Robert	Lnc 880	Robert	Orn 539
Jerimiah	Wrr 833	Silas	Crv 309	Sampson	Glf 664
John	Prq 651	Thomas	Crv 309	Samuel	Cht 214
Joseph	Rth 145	William	Ird 613	Samuel	Glf 656
Martha	Prq 658	William	Nrt 473	Samuel, (Wil-	
Saml.	Wrr 832	Stevinson, John	Glf 627	liam)	Orn 537
Silas	Jns 811	John	Jhn 765	Spencer	Cht 157
Thomas	Prq 649	Steward, Affiah	Crr 156	Thomas	Ans 236
Thomas	Prq 657	Ben.	Frn 464	Thomas	Csw 117
William	Brk 797	Charles	Crv 251	Tinley	Glf 630
William (2)	Ird 642	Charls	Rnd 340	Will.	Prs 198
Stepney, William	Prq 642	Daniel	Crv 333	William	Ans 208
Stepp, Joshua	Prs 214	George	Rnd 340	William	Edg 243
Steptoe, John	Gts 279	Moses	Rnd 341	William	Glf 622
Sterlery, John	Brt 797	William	Dpl 439	William	Hlf 342
Sterling, Abraham	Wne 857	Stewart, Agniss	Prs 198	William	Nrt 475
Stern, Benjamin	Ird 645	Allen	Rch 252	William	Nrt 479
Sterper, Joshua	Lnc 872	Allen	Smp 523	William	Rth 143
Sterret, Wm.	Lnc 826	Alexander	Crt 69	William	Wke 765
Sterrit, Daniel	Mck 573	Alexander	Cmb 362	William Samuel	Orn 537
Steudewant, Randle	Cbr 711	Alexander	Cmb 384	Wm.	Csw 117
Stevens, Abram	Bld 21	Alexander	Orn 539	Stewarts Mill	Wsh 710
Absalom	Lnr 23	Archabald	Rbs 419	Stichleather,	
Barnebas	Smp 522	Archd.	Rbs 432	George	Cbr 717
Benjamin	Jhn 749	Charles	Wke 764	Stieckey, James	Jhn 747
Benjamin	Lnr 23	Charles	Wrr 832	Stier, Daniel	Rck 478
Charles	Jhn 750	Daniel	Cht 226	Stierbagger, George	Stk 604

Stierwalt see Stirewatt	Hannah Crt 62	Tully Prq 657
Stigner, Curtiss Stk 574	John Crt 62	William Ans 234
Stile, Christian Cht 195	Lemuel, jr. Crt 60	William Nrt 475
Stiles, Britton Ons 177	Lemuel, Snr. Crt 60	Young Mnt 503
George Mnt 519	Lemuel, sr. Crt 61	see Stocks
John Bnc 189	Richard Crt 60	Stokesbury, John
John Ons 175	Sabia Crt 57	P. Bld 6
John Rnd 343	Wallace Crt 59	Stoks, Thomas,
William Mnt 519	Stitez, Andrew Lnc 871	Senior Ptt 244
William Ons 177	Stith, Bassett Hlf 344	Stoltz, Philip Stk 596
Still, Benja.,	Bassett Hlf 358	Stone, Benjamin Brt 74
Lisle Mnt 499	Jesse Stk 611	Burges Rck 457
Booz Rth 144	Stitler, Peter Rwn 314	Conaway Rnd 342
James Mck 600	Stitwell, John Mnt 515	Cornelious Prq 646
John Cbr 704	Stoaks, Andrew Dpl 424	Cuthberth Wlk 62
John Jns 785	William Dpl 400	David Brt 78
John Mck 599	Stochdon, Joseph Srr 690	David Orn 492
John Wke 765	Stockard, Rachel Glf 689	David Rbs 420
Samuel Rck 474	Stockart, James Orn 535	Edward Brt 76
William Mck 599	William Orn 535	Edward Bnc 189
Stilley, Fountain Bfr 17	Stocker, Thomas Rnd 343	Enoch Srr 688
Fountaine Crv 283	Stockinger, Chris-	Ephiodius Csw 102
Lazarus Bnc 188	tian Rwn 401	Francis Cht 164
Levi Crv 281	Stockly, John Nwh 10A	James Frn 493
Stilly, Epraim Ons 161	Stocks, Hillory Crv 269	James Ons 166
Stilton, Micajah Rch 248	Sarey Ptt 244	James Rbs 419
Stilwell, David,	Starey, junior Ptt 244	Jesse Brt 74
Junr. Mnt 521	William Crv 271	John Ans 205
David, (Senr. Mnt 519	see Stoks	John Cmb 376
Elijah Mck 581	Stockstil, Rachel Rwn 454	John Frn 488
Elisha Mck 581	Stockstill, Wor-	John Glf 626
Jesse Mck 581	nell Rwn 454	John Rth 146
John Brk 794	Zebediah Rwn 454	John Stk 571
John Mck 606	Stockton, Davis Rth 143	John, Jur. Stk 570
John Mnt 519	Davis Rth 145	John, Sypher Wlk 64
Shaderick Brk 792	Samuel Rth 143	Joseph Cmb 374
Stinchicomb, John Rwn 434	Thomas Rth 143	Joseph, Sypper Ash 88
Stine, Elias Lnc 881	Stogdal, Mathew Edg 240	Lemuel Psq 627
Stinen, Wm. Crr 169	Stogdil, Zebedee Lnc 893	Mary Orn 532
Stinnet, Jerusha Rth 143	Stogdon, Daniel Stk 621	Mary Psq 627
Stinson, Aaron Srr 706	Daughety Stk 621	Mary Prs 198
Alexander Mck 552	Stogner, Benjamin Mnt 494	Merett Prs 189
Berdit Wke 764	George Mnt 494	Moses Prq 654
Clement Wke 764	Stognor, John Mnt 492	Nicholas Rch 256
David Mck 556	Stogsdale, Edward Ash 89	Randal Ans 206
Deby Cht 182	Stoic see Stow	Richard Ans 228
Hugh Mck 535	Stokely, Isaac Psq 638	Salathiel Glf 675
John Cht 221	Joseph Psq 638	Samuel Rbs 418
John Mck 530	Stoker, Ambrose Mnt 512	Sparkman Mrt 388
John Mck 550	Richard Mnt 512	Thomas Ans 205
John Mck 590	Stokes, Abner Mnt 503	Thomas Cht 170
John Mck 600	Allin Brk 792	Thomas Rth 143
John Wke 767	Anne Nrt 475	Uriah Mnt 497
Joshua Mck 554	Christopher Rwn 383	Will. Prs 206
Joshua Rwn 460	David Edg 241	William Ans 206
Louel Wke 764	Dempsey Edg 240	William Ans 228
M. Srr 706	Edward Glf 657	William Brt 78
Michael Mck 549	Elisha Ans 236	William Frn 488
Robert Cht 171	Frederick Prq 657	William Stk 571
Samuel Mck 549	James Ptt 248	William, Ser. Srr 688
Stipe, Charles Stk 603	James Ptt 289	Zeakel Srr 688
Stipons, Joshua Wlk 63	Joel Ptt 274	Stoner, Henry Brk 798
Welcom Wlk 63	John Ans 219	Henry, Junr. Brk 798
Stire, Philip Rth 144	John Mnt 502	Isaac Brk 798
Stiren, Adonijah Crv 291	John Nrt 475	John Abraham Rwn 402
Samuel Crv 337	John Ptt 242	Peter Orn 533
Stirewalt, Adam Rwn 342	John, junior Ptt 248	Stonestreet, But-
Frederick Rwn 344	Jonas Brk 792	tler Rwn 362
John Rwn 342	Margaret Ptt 247	Margery Rwn 445
Michael Rwn 342	Montfort, Esqr. Rwn 291	Stoolsman, John Rwn 358
Peter Rwn 342	Nathan Prq 657	Stoolsmon, Jacob Rnd 341
Stirewatt, Tobius Cbr 716	Reading Ptt 266	Joseph Rnd 341
Stiron, Abigail Crt 62	Richard Wke 764	Stoots, Peter Srr 690
Cason Crt 61	Samuel Lnc 850	Storch, Charles Rwn 278
Christopher Crt 60	Thomas Cht 197	Storke, Charles Rwn 291
Elisha Wsh 712	Thomas Glf 658	Storkey, Jonan. Csw 120
Francis Crt 65	Thomas Mnt 520	Storm, John Rbs 419

Mary	Bld 37	John	Rck 489	William	Nrt 477
Stors, Roger	Cmd 96	Josiah	Grv 562	Wm.	Wke 762
Story, Benjamin	Mck 582	Owen	Rwn 401	Stricklen, Breton	Wne 855
Benjamin	Mck 597	Stratten, Lewis	Stk 582	Hyman	Jns 789
Caleb	Stk 618	Straughan, Bindal	Cht 193	Joseph	Wne 847
Daniel	Ans 231	Crespin	Cht 199	Matthew	Rch 269
Edward	Mck 582	Hosea	Cht 155	Stricklin, Benja-	
Elizabeth	Glf 631	John	Cht 174	min	Jhn 750
George	Mck 602	Reuben	Cht 165	David	Jhn 749
James	Cht 221	Richard	Cht 156	Harmond	Ans 213
James	Mck 581	Richard	Cht 224	Jacob	Ans 234
James	Mnt 464	Richard, jr.	Cht 224	Jesse	Ans 199
John	Cht 221	Stephen	Cht 156	John	Wne 856
John	Hrt 733	Straughn, Eli	Rch 248	Joseph	Wne 856
Joshua, junr.	Wlk 64	Strawbridge, Wm.,		Lott	Ans 199
Joshua, Senr.	Wlk 64	Junr.	Mrt 410	Marmaduke	Jhn 755
Mary	Bfr 23	Wm., Senr.	Mrt 410	Micajah	Jhn 756
Samuel	Ans 220	Strawn, David	Stk 570	Samuel	Jhn 757
William	Mck 597	Larkin	Srr 693	Uriah	Jhn 749
Stot, Henry	Bfr 24	Larkin	Srr 711	Strickling, Abso-	
Stotcup, Peter	Brk 794	Strayhorn, Charles	Orn 540	lam	Dpl 399
Stotker, John	Rnd 342	David	Orn 536	Hamon	Smp 496
Stott, Patrick	Rth 142	Gilbert	Orn 536	Holly	Smp 496
William E.	Rth 142	James	Orn 536	Isaac	Smp 503
see Scott		John	Orn 538	John	Smp 497
Stotts, Adam	Stk 597	Streater, John	Wke 762	Mathew	Smp 496
Gasper, Senr.	Stk 597	Strechlen, Archi-		Mathew	Smp 517
Gesper	Stk 597	bald	Ans 214	Samuel	Smp 496
Godfrey	Stk 599	Streef, Peter	Lnc 823	Samuel	Smp 500
Samuel	Stk 599	Street, Anthony	Bnc 188	Thomas	Smp 500
Samuel	Stk 625	Anthony	Rth 143	William	Smp 497
Stough, Andrew	Cbr 710	Betsey	Rth 143	Wm.	Smp 496
Stout, Charles	Orn 534	Jas.	Csw 139	Strider, Jacob	Rnd 340
Ellener	Glf 627	John	Bnc 190	Strikland, Jacob,	
John	Cht 216	John	Rth 143	Jur.	Nsh 120
John	Orn 534	Moses	Prs 193	Noah	Nsh 119
John	Rnd 342	Richd.	Nwh 2	Stringer, Francis	Crv 233
Joseph	Orn 534	Simon	Rth 143	John	Edg 239
Joseph	Rnd 342	Will	Prs 196	John	Nwh 4A
Peter	Orn 534	William	Rth 145	Kiah	Nwh 12A
Samuel	Brk 798	Streeter, Mathew	Grn 597	Lawrence	Edg 239
Samuel (2)	Rnd 342	Streets, Mary	Dpl 421	Leonard	Orn 532
William	Orn 534	Nathaniel	Crv 243	Mary	Wke 764
Stouthard, William	Stk 573	Samuel	Crv 243	Rueben	Ash 88
Stovall, ...	Grv 539	Streter, Edward	Ans 198	William	Edg 241
George	Csw 98	Strett, Alexander	Bnc 188	Stringfellow,	
John	Grv 539	Stricker, Daniel	Lnc 822	Enoch	Rch 256
William	Grv 541	Strickland, Abel	Frn 469	Henry	Rch 244
Stover, Francis	Stk 571	Alexander	Mck 536	William, Sr.	Mnt 464
Jacob	Rth 142	Aron	Rbs 417	Stringfelow, William,	
Lewis	Bnc 188	Aron	Rbs 420	Junr.	Mnt 464
Stow, Abraham	Srr 688	Benjamin	Nrt 477	Stroade, Arthur	Cmb 358
Jacob	Lnc 835	Brasil	Frn 469	Stroder, Alexr.	Lnc 829
Jeremiah	Crr 166	David	Bld 16	Henry	Glf 639
John	Crr 168	Duke M.	Hlf 344	Strong, Elizabeth	Rck 458
Richard	Ird 644	Hardy	Nsh 121	James	Rck 463
Saml.	Crr 169	Henry	Nsh 121	James	Stk 608
Solomon	Mck 602	Isaac	Frn 472	John	Rck 475
William	Cbr 693	Ishmel	Nsh 120	Mary	Rck 475
Wm.	Crr 168	Jacob	Bld 13	Sneed	Rck 476
Stowman, Thomas	Brk 790	Jno., Jr.	Hlf 344	Thomas	Rck 488
Straden, Lewis	Csw 123	Jno., Jur.	Wke 762	Stroop, Jacob	Rwn 290
Strader, Adam	Glf 665	Jno., Senr.	Wke 763	see Stroupe	
Coonrod	Csw 142	Jno., Sr.	Hlf 344	Strother, James	Frn 470
Stradford, Sarah	Nwh 1A	Joseph	Nsh 121	John	Frn 460
Straghorn, Andrew	Brk 791	Joseph	Rbs 417	Judd	Frn 467
Strahan, Alexr.	Bld 50	Lazarus	Nsh 120	Owen	Rch 245
Straigter, Adam	Grv 571	Lazarus, Jur.	Nsh 120	Stroud, Anderson	Orn 535
Henry	Grv 556	M. Duke	Hlf 344	Arthur	Cmb 371
Straily, Gotlip	Stk 577	Mark	Nsh 121	Hannah	Dpl 402
Gotlieb	Stk 626	Matthew	Wke 767	Jesse	Rnd 341
Strain, Alexander	Orn 537	Nathan	Nrt 479	Jesse	Rth 144
John	Orn 537	Obediah	Frn 469	John	Orn 535
Stramy, Henry	Lnc 906	Orsbon	Nsh 120	John	Rnd 344
Strange, Charrity	Ons 156	Philip	Bld 16	Jorden	Brk 791
James	Rck 489	Simon	Nsh 120	Mark	Ash 87
John	Ons 156	Sion	Rbs 420	Peter	Brk 791

Peter, Senr.	Brk 795	
Stephen	Ans 222	
Thomas	Ird 669	
Thomas	Orn 535	
Thomas	Rnd 344	
William	Bnc 190	
William	Orn 535	
Strough, Andrew	Cbr 693	
Stroup, Adam	Lnc 857	
Adam	Stk 571	
George	Lnc 857	
Jacob (2)	Lnc 857	
John	Lnc 858	
Joseph	Lnc 858	
Michael	Lnc 858	
Philip	Lnc 857	
Samuel	Stk 627	
Stroupe, Samuel	Stk 572	
Strubeck see Stanbeck		
Strudwick, Martha	Nwh 12	
Strum, Bartholomew	Grv 534	
Christian	Grv 533	
Strunk, Daniel	Ash 88	
Strutton, Absalom	Wlk 62	
Hezekiah	Wlk 62	
Stuart, Alexander	Mck 604	
Andrew	Crv 299	
Daniel	Mre 61	
David	Stk 607	
David, Ser.	Stk 607	
Duncan	Ird 652	
Edwurd	Rwn 439	
James	Ird 613	
James	Ird 652	
James	Mck 600	
James	Mre 42	
James	Rwn 314	
John	Cbr 693	
John	Ird 641	
John	Mck 604	
John	Rwn 343	
John	Rwn 419	
John	Srr 710	
John	Srr 711	
John, Senr.	Mnt 480	
Joseph	Mck 594	
Joseph	Srr 709	
Joshua	Rwn 419	
Matthew	Mck 578	
Matthew	Rwn 318	
Reubin	Stk 608	
Robert	Rwn 314	
Samuel	Mre 52	
Samuel	Stk 607	
Silas	Mnt 481	
Stuart	Srr 709	
William	Mck 544	
William	Mck 563	
William	Mck 602	
William	Mnt 481	
William	Rwn 419	
see Huart, Sturt		
Stubbins, Joseph	Orn 532	
Joseph, Junr.	Orn 532	
Stubblefield,		
Jere.	Rck 448	
Nathan	Rck 449	
Richd.	Rck 448	
Richd.	Rck 449	
Wyatt	Csw 99	
Wyatt, Jur.	Csw 148	
Stubbs, George	Bld 11	
George	Mrt 411	
James	Wsh 710	
John	Wsh 710	
Levi	Wsh 710	
Micajah	Wsh 710	
Richard	Bld 12	
Samuel	Hde 376	
Thomas	Wsh 710	
William	Hde 376	
William	Wsh 710	
Stubs, John	Bld 6	
Stucker, James	Mnt 512	
Michael	Ash 87	
Stuckey, Sam.	Nwh 5A	
John	Hrt 733	
Studard, John	Srr 708	
Studham, Woolham	Srr 692	
Studivant, Holimon	Wke 761	
Lucy	Wke 761	
William	Wke 761	
Studwick, William	Orn 532	
Stugel, John	Ash 88	
Stule, Thomas	Orn 539	
William	Orn 534	
Stultz, Abraham	Stk 607	
Henry	Stk 607	
Sturdevant, Ander-		
son	Edg 241	
Sturdevent, Sarah	Wrr 833	
see Steudewant		
Sturdivant, Antho-		
ny	Nrt 479	
James	Nrt 477	
Jesse	Hlf 342	
Sturgeon, Henry	Mck 545	
Sturgin, Elizabeth	Rwn 314	
John	Mck 545	
Sturling, James	Mck 524	
Sturrel, Peter	Rwn 419	
Sturt, Thos.	Prs 195	
Stute, Francis	Stk 588	
Stuther, David	Cbr 699	
Stutman, Elizabeth	Srr 690	
Stuts, Christian	Mre 69	
Hennery	Mre 47	
Leonard	Mre 48	
Styers, Samuel	Stk 600	
Style, Benjamin	Lnc 863	
Styles, John	Frn 481	
see Stiles		
Styne, John	Lnc 880	
John	Lnc 881	
Sual, Richard	Mre 42	
Suat see Sual		
Sucus, William	Glf 658	
Suell, Alexander	Cmb 371	
Sugart, Zachary	Srr 709	
Sugg, Aaron	Wke 761	
Absalom	Grn 607	
Aquila	Grn 607	
John, junior	Grn 608	
John, Senior	Grn 608	
John, Son of		
Absalom	Grn 608	
Joshua	Wke 761	
Joshua, Junr.	Wke 761	
Josiah, junior	Grn 608	
Mary	Edg 239	
Michael	Lnr 23	
Moses	Wke 761	
Peter	Ptt 291	
Toshoud	Lnr 21	
William	Mnt 513	
William	Wke 765	
Suggs, Absalom	Rbs 418	
Allegood	Bld 43	
Aquilla	Mnt 473	
Curtis	Rbs 418	
Ezekiel	Brn 18A	
Harbert	Mnt 473	
James	Rbs 418	
John	Mnt 480	
John H.	Mnt 512	
Thomas	Mnt 473	
Timothy	Mnt 512	
William	Mnt 503	
Sugor see Seegoe		
Suit, James	Hlf 342	
Suiter, Henry	Nrt 479	
John	Nrt 477	
Sukman see George		
Sulavan, Hampton	Dpl 439	
John	Dpl 439	
Mildred	Dpl 427	
Sulemire, Adam	Lnc 907	
Sulgrove, James	Glf 686	
Sulivan, Daniel	Glf 622	
Florence	Glf 622	
Samuel	Glf 623	
Thomas	Rnd 342	
Sulivant, Joseph	Mre 68	
Sullavan, Leven	Orn 532	
Martha	Brn 14A	
Sullenger, James	Glf 642	
Sullevant, Corne-		
lious	Frn 481	
Drury	Frn 448	
Sullion, George	Stk 593	
Sullivan, Andrew	Rwn 382	
Ayel	Glf 678	
Cabb	Glf 679	
Caleb	Mck 578	
Charles	Glf 648	
Comfort	Lnr 21	
Daniel	Brk 798	
Davis	Cmb 358	
Edward	Glf 672	
Edwd.	Brn 15	
Fetcher	Glf 648	
Florance	Glf 669	
Florence	Glf 676	
Ginkin	Glf 627	
Isaac	Nrt 479	
Jacob	Glf 648	
James	Cbr 684	
James	Lnc 822	
Jesse	Glf 679	
John	Glf 627	
Keziah	Rth 146	
Levy	Glf 677	
Pattrick	Mck 534	
Polly	Bnc 190	
Robert	Cbr 703	
Samuel	Glf 623	
Samuel	Glf 628	
Samuel	Lnc 822	
Sarah	Brt 78	
Thomas	Lnc 822	
William	Glf 623	
William	Glf 674	
William	Mck 583	
Sullivant, Isaac	Hlf 344	
Jesse	Hlf 340	
John	Hlf 340	
John	Nwh 9A	
William, Jr.	Hlf 340	
William, Sr.	Hlf 340	
Zachary	Hlf 340	
Sulliven, John	Crt 56	
Sullivent, Owen	Nsh 119	
Sullum, Isom	Brn 21A	
Sullvan, John	Jhn 752	
Sult, John	Wlk 64	
Sultruth, John	Glf 686	
Sumerlin, Winborn	Wlk 64	
Sumers, Michael	Lnc 823	
Sumlin, Thomas	Ptt 293	
Summarel, Barron	Edg 240	

Benjamin	Edg 239	Francis	Ons 159	Sutton, Bailey,	
Edward	Edg 239	Isaac	Nrt 473	Esqr.	Bld 47
Hardee	Edg 239	James	Hrt 718	Bartholomew	Ptt 287
Henry	Edg 239	James	Nrt 473	Beaumont	Bld 47
Jacob	Edg 239	James	Prq 649	Benjamin	Lnr 23
Micajah	Edg 239	James B.	Gts 278	Benjamin	Ptt 257
Sarah	Edg 241	Jethro	Gts 278	Benjn.	Nwh 5A
Summent, Valentine	Glf 662	John	Bnc 189	Campbell	Orn 538
Summerhill,		John	Gts 279	Christr.	Bld 46
Charles	Grv 550	Joseph	Hrt 707	David	Bfr 18
William	Grv 548	Joseph H.	Gts 278	Dempsey	Grv 524
Summerille, Samuel	Nrt 475	Josiah	Gts 279	Elias	Dpl 419
Summerlin, Jacob	Dpl 404	Judith	Gts 278	Elijah	Ptt 245
Jacob, Sr.	Dpl 404	Martha	Edg 243	Ephraim	Brn 16
James	Ptt 260	Mathew	Dpl 413	Freeland	Orn 531
Reading	Dpl 438	Moses	Hrt 718	George	Nsh 119
Thos.	Lnr 21	Moses, jr.	Hrt 707	George	Prq 649
Summermon, John	Stk 605	Richard	Bnc 190	Isaac	Ptt 257
Summers, Alexander	Ptt 237	Richard	Nrt 473	James	Chw 120
Allen	Bnc 188	Thomas E.	Wrr 829	Jeremiah	Prq 652
Barsil	Ird 622	Wm. Duke	Edg 239	Jesse	Rch 246
Benjamin	Ird 622	Sumney, John	Rnd 342	Jesse	Rbs 418
Caleb	Stk 572	Sumpter, Fielding	Brk 793	Jesse	Rth 141
Charles	Ird 665	Henry	Brk 792	John	Bld 49
Fetty	Glf 637	James	Brk 797	John	Cmb 366
George	Csw 98	Livingston	Brk 793	John	Prq 655
George	Csw 121	Thomas	Brk 792	John (2)	Rth 141
George	Ird 674	see Lumpter		Joshua	Nwh 5A
James	Rck 450	Sumter, William,		Lemuel	Wsh 710
John	Csw 98	Senr.	Brk 793	Moses	Ptt 245
John	Ird 622	Sunford, Ephraim	Rch 267	Patrick	Cmb 367
John	Lnc 879	Supler, Jacob	Crr 153	Perry	Orn 531
John	Rwn 454	Suret, Simon	Rwn 382	Philip	Bnc 189
John, Se.	Srr 691	Surgeloe, James	Rch 243	Richard	Lnr 23
Johnston	Bnc 189	John	Rch 257	Samuel	Lnc 858
Jonathan	Orn 531	Surles, Major	Dpl 426	Sarah	Prq 646
Joseph	Stk 573	Robert	Lnr 22	Simon	Lnr 21
Levy	Csw 99	Robert	Lnr 23	Solomon	Ptt 245
Major	Orn 531	Surlevent, Jesse	Wrr 831	Tab	Crt 61
Mannering	Srr 689	Surls, Henry	Wke 763	Theophilus	Ptt 245
Margret	Brk 790	William	Lnr 21	Thomas	Brt 76
Nancy	Hrt 702	Surman, Calia	Ptt 286	Thomas	Orn 538
Paul	Ird 673	John	Ptt 250	Thomas	Prq 657
Peter	Glf 637	Nancy	Ptt 286	Thomas	Smp 521
Reuben	Stk 591	Thomas	Ptt 289	William	Brt 76
Samuel	Brk 799	Surmons, Ephraim	Crv 303	William	Bld 47
Thomas	Brk 790	Surratt, John	Prs 205	William	Crt 89
Thomas	Brk 794	Sute, John	Prs 187	William	Rwn 363
Thomas	Ird 669	Ralph	Grv 554	William	Wsh 712
Thomas	Stk 572	William	Csw 112	William, Jur.	Bld 48
Thomas	Srr 691	Suter, John	Rck 483	Zacheriah	Rth 141
Widow	Mck 533	Wm.	Nsh 121	Sutts, Christian	Glf 646
William	Brk 792	Suthard, Micaijah	Lnc 880	Jacob	Glf 646
William	Brk 795	Suthards, Thomas	Brk 793	Thomas	Brk 795
William	Ird 622	Sutherland, Anne	Cmb 358	Suty, John	Brn 15A
William	Ird 674	Findel	Brk 794	Swace, John	Ans 212
William	Rwn 449	Mordeca	Orn 599	Swaddle, Catherine	Bld 26
William	Srr 690	Ransom	Wke 766	Swafford, James	Rth 145
Summerville, John,	& oves.	William	Brk 790	William	Rth 145
together	Grv 517	William	Edg 240	Swaford, John	Rdn 341
Summey, Blandina	Lnc 822	Sutherlin, Daniel	Wlk 64	William	Rnd 341
Henry	Lnc 822	Suthern, John	Cbr 697	William	Rnd 343
Jacob	Lnc 822	Sutimore, Jacob	Brk 796	Swaim, Christopher	Rnd 344
Petter	Rwn 388	Sutliff, Joseph	Rwn 358	John	Rnd 344
Summit, Francis	Lnc 857	Sutril, Presly	Csw 148	Joshua	Rnd 344
Summon, Neill	Cmb 360	Sutten, Elliott	Rck 467	William	Rnd 344
Summons, Abm.	Csw 138	James	Lnr 23	Swain, Abram	Trl 686
Daniel	Stk 571	John	Lnr 23	David	Brn 18
James	Hlf 344	John	Rck 467	Eleazer	Wsh 710
Jesse	Stk 571	Wm.	Rck 469	Eliakim	Trl 686
John	Brn 18	Suttin, William	Lnr 21	George	Bnc 189
Summy, Christian	Lnc 823	Suttle, Benjamin	Rth 144	George	Glf 689
Michael	Rwn 401	Bushrod	Rth 141	Henrietta	Brt 76
Peter, Senr.	Rwn 388	George	Rth 141	James	Ptt 235
Sumner, Abraham	Chw 123	Isaac	Rth 142	James	Wsh 710
Demcey	Nrt 473	Matthew	Hlf 342	James, Senr.	Trl 686
Edwin	Nrt 473	Reuben	Wlk 61	Jas.	Mrt 408

Name	Ref	Name	Ref	Name	Ref
Jeremiah	Trl 686	Swicegood, Adam	Rwn 412	Jacob	Rwn 290
Job	Mrt 408	see Smicegood		John	Glf 640
John (2)	Brn 15A	Swift, Anthony	Csw 143	Sykes, Allen	Orn 537
John	Brn 18	David	Glf 619	Anne	Nrt 475
John	Mrt 408	David	Glf 621	Arther	Ans 216
John	Trl 672	Elias	Rnd 343	Britain	Nrt 475
John	Wsh 710	Ephraim	Ons 136	Israel	Bld 36
John	Wsh 712	John	Csw 109	James	Orn 537
Joshua	Trl 682	John	Csw 147	Jethro	Nrt 475
Levi	Brn 16A	Parks	Csw 143	John	Bld 47
Mary	Rbs 418	Richd.	Csw 143	John	Bld 48
Paul	Ird 627	Thomas	Rnd 343	John	Orn 537
Richard	Brt 76	Thos.	Csw 147	Jona.	Bld 46
Stephen	Wsh 712	William	Csw 143	Joseph	Nrt 475
Sylvanius	Glf 674	William	Jns 803	Joshua	Psq 633
Thomas	Glf 625	Swilley, Ziners	Jns 819	Josiah	Bld 47
William	Brt 76	Swim, John	Srr 692	Josiah, Senr.	Bld 48
Wm.	Mrt 410	Jonathan	Stk 618	Mary	Bld 47
Swainey, John	Bnc 190	Marmaduke	Glf 678	Mary	Nwh 7
Swales, John	Cmb 373	Michael	Glf 678	Thomas	Nrt 475
Swallow, John	Stk 616	Moses	Srr 673	William	Nrt 475
Saml.	Srr 708	William	Stk 618	Syllavant, Martha	Brt 78
Swan, Henry	Prq 657	Swims, Michael	Wlk 65	Sylon, Fredrick	Mre 76
Jane	Nwh 12A	Swin, William	Glf 677	Sylvester, James	Prq 651
John	Nwh 11A	Swindell, Ananias	Hde 377	Samuel	Prq 656
Samuel	Rth 141	Benjamin	Hde 376	Thos.	Psq 633
William	Cmd 108	Caleb	Hde 377	Zacharia	Psq 624
Zachariah	Rwn 333	Casen	Hde 377	Sylvestr, Nathan	Ons 156
Swaner, Wm.	Mrt 408	Christopher	Bfr 17	Symons, Benn.	Psq 625
Swangham, Van	Ans 202	Elizabeth	Hde 377	David	Psq 636
Swann, Asa	Ird 669	Ellender	Hde 376	Sympson, Mary	Wsh 712
Charles	Rwn 334	Henry	Bld 11	Salathiel	Trl 682
Ecen	Csw 109	Isaac	Hde 377	Sarah	Wsh 710
Elisabeth	Crv 343	Jacob	Hde 376	Sypherstone see Stone	
Essry	Rwn 449	Job	Hde 377	Sypper see Stone	
James	Lnc 826	Joel	Hde 377	Syps, Abraham	Lnc 879
Jno.	Lnc 826	John	Hde 376		
John	Mck 543	Jonathan	Hde 377		
John, Jun.	Mck 546	Joseph	Hde 377	-- T --	
Joseph	Mck 547	Joshua	Hde 377		
Matthew	Rwn 338	Josiah	Hde 377		
Rachel	Crv 343	Nathan	Bfr 17	T..., William	Ans 198
Robert	Rwn 445	Robert	Hde 376	Tabb, Thomas	Hlf 346
Taphenia	Ird 637	Saml.	Bld 11	Taber, Jacob	Rth 148
Thomas	Csw 98	Saml., Ser.	Bld 17	James	Rth 148
William	Mck 543	Samuel	Hde 376	Jeconias	Rth 148
William	Mck 544	Thomas	Hde 377	John	Rth 147
Zapheniah	Ird 669	Valentine	Hde 377	John	Rth 148
Swanner, Henry	Wsh 710	Waide	Hde 377	Jonathan	Rth 147
Jesse	Bfr 17	William	Hde 377	Solomon	Rth 148
Matthias	Bfr 17	Willis	Bld 9	Tabern, Demsey	Wke 768
Swanson, Elizabeth	Wke 764	Willis	Hde 378	Elisha	Wke 767
John	Lnc 850	Swindle, John	Rck 484	James	Wke 769
Richard	Frn 475	Swinea, Jno.,Junr.	Prs 189	Henry	Nsh 123
William	Wlk 65	Jno., Senr.	Prs 189	William	Wke 768
Swaringam, John	Mnt 497	Sarah	Chw 113	Taborn, Burrl	Nsh 122
Swathlander, Phi-		Swing, John	Glf 647	Jessey	Frn 471
lip	Rwn 445	Mathias	Glf 647	Nathan	Nrt 481
Sweaney, Betha	Wke 777	Swink, Abraham	Rwn 291	Solomon	Nsh 122
Sweany, James	Rnd 343	Barbary	Rwn 291	Tacker, Joshua	Rwn 358
Joseph	Rnd 342	George	Rwn 333	Seaborn	Rwn 359
Swearinggame, Jo-		John	Brk 797	Tade, John	Orn 598
siah	Smp 517	John, Senr.	Rwn 290	Joseph	Orn 601
Swearingham, Cheek	Lnc 891	Leonard	Rwn 290	Tadlock, Jesse	Prq 658
Samuel	Lnc 891	Swinney, Daniel	Rwn 412	Joshua	Prq 658
Sweat, Allin	Wke 761	Thomas	Wrr 828	Tadlocke, Absalom	Brt 80
William	Srr 691	Swinson, Ebineger	Nwh 6A	Tagert, James,	
Sweatman, John J.	Rwn 393	Jesse	Dpl 436	Esqr.	Mck 529
Sweatt, William	Nrt 477	John	Nwh 4	John	Cbr 701
Sweden, Robert	Brk 792	John	Wsh 710	Tague, Francis	Ird 632
Sweet, John	Glf 679	John A.	Dpl 440	William	Ird 632
Sweney, Levie	Grv 559	Richard	Dpl 402	see Teague	
Swenny, Miles	Jhn 762	Richard	Wsh 710	Tailor, John (2)	Rnd 345
Swery, Samuel	Hrt 733	Theophilus	Dpl 419	Luke	Srr 696
Swet, Abraham	Hlf 344	Thos.	Mrt 145	Matthew	Srr 696
Swetman, William	Dpl 440	Swiny, Daniel	Rth 145	Matthisas	Stk 602
Swezy, Rachael	Rth 145	Swisher, George	Glf 665	William, Jr.	Stk 572

William, Sr.	Stk 572	Tarbe, Peter A.	Nwh 2	William	Wke 767
see Sailor		Tarber, Samuel	Wke 767	William	Wke 768
Talant, Aaron	Rth 148	Tarbutton, Joseph	Rch 267	William, Junr.	Orn 600
Talby, Samuel	Wlk 65	Tarkenton, Benja-		Wm.	Csw 146
William	Wlk 65	min	Trl 674	Zachariah	Csw 96
Tale, Vinsen	Rwn 405	Benjn.	Mrt 411	Zaphaniah	Csw 127
Tallar, Absalom	Nrt 481	Isaac	Trl 692	Tatem, Benj.	Crr 145
Tallent, Richard	Ans 202	Jeremiah	Trl 674	Caleb	Crr 146
Richd.	Ans 200	John	Trl 682	Holloway	Crr 145
Thomas	Ans 202	Joseph	Trl 692	John	Crr 145
Talley, Fredrick	Wrr 835	Joseph, Senr.	Trl 674	Wm.	Crr 145
Friar	Ans 209	Joseph, (son of		Tatesnider, Andrew	Lnc 885
Joel	Wrr 835	Josh.)	Trl 674	Tatom, Absalom	Orn 493
Tallman, John	Ons 137	William	Trl 674	Haly	Rwn 434
Tally, Dyer	Grv 537	Zebulun	Trl 674	Jesse	Smp 520
Fredk.	Cht 185	Tarland, Jonathan	Rth 146	Joshua	Smp 530
George	Mnt 492	Tarleton, Arther	Jhn 746	Laban	Smp 519
John	Cht 198	John	Ans 231	Richard	Bld 16
John	Glf 686	Thomas	Ans 231	see Taytom, Thatom	
Pleasant	Cht 184	William	Jhn 751	Tattom, James	Rwn 429
Reuben	Grv 538	Tarliton, James	Jhn 747	Tatton, Joshua	Prq 644
Thornton	Mnt 508	Tarlton, Benjamin	Brt 82	Tatum, Fiby	Rck 467
Talow, Baltsor	Rwn 429	Tarner see Turner		Henry	Hlf 344
Talton, Abner	Ans 240	Tarr, Lewis	Rwn 358	Keziah	Orn 596
Briton	Ans 240	Melchor	Rwn 359	Osburn	Rck 456
Hardy	Jhn 751	Tarrant, Henry	Csw 148	William	Orn 596
James	Ird 653	Tarrbarr, Thomas	Grn 614	Taunt, Isaac	Bfr 18
Thomas, Senr.	Ans 240	Tarrell, Henry	Wne 849	Thomas	Crv 321
Taly, John	Cht 222	Tarrence, Adam	Ird 658	Tawmey, Dennis	Glf 674
Tamer see Abram		Alexander	Ird 658	Taylaur, Samuel	Wrr 834
Tammer, George	Rwn 454	George	Mck 565	Tayler, Balantine	Cht 177
Tammerlin, Alexan-		Tart, Enos	Edg 245	Francis	Frn 495
der	Srr 696	James	Brt 80	Moses	Ons 137
Tamson, Alisander	Nsh 122	Nathan, Junr.	Brt 80	Sally	Cht 225
Tancasly, William	Rth 147	Nathan, Senr.	Brt 80	Samuel	Frn 480
Tankard, George	Bfr 19	Thomas	Smp 506	Simeon	Cht 206
John	Bfr 19	Tarter, John	Brk 800	William	Cht 206
Tankisley, John	Mnt 520	Tarver, Benjamin	Nrt 481	Wright	Frn 483
Tann, Benjamin	Nsh 122	Benjamin	Wke 768	Tayloe, Laban	Smp 528
Benjamin, Sr.	Nsh 122	Billison	Nrt 479	see Tayler	
Drew	Hrt 722	James	Nrt 479	Taylor, Abel	Brn 21A
Tannel, Samuel	Hlf 346	Lucy	Nrt 479	Abel	Crv 309
Tanner, Benjamin	Nrt 481	Mary	Nrt 479	Abraham	Crv 311
Benjamin	Ons 141	Micajah	Nrt 479	Abraham	Glf 636
Daniel	Rth 147	Samuel	Nrt 481	Abram	Brt 80
Edward	Wrr 835	Tasey, Elizabeth	Cbr 681	Abram	Edg 246
Federick	Srr 696	Tash, Adam	Rwn 419	Absolum	Nwh 9
James	Cbr 684	Andrew	Rwn 419	Adam	Dpl 417
Joel	Stk 572	George	Rwn 419	Allen	Ans 208
John	Frn 480	Tassley, Mason	Rnd 345	Andw.	Lnc 827
John	Rbs 422	Tate, Adam	Rck 474	Ann	Crv 307
John	Srr 695	Arthor	Stk 572	Ann	Hrt 733
John	Wrr 834	Caswell	Glf 662	Ann	Jns 807
Joseph	Brk 799	David	Brk 798	Aron	Ons 141
Joseph	Nrt 479	David	Brk 279	Arther	Ans 208
Joseph	Wrr 834	Francis	Hlf 346	Benja.	Nsh 123
Ludwick	Grv 569	George	Orn 601	Benjamin	Lnc 882
Michael	Rth 146	Henry	Rth 146	Benjn. (2)	Brn 21A
Michael	Rth 147	Hugh	Brk 798	Benjn.	Crr 138
Thomas	Cht 172	James	Orn 595	Benjn.	Crr 148
Thomas	Mck 579	James	Orn 600	Benjn., Ser.	Crr 165
Thomas	Srr 695	James, (W.)	Orn 600	Blake	Rbs 423
Thomas, Ser.	Cht 177	Jesse	Rth 147	Boaz	Hrt 702
Tansy, William	Srr 695	John	Orn 595	Burwell	Lnr 24
Tant, Amey	Frn 470	Joseph	Orn 595	Canon	Mnt 481
James	Frn 485	Joseph	Orn 595	Charles	Ans 234
Sion	Frn 471	Owen	Stk 572	Charles	Crv 273
Sion	Frn 485	Randle	Rth 147	Charles	Grv 525
William	Ptt 257	Sally	Csw 130	Charles	Rwn 383
Tapley, James	Rnd 345	Sampson	Orn 595	Christing	Crr 163
Tapp, Abnen	Orn 597	Samuel	Brk 800	Christopher	Nsh 122
George	Prs 209	Samuel	Lnc 899	Christopher	Nrt 481
Lewis	Prs 202	Thomas	Orn 594	Cornealius	Nsh 124
Will.	Prs 191	Valentine	Orn 595	Daniel	Nsh 124
Tapscott, Ednea	Csw 145	William	Brk 798	Daniel	Rbs 422
Henry (2)	Csw 145	William	Brk 279	Daniel	Wke 769
Wm.	Csw 145	William	Orn 600	Danl.	Bld 20

David	Brt 80	James	Grv 544	Joseph	Crr 140
David	Cbr 676	James	Grn 612	Joseph (2)	Edg 245
David	Csw 146	James	Hlf 346	Joseph	Gts 279
David	Edg 247	James	Hrt 738	Joseph	Grv 547
David	Hlf 346	James	Ird 669	Joseph	Grv 584
Deborah	Trl 694	James	Lnr 24	Joseph	Lnr 25
Demcey	Nrt 481	James	Psq 641	Joseph	Nrt 479
Dempsey	Cht 205	James	Ptt 237	Joseph	Orn 597
Dempsey	Dpl 435	James	Ptt 284	Joseph, Jur.	Lnr 25
Demsey	Nsh 122	James	Rbs 423	Joseph, Senr.	Edg 245
Demsey, Sr.	Nsh 122	James	Rck 438	Joshua	Crt 84
Dorcas	Lnr 22	James	Rwn 343	Joshua	Crr 146
Drewry	Nsh 123	James	Rwn 449	Joshua	Lnr 24
Drury	Rth 147	James	Wlk 66	Joshua	Mrt 411
Edmond	Mnt 503	James, Junr.	Crv 335	Joshua	Ptt 262
Edmund	Grv 534	James, Jur.	Lnr 25	Joshua	Rth 146
Edward	Crr 137	James, Senr.	Crv 335	Josiah	Crv 311
Edward	Grv 524	Jeremiah	Bnc 191	Josiah	Rbs 424
Edward	Grv 544	Jeremiah	Ptt 260	Katon	Grn 594
Edward	Grn 594	Jesse	Crr 137	Keze	Hlf 346
Edward	Rwn 383	Jesse (2)	Gts 280	Keziah	Mrt 411
Edward	Srr 696	Jesse	Jns 785	Kinchen	Grn 612
Elijah	Lnc 823	Jno.	Lnc 825	Leml.	Crr 141
Elisabeth	Jns 809	Joel	Grn 598	Lemuel	Rbs 423
Elizabeth	Crt 85	John	Ash 89	Leuer	Orn 594
Elizabeth	Dpl 430	John	Bfr 19	Leven	Crt 83
Elizabeth	Edg 246	John	Bld 25	Lewis	Grv 558
Elizabeth	Lnr 25	John	Brk 800	Lewis	Rth 147
Elizabeth	Nrt 481	John	Cmd 100	Lydia	Cmd 94
Elizebeth	Crr 166	John	Cmd 108	Mary	Bfr 18
Emanuel	Bfr 19	John	Chw 118	Mary	Csw 145
Emanuel	Jhn 773	John	Crv 339	Mary	Crv 243
Etheldred	Nrt 481	John	Cmb 358	Mary	Gts 281
Francis	Ptt 262	John	Cmb 386	Mary	Ptt 237
Frederick	Ans 221	John	Crr 143	Mary	Rck 451
Frederick	Lnc 885	John (2)	Edg 245	Milicent	Psq 640
Frederick	Orn 599	John	Grv 525	Mills	Rbs 423
Frederick	Wke 768	John	Grv 545	Morisem	Crr 142
Gabriel	Cmd 94	John	Grn 615	Moses	Cmb 359
Geo.	Csw 108	John	Glf 685	Nancy, (TC)	Edg 245
George	Grv 523	John	Hlf 346	Nathan	Ash 89
George	Grv 525	John	Lnc 886	Nathaniel	Gts 279
George	Lnc 872	John	Mrt 411	Nedey	Crr 143
George	Rwn 434	John	Nsh 122	Nehemiah	Wne 867
George	Smp 527	John	Nwh 1A	Neill	Cmb 386
George	Wlk 65	John	Nwh 9A	Nice Ann	Rwn 278
Grace	Lnr 24	John	Nwh 11	Niecy Ann	Rwn 339
Harford	Rck 474	John	Nrt 479	Pharilise	Nsh 123
Harris	Rbs 423	John	Orn 495	Prudence	Dpl 428
Henry	Grn 612	John	Orn 596	Reuben	Nsh 122
Henry	Mnt 503	John	Orn 598	Reubin	Csw 108
Henry	Nwh 6	John	Orn 599	Reubin	Rck 448
Henry	Rbs 423	John	Psq 624	Richard	Edg 246
Hilary	Grn 601	John	Prs 214	Richard	Mnt 503
Hill	Cht 155	John	Rch 243	Richard	Stk 572
Hillery	Grn 597	John	Rch 264	Richard, Senr.	Edg 245
Hudson	Hlf 346	John	Rbs 424	Richd.	Mrt 411
Hudson	Mnt 503	John	Rwn 449	Richd., Junr.	Edg 245
Isaac	Ash 89	John	Rth 146	Robert	Brn 21A
Isaac	Crt 56	John	Rth 147	Robert	Grv 529
Isaac	Crv 237	John	Wke 768	Robert	Orn 598
Isaac	Hrt 702	John	Wne 873	Robert	Orn 599
Isaac	Lnr 24	John, B.	Grv 513	Robert (2)	Rth 146
Isaac	Lnr 25	John, D Creek	Bfr 19	Robert	Rth 147
Isdress	Cmd 94	Johh, Esqr.	Mrt 411	Ruben	Crr 144
Jacob	Cmb 359	John, Junior	Grn 601	Salley	Crr 145
Jacob	Lnr 24	John, Senior	Grn 605	Sam	Brn 17
Jacob	Mck 583	John, Senior	Ptt 260	Saml.	Mrt 411
Jacob	Rwn 419	John, Senr.	Mnt 481	Samuel	Ash 89
James	Bfr 18	John, Sr.	Nsh 123	Samuel	Bfr 19
James	Bfr 19	John L.	Crv 249	Samuel	Bnc 191
James	Brt 80	Jocie	Gts 279	Samuel	Cmb 358
James	Bnc 190	Jonathan	Ans 235	Samuel	Glf 621
James	Crt 58	Jonathan	Crr 143	Samuel, Junr.	
James	Cht 153	Jonathan	Mrt 411	(2)	Gts 280
James	Crv 335	Jonathan	Rbs 423	Samuel, Senr.	Gts 280
James	Edg 246	Jonathan	Wne 858	Sarah	Nwh 11

Sarah	Prs 190	Jacob	Rwn 369	Freck.	Ans 228
Siah	Crr 144	Jacob	Rwn 370	John	Ans 228
Simon	Bfr 19	James	Rwn 370	Needham	Rwn 419
Solomon	Brn 13	John	Brk 801	Samuel	Cht 198
Stephen	Edg 246	John	Stk 615	Templeton, Archi-	
Stephen	Orn 597	Mary	Cht 213	bald	Brk 800
Stephen	Wne 866	Morris	Rwn 370	David	Cbr 684
Susanna	Crv 333	Moses	Brk 801	David	Ird 645
Tabitha	Mrt 411	Nimrod	Ird 632	George	Ird 658
Tabitha	Nsh 123	Widow	Rwn 370	James	Brk 799
Teagle	Edg 246	William	Brk 801	James	Ird 658
Tekle	Rbs 423	see Tague, Teauge,		John (2)	Brk 800
Thomas	Bld 37	Tegue		John	Crv 235
Thomas	Cmd 108	Teagur, Michal	Stk 613	John	Ird 615
Thomas	Chw 118	Teal, Jacob	Ptt 289	Joseph	Ird 658
Thomas	Edg 245	James	Ptt 289	Moses	Brk 800
Thomas	Grv 547	Jas.	Mrt 411	Robert	Ird 615
Thomas	Rbs 422	Lewis	Jhn 749	Robert	Ird 658
Thomas	Wne 867	Moses	Ptt 289	Thomas	Lnc 898
Thomas, Ser.r.	Mnt 482	Phabe	Ptt 289	Teneson, Jno.	Csw 126
Thos.	Crr 144	William	Jhn 746	Tenison, Abraham	Rwn 449
Thos.	Crr 145	Teale, Caley	Ptt 231	Benjamin	Rwn 450
Timothy	Ans 219	Jacob	Rwn 343	Tenneson, Igna-	
Treasey	Nsh 122	William	Ptt 278	tious	Csw 99
Widow	Mck 538	Yoest	Rwn 343	Tennessee, Jacob	Bnc 191
Wilie	Nsh 122	Teame, Peter	Cbr 692	Tennison, Abraham	Rwn 434
Will.	Nsh 123	Teasley, Abraham	Orn 597	Samuel	Rwn 450
William	Ans 222	George	Orn 596	Tenor, John	Grv 562
William	Ans 230	Teastor, Robert	Mre 73	Keziah	Grv 562
William	Bfr 18	Sarah	Mre 73	Tensly, Thomas	Wlk 65
William	Cmd 95	Teat, Thomas B.	Ans 201	Teplow, Johnathan	Brk 800
William	Cmd 108	Teater, George	Cbr 693	Terlington, Eliza-	
William	Crt 83	Teatham, Thomas	Bnc 190	beth	Nsh 121
William	Crv 229	Teauge, William	Stk 615	Terpen, Obediah	Rth 146
William	Crv 341	Tebathson, Sarah	Cmb 358	William	Rth 147
William	Cmb 385	Tedder, Benjamin	Rch 245	Terrel, Jeptha,	
William	Dpl 417	Harman	Cht 168	Jur.	Grv 525
William	Dpl 429	James	Cht 152	Terrell, Henry	Orn 491
William	Edg 245	John	Cht 173	Joel	Frn 487
William	Edg 246	John	Cmb 373	John	Wke 769
William	Gts 280	Martha	Edg 175	Joseph	Orn 601
William	Grv 517	Martha	Edg 245	Micajah	Cmb 369
William	Grn 615	Mary	Bld 39	Nancy	Csw 131
William	Jns 787	Morris	Ans 203	Patrick	Wke 768
William	Mck 581	Samuel	Bld 39	Solomon	Wke 768
William	Mnt 481	Selviar	Grn 616	see Ferrell	
William	Ons 176	Solomon	Wke 767	Terrey, Benjamin	Wrr 834
William	Psq 641	Stephen	Bld 29	James	Wrr 833
William	Ptt 255	William	Bld 38	Joseph	Prs 187
William	Ptt 284	William	Cht 209	Terril, John	Csw 119
William	Rwn 419	Teder, Jesse	Cmb 381	Presly	Rwn 339
William	Rwn 449	Tedrick, Michael	Wke 767	Terrill, Henry	Csw 148
William, (S)	Grv 517	Teel, Emanuel	Ans 215	Jonan.	Csw 119
William B.	Wrr 833	Lodereck	Ans 215	Terry, Chance	Rch 268
William W.	Ons 146	Patience	Cht 210	David	Crv 237
Willis	Rbs 423	Richd.	Ans 215	Eli	Rch 269
Wilson, Jur.	Nsh 123	Teer, Luke	Orn 601	Elijah	Hrt 733
Wilson, Sr.	Nsh 123	Teete, Dorcas	Edg 247	James	Cht 211
Windal	Lnr 25	Teevnen see Tewnen		James	Grv 511
Winifred	Hrt 702	Tegue, Isaac	Wlk 66	James	Grv 549
Zachariah	Crr 143	Telfare, Paulina	Edg 246	James	Grv 580
see Harris, Staplefoot,		Tellet see Fillet		James	Rch 267
Taylaur, Tayler		Tellett see Fellett		James	Rbs 423
Taytom, John	Crr 143	Telwell, Thomas	Jhn 747	James, Junr.	Rch 269
Teabaugh see Leabaugh		Tempels, Lewis	Mre 43	Jno.	Csw 127
Teachy, Daniel	Dpl 423	Temple, Daniel	Nrt 481	John	Grv 535
Jacob	Dpl 423	Darkis	Crt 85	John	Hrt 733
Timothy	Dpl 422	Elisabeth	Jhn 772	John	Stk 590
Teag, Mattathias	Mre 76	Henry	Wke 769	John	Stk 594
Teague, Aaron	Rwn 370	James	Psq 638	John	Wke 769
David	Cht 168	Jos.	Psq 639	John	Wke 778
Edward	Brk 801	Robert	Wke 769	Joseph	Cht 211
Edward	Cht 195	Solomon	Psq 637	Matthew	Rch 242
Elijah	Cht 195	Thomas	Crt 85	Moses	Brk 800
Ezekiel	Rwn 370	Thomas	Psq 630	Nancy	Rck 471
Hannah	Rwn 369	William	Crt 85	Offy	Rch 269
Jacob	Cht 213	Temples, Benjn.	Cht 180	Peter	Rck 481

Thomas	Edg 246	Samuel	Cmb 381	Jeams	Crr 150
Thomas	Grv 582	Thomas	Cmb 380	Jesse	Crt 74
William	Wke 768	William	Cmb 382	Jesse	Dpl 426
William, Jr.	Rch 243	Theams, Elizabeth	Cmb 383	Jesse	Hde 379
William, Senr.	Rch 243	Thear, James	Rnd 348	Jesse	Nsh 123
Wm.	Csw 117	Theatch, Mary	Prq 656	Jesse	Rwn 291
see Tury		Thetwood, Stephen	Ons 169	Jessee	Orn 594
Tervathan, Henry	Edg 247	They, Thomas	Cht 159	Jethro	Nsh 121
Robert	Edg 247	Thigpen, Cyphean	Edg 246	John	Ans 200
Sion	Edg 247	Dennis	Edg 245	John	Ans 212
William	Edg 247	Galead	Edg 246	John	Brt 80
Testament, Thomas	Ash 89	James	Edg 245	John	Bld 40
Tester, Samuel	Mnt 465	Job	Dpl 416	John	Brn 19
Stephen	Bld 43	John	Dpl 412	John	Brn 19A
see Teastor		Lemuel	Edg 245	John	Bnc 190
Tetam, David	Psq 629	Mary	Edg 246	John	Csw 144
Tetterton, Benja-		Thigpin, Dread	Ptt 275	John	Cht 156
min	Lnr 24	James	Grn 593	John	Crv 295
Jesse	Bfr 19	John	Grn 593	John	Crv 303
Joseph	Bfr 18	Jonathan	Grn 593	John	Crv 339
Kizia	Bfr 19	Joseph	Grn 593	John	Cmb 385
Stephen	Bfr 19	Martha	Grn 593	John	Frn 476
Thomas	Dpl 403	Thom, John	Glf 633	John	Grv 505
William	Wsh 712	Thomas, Aaron	Rth 148	John	Hde 379
William, Jur.	Bfr 19	Abel	Crv 319	John	Ird 645
William, Sr.	Bfr 19	Abel	Ptt 263	John	Jhn 756
Tew, Jean	Smp 524	Allender	Rwn 370	John	Jns 793
Jeremiah	Smp 496	Andrew	Rwn 370	John	Orn 595
John	Smp 524	Archible	Rch 253	John	Rck 482
Joseph	Smp 504	Arnold	Rch 250	John	Rwn 405
Lewis	Smp 495	Asa	Csw 110	John	Rth 147
Marmaduke	Smp 494	Athanatious	Frn 461	John	Smp 506
Philip	Smp 496	Barney	Cht 210	John	Wrr 833
Tewnen, Bartholo-		Benjamin	Ans 217	John, jr.	Bnc 190
mew	Ans 215	Benjamin	Edg 246	John, Junr.	Mnt 498
George	Ans 239	Benjamin	Frn 473	John, Senr.	Mnt 498
Thach, Joseph	Prq 652	Benjamin	Hrt 707	John R.	Lnr 20
Leven	Prq 652	Daniel	Rch 256	John W.	Ans 208
Spencer	Prq 642	David	Ans 217	Jona.	Bld 39
Thacher, Charles	Rck 473	David	Csw 98	Jonah	Brt 80
Thacker, Charles	Nrt 481	David	Csw 108	Jonathan	Dpl 438
Mary	Bnc 191	David	Crv 283	Jonathan	Edg 245
Nathan	Bnc 191	David	Wrr 835	Jonathan	Edg 246
Thackery, Oliver	Psq 638	Demcy	Hrt 719	Jonathan	Frn 464
Thagud, George	Cmb 381	Edmond	Ans 216	Jordan	Brt 80
Thally, Andrew	Dpl 410	Edward	Orn 595	Jordan	Frn 473
John	Dpl 419	Eli	Rch 256	Joseph	Brk 801
Thaneas see Thomas		Elijah	Rch 255	Joseph	Mre 63
Tharp, Aron	Glf 650	Elisabeth	Frn 464	Josiah	Frn 463
Benjamin	Frn 447	Elisha	Jhn 758	Josiah	Hrt 718
Charles	Brn 18	Evan	Crv 265	Josiah	Orn 593
Henry	Nsh 124	Ezekiel	Ans 218	Laben	Crr 149
James	Brn 17	Ezekiel	Brt 80	Lewis	Dpl 433
James	Glf 651	Gentry	Rck 471	Lewis	Ird 645
Jeremh.	Glf 651	Geoge	Orn 594	Lewis	Rbs 424
Job	Bfr 18	George	Brt 80	Lewis	Rck 488
John	Rwn 358	George	Mnt 475	Luke	Rwn 369
Joseph	Glf 650	George	Wne 873	Luke	Smp 513
Laban	Glf 651	Hannah	Orn 600	Manzy	Rth 147
Thomas	Glf 652	Henry	Bld 44	Margan	Cht 182
Thomas	Jhn 765	Hezekiah	Ans 213	Margaret	Bld 40
Thomas	Rwn 369	Hugh	Rch 253	Martha	Nsh 121
Timothy	Frn 472	Isaac	Dpl 412	Martin	Crv 281
William	Brn 17	Isaac	Hrt 719	Mary -	Edg 245
William	Nwh 5	Isaac	Rch 271	Menzy	Rth 147
Tharpe, William		Ichabud	Edg 245	Michael	Bld 44
(2)	Ird 637	Jack	Frn 465	Michal.	Rck 444
Zadock	Ird 637	Jacob	Csw 105	Nancy	Chw 117
Tharrington, Eley	Frn 460	Jacob	Edg 245	Nathan	Mre 44
Thatem, John, Sr.	Stk 612	Jacob	Nsh 123	Nathan	Rch 255
Thatom, John	Stk 612	James	Brt 80	Nathaniel	Hde 379
Thomas	Stk 612	James	Cht 206	Oliver	Wke 778
Thaxton, John	Wlk 66	James	Gts 280	Philip	Cmb 392
Theames, David	Cmb 381	James	Hde 379	Rachel	Brt 80
John	Cmb 380	James	Mnt 498	Rachel	Rch 255
Joseph	Cmb 379	James	Rnd 348	Reubin	Crv 303
Martha	Cmb 379	James	Wke 768	Richard	Cht 184

Name	Ref	Name	Ref	Name	Ref
Richard	Rbs 424	David	Srr 695	John (2)	Orn 596
Richd.	Rck 448	Drewry	Wrr 834	John (2)	Orn 598
Robert	Csw 116	Duncan	Cmb 372	John	Orn 601
Ross	Hde 378	Ealinor	Rth 147	John	Orn 602
Saml.	Wne 851	Edwd.	Rck 450	John	Rnd 345
Samuel	Crt 78	Elijah	Srr 696	John	Rbs 422
Samuel	Stk 600	Elisha	Mnt 487	John	Rbs 423
Samuel	Stk 626	Elizabeth	Brt 80	John	Rwn 402
Samuel, Junr.	Edg 246	Elizabeth	Ons 166	John	Rth 147
Samuel, Senr.	Edg 245	Elizabeth	Rth 146	John	Stk 621
Simeon	Rch 249	Elizabeth	Stk 591	John	Srr 695
Simeon	Rch 256	Elutious	Mnt 474	John	Wke 767
Simon	Cmb 385	Ely	Orn 599	John	Wke 768
Solomon	Ans 210	Elzabeth	Dpl 403	John	Wne 870
Solomon	Ans 231	Etheldred	Nrt 481	John, Jr.	Stk 621
Stephen	Ans 199	Francess	Wne 843	John, Junior	Rbs 422
Theophilus	Edg 246	George	Bnc 191	John, Jur.	Srr 695
Thomas	Ans 200	George	Cmb 358	John C.	Dpl 438
Thomas	Csw 119	George	Ird 613	John F.	Glf 639
Thomas	Orn 600	George	Rbs 422	Johnathan	Orn 601
Thos.	Prs 215	George	Stk 619	Jonathan	Wke 768
William	Bnc 190	George	Wke 769	Joseph	Mck 535
William	Crt 76	Gideon	Mck 551	Joseph	Mck 598
William	Cht 156	Gideon	Rth 146	Joseph	Orn 596
William	Cht 184	Hannah	Cht 184	Joseph (2)	Orn 601
William	Crv 325	Henry	Mck 552	Joseph	Rwn 319
William	Dpl 413	Henry	Orn 599	Joseph (2)	Srr 696
William	Frn 465	Henry	Rbs 423	Joshua	Orn 597
William	Ptt 291	Henry, Junr.	Nrt 479	Joshua	Orn 600
William	Rch 248	Henry, Senr.	Nrt 481	Josiah	Orn 601
William	Rch 260	Hezekiah	Brt 80	Lemuel	Rbs 422
William	Rck 458	Hudson	Nrt 481	Leonard	Wke 768
William	Wrr 835	Isaac	Brk 799	Lewis	Brt 82
William	Wne 868	Isham	Prs 191	Little B.	Wke 769
William, jr.	Cht 184	Isteal	Brk 763	M.	Rbs 423
Thomason, Benjamin	Bfr 18	Jacob	Brn 19	Malcolm	Cmb 368
George	Rwn 395	James	Brt 80	Mary	Crr 146
Joseph	Mnt 505	James	Brk 800	Mary	Lnc 866
Landy	Rwn 334	James	Cht 168	Mary	Wne 852
Mary	Rwn 334	James	Glf 680	Mayton	Wke 767
Richard	Mnt 503	James	Ird 614	Moses	Brk 799
Richard	Grv 530	James	Mck 553	Moses	Mck 603
Richard	Rwn 334	James	Ons 155	Moses, Junr.	Rwn 334
Richard, Senr.	Mnt 505	James	Ons 157	Moses, Senr.	Rwn 334
Richard P.	Grv 529	James (2)	Orn 596	Nathaiel	Bnc 190
Samuel	Rth 148	James	Orn 597	Neill	Rbs 424
William (2)	Rth 146	James	Orn 599	Nicholas	Nsh 122
Zachariah	Rwn 334	James	Orn 601	Obadiah	Mck 585
Thomasson, Jane	Bfr 18	James	Rnd 345	Owen	Cht 185
Thomison, George	Grv 543	James	Rwn 434	Peter	Brk 799
Thomas	Grv 545	James	Rth 147	Randol	Cht 201
William (2)	Grv 543	James	Smp 510	Rebeca	Wke 768
Thomlinson, Richd.	Wke 769	James	Srr 696	Richard	Orn 596
Thompson, Aaron	Mck 603	James	Wrr 834	Richard	Orn 599
Achabald	Edg 175	James	Wne 871	Richard, (of T)	Orn 595
Adam	Rth 146	Jane	Srr 695	Robbert	Rnd 345
Alexander	Rbs 422	Jesse	Orn 600	Robert	Csw 138
Andrew	Rnd 345	Jethro	Wne 870	Robert	Cht 162
Andy	Crr 137	John	Bfr 18	Robert	Glf 650
Anmarlen	Bfr 19	John	Brn 15A	Saml.	Crr 140
Ann	Csw 130	John (2)	Brk 798	Samuel	Cht 214
Anthony	Orn 595	John	Cht 178	Samuel	Glf 665
Archabald	Edg 245	John	Cht 181	Samuel	Lnc 850
B. Little	Wke 769	John	Cht 185	Samuel	Lnc 863
Bartholomew	Lnc 858	John	Cmb 359	Samuel	Orn 597
Benja.	Wke 768	John	Crr 145	Samuel	Orn 599
Benjamin	Mck 597	John	Glf 653	Samuel	Orn 601
Charitylite	Cht 186	John	Hlf 344	Samuel	Srr 695
Charles	Brt 80	John	Ird 632	Sarah	Brn 16
Charles	Lnc 893	John	Ird 642	Sarah	Orn 597
Charles	Ons 155	John (2)	Ird 658	Sarah	Orn 600
Charles	Rbs 422	John	Jhn 747	Stephen	Orn 601
Charles	Rbs 423	John	Lnr 22	Swan	Wke 768
Charles, Junr.	Nrt 481	John	Mck 547	Sylvester	Stk 606
Charles, Senr.	Nrt 479	John	Mck 594	Theophilus	Orn 595
Corben	Bnc 191	John	Mnt 499	Theophilus	Rbs 422
David	Rbs 422	John	Nrt 481	Thomas	Brt 80

Thomas	Mnt 483	min	Edg 246	Tilley, David	Stk 572
Thomas	Mre 60	Thornton, Aaron	Wlk 65	Edmond	Stk 592
Thomas	Ons 170	Benjamin	Smp 500	John	Stk 588
Thomas	Orn 601	Benjamin	Wrr 834	Tillman, Ann	Lnr 24
Thomas	Rch 256	Clarky	Hde 379	John	Crv 273
Thomas	Rck 443	Elizabeth	Smp 504	John	Lnr 24
Thomas	Rth 147	F., (decd.)	Wrr 812	Joseph	Lnr 24
Tobias	Srr 696	Henry	Hlf 346	Richard	Lnr 25
Trimigan	Rbs 422	John	Rch 269	see Tilmon	
Washington	Nrt 481	John	Smp 498	Tilly, Edmund	Wlk 66
Widow	Mck 535	John	Smp 530	Elijah	Orn 596
Widow	Rwn 319	Joseph	Prq 663	George	Orn 597
William (2)	Brt 80	Mary	Smp 504	Henry	Stk 587
William	Brk 799	Mosses	Wlk 65	Henry	Wlk 66
William	Hlf 346	Nancy	Hde 379	John	Orn 596
William	Ird 613	Nathaniel	Smp 500	John, junr.	Orn 597
William	Lnc 850	Needham	Smp 506	Lazarus	Orn 597
William	Mnt 509	Theophilus	Ird 673	Margret	Wlk 66
William	Nrt 479	Thomas (2)	Smp 500	William	Orn 597
William	Orn 595	William	Brk 801	Tilman, Ann	Mnt 487
William	Orn 601	William	Hde 379	George	Mck 541
William (2)	Rnd 345	William	Mck 583	Henry	Crv 285
William	Rbs 422	William	Srr 695	Stephen	Mck 541
William	Rbs 424	Thoroughgood, Ann	Hde 379	Tilmon, Joshua	Cht 219
William	Rwn 402	Paul	Trl 682	Roger	Prs 211
William	Smp 505	Thorp, Jahue	Rwn 369	Timberlake, Richd.	Wke 767
William	Srr 695	Zacheriah	Stk 594	Timberluk, Frank	Frn 453
William	Wrr 834	Thrailkill, Jessee	Cht 208	Timbertain, Ste-	
Thomson, Alexander	Mck 589	William	Cht 211	phen	Wke 769
Alexr.	Ash 89	Thrash, Joseph	Rwn 419	Timmons, Elisha	Jns 793
Benjamin	Bld 18	Volentine	Bnc 191	Honor	Bfr 19
Charles	Ans 233	Thrasher, Sarah	Brk 800	William	Brk 801
Elijah	Jhn 749	Thredgell, William	Ans 206	Timpleton see Templeton	
Elisabeth	Crv 247	Thredgill, George	Ans 205	Tindal, Charles	Grn 609
Enock	Ons 169	John	Ans 213	John	Cmd 108
Hardy	Wne 869	Randal	Ans 213	John	Crv 319
Henry	Orn 492	Thomas	Ans 205	John	Crv 333
John	Crv 239	Thrift, John	Ird 674	Joshua	Smp 496
John	Wne 869	Nathaniel	Nrt 481	Lucretia	Grn 609
Peter	Wne 869	Throckmorton, Jo-		Mary	Crv 247
Robert	Orn 601	siah	Mnt 503	Ruel	Crv 263
Samuel	Orn 598	William	Mnt 504	Samuel	Grn 610
Susanna	Jhn 749	Throgmorton, Ro-		Tindle, George	Rth 148
Thomas	Crv 249	bert	Ans 227	Richard	Mnt 519
Thomas	Wne 869	Thrower, Henry	Wke 767	Thomas	Rth 146
Thos. W.	Chw 122	Jesse	Wke 768	William	Ird 645
Timothy	Chw 122	Mason	Hlf 346	Tiner, Benjamin	Rch 255
William	Crt 75	Thunderburk, Fran-		Etheldred	Wne 868
William	Chw 122	cis	Cbr 692	James	Wne 858
Zadoch	Wne 870	Thurmon, Benjamin	Wrr 834	Jesse	Jhn 749
Thorn, Hardy	Wne 862	Thurmond, Thomas	Wlk 65	Lewis	Rbs 424
John	Ird 622	Thurston, Benjn.	Wlk 65	Nicholas	Jhn 748
Martin, (T		Samuel J.	Rbs 424	William	Wne 868
Creek)	Edg 245	Samuel J.	Rbs 432	Willis	Jhn 749
Nicholas	Nsh 124	William	Chw 130	Tingal, James	Crv 265
Peggy Ozina	Hrt 732	Tice, Abram	Mrt 411	Joshua	Crv 265
Samuel	Hlf 346	Jacob	Mrt 411	Tingle, David	Crv 277
Theophilus	Edg 247	Jacob	Rwn 376	Israel	Crv 285
Thomas	Rch 251	William	Ans 203	Joseph	Crv 279
William	Edg 247	Tickle, Peter	Orn 599	Mary	Crv 279
William	Wke 767	Tidwell, Robert	Rth 147	Tining, James	Orn 596
Wm., Jur.	Wke 767	Tieer, Lewis	Cht 193	John	Orn 597
Thornberry, David	Ash 89	Tiefeteller, Mi-		Tinker, Faney	Crv 247
Edward	Glf 680	chael	Lnc 884	Sarah	Crv 255
Isaac	Glf 680	Tigart, Andrew	Rwn 449	Tinning, Carns	Orn 600
James	Glf 678	John	Brk 799	Catharine	Orn 600
James	Glf 680	Tigert, Thomas	Brk 799	James	Orn 596
Joseph	Glf 635	Tignall, Isaac	Nrt 481	John	Orn 600
Richard	Glf 681	Tignor, William	Crv 245	Robert	Orn 597
Thomas	Glf 678	Tiler, John	Crt 67	Robert	Orn 600
William	Glf 635	Tilgo see Filgs		Tipper, John	Wke 768
Thornbury, Edward	Rnd 348	Tillary see Fillary		William	Wke 767
Marthy	Rnd 348	Tillery, George	Rnd 345	Tippett, John	Grv 575
Mary	Rnd 348	John	Hlf 346	Luke	Grv 575
Thomas	Rnd 345	Parismus	Hlf 346	Tippit, Erasmus	Ons 170
William (2)	Rnd 348	Viley	Hlf 346	John	Jns 813
Thornhill, Benja-		Tillet, Reuben	Cmd 104	Joseph	Jns 811

Scenah	Jns	813	John	Ird	622	Tommey, Jacob	Lnc	858
Susanna	Rwn	383	John	Mck	534	Tommilson, Elisa-		
William	Jns	811	Joseph	Mck	533	beth	Crv	245
William	Rwn	383	Joshua	Wke	769	Tommy	Cmb	369
Tippitt see Fippitt			Moses	Wke	769	Tompkins, Benjamin	Ash	90
Tips, Jacob	Brk	799	Moses, Jur.	Wke	769	Gersham	Ash	90
Conrod	Lnc	870	Nathan	Ird	622	Jonathan	Wlk	66
Tire, Council	Glf	638	Solomon	Wke	769	Tompson, John	Cht	213
Fredrk.	Glf	638	William	Brt	80	John	Psq	636
Tirlington, Elisha	Smp	515	William	Mck	529	Tomson see Tamson		
James	Smp	515	William	Mck	533	Toney, John	Hlf	344
Tisdale, Edward	Edg	246	William	Rck	488	Steptento	Rck	476
Henry	Nsh	123	William	Rwn	376	Wimberly	Nsh	124
Nathan	Crv	249	Tolaver, Charles	Srr	710	Tooke, John	Crv	327
Philander	Nsh	121	Tolbert, Josiah	Rnd	348	Tool, Elizabeth	Edg	175
Renison	Edg	246	Samuel	Mnt	481	Elizabeth	Edg	245
Robert	Mnt	474	Thomas	Rnd	345	Garraldus	Frn	448
Will.	Nsh	123	Zedekiah	Mnt	482	Garrott	Orn	595
Tish see Tush			Tolbort, Thomas	Prs	211	Geralders	Edg	246
Tison, Aaron	Hde	378	Tolbott, Joshua	Srr	696	Tooley, Abel	Hde	378
Allen	Ptt	280	Toler, Caleb	Crr	149	Anthony	Hde	378
Ann	Ptt	281	Edward	Crv	285	Bryan	Hde	378
Benjamin	Ptt	278	Jeams	Crr	145	Dinah	Hde	379
Cornelius	Ptt	280	John	Cmb	383	Elisha	Hde	378
Elijah	Ans	213	John, Jr.	Cmb	381	Elizabeth	Hde	378
Elizabeth	Ptt	283	Mathias	Crr	146	Ephraim	Hde	379
Ferebee	Ptt	278	Matthias	Wsh	716	George	Srr	708
Frederick	Ptt	267	Robert	Jhn	751	Henry	Hde	378
George	Ptt	279	William	Crv	281	Jacob, Jur.	Hde	378
George, Junior	Ptt	279	William	Crv	285	Jacob, Ser.	Hde	378
Henry	Ptt	279	Toleson, Lydda	Edg	245	James	Crv	259
Hezekiah	Ptt	281	Tolliver, Charles	Ash	89	Job	Hde	379
Honor	Ptt	279	Jesse	Ash	89	Jones	Hde	378
Ichabud	Ptt	268	John	Ash	89	Laban	Hde	378
Jacob	Ans	205	Moses	Ash	89	Lot	Hde	378
Jacob	Ptt	279	Tolly, Elkanah	Rth	148	Major, Jur.	Hde	378
Jesse	Ans	205	Tolmon, John	Mre	70	Major, Ser.	Hde	379
Joab	Ptt	279	Tolson, Daniel	Ans	229	Nathaniel, Jur.	Hde	379
Manoah	Ptt	283	Daniel	Crr	167	Nathaniel, Senr.	Hde	378
Margaret	Ptt	289	Daniel	Crr	168	Ormond	Hde	378
Melley	Ans	206	Elizabeth	Crt	57	Rhoda	Hde	378
Moses	Ptt	279	George	Crv	339	Richard	Hde	378
Moses, Senior	Ptt	282	Isaac	Prq	647	Solomon	Hde	379
Richard	Grn	595	Jesse	Crt	58	Thomas	Hde	378
Richard	Hde	379	Nancy	Crt	85	Tootle, Abselom	Bfr	18
Samuel	Ans	206	Rebeca	Ans	198	Amos	Bfr	19
Sarah	Hde	378	Thomas, jr.	Crt	58	Elizabeth	Brt	82
Thomas	Ptt	276	Thomas, sr.	Crt	58	Topp, George	Wrr	835
Uriah	Ans	205	William	Crt	58	Toppin, Samuel	Chw	127
William	Ans	206	William	Crv	231	William	Chw	119
William	Ans	227	William	Prq	647	Topping, Thomas	Hde	378
William	Ptt	282	Zachariah	Crt	58	Torksey, John	Cmd	106
Zachariah	Hde	378	Tom, ...	Hlf	346	Noah	Cmd	105
Titus, John	Mck	593	Tomberlen, Lewis	Rth	148	Phillip	Cmd	105
Toby, Nanny	Crt	73	Tomberlin, Moses	Rth	148	Tornsly, Moses	Ans	208
Tocksey see Torksey			Stephen	Wne	862	Torrance, Barnabas	Ird	658
Tod, Aron H.	Ons	152	Tomberlinson, Wil-			Hugh	Mck	561
Hardy	Wsh	712	liam	Wne	863	see Tarrence		
John	Wsh	712	Tombleston, Josiah	Rnd	345	Torrans, Alexander	Crv	233
Lewis, (Capt.)	Edg	245	William	Rnd	345	Alexander	Cmb	358
Samuel	Edg	246	see Tumbleston			Walter	Cmb	359
Todd, Adam	Mck	551	Tombolin, John	Rck	437	Torrence, Albert	Rwn	278
Anne	Rwn	334	Tombs, John	Prq	649	Albert	Rwn	291
Elisha	Brt	80	Joseph	Prq	658	Hugh	Lnc	840
George	Mck	533	Tombuslin, Edmund	Rth	146	Torrens, Elizabeth	Dpl	441
George	Wrr	835	Tomelson, William	Wne	872	Torrentine, James		
Hardy	Brt	80	Tomely see Tornsly			(2)	Orn	598
James	Brt	80	Tomkins, Thomas	Cht	194	John	Orn	598
James	Grn	608	Tomlentonson,			Samuel	Orn	598
James	Mck	534	Archd.	Wlk	66	Samuel	Rwn	429
James	Mck	569	Tomlinson, Edmond	Jhn	763	Torrie, David	Rbs	424
James	Rwn	334	Harris	Jhn	769	Torry, James	Cmb	363
James	Rwn	370	Moses	Cht	166	Toter, Molley	Crr	150
James	Srr	696	Thomas	Crv	237	Totewine, Spence	Lnr	25
James, Junr.	Mck	533	Thomas	Mnt	498	Totty, Francis	Hlf	344
Jesse	Brt	80	Thomas	Ons	153	Robert	Hlf	344
Jesse	Ird	674	see Tumlinson			William	Orn	596

Totum, William	Crr 143	Peter	Rwn 298	Seth	Gts 279
Touchstone, Jonas	Glf 651	William	Rwn 298	Thomas	Gts 279
Touchton, Stephen	Mnt 465	Treesinger, Freder-		Trott, Abraham	Ons 140
Tounsend, Aaron	Cbr 678	ick	Rwn 389	Abram	Rwn 319
Charles	Cbr 689	Trencham, Lazarus	Grv 548	Adam	Ons 138
Daniel	Mnt 487	Trent, Simon	Ans 221	Henry	Rwn 334
Dudly	Cbr 699	William	Mck 528	Jacob	Rwn 429
James, Overseer	Mck 525	Trentham, Martin	Rwn 419	James	Ons 138
John	Mnt 487	Trett, Henry	Lnc 882	James	Rwn 334
Lewis	Cbr 688	Trevatham, Williss	Nsh 122	John	Ons 138
William	Cbr 687	Trevathan, Elisha	Gts 279	Richard	Ons 145
see Townsend		James	Gts 279	Samuel	Rwn 334
Tounsly, Oliver	Rwn 291	Trexeller, John	Rwn 291	Winnefreed	Ons 147
Tow, Abegail	Ons 152	Lawrence	Rwn 304	Trotter, Benjamin	Rnd 345
Deborah	Prq 651	Peter	Rwn 304	Ephraim	Glf 675
John	Prq 650	Peter	Rwn 310	George	Glf 674
Joseph	Prq 649	Trexler, John	Rwn 278	Joseph	Grv 513
Towel, Jessee	Orn 596	Tribble, Amos	Brk 801	Joseph	Glf 673
John	Orn 596	Trible, William	Wlk 66	Richard	Rwn 278
Towler, Benjm.	Prs 196	Tribute, Richard	Rwn 454	Richard	Rwn 291
Towning, James	Nwh 11A	Trice, Ann	Orn 602	Thomas	Trl 674
Townly, Joseph	Orn 597	Charles	Orn 598	Will.	Prs 210
Towns, Hanner	Wrr 835	Edward	Orn 598	William, P.M.	Orn 599
James	Wrr 835	Eliza	Orn 598	see Troller	
Richard	Wrr 835	Ezekiel	Orn 598	Troublefield,	
Townsend, David	Ans 212	Harrison	Orn 598	James	Smp 506
John	Ans 212	Henry	Orn 598	Trousdale, James	Orn 596
John	Brk 800	Henry	Orn 599	Trout, Henry	Lnc 890
Josiah	Prq 646	James	Orn 598	Jacob	Rwn 454
Lawrence	Cmb 370	Joseph	Orn 598	Joshua	Ans 214
Thomas	Rbs 423	William	Orn 602	Michael	Lnc 890
William	Prq 642	Trickey, Giles	Prs 199	Troutman, Adam,	
William	Rbs 424	Triflesteat, Freder-		Jur.	Rwn 304
Townsill, Thomas	Frn 480	ick	Lnc 882	Adam, Senr.	Rwn 304
Townson, John	Wlk 65	Peter	Lnc 882	Jacob	Ird 653
Towree, Adam	Lnc 898	Triftestal, John	Lnc 886	Jacob	Rwn 304
Towry, Edward	Lnc 891	Triggs, Samuel	Smp 524	Michael	Rwn 304
Towsey, Ellick	Chw 119	Trim, Charles	Prs 204	Peter	Cbr 714
Towson, Charles	Rch 263	Trimble, John	Orn 598	Troxler, Jacob	Orn 599
Toxey, Jacob	Trl 682	Trip, John	Cht 191	Troy, Jane	Rwn 278
Joseph	Cmd 108	Jonathan	Cht 190	Jean	Rwn 291
Toy, Francis A.	Bfr 23	Reubin	Cht 190	Michael	Rwn 278
Tracey, John	Jns 799	Robert	Bfr 18	Michael	Rwn 291
Tracy, Michael	Rwn 395	Triplet, Thomas	Brk 801	Trueblood, Caleb	Psq 626
Trady, Charles	Srr 695	Triplite, Eliza-		Caleb	Psq 631
Tramble, John	Brk 800	beth	Wlk 66	Jno.	Psq 632
Transaw, John	Stk 627	Ellender	Wlk 66	Jonathan	Psq 633
Rozania	Stk 626	Jesse	Wlk 65	Joshua	Psq 631
Trap, John	Rth 146	Mary	Wlk 66	Joshua	Psq 634
Robert	Rth 146	Thomas	Ash 89	Josiah	Psq 632
Trapnal, William	Cmb 386	William	Wlk 66	Samuel	Psq 634
Trausdale, William	Orn 595	Tripp, Avarella	Ptt 288	Thos.	Psq 633
see Trousdale		Caleb	Ptt 288	Timothy	Psq 627
Travers, Arthur	Brk 800	John	Bfr 18	Willi	Rnd 345
Charles	Mnt 520	Rhoda	Ptt 288	Truelock, Eliza-	
Henry	Mnt 519	William	Crv 245	beth	Ptt 243
Jane	Cmb 359	Trissel, Nathan	Ans 236	Truelove, Ladon	Cmb 389
John	Mnt 520	Trogdon, John	Rnd 348	Mitcherner	Chw 121
Traverse, William	Ird 616	Samuel	Rnd 348	Timothy	Cmb 389
Travis, Josiah	Rwn 383	William	Rnd 348	Truesdale, James	Grv 515
Traxler, Bennett	Orn 595	Trolenger, Henry	Glf 637	see Trausdale	
Traylor, Joseph	Prs 187	Henry	Orn 601	Truet, Nancy	Lnr 24
Joseph	Prs 196	John	Glf 637	Truett, Joseph	Lnr 24
Traywick, Moorre	Wke 767	Michal.	Rck 443	Truit, Collans	Srr 695
Othniel	Wke 767	Trolinger, Adam	Rck 454	Eli	Srr 695
Othoneil	Rbs 422	Saml.	Rck 454	James	Rwn 405
Robert	Wke 767	Troller, Robert	Orn 602	Joseph	Srr 695
Treadaway, Daniel	Ans 204	William, H.R.	Orn 602	Levi	Crv 315
Richard	Ans 204	Trorebaugh, George	Lnc 823	Levi	Rwn 389
Treadwell, John	Smp 516	William	Lnc 823	Truitt, Samuel	Srr 695
John, Sr.	Smp 516	Trosper, Elijah	Brk 800	Saragath	Srr 695
Treasurer, Richd.	Rck 449	Nicholas	Brk 800	William	Crv 305
Tredway, William	Bnc 190	Trotman, Elisha	Gts 279	Trull, Allen	Ans 231
Tredwell, Samuel	Chw 113	Ezekel	Gts 279	James	Mnt 513
Stephen	Mnt 519	Hannah	Chw 129	Stephen	Ans 231
Treece, Jacob	Rwn 304	Noah	Gts 279	Trulove, William	Frn 453
John	Rwn 304	Riddick	Gts 279	Trumbell, Jethro	Brt 80

Truss, Joel	Ptt 271	Sarah	Rnd 345	William H.	Wke 767	
Samuel, Junior	Ptt 271	Shaderick	Rck 457	Turnbull, James	Wlk 65	
Samuel, Senior	Ptt 271	Shadk.	Rck 482	John	Wlk 65	
Trusty, David	Rwn 383	Sion	Nsh 123	Turner, Abraham	Ptt 283	
John	Rwn 383	Starling	Lnc 885	Abraham	Wlk 65	
John	Rwn 389	Thomas	Ird 617	Agness	Orn 600	
William	Mnt 499	Thomas	Lnc 864	Amey	Brn 13A	
Trwood, Thomas	Lnc 886	Thomas	Rnd 345	Amos	Brt 80	
Tucker, Aaron	Rwn 439	Thomas	Stk 574	Ann	Nsh 122	
Amos	Dpl 420	Thos.	Lnr 24	Anna	Brt 80	
Anderson	Wrr 833	William	Brk 799	Aron	Rch 259	
Andrew	Rwn 439	William	Cht 171	Augustus	Wke 767	
Anne	Lnc 898	William	Hlf 346	Bartholomew	Bnc 190	
Anthony	Nrt 481	William	Rnd 345	Benjamin	Cmb 359	
Arch	Srr 709	William	Smp 533	Benjamin	Hde 379	
Benja.	Nsh 123	William	Srr 695	Benjamin	Prq 656	
Benjamin	Hlf 346	William	Wrr 834	Benjamin	Prq 658	
Benjamin	Rwn 429	Willis	Lnc 885	Bethlehem	Hlf 346	
Branch	Srr 710	Winney	Nsh 124	Betty	Rnd 345	
Campbell	Glf 655	Tuder, Owen	Cmb 392	Caleb	Nrt 481	
Carner	Srr 709	Tudor, Eltheldred	Rbs 424	Charles	Grv 570	
Charles	Glf 647	Tuel, James	Nsh 124	Daniel	Cmd 106	
Corbin	Nsh 124	Tugal, James	Ptt 269	David	Brt 80	
Curle	Nrt 481	Tuggle, Griffin	Csw 148	David	Wke 768	
Daniel	Grv 582	Tugman, Edward	Wlk 66	Dawson	Jns 787	
Daniel	Jhn 763	James	Wlk 66	Edward	Orn 595	
David	Dpl 420	Tugwell, James	Gts 280	Edward	Orn 599	
David	Ird 669	Tull, Agnes	Glf 657	Elias	Orn 597	
Dircah	Nsh 123	Charles	Lnr 22	Elias	Orn 599	
Edward	Rwn 434	George	Stk 608	Elias	Srr 695	
Elijah	Dpl 440	John	Lnr 24	Elias, junr.	Orn 597	
Frances	Hlf 346	William	Lnr 22	Elias, junr.	Orn 599	
Francis	Wrr 834	William	Srr 695	Elsbury	Prq 644	
Frederick	Hlf 346	Winifred	Lnr 27	Ezekiel	Hde 379	
George	Rnd 345	Tulley, John	Lnr 25	George	Prq 657	
George	Srr 695	Tullock, David	Csw 120	Henry	Csw 106	
George, (Junr.)	Cbr 696	Tully, Starling	Grv 567	Henry	Csw 135	
George, Senr.	Brk 799	Tumbleston, James	Glf 655	Henry	Mrt 411	
George, Senr.	Cbr 697	James	Lnc 907	Henry	Prq 649	
Gray	Hlf 346	James, Junr.	Lnc 907	Henry	Prq 659	
Henry	Lnr 24	John	Brk 799	Jacob	Lnr 25	
Hezh.	Csw 108	John	Glf 655	James (2)	Brt 80	
Jacob	Mnt 481	Zadoc	Glf 655	James	Csw 122	
Jacobs	Cbr 697	Tumlinson, Archd.	Ird 622	James	Csw 124	
James	Brt 80	Becket	Ird 616	James	Csw 133	
Jarrot	Mre 58	John	Ird 622	James	Csw 136	
Joab	Nsh 123	Josiah	Rwn 358	James	Cmb 373	
John	Brk 801	Samuel	Rwn 358	James	Hlf 344	
John	Cbr 694	Tummans, Samuel	Brk 799	James (2)	Hlf 346	
John	Cht 223	William	Brk 799	James	Jns 789	
John	Ird 669	Tummire, Samuel	Brk 798	James	Nsh 122	
John	Lnc 898	see Tunmire		James	Orn 601	
John	Prs 196	Tunmire, Peter	Brk 799	James	Rch 266	
John	Rwn 454	Tunnage, Michal	Stk 610	James	Wrr 833	
John	Srr 696	Tunnel, William	Hlf 346	James, jr.	Orn 601	
John	Wrr 834	Tunstall, Eliza-		James, Senr.	Csw 105	
John	Wrr 835	beth	Brt 80	James, Senr.	Mnt 465	
John E.	Wrr 834	George	Frn 484	James, Sr.	Wrr 833	
Joseph	Wke 769	Payton R.	Hlf 346	Jesse	Bnc 190	
Joshua	Ptt 226	Richard	Wrr 833	Jesse	Mnt 499	
Kelly	Ptt 283	Tunus, Hoglan	Wlk 66	John	Ans 212	
Levy	Glf 623	Tupper, Samuel	Chw 114	John	Bld 32	
Mary	Jhn 761	Turbush, Luke	Cmd 101	John	Bnc 190	
Nethaniel (2)	Rnd 345	Turbyfill, John	Lnc 863	John	Edg 175	
Obadiah	Csw 102	Ludwick	Lnc 863	John	Edg 245	
Pascal	Jhn 763	Turher, Miel	Ons 163	John	Grv 566	
Peter	Cbr 693	Turke, John	Bnc 158	John (2)	Jhn 763	
Pharaby	Nsh 123	Turley, Richard	Jhn 750	John	Jns 787	
Prissilla	Nsh 122	Turnage, Abraham	Grn 593	John	Psq 628	
Redick	Ptt 226	Daniel	Grn 596	John	Prs 196	
Right	Ptt 225	Emanuel	Ptt 264	John	Rwn 334	
Robert	Jhn 758	Jesse	Dpl 427	John	Smp 518	
Robey	Ird 669	John	Grn 600	John	Smp 527	
Robt.	Nsh 124	Josiah	Crv 329	John	Smp 530	
Samuel	Lnc 891	Luke	Grn 600	Jonathan	Wke 767	
Samuel	Rth 147	William	Grn 593	Joseph	Bnc 190	
Sarah	Prq 649	William, junr.	Grn 600	Joseph	Psq 629	

Joseph	Prq 644	William	Hde 379	Jacob	Ons 180
Joseph	Prs 194	Tuvnen see Tewnen		John	Ons 157
Joseph	Rth 148	Tweedy, Jonathan	Psq 631	Joseph	Ons 180
Juda	Mnt 503	Twiddy, Benjamin	Trl 682	William	Ons 166
Lazarus	Bld 19	David	Trl 682	Umphrig, Daniel	Crv 237
Mabrey	Ons 162	Devotion	Trl 682	Umphrys, James	Brk 801
Martha	Nrt 481	Jessy	Ons 139	William	Brk 801
Mathias	Rth 147	John	Trl 682	Umpstead, John	Orn 571
Matiah	Cht 186	John, Junr.	Trl 682	Umstead, Daniel	Orn 619
Matthew	Ans 204	Samuel	Trl 682	David	Orn 619
Matthew	Ans 205	Twiford, Leven	Crr 148	Richard	Orn 619
Matthew	Ans 207	William	Trl 682	Underdew, Polley	Hlf 346
Matthew	Wke 768	Twigs, Timothy	Rth 148	Underhill, John	Rnd 348
Matthew	Wne 861	Twilly, Robert	Dpl 441	William	Dpl 400
Minus	Crr 147	Twine, Abraham	Prq 659	William	Smp 514
Myles	Prq 649	Elisha	Prq 661	Underwood, Abner	Csw 148
Nathan	Wrr 833	Jesse	Prq 643	Alex.	Mnt 509
Nathl.	Ans 204	John	Chw 117	Arthur	Cbr 692
Nathl.	Ans 230	Thomas	Prq 661	Daniel	Cht 180
Nei...n	Nwh 10	William	Psq 640	Eml.	Nsh 125
Nelson	Hlf 346	Twinmire, David	Mck 571	George	Mre 67
Peter	Hlf 346	Twitty, Allen	Rth 146	Hamblet	Mnt 508
Pheroby	Hlf 346	Russel	Rth 147	Hanah	Nsh 125
Rachael	Ptt 283	William	Rth 146	Henry	Mnt 509
Robert	Bnc 191	Tyce, Thomas	Crv 343	Henry	Mnt 510
Robert	Mnt 503	Tye, John	Mnt 504	Henry	Orn 600
Roger	Wlk 65	William	Ans 217	Howel	Nsh 125
Salley	Wke 768	Tyleman, Jno.	Lnc 832	Isham,(Mulatto)	Edg 249
Sampson	Brt 80	Tyler, Aaron	Cmb 378	James	Cht 181
Samuel (2)	Rth 147	Edward D.	Mnt 474	James	Cht 214
Sarah	Bld 32	Eliza.	Lnr 22	James	Orn 600
Sarah	Bnc 190	Moses	Bld 15	Jesse	Nrt 481
Simon	Nrt 481	Thomas	Edg 246	Joel	Srr 710
Simon	Wke 767	Tylman, Elisha	Bld 14	John	Cht 180
Solomon	Hlf 346	Tylor, Bartlet	Wrr 835	John	Nrt 481
Susanna	Prs 198	Needham	Smp 523	Joseph	Bnc 191
Susanna	Wrr 834	Owen	Smp 530	Joseph	Glf 660
Swisher	Wrr 834	Tyner, John	Nrt 481	Joseph	Mnt 508
Thomas	Bld 10	Nicholas	Nrt 481	Joshua	Glf 662
Thomas	Csw 106	William	Nrt 481	Lewis	Wlk 66
Thomas	Csw 135	Tynes, John	Hlf 346	Malici	Nsh 125
Thomas	Crv 239	Tynor, Thomas	Mre 77	Nancy	Cht 196
Thomas	Hlf 346	Tyre, George	Ash 89	Reubin	Glf 662
Thomas	Mnt 498	George	Ptt 285	Rubin	Lnc 858
Thomas	Srr 696	James	Ptt 265	Samuel	Mnt 508
Thomas	Wlk 65	Jesse	Crv 271	Simon	Wke 769
Titus	Wke 768	John	Ash 89	Stephen	Brk 801
Will.	Nsh 124	John	Crv 321	Thomas	Hlf 346
William	Ans 204	Thomas	Ash 89	Thomas	Smp 517
William	Cmb 382	Thomas	Crv 269	William	Nrt 481
William	Cmb 385	William	Ash 89	William	Rch 257
William	Hrt 714	William	Crv 271	William	Wlk 66
William	Jns 789	William	Crv 285	Wm.	Csw 147
William	Orn 597	Tyrlington, Southy	Smp 529	UnderWood, Samuel	Rnd 348
William	Orn 599	Tyrrell, Soloman	Cht 154	Unthank, Allen	Glf 679
William	Ptt 283	Tyrry, David	Smp 522	James	Glf 680
William	Rwn 334	Tyson, Aaron	Mre 59	Joseph	Glf 665
William	Smp 522	Benjamine	Mre 60	Josiah	Glf 681
William	Wke 768	Charles	Bld 22	Up, Jacob	Stk 573
William	Wrr 834	Moses	Bld 22	Nu.	Stk 573
Wilson	Ird 637	Richard	Cht 222	Upchurch, Abel	Frn 469
Zekel	Srr 695	Thomas	Mre 44	Anny	Cht 208
see Povel, Ray				Benjamin	Frn 469
Turnge, Zacheriah	Dpl 427			Buckner	Frn 467
Turrentine, Samuel	Orn 493	-- U --		Charles	Frn 472
Turry, Jno.	Csw 137			David	Rth 148
Turton, Arther	Crr 164			George	Ird 627
Tury, Nancy	Csw 103	Uery, George	Cbr 710	James	Frn 467
Tush, Adam	Rwn 376	Uety, Godfred	Cbr 711	James	Frn 477
Tusney, Gilbert	Srr 710	Umfleet, Benjamin	Hrt 719	John	Grv 543
Tussey, John	Rwn 405	Joseph	Wne 862	Joseph	Rth 148
Tuten, William	Lnr 24	Umphlet, William	Gts 280	Jubal	Frn 469
Tuton, Shadrach	Ptt 256	Umphrey, Daniel	Ons 175	Martha	Wke 770
William	Ptt 287	David	Ons 179	Moses	Frn 471
William	Smp 527	Francis	Ons 181	Richard	Frn 467
Tuttle, John	Stk 572	Jacob	Jns 813	Samuel	Cht 209
Peter	Hlf 346	Jacob	Ons 174	Wm.	Wke 769

UpChurch, William	Grv 543	
Upright, Samuel	Rwn 310	
Uptergrove, George	Rth 148	
Solomon	Rth 148	
William	Rth 148	
Upton, David	Cht 197	
Edward	Cmd 97	
Edward	Mre 49	
Edward	Rth 148	
Hillery	Cmd 94	
Jesse	Mre 49	
John	Cmd 101	
John	Mre 76	
John	Rbs 425	
Major	Crv 337	
Mark	Cmd 100	
Need	Cht 223	
Nicholas	Rth 148	
Robert	Rbs 425	
Thomas	Cmd 107	
Thomas	Rth 148	
William	Cmd 107	
Ure, Andrew	Nwh 2A	
Urghuart, Mary	Crv 245	
Urquhart, Alexan-		
der	Brt 90	
Alexander	Cmb 374	
Henry	Nwh 2	
John	Cmb 390	
Norman	Cmb 374	
Usenam, Charles	Rwn 395	
Usher, Samuel	Rch 248	
Thomas	Rch 250	
Uslun, Sally	Brk 801	
Usrey, Martin	Cbr 716	
Usry, Nathan	Cht 195	
Rebeckah	Rth 149	
Ussarry, Elizabeth	Cmb 359	
Ussery, David	Mnt 495	
Elijah	Mnt 492	
James	Mnt 494	
John	Mnt 492	
Martin	Mnt 465	
Thomas	Mnt 465	
William	Brk 801	
Utley, Allen	Cmb 391	
Britain	Wke 770	
Burwell	Wke 769	
Isham	Wke 769	
Jacob	Cmb 391	
John, Jur.	Wke 769	
John, Senr.	Wke 769	
John L.	Wke 769	
Jonathan	Wke 769	
L. John	Wke 769	
Merrill	Wke 769	
Phebea	Wke 769	
William	Cmb 391	
William	Wke 769	
Utzman, Jacob	Rwn 291	
Uzzel, Major	Wne 843	
Ison	Lnr 27	
Uzzell, Thomas	Lnr 25	
-- V --		
Vaceshu, James	Csw 98	
Vail, Benners	Crv 287	
Bond	Crv 293	
Elijah	Hde 379	
Elisabeth	Crv 229	
Richard	Brt 82	
Thomas	Brt 82	
Thomas	Chw 127	
Vaill, John	Crv 251	

Vails, James	Rwn 310	
Valantine, Rigdan	Wrr 835	
Vale, John	Nrt 483	
Mary	Bfr 19	
Valentine, Alexan-		
der	Hrt 702	
Clary	Nrt 483	
David	Hrt 702	
David	Wke 770	
Paul	Hrt 702	
William	Grv 524	
Valiant, Ancil	Glf 672	
Vallentine, Benja.	Bld 46	
Hardy	Bld 46	
Vallett, Francis	Chw 115	
Vanata, Peter	Lnc 826	
Vance, Anne	Edg 251	
Daniel	Rch 248	
David	Bnc 191	
John	Hlf 348	
Samuel	Cmb 359	
Widow	Mck 539	
William	Hlf 348	
Vandagriff, Archd.	Wke 770	
Ells	Wke 770	
Vandeford, George	Lnc 892	
James	Ans 202	
John	Ans 202	
John	Cht 222	
John, Jr.	Ans 202	
Minta	Cht 222	
William	Cht 222	
Vanderpoll, Josiah	Srr 697	
Abraham	Ash 90	
Anthony	Ash 90	
Isaac	Wlk 67	
Jesse	Brk 802	
John (2)	Ash 90	
John	Wlk 67	
Samuel	Ash 90	
Winen	Ash 90	
Vandever, John	Srr 697	
Vandike, John	Grv 517	
Vandyke, James	Lnc 834	
Joseph	Lnc 844	
Richd.	Lnc 828	
Vane, John	Stk 558	
Van Eltin, Samuel	Rwn 450	
Van Etlin see Van Eltin		
Vangan, Zebulon	Stk 574	
Vanghan see Vaughn		
Vanhaus, John	Rth 149	
Vanhook, Isaac	Prs 192	
Jacob	Prs 218	
Kindle	Prs 211	
Lawrence	Csw 115	
Loyd	Prs 213	
Lucey	Prs 202	
Robert	Prs 203	
Vanhorn, Christian-		
na	Lnc 823	
Isaac	Brk 801	
John	Lnc 870	
Vanhouse, Vasel	Mnt 498	
Vanhoy, Jeremiah	Stk 620	
Vanlandingham, Dan-		
iel	Rck 460	
Dawson	Wrr 835	
John	Wrr 835	
Peter	Edg 251	
Richd.	Rck 477	
Vann, Charity	Smp 516	
Elisha	Edg 251	
James	Gts 280	
Jesse	Gts 280	
John	Bnc 191	
John	Smp 533	

John	Smp 534	
John,(of Isaac)	Gts 280	
John, Senr.	Gts 280	
King	Smp 513	
Mary	Cmb 359	
Needham	Smp 526	
Rachel	Gts 280	
Stephen	Dpl 418	
Thomas	Smp 516	
Thos.	Mrt 413	
William	Cmb 369	
William	Edg 251	
William	Smp 512	
William	Smp 514	
Van Noorden, Had	Ptt 239	
Vannoy, Andrew	Wlk 66	
Francis	Wlk 66	
John	Wlk 66	
Nathanl.	Wlk 66	
Vanover, Mathew	Wlk 67	
Vanoy, Edward	Stk 558	
Jamima	Stk 575	
Vanpelt, Daniel	Hrt 707	
Harmon	Hrt 714	
James	Brt 82	
John	Edg 251	
Luke	Hrt 714	
Peter	Brt 82	
Simon	Mck 522	
Van Pelt, Anthony	Grn 594	
John	Ptt 249	
Vanpool, Henry	Rwn 314	
Widow	Rwn 297	
Van Pool, Jacob	Rwn 303	
John	Rwn 303	
Vanstray, John	Glf 665	
Vanwinkle, Benja-		
min	Ash 90	
James	Ash 90	
Vardin, Moses	Psq 637	
Tully	Psq 637	
Varnal, Benjamin	Edg 251	
John	Edg 251	
Varner, John	Rnd 353	
Varnon, James	Stk 595	
Varnor, Henry	Rwn 298	
John	Rwn 383	
Widow	Mck 528	
Varnum, Jacob	Rnd 346	
John	Rbs 425	
Varzant, Barnabas	Srr 697	
Vass, Greenberry	Csw 100	
Thomas (2)	Grv 542	
Thomas	Stk 614	
Thomas, Senr.	Grv 550	
Vincent	Rck 474	
Vasser, Dawson	Edg 251	
James	Nrt 483	
Sally	Hrt 732	
Vaugh, Ishmael	Orn 609	
Vaughan, A.	Srr 707	
Abe	Srr 706	
David	Nrt 481	
Elijah	Hrt 736	
Frederick	Stk 587	
Henrietta	Cmb 359	
Henry	Rck 461	
Honor	Nrt 483	
James	Grv 517	
James, Junr.	Nrt 483	
James, Senr.	Nrt 483	
Jeremiah	Hlf 348	
John	Csw 121	
John	Hrt 736	
John (4)	Nrt 483	
John	Stk 593	
Joseph	Stk 590	

Name	Ref		Name	Ref		Name	Ref
Joshua	Hlf 348		Verdier, Francis	Nwh 3A		Jehue	Rnd 348
Lewis	Csw 112		Verell, William	Frn 447		John	Rnd 348
Lewis	Csw 127		Vermilion, Guy	Rck 476		Vicks, John	Rth 149
Martha	Nrt 483		Vernelson, Charles	Mrt 413		Samuel	Srr 697
Mary	Cmb 359		Nehemiah	Mrt 413		Vickus see Vickers	
Salley	Hlf 348		Vernon, Isaac	Rck 461		Vicus, Elijah	Wlk 67
Sarah	Hrt 737		Isaac	Rck 487		Vidito, Stephen	Rwn 359
Sarah	Nsh 124		Isaac, Senr.	Rck 487		Vill see Fum. Vill	
Stephen	Nsh 124		James	Rck 483		Vincen, Grove	Mck 586
Thomas	Csw 133		John	Rck 487		Obadiah	Mck 586
Thomas	Nrt 483		Jonan.	Rck 487		Thomas	Mck 586
Thomas, Jur.	Csw 133		Nehemiah	Rck 488		Vincent, Alexander	Grv 523
Vinsent	Wrr 835		Richd.	Rck 484		Ann	Csw 140
William (2)	Hlf 348		Richd., Senr.	Rck 487		Drury	Hrt 737
William, jr.	Hrt 737		Vernor, Henry	Lnc 840		Elizabeth	Hrt 736
Vaughhan, William	Stk 578		Wm.	Lnc 840		Jacob	Grv 557
Vaughn, Duella	Prs 189		Vernum, Jonathan	Stk 589		James	Csw 145
George	Prs 201		Versor, William	Wrr 836		Joseph	Wke 770
Granvil	Prs 190		Vesall, David	Cht 184		Maccalester	Hlf 348
John	Wlk 66		see Veasal			Moses	Rck 474
Joshua	Brk 802		Vest, Charles	Stk 574		Moses	Rck 476
Mastin	Hfl 348		Isham	Stk 574		Orias	Wke 770
Sherewood	Brk 801		Samuel	Stk 574		Peter	Rwn 383
Thomas	Lnc 851		William, Jun.	Stk 574		Rachel	Rwn 383
William (2)	Rth 149		William, Ser.	Stk 574		Richard	Grv 522
Vaulx, Daniel	Wrr 836		Vestal, Benjn.	Cht 195		Telitha	Ptt 284
Vaun, William	Ans 214		David	Cht 194		Thomas	Orn 609
William	Jhn 755		David	Cht 216		William	Mnt 509
Vause, Ephraim	Lnr 27		Isaac	Srr 697		Vines, John	Brn 13
William	Lnr 27		James	Srr 697		Samuel	Brn 13A
Wm., Jur.	Lnr 27		Jesse	Rnd 348		Samuel	Ptt 278
Vaws, John	Lnr 27		John	Srr 697		Sarah	Wlk 67
Vawter, John	Stk 593		Nathan	Srr 709		Thomas	Bfr 19
Vawters, Russel	Stk 592		Silas	Cht 195		William	Bfr 19
Veach, Elijah	Rwn 434		Thomas	Cht 194		Winnifrid	Bfr 19
John	Rwn 359		Thomas	Srr 697		Vinsant, Abraham	Rth 149
John	Rwn 450		William	Cht 194		Jacob	Rth 149
Richard	Ird 637		see Visal			James	Rth 149
Richard	Rwn 450		Vestall, Daniel	Srr 704		Vinson, Abner	Nrt 483
Veache, John	Ird 637		Thomas	Srr 709		Allen	Cht 201
Veale, Dempsey	Crr 140		Vestel, Jesse	Srr 697		Archble.	Jhn 770
Veark, Henry	Nwh 7		Vester, Elzabeth			Benjamin	Rth 149
Veasal, Elijah	Grv 567		Mical	Nsh 124		Benjamin	Wne 844
see Vesall			Solomon	Nsh 124		David	Frn 476
Veasey see Veisey			William, Sr.	Nsh 125		David	Nrt 483
Vechine, Everyhart	Ans 205		Viar, William	Wlk 66		Drury	Jhn 777
Veisey, Abner	Orn 609		Vicars, John	Rth 149		Groves	Ans 237
Veitch, William	Cbr 680		Vick, Benja.	Nsh 125		Henry	Nrt 483
Venable, John	Stk 574		Henry	Nsh 125		Jacob	Edg 251
William	Bnc 191		Jacob	Hrt 738		James	Frn 477
William	Stk 574		Jacob	Nsh 125		James	Nrt 483
Vendrick, Abraham	Crv 289		Joel	Nsh 125		John	Jhn 759
Ann	Crv 289		John	Ptt 231		Leticius	Hlf 348
James	Crv 287		John, Jur.	Nsh 125		Moses	Ans 209
James	Crv 307		John, Sr.	Nsh 125		Paton	Jhn 769
Jesse	Crv 287		Jordan	Ans 232		Peter	Nrt 483
John	Crv 289		Joseph	Smp 503		Philip	Hlf 348
William	Crv 287		Joshua	Nsh 125		Reuben	Ans 209
Vendricks, Rebecca	Crv 263		Josiah	Hlf 348		Samuel	Rnd 348
Veneble, Jno.	Lnc 840		Lewis	Nsh 125		Silas	Nrt 481
Venson, Salmon	Wne 855		Mary	Hlf 348		Thomas	Cht 201
Venters, Arther	Ons 163		Moses	Rwn 376		Thomas	Nrt 483
Benjamin	Ptt 258		Nathan	Nsh 125		William	Nrt 483
Daniel	Ptt 258		Providence	Edg 251		Willis	Hlf 348
Francis	Ons 152		Robert	Grn 587		Vinters, Asa	Jns 795
James	Jns 809		Robert	Nsh 125		Virgin, Jas.	Mrt 388
Mack	Ons 156		Robert	Smp 529		Virginia, Wm. Jor-	
Moses	Hde 379		Vickers, Alexander	Rwn 292		dan	Psq 634
Ventourse, Grace	Crr 154		Charles	Cht 157		Visal, William	Cht 216
Ventress, Edward	Rnd 348		Ralph	Edg 251		Visson, Thomas G.	Crv 237
Frederick	Rnd 346		Rylie, (Vick)	Orn 609		Vistal see Vestal	
Stephen	Wsh 716		Vickorey, Marma-			Viviet, Lancelot	Edg 251
Verble, Henry	Rwn 292		duke	Bnc 191		Vivirett, Micajah	Nsh 125
Jacob	Rwn 298		Vickory, Abner	Rnd 348		Vodin, Lodwick	Wke 770
John	Rwn 298		Absolom	Rnd 348		William	Wke 770
Vercer, Nathan	Wke 770		Christopher	Rnd 348		Voight, John W.	Gts 280
Verden, David	Edg 251					Voik see Vick	

Voiles, George	Cbr 689	Micajah	Grv 569	Waite, John	Psq 629
Hannah	Cbr 688	Moses	Rck 464	Parker	Psq 628
Roland	Cbr 688	Obediah	Dpl 440	Waitman, Daniel	Rth 154
Thomas	Cbr 685	Robert	Grv 509	Wakefield, Alexan-	
Voille, John	Rth 149	Robert	Rnd 347	der	Brk 805
Volentine, Joseph	Gts 280	Sarah	Brn 16	Charles, Junr.	Brk 804
Thos.	Nsh 125	Seth	Rnd 352	Charles, Sn.	Brk 804
Volick, John	Rwn 323	Theodore	Crt 71	John	Brk 805
Vollentine, Richd.	Bld 29	Widow	Ans 241	Thomas	Brk 805
Volloway, Elisha	Trl 692	William	Crt 68	Thomas	Stk 576
Joseph, Junr.	Trl 692	William	Rnd 352	Wakiser, Jacob	Rwn 390
Joseph, Senr.	Trl 692	Wadford, John	Edg 254	Wakser, Jacob,	
Volluntine, Penny	Ons 159	Wadkins, David	Wlk 67	Junr.	Rwn 389
Voris, Aaron	Rwn 338	Gillam	Frn 484	Walace, Matthew	Mck 554
Vose, Thomas	Brt 82	John	Frn 477	Walbert, John	Rth 153
Voss, John	Mck 597	Matthew	Bld 15	Walden, David	Wke 772
William	Mck 579	Nancy	Rck 486	Drury	Nrt 483
Vossel, Johen	Cbr 695	Phillip	Prs 214	Eaton	Wrr 837
Voswinkle, Jatus		Richard	Wrr 837	Harwood	Nrt 487
K.	Nwh 2A	Wiley	Jhn 753	John	Ans 236
Vowell, William	Glf 645	Willis	Wke 773	John	Cht 172
Vowels, Cenah	Hde 379	Wadsworth, Archd.	Mre 74	John	Wrr 837
Vukins, Ratrigh	Csw 140	Ignatius	Crv 315	Michael	Nrt 485
Vuncannon, Martin	Rnd 348	Jason (2)	Mre 52	Richard	Ans 235
Peter (2)	Rnd 348	John	Mre 58	Samuel	Jhn 748
		Thomas	Crv 229	Walder, John	Dpl 413
		Thos.	Mre 74	Nathan	Dpl 413
-- W --		William	Crv 315	Nathaniel	Dpl 412
		see McWadsworth		Waldin, David	Mre 59
		Waff, Thomas	Chw 115	Walding, John	Ons 175
W...esly, Mary	Nwh 6A	William	Chw 115	John	Ons 179
Wace, Jacob	Rth 153	Wafford, Abram	Rwn 405	Rebh.	Ons 179
Wadall, Edmond	Rnd 351	Samuel	Rwn 405	Waldrope, Daniel	Rth 152
Waddel, Thomas	Cht 180	Widow	Rwn 405	Isiah	Rth 152
Waddell, Hu.,Esqr.	Bld 28	Waganer, John	Srr 699	John	Rth 152
Jacob	Frn 447	Wageman, George	Stk 601	Johonias	Rth 152
John, Esqr.	Bld 23	Waggley, John	Brk 805	Luke	Rth 152
Wadden, Richard	Jhn 754	Waggoner, Adam	Stk 608	Waler, Jacob	Rwn 420
Waddington, Samuel	Cbr 705	Adam	Srr 700	Wales, George	Ird 637
Waddle, Charles	Glf 669	Benjamin	Hde 379	Richard	Mnt 487
David	Ird 666	Catharine	Orn 605	Samuel	Ird 637
Elizabeth	Glf 644	Daniel, Cap.	Rwn 350	Waley, Charles	Cmd 97
Hugh	Brn 18	Daniel, Senr.	Rwn 350	Walfinton, Jas.	Rck 453
James	Mck 528	Edmond	Lnc 863	Walk, Elizabeth	Rwn 420
Joel	Cmb 391	Gabirl	Stk 576	Jonathan	Rwn 412
John	Ird 669	Henry	Ash 90	Joseph	Rwn 420
William	Mck 560	Henry	Orn 605	Samuel	Rwn 420
Waddleton, Edwd.	Csw 101	Isaac	Rth 152	Walker, Aaron	Wrr 840
Edwd.	Csw 107	Jacob	Bnc 191	Abraham	Ird 627
Waddy, Spence	Frn 449	Jacob	Orn 605	Adley	Crr 137
Wade, Abram	Crt 66	Jacob	Rwn 350	Alex.	Csw 147
Amos	Crv 255	John	Glf 665	Alex.	Rck 481
Andrew	Ans 214	John	Orn 605	Allen	Rck 442
Andrew	Rnd 352	John	Rwn 350	Allen	Rck 466
Ann	Crv 293	Joseph	Stk 575	Andrew	Mck 545
Archable	Ons 136	Leonard	Orn 605	Andrew	Orn 607
Barney	Crt 66	Peter	Glf 639	Andrew, Esqr.	Mck 588
Benja., Jur.	Wke 772	Peter	Glf 665	Archd., (Cap.	Mck 604
Benjamin	Wke 772	Samuel	Stk 576	Arthur	Ird 653
Benjamin	Wke 773	Thomas	Lnc 864	Asawell	Crr 148
Charles	Grv 568	William	Srr 707	Baker	Smp 532
David	Crt 66	William, Jr.	Stk 577	Benjamin	Brk 802
Edmond	Mre 42	William, Ser.	Stk 577	Benjamin	Lnc 851
Elisabeth	Ans 200	Waggonor, Hannah	Lnc 872	Benjamin	Rwn 439
Elisha	Nrt 483	Michael	Lnc 871	Caleb	Crr 144
Elisha	Rck 444	Wagley, Abraham	Bnc 193	Cathrine	Rth 151
George	Crt 68	Wagoner, William	Cbr 699	Celia	Rwn 338
Henry F.	Rnd 346	Wagster, David	Mnt 508	Charles	Brk 807
Howell	Nrt 485	William	Mnt 508	Charles	Rbs 425
Isaac	Crt 66	Wahob, Thomas	Crt 59	Charles	Wlk 69
Jeremiah	Stk 550	Waid, Andrew	Frn 455	Daniel	Bfr 20
John	Nrt 483	Thomas	Ash 91	Daniel	Nsh 127
Joseph	Crv 253	Waide, Thomas	Bfr 24	Daniel	Rth 151
Joseph	Grn 611	Wailon, Peter	Rwn 350	Daniel	Rth 153
Lemuel	Grn 611	Wainright, Ann	Hrt 733	David	Dpl 426
Lidia	Ans 200	Wainwright, James	Ptt 281	David	Stk 575
Memucom	Grv 568	William	Ptt 280	David	Srr 698

Name	Code	Name	Code	Name	Code
Dempsey	Crr 148	Major	Jhn 759	Jacob	Wlk 67
E.	Lnc 887	Martha	Rth 151	Jeremiah	Rbs 425
Edward	Psq 628	Mary	Cmb 359	Jesse	Jhn 761
Eleanor	Wsh 712	Mary Ann	Nwh 7A	Jesse	Wke 773
Eliza.	Rck 453	Matthew	Mck 553	John	Cht 219
Elizabeth	Crr 143	Maxey	Crr 144	John	Glf 620
Elizabeth	Rth 150	Michael	Cbr 718	John	Jhn 761
Ephamia	Bld 49	Milly	Rck 445	John	Mnt 498
Ezeriah	Crr 144	Mitchel	Crr 142	John	Rnd 349
Felix	Rth 150	Patsey	Hrt 719	John	Rck 436
Francis (2)	Cmb 360	Peter	Wrr 839	John	Rth 156
Francis	Prs 195	Pricilla	Crr 164	John	Wke 773
George	Cmb 359	Rebecah	Wrr 836	Joseph	Bfr 21
George	Rth 151	Richard	Lnc 892	Joseph	Wlk 67
Green	Frn 464	Robert	Bnc 194	Mack	Nsh 130
Hadley	Crr 147	Robert	Mck 532	Mial	Nwh 5A
Harburt	Wrr 838	Robert	Mnt 513	Michael	Wke 773
Henry	Cbr 718	Robert	Orn 607	Peter	Rck 437
Henry	Grv 578	Robert	Rnd 347	Peter	Rck 478
Henry	Wlk 68	Robert	Rck 471	Randle	Mnt 487
Howard	Wlk 68	Robert	Srr 700	Richard	Mnt 498
Hugh	Mck 536	Rubin	Brk 803	Richd.	Rck 485
Jacob	Glf 651	Saml.	Wrr 838	Robert	Rck 466
Jacob	Rth 150	Samuel	Grv 526	Robert	Wke 773
James	Brk 807	Samuel (2)	Rnd 347	Samuel	Wke 773
James	Cbr 707	Sarah	Orn 608	William	Cht 219
James	Csw 146	Silvanus	Mck 540	William	Nrt 485
James	Cmb 394	Solomon	Cmb 377	William	Srr 698
James	Glf 646	Solomon	Edg 257	William	Wke 773
James	Glf 681	Solomon	Wrr 839	William, Jr.	Jhn 761
James	Ird 614	Spine	Crr 142	William, Sr.	Jhn 761
James	Mck 529	Stewart	Wsh 712	Willis	Wke 773
James	Mck 544	Tandy	Cht 159	Zachariah	Rck 485
James	Mck 554	Thaddias	Rth 156	see Waul	
James	Nwh 3	Thomas	Bfr 20	Wallace, Adam	Crt 76
James	Orn 605	Thomas	Edg 257	Anthony	Ptt 270
James	Rck 489	Thomas	Mck 561	Archibald	Crv 293
James	Rth 151	Thomas	Mck 590	Asa	Jns 805
James	Wke 771	Thomas	Wsh 712	Benjamin	Crv 301
James	Wlk 69	Thomas, B.Creek	Bfr 20	Benjamin	Ons 157
James W.	Nwh 1A	Thos.	Crr 142	Beverly	Crv 245
Jeremiah	Rth 151	Thos.	Crr 143	David, jr.	Crt 58
Jesse	Rwn 435	William	Bfr 19	David, sr.	Crt 58
Joab	Rth 151	William	Brk 803	Etherldred	Mrt 414
Job	Grv 573	William	Grv 526	George	Ptt 278
Job	Prs 205	William	Ird 653	Hannah	Crt 58
Joel	Nsh 130	William	Mnt 515	Isham	Mnt 484
Joel	Rck 466	William	Nrt 487	James	Bnc 192
John	Bnc 192	William	Rnd 347	James	Csw 118
John	Cmb 362	William	Rck 452	James	Dpl 418
John	Grv 576	William	Rck 472	Jane	Crt 73
John	Grv 580	William	Rck 481	Jeremiah	Hlf 350
John	Glf 656	William	Rwn 435	Jno.	Csw 118
John	Lnc 851	William	Rwn 440	Jno., Jur.	Csw 118
John	Mck 529	William	Stk 575	Jodiah	Cbr 681
John	Mck 544	William	Wke 771	John	Crt 59
John	Mck 590	William	Wke 774	John	Edg 254
John	Mnt 513	William, Jr.	Stk 576	John	Ird 614
John	Nwh 1A	William, Jur.	Wke 773	John	Rth 153
John	Nwh 6A	William L.	Cmb 367	Joseph	Crt 62
John	Orn 604	Willes	Crr 144	Joseph	Crv 293
John	Orn 609	Wm.	Crr 144	Ludwick	Cbr 680
John	Rnd 347	Walkins, Ledwill	Brk 805	Martha	Hlf 348
John	Rck 440	Walkup, Isaac	Mck 590	Mary	Mnt 484
John	Rck 481	Joseph	Mck 590	Mary	Nwh 11A
John	Rth 150	Wall, Abraham,		Matthew	Ird 614
John	Rth 156	Junr.	Nrt 483	Nancy	Hlf 350
John	Srr 698	Abraham, Senr.	Nrt 487	Rachl.	Csw 116
John	Wke 774	Amos	Rth 155	Reuben	Crt 57
John	Wsh 712	Arthur	Wke 773	Richard M.	Crv 295
John	Wlk 68	Bird	Prs 207	Robert	Crt 62
John, Senr.	Mck 577	Burwell	Wke 773	Robert	Crv 295
Joseph	Bnc 194	Clabourn	Rck 437	Robert	Dpl 409
Joseph	Srr 698	Clement	Glf 673	Robert	Mck 558
Joseph	Wrr 838	David	Hlf 352	Robert	Smp 513
Justice	Grv 528	David	Rck 455	Ruth	Rth 153
Leml.	Crr 144	Edward	Bld 3	Soloman	Crv 293

Stephen	Jns 801	John	Grn 589	Wanuch, Daniel	Glf 665
Thomas	Crv 295	Jonas	Edg 253	Warburton, John	Nsh 127
Thomas	Ptt 277	Philip	Grn 589	Susannah	Wsh 712
Thomas	Rth 153	Sarey	Ptt 269	Thomas	Mnt 512
William	Cbr 680	Silas	Edg 254	Ward, Abigail	Ons 150
William	Crt 57	Thomas	Cmd 103	Allen	Nrt 487
William	Crv 277	Winnifred	Brt 86	Ann	Brt 88
William	Mck 558	Walter, Daniel	Ptt 240	Ann	Grn 589
William	Orn 608	Frederick	Rwn 413	Anne	Trl 688
William	Ptt 263	James	Ons 161	Aron	Chw 122
Wm.	Csw 118	see Wattee		Benjamin	Ash 91
Wm., Esqr.	Mrt 412	Walters, Abrm.	Prs 197	Benjamin	Hlf 350
Wallen, Edwd.	Rck 446	Isaac	Gts 281	Benjamin	Ons 151
Waller, Adam	Rth 155	Isreal	Wlk 67	Benjamin	Rnd 346
Frederick	Rwn 298	Lewis	Gts 281	Benjamin	Wrr 836
Jacob	Ptt 283	Lewis	Hrt 707	Best	Grn 599
Jacob	Stk 575	Mary	Gts 281	Bridget	Dpl 431
James	Edg 253	Paul	Prs 197	Burrell	Grn 613
James	Mck 548	Stephen	Gts 281	Champion	Brt 82
James	Mck 571	William	Ash 90	Charles	Dpl 423
John	Rwn 298	William	Gts 281	Charles	Lnc 887
Lucy	Edg 254	William	Ird 645	Conrod	Lnc 882
Martin	Rwn 413	see Watters		Daniel	Grn 613
Nathaniel	Grv 569	Walthall, Branch	Wke 770	Daniel	Jhn 754
Philip	Rwn 420	Walton, Amos	Ons 161	Daniel	Mrt 412
Robert	Wrr 840	Ann	Gts 280	David	Crt 84
Sterling	Edg 254	Benjamin	Rwn 298	David	Wsh 716
William	Gts 281	Elizabeth	Wke 770	Demdy	Brt 82
Wm.	Srr 707	George	Brk 802	Dia Dama	Grn 609
Walles, Polley	Crr 164	George	Prq 660	Drury	Stk 591
Wallice, James,		Henry	Brk 805	Duke	Ash 91
Revd.	Mck 599	Henry	Gts 280	Edward	Ons 153
Wallis, Aaron	Cbr 707	Holleyday	Chw 120	Edy	Mre 68
Alexander	Mck 572	James	Gts 280	Elizabeth	Trl 692
Aron	Rch 259	Jas.	Prs 204	Elizabeth	Wsh 712
Crecey	Wke 772	Jno.	Ons 170	Ezekiel	Grn 613
Deep	Brk 803	John	Glf 630	Feribee	Grn 590
Edward	Wke 774	John	Ons 171	Frederick	Lnc 882
Elisha	Rch 259	John	Rwn 298	Frederick	Nrt 485
Everit	Mre 57	John B.	Gts 280	George	Lnc 882
Ezekiel	Mck 556	Jonathan	Jhn 758	George	Ons 153
George	Mck 552	Loftin	Prs 217	George	Ptt 284
Hannah	Hde 380	Margret	Rwn 298	Gilburd	Wrr 839
John	Ans 209	Meshack	Rth 150	H. Isaac	Brt 84
John	Ird 646	Miles	Gts 280	Hannah	Ptt 235
John	Mck 572	Nathal.	Glf 630	Hardy	Chw 130
John	Rnd 349	Paul	Cbr 704	Henry	Mrt 412
John	Rch 259	Richard	Rwn 298	Henry	Wsh 716
Joshua	Hde 379	Thomas	Ons 161	Humphrey	Chw 129
Josiah	Rnd 349	Tilmon	Brk 802	Isaac	Chw 130
Mary	Rch 259	Timothy	Brt 84	Isaac	Grn 609
Matthew	Mck 553	Timothy	Gts 280	Isaac	Ptt 291
Richard	Ans 239	Tymothy	Wke 772	Isaac H.	Brt 84
Sarah	Crt 89	William	Brk 802	Jacob	Chw 130
Thomas	Ans 238	William	Brk 279	Jacob	Hrt 703
Thomas	Bfr 21	William	Rth 150	James	Brt 84
Thomas	Rnd 349	William	Wke 770	James	Brt 86
William	Cbr 684	William, Senr.	Brk 807	James	Brn 21A
William	Gts 281	Wamack, Josiah	Csw 131	James	Chw 127
William	Ird 663	Nancy	Cmb 392	James	Glf 654
William	Ptt 282	Wammack, Josiah	Rth 150	James	Psq 624
Wallon see Walton		Wammock, Abner	Rth 150	James	Prq 642
Wallons, George	Srr 700	Abraham	Rth 150	James J.	Bnc 193
Wallow, Moses	Mck 524	Anderson	Rth 150	Jas.	Mrt 413
Walls, Absalom	Crt 86	Brittan	Mre 68	Jeremiah	Chw 129
Isel	Crv 271	James	Rth 150	Jesse	Brn 19A
James	Wlk 69	Louisa	Rth 150	Jesse	Smp 508
Thomas	Ans 238	William	Rth 150	Jessy	Ons 159
Walpole, Rebecca	Nrt 487	Wamock, Richard	Rwn 405	Job	Cht 172
Walrick, Moses	Smp 505	Wamsley, John	Crr 161	Job, Ser.	Cht 172
Walser, Frederick	Rwn 421	Wanderweedle,		John (2)	Brn 21A
Jacob	Rwn 413	Keziah	Rbs 429	John	Chw 126
Philip	Rwn 413	Wane, Edward	Wke 778	John	Chw 127
Walsh, John	Crt 91	John	Nwh 4A	John	Chw 130
Walston, Barbara	Ptt 269	Wanich, Ludwick	Glf 662	John	Dpl 434
George	Ptt 269	Wanns, Edward	Ird 614	John	Lnr 35
Henry	Edg 256	William	Ird 614	John	Mrt 412

John	Mnt 476	William	Lnc 887	Anne	Nrt 487
John	Mre 66	William	Mck 552	Benjamin	Bld 7
John	Orn 604	William	Ptt 235	Benjamin	Csw 135
John	Orn 607	William	Rnd 349	Bosdell	Csw 118
John	Ptt 235	William	Rbs 428	Edward	Bfr 20
John	Rnd 347	William	Rck 478	Edward	Cht 223
John	Rnd 349	William	Rwn 384	Elijah	Jhn 748
John	Smp 503	William	Smp 535	Elizabeth	Hrt 738
John	Trl 674	William	Wke 771	Ervin	Hrt 737
John	Wsh 712	William, Jun.	Chw 119	Etheldred	Ptt 292
John, Junr.	Rwn 390	William, Jun.	Chw 129	George	Wke 770
John, Sen.	Chw 117	William, Sen.	Chw 130	Goodle	Prs 206
John, Senr.	Rwn 383	Willie	Wrr 839	Hankley	Csw 129
John, Sr.	Dpl 434	Wm., Senr.	Mrt 412	Harry	Nsh 129
John L.	Wrr 839	Zephaniah	Ons 169	Henry	Bfr 21
Jonathan	Bfr 20	Warde, Richard	Crr 149	Henry	Nsh 129
Jonathan	Mrt 412	Wm.	Crr 155	Henry	Rnd 346
Jordan	Ptt 236	Warden, Elijah	Srr 699	Henry	Wke 771
Joseph	Brn 19A	Wardex, Samuel	Mck 591	Henry, Jur.	Wke 771
Joseph	Chw 130	Wardin, William	Cht 225	Hossington	Crv 323
Joseph	Grv 568	Wardlow, John	Rck 478	Isaiah	Smp 509
Joseph	Hlf 350	Wardrope, Edwd.	Csw 148	James	Csw 118
Joseph	Hde 380	Youngen	Mnt 514	James	Csw 135
Joseph	Ons 146	Ware, Amelia	Brt 86	James	Orn 608
Joshua	Brt 84	George	Brt 88	James, Jur.	Csw 119
Josiah	Chw 130	Peater	Mre 47	Jeremiah	Crv 273
Josiah	Wsh 716	Peter	Mre 48	Jeremiah	Crv 323
Leven	Rwn 445	Roland	Mnt 519	John (2)	Csw 118
Lewis	Rnd 346	Thomas	Csw 124	John	Hlf 352
Luke	Mrt 413	William	Brt 86	John	Ptt 293
Malchor	Lnc 882	William	Csw 102	Jordan	Hrt 737
Mark	Brn 20	Warford, John	Rck 439	Joseph	Bnc 192
Marthy	Mrt 414	Warham, John	Mck 567	Joseph	Wsh 712
Mary	Cmb 394	Warington, Thomas	Psq 626	Joshua	Edg 256
Mathew	Dpl 438	Wark see Veark		Joshua	Nrt 487
Messer	Ans 225	Warker, Buckler	Prs 195	Larkin	Csw 118
Mial	Hrt 703	Elizebeth	Prs 195	Margarett	Rnd 346
Michael	Brt 84	Moses, Senr.	Prs 196	Mary	Gts 281
Michael	Hrt 707	Robert	Prs 203	Mary	Prs 208
Moses	Brt 82	Warleck, Daniel	Lnc 898	Mary, Junr.	Mrt 412
Moses	Brn 21A	Warley, Robert	Nsh 133	Mary, Senr.	Mrt 412
Nathaniel	Wke 771	Warlick, Daniel	Lnc 823	Needham	Smp 509
Needham	Grn 589	Lewis	Lnc 908	Prisscilla	Ptt 269
Palser	Lnc 882	Warlow, Jacob	Rwn 376	Richard	Jhn 748
Philip	Bld 22	Mary	Hlf 352	Richard	Smp 510
Rebeccah	Gts 280	Peter	Rwn 420	Saml.	Csw 115
Richard	Wrr 840	Stutdel	Rwn 376	Saml.	Csw 135
Ricd.	Ons 153	William	Hlf 354	Steward	Csw 104
Robert	Cht 170	Warmouth, John	Frn 457	Thomas	Nsh 127
Robert	Gts 280	Meredith	Wke 772	William	Orn 605
Samuel	Bfr 21	Thomas	Frn 457	William	Wke 771
Samuel	Brt 82	William	Wke 772	William, Sen.	Gts 281
Samuel	Dpl 401	Willie	Wke 772	Williss	Nsh 130
Sarah	Nsh 130	Warnen, Edward	Gts 281	Wm.	Csw 135
Shadrick	Chw 130	Warner, Hardin	Cmb 376	see Worren	
Solomon	Crt 77	James	Hde 379	Warrick, Andw.	Csw 115
Solomon	Chw 118	John	Rwn 420	Elizabeth	Smp 500
Solomon	Edg 254	Samuel	Psq 632	Wiat	Wne 872
Solomon	Ons 169	William	Rwn 420	Wiley	Ans 200
Spellar	Mrt 412	Warnier, Angel	Prq 652	Warrin, Jas.	Prs 207
Stephen	Ans 210	Warnor, John	Mre 44	Jas., Junr.	Prs 207
Stephen	Rnd 352	John	Grn 612	John	Prs 219
Swain	Ptt 235	Lemuel	Nrt 487	Joseph	Stk 621
Thomas	Ans 231	Mildred	Nrt 487	Molly	Ons 179
Thomas	Brt 82	Warran, John	Rck 444	Saml.	Prs 206
Thomas	Brt 88	Solomn.	Rck 444	Starling	Prs 219
Thomas	Brn 19A	see Warren		Will.	Prs 207
Thomas	Crt 78	Warrel, Alexr.	Wne 871	Will.	Prs 211
Thomas	Cht 216	Solomon	Rnd 349	Warring, Ann	Chw 113
Thomas	Grn 613	Warrell, James	Wne 869	Warrington, Elijah	Trl 674
Thomas	Mre 72	Jesse	Wne 869	John	Psq 635
Thomas	Rnd 347	John	Wne 863	Warson, Archd.	Ird 642
Thomas	Wke 771	John	Wne 869	John	Ird 642
William	Ans 210	see Worrell		John	Rwn 323
William	Ans 225	Warren, Abraham	Crv 283	Joseph	Ird 642
William	Brk 807	Allen	Hrt 737	Robert	Rwn 319
William	Cht 164	Allen	Ptt 291	Robert	Rwn 328

Samuel	Ird 673	Zachariah	Bfr 21	Elija	Wke 772
Samuel	Rwn 338	see Watters		Elisebeth	Prs 206
Widow	Rwn 323	Waterson, John	Lnc 898	Elizabeth	Rck 484
Wilie	Ird 659	Watford, William,		Elizabeth	Rth 153
William	Ird 658	Junr.	Brt 84	Ephraim	Jhn 753
William	Rwn 323	William, Senr.	Brt 86	Ezekiel	Dpl 418
Warters, Walter	Wlk 68	Watker, Charles	Rbs 425	Ezekiel	Dpl 419
Wartham, Benjamin		Watkins, Allen	Jhn 753	George	Orn 605
H.	Wrr 838	Ambrose	Rth 151	George	Rth 151
John, jr.	Wrr 837	Amos	Jhn 754	Grey	Mrt 414
Warwell, William	Wrr 841	Charles	Stk 610	Henry D.	Ans 214
Warwick, Barnabas	Rbs 429	Cristopher	Ans 211	Hugh	Rth 151
Benjamin	Nrt 487	Daniel	Smp 509	Isaac	Jhn 754
Job	Nrt 487	David	Smp 514	Isham	Ans 240
Sarah	Nrt 487	Dicy	Edg 256	Isham	Jhn 753
Wasdon, Augustin	Grn 609	Eleven	Dpl 428	Israel	Hde 380
Washburn, Gabriel	Rth 156.	George	Srr 699	Jacob	Rwn 402
Washer, Peter	Mnt 499	Henry	Nsh 126	James	Cmb 367
Washington, Bar-		Isaac	Smp 509	James	Hde 380
bard	Grv 582	Israel	Rch 243	James	Jhn 753
John	Grv 560	James	Ans 203	James	Orn 607
John	Lnr 35	James	Dpl 430	James	Orn 608
Lucy	Nrt 487	James	Mnt 499	James	Rch 242
Selemachus	Nrt 487	James	Stk 582	James	Wke 771
Wm.	Bld 11	James	Srr 698	James, Jur.	Orn 607
Wason, Conrod	Rth 156	Jesse	Cmb 369	Jane	Glf 631
John	Lnc 824	Jesse	Stk 583	Jas.	Prs 217
Wassen, Henry	Bnc 192	Jewell	Brk 805	Jeremiah	Jns 807
Wasterfield, John	Crr 154	John	Cmd 109	Jesse	Crv 287
Wrightmon	Crr 155	John	Nsh 126	Jesse	Prs 217
Wate, Will.	Prs 208	John	Nrt 483	Jno.	Prs 196
Waterfield, Abra-		John	Ons 171	Joel	Stk 558
ham	Crr 155	John	Ptt 253	Joel	Stk 577
Abraham, Jur.	Crr 155	John	Rch 243	John	Ans 205
Abraham, Jur.	Crr 158	Joseph	Srr 698	John	Bfr 20
Abraham, Ser.	Crr 158	Kesiah	Rch 252	John	Brt 86
Benjn.	Crr 155	Kinchen	Wne 864	John	Cmb 371
Elizebeth	Crr 159	Lydia	Wne 865	John	Jhn 761
John	Csw 125	Mary	Rck 465	John	Mre 64
John	Crr 158	Peter	Dpl 435	John	Orn 536
John	Crr 159	Peter	Rth 151	John	Rch 269
Mary	Crr 158	Samuel	Rch 257	John	Rbs 425
Michel	Crr 158	Thomas	Brk 805	John	Rbs 429
Michel	Crr 159	Thomas	Ptt 254	John	Rck 489
Suthey	Crr 158	William	Brk 807	John	Rth 151
Wm.	Crr 155	William	Rch 252	John	Rth 153
see Wasterfield		William	Rth 151	John	Smp 494
Wateridge, Abram	Hrt 702	see Walkins		John (2)	Wrr 836
Waterman, William	Dpl 424	Wats, Elias	Srr 701	Jordon	Mrt 413
Waters, Absalom	Rth 154	Watson, Abigail	Ons 142	Joseph	Crv 311
Amos	Bfr 21	Adam	Rth 151	Joseph	Rch 253
Benjamin	Smp 513	Addison	Mrt 414	Joseph	Smp 512
Catharine	Chw 115	Alex	Ans 213	Leaven	Ans 227
Danl.	Lnr 28	Alex.	Ans 215	Lemuel	Hlf 352
David	Bfr 21	Alexander	Cmb 371	Levan	Bld 39
Hezekiah	Edg 254	Alexander	Rbs 429	Martha	Cbr 705
Isaac	Bfr 19	Alexr.	Rch 262	Mary	Hlf 358
Jeremiah	Bfr 21	Alon	Stk 576	Mary, Junr.	Mrt 414
John	Bfr 21	Andraw	Orn 607	Mary, Senr.	Mrt 414
John	Edg 253	Anne	Bld 32	Matthew	Rbs 429
John	Glf 675	Archble	Rch 268	Micajah	Hrt 737
John (2)	Lnr 28	Arthur	Mrt 413	Moses, Senr.	Jns 805
John	Ons 146	Balaam	Jhn 753	Neill	Crv 313
John	Stk 594	Benjamin	Cht 167	Neill	Jns 783
John, Jur.	Stk 594	Benjamin	Crv 313	Neill	Jns 785
John P.	Wlk 67	Catharine	Mre 63	Noah	Ird 646
Mosses	Wlk 68	Charity	Rch 259	Obadiah	Jhn 754
Needham	Lnr 28	Clabourn	Glf 666	Patrick	Rth 151
Regimelick	Lnr 28	Daniel	Orn 604	Richard, Junr.	Crv 313
Samuel	Mck 569	Daniel	Rnd 346	Richard, Senr.	Crv 313
Seathy	Ons 145	David	Bfr 20	Robert	Cht 151
Suthey	Ons 149	David	Nrt 485	Robert	Mre 63
Thomas	Bfr 21	David	Rck 466	Roberts	Jhn 753
Thomas	Rbs 425	David	Rth 151	Saml.	Wne 861
William	Bfr 21	Earnest	Jns 779	Solomon	Jhn 750
William	Rbs 425	Edward	Brt 86	Thomas	Cht 183
Winfield	Bfr 19	Edward	Cht 201	Thomas	Hlf 354

Name	Ref	Name	Ref	Name	Ref
Thos., Junr.	Mrt 413	Seth	Crt 77	Henry, Senr.	Nrt 487
Thos., Senr.	Mrt 414	William	Crt 91	Isaac	Ash 90
William	Bld 39	Weant, John	Rwn 292	Isaac	Grv 577
William	Brn 14A	Wear, John	Lnc 898	Jacob	Cbr 710
William	Cht 204	Robert	Lnc 898	Jacob	Lnc 908
William	Dpl 418	Weare, Thomas	Mnt 487	James	Gts 280
William	Hlf 352	Wease, Adam	Bnc 193	James	Hlf 350
William	Jns 791	Weatherford,		James	Hrt 727
William	Mre 63	Charles	Ans 228	Jesse	Hrt 727
William	Nrt 485	Helkiah	Mnt 509	John	Bnc 191
William	Rck 482	Irehble.	Ans 199	John	Edg 256
William	Rwn 370	William	Ans 199	Joshua	Ash 91
William	Rth 151	William	Mnt 509	Joshua	Mnt 504
William	Stk 577	Weatherington, Fred-		Mark	Ash 90
William, Ser.	Hde 380	erick	Lnr 8	Martha	Frn 485
Willis	Jhn 751	Nathan	Lnr 27	Mary	Hrt 733
Wm.	Mrt 414	Weatherly, Abner	Glf 659	Penny	Orn 605
Watt, Hugh	Bld 21	Andrew	Glf 660	Peter	Cbr 715
John	Rck 475	Curtis	Glf 644	Sarah	Nrt 487
John	Rwn 439	Edward	Glf 656	Shaderick	Srr 698
Samuel	Rck 474	Edward, Senr.	Glf 656	Stephen	Srr 698
Wattee, Ezekiel	Rck 456	Isaac	Hrt 732	Thomas	Srr 698
Watters, Henry	Nwh 11	Isaiah	Glf 676	Timothy	Orn 602
Henry	Orn 494	Jesse	Glf 644	Welson	Nsh 130
Jacob	Grv 513	Job	Glf 681	William	Ash 91
John	Bld 15	Levy	Glf 660	William	Mnt 505
Michael	Cbr 695	Thomas	Trl 692	William	Rch 268
Watton, Leah	Chw 128	William	Glf 660	William	Rwn 440
Watts, Andrew	Cbr 693	Wm.	Glf 659	William	Srr 698
Andrew	Mnt 509	Weathermon, Christo-		William	Wrr 836
Benjamin	Ans 234	pher	Srr 699	Zadock	Orn 605
Berriman	Bld 15	Christopher,		see Wever	
George	Brk 806	Ser.	Srr 700	Weavle, George	Rwn 350
Jacob	Mnt 510	John	Srr 700	Stephen	Rwn 350
John	Cbr 693	Saml.	Srr 699	Web, Jesse	Rnd 351
John	Ird 643	Weathernton, Jos.	Mrt 413	John	Crt 82
John	Ird 673	Weathers, Elisha	Lnc 844	Webb, Abraham	Jhn 771
John	Mrt 388	Elizabeth	Wke 773	Benjamin	Ash 91
John	Rth 154	James	Grv 521	Benjamin	Rck 469
John	Wke 771	James	Lnc 844	Caleb	Ird 666
Jonathan	Rbs 428	James	Wke 773	Chesly	Rth 149
Lewis	Mrt 415	John	Lnc 844	Cutliff	Wlk 68
Malachi	Ans 239	Willis	Mck 526	Daniel	Rwn 450
Richard	Bld 16	Weathersbee, Bar-		Daniel	Rth 150
Spence	Wke 771	tholemen	Mrt 413	Darling	Rth 149
Thomas	Ird 673	John	Mrt 413	David	Bnc 193
Thomas	Orn 492	Thos.	Mrt 414	David (2)	Rth 149
Valentine	Cbr 693	Weathersby, Isham	Bld 43	Dilstrap	Rck 469
William	Ird 643	Shadch.	Bld 46	Elisabeth	Bld 27
William	Ird 663	Weatherspoon,James	Lnc 832	Ellis	Rth 149
William	Ird 674	Jesse	Wke 771	Etheldred	Nrt 487
Winiford	Wke 771	John	Wke 771	Frank	Wlk 68
see Jones		William	Mck 543	George	Hlf 350
Wattson, Bennett	Orn 495	Wm.	Wke 771	George	Wrr 840
Waugh, William	Ird 642	Wm., Jur.	Wke 771	Harmon	Wsh 712
Waul, John	Rch 248	Weaver, Abraham	Orn 605	Henry	Lnc 885
Widow	Rch 268	Absalom	Orn 605	Henry	Rch 267
William	Ans 201	Adam	Rwn 376	Hill	Nrt 485
William	Rch 243	Alexander	Orn 606	Jacob	Rth 150
William	Rch 268	Andrew	Stk 576	James	Orn 493
Way, Amos	Cht 217	Ashwell	Grn 590	James	Rwn 445
Benjamin	Rnd 346	Benjamin	Edg 255	James	Rth 149
Henry	Glf 674	Benjamin	Hlf 358	James	Wlk 67
John, Jur.	Glf 681	Charles	Hrt 715	James C.	Brk 733
Joseph	Cht 218	Charles	Hrt 722	Jesse	Chw 131
Nathaniel	Cht 217	Charles	Stk 576	Jesse	Nrt 487
William	Glf 630	Conrod	Lnc 908	Jesse	Rth 149
Waymire, Daniel	Rnd 346	Craven	Hlf 350	Jessey	Frn 481
Frederick	Rnd 351	David	Lnc 824	Jessy	Ons 170
Rudolph	Rnd 346	David	Rth 156	Joel	Rth 150
Volentine	Rnd 351	Edward	Hrt 719	John	Brt 82
Wayne, Levi	Crv 263	Elizabeth	Hlf 350	John	Bld 9
Wea see Wed		George	Rwn 420	John	Bnc 192
Weaks, Benjamin	Crt 91	George, Jur.	Stk 576	John	Bnc 193
Jabez	Crt 91	George, Ser.	Stk 576	John	Brk 802
Rhodes	Crt 91	Henry	Brk 804	John	Edg 253
Sarah	Crt 87	Henry	Hlf 352	John	Grv 506

Name	Ref	Name	Ref	Name	Ref
John	Prq 656	John	Smp 502	Well, William	Ash 91
John	Prq 663	Joseph W.	Prq 658	Welles, Thomas	Rwn 405
John	Rch 243	Julian	Smp 502	Welling, Thomas	Ptt 247
John	Rch 264	Lemuel	Prq 657	Wells, Aaron	Lnc 899
John B.	Rth 149	Philip	Mck 545	Anne	Nrt 483
John, Revd.	Rth 150	Samuel, Sen.	Prq 655	Benj.	Prs 204
Johnson	Orn 595	Samuel, Sen.	Prq 658	Daniel	Jns 797
Jonathan	Rth 149	Shaderick	Prq 651	Elisha	Csw 131
Joshua	Rth 149	Stephen	Ons 170	Fedrick	Dpl 419
Joiles	Mrt 412	Thomas	Prq 657	Francis	Rwn 455
Laurence	Brt 84	William	Prq 659	Frank, Jur.	Frn 475
Leonard	Ans 227	Wilson	Prq 657	Frank, Ser.	Frn 475
Lewis	Frn 485	Weere, John	Rwn 376	Hardy	Nsh 130
Mary	Chw 131	Weerick, Martin	Glf 661	Humphrey	Rth 155
Micjah	Nsh 130	Weggings, Abraham	Brk 802	Isaac	Rnd 346
Moses	Chw 131	Weighman, Johm	Rwn 359	Jacob	Dpl 409
Penny	Srr 705	Weisner, David	Cbr 694	Jacob	Dpl 420
Richard	Edg 256	Welborn, William	Rnd 351	Jacob	Dpl 421
Richard	Frn 485	Welbourn, John	Orn 605	James	Csw 131
Richard	Frn 490	Welch, Andrew	Bnc 192	James	Lnc 844
Richard	Prq 652	Andrew	Wlk 68	James	Rwn 455
Robert	Rch 248	David	Chw 130	Jessy	Ons 150
Robert	Rth 149	David	Rth 155	Joab	Bld 15
Stephen	Wlk 68	David	Stk 626	John	Bnc 192
Thomas	Grv 505	David	Srr 699	John	Csw 133
Thomas (2)	Rth 149	David, Ser.	Srr 699	John	Jns 797
Turner	Rch 258	Demcy	Hrt 703	John	Nsh 130
Watson	Rch 264	Edward	Chw 125	Joseph	Prq 650
William	Bld 9	Ephraim	Srr 699	Leonard	Edg 256
William	Brk 802	Hananah	Ans 214	Martin	Dpl 423
William	Frn 485	Henry	Ans 233	Mathew	Edg 256
William	Grv 577	Henry	Cht 185	Micajah	Nsh 126
William	Rch 242	Isaac	Chw 118	Miles	Csw 131
William	Rch 250	Isham	Srr 699	Nathaniel	Wke 778
William	Rth 150	Jacob	Chw 124	Richd.	Brn 16
William, Jun.	Chw 128	James	Cht 168	Robert	Rth 154
William, Junr.	Brk 804	John	Ans 233	Samuel	Grv 582
William, Sen.	Chw 129	John	Bnc 193	Samuel	Hrt 719
Willis	Frn 488	John	Brk 807	Stephen	Prs 216
Wilson	Chw 131	John	Rth 153	Stephen, Sr.	Nsh 128
Zachariah	Chw 116	John	Rth 155	Thomas	Bnc 192
Webber, Daniel	Grn 604	John	Stk 586	Thomas	Dpl 410
David	Rth 156	John, jr.	Grv 555	Thomas	Edg 254
Thomas	Crv 239	John, Senr.	Grv 557	Thomas	Hlf 352
William	Rth 153	Joseph	Rth 156	Thomas, Senr.	Edg 256
Webster, James	Csw 142	Joshua	Orn 607	William	Dpl 442
James	Cht 195	Margaret	Chw 128	William	Edg 256
James	Rck 467	Mary	Crt 79	William	Rth 154
John	Bnc 193	Mathew	Cht 185	Willoughby	Edg 257
John	Cht 194	Michael	Cht 183	see Wills	
John	Hde 380	Michael	Cht 186	Wels, William	Ons 155
John	Rck 489	Robert	Crt 77	Welsh, Edward	Cmb 359
Margaret	Hde 380	Robt.	Cht 205	James	Rwn 420
Moses	Bnc 193	Samuel	Prq 659	John	Ird 615
Richard	Cht 167	Thomas	Bnc 193	John	Rwn 429
Shaderick	Stk 576	Thomas	Rth 155	Joseph	Cbr 678
William	Cmd 106	Thomas	Wlk 68	Mathias	Rwn 389
William	Glf 636	Walter (2)	Cht 185	Roland	Mnt 488
Wed, Martha	Stk 585	William	Bfr 20	Samuel	Ird 619
Weden, Hartwell	Rch 267	William	Bnc 191	Thomas	Lnc 892
Wedinhouse, Martin	Cbr 692	William	Bnc 193	Thomas, Senr.	Lnc 892
Weeaks, Shoebal	Rch 250	William	Glf 632	Welton, Angillies	Frn 495
Weeden, Benjamin	Rth 151	William	Glf 686	see Weldon	
Weedings, John	Brn 16A	Welcher, Charles	Brk 804	Wenget, William	Wrr 838
Weedon, John	Mck 548	George (2)	Glf 627	Wenningham, James	Rnd 346
Week, Jacob	Lnc 884	Weld see Wild		Wersner, John	Stk 605
Weeks, Cornelius	Crv 247	Weldon, Benjamin	Hlf 348	Wesley, Robert	Brk 803
Elijah	Rth 155	Daniel	Frn 475	Wesner, Micajah	Stk 617
Elisa	Ons 136	Daniel	Hlf 352	Wesson, Reuben	Nrt 487
Elizabeth	Edg 257	Mrs.	Frn 495	West, Acquilla	Orn 602
Huet	Mnt 512	William (2)	Wrr 836	Andrew	Jns 807
James, Junr.	Edg 257	Williams	Hlf 348	Anna	Crv 295
James, Senr.	Edg 257	see Welton		Arther	Ans 213
Jesse	Prq 658	Welker, Daniel	Rwn 292	Arther, Senr.	Ans 233
John	Lnc 844	Leonard	Lnc 884	Barney	Lnc 833
John	Mck 545	Samuel	Stk 590	Berry	Cht 196
John	Nwh 8	Welkor, Adam	Rwn 363	Caleb	Crr 157

Charles	Cht 175	William	Rbs 425	Thomas	Rck 465
Charles	Psq 635	William	Rwn 298	Whaley, Isaac	Dpl 412
Daniel	Crv 307	William	Rth 153	John	Ird 646
Daniel	Crv 311	William	Srr 701	John C.	Crv 339
Daniel	Rwn 359	William	Trl 692	Marey	Ptt 229
Daniel	Rwn 390	William	Wrr 838	Nathan	Cmd 93
David	Crv 259	Willis	Smp 509	Samuel	Dpl 413
Delila	Dpl 407	Westbrook, Benja-		William	Crv 339
Edward	Crr 164	min	Jns 813	William	Dpl 413
Edwd.	Rck 469	Burrel	Grn 606	William	Dpl 441
Elisabeth	Ans 232	Charles	Lnr 26	Whalin, Mary	Crt 84
Ezekiel	Rwn 455	Gray	Lnr 35	Whaly, Ezekiel	Lnr 35
George	Ash 91	Henry	Rck 453	Wharey, George	Rth 150
George	Brt 86	James	Lnr 28	John	Rth 150
Henery	Crr 161	James	Smp 509	Thomas	Rth 150
Henry	Bnc 192	Jno.	Csw 125	Wharton, Edmond	Ons 138
Ignatious	Cht 174	John	Jns 817	Isaac	Ons 137
Ignatious	Mnt 465	John	Wne 854	Samuel	Psq 634
Isaac	Brk 807	Joseph	Smp 528	Thomas	Ons 139
Isaac	Lnc 827	Moses	Lnr 26	see Whorton	
Isaac	Rwn 298	Moses	Smp 503	Whealass, Luis	Srr 700
Isaiah	Rwn 455	Samuel	Jns 817	Whealen, John	Srr 705
Jacob	Ons 148	Thomas	Nrt 483	John, Jr.	Srr 705
James	Bld 45	Thomas	Rck 453	Richard	Srr 710
James	Crv 313	Thomas	Rck 479	Whealer, Mary	Ons 162
James	Mck 602	William	Smp 503	Wheart, Jacob	Glf 640
James	Ons 154	William	Smp 506	Wheateker, Jona-	
Jenkin	Rwn 299	Westcoat, Jeremiah	Brn 17	than	Srr 698
Jeptha	Cht 151	John	Brn 15A	Wheatfeild, John	Mrt 414
Jereh.	Rck 469	Westcoate, John	Crr 149	Milley	Mrt 414
Jessee	Cht 151	Stephen	Crr 151	Willis	Mrt 412
John	Ans 229	Weste, Willoughby	Crr 157	Wheaticer, Ephraim	Srr 701
John	Bnc 193	Westen, Reuben	Dpl 424	Wheatley, Elisa-	
John	Crv 263	Reuben	Dpl 426	beth	Mrt 414
John	Crv 311	Wester, ..., Mrs.	Hrt 715	Elisabeth	Mrt 415
John (2)	Crv 337	Daniel	Frn 489	George (2)	Wlk 67
John	Ird 666	Henry	Ird 659	George, junr.	Wlk 68
John	Rbs 425	Julias	Ird 659	Hardy	Mrt 412
John	Trl 686	John	Smp 508	Henry	Mrt 412
John S.	Crv 327	Simon	Frn 490	Jesse	Ptt 260
Jolly	Brk 803	Westerdaw, Francis	Edg 253	John	Wlk 67
Jonathan	Crr 164	Westerfield see Waster-		Mason	Wlk 67
Joseph	Crv 305	field		Saml.	Mrt 414
Joseph	Crv 313	Western, Amos	Brt 86	Samuel	Ptt 264
Joseph	Stk 577	Benjamin	Hde 380	Simon	Edg 256
Joshua	Crr 164	Ephraim, Junr.	Brt 84	Thomas	Ptt 260
Joshua	Psq 635	Ephraim, Senr.	Brt 84	Wheatmell	Mrt 412
Josiah	Brt 86	John	Brt 84	William	Bfr 20
Kear	Ons 152	Malichi	Brt 84	Wm.	Crr 160
Levi	Ans 218	Samuel	Hde 380	Wm.	Mrt 412
Levi	Crv 315	Westmoreland,		Wheatly, Curtis	Glf 649
Martin	Mck 541	Reaves	Ird 658	Jas.	Rck 467
Mary	Ons 150	David	Stk 576	Johnson	Glf 649
Mathew	Cht 169	Sarah	Stk 576	Wheaton, Danl.	Nwh 7A
Nancey	Crr 150	Weston, Benjamin	Hrt 715	John	Csw 140
Obediah	Crr 144	James	Hrt 722	Sterling	Wke 778
Penelope	Brt 82	Jeremiah	Hrt 715	Thomas	Mck 603
Peter	Wlk 69	Robert	Prq 642	William	Prq 643
Phillip	Cht 154	Robert	Prq 652	Whedbee, Elizabeth	Prq 649
Randolph	Hlf 350	Thomas	Hrt 715	James	Prq 655
Richard	Cht 193	Westray, Benjamin	Cht 158	Lemuel	Prq 655
Robert	Brt 82	Sam.	Nsh 126	Thomas, sen.	Prq 649
Robert	Lnc 883	William	Nsh 127	William	Prq 649
Samson	Frn 489	Wetherow, Awalt	Rwn 298	Whedon, John	Crv 275
Samuel	Dpl 401	Wethers, Rubin	Mck 540	Wheelar, Boon	Nrt 483
Stephen	Lnc 827	Wettel, Russell	Cht 165	Celia	Nrt 487
Stevens	Brt 86	Wever, Adam	Cht 180	Henry	Nrt 483
Tart	Cmb 359	Edward	Grv 518	Hezekiah	Nrt 487
Thomas	Cht 180	John	Mre 56	Wheelas, James	Hlf 350
Thomas	Jns 807	Manus	Grv 520	Joiner	Hlf 354
Thomas	Rwn 445	Shadrack	Cht 169	Joseph	Hlf 352
Thomas	Rwn 455	Thomas	Cht 210	Kinchin	Hlf 354
Thomas	Rth 152	Wewcomb, Wm.	Orn 590	Wheeler, Ann	Grv 570
William	Ans 232	Weyman, Henry	Rwn 402	Anthony	Rck 472
William	Brt 82	Weymouth, Caben	Psq 631	Benjamin	Grv 568
William	Bld 41	Thomas	Psq 630	Benjamin	Wke 774
William	Cht 174	Whalebone, James	Csw 100	Elizabeth	Glf 688

Ezekiah	Glf 638	Elizabeth	Hlf 354	George	Ans 217
Ezekiah, Senr.	Glf 640	Hawkins	Hlf 354	George	Brt 86
Henry	Edg 254	Israel	Rwn 460	George	Bld 50
Henry	Smp 516	John	Hlf 354	George	Csw 130
James	Glf 619	John	Rwn 460	George	Chw 123
John	Glf 679	John	Wke 771	George	Grn 613
John	Hrt 738	Joshua	Rwn 395	George	Glf 663
John	Nwh 8A	Lunsford	Hlf 352	George	Ird 674
John	Wke 773	Mary	Rwn 395	George	Ons 157
John	Wke 774	Matthew	Hlf 352	George, Sen.	Chw 118
Joseph	Wke 774	Noah	Rwn 395	Guly	Nsh 127
Manlove	Glf 693	Peter, Junr.	Rwn 395	Hannah	Bld 33
Martin	Grv 570	Richard	Hlf 354	Hannah	Nrt 487
Richard	Glf 674	Richard	Nrt 485	Henery	Crr 159
Samuel	Glf 644	Robert	Frn 466	Henry	Ans 217
Samuel	Rth 155	Robert	Hlf 352	Henry	Hde 379
Sarah	Rck 472	Robert	Wke 771	Henry	Psq 641
Vincent	Rck 436	Tabetha	Hlf 354	Henry	Rth 155
William	Rbs 428	Thomas	Rwn 455	Isaac	Ash 91
Wm.	Rbs 432	Thomas	Rwn 460	Isaac	Rth 154
Wheelington, Levan	Crv 279	William	Rwn 460	Isaac, (of Wil-	
Wheelor, John	Lnc 864	William	Srr 698	liam)	Prq 646
Thomas	Lnc 863	White, Abigail	Crv 245	Isaiah	Rnd 347
William	Rwn 405	Adam	Mre 41	Jacob	Rwn 420
Wheiler, Benjn.	Prs 205	Adam	Mre 73	Jacob	Wke 770
Saml.	Prs 205	Adml.	Csw 120	Jacob, Sen.	Prq 655
Whelas, Isaac	Cht 168	Andrew	Mre 39	James	Ans 217
Wheler, Dred	Cht 205	Archibald	Cbr 705	James	Brt 86
Jessee	Cht 204	Arnold	Prq 662	James	Bld 32
John	Cht 204	Augusten	Rth 155	James	Brn 20
Whelis, John	Wrr 839	Benajah	Lnr 27	James	Bnc 191
Wheliss, Hardy	Cht 210	Benjamin	Brk 803	James	Brk 807
William	Nsh 126	Benjamin	Edg 254	James	Crv 309
Whelley, John	Crr 160	Benjamin, Sen.	Prq 646	James	Ird 646
Whelon, Jordon	Csw 125	Benjamin, Senr.	Crv 333	James	Lnc 898
Whennery, Robt.	Cht 212	Benn.	Psq 624	James	Mck 563
Whetherton, Clever-		Benn.	Psq 627	James	Mck 593
ly	Crv 327	Benn.	Psq 633	James (2)	Psq 633
Reubin	Crv 327	Betty	Rnd 351	James	Prq 645
Richard	Crv 331	Bitlebrey L.	Nsh 179	James	Prq 648
Robert	Crv 327	Caleb	Crr 155	James	Rth 154
William	Crv 327	Calib	Prq 658	James	Wrr 840
Willis	Crv 329	Carr	Rwn 419	James, Jun.	Prq 662
Whetsett see Whitsell		Charles	Cht 181	James B.	Nwh 2A
Whicher, Thomas	Stk 574	Charles	Cht 182	Jarrott	Grv 555
Whicker, Caleb	Glf 685	Charles	Prq 645	Jeams	Crr 145
Robert	Cht 198	Charles	Wrr 840	Jean	Cbr 706
Thomas	Stk 558	Charlotty	Crr 155	Jeffrey	Grn 596
William	Glf 685	Clemon	Grv 555	Jemima	Ptt 287
Whidbee, Thomas	Prq 643	Cornelius	Cmd 103	Jeremiah	Gts 280
see Whedbee		D. John	Brt 86	Jeremiah	Rth 155
Whidbey, Elizebeth	Crr 168	David	Cbr 678	Jesse	Chw 130
Mager	Crr 168	David	Ird 674	Jesse, Jun.	Prq 647
Whiker, Joseph	Crv 255	David	Rwn 420	Jesse, Sen.	Prq 647
Whiliss, Milbra	Nsh 127	Deborah	Psq 638	Jessee	Cht 182
Whilworth, Suther-		Dorothy	Edg 255	Joel	Ans 219
lin	Bnc 191	Ealenor	Rth 154	Joel	Ans 231
Whinery, Abraham	Orn 603	Edith	Bld 9	Joel	Hrt 703
John	Srr 700	Edmund	Psq 633	John	Ans 238
Whipple, David	Rth 151	Edward	Lnc 900	John	Brt 86
Whirly, Silas	Rth 152	Edward	Ons 179	John	Bld 31
Whisenhunt, Adam	Rnd 349	Elias	Lnc 882	John	Cbr 707
George	Lnc 898	Elisha	Ans 201	John	Crt 74
George M.	Rnd 351	Elisha	Ans 227	John	Csw 146
Henry	Rnd 346	Eliza	Glf 654	John	Cht 152
Jacob	Rnd 349	Elizabeth	Glf 622	John	Crv 333
Whisht, James	Cmd 101	Elizabeth	Nrt 485	John	Crr 155
Whisong, Philip	Srr 700	Elizabeth	Prq 643	John	Frn 455
Whitacker, James	Edg 253	Ephraim	Brt 86	John	Frn 477
Whitacur, Abraham	Orn 608	Esther	Nrt 485	John	Grv 556
John	Orn 608	Ezekiel	Brt 88	John	Glf 665
William	Orn 608	Francis	Bfr 19	John	Ird 642
Whitaker, B. Eli	Hlf 352	Francis	Psq 629	John	Mnt 465
Cary	Hlf 352	Francis	Prq 658	John	Nwh 7
Dudley	Hlf 352	Frederick	Brt 86	John	Nrt 483
Edward	Hlf 354	Frederick	Ptt 273	John	Psq 629
Eli B.	Hlf 352	Gabriel	Prq 656	John	Prq 655

John	Ptt 283	Philip	Grv 533	William	Ans 219
John	Rnd 347	Philip	Rwn 420	William	Brt 82
John (2)	Rnd 351	Phillip	Mre 57	William	Brt 84
John	Rwn 421	Polley	Wke 773	William	Brt 86
John	Wrr 838	Rachael	Cmb 362	William	Bld 40
John, Capt.	Ans 226	Rachel	Psq 633	William	Brk 802
John, Jr.	Wrr 838	Reuben	Ans 219	William	Crv 309
John, Jun.	Prq 649	Reuben	Brt 84	William (2)	Edg 253
John, Jun.	Prq 659	Reuben	Psq 636	William	Glf 630
John, Junr.	Cbr 705	Reubin	Brk 807	William	Ird 642
John, Junr.	Cbr 707	Richard	Grn 594	William	Ird 659
John, Senr.	Edg 255	Rigdon	Jns 817	William	Rck 485
John D.	Brt 86	Robert	Ans 219	William	Rwn 419
Jonan.	Rck 486	Robert	Cbr 706	William	Rth 154
Jonathan	Rwn 420	Robert	Grn 591	William	Rth 155
Jonathan	Trl 692	Robert	Glf 678	William	Stk 576
Jordon	Psq 636	Robert	Ird 658	William	Wke 773
Joseph	Ans 219	Robert	Lnr 33	William	Wke 778
Joseph	Cbr 688	Robert	Lnc 899	William	Wrr 838
Joseph	Cmd 104	Robert	Mck 576	William	Wsh 712
Joseph	Cmb 359	Robert	Psq 627	William, Junr.	Edg 253
Joseph	Grv 558	Robert	Rck 450	William, Senr.	Edg 255
Joseph	Grv 565	Robert	Srr 699	William, (Wh.)	Orn 608
Joseph	Orn 608	Samuel	Cbr 705	William W.	Crv 333
Joseph	Prq 643	Samuel	Crv 333	Willis	Wrr 840
Joseph	Trl 682	Samuel	Ird 642	Willoughby	Crr 146
Joseph	Trl 692	Samuel	Ird 653	Windsor	Bfr 20
Joseph, Jun.	Prq 660	Samuel	Prq 661	Wm.	Crr 142
Joseph, Senr.	Ans 219	Samuel	Rwn 323	Zachariah	Ans 220
Joshua	Bfr 21	Sarah	Grn 602	Zedekiah	Ans 220
Joshua	Chw 130	Sarah	Nsh 127	Whiteaker, Abram	Bfr 19
Joshua	Edg 255	Saul	Jhn 767	Isom	Mrt 413
Joshua	Grv 555	Sherwood	Cht 162	Whitehall, Thos.	Crr 141
Joshua	Hlf 348	Simion	Cht 192	Whitehart, John	Cmd 110
Joshua	Lnc 882	Soloman	Hrt 703	Whitehead, Abrahm.	Hlf 352
Joshua	Psq 628	Solomon	Bfr 20	Allen	Hlf 352
Joshua	Prq 643	Solomon	Grv 544	Arthur	Cht 211
Joshua, Sen.	Prq 646	Starling	Glf 653	Augustin	Edg 254
Josiah	Ans 219	Stephen	Brn 20	B. William	Edg 255
Josiah	Bld 10	Stephen	Cht 180	Benja.	Nsh 127
Josiah	Psq 636	Stephen	Orn 603	Burril	Rwn 455
Josiah, Sen.	Prq 654	Stephen	Rth 155	Cole	Edg 255
Jourdan	Prq 650	Stevens	Brt 86	Cullen	Hlf 352
Kider	Bfr 23	Surrell	Jhn 767	David	Prq 644
King	Brt 84	Susanna	Hrt 715	Edwin	Smp 503
Leer	Crt 71	Susanna	Ptt 254	Elizebeth	Prs 211
Leml.	Crr 138	Theofilas	Prq 643	Henry	Nsh 130
Litlebrey	Nsh 129	Thomas	Bld 3	Iaac	Nsh 128
Lizy	Cht 186	Thomas	Brk 803	James	Edg 256
Luke	Ash 91	Thomas	Cbr 689	John	Cht 211
Luke	Brt 82	Thomas	Chw 120	John	Crv 335
Luke	Bld 50	Thomas	Cmb 359	John	Crv 341
Luke	Prq 652	Thomas	Gts 280	John	Dpl 426
Luke	Smp 535	Thomas	Grv 540	John	Hlf 352
Luke H.	Wsh 712	Thomas	Mck 603	John, Jr.	Hlf 352
Margaret	Bld 29	Thomas	Nrt 485	Jonathan	Nsh 128
Mark	Frn 458	Thomas	Psq 640	Jonathan	Nsh 130
Mary	Brt 84	Thomas	Prq 645	Joshua	Ird 614
Mary	Cbr 688	Thomas	Ptt 240	Josiah	Cht 211
Mary	Edg 254	Thomas	Rnd 347	Keeling	Hde 381
Mary	Ird 658	Thomas	Rth 154	Lazarus	Cmb 372
Mary	Psq 629	Thomas	Rth 155	Lazarus	Hlf 350
Matthew	Bld 32	Thomas	Wsh 712	Lazarus	Nsh 128
Mede	Brt 86	Thomas	Wne 853	Lazerus	Rwn 455
Milly	Rck 440	Thomas, Jun.	Prq 647	Lewis	Hlf 354
Nathan	Psq 640	Thomas, Sen.	Prq 647	Mary	Ons 153
Nathan	Prq 648	Thomas, Sen.	Prq 654	Mathew	Edg 254
Nathaniel	Lnc 893	Thomas, Senr.	Cbr 706	Mrs.	Ons 159
Nehemiah	Trl 682	Thos.	Crr 137	Nathan	Hde 379
Nicholas	Rnd 346	Thos.	Prs 207	Nathan	Nsh 126
Noah	Brt 86	Timothy	Rnd 347	Robert	Jhn 770
Patrick	Crr 157	Toms	Psq 635	Robert	Orn 603
Peter	Brt 84	Valentine	Grv 533	Saml.	Nsh 130
Peter	Rth 155	Valentine, Jur.	Grv 536	Thomas	Cht 211
Peter	Srr 698	Vinson	Crr 157	Thomas	Cht 216
Philemon	Grv 555	Whitchcoat	Crv 333	Thomas	Orn 603
Philip	Ans 209	Will.	Brn 17A	Thos.	Nsh 126

Thos., Jur.	Nsh 126	Whitford, David	Crv 281	see Whitsett			
Will.	Nsh 127	John, Junr.	Crv 283	Whitsett, John	Orn 603		
William	Hlf 352	John, Senr.	Crv 279	Whitston, David	Lnc 824		
William	Orn 605	Martin	Crv 285	Whitt, Jesse	Orn 604		
William	Ptt 227	William	Jns 793	Mary	Glf 638		
William	Srr 701	Whitherton, James	Crv 309	Whitted, John	Orn 490		
William, Jr.	Hlf 352	Joseph	Crv 309	William	Orn 491		
William, Sr.	Hlf 352	Solomon	Crv 307	Whitteker, John	Bnc 193		
William B.	Edg 255	Thomas	Crv 309	William	Bnc 193		
Williams	Jhn 773	William	Crv 309	Whitten, Noah	Hrt 719		
Willis	Hde 380	Whithouse, Gidion	Crr 145	Whittenton, Faddy	Jhn 769		
Whitehouse, Antho-		Whithurst, Arthur	Ptt 263	James	Jhn 772		
ny	Psq 639	Batson	Ptt 263	John	Ash 91		
Gideon	Psq 629	Batson, junr.	Ptt 264	Leonard	Wlk 68		
Henry	Psq 639	Lanfare	Ptt 264	Richard	Jhn 772		
Jeams	Crr 153	Richard	Ptt 264	Robert	Jhn 770		
John	Nsh 126	Samuel	Ptt 264	Whittey, Edward	Jns 793		
see Whiteouse		Whiticker, Abraham	Rth 156	Whittle, James	Rnd 351		
Whitehurst, Batson	Bfr 20	Whitley, Ambrose	Jns 789	Jesse	Cmb 369		
Frederick	Cmd 95	Ann	Hlf 354	Whitton, Thomas	Wlk 69		
Henry	Bfr 20	Arthur, Jur.	Bfr 20	Thos.	Wlk 69		
Hillery	Bfr 20	Arthur, Ser.	Bfr 20	Whittson, John	Bnc 192		
John	Cmd 97	Cager	Mnt 509	William	Bnc 194		
Richard	Crt 70	David	Hrt 732	Whitty, William	Crv 305		
Robert	Crt 70	Drury	Wne 872	Whitus, Johnen	Crv 293		
Whiteman, Freder-		Enoch	Jhn 761	Nelson	Ons 169		
ick	Chw 120	Exodus	Mnt 509	Rheubin	Crv 295		
Mathias	Glf 646	George	Mnt 506	Richard	Ons 168		
Matthew	Chw 120	James	Hrt 732	Samuel	Crv 295		
Whitemore, Clemt.	Rck 446	James	Rbs 428	Simon	Crv 267		
Gower	Csw 144	Jesse	Bfr 20	Thomas	Ons 169		
Sepin	Cmd 103	Jesse	Hrt 733	William	Crv 299		
Whiten, Martha	Edg 256	Jesse	Smp 500	Whitworth, Isaac	Rck 476		
Whitener, Henry	Lnc 908	John	Jhn 746	Jacob	Rck 484		
Philip	Lnc 908	Joseph	Grn 607	John	Rck 488		
Whitens, Christo-		Josiah	Nsh 128	Thomas	Rck 466		
pher	Cmd 97	Mary	Nsh 130	William	Lnc 898		
Whitenton, Joseph	Glf 639	Micajah	Wne 872	Whorten, John	Glf 659		
Whiteous, Saml.	Crr 160	Mills	Hlf 350	Whorton, Abram	Crt 93		
Whiteside, Jno.	Lnc 840	Needham	Jhn 748	David	Crv 277		
John	Rth 153	Randolph	Hlf 350	Ebenezer	Crt 73		
Thos.	Lnc 840	Sarah	Bfr 20	Elam	Glf 659		
Whitesides, Adam	Rth 152	Sion	Nsh 127	Elisha	Glf 659		
James	Rck 482	Solomon	Nsh 127	John	Glf 621		
Thomas	Rth 152	Solomon	Rbs 428	Watson	Glf 659		
William F.	Rth 152	William	Mnt 504	William	Crv 277		
Whitesil, Tobias	Glf 637	William	Mnt 510	Whotan, George	Srr 698		
Whitfeild, John	Lnr 35	Whitlock, Charles		George, Jur.	Srr 698		
Whitfeld, Will.,		(2)	Stk 585	Isaac	Srr 698		
Sr.	Nsh 128	James	Srr 700	Jeremiah	Srr 698		
Whitfield, Benja-		John	Srr 701	Thomas, Jr.	Srr 698		
min	Nsh 127	Thomas	Srr 699	Thomas, Ser.	Srr 698		
Benjamin	Ptt 261	William	Stk 585	Whoton, John	Srr 700		
Bryan	Lnr 26	William	Srr 699	Moses	Srr 700		
Bryan, Jur.	Lnr 26	Whitlow, Henry	Ird 658	Richard	Srr 700		
C. Wm.	Hlf 354	Joseph	Psq 641	Wiatt, John	Hlf 352		
Elzabeth	Nsh 128	Nathan	Grv 536	Sarah	Hlf 352		
George	Prs 215	Whitly, Benja.	Nsh 129	Wice, George	Crv 235		
Jaccob	Nsh 127	Elijah	Smp 505	John	Jns 781		
James	Orn 607	Jonas	Edg 257	Wicker, Benjn.	Mre 63		
John	Ans 233	Titas	Mnt 510	Elizebeth	Crr 158		
John	Grv 537	William	Smp 499	James	Stk 618		
Joseph	Dpl 426	Whitman, John	Dpl 401	Joel	Crr 155		
Lewis	Lnr 26	Whitmill, Ann	Hlf 354	Jonathan	Mre 63		
Lewis	Wne 871	Whitmon, Jessee	Orn 603	Marthew	Mre 63		
Matthw	Nsh 128	Whitmus, Withery	Jns 813	Milly	Cht 197		
Needham	Wne 873	Whitmer, Benjamin	Lnc 908	Plesant	Mre 64		
Rachel	Crv 253	Daniel	Lnc 908	Robert	Cht 161		
Reuben	Nsh 126	Elizath.	Rck 469	Thomas	Cht 159		
Robert	Ptt 286	Whitney, Abner	Psq 637	William	Stk 619		
Solomon	Nsh 127	Ebenezer	Rnd 349	Wm.	Crr 158		
Will., Jur.	Nsh 128	Josiah	Smp 502	Wickersham, Jehu	Glf 689		
William	Dpl 441	Whitsel, John	Mck 539	Wickery, Benjamin	Chw 114		
William	Orn 607	Samuel	Mck 547	Widdick, William	Glf 693		
William	Stk 591	Whitsell, Adam	Orn 603	Widows, Isaac	Glf 689		
William	Wne 858	Adam, Jr.	Orn 603	Isaac, Jur.	Glf 689		
Wm. C.	Hlf 354	Jacob	Orn 603	Peter	Glf 691		

William	Glf 691	Wilborne, Rebeckah	Stk 575	George	Cbr 690
Wier, Thomas	Mck 556	Wilbourn, Lewis	Jhn 762	Wilhide, Jacob	Orn 603
Thomas	Mck 557	Wilburn, Isaac	Srr 701	Wilhite, Abraham	Orn 603
Wiere, William	Mck 560	James	Rwn 370	Lewis	Frn 478
Wiett, Jeremiah	Rth 153	Joshua	Rwn 371	Phillip	Frn 476
Wiggans, Jane	Bld 21	Samuel	Rwn 370	William	Frn 487
John	Gts 281	Samuel, Senr.	Rwn 370	Wilis, Robert P.	Csw 114
Willis	Gts 281	Wilcher, Alex	Stk 578	Wilkenson, Benja-	
Wiggens, Arthur	Brt 86	Wilcocks, James	Crv 277	min	Rth 155
Wiggins, Archibald	Frn 451	Stephen	Trl 682	Richard	Jhn 746
Arthur	Hlf 354	Wilcork, David	Rth 152	Wilkerow, James	Bnc 194
Benjn.	Hrt 733	Wilcox, Benjamin	Jns 795	Wilkerson, Angus	Rbs 425
Blake B., Esqr.	Mrt 415	David	Rbs 428	Benja.	Wke 770
Edmond	Crv 269	John	Cht 178	Benjamin	Rnd 349
Edward	Nrt 483	Joshua	Rwn 376	Charls	Rnd 346
Ezekiel	Brk 807	Samuel	Ash 91	Daniel	Rbs 425
Francis	Grv 519	Soloman	Cht 182	David	Grv 507
Frederick	Grv 520	Squire	Ash 91	David, Jur.	Grv 508
Frederick	Hlf 350	Stephen	Jns 825	Duncan	Rbs 429
George	Smp 521	Thomas	Cht 179	Francis	Grv 553
Gershom	Lnr 26	see Wilson		George	Grv 508
Hardin	Cbr 690	Wilcoxon, William	Rwn 429	James	Orn 606
James	Edg 254	Wilcoxson, Daniel	Wlk 68	John	Cht 218
Jas.	Mrt 414	William	Wlk 67	John	Grv 506
Jesse	Mrt 415	Wild, Phelix	Brk 803	John	Orn 607
John	Edg 257	Wilder, Cullin	Jhn 760	John	Rnd 349
John	Lnr 26	Francis	Chw 120	Mary	Cht 183
John	Mrt 414	James	Jhn 760	Neill	Rbs 429
Joseph	Crv 325	Jessy	Ons 179	Peter	Rbs 425
Joseph	Hlf 350	John	Chw 122	Polley	Mrt 414
Joshua	Hrt 722	John	Jhn 769	Robert	Cht 213
Joshua, Jun.	Hrt 722	Mary	Cmb 376	Sarah	Rbs 429
Leml.	Mrt 412	Matthew	Jhn 760	William	Cht 183
Mary	Smp 512	Michael	Chw 121	William	Grv 507
Matthew	Bfr 21	Moses	Nsh 128	Wm.	Csw 110
Patsey	Smp 521	Nathaniel	Chw 122	Wilkes, James	Brt 88
Samuel	Crv 271	Robert	Nsh 129	John	Rbs 429
Samuel	Hrt 727	Samuel	Crt 89	Mary	Brt 88
Sarah	Hrt 727	Samuel, Jr.	Jhn 760	Micajah	Brt 88
Thomas	Hlf 350	Sarah	Crt 89	Sarah	Crv 307
Thomas	Hrt 707	William	Cmb 374	Tabitha	Rbs 430
Thomas	Smp 508	William	Jhn 760	Wilkie, George	Cht 192
Thos.	Mrt 413	Willis	Chw 128	George S.	Cht 193
William	Crv 319	Willis	Wke 770	John	Cht 192
William	Hlf 354	Wildman, Elias	Bnc 192	Wilkin, Henry	Stk 583
William	Hrt 732	William	Bnc 192	Wilkings, David	Dpl 412
William	Smp 507	Wildner, Ann	Brt 86	John	Nwh 3
William	Smp 533	Wildon, John	Frn 449	Michael	Dpl 425
Willis	Wne 853	Wiles, Annis	Hrt 722	Michael	Dpl 429
Winefred	Edg 257	John	Srr 701	Nicy	Smp 514
Wright	Hrt 727	Luis	Srr 701	Richard	Smp 529
Wiggons, Elias	Frn 451	Pinson	Srr 700	William	Dpl 426
Samson	Frn 451	Thomas, Sr.	Srr 701	Wilkins, Alexr.	Cht 170
Wiggs, Arther	Wne 866	Wiley, Alexander	Glf 631	Allice	Brk 805
Henry	Wne 870	David (2)	Glf 632	Arthur	Cmd 95
Henry, Senr.	Wne 866	Hugh	Glf 632	Charles	Rth 152
John (2)	Wne 866	Isaac	Wsh 712	Elijah	Hlf 352
John	Wne 867	James	Mck 601	Elisha	Cmb 380
Jordan	Nsh 129	James	Wsh 712	George	Chw 131
Obediah	Nsh 129	John	Cbr 688	George	Orn 603
Radford	Smp 522	John	Glf 631	George	Rwn 455
Thomas	Wne 867	John	Mck 564	Jacob	Cht 154
William	Wne 865	Moses	Cbr 676	Jacob	Gts 281
Wigins, John	Nsh 130	Oliver	Cbr 676	Jacob	Hde 380
Williss	Nsh 128	Thomas	Glf 631	James	Edg 253
Wikers see Aberella		Thomas	Wsh 712	James, Senr.	Mnt 505
Wikle, John	Rth 155	William	Cbr 681	Jesse	Rbs 428
Wilban, William	Csw 103	William	Mck 564	John	Cmd 95
Wilborn, Edward	Srr 698	William	Ons 168	John	Cht 193
Gideon	Ash 91	Wilfong, John	Lnc 908	John	Hlf 350
Jean	Rnd 347	George	Lnc 907	John	Hde 380
John	Rnd 347	George	Lnc 908	John	Ons 164
John	Stk 613	Jacob	Orn 493	John	Stk 584
Lydia	Rnd 347	Jacob	Wke 778	Jonas	Rbs 428
Richard	Srr 698	Wilhelm, Lewis	Rwn 315	Kinchen	Ans 203
Richard, Jr.	Srr 698	Wilhelom, Eve	Cbr 690	Lewis	Hlf 354
William	Stk 576			Matthew	Rbs 429

Michl.	Wne 873	Willcox, Littleber-			Benjamin	Crt 60
Morning	Wlk 68	ry	Hlf 348		Benjamin	Edg 255
Patrick	Hde 380	Willeford, Benja-			Benjamin	Hlf 348
Richard	Rth 152	min	Edg 255		Benjamin	Hlf 350
Robt.	Cht 220	Jacob	Edg 253		Benjamin	Jns 791
Samuel	Cmd 100	James	Edg 253		Benjamin	Mnt 492
Samuel	Crv 231	John (2)	Edg 255		Benjamin	Rnd 351
West	Hlf 354	Thomas	Edg 255		Benjamin	Rnd 352
Whitmill	Hlf 354	Will.	Nwh 11A		Benjamin	Rch 266
William	Ans 200	Willes, Jeremiah	Cmb 382		Benjamin	Rck 445
William	Bld 29	Luke	Srr 701		Benjamin	Rwn 460
William	Nrt 485	Thomas, Jur.	Srr 701		Benjamin	Rth 153
William	Wke 773	Willet, Demsey	Mnt 466		Benjamin (2)	Smp 505
Zilpha	Grn 598	Henry	Brn 15A		Benjamin	Stk 626
Wilkinsin, Abraham	Hde 380	John	Brn 15A		Benjamin	Srr 700
Wilkinson, Abram	Bfr 20	Willett, James	Cht 173		Benjamin	Wrr 836
Angus	Cmb 365	John	Cht 224		Benjamin	Wrr 839
Archibald	Rch 253	William	Cht 169		Benjn.	Brn 16A
Benjamin	Ptt 263	Willey, Elizabeth	Hlf 352		Benjn.	Brn 21
Charles	Jhn 758	Hilry	Gts 281		Benjn.	Mre 43
Coleman	Hde 380	James	Mre 44		Bennett	Rck 439
David	Crv 295	John	Hlf 352		Billey	Nsh 129
Dawkins	Jns 805	John	Ons 158		Bird	Dpl 410
Edward	Rch 260	Matthias	Hlf 354		Bridges	Grv 520
Elizabeth	Dpl 434	Purdy	Ons 181		Buckner	Nrt 485
Elizabeth	Hde 380	Thomas	Hlf 352		Burwell	Cht 207
Francis	Ptt 262	William, Jr.	Hlf 352		Burwell	Edg 254
Frederick	Hde 381	William, Sr.	Hlf 352		Caleb	Grv 534
George	Chw 116	Willford, Archi-			Caleb	Grv 549
George	Mck 526	bald	Brt 84		Calib	Cmd 103
Isaac	Hde 380	Isham	Brt 86		Cary	Prs 197
Israel	Hde 381	James	Brt 86		Catharine	Smp 518
Jacob	Hde 380	Wright	Brt 84		Charity	Dpl 437
James	Hde 380	William, Elizabeth	Orn 603		Charles	Crv 283
James	Lnc 863	John, Senior	Grn 614		Charles	Frn 470
Jehu	Dpl 436	Kenney	Rwn 380		Charles	Frn 483
John	Bfr 20	Mackey	Brk 771		Charles	Grv 553
John	Brn 13A	Simison	Rwn 404		Charles	Lnc 851
John	Cmb 372	Williams, A. John	Wke 778		Charles	Orn 604
John	Dpl 435	Aaron	Dpl 410		Charles	Rck 445
John	Nrt 485	Abner	Prs 187		Charles	Stk 595
John	Prs 194	Absalom	Crv 339		Charles	Wrr 839
John	Ptt 228	Absalom	Grv 578		Charles	Wrr 840
John	Rwn 439	Absolem	Crr 148		Christian	Dpl 411
Joshua	Ptt 262	Absolom	Rnd 352		Christopher	Crr 159
Lewis	Prs 195	Absolum	Wne 845		Cooper	Nsh 127
Marvel	Hde 381	Ailce	Crv 245		Crafton	Csw 112
Moses	Brk 803	Alanson	Wrr 837		Daniel	Bfr 20
Nathan	Jhn 759	Alexander	Cmd 99		Daniel	Cht 217
Oden	Hde 381	Allen	Brt 86		Daniel	Hrt 732
Reuben	Jhn 759	Allen	Rck 463		Daniel	Ons 176
Richard	Crv 293	Allin	Wke 774		Daniel	Psq 637
Robert	Hde 381	Amey	Wrr 838		Daniel	Rnd 347
Rowland	Jhn 758	Amos	Mnt 489		Daniel	Smp 521
Samuel	Mnt 494	Amos	Rnd 352		David	Ans 228
Samuel	Rwn 292	Anderson	Csw 124		David	Cht 155
Shadrach	Hde 381	Andrew	Glf 683		David	Dpl 431
Thomas	Hde 380	Andrew	Glf 693		David	Glf 649
Will.	Nwh 3A	Ann	Brt 84		David	Lnc 851
William	Hlf 352	Anney	Crr 160		David	Nwh 5A
William	Ptt 260	Archilus	Rck 464		David	Orn 604
William	Rwn 343	Ars.	Ons 177		David	Psq 637
William	Rwn 420	Arthur	Edg 255		David	Rnd 351
William	Rwn 440	Arthur	Nrt 485		David	Rck 476
William S.	Jns 807	Asa	Hrt 727		Demcy (2)	Gts 281
Wilkison, Elkanah	Bld 12	Ashkenus	Wrr 837		Denton	Mnt 492
Neill	Cmb 370	Austin	Hlf 348		Derrell	Cht 160
Robert	Mre 59	Bartholw.	Rwn 370		Dilly	Mnt 520
William	Bld 7	Barton	Stk 605		Dixon	Mrt 415
William	Cmb 380	Benedict	Bld 4		Drewry	Edg 255
Wilks, Francis	Wke 773	Bengt	Prs 204		Drewry	Nsh 129
Willard, Auguston	Srr 700	Benja.	Crv 343		Drury	Brk 803
George	Stk 576	Benja.	Nsh 129		E. William	Nrt 485
George	Stk 614	Benja.	Wke 778		Edward	Cmd 100
Willborn, James	Wlk 68	Benjamin	Brt 84		Edward	Lnr 35
Lewis	Wlk 69	Benjamin	Cmd 96		Edward	Lnc 883
Willcher, Thomas	Brk 803	Benjamin	Crt 59		Edward	Cmd 100

Edward	Ptt 273	Henry	Wrr 836	John		Bnc 194
Edward	Stk 595	Henry	Wrr 837	John		Bnc 192
Edwd.	Mrt 412	Herbert	Rch 265	John		Brk 802
Edwd.	Rck 444	Herrod	Nsh 133	John		Brk 807
Eleaney	Nsh 128	Herry	Nsh 128	John		Brk 279
Eley	Nsh 130	Hesekiah	Smp 528	John		Cmd 98
Elijah	Brk 279	Hickman	Frn 468	John		Cmd 106
Elixabeth	Brk 806	Hilson	Hrt 727	John		Crt 59
Elisha	Brt 82	Hockins	Srr 700	John		Csw 96
Elisha	Brk 802	Hosea	Ons 173	John		Cht 174
Elisha	Frn 466	Hubbard	Rch 267	John		Cht 191
Elisha	Mrt 388	Huggans	Jns 791	John		Chw 117
Elixabeth	Ptt 229	Hugh	Rck 445	John		Crv 307
Eliza	Orn 602	Humphrey	Orn 602	John		Crv 323
Elizabeth	Bfr 19	Humphry	Rwn 390	John		Crv 335
Elizabeth	Brt 84	Hyram	Brk 804	John		Crv 339
Elizabeth	Csw 128	Isaac	Bnc 194	John		Crr 140
Elizabeth	Chw 113	Isaac	Csw 142	John		Crr 145
Elizabeth	Chw 117	Isaac	Cmb 373	John		Crr 157
Elizabeth	Hde 380	Isaac	Glf 680	John		Dpl 409
Elizabeth	Ons 177	Isaac	Jhn 774	John	(2)	Dpl 410
Elizabeth	Orn 492	Isaac	Psq 640	John		Dpl 411
Elizabeth	Prq 645	Isaac	Prq 650	John		Edg 256
Elizabeth	Smp 522	Isaac	Rch 259	John		Frn 445
Elizebeth	Crr 137	Isaac	Rch 266	John		Frn 452
Elizebeth	Wrr 840	Isaac	Smp 509	John		Frn 472
Enion	Rnd 349	Isham	Cht 202	John	(2)	Frn 487
Ephraim	Mnt 487	Jacob	Bld 22	John		Grv 526
Ephraim	Srr 701	Jacob	Crr 167	John		Grv 548
Etheldred	Brt 84	Jacob	Dpl 405	John		Grv 566
Evan	Lnr 33	Jacob	Dpl 424	John		Grv 582
Ewd.	Ons 174	Jacob	Mck 584	John		Grn 596
Ezekiel	Cht 218	Jacob	Rch 248	John		Glf 625
Ezekiel	Dpl 413	James	Ash 91	John		Hlf 348
Fanney	Crr 162	James	Bfr 20	John		Hrt 707
Fedrick	Dpl 408	James	Brt 82	John		Jhn 764
Feribe	Wne 848	James	Brt 86	John		Lnr 27
Floyd	Frn 470	James	Brn 14	John		Lnr 33
Fountaine	Jns 785	James	Cmd 99	John		Lnr 35
Francis	Brt 84	James	Cmd 106	John		Mck 586
Francis	Hlf 348	James	Frn 470	John		Mck 592
Francis	Mnt 493	James	Ird 627	John		Nsh 130
Francis, Cap.	Rwn 420	James	Mnt 492	John		Ons 181
Frankey	Crr 158	James	Mre 48	John		Orn 604
Frankey	Crr 163	James	Nsh 126	John		Orn 607
Frederick	Lnc 851	James	Nsh 127	John		Prs 197
Frederick	Wke 772	James	Ons 167	John		Rnd 347
Fredk.	Cht 192	James	Orn 494	John		Rnd 351
Geoarge	Rth 153	James	(2)	Orn 602	John	Rch 266
George	Cht 203	James	Rnd 347	John		Rbs 429
George	Dpl 424	James	Rnd 351	John		Rck 471
George	Gts 281	James	Rwn 429	John		Rwn 298
George	Hde 380	James	Wke 772	John		Rth 151
George	Lnc 851	James, Junior	Ptt 272	John		Rth 152
George	Mck 548	James, Senior	Ptt 272	John		Smp 528
George	Ptt 251	James M.	Csw 113	John		Srr 699
George	Rnd 352	Jams	Orn 558	John		Wke 772
George	Rwn 429	Jeams	Crr 150	John		Wke 774
George	Rwn 445	Jenny	Nrt 485	John	(2)	Wrr 836
George, Senr.	Gts 280	Jeremiah	Dpl 416	John		Wrr 839
Gideon	Grv 534	Jeremiah	Mre 70	John		Wsh 712
Giles	Wne 845	Jesse	Bnc 194	John		Wne 847
Gilstrap	Hrt 719	Jesse	Dpl 405	John, junior		Ptt 268
Godfray	Mck 532	Jesse	Glf 664	John, Junr.		Mrt 415
Godfrey	Bfr 19	Jessy	Ons 177	John, Junr.		Prs 198
H. Hampton	Edg 253	Jethro	Gts 281	John, (SC)		Edg 253
Halon	Gts 281	Jethro	Hrt 727	John, Senior		Ptt 289
Hampton H.	Edg 253	Jno. Jos., Jur.	Hlf 350	John, Senr.		Mrt 412
Hannah	Smp 498	Job	Lnr 26	John, Son of		
Harris	Frn 470	Job	Lnr 33	Edward		Ptt 270
Harrod	Edg 256	Joel	Cmb 368	John, Son of		
Henry	Csw 128	Joel	Lnc 851	John		Ptt 274
Henry	Edg 256	Joel	Nsh 129	John, terts.		Mrt 414
Henry	Frn 468	John	(2)	Ash 90	John A.	Wke 778
Henry	Grv 526	John		Brt 82	John D.	Mrt 414
Henry	Nwh 5A	John	(2)	Brt 84	John Jos., Sr.	Hlf 350
Henry	Smp 533	John		Brt 88	John P.	Nwh 7A

Jonas	Grn 595	Nathan	Csw 127	Samuel	Ird 627
Jonas	Nsh 129	Nathan	Csw 128	Samuel	Prq 653
Jonathan	Gts 281	Nathan	Dpl 411	Samuel	Ptt 251
Jonathan	Nwh 5	Nathan	Hrt 719	Samuel, Junr.	Nrt 487
Jonathan (2)	Rnd 349	Nathan	Mck 594	Samuel, Senr.	Nrt 485
Jones	Rth 153	Nathan	Mck 598	Samuel F.	Grv 517
Jones	Wrr 838	Nathan	Ptt 263	Sarah	Jhn 774
Jordan	Nsh 130	Nathan	Smp 504	Sarah (2)	Nwh 5
Jos. Jno., Jur.	Hlf 350	Nathanial	Grv 584	Sarah	Smp 499
Jos. John, Sr.	Hlf 350	Nathl.	Lnr 28	Seth	Psq 639
Joseph	Bld 22	Nathl.	Rck 479	Simeon	Ptt 273
Joseph	Cmd 99	Nathal., Senr.	Rck 445	Simon	Edg 257
Joseph	Crt 59	Nehemiah	Frn 483	Simon	Frn 463
Joseph (2)	Crr 166	Nh.	Ons 146	Simon	Wrr 837
Joseph	Dpl 408	Noah	Edg 255	Smith	Bnc 194
Joseph	Dpl 410	Obed.	Ons 178	Soloman	Crv 323
Joseph	Edg 254	Obediah	Rnd 346	Solomon	Grv 581
Joseph	Frn 449	Owen	Stk 616	Solomon	Mnt 489
Joseph	Grn 595	Parrot	Smp 533	Stephen	Bnc 193
Joseph	Glf 671	Peter	Jhn 764	Stephen	Dpl 410
Joseph	Hde 380	Peter	Orn 604	Stephen	Jns 801
Joseph	Mnt 492	Peter	Rck 445	Stephen	Ons 174
Joseph	Nsh 133	Philip	Ird 627	Stephen	Ons 180
Joseph	Rwn 429	Phillip	Brn 16A	Susanna	Rch 255
Joseph	Smp 525	Pilgram	Nsh 133	Sylviah	Hlf 350
Joseph	Srr 700	Ralph	Prs 204	Temperance	Dpl 424
Joseph	Wrr 839	Reason	Rwn 292	Theophilus	Dpl 403
Joseph, Sr.	Smp 533	Reason	Stk 604	Thomas	Bfr 19
Joshua	Ans 207	Rebekah	Orn 608	Thomas (2)	Bnc 192
Joshua	Bld 5	Reece	Rwn 405	Thomas	Brk 805
Joshua	Bld 22	Reuben	Smp 504	Thomas	Cmd 99
Joshua	Bnc 191	Richard	Crt 80	Thomas	Cmd 103
Joshua	Glf 659	Richard	Glf 682	Thomas	Cmb 374
Joshua	Smp 506	Richard	Hrt 715	Thomas	Dpl 404
Josiah	Ans 200	Richard	Lnc 851	Thomas	Edg 255
Josiah	Hrt 732	Richard	Orn 607	Thomas	Grv 549
Judith	Lnc 858	Richard	Ptt 273	Thomas	Grv 570
Judy	Psq 640	Richard	Rwn 363	Thomas	Glf 681
Lam	Ons 175	Richd.	Ash 90	Thomas	Lnc 858
Lawrence	Rwn 429	Richd.	Bnc 193	Thomas	Ons 181
Leas	Crr 158	Richd.	Crv 339	Thomas	Psq 624
Leonard	Cmd 98	Richd.	Crr 160	Thomas	Rch 249
Leonard	Wrr 837	Richd.	Mrt 388	Thomas	Rck 482
Levey	Hrt 727	Richd.	Ons 165	Thomas	Rwn 292
Levin	Glf 675	Roderick	Ptt 273	Thomas	Rwn 389
Lewis	Frn 453	Roger	Rnd 347	Thomas	Rth 152
Lias	Srr 701	Robert	Cbr 710	Thomas	Srr 700
Lightfoot	Lnc 908	Robert	Cmd 103	Thomas	Srr 701
Lodwick	Cmd 100	Robert	Crt 59	Thomas	Trl 674
Lodwick	Psq 639	Robert	Crv 241	Thomas	Wsh 712
Lodwik, Sen.	Psq 637	Robert	Crv 257	Thomas, Junr.	Nrt 487
Lovey	Crt 80	Robert	Crv 303	Thomas, Senr.	Nrt 485
Luke	Csw 96	Robert	Dpl 424	Thomas C.	Mnt 485
Mack	Hrt 732	Robert	Lnc 851	Thos.	Crr 143
Margreat	Brn 14	Robert	Mck 578	Thos.	Crr 157
Margret	Wrr 837	Robert	Nsh 129	Thos.	Mrt 413
Mark	Lnr 35	Robert	Nrt 485	Thos.	Prs 217
Marmaduke	Csw 120	Robert	Ons 160	Thos., T. Creek	Bfr 19
Mary	Crr 150	Robert	Ptt 259	Thos. P.	Crr 139
Mary	Edg 255	Robert	Ptt 263	Timothy	Smp 504
Mary	Nwh 4	Robert	Rck 444	Tobeas	Prs 208
Mary	Ptt 259	Robert	Smp 526	Tolbert	Crv 271
Mary	Smp 501	Robert	Wke 778	Trimgan	Psq 635
Mathias	Rth 152	Roland	Nsh 129	Uriah	Prq 642
Michael	Edg 256	Roland	Rck 463	Whitmill	Hrt 715
Michael	Mck 604	Rowlen	Ans 234	Widow	Mck 529
Mildred	Dpl 405	Rubin	Mck 536	William	Ans 216
Mr.	Ons 176	Sally	Mck 540	William	Bfr 20
Mr.	Ons 178	Saml.	Brn 21	William	Bfr 24
Moses	Brt 82	Saml.	Mrt 413	William	Brt 82
Moses	Brn 20	Saml.	Wrr 836	William	Brt 84
Moses	Mck 547	Saml., Esqr.	Mrt 414	William	Bnc 191
Moses	Rch 262	Samuel	Brt 84	William	Bnc 192
Moses	Srr 701	Samuel	Bnc 192	William	Cmd 96
Mourning	Edg 254	Samuel	Cmb 367	William	Chw 119
Nancy	Glf 683	Samuel	Gts 280	William	Crv 339
Nancy	Hrt 722	Samuel	Hlf 350	William	Crr 140

Name	Ref	Name	Ref	Name	Ref
William	Crr 161	Jeams	Crr 144	James	Rwn 413
William	Frn 458	Jereh.	Rck 437	James	Rth 154
William	Frn 492	Jesse	Smp 532	James	Rth 155
William	Gts 280	Jessey	Frn 449	James	Stk 619
William	Gts 281	John	Brn 20	Jeremiah	Crv 275
William	Grv 563	John	Ptt 290	Joab	Rbs 425
William	Grv 564	Joseph	Nsh 130	Joel	Glf 664
William	Grv 566	Joseph	Nrt 487	John	Bfr 21
William	Grn 594	Joseph	Smp 532	John	Cht 152
William	Glf 653	Joseph	Wne 871	John	Cmb 359
William	Glf 659	Lewis	Mck 547	John	Lnc 871
William	Hlf 348	Littleton	Nrt 487	John	Rbs 428
William	Lnc 898	Mary	Bld 13	John	Wrr 840
William	Jhn 775	Nathan	Bld 37	Jonathan	Dpl 408
William	Mnt 493	Nathaniel	Smp 520	Joseph	Crv 283
William	Orn 608	Peter C.L.	Hde 380	Joseph	Rth 154
William	Prq 653	Pulliam	Prs 205	Joshua	Crv 281
William	Ptt 255	Richd.	Bld 15	Joshua	Orn 608
William	Rnd 351	Richd.	Bnc 193	Joshua, Senr.	Crv 285
William	Rnd 352	Right	Smp 527	Lewis	Hlf 348
William	Rch 262	Robert	Bnc 191	Major	Crv 325
William	Rck 485	Salley	Crr 162	Martha	Rbs 425
William	Rwn 413	Samuel	Hde 380	Mary	Crv 325
William	Rth 152	Sarah	Jns 781	Nancy	Orn 603
William (2)	Rth 153	Shadrick	Dpl 419	Nathaniel	Ons 151
William	Smp 505	Stephen	Nwh 6	Norman	Crv 285
William	Smp 530	Thomas	Hde 380	Owen	Cht 205
William	Stk 581	Thos.	Nsh 130	Peggy	Rth 154
William	Stk 605	Thos. H.	Mnt 476	Peter	Rth 152
William	Stk 616	Timothy	Smp 520	Plummer	Wrr 840
William	Wke 772	Upton	Mck 532	Porge	Rbs 432
William	Wrr 836	Urbane	Jns 807	Richard	Crv 281
William	Wrr 837	William	Mre 73	Richard	Cmb 382
William	Wrr 839	William	Mre 74	Robert	Rbs 428
William	Wlk 67	William	Rwn 335	Roger	Glf 651
William, Sen.	Mnt 493	William	Smp 533	Samuel	Bfr 24
William, Senr.	Crv 323	Wm.	Crr 157	Samuel	Crv 285
William E.	Nrt 485	Willias, Henry	Stk 619	Samuel	Rbs 428
Williams	Rnd 346	Willie, Rufus	Crv 229	Sherwood	Cht 164
Willey	Wrr 839	see Willis		Sherwood	Cht 203
Willoughby	Brt 88	Williford, Abner	Brt 84	Simon	Rbs 429
Willoughby	Grn 616	Elisha	Dpl 422	Stephen	Rth 151
Wilson	Nsh 128	John	Brt 84	Vinson	Cht 163
Wm.	Csw 104	Jordan	Bld 22	White	Wrr 840
Wm.	Crr 158	Micajah	Smp 495	William	Crv 275
Wm.	Crr 165	Polley	Wke 778	William, Jur.	Glf 644
Wm.	Crr 168	Rebecca	Bld 14	William, Senr.	Glf 644
Wm.	Lnr 28	Richd.	Bld 9	Wilson	Cht 176
Wm.	Lnr 33	Sion	Smp 497	Wood	Wrr 840
Wm.	Mrt 414	Theosppelus	Prs 189	see Wheliss, Willie	
Wm., Junr.	Mrt 413	Thomas	Nrt 487	Willison, Benjamin	Cmd 106
Wyatt	Wrr 839	William	Smp 497	John	Prq 645
see Willias		William	Wke 773	Williss, Sarah	Nsh 127
Williamson, Anderson	Rth 155	Willingham, Elijah	Grv 525	Williston, Abner	Crt 75
Ann	Rck 443	Willings, Charles	Jhn 748	Alphius	Crt 67
Benjamin	Nrt 487	Willis, Adgerton	Rbs 428	Andrew	Crt 67
C.L. Peter	Hde 380	Adn.	Rbs 432	Benjamin	Crt 85
Charles	Bnc 193	Andw.	Lnc 827	Daniel	Crt 66
David	Hlf 350	Ann	Hlf 348	Daniel	Crt 67
Dempsey	Hde 380	Benjamin	Bld 34	Elijah	Crt 65
Elijah	Bnc 192	Benjamin	Rbs 430	George	Crt 63
Fancis	Crr 156	Benjamin	Rth 154	James	Crt 67
Francis	Hrt 729	Conrod	Lnc 829	Joseph	Crt 64
Gemima	Hlf 354	David	Bld 37	Josiah	Crt 67
George, Jr.	Hlf 350	David	Rth 154	Reuben, jr.	Crt 64
George, Sn.	Hlf 350	Elisha	Hlf 348	Reuben, Sr.	Crt 64
Green	Frn 475	Enock	Wrr 840	Sarah	Crt 66
Hardy	Jhn 751	Ephraim	Crv 281	Seth	Crt 65
Henry	Hde 379	Ezekiah	Crv 283	Thomas	Crt 66
Henry	Ptt 269	George	Rbs 428	Thomas, Sr.	Crt 66
James	Csw 120	George	Rbs 432	Wallace	Crt 67
James	Dpl 399	George, Ser.	Rbs 428	William	Crt 85
James	Mck 567	Henry	Csw 107	Willits, Gabril	Stk 614
James	Mre 73	Henry	Rth 154	Willitt, James	Prq 658
James	Smp 520	Icabod	Mrt 413	Willitts, Stephen	Stk 614
Jas.	Prs 202	Isaac	Crv 325	Willkins, Allen	Grv 570
		James	Ptt 285	Willman, William	Rth 155

Willoby, Edlene	Rch 264	Clement	Bld 24	John	Bld 38		
Kedar	Jhn 769	Conrod	Orn 604	John (2)	Bnc 194		
Solomon	Jhn 764	Daniel	Cht 178	John (3)	Brk 806		
Willoughby, Arther	Crr 161	David	Crv 289	John	Cbr 685		
John	Ans 204	David	Mck 560	John	Csw 114		
John	Hrt 714	Edward	Bld 3	John	Cmb 359		
John	Ptt 277	Edward	Brk 804	John	Dpl 419		
John	Rwn 359	Edward	Jhn 762	John	Edg 254		
Thos., Jur.	Crr 160	Edward, Junr.	Brt 86	John	Grv 517		
Thos., Ser.	Crr 161	Edward, Senr.	Brt 86	John	Glf 671		
William	Hrt 715	Edward, Ser.	Bld 5	John	Glf 676		
Willis	Hrt 715	Elishamore	Smp 500	John	Hde 381		
Wills, Archibald	Wke 770	Ephraim	Crv 339	John	Jhn 748		
Burrel	Lnc 832	Genvial	Brk 804	John	Lnc 901		
Featherston	Lnc 832	George	Bld 38	John	Lnc 907		
Hardy	Srr 701	George	Bnc 191	John	Mck 526		
Henry	Chw 113	George	Hrt 703	John	Mck 532		
James	Chw 113	George	Orn 607	John	Orn 604		
James	Srr 699	George	Rnd 347	John	Orn 605		
John	Frn 485	Henry	Grv 553	John	Orn 608		
John	Lnc 898	Henry	Wrr 837	John	Psq 635		
Micajah	Wne 844	Henry	Wrr 838	John	Prs 193		
Paschal	Wke 778	Isaac	Mck 524	John	Rnd 346		
William	Ons 182	Isaac	Rwn 395	John	Rck 451		
Willson, Amos	Ptt 284	Isaac, Jun.	Prq 647	John	Rck 472		
Ann	Ptt 285	Isaac, Jun.	Prq 653	John	Rwn 405		
Augustin	Grn 606	Isaac, Sen.	Prq 647	John	Rwn 429		
Benjamin	Hlf 350	Isabellah	Orn 494	John (2)	Rth 153		
Boyd	Rwn 393	Jacob	Lnc 907	John	Smp 494		
Buckna	Grn 606	Jacob	Prq 648	John	Smp 524		
Elizabeth	Ptt 246	Jacob, Jun.	Prq 653	John	Stk 589		
Henry	Grn 608	James	Brt 82	John	Wlk 68		
James	Hlf 352	James	Bld 12	John, Jr.	Grv 553		
James	Ons 151	James	Bld 29	John, Senr.	Grv 553		
James	Orn 608	James	Brk 807	Jonathan	Glf 636		
John	Dpl 408	James	Csw 111	Jonathan	Stk 578		
John	Ons 151	James	Csw 112	Joseph	Brk 804		
John	Ptt 246	James	Csw 135	Joseph	Brk 805		
Joshua	Hlf 350	James	Crv 241	Joseph	Brk 806		
Josiah	Ons 152	James	Cmb 359	Joseph	Lnr 28		
Samuel	Orn 604	James	Dpl 431	Joseph	Mck 538		
Sanford	Hlf 348	James	Glf 675	Joseph	Mnt 492		
Widow	Rwn 395	James	Ird 627	Joseph	Psq 624		
William	Grn 606	James	Ird 633	Joseph	Prs 217		
William	Hlf 348	James	Ird 666	Joseph	Smp 502		
William	Ptt 238	James	Jns 795	Joseph	Wlk 68		
Willis	Ptt 246	James	Lnr 27	Joshua	Brt 84		
Willy, Eliz.	Ons 154	James	Lnr 33	Joshua	Lnc 824		
Francis	Ons 156	James	Lnc 823	Joshua	Rth 154		
Wilman, Jeromiah	Rwn 460	James	Lnc 882	Josiah	Brt 86		
Wilmore, Edy	Cht 204	James	Lnc 892	Leml.	Crr 156		
Wilmoth, Teakle	Srr 699	James	Mck 540	Levan	Jns 781		
William	Brk 804	James	Mck 555	Lewis Felte	Ird 642		
Wilmuth, John	Rth 151	James	Mck 556	Lucy	Frn 490		
Wiloughby, John	Rwn 350	James	Mck 576	Lydia	Prq 662		
Wilson, Aaron	Mck 547	James	Mck 604	Margret	Lnc 823		
Abner	Csw 114	James	Nwh 10A	Mary	Wrr 840		
Abraham	Rnd 346	James	Orn 607	Mary	Wlk 68		
Alexander	Ird 666	James	Orn 608	Mathew	Bld 3		
Andrew	Glf 640	James	Rbs 429	Matthew	Lnc 823		
Amos	Glf 660	James	Rck 464	Meshach	Bld 3		
Andrew	Glf 666	James	Rwn 445	Michael	Brk 806		
Andrew	Glf 667	James	Rth 154	Michael	Cht 208		
Andrew	Glf 672	James	Wrr 839	Michael	Glf 625		
Andrew	Lnc 907	James	Wne 851	Michael	Rwn 445		
Andrew	Mck 545	Jas.	Prs 206	Moses	Lnc 823		
Andrew	Ons 136	Jasper	Glf 625	Nancy	Rth 155		
Aquilla	Rck 443	Jeremiah	Mre 46	Nancy	Wrr 837		
Archabald	Glf 654	Jesse	Brk 803	Penelope	Edg 254		
Archibald	Orn 607	Jesse	Rnd 351	Peter	Rck 485		
Benjamin	Cmd 110	Jms.	Lnc 840	Philip	Rck 464		
Benjamin	Glf 661	Jno. (3)	Lnc 840	Philip	Stk 588		
Benjamin	Rwn 429	Joel	Mnt 493	Pleasant	Wrr 837		
Benjn.	Cht 204	Joel	Smp 506	Richard	Glf 669		
Bloomer	Cht 208	Joel	Smp 509	Richard	Ird 633		
Charles	Cmb 363	John	Bfr 20	Richard	Rwn 413		
Christopher	Prq 649	John	Bld 3	Richard	Rth 154		

Richard	Wrr 838	Wm. J.	Lnc 840	Obediah	Srr 701
Robert	Brk 804	Zachariah	Prq 663	Winfield, Ammy	Hde 379
Robert	Brk 805	see Wolson		Bryan	Hde 379
Robert	Csw 112	Wilton, Robert	Jns 795	Edward	Ans 205
Robert	Crv 255	Wily, Miriam	Psq 624	Jesse	Hde 381
Robert	Grv 553	Wimberley, George	Jhn 760	John	Hde 379
Robert	Mck 560	James	Ans 238	Martha	Hde 380
Robert	Nwh 10A	Malachi	Jhn 760	Richard	Hde 379
Robert	Orn 606	Winberly, Benjamin	Brt 86	Robert	Hde 380
Robert	Rch 242	David	Cht 203	Winnifrid	Bfr 20
Robert	Rwn 413	George	Edg 257	Winford, Charles	Wke 774
Robt.	Cht 222	Jacob	Cht 202	Joshua	Brk 806
Saml.	Lnc 844	Levi, Junr.	Brt 86	Winfrey, David	Grv 541
Samuel	Ans 200	Levi, Senr.	Brt 86	Wingants, Mrs.	Chw 117
Samuel	Ash 90	Marke	Cht 202	Wingate, Cornelius	Cmb 359
Samuel	Bnc 192	Wimbly, Moses	Mnt 504	Elizabeth	Ptt 242
Samuel	Glf 625	Winagim, John	Prs 201	Hannah	Bld 5
Samuel	Ird 653	Winants, Mary	Brt 82	Isaac	Crv 269
Samuel	Mck 560	Penelope	Chw 116	Jackson	Lnc 851
Samuel	Orn 607	Winbord, David	Nsh 128	Joel	Ptt 243
Samuel (2)	Wlk 68	Winborn, Abraham	Nsh 129	John	Bld 5
Samuel, Senr.	Jhn 761	John	Nsh 129	Jonathn.	Brn 20A
Samuel C.	Cmb 381	Pharaby	Nsh 129	Joseph	Cmb 359
Sarah	Nsh 133	Thomas	Hrt 727	Michael	Cht 196
Seth	Bfr 19	Winborne, David	Nrt 483	Peter	Crv 319
Shadrach	Bld 4	Demcey	Nrt 485	Reuben	Ans 217
Sherwood	Wrr 841	Elias	Nrt 487	Reuben	Ans 223
Simon	Crr 153	Henry	Nrt 485	Thomas	Crv 343
Solomon	Ans 200	James	Hrt 727	Walter	Brn 16A
Spencer	Rck 473	James	Nrt 485	William	Ans 223
Spensor	Wrr 838	Jesse	Nrt 485	William	Brn 18A
Stephen	Cht 208	John	Hrt 727	Winget, Demsey	Prq 642
Stephen	Orn 605	John	Nrt 485	John	Prq 644
Sylvanos	Frn 494	Phillip	Nrt 483	Levy	Prq 643
Sylvans	Cmb 382	William, Junr.	Nrt 485	Winhorn, Isaac	Brk 806
Tatem	Crr 156	William, Senr.	Nrt 485	Winifred, Tull	Lnr 27
Tenneson	Rck 463	William, Ters.	Nrt 485	Winkfield, Joseph	Wne 873
Thomas	Cmd 108	Winborough, Mi-		Thomas	Ird 663
Thomas	Crt 89	chael	Edg 257	Peter	Ans 206
Thomas	Csw 114	Winbray, Jesse	Mrt 412	Winkle, Conrod,	
Thomas	Frn 479	John, Esqr.	Mrt 412	Junr.	Brk 802
Thomas	Grv 547	Winbun, Thomas	Hlf 354	Thomas	Brk 802
Thomas	Lnc 907	Winbury, Enoch	Psq 632	Winkler, Abraham	Brk 803
Thomas	Mck 606	Winchester, Cole-		Adam	Rwn 420
Thomas	Orn 606	man	Rck 457	Conrod	Brk 804
Thomas	Rck 464	Daniel	Mck 594	Conrod	Brk 806
Thomas	Rth 156	Douglass	Cbr 696	Francis	Rwn 395
Thomas	Srr 701	Francis	Brk 803	Henry	Rwn 395
Thomas	Wrr 838	John	Rck 457	Jacob, Senr.	Brk 804
Thomas	Wne 851	Thomas	Mck 598	Joseph	Brk 806
Thomas, Junr.	Mck 576	Winders, Adan	Rck 471	Lawrence	Brk 806
Timy.	Nwh 11	Edward	Dpl 436	Mathias	Brk 804
Widow	Mck 561	Epenetus	Prs 207	Peter	Rwn 412
Widow	Mck 589	James	Dpl 433	Thomas	Brk 806
William	Brt 82	James	Wlk 69	Thomas, Junr.	Brk 807
William	Bnc 193	John	Dpl 427	Winley, Churchman	Hde 380
William	Brk 805	John	Dpl 436	Elijah	Hde 379
William	Csw 104	Windham, Isaac	Bld 34	Israel	Bfr 20
William	Crv 245	John	Wne 872	John	Bfr 21
William	Edg 256	Windle, Henry	Stk 610	Levi	Hde 380
William	Glf 633	Windom, Green	Ptt 275	Maple	Hde 380
William	Ird 642	Isaaiah	Ptt 260	Moses	Bfr 21
William	Mck 526	John	Ptt 262	Shadrach	Hde 380
William	Mck 533	Micajah	Ptt 274	Thomas	Bfr 20
William	Mck 563	Windsor, Jno.	Csw 145	Thomas	Hde 380
William	Mre 76	John	Rck 477	William	Bfr 21
William	Ons 136	Molly	Crt 56	Winn, Joseph	Cmb 359
William	Psq 628	Thomas	Csw 145	William	Brk 806
William	Rck 463	Wine, Andrew	Crr 148	William	Wke 771
William (2)	Rth 154	Clarett	Lnr 26	Winningham, John	Cmb 359
William	Rth 156	John	Crr 153	Richard	Rnd 347
William	Stk 589	Winebarger, Conrod	Lnc 882	Winns, Thomas	Ans 227
William	Wne 871	Winecough, John	Cbr 699	Winock, Carter	Hlf 354
William (2)	Wlk 68	Winegardner, James	Glf 637	Wins, John	Brk 802
Willie	Edg 256	Wineser, Robert	Mck 606	Winscot, Christo-	
Wm.	Crr 156	Winfery, Caleb	Srr 699	pher	Brk 803
Wm.	Lnc 840	Isaac	Srr 701	Winseth, Joseph	Jns 785

Name	Ref
Robert	Jns 789
William	Jns 785
Winslew, Jesse	Prq 643
Winsloe, Joseph	Edg 256
Winslow, Calib	Prq 654
Fany	Rnd 350
Henry	Rnd 346
Jabob	Chw 119
Jacob, Jun.	Prq 661
Jesse, Jun.	Prq 661
Jesse, Sen.	Prq 660
Jesse, (the younger)	Prq 660
Jobe	Chw 130
John	Chw 124
John	Cmb 359
John	Psq 640
John	Rnd 352
John	Rnd 352
Joseph	Rnd 352
Moses	Ird 659
Phillip	Rnd 350
Pleasant	Prq 648
Samuel	Chw 124
Thomas	Rnd 352
Thomas	Wne 869
William	Chw 119
Winsor, Isaac	Srr 699
Winstead, David	Nsh 129
Ezikiel	Nsh 126
Francis	Edg 255
Jeremiah, Junr.	Edg 255
Jeremiah, Senr.	Edg 255
Joseph	Edg 254
Peter	Edg 255
Thomas	Nsh 129
Winsted, Cattance	Prs 192
Charles	Prs 211
Manley	Prs 192
Saml.	Prs 192
Will.	Prs 192
Winston, Antony	Frn 457
Antony, Jur.	Frn 458
George	Frn 459
Isaac	Frn 458
Isaac, Capt.	Frn 458
John	Frn 458
Joseph	Stk 576
Thomas	Rck 436
William	Frn 460
Winstone, Nathaniel	Grv 557
Winter, James	Hlf 348
Ambrose	Hlf 348
Winters, John	Csw 126
John, Jur.	Frn 461
John, Jur.	Frn 472
John, Ser.	Frn 461
John, Ser.	Frn 472
Joseph	Frn 472
Joseph	Hlf 348
Ritter	Hlf 350
Walson	Csw 122
Walter	Csw 110
William	Hlf 352
William	Lnc 900
Wm.	Csw 110
Wintz, Valentine	Mck 606
Wipper, Jacob	Wne 845
Wires, James	Rnd 347
Wisdom, Abner	Csw 118
Anne	Wlk 69
James	Csw 118
John	Csw 118
Larkin	Csw 116
Thomas	Ans 227
William	Ans 240
Wise, Alexander	Brk 805
Benjamin	Rth 153
Jacob	Rwn 298
James	Jhn 776
John	Wne 867
Joseph	Bfr 21
Joshua	Hrt 738
Josiah	Wne 873
Lemuel	Ons 136
Mary	Bfr 21
Mathew	Ons 143
Peter	Brk 803
Thomas	Ons 143
William	Cmb 369
Wiseman, Isaac	Rwn 405
Jacob	Rwn 405
Martin	Brk 806
William	Brk 803
William	Brk 805
William	Rwn 395
Wisener, Andrew	Rwn 421
Jacob	Rwn 420
John	Cbr 697
Wisenhunt, Adam	Lnc 893
Wiser, Michael	Cbr 521
Wishart, Jonathan	Rbs 428
Widow	Mck 525
Widow	Mck 606
Wishong, Lenard	Srr 700
Wislock, James	Wlk 68
Wiss, Peter	Nwh 2
Witchard, John	Ptt 239
Philip	Ptt 229
Prisscilla	Ptt 225
Witenbarger, Henry	Lnc 882
John	Lnc 882
Witherby, Aaron	Rth 152
Witherington, Ambrose	Ptt 287
Benja.	Lnr 27
Charlton	Hrt 703
Danl.	Lnr 27
Eliza	Lnr 27
Robert	Ptt 287
Stephen	Lnr 27
Witherspoon, David	Crv 341
David	Wlk 68
John	Ird 653
John	Wlk 68
William	Ird 653
Witherton, John	Crv 269
Withrow, James	Rth 154
John	Rth 154
Mary	Rth 152
Sidney	Rth 153
William	Rth 153
Witson, Elisabeth	Stk 582
Witt, Ann	Stk 576
Mary	Glf 662
see Whitt	
Wittenton, Wm. (2)	Ash 91
Wittie, Andrew	Glf 650
Elijah	Rck 456
John	Glf 650
see Wattee	
Wittiker, Isaac	Ash 90
Witty, Thomas	Csw 125
Witworth, Elizabeth	Stk 576
Wix, John	Rnd 351
Wize, David	Lnc 824
Henry	Lnc 824
Jacob	Lnc 824
John	Lnc 824
Wobbleton, William	Orn 604
Woblison, Susanah	Rnd 347
Woddle, Noel	Srr 699
Wold, William	Srr 700
Wolderage, William	Srr 706
Wolf, Adam	Stk 575
Charles	Wne 853
Daniel	Stk 614
George	Wne 853
Jacob	Rth 152
Jesse	Dpl 440
Lewis	Stk 575
Michael	Bnc 193
William	Orn 603
Wolfenden, John	Brt 86
Wolfinsporger, John	Srr 701
Wolford, Jacob	Stk 601
Wollard, Absalom	Bfr 19
Absalom, Ser.	Bfr 21
Allegood	Bfr 21
Benjamin	Ptt 238
Coleman	Bfr 21
Covernton	Bfr 20
Elizabeth	Bfr 21
Jasper	Bfr 19
Jeremiah	Bfr 21
Jesse	Bfr 19
Jno., son Micl.	Bfr 21
John, Jur.	Bfr 21
John, Sr.	Bfr 20
Michael	Bfr 19
Michael, Jur.	Bfr 21
Noah	Bfr 21
Richd.	Mrt 414
Samuel	Bfr 20
William	Bfr 20
Willibough	Bfr 20
Willie	Bfr 19
Wolley, James	Orn 602
Wolsington, John	Glf 678
Wolson, James	Ptt 281
Womack, Britain	Cht 210
David	Prs 208
John	Prs 202
Womble, John	Cht 163
John	Edg 175
John	Edg 253
John	Jns 781
Josiah	Hlf 348
Mary	Jns 789
Nathan	Smp 507
Samuel	Mre 42
William	Wke 772
Wombwell, Benjamin	Ptt 276
Benjamin, Senior	Ptt 276
Lucretia	Ptt 275
Wommack, John	Cht 159
Wommock, John, Sr.	Cht 159
Wonderweedle, Keziah	Rbs 432
Wood, Aaron	Ird 663
Andrw	Brk 802
Anna	Prs 201
Anne	Edg 253
Archibald	Lnc 893
Asa	Brt 84
Bennit	Mck 537
Burges	Wke 772
Burril	Rwn 384
Charles	Rwn 278
Charles	Rwn 292
Clement	Rnd 351
Cornelius	Rwn 460
Cullen	Wne 844
Daniel	Edg 255
Daniel	Rwn 412
David	Rnd 349
Elizabeth	Grn 612
F. Isaac	Nrt 485
Federick	Ons 144

Name	Loc	Name	Loc	Name	Loc
Frame	Ans 224	Soloman	Cht 165	Matthew	Rch 262
Gracey	Grn 611	Stephen	Wlk 67	Mark	Rch 257
Henry	Bnc 193	Thomas	Psq 624	Mark	Rch 262
Henry	Brk 804	Thomas	Psq 641	Woodley, Phillip	Frn 449
Henry	Cht 188	Vinson	Rwn 421	Samuel	Trl 674
Henry	Cht 200	Walter	Rwn 435	Stephen	Trl 674
Isaac	Rnd 349	Walter	Srr 699	Willis	Gts 281
Isaac F.	Nrt 485	Widow	Rwn 335	Woodring, Daniel	Lnc 882
Isham	Rwn 413	Will.	Nsh 128	Woodroof, Gideon	Srr 700
Jacob	Ons 178	Will.	Prs 200	Moses	Srr 699
Jacob	Wke 771	William	Ans 200	Richard	Stk 611
James	Brt 84	William	Frn 464	Woodruff, John A.	Ash 90
James	Brk 804	William	Hlf 350	Moses	Ash 90
James	Frn 478	William	Nrt 487	Woods, Benjamin	Crv 249
James	Jns 819	William	Rnd 349	David	Orn 606
James	Rwn 413	William	Rwn 413	David	Rwn 338
James	Wlk 69	William	Rth 149	Dempsey	Orn 608
James, Jun.	Prq 646	William	Rth 155	Dorset	Brk 807
James, Sen.	Prq 653	William	Smp 498	Elihu	Orn 606
Jane	Prq 654	William	Smp 508	Elizabeth	Grv 541
Jessee	Cht 188	William, Ser.	Cht 200	Ezekiel	Grv 560
Jessy	Ons 176	Willis	Wrr 840	Freeman	Crv 243
John	Bnc 192	Zacheriah	Rth 151	Harrison	Orn 605
John	Bnc 193	Zebedee (2)	Rnd 351	Henry	Smp 516
John	Dpl 441	Woodal, Absalom	Jhn 773	James	Brk 805
John	Ird 666	Jacob	Jhn 771	James	Ird 673
John	Jhn 773	Jacob	Jhn 772	James	Orn 605
John	Mnt 487	Martin	Jhn 771	James, B.S.	Orn 606
John	Nrt 483	Woodard, Britain	Nrt 487	John	Grv 582
John	Psq 637	Catharine	Dpl 410	John	Lnc 898
John	Prq 643	Corbel	Wke 771	John, (shff.)	Orn 606
John (2)	Rnd 349	David	Hlf 348	John, W	Orn 606
John	Rwn 413	Demsey	Wke 771	Jos.	Prs 200
John (2)	Rwn 435	Elisha	Edg 253	Joseph	Jns 793
John (2)	Wlk 67	Elizabeth	Edg 256	Joseph	Orn 606
Jonas	Mrt 413	Franky	Dpl 410	Joseph	Orn 608
Jonas	Nrt 485	Gofdin	Rnd 349	Leven	Orn 603
Joseph (2)	Psq 628	Isaiah	Bfr 20	Margarett	Orn 604
Joseph	Psq 637	James	Dpl 427	Mary	Orn 493
Joseph	Prq 646	James	Wke 772	Mary	Orn 606
Joseph	Prq 660	John	Bfr 20	Matthew	Rwn 323
Joseph	Rbs 429	Jordan	Wke 772	Misael, jr.	Grv 536
Joseph	Stk 585	Joseph	Wke 772	Payton	Grv 553
Joseph	Wlk 67	Lewis	Nrt 485	Peter	Jns 781
Joseph, (Junr.	Rwn 435	Martha	Rnd 351	Rabecca	Brk 806
Joseph, Sen.	Prq 662	Oliver	Nrt 485	Rchard	Grv 581
Joseph, (Senr.	Rwn 435	Penny	Wke 773	Robert	Rwn 323
Josiah	Rwn 413	Peter	Rth 152	Sampson	Orn 606
Judah	Chw 129	Pleasant	Wke 771	Samuel	Orn 606
Kenchion	Wke 772	Richard	Wke 771	Simon	Dpl 410
Laurence	Nrt 485	Thomas	Nrt 485	Thomas	Orn 606
Loudrick	Chw 130	William	Frn 474	Widow	Mck 526
Lucy	Bld 36	William	Hlf 350	Widow	Mck 550
Margret	Mre 71	Woodards, Peter	Rth 153	William	Grv 566
Mark	Ons 171	Woodburn, David	Glf 642	William (2)	Orn 606
Mark	Psq 637	Thomas	Glf 682	William	Rwn 343
Mary	Brt 84	William	Glf 642	Woodsides, Archd.	Rwn 338
Mary	Csw 120	Woodcock, Robt.	Nwh 9	John	Ird 615
Mathew	Dpl 417	Wooddle, Matthew	Rch 257	Robert	Ird 642
Moses	Ans 230	Woodel, William	Rch 258	Robt.	Brn 16A
Moses	Jns 801	Woodell, Jeromiah	Mnt 492	William	Ird 614
Moses	Wke 772	John	Mnt 493	Woodsin see Woodfen	
Nathan	Prq 660	Joseph	Cht 207	Woodsock, Richard	Rwn 369
Penawell	Rnd 349	Wooderoofe, David	Nrt 485	Woodson, Booker	Nrt 487
Peter	Dpl 417	Richard	Nrt 485	David	Rwn 278
Peter	Stk 585	Woodfen, Nicholas	Bnc 192	David, Junr.	Rwn 292
Phurny	Smp 506	Woodfin, Thomas	Bnc 192	David, Senr.	Rwn 310
Rachel	Rwn 413	Woodford, James	Lnr 26	Woodwald see Woodward	
Reuben	Rnd 346	Woodfork, Joseph	Wlk 67	Woodward, Aron	Nsh 127
Richard	Prq 646	William	Stk 608	Azariah	Brk 807
Richard	Stk 585	Woodhouse, Hadley	Crr 137	Benjamin	Jhn 748
Richard	Trl 674	Hezekiah	Crr 141	Daniel	Nsh 128
Robert	Rnd 351	Wilson	Crr 145	David	Nsh 126
Robert	Stk 585	Wm.	Crr 137	Edward	Chw 126
Sally	Rth 153	Woodington, John	Cbr 700	James	Chw 129
Seth	Chw 130	Woodland, John	Trl 674	James	Jhn 771
Sidney	Jns 781	Woodle, James	Orn 604	James	Nsh 126

Jesse	Wne 864	Robert	Ird 658	Absalom	Mnt 466
John	Wne 860	Workman, Isaac	Cbr 702	Alexander	Rck 488
Luke	Wne 859	John	Orn 606	Anderson	Wrr 841
Luke	Wne 862	Richard	Orn 604	Ann	Crv 285
Mary	Wne 861	Richard	Orn 606	Archl.	Nwh 9A
Richard	Chw 119	Thomas	Cht 175	Arthur	Cmd 104
Samuel	Wne 861	Works, Joseph	Orn 604	Augustin	Cht 206
Samuel	Wne 862	Worldly, Jacob	Srr 699	Barnaby	Cmd 105
Thomas	Jhn 752	Loftus	Dpl 440	Benjamin	Jhn 771
William	Bnc 192	Mary	Hlf 350	Benjamin	Rnd 351
Woody, Hugh	Cht 212	Nathan	Srr 699	Benjamin	Wke 773
John	Orn 602	Stephen	Srr 699	Caled	Csw 108
Joseph	Orn 602	Worley, Daniel	Brt 84	Charles	Lnc 849
Lewis	Orn 604	Henry	Stk 576	Charles	Mck 522
Samuel	Orn 602	John	Jhn 749	Charles	Mnt 465
Samul	Orn 604	Nicholas	Bld 2	Charles	Rck 464
Talton	Ash 90	William	Jhn 749	Claibourn	Wke 774
William	Bnc 193	William	Jhn 750	David	Bld 7
William	Orn 604	Wormington, Edward	Hde 380	David	Dpl 401
Woolard, Daniel	Prq 662	Wornum, Samuel	Nrt 485	David	Hde 380
James	Ptt 236	Worran, Josiah	Orn 608	Duncan	Cmb 360
John	Ptt 224	Worrel, Amos	Hlf 354	Edward	Mnt 465
Martin	Prq 645	Richard	Hrt 729	Esau	Rwn 388
Simon (2)	Ptt 238	Worrell, Benjamin	Bld 4	Ezekiel	Cbr 681
Woolbrook, John	Brk 807	Levi	Wne 872	Francis	Rck 439
Woolever, Joseph	Cbr 713	Stephen	Wne 871	George	Grv 574
Woolf, Daniel	Srr 701	see Warrel		George	Mck 566
John Charles	Grn 608	Worren, John	Orn 606	George	Rnd 347
Woolfe, Calib	Cbr 707	Worret, William	Wne 846	George	Rch 258
Henry	Mck 597	Worrill, Dempsey	Rbs 429	Green	Rnd 347
Philip	Mck 594	Worsley, Dicy	Edg 254	Griffin	Frn 448
Philip, Senr.	Mck 597	Jesse	Bfr 23	Grove	Ptt 294
Woolford, Arthur	Brt 90	John	Bfr 20	Henry	Cmd 107
Tubman	Ptt 293	Joseph	Bfr 21	Henry	Nwh 8
Wooling, Edwd.	Rck 468	Thomas	Bfr 20	Isaac	Glf 667
Woollard, Masa	Wsh 716	Thos., Bay		Isaac	Rnd 347
Wooten, Abner	Wlk 68	River	Bfr 20	Isaac	Smp 526
Benjn.	Bnc 193	William	Bfr 20	Jacob	Csw 105
Britain	Smp 517	Worth, Danl.	Glf 626	Jacob	Csw 108
Elizabeth	Wlk 67	David	Glf 626	Jacob	Cmb 359
James	Mnt 499	Jobe	Glf 626	James	Bld 8
James	Smp 496	Joseph	Rnd 351	James	Cht 158
Jesse	Jhn 761	Silas	Stk 618	James	Dpl 434
John	Frn 450	Zeno	Glf 626	James	Grv 574
John	Lnr 26	Wortham, Charles	Orn 607	James	Glf 644
Moses	Frn 460	Edward	Orn 605	James	Glf 654
Thomas	Smp 499	James	Grv 512	James	Hlf 348
see Hooten		John	Wrr 836	James	Hde 380
Wooters, Markland	Lnr 27	Jordan	Wke 773	James	Rch 263
Wootes, Jesse	Lnr 26	Thomas	Rck 464	James	Rck 464
Wootin, Britain	Smp 496	William	Stk 619	James	Rck 483
Wooton, Absolom	Edg 253	William	Wrr 837	James	Rck 490
Amos	Edg 253	see Wartham		James	Rwn 388
Anne	Edg 253	Worthington, John	Rnd 351	James	Wrr 840
James	Edg 253	Worthinton, Jacob	Rnd 349	James	Wlk 67
John	Ird 638	Worthy, John	Mre 61	James, Jun.	Prq 656
Jonathan	Ird 638	Wortman, Henry	Rwn 402	Jeptha	Frn 472
Josiah	Ptt 271	Peter	Rwn 402	Jess	Wrr 841
William	Edg 253	Philip	Rwn 359	Jms.	Lnc 840
William	Wne 860	Thomas	Rwn 402	John	Brk 787
Wootten, William	Hlf 348	William	Rwn 402	John	Cmb 377
Worcely, Stephen	Crv 319	Wosen, Alex.	Csw 147	John	Hde 380
Stephen	Crv 343	Woten, James	Rch 245	John	Rwn 359
Word, A. Thomas	Srr 699	Wotton, William	Ptt 258	John	Rwn 395
Fanny	Ons 153	Wowden, Benj.	Prs 213	John	Smp 520
John	Stk 576	Wrann, Joel	Rwn 363	John	Stk 579
Randolph	Stk 576	Wray, Darling S.	Ptt 240	John	Wrr 839
Thomas	Csw 149	James	Rck 457	John, Jun.	Hlf 350
Thomas A.	Srr 699	John	Cht 155	John, Junr.	Ans 229
Worden, Michal	Srr 698	Wren, Benjm.	Prs 188	John, Sen.	Hlf 350
Wordley, Francis	Bnc 191	Eliz.	Ons 156	Jos. G.	Nwh 3
Worford, John	Rck 469	Elizebeth	Wrr 841	Joseph	Cht 179
Work, Alexander	Ird 659	John	Cht 165	Joseph	Hlf 350
Ann	Glf 648	Richard	Edg 256	Joseph	Mck 522
John	Glf 649	Wrenn, Elias	Frn 485	Kenan	Smp 527
John, Senr.	Glf 649	Wrey, William	Rbs 428	Lucey	Rnd 349
Margarett	Glf 648	Wright, Abner	Wke 772	Martin	Rck 439

Matthew P.	Cmd 106	Wyatte, John	Bnc 192	Henry	Rwn 395
Matthias	Hrt 727	Simmons	Mrt 413	Jacob	Rnd 352
Nathan	Wke 774	Sollomon	Mrt 413	James	Orn 491
Newton	Glf 658	Wm.	Mrt 413	Jas.	Hlf 354
Nicoll	Cmb 379	Wyce, Nicey	Crv 253	Jno., Jr.	Hlf 354
Peter	Rnd 346	Wyett, John	Rth 155	John	Mnt 465
Philbert	Rwn 359	see Wiett		Jon, Ser.	Hlf 354
Philip	Rwn 389	Wylie, James	Mck 556	Joseph	Cmb 378
Prudence	Rck 488	Robert	Glf 669	Joshua	Mck 586
Richard	Rwn 389	Robert	Mck 556	Joshua, Senr.	Mck 586
Richard	Rth 152	William	Glf 669	Judith	Rwn 396
Robert	Smp 519	Wynens, Widow	Mck 557	Noah	Rwn 395
Salley	Hde 379	Wynn, James	Orn 608	Richd.	Hlf 354
Samuel	Wke 772	James B.	Brt 82	Thomas	Rwn 395
Samuel, Jur.	Wke 772	Thomas	Orn 608	Wm.	Hlf 354
Sarah	Crr 141	William	Crv 337	Yarborow, Elisha	Mre 68
Simon	Rwn 411	William	Wke 770	Yarbro, Benjamin	Mck 528
Solomon	Brk 788	Wynne, Anne	Trl 674	Humphrey, Jr.	Ans 207
Sterling	Hlf 350	Benjamin	Trl 684	Yarbrough, Ambrous	Ans 234
Thomas	Ans 224	Charles	Frn 466	Charles	Frn 484
Thomas	Brk 788	Daniel	Brt 84	David	Ans 234
Thomas	Dpl 432	George	Trl 682	Edmond	Mck 590
Thomas	Glf 668	Jeremiah	Trl 674	Edward	Rwn 278
Thomas	Rck 481	Jesse	Trl 682	Humphrey, Jr.	Ans 207
Thomas	Srr 700	John	Brt 84	Humphrey, Junr.	Ans 235
W. John	Brk 787	Joseph	Trl 674	Gideon	Mck 589
Wiley	Stk 578	Robert	Trl 674	James	Ans 234
Will.	Nwh 11	Wynns, John	Mrt 412	James	Frn 457
William	Hlf 350	John A.	Hrt 714	Jeptha	Mck 586
William	Hde 379	Matthew	Hrt 722	John	Prs 193
William	Prq 648	Thomas, Esqr.	Hrt 715	Jonathan	Ans 235
William	Prq 659	Watkin Wm.	Mrt 412	Joseph	Cht 159
William	Rch 258	William	Hrt 727	Lea	Ans 207
William	Rck 442	Wyre, Adam	Rwn 370	Levi	Ans 235
William	Rck 485	Jacob	Rwn 370	Lewis	Cht 225
William	Smp 519	Wyrich, Jacob	Stk 603	Micajah, Jur.	Frn 479
William	Stk 576	Wyrick, Jacob	Rwn 370	Micajah, Ser.	Frn 479
William	Wke 774			Nathan	Cht 160
Williams	Srr 700			Nathaniel	Frn 457
Willis	Glf 621	-- X --		Rubin	Mck 585
Willis	Glf 644			Saml.	Prs 192
Willis	Mnt 476	Xavia, Francis	Bfr 24	Shadrick	Frn 462
Zackeriah	Wrr 840			Thomas	Frn 448
see Matthew & Wright				Will.	Prs 191
Wrightman, Peter	Orn 607	-- Y --		William	Ans 240
Wrights, John	Stk 625			William	Mnt 488
Write, William	Mre 47			Yarnnold, Mordecia	Wlk 69
Writenhower, John	Mnt 515			Yarnold, Aaron	Wlk 69
Writesmon, David	Rnd 346	Yallowley, Edwd.	Mrt 388	Joseph	Wlk 69
Mary	Rnd 346	Yalock, Will.	Prs 214	Yarrell, Matthew	Mrt 415
Writley, John	Bfr 19	Yance, Fredrick	Ash 91	Thos.	Mrt 415
Writtor, Averit	Mre 77	John	Ash 91	Yates, Auley	Cht 203
Jesse	Mre 49	Yancey, Charles	Rbs 430	Benjamin	Ash 92
Thomas	Mre 40	Yancy, Anne	Csw 130	Benjamin	Ons 164
Wroten, James	Ash 91	Charles	Grv 540	Benjamin	Ons 168
Wurrel, Mary	Edg 255	James	Csw 130	Bennet	Ons 138
Wutt, Sarah	Hlf 352	Jechonias	Grv 540	Charles	Crt 56
Wyat, Isaac	Psq 632	John	Csw 130	Daniel	Ons 175
Wyatt, Aaron	Rwn 434	Lewis	Grv 540	Isaac	Rch 262
Cornelius	Rwn 434	Philip	Grv 541	James (2)	Ons 147
Daniel	Lnc 844	Sterling	Grv 508	James	Rnd 352
Demsey	Nsh 133	Thomas	Csw 105	James	Rch 243
James	Lnc 844	Tryon	Grv 541	John	Lnc 866
James	Prq 651	William	Grv 541	John (2)	Wlk 69
James	Rwn 384	William	Grv 542	John, Esqr.	Bld 2
John	Prq 646	Yandel, Widow	Mck 553	John, Jur.	Bld 2
John	Rwn 383	Yandle, Samuel	Mck 581	Luke	Bld 2
John	Rwn 434	Samuel, Jun.	Mck 545	Mathew	Cht 202
John, Junr.	Rwn 384	William, Jun.	Mck 545	Penelepy	Ons 178
Joseph	Trl 674	Yarboraugh, Jesse	Wrr 841	Peter	Rnd 352
Richard	Orn 603	Wm. (3)	Wrr 841	Richd.	Wlk 69
Silvester	Mck 601	Yarborough,		Thomas	Chw 129
Thomas	Lnc 844	Charles	Lnc 825	William	Csw 112
Thomas	Rwn 384	Charles	Mnt 465	William	Cht 202
William	Ash 90	Daniel	Hlf 356	William	Rnd 352
William	Rwn 434	Edwd.	Rwn 292	William (2)	Wlk 69
William, Senr.	Rwn 434	Eliza.	Hlf 354	William, Sr.	Cht 202

Yawbanks, John	Ptt 236	Nethaniel	Rnd 352	Joshua	Stk 589
Mary	Ptt 234	Philemon	Grv 530	Katey	Grn 599
Yearby, Henry	Hlf 354	Richard	Srr 703	Marling	Srr 703
William	Hlf 354	Samuel	Rnd 352	Mary	Hlf 356
Yearly, Benjamin	Brk 808	Shuble	Rnd 350	Micajah	Ans 203
Yearrell, Maria	Stk 600	Thomas	Grv 531	Michael	Cbr 698
Yearrill, Maria	Stk 626	Thomas	Rnd 350	Michael	Rwn 413
Yeates, Abraham	Crv 343	Thomas	Rnd 352	Molley	Frn 456
Daniel	Jns 807	Thomas	Rth 156	Moses	Brk 808
David	Jns 797	Thomas H.	Crv 275	Nelly	Wne 873
Edward	Nrt 487	William	Rnd 350	Patty	Rck 456
Isma	Brt 88	William (2)	Rth 156	Rachel	Brk 808
James	Brt 88	Young, Absalom	Rck 444	Rachel	Grv 540
John B., Junr.	Jns 801	Alexander	Ird 663	Robert	Frn 472
John B., Senr.	Jns 803	Archibald	Ird 674	Samuel	Bfr 24
Melchisedec	Crv 343	Barnabas	Rwn 413	Samuel	Bnc 194
Peter R.	Jns 797	Benjamin	Ird 663	Samuel	Frn 466
William	Brt 88	Benjamin	Stk 578	Samuel	Frn 493
William	Jns 803	Benjamin	Stk 589	Samuel	Mck 602
Yeats, Jesse	Hrt 727	Caclia	Grn 599	Samuel	Rck 484
Thomas	Bfr 21	Cathrine	Wlk 69	Samuel (3)	Rth 156
Yeilding, Richd.	Rth 156	Daniel	Brt 90	Samuel	Stk 589
Yelvingston, Shad-		David	Bld 35	Samuel	Wke 774
rach	Jhn 759	David	Glf 670	Samuel	Wsh 712
Yelvington, Elisa-		Demetrus	Frn 467	Sarah	Hlf 354
beth	Wne 872	Dobbs	Smp 507	Steven	Frn 491
Hardy	Wne 872	Dorrell	Nrt 487	Strob	Brk 808
Noah	Wne 872	Elisabeth	Cbr 704	Temperence	Frn 453
Yeoman, Shadrach	Rck 443	Elisabeth	Crv 301	Thomas	Brk 808
Stokes	Rck 443	Elizabeth	Bfr 24	Thomas	Hlf 356
Yeomands, Stokes	Ans 219	Ellarson	Rck 454	Thomas (2)	Ird 638
Young	Ans 219	Fountain	Rck 438	Thomas	Wke 774
Yeomans, James	Chw 115	Francis	Hlf 356	Wiley	Ans 203
Joseph	Crt 61	Francis	Mnt 481	William	Bfr 21
Yeost, Jacob	Rwn 310	Francis	Wke 774	William (2)	Bnc 194
Philip	Rwn 304	Frederick	Rwn 402	William	Cbr 681
Yerbie, Everet	Mck 588	Harriott	Hlf 356	William	Ird 653
James	Mck 588	Henry	Crv 235	William	Ird 674
Yerby, Henry	Bld 38	Henry	Rnd 352	William	Rck 470
John	Ans 236	Henry	Stk 626	William	Rwn 329
William	Ans 237	Henry	Srr 703	William	Stk 589
Yergen, Benjamin	Orn 602	Holley	Wke 774	Willis	Mnt 481
Jarrott	Orn 602	Isham	Srr 703	Youngblood, Judith	Cht 199
Yewell, Solomon S.	Srr 703	Jacob	Brk 808	Thomas	Jhn 765
Yews, Martha	Rck 483	Jacob	Rck 468	Younge, Archibald	Ird 675
Yoap, Abegail	Ons 164	Jacob	Rwn 402	William	Ird 675
Jeremiah	Ons 161	James	Brk 808	Younger, Gilbert	Bfr 21
John	Ons 164	James	Cmb 359	Henry	Orn 602
Yoder, David	Lnc 908	James	Frn 470	Joseph	Orn 602
Elias	Lnc 908	James	Frn 492	Joseph	Wlk 69
Jacob	Lnc 908	James	Grn 599	Madam	Chw 114
John	Lnc 908	James	Ird 663	Yount, Daniel	Rnd 350
Yokely, Griffin	Rwn 361	James	Mck 558	George	Rnd 352
William	Rwn 359	James	Mnt 481	Henry	Rnd 350
Yoman, John	Cbr 704	James	Rwn 329	John	Rnd 352
Yondel, Samuel	Mck 544	James	Stk 585	Peter	Brk 808
Yondle, William	Mck 542	James	Wlk 69	Yow, Andrew	Mre 75
Yons, Rudolph	Rwn 351	Jean	Smp 502	Christopher	Mnt 507
Yont, Abraham	Lnc 883	John	Bfr 24	Christopher	Mre 75
Andrew	Lnc 883	John	Brt 88		
George	Lnc 883	John	Bld 6		
Henry	Lnc 883	John	Frn 493	-- Z --	
York, Abner	Rnd 352	John	Grv 540		
Aron	Rck 465	John	Psq 636		
Caty	Rnd 350	John	Rck 444	Zachakay, Barthow.	Csw 145
Edward	Nsh 133	John	Rwn 329	Zachery, Wm.	Srr 703
Elisha	Rnd 352	John	Wke 774	Zegler, Christo-	
Isaac	Rnd 350	John, Jur.	Wke 774	pher	Stk 578
James	Srr 703	John, Sen.	Wke 774	George	Stk 601
Jerry	Rnd 352	Joseph	Brk 808	James	Stk 591
Jesse	Rnd 350	Joseph	Cbr 680	Zimmerman, David	Lnc 824
Jinny	Edg 259	Joseph	Frn 487	Michael	Lnc 908
John	Grv 527	Joseph	Rwn 329	Samuel	Lnc 824
John (2)	Rnd 350	Joshua	Brk 808	Zollowffer, George	Hlf 356
Jonathan	Srr 703				

.

www.ingramcontent.com/pod-product-compliance
Lightning Source LLC
Chambersburg PA
CBHW071846270326
41929CB00013B/2121